D1530145

Social Sciences

An international bibliography of serial literature, 1830–1985

JAN WEPSIEC

MANSELL

First published 1992 by
Mansell Publishing Limited, *A Cassell imprint*
Villiers House, 41/47 Strand, London WC2N 5JE, England
125 East 23rd Street, Suite 300, New York 10010, U.S.A.

British Library Cataloguing in Publication Data
Wepsiec, Jan
Social sciences: an international bibliography of serial literature, 1830–1985.
1. Social sciences – Bibliographies
I. Title
016.3005

ISBN 0–7201–2109–4

Library of Congress Cataloging-in-Publication Data
Wepsiec, Jan, 1909–
Social sciences: an international bibliography of serial literature, 1830–1985 / Jan Wepsiec.
p. cm.
Includes index.
ISBN 0–7201–2109–4
1. Social sciences—Periodicals—Bibliography. I. Title.
Z7161.A15W38 1991
[H85]
016.3′005—dc20 90–20252
CIP

Printed and bound in Great Britain
by Bookcraft (Bath) Ltd

Contents

Introduction

The large and ever increasing number of serial publications in the social sciences, as already demonstrated by the study made by the Library of the University at Bath under the direction of Dr. Maurice Line[1], has created a need for bibliographic control which provides easy access to such publications. As examples of bibliographies one may mention: Unesco's *World List of Social Science Periodicals* (1st ed., 1953; 8th ed., 1982), international in scope and listing current publications; works covering a group of countries, e.g. I. Zimmerman's *A Guide to Current Latin American Periodicals; Humanities and Social Sciences* (1961); works covering one country, e.g. *Bibliografia brasileira de ciências sociais* (v.1–, 1954–, Rio de Janeiro); or works limited to one discipline but international in scope, e.g. Tax, Sol and Fr. Francis X. Grollig, eds. *Serial Publications in Anthropology* (2nd ed., 1982), or Harris, Chauncy D. and Jerome Fellmann. *International List of Geographical Serials* (2nd ed., 1973).

The interdisciplinary research revealed relations among the social sciences and other disciplines and broadened the range of sources of information in serials.

Scope

Following the establishment of individual social sciences in the eighteenth and nineteenth centuries the boundaries of individual disciplines were considered as clearly separating individual sciences. But some scholars in their research combined two fields, as one learns from the contributions by Luther L. Bernard[2] and Frank H. Hankins[3]. The relationship between individual social sciences was presented in greater detail in the *Interdisciplinary Relationships in the Social Sciences*, edited by Sherif Muzafer[4], and in the "Conditions Favoring Major Advances in Social Science" by Karl W. Deutsch, John Platt and Dieter Senghaas[5] and in a more detailed presentation titled *Major Advances in Social Science since 1900* by the same authors[6]. Another analysis of interrelationships among the social sciences was made by Piaget in his two contributions: "The Place of Sciences of Man in the System of Sciences" and "General Problems of Interdisciplinary Research and Common Mechanisms".[7] One may conclude this short review of analyses of the development in social sciences by citing the contribution by Daniel Bell, who listed advances and some failures, e.g. lack of explanation of the occurrence of inflation in the theory of full employment[8].

Two primary considerations had to be solved before compilation of this work started: what social science disciplines should be included and which event in the development of social sciences should be taken as the starting date. The decision concerning the latter was to a degree arbitrary. The year 1830 was selected because the first journal on economics, the first established discipline, was published in that year. Social philosophy, sometimes called moral philosophy at that period, was in the intellectual atmosphere but the first positivistic ideas already pervaded the old atmosphere of non-empirical thinking. The second question, namely that of the inclusion of individual disciplines, could not follow any accepted system because of lack of agreement on the subject matter. Taking into account the present situation and relations among individual disciplines the following sciences are taken as forming the main group: economics, political science, cultural anthropology, sociology, international public law (related to international relations) and comparative law (this is not a code of law but a method of studying the infrastructures of various families of law, their traditions and relations between laws and social standards and values).

In addition to these six sciences four other disciplines are also considered as minor members of the social sciences group: education (its function is a formal socialization of the younger generation), psychology (and social psychology especially is applied by various sciences and in various ways), history (its subdivisions deal with economic, social and cultural phenomena of the past time) and geography (social and economic geography throws light on social behavior).

The formation of two groups of disciplines in this bibliography leads to the exclusion of one rule of selecting in the same way publications from all the disciplines considered; a kind of differentiation is advisable.

Criteria for Selecting Publications

1. Publications of scholarly level on the social sciences in the main group when they contain information about theories or methods or when they contain information about social, political, economic and cultural systems of any society are selected comprehensively regardless of the country or language of such publications. However, if publications are limited geographically either to a region smaller than a state in the United States or to corresponding political entities in large counries, such publications are not included, unless their theoretical orientation or methodology is important. An exception to this rule is made with a small number of popular but long-living publications because they reflect the degree of diffusion and time-lag in the adoption of scholarly ideas which were presented first in scholarly publications.
2. Publications of international organizations, such as the League of Nations, United Nations, Organisation for Economic Co-operation and Development, European Economic Community and Organization of American States, are selected comprehensively including their statistical publications although statistical publications of individual countries are not selected. Statistical data in publications of international organizations are created on the basis of adopted models and they can be used without adjustments in comparative studies.
3. Publications dealing with failures in the functioning of various sectors of human societies are included selectively if they deal with origin, evaluation, impact and prevention, but not with medical treatment or techniques of rehabilitation. Publications dealing with the forecasting of social development, social aspects of the aged and similar others are included selectively.
4. Short-lived publications, if they are not continued by successors, are not included unless their content is relevant to the theory and methodology, or their content is relevant to the area about which there is not much information.
5. Publications on sciences listed in the second group (education, psychology, history and geography) are included more selectively than those on the sciences in the main group.
6. For publications published in several language-versions one in a world-language is selected for description; the titles of other versions are listed in the description of the selected publication and cross-references from other titles to the one listed are provided.
7. Numbered series of monographs or research papers, the latter having their own distinctive titles, are listed if they were or continued to be published for a long period of time.
8. Serial publications of secondary information sources, i.e. bibliographies, indexing and abstracting journals, are listed if they are in the field of the social sciences.
9. The selection of serials on international public law differs from the selection in other disciplines. Usually journals on this discipline are broader than just international public law and contain information on other kinds of international law; all such publications are included in this bibliography.
10. Excluded are serial publications which, although published regularly, in fact are series of papers or pamphlets written by one person, e.g. *Organisateur* written by Saint-Simon. These are very rare cases.

Form of Entry and Description of Publications

The type of entry is not entirely consistent in this compilation owing to the change in the Anglo-American cataloging rules. Some old and ceased publications which had changed their titles were listed in library catalogs under the latest title with cross-references from earlier titles. They were bound and sometimes microfilmed as one publication. They are listed as one publication in this bibliography. But when the title was changed in recent years, then both the predecessor and successor to the change are listed as separate publications. If the successor continues the volume numbering of its predecessor, then in its description the term "Continues:" followed by the title of its predecessor is used. If, however, the succeeding publication starts its volume number with "v.1" or "no.1", then in its description the term "Supersedes:" is used followed by the title of its predecessor; in the description of the predecessor the term "Superseded by:" followed by the title of its successor is used. In a few cases when the period of publishing the preceding publication was short and its description is not complex, the statement "Supersedes:" is followed by the title and numbers of volumes published and the years of publication.

All publications which according to the old rules of cataloging were listed under a place name, followed by the name of the issuing institution and title, are listed in this bibliography under the names of issuing bodies. For example *Memoirs of the Francis Galton Laboratory* of the University of London is listed in this compilation as follows:

University of London. University College.
Francis Galton Laboratory of Eugenics.
MEMOIRS.

Cross-references from the title to the corporate entry are provided.

The names of institutions changed sometimes. Old publications where the names of issuing bodies changed some years ago are entered under the most recent name and title, and appropriate cross-references are provided. But in the case of a recent change the publication carrying the new name of the issuing body is listed as a separate publication and information pertinent to such a change is included in the description of both publications. The language of the text other than English is always listed. The languages of summaries and tables of contents are listed if other than the language of the text. The entire text of some publications is in two languages: this is indicated in the description by the phrase "parallel text in . . . and . . .", e.g. English and French. If the publication is a statistical one the phrase used is: e.g. French and German.

The publishing of supplements to journals has a long tradition. They can be called by various terms, e.g. "Suplemento", "Beiheft", "Annexe" or other term, or a distinctive title. If a supplement with a distinctive title is published regularly a cross-reference to it is provided or a separate entry may be given.

Indexes

Many journals provide an annual table of contents; some also provide an annual subject index. But fewer serials issue cumulative subject indexes covering a few years or an even longer period of time. A record of publishing such indexes is made in the description of the parental journal with an indication whether it is included in one of the issues or published separately.

Indexing and/or Abstracting the Contents

Indexing or abstracting the contents of a given journal in secondary information journals in the social sciences is recorded selectively in this compilation using abbreviations of which a list follows this introduction.

Arrangement

Entries are arranged alphabetically word-by-word in one sequence. Definite or indefinite articles used at the beginning of titles are disregarded in all languages. Titles with acronyms are listed at the beginning of the appropriate letter group and are usually used as references to full titles. There are no titles beginning with numbers listed in this bibliography. Titles beginning with hyphenated words follow titles consisting of the same words but not hyphenated, and precede titles beginning with words consisting of the same morphemes but written as one word. An example of such arrangement occurs when the title begins with "Inter American", "Inter-American" and "Interamerican".

Romanization

Titles of publications in languages not using the Roman alphabet are transliterated into the Roman alphabet according to the established rules for a given language. But sometimes there are more than one set of rules for a given non-Roman alphabet. Collecting information and using catalogs in libraries other than those in the United States was done following rules different from those used in the Library of Congress. In order to provide a consistency of approach the rules used by the Library of Congress have been applied bearing in mind the wide variety of reference works it publishes and distributes.

Acknowledgements

The following libraries were used most frequently: the British Library, London; the British Library Document Supply Centre, Boston Spa; and the University of London Library. Occasionally the University of Leeds Library was used. In the early years of gathering information the

National Library of Canada, the University of Toronto Library and the McGill University Library were used extensively.

The most important library as a source of information in my work was the Library of Congress, which offered me unique facilities by granting me access to its stacks of bound and unbound publications and some records from which I could obtain information not published in bibliographic sources.

I am greatly indebted to friendly librarians on both sides of the Atlantic Ocean. The completion of this work has been to a degree a result of facilities offered to me by those libraries.

References

1. *Size, Growth and Composition of Social Science Literature*. Bath, 1975. University, Bath. Library. Design of Information Systems in the Social Sciences. *Research Report. Series A*, no.2.
2. Bernard, Luther L., *Encyclopaedia of the Social Sciences*, v.1, pp.343–346 (1930).
3. Hankins, Frank H., "Sociology", in: Barnes, Harry E., ed. *History and Prospects of the Social Sciences*. New York, 1975, pp.314–331.
4. Muzafer, Sherif and Carolyn W. Muzafer, eds. *Interdisciplinary Relationships in the Social Sciences*. Chicago, Aldine Pub. Co., 1969.
5. Karl W. Deutsch, John Platt and Dieter Senghaas, "Conditions Favoring Major Advances in Social Science", *Science*, Feb. 1971, pp.450–459.
6. Karl W. Deutsch, John Platt and Dieter Senghaas. *Major Advances in Social Science since 1900*. New York, University Press of America, 1986.
7. *Main Trends of Research in the Social and Human Sciences. Part 1. Social Sciences*. Paris, Mouton, Unesco, 1970, pp.1–57, 467–528.
8. Bell, Daniel, "The Social Sciences since the Second World War. Part 1", *The Great Ideas Today*, 1979, pp.139–181; "Part 2", *The Great Ideas Today*, 1980, pp.184–232.

Abbreviations for Titles of Abstracting and Indexing Journals

ABC POL SCI
ABC Political Science (1969–)
Abst. Anth.
Abstracts in Anthropology (1970–)
Abst. Soc. Work
Abstracts for Social Workers (1965–1977). Continued by: *Social Work Research & Abstracts*.
Am. His. Life
America; History and Life (1964–)
APAIS
Australian Public Affairs Information Service Index to Current Literature (1945–)
Brit. Arch. Abst.
British Archaeological Abstracts (1968–)
Brit. Hum. Ind.
British Humanities Index (1915–)
Bull. Anal. Pol. Ec. Soc.
Bulletin Analytique de Documentation Politique, Économique, Social
Bull. Sig. Soc. Eth.
Bulletin Signalétique. 521. Sociologie–Ethnologie (1961–)
Curr. Cont. Soc. Beh. Sc.
Current Contents. Social and Behavioral Sciences (1961–)
Eco. Abst.
Economic Abstracts, The Hague (1963–1968). Continued by: *Key to Economic Science* (1976–1977), and *Key to Economic Science and Managerial Sciences* (1978–1987)
Geo. Abst.
Geographical Abstracts (1966–)
His. Abst.
Historical Abstracts (1955–)
HRA
Human Resources Abstracts (1975–). Continues: PHRA.
Ind. For. Leg. Per.
Index to Foreign Legal Periodicals (1960–)
Ind. Leg. Per.
Index to Legal Periodicals (1908–). Continues: *Index to Legal Periodicals and Law Library Journal* (1908–1935)
Ind. Per. Art. Law
Index to Periodical Articles Related to Law (1958–)
Int. Bibl. Eco.
International Bibliography of Economics (1952–)
Int. Bibl. Pol. Sc.
International Bibliography of Political Science (1953–)
Int. Bibl. Soc.
International Bibliography of Sociology (1951–)
Int. Bibl. Soc. Cul. Anth.
International Bibliography of Social and Cultural Anthropology (1955–)
Int. Lab. Doc.
International Labour Documentation (1951–)
Int. Pol. Sc. Abst.
International Political Science Abstracts (1951–)
J. Eco. Lit.
Journal of Economic Literature (1969–)
LLBA
Language and Language Behavior Abstracts (1967–)
PAIS
Public Affairs Information Service Bulletin (1915–)
PAISFL
Public Affairs Information Service. Foreign Language Index (1968/1971–)
Peace Res. Abst. J.
Peace Research Abstracts Journal (1964–)
PHRA
Poverty and Human Resources Abstracts (1966–1974). Continued by: HRA.
Pop. Ind.
Population Index (1935–)
Psych. Abst.
Psychological Abstracts (1927–)
Sage Fam. Stu. Abst.
Sage Family Studies Abstracts (1979–)
Sage Pub. Adm. Abst.
Sage Public Administration Abstracts (1974–)
Sage Race Rel. Abst.
Sage Race Relations Abstracts (1975–)
Sage Urb. Stu. Abst.
Sage Urban Studies Abstracts (1973–)

Soc. Abst.
Sociological Abstracts (1952–)
Soc. Beh. Sc.
See Curr. Cont. Soc. Beh. Sc.
Soc. Sc. Ind.
Social Sciences Index (1974/1975–). Supersedes, in part: *Social Sciences and Humanities Index*
Soc. Work Res. Abst.
Social Work Research and Abstracts (1977–)
SSCI
Social Sciences Citation Index (1973–)
SSHI
Social Sciences and Humanities Index (1913–1974). Superseded by: *Social Sciences Index* (1974/1975–), and *Humanities Index*.
Urb. Aff. Abst.
Urban Affairs Abstracts (1972–)
Wom. Stu. Abst.
Women Studies Abstracts (1972–)

AAUN
See UNA NEWS

ABC AMERICAN BEHAVIORAL SCIENTIST
See AMERICAN BEHAVIORAL SCIENTIST

1
ABC POL SCI; ADVANCED BIBLIOGRAPHY OF CONTENTS: POLITICAL SCIENCE AND GOVERNMENT. v.1– , Mar. 1969– . Santa Barbara, Calif., ABC-Clio. Eight no. a year.

ACA
See ADVANCES IN COMPUTER ARCHAEOLOGY

ACP ANNUAIRE DES STATISTIQUES DU COMMERCE EXTÉRIEUR
See Statistical Office of the European Communities. ACP YEARBOOK OF FOREIGN TRADE STATISTICS

ACP COUNTRIES
See YEARBOOK OF FOREIGN TRADE STATISTICS. THIRD COUNTRIES (VOLUME A)

ACP YEARBOOK OF FOREIGN TRADE STATISTICS
See Statistical Office of the European Communities. ACP YEARBOOK OF FOREIGN TRADE STATISTICS

2
A.E. & R.S. [i.e. Agriculture: Economics & Rural Sociology] no.1– , 1956– . University Park, Pa. Irreg.
Issued by: Department of Agricultural Economics and Rural Sociology, Pennsylvania State University. No.74 never published.

3
AEDC JOURNAL. v.16– , fall 1981– . Kansas City, Mo. Quarterly.
Issued by: American Development Economic Council.
Continues: *A.I.D. Journal.*

AEHR
See AUSTRALIAN ECONOMIC HISTORY REVIEW

4
AEI FOREIGN POLICY AND DEFENSE REVIEW. v.1– , 1980– . Washington, D.C. Six no. a year.
Issued by: American Enterprise Institute for Public Policy Research.
Supersedes: American Enterprise Institute for Public Policy Research. *AEI Defense Review.*
Indexed: Int. Pol. Sc. Abst.

AICC ECONOMIC REVIEW
See POLITICAL AND ECONOMIC REVIEW

5
A.I.D. RESEARCH AND DEVELOPMENT ABSTRACTS. v.1– , 1975– . Washington, D.C., U.S. Agency for International Development.
Issued by: Bureau for Technical Assistance, subsequently the Division of Documentation and Information, Office of Development Information and Utilization, Bureau for Development Support. Other title: *ARDA*. (Sup. of Docs. no.S 18.47)
Supersedes: *A.I.D. Research Abstracts.*

A.I.S.C.
See ARCHIVES INTERNATIONALES DE SOCIOLOGIE DE COOPÉRATION ET DU DÉVELOPPEMENT

AKD QUARTERLY; ALPHA KAPPA DELTA QUARTERLY
See SOCIOLOGICAL INQUIRY

AMRI
See ANUARIO MEXICANO DE RELACIONES INTERNACIONALES

AQ THE AUSTRALIAN QUARTERLY
See THE AUSTRALIAN QUARTERLY

ARDA
See A.I.D. RESEARCH AND DEVELOPMENT ABSTRACTS

ARPA
See AMERICAN REVIEW OF PUBLIC ADMINISTRATION

A.S.I. COMMUNICATION
See University of the Witwatersrand, Johannesburg. African Studies Institute. A.S.I. COMMUNICATION

ASPAC QUARTERLY OF CULTURE AND SOCIAL AFFAIRS
See Asian and Pacific Council. Cultural and Social Centre. ASPAC QUARTERLY OF CULTURE AND SOCIAL AFFAIRS

6
ABBIA; REVUE CULTURELLE CAMEROUNAISE. v.1– , 1963– . Yaoundé, Centre de Production de Manuelles et d'Auxiliaires de l'Enseignement. Four no. a year.
Issued by: Ministère de l'Éducation Nationale. In English or French.
Indexed: Bull. Anal. Pol. Ec. Soc.; Int. Bibl. Soc.; Int. Bibl. Soc. Cul. Anth.

ABHANDLUNGEN
See Akademie der Wissenschaften, Berlin. Klasse für Gesellwissenschaften. ABHANDLUNGEN

ABHANDLUNGEN
See Akademie der Wissenschaften, Berlin. Philosophisch-Historische Klasse. ABHANDLUNGEN

ABHANDLUNGEN
See Akademie der Wissenschaften und Literatur, Mainz. Geistes- und Sozialwissenschaftliche Klasse. ABHANDLUNGEN

ABHANDLUNGEN
See Österreichisches Kulturinstitut, Rome. Abteilung für Historische Studien. PUBLIKATIONEN. I. ABTEILUNG. ABHANDLUNGEN

ABHANDLUNGEN DER GEISTES- UND SOZIALWISSENSCHAFTLICHEN KLASSE
See Akademie der Wissenschaften und Literatur, Mainz. Geistes- und Sozialwissenschaftliche Klasse. ABHANDLUNGEN

7
ABHANDLUNGEN ZUR FORTSCHREITENDEN KODIFIKATION DES INTERNATIONALEN RECHTS. no.1– , 1927– . Berlin, Duncker & Humblot. Irreg.
Issued by: Institut für Internationales Recht, Universität zu Kiel. In German. Includes the institute's "Veröffentlichungen".

8
ABHANDLUNGEN ZUR HANDELS- UND SOZIALGESCHICHTE. v.1– , 1958– . Weimar, Böhlaus. Irreg.
Issued by: Hansische Arbeitsgemeinschaft der Historischen Gesellschaft der Deutschen Demokratischen Republik. In German. Monograph series.

9
AL-ABḤĀT AL-IJTIMĀ'ĪYAH. v.1– , 1948– . Beirut, Lebanon. Quarterly.
Issued by: American University in Beirut. In Arabic; summaries in English. Other title: *Social Studies*.

10
ABORIGINAL HISTORY. v.1– , 1977– . Canberra. Annual.
Issued by: Department of Pacific and Southeast Asian History, Australian National University.

11
ABRAXAS. v.1– , 1970– . Southampton, N.Y. Quarterly.
Issued by: Humanities Division, Southampton College. Subtitle reads: "Journal for the theoretical study of philosophy, the humanities and the social sciences".

11a
ABSEES. no.1 (27)– , July 1970– . Glasgow (1970–1976), Oxford, Oxford Microform Publications. Quarterly, 1970–76; three no. a year.
Issued by: National Association for Soviet and East European Studies (NASEES), and the Institute of Soviet and East European Studies. Beginning with Jan. 1978 published on microfiche.

12
ABSTRACTS FOR SOCIAL WORKERS. v.1–13, no.1, spring 1965–1977. Albany, N.Y.
Issued by: National Association of Social Workers.
Continued by: *Social Work Research & Abstracts.*

13
ABSTRACTS IN ANTHROPOLOGY. v.1– , Feb. 1970– . Farmingdale, N.Y., Baywood Pub. Co. Quarterly.
Indexed: Brit. Arch. Abst.

14
ABSTRACTS IN GERMAN ANTHROPOLOGY. no.1– , autumn 1980– . Göttingen, Edition Herodot. Semi-annual.
Issued by: Arbeitskreis für Internationale Wissenschaftskommunikation. Works by Austrian, German and Swiss authors in English; abstracts of other authors are in other languages.

15
ABSTRACTS IN HUMAN EVOLUTION. v.1, no.1/2– , Jan./Feb. 1975– . Los Angeles, Calif., Bibliographics Information Resources. Bimonthly.

16
ABSTRACTS OF BULGARIAN SCIENTIFIC LITERATURE. ECONOMICS AND LAW. BULLETIN D'ANALYSES DE LA LITTÉRATURE SCIENTIFIQUE BULGARE. ÉCONOMIE ET DROIT. 1– , 1958– . Sofia. Four no. a year.

Issued by: Scientific Information Center for Natural Mathematical and Social Sciences, Bulgarian Academy of Sciences. Abstracts of work on economics are in English; of works on law in French. Another edition is published in Russian. Other title: *Referativnyĭ Biulleten' Bolgarskoĭ Nauchnoĭ Literatury. Ekonomika i Pravo*. Processed.

17
ABSTRACTS OF BULGARIAN SCIENTIFIC LITERATURE: HISTORY, ARCHAEOLOGY AND ETHNOGRAPHY. v.1– , 1958– . Sofia. Semi-annual.
Issued by: 1958–July/Sept. 1969, Department of Scientific Information and Documentation, Central Library of the Bulgarian Academy of Sciences; Oct./Dec. 1959–July/Sept. 1962, Centre of Scientific Information and Documentation, Bulgarian Academy of Sciences. In French and German.

18
ABSTRACTS OF BULGARIAN SCIENTIFIC LITERATURE: PHILOSOPHY, PSYCHOLOGY AND PEDAGOGICS. v.1– , 1958– . Sofia. Semi-annual.
Issued by: Scientific Information Centre for Natural, Mathematical and Social Sciences. Title varies: v.1–8, 1958–65, *Philosophy and Pedagogics*. With: *Abstracts of Bulgarian Scientific Literature; Scientific Communism, Philosophy, Sociology, Science of Science, and Scientific Information*, continues: *Abstracts of Bulgarian Scientific Literature; Philosophy, Sociology, Science of Science, Psychology and Pedagogics*.

19
ABSTRACTS OF BULGARIAN SCIENTIFIC LITERATURE; PHILOSOPHY, SOCIOLOGY, SCIENCE OF SCIENCE, PSYCHOLOGY AND PEDAGOGICS. v.1–21, 1958–1979. Sofia, Publishing House of the Bulgarian Academy of Sciences. Semi-annual.
Issued by: Scientific Information Centre for Natural, Mathematical and Social Sciences, Bulgarian Academy of Sciences. In English. Published also in Russian.
Continued by: *Abstracts of Bulgarian Scientific Literature; Philosophy and Pedagogics*, and: *Abstracts of Bulgarian Scientific Literature; Scientific Communism, Philosophy, Sociology, Science of Science and Scientific Information*.

20
ABSTRACTS OF BULGARIAN SCIENTIFIC LITERATURE; SCIENTIFIC COMMUNISM, PHILOSOPHY, SOCIOLOGY, SCIENCE OF SCIENCE AND SCIENTIFIC INFORMATION. v.22– , July/Oct. 1979– . Sofia, Publishing House of the Bulgarian Academy of Sciences.
Issued by: Scientific Information Centre for Natural, Mathematical and Social Sciences, Bulgarian Academy of Sciences. In English. Published also in Russian.
Continues, in part: *Abstracts of Bulgarian Scientific Literature; Philosophy, Science of Science, Psychology and Pedagogics*.

ABSTRACTS OF CURRENT STUDIES
See World Bank. World Bank Research Program. ABSTRACTS OF CURRENT STUDIES

21
ABSTRACTS OF FOLKLORE STUDIES. v.1– , Jan. 1963– . Austin, Tex. Four no. a year.
Issued by: American Folklore Society.

22
ABSTRACTS OF POPULAR CULTURE. v.1– , 1976/77– . Bowling Green, Ohio, Bowling Green University Popular Press. Biennial.
Issued by: Center for the Study of Popular Culture, State University at Bowling Green.

23
ABSTRACTS ON CRIMINOLOGY AND PENOLOGY. v.1–19, Jan./Feb. 1961–1979. Deventer, Kluwer. Bimonthly.
Issued by: Excerpta Criminologica Foundation. In English. Title varies: v.1–8, 1961–68, *Excerpta Criminologica*.
Continued by: *Criminology and Penology Abstracts*.
Indexed: Ind. Per. Art. Law

24
Academia de Ciencias Políticas y Sociales, Caracas. BOLETÍN. v.1– , Apr./June 1936–. Caracas. Quarterly, 1936–78; three no. a year.
In Spanish.

25
Academia de Ştiinţe Sociale şi Politice a Republicii Socialiste România. Centrul de Informare in Ştiinţele Sociale şi Politice. ISTORIE-ARHEOLOGIE. v.–1 , 1964– . Bucureşti. Bimonthly.
Vols. 1–6 issued by: the academy's Filiala, Iaşi. In Romanian; summaries in French. Monographic supplements accompany some issues.

26
Academia de Ştiinţe Sociale şi Politice a Republicii Socialiste România. Institutul de Istorie "N. Iorga". STUDII ŞI MATERIALE DE ISTORIE MODERNE. v.4– , 1973– . Bucureşti.
In Romanian; summaries in French.
Continues: Academia Republicii Populare Romine. Institutul de Istorie. *Studii şi Materiale de Istorie Moderne*.

27
Academia de Ştiinţe Sociale şi Politice a Republicii Socialiste România. Institutul de Arheologie. MATERIALE ŞI CERCETĂRI ARHEOLOGICE. 1– , 1955– . Bucureşti, Editura Academiei Republicii Socialiste România.
Early volumes issued by: Academia Republicii Populare Romîne. In Romanian; summaries in French and Russian. Tables of contents in French.

28
Academia de Ştiinţe Sociale şi Politice a Republicii Socialiste România. Institutul de Istorie şi Archeologie, Cluj. ANUARUL. v.1– , 1958– . Bucureşti, Editura Academiei Republicii Socialiste România.
In Romanian.

29
Academia Dominicana de la Historia. PUBLICACIONES. v.1– , 1955– . San Domingo. Irreg.
In Spanish. Monograph series.

30
Academia Mexicana de la Historia. MEMORIAS. v.1– , Jan./Apr. 1942– . Mexico, D.F. Quarterly.
In Spanish. Monograph series.

31
Academia Nacional de Ciencias Morales y Políticas. ANALES. 1972– . Buenos Aires. Annual.
In Spanish.

32
Academia Portuguêsa de Historia. ANAIS. v.1– , 1940– . Lisboa. Annual.
In Portuguese.

33
Academia Republicii Socialiste România. Centrul de Documentare Ştiinţifica. BULETIN DE INFORMARE ŞTIINŢIFICA: FILOZOFIE, LOGICA, SOCIOLOGIE, PSIHOLOGIE. v.1– , 1964– . Bucureşti.
In Romanian.

34
Academia Republicii Socialiste România. Centrul de Informare Ştiinţifica. BULETIN DE INFORMARE ŞTIINŢIFICA. ŞTIINŢE ECONOMICE. v.1– , Jan./Feb. 1964–. Bucureşti. Monthly.
Later, issued under the changed name of the center: Centrul de Informare şi Documentare in Ştiinţele Sociale şi Politice. Title varies: v.1–2, 1964–65, *Revista de Referati şi Recenzii; Ştiinţe Economice*. In Romanian.

Academia Republicii Socialiste România. Centrul de Informare şi Documentare in Ştiinţele Sociale şi Politice
See ROMANIAN SCIENTIFIC ABSTRACTS. SOCIAL SCIENCES

35
Academia Republicii Socialiste România. Institutul de Istorie. STUDII: REVISTA DE ISTORIE. v.8– , 1955– . Bucharest. Bimonthly, 1955–73; monthly.
In Romanian; summaries in French.
Continues: *Studii: Revista de Istorie e Filosofie*, issued by Academia Republicii Populare Romîne.

ACADEMIC JOURNAL. GRADUATE SCHOOL, CHINESE ACADEMY OF SOCIAL SCIENCES
See CHUNG-KUO SHE HUI K'O HSÜEH YUAN YEN CHIN SHENG YÜAN HSÜEH PAO

36
Académie de Droit International, The Hague. RECUEIL DES COURS. v.1– , 1953– . Leiden, Sijthoff. Three no. a year.
In French.
Indexes: vols. 1–20, 1923–27; 1v; v.21–42, 1928–32, 1v; v.1–62, 1923–37, 1v; v.1–84, 1923–53, 1v; v.1–101, 1923–60, 1v; v.102–125, 1961–68, 1v. v.126–151, 1969–76, 1v.

37
Académie des Sciences Coloniales. ANNALES. v.1–9, 1925–1938. Paris, Société d'Éditions.
In French.

Académie des Sciences Coloniales
See also Académie des Sciences d'Outre-Mer

38
Académie des Sciences d'Outre-Mer. COMPTES RENDUS TRIMESTRIELLES DES SÉANCES. v.1–37, 1922/23–1977. Paris. Frequency varies.
Volumes through June 1957 issued by the academy under its earlier name: Académie des Sciences Coloniales. Title varies: 1922/23–1928/29, *Comptes Rendus des Séances*: 1929/30–1931, *Comptes Rendus des Séances. Communications*; 1931–40, *Communications*; Jan. 1946–Dec. 1970, *Comptes Rendus Mensuels des Séances*. In French.
Continued by: *Mondes et Cultures*.

39
Académie des Sciences d'Outre-Mer. TRAVAUX ET MÉMOIRES, n. ser. no. 1– , 1972– . Paris. Irreg.
In French. Monograph series. Subseries of the academy's *Publications*.

40
Académie des Sciences Morales et Politiques. REVUE DES TRAVAUX ET COMPTES RENDUS DE SES SÉANCES. 1842– . Paris, Sirey. Monthly (irreg.); two volumes per year except for the years 1853–70 when the numbers formed four volumes annually; semi-annual.
In French. Title varies: 1842–1935, *Séances et Travaux.*
Continued by: *Revue des Sciences Morales et Politiques.*

41
Académie des Sciences Morales et Politiques, Montréal. TRAVAUX ET COMMUNICATIONS. v.1– , 1973– . Sherbrooke, later Montréal, Les Éditions Bellarmin. Annual (irreg.)
In French.

42
Académie Royale des Sciences d'Outre-Mer. Classe des Sciences Morales et Politiques. BULLETIN DES SÉANCES. MEDEDELINGEN DER ZITTINGEN. [v.1]–75, 1930–1954; n. ser. v.1– , 1955– . Bruxelles. Two no. a year.
Early volumes issued under the academy's earlier name: Institut Royal Colonial Belge (Koninklijke Belgisch Koloniaal Instituut). In French or Flemish, or occasionally in English.

43
Académie Royale des Sciences d'Outre-Mer. Classe des Sciences Morales et Politiques. MÉMOIRES. 29– , 1964– . Bruxelles. Irreg.
In French. Other title: *Verhandelingen.*
Continues: Académie Royale des Sciences d'Outre-Mer. Classe des Sciences Morales et Politiques. *Mémoires: in 8°.*

44
Académie Royale des Sciences d'Outre-Mer. Classe des Sciences Morales et Politiques. MÉMOIRES. VERHANDELINGEN. In 4°. v.1–5, 1938–1950. Bruxelles. Irreg.
Issued under the academy's earlier name: Institut Royal Colonial Belge. In French or Flemish. Monograph series.

45
Académie Royale des Sciences d'Outre-Mer. Classe des Sciences Morales et Politiques. MÉMOIRES. VERHANDELINGEN. In 8°. v.1–38, 1933–1954; n. ser. v.1–28, 1955–1963. Bruxelles. Irreg.
In French, Flemish, or German. Other title: *Verzameling.* Monograph series.
Continued by the academy's: *Mémoires. Verhandlingen* (v.29– , 1964–)

46
The Academy of Management. THE ACADEMY OF MANAGEMENT REVIEW. v.1– , Jan. 1976– . Mississippi State, Miss. Quarterly.
Indexed: SSCI

THE ACADEMY OF MANAGEMENT REVIEW
See The Academy of Management. THE ACADEMY OF MANAGEMENT REVIEW

47
Academy of Marketing Science. JOURNAL. v.1– , spring 1973– . Greenvale, N.Y. Quarterly.
Co-sponsored by: G.W. Post Center, Long Island University, and School of Business Administration, University of Miami.
Indexed: PAIS.

48
Academy of Political Science. PROCEEDINGS. v.1– , 1910– . New York. Irreg.
Indexed: Abst. Soc. Work; Int. Bibl. Soc. Cul. Anth.; Int. Pol. Sc. Abst.; PAIS; Soc. Sc. Hum. Ind.

49
Academy of the Social Sciences in Australia. ANNUAL REPORT. 1971-72– . Canberra.
Continues: *Annual Report* issued by the academy under its earlier name: Social Science Council of Australia.

50
ACCOUNTING, ORGANIZATION AND SOCIETY. 1976– . Oxford, Pergamon Press. Quarterly.

51
ACRACIA; REVISTA SOCIOLÓGICA. v.1, no.1–30, Jan. 1886–1888. Barcelona. Weekly (irreg.)
In Spanish.

ACTA ACADEMIAE UNIVERSALIS JURISPRUDENTIARUM COMPARATIVAE
See International Academy of Comparative Law. ACTA ACADEMIAE UNIVERSALIS JURISPRUDENTIARUM COMPARATIVAE

ACTA AFRICANA
See GENÈVE-AFRIQUE

52
ACTA ANTHROPOLOGICA. 1–3, 1945–1948; epoca 2, v.1– , 1956– . Mexico, D.F.
Issued by: Escuela Nacional de Antropología e Historia, which in 1945–48 was called Escuela Nacional de Antropología. In Spanish. Publication was suspended in 1949–55.

53
ACTA ANTHROPOLOGICA LODZIENSIA. v.1– , 1949– . Łódź. Irreg.
Issued by: Uniwersytet Łódzki. In Polish; summaries in French. Title varies: v.1–5, 1949–58, *Acta Anthropologica Universitatis Lodziensis*. Subseries of: Łódzkie Towarzystwo Naukowe. Wydział III: Nauk Matematyczno-Przyrodniczych. *Prace*.

ACTA ANTHROPOLOGICA SINICA
See JEN LEI HSÜEH HSÜEH PAO

ACTA ANTHROPOLIGICA UNIVERSITATIS LODZIENSIS
See ACTA ANTHROPOLOGICA LODZIENSIA

54
ACTA ANTIQUA ET ARCHAEOLOGICA. v.1– , 1958– . Szeged. Irreg.
In English or German. Includes subseries: *Opuscula Byzantina*. Title varies: v.1–4, 1958–61, *Acta Universitatis Szegedensis. Sectio Antiqua*. (Acta Universitatis de Attila Jozsef nominatae)

55
ACTA ARCHAEOLOGICA. v.1– , 1930– . Copenhagen, Munksgaard. Annual.
In English or German.
Indexed: Int. Bibl. Soc. Cul. Anth.

56
ACTA ARCHAEOLOGICA. v.1– , 1951– . Budapest, Akadémiai Kiadó. Four no. a year. Some nos. are combined.
Issued by: Magyar Tudományos Akadémia. In English, French, German, or Russian.
Indexed: SSCI.

57
ACTA ARCHAEOLOGICA CARPATHICA. v.1– , 1958– . Wrocław, Zakład Narodowy im. Ossolińskich. Irreg.
Issued by: Komisja Archeologiczna, Oddział w Krakowie of Polska Akademia Nauk. In Polish; occasionally in English, German, or Russian; summaries in French or in a language other than that of text. Tables of contents also in French and Russian.

58
ACTA ARCHAEOLOGICA LODZIENSIA. v.1– , 1949– . Łódź. Irreg.
Issued by: Uniwersytet Łódzki. In Polish; summaries in English. Title varies: v.1, 1949, *Acta Praehistorica Universitatis Lodziensis*; v.2–10, 1949–61, *Acta Archaeologica Universitatis Lodziensis*. Subseries of: Łódzkie Towarzystwo Naukowe. Wydział II: Nauk Historycznych i Społecznych. *Prace*.

59
ACTA ARCHAEOLOGICA LUNDENSIA. SERIES IN 8°. no.1– , 1957– . Lund, C.W.K. Gleerup. Irreg.
In English, German, or a Scandinavian language. Monograph series.

ACTA ARCHAEOLOGICA UNIVERSITATIS LODZIENSIS
See ACTA ARCHAEOLOGICA LODZIENSIA

60
ACTA ASIATICA. v.1– , 1960– . Tokyo. Two no. a year.
Issued by: Tōhō Gakkai. In Japanese.
Indexed: Bul. Sig. Soc. Eth; Abst. Anth.

61
ACTA CRIMINOLOGICA. ÉTUDES SUR LA CONDUITE ANTISOCIALE. STUDIES OF ANTISOCIAL BEHAVIOR. v.1–7, 1968–74. Montréal, Presses Universitaires de Montréal. Annual.
Issued by: Département de Criminologie, Université de Montréal. In English or French; summaries in English, French, German, Russian, or Spanish.
Indexed: Soc. Abst.

ACTA DE LA SESIÓN
See Organization of American States. Permanent Council. ACTA DE LA SESIÓN

ACTA DE LA SESIÓN EXTRAORDINARIA
See Organization of American States. Permanent Council. ACTA DE LA SESIÓN

ACTA DE LA SESIÓN ORDINARIA
See Organization of American States. Permanent Council. ACTA DE LA SESIÓN

62
ACTA ETHNOGRAPHICA. v.1– , 1950– . Budapest, Akadémiai Kiadó. Four no. a year.
Issued by: Magyar Tudományos Akadémia. In English, French, German, or Russian.
Indexed: Bull. Sig. Soc. Eth.; Int. Bibl. Soc. Cul. Anth.; SSCI.

ACTA ETHNOLOGICA ET FOLKLORISTICA EUROPEA
See FOLK-LIV

63
ACTA GEOGRAPHICA. no.1–80, Feb. 1947–1969; 3. ser. no.1– , Jan./Mar. 1970– . Paris. Quarterly.
Issued by: Société de Géographie. In French.
Indexed: Int. Bibl. Soc. Cul. Anth.; SSCI.

64
ACTA GEOGRAPHICA LOVANIENSIA. v.1– , 1961– . Louvain. Irreg.
Issued by: Institut de Géographie, Université Catholique de Louvain. In Flemish or French. Monograph series.

65
ACTA HISTORIAE NEERLANDICA. v.1–5, 1966–1973. The Hague, Nijhoff.
Issued under the auspices of the Netherlands Committee of Historical Sciences. In Dutch, English, French, or German.
Continued by: *Acta Historiae Neerlandicae.*

66
ACTA HISTORIAE NEERLANDICAE. STUDIES IN THE HISTORY OF NETHERLANDS. v.6– , 1973– . The Hague, Nijhoff.
Published under the auspices of the Dutch Historical Society. In Dutch or English.
Continues: *Acta Historiae Neerlandica.*

67
ACTA HISTORICA. v.1– , 1951– , Budapest, Akadémiai Kiadó. Two no. a year.
Issued by: Magyar Tudományos Akadémia. In English, French, German, or Russian; summaries in one of these languages.

68
ACTA HISTORICA. v.1– , 1957– . Szeged. Annual.
Issued by: University of Szeged. In Hungarian. V.1–7 published as *Acta Universitatis Szegedensis. Sectio Historica*; v.8–16, as *Acta Universitatis Szegedensis.*

69
ACTA HISTORICO-OECONOMICA IUGOSLAVIAE. 1974– . Zagreb. Annual.
Issued by: Komisija za Ekonomsku Historije Jugoslavije. In Serbo-Croatian; summaries in English and German.

70
ACTA HUMBOLTIANA. SERIES GEOGRAPHICA ET ETHNOGRAPHICA. no.1– , 1959– . Wiesbaden, Steiner Verlag.
Issued by: Deutsche Iberoamerika-Stiftung. In English, German, or Portuguese.

71
ACTA JURIDICA ET POLITICA. v.1– , 1955– . Szeged. Irreg.
Issued by: University of Szeged. In Hungarian; occasionally in French or Russian; summaries in French, German, or Russian. Monograph series. Subseries of: *Acta Universitatis Szegedensis de Attila Jozsef nominatae.*

72
ACTA MANILANA. SERIES B: SOCIO-ECONOMIC AND HISTORICAL SCIENCES. 1– , Aug. 1965– . Manila.
Issued by: Research Center, University of Santo Tomas.
Supersedes, in part: *Acta Manilana.*

73
ACTA MARXISTICA DEBRECINA. v.9– , 1963– . Debrecen. Annual.
Issued by: Kossuth Lajos Tudományegyetem at Debrecen. In Hungarian. Other title: *Acta Universitatis Debrecensis de Ludovico Kossuth nominatae. Series Marxistica-Leninistica.*
Continues, in part: *Acta Marxistica et Pedagogica Debrecina*, and continues its volume numbering.

74
ACTA MEDICA ET SOCIOLOGICA. v.1– , 1962– . [Place of publication varies]
Issued by: International Medical Association for the Study of Living Conditions and Health. Includes papers read at the sessions of congresses of the International Medical Association. Text and summaries in English, French, or Russian.

75
ACTA MEDIEVALIA. 1973– . Lublin. Irreg.
Issued by: Towarzystwo Naukowe Katolickiego Uniwersytetu w Lublinie. In Latin or Polish.

76
ACTA MEXICANA DE CIENCIAS SOCIALES. v.1– , 4th quarter of 1978– . Mexico, D.F. Quarterly.
Issued by: Instituto Politécnico Nacional. In Spanish.

77
ACTA MONETARIA. 1–4, 1977–1980. Frankfurt am Main, F. Knapp. Annual.
In English or German.

78
ACTA OECONOMICA. v.1– , 1966– . Budapest, Akadémiai Kiadó. Quarterly, 1966–70; eight no. a year in 1971; semi-annual.
Issued by: Magyar Tudományos Akadémia. In English, French, German, or Russian; summaries in one of these languages.
Indexes: Vols. 1–5, 1966–70, 1v; 6–10, 1967–73, 1v.
Indexed: Eco. Abst.; Int. Bibl. Eco.; Int. Bibl. Pol. Sc.; Int. Bibl. Soc.; Int. Bibl. Soc. Cul. Anth.; PAIS; SSCI.

79
ACTA ORIENTALIA. v.1– , 1950– . Budapest, Akadémiai Kiadó. Three no. a year.
Issued by: Orientalisztikai Közleményei, Magyar Tudományos Akadémia. In English, French, German, or Russian.

80
ACTA POLITICA. 1965/66– . Meppel, Boompersboeken en Tijdschriften Uitgeverij. Quarterly.
Issued by: Nederlands Kring voor Wetenschapp der Politiek. In Dutch or English; summaries in English.
Indexed: ABC POL SCI; Bull. Sig. Soc. Eth.; Int. Bibl. Eco.; Int. Bibl. Pol. Sc.; Int. Bibl. Soc.; Int. Bibl. Soc. Cul. Anth.; Int. Pol. Sc. Abst.

81
ACTA POLONIAE HISTORICA. v.1– , 1958– . Warszawa, Zakład Narodowy im. Ossolińskich. Annual.
Issued by: Instytut Historii, Komitet Nauk Historycznych, Polska Akademia Nauk. In English, French, German, or Polish.
Indexed: His. Abst.; Peace Res. Abst. J.

ACTA PRAEHISTORICA UNIVERSITATIS LODZIENSIS
See ACTA ARCHAEOLOGICA LODZIENSIA

ACTA SCANDINAVICA IURIS GENTIUM
See NORDISK TIDSKRIFT FOR INTERNATIONAL RET OG JUS GENTIUM

82
ACTA SCIENTIARUM SOCIALIUM. v.1– , 1959– . Roma. Irreg.
Issued by: Societa Academica Romana. In English, French, German, or Italian.

ACTA. SECTIO POLITICO-JURIDICA
See ACTA JURIDICA ET POLITICA

ACTA SILESIACA
See SLEZSKÝ SBORNIK

83
ACTA SOCIO-MEDICA SCANDINAVICA. 1–4, 1969–1972. Stockholm, Svenska Bokfoerlag. Three no. a year (irreg)
Issued by: Nordic Social Medical Association. In English, French, or German. Includes supplements.

84
ACTA SOCIOLOGICA. SCANDINAVIAN REVIEW OF SOCIOLOGY. SCANDINAVISCHE ZEITSCHRIFT FÜR SOZIOLOGIE. REVUE SCANDINAVE DE SOCIOLOGIE. v.1– , 1955– . Copenhagen, Munksgaard. Quarterly.
Issued by: Danish Sociological Society, Norwegian Sociological Society, Lund Sociological Society, and Westermarck Society. In English, French, German, or occasionally in one of the Scandinavian languages.
Indexed: ABC POL SCI; Bull. Anal. Eco. Soc.; Bull. Sig. Soc. Eth.; Int. Bibl. Soc.; Int. Bibl. Soc. Cul. Anth.; Int. Pol. Sc. Abst.; PAIS; Sage Urb. Abst.; Soc. Abst.; Soc. Sc. Ind.; SSCI.

85
ACTA SOCIOLOGICA. SERIE B: CIUDAD. 1– , 1969– . Mexico, D.F. Irreg.
Issued by: Centro de Estudios del Desarrollo, Universidad Autónoma Nacional de México. In Spanish.

86
ACTA SYMBOLICA. v.1– , spring 1970– . Akron, Ohio, later Memphis, Tenn. Annual.
Issued by: International Association for Symbolic Analysis. Subtitle reads: "An interdisciplinary journal of theory and research on symbolic processes, communication disorders, and behavioural science".

ACTA UNIVERSITATIS DEBRECENSIS DE LUDOVICO KOSSUTH NOMINATAE. SERIES MARXISTICA-LENINISTICA
See ACTA MARXISTICA DEBRECINA

ACTA UNIVERSITATIS LODZIENSIS. ZESZYTY NAUKOWE UNIWERSYTETU ŁÓDZKIEGO. SERIA 1. NAUKI HUMANISTYCZNO-SPOŁECZNE
See NAUKI HUMANISTYCZNO-SPOŁECZNE

87
ACTA UNIVERSITATIS STOCKHOLMIENSIS. STOCKHOLM STUDIES IN HUMAN GEOGRAPHY. v.1– , 1980– . Stockholm, Almqvist & Wiksell.
In English or Swedish.

ACTA UNIVERSITATIS SZEGEDENSIS DE ATTILA JOZSEF NOMINATAE. ACTA JURIDICA ET POLITICA
See ACTA JURIDICA ET POLITICA

ACTA UNIVERSITATIS SZEGEDENSIS. SECTIO ANTIQUA
See ACTA ANTIQUA ET ARCHAEOLOGICA

ACTAS
See International Congress of Americanists. PROCEEDINGS

ACTES
See Congrès International d'Anthropologie Criminelle. BERICHT

88
ACTES DE LA RECHERCHE EN SCIENCES SOCIALES. no.1– , Jan. 1975– . Paris, Service des Publications de la Maison de l'Homme. Bimonthly.
Issued by: La Maison des Sciences de l'Homme in cooperation with École des Hautes Études en Sciences Sociales. In French; summaries in English and German.

Indexed: Bull. Anal. Pol. Ec. Soc.; Int. Bibl. Pol. Sc.; Int. Pol. Sc. Abst.; SSCI.

89
Action Populaire. DOSSIERS DE L'ACTION POPULAIRE. Jan. 1934–Mar. 1938. Paris. Semimonthly.
In French.

90
Action Populaire. REVUE. 1945–1961?. Paris, Spes. Monthly.
In French. Title varies: 1945–Dec. 1949, *Travaux*.

ACTIVITÉS DE L'ADMINISTRATION FÉDÉRALE EN SCIENCES HUMAINES
See Canada. Statistics Canada. FEDERAL GOVERNMENT ACTIVITIES IN HUMAN SCIENCES

91
ACTUALIDAD ANTROPOLÓGICA. no.1– , July/Dec. 1967– . Alavaria. Two no. a year.
Issued by: Museo Ethnográfico Municipal "Damaso Arce". Published as a supplement to *Etnia*. In Spanish.
Indexed: Bull. Sig. Soc. Eth.

ACTUALITÉ D'HISTOIRE
See LE MOUVEMENT SOCIAL

92
ACTUALITÉ ÉCONOMIQUE. v.1– , Apr. 1925– . Montréal. Four no. a year.
Issued by: Société Canadienne de Science Économique in cooperation with École des Hautes Études Commerciales. In French.
Indexed: Bull. Anal. Pol. Ec. Soc.; His. Abst.; Int. Bibl. Eco.; PAISFL; SSCI.

93
ADELPHI PAPERS. no.1– , 1964?– , London. Irreg.
Issued by: International Institute for Strategic Studies.

94
ADMINISTRACIÓN PÚBLICA. no.1– , 1978– . Barcelona, Servicio de Publicaciones de la Universidad Autónoma de Barcelona. In Spanish.
Indexed: Int. Bibl. Soc. Cul. Anth.; Int. Pol. Sc. Abst.

95
ADMINISTRACIÓN Y DESARROLLO. v.1–16, 1962–1976. Bogotá. Quarterly.
Issued by: Escuela Superior de Administración Pública.
Continued by: *Revista de Administración y Desarrollo*.
Indexed: Bull. Anal. Pol. Ec. Soc.

96
ADMINISTRASI NEGARA. THE INDONESIAN JOURNAL OF PUBLIC ADMINISTRATION. v.10– , May 1970– . Djakarta. Quarterly.
Issued by: Lembaga Administrasi Negara. In Indonesian.
Continues: *Madjalah Administrasi Negara*.

97
ADMINISTRATION. v.1– , 1953– . Dublin. Quarterly.
Issued by: Institute of Public Administration.
Indexes: Vols. 1–10, 1953–62, 1v.
Indexed: Bull. Anal. Pol. Ec. Soc.; Int. Bibl. Eco.; Int. Bibl. Pol. Sc.; Int. Bibl. Soc. Cul. Anth.; Int. Pol. Sc. Abst.; Sage Urb. Stu. Abst.

98
ADMINISTRATION. 79– , 1980– . Paris. Annual.
Issued by: Institut International d'Administration Publique. In French.
Indexed: Bull. Anal. Pol. Ec. Soc.; Int. Bibl. Pol. Sc.; Int. Pol. Sc. Abst.

99
ADMINISTRATION & SOCIETY. v.6– , May 1974– . Beverly Hills, Calif., Sage Publications. Quarterly.
Continues: *Journal of Comparative Administration*.
Published in cooperation with the Comparative Administration Group, American Society for Public Administration.
Indexed: ABC POL SCI; Hum. Res. Abst.; Int. Bibl. Eco.; Int. Bibl. Soc.; Int. Pol. Sc. Abst.; PAIS; Sage Pub. Adm. Abst.; Sage Urb. Stu. Abst.; SSCI.

100
ADMINISTRATION FOR DEVELOPMENT. no.1– , Jan. 1974– . Boroko. Two no. a year.
Issued by: Administrative College Papua New Guinea.

101
ADMINISTRATION IN KENYA. 1965– . Lower Kabete. Irreg.
Issued by: Kenya Institute of Administration.

102
ADMINISTRATION IN SOCIAL WORK. v.1– , spring 1977– . New York, Haworth Press. Quarterly.
Issued by: School of Social Administration, Temple University.

Indexed: Bull. Sig. Soc. Eth.

103
L'ADMINISTRATION LOCALE. no.1–30, Jan. 1933–Aug. 1948. Bruxelles.
Formed by the merger of: *Administration Locale* (1925–32) and *Tablettes Documentaires Municipales*. Superseded by: *IULC Bulletin* called later *IULC Quarterly*.

104
ADMINISTRATION PUBLIQUE. 1– , Sept. 1976– . Bruxelles. Quarterly.
Issued by: Institut Belge des Sciences Administratives. In French.

ADMINISTRATION PUBLIQUE DU CANADA *See* CANADIAN PUBLIC ADMINISTRATION

105
ADMINISTRATION YEARBOOK & DIARY. 1974– . Dublin.
Issued by: Institute of Public Administration.

106
ADMINISTRATIVE AFFAIRS IN BANGLADESH. 1979– . Dacca. Annual.
Issued by: Centre for Administrative Studies, University of Dacca.

107
ADMINISTRATIVE CHANGE. v.1– , 1973– . Jaipur.
Indexed: Bull. Anal. Pol. Ec. Soc.; Int. Pol. Sc. Abst.

108
ADMINISTRATIVE HISTORY SERIES. 1– , 1971– . Dublin. Irreg.
Monograph series.

109
ADMINISTRATIVE SCIENCE QUARTERLY. v.1– , June 1956– . Ithaca, N.Y. Quarterly.
Issued by: Graduate School of Business and Public Administration, Cornell University.
Indexes: Vols. 1–12, 1956–67, 1v.
Indexed: ABC POL SCI; Eco. Abst.; Hum. Res. Abst.; Int. Bibl. Eco.; Bull. Sig. Soc. Eth.; Int. Bibl. Soc.; Int. Pol. Sc. Abst.; PAIS; Psych. Abst.; Sage Pub. Adm. Abst.; Soc. Abst.; SSCI.

110
ADMINISTRATIVE SCIENCE REVIEW. v.1– , Mar. 1967– . Dacca.
Issued by: National Institute of Public Administration.
Supersedes: the institute's *Guide*.

111
THE ADMINISTRATOR. v.21– , spring 1976– . Mussori.
Issued by: Lal Bahadur Shastri National Academy of Administration.
Continues: Lal Bahadur Shastri National Academy of Administration. *Journal*.

112
ADOLESCENCE. v.1– , spring 1966– . Roslyn Heights, N.Y., Librae Publishers. Quarterly.
Indexed: Abst. Anth.; Bull. Sig. Soc. Eth.; Int. Bibl. Soc. Cul. Anth.; Psych. Abst.; Wom. Stu. Abst.

113
ADVANCED MANAGEMENT JOURNAL. v.39, no.2– , Apr. 1974– . New York. Quarterly.
Issued by: Society for Advancement of Management.
Continues: *S.A.M. Advanced Management Journal*.

114
ADVANCES DE INVESTIGACIÓN. 1975– . San José.
Issued by: Instituto de Investigaciones Sociales, Faculdad de Ciencias Sociales, Universidad de Costa Rica. In Spanish.

115
ADVANCES IN ANALYSIS OF BEHAVIOUR. 1979– . Chichester, New York, Wiley. Irreg.

116
ADVANCES IN APPLIED SOCIAL PSYCHOLOGY. v.1– , 1980– . Hillsdale, N.J., Lawrence Erlbaum Associates. Annual.

117
ADVANCES IN ARCHAEOLOGICAL METHOD AND THEORY. v.1– , 1978– . New York, Academic Press. Irreg.

118
ADVANCES IN BEHAVIORAL MEDICINE. v.1– , 1981– . Sydney. Annual.
Issued by: Cumberland College of Health Science.

119
ADVANCES IN COMPUTER ARCHAEOLOGY. fall 1983– . Tempe, Ariz. Semi-annual.
Issued by: Department of Anthropology, State University of Arizona, in cooperation with the Branch of Cultural Data Processing, Southwest Region, National Park Service. Other title: ACA.

Continues: *Newsletter of Computer Technology.*

120
ADVANCES IN ECONOMETRICS. v.1– , 1980– . Greenwich, Conn., JAI Press. Annual.

121
ADVANCES IN EXPERIMENTAL SOCIAL PROCESSES. 1978– . Chichester, New York, Wiley. Irreg.
Monograph series.

122
ADVANCES IN EXPERIMENTAL SOCIAL PSYCHOLOGY. v.1– , 1964– . New York, Academic Press. Annual (irreg.)

123
ADVANCES IN GROUP PROCESSES. v.1– , 1984– . Greenwich, Conn., JAI Press. Annual.

124
ADVANCES IN HUMAN GENETICS. v.1– , 1970– . New York, Plenum Press. Annual.

125
ADVANCES IN INDUSTRIAL AND LABOR RELATIONS. v.1– , 1983– . Greenwich, Conn., JAI Press. Annual.

126
ADVANCES IN NONPROFIT MARKETING. v.1– , 1985– . Greenwich, Conn., JAI Press. Annual.

127
ADVANCES IN POLITICAL SCIENCE. 1– , 1982– . Beverly Hills, Calif., Sage Publications.
Published in cooperation with the International Political Science Association.

128
ADVANCES IN PSYCHOLOGY. v.1– , 1978– . Amsterdam, North-Holland Pub. Co. Irreg.
Monograph series.

129
ADVANCES IN SPECIAL EDUCATION. v.1– , 1980– . Greenwich, Conn., JAI Press. Annual.

130
ADVANCES IN STRATEGIC MANAGEMENT. v.1– , 1983– . Greenwich, Conn., JAI Press. Annual.

131
ADVANCES IN THE ECONOMICS OF ENERGY AND RESOURCES. v.1– , 1979– . Greenwich, Conn., JAI Press. Annual.

ADVANCES IN THE SOCIOLOGY OF LANGUAGE
See CONTRIBUTIONS TO THE SOCIOLOGY OF LANGUAGE

132
ADVANCES IN WORLD ARCHAEOLOGY. v.1– , 1982– . New York, Academic Press. Annual.
Summaries in French, German and Russian.
Indexed: Brit. Arch. Abst.

ADVOCATE OF PEACE
See WORLD AFFAIRS (Washington)

AEI FORUM
See American Enterprise Institute for Public Policy Research. AEI FORUM

133
AEI–HOOVER POLICY STUDIES. no.1– , 1971– . Washington, D.C. Irreg.
Issued by: American Enterprise Institute for Public Policy Research and co-sponsored by the Hoover Institution on War, Revolution and Peace. Subseries of: *Hoover Institution Studies.*

134
AFFAIRES ÉTRANGÈRES. v.1–9, no.7, Mar. 1931–July 1939. Paris. Monthly.
In French.

135
AFFARI ESTERI. v.1– , Jan. 1969– . Roma. Quarterly.
Issued by: Associazione Italiana per gli Studi di Politica Estera. In Italian.
Indexed: Bull. Anal. Pol. Ec. Soc.; Int. Bibl. Pol. Sc.; Int. Pol. Sc. Abst.; PAISFL.

136
AFFARI SOCIALI INTERNAZIONALI. v.1– , Mar. 1973– . Milano, Franco Angeli Editore. Quarterly.
In Italian.
Indexed: Bull. Anal. Pol. Ec. Soc.; Int. Bibl. Eco.

137
AFRICA. no.1– , Apr. 1928– . London, Oxford University Press. Quarterly.
Issued by: International African Institute (called Jan. 1928–Dec. 1945, International Institute of African Languages and Cultures). In English, French, or German. Publication suspended Oct. 1940–Oct. 1942. Supplements accompany some numbers.
Indexed: Abst. Anth.; Bull. Anal. Pol. Ec. Soc.; His. Abst.; Int. Bibl. Eco.; Int. Bibl. Soc. Cul. Anth.; Soc. Abst.; SSCI.

138
AFRICA. 1946– . Roma. Monthly, 1946–56; bimonthly; three no. a year.
Issued by: Istituto Italo-Africano. In Italian. Title varies: *Notiziario della Associazione Frale*; *Impresse Italiane in Africa*.
Indexed: Bull. Anal. Pol. Ec. Soc.; Bull. Sig. Soc. Eth.; His. Abst.; Int. Bibl. Pol. Sc.; Int. Bibl. Soc. Cul. Anth.; Int. Pol. Sc. Abst.; PAISFL.

139
AFRICA. 1– , 1978– . Senri Expo Park, Sito. Irreg.
Issued by: National Museum of Ethnology. In English, French, or Spanish.
Supersedes: *Kyoto University African Studies*.

140
AFRICA CONTEMPORARY RECORD; ANNUAL SURVEY AND DOCUMENTS. 1968/69– . London, Rex Collins. Annual.

141
AFRICA CURRENTS. 1– , spring 1975– . London, The Africa Publications Trust. Quarterly.
Supersedes: *Africa Digest* (1952–55)

142
AFRICA DEVELOPMENT. AFRIQUE ET DÉVELOPPEMENT. v.1– , May 1976– . Dakar.
Issued by: Council for the Development of Economic and Social Research in Africa. In English or French.
Indexed: Bull. Anal. Pol. Ec. Soc.

143
AFRICA IN SOVIET STUDIES. 1968– . Moskva. Annual.
Issued by: Institut Afriki, Akademii͡a Nauk SSSR. In English. Articles included are translations from *Afrika v Sovetskikh Issledovanii͡akh*.

144
AFRICA INDEX: SELECTED ARTICLES ON SOCIO-ECONOMIC DEVELOPMENT. CATALOGUE AFRIQUE. ARTICLES CHOISIS SUR LE DÉVELOPPEMENT ÉCONOMIQUE ET SOCIAL. no.1– , Apr. 1971– . New York. Three no. a year.
Issued by: Economic Commission for Africa, United Nations (United Nations [Document] E/CN.14/LIB/ Ser. E/1)

145
AFRICA INDEX TO CONTINENTAL PERIODICAL LITERATURE. no.2– , 1977– . Oxford, Hans Zell. Annual.
Continues: *Africa Index* (no.1, 1976. Dar es Salaam)

146
AFRICA INSIGHT. v.10– , 1980– . Pretoria. Three no. a year.
Issued by: Africa Institute of South Africa.
Continues: *South African Journal of African Affairs* (1971–79)

147
AFRICA QUARTERLY. v.1– , Apr./June 1961– . New Delhi.
Issued by: Indian Council for Cultural Relations.
Indexed: ABC POL SCI.; Int. Bibl. Eco.; Int. Bibl. Pol. Sc.; Int. Bibl. Soc.; Int. Bibl. Soc. Cul. Anth.; Int. Pol. Sc. Abst.; Ind. Per Art. Law; PAIS.

148
AFRICA REPORT. July 5, 1956– . Washington, D.C., later New Brunswick, N.J., Transaction Periodicals Consortium. Bimonthly.
Issued by: African–American Institute (June 1956–June 1957, called Institute of African American Relations)
Indexed: ABC POL SCI.; PAIS; Pop. Ind.; Wom. Stu. Abst.

AFRICA SERIES
See PAPERS IN INTERNATIONAL RELATIONS. AFRICA SERIES

149
AFRICA SOUTH OF THE SAHARA. 1971– . London, Europa Publications. Annual.

150
AFRICA—TERVUREN. v.1– , 1955– . Tervuren. Quarterly.
Issued by: Amis du Musée Royal d'Afrique Centrale. In French, occasionally in Flemish; summaries in French or Flemish.
Indexed: Bull. Sig. Soc. Eth.; Int. Bibl. Soc. Cul. Anth.

151
AFRICA TODAY. v.1– , Apr. 1954– . Denver, Colo., Africa Today Associates. Quarterly.
Indexed: ABC POL SCI.; Bull. Anal. Pol. Ec. Soc.; His. Abst.; Int. Bibl. Eco.; Peace Res. Abst. J.; PAIS; SSCI.

152
AFRICAN ABSTRACTS. v.1–23, 1950–Oct. 1972. London, Macmillan. Quarterly.
Issued by: International African Institute. English edition of *Analyses Africanistes*.

153
AFRICAN ADMINISTRATIVE ABSTRACTS. 1– , 1974– . Tangier. Quarterly.
Issued by: Centre Africain de Formation et de Recherche Administrative pour le Développement. In Arabic, English, or French.

AFRICAN ADMINISTRATIVE STUDIES
See CAHIERS AFRICAINS D'ADMINISTRATION PUBLIQUE

154
AFRICAN AFFAIRS. v.[1]– , Oct. 1901– . London, Macmillan. Quarterly.
Issued by: Royal African Society (called, 1901–Apr. 1935, The African Society). Each issue includes a bibliography of literature on Africa. Title varies: 1901–Apr. 1944, *Journal of the African Society*, or *Journal of the Royal African Society*. Supplements accompany some issues.
Indexed: Bull. Anal. Pol. Ec. Soc.; His. Abst.; Ind. Per. Art. Law; Int. Bibl. Eco.; Int. Bibl. Pol. Sc.; Int. Bibl. Soc.; Int. Bibl. Soc. Cul. Anth.; Peace Res. Abst. J.; Soc. Abst.; SSCI.

155
AFRICAN ARCHAEOLOGICAL REVIEW. v.1– , 1985– . Cambridge, Press Syndicate of the University of Cambridge. Annual.

156
African Development Bank. Board of Governors. ANNUAL REPORT. 1st– , 1964/65– . Abidjan. Annual.
In English and parallel French.

157
AFRICAN ECONOMIC HISTORY. no.1– , spring 1976– . Madison, Wis. Two no. a year.
Issued by: African Studies Program, University of Wisconsin.
Continues: *African Economic History Review* (spring 1974–75)
Indexed: Int. Bibl. Soc. Cul. Anth.; SSCI.

AFRICAN ECONOMIC INDICATORS
See United Nations. Economic Commission for Africa. AFRICAN SOCIO-ECONOMIC INDICATORS

AFRICAN ENVIRONMENT
See ENVIRONNEMENT AFRICAIN

158
AFRICAN FORUM. v.1– , 1965– . New York. Quarterly.
Issued by: American Society of African Culture.
Indexed: Ind. Per. Art. Law; Int. Bibl. Eco.; Int. Bibl. Pol. Sc.; Int. Bibl. Soc.; Int. Lab. Doc.; Peace Res. Abst. J.

159
AFRICAN HISTORICAL STUDIES. v.1–4, 1969–1971. Boston, Mass.
Issued by: African Studies Center, Boston University.
Continued by: *International Journal of African Historical Studies*.

AFRICAN HISTORY. STUDIES AND PUBLICATIONS
See ISTORIIA AFRIKI

160
AFRICAN JOURNAL OF SOCIOLOGY. v.1– , May 1981– . Nairobi. Semi-annual.
Issued by: Department of Sociology, University of Nairobi.
Indexed: Int. Bibl. Soc. Cul. Anth.; LLBA.

161
AFRICAN PERSPECTIVES. 1976– . Leiden. Two no. a year.
Issued by: Afrika-Studiecentrum. In English or French. Some numbers have also distinctive titles.
Continues: *Kroniek van Afrika*.
Indexed: Bull. Anal. Pol. Ec. Soc.

162
THE AFRICAN REVIEW. v.1– , Mar. 1971– . Dar es Salaam. Quarterly.
Issued by: Department of Political Science, University of Dar es Salaam. Subtitle reads: "A journal of politics, development and international relations".
Indexed: Ind. Per. Art. Law; Int. Bibl. Soc. Cul. Anth.; Int. Pol. Sc. Abst.; PAIS.

163
THE AFRICAN SCHOLAR. v.1– , Aug./Nov. 1968– . Washington, D.C. Quarterly.
Issued by: African Academy of Political and Social Sciences.

164
AFRICAN SCIENTIST. 1– , Aug. 1969– . Nairobi, East Africa Pub. House.
Indexed: Int. Lab. Doc.

165
AFRICAN SOCIAL RESEARCH. no.1– , June 1966– . Manchester, Manchester University Press. Semi-annual.
Issued by: Institute for African Studies, University of Zambia.

Supersedes: *Rhodes–Livingstone Journal* (no.1–38, 1944–65)
Indexed: Abst. Anth.; Bull. Sig. Soc. Eth.; His. Abst.; Int. Bibl. Soc. Cul. Anth.; SSCI.

AFRICAN SOCIO-ECONOMIC INDICATORS
See United Nations. Economic Commission for Africa. AFRICAN SOCIO-ECONOMIC INDICATORS

166
AFRICAN STATISTICAL YEARBOOK. ANNUAIRE STATISTIQUE POUR L'AFRIQUE. 1974– . Addis Ababa. Annual.
Issued by: Economic Commission for Africa, United Nations. In English and French.
Continues: United Nations, Economic Commission for Africa. *Statistical Yearbook* (1970–73)

167
AFRICAN STUDIES. v.1– , May 1942– . Johannesburg, Witwatersrand University Press. Quarterly, 1942–75; two no. a year.
Issued by: Department of African Languages, Political Studies and Social Anthropology, Witwatersrand University. In Afrikaans, English, French, or Portuguese. Some nos. processed.
Supersedes: *Bantu Studies*.
Indexed: ABC POL SCI; Abst. Anth.; Bull. Sig. Soc. Eth.; Ind. Per. Art. Law; His. Abst.; Int. Bibl. Eco.; Int. Pol. Sc. Abst.; Int. Pol. Sc. Abst.; LLBA; Peace Res. Abst. J.

168
AFRICAN STUDIES BULLETIN. v.1–12, Apr. 1958–1969. [Place of publication varied]. Quarterly, 1958–64; three no. a year.
Issued by: African Studies Association, 1958–69; Hoover Institution on War, Revolution and Peace, Stanford University, Institute of International Studies, University of California, and Columbia University.
Indexed: Int. Bibl. Soc.; Int. Bibl. Soc. Cul. Anth.

169
AFRICAN STUDIES REVIEW. v.13– , Apr. 1970– . Los Angeles, Calif., later East Lansing, Mich. Three no. a year.
Organ of the African Studies Association. Edited by: African Studies Center, State University of Michigan.
Continues, in part: *African Studies Bulletin*.
Indexed: ABC POL SCI; Bull. Anal. Pol. Ec. Soc.; Int. Bibl. Eco.; Int. Bibl. Pol. Sc.; Int. Bibl. Soc. Cul. Anth.; Pop. Ind.; Soc. Abst.; Wom. Stu. Abst.

170
AFRICAN TARGET. OBJETS AFRICAINS. v.4– , 1970– . Addis Ababa. Quarterly.
Issued by: Economic Commission for Africa, United Nations. In English and French.

AFRICAN TRADE
See COMMERCE AFRICAIN

AFRICAN TRADE STATISTICS. SERIES A. DIRECTION OF TRADE
See United Nations. Economic Commission for Africa. FOREIGN TRADE STATISTICS. SERIES A. DIRECTION OF TRADE

AFRICAN TRADE STATISTICS. STATISTICAL BULLETINS. SERIES B
See United Nations. Economic Commission for Africa. FOREIGN TRADE STATISTICS FOR AFRICA. SERIES B. TRADE BY COMMODITIES

171
AFRICAN URBAN STUDIES. n. ser. no.1– , spring 1980– . East Lansing, Mich. Three no. a year.
Issued by: African Studies Center, Michigan State University.
Continues: *Urban Studies Notes* (spring 1978–79)

AFRICANA. AFRIKANSKIĬ ETNOGRAFICHESKIĬ SBORNIK
See Akademii͡a Nauk SSSR. Institut Etnografii. TRUDY. n. ser.

172
AFRICANA BULLETIN. v.1– , 1964– . Warszawa. Semi-anual.
Issued by: Studium Afrykanistyczne, Uniwersytet Warszawski. In English or French.
Indexed: Bull. Anal. Pol. Ec. Soc.; Int. Bibl. Eco.; Int. Bibl. Soc. Cul. Anth.

173
Africana Society of Pretoria. YEARBOOK. JAARBOEK. 1– , 1975– . Pretoria. Annual.
In Afrikaans or English.

Africana Vereniging van Pretoria
See Africana Society of Pretoria

174
AFRIKA—RECHT & WIRTSCHAFT. 1– , 1980– . Wiesbaden, Intrapress. Quarterly.
Issued by: Deutsch–Südafrikanische Juristen Vereinigung e.V. In English or German.
Continues: *Afrika-Recht* (1976–79)

175
AFRIKA SPECTRUM. 1– , 1966– . Hamburg, Vertrieb Afrika-Verlag. Three no. a year.
Issued by: Deutsches Institut für Afrika-Forschung, and Deutsches Übersee-Institut, Hamburg. In German.
Indexed: Ind. Bibl. Eco.; PAIS; PAISFL.

176
AFRIKA UND ÜBERSEE; SPRACHEN, KULTUREN. v.1– , Oct. 7, 1910– . Berlin, D. Reimer. Irreg., 1910–23; four no. a year.
In German or English. Publication suspended Oct. 1944–Feb. 1949, July 1950–Feb. 1952. Title varies: 1910–Jan. 1920, *Zeitschrift für kolonial Sprachen*; Mar. 1920–June 1950, *Zeitschrift für Eingeborenen Sprachen*.
Indexed: Abst. Anth.; Int. Bibl. Soc. Cul. Anth.

177
AFRIKANO-AZIATSKI PROBLEMI. 1– , 1970– . Sofiia, Izd-vo na Bulgarskata Akademiia na Naukite. Irreg.
Issued by: Tsentur za Aziia i Afrika, Bulgarska Akademiia na Naukite. In Bulgarian; summaries in English and Russian. Tables of contents also in English and Russian.

AFRIKANSKIĬ ETNOGRAFICHESKIĬ SBORNIK
See Akademiia Nauk SSSR. Institut Etnografii. TRUDY. n. ser.

178
L'AFRIQUE CONTEMPORAINE; DOCUMENTS D'AFRIQUE NOIRE ET DE MADAGASCAR. 1962– . Paris. Bimonthly.
Issued by: Centre d'Études et de Documentation sur l'Afrique et l'Outre-Mer. In French.
Indexed: Abst. Anth.; Bull. Sig. Soc. Eth.; Int. Bibl. Pol. Sc.; Int. Bibl. Soc. Cul. Anth.; Peace Res. Abst. J.

AFRIQUE ET DÉVELOPPEMENT
See AFRICA DEVELOPMENT

179
AFRIQUE ET L'ASIE. no.1–99, 1949–1982. Paris, Peyronet. Quarterly.
Issued by: Centre des Hautes Études sur l'Afrique et l'Asie Modernes in cooperation with Anciens du C.H.E.A.M. In French.
Continued by: *Afrique et l'Asie Modernes*.
Indexed: Bull. Anal. Pol. Ec. Soc.; Int. Bibl. Pol. Sc.; Int. Bibl. Soc. Cul. Anth.; Int. Pol. Sc. Abst.; PAISFL.

180
AFRIQUE INDUSTRIE. no.1–43, Oct. 1970–Nov. 1972. Paris, Ediafric. Frequency varies.
In French.
Continued by: *Afrique Industrie Infrastructures*.

181
AFRIQUE INDUSTRIE; AI. v.12(no.240)– , Oct. 15, 1981– . Paris, Ediafric. Semimonthly.
In French.
Continues: *Afrique Industrie Infrastructures*.
Indexed: PAISFL.

182
AFRIQUE INDUSTRIE INFRASTRUCTURES. no.44–v.11(no.239), Dec. 1972–Sep. 1981. Paris, Ediafric. Monthly.
In French.
Continues: *Afrique Industrie*. Continued by: *Afrique Industrie; AI*
Indexed: Bull. Pol. Ec. Soc.; PAISFL.

183
AFRIQUE NOIRE POLITIQUE ET L'ÉCONOMIQUE. 1st ed.– , 1977– . Paris, Ediafric—La Documentation Africaine. Annual (irreg.)
In French. Occasionally accompanied by supplements called "Numéro spécial du Bulletin d'Afrique Noire". Processed.

184
AFRO-AMERICAN CULTURE AND SOCIETY. v.1– , 1979– . Los Angeles, Calif. Irreg.
Issued by: Center for Afro-American Studies, University of California at Los Angeles (UCLA Latin American Center Publications)

185
AFRO-AMERICAN STUDIES. v.1–3, May 1970–1975. London, Gordon and Breach. Bimonthly.
Superseded by: *Ethnic Groups*.
Indexed: Psych. Abst.

186
AFRO-ASIA. no.1– , Dec. 1965– . Salvador. Three no. a year.
Issued by: Centro de Estudos Afro-Orientais, Universidade Federal de Bahia. In Portuguese.

187
AFRO-ASIAN AFFAIRS. no.1–83, 1975–1979. London, Afro-Asian Publications Ltd.
Continued by: *Arab–Asian Affairs*.

188
AFRO-ASIAN AND WORLD AFFAIRS. v.1– , Mar. 1964– . New Delhi. Quarterly.
Issued by: Institute of Afro-Asian and World Affairs.

189
AFRO-ASIAN ECONOMIC REVIEW. 1959– . Cairo. Monthly.
Issued by: Afro-Asian Organization for Economic Cooperation.

190
AFRYKA, AZJA, AMERYKA ŁACIŃSKA; STUDIA I MATERIAŁY. no.1/2(58/59)– , 1980– . Warszawa, Wydawnictwo Uniwersytetu Warszawskiego. Irreg.

Issued by: Instytut Krajów Rozwijających sie Uniwersytet Warszawski. In Polish; summaries in English or French. Tables of contents also in English and French. Processed.

Continues: *Przegląd Informacji o Afryce* (no.1–57, 1965–79)

191
AFURIKA KENKYŪ. JOURNAL OF AFRICAN STUDIES. 1964– . Tokyo. Annual, 1964–66; semi-annual.
Issued by: Nihon Afurika Gakkai.
Indexed: Int. Bibl. Soc. Cul. Anth.

192
AGEING AND SOCIETY. v.1– , Mar. 1981– . Cambridge, New York, Cambridge University Press. Three no. a year.
Issued by: The Centre for Policy on Ageing, and the British Society of Gerontology.

193
AGEING INTERNATIONAL. v.1– , winter 1973/74– . Washington, D.C. Quarterly.
Issued by: International Federation on Ageing.

AGENDA ITEMS
See United Nations. Dag Hammarskjöld Library. INDEX TO PROCEEDINGS OF THE ECONOMIC AND SOCIAL COUNCIL

194
AGGIORNAMENTI SOCIALI. 1– , 1950– . Milano. Monthly.
Issued by: Centro di Studi Sociali. In Italian.
Indexes: Vols. 1950–69.
Indexed: Bull. Anal. Pol. Ec. Soc.; Bull. Sig. Soc. Eth.; Int. Bibl. Eco.; Int. Bibl. Pol. Sc.; Int. Bibl. Soc.; Int. Pol. Sc. Abst.

195
AGING AND WORK. v.1– , winter 1978– . Washington, D.C. Quarterly.
Issued by: National Council on the Aging.

196
AGORA. v.1– , Apr. 1980– . Potsdam, N.Y.
Issued by: College at Potsdam, State University of New York. Subtitle reads: "Journal of the humanities and the social sciences".

197
Agrarsoziale Gesellschaft. MATERIALSAMMLUNG. no.1– , 1954– . Göttingen. Irreg.
In German.

198
AGRICULTURAL ECONOMICS RESEARCH. v.1–39, no. 1, winter 1987, Jan. 1949– . Washington, D.C. Quarterly.
Issued by: U.S. Bureau of Agricultural Economics, 1949–Oct. 1953; Agricultural Marketing Service (with the Agricultural Research Service), 1954, and U.S. Department of Agricultural Economics, 1955– .
Indexed: Int. Bibl. Eco.; Int. Lab. Doc.; PAIS.

199
AGRICULTURAL FINANCE REVIEW. v.1– , May 1938– . Washington, D.C. Semi-annual, 1938–41; four no. a year.
Issued by: 1938–52, Bureau of Agricultural Economics; 1953–55, Agricultural Research Service; Economics, Statistics and Cooperative Service, U.S. Department of Agriculture.

200
AGRICULTURAL HISTORY. v.1– , June 1927– . Chicago, Ill., Baltimore, Md. and Washington, D.C. Semi-annual, 1927; quarterly.

201
AGRICULTURAL HISTORY REVIEW. v.1– , 1953– . London. Two no. a year.
Supplements accompany some issues.
Indexed: His. Abst.

202
AGRICULTURE AND HUMAN VALUES. v.1– , winter 1984– . Gainesville, Fla. Quarterly.
Issued by: Humanities and Agriculture Program, Center for Applied Philosophy and Ethics in the Professions, University of Florida.

AIAS INFORMATIONEN
See ANGEWANDTE SOZIALFORSCHUNG

203
Aichi Gakukei Daigaku, Okazaki. KENKYŪ HOKŌKU; SHAKAI KAGAKU. v.7–15, 1953–1966. Okazaki. Annual.
In Japanese; some articles in English; summaries in English. Other title: *Bulletin of the Aichi Gakukei University; Social Science*. Vols. 1–6 never published.
Continued by a publication of the same title under the new university's name.

204
Aichi Gakukei Daigaku, Okazaki. KENKYŪ HOKŌKU; SHAKAI KAGAKU. v.16–18, 1967–1971. Okazaki. Annual.
In Japanese; summaries in English. Vols. 16–18 have added title: *Bulletin of the Aichi University of Education; Social Science*.
Continues publication of the same title issued by the university under its earlier name.

205
AJIA AFURIKA GENGO BUNKA KENKYŪ. 1968– . Tokyo. Annual, 1968–76; two no. a year.
Issued by: Gaikokugo Daigaku. In Japanese; some articles and summaries in English. Other title: *Journal of Asian and African Studies.*

206
AJIA BUNKA KENKYŪ. ASIAN CULTURAL STUDIES. 1– , Oct. 1958– . Mitaka. Irreg.
Issued by: Kokusai Kirisutokyo Daigaku. In English or Japanese. No.2 issued as the university's *Publication*, 3-A. Title varies: no.1, Oct. 1958, *Ajia Bunka Kenkyū Ronso.*

AJIA BUNKA KENKYŪ RONSO
See AJIA BUNKA KENKYŪ.

207
AJIA KEIZAI. v.1– , May 1960– . Tokyo. Bimonthly.
Issued by: Ajia Keizai Kenkyūjo. In Japanese. Tables of contents also in English. Other title: *Monthly Journal of Institute of Developing Economies.*
Indexed: His. Abst.; Int. Bibl. Soc.; Int. Bibl. Soc. Cul. Anth.

208
Akademia de Shtiin͡tse a RSS Moldovenest. BULETINUL. IZVESTII͡A. SERII͡A OBSHCHESTVENNYKH NAUK. 1968– . Kishenev, Redakt͡sionno-izdavatel'skiĭ Otdel. Three no. a year.
In Russian.
Continues, in part: Akademia de Shtiin͡tse a RSS Moldovenest. *Buletinul. Izvestii͡a.*

209
Akademie der Wissenschaften, Berlin. Institut für Deutsche Volkskunde. VERÖFFENTLICHUNGEN. v.1– , 1953– . Berlin. Irreg.
In German. Early volumes issued under the name of Kommission für Volkskunde.

210
Akademie der Wissenschaften, Berlin. Klasse für Gesellwissenschaften. ABHANDLUNGEN. 1950–1953. Berlin, Akademie-Verlag. Irreg.
In German. Monograph series.
Continued by: Akademie der Wissenschaften, Berlin. Klasse für Philosophie, Geschichte, Staats-, Reichts- und Wirtschaftswissenschaften. *Abhandlungen.*

211
Akademie der Wissenschaften, Berlin. Philosophisch-Historische Klasse. ABHANDLUNGEN. v.1–37, 1908–1949. Berlin.
In German. Vols for 1908–18 were issued by the academy under its earlier name: Königlich Preussische Akademie der Wissenschaften; 1919–1944 under Preussische Akademie der Wissenschaften; 1945–49 by Deutsche Akademie der Wissenschaften. Monograph series.

212
Akademie der Wissenschaften, Wien. ARCHIV FÜR ÖSTERREICHISCHE GESCHICHTE. 1848– . Wien, Verlag der Österreichischen Akademie der Wissenschaften.
In German.

213
Akademie der Wissenschaften, Wien. Ethnologische Kommission. VERÖFFENTLICHUNGEN. no.1– , 1966– . Wien, H. Böhlaus Nachfolger. Irreg.
In German. (Österreichische Akademie der Wissenschaften. Philosophisch-Historische Klasse. *Sitzungsberichte*)

214
Akademie der Wissenschaften, Wien. Kommission für Sozial- und Wirtschaftswissenschaften. VERÖFFENTLICHUNGEN. no.1– , 1973– . Wien, Verlag der Österreichischen Akademie der Wissenschaften. Irreg.
In German. (Österreichische Akademie der Wissenschaften. Philosophisch-Historische Klasse. *Sitzungsberichte*)

215
Akademie der Wissenschaften, Wien. Kommission für Wirtschafts-, Sozial- und Stadtgeschichte. VERÖFFENTLICHUNGEN. 1– , 1973– . Wien. Irreg.
In German. Monograph series.

216
Akademie der Wissenschaften, Wien. Prähistorische Kommission. MITTEILUNGEN. v.1– , 1887– . Wien, Verlag der Österreichischen Akademie der Wissenschaften. Irreg.
In German.

217
Akademie der Wissenschaften der DDR. ABHANDLUNGEN. GESELLWISSENSCHAFTEN. 1– , 1975– . Berlin, Akademie-Verlag. Irreg.
In German.

218
Akademie der Wissenschaften der DDR. JAHRBUCH. 1973– . Berlin, Akademie-Verlag. Annual.

In German. Earlier names of the academy were: Königlich Preussische Akademie der Wissenschaften, 1908–18; Preussische Akademie der Wissenschaften, 1919–44; Deutsche Akademie der Wissenschaften, 1945–49.

219
Akademie der Wissenschaften der DDR. Zentralinstitut für Alte Geschichte und Archäologie. VERÖFFENTLICHUNGEN. v.1– , 1974– . Berlin, Akademie-Verlag. Irreg.
In German. Each volume has also a distinctive title.

220
Akademie der Wissenschaften der DDR. Zentralinstitut für Geschichte. SCHRIFTEN. v.1– , 1957– . Berlin, Akademie-Verlag. Irreg.
In German. Vols. 1–37, 1957–72 issued with the subtitle: "Reihe 1: Allgemeine und Deutsche Geschichte". Monograph series.

221
Akademie der Wissenschaften und der Literatur, Mainz. Geistes- und Sozialwissenschaftliche Klasse. ABHANDLUNGEN. no.1– , 1950– . Wiesbaden, F. Steiner Verlag. Irreg.
In German. Monograph series.

222
Akademie van Wetenschappen, Amsterdam. Sociaal-Wetenschappelijke Informatie- en Dokumentatiecentrum. REGISTER VAN SOCIAAL-WETENSCHAPPELIJKE ONDERZOEK. REGISTER OF SOCIAL SCIENCE RESEARCH IN THE NEDERLANDS. 1964–1974/1975– . Amsterdam. Irreg.
Title varies: *Register van Lopend Onderzoek in de Sociaal Wetenschappen*. In Dutch.

223
Akademie van Wetenschappen, Amsterdam. Sociaal Wetenschappelijke Raad. HANDELINGEN. n. ser. no.1– , Feb. 1965– . Amsterdam, Nord-Hollandische Uitgivers Maatschappij. Irreg.
In Dutch. Monograph series.

224
Akademii͡a Nauk Armi͡anskoĭ SSR. IZVESTII͡A. OBSHCHESTVENNYE NAUKI. 1945–1965. Erivan. Monthly.
In Armenian; occasionally summaries in Russian. Tables of contents in English and Russian.
Continued by its: *Vestnik Obshchestvennykh Nauk*.

225
Akademii͡a Nauk Armi͡anskoĭ SSR. VESTNIK OBSHCHESTVENNYKH NAUK. 1966– . Erivan. Monthly.
In Armenian or Russian.
Continues: Akademii͡a Nauk Armi͡anskoĭ SSR. *Izvestii͡a. Obshchestvennye Nauki*.
Indexed: Int. Bibl. Eco.; Int. Bibl. Pol. Sc.; Int. Bibl. Soc.; Int. Bibl. Soc. Cul. Anth.

226
Akademii͡a Nauk Azerbaĭdzhanskoĭ SSR, Baku. IZVESTII͡A. SERII͡A EKONOMIKI. 1– , 1966– . Baku. Four no. a year.
In Russian. Tables of contents and the title also in Azerbaidzhani.

227
Akademii͡a Nauk Azerbaĭdzhanskoĭ SSR, Baku. IZVESTII͡A. SERII͡A ISTORII, FILOSOFII I PRAVA. 1– , 1966– . Baku, Izd-vo Akademii Nauk Azerbaĭdzhanskoĭ SSR. Four no. a year.
In Azerbaidzhani. Title in Azerbaidzhani precedes the title in Russian.
Continues: Akademii͡a's *Izvestii͡a. Serii͡a Obshchestvennykh Nauk*.

228
Akademii͡a Nauk Azerbaĭdzhanskoĭ SSR. SERII͡A OBSHCHESTVENNYKH NAUK. 1958–1965. Baku, Izd-vo Akademii Nauk Azerbaĭdzhanskoĭ SSR. Six no. a year, 1958–60, 1963–65; monthly, 1961–62.
In Azerbaidzhani or Russian; summaries in the other language.
Continued by: Akademii͡a's *Izvestii͡a. Serii͡a Istorii, Filosofii i Prava*.

229
Akademii͡a Nauk Azerbaĭdzhanskoĭ SSR. Baku. Institut Istorii. AZERBAĬDZHANSKIĬ ETNOGRAFICHESKIĬ SBORNIK; ISSLEDOVANII͡A I MATERIALY. no.1– , 1964– . Baku, Izd-vo Akademii Nauk SSR.
In Russian.

Akademii͡a Nauk Estonskoĭ SSR
See Eesti NSV. Teaduste Akademia

230
Akademii͡a Nauk Gruzinskoĭ SSR. Tiflis, Institut Istorii, Arkheologii i Etnografii. MATERIALY PO ARKHEOLOGII GRUZII I KAVKAZA. no.1– , 1955– . Tiflis. Irreg.
In Georgian or Russian; summaries in Russian. Tables of contents also in English.

231
Akademii͡a Nauk Gruzinskoĭ SSR. Otdelenie Obshchestvennykh Nauk. MATSUE. 1964– . Tiflis.
In Georgian or Russian.
Indexed: Int. Bibl. Soc. Cul. Anth.

232
Akademiia Nauk Kazakhskoi SSR.
IZVESTIIA. SERIIA EKONOMIKI, FILOSOFII I PRAVA. no.1–15, 1958–1961. Alma-Ata, Izd-vo Akademii Nauk Kazakhskoi SSR.
In Russian; summaries in Kazakh. Tables of contents also in Kazakh.
Supersedes, in part: Akademiia's *Izvestiia. Seriia Istorii Ekonomiki, Filosofii i Prava*.

233
Akademiia Nauk Kazakhskoi SSR.
IZVESTIIA. SERIIA ISTORII, ARKHEOLOGII I ETNOGRAFII. 1958–1961. Alma-Ata, Izd-vo Akademii.
In Russian; summaries in Kazakh.
Merged with: Akademiia's *Izvestiia. Seriia Filologii i Iskustvodedeniia* to form: Akademiia Nauk Kazakhskoi SSR. *Izvestiia. Seriia Obshchestvennykh Nauk*.

234
Akademiia Nauk Kazakhskoi SSR.
IZVESTIIA. SERIIA ISTORII, EKONOMIKI, FILOSOFII I PRAVA. 1–5, 1954–1957. Alma-Ata, Izd-vo Akademii.
In Kazakh or Russian. No.1 also numbered as no.137 of the Akademiia's *Izvestiia*.
Split into: Akademiia Nauk Kazakhskoi SSR. *Izvestiia. Seriia Ekonomiki, Filosofii i Prava*, and: Akademiia Nauk Kazakhskoi SSR. *Izvestiia. Seriia Istorii, Arkheologii i Etnografii*.

235
Akademiia Nauk Kazakhskoi SSR.
IZVESTIIA. SERIIA OBSHCHESTVENNAIA. 1966–1973. Alma-Ata, Izd-vo Nauka Kazakhskoi SSR. Bimonthly.
Chiefly in Russian; occasionally in Kazakh; summaries in the other language. Tables of contents in Kazakh.
Continues: Akademiia's *Izvestiia. Seriia Obshchestvennykh Nauk*. Continued by: Akademiia's *Izvestiia. Seriia Obshchestvennykh Nauk*.

236
Akademiia Nauk Kazakhskoi SSR.
IZVESTIIA. SERIIA OBSHCHESTVENNYKH NAUK. 1963–1965. Alma-Ata, Izd-vo Nauka Kazakhskoi SSR. Bimonthly.
Chiefly in Russian; occasionally articles in Kazakh; summaries in the other language. Tables of contents also in Kazakh.
Formed by the merger of: Akademiia's *Izvestiia. Seriia Filologii i Iskustvovedeniia*, and: *Izvestiia. Seriia Istorii, Arkheologii i Etnografii*.
Continued by: Akademiia Nauk Kazakhskoi SSR. *Izvestiia. Seriia Obshchestvennaia*.

237
Akademiia Nauk Kazakhskoi SSR.
IZVESTIIA. SERIIA OBSHCHESTVENNYKH NAUK. 1974– . Alma-Ata, Izd-vo Nauka Kazakhskoi SSR.
Chiefly in Russian; occasionally articles in Kazakh; summaries in the other language.
Continues: Akademiia Nauk Kazakhskoi SSR. *Izvestiia. Seriia Obshchestvennaia*.

Akademiia Latviiskoi SSR
See Latvijas Padomju Socialistikas Republikas Zinatnu Akademija

Akademiia Nauk Litovskoi SSR
See Lietuvos TSR. Mokslų Akademija, Vilna

Akademiia Nauk Moldavskoi SSR
See Akademia de Șiintse a RSS Moldovenest

238
Akademiia Nauk SSSR. IZVESTIIA. SERIIA; OTDELENIE OBSHCHESTVENNYKH NAUK. 1926–1935; n. ser. 1936–1938. Moskva. Ten no. a year, 1928–35; monthly (irreg.)
In Russian. Title varies: 1928–30, *Izvestiia. Seriia; Otdelenie Obshchestvennykh Nauk*.
Supersedes, in part: *Izvestiia: V Seriia*.

239
Akademiia Nauk SSSR. IZVESTIIA. SERIIA EKONOMICHESKAIA. 1970– . Moskva, Nauka. Bimonthly.
In Russian.
Indexed: Int. Bibl. Eco.; Int. Bibl. Soc. Cul. Anth.

240
Akademiia Nauk SSSR. Institut Etnografii. TRUDY. n. ser. 1947– . Moskva. Irreg.
In Russian. Includes subseries: *Afrikanskii Etnograficheskii Sbornik*; *Antropologicheskii Sbornik*; *Kavkazskii Etnograficheskii Sbornik*; *Ocherki Istorii Russkoi Etnografii*; *Sibirskii Etnograficheskii Sbornik*; and *Vostochnoi Aziatskii Etnograficheskii Sbornik*. Other title: *Travaux de l'Institut d'Ethnographie*.

241
Akademiia Nauk SSSR. Irkutskii Filial. TRUDY. OBSHCHESTVENNYE NAUKI. 1– , 1958– . Irkutsk. Irreg.
In Russian.

242
Akademiia Nauk SSSR. Sibirskoe Otdelenie. IZVESTIIA. SERIIA EKONOMIKI I PRIKLADNOI SOTSIOLOGII. no.1– , Jan. 1984– . Novosibirsk, Izd-vo Sibirskogo Otdeleniia AN SSSR. Three no. a year.

In Russian. Tables of contents also in English.
Supersedes, in part: Akademiia Nauk SSSR. Sibirskoe Otdelenie. *Izvestiia. Seriia Obshchestvennykh Nauk.*

243
Akademiia Nauk SSSR. Sibirskoe Otdelenie. IZVESTIIA. SERIIA OBSHCHESTVENNYKH NAUK. 1963–1983. Novosibirsk, Izd-vo Sibirskogo Otdeleniia AN SSSR. Three no. a year.
Supersedes, in part: Akademiia Nauk SSSR. Sibirskoe Otdelenie. *Izvestiia*. Continued by: Akademiia Nauk SSSR, Sibirskoe Otdelenie. *Izvestiia. Seriia Istorii, Filologii i Filosofii*, and: *Izvestiia. Seriia Ekonomiki i Prikladnoĭ Sotsiologii.*
Indexed: Int. Bibl. Eco.; Int. Bibl. Soc. Cul. Anth.; LLBA.

244
Akademiia Nauk SSSR. Muzeĭ Antropologii i Etnografii. SBORNIK MUZEIA. 1900– . Leningrad.
In Russian. Other title: *Publications du Musée d'Anthropologie et d'Ethnographie*. Title varies: *Sbornik Muzeia Antropologii i Etnografii pri Imperatorskoĭ Akademii Nauk*; *Sbornik Muzeia i Etnografii imeni Petra Velikogo pri Akademii Nauk Soiuza Sovetskikh Sotsialisticheskikh Respublik.*

Akademiia Nauk SSSR. Turkmenskiĭ Filial
See Akademiia Nauk Turkmenskoĭ SSR

245
Akademiia Nauk Tadzhikskoĭ SSR, Dushanbe. Otdel Ekonomiki. TRUDY. v.3– , 1960– . Dushanbe. Annual.
In Russian.

246
Akademiia Nauk Turkmenskoĭ SSR. IZVESTIIA. SERIIA OBSHCHESTVENNYKH NAUK. 1952?– , Ashabad. Six no. a year.
In Russian.
Continues: Akademiia Nauk SSSR. Turkmenskiĭ Filial. *Izvestiia.*
Indexed: Bull. Sig. Soc. Eth.; Int. Bibl. Soc. Cul. Anth.

247
Akademiia Navuk Belarusskoĭ SSR. VESTSI. SERYIA HRAMADSKIKH NAVUK. 1956– . Minsk. Four no. a year, 1956–76; six no. a year.
In White Russian or Russian; summaries in Russian. Other title: *Izvestiia. Seriia obshchestvennykh nauk.*
Continues, in part: the Akademiia's *Vestsi.*

248
Akademiia Navuk Belarusskoi SSR. Institut Mastatvaznavstva, Fol'kloru i Etnografiĭ. PRATSY. SERYIA ETNOGRAFII I FOL'KLORU. no.1– , 1958– . Minsk, Vyd-vo Akademii Navuk BSSR.
In White Russian.

249
Akademiia za Obshchestveni Nauki i Sotsialno Upravlenie pri TsK NH BKR. NAUCHNI TRUDOVE. 44– , 1970– . Sofiia, Izd-vo na BKP.
In Bulgarian; summaries chiefly in Russian, occasionally in English or French. Processed.

Akademija Nauka i Umetnosti
See Srpska Akademija Nauka i Umetnosti

250
Akademija Nauka i Umjetnosti Bosne i Hercegovine. Centar za Balkanoloska Ispitivanja. GODISNJAK. v.1– , 1965– . Sarajevo.
In Serbo-Croatian.

251
Akademija Nauka i Umjetnosti Bosne i Hercegovine. Odeljenie Društvenih Nauka. [RADOVI]. v.1– , 19??– . Sarajevo. Irreg.
In Serbo-Croatian; summaries in English, French, or German. Subseries of: Akademija Nauka i Umjetnosti Bosne i Hercegovine. [*Radovi*]

252
AKADEMIKA. 1– , July 1972– . Kuala Lumpur. Semi-annual.
Issued by: Jawatankuasa Penerbitan Universiti Kebangsaan. In English or Malay. Other title: *Journal of Humanities and Social Sciences.*

AKTEN
See International Congress of Americanists. PROCEEDINGS

253
ALASKA REVIEW OF SOCIAL AND ECONOMIC CONDITIONS. v.14, no.3– , Dec. 1977– . Fairbanks, Alaska.
Issued by: Institute of Social and Economic Research, University of Alaska.
Continues: *Alaska Review of Business and Economic Conditions.*

AL-ALAM AL-'ARABI; AL MAGRIB WA-AL-MASHRIQ
See MAGHREB MACHREK

254
ÁLLAM-ÉS IGAZGATÁS. 1– , May 1949– . Budapest. Monthly.
In Hungarian. Title varies: 1949–July/Aug. 1951, *Állam-és Kozigazgatas.*

Indexed: Int. Bibl. Pol. Sc.; Int. Bibl. Soc. Cul. Anth.

255
ÁLLAM-ÉS JOGTUDOMÁNYI. POLITICAL SCIENCE AND JURISPRUDENCE. v.1– , 1957– . Budapest, Akadémiai Kiadó. Four no. a year.
Issued by: Alames Jogtudomány Intézet, Magyar Tudományos Akadémia. In Hungarian. Title varies: 1957–61, *Az Állam-és Jogtudományi Intézet Értesitöje*.
Indexed: Int. Bibl. Eco.; Int. Bibl. Pol. Sc.

AZ ÁLLAM-ÉS JOGTUDOMÁNYI INTÉZET ÉRTESTITÖJE
See ÁLLAM-ÉS JOGTUDOMÁNYI

ÁLLAM-ÉS KOZIGAZGATÁS
See ALLAM-ES IGAZGATAS

256
ALLEMAGNES D'AUJOURD'HUI. n. ser. Dec. 1952/Jan. 1953– . Paris. Bimonthly.
Issued by: Association pour la Connaissance de l'Allemagne Aujourd'hui. In French. Subtitle reads: "Revue sur les deux Allemagnes".
Formed by the union of: *Allemagne Aujourd'hui*, and: *Réalités Allemandes*.

257
ALLENSBACHER JAHRBUCH DER DEMOSKOPIE. 1947/55–1974/76. Wien, Verlag F. Molden. Irreg.
Issued by: Institut für Demoskopie. In German.
Continues: *Jahrbuch der Öffentlichen Meinung*.

258
ALLIED HEALTH AND BEHAVIORAL SCIENCES. v.1–3, no.1, 1978–1980. Milwaukee, Wis. Quarterly.
Issued by: School of Allied Health Professions, University of Wisconsin-Milwaukee.

ALMANAC OF CHINA'S ECONOMY
See CHUNG-KUO CHING CHI NIEN CHIEN

259
ALMANACH DE LA QUESTION SOCIALE. REVUE ANNUELLE DU SOCIALISME INTERNATIONAL. 1891– . Paris.
In French.

260
ALTERNATIVA LATINOAMERICANA. AL. 1– , Jan./Feb. 1983– . Mendoza. Quarterly.
Issued by: Secretaría de Estudios de APE. In Spanish.

261
ALTERNATIVAS. 1– , Sept./Dec. 1983– . Santiago, Chile.
Issued by: Centro de Estudios de la Realidad Contemporánea, Academia de Humanismo Cristiano. In Spanish. Occasionally additional issues called "Número Special" are published.

262
ALTERNATIVE LIFESTYLES. v.1– , Feb. 1978– . New York, Human Sciences Press, later Beverly Hills, Calif., Sage Publications. Quarterly.
Issued by: Department of Sociology and Anthropology, University of New Hampshire. Subtitle reads: "Changing patterns in marriage, family & intimacy".

263
ALTERNATIVE PRESS DIGEST. no.1– , 1974– . London. Annual.

264
ALTERNATIVE PRESS INDEX. v.1, no.1/2– , July/Dec. 1969– . Northfield, Minn., subsequently Baltimore, Md. Quarterly.
Issued by: Radical Research Center, Carleton University, subsequently by: Alternative Press Center.
Superseded by: *The British Alternative Press Index*.

265
ALTERNATIVES. 1971– , Peterborough, Canada. Quarterly.
Issued by: Department of Politics, Trent University (Ontario)

266
ALTERNATIVES. v.1– , 1975– . New Delhi. Quarterly.
Issued by: Centre for the Study of Developing Societies, Delhi, Institute of World Order, and World Policy Institute. Published also in American edition (v.8– , 1982–)
Indexed: Int. Pol. Sc. Abst.

267
ALTERNATIVES. v.8– , summer 1982– . New York. Quarterly.
Issued by: Institute of World Order, 1982–winter 1983; subsequently by the World Policy Institute.
Indexed: Bull. Anal. Pol. Ec. Soc.; Int. Bibl. Eco.; Int. Bibl. Pol. Sc.; Int. Bibl. Cul. Anth.; PAIS.

268
ALTERNATIVES IN PRINT. 1971– . New York, Neal-Schuman Pub. Annual.
Issued by: Task Force on Alternatives in Print, Social Responsibilities Round Table, American Library Association. Published also in London by: Mansell Pub. Ltd.

269
ALTORIENTALISCHE FORSCHUNGEN. 1– , 1974– . Berlin, Akademie-Verlag. Annual, 1974–82, two no. a year.
In English, German, Italian, or Russian. (Schriften zur Geschichte und Kultur des Alten Orients)

ALUMNUS
See THE EDUCATIONAL TRENDS

270
AMBIO. v.1– , Feb. 1972– . Oxford, Pergamon Press. Quarterly.
Issued by: Royal Swedish Academy of Science and sponsored by a number of Swedish institutions.
Indexed: Sage Urb. Stu. Abst.

271
AMÉNAGEMENT DU TERRITOIRE ET DÉVELOPPEMENT RÉGIONAL. [1]–6, 1965/66–1973. Grenoble. Annual.
Issued by: Institut d'Études Politiques, Université de Grenoble, 1965/66–1970/71; Centre d'Étude et de Recherche sur l'Administration Économique et l'Aménagement du Territoire (C.E.R.A.T.) of the Institut d'Études Politiques, Université de Grenoble. In French.
Continued by: *Annuaire de l'Aménagement du Territoire.*
Indexed: Bull. Anal. Pol. Ec. Soc.; Int. Bibl. Eco.; Int. Bibl. Soc.; Int. Pol. Sc. Abst.

272
AMERASIA JOURNAL. v.1– , Mar. 1971– . Los Angeles, Calif. Semi-annual.
Issued by: Asian American Studies Center, University of California at Los Angeles.
Indexed: His. Abst.; Sage Urb. Stu. Abst.

273
AMERICA AND THE WORLD. 1978– . New York, Pergamon Press. Annual.

274
AMERICA EN CIFRAS. 1960– . Washington, D.C. Irreg.
Issued by: Inter-American Statistical Institute, Department of Statistics, Pan American Union. Subtitle reads: "Situación demográfica, social, cultural".
In Spanish.

275
AMERICA: HISTORY AND LIFE. v.1–10, 1964–1973. Santa Barbara, Calif., Clio Press.
Continued by a publication of the same title divided into four parts.
Indexes: Vols. 1–5, 1964–69, 1v.; v.6–10, 1969–73, 1v.

276
AMERICA: HISTORY AND LIFE. v.11– , 1974– . Santa Barbara, Calif., Clio Press.
Issued by: American Bibliographic Center. Consists of four parts called: *Part A. Article Abstracts and Citations*, three no. a year; *Part B. Index to Book Reviews*, two no. a year; *Part C. American History Bibliography (Books, Articles and Dissertation)*, annual; *Part D. Annual Index*, annual.
Continues: *America: History and Life.*

277
AMÉRICA INDÍGENA. v.1– , Oct. 1941– . Mexico, D.F. Quarterly.
Issued by: Instituto Indigenista Interamericano. In Spanish; beginning with v.22 (1962) in English or Spanish; summaries in English. Includes annual supplement: *Boletín Indigenista.*
Indexed: Abst. Anth.; Bull. Anal. Pol. Ec. Soc.; Bull. Sig. Soc. Eth.; His. Abst.; Int. Bibl. Soc. Cul. Anth.; Int. Lab. Doc.; Psych. Abst.; Soc. Abst.; Wom. Stu. Abst.

278
AMÉRICA LATINA. v.1– , 1958– . Rio de Janeiro. Four no. a year.
Issued by: Centro Latino-Americano de Pesquisas em Ciências Sociais, 1958–61, subsequently by: Centro Latino-Americano de Investigaciones em Ciências Sociais, and Centro Latinoamericano em Ciências Sociais. In English, Portuguese, or Spanish. Some nos. are combined. Title varies: v.1–41, 1958–61, *Boletim.*
Indexed: Bull. Anal. Pol. Ec. Soc.; Pop. Ind.

279
AMERICA LATINA. 1970– . Moskva. Monthly.
Edition in English of: *Latinskaīa Amerika.*

280
AMÉRICA LATINA; REVISTA TEÓRICA-POLÍTICA. 1– , 1968– . Montevideo, Corporación Gráfica.
In Spanish.
Indexed: ABC POL SCI; Bull. Sig. Soc. Eth.; His. Abst.

281
American Academy of Political and Social Science. ANNALS. v.1– , July 1890– . Philadelphia, Pa. Two vols. a year.
Indexes: Vols. 1–63, July 1890–Jan. 1916, as a supplement to the Mar. 1916 issue, 1v.; v.64–96, Mar. 1916–July 1921, 1v.; v.97–126, Sept. 1921–July 1926, 1v.; v.127–152, 1926–Nov. 1930, 1v. issued as v. 159, pt. 2; v.153–182, 1931–35, 1v.; v.183–212, 1936–40, 1v.; v.213–242, 1941–45, 1v.; v.303–332, 1956–60, 1v.

282
American Academy of Political and Social Science. MONOGRAPH. 1– , 1962– . Philadelphia, Pa. Irreg.
Monograph series.

283
American Anthropological Association. BULLETIN. v.1– , Apr. 1953– . Menasha, Wis. Quarterly.
Supersedes: the association's *News Bulletin*.
Index to this publication is listed under *American Anthropologist*.

284
American Anthropological Association. MEMOIRS. 1906–1919, 1923. Lancaster, Pa., subsequently Washington, D.C.

285
AMERICAN ANTHROPOLOGIST. v.1–11, 1888–Nov. 1898; n. ser. v.1– , 1899– . Washington, D.C. Bimonthly.
Indexes: 1888–1928 issued by: American Anthropological Association, as *General Index*. It includes also indexes to: *Current Anthropological Literature* and the association's *Memoirs*. Issued as: v.32, no.3, pt. 2.
Indexed: ABC POL SCI; Abst. Anth.; Bull. Anal. Pol. Ec. Soc.; Bull. Sig. Soc. Eth.; His. Abst.; Hum. Res. Abst.; LLBA; Peace Res. Abst. J.; Psych. Abst.; Soc. Abst.; SSCI.

286
AMERICAN ANTIQUITY. v.1– , July 1935– . Menasha, Wis. Quarterly.
Issued by: Society for American Archaeology.
Indexes: Vols. 1–30, 1935–65, 1v.
Indexed: Abst. Anth.; Bull. Sig. Soc. Eth.; His. Abst.; Int. Bibl. Soc. Cul. Anth.

287
AMERICAN APPEAL. v.1–18, July 15, 1920–Nov. 26, 1927. Chicago, Ill. Weekly.
Issued by: Socialist Party of America.

288
AMERICAN–ARAB AFFAIRS. no.1– , summer 1982– . Washington, D.C. Quarterly.
Issued by: American–Arab Affairs Council.
Indexed: PAIS.

289
THE AMERICAN BEHAVIORAL SCIENTIST. Sept. 1960– . New York, subsequently Beverly Hills, Calif., Sage Publications. Monthly except July-Aug., 1960–67; bimonthly.
Title varies: 1960–64, *PROD*. Other title: *ABS American Behavioral Scientist*.
Indexed: ABC POL SCI; Abst. Anth.; Bull. Sig. Soc. Eth.; Eco. Abst.; Hum. Res. Abst.; Int. Bibl. Eco.; Int. Bibl. Pol. Sc.; Ind. Per. Art. Law; Int. Pol. Sc. Abst.; Peace Res. Abst. J.; Psych. Abst.; Soc. Sc. Hum. Ind.; SSCI; PAIS; Wom. Stu. Abst.

290
THE AMERICAN BIBLIOGRAPHY OF RUSSIAN AND EAST EUROPEAN STUDIES. 1957– . Columbus, Ohio; 1978– . Stanford, Calif. Annual; occasionally biennial.
Prepared at the Library of Congress for the American Association for the Advancement of Slavic Studies, Ohio State University, with the support of The National Council for Soviet and East European Research.
Title varies: 1960–67, *American Bibliography of Slavic and Eastern European Studies*.

THE AMERICAN CATHOLIC SOCIOLOGICAL REVIEW
See SOCIOLOGICAL ANALYSIS

291
THE AMERICAN CITY & COUNTY. v.90, no.9– , Sept. 1979– . Pittsfield, Mass., Morgan-Grampian Pub. Co. Monthly.
Continues: *The American City* (Sept. 1909–Aug. 1975)
Indexed: Urb. Aff. Abst.

292
THE AMERICAN COUNTY. v.35– , Jan. 1970– . Washington, D.C. Monthly.
Issued by: National Association of Counties.
Continues: *American County Government* (v.31–34, 1966–69)

293
AMERICAN DEMOGRAPHICS. v.1– , Jan. 1979– . Albany, N.Y., American Demographics, Inc. Monthly (except July/Aug. and Nov./Dec. when bimonthly).
Indexed: PAIS; Pop. Ind.

294
AMERICAN ECONOMIC REVIEW. 1886–1910. Nashville, Tenn. Bimonthly.
Issued by: American Economic Association. Includes "Papers and Proceedings of the Annual Meeting of the AEA".
Continued, in part, by: *The American Economic Review*.
Indexes: 1886–1910, in v.7, no.4 supplement titled: "Index to the Publications of the American Economic Association in the *American Economic Review*".

295
THE AMERICAN ECONOMIC REVIEW. v.1– , Mar. 1911– . Princeton, N.J. Five no. a year and one no. of *Proceedings of the Annual Meeting*.
Issued by: American Economic Association. Includes "Survey of National Economic Policy Issues and Policy Research", "Directory" and occasionally other supplements. Some nos. are thematic.

Indexed: ABC POL SCI; Abst. Soc. Work; Bull. Anal. Pol. Ec. Soc.; Eco. Abst.; His. Abst.; Hum. Res. Abst.; Ind. Per. Art. Law; Int. Bibl. Eco.; Int. Bibl. Pol. Sc.; Int. Bibl. Soc.; PAIS; Pop. Ind.; Psych. Abst.; SSCI; Urb. Aff. Abst.; Wom. Stu. Abst.

296
AMERICAN ECONOMIC SECURITY. Jan. 1944– . Washington, D.C. Monthly (irreg.)
Issued by: Chamber of Commerce of the United States.

297
THE AMERICAN ECONOMIST. v.1–81, no.7, 1887–July 1930. New York, American Tariff League. Weekly, 1887–July 2, 1926; monthly.
Title varies: 1887–June 1891, *American Economist and Tariff League Bulletin*; July 1891–July 1926, *American Economist*; 1927–July 1930, *The Tariff Review*.

298
THE AMERICAN ECONOMIST. v.1– , Feb. 1944– . Chicago, Ill. Monthly.
Issued by: Institute of American Economics.
Indexed: Bull. Anal. Pol. Ec. Soc.; Int. Bibl. Eco.; Int. Bibl. Pol. Sc.; Int. Bibl. Soc.; PAIS; SSCI.

299
THE AMERICAN ECONOMIST. v.1– , 1957– . Los Angeles, Calif. Semi-annual.
Issued by: Omicron Delta Epsilon Honor Society in Economics and the Department of Economics, University of Southern California. Includes some dissertation abstracts.
Indexed: Int. Bibl. Eco.; PAIS.

AMERICAN ECONOMIST AND TARIFF LEAGUE BULLETIN
See AMERICAN ECONOMIST (New York)

300
AMERICAN EDUCATION. v.1– , Jan. 1965– . Washington, D.C. Ten no. a year.
Issued by: U.S. Department of Health, Education and Welfare, Office of Education, 1965–Apr. 1980; Department of Education, May 1980– . (Sup. Docs. no.ED1.10)
Supersedes: *Higher Education* (1945–64), and *School Life* (1918–64)
Indexed: His. Abst.; PHRA; Wom. Stu. Abst.

301
AMERICAN EDUCATIONAL RESEARCH JOURNAL. v.1– , Jan. 1964– . Washington, D.C. Quarterly.
Issued by: American Education Association.
Indexed: LLBA; Psych. Abst.

302
American Enterprise Institute for Public Policy Research. AEI FORUM. 1– , 1977– . Washington, D.C. Irreg.
Monograph series.

303
American Ethnological Society. BULLETIN OF PROCEEDINGS. Sept. 1860–Jan./Mar. 1863. New York. Monthly (Irreg.)
Title varies: 1860–61, *Bulletin*.
Supersedes: *Bulletin* (Jan. 1859–May 1960)

304
American Ethnological Society. MONOGRAPHS. 1– , 1940– . St. Paul, Minn., West Pub. Co. Irreg.
Monograph series.

305
American Ethnological Society. PUBLICATIONS. 1970–1917. Leiden, E.J. Brill. Irreg.
Monograph series.

306
AMERICAN ETHNOLOGIST. v.1– , Feb. 1974– . Washington, D.C. Quarterly.
Issued by: American Anthropological Association.
Indexed: Bull. Sig. Soc. Eth.; Int. Bibl. Soc. Cul. Anth.; SSCI.

AMERICAN FOREIGN POLICY; CURRENT DOCUMENTS
See United States. Department of State. Historical Division. AMERICAN FOREIGN POLICY: CURRENT DOCUMENTS. 1981– .

AMERICAN FOREIGN POLICY; CURRENT DOCUMENTS
See United States. Department of State. Historical Office. AMERICAN FOREIGN POLICY; CURRENT DOCUMENTS. 1956–1980.

307
AMERICAN FOREIGN RELATIONS—A DOCUMENTARY RECORD. 1939– . New York, New York University Press. Annual.
Issued by: Council on Foreign Relations.
Incorporates: *United States in World Affairs*.
Continues: *Documents on American Foreign Relations*.

THE AMERICAN FOREIGN SERVICE JOURNAL
See FOREIGN SERVICE JOURNAL

308
AMERICAN GOVERNMENT ANNUAL. 1958/59–1965/66. New York, Holt, Rinehart & Winston.

309
THE AMERICAN HISTORICAL REVIEW. v.1– , Oct. 1895– . New York. Quarterly.
Issued by: American Historical Association.
Indexes: Vols. 1–10, 1895–July 1905; v.11–20, Oct. 1905–July 1915; v.21–30, Oct. 1915–July 1925; v.31–40, Oct. 1925–July 1935; v.61–70, Oct. 1955–July 1965.
Indexed: His. Abst.; Ind. Per. Art. Law; Peace Res. Abst. J.; SSCI; Wom. Stu. Abst.

310
THE AMERICAN INDIAN. v.1–8, no.2, Nov. 1943–1958. Troy, N.Y. Quarterly.
Issued by: American Association of Indian Affairs.
Supersedes: *Newsletter* of the American Association of Indian Affairs.

311
AMERICAN INDIAN CULTURE AND RESEARCH JOURNAL. v.1– , Sept. 1974– . Los Angeles, Calif. Quarterly.
Issued by: American Indian Culture and Research Center, University of California.
Supersedes: American Indian Culture Center. *Journal.*
Indexed: Bull. Sig. Soc. Eth.; Int. Bibl. Soc. Cul. Anth.

312
AMERICAN INDIAN JOURNAL. Oct. 1975– . Washington, D.C. Monthly.
Issued by: Institute for the Development of Indian Law.
Formed by the union of: *Educational Journal* and *Legislative Review*, both of the Institute for the Development of Indian Law.

313
AMERICAN INDIAN LAW REVIEW. v.1– , winter 1973– . Norman, Okla. Annual.
Issued by: College of Law, University of Oklahoma.

314
AMERICAN INDIAN QUARTERLY. v.1– , spring 1974– . Berkeley, Calif., Southwestern American Indian Society.
Issued by: Native American Studies, University of California at Berkeley.

315
American Institute for Marxist Studies. BIBLIOGRAPHICAL SERIES. no.1–6, 1965–1969. New York. Irreg.
Each no. has a distinctive title.

316
American Institute for Marxist Studies. OCCASIONAL PAPERS. no.1– , 1965– . New York. Irreg.
Each no. has also a distinctive title.

317
American Institute of Planners. JOURNAL. v.1–44, May/June 1935–1978. Cambridge, Mass., later Washington, D.C. Bimonthly, 1935–Feb. 1939; quarterly.
Early volumes published under the institute's earlier name: American City Planning Institute. Publication suspended: Apr. 1943–1944. Title varies: 1935–43, *The Planner's Journal.*
Continued by: American Planning Association. *Journal.*
Indexes: Vols. 1–24, 1935–58, in v.24; v.24–27, 1958–64, in v.27; v.24–30, 1958–64, in v.30; v.31–33, 1965–67, 1v.; v.34–36, 1968–70, 1v.
Indexed: Abst. Soc. Work; ABC POL SCI; Bull. Sig. Soc. Eth.; His. Abst.; Curr. Cont. Soc. Beh. Sc.; Ind. Per. Art Law 1970; Int. Bibl. Eco.; Int. Bibl. Pol. Sc.; PAIS; PHRA; Urb. Aff. Abst.

318
AMERICAN JEWISH HISTORICAL QUARTERLY. no.1–61, 1893–1978. Waltham, Mass. Annual, 1893–1947 (irreg.); quarterly.
Issued by: American Jewish Historical Society. Some nos. are monographs. Title varies: 1893–June 1951, *Publications*; Sept. 1951–June 1961, *Publication.*
Continued by: *American Jewish History.*
Indexes: no.1–20, 1893–1911, 1v.
Indexed: His. Abst.

319
AMERICAN JEWISH HISTORY. v.68– , Sept. 1978– . Waltham, Mass. Quarterly.
Issued by: American Jewish Historical Society.
Continues: *American Jewish Historical Quarterly.*
Indexed: His. Abst.

320
AMERICAN JEWISH YEARBOOK. [v.1]– , 1899/1900– . Philadelphia, Pa., New York.
Issued by: American Jewish Committee. Issues for 1899/1900–1948/49 called also 5660–5709.
Indexes: Vols. 1–35, 1899/1900–1933/34, in v.36; 1–40, 1899/1900–1938/39, in v.40; v.1–45, 1899/1900–1943/44, in v.45; v.1–46, 1899/1900–1945/46, in v.46; v.1–50, 1899/1900–1948/49, in v.50.

321
AMERICAN JOURNAL OF AGRICULTURAL ECONOMICS. v.1– , 1919– . Lexington, Ky. Five no. a year.
Issued by: American Agricultural Economics Association. Includes lists of doctoral dissertations in agricultural economics in the United States.
Indexed: Int. Bibl. Eco.; Int. Bibl. Pol. Sc.; Int. Bibl. Soc.; PAIS; SSCI

322
AMERICAN JOURNAL OF ARCHAEOLOGY. v.1–11, 1885–1896; n. ser. v.1– , 1897– . Baltimore, Md. Bimonthly, 1897–99; quarterly, 1885–1896, 1900– .
Title varies: 1885–96, *The American Journal of Archaeology and of the History of Fine Arts*.
Indexes: Vols. 1–11, 1885–96; 1897–1906; v.11–70, 1907–1966.

THE AMERICAN JOURNAL OF ARCHAEOLOGY AND OF THE HISTORY OF FINE ARTS
See AMERICAN JOURNAL OF ARCHAEOLOGY

323
AMERICAN JOURNAL OF COMMUNITY PSYCHOLOGY. v.1– , Jan./Mar. 1973– . Washington, D.C., V.H. Vinston. Quarterly.
Issued by: Association of Community Psychology in cooperation with the American Psychological Association.
Indexed: Psych. Abst.; SSCI; Sage Urb. Stu. Abst.

324
AMERICAN JOURNAL OF COMPARATIVE LAW. v.1– , winter/spring 1952– . Baltimore, Md. Quarterly.
Issued by: American Association for Comparative Law.
Indexes: Vols. 1–10, 1952–61, 1v.; v.11–15, 1962–67, 1v.; v.16–25, 1968–77, 1v.
Indexed: ABC POL SCI; Ind. For. Leg. Per.; PAIS; SSCI.

325
AMERICAN JOURNAL OF ECONOMICS AND SOCIOLOGY. v.1– , Oct. 1941– . New York. Quarterly.
Sponsored by: Robert Schalkenback Foundation; co-sponsored by the Francis Neilson Fund.
Indexed: ABC POL SCI; Abst. Soc. Work; Bull. Sig. Soc. Eth.; Ind. Per. Art. Law; Ind. Per. Art. Law 1970; Int. Bibl. Eco.; Int. Bibl. Soc.; Int. Lab. Doc.; PAIS; Peace Res. Abst. J.; PHRA; Pop. Ind.; Sage Urb. Stu. Abst.; Soc. Abst.; SSCI.

326
AMERICAN JOURNAL OF EDUCATION. v.88– , Nov. 1979– . Chicago, Ill., The University of Chicago Press. Quarterly.
Issued by: Department of Education, University of Chicago.
Continues: *School Review*.
Indexed: Psych. Abst.; Soc. Abst.; SSCI

327
THE AMERICAN JOURNAL OF FAMILY THERAPY. v.7– , spring 1979– . New York, Mazel Brunner. Quarterly.
Continues: *International Journal of Family Counselling*.

328
AMERICAN JOURNAL OF HUMAN GENETICS. v.1– , Sept. 1949– . Chicago, Ill., The University of Chicago Press. Two no. a year, 1949; quarterly, 1950– ; bimonthly.
Issued by: American Society of Human Genetics.
Indexed: Abst. Anth.; Int. Bibl. Soc. Cul. Anth.; LLBA; Peace Res. Abst. J.; Pop. Ind.; Wom. Stu. Abst.

THE AMERICAN JOURNAL OF INSANITY
See AMERICAN JOURNAL OF PSYCHIATRY

329
AMERICAN JOURNAL OF INTERNATIONAL LAW. v.1– , Jan. 1907– . Washington, D.C. Quarterly.
Issued by: American Society of International Law. The edition in Spanish titled: *Revista Americana de Derecho Internacional*. Absorbed: *Proceedings* of the American Society of International Law.
Indexes: Parts 1–14, 1907–20, includes the Cumulative Analytical Index to the American Journal of International Law and supplements to the *Proceedings* of the American Society of International Law; vols. 15–34, 1921–40, 1v.; v.35–54, 1941–60, 1v.; v.55–74, 1961–70, 1v.
Indexed: ABC POL SCI; Bull. Anal. Pol. Ec. Soc.; Ind. Leg. Per.; Int. Bibl. Eco.; Int. Bibl. Pol. Sc.; Int. Bibl. Soc.; Int. Lab. Doc.; His. Abst.; PAIS; Peace Res. Abst. J.; Int. Pol. Sc. Abst.; Soc. Sc. Hum. Ind.; SSCI.

330
THE AMERICAN JOURNAL OF ISLAMIC SOCIAL SCIENCES. v.2– , July 1985– . Silver Spring, Md. Two no. a year.
Published jointly by the Association of Muslim Social Scientists, and International Institute of Islamic Thought.
Continues: *American Journal of Islamic Studies* (v.1, 1984)

331
AMERICAN JOURNAL OF ORTHOPSYCHIATRY. v.1– , Aug. 1930– . Menasha, Wis., later New York. Quarterly.
Issued by: American Orthopsychiatric Association. Subtitle reads: "A journal of human behavior".
Indexes: Vols. 1–10, 1930–40.
Indexed: Abst. Soc. Work.; Ind. Per. Art. Law; Ind. Per. Art. Law 1970; Int. Bibl. Soc. Cul. Anth.; LLBA; Peace Res. Abst. J.; Psych. Abst.; Wom. Stu. Abst.

332
AMERICAN JOURNAL OF POLITICAL SCIENCE. v.17– , Feb. 1973– . Austin, Tex., University of Texas Press. Quarterly.
Issued by: Midwest Political Science Association.
Continues: *Midwest Journal of Political Science*.
Indexed: ABC POL SCI; Bull. Anal. Pol. Ec. Soc.; Bull. Sig. Soc. Eth.; Int. Bibl. Pol. Sc.; PAIS; Sage Pub. Adm. Abst.; Sage Urb. Stu. Abst.; SSCI; Urb. Aff. Abst.

333
AMERICAN JOURNAL OF PSYCHIATRY. v.1– , July 1844– . Baltimore, Md. Bimonthly, 1844–June 1947; monthly.
Official organ of: American Psychiatric Association. Title varies: 1844–spring 1921, *The American Journal of Insanity*.
Indexes: Vols. 1–45, 1844–89, iv.
Indexed: Abst. Soc. Work; LLBA; Psych. Abst.; SSCI; Wom. Stu. Abst.

334
AMERICAN JOURNAL OF PSYCHOANALYSIS. v.1– , 1941– . New York. Semi-annual.
Issued by: Association for the Advancement of Psychoanalysis.
Indexes: Vols. 1–25, 1941–65, 1v.
Indexed: Abst. Anth.; ABC POL SCI; Bull. Sig. Soc. Eth.; Ind. Per. Art. Law; Int. Bibl. Soc.; LLBA; Peace Res. Abst. J.; Soc. Sc. Hum. Ind.; Psych. Abst.; SSCI; Wom. Stu. Abst.

335
AMERICAN JOURNAL OF PSYCHOLOGY. v.1– , Nov. 1887– . Ithaca, N.Y. Quarterly.
Issued by: Cornell University.
Indexes: Vols. 1–30, 1887–1919; v.31–50, 1920–37.
Indexed: LLBA; Psych. Abst.

THE AMERICAN JOURNAL OF RELIGIOUS PSYCHOLOGY AND EDUCATION
See JOURNAL OF RELIGIOUS PSYCHOLOGY, INCLUDING ITS ANTHROPOLOGICAL AND SOCIOLOGICAL ASPECTS

336
AMERICAN JOURNAL OF SMALL BUSINESS. v.1–10, no. 2, July 1976–1985. Baltimore, Md. Quarterly.
Continued by: *Entrepreneurship. Theory and Practice*.
Indexed: PAIS.

337
THE AMERICAN JOURNAL OF SOCIAL PSYCHIATRY. v.1– , Apr. 1981– . Santa Barbara, Calif. Quarterly.
Issued by: American Association for Social Psychiatry.
Supersedes: *Bulletin* of the American Association for Social Psychiatry.
Indexed: Psych. Abst.

338
AMERICAN JOURNAL OF SOCIOLOGY. v.1– , July 1985– . Chicago, Ill., The University of Chicago Press. Bimonthly.
Indexed: ABC POL SCI; Abst. Anth.; Abst. Soc. Work; Bull. Sig. Soc. Eth.; His. Abst.; Ind. Per. Art. Law 1970; Int. Bibl. Soc. Cul. Anth.; Int. Lab. Doc.; Int. Pol. Sc. Abst.; LLBA; Peace Res. Abst. J.; Soc. Sc. Hum. Ind.; Soc. Abst.; Psych. Abst.; Wom. Stu. Abst.

THE AMERICAN LEGISLATOR
See STATE GOVERNMENT

339
AMERICAN MEN AND WOMEN OF SCIENCE: SOCIAL AND BEHAVIORAL SCIENCES. 13th ed.– , 1978– . New York, R.R. Bowker.
Continues: second section of the 12th ed. of: *American Men and Women of Science*.

340
American Museum of Natural History, New York. ANTHROPOLOGICAL PAPERS. 1– , 1908– . New York. Irreg.
Monograph series.
Indexed: Bull. Sig. Soc. Eth.

341
AMERICAN OPINION. v.1–28, no.7, Feb. 1958–July/Aug. 1985. Belmont, Mass., R. Welch. Eleven no. a year (monthly except July)
Supersedes: *One Man's Opinion*. Merged with: *The Review of the News* to form: *The New American*.
Indexed: Ind. Per. Art. Law 1970; Peace Res. Abst. J.

342
American Oriental Society. JOURNAL. v.1– , 1843/49– . New Haven, Conn. Frequency varied; quarterly, 1911– .

Includes *Proceedings* of the American Oriental Society and some supplements.
Indexes: Vols. 1–20, 1843–1900; v.21–60, 1901–40.
Indexed: Ind. Per. Art. Law; Int. Bibl. Soc. Cul. Anth.; Soc. Sc. Hum. Ind.

343
AMERICAN PERSPECTIVE. v.1–4, Apr. 1947–Sept. 1950. Washington, D.C.
Issued by: Foundation for Foreign Affairs.

344
American Philosophical Association. TRANSACTIONS. 1789–1809; 1818– . Philadelphia, Pa. Bimonthly.
Indexed: Abst. Anth.; His. Abst.; Ind. Per. Art. Law 1970; LLBA; PAIS.

345
American Planning Association. JOURNAL. v.45– , Jan. 1979– . Washington, D.C., later Chicago, Ill. Quarterly.
Continues: American Institute of Planners. *Journal.*
Indexed: ABC POL SCI; Bull. Sig. Soc. Eth.; His. Abst.; Ind. Per. Art. Law 1970; Int. Bibl. Eco.; Int. Bibl. Pol. Sc.; PHRA; PAIS.

346
American Political Science Association. PROCEEDINGS. 1–10, Dec. 1904–Jan. 1914. Menasha, Wis.
Vols. 8–10 issued as supplements to: *American Political Science Review.* Subsequently incorporated into *The American Political Science Review.*

347
THE AMERICAN POLITICAL SCIENCE REVIEW. v.1– , Nov. 1906– . Menasha, Wis. Bimonthly, 1932–49; quarterly, 1906–31, 1950– .
Issued by: American Political Science Association. Vols. 6–8 include *Proceedings* of the American Political Science Association at its 8–10th annual meetings, 1911–1913/14. Vol. 24, no.1 accompanied by Report of the Committee on Policy of the Association.
Indexes: Vols. 1–10, 1906–16, a supplement to v.11, no.3; this index includes index to the Association's Proceedings, 1904–14; v.1–57, 1906–63, 1v.
Indexed: ABC POL SCI; Bull. Sig. Soc. Eth.; Ind. Per. Art. Law 1970; Int. Bibl. Pol. Sc.; Int. Bibl. Soc. Cul. Anth.; His. Abst.; Peace Res. Abst. J.; Pop. Ind.; SSCI; Soc. Sc. Hum. Ind.

348
AMERICAN POLITICS QUARTERLY. 1– , Jan. 1973– . Beverly Hills, Calif., Sage Publications. Quarterly.
Indexed: ABC POL SCI; Bull. Anal. Pol. Ec. Soc.; Int. Bibl. Pol. Sc.; Int. Pol. Sc. Abst.; PAIS; SSCI.

349
AMERICAN POLITICS YEARBOOK. 1982/83– . New York, Longman. Annual.

AMERICAN POPULATION ABSTRACTS
See RESUMENES SOBRE POBLACIÓN EN AMÉRICA LATINA

350
AMERICAN PSYCHOLOGIST. v.1– , 1946– . Washington, D.C. Monthly.
Issued by: American Psychological Association.
Indexed: Bull. Anal. Pol. Ec. Soc.; Psych. Abst.; SSCI

351
AMERICAN QUARTERLY. v.1– , spring 1949– . Minneapolis, Minn., University of Minnesota Press.
Indexed: Abst. Soc. Work; His. Abst.; Ind. Per. Art. Law; Soc. Sc. Hum. Ind.; Wom. Stu. Abst.

352
THE AMERICAN REVIEW OF CANADIAN STUDIES. v.3– , spring 1973– . Washington, D.C. Semi-annual, 1973–81; three no. a year.
Issued by: Association for Canadian Studies in the United States.
Continues: ACSUS. *Newsletter.*

353
AMERICAN REVIEW OF EAST–WEST TRADE. v.1– , Jan. 1968– . White Plains, N.Y. Monthly.
Indexed: Ind. Per. Art Law 1970; Int. Bibl. Eco.; Int. Bibl. Soc. Cul. Anth.

354
AMERICAN REVIEW OF PUBLIC ADMINISTRATION. v.15– , spring 1981– . Parkville, Mo. Quarterly.
Issued by: Greater Kansas City Chapter, American Society for Public Administration. Other title: ARPA.
Continues: *Midwest Review of Public Administration.*
Indexed: ABC POL SCI; Int. Pol. Sc. Abst.; PAIS.

AMERICAN REVIEW OF SOVIET AND EASTERN EUROPEAN FOREIGN TRADE
See SOVIET AND EASTERN EUROPEAN TRADE

AMERICAN SCANDINAVIAN REVIEW
See SCANDINAVIAN REVIEW

355
THE AMERICAN SCHOLAR. v.1– , 1932– . Concord, N.H., Rumford Press. Quarterly.
Supersedes: *The Phi Beta Kappa Key.*
Indexed: His. Abst.; Ind. Per. Art Law 1970; Bull. Anal. Pol. Ec. Soc.; Int. Bibl. Eco.; Int. Bibl. Pol. Sc.; Int. Bibl. Soc.; Ind. Per. Art. Law; PAIS; Peace Res. Abst. J.; Soc. Abst.; Sage Urb. Stu. Abst.; SSCI; Int. Pol. Sc. Abst.

AMERICAN SLAVIC AND EAST EUROPEAN REVIEW
See SLAVIC REVIEW

AMERICAN SOCIALIST MONTHLY
See SOCIALIST REVIEW (New York)

AMERICAN SOCIALIST QUARTERLY
See SOCIALIST REVIEW (New York)

American Society of International Law. OCCASIONAL PAPERS
See STUDIES IN TRANSNATIONAL LEGAL POLICY

356
American Society of International Law. PROCEEDINGS OF THE ANNUAL MEETING. 1907–1914; 1974– . [Place of publication varies]
Proceedings were incorporated into the *American Political Science Review*. They became an independent publication in 1974.
Indexed: Ind. Leg. Per.

357
AMERICAN SOCIOLOGICAL REVIEW. v.1– , Feb. 1936– . Albany, N.Y. Bimonthly.
Official organ of: American Sociological Society, 1936–Oct. 1959, of American Sociological Association, Dec. 1959– . Sections: "Book Reviews" and "Periodical Literature" were separated from and have appeared as *Contemporary Sociology* since 1972.
Indexes: Vols. 1–25, 1936–60, 1v.; v.26–30, 1961–65, 1v.
Indexed: Abst. Anth.; ABC POL SCI; Bull. Anal. Pol. Ec. Soc.; Bull. Sig. Soc. Eth.; His. Abst.; Hum. Res. Abst.; Int. Bibl. Eco.; Int. Bibl. Pol. Sc.; Int Bibl. Soc.; Int. Bibl. Soc. Cul. Anth.; Int. Lab. Doc.; PAIS; Psych. Abst.; SSCI; Sage Urb. Stu. Abst.; Soc. Sc. Hum. Ind.; Soc. Abst.; Wom. Stu. Abst.

358
THE AMERICAN SOCIOLOGIST. v.1– , Nov. 1965– . Not published 1983–86. Albany, N.Y., subsequently Washington, D.C. Quarterly.
Issued by: American Sociological Association.
Indexed: Bull. Anal. Pol. Ec. Soc.; Bull. Sig. Soc. Eth.; Int. Bibl. Pol. Sc.; Int. Bibl. Soc.; Int. Pol. Sc. Abst.; Soc. Abst.; SSCI; Wom. Stu. Abst.

359
AMERICAN STATISTICS INDEX. 1973– . Washington, D.C., Congressional Information Service. Annual.
Issued in two parts: Part 1. Index; Part 2. Abstracts.

360
AMERICAN STUDIES. 1– , 1960– . Lawrence, Kans. Semi-annual.
Issued by: Midcontinent American Studies Association, and American Studies Department, University of Kansas.
Indexed: His. Abst.; PAIS.

AMERICAN STUDIES
See AMERIKA STUDIEN

361
AMERICAN STUDIES INTERNATIONAL. v.14– , autumn 1975– . Washington, D.C. Quarterly.
Issued by: Advisory Committee on American Studies, a subcommittee on International Exchange of Persons of the Conference Board of Associated Research Councils. Supplement to: *American Quarterly*. Published with the support of the International Communication Agency.

362
American Universities Field Staff. POPULATION PERSPECTIVES. 1971– . San Francisco, Calif., Freeman, Cooper.

363
American Universities Field Staff. REPORTS SERVICE. CENTRAL & SOUTHERN AFRICA SERIES. v.1–11, 1952–1964. New York. Irreg.
Continued by: *Central & Southern Africa Series*.

364
American Universities Field Staff. REPORTS SERVICE. EAST AFRICA SERIES. v.1–6, no.1, Sept. 1952–Apr. 1963. New York. Irreg.
Reports until July 1958 issued without series title and volume numbering.
Continued by: *East Africa Series*.

365
American Universities Field Staff. REPORTS SERVICE. EAST ASIA SERIES. v.1–14, Aug. 1952–196?. New York. Irreg.
Some reports until May 1959 issued without series title and volume numbering.
Continued by: *East Asia Series*.

366
American Universities Field Staff. REPORTS SERVICE. EAST COAST SOUTH AMERICA SERIES. v.1–13, 195?–1967. New York. Irreg.
Continued by: *East Coast South America Series*.

367
American Universities Field Staff. REPORTS SERVICE. MEXICO & CARIBBEAN AREA SERIES. v.1–5, 1954–1960. New York. Irreg.
Reports until July 1957 issued without series title and volume numbering.

Continued by: *Mexico & Caribbean Area Series.*

368
American Universities Field Staff. REPORTS SERVICE. NORTH AFRICA SERIES. v.1–13, Jan. 1955–1967. New York. Irreg.
Reports for Jan.–June 1955 issued without series title and volume numbering.
Continued by: *North Africa Series.*

369
American Universities Field Staff. REPORTS SERVICE. NORTHEAST AFRICA SERIES. v.1–14, no.3, Sept. 1953–Sept. 1967. New York. Irreg.
Continued by: *Northeast Africa Series.*

370
American Universities Field Staff. REPORTS SERVICE. SOUTH ASIA SERIES. v.1–21, no.1, Oct. 1956–1977. New York. Irreg.
Continued by: *Southwest Asia Series.*

371
American Universities Field Staff. REPORTS SERVICE. SOUTHEAST EUROPE SERIES. [v.1]–19, Sept. 1952–1972. New York. Irreg.
Continued by: *Southeast Europe Series.*

372
American Universities Field Staff. REPORTS SERVICE. SOUTHWEST ASIA SERIES. [v.1]–16, 1952–196?. New York. Irreg.
Reports for July 1952–Sept. 1958 issued without series title and volume numbering.
Continued by: *Southwest Asia Series.*

373
American Universities Field Staff. REPORTS SERVICE. WEST AFRICA SERIES. [v.1]–17, Feb. 5, 1955–1977. New York. Irreg.
Early reports issued without series title and volume numbering.
Continued by: *West Africa Series.*

374
American Universities Field Staff. REPORTS SERVICE. WEST COAST SOUTH AMERICA SERIES. [v.1]–14, no.5, Aug. 24, 1954–1967. New York. Irreg.
Reports for Aug. 1954–June 1959 issued without series title and volume numbering.
Continued by: *West Coast South America Series.*

375
THE AMERICAN YEARBOOK: A RECORD OF EVENTS AND PROGRESS. 1910–1919, 1925–1950. New York, Nelson. Annual.
Publication suspended 1920–24.

376
THE AMERICAS. v.1– , July 1944– . Washington, D.C. Quarterly.
Issued by: Academy of Franciscan History.
Indexed: Bull. Sig. Soc. Eth.; His. Abst.; Int. Bibl. Soc.; Int. Bibl. Soc. Cul. Anth.; Soc. Sc. Hum. Ind.

377
THE AMERICAS. v.1– , Mar. 1949– . Washington, D.C. Monthly.
In Spanish. Issued by: Union Pan-Americana. Published also in English and Portuguese.
Supersedes, in part: Union's *Bulletin.*
Indexed: His. Abst.; Soc. Sc. Hum. Ind.

378
AMERIKA STUDIEN. AMERICAN STUDIES. v.19– , 1974– . Stuttgart, J.B. Metzlerische Verlagsbuchhandlung. Two no. a year.
Issued under the auspices of: Deutsche Gesellschaft für Amerikastudien. In English or German; summaries in English.
Continues: *Jahrbuch für Amerikastudien* (v.1–18, 1956–73)
Indexed: His. Abst.; Int. Bibl. Soc.

379
AMERIKANSKIĬ EZHEGODNIK. 1971– . Moskva, Nauka. Annual.
Issued by: Institut Vseobshcheĭ Istorii, Akademii͡a Nauk SSSR. In Russian. Other title: *Annual Studies of America.*

380
AMERINDIA. no.1– , 1962– . Montevideo. Irreg.
Issued by: Centro de Estudios Arqueológicos y Antropológicos Americanos. In Spanish.

381
AMERINDIA. v.1– , 1976– . Paris, SELAF.
In French or Spanish; summaries in English, German, Portuguese, and Russian.
Indexed: Int. Bibl. Soc. Cul. Anth.

382
AMÉRIQUE LATINE. no.1– , 1980– . Paris. Quarterly.
Issued by: Centre de Recherche sur l'Amérique Latine et de Tiers Monde. In French. Numbers are thematic.
Indexed: Ind. Bibl. Eco.; Int. Bibl. Soc. Cul. Anth.

383
AMMINISTRARE. 1963– . Milano. Quarterly.
Issued by: Istituto per la Scienza dell'Amministrazione Pubblica. In Italian.
Indexed: Bull. Anal. Pol. Ec. Soc.; Int. Bibl. Pol. Sc.; Int. Pol. Sc. Abst.; Soc. Abst.

384
AMNESTY INTERNATIONAL REPORT. 1970– . London, Amnesty International Publications. Annual.
Continues: Amnesty International. *Annual Report*.

385
AMSTERDAM SOCIOLOGISCH TIJDSCHRIFT. v.1– , May 1974– . Groningen, Wallers-Noordhoff. Annual.
In Dutch.

ANAIS
See Academia Portuguêsa da História. ANAIS

ANAIS
See International Congress of Americanists. PROCEEDINGS

386
ANALELE ROMANO-SOVIETICE. SERIA ECONOMIE, DREPT. 1–11, Oct./Dec. 1949–Dec. 1951. Bucureşti, Carta Rusa. Quarterly, 1949–50; bimonthly.
Issued by: Institutul di Studii Romano-Sovietice, 1949–Mar./Apr. 1951; the Institutul's Sectile Economie şi Drept, Academia Republicii Populare Romîne. In Romanian.
Supersedes, in part: *Analele Romano-Sovietice*; in addition to its own volume numbering, continues also the volume numbering of *Analele Romano-Sovietice*.
Superseded by: *Analele Romano-Sovietice. Seria Economie*, and: *Analele Romano-Sovietice. Seria Drept*.

ANALELE. SOCIOLOGIE
See Universitatea Bucureşti. ANALELE. SOCIOLOGIE

ANALELE ŞTIINŢIFICE. SERIA NOVA. SECTIUNEA III A: ISTORIE
See Universitatea din Iaşi. ANALELE ŞTIINTIFICE. SERIA NOVA. SECTIUNEA III A: ISTORIE

ANALELE ŞTIINŢIFICE DE UNIVERSITATEI DIN IAŞI. B.I. ŞTIINŢE FILOZOFICE, ECONOMICE ŞI JURIDICE
See Universitatea din Iaşi. ANALELE ŞTIINŢIFICE B 1. ŞTIINŢE FILOZOFICE, ECONOMICE ŞI JURIDICE

ANALELE ŞTIINŢIFICE. SECTIUNEA III C. ŞTIINTE ECONOMICE
See Universitatea din Iaşi. ANALELE ŞTIINŢIFICE. SECTIUNEA III C. ŞTIINŢE ECONOMICE

ANALES
See Academia Nacional de Ciencias Morales y Políticas. ANALES

ANALES
See ANALES JURÍDICO-SOCIALES

ANALES
See Instituto Nacional de Antropología e Historia. ANALES

ANALES
See Universidad de Chile, Santiago. Faculdad de Ciencias Jurídicas y Sociales. ANALES

ANALES
See Universidad de Chile, Santiago. Faculdad Latinoamericana de Ciencias Sociales. ANALES

ANALES
See Universidad Nacional de la Plata. Faculdad de Ciencias Jurídicas y Sociales. ANALES

387
ANALES DE ANTROPOLOGÍA. v.1– , 1964– . Mexico, D.F. Annual.
Vols. 1–11 were issued by: Instituto de Investigaciones Históricas; v.12– by Instituto de Investigaciones Antropológicas, Universidad Nacional Autónoma de México. Beginning with v.17 volumes are thematic and subtitled: "Tomo 1. Arqueología y Antropología Física", and Tomo II. "Etnología y Lingüística", the latter issued by: Sección de Antropología y Lingüística. The volume numbering of both subseries is kept in order.
Indexed: Abst. Anth.; His. Abst.; Int. Bibl. Soc. Cul. Anth.

ANALES DE ANTROPOLOGÍA. TOMO I. ARQUEOLOGÍA Y ANTROPOLOGÍA FÍSICA
See ANALES DE ANTROPOLOGÍA

ANALES DE ANTROPOLOGÍA. TOMO II. ETNOLOGÍA Y LINGÜÍSTICA
See ANALES DE ANTROPOLOGÍA

388
ANALES DE ARQUEOLOGÍA Y ETNOLOGÍA. v.1– , 1947– . Mendoza. Irreg.
Issued by: Instituto de Arqueología y Etnología, Faculdad de Filosofía y Letras, Universidad de Cuyo. In Spanish. Title varies: 1940–44, *Anales del Instituto de Etnografía Americana*; 1945–46, *Anales del Instituto del Etnología Americana*.
Indexed: Abst. Anth.; His. Abst.; Int. Bibl. Soc. Cul. Anth.

389
ANALES DE CIENCIAS SOCIALES. no.1– , Dec. 1971– . Panama City, Editoriale Universitaria. Semi-annual.
Issued by: Centro de Investigaciones Sociales y Económicas, Universidad de Panamá. In Spanish.

390
ANALES DE ECONOMÍA. v.1– , Jan./Mar. 1941– . Madrid. Quarterly.
Issued by: Consejo Superior de Investigaciones Científicas. Instituto de Economía Sancho de Moncada Duque de Medinaceli. In Spanish.

391
ANALES DE INVESTIGACIÓN HISTÓRICA. v.1– , Jan./Mar. 1974– . Rio Piedras, P.R. Semi-annual.
Issued by: Departamento de Historia, Faculdad de Humanidades, Universidad de Puerto Rico. In Spanish. Some numbers are in combined form.

ANALES DE LA FACULDAD DE CIENCIAS JURIDICAS Y SOCIALES
See Universidad de Chile. Faculdad de Ciencias Juridicas y Sociales. ANALES

ANALES DE LA FACULDAD DE CIENCIAS JURÍDICAS Y SOCIALES DE LA UNIVERSIDAD DE LA PLATA
See Universidad Nacional de la Plata. Faculdad de Ciencias Jurídicas y Sociales. ANALES

392
ANALES DE MORAL SOCIAL Y ECONOMÍA. v.1– , 1962– . Madrid. Irreg.
Issued by: Centro de Estudios Sociales de la Santa Cruz del Valle de los Caidos. In Spanish. Monograph series.

393
ANALES DE SOCIOLOGÍA. v.1– , June 1966– . Barcelona. Two no. a year.
Issued by: Departamento de Sociología del Centro de Estudios Económicos y Sociales de la Delegación del Consejo Superior de Investigaciónes Científicas en Barcelona. In Spanish.
Indexed: His. Abst.; Soc. Abst.

ANALES DEL INSTITUTO DE ETNOGRAFÍA AMERICANA
See ANALES DE ARQUEOLOGÍA Y ETNOLOGÍA

ANALES DEL INSTITUTO NACIONAL DE ANTROPOLOGÍA E HISTORIA
See Instituto Nacional de Antropología e Historia, Mexico. ANALES

ANALES INTERNACIONALES DE CRIMINOLOGÍA
See ANNALES INTERNATIONALES DE CRIMINOLOGIE

394
ANALES JURÍDICO-SOCIALES. 1915– . Santiago, Chile. Annual.
Issued by: Faculdad de Ciencias Jurídicas, Políticas y Sociales, Universidad Católica de Chile. In Spanish.

ANALI
See Jugoslovenska Akademija Znanosti i Umjetnosti. Historijski Institut, Dubrovnik. ANALI

395
ANALISE SOCIAL. v.1– , Jan. 1962– . Lisboa, Editorial Imperio. Annual.
Issued by: Instituto Superior de Ciências Econômicas y Finanzieras. Cabinete de Investigações Sociais. In Portuguese; summaries in English and French. Tables of contents also in English and French.
Indexed: Bull. Anal. Pol. Ec. Soc.; Bull. Sig. Soc. Eth.; Int. Bibl. Eco.; Int. Bibl. Soc. Cul. Anth.; Int. Pol. Sc. Abst.; Peace Res. Abst. J.; Soc. Abst.

396
ANALISI; CUADERNOS DE COMUNICACIÓ Y CULTURA. 1– , 1980– . Belaterra. Annual.
Issued by: Faculdad de Ciencias de la Información, Departamento de Teoría de la Comunicació, Universidad Autónoma de Barcelona. In Spanish.

397
ANÁLISIS. no.1– , Jan./Mar. 1977– . Lima, Perugraph Editores S.A. Annual.
In Spanish.

398
ANALIZY I PRÓBY TECHNIK BADAWCZYCH W SOCJOLOGII. v.1– , 1975– . Wrocław, Zakład Narodowy im. Ossolińskich. Irreg.
Issued by: Instytut Filozofii i Socjologii, Polska Akademia Nauk. In Polish; summaries in English and Russian.

ANALYSE DE POLITIQUES
See CANADIAN PUBLIC POLICY

399
ANALYSE & [i.e. et] PRÉVISION. 1–8, no.4/6, 1966–Oct./Dec. 1974. Paris. Bimonthly.
Issued by: Société d'Études et de Documentation Économiques, Industrielles et Sociales.
Supersedes, in part: the society's *Études Futuribles*, and *Revue Critique*.

Indexed: Bull. Sig. Soc. Eth.; Int. Bibl. Eco.; Int. Bibl. Pol. Sc.; Int. Bibl. Soc.; Int. Bibl. Soc. Cul. Anth.; Int. Lab Doc.; Int. Pol. Sc. Abst.; Peace Res. Abst. J.; Pop. Ind.

400
ANALYSE & [i.e. und] KRITIK. v.1– , 1979– . Wiesbaden, Westdeutscher Verlag. Semi-annual.
Issued by: Institut für Zukunft Forschung, Berlin, Gesellschaft für Zukunftsfragen e.V., Bonn, in cooperation with Österreichische Gesellschaft für Lanfrüstige Entwicklungsforschung (Zukunftforschung), Wien. In German.

401
ANALYSES SOCIALES. v.1– , Jan./Feb. 1984– . Kinshasa. Bimonthly.
Issued by: Laboratoire d'Analyses Sociales de Kinshasa. In French.

ANALYTICAL TABLES OF FOREIGN TRADE
See ANALYTISKE TABELLER VERDRØRENDE UDENRIGSHANDEL (NIMEXE)

ANALYTICAL TABLES OF FOREIGN TRADE. STTC/CTCI. REV.2. EXPORT
See ANALYTISKE TABELLER VERDRØRENDE UDENRIGSHAN

ANALYTICAL TABLES OF FOREIGN TRADE, STTC/CTCI. REV.2. IMPORT
See ANALYTISKE TABELLER VERDRØRENDE UDENRIGSHANDEL

ANALYTIKOI PINAKES ESOTEPIKOY EMPORIOY
See ANALYTISKE TABELLER VERDRØRENDE UDENRIGSHANDEL (NIMEXE)

ANALYTISCHE TABELLEN VAN BUITENLANDSE HANDEL
See ANALYTISKE TABELLER VERDRØRENDE UDENRIGSHANDEL (NIMEXE)

ANALYTISCHE ÜBERSICHTEN DES AUSSENHANDELS CITC/CTCI. REV. 2.IMPORT
See ANALYTISKE TABELLER VERDRØRENDE UDENRIGSHANDEL

ANALYTISCHE ÜBERSICHTEN DES AUSSENHANDELS SITC/CICO. REV. 2. EXPORT
See ANALYTISKE TABELLER VERDRØRENDE UDENRIGSHANDEL

402
ANALYTISKE TABELLER VERDRØRENDE UDENRIGSHANDEL (NIMEXE). ANALYTISCHE ÜBERSICHTEN DES AUSSENHANDELS (NIMEXE). ANALYTICAL TABLES OF FOREIGN TRADE (NIMEXE). 1976– . Luxembourg, Eurostat. Annual.
Issued by: Statistical Office of the European Communities. Text in French and German; title and introduction in Danish, Dutch, English, French, German, Greek, Italian and Spanish. Other titles: *Analytikoi Pinakes Esotepikoi Emporioy*; *Tableaux Analytiques du Commerce Extérieur*; *Tavole Economiche de Commercio Estero*; *Analytische Tabellen van de Buitenlandse Handel*; *Tablas Analíticas de Comercio Exterior*. The annual publication consists of 13 volumes.

403
ANCIENT SOCIETY. 1– , 1970– . Leuven. Annual (irreg.)
Issued by: Katholieke Universiteit te Leuven. In Dutch, English, French, German, or Italian.

404
ANGEWANDTE SOZIALFORSCHUNG. 1– , 1968– . Wien.
Issued by: Arbeitsgemeinschaft für Interdisziplinare Angewandte Sozialforschung. In German. Title on cover: *AIAS Informationen*.

405
ANGEWANDTE SOZIALFORSCHUNG JOURNAL. 1– , 1961– . Wien. Quarterly.
Issued by: Sozialwissenschaftliche Studiengesellschaft. In German.
Indexes: cumulative indexes every five years.

ANNALEN DER GEMEINWIRTSCHAFT
See ANNALS OF PUBLIC AND COOPERATIVE ECONOMY

ANNALEN DES DEUTSCHEN REICHS (VORMALS DES NORD-DEUTSCHEN BUNDES UND DES DEUTSCHEN ZOLLVEREINS) FÜR GESETZGEBUNG, VERWALTUNG UND STATISTIK
See ANNALEN DES DEUTSCHEN REICHS FÜR GESETZGEBUNG, VERWALTUNG UND VOLKSWIRTSCHAFT

406
ANNALEN DES DEUTSCHEN REICHS FÜR GESETZGEBUNG, VERWALTUNG UND VOLKSWIRTSCHAFT. v.1– , 1868– . Berlin. Eight no. a year, 1868–71; monthly.

In German. From 1901 to 1906 includes monthly supplement: "Literarische Mitteilungen für Annalen des Deutschen Reichs" (formerly issued as *Literarische Mitteilungen für Juristen und Verwaltungsbeamte*). Subtitle reads: "Rechts- und Staatswissenschaftliche Zeitschrift und Materialsammlung". Title varies: 1868–69, *Staatshandbuch für Gesetzgebung, Verwaltung und Statistik des Norddeutschenbundes und des Deutschen Zollverein*; 1870, *Annalen des Deutschen Reichs (Vormals des Nord Deutschen Bundes und des Deutschen Zollverein) für Gesetzgebung, Verwaltung und Statistik.*
Indexes: 1868–1902 titled "Systematische Gesamtregister zu den Jahrgängen 1868–1902".

ANNALEN VOOR RECHTSGELEERDHEID EN STAATSWETENSCHAPPEN
See ANNALES DE DROIT ET DES SCIENCES POLITIQUES

ANNALES
See Académie des Sciences Coloniales. ANNALES

ANNALES
See Musée Social, Paris. ANNALES

ANNALES
See SCIENCES POLITIQUES

ANNALES
See Université d'Aix-Marseille. Faculté de Droit et de Science Politique. ANNALES

ANNALES
See Université d'Aix-Marseille. Faculté de Droit et des Sciences Économiques. ANNALES

ANNALES
See Université de Toulouse I. Sciences sociales. ANNALES

ANNALES
See Université de Bordeaux III. Centre de Recherches sur l'Amérique Anglophone. ANNALES

ANNALES
See Université de Yaoundé. Faculté des Lettres et Sciences Humaines. ANNALES

407
ANNALES AFRICAINES. v.1– , 1954– . Paris, A. Pedone. Annual.
Issued by: Faculté de Droit et des Sciences Économiques, Université de Dakar. In French.
Indexed: Bull. Anal. Pol. Ec. Soc.; His. Abst.; Int. Bibl. Soc.; Int. Pol. Sc. Abst.

408
ANNALES ARCHÉOLOGIQUES ARABES SYRIENNES. v.16– , 1965– . Damas.
Issued by: Direction Générale des Antiquités de Syrie. In Arabic, English, French, or German. Other title: *Revue d'Archéologie et d'Histoire Syriennes.*
Continues: *Les Annales Archéologiques de Syrie.*

409
LES ANNALES ARCHÉOLOGIQUES DE SYRIE. v.1–15, pt.2, 1951–1965. Damas. Annual, 1951–64; semi-annual.
Issued by: Direction Générale des Antiquités de Syrie. In Arabic, English, or French.
Continued by: *Annales Archéologiques Arabes Syriennes.*

ANNALES CRIMINOLOGIAE JAPONICAE
See HANZAI GAKU NENPŌ

410
ANNALES D'ÉCONOMIE ET DE SOCIOLOGIE RURALES. 1– , 1972– . Versailles. Three or four no. a year.
Issued by: Institut National de la Recherche Économique. Département d'Économie et de Sociologie Rurales. In French; summaries in English.
Supersedes: *Recherches d'Économie et de Sociologie Rurales.*

411
ANNALES D'ÉTUDES INTERNATIONALES. ANNALS OF INTERNATIONAL STUDIES. 1970– . Genève. Annual.
Issued by: Associations des Anciens de l'Institut Universitaire des Hautes Études Internationales. In English or French.
Indexed: Bull. Anal. Pol. Ec. Soc.; Int. Bibl. Pol. Sc.; Int. Bibl. Soc.; Int. Pol. Sc. Abst.

412
ANNALES D'HISTOIRE ÉCONOMIQUE ET SOCIALE. v.1–10(no.1–54), Jan. 15, 1929–Nov. 30, 1938. Paris, A. Colin. Quarterly, 1929–31; bimonthly.
In French.
Superseded by: *Annales d'Histoire Sociale.*
Indexes: Vols. 1–10, in v.10.

413
ANNALES D'HISTOIRE SOCIALE. v.1–3, no.3/4, Jan. 1939–July/Dec. 1941. Paris.
In French.

Supersedes: *Annales d'Histoire Économique et Sociale.*

ANNALES D'HISTOIRE SOCIALE ET ÉCONOMIQUE
See ROCZNIKI DZIEJÓW SPOŁECZNYCH I GOSPODARCZYCH

414
ANNALES DE DÉMOGRAPHIE HISTORIQUE. 1964– . Paris, Éditions de l'École des Hautes Études en Sciences Sociales. Annual.
Issued by: Société de Démographie Historique. In French. Monograph series. Title varies: 1964, *Études et Chronique de Démographie Historique.*

415
ANNALES DE DROIT ET DES SCIENCES POLITIQUES. ANNALEN VOOR RECHTSGELEERDHEID EN STAATSWETENSCHAPPEN. v.1– , 1931– . Bruxelles. Quarterly.
Issued by: Association des Anciens Étudiants de la Faculté de Droit de l'Université Catholique de Louvain up to Apr. 1948; later by: Fédération des Anciens Étudiants de la Faculté de Droit et de l'École des Sciences Politiques et Sociales de l'Université de Louvain. In French. Publication suspended July 1940–July 1948.

416
ANNALES DE FINANCES PUBLIQUES COMPARÉES. no.1– , 1936– . Paris. Annual.
Issued by: Section de Finances Publiques, Institut de Droit Comparée, Université de Paris. In French. Not published 1940–44.

417
ANNALES DE GÉOGRAPHIE. v.1– , Oct. 1891– . Paris, A. Colin. Bimonthly.
In French. Vols. 1–23/24 (1891/92–1914/15) include "Bibliographie Géographique Annuelle" for 1891–1913/14. Beginning with Jan. 1941 issued as the *Bulletin* of the Société de Géographie. Not published Sept. 1914–July 1915, and 1944.
Indexed: Bull. Sig. Soc. Eth.; Int. Bibl. Eco.; Int. Bibl. Soc.

ANNALES DE L'ÉCOLE LIBRE DES SCIENCES POLITIQUES
See SCIENCES POLITIQUES

ANNALES DE L'ÉCONOMIE COLLECTIVE
See ANNALS OF COLLECTIVE ECONOMY

ANNALES DE L'ÉCONOMIE PUBLIQUE, SOCIALE ET COOPÉRATIVE
See ANNALS OF PUBLIC AND COOPERATIVE ECONOMY

ANNALES DE L'UNIVERSITÉ D'ABIDJAN. SÉRIE K. SCIENCES ÉCONOMIQUES
See Université d'Abidjan. ANNALES. SÉRIE K. SCIENCES ÉCONOMIQUES

ANNALES DE LA FACULTÉ DE DROIT, D'ÉCONOMIE, ET DE SCIENCES SOCIALES
See Université de Liège. Faculté de Droit, d'Économie et de Sciences Sociales. ANNALES

ANNALES DE LA FACULTÉ DE DROIT ET DES SCIENCES ÉCONOMIQUES D'AIX-EN-PROVENCE
See Université d'Aix-en-Provence. Faculté de Droit et des Sciences Économiques. ANNALES

418
ANNALES DE LA RECHERCHE URBAINE. no.1– , Oct. 1978– . Paris. Quarterly.
Issued by: Centre de Recherche d'Urbanisme. In French.

ANNALES DE LA RÉGIE COLLECTIVE DIRECTE
See ANNALS OF COLLECTIVE ECONOMY

419
ANNALES DE PHILOSOPHIE POLITIQUE. 1956– . Paris, Presses Universitaires de France.
In French.

ANNALES DE RECHERCHES ET DE DOCUMENTATION SUR LE CONSOMMATION
See CONSOMMATION

420
ANNALES DE SOCIOLOGIE. v.1–6, 1900–1910. Paris, and Bruxelles.
Issued by: Société Belge de Sociologie. In French. Title varies: v.1, 1900, *Annales de Sociologie et Mouvement Sociologique Internationale.*

ANNALES DE SOCIOLOGIE ET MOUVEMENT SOCIOLOGIQUE INTERNATIONALE
See ANNALES DE SOCIOLOGIE

421
ANNALES DES SCIENCES ÉCONOMIQUES APPLIQUÉES. 1937– . Louvain. Five no. a year.
Issued by: Institut des Sciences Économiques Appliquées. In French.

ANNALES DES SCIENCES POLITIQUES
See SCIENCES POLITIQUES

ANNALES DES SCIENCES SOCIALES
See ROCZNIKI NAUK SPOŁECZNYCH

422
LES ANNALES DIPLOMATIQUES & CONSULAIRES. v.1– , Aug. 5, 1903–Dec. 20, 1966. Paris. Monthly, 1903–Aug. 1904; semimonthly.
In French. Subtitle reads: "Revue bi-mensuelle des questions extérieurs, organ des ambassades, légations, chancelleries, consultants et commerce, industrie, droit international".

423
ANNALES DU DROIT ET DES SCIENCES SOCIALES. v.1–4, no.6, 1933–1936. Paris, Sirey.
Organ of: Association des Candidates à l'Agrégation des Facultés de Droit. In French.

424
LES ANNALES DU MARCHÉ COMMUN. 1– , Feb. 1958– . Bruxelles. Bimonthly.
Issued by: Chambre de Commerce Belge pour le Marché Commun. In French.

425
ANNALES DU MIDI. v.1– , 1889– . Toulouse, Éditions Eduard Privat. Quarterly.
Issued by: Universités de Toulouse et de Bordeaux, Aix-Marseille, Montpellier et Venise. In French. Subtitle reads: "Revue archéologique, historique et philologique de la France Méridionale"; later "Revue de la France Méridionale".
Indexes: Vols. 1919–58, 1v.

426
ANNALES: ÉCONOMIES, SOCIÉTÉS, CIVILISATIONS. 1– , Jan./Mar. 1946– . Paris, A. Colin. Bimonthly.
In French.
Supersedes: *Annales d'Histoire Sociale.*
Indexed: Bull. Anal. Pol. Ec. Soc.; Bull. Sig. Soc. Eth.; Geo. Abst.; His. Abst.; Int. Bibl. Eco.; Int. Bibl. Pol. Sc.; Int. Bibl. Soc.; Int. Bibl. Soc. Cul. Anth.; LLBA; Peace Res. Abst. J.; Pop. Ind.; SSCI; Wom. Stu. Abst.

427
ANNALES INTERNATIONALES DE CRIMINOLOGIE. INTERNATIONAL ANNALS OF CRIMINOLOGY. ANALES INTERNACIONALES DE CRIMINOLOGÍA. v.1– , 1952– . Paris. Semi-annual.
Issued by: Société Internationale de Criminologie. In English or French; summaries in English, French and Spanish. Some no. are combined.
Supersedes: Société Internationale de Criminologie. *Bulletin.*
Indexed: Bull. Anal. Pol. Ec. Soc.; Bull. Sig. Soc. Eth.; Int. Bibl. Soc.; PAISFL.

428
ANNALES JURIDIQUES, POLITIQUES, ÉCONOMIQUES ET SOCIALES. v.1– , 1955?– . Alger, Librairie Ferraris.
Issued by: Faculté de Droit d'Alger. In French.

ANNALES MALGACHES
See Université de Madagascar. Faculté de Droit et des Sciences Économiques. ANNALES. SÉRIE LETTRES ET SCIENCES HUMAINES

429
ANNALES MAROCAINES DE SOCIOLOGIE. 1968– . Rabat. Annual.
Issued by: Institut de Sociologie de Rabat. In Arabic, English, or French; summaries in two of these languages, other than the language of text. Other title: *Moroccan Annals of Sociology.* 1970 issue last examined.
Indexed: Soc. Abst.

ANNALES MUSEI ARCHAEOLOGICI POSNANIENSIS
See FONTES ARCHAEOLOGICI POSNANIENSES

ANNALES MUSEI NATIONALIS HUNGARICI
See FOLIA ARCHAEOLOGICA

ANNALES POLITIQUES
See ḤAWLĪYĀT, SIYĀSĪYA-AL-SAMAH

430
ANNALES RÉVOLUTIONAIRES. v.1–15, 1908–1923. Paris. Annual.
In French. Vols. 8–15, 1916–23 called also "Nouvelle série". None published in 1915.
Indexes: 1908–18, 1v.; 1919–23, 1v.

ANNALES. SECTIO PHILOSOPHICA ET SOCIOLOGICA
See Tudományegyetem, Budapest. ANNALES. SECTIO PHILOSOPHICA ET SOCIOLOGICA

ANNALES. SÉRIE F. ETHNOSOCIOLOGIE
See Université d'Abidjan. ANNALES. SÉRIE F. ETHNOSOCIOLOGIE

ANNALES. SÉRIE G. GÉOGRAPHIE
See Université d'Abidjan. ANNALES. SÉRIE G. GÉOGRAPHIE

ANNALES. SÉRIE K. SCIENCES ÉCONOMIQUES
See Université d'Abidjan. ANNALES. SÉRIE K. SCIENCES ÉCONOMIQUES

ANNALES. SÉRIE LETTRES ET SCIENCES HUMAINES
See Université de Madagascar. Faculté de Droit et des Sciences Économiques. ANNALES. SÉRIE LETTRES ET SCIENCES HUMAINES

ANNALES. SERIES A. SECTION 5. MEDICA ANTHROPOLOGICA
See Soumalainen Tiedeakademia, Helsingfors. TOIMITUKSIA

431
ANNALES SILESIAE. v.1– , 1960– . Wrocław, Państwowe Wydawnictwo Naukowe. Quarterly.
Issued by: Wrocławskie Towarzystwo Naukowe. In English or Polish.

ANNALI
See Fondazione Giangiacomo Feltrinelli. ANNALI

ANNALI
See Fondazione Italiana per la Storia Amministrativa. ANNALI

ANNALI
See Universita di Palermo. Facoltà di Economia e Commercio. ANNALI

ANNALI DI DIRITTO INTERNAZIONALE
See DIRITTO INTERNAZIONALE

ANNALI DI ECONOMIA
See GIORNALE DEGLI ECONOMISTI E ANNALI DI ECONOMIA

ANNALI DI SCIENZE POLITICHE
See IL POLITICO

432
ANNALI DI SOCIOLOGIA. v.1– , 1964– . Milano. Annual.
Issued by: Centro di Studi Sociologici. In Italian.
Indexed: Bull. Anal. Pol. Ec. Soc.; Bull. Sig. Soc. Eth.; Int. Bibl. Soc.; Soc. Abst.

433
ANNALI LATERANENSI. v.1– , 1937– . Città del Vaticano, Poligrafia Poliglotta Vaticana. Annual.
Issued by: Pontificio Museo Missionario Etnologico. In English, French, German, Italian, or Spanish.

ANNALS
See Association of American Geographers. ANNALS

ANNALS
See Hitotsubashi Daigaku. ANNALS

ANNALS
See Organization of American States. ANNALS

THE ANNALS
See Philippine Chinese Historical Association. THE ANNALS

ANNALS
See Southeastern Conference on Latin American Studies. ANNALS

434
ANNALS OF ARCHAEOLOGY AND ANTHROPOLOGY. 1–28, 1908–Nov. 1940. Liverpool, University Press of Liverpool.
Publication suspended: Oct. 1916–1919.
Indexes: Vols. 1–28, in 28.

435
ANNALS OF COLLECTIVE ECONOMY. v.1–34, Jan./Dec. 1925–1963. Geneva.
Issued by: International Centre of Research and Information on Collective Economy. Published also in French edition: *Les Annales de l'Économie Collective*, and Spanish: *Anales de la Régie Collective Directe*. Publication suspended Nov./Dec. 1942–Jan./Mar. 1948.
Supersedes: *Annales de la Régie Directe* (v.1–16, 1908–Dec. 1924)
Continued by: *Annals of Public and Cooperative Economy*.
Indexes: 1925–37, in v.14.

436
ANNALS OF ECONOMIC AND SOCIAL MEASUREMENT. v.1–6, no.5, Jan. 1972–winter/spring 1977/78. New York. Quarterly.
Organ of: National Bureau of Economic Research. Subtitle reads: "Journal of computer, information retrieval and research methodology".
Indexed: Int. Bibl. Eco.; Int. Bibl. Pol. Sc.; Int. Bibl. Soc.; PAIS; Pop. Ind.; SSCI.

ANNALS OF EUGENICS
See ANNALS OF HUMAN GENETICS

437
ANNALS OF HUMAN GENETICS. v.1– , Oct. 1925– . London, Cambridge University Press. Semi-annual.
Issued by: Galton Laboratory, University College, London. Title varies: v.1–18, 1925–54, *Annals of Eugenics.*
Indexes: Vols. 1–14, 1925–June 1950, 1v.
Indexed: Abst. Anth.; Int. Bibl. Pol. Sc.; Int. Bibl. Soc. Cul. Anth.; Int. Pol. Sc. Abst.; Pop. Ind.

ANNALS OF INTERNATIONAL STUDIES
See ANNALES D'ÉTUDES INTERNATIONALES

438
THE ANNALS OF PHENOMENOLOGICAL SOCIOLOGY. v.1–2, 1976–1977. Dayton, Ohio.
Issued by: Wright State University.
Continued by: *Phenomenology and Human Sciences.*

439
ANNALS OF PUBLIC AND COOPERATIVE ECONOMY. ANNALES DE L'ÉCONOMIE PUBLIQUE, SOCIALE ET COOPÉRATIVE. ANNALEN DER GEMEINWIRTSCHAFT. Jan./Mar. 1964– . Liège. Irreg.
Issued by: International Centre of Research and Information on Public and Cooperative Economy. Issued also in French and German editions.
Continues: *Annals of Collective Economy.*
Indexed: Bull. Anal. Pol. Ec. Soc.; Int. Bibl. Eco.; Int. Lab. Doc.; PAIS; PAISFL; SSCI.

440
ANNALS OF REGIONAL SCIENCE. v.1– , Dec. 1967– . Bellingham, Wash. Annual, 1967–??; two no. a year, 19??–73; three no. a year.
Issued by: Western Regional Science Association in cooperation with the Western Washington University (earlier called Western Washington State College).
Supersedes: Regional Science Association. Western Section. *Papers and Proceedings.*
Indexes: Vols. 1–5, 1967–71, 1v.; v.6–10, 1972–76, 1v.
Indexed: ABC POL SCI; PAIS; Pop. Ind.: SSCI.

ANNALS OF SOCIAL SCIENCES
See ROCZNIKI NAUK SPOŁECZNYCH (Lublin)

THE ANNALS OF THE AMERICAN ACADEMY OF POLITICAL AND SOCIAL SCIENCE
See The American Academy of Political and Social Science. ANNALS

THE ANNALS OF THE CHINESE ASSOCIATION OF POLITICAL SCIENCE
See CHENG-CHIH HSÜEH PAO

THE ANNALS OF THE CHINESE SOCIETY OF INTERNATIONAL LAW
See CHUNG-KUO KUO CHI FA HSÜEH HUI

ANNALS OF THE DEMOGRAPHIC RESEARCH INSTITUTE OF THE CENTRAL STATISTICAL OFFICE
See Nepessegtudományi Kutato Intézet. ANNALS OF THE DEMOGRAPHIC RESEARCH INSTITUTE OF THE CENTRAL STATISTICAL OFFICE

441
ANNALS OF THE FRENCH REVOLUTION. 1– , 1978– . Lafayette, La. Annual.
Issued by: Institute of French Studies, University of Southwestern Louisiana, in cooperation with the Société des Études Robespierristes. An English edition of selected articles from the *Annales Historiques de la Révolution Française* (v.47–).

ANNALS OF THE HITOTSUBASHI ACADEMY
See Hitotsubashi Daigaku. Hitotsubashi Gakkai. ANNALS

ANNALS OF THE HITOTSUBASHI ACADEMY
See HITOTSUBASHI JOURNAL OF LAW AND POLITICS

ANNALS OF THE INSTITUTE OF SOCIAL SCIENCE
See Tokyo Daigaku. Shakai Kagaku Kenkyūjo. ANNALS

ANNALS OF THE JAPANESE SOCIETY OF PUBLIC ADMINISTRATION
See NENPŌ GYŌSEI KENKYŪ

ANNALS OF THE SOCIETY FOR THE HISTORY OF SOCIAL THOUGHT
See SHAKAI SHISO SHI KENKYŪ

442
ANNALS OF TOURISM RESEARCH. v.1– , Sept. 1974– . Menomonie, Wis., Oxford, Pergamon Press, 1982– . Five no. a year.
Issued by: Department of Habitational Resources, Tourism, University of Wisconsin–Stout. Until May/June 1975 issued jointly with the Society for the Advancement of the Tourism Industry.

Indexed: PAIS; SSCI.

443
L'ANNÉE ADMINISTRATIVE. 1903–1904. Paris, V. Giard & E. Briere.
In French.

444
ANNÉE AFRICAINE. 1963– . Paris, A. Pedone. Annual.
Issued by: Centre d'Études d'Afrique Noire, Institut d'Études Politiques, Université de Bordeaux. In French.
Indexed: Bull. Anal. Pol. Ec. Soc.; Int. Pol. Sc. Abst.

445
L'ANNÉE COLONIALE. v.1–4, 1899–1903. Paris, Librairie C. Tallandier.
In French.

446
L'ANNÉE ÉCONOMIQUE ET SOCIALE À GENÈVE. 1982– . Genève, Promoedition.
In French.

447
L'ANNÉE POLITIQUE. POLITIEK JAARBOEK. 1976– . Bruxelles, Res Publica.
In Flemish or French; summaries in English.

448
L'ANNÉE POLITIQUE AFRICAINE. 1965– . Dakar, Société Africaine d'Éditions.
In French.

L'ANNÉE POLITIQUE, ÉCONOMIQUE ET COOPÉRATIVE
See L'ANNÉE POLITIQUE ET ÉCONOMIQUE

449
L'ANNÉE POLITIQUE ET ÉCONOMIQUE. v.1– , 1925– . Paris, Presses Universitaires de France. Four no. a year, 1925–40; bimonthly (some numbers combined)
In French. Title varies: 1925–Apr. 1935, *L'Année Politique Française et Étrangère*. In Nov. 1947 united with *La Revue des Études Coopératives*, and *Res Publica* to form: *L'Année Politique et Revue des Études Coopératives [et] Res Publica* in Nov./Dec. 1947–May/July 1948, and *L'Année Politique, Économique et Coopérative* in Aug./Oct. 1948–Jan./Feb. 1950. It assumed its present title with no. for Mar./Apr. 1950.

450
L'ANNÉE POLITIQUE ET ÉCONOMIQUE AFRICAINE. 1981– . Dakar, Société Africaine d'Éditions.
In French.

L'ANNÉE POLITIQUE ET REVUE DES ÉTUDES COOPÉRATIVES [ET] RES PUBLICA
See L'ANNÉE POLITIQUE ET ÉCONOMIQUE

L'ANNÉE POLITIQUE FRANÇAISE ET ÉTRANGÈRE
See L'ANNÉE POLITIQUE ET ÉCONOMIQUE

451
L'ANNÉE POLITIQUE SUISSE. SCHWEIZERISCHE POLITIK IN JAHRE. . . 1967– . Bern. Annual.
Issued by: Forschungszentrum für Schweizerische Politik, and Universität Bern. In French or German.

452
L'ANNÉE PSYCHOLOGIQUE. v.1– , 1894– . Paris, Presses Universitaires de France. Annual.
Issued by: Laboratoire de Psychologie Physiologique de la Sorbonne (1894–1903). In French.
Indexes: Vols. 1–25, 1894–1924, with v.26.
Indexed: LLBA; Psych. Abst.; SSCI.

453
L'ANNÉE SOCIALE. 1960– . Bruxelles, Éditions de l'Université de Bruxelles. Irreg.
Issued by: Institut de Sociologie, Université Libre. In French.

454
L'ANNÉE SOCIOLOGIQUE. 1–12, 1896/97–1909/12; n. ser. v.1–2, 1923/24–1924/25; ser. 3. v.1– , 1940/48– . Paris, Presses Universitaires de France. Annual.
In French. Absorbed: *Annales Sociologiques*. Série A, B, C, D, and E (v.1–3/4).
Indexed: Bull. Sig. Soc. Eth.; Int. Bibl. Eco.; Int. Bibl. Soc.; Int. Pol. Sc. Abst.; Soc. Abst.

ANNOTATED BIBLIOGRAPHY
See Smithsonian Institution, Washington, D.C. International Program for Population Analysis. Interdisciplinary Communications Program. ANNOTATED BIBLIOGRAPHY.

455
ANNOTATED INDEX OF BEHAVIORAL SCIENCES AND COMMUNITY DEVELOPMENT. v.1–7, 1967–1973.
Issued by: National Institute of Community Development.

ANNUAIRE
See Economic and Social Committee of the European Communities.

ANNUAIRE
See Schweizerische Gesellschaft für Urgeschichte. JAHRBUCH

ANNUAIRE
See Statistical Office of the European Communities. ASSOCIÉS. STATISTIQUE DU COMMERCE EXTÉRIEUR. ANNUAIRE

456
ANNUAIRE ADMINISTRATIF. 1980– . Abidjan.
Issued by: Ministère de l'Information, République de Côte d'Ivoire. In French.
Continues: *Répertoire Politique et Administratif.*

457
ANNUAIRE CNRS. SCIENCES DE L'HOMME. 1980?– . Paris. Annual.
Issued by: Centre de Documentation Sciences Humaines. Centre National de la Recherche Scientifique. In French.
Continues: *Annuaire des Sciences de l'Homme.*

ANNUAIRE CANADIENNE DES DROITS DE LA PERSONNE
See CANADIAN HUMAN RIGHTS YEARBOOK

ANNUAIRE DE DOCUMENTATION COLONIALE COMPARÉE
See International Institute of Differing Civilizations. ANNUAIRE DE DOCUMENTATION COLONIALE COMPARÉE

ANNUAIRE DE DROIT AFRICAIN
See JAHRBUCH FÜR AFRIKANISCHE RECHT

ANNUAIRE DE DROIT COMPARÉ ET D'ÉTUDES LÉGISLATIVES
See ANNUARIO DI DIRITTO E DI STUDI LEGISLATIVI

ANNUAIRE DE DROIT INTERNATIONAL
See CANADIAN YEARBOOK OF INTERNATIONAL LAW

458
ANNUAIRE DE L'AFRIQUE DU NORD. 1– , 1962– . Paris, Centre Nationale de la Recherche Scientifique.
Issued by: Centre Nationale de Recherches sur l'Afrique Mediterranéenne, Aix-en-Provence. In French.
Indexed: Bull. Anal. Pol. Ec. Soc.; Bull. Sig. Soc. Eth.; Int. Bibl. Soc. Cul. Anth.; Int. Pol. Sc. Abst.

ANNUAIRE DE L'ASSOCIATION SUISSE DE SCIENCE POLITIQUE
See ANNUAIRE DE SCIENCE POLITIQUE

ANNUAIRE DE L'INSTITUT INTERNATIONAL
See Institute of International Law. ANNUAIRE DE L'INSTITUT DE DROIT INTERNATIONAL

459
ANNUAIRE DE L'U.R.S.S.: DROIT, ÉCONOMIE, SOCIOLOGIE, POLITIQUE, CULTURE. 1965–1969. Paris. Quarterly.
Issued by: Centre de Recherches sur l'U.R.S.S. et des Pays de l'Est, Université des Sciences Juridiques, Politiques et Sociales. In French.
Supplements: a two-volume publication: *L'U.R.S.S.: Droit, Économie, Sociologie, Politique, Culture.*
Continued by: *Annuaire de l'U.R.S.S. et des Pays Socialistes Européens.*
Indexed: Int. Pol. Sc. Abst.

460
ANNUAIRE DE L'U.R.S.S. ET DES PAYS SOCIALISTES EUROPÉENS. 1972/73– . Strasbourg, Librairie Iska.
Issued by: Centre de Recherches sur l'U.R.S.S. et les Pays de l'Est, Université de Strasbourg. In English or French.
Continues: *Annuaire de l'U.R.S.S.: Droit, Économie, Sociologie, Politique, Culture.*
Indexed: Bull. Anal. Pol. Ec. Soc.; Int. Bibl. Eco.; Int. Bibl. Pol. Sc.; Int. Pol. Sc. Abst.

ANNUAIRE DE L'ASSOCIATION SUISSE DE SCIENCE POLITIQUE
See ANNUAIRE SUISSE DE SCIENCE POLITIQUE

ANNUAIRE DE LA CONVENTION EUROPÉENNE DES DROITS DE L'HOMME
See YEARBOOK OF THE EUROPEAN CONVENTION ON HUMAN RIGHTS

461
ANNUAIRE DE LA FRANCE POLITIQUE. May 1981/May 1983– . Paris, Presses de la Fondation Nationale des Sciences Politiques, [publ. 1984–]. Irreg.
In French.

462
ANNUAIRE DE STATISTIQUE INTERNATIONALE DES GRANDES VILLES. INTERNATIONAL STATISTICAL YEARBOOK OF LARGE TOWNS. 1961–1972. The Hague. Biennial.
Issued by: International Statistical Institute in

cooperation with the International Union of Local Authorities. In English and French.

ANNUAIRE DÉMOGRAPHIQUE
See DEMOGRAPHIC YEARBOOK

ANNUAIRE DE STATISTIQUES DES COMPTABILITÉS NATIONALES
See United Nations. Statistical Office. YEARBOOK OF THE NATIONAL ACCOUNTS STATISTICS

ANNUAIRE DE STATISTIQUES RÉGIONALES
See Statistical Office of the European Communities. REGIONAL STATISTISK ÅRBOG

ANNUAIRE DE STATISTIQUES SOCIALES
See Statistical Office of the European Communities. SOZIALSTATISTIK

ANNUAIRE DE STATISTIQUES DU COMMERCE EXTÉRIEUR. PAYS TIERS
See YEARBOOK OF FOREIGN TRADE STATISTICS. THIRD COUNTRIES

ANNUAIRE DES ORGANISATIONS INTERNATIONALES
See YEARBOOK OF INTERNATIONAL ORGANIZATIONS

463
ANNUAIRE DES PAYS DE L'OCÉAN INDIEN. v.1– , 1974– . Aix-en-Provence, Presses Universitaires d'Aix-Marseille. Annual.
In French; summaries in English.
Indexed: Bull. Anal. Pol. Ec. Soc.; Bull. Sig. Soc. Eth.; Int. Pol. Sc. Abst.; Int. Bibl. Soc. Cul. Anth.

464
ANNUAIRE DU TIERS-MONDE. 1– , 1974/75– . Paris, Berger-Levrault. Annual.
Issued by: Association Française pour l'Étude du Tiers-Monde in cooperation with the Centre d'Études Politiques et Juridiques du Tiers-Monde, Université de Paris I (Panthéon-Sorbonne) and Centre d'Études des Relations Internationales de la Faculté de Droit de Rheims. In French.
Indexed: Bull. Anal. Pol. Ec. Soc.; Int. Bibl. Eco.; Int. Pol. Sc. Abst.

ANNUAIRE ÉCONOMIQUE
See STATE OF THE WORLD ECONOMY

465
ANNUAIRE ÉCONOMIQUE DE LA TUNISIE. ECONOMIC YEARBOOK OF TUNISIA. 1964– . Tunis. Annual.
Issued by: Union Tunisienne de l'Industrie, du Commerce et de la Artisanat. In Arabic, English, or French.

ANNUAIRE EISS
See EISS YEARBOOK

466
ANNUAIRE EUROPÉEN. EUROPEAN YEARBOOK. v.1– , 1955– . The Hague, M. Nijhoff. Annual.
Issued under the auspices of the Conseil de l'Europe. In English and French.
Indexed: Bull. Anal. Pol. Ec. Soc.; Ind. For. Leg Per.; Int. Pol. Sc. Abst.

467
ANNUAIRE EUROPÉEN D'ADMINISTRATION PUBLIQUE. 1– , 1978– . Paris, Éditions du Centre National de la Recherche Scientifique, [pub. 1979] Annual
Issued by: Centre de Recherches Administratives, Université de Droit, d'Économie et des Sciences d'Aix-Marseille. In French.

468
ANNUAIRE FRANÇAISE DE DROIT INTERNATIONAL. v.1– , 1955– . Paris, Éditions CNRS. Annual.
Issued by: Groupe Français des Anciens Auditeurs de l'Académie de Droit International de la Haye, and Centre National de la Recherche Scientifique. In French.
Indexes: Vols. 1–10, 1955–61, 1v.; "Tables quinquennales", 1975–79.
Indexed: Bull. Anal. Pol. Ec. Soc.; Int. Bibl. Pol. Sc.; Int. Pol. Sc. Abst.

ANNUAIRE INTERNATIONAL DE L'ÉDUCATION
See INTERNATIONAL YEARBOOK OF EDUCATION

ANNUAIRE INTERNATIONAL DE L'ÉDUCATION ET DE ENSEIGNEMENT
See INTERNATIONAL YEARBOOK OF EDUCATION

469
ANNUAIRE INTERNATIONAL DE LA FONCTION PUBLIQUE. 1970/71– . Paris. Annual.
Issued by: Centre de Recherche et de Documentation sur la Fonction Publique. Published as a supplement to: Institut International d'Administration Publique. *Bulletin*. In French.

470
ANNUAIRE INTERPARLEMENTAIRE. v.1–2, 1931–1932. Paris. Annual.
In French.

ANNUAIRE POLONAIS DE DROIT INTERNATIONAL
See THE POLISH YEARBOOK OF INTERNATIONAL LAW

471
ANNUAIRE ROUMAIN D'ANTHROPOLOGIE. v.1– , 1964– . Bucureşti, Éditions de la Académie de la République Populaire Roumaine. Annual.
In French.
Indexed: Int. Bibl. Soc. Cul. Anth.

ANNUAIRE STATISTIQUE
See United Nations. Economic Commission for Africa. STATISTICAL YEARBOOK

ANNUAIRE STATISTIQUE
See United Nations. Statistical Office. STATISTICAL YEARBOOK

ANNUAIRE STATISTIQUE
See United Nations Educational, Scientific and Cultural Organization. STATISTICAL YEARBOOK

472
ANNUAIRE STATISTIQUE DE LA SÉCURITÉ SOCIALE. 1981– . Bruxelles. Annual.
Issued by: Ministère de la Prévoyance Sociale. In French. Issued also in Flemish under the title: *Statistisch Jaarboek van Sociale Zekerheid.*
Continues, in part: *Annuaire Statistique de la Sécurité Sociale.*

ANNUAIRE STATISTIQUE DU COMMERCE INTERNATIONAL
See INTERNATIONAL TRADE STATISTICS YEARBOOK

ANNUAIRE STATISTIQUE POUR L'AFRIQUE
See AFRICAN STATISTICAL YEARBOOK

ANNUAIRE SUISSE DE DROIT INTERNATIONAL
See SCHWEIZERISCHES JAHRBUCH FÜR INTERNATIONALES RECHT

ANNUAIRE SUISSE DE LA VIE PUBLIQUE
See SCHWEIZER JAHRBUCH DES ÖFFENTLICHEN LEBENS

473
ANNUAIRE SUISSE DE SCIENCE POLITIQUE. SCHWEIZERISCHES JAHRBUCH FÜR POLITISCHE WISSENSCHAFT. 1961– . Bern, Verlag Paul Haupt. Annual.
Issued by: Association Suisse de Science Politique. In French or German; summaries in both languages. Title varies: 1961–63, *Annuaire de l'Association Suisse de Science Politique. Jahrbuch der Schweizerischen Vereinigung für Politische Wissenschaft.*
Indexed: Bull. Anal. Pol. Ec. Soc.; Int. Pol. Sc. Abst.

474
ANNUAIRE SUISSE TIERS-MONDE. JAHRBUCH SCHWEIZ DRITTE WELT. 1981– . Genève. Annual.
Issued by: Institut Universitaire d'Études du Développement. In French or German.

ANNUAIRE TÜRC SUR LES DROITS DE L'HOMME
See TURKISH YEARBOOK OF HUMAN RIGHTS

ANNUAL BULLETIN FOR ARAB COUNTRIES FOREIGN TRADE STATISTICS ACCORDING TO SITC, R. DIVISIONS
See AL-NASRAH AL-SANAWĪYAH LIL-IHSA AL-TĪJARAH AL-KHĀRIJĪYAH LIL-BĪLAU AL-ARABĪYAH 'ALA MUSTAWA FUṢŪL AL-TASNĪF AL-DUWALĪ AL-MU'UD

ANNUAL BULLETIN OF SOCIOLOGY
See SHAKAI-GAKU NENSHI

ANNUAL DIGEST AND REPORTS OF PUBLIC INTERNATIONAL LAW CASES
See INTERNATIONAL LAW REPORTS

ANNUAL ECONOMIC REPORT ON CHINA
See CHUNG-KUO CHING CHI NIEN CHIEN

475
ANNUAL LEISURE REVIEW. 1982– . Sudbury, Leisure Consultants.

ANNUAL MEETING OF THE BOARD OF DIRECTORS. REPORT OF THE EXECUTIVE DIRECTORS AND SUMMARY PROCEEDINGS
See International Monetary Fund. SUMMARY PROCEEDINGS OF THE ANNUAL MEETING OF THE BOARD OF GOVERNORS

476
ANNUAL OF POWER AND CONFLICT. 1971– . London. Annual.
Issued by: Institute for the Study of Conflict, jointly with the National Strategy Information Center, New York.

477
ANNUAL OF PSYCHOANALYSIS. v.1– , 1973– . New York, International Universities Press. Annual.
Issued by: Chicago Institute for Psychoanalysis.

ANNUAL REPORT
See Academy of the Social Sciences in Australia. ANNUAL REPORT

ANNUAL REPORT
See African Development Bank. Board of Governors. ANNUAL REPORT

ANNUAL REPORT
See Caisse Centrale de Coopération Économique. RAPPORT D'ACTIVITÉ

ANNUAL REPORT
See Canada. Indian and Northern Affairs. ANNUAL REPORT

ANNUAL REPORT
See Canadian Human Rights Commission. ANNUAL REPORT

ANNUAL REPORT
See Central African States Development Bank. ANNUAL REPORT

ANNUAL REPORT
See International Institute for Population Studies. ANNUAL REPORT

ANNUAL REPORT
See International League for Human Rights. ANNUAL REPORT

ANNUAL REPORT
See Islamic Development Bank. ANNUAL REPORT

ANNUAL REPORT
See Jugoslovenska Banka za Medunarodnu Ekonomensku Sarandju. ANNUAL REPORT

ANNUAL REPORT
See Social Science Federation of Canada. ANNUAL REPORT

ANNUAL REPORT
See University of Sussex. Institute of Development Studies. ANNUAL REPORT. HANDBOOK

ANNUAL REPORT
See University of Toronto. Institute for the Quantitative Analysis of Social and Economic Policy. ANNUAL REPORT

ANNUAL REPORT AND PROCEEDINGS OF THE ANNUAL CONFERENCE
See National Council on Crime and Delinquency. YEARBOOK

ANNUAL REPORT OF THE INSTITUTE OF POPULATION PROBLEMS
See JINKO MONDAI KENKYŪ

ANNUAL REPORT ON EXCHANGE ARRANGEMENTS AND EXCHANGE RESTRICTIONS
See International Monetary Fund. ANNUAL REPORT ON EXCHANGE ARRANGEMENTS AND EXCHANGE RESTRICTIONS

ANNUAL REVIEW
See COMMONWEALTH INSTITUTE JOURNAL

ANNUAL REVIEW
See Nihon Kokusai Kenkyūjo. ANNUAL REVIEW

478
ANNUAL REVIEW OF ANTHROPOLOGY. v.1– , 1972– . Palo Alto, Calif., Annual Reviews. Annual.
Supersedes: *Biennial Review of Anthropology*.
Indexed: Int. Bibl. Soc. Cul. Anth.; Int. Pol. Sc. Abst.; Psych. Abst.; SSCI

479
ANNUAL REVIEW OF GOVERNMENT ADMINISTRATION. 1975– . Taipei. Annual.
Issued by: Research, Development and Evaluation Commission.
Continues: *A Review of Public Administration in the Republic of China*.

480
ANNUAL REVIEW OF MONETARY AND ECONOMIC DEVELOPMENTS. 1979– . Tokyo. Annual.
Issued by: Research and Statistics Department, The Bank of Japan.

481
ANNUAL REVIEW OF POPULATION LAW. 1974– . New York.
Issued by: International Advisory Committee on Population and Law, 1974–76; Committee on Population and Law, 1977–; United Nations Fund for Population Activities, 1974–75. (Law and Population Monograph Series, no.30, 39, 1976; Law and Population Book Series, no.20)

482
ANNUAL REVIEW OF PSYCHOLOGY. v.1– , 1950– . Stanford, Calif. Annual.
Issued by: Stanford University.
Indexed: Psych. Abst.; SSCI.

483
ANNUAL REVIEW OF SOCIOLOGY. 1– , 1975– . Palo Alto, Calif., Annual Reviews. Annual.
Indexed: Bull. Anal. Pol. Ec. Soc.; Int. Bibl. Eco.; Int. Bibl. Soc. Cul. Anth.; Int. Pol. Sc. Abst.; SSCI.

484
THE ANNUAL REVIEW OF THE SOCIAL SCIENCES OF RELIGION. v.1–6, 1977–1982. The Hague, New York, Mouton. Annual.
Chiefly in English; some articles in French or German.

ANNUAL STUDIES OF AMERICA
See AMERIKANSKIĬ EZHEGODNIK

ANNUAL SUPPLEMENT
See Council of State Governments. INDEX TO RECENT POLICY POSITIONS OF THE GOVERNING BOARD OF STATE GOVERNMENTS, GENERAL ASSEMBLY OF THE STATES AND ORGANIZATIONS AFFILIATED WITH THE COUNCIL OF STATE GOVERNMENTS. ANNUAL SUPPLEMENT

485
ANNUAL SURVEY OF PSYCHOANALYSIS. v.1–10, 1950–1959. New York, International Universities Press. Annual.

486
ANNUARIO DI DIRITTO COMPARATO E DI STUDI LEGISLATIVI. v.1– , 1927– . Milano, later Roma, Edizioni dell'Istituto. Annual.
Issued by: Istituto Italiano di Studi Legislativi. In English, French, or Italian; summaries in French, German, and Italian. Other titles: *Annuaire de Droit Comparé et d'Études Législatives*; *Yearbook of Comparative Law and Legislative Studies*, and *Jahrbuch für Rechtsvergleichung und Gesetzgebungstudien*. Includes some supplements.

487
ANNUARIO DI POLITICA INTERNAZIONALE. v.1– , 1935– . Milano. Annual.
Issued by: Istituto per gli Studi di Politica Internazionale. In Italian.
Indexed: Bull. Anal. Pol. Ec. Soc.

ANNUARIO DI STATISTICHE REGIONALI
See Statistical Office of the European Communities. REGIONAL STATISTISK ÅRBOG

488
ANNUARIO POLITICO ITALIANO. 1963–1965. Milano, Edizioni di Comunità.
Issued by: Centro Italiano Ricerche e Documentazione. In Italian.
Superseded by: *Italia; Annuario del Economia, della Politica, della Cultura.*

489
ANTHROPINES SCHESEIS. v.1– , July 1972– . Athenae, Voukourestoin.
In Greek.

490
ANTHROPOLOGIA. v.1–, no.1–4, Oct. 1873–Apr. 1875. London.
Issued by: London Anthropological Society.

491
ANTHROPOLOGIAI KÖZLEMÉNYEK. v.1– , 1957– . Budapest, Akadémiai Kiadó. Four no. a year, 1957–70; two no. a year.
Chiefly in Hungarian; some articles in English, French, German, or Russian; summaries in Hungarian. Prior to 1957 published as a section of *Biologiai Közlemények*, a subseries of *Magyar Biologiai Társaság Embertani Szakosztályának Folyóirata*.
Indexed: Int. Bibl. Soc. Cul. Anth.

492
ANTHROPOLOGICA. no.1–8, 1955–1959; n. ser. v.1– , 1959– . Ottawa. Semi-annual.
Issued by: Research Centre for Amerindian Anthropology (1st ser.), Canadian Research Centre for Anthropology, University of Ottawa (n. ser.). In English or French.
Indexed: Int. Bibl. Soc. Cul. Anth.

493
ANTHROPOLÓGICA. v.1– , 1983– . Lima. Annual.
Issued by: Departamento de Ciencias Sociales, Pontificia Universidad Católica del Perú. In Spanish. Other title: *Revista Anthropológica.*
Supersedes: *Debates en Antropología.*

494
ANTHROPOLOGICAL FORUM. v.1– , 1963– . Nedlands, University of Western Australia Press. Annual (irreg. –1970/71); quarterly.
Indexed: Abst. Anth.; APAIS; Int. Bibl. Soc. Cul. Anth.

495
ANTHROPOLOGICAL INDEX. 1– , Jan./Mar. 1963– . London. Quarterly.
Issued by: Library of the Royal Anthropological Institute, v.1–14, 1963–76; Library of the Museum of Mankind, v.15–20, 1977–82; Commission on Documentation of the International Union of Anthropological and Ethnological Sciences. Title varies: v.1–14, 1963–76, *Anthropological Index to Current Periodicals Received in the Library*; v.15–20, 1977–82, *Anthropological Index to Current Periodicals in the Museum of Mankind Library.*

ANTHROPOLOGICAL INDEX TO CURRENT PERIODICALS IN THE MUSEUM OF MANKIND LIBRARY
See ANTHROPOLOGICAL INDEX

ANTHROPOLOGICAL INDEX TO CURRENT PERIODICALS RECEIVED IN THE LIBRARY
See ANTHROPOLOGICAL INDEX

496
ANTHROPOLOGICAL JOURNAL OF CANADA. 1963– . Ottawa, Anthropological Association of Canada. Quarterly.
Issued by: Guild of American Prehistorians.
Indexed: Abst. Anth.; Bull. Sig. Soc. Eth.

497
ANTHROPOLOGICAL LINGUISTICS. v.1– , Jan. 1959– . Bloomington, Ind. Nine no. a year.
Issued by: Archives of the Languages of the World, Anthropology Department, Indiana University.
Indexed: Abst. Anth.; Bull. Sig. Soc. Eth.; Int. Bibl. Soc. Cul. Anth.; LLBA; SSCI; Wom. Stu. Abst.

498
ANTHROPOLOGICAL LITERATURE. v.1– , winter 1979– . Pleasantville, N.Y., Readgrave Pub. Co, 1979–83; Cambridge, Mass., 1984– . Quarterly with annual cumulation.
Compiled by: Tozzer Library, Peabody Museum of Archaeology, Harvard University. Beginning with v.6 published in microform.

ANTHROPOLOGICAL PAPERS
See American Museum of Natural History, New York. ANTHROPOLOGICAL PAPERS.

499
ANTHROPOLOGICAL QUARTERLY. v.1– , Jan. 1928– . Washington, D.C., Catholic University of America Press. Quarterly.
Issued by: Department of Anthropology, Catholic University of America. Nos for 1953 called also n. ser. v.1. Title varies: V.1–25, 1928–52, *Primitive Man*.
Indexes: Vols. 1–10, 1928–37, 1v.; v.26–35, 1953–63, 1v.
Indexed: Abst. Anth.; Bull. Sig. Soc. Eth.; Int. Bibl. Soc. Cul. Anth.; LLBA; SSCI

500
ANTHROPOLOGICAL REVIEW. v.1–8, May 1863–Apr. 1970. London, Trübner.
Issued by: Anthropological Society of London. With v.4 of the *Anthropological Review* was issued also *Popular Magazine of Anthropology*.
Superseded by: *Journal of Anthropology*.

ANTHROPOLOGICAL SERIES
See FIELDIANA; ANTHROPOLOGY

501
Anthropological Society of Bombay. JOURNAL. v.1–15, 1886–1936; n. ser. v.1– , 1946– . Bombay.
Indexes: Vols. 1–15, 1886–1936.

502
Anthropological Society of London. JOURNAL. v.1–8, Apr. 1863–1870/71. London.

503
Anthropological Society of London. MEMOIRS. v.1–3, 1863/64–1867/69. London [publ. 1865–70]

504
Anthropological Society of Oxford. JOURNAL. 1970– . Oxford. Three no. a year.
Other title: *JASO*.
Indexed: Abst. Anth.

505
ANTHROPOLOGICAL STUDIES OF BRITAIN. no.1– , 1982– . Manchester, Manchester University Press.

506
ANTHROPOLOGIE. v.1– , 1890– . Paris, Masson. Bimonthly, 1890–1971; eight no. a year, 1972–73; quarterly.
In French. Formed by the union of: *Matériaux pour l'Histoire de l'Homme*, and: *Revue d'Ethnographie*. Table of contents of vols. 21–40, 1910–30, in v.40, pp. 545–806.
Indexed: Bull. Sig. Soc. Eth.

507
ANTHROPOLOGIE. 1923–1938. Praha. Quarterly.
Issued by: Antropologický Ústav, Universita Karlova, Prague.

508
ANTHROPOLOGIE. 1– , 1962– . Brno. Three no. a year.
Issued by: Ústav Anthropos, Moravské Museum. In Czech, English, French, German, or Russian; summaries in any language other than the text.

509
Anthropologische Gesellschaft in Wien. MITTEILUNGEN. 1– , Mar. 1870– . Wien, F. Berger. Annual.

In 1870–1949 issued by the Society under its earlier name: Österreichische Gesellschaft für Anthropologie, Ethnologie und Prähistorie. In German. Publication suspended in 1943–46; v. 73/77 published in 1947. Vols. 11–26, 1881–96 called also "neue Folge", v.1–16; v.31– , 1901– , also called "dritte Folge".
Indexes: Vols. 1–10, 1870–81, in v.10; v.11–20, 1881–90, with v.20; v.21–30, 1891–1900.

510
ANTHROPOLOGISCHER ANZEIGER. 1– , Mar. 1924– . Stuttgart, E. Schweizerbart'sche Verlagsbuchhandlung. Quarterly.
In English or German; occasionally in French or Italian. Publication suspended between v.19, no.1/2, 1943/44 and v.20, no.1, Apr. 1956. Includes supplement "Sonderheft".
Indexed: Bull. Sig. Soc. Eth.; Int. Bibl. Soc. Cul. Anth.

511
THE ANTHROPOLOGIST. v.1– , 1954– . Delhi. Semi-annual.
Issued by: Department of Anthropology, University of Delhi.

512
ANTHROPOLOGY. v.1– , May 1977– . Stony Brook, N.Y. Semi-annual.
Indexed: Bull. Sig. Soc. Eth.; Int. Bibl. Soc. Cul. Anth.

513
ANTHROPOLOGY AND EDUCATION QUARTERLY. v.7, no.3– , Aug. 1976– . Washington, D.C.
Issued by: Council on Anthropology and Education. Absorbed the Council's *Newsletter*.
Continues: Council on Anthropology and Education. *Quarterly*.
Indexed: Abst. Anth.; Bull. Sig. Soc. Eth.; Int. Bibl. Soc. Cul. Anth.; SSCI

514
ANTHROPOLOGY AND HUMANISM QUARTERLY. v.1– , Apr. 1976– . Tallahassee, Fla. Quarterly.
Issued by: Society of Anthropology and Humanism, 1976–77, and Society for Humanistic Anthropology, 1978– . Some nos. are combined.
Indexed: Abst. Anth.; Int. Bibl. Soc. Cul. Anth.

515
ANTHROPOLOGY AND SOCIOLOGY SERIES. no.1–31, 1950–1965. Missoula, Mont. Irreg.
Issued by: Department of Anthropology and Sociology, Montana State University. Monograph series.

516
ANTHROPOLOGY OF THE NORTH: TRANSLATIONS FROM RUSSIAN SOURCES. no.1– , 1961– . Toronto, University of Toronto Press.
Issued by: Arctic Institute of North America.

517
ANTHROPOLOGY OF WORK REVIEW; AWR. v.4– , Feb. 1983–. Stewartsville, N.J. Quarterly.
Issued by: Society for Anthropology of Work.
Continues: *Anthropology of Work Newsletter* (v.1–3, Mar. 1980–1982)

518
ANTHROPOLOGY TODAY. v.1– , Feb. 1985– . London. Bimonthly.
Issued by: Royal Anthropological Institute of Great Britain and Ireland.
Supersedes: *Royal Anthropological Institute News*.

519
ANTHROPOLOGY UCLA. v.1– , Jan. 1969– . Los Angeles, Calif. Two no. a year.
Indexed: Int. Bibl. Soc. Cul. Anth.; SSCI.

520
ANTHROPOS. v.1– , 1906– . St. Augustin. Four no. a year, –1959; six no. a year (frequently two nos. combined).
Issued by: Anthropos Institute. In English, French, German, Italian, or Spanish. Subtitles read: *Revue Internationale d'Ethnologie et de Linguistique*; *Revista Internacional de Etnología e de Lingüística*.
Indexed: Abst. Anth.; Bull. Sig. Soc. Eth.; Int. Bibl. Soc. Cul. Anth.

521
ANTHROPOS. v.1– , Feb. 1974– . Athenai.
Issued by: Hellenike Anthropologike Hetaireia. In English or Greek.

522
ANTIQUITY. v.1– , Mar. 1927– . Cambridge. Quarterly, 1927–75; three no. a year.
Indexes: Vols. 1–25, 1927–51, 1v.; v.26–50, 1952–70, 1v.
Indexed: Abst. Anth.; Int. Bibl. Soc. Cul. Anth.

523
ANTROPOLOGÍA. n. epoca no.1– , Jan./Feb. 1935– ; epoca 3., no.20– , Oct./Dec. 1977– . Mexico, D.F. Bimonthly.
Issued by: Instituto Nacional de Antropología e Historia. In Spanish.

524
ANTROPOLOGÍA. v.1– , 1963– . Santiago, Chile. Semi-annual.
Issued by: Centro de Estudios Antropológicos, Universidad de Chile. In Spanish.

525
ANTROPOLOGÍA. no.1– , 1965– . Bogotá.
Issued by: Universidad de los Andes. In Spanish.

526
ANTROPOLOGÍA. v.1– , first semester 1979– . La Paz.
Issued by: Instituto Nacional de Antropología. In Spanish. Other title: *Revista del Instituto Nacional de Antropología*.

527
ANTROPOLOGÍA. 1– , July 1983– . Quito. Semi-annual.
Issued by: Departamento de Antropología, Pontificia Universidad Católica del Ecuador. In Spanish.

528
ANTROPOLOGIA CONTEMPORANEA. v.1– , 1978– . Torino. Quarterly.
Issued by: Unione Antropologica Italiana, and Federazione delle Istituzioni Antropologiche Italiane. In Italian.

529
ANTROPOLOGÍA E HISTORIA. 1. epoca, 1960–70; 2. epoca Apr./June 1972–1977; 3. epoca, no.20– , Oct./Dec. 1977– . Mexico, D.F. Irreg.
Issued by: Instituto Nacional de Antropología e Historia. In Spanish. Title varies: 1.–2. epoca, 1960–77, *Boletín*.

530
ANTROPOLOGÍA E HISTORIA DE GUATEMALA. v.1– , Jan. 1949– . Guatemala City. Semi-annual.
Issued by: Instituto de Antropología e Historia de Guatemala. In Spanish.

531
ANTROPOLOGIA PORTUGUESA. v.1– , 1983– . Coimbra. Annual.
Issued by: Instituto de Antropologia, Universidade de Coimbra. In Portuguese.

532
ANTROPOLOGÍA Y MARXISMO. v.1– , May 1979– . Mexico, D.F., Ediciones de Cultura Populare.
In Spanish.

533
ANTROPOLÓGICA. no.1– , Sept. 1956– . Caracas, Editorial Sucre. Irreg.
Issued by: Sociedad de Ciencias Naturales La Salle (1956–Aug. 1962); subsequently by Instituto Caribe de Antropología y Sociología of the Fundación La Salle Ciencias Naturales. In English, German, or Spanish.

ANTROPOLOGICA
See BIJDRAGEN TOT DE TAALLAND EN VOLKENKUNDE

ANTROPOLOGICHESKIĬ SBORNIK
See Akademii͡a Nauk SSSR. Institut Etnografii. TRUDY. n.ser.

534
ANTROPOLOGICHESKIĬ ZHURNAL. 1932–1937. Moskva.
In Russian.
Continues: *Russkiĭ Antropologicheskiĭ Zhurnal*.

535
ANTROPOLOGISKA STUDIER. 1971– . Stockholm. Four no. a year.
Issued by: Antropologföreningen, Socialantropologiska Institutionen, Stockholm Universitet. No.30–31 also called *Women's Work and Household Systems*. In English or Swedish.
Continues: *Antropolognytt*.

ANUARIO
See Pontificia Universidad Católica, Rosario. Facultad de Derecho y Ciencias Sociales. ANUARIO

ANUARIO
See United Nations. International Law Commission. YEARBOOK

ANUARIO
See Universidad Central de Venezuela. Instituto de Antropología e Historia. ANUARIO

ANUARIO
See Universidad Central de Venezuela. Instituto de Estudios Hispanoamericanos. ANUARIO

ANUARIO COMERCIAL DE LAS ANTILLAS Y PAÍSES DE CARIBE
See THE WEST INDIES YEARBOOK

536
ANUARIO COLOMBIANO DE HISTORIA SOCIAL Y DE LA CULTURA. v.1– , 1963– . Bogotá. Irreg.

Issued by: Facultad de Ciencias Humanas, and Sección de Historia de Colombia y América, Facultad de Filosofía y Letras, Universidad Nacional de Colombia. In Spanish.

537
ANUARIO DE DERECHO INTERNACIONAL. 1– , 1974– . Pamplona, Ediciones Universidad de Navarra. Annual.
Issued by: Departamento de Derecho Internacional, Universidad de Navarra. In Spanish.
Indexed: Bull. Anal. Pol. Ec. Soc.

538
ANUARIO DE ESTUDIOS CENTROAMERICANOS. 1– , 1974– . San José, Departamento de Publicaciones, Universidad de Costa Rica.
Issued by: Instituto de Estudios Centroamericanos, Universidad de Costa Rica. In Spanish.

539
ANUARIO DE ESTUDIOS MEDIEVALES. 1– , 1964– . Barcelona. Annual.
Issued by: Instituto de Historia Medievale, Universidad de Barcelona. In Romance languages; summaries in English and French.

540
ANUARIO DE LOS PUEBLOS IBÉRICOS. 1955–1967. Madrid, Instituto de Estudios Sindicales, Sociales y Cooperativos. Annual.
Issued by: Asociación de Sociólogos de Langua Española y Portuguesa (ASLEP), and Instituto de Cultura Hispánica. In Spanish.

541
ANUARIO DE SOCIOLOGÍA ESPAÑOLA. v.1– , winter 1980– . Madrid, Euramerica. Annual.
Issued by: Fundación Foessa. In Spanish. (Colección FF. Serie Sintesis)

542
ANUARIO DE SOCIOLOGÍA Y PSICOLOGÍA JURÍDICAS. 1975– . Barcelona. Annual.
Issued by: Instituto de Psicología y Sociología Jurídicas. In Spanish.

543
ANUARIO ECUATORIANO DE DERECHO INTERNACIONAL. 1– , 1964/65– . Quito. Annual.
Issued by: Instituto Ecuatoriano de Derecho Internacional, Universidad Central del Ecuador. In Spanish.

544
ANUARIO ESTADÍSTICO CENTROAMERICANO DE COMERCIO EXTERIOR. 1964– . Guatemala City. Annual.
Issued by: Secretaría Permanente del Tratado General de Integración Económica Centroamericana. In Spanish.

ANUARIO ESTADÍSTICO DE AMÉRICA LATINA
See ANUARIO ESTADÍSTICO DE AMÉRICA LATINA Y DEL CARIBE

545
ANUARIO ESTADÍSTICO DE AMÉRICA LATINA Y DEL CARIBE. 1973– . Santiago, Chile. Annual.
Issued by: Economic Commission for Latin America and the Caribbean, United Nations. Other title: *Statistical Yearbook of Latin America and the Caribbean*. In English and Spanish. Title varies: 1973/74, *Statistical Yearbook of Latin America*.
Supersedes: United Nations. Economic Commission for Latin America. *Boletín Estadístico de América Latina*. (E/CEPAL)

546
ANUARIO FINANZIERO DE MÉXICO. v.1– , 1940– . Mexico, D.F., Editorial Cultura. Annual.
Issued by: Asociación de Banqueros de México. In Spanish.

547
ANUARIO IBEROAMERICANO. 1962– . Madrid. Annual.
Issued by: Servicio de Documentación Iberoamericana, Instituto de Cultura Hispánica. In Spanish. Subtitle reads: "Hechos y documentos".

548
ANUARIO INDIGENISTA. v.22– , Dec. 1962– . Mexico, D.F. Annual.
Issued by: Instituto Indigenista Interamericano. In Spanish. It is a supplement to *América Indigena*. Other title: *Indianist Yearbook*.
Continues: *Boletín Indigenista*.
Indexed: Bull. Anal. Pol. Ec. Soc.; Int. Bibl. Soc. Cul. Anth.; Int. Lab. Doc.

549
ANUARIO INTERAMERICANO DE ARCHIVOS. v.9/10– , 1983– . Córdoba. Annual.
Issued by: Centro Interamericano de Desarrollo de Archivos. In Spanish. Some numbers are combined.
Continues: *Boletín Interamericano de Archivos*.

550
ANUARIO INTERAMERICANO DE DERECHOS HUMANOS. INTER-AMERICAN YEARBOOK OF HUMAN RIGHTS. 1968– . Washington, D.C., Department of Publications, Organization of American States. Biennial.
Issued by: Inter-American Commission on Human Rights. In English and Spanish.

551
ANUARIO MEXICANO DE RELACIONES INTERNACIONALES. AMRI. v.1– , 1980– . Mexico, D.F. [publ. in 1981]. Annual.
Issued by: Escuela Nacional de Estudios Profesionales Acatlan, Universidad Nacional Autónoma de México. In Spanish.

552
ANUARIO POLÍTICO DE AMÉRICA LATINA. 1974– . Mexico, D.F. Annual.
Issued by: Facultad de Ciencias Políticas y Sociales, Universidad Nacional Autónoma de México. In Spanish.

ANUARIO POLÍTICO ESPAÑOL
See CAMBIO SOCIAL Y MODERNIZACIÓN POLÍTICA

553
ANUARIO URUGUAYO DE DERECHO INTERNACIONAL. 1962– . Montevideo. Annual.
Issued by: Facultad de Derecho y Ciencias Sociales, Universidad de la República. In Spanish. (Biblioteca de Publicaciones de la Facultad de Derecho y Ciencias Sociales de la Universidad de la República. Sección 3)

ANUARUL
See Academia de Ştiinţe Sociale şi Politice a Republicii Socialiste România. Institutul de Istorie şi Archeologie, Cluj-Napoca. ANUARUL

AOYAMA JOURNAL OF SOCIAL SCIENCES
See AOYAMA SHAKAI KAGAKU KIYŌ

554
AOYAMA SHAKAI KAGAKU KIYŌ. no.1– , 1973– . Tokyo. Two no. a year.
Issued by: Graduate School, Aoyama Gakuin University. In Japanese. Tables of contents also in English. Other title: *Aoyama Journal of Social Sciences* and *Aoyama Shakaigakkai Kiyō.*

555
APORTES. no.1–25, July 1966–July 1972. Paris. Quarterly.
Issued by: Instituto Latinoamericano de Relaciones Internacionales. In Spanish. Subtitle reads: "Cuadernos de información política y económica".
Indexed: Bull. Sig. Soc. Eth.; Int. Bibl. Soc. Cul. Anth.; Int. Pol. Sc. Abst.; Int. Lab. Doc.

APORTES A LA ETNOLOGÍA Y LINGÜÍSTICA, ARQUEOLOGÍA Y ANTROPOLOGÍA DE LA AMÉRICA INDÍGENA
See INDIANA

APPLIED ANTHROPOLOGY
See HUMAN ORGANIZATION

556
APPLIED ECONOMICS. v.1– , Jan. 1969– . Oxford, New York, Pergamon Press. Quarterly.
Issued by: Queen Mary College, University of London.
Indexed: Bull. Anal. Pol. Ec. Soc.; Int. Bibl. Eco.; Int. Bibl. Pol. Sc.; Int. Bibl. Soc.; Int Lab. Doc.; PAIS; SSCI.

557
APPLIED GEOGRAPHY AND DEVELOPMENT. v.15– , 1980– . Tübingen. Biennial.
Issued by: Institute for Scientific Cooperation.
Continues: *Applied Sciences and Development.*
Indexed: Int. Bibl. Eco.; PAIS

558
APPLIED MATHEMATICAL MODELLING. v.1– , June 1976– . Guildford, IPC Science and Technology Press. Bimonthly.
Subtitle reads: "Environmental, social and engineering systems".

559
APPLIED PSYCHOLOGICAL MEASUREMENT. v.1– , winter 1977– . Minneapolis, Minn., West Pub. Co. Quarterly.

560
APPLIED SOCIAL PSYCHOLOGY ANNUAL. 1– , 1980– . Beverly Hills, Calif., Sage Publications.
Sponsored by: The Society for the Psychological Study of Social Issues, Division of the American Psychological Association. CSPSSI.
Indexed: Psych. Abst.

561
APPLIED SOCIAL SCIENCES BIBLIOGRAPHIES. v.1– , 1984– . New York, Garland Press. Irreg.

562
APPLIED SOCIAL STUDIES. v.1– , 1969– . Oxford, Elmsford, N.Y., Pergamon Press. Three no. a year.

Indexed: Abst. Soc. Work; Psych. Abst.; Wom. Stu. Abst.

563
APPLIED STATISTICS. v.1– , Mar. 1952– . London, Oliver and Boyd. Three no. a year.
Issued by: Royal Statistical Society.

564
ARAB–ASIAN AFFAIRS. no.84– , Jan. 1980– . London, World Reports. Monthly.
Continues: *Afro-Asian Affairs.*
Indexes: Vols. 1–5, no.1–10, a supplement to no.11 (1980)

565
ARAB COOPERATION WITH AFRICA: A SURVEY. MAṢRIF-AL-‘ARABĪ LIL-TAUMĪYAH AL-AL-IQTIṢĀDĪYAH FI AFRIQ’UJA. 14th ed., 1983– . Khartoum, BADEA. Annual.
Continues: *Survey of Arab Programme of Cooperation with Africa.*

566
ARAB ECONOMIST. no.25– , Jan. 1971– . Beirut. Monthly.
Issued by: Center for Economic, Financial and Social Research and Documentation.
Continues: *Monthly Survey of Arab Economies* (no.1–24, 1969–70)

567
THE ARAB GULF JOURNAL. v.1– , Oct. 1981– . London, MD Research and Services, Ltd. Semi-annual.
Vol. 3 (1983) has special issue called “Supplement: Arab Banking and International Finance”.
Indexed: PAIS.

ARAB HISTORIAN
See MAJALLAT AL-MU’ARKIKH AL-‘ARABI

ARAB JOURNAL FOR SOCIOLOGICAL DEFENCE
See AL-MAJALLAH AL-‘ARABĪYAH LIL-DIFĀ’ AL IJTIMĀ’Ī

ARAB STUDIES
See DIRĀSĀT ĀRABĪYAT

568
ARAB STUDIES QUARTERLY. v.1– , winter 1979– . Detroit, Mich.
Issued by: Association of Arab-American University Graduates, and the Institute of Arab Studies.
Indexed: Bull. Sig. Soc. Eth.; Int. Bibl. Pol. Sc.; Int. Pol. Sc. Abst.; PAIS.

569
ARABIAN STUDIES. 1– , 1974– . London, C. Hurst & Co.; Totowa, N.J., Rowman and Littlefield. Annual.
Issued by: Middle East Centre, Cambridge University.

ARBEIDSBLAD
See REVUE DU TRAVAIL

570
ARBEIT UND LEISTUNG. 1–28, 1947–1974. München, Bartman. Quarterly.
Issued by: Gesellschaft für Arbeitswissenschaft. In German. Title varies: 1947–62, *Zentralblatt für Arbeitswissenschaft und Soziale Betriebspraxis.*
Continued by: *Zeitschrift für Arbeitswissenschaft.*
Indexes: 1947–1967, 1v.

571
ARCHAEOLOGIA AUSTRIACA. no.1– , 1948– . Wien, F. Deuticke. Three no. a year, 1948–52; quarterly, 1953–78; annual.
Issued by: Anthropologisches Institut, and Urgeschichtliches Institut of the Universität Wien. In German. Some numbers accompanied by supplement called “Beiheft” (no.1, 1957).
Indexed: Brit. Arch. Abst.; Int. Bibl. Soc. Cul. Anth.

572
ARCHAEOLOGIA GEOGRAPHICA. v.1– , 1950– . Hamburg, Flemingsverlag. Four no. a year, 1950–52; annual.
Issued by: Hamburgisches Museum für Völkerkunde und Geschichte, 1950–52; Kartographisches Institut. In German.

573
ARCHAEOLOGIA IUGOSLAVICA. 1– , 1954– . Beograd.
Issued by: Societas Archaeologica Iugoslaviae. In English, French, or German.

ARCHAEOLOGIA JAPONICA
See Nihon Koko-gaku Kyokai. NIHON KOKO-GAKU NEMPŌ

574
ARCHAEOLOGIA POLONA. 1– , 1958– . Wrocław, Zakład Narodowy im. Ossolińskich. Annual.

Issued by: Instytut Historii Kultury Materialnej, Polska Akademia Nauk. In English, French, or German.
Indexed: Int. Bibl. Soc. Cul. Anth.

575
ARCHAEOLOGIA TRANSATLANTICA. 1– , 1981– . Louvain-la-Neueve.
Issued by: Institut Supérieur d'Archéologie et d'Histoire d'Art, Collège Erasme. In French.

576
ARCHAEOLOGIAI ÉRTESITÖ. ARCHAEOLOGICAL BULLETIN. v.1–14, Nov. 1868–1880; 1– , 1887– . Budapest, Akadémiai Kiadó. Semi-annual.
Issued by: A. Magyar Tudományos Akadémia. In Hungarian; summaries in English, French, German, Italian, or Russian. Tables of contents also in English and Russian.

577
ARCHAEOLOGICA. 1– , 1968– . Toruń. Irreg.
Issued by: Uniwersytet Mikołaja Kopernika at Toruń. In Polish; summaries in German. Subseries of: *Zeszyty Naukowe Uniwersytetu Mikołaja Kopernika. Nauki Humanistyczno-Społeczne.*

ARCHAEOLOGICA HUNGARICA
See FOLIA ARCHAEOLOGICA

ARCHAEOLOGICAL BULLETIN
See ARCHAEOLOGIAI ÉRTESITÖ

578
ARCHAEOLOGICAL JOURNAL. 1844– . London. Annual.
Issued by: Council of the Royal Archaeological Institute (formerly called: Royal Archaeological Institute of Great Britain and Ireland).
Indexes: Vols. 1–25, 1844–68, 1v.; v.26–50, 1869–93, 1v.

579
Archaeological Survey of Canada. PAPER. no.1– , 1971– . Ottawa. Irreg.
Issued by: National Museum of Man. In English or French. Other title: *Dossier.* Monograph series. (Mercuri Series. Collection Mercuri)

580
ARCHAEOLOGY. v.1– , Mar. 1948– . New York. Quarterly, 1948–76; bimonthly.
Issued by: Archaeological Institute of Amerika.
Indexed: Abst. Anth.; Bull. Sig. Soc. Eth.; Int. Bibl. Soc. Cul. Anth.; SSCI.

581
ARCHAEOLOGY & PHYSICAL ANTHROPOLOGY IN OCEANIA. v.1–15, no.3, Apr. 1966–Oct. 1980. Sydney.
Issued by: University of Sydney.
Indexed: Bull. Sig. Soc. Eth.; Int. Bibl. Soc. Cul. Anth.

582
ARCHAEOLOGY IN OCEANIA. v.16– , Apr. 1981– . Sydney. Three no. a year.
Issued by: University of Sydney.
Continues: *Archaeology & Physical Anthropology in Oceania.*

ARCHAEOLOGY, LINGUISTIC STUDIES, HISTORY
See Royal Irish Academy. PROCEEDINGS. SECTION C: ARCHAEOLOGY, LINGUISTIC STUDIES, HISTORY

583
ARCHAEOLOGY MONOGRAPHS. 1– , 1974– . Toronto. Irreg.
Issued by: Royal Ontario Museum. Other title: *Royal Ontario Museum Archaeology Monograph.* Monograph series.

ARCHAEOLOGY SERIES
See OCCASIONAL PUBLICATIONS IN ANTHROPOLOGY. ARCHAEOLOGY SERIES

584
ARCHAEOMETRY. v.1– , spring 1958– . Oxford. Annual.
Issued by: Research Laboratory for Archaeology and the History of Art.
Indexed: Abst. Anth.; SSCI.

ARCHAIOLOGIKĒ EPHĒMERIS
See Archaiologike Hetaireia en Athenais. ARCHAIOLOGIKĒ EPHĒMERIS

585
Archaiologikē Hetaireia en Athenais. ARCHAIOLOGIKĒ EPHĒMERIS. ser. 2, v.1–17, 1862–1874; 1883– . Athens.
In Greek. Not published July 1843–Oct. 1852. Title varies: 1837–60, 1883–1909, *Ephēmeris Archaiologikē.*

586
ARCHÄOLOGIE UND NATURWISSENSCHAFTEN. 1– , 1977– . Mainz, Verlag des Römisch-Germanisches Zentralmuseums in Kommission bei R. Habelt. Irreg.
Issued by: Römisch-Germanisches Zentralmuseum. Forschungsinstitut für Vor- und Frühgeschichte. In German.

587
ARCHEOLOGIA. ETNOGRAFIA. no.1– , 1958– . Poznań, Państwowe Wydawnictwo Naukowe. Irreg.
Issued by: Uniwersytet in Poznań. In Polish; summaries in German. Subseries of: *Zeszyty Naukowe Uniwersytetu im. A. Mickiewicza.*

588
ARCHEOLOGIA POLSKI. v.1– , 1957– . Warszawa, Zakład Narodowy im. Ossolińskich. Two no. a year.
Issued by: Instytut Historii Kultury Materialnej, Polska Akademia Nauk. In Polish; summaries in English, French, German, or Russian.

589
ARCHEOLOGICKÉ ROZHLEDY. [1]– , 1949– . Praha. Six no. a year.
Issued by: Státni Archeologický Ústav. In Czech; summaries in Czech, French, German, or Russian. Tables of contents also in French. Other title: *Nouvelles Archéologiques.*
Indexed: Int. Bibl. Soc. Cul. Anth.

590
ARCHÉOLOGIE. 1– , Nov./Dec. 1964– . Paris. Bimonthly.
In French.

ARCHEOLOGIJA UN ETNOGRAFIJA
See ARHEOLOGIJA UN ETNOGRĀFIJA

591
ARCHIPEL. 1– , 1971– . Bandung, Paris, SECMI. Semi-annual.
Issued by: Société pour l'Étude et la Connaissance du Monde Insulindien with the cooperation of Centre National de la Recherche Scientifique and Institut National des Langues et Civilisations Orientales. In English, French, or Indonesian. Subtitle reads: "Études interdisciplinaires sur le monde insulindien".
Indexed: Bull. Anal. Pol. Ec. Soc.; Bull. Sig. Soc. Eth.; Int. Bibl. Soc. Cul. Anth.; Int. Pol. Sc. Abst.

ARCHIV FÜR ANTHROPOLOGIE
See ARCHIV FÜR ANTHROPOLOGIE, VÖLKERFORSCHUNG UND KOLONIALEN KULTURWANDEL

592
ARCHIV FÜR ANTHROPOLOGIE, VÖLKERFORSCHUNG UND KOLONIALEN KULTURWANDEL. v.1–56, 1866–1943. Braunschweig, Verlag von Vieweg. Annual.
Title varies: 1866–1936, *Archiv für Anthropologie*; 1937–38, *Archiv für Anthropologie und Völkerforschung.* In German. V.29, 1900, also as n. ser. v.1.
Superseded by: *Sociologus*, n. ser.
Indexes: Vols. 1–22, in v.22.

ARCHIV FÜR BEVÖLKERUNGSPOLITIK, SEXUALPOLITIK UND FAMILIENKUNDE
See ARCHIV FÜR BEVÖLKERUNGSWISSENSCHAFT (VOLKSKUNDE) UND BEVÖLKERUNGSPOLITIK

593
ARCHIV FÜR BEVÖLKERUNGSWISSENSCHAFT (VOLKSKUNDE) UND BEVÖLKERUNGSPOLITIK. 1– , 1931– . Berlin.
In German. Title varies: 1931–32, *Archiv für Bevölkerungspolitik, Sexualpolitik und Familienkunde.*

ARCHIV FÜR DIE GESAMTE PSYCHOLOGIE
See ARCHIV FÜR PSYCHOLOGIE

594
ARCHIV FÜR DIE GESCHICHTE DES SOZIALISMUS UND DER ARBEITSBEWEGUNG. v.1–15, 1910–1930. Leipzig, C.L. Hirschfeld. Three no. a year.
In German. Supplements (no.1–5, 1923–30) are called "Beiheft".
Continued by: *Zeitschrift für Sozialforschung.*

595
ARCHIV FÜR KOMMUNALWISSENSCHAFTEN. v.1– , 1962– . Stuttgart, Kohlhammer. Semi-annual.
Issued by: Deutsches Institut für Urbanistik. In German; summaries in English and French.
Indexed: ABC POL SCI; Bull. Anal. Pol. Ec. Soc.; His. Abst.; Int. Bibl. Eco.; Int. Bibl. Pol. Sc.; Int. Bibl. Soc. Cul. Anth.; Int. Pol. Sc. Abst.; PAISFL; Peace Res. Abst. J.

ARCHIV FÜR KULTUR-GESCHICHTE
See ARCHIV FÜR KULTURGESCHICHTE

596
ARCHIV FÜR KULTURGESCHICHTE. v.1–16, 1903–1925/26. Cologne, Böhlau Verlag. Quarterly (irreg.), 1903–23; three no. a year, 1925–49; two no. a year.
In German. Includes supplements called "Beihefte". Other title: *Archiv für Kultur-Geschichte.*
Supersedes: *Zeitschrift für Kulturgeschichte.*

ARCHIV FÜR ÖSTERREICHISCHE GESCHICHTE
See Akademie der Wissenschaften, Wien. ARCHIV FÜR ÖSTERREICHISCHE GESCHICHTE

597
ARCHIV FÜR PSYCHOLOGIE. v.122– , July 1970– . Frankfurt am Main, Akademische Verlagsgesellschaft. Irreg.

Issued by: Deutsche Gesellschaft für Psychologie. In German.

Continues: *Archiv für die Gesamte Psychologie.*

Indexed: Psych. Abst.

598
ARCHIV FÜR RASSEN- UND GESELLSCHAFTSBIOLOGIE, EINSCHLIESSLICH RASSEN- UND GESELLSCHAFTS-HYGIENE. v.1–37, no.4, 1904–1944. Berlin, Verlag für Archiv-Gesellschaft.

In German. Subtitle reads: "Zeitschrift für die Erforschung des Wesen von Rasse und Gesellschaft und ihres gegenseitigen Verhaltnisses für die biologischen Bedingungen ihre Erhaltung und Entwicklung, sowie für die Grundlegen-Probleme der Entwicklungslehre".

ARCHIV FÜR RECHTSPHILOSOPHIE
See ARCHIV FÜR RECHTS- UND SOZIALPHILOSOPHIE

599
ARCHIV FÜR RECHTS- UND SOZIALPHILOSOPHIE. v.1– , Oct. 1907– . Wiesbaden, F. Steiner Verlag. Quarterly.

Issued by: Internationale Vereinigung für Rechts- und Wirtschaft. In English, French, or German. Other titles: *Archives de Philosophie du Droit et de Philosophie Social, Archives for Law and Social Philosophy*. Title varies: 1907–Apr. 1933, *Archiv für Wirtschaftsphilosophie mit besonderer Berücksichtigung der Gesetzgebungfragen*; July 1933, *Archiv für Rechtsphilosophie*.

Indexed: Bull. Anal. Pol. Ec. Soc.; Bull. Sig. Soc. Eth.; Ind. For. Leg. Per.; Ind. Per. Art. Law 1970; Int. Bibl. Pol. Sc.; Int. Pol. Sc. Abst.; Soc. Abst.

600
ARCHIV FÜR REFORMATIONSGESCHICHTE. v.1– , 1903/04– . Gütersloh, Gütersloher Verlagshaus Mohn. Four no. a year, 1903–38; three no. a year, 1939–52; two no. a year, 1953–71; annual.

Published in cooperation with Verein für Reformationsgeschichte, and Society for Reformation Research. In English, French, or German. Other title: *Archive for Reformation History* (1968–). Publication suspended 1944–47, 1949–50. Subtitle varies. Supplements called "Ergänzungsband" (1–4, 1906–11).

Indexes: 1903–24.

601
ARCHIV FÜR REFORMATIONSGESCHICHTE. BEIHEFT. LITERATURBERICHT. 1972– . Gütersloh, Gütersloher Verlagshaus Gehrd Mohn. Irreg.

Published under the auspices of the Verein für Reformationsgeschichte and the American Society for Reformation Research. In English, French, German, or Italian. Other title: *Archive for Reformation History; Literature Review.*

ARCHIV FÜR SOZIALE GESETZGEBUNG UND STATISTIK
See ARCHIV FÜR SOZIALWISSENSCHAFT UND SOZIALPOLITIK

602
ARCHIV FÜR SOZIALGESCHICHTE. 1– , 1961– . Hannover, Verlag für Literatur und Zeitgeschehen; later Verlag Neue Gesellschaft. Annual.

Issued by: Friedrich-Ebert-Stiftung in collaboration with the Institut für Sozialgeschichte, Braunschweig–Bonn. In German. Includes supplement "Beiheft" (1– , 1974–).

Indexed: Bull. Anal. Pol. Ec. Soc.; Bull. Sig. Soc. Eth.; Int. Bibl. Eco.

603
ARCHIV FÜR SOZIALWISSENSCHAFT UND SOZIALPOLITIK. v.1–69, no.5/6, 1888–Aug./Sept. 1933. Tübingen, J.C.B. Mohr. Four no. a year, 1888–96; irreg. 1897–1925; bimonthly, 1926–31; monthly, 1932–33.

In German. Title varies: 1888–1903, *Archiv für Soziale Gesetzgebung und Statistik.*

Indexes: Vols. 1–8, 1888–1903, in v.18; v.1–50, 1888–1923, 1v.

604
ARCHIV FÜR VÖLKERKUNDE. v.1– , 1946– . Wien. Annual.

Issued by: Verein "Freunde der Völkerkunde" and Museum für Völkerkunde, Wien. In German.

Indexed: Abst. Anth.; Bull. Sig. Soc. Eth.; Int. Bibl. Soc. Cul. Anth.

605
ARCHIV FÜR VÖLKERRECHTS. v.1– , July 1948– . Tübingen, J.C.B. Mohr (Paul Siebeck). Four no. a year.

In German; some articles in English.

Indexes: Vols. 1–5, 1948–1955/56, with v.7.

Indexed: Bull. Anal. Pol. Ec. Soc.

ARCHIV FÜR WIRTSCHAFTSPHILOSOPHIE MIT BESONDERER BERÜCKSICHTIGUNG DER GESETZGEBUNGSFRAGEN
See ARCHIV FÜR RECHTS- UND SOZIALPHILOSOPHIE

606
ARCHIV FÜR ZENTRAL ASIATISCHE GESCHICHTSFORSCHUNG. no.1– , 1983– . Sankt Augustin, Wissenwirtschaftsverlag.

In English or German.

607
ARCHIV ORIENTÁLNI. v.1– , 1929– . Praha. Quarterly.
Issued by: Oriental Institute, Czechoslovak Academy of Sciences. In English, German, or Russian.

ARCHIVE FOR REFORMATION HISTORY
See ARCHIV FÜR REFORMATIONSGESCHICHTE

ARCHIVE FOR REFORMATION HISTORY: LITERATURE REVIEW
See ARCHIV FÜR REFORMATIONSGESCHICHTE. BEIHEFT. LITERATURBERICHT

608
ARCHIVES AFRICAINES DE SOCIOLOGIE. v.1– , Paris, Éditions Classiques d'Expression Française. Irreg.
Issued by: Centre de Recherche et d'Information Socio-Politique. In French. Monograph series.

609
ARCHIVES D'ANTHROPOLOGIE. 16– , 1972– . Tervuren.
Issued by: Musée Royal d'Afrique Centrale, Tervuren. In French.
Continues: *Archives d'Ethnographie.*

610
ARCHIVES D'ANTHROPOLOGIE CRIMINELLE. v.1–29, 1886–1914. Paris.
In French. Title varies: 1886–92, *Archives d'Anthropologie Criminelle et des Sciences Pénales.*
Indexes: Vols. 1–25, 1886–1910, in v.25.

ARCHIVES D'ANTHROPOLOGIE CRIMINELLE ET DES SCIENCES PÉNALES
See ARCHIVES D'ANTHROPOLOGIE CRIMINELLE

611
ARCHIVES D'ETHNOLOGIE FRANÇAISE. 1– , 1970– . Paris. Irreg.
Issued by: Musée National des Arts et Traditions Populaires, Centre d'Ethnologie Française, and Laboratoire Associé au Centre National de la Recherche Scientifique. In French. Monograph series.

ARCHIVES DE PHILOSOPHIE DE DROIT ET DE PHILOSOPHIE SOCIAL
See ARCHIV FÜR RECHTS- UND SOZIALPHILOSOPHIE

612
ARCHIVES DE POLITIQUE CRIMINELLE. no.1– , 1975– . Paris, A. Pedone. Annual.
Issued by: Centre de Recherches de Politique Criminelle. In French.
Indexed: PAISFL.

613
ARCHIVES DE PSYCHOLOGIE. 1901– . Genève. Four no. per volume. Irreg.
In English or French.

614
ARCHIVES DES SCIENCES SOCIALES DE LA COOPÉRATION ET DU DÉVELOPPEMENT. no.43– , Jan./Mar. 1978– . Paris. Quarterly.
Issued by: Bureau d'Études Coopératives et Communautaires. In French.
Continues: *Archives Internationales de Sociologie de la Coopération et du Développement.*
Indexed: Bull. Sig. Soc. Eth.; Int. Lab. Doc.

615
ARCHIVES DES SCIENCES SOCIALES DES RELIGIONS. v.18(no.35)– , Jan./June 1973– . Paris, Centre National de la Recherche Scientifique. Semi-annual.
Issued by: Institut des Sciences des Religions. In French.
Continues: *Archives de Sociologie des Religions* (1956–72)
Indexed: Bull. Anal. Pol. Ec. Soc.; Bull. Sig. Soc. Eth.; Int. Bibl. Pol. Sc.; Int. Bibl. Soc. Cul. Anth.; Soc. Abst.

616
ARCHIVES DIPLOMATIQUES. v.1–62, 1861–79; 2. ser. v.1–76, 1880–1900; 3. ser. v.77–129, 1901–13; v. ser. v.130–131, Jan./Apr./May 1914.
In French. Not published in July-Dec. 1870. In 1871–72, 1876–83 the issues were combined, giving four volumes for two years in place of four volumes annually. Includes section "Bibliographie".

617
ARCHIVES ÉCONOMIQUES ET FINANCIÈRES. no.1– , Jan. 15, 1948– . Paris, Agence International Pharos. Semimonthly (irreg.), 1948–Aug. 1949; bimonthly.
In French.

618
ARCHIVES EUROPÉENNES DE SOCIOLOGIE. v.1– , 1960– . Paris, G.P. Maisonneuve et Larose. Semi-annual.

Issued by: 6e Section des Sciences Économiques et Sociales, École Pratique des Hautes Études. In French. Other titles: *European Journal of Sociology*, *Europäisches Archiv für Soziologie*.
Indexed: Bull. Anal. Pol. Ec. Soc.; Bull. Sig. Soc. Eth.; Int. Bibl. Pol. Sc.; Int. Bibl. Soc.; Int. Lab. Doc.; Sage Urb. Abst.; SSCI; Wom. Stu. Abst.

ARCHIVES FOR LAW AND SOCIAL PHILOSOPHY
See ARCHIV FÜR RECHTS- UND SOZIALPHILOSOPHIE

ARCHIVES INTERNATIONALES D'ETHNOGRAPHIE
See INTERNATIONAL ARCHIVES OF ETHNOGRAPHY

619
ARCHIVES INTERNATIONALES DE SOCIOLOGIE DE LA COOPÉRATION. ARCHIVIO INTERNAZIONALE DI SOCIOLOGIA DELLA COOPERAZIONE. INTERNATIONAL ARCHIVES OF SOCIOLOGY OF COOPERATION. no.1–41/42, Jan./June 1957–1977. Paris. Semi-annual.
Issued by: Centre de Recherches Coopératives, Bureau d'Études Coopératives et Communautaires, International Council for Research in Sociology of Cooperation. In French; some articles in English. Issued as a supplement to *Communauté*. Other title: *A.I.S.C.*
Continued by: *Archives des Sciences Sociales de la Coopération et du Développement.*
Indexed: Bull. Sig. Soc. Eth.; Int. Bibl. Soc.; Soc. Abst.

620
ARCHIVES MAROCAINES. v.1–34, 1904–1934. Paris, H. Champion.
Issued by: Direction des Affaires Indigènes. Section Sociologique. In French. Vol. 5 never published.

621
ARCHIVES OF THE BEHAVIORAL SCIENCES. no.44– , Apr. 1975– . Brandon, Clinical Psychology Pub. Co.
Continues: *Journal of Clinical Psychology. Monograph Supplement.*

622
ARCHIVES SUISSES D'ANTHROPOLOGIE GÉNÉRAL. v.1– , 1914/15– . Genève. Annual.
Issued by: Institut Suisse d'Anthropologie Général. In French.
Indexed: Bull. Sig. Soc. Eth.; Int. Bibl. Soc. Cul. Anth.

ARCHIVIO
See Fondazione Italiana per la Storia Amministrativa. ARCHIVIO

ARCHIVIO
See Istituto per la Scienza dell'Amministrazione Pubblica. ARCHIVIO

623
ARCHIVIO DI STUDI URBANI E REGIONALI. 1968– . Milano. Ten no. a year.
Issued by: Studi Urbani e Regionali. In Italian; summaries in English. Monograph series.

624
ARCHIVIO FINANCIERO. v.1– , 1950– . Padova, CEDAM. Annual.
Issued by: Istituto di Finanza Pubblica, Università di Ferrara. In English, French, German, Italian, or Spanish; with summaries in at least two other languages. Includes some abstracts and bibliography.

625
ARCHIVIO INTERNAZIONALE DI ETNOGRAFIA E PREHISTORIA. v.1– , 1958– . Torino, Editrice S.A.I.E.
In English, French, German, Italian, or Spanish.

ARCHIVIO INTERNAZIONALE DI SOCIOLOGIA DELLA COOPERAZIONE
See ARCHIVES INTERNATIONALES DE SOCIOLOGIE DE LA COOPÉRATION

ARCHIVIO ITALIANO DI PSICOLOGIA GENERALE E DEL LAVORO
See RIVISTA DI PSICOLOGIA SOCIALE E ARCHIVIO ITALIANO DI PSICOLOGIA GENERALE E DEL LAVORO

626
ARCHIVIO ITALIANO DI SOCIOLOGIA. v.1– , 1978– . Milano, Franco Angeli.
Issued by: Istituto di Scienze Politiche, Università di Torino. In Italian.

627
ARCHIVIO ITALIANO DI SOCIOLOGIA DEL DIRITTO. 1– , 1977– . Roma, Beniamino Carucci Editore. Annual.
In Italian.

628
ARCHIVIO PER L'ANTROPOLOGIA E LA ETNOLOGIA. v.1– , 1871– . Firenze. Annual.
Issued by: Società Italiana di Antropologia e di Psicologia Comparata (until 1878 called Società Italiana di Antropologia e di Etnologia). In Italian.
Indexes: 1871–1970, 1v.
Indexed: Bull. Sig. Soc. Eth.; Int. Bibl. Soc. Cul. Anth.

629
ARHEOLOGIJA UN ETNOGRĀFIJA. 1957– . Latvijas PSR Zinātņu Akadēmijas Izdevniecība. Irreg.
Issued by: Vēstures Instituts, PSR Zinātnu Akadēmija. In Latvian; summaries in Russian. Title varies: v.1, *Archeologija un Etnogrāfija.*

ARHEOLOGINE KOGUMIK
See Eesti NSV. Teaduste Akademija. Ajaloo Instituut. ARHEOLOGINE KOGUMIK

630
ARHIV ZA PRAVNE I DRUSTVENE NAUKE. v.1– , 1906– . Beograd, Izdanje Saveza Udruženja Pravnika Jugoslavije. Four no. a year.
Issued by: Pravni Fakultet, Univerzitet u Beogradu, 1906–47; Udruženje Pravnika FNRJ, 1948–June 1951; Savez Udruženja Pravnika Jugoslavije. In Serbo-Croatian. Vols. 1906–80 in the Cyrillic alphabet. Summaries in English. Some no. are combined. Not published Aug. 1914–1919; Apr. 1941–1944.

631
ARIZONA JOURNAL OF INTERNATIONAL AND COMPARATIVE LAW. v.1– , 1982– . Tucson, Ariz. Two no. a year.
Issued by: College of Law, University of Arizona. Other title: *Revista de Derecho Internacional y Comparado de Arizona.*

ARKEOLOGISKE RAPPORTER
See Universitet i Bergen. Historisk Museum. ARKEOLOGISKE RAPPORTER

ARKEOLOGISKE RAPPORTER FRA HISTORISK MUSEUM
See Universitet i Bergen. Historisk Museum. ARKEOLOGISKE RAPPORTER

632
ARKHEOLOGICHESKIE OTKRYTIIA. 1965– . Moskva, Nauka. Annual.
Issued by: Institut Arkheologii, Akademiia Nauk SSSR. In Russian.

633
ARKHEOLOGICHESKIĬ EZHEGODNIK. 1957– . Moskva, Izd-vo Akademii. Annual.
Issued by: Arkheologicheskaia Komissiia, Otdelenie Istoricheskikh Nauk, Akademiia Nauk SSSR. In Russian.

634
ARKHEOLOGIIA. v.1– , 1959– . Sofiia. Quarterly.
Issued by: Arkheologicheski Institut, Bulgarska Akademiia na Naukite. In Bulgarian; summaries in French.

635
ARKHEOLOGIIA I ETNOGRAFIIA BASHKIRII. 1– , 1962– . Ufa, Bashkirskoe Knizhnoe Izd-vo. Irreg.
Issued by: Ufimskiĭ Institut Istorii, IAzika i Literatury, Akademiia Nauk SSSR. In Russian.

636
ARKHEOLOGIIA SSSR. SVOD ARKHEOLOGICHESKIKH ISTOCHNIKOV. 1964– . Moskva, Izd-vo Nauka.
In Russian.

637
ARKHEOLOHIIA. 1– , 1971– . Kiiv, Naukova Dumka. Four no. a year.
Issued by: Institut Arkheolohii, Akademiia Nauk Ukrainskoi SSR, and Ukrainske Tovaristvo Okhrany Pam'iatnikov Istorii ta Kultury. In Ukrainian; summaries in Russian.

638
ARKHIV K. MARKSA I ENGELSA. v.1–5, 1924–1930. Moskva. Four no. a year.
Issued by: Institut Karla Marksa i Friderika Engelsa. In Russian.

639
ARMED FORCES AND SOCIETY. v.1– , fall 1974– . Chicago, Ill. Quarterly.
Issued by: Inter-University Seminar on Armed Forces & Society.
Indexed: Bull. Anal. Pol. Ec. Soc.; PAIS; SSCI.

640
Armianskiĭ Gosudarstvennyĭ Pedagogicheskiĭ Institut. NAUCHNYE TRUDY. SERIIA OBSHCHESTVENNYKH NAUK. no.1– , 1966– . Erivan.
In Russian. Title varies: *Sbornik Nauchnykh Trudov. Seriia Obshchestvennykh Nauk.*

641
ARMS CONTROL. v.1– , May 1980– . London, Frank Cass. Three no. a year.
Indexed: Int. Pol. Sc. Abst.

642
ARMS CONTROL & DISARMAMENT. v.1– , winter 1964/65– . Washington, D.C., Government Printing Office. Quarterly.
Compiled by: Arms Control and Disarmament Bibliography Section.
Indexed: PAIS.

643
ARMS CONTROL AND DISARMAMENT. v.1– , 1968– . Croton-on-Hudson, N.Y.
Issued jointly by: Hudson Institute and Pergamon Press.

644
ARQUEOLOGÍA BOLIVIANA. no.1– , 1984– . La Paz.
Issued by: Instituto Nacional de Arqueología. In Spanish.

645
ARQUEOLOGIA E HISTÓRIA. 1–10, 1922–1932; n. ser. 1– , 1945– ; ser. 3. v.1– , 1968– . Lisboa.
Issued by: Associação dos Arqueólogos Portugueses. In Portuguese.
Supersedes: the Associação's *Boletim* (1874–1921). (Subseries of: Publicações da Associação dos Arqueólogos Portugueses)

646
ARQUEOLOGÍA Y SOCIEDAD. 1– , Mar. 1970– . Lima. Quarterly.
Issued by: Museo de Arqueología y Etnología, Universidad de San Marco. In Spanish.

ARQUIVO DO INSTITUTO GULBENKIAN DE CIÊNCIA. B. ESTUDOS DE ECONOMIA E FINANÇAS
See Instituto Gulbenkian de Ciência, Centro de Economia e Finanças. ARQUIVO. B. ESTUDOS DE ECONOMIA E FINANÇAS

647
ARQUIVOS BRASILEIROS DE PSICOLOGIA. 1949– . Rio de Janeiro. Quarterly.
Issued by: Fundação Getulio Vargas. Instituto de Selecaçõe Orientação Profesional. In Portuguese. Title varies: 1949–68, *Arquivos Brasileiros de Psicotécnica*; 1969–78, *Arquivos Brasileiros de Psicologia Aplicada*.

ARQUIVOS BRASILEIROS DE PSICOLOGIA APLICADA
See ARQUIVOS BRASILEIROS DE PSICOLOGIA

ARQUIVOS BRASILEIROS DE PSICOTÉCNICA
See ARQUIVOS BRASILEIROS DE PSICOLOGIA

ART ET ARCHÉOLOGIE PROCHE-ORIENT, ASIE, AMÉRIQUE
See BULLETIN SIGNALÉTIQUE. 526. ART ET ARCHÉOLOGIE PROCHE-ORIENT, ASIE, AMÉRIQUE

648
ARTES POPULARES. 1– , 1970– . Budapest. Annual.
Issued by: A Folklore Tauszek Evkönyve, Eotvös Lorand Tudomány Egyetem. In French or Hungarian; summaries in English, German, Russian, and Spanish. Other title: *Yearbook of the Department of Folklore*. (Publicationes Instituti Folklori Universitatis Rolando Eotvös naminatae)

649
ARTHA VIJNANA. 1– , Mar. 1959– . Poona. Quarterly.
Issued by: Gokdale Institute of Politics and Economics. In English; some articles in Indian languages; summaries in English and Hindi.
Indexed: Bull. Anal. Pol. Ec. Soc.; Int. Bibl. Soc. Cul. Anth.; Int. Lab. Doc.

ARTICLES CHOISIS SUR LE DÉVELOPPEMENT ÉCONOMIQUE ET SOCIALE
See AFRICA INDEX; SELECTED ARTICLES ON SOCIO-ECONOMIC DEVELOPMENT

ARTS AND SCIENCES STUDIES. SOCIAL STUDIES SERIES
See Oklahoma State University of Agriculture and Applied Science, Stillwater. ARTS AND SCIENCES STUDIES. SOCIAL STUDIES SERIES

650
ARTS ET TRADITIONS POPULAIRES. 1953– . Paris. Quarterly.
In French.
Indexed: Bull. Sig. Soc. Eth.; Int. Bibl. Soc. Cul. Anth.

651
THE ASAHI ASIA REVIEW. 1– , 1970– . Tokyo. Quarterly.
Issued by: Asahi Shimbun. In Japanese.

652
ASEIA YEUMKU. JOURNAL OF ASIATIC STUDIES. 1– , 1958– . Seoul. Quarterly.
Issued by: Aseia Munje Yeunkkuso, Koro Daihakkyo. In Korean; summaries and tables of contents in English.

653
ASIA AND THE AMERICAS. v.1– , July 1898– . New York. Irreg. 1898–Jan. 1917; monthly.
Beginning with Nov. 1942 includes "Monthly Review of the East and West Association". Title varies: 1898–Jan. 1917, *Journal of the American Asiatic Association*.

654
ASIA PACIFIC COMMUNITY. no.1– , summer 1978– . Tokyo, Japan Asian Club. Quarterly.
Supersedes: *Pacific Community*.
Indexed: Bull. Anal. Pol. Ec. Soc.; Int. Bibl. Eco.; Int. Bibl. Soc. Cul. Anth.; SSCI.

655
ASIA QUARTERLY. no.1– , 1971– . Bruxelles, Éditions de l'Institut de Sociologie. Four no. a year.
Issued by: Centre d'Étude du Sud-East Asiatique et de l'Extrême-Orient, Institut de Sociologie, Université Libre. In French.

Supersedes: *Revue du Sud-Est Asiatique et de l'Extrême-Orient. Journal of Southeast Asia and the Far East.*
Indexed: Bull. Anal. Pol. Ec. Soc.; Int. Bibl. Pol. Sc.; Int. Bibl. Soc.; Int. Pol. Sc. Abst.; PAIS; Soc. Abst.

656
ASIA YEARBOOK. 1973– . Hong Kong, Far Eastern Economic Review. Annual.
Continues: *Yearbook* issued by the Far Eastern Economic Review.

657
ASIAN AFFAIRS. v.57– , Feb. 1970– . London. Three no. a year.
Issued by: Royal Central Asian Society.
Continues: Royal Central Asian Society. *Journal.*
Indexed: Bull. Anal. Pol. Ec. Soc.; Bull. Sig. Soc. Eth.; Int. Bibl. Pol. Sc.; Int. Pol. Sc. Abst.; PAIS

658
ASIAN AFFAIRS. v.1– , Jan./June 1980– . Dacca. Semi-annual.
Issued by: Study Group.
Indexed: Int. Bibl. Soc. Cul. Anth.; Int. Pol. Sc. Abst.

659
ASIAN AFFAIRS; AN AMERICAN REVIEW. Sept./Oct. 1973– . New York, Crane, Russak and Co. for the American Asian Educational Exchange, subsequently Heldref Publications of the Helen Dwight Reid Educational Foundation. Bimonthly.
Indexed: ABC POL SCI; Bull. Anal. Pol. Ec. Soc.; Int. Bibl. Pol. Sc.; Int. Pol. Sc. Abst.; PAIS.

660
ASIAN AND AFRICAN STUDIES. v.1– , 1965– . Bratislava, Vydavatelstvo Slovenskej Akademie Vied.
In English, French, German, or Russian.

661
Asian and Pacific Council. Cultural and Social Centre. ASPAC QUARTERLY OF CULTURAL AND SOCIAL AFFAIRS. v.1–2, summer 1969–1970. Seoul.
Issued by: Public Relations and Information Office, Cultural and Social Center for Asian and Pacific Region.
Continued by: *Asian and Pacific Quarterly of Cultural and Social Affairs.*
Indexed: Bull. Anal. Pol. Ec. Soc.

662
ASIAN BUSINESS. v.5, no.6– , June 1979– . Hong Kong, Far East Trade Press. Monthly.
Continues: *Asian Business and Industry.*

ASIAN CULTURAL STUDIES
See AJIA BUNKA KENKYŪ

663
ASIAN DEVELOPMENT REVIEW. v.1– , 1983– . Manila. Semi-annual.
Issued by: Asian Development Bank.
Indexed: PAIS.

664
ASIAN ECONOMIC AND SOCIAL REVIEW. v.1– , Nov. 1976– . Bombay. Quarterly.
Issued by: Indian Institute of Asian Studies.
Absorbed: IFCEP *Journal*, and *Quarterly Journal of Indian Studies in Social Sciences.*

665
ASIAN ECONOMIC REVIEW. v.1– , Nov. 1958– . Hyderabad. Three no. a year.
Issued by: Indian Institute of Economics.
Indexed: Int. Bibl. Eco.

666
ASIAN ECONOMICS. v.1– , 1972– . Seoul. Quarterly.
Issued by: Research Institute of Asian Economies.
Indexed: Bull. Anal. Pol. Ec. Soc.; Int. Bibl. Eco.; PAIS.

667
ASIAN EDUCATION. L'ÉDUCATION EN ASIE. v.1– , 1964– . Bangkok. Quarterly.
Issued by: Regional Office for Education in Asia, United Nations Educational, Scientific and Cultural Organization. In English and French.

668
ASIAN FINANCE. v.1– , July 1975– . Hong Kong, Asian Finance Publications. Monthly.

669
ASIAN FINANCE & DEVELOPMENT. v.1– , 1976– . Kuala Lumpur, Dion Jackson Publications. Bimonthly.

670
ASIAN FOLKLORE STUDIES. v.22– , 1963– . Nagoya, Sain Folklore Institute. Annual.
Issued by: Society for Asian Folklore, 1963–72; Sain Folklore Institute, 1973– . Other title: *Minzokugakushi.*
Supersedes: *Folklore Studies.*

671
ASIAN FORUM. v.1– , Jan. 1969– . Washington, D.C. Frequency varies.
Issued by: Pan-Asian Foundation.

Indexed: His. Abst.; PAIS.

672
THE ASIAN JOURNAL OF ECONOMICS. v.1– , Jan. 1982– . Meerut. Quarterly.
Issued by: Department of Economics, Meerut University on behalf of the Society for Asian Development.

673
ASIAN JOURNAL OF PSYCHOLOGY & EDUCATION. v.1– , Mar. 1976– . Agra. Three no. a year.
Issued by: Agra Psychological Research Cell.
Indexed: Psych. Abst.

674
ASIAN JOURNAL OF PUBLIC ADMINISTRATION. YACHOU KUNG KUNG HSING CHENG HSÜEH. v.5– , June 1983– . Hong Kong. Semi-annual.
Issued by: Department of Political Science, University of Hong Kong.
Continues: *Hong Kong Journal of Public Administration.*

675
ASIAN LABOUR. v.1– , Oct. 1948– . New Delhi. Bimonthly.
Issued by: Indian Labour Forum.
Indexed: Int. Lab. Doc.

676
ASIAN LABOUR. 1– , 1950– . Bangalore, Delhi. Monthly.
Issued by: Asian Regional Organization, International Confederation of Free Trade Unions (ICFTU)

677
ASIAN-PACIFIC POPULATION PROGRAMME NEWS. v.7– , 1978– . Bangkok. Quarterly.
Issued by: Economic and Social Commission for Asia and the Pacific, United Nations.
Continues: *Asian Population Programme News* (v.1–6)

678
ASIAN PERSPECTIVES. v.1– , summer 1957– . Tucson, Ariz., later Hong Kong, Hong Kong University Press. Semi-annual.
Issued by: American Branch, Far-Eastern Prehistory Association. Subtitle reads: "A journal of archaeology and prehistory of Asia and the Pacific".
Indexed: Bull. Sig. Soc. Eth.; Int. Bibl. Soc. Cul. Anth.

679
ASIAN POPULATION STUDIES SERIES. no.1– , Nov. 1966– . New York. Irreg.
Issued by: Economic and Social Commission for Asia and the Pacific, United Nations. Monograph series. (E/CN–11)
Indexed: Pop. Ind.

680
ASIAN PROFILE. 1– , Aug. 1973– . Hong Kong, Asian Research Service. Bimonthly.
Indexed: Bull. Anal. Pol. Ec. Soc.; Int. Bibl. Eco.; Int. Bibl. Pol. Sc.; Int. Pol. Sc. Abst.

681
ASIAN REVIEW. v.1–10(no.1–20), Jan. 1886–Oct. 1890; 2d ser. v.1–10(no.1–20), Jan 1891–Oct. 1895; 3d ser. v.1–34(no.1–68), Jan. 1896–Oct. 1912; n. ser. v.1–60(n.1–221), Jan. 1913–Jan. 1966; London, East & West. Quarterly, 1886–Jan. 1964 (every six weeks, 1914–17); three no. a year.
Issued by: East India Association, and Royal India, Pakistan and Ceylon Society. Title varies: 1886–90, 1913, *The Asiatic Quarterly Review*; 1891–1912, *The Imperial and Asiatic Quarterly Review and Colonial Record*; 1914–52, *The Asiatic Review*. Absorbed: *Journal of the East India Association*, and *Art and Letters*, in Apr. 1964. Beginning with 1895 includes the *Proceedings of the East India Association.*
Superseded by: *Asian Review.*
Indexed: Int. Bibl. Soc. Cul. Anth.

ASIAN REVIEW
See SOUTH ASIAN REVIEW

682
ASIAN SECURITY. 1979– . Tokyo, later Washington, D.C., Brassey's Defence Publishers. Annual.
Issued by: Research Institute for Peace and Security. Other title: *Kigyo Keiei Kenkyū Nenpō.*

683
ASIAN SOCIAL SCIENCE BIBLIOGRAPHY WITH ANNOTATIONS AND ABSTRACTS. v.1– , 1952– . Delhi, Vikas Publishing House. Annual.
Issued by: Research Centre on the Social Implications of Industrialization in Southern Asia, Unesco.
Title varies: 1952–56, *Social Science Bibliography, India*; 1957, *Social Science Bibliography, India, Pakistan*; 1958, *South Asia Social Science Bibliography (with Annotations and Abstracts)*. Absorbed: *South Asia Social Science Bibliography*, in 1959.

684
ASIAN STUDIES. v.1– , 1963– . Quezon City, University of the Philippines Press. Three no. a year, 1963–75; annual.
Issued by: Institute of Asian Studies, University of the Philippines.
Indexed: Bull. Anal. Pol. Ec. Soc.; Bull. Sig. Soc. Eth.; Int. Bibl. Eco.; Int. Bibl. Soc. Cul. Anth.

685
ASIAN STUDIES. 1– , 1979– . Dacca. Annual.
Issued by: Centre for Asian Studies, Department of Government and Politics, Jahangirnagar University. Vol. 3, 1981, last examined.

686
ASIAN STUDIES AT HAWAII. no.1– , 1965– . Honolulu, The University Press at Hawaii. Irreg.
Issued by: Asian Studies Program, University of Hawaii. Includes subseries: *East Asian Occasional Papers*.

687
ASIAN SURVEY. v.1– , Mar. 1961– . Berkeley, Calif., University of California Press. Monthly.
Issued by: Institute of International Studies, University of California, Berkeley (Oct. 1961–1969)
Supersedes: *Far Eastern Survey*.
Indexed: Abst. Anth.; ABC POL SCI; Int. Bibl. Eco.; Int. Bibl. Pol. Sc.; Int. Pol. Sc. Abst.; Pop. Ind.; Sage Urb. Stu. Abst.

688
ASIAN THOUGHT AND SOCIETY. v.1– , Apr. 1976– . Oneonta, N.Y., East–West Pub. Three no. a year.
Issued by: State University of New York, Oneonta.
Indexed: Abst. Anth.; ABC POL SCI; Bull. Anal. Pol. Ec. Soc.; His. Abst.; Int. Bibl. Soc. Cul. Anth.; Int. Lab. Doc.; Peace Res. Abst. J.; Wom. Stu. Abst.

THE ASIATIC QUARTERLY REVIEW
See ASIAN REVIEW

THE ASIATIC REVIEW
See ASIAN REVIEW

689
Asiatic Society. JOURNAL. v.1–75, 1832–1904?; n. ser. v.1–30, 1905–1934; 3d ser. v.1– , 1959– . Calcutta. Quarterly.
The society's earlier names were: 1832–1935, Asiatic Society of Bengal; 1936–July 1951, Royal Asiatic Society of Bengal. Some no. are combined. Title varies: 1832–1904, *Proceedings*; 1865–1904, *Journal and Proceedings*; 1905–34, *Letters and Proceedings*; 1935–58, *Letters and Science*.
Supersedes: *Gleanings in Science*.
Indexes: Vols. 1–25, 1832–54, with v.26.
Indexed: His. Abst.

690
Asiatic Society of Bangladesh. JOURNAL. HUMANITIES. v.24/26– . Dacca. Three no. a year; 1979/81– , two no. a year.
Continues: Asiatic Society of Bangladesh. *Journal*, v.16,no.3–v.23, 1975–78, which continues Asiatic Society of Pakistan. *Journal*, 1956–71.

691
Asiatic Society of Japan. TRANSACTIONS. v.1–50, 1872/73–Dec. 1922; ser. 2. v.1–19, Dec. 1924–1940; 3d ser. v.1– , 1948– . Tokyo.
Indexes: General, v.1–12, 1872/73–1883/85, in v.12; v.1–23, 1872/73–1895, in v.23. Subject index: v.1–50, in ser. 2, v.5.

692
ASIATISCHE STUDIEN. ÉTUDES ASIATIQUES. 1– , 1947– . Bern, A. Francke. Four no. a year.
Issued by: Schweizerische Gesellschaft der Freunde Ostasiatischer Kultur. In English, French, German, or Italian.
Supersedes: Gesellschaft's *Mitteilungen*.

693
ASIE DU SUD-EST ET DE MONDE INSULINDIEN. v.2, no.3– , spring 1971– . Paris, Mouton. Quarterly.
Issued by: Centre de Documentation et de Recherche (CEDRA-SEMI), 6e Section Sciences Économiques et Sociales, École Pratique des Hautes Études—Sorbonne. In French.
Continues: *Asie du Sud-Est & Monde Insulindien* (v.1–2, no.2)
Indexed: Bull. Sig. Soc. Eth.; Int. Bibl. Soc. Cul. Anth.

694
ASIEN. v.1–16, no.12, Oct. 1901–Sept. 1919. Berlin, H. Paetal. Monthly.
Issued by: Deutsch–Asiatische Gesellschaft, and Münchner Orientalische Gesellschaft. In German. Includes, beginning with Oct. 1903, supplement called: "Das Wirtschaftliche Asien. Beilage zu Asien".

695
ASIEN, AFRIKA, LATEINAMERIKA. 1966–1973. Berlin, Deutscher Verlag der Wissenschaften. Annual.
Issued by: Sektion Asien, Afrika und Lateinamerika Wissenschaften, Universität Leipzig, 1966–68; Sektion Afrika–Nachost-Wissenschaften, Universität Leipzig, 1969; Zentral Rat für Asien, Afrika und Lateinamerika Wissenschaften, Universität Leipzig, 1970. In German. Includes monographic supplements called "Sonderheft".

Indexed: Int. Bibl. Soc. Cul. Anth.

696
ASPECTOS FINANZIEROS DE LAS ECONOMÍAS LATINOAMERICANAS. 1956–1964. Mexico, D.F.
Issued by: Centro de Estudios Monetarios Latinoamericanos. In Spanish.
Continued by: *Aspectos Monetarios de las Economías Latinoamericanas*.

ASPECTOS MONETARIOS LATINOAMERICANOS
See Centro de Estudios Monetarios Latinoamericanos. BOLETIN QUINCENAL

697
ASPECTS ET PERSPECTIVES DE L'ÉCONOMIE TUNISIENNE. 1– , 1960– . Tunis.
Issued by: Circle d'Études Économiques, Comité des Associations Culturelles. In French.

ASSEMBLÉE PARLEMENTAIRE EUROPÉENNE
See European Parliament. DEBATS: COMPTE RENDU IN EXTENSO DES SÉANCES

698
Associated University Bureaus of Business and Economic Research. BIBLIOGRAPHY OF PUBLICATIONS OF UNIVERSITY BUREAUS OF BUSINESS AND ECONOMIC RESEARCH. v.[1]– , 1950/56– . Eugene, Oreg., later Boulder, Colo. Annual.
Title varies: 1950/56–1962, *Bibliography of Publications of Business and Economic Research*. Vols. for 1957–62 issued as supplement to the volume 1950/56. Title on spine: *AUBER Bibliography of Publications of Bureaus of Business and Economic Research*.

ASSOCIATION CATHOLIQUE
See MOUVEMENT SOCIAL (Paris, 1876–)

699
Association of American Geographers. ANNALS. v.1– , 1911– . Lancaster, Pa. Annual, 1911–22; quarterly.
Some issues are thematic.
Indexes: Vols. 1–25, 1911–35, 1v.
Indexed: Abst. Anth.; His. Abst.; Ind. Per. Art. Law 1970; Int. Bibl. Soc. Cul. Anth.; Int. Pol. Sc. Abst.; Soc. Sc. Hum. Ind.; SSCI.

ASSOCIÉS. STATISTIQUE DU COMMERCE EXTÉRIEUR. ANNUAIRE
See Statistical Office of the European Communities. ASSOCIÉS. STATISTIQUE DU COMMERCE EXTÉRIEUR. ANNUAIRE

ASYLUM JOURNAL OF MENTAL SCIENCE
See BRITISH JOURNAL OF PSYCHIATRY

700
'ATIQOT. ENGLISH SERIES. v.1– , 1955– . Jerusalem. Irreg.
Issued by: Department of Antiquities and Museums, Ministry of Education and Culture, Department of Archaeology, Hebrew University, and Israel Exploration Society. Some vols. are accompanied by supplements. A Hebrew edition, *Atikoth*, published also.

701
THE ATLANTIC. v.150–222, July 1932–June 1971. Boston, Mass., Atlantic Monthly Co. Monthly.
Continues: *Atlantic Monthly* (v.1–149, 1857–June 1932)
Continued by: *Atlantic Monthly* (v.223– , July 1971–)
Indexed: Bull. Anal. Pol. Ec. Soc.; His. Abst.; Ind. Per. Art. Law; Peace Res. Abst. J.

702
ATLANTIC COMMUNITY QUARTERLY. v.1– , Mar. 1963– . Washington, D.C. Quarterly.
Issued by: Atlantic Council of the United States.
Indexed: ABC POL SCI; Bull. Anal. Pol. Ec. Soc.; His. Abst.; Int. Bibl. Pol. Sc.; Int. Bibl. Soc. Cul. Anth.; Int. Lab. Doc.; Int. Pol. Sc. Abst.; Peace Res. Abst. J.; PAIS; Soc. Sc. Hum. Ind.

703
ATLANTIC ECONOMIC JOURNAL. v.1– , Nov. 1973– . Edwardsville, Ill. Semi-annual, 1973–75; three no. a year, 1976– ; quarterly.
Issued by: Atlantic Economic Society.
Indexed: PAIS.

704
THE ATLANTIC PAPERS ANNUAL. v.1– , 1970– . New York, Dunelen.
Issued by: Atlantic Institute.

ATTI
See RIVISTA DI ANTROPOLOGIA

ATTI DELLA SOCIETÀ ROMANA DI ANTROPOLOGIA
See RIVISTA DI ANTROPOLOGIA

AUBER BIBLIOGRAPHY OF PUBLICATIONS
See Associated University Bureaus of Business and Economic Research. BIBLIOGRAPHY OF PUBLICATIONS OF UNIVERSITY BUREAUS OF BUSINESS AND ECONOMIC RESEARCH

705
AUSSENPOLITIK. 1– , May 1950– . Stuttgart, later Hamburg, Interpress Verlag. Bimonthly, 1950–51; monthly.
In German.
Indexed: Bull. Anal. Pol. Ec. Soc.; Int. Bibl. Eco.; Int. Pol. Sc. Abst.; Int. Bibl. Pol. Sc.; PAISFL; Peace Res. Abst. J.; SSCI.

706
AUSSENWIRTSCHAFT. v.1– , Mar. 1946– . Bern, A. Francke. Quarterly.
Issued by: Schweizerisches Institut für Aussenwirtschafts- und Marktforschung at the Handels-Hochschule, St. Gall. In English or German. Some nos. are thematic. Other titles: *Schweizerische Zeitschrift für Internationale Wirtschaftsbeziehungen*; *The Swiss Review of International Relations*.
Indexed: Bull. Anal. Pol. Ec. Soc.; Int. Bibl. Eco.; PAIS; PAISFL.

707
Australia. Bureau of Statistics. SOCIAL INDICATORS. AUSTRALIA. 1976– . Canberra. Annual.

708
AUSTRALIAN ABORIGINAL STUDIES. no.1– , 1963– . Canberra. Irreg.
Issued by: Australian Institute of Aboriginal Studies. This publication includes subseries: *Bibliography Series*; *Ethnohistory Studies*; *Human Biology Series*; *Linguistic Series*; *Prehistory and Culture Series*; *Social Anthropology Series*; *Monograph Series*. Title varies: *Occasional Papers in Aboriginal Studies*.
Indexed: Abst. Anth.

709
AUSTRALIAN AND NEW ZEALAND JOURNAL OF CRIMINOLOGY. v.1– , Mar. 1968– . Melbourne, Southdown Press. Quarterly.
Issued by: Australian and New Zealand Society of Criminology.
Indexed: Ind. Per. Art. Law; PAIS; SSCI.

710
THE AUSTRALIAN AND NEW ZEALAND JOURNAL OF SOCIOLOGY. v.1– , Apr. 1965– . Melbourne, Pitman. Three no. a year.
Issued by: Sociological Association of Australia and New Zealand. Processed.
Indexes: Vols. 1–2, with v.2.
Indexed: Bull. Anal. Pol. Ec. Soc.; Int. Bibl. Eco.; Int. Bibl. Pol. Sc.; Int. Bibl. Soc.; Int. Pol. Sc. Abst.; Soc. Abst.; SSCI.

711
AUSTRALIAN DEMOGRAPHIC REVIEW. no.1– , Jan. 1951– . Canberra. Irreg.
Issued by: Bureau of Census and Statistics.

712
AUSTRALIAN ECONOMIC HISTORY REVIEW. v.7– , Mar. 1967– . Sydney, Sydney University Press. Semi-annual.
Published in association with: Department of Economic History, 1967–74; Department of Economics, University of Sydney, and Economic History of Australia and New Zealand, Sept. 1974– . Other title: AEHR.
Continues: *Business Archives and History* (v.1–6, 1962–66)
Indexed: Int. Bibl. Soc.; SSCI.

713
AUSTRALIAN ECONOMIC PAPERS. v.1– , Sept. 1962– . Adelaide. Semi-annual.
Issued by: University of Adelaide with the Flinders University of South Australia.
Indexed: APAIS; Int. Bibl. Eco.; Int. Bibl. Soc.

714
AUSTRALIAN ECONOMIC REVIEW. 1– , 1968– . Melbourne, F.W. Cheshire Pub. Quarterly.
Issued by: Institute of Applied Economics and Social Research, University of Melbourne.
Indexed: PAIS.

715
AUSTRALIAN FOREIGN AFFAIRS RECORD. v.44– , Jan. 1973– . Canberra, Gov. Pub. Service. Monthly.
Issued by: Department of Foreign Affairs.
Continues: *Current Notes on International Affairs*.
Indexed: APAIS; Bull. Anal. Pol. Ec. Soc.; Int. Lab. Doc.; PAIS.

716
AUSTRALIAN GEOGRAPHICAL STUDIES. v.1– , Apr. 1963– . Melbourne. Semi-annual.
Issued by: Institute of Tasmanian Geographers, later by the Institute of Australian Geographers.

717
Australian Institute of Aboriginal Studies. NEWSLETTER. v.1–3, Jan. 1963–1973; n. ser. no.1–18, 1974–1982. Canberra. Semi-annual.
Continued by: *Australian Aboriginal Studies*.
Indexes: Vols. 1–3, 1963–73, 1v.

718
THE AUSTRALIAN JOURNAL OF AGRICULTURAL ECONOMICS. v.1– , 1957– . Sydney. Semi-annual, 1957–72; three no. a year.
Issued by: Australian Agricultural Economics Society. Vols. for 1957–59 include *Proceedings of the Conference* of the Australian Agricultural Economics Society.
Indexes: Vols. 1–5, 1957–61.
Indexed: Ind. Per. Art. Law 1970; Int. Bibl. Eco.; SSCI.

719
AUSTRALIAN JOURNAL OF EDUCATION. 1– , 1957– . Hawthorn. Three no. a year.
Issued by: Australian Council for Educational Research.
Indexed: APAIS; SSCI.

720
AUSTRALIAN JOURNAL OF HIGHER EDUCATION. v.1– , Nov. 1961– . Perth, University of Australia Press. Annual.
Issued by: Faculty of Education, University of Western Australia.
Superseded by: *Education Research and Perspectives*.

721
AUSTRALIAN JOURNAL OF POLITICS AND HISTORY. v.1– , 1955– . Brisbane, later St. Lucia, University of Queensland Press. Three no. a year.
Issued by: Department of History and Political Science, University of Queensland.
Indexed: ABC POL SCI; APAIS; Bull. Anal. Pol. Ec. Soc.; His. Abst.; Ind. Per. Abst. Law 1970; Int. Bibl. Pol. Sc.; Int. Bibl. Soc.; Int. Lab. Doc.; Int. Pol. Sc. Abst.; Peace Res. Abst. J.; SSCI; Soc. Abst.

722
AUSTRALIAN JOURNAL OF PSYCHOLOGY. v.1– , June 1949– . Melbourne, Melbourne University Press. Semi-annual, 1949–61; three no. a year.
Issued by: Australian Branch, British Psychological Society.
Indexed: APAIS; Bull. Sig. Soc. Eth.; His. Abst.; Int. Pol. Sc. Abst.; Psych. Abst.; Wom. Stu. Abst.

723
AUSTRALIAN JOURNAL OF PUBLIC ADMINISTRATION. v.35– , May 1976– . Sydney. Quarterly.
Issued by: regional groups of the Royal Institute of Public Administration.
Continues: *Public Administration*.
Indexed: APAIS; Bull. Anal. Pol. Ec. Soc.; Sage Pub. Adm. Abst.

724
AUSTRALIAN JOURNAL OF SEX, MARRIAGE & FAMILY. v.1– , Feb. 1980– . Concord, Family Life Movement. Quarterly.

725
AUSTRALIAN JOURNAL OF SOCIAL ISSUES. v.1– , spring 1961– . Sydney. Semi-annual.
Issued by: University of Sydney, and the New South Wales Branch of the Australian Association of Social Workers.
Indexed: APAIS; SSCI; Soc. Abst.

726
AUSTRALIAN LEFT REVIEW. June/July 1966– . Sydney, D.B. Young Pty. Bimonthly.
Subtitle reads: "Marxist journal of information and discussion".

727
Australian National University. Development Studies Centre. OCCASIONAL PAPER. no.38– , 1984– . Canberra. Irreg.
Continues: Australian National University. Development Studies Centre. *Working Paper* (no.1–37, 1975–83)

728
Australian National University. Faculty of Asian Studies. OCCASIONAL PAPERS. 1– , 1963– . Canberra. Irreg.
Supersedes: Australian National University. Centre of Oriental Studies. *Occasional Papers*.

729
Australian National University. Research School of Pacific Studies. Department of Human Geography. PUBLICATION HG. 1– , 1969– . Canberra. Irreg.
Supersedes, in part: *Publications Series* of the School's Department of Geography. Monograph series.

730
THE AUSTRALIAN OUTLOOK. v.1– , Mar. 1947– . Sydney. Three no. a year.
Issued by: Institute of International Affairs. Incorporates: *Australian Asiatic Bulletin*.
Indexed: ABC POL SCI; APAIS; Bull. Anal. Pol. Ec. Soc.; His. Abst.; Ind. Per. Art. Law; Int. Bibl. Eco.; Int. Bibl. Pol. Sc.; Int. Pol. Sc. Abst.; Peace Res. Abst. J.; Pop. Ind.; PAIS; SSCI.

731
Australian Planning Institute. JOURNAL. v.1– , 1958– . Sydney, West Pub. Co. Four no. a year.
Indexed: APAIS; Ind. Per. Art. Law.

732
Australian Public Affairs Information Service. SUBJECT INDEX TO CURRENT LITERATURE. no.1– , July 1945– . Canberra. Monthly, cumulated annually.
Issued by: Commonwealth National Library.

733
THE AUSTRALIAN QUARTERLY. no.1–32, Mar. 1929–1936; v.9– , 1937– . Sydney.
Issued by: Australian Institute of Political Science. Issues for 1929–36 constitute v.1–8. Title on cover: *AQ The Australian Quarterly*.
Indexes: 1929–53.
Indexed: ABC POL SCI; APAIS; Bull. Anal. Pol. Ec. Soc.; His. Abst.; Int. Bibl. Eco.; Int. Bibl. Pol. Sc.; Int. Bibl. Soc.; Int. Lab. Doc.; PAIS; Peace Res. Abst. J.; Int. Pol. Sc. Abst.; Pop. Ind.; Soc. Abst.

734
AUSTRALIAN SOCIAL SCIENCE ABSTRACTS. no.1–18, Mar. 1946–Nov. 1954. Melbourne. Semi-annual.
Issued by: Committee on Research on the Social Sciences, Australian National Council, 1946–Oct. 1951; Social Science Research Council of Australia, May 1952–Nov. 1954.

735
AUSTRALIAN SOCIETY. v.1– , Oct. 1982– . Fitzroy, Australian Society Pub. Co. Semi-annual.

736
THE AUSTRALIAN YEAR BOOK OF INTERNATIONAL LAW. 1965– . Sydney, Australian Butterworth. Annual.
Issued by: Faculty of Law, The Australian National University.
Indexed: Ind. Leg. Per.; Ind. For. Leg. Per.

737
AUSTRALIA'S POPULATION TRENDS AND PROSPECTS. 1984– . Canberra, Government Publishing Service.
Issued by: Department of Immigration and Ethnic Affairs. Formed by merger of: *Review of Australia's Demographic Trends* (1981–83) and *Population Trends*.

738
AUSTRIACA. 1– , 1975– . Mont-Saint-Aignan. Semi-annual.
Issued by: Centre d'Études et des Recherches Autrichiennes, Université de Rouen. In French.
Indexed: Bull. Anal. Pol. Ec. Soc.

AUSTRIAN HISTORICAL BIBLIOGRAPHY
See ÖSTERREICHISCHE HISTORISCHE BIBLIOGRAPHIE

739
AUSTRIAN HISTORY YEARBOOK. v.1– , 1965– . Houston, Tex. Annual.
Issued by: Rice University at Houston. Co-sponsored by: Conference Group for Central European History.
Supersedes: *Austrian History Newsletter*.
Indexed: His. Abst.

740
AUSWÄRTIGE POLITIK. v.[1]–11, no.5/6, July 1934–May/June 1944. Berlin, A. Limbach. Monthly.
Organ of: Hamburger Institut für Auswärtige Politik, and, May 1937– , Deutsches Institut für Aussen-politische Forschung, Berlin. In German. Includes supplements called "Monatshefte für Auswärtige Politik".

741
AUTONOMOUS GROUPS. v.1–15, Feb. 1945–winter 1960. New York. Quarterly.
Issued by: Committee on Autonomous Groups. Title varies: 1945–summer 1955, *Autonomous Groups Bulletin*.

AUTONOMOUS GROUPS BULLETIN
See AUTONOMOUS GROUPS

742
AUTREMENT. no.1– , spring 1975– . Paris. Four no. a year.
Issues are thematic.
Indexed: Bull. Anal. Pol. Ec. Soc.; Bull. Sig. Soc. Eth.

743
AVANCES DE INVESTIGACIÓN. 1975– . San José. Irreg.
Issued by: Faculdad de Ciencias Sociales, Universidad de Costa Rica. In Spanish.

744
'AVARYYANUTH VE-ḤEVRAH. DELINQUENCY AND SOCIETY. 1– , 1966– . Jerusalem. Irreg.
Issued by: Israel Society of Criminology, and Institute of Criminology, Faculty of Law, Hebrew University. In Hebrew; summaries and table of contents in English.

745
AZANIA. v.1– , 1966– . Nairobi, Oxford University Press. Annual.
Issued by: British Institute of History and Archaeology in East Africa, 1966–70; British Institute in Eastern Africa, 1971– .

Indexed: Abst. Anth.; Int. Bibl. Soc. Cul. Anth.

746

AZERBACHAN KOOMUNISTI. KOMMUNIST AZERBAĬDZHANA. 1920– . Baku, Ob'dinnoe Izdatel'stvo. Monthly.

Issued by: Komitet Kommunisticheskoĭ Partii Azerbaĭdzhanskoĭ SSR. In Russian. Title varies: 1939–57, *Propagandist.*

AZERBAĬDZHANSKIĬ ETNOGRAFICHESKIĬ SBORNIK; ISSLEDOVANIIA I MATERIALY *See* Akademiia Nauk Azerbaĭdzhanskoĭ SSR, Baku. Institut Istorii. AZERBAĬDZHANSKIĬ ETNOGRAFICHESKIĬ SBORNIK: ISSLEDOVANIIA I MATERIALY

747

AZIIA I AFRIKA SEGODNIA. 1957– . Moskva, Nauka. Monthly.

Issued by: Institut Narodov Azii i Institut Afriki, Akademiia Nauk SSSR. In Russian. Title varies: 1957–61, *Sovremennyĭ Vostok.*

Indexed: Bull. Sig. Soc. Eth.; Bull. Anal. Pol. Ec. Soc.; Int. Bibl. Soc. Cul. Anth.

748

AZTLAN. spring 1970– . Los Angeles, Calif. Three no. a year.

Issued by: Mexican–American Cultural Center, University of California at Los Angeles. Subtitle reads: "International journal of Chicano studies research".

Indexed: PAIS; Soc. Abst.

B

BACKGROUND ON FOREIGN POLITICS
See INTERNATIONAL STUDIES QUARTERLY

749
BADANIA OŚWIATOWE. ISSLEDOVANIIA V OBLASTI PROSVESHCHENIIA. RECHERCHES SUR L'ÉDUCATION. no.1–28, 1976–1982. Warszawa, Wydawnictwa Szkolne i Pedagogiczne.
Issued by: Instytut Badań Pedagogicznych. In Polish.
Continued by: *Edukacja.*

750
BADANIA Z DZIEJÓW SPOŁECZNYCH I GOSPODARCZYCH. v.1–35, 1925–1939; v.36– , 1948– . Poznań, Państwowe Wydawnictwo Naukowe.
Issued by: Wydział II. Historii i Nauk Społecznych, Poznańskie Towarzystwo Przyjaciół Nauk. In Polish; summaries in English, French, and German.

751
BAESSLER ARCHIV; BEITRÄGE ZUR VÖLKERKUNDE. v.1–25, no.2, 1910–1943; n. ser. v.1– , 1952– . Berlin, D. Reimer. Quarterly.
In German.
Indexed: Abst. Anth.; Bull. Sig. Soc. Eth.; Int. Bibl. Soc. Cul. Anth.

BALANCE OF PAYMENTS. YEARBOOK
See International Monetary Fund. BALANCE OF PAYMENTS. YEARBOOK

BALANCES DES PAIEMENTS. VENTILATION GÉOGRAPHIQUE
See Statistical Office of the European Communities. BALANCES OF PAYMENTS. GEOGRAPHICAL BREAKDOWN

BALANCES DES PAIEMENTS. DONNÉES GLOBALES
See Statistical Office of the European Communities. GLOBAL DATA

BALANCES OF PAYMENTS
See League of Nations. BALANCES OF PAYMENTS

BALANCES OF PAYMENTS. GEOGRAPHICAL BREAKDOWN
See Statistical Office of the European Communities. BALANCES OF PAYMENTS. GEOGRAPHICAL BREAKDOWN

BALANCES OF PAYMENTS. GLOBAL DATA
See Statistical Office of the European Communities. GLOBAL DATA

752
BALANÇO FINANCEIRO. v.1– , 1979– . São Paulo, Gazeta Mercantil. Annual.
Issued by: Bank for International Settlements.

753
BALCANICA POSNANIENSIA. 1– , 1984– . Poznań. Irreg.
Issued by: Uniwersytet in Poznań. In Polish.

754
BALKAN STUDIES. v.1– , 1960– . Thessaloniki. Semi-annual.
Issued by: IDPMA Meleton Hereonie oy toy Aimoy. In English; occasionally in French, German, or Italian.
Indexed: Bull. Anal. Pol. Ec. Soc.

755
LES BALKANS. v.1–11, 1930–1940. Athènes.
In French.

756
BALKANSKIE ISSLEDOVANIIA. 1974– . Moskva, Izd-vo Nauka. Irreg.
Issued by: Institut Slavianovedeniia i Balkanistiki, Akademiia Nauk SSSR. In Russian. Monograph series.

757
BALTISCHE STUDIEN. v.1–46, 1832–1896; n. ser. v.1–42, 1897–1940; 1955– . Hamburg.
Issued by: Gesellschaft für Pommersche Geschichte und Altertumskunde. In German.

BĀMLĀDESA ESIYĀTICA SOSĀITI PATRIKĀ
See Asiatic Society of Bangladesh. JOURNAL OF THE ASIATIC SOCIETY OF BANGLADESH

758
Banca Nazionale del Lavoro. QUARTERLY REVIEW. 1– , 1947– . Roma.
Issued by: the Banca's Ufficio Studi. In English.
Indexed: Int. Lab. Doc.; PAIS.

759
BANCARIA. v.1– , 1945?– . Roma. Monthly.
Issued by: Associazione Bancaria Italiana. In Italian.
Indexed: Bull. Anal. Pol. Ec. Soc.; Int. Bibl. Eco.; PAISFL.

760
BANGLADESH ARCHAEOLOGY. v.1– , 1979– . Dacca.
Issued by: Department of Archaeology and Museums, Ministry of Sports and Culture.

761
BANGLADESH DEVELOPMENT STUDIES. v.1– , 1955– . Dacca. Quarterly.
Issued by: Bangladesh Institute of Development Studies. Title varies: 1955–60, *Economic Digest*; 1961–71, *Pakistan Development Review*; 1972–73, *Bangladesh Economic Review*.
Indexed: Bull. Anal. Pol. Ec. Soc.; Int. Bibl. Eco.; PAIS; Pop. Ind.

BANGLADESH ECONOMIC REVIEW
See BANGLADESH DEVELOPMENT STUDIES

762
BANGLADESH JOURNAL OF POLITICAL ECONOMY. v.5– , 1981– . Dacca. Irreg.
Issued by: Bangladesh Economic Association. In Bengali or English.
Continues: *Political Economy* (v.1–4, 1974–79)

763
BANGLADESH JOURNAL OF SOCIOLOGY. v.1– , 1983– . Dacca. M. Afsarudin. Annual.

764
BANGLADESH POLITICAL STUDIES. v.1– , 1978– . Chittagong. Annual.
Issued by: Department of Political Science, University of Chittagong. In Bengali or English.

765
BANGLADESH POLITICS. [1]– , 1980– . Dacca. Annual.
Issued by: Centre for Social Studies. First volume unnumbered and undated.

766
Bank of Japan. MONETARY AND ECONOMIC STUDIES. v.1– , June 1983– . Tokyo, Institute for Monetary and Economic Studies. Two no. a year.
Published also in Japanese.

767
THE BANKER. v.1– , Jan. 1926– . London, Financial Times Business Publication. Monthly.

Banque Africaine de Développement
See African Development Bank

768
Banque des États de l'Afrique Centrale. ÉTUDES ET STATISTIQUES. no.1– , Apr. 1973– . Paris. Monthly.
In French.
Continues a publication with the same title issued by the bank under its earlier name: Banque Central des États de l'Afrique Équatoriale et du Cameroun.

769
BANTOE-ONDERWYSBLAD, BANTU EDUCATION JOURNAL. v.1–24, no.3, Nov. 1954–Apr. 1978. Pretoria, Government Printer. Monthly (except January and July).
Issued by: Department of Information. In Afrikaans, Bantu, or English. Supplements accompany some numbers.

770
BANTU. v.7–25, no.6, 1960–June 1978. Pretoria. Monthly.
Issued by: Department of Information, Government of South Africa. In Afrikaans, Bantu, or English.
Continues: *Bantoe*. Continued by: *Progress*.

BANTU EDUCATION JOURNAL
See BANTOE-ONDERWYSBLAD

771
BANTU STUDIES. 1921–1941. Johannesburg, Witwatersrand University Press. Irreg., 1921–1929; quarterly.
Title varies: v.1, 1921, *Bantu Studies and General South African Anthropology*.
Superseded by: *African Studies*.
Indexed: Int. Bibl. Soc. Cul. Anth.

BANTU STUDIES AND GENERAL SOUTH AFRICAN ANTHROPOLOGY
See BANTU STUDIES

772
BAR RASIHÂYE TÂRIKHI. no.1– , Sept. 1971– . Tehran.
Issued by: Supreme Commander's Staff (English form of name). Translations of Articles into English. Other title: *Historical Studies of Iran*. Volume for 1979 last examined. Ceased publication.

773
BARCLAYS INTERNATIONAL REVIEW. Oct. 1972– . London, Barclays Bank International. Monthly.

774
Barnaul'skiĭ Gosudarstvennyĭ Pedagogicheskiĭ Institut. TRUDY KAFEDR OBSHCHESTVENNYKH NAUK. no.1– , 1966– . Barnaul. Irreg.
In Russian.

BAROMETRO ECONOMICO
See BAROMETRO ECONOMICO ITALIANO

775
BAROMETRO ECONOMICO ITALIANO. 1– , Feb. 1923– . Roma, Agenzia d'Informazioni per la Stampa "Alessandro Volta".
Includes supplement called "Bolletino". Title varies: 1923–Nov. 1933, "Bolletino". In Italian.

776
BASIC AND APPLIED SOCIAL PSYCHOLOGY. v.1– , Mar. 1980– . Hillsdale, N.J., Lawrence Erlbaum Associates. Quarterly.
Indexed: Psych. Abst.

BASIC DOCUMENTATION
See World Fertility Survey. BASIC DOCUMENTATION

777
Battelle Population and Development Policy Program. PDP WORKING PAPER SERIES. no.1– , 1978– . Washington, D.C. Irreg.
Issued by: Battelle Human Affairs Research Center. International Development Study Center.

BAYERISCHE VERWALTUNGSBLÄTTER FÜR ADMINISTRATIVE PRAXIS
See DEUTSCHE VERWALTUNGSBLÄTTER; BLÄTTER FÜR ADMINISTRATIVE PRAXIS

778
BE'AYOT BENLEIUMIYOT. 1– , 1963– . Tel-Aviv, Aldershot.
Issued by: The Israeli Institute for the Study of International Affairs. In English, French, or Hebrew. Other title: *International Problems*.
Indexed: PAIS.

779
BEBJONG-HAKPO. LAW AND POLITICAL REVIEW. 1– , 1958– . Seoul. Annual.
Issued by: EWHA Yoja Daihakkyo. Bobjonk Dalhak. In Korean. Tables of contents also in English.

780
BEHAVIOR GENETICS. v.1– , Feb. 1970– . New York, London, Plenum Press. Quarterly, 1970–78; bimonthly.
Published in cooperation with the Behavior Genetics Association.
Indexed: Abst. Anth.

781
BEHAVIOR RESEARCH METHODS AND INSTRUMENTATION. v.1–15, Sept. 1968–1983. Austin, Tex. Bimonthly.
Issued by: Psychonomic Society.
Continued by: *Behavior Research Methods, Instruments & Computers*.

782
BEHAVIOR RESEARCH METHODS, INSTRUMENTS & COMPUTERS. v.16– , Feb. 1984– . Austin, Tex. Bimonthly.
Issued by: Psychonomic Society.
Continues: *Behavior Research Methods and Instrumentation*.

783
BEHAVIOR SCIENCE NOTES. v.1–8, 1966–1973. New Haven, Conn., Human Relations Area Files. Quarterly.
Supersedes: *HRAF News*. Continued by: *Behavior Science Research*.
Indexed: Abst. Anth.

784
BEHAVIOR SCIENCE OUTLINES. v.1–3, 1950–1972. New Haven, Conn., Human Relations Area Files. Irreg.
Monograph series.

785
BEHAVIOR SCIENCE RESEARCH. v.9– , 1974– . New Haven, Conn., Human Relations Area Files. Four no. a year, frequently combined in one issue.
Continues: *Behavior Science Notes*.
Indexed: Bull. Anal. Pol. Ec. Soc.; Int. Bibl. Soc. Cul. Anth.; Int. Pol. Sc. Abst.

786
BEHAVIORAL ANALYSIS AND MODIFICATION. v.2– , Nov. 1977– . Munich, Baltimore, Md., Urban & Schwarzenberg.
Summaries in French and German.
Continues: *European Journal of Behavioral Analysis and Documentation*.

787
BEHAVIORAL AND BRAIN SCIENCES. v.1– , 1978– . New York, Cambridge University Press. Quarterly.

BEHAVIORAL AND SOCIAL SCIENCES
See NATO ADVANCED STUDY INSTITUTES SERIES. SERIES B. BEHAVIORAL AND SOCIAL SCIENCES

788
BEHAVIORAL ASSESSMENT. v.1– , 1979– . Oxford, Elmsford, N.Y., Pergamon Press. Annual, 1979; quarterly.
Issued under the auspices of the Association for the Advancement of Behavior.

Indexed: Psych. Abst.

789
BEHAVIORAL COUNSELLING QUARTERLY. v.1– , spring 1981– . New York, Human Sciences Press. Quarterly.

790
BEHAVIORAL ECOLOGY. Feb. 1976– . New York, Springer-Verlag. Quarterly.

791
BEHAVIORAL GROUP THERAPY. 1979– . Champaign, Ill., Research Press. Annual.

792
BEHAVIORAL SCIENCE. v.1– , Jan. 1956– . Baltimore, Md. Bimonthly, 1966–1980; quarterly, 1956–65, 1981– .
Issued by: Mental Health Research Institute, University of Michigan, 1956–1966; sponsored by the Institute of Management Sciences, 1967–72; Society for General Systems Research, 1973– .
Indexed: Abst. Anth.; ABC POL SCI; Abst. Soc. Work; Bull. Sig. Soc. Eth.; Curr. Cont. Soc. Beh. Sc.; Int. Bibl. Eco.; Int. Bibl. Pol. Sc.; Int. Bibl. Soc.; Int. Pol. Sc. Abst.; PAIS; Peace Res. Abst. J.; Psych. Abst.; Sage Pub. Adm. Abst.; Sage Urb. Stu. Abst.; Soc. Abst.; SSCI; Wom. Stu. Abst.

793
BEHAVIORAL SCIENCE & THE LAW. v.1– , 1983– . New York, Van Nostrand Reinhold. Quarterly.
Issues are thematic.

794
BEHAVIORAL SCIENCE IN PROGRESS. 1– , 1971– . Washington, D.C.
Issued by: American Psychological Association.

795
BEHAVIOROMETRIC. 1970– . Bihar. Semi-annual.
Issued by: Council of Behavioral Research.
Indexed: Psych. Abst.

796
BEHAVIOUR ANALYSIS LETTER. v.1– , Jan. 1981– . Amsterdam, Elsevier/North-Holland. Six no. a year.

797
BEHAVIOUR RESEARCH AND THERAPY. v.1– , May 1963– . Oxford, Pergamon Press. Four no. a year.
Indexed: Abst. Soc. Work.; LLBA; Psych. Abst.; Soc. Abst.

798
BEHAVIOURAL ABSTRACTS. v.1– , 1983– . Abingdon. Quarterly.
Abstracts of articles and monographs.

799
BEHAVIOURAL PROCESSES. 1976– . Amsterdam, Elsevier Pub. Co. Quarterly, 1976–84; eight no. a year, forming two volumes.
Issued by: Centre de Psychologie Expérimentelle et Comparé, Université de Louvain. In French. Subtitle reads: "An international journal of comparative and physiological ethology".
Indexed: Psych. Abst.

800
BEHAVIOURAL SCIENCES AND COMMUNITY DEVELOPMENT. v.1–11, no.2, Mar. 1967–Sept. 1977. Hyderabad. Semi-annual.
Issued by: National Institute of Community Development.
Superseded by: *Behavioural Sciences and Rural Development.*
Indexed: Bull. Anal. Pol. Ec. Soc.; Int. Bibl. Soc.; Int. Pol. Sc. Abst.; Soc. Abst.

801
BEHAVIOURAL SCIENCES AND RURAL DEVELOPMENT. v.1–4, Jan. 1978–July 1981. Hyderabad. Semi-annual.
Issued by: National Institute of Rural Development.
Supersedes: *Behavioural Sciences and Community Development.*
Merged with: *Rural Development Digest* to form: *Journal of Rural Development.*

BEIHEFT
See ZEITSCHRIFT FÜR GESCHICHTSWISSENSCHAFT

BEIHEFT. LITERATURBERICHT
See ARCHIV FÜR REFORMATIONSGESCHICHTE. BEIHEFT. LITERATURBERICHT

802
BEITRÄGE ZUR AUSWÄRTIGEN UND INTERNATIONALES POLITIK. v.1– , 1966– . Berlin, W. de Gruyter. Annual.
In German. Monograph series.

803
BEITRÄGE ZUR DEMOGRAPHIE. no.1– , 1977– . Berlin, Akademie-Verlag. Irreg.
Issued by: Lehrstuhl Demographie, Humboldt Universität zu Berlin. In German.

804
BEITRÄGE ZUR GANZHEITLICHEN WIRTSCHAFTS- UND GESELLSCHAFTSLEHRE. v.1– , 1966– . Berlin, Duncker & Humblot. Irreg.

In German. Monograph series.

805
BEITRÄGE ZUR GESCHICHTE DER DEUTSCHEN ARBEITERBEWEGUNG. v.1– , 1959– . Berlin, Dietz Verlag. Bimonthly.
In German. Supplements called "Sonderhefte" accompany some issues.

806
BEITRÄGE ZUR GESCHICHTE DES PARLAMENTARISMUS UND DER POLITISCHEN PARTEIEN. v.1– , 1952– . Düsseldorf, Droste Verlag. Irreg.
Issued by: Kommission für Geschichte des Parlamentarismus und der Politischen Parteien, Bonn. In German.

807
BEITRÄGE ZUR GESCHICHTE DER SOZIALWISSENSCHAFTEN. no.1– , 1959– . Berlin, Duncker & Humblot. Irreg.
In German. Monograph series.

BEITRÄGE ZUR GESCHICHTE DES SOZIALISMUS
See PRILOZI ZA ISTORIJU SOCIJALIZMA

808
BEITRÄGE ZUR HISTORISCHEN SOZIALKUNDE. 1971– . Salzburg. Quarterly.
Issued by: Arbeitsgemeinschaft für Historische Sozialkunde. In German.

BEITRÄGE ZUR KOLONIALPOLITIK UND KOLONIAL WIRTSCHAFT
See KOLONIALE MONATSBLÄTTER

809
BEITRÄGE ZUR KONFLIKTFORSCHUNG. v.1, no.1/2– , 1971– . Köln, Markus-Verlags-Gesellschaft. Quarterly.
In German.
Indexed: Bull. Anal. pol. Ec. Soc.; Int. Bibl. Eco.; Int. Bibl. Pol. Sc.; Int. Pol. Sc. Abst.

BEITRÄGE ZUR RELIGIONSSOZIOLOGIE
See BEITRÄGE ZUR WISSENSSOZIOLOGIE

810
BEITRÄGE ZUR SOZIAL- UND WIRTSCHAFTSGESCHICHTE. v.1– , 1970– . Kiel, Verlag Walter G. Mühlau. Annual.
In German. Some volumes are originally theses.

811
BEITRÄGE ZUR SOZIALFORSCHUNG. no.1– , 1969– . Köln, Markus-Verlags-Gesellschaft. Irreg.
Issued by: Hochschule für Sozial- und Wirtschaftswissenschaften. In German. Monograph series.

812
BEITRÄGE ZUR SOZIALWISSENSCHAFTLICHEN FORSCHUNG. 1– , 1968– . Opladen, Westdeutscher Verlag. Irreg.
In German. Monograph series. Title varies: 1–8, 1968–72, *Beiträge zur Sozialogischen Forschung*.

813
BEITRÄGE ZUR SOZIOLOGIE AFRIKAS. 1– , 1976– . Freiburg, Klaus Schwartz Verlag. Irreg.
In German. Monograph series.

814
BEITRÄGE ZUR SOZIOLOGIE DES BILDUNGSWESEN. v.1– , 1960– . Heidelberg, Quelle & Meyer. Irreg.
In German. Monograph series. Includes some translations.

815
BEITRÄGE ZUR SOZIOLOGIE UND SOZIALKUNDE LATEINAMERIKAS. v.1–10, 1967–1971. Berlin, Gehlin. Irreg.
In German. Monograph series. Includes some translations.

816
BEITRÄGE ZUR SOZIOLOGIE UND SOZIALPHILOSOPHIE. v.1–13, 1946–1967. Bern, Regio Verlag. Irreg.
In German. Monograph series.

BEITRÄGE ZUR SOZIOLOGISCHEN FORSCHUNG
See BEITRÄGE ZUR SOZIALWISSENSCHAFTLICHEN FORSCHUNG

BEITRÄGE ZUR UKRAINISCHEN ETHNOLOGIE
See MATERIALY DO UKRAINSKOÏ ETHNOLOGII

817
BEITRÄGE ZUR SUDASIEN FORSCHUNG. v.1– , 1974– . Wiesbaden, Franz Steiner Verlag. Irreg.
Issued by: Südasien Institut, Universität Heildelberg. In German.

BEITRÄGE ZUR VÖLKER- UND SPRACHENKUNDE DES INDIANISCHEN AMERIKA
See INDIANA

818
BEITRÄGE ZUR WISSENSSOZIOLOGIE. BEITRÄGE ZUR RELIGIONSSOZIOLOGIE. CONTRIBUTIONS TO THE SOCIOLOGY OF KNOWLEDGE. CONTRIBUTIONS TO THE SOCIOLOGY OF RELIGION. v.1– , 1975– . Opladen, Westdeutscher Verlag. Irreg.
In English, French, or German; summaries in English or German (Internationales Jahrbuch für Wissens- und Religionssoziologie. International Yearbook of Sociology of Knowledge and Religion)

819
BELFAGOR. v.1– , Jan. 1946– . Messina, later Firenze, Olschi. bimonthly.
In Italian. Subtitle reads: "Rassegna di varia umanità".
Indexed: Bull. Anal. Pol. Ec. Soc.

BELGIAN REVIEW OF INTERNATIONAL LAW
See REVUE BELGE DE DROIT INTERNATIONALE

BELGISCH TIJDSCHRIFT VOOR INTERNATIONAL RECHT
See REVUE BELGE DE DROIT INTERNATIONALE

820
BELL JOURNAL OF ECONOMICS. v.6– , spring 1975– . New York, American Telephone and Telegraph Co. Semi-annual.
Continues: *The Bell Journal of Economics and Management Science* (v.1–5, spring 1970–1974)
Indexed: ABC POL SCI; Bull. Anal. Pol. Ec. Soc.; Ind. Per. Art. Law; Int. Bibl. Eco.; Int. Pol. Sc. Abst.; SSCI; Sage Urb. Stu. Abst.; PAIS.

821
BENELUX; BULLETIN TRIMESTRIELLE DE STATISTIQUE. STATISTISCH KVARTAALBERICHT. 1954–1965. Bruxelles. Quarterly.
Issued by: Union Doanière. In Dutch and French.
Continues: *Benelux; Economische en Statistisch Kvartaalbericht.*
Continued by: *Benelux; Economisch en Statistisch Kvartaalbericht.*
Indexed: PAISFL.

822
BENELUX; ECONOMISCHE EN STATISTISCH KVARTAALBERICHT. BULLETIN TRIMESTRIELLE ÉCONOMIQUE ET STATISTIQUE. 1966– . Bruxelles. Quarterly.
Issued by: Secretariat Général, Union Économique Benelux.
Continues: *Benelux; Bulletin Trimestrielle de Statistique. Statistisch Kvartaalbericht.*
Indexed: Bull. Anal. Pol. Ec. Soc.

BERICHT
See Congrès International d'Anthropologie Criminelle. BERICHT

BERICHT
See Inter-Parliamentary Union. Conference. COMPTE RENDU DE LA CONFÉRENCE

BERICHTE
See Österreichische Gesellschaft für Raumforschung und Landesplanung. BERICHTE

BERICHTE UND INFORMATIONEN
See Österreichisches Forschungsinstitut für Wirtschaft und Politik. BERICHTE UND INFORMATIONEN

BERICHTE ZUR LANDESFORSCHUNG UND LANDESPLANUNG
See Österreichische Gesellschaft für Raumforschung und Raumplanung. BERICHTE

823
BERITA ANTROPOLOGI; MADJALAH DJURASAN ANTROPOLOGI UNIVERSITAS INDONESIA. v.1– , Feb. 1969– . Djakarta. Frequency varies.
Issued by: Fakultas Sastra, Universitas Indonesia. In Indonesian. Publication suspended with v.1, no.3, June 1969; resumed with v.2, no.4, Aug. 1971.

824
Berliner Gesellschaft für Anthropologie, Ethnologie und Urgeschichte. MITTEILUNGEN. 1– , 1967– . Berlin. Irreg.
In German.

825
BERLINER JAHRBUCH FÜR VOR- UND FRÜHGESCHICHTE. v.1– , 1961– . Berlin, Hessling. Annual.
Issued by: Museum für Vor- und Frühgeschichte, Berlin. Stiftung Preussischer Kulturbesitz der Bodendenkmalpflege des Landes, Berlin.
Indexed: Int. Bib. Soc. Cul. Anth.

826
BERKELEY JOURNAL OF SOCIOLOGY: A CRITICAL REVIEW. v.1– , 1955– . Berkeley, Calif. Annual (irreg.)
Title varies: v.1–4, 1955–58, *Berkeley Publications in Society and Institutions.*
Indexed: Bull. Anal. Pol. Ec. Soc.; Bull. Sig. Soc. Eth.; Int. Bibl. Eco.; Int. Bibl. Soc.; Int. Bibl. Soc. Cul. Anth.; Int. Pol. Sc. Abst.; Soc. Abst.

BERKELEY PUBLICATIONS IN SOCIETY AND INSTITUTIONS
See BERKELEY JOURNAL OF SOCIOLOGY: A CRITICAL REVIEW

BERNER BEITRÄGE ZUR SOZIOLOGIE
See BERNESE STUDIES IN SOCIOLOGY

827
BERNESE STUDIES IN SOCIOLOGY. 1– , 1959– . Bern, Stuttgart. Irreg.
Issued by: Institut für Soziologie, und Sozio-ökonomische Entwicklungsfragen, Universität Bern. In German.
Title varies: 1–15, 1959–75, *Berner Beiträge zur Soziologie*.

828
BEVOLKING EN GEZIN. 1– , 1976– . Bruxelles. Three no. a year.
Issued by: Centrum voor Bevolkings- en Gezinsstudien, Ministere van Volksgezondheid en Gezin, and Nederlands Interuniversitair Demografisch Instituut den Haag. In Flemish.
Continues publication of the same title.

829
BEVOLKING EN GEZIN. POPULATION ET FAMILLE. 1–36, Oct. 1963–1973. Bruxelles. Three no. a year.
Issued by: Centrum voor Bevolkings- en Gezinsstudien. In Flemish or French; summaries in the other language, and English, German, and Italian. Title in Flemish is reversed on some issues; title in French is used for some issues.
Continued by: *Bevolking en Gezin*.
Indexed: Int. Bibl. Soc.; Soc. Abst.

830
BIBLICAL ARCHAEOLOGIST. v.1– , Feb. 1938– . New Haven, Conn. Quarterly.
Issued by: American School of Oriental Research (Jerusalem and Baghdad).
Indexes: v.1–5, 1938–42, in v.5.
Indexed: Abst. Anth.; Int. Bib. Soc. Cul. Anth.

BIBLIOGRAFIA
See Centro Latinoamericano de Pesquisas em Ciências Sociais. BIBLIOGRAFIA

831
BIBLIOGRAFÍA ARGENTINA DE CIENCIAS SOCIALES. ARGENTINE BIBLIOGRAPHY OF THE SOCIAL SCIENCES. 1982– . Buenos Aires. Annual.
Issued by: Fundación Aragon. In English or Spanish.

832
BIBLIOGRAFIA BRASILEIRA DE CIÊNCIAS SOCIAIS. v.1– , 1954– . Rio de Janeiro. Annual (irreg.)
Issued by: Instituto Brasileiro de Bibliografia e Documentação, 1954–55; Conselho Nacional de Pesquisas, Instituto Brasileiro de Bibliografia e Documentação, and Conselho Nacional de Desenvolvimento Científico e Tecnológico. Instituto Brasileiro de Informação em Ciência e Tecnologia. In Portuguese.
Supersedes: *Bibliografia Economico-Social*.

833
BIBLIOGRAFIA CIENTÍFICA DA JUNTA INVESTIGAÇÕES DO ULTRAMAR. 1–16, 1960–1973. Lisboa. Irreg.
Issued by: Centro de Documentação Científica Ultramarina, and Junta da Investigações do Ultramar. In Portuguese.
Continued by: *Bibliografia Científica da Junta de Investigações Científicas do Ultramar* (v.17– , 1974–)

834
BIBLIOGRAFIA HISTORII POLSKIEJ. 1944– . Wrocław, Zakład Narodowy im. Ossolińskich. Annual.
Issued by: Instytut Historii, Polska Akademia Nauk. In Polish.

835
BIBLIOGRAFIA ITALIANA DELLE SCIENZE SOCIALI. [1]– , 1957– . Milano, Società Editrice "Vita e Pensiero" [pub. 1958]. Annual.
Prepared by: Istituto di Scienze Economiche, Università Cattolica del Sacro Cuore di Milano. In Italian. Volumes for 1957–58 are extracts from *Rivista di Scienze Sociali*, fasc. 6, Nov.–Dec. 1958, and fasc. 6, Nov.–Dec. 1959.

BIBLIOGRAFÍA MÉXICO–ESTADOS UNIDOS
See RELACIONES MEXICO–ESTADOS UNIDOS

BIBLIOGRAFÍA MUNDIAL DE SEGURIDAD SOCIAL
See BIBLIOGRAPHIE UNIVERSELLE DE SÉCURITÉ SOCIAL

BIBLIOGRAFIAS
See Pan American Institute of Geography and History. Commission on History. BIBLIOGRAFIAS.

836
BIBLIOGRAFIE NEDERLANDS SOCIOLOGIE. 1970– . Utrecht. Annual.
Issued by: Afdeling Bibliothek en Documentatie, Sociologisch Instituut, Rijksuniversiteit te Utrecht. In Dutch.

837
BIBLIOGRAFIJA JUGOSLAVIJE. SERIJA A. DRUSTVENE NAUKE. ČLANCI I KNJIŽEVNI PRILOŽI U CASOPISMA I NOVINAMA. Jan./Mar. 1952– . Beograd.
Issued by: Bibliografski Institut. In Serbo-Croatian. Continues, in part, and continues the volume numbering of *Bibliografija Jugoslavije. Članci i Književni Priloži u Casopisma i Novinama.*

838
BIBLIOGRAPHIC GUIDE TO LATIN AMERICAN STUDIES. 1978– . Boston, Mass., G.K. Hall. Annual.
Continues: *Benson Latin American Collection. Catalog of the Nettie Lee Benson Collection. Supplement.*

839
BIBLIOGRAPHIC GUIDE TO SOVIET AND EAST EUROPEAN STUDIES. 1978– . Boston, Mass., G.K. Hall. Annual.
Continues: New York (City). Public Library. Slavonic Division. *Dictionary Catalog of the Slavonic Collection.*

BIBLIOGRAPHIC SERIES
See American Institute for Marxist Studies. BIBLIOGRAPHIC SERIES

840
BIBLIOGRAPHIC SURVEY; THE NEGRO IN PRINT. v.1– , May 1965– . Washington, D.C. Bimonthly.
Issued by: Negro Bibliographic and Research Center.

841
BIBLIOGRAPHIE AMÉRICANISTE; ARCHÉOLOGIE ET PRÉHISTOIRE. ANTHROPOLOGIE ET ETHNOHISTOIRE. 1965/66– . Paris, Musée de l'Homme.
Issued by: Société des Américanistes de Paris. In French. Vol. for 1965/66 has subtitle: "Anthropologie, physiologie, pathologie".

842
BIBLIOGRAPHIE D'ÉTUDES BALCANIQUES. [1]– , 1966– . Sofia. Annual.
Issued by: Institut d'Études Balcaniques, Centre International de Recherches Scientifiques et de Documentation, Académie Bulgare des Sciences. In French. Includes periodical articles and monograph series.

843
BIBLIOGRAPHIE DE L'AFRIQUE SUB-SAHARIENNE. SCIENCES HUMAINES ET SOCIALES. 1979– . Tervuren. Annual [publ. 1983–]
Issued by: Musée Royal d'Afrique Centrale. In French.
Continues: *Bibliographie Ethnographique de l'Afrique Sud-Saharienne.*

844
BIBLIOGRAPHIE DER SOZIALETHIK. 3–11, 1961–1977/79. Freiburg, New York, Herder. Biennial.
Issued by: Union de Fribourg, Internationales Institut für Sozial- und Politikwissenschaften. In English, French, German, or Spanish. Continues: *Grundsatzfragen des Deutschen Lebens.*

845
BIBLIOGRAPHIE DER SOZIALWISSENSCHAFTEN. 1– , 1905– . Dresden, later Berlin.
In German. Vols. 1–3, 1905–07, published as supplements to *Kritische Blätter für die Gesamten Sozialwissenschaften.* Title varies: 1921–24, *Sozialwissenschaftliches Literaturblatt*; 1937–43, *Bibliographie der Staats- und Wirtschaftswissenschaften.* Publication suspended: 1944–49; resumed with v.42, 1950, covering 1948–50. Absorbed: *Bibliographie des Sciences Économiques, Politiques et Sociales* (v.1–2, 1909–10).

BIBLIOGRAPHIE DER STAATS- UND WIRTSCHAFTSWISSENSCHAFTEN
See BIBLIOGRAPHIE DER SOZIALWISSENSCHAFTEN

BIBLIOGRAPHIE DES PUBLICATIONS STATISTIQUES AFRICAINES
See BIBLIOGRAPHY OF AFRICAN STATISTICAL PUBLICATIONS

846
BIBLIOGRAPHIE DES TRAVAUX EN LANGUE FRANÇAISE SUR L'AFRIQUE AU SUD DU SAHARA. SCIENCES HUMAINES ET SOCIALES. 1977– . Paris. Annual.
Issued by: Centre d'Études Africaines, École des Hautes Études en Sciences Sociales. Formed by the merger of: Centre d'Analyse et de Recherche Documentaire pour l'Afrique Noire. *Fiches d'Ouvrages. Sciences Humaines Africanistes*, and: *Bibliographie Française sur l'Afrique au Sud du Sahara.*

847
BIBLIOGRAPHIE ETHNOGRAPHIQUE DE L'AFRIQUE SUD-SAHARIENNE. 1925/30– . Tervuren. Annual (irreg.)
Issued by: Musée Royal d'Afrique Centrale (1925/30–1957, called Musée du Congo Belge, and Musée Royal du Congo Belge). In French. Title varies: 1925/30–1959, *Bibliographie Ethnographique du Congo Belge et des Régions Avoisinantes.*

BIBLIOGRAPHIE ETHNOGRAPHIQUE DU CONGO BELGE ET DES RÉGIONS AVOISINANTES
See BIBLIOGRAPHIE ETHNOGRAPHIQUE DE L'AFRIQUE SUD-SAHARIENNE

BIBLIOGRAPHIE INTERNATIONALE AFRICAINE
See INTERNATIONAL AFRICAN BIBLIOGRAPHY

BIBLIOGRAPHIE INTERNATIONALE D'ANTHROPOLOGIE SOCIALE ET CULTURELLE
See INTERNATIONAL BIBLIOGRAPHY OF SOCIAL AND CULTURAL ANTHROPOLOGY

BIBLIOGRAPHIE INTERNATIONALE DE L'HISTOIRE DES RELIGIONS
See INTERNATIONAL BIBLIOGRAPHY OF THE HISTORY OF RELIGIONS

848
BIBLIOGRAPHIE INTERNATIONALE DE LA DEMOGRAPHIE HISTORIQUE. INTERNATIONAL BIBLIOGRAPHY OF HISTORICAL DEMOGRAPHY. 1977– . Liège.
Issued by: Comité International des Sciences Historiques, and similar agencies. In various languages.

849
BIBLIOGRAPHIE INTERNATIONALE DE PSYCHOLOGIE. 1963– . Paris. Annual.
Issued by: Comité International pour la Documentation des Sciences Sociales. Other title: *International Bibliography of Psychology*.

BIBLIOGRAPHIE INTERNATIONALE DE SCIENCE ADMINISTRATIVE
See BULLETIN SIGNALÉTIQUE. 528. BIBLIOGRAPHIE INTERNATIONALE DE SCIENCE ADMINISTRATIVE

BIBLIOGRAPHIE INTERNATIONALE DE SCIENCE POLITIQUE
See INTERNATIONAL BIBLIOGRAPHY OF POLITICAL SCIENCE

BIBLIOGRAPHIE INTERNATIONALE DE SOCIOLOGIE
See INTERNATIONAL BIBLIOGRAPHY OF SOCIOLOGY

BIBLIOGRAPHIE INTERNATIONALE DES SCIENCES ÉCONOMIQUES
See INTERNATIONAL BIBLIOGRAPHY OF ECONOMICS

BIBLIOGRAPHY INTERNATIONALE DES SCIENCES SOCIALES
See INTERNATIONAL BIBLIOGRAPHY OF THE SOCIAL SCIENCES

850
BIBLIOGRAPHIE UNIVERSELLE DE SÉCURITÉ SOCIALE. WORLD BIBLIOGRAPHY OF SOCIAL SECURITY. BIBLIOGRAFÍA MUNDIAL DE SEGURIDAD SOCIAL. WELTBIBLIOGRAPHIE DER SOZIALEN SICHERKEIT. v.1– , 1963– . Geneva. Quarterly.
Issued by: International Social Security Association.
Supersedes: *World Bibliography of Social Security* issued by the Section of the Association.
Indexed: PAIS.

851
BIBLIOGRAPHIES IN SOCIAL RESEARCH. 1– , 1974– . Bundora. Irreg.
Issued by: Department of Sociology, La Trobe University.

BIBLIOGRAPHISCHE MITTEILUNGEN
See Freie Universität, Berlin. Osteuropa Institut. BIBLIOGRAPHISCHE MITTEILUNGEN

852
BIBLIOGRAPHY OF AFRICAN STATISTICAL PUBLICATIONS. BIBLIOGRAPHIE DES PUBLICATIONS STATISTIQUES AFRICAINES. 1962– . New York, United Nations. Irreg.
In English and French.

BIBLIOGRAPHY OF PUBLICATIONS OF UNIVERSITY BUREAUS OF BUSINESS AND ECONOMIC RESEARCH
See Associated University Bureaus of Business and Economic Research. BIBLIOGRAPHY OF PUBLICATIONS OF UNIVERSITY BUREAUS OF BUSINESS AND ECONOMIC RESEARCH

853
BIBLIOGRAPHY OF SOCIO-LEGAL STUDIES. no.1– , 1980– . Oxford. Irreg.
Issued by: Center for Socio-Legal Studies, Wolfson College.

BIBLIOGRAPHY SERIES
See AUSTRALIAN ABORIGINAL STUDIES

BIBLIOTHÈQUE COLONIALE INTERNATIONALE
See International Institute of Differing Civilizations. COMPTE RENDU

854
BIBLIOTHÈQUE GÉNÉRALE DES SCIENCES SOCIALES. 1–51, 1898–1914; n. ser. v.1–2, 1917. Paris. Irreg.

In French. Monograph series.

855
BIBLIOTHÈQUE INTERNATIONALE DES SCIENCES SOCIOLOGIQUES. v.1–11, 1890–1901. Paris. Irreg.
In French. Monograph series.

856
BIENNIAL REVIEW OF ANTHROPOLOGY. v.1–13, 1959–1971. Stanford, Calif., Stanford University Press. Biennial.
Continued by: *Annual Review of Anthropology*.
Indexed: Int. Bibl. Soc. Cul. Anth.

857
BIJDRAGEN TOT DE TAAL-, LAND- EN VOLKENKUNDE VAN NEDERLANDSCH-INDIE. 1– , 1853– . 's-Gravenhage, M. Nijhoff.
Issued by: Koninklijk Instittuut voor de Taal-, Land- en Volkenkunde van Nederlandsch-Indie. In Dutch. Some no. are called *Anthropologie*; in such no. the title *Bijdragen* is used as subtitle. V.1–4, 1853–56; n. ser. v.1–8, 1956–64; ser. 3, v.1–12, 1866–76; ser. 4, v.1–10, 1877–85; ser. 5, v.1–10, 1886–94; ser. 6, v.1–10, 1895–1902; ser. 7, v.1–10, 1903–10; ser. 8, v.1–10, 1910–1918.
Indexes: vols. 1–90, 1853–1933, 1v.; v.91–100, 1934–41, 1v.
Indexed: Int. Bibl. Soc. Cul. Anth.

BILTEN ODELJENIA ZA ANALIZE I EKONOMSKA IZUČIVANJA NARODNE BANKE FNRJ
See Narodna Banka FNRJ. Odeljenie za Analize i Ekonomska Izučivanja. BILTEN

858
BIOLOGY AND HUMAN AFFAIRS. v.44, no.2– , 1979– . London. Three no. a year.
Issued by: Educational Advisory Board, British Social Biology Council.
Continues: *Biology*.

BIULETYN BIURA HISTORYCZNEGO CRZZ
See KWARTALNIK HISTORII RUCHU ZAWODOWEGO

BIULLETEN' GOSPLANA
See PLANOVOE KHOZIAĬSTVO

859
THE BLACK SCHOLAR. v.1– , Nov. 1969– . San Francisco, Calif., Black World Foundation. Monthly, except July and August, 1969–80; bimonthly.
Indexed: Hum. Res. Abst.; PAIS; PHRA; Sage Pub. Adm. Abst.; Sage Urb. Stu. Abst.; Soc. Abst.; Wom. Stu. Abst.

860
BLÄTTER FÜR DEUTSCHE UND INTERNATIONALE POLITIK. 1– , 1965– . Cologne, Paul Regenstein Verlag. Monthly.
Indexed: Bull. Anal. Pol. Ec. Soc.; Int. Bibl. Pol. Sc.; Int. Pol. Sc. Abst.; PAIS.

861
BOGAZICI UNIVERSITESI DERGISI. IDARI BILIMLER. ADMINISTRATIVE SCIENCE. v.2– , 1974– . Istanbul. Annual.
Issued by: Bogazici University. In English or Turkish.
Continues, in part: *Bogazici Universitesi Dergisi. Sosyal Bilimler*.

862
BOGAZICI UNIVERSITESI DERGISI; SOSYAL BILIMLER. BOGAZICI UNIVERSITY JOURNAL: SOCIAL SCIENCES. v.1–, 1973. Istanbul. Annual.
Issued by: Bogazici University. In English or Turkish.
Continued by: *Bogazici Universitesi Dergisi, Yonetilicik, Ekonomi ve Sosyal Bilimler*, and *Bogazici Universitesi Dergisi. Idari Bilimler*.

863
BOGAZICI UNIVERSITESI DERGISI. YONETILICIK, EKONOMI VE SOSYAL BILIMLER. BOGAZICI UNIVERSITESI JOURNAL: MANAGEMENT, ECONOMICS AND SOCIAL SCIENCES. v.2– , 1974– . Istanbul. Annual.
Issued by: Bogazici University. In English or Turkish.
Continues: *Bogazici Universitesi Dergisi. Sosyal Bilimler*.

BOGAZICI UNIVERSITY JOURNAL: MANAGEMENT, ECONOMICS AND SOCIAL SCIENCES
See BOGAZICI UNIVERSITESI DERGISI. YONETILICIK, EKONOMI VE SOSYAL BILIMLER

BOGAZICI UNIVERSITY JOURNAL; SOCIAL SCIENCES
See BOGAZICI UNIVERSITESI DERGISI; SOSYAL BILIMLER

BOLETIM
See AMERICA LATINA

BOLETIM DA AGÊNCIA GERAL DAS COLÔNIAS
See BOLETIM GERAL DO ULTRAMAR

864
BOLETIM DE ANTROPOLOGIA. 1956– . Ceará. Irreg.
Issued by: Instituto de Antropologia, Universidade do Ceará. In Portuguese.

BOLETIM DO INSTITUTO JOAQUIM NABUCO DE PESQUISAS SOCIAIS
See Instituto Joaquim Nabuco de Pesquisas Sociais. BOLETIM DO INSTITUTO JOAQUIM NABUCO DE PESQUISAS SOCIAIS

BOLETIM GERAL DAS COLONIAS
See BOLETIM GERAL DO ULTRAMAR

865
BOLETIM GERAL DO ULTRAMAR. v.1– , July 1925– . Lisboa. Monthly.
Issued by: Agencia Geral das Colonias, 1925–July 1951; Agencia Geral do Ultramar, 1951– . In Portuguese. Title varies: 1925–31, *Boletim da Agência Geral das Colônias*; 1932–July 1951, *Boletim Geral das Colônias*.

BOLETÍN
See Academia de Ciencias Políticas y Sociales, Caracas. BOLETIN

BOLETÍN
See ANTROPOLOGÍA E HISTORIA

BOLETÍN
See Universidad Nacional de Córdoba. BOLETIN

BOLETÍN BIBLIOGRÁFICO DE ANTROPOLOGÍA AMERICANA
See Pan American Institute of Geography and History. BOLETÍN BIBLIOGRÁFICO DE ANTROPOLOGÍA AMERICANA

866
BOLETÍN CENTROAMERICANO Y DEL CARIBE. v.1– , Aug. 1981– . Mexico, D.F.
Issued by: Universidad Iberoamericano. In Spanish.

867
BOLETÍN DE CIENCIAS ECONÓMICAS Y SOCIALES. no.1– , May 1978– . San Salvador. Monthly.
Issued by: Departamento de Economía, Universidad Centroamericana José Simeon Canas. In Spanish.

868
BOLETÍN DE CIENCIAS POLÍTICAS Y SOCIALES. no.1– , 1951– . Mendoza. Annual.
Issued by: Facultad de Ciencias Políticas y Sociales, Universidad Nacional de Cuyo. In Spanish. Title varies: 1951–61, *Boletín de Estudios Políticos y Sociales*.
Indexed: Bull. Anal. Pol. Ec. Soc.; Int. Bibl. Soc. Cul. Anth.

869
BOLETÍN DE ECONOMÍA INTERNACIONAL. v.11– , Jan./Mar. 1985– . Mexico, D.F. Quarterly.
Issued by: Banco de Mexico. In Spanish. Other title: *Boletín de Economía Internacional del Banco de México*.
Continues: *Boletín de Indicadores Económicos Internacionales*.

BOLETÍN DE ECONOMÍA INTERNACIONAL DEL BANCO DE MÉXICO
See BOLETÍN DE ECONOMÍA INTERNACIONAL

870
BOLETÍN DE ESTUDIOS LATINOAMERICANOS. no.1–15, 1950–73. Amsterdam. Two no. a year.
Issued by: Centro de Estudios y Documentación Latinoamericana in Amsterdam (CEDLA) in cooperation with the Sección de Estudios del Caribe del Instituto de Lingüística y Antropología at Leiden. In Spanish; occasionally papers in English. Title varies: no.1–9, 1950–69, *Boletín Informativo sobre Estudios Latinoamericanos en Europa*.
Continued by: *Boletín de Estudios Latinoamericanos y del Caribe*.
Indexed: Bull. Anal. Pol. Ec. Soc.; Int. Bibl. Eco.; PAIS.

871
BOLETÍN DE ESTUDIOS LATINOAMERICANOS Y DEL CARIBE. no.16– , June 1974– . Amsterdam. Semi-annual.
Issued by: Centro de Estudios y Documentación Latinoamericanos (CEDLA). Cover title: *Journal of Latin American and Caribbean Studies*. In English or Spanish.
Continues: *Boletín de Estudios Latinoamericanos*.
Indexed: Bull. Anal. Pol. Ec. Soc.; Int. Bibl. Eco.; PAIS.

872
BOLETÍN DE ESTUDIOS POLÍTICOS Y SOCIALES. 1– , 1980– . Madrid. Four no. a year.
In Spanish.

BOLETÍN DE ESTUDIOS POLÍTICOS Y SOCIALES
See BOLETÍN DE CIENCIAS POLÍTICAS Y SOCIALES

BOLETÍN DE I.T.A.T.
See REVISTA MEXICANA DEL TRABAJO

873
BOLETIN DE INVESTIGACIONES Y DE ESTUDIOS SOCIALES Y ECONÓMICOS. 1– , 1938– . Quito. Four no. a year (in two double issues)

Issued by: Instituto Nacional de Previsión. In Spanish.

BOLETÍN DEL CONSEJO DE ARQUEOLOGÍA
See Consejo de Arqueología. BOLETÍN

BOLETÍN DEL FMI
See International Monetary Fund. IMF SURVEY

BOLETÍN ESTADÍSTICO DE AMÉRICA LATINA
See United Nations. Economic Commission for Latin America. BOLETÍN ESTADÍSTICO DE AMÉRICA LATINA

BOLETÍN ESTADÍSTICO DE AMÉRICA LATINA
See Organization of American States. BOLETÍN ESTADÍSTICO DE AMÉRICA LATINA

BOLETÍN ESTADÍSTICO DE LA OEA
See Organization of American States. BOLETÍN ESTADÍSTICO DE AMÉRICA LATINA

874
BOLETÍN INDIGENISTA. v.1–21, Sept. 1941–Dec. 1961. Mexico, D.F. Bimonthly, 1941; quarterly.
Issued by: Instituto Indigenista Interamericano. In English or Spanish. Published as a supplement to *América Indígena.*
Continued by: *Indianist Yearbook (Anuario Indigenista*, 22– , 1962–)
Indexes: Vols. 1–13, 1941–53, 1v.
Indexed: His. Abst.

BOLETÍN INFORMACIÓN ECONÓMICA
See ECONOMÍA Y ADMINISTRACIÓN (Quito)

BOLETÍN INFORMATIVO SOBRE ESTUDIOS LATINOAMERICANOS EN EUROPA
See BOLETÍN DE ESTUDIOS LATINOAMERICANOS

BOLETÍN MENSUAL
See Centro de Estudios Monetarios Latinoamericanos. BOLETÍN QUINCENAL

875
BOLETÍN MEXICANO DE DERECHO COMPARADO. v.1– , Jan./Mar. 1968– . Mexico, D.F. Three no. a year.
Issued by: Instituto de Investigaciones Jurídicas. In Spanish.
Supersedes: *Boletín del Instituto de Derecho Comparado de México.*

BOLETÍN QUINCENAL
See Centro de Estudios Monetarios Latinoamericanos. BOLETÍN QUINCENAL

BOLETIN TRIMESTRAL DE INFORMACIÓN ECONÓMICA
See ECONOMÍA Y ADMINISTRACIÓN (Quito)

BOL'SHEVIK
See KOMMUNIST (Moskva)

BOL'SHEVIK
See TURKMENISTAN KOMUNISTI

BOL'SHEVIK BELARUSSI
See KOMMUNIST BELORUSSI

BOL'SHEVIK ESTONII
See KOMMUNIST ESTONII

BOL'SHEVIK SOVETSKOĬ LATVII
See KOMMUNIST SOVETSKOĬ LATVII

BOL'SHEVIK TADZHIKISTANA
See KOMMUNIST TADZHIKISTANA

BOL'SHEVIK UKRAINY
See KOMMUNIST UKRAINY

THE BOMBAY COOPERATIVE QUARTERLY
See THE MAHARASHTRA CO-OPERATIVE QUARTERLY

876
BORNEO RESEARCH BULLETIN. v.1– , Mar. 1969– . Williamsburg, Va. Semi-annual.
Issued by: Department of Anthropology, The College of William and Mary, and the Borneo Research Council.
Indexed: Int. Bibl. Soc. Cul. Anth.

877
BOSTON COLLEGE INTERNATIONAL AND COMPARATIVE LAW JOURNAL. v.1–2, no.1, 1977–1978. Newton Centre, Mass. Semi-annual.
Issued by: School of Law, Boston College.
Continued by: *Boston College International and Comparative Law Review.*

878
BOSTON COLLEGE INTERNATIONAL AND COMPARATIVE LAW REVIEW. v.2, no.2– , 1979– . Newton Centre, Mass. Semi-annual.
Issued by: School of Law, Boston College.
Continues: *Boston College International and Comparative Law Journal.*
Indexed: ABC POL SCI; Ind. Leg. Per.

879
Boston University. African Studies Center. WORKING PAPERS. no.1– , 1978– . Boston, Mass. Irreg.
Supersedes: *Working Papers in African Studies* (Brookline)

880
BOSTON UNIVERSITY INTERNATIONAL LAW JOURNAL. v.1– , spring 1982– . Boston, Mass. Semi-annual.
Issued by: School of Law, Boston University.
Indexed: Ind. Leg. Per.

BOSTON UNIVERSITY PAPERS IN AFRICAN HISTORY
See BOSTON UNIVERSITY PAPERS ON AFRICA

881
BOSTON UNIVERSITY PAPERS ON AFRICA. no.1– , 1964– . Boston, Mass. Irreg.
Issued by: African Studies Center, Boston University. Title varies: no.1, *Boston University Papers in African History*.

882
BOTSWANA NOTES AND RECORDS. v.1– , 1968– . Gaborone. Irreg.
Issued by: Botswana Society. Some volumes processed.
Indexed: Int. Bibl. Soc. Cul. Anth.

883
BRASIL: PERSPECTIVAS INTERNACIONAIS. v.1– , Jan./June 1984– . Rio de Janeiro. Bimonthly.
Issued by: Instituto de Relações Internacionais, Pontifícia Universidade Católica do Rio de Janeiro. In Portuguese.

884
BRAZILIAN AMERICAN SURVEY. no.1–30, 1953/54–Dec. 1966. Rio de Janeiro. Two no. a year.

885
BRITISH ARCHAEOLOGICAL ABSTRACTS. v.1– , Apr. 1968– . London. Semi-annual.
Issued by: Council for British Archaeology.
Indexed: Int. Bibl. Soc. Cul. Anth.

886
BRITISH EDUCATION INDEX. 1961– . London. Three no. a year with annual cumulation.
Issued by: Bibliographic Services Division, British Library.

887
BRITISH EDUCATIONAL RESEARCH JOURNAL. v.4– , Apr. 1978– . Oxford, Carfax Pub. Co. Semi-annual.
Continues: *Research Intelligence*.

888
THE BRITISH EMPIRE REVIEW. v.1–28, no.8, July 1899–July/Sept. 1939. London. Monthly.
Issued by: British Empire League.

889
THE BRITISH JOURNAL OF CRIMINOLOGY. v.14– , 1974– . London, Stevens. Quarterly.
Issued by: Institute for the Study and Treatment of Delinquency.
Continues: *British Journal of Criminology, Delinquency and Deviant Social Behaviour* (v.1–13, 1961–73).
Indexed: Soc. Abst.

890
BRITISH JOURNAL OF DELINQUENCY. v.1–10, July 1950–Apr. 1960. London. Quarterly.
Superseded by: *British Journal of Criminology, Delinquency and Deviant Social Behaviour*.
Indexes: Vols. 1–10, included in the index to *British Journal of Criminology, Delinquency and Deviant Social Behaviour*.

891
BRITISH JOURNAL OF EDUCATIONAL STUDIES. v.1– , Nov. 1952– . London, later Oxford, B. Blackwell. Semi-annual, 1952–May 1965; three no. a year.
Issued by: Department of Education, King's College, Oxford.

892
BRITISH JOURNAL OF INDUSTRIAL RELATIONS. Feb. 1963– . Clevedon. Three no. a year.
Issued by: London School of Economics and Political Science.
Indexed: Bull. Anal. Pol. Ec. Soc.; Bull. Sig. Soc. Eth.; Ind. Per. Art. Law; Ind. Per. Art. Law 1970; Int. Bibl. Eco.; Int. Bibl. Pol. Sc.; Int. Bibl. Soc.; Int. Bibl. Soc. Cul. Anth.; Int. Lab. Doc.

893
BRITISH JOURNAL OF INTERNATIONAL STUDIES. v.1–6, Apr. 1975–Oct. 1980. Harlow, Longman. Three no. a year.
Issued by: British International Studies Association.
Continued by: *Review of International Studies*.
Indexed: Bull. Anal. Pol. Ec. Soc.; Int. Bibl. Pol. Sc.

894
BRITISH JOURNAL OF LAW AND SOCIETY. v.1–8, no.2, summer 1974–winter 1981. London, Professional Books. Quarterly.
Continued by: *Journal of Law and Society*.
Indexed: Bull. Anal. Pol. Ec. Soc.; Int. Bibl. Pol. Sc.; Int. Pol. Sc. Abst.; Soc. Work. Res. Abst.; Soc. Abst.

Indexes: Vols. 1–3, 1974–76, with the 1976 volume of the *British Research Directory of Law and Society*.

895
THE BRITISH JOURNAL OF MATHEMATICAL & STATISTICAL PSYCHOLOGY. v.18– , May 1965– . Bristol, J. Wright. Two no. a year.
Issued by: British Psychological Society.
Continues: *British Journal of Statistical Psychology*.
Indexed: Bull. Sig. Soc. Eth.; LLBA; Psych. Abst.; SSCI; Soc. Abst.

896
BRITISH JOURNAL OF POLITICAL SCIENCE. v.1– , Jan. 1971– . London, Cambridge University Press. Quarterly.
Issued by: Department of Government, University of Essex.
Indexed: ABC POL SCI; Ind. Per. Art. Law; Int. Bibl. Pol. Sc.; Int. Bibl. Eco.; Int. Bibl. Soc.; Int. Pol. Sc. Abst.; Soc. Abst.; SSCI.

BRITISH JOURNAL OF PSYCHOLOGY [STATISTICAL SECTION]
See BRITISH JOURNAL OF STATISTICAL PSYCHOLOGY

897
BRITISH JOURNAL OF PSYCHIATRY AND COMMUNITY HEALTH. v.4– , 1970– . London, Avenue Pub. Co. Quarterly.
Issued by: British Association of Social Psychiatry.
Continues: *British Journal of Social Psychiatry*.
Indexed: Int. Bibl. Soc.; SSCI.

898
THE BRITISH JOURNAL OF SOCIAL AND CLINICAL PSYCHOLOGY. v.1–19, Feb. 1962–1980. London, Cambridge University Press. Three no. a year.
Issued by: British Psychological Society, and Institute of Experimental Psychology.
Continued, in part, by: *The British Journal of Social Psychology*.
Indexed: Bull. Sig. Soc. Eth.; Int. Bibl. Soc.; Soc. Abst.; Wom. Stu. Abst.

899
THE BRITISH JOURNAL OF SOCIAL PSYCHOLOGY. v.20– , Feb. 1981– . Letchworth. Quarterly.
Issued by: British Psychological Association.
Continues: *British Journal of Social and Clinical Psychology*.

900
THE BRITISH JOURNAL OF SOCIOLOGY. v.1– , Mar. 1950– . London, Routledge & Kegan Paul. Quarterly.
Issued by: London School of Economics and Political Science (until Mar. 1957 called London School of Economics)
Indexes: Vols. 1–10, 1950–59, in v.10, no.5.
Indexed: Bull. Anal. Pol. Ec. Soc.; Bull. Sig. Soc. Eth.; Int. Bibl. Eco.; His. Abst.; Int. Bibl. Pol. Sc.; Int. Bibl. Soc.; Int. Bibl. Soc. Cul. Anth.; Int. Pol. Sc. Abst.; Ind. Per. Art. Law; PAIS; Pop. Ind.; Psych. Abst.; SSCI; Soc. Sc. Hum. Ind.; Soc. Work. Res. Abst.; Wom. Stu. Abst.

901
BRITISH JOURNAL OF SOCIOLOGY OF EDUCATION. v.1– , 1980– . Oxford, Carfax Pub. Co. Three no. a year.
Indexed: Int. Bibl. Soc. Cul. Anth.; Soc. Abst.

902
BRITISH JOURNAL OF STATISTICAL PSYCHOLOGY. v.1–17, pt.2, Oct. 1947–Nov. 1964. Bristol, J. Wright. Three no. a year, 1947–52; two no. a year.
Issued by: British Psychological Society. Title varies: v.1–5, no.3, Oct. 1947–Nov. 1952, *British Journal of Psychology*.
Continued by: *British Journal of Mathematical and Statistical Psychology*.
Indexes: Vols. 1–14, 1947–61, 1v.

903
British Library. Lending Division. INDEX TO CONFERENCE PROCEEDINGS RECEIVED. no.69– , June 1973– . Boston Spa. Monthly with annual cumulation.
Continues: Lending Division for Science and Technology. *Index to Conference Proceedings*.

904
BRITISH POLITICAL SOCIOLOGY YEARBOOK. v.1– , 1974– . New York, Halstead Press. Annual.
Indexed: Bull. Anal. Pol. Ec. Soc.; Int. Pol. Sc. Abst.

905
BRITISH POLITICAL SOURCES; POLITICAL PARTY YEARBOOKS. 1– , 1970– . Brighton, Harvester Press.

906
BRITISH PRACTICE IN INTERNATIONAL LAW. Jan./June 1962– . London. Semi-annual.
Issued by: British Institute of International and Comparative Law. Title varies: v.1, 1962, *Contemporary Practice of the United Kingdom in the Field of International Law*.

907
BRITISH PUBLIC OPINION QUARTERLY. 1– , 1979– . London. Quarterly.

908
BRITISH REVIEW OF ECONOMIC ISSUES. no.1– , Nov. 1977– . Kingston.
Issued by: Association of Polytechnic Teachers in Economics.
Indexed: PAIS.

909
BRITISH YEAR BOOK OF INTERNATIONAL LAW. [1]– , 1920/21– . London, New York, Oxford University Press. Annual.
Vols. for 1920/21–1927 published under the auspices of the British Institute of International Affairs; 1928–, Royal Institute of International Affairs. Publication suspended 1940–43. Vols. 1955/56, 1965/68 and 1968/69 combined.
Indexes: Vols. 1–10, 1920/21–1929, in v.10; v.11–20, 1930–39, in v.20; v.1–36, 1920/21–1960, 1v.
Indexed: Bull. Anal. Pol. Ec. Soc.; Ind. For. Leg. Per.; Ind. Leg. Per.; Int. Bibl. Eco.; Int. Pol. Sc. Abst.

910
Brnenske Univerzita. Filozofická Fakulta. SBORNIK PRACI. RADA G. SOCIAINI VĚDY. v.1– , 1957– . Praha.
In Czech; summaries in German and Russian. Tables of contents also in German and Russian. (Subseries of: Univerzita's *Sbornik Praci*)

911
BROOKINGS PAPERS ON ECONOMIC ACTIVITY. 1970– . Washington, D.C. Three no. a year.
Issued by: The Brookings Institution.
Indexed: Bull. Anal. Pol. Ec. Soc.; Curr. Cont. Soc. Beh. Sc.; Int. Bibl. Eco.; Int. Bibl. Pol. Sc.; Int. Pol. Sc. Abst.; PAIS: SSCI.

912
BROOKINGS RESEARCH REPORT. 1– , 1962– . Washington, D.C. Irreg.
Issued by: The Brookings Institution.
Indexed: PAIS; SSCI.

913
THE BROOKINGS REVIEW. fall 1982– . Washington, D.C. Four no. a year.
Issued by: The Brookings Institution.
Continues: *Brookings Bulletin* (1962–81)
Indexed: PAIS.

914
BROOKLYN JOURNAL OF INTERNATIONAL LAW. v.1– , spring 1975– . Brooklyn, N.Y. Semi-annual.
Issued by: Brooklyn Law School.

BUDGETING
See PUBLIC BUDGETING & FINANCE

915
BUḤŪTH. 1– , 1974– . Khartoum, Khartoum University. Quarterly.
Issued by: National Council for Research. Issues for 1979 last available for examination.

BUḤŪTH AL-QĀHIRAH FĪ AL-'ULŪM AL-IJTIMĀ' ĪYAH
See CAIRO PAPERS IN SOCIAL SCIENCE

BULETIN DE INFORMARE ŞTIINŢIFICA: FILOZOFIE, LOGICA, SOCIOLOGIE, PSIHOLOGIE
See Academia Republicii Socialiste România. Centrul de Documentare Ştiinţifica: BULETIN DE INFORMARE ŞTIINŢIFICA: FILOZOFIE, LOGICA, SOCIOLOGIE, PSIHOLOGIE

BULETIN DE INFORMARE ŞTIINŢIFICA: FILOZOFIE, LOGICA, SOCIOLOGIE, PSIHOLOGIE
See Universitatea Bucureşti. BULETIN INFORMARE ŞTIINŢIFICA: FILOZOFIE, LOGICA, SOCIOLOGIE, PSIHOLOGIE

BULETIN INFORMARE ŞTIINŢIFICA: ŞTIINŢE ECONOMICE
See Academia Republicii Socialiste România. Centrul de Informare Ştiinţifica. BULETIN DE INFORMARE ŞTIINŢIFICA: ŞTIINŢE ECONOMICE

BULETINUL. IZVESTIIA. SERIIA OBSHCHESTVENNYKH NAUK
See Akademia de Shtiintse a RSS Moldovenest. BULETINUL. IZVESTIIA. SERIIA OBSHCHESTVENNYKH NAUK

BULETINUL. ŞTIINŢE SOCIALE ŞI UMANISTE
See Universitatea din Galati. BULETINUL. ŞTIINŢE SOCIALE ŞI UMANISTE

BULGARIAN ETHNOGRAPHY
See BULGARSKA ETNOGRAFIIA

916
BULGARIAN HISTORICAL REVIEW. REVUE BULGARE D'HISTOIRE. 1973– . Sofia.
Issued by: Bulgarska Akademiia na Naukite. In English, French, German, or Russian.

917
BULGARIAN JOURNAL OF SOCIOLOGY. 1– , 1978– . Sofia, Bulgarian Academy of Sciences Press. Annual.
Issued by: Institute of Sociology, Bulgarian Academy of Sciences, and the Bulgarian Sociological Association.

918
BULGARIAN TRADE UNIONS. 1947– . Sofia. Bimonthly.
Issued by: Tsentralen Suvet na Profesionalnite Suiuzi. In Bulgarian. Published also in Arabic, French, Russian and Spanish.

919
Bulgarska Akademii͡a na Naukite. Etnografski Institut. IZVESTII͡A NA ETNOGRAFSKI INSTITUT E MUZEI. 1953–1974. Sofii͡a.
In Russian; summaries in French and Russian. Other title: *Bulletin de l'Institut d'Ethnographie et Musée.*
Superseded by: *Bulgarska Etnografii͡a.*

920
Bulgarska Akademii͡a na Naukite. Geografski Institut. IZVESTII͡A. 1951– . Sofii͡a, Izd-vo na Bulgarskata Akademii͡a na Naukite. Irreg.
In Bulgarian; summaries in French and Russian. Tables of contents also in French and Russian. Other title: *Bulletin de l'Institut de Géographie.*

921
Bulgarska Akademii͡a na Naukite. Institut za Istorii͡a. IZVESTII͡A. 1/2– , 1951– . Sofii͡a, Izd-vo na Bulgarskata Akademii͡a na Naukite. Irreg.
In Bulgarian; summaries in various languages. Tables of contents also in French and Russian.

922
BULGARSKA ETNOGRAFII͡A. 1975– . Sofii͡a, Izd-vo na Bulgarskata Akademii͡a na Naukite. Four no. a year.
Issued by: Etnografski Institut e Musei, Bulgarska Akademii͡a na Naukite. In Bulgarian; summaries in English and Russian. Other title: *Bulgarian Ethnography.*
Supersedes: Bulgarska Akademii͡a na Naukite. Etnografski Institut. *Izvestii͡a na Etnografii͡a.*

923
Bulgarsko Istorichesko Druzhestvo. IZVESTII͡A. BULLETIN. v.1– , 1905– . Sofii͡a, Izd-vo na Bulgarskata Akademii͡a na Naukite.
In Bulgarian; summaries in French.

BULLETIN
See American Anthropological Association. BULLETIN

BULLETIN
See American Ethnological Society. BULLETIN

BULLETIN
See Bulgarsko Istorichesko Druzhestvo. IZVESTII͡A

BULLETIN
See THE BUSINESS HISTORY REVIEW

BULLETIN
See École Française de l'Extrême-Orient. BULLETIN

BULLETIN
See Economic and Social Committee of the European Communities. BULLETIN

BULLETIN
See ÉTUDES & EXPANSION

BULLETIN
See France. Agence Générale des Colonies. BULLETIN

BULLETIN
See Institut Fondamental d'Afrique Noire. BULLETIN

BULLETIN
See Institut International d'Administration Publique. BULLETIN

BULLETIN
See Institut International d'Études Sociales. BULLETIN

BULLETIN
See International Bureau of Education. BULLETIN [English edition]

BULLETIN
See International Institute of Social History. BULLETIN

BULLETIN
See Public Affairs Information Service. BULLETIN

BULLETIN
See RELIGION AND SOCIETY

BULLETIN
See REVUE ÉCONOMIQUE FRANÇAISE

BULLETIN
See Social Science Research Council (U.S.A.). BULLETIN

BULLETIN
See Société Belge d'Études Coloniales. BULLETIN

BULLETIN
See Société Belge d'Études Géographiques. BULLETIN

BULLETIN
See Société d'Économie et des Sciences Sociales. BULLETIN

BULLETIN
See Société des Études Indochinois. BULLETIN

BULLETIN
See Society for the Psychological Study of Social Issues. BULLETIN

BULLETIN
See Society for the Study of Labour History. BULLETIN

BULLETIN ANALYTIQUE AFRICANISTE
See ANALYSES AFRICANISTES

924
BULLETIN ANALYTIQUE DE DOCUMENTATION POLITIQUE, ÉCONOMIQUE ET SOCIALE CONTEMPORAINE. v.1– , May 1946– . Paris, Presses Universitaires de France. Monthly, May–Oct. 1946; bimonthly.
Organ of: Fondation Nationale des Sciences Politiques. In French.
Indexed: PAISFL.

BULLETIN ANALYTIQUE SUR LE DÉVELOPPEMENT
See DEVELOPMENT INFORMATION ABSTRACTS

BULLETIN ANALYTIQUE. TROISIÈME PARTIE. PHILOSOPHIE
See BULLETIN SIGNALÉTIQUE; SCIENCES HUMAINES

BULLETIN ARCHÉOLOGIQUE POLONAIS
See WIADOMOŚCI ARCHEOLOGICZNE

925
BULLETIN BIBLIOGRAPHIQUE DE DOCUMENTATION INTERNATIONALE CONTEMPORAINE. BULLETIN ON INTERNATIONAL AFFAIRS. 1–3, Jan./Feb. 1926–Dec. 1928; n. ser. 4–6; 1929–Dec. 1931; 3. ser., 7–9, 1932–Dec. 1934; 4. ser., v.10– , 1935– . Paris, Presses Universitaires de France.
In French.
Supersedes: *Bulletin de l'Office de Documentation Internationale*.

BULLETIN D'ANALYSES DE LA LITTÉRATURE SCIENTIFIQUE BULGARE. ÉCONOMIE ET DROIT
See ABSTRACTS OF BULGARIAN SCIENTIFIC LITERATURE. ECONOMICS AND LAW

BULLETIN D'ANALYSES DE LA LITTÉRATURE SCIENTIFIQUE BULGARE. HISTOIRE ET ARCHÉOLOGIE
See ZENTRALBLATT DER BULGARISCHEN LITERATUR. GESCHICHTE, ARCHÄOLOGIE UND ETHNOGRAPHIE

926
BULLETIN D'ARCHÉOLOGIE MAROCAINE. v.1– , 1956– . Casablanca. Irreg.
Issued by: Centre National de la Recherche Scientifique in Paris, subsequently by: Service de l'Archéologie, Division d'Archéologie des Monuments Historiques et des Sites et des Musées, Morocco. In French.
Indexed: Int. Bibl. Soc. Cul. Anth.

927
BULLETIN D'ARCHÉOLOGIE SUD-EST EUROPÉENNE. 1– , 1969– . Bucarest. Irreg.
Issued by: Association Internationale d'Études du Sud-Est Européen. In French.

BULLETIN D'ÉTUDES ET D'INFORMATIONS
See VIE ÉCONOMIQUE ET SOCIALE

928
BULLETIN D'HISTOIRE ÉCONOMIQUE ET SOCIALE DE LA RÉVOLUTION FRANÇAISE. 1961– . Paris, Imprimerie Nationale. Annual.
Issued by: Commission d'Histoire Économique et Sociale de la Révolution Française. In French.
Indexes: Vols. 1907–21.

BULLETIN D'INFORMATION
See SERVICE SOCIAL DANS LE MONDE

BULLETIN D'INFORMATION
See SONDAGES

BULLETIN D'INFORMATION DE LA FRANCE D'OUTRE-MER
See EUROPE, FRANCE D'OUTRE-MER

BULLETIN D'INFORMATION STATISTIQUE ET ÉCONOMIQUE POUR L'AFRIQUE
See United Nations. Economic Commission for Africa. STATISTICAL AND ECONOMIC INFORMATION BULLETIN FOR AFRICA

929
BULLETIN D'INFORMATIONS SOCIALES. 1– , 1974– . Genève. Four no. a year.
Issued by: Bureau International du Travail. In French.

BULLETIN DE L'INSTITUT FRANÇAIS D'HISTOIRE SOCIALE
See LE MOUVEMENT SOCIALE

BULLETIN DE DOCUMENTATION FISCALE INTERNATIONALE
See International Bureau of Fiscal Documentation, Amsterdam. BULLETIN FOR INTERNATIONAL FISCAL DOCUMENTATION

BULLETIN DE L'ÉCOLE FRANÇAISE D'EXTRÊME-ORIENT
See École Française de l'Extrême-Orient. BULLETIN

BULLETIN DE L'ENSEIGNEMENT DE L'AFRIQUE OCCIDENTALE
See L'ÉDUCATION AFRICAINE

BULLETIN DE L'INSTITUT D'ETHNOGRAPHIE ET MUSÉE
See Bulgarska Akademiia na Naukite. Etnografski Institut. IZVESTIIA NA ETNOGRAFSKI INSTITUT E MUZEI

BULLETIN DE L'INSTITUT DE GÉOGRAPHIE
See Bulgarska Akademiia na Naukite. Geografski Institut. IZVESTIIA

BULLETIN DE L'INSTITUT DE RECHERCHES ÉCONOMIQUES
See RECHERCHES ÉCONOMIQUES DE LOUVAIN

BULLETIN DE L'INSTITUT DE RECHERCHES ÉCONOMIQUES ET SOCIALES
See RECHERCHES ÉCONOMIQUES DE LOUVAIN

BULLETIN DE L'INSTITUT DES HAUTES ÉTUDES D'OUTRE-MER
See REVUE FRANÇAISE D'ADMINISTRATION PUBLIQUE

BULLETIN DE L'INSTITUT DES SCIENCES ÉCONOMIQUES
See RECHERCHES ÉCONOMIQUES DE LOUVAIN

BULLETIN DE L'INSTITUT INTERNATIONAL D'ADMINISTRATION PUBLIQUE
See Institut International d'Administration Publique. BULLETIN

BULLETIN DE L'INSTITUT FONDAMENTAL D'AFRIQUE NOIRE. SÉRIE B.
See Institut Fondamental d'Afrique Noire. BULLETIN. SÉRIE B. SCIENCES HUMAINES

BULLETIN DE L'INSTITUT FRANÇAIS D'AFRIQUE NOIRE. SÉRIE B. SCIENCES HUMAINES
See Institut Fondamental d'Afrique Noire. BULLETIN. SÉRIE B. SCIENCES HUMAINES

BULLETIN DE L'INSTITUT POUR L'ÉTUDE DE L'EUROPE SUD-ORIENTALE
See Institutul de Studii Sud-Est Europene. BULLETIN DE L'INSTITUT POUR L'ÉTUDE DE L'EUROPE SUD-ORIENTALE

BULLETIN DE LA SOCIÉTÉ DES ÉTUDES INDOCHINOISES
See Société des Études Indochinoises. BULLETIN

BULLETIN DE LA SOCIÉTÉ PRÉHISTORIQUE FRANÇAISE
See Société Préhistorique Française. BULLETIN. ÉTUDES ET TRAVAUX

930
BULLETIN DE LIAISON DE DÉMOGRAPHIE FRANÇAISE. no.29– , Mar./Apr. 1979– . Yaoundé. Three no. a year.
Issued by: Institut de Formation et de Recherches Démographiques. In French. Cover title: *Démographie Africaine*.
Continues: *Démographie Africaine*.

931
BULLETIN DE MADAGASCAR. no.1– , Jan. 16, 1950– . Tananarive. Semi-monthly, 1950–52; monthly.
Issued by: Direction de l'Information (called 1950–Mar. 1966, Service Générale de l'Information). In French.
Indexed: Abst. Anth.; Int. Bibl. Soc. Cul. Anth.

BULLETIN DE SOCIOLOGIE ET DE RELIGION COMPARÉS
See JOURNAL OF COMPARATIVE SOCIOLOGY AND RELIGION

BULLETIN DE STATISTIQUE POUR L'AFRIQUE
See United Nations. Economic Commission for Africa. STATISTICAL YEARBOOK

BULLETIN DES DROITS DE L'HOMME
See CAHIERS DES DROITS DE L'HOMME

BULLETIN DES SÉANCES
See Académie Royale des Sciences d'Outre-Mer. Classe des Sciences Morales et Politiques. BULLETIN DES SÉANCES

BULLETIN DU BUREAU NATIONAL D'ETHNOLOGIE
See Bureau National d'Ethnologie. BULLETIN

BULLETIN DU CENTRE D'ÉTUDE DES PAYS DE L'EST ET DU CENTRE NATIONAL POUR L'ÉTUDE DES ÉTATS DE L'EST
See REVUE DES PAYS DE L'EST

BULLETIN DU CENTRE D'ÉTUDES DES PROBLÈMES SOCIAUX INDIGÈNES
See PROBLEMES SOCIAUX ZAÏROIS

BULLETIN DU FMI
See International Monetary Fund. IMF SURVEY

BULLETIN ÉCONOMIQUE DU MAROC
See BULLETIN ÉCONOMIQUE ET SOCIALE DU MAROC

932
BULLETIN ÉCONOMIQUE ET SOCIALE DU MAROC. July 1933– . Rabat. Quarterly (irreg.)
Issued by: Société d'Études Économiques, Sociales et Statistiques. In French. Title varies: 1933–39, *Bulletin Économique du Maroc*. Not published Oct. 1939–Apr. 1945.
Indexed: Bull. Anal. Pol. Ec. Soc.; Int. Lab. Doc.; PAISFL.

BULLETIN FOR INTERNATIONAL FISCAL DOCUMENTATION
See International Bureau of Fiscal Documentation, Amsterdam. BULLETIN FOR INTERNATIONAL FISCAL DOCUMENTATION

BULLETIN FROM THE EUROPEAN COMMUNITY
See EUROPEAN COMMUNITY [American Edition]

BULLETIN FROM THE EUROPEAN COMMUNITY FOR COAL AND STEEL
See EUROPEAN COMMUNITY [American Edition]

BULLETIN INTERPARLEMENTAIRE
See Inter-Parliamentary Union. BULLETIN INTERPARLEMENTAIRE

BULLETIN MENSUELLE DE STATISTIQUE
See United Nations. Statistical Office. MONTHLY BULLETIN OF STATISTICS

BULLETIN MENSUELLE DES TRAVAUX ET DÉCOUVERTES CONCERNANT ANTHROPOLOGIE, LES TEMPS PRÉHISTORIQUES, L'ÉPOQUE QUATERNAIRE, LES QUESTIONS DE L'ESPACE ET DE LA GÉNÉRATION SPONTANÉE
See MATÉRIAUX POUR L'HISTOIRE PRIMITIVE DE L'HOMME

933
BULLETIN OF COMPARATIVE LABOUR RELATIONS. 6– , 1975– . Deventer, Kluwer. Annual.
In Dutch, English, French, or German.
Continues: Katholieke Universiteit Leuven. Instituut voor Arbeids Recht. *Bulletin*.

934
BULLETIN OF ECONOMIC RESEARCH. v.23– , May 1971– . Hull. Semi-annual.
Issued jointly by: departments of economics of the University of Hull, Leeds, Sheffield, York, and Brighton.
Continues: *Yorkshire Bulletin of Economic Research. Occasional Paper*.
Indexed: Bull. Anal. Pol. Ec. Soc.; Int. Bibl. Eco.

935
BULLETIN OF INDONESIAN ECONOMIC STUDIES. no.1– , June 1965– . Canberra. Three no. a year.
Issued by: Department of Economics, Research School of Pacific Studies, Australian National University. Issues for 1965–68, called no.1–11, constitute v.1–4.
Indexes: Vols. 1–11, no.3, 1965–Nov. 1975, 1v.
Indexed: APAIS; Bull. Anal. Pol. Ec. Soc.; Int. Lab. Doc.; PAIS.

936
BULLETIN OF LATIN AMERICAN RESEARCH. v.1– , Oct. 1981– . Oxford, Oxford Microform Publications. Semi-annual.
Issued by: Society for Latin American Studies.
Supersedes: *Bulletin* of the same society.
Indexed: ABC POL SCI.

937
BULLETIN OF PEACE PROPOSALS. v.1– , 1970– . Oslo, Universitetsforlaget. Quarterly.
Issued by: International Peace Research Institute (Oslo), under the auspices of the International Peace Research Association (Groningen), World Policy Institute, and the Berglof Foundation for Conflict Research. First printed issue was preceded by two mimeographed issues in spring and autumn 1969.
Indexed: Bull. Anal. Pol. Ec. Soc.; Int. Bibl. Pol. Sc.; Int. Pol. Sc. Abst.

BULLETIN OF PROCEEDINGS
See American Ethnological Society. BULLETIN OF PROCEEDINGS

938
BULLETIN OF RURAL ECONOMICS AND SOCIOLOGY. v.1–8, no.1, 1964–1973. Ibadan.
Issued by: Department of Agricultural Economics, University of Ibadan.
Continued by: *Journal of Rural Economic Development*.

939
BULLETIN OF SCIENCE, TECHNOLOGY & SOCIETY. v.1–, no.1/2– , 1981– . New York, Pergamon Press. Bimonthly.

BULLETIN OF SUDANESE STUDIES
See MAJALLAT AL-DIRĀSĀT AL-SŪDĀNĪYAH

BULLETIN OF THE ACADEMY OF MEDICINE
See JOURNAL OF SOCIOLOGIC MEDICINE

BULLETIN OF THE AICHI GAKUKEI UNIVERSITY; SOCIAL SCIENCE
See Aichi Gakukei Daigaku, Okazaki. KENKYŪ HOKŌKU; SHAKAIGAKU

BULLETIN OF THE ANTHROPOLOGICAL INSTITUTE
See Nanzan Daigaku, Nagoya. Jinruigaku Kenkyūjo. JINRUIGAKU KENKYUJO KIYŌ—NANZAN DAIGAKU JINRUIGAKU KENKYŪ

BULLETIN OF THE ATOMIC SCIENTIST OF CHICAGO
See BULLETIN OF THE ATOMIC SCIENTISTS

940
BULLETIN OF THE ATOMIC SCIENTISTS. v.1– , Dec. 10, 1945– . Chicago, Ill. Monthly.
Issued by: Atomic Scientists of Chicago. Title varies: v.1, no.1–6, *Bulletin of the Atomic Scientist of Chicago.*
Indexed: ABC POL SCI; Bull. Anal. Pol. Ec. Soc.; His. Abst.; Ind. Per. Art. Law 1970; Int. Lab. Doc.; Peace Res. Abst. J.; Soc. Abst.; Wom. Stu. Abst.

BULLETIN OF THE AUSTRALIAN SOCIETY FOR THE STUDY OF LABOUR HISTORY
See LABOUR HISTORY

941
BULLETIN OF THE EUROPEAN COMMUNITIES. v.1– , Jan. 1968– . Luxembourg. Monthly, 1968–74; eleven no. a year.
Issued by: Secretariat General of the Commission of European Communities. Supplements called "Beilage" accompany some issues.
Continues: European Coal and Steel Community High Authority. *Bulletin from the European Community for Coal and Steel*, and: European Economic Community. *Bulletin.*

BULLETIN OF THE INTERNATIONAL BUREAU OF EDUCATION
See International Bureau of Education. BULLETIN

BULLETIN OF THE INTERNATIONAL INSTITUTE FOR SOCIAL HISTORY
See International Institute for Social History. BULLETIN

BULLETIN OF THE INTERNATIONAL INSTITUTE OF SOCIAL HISTORY
See International Institute for Social History. BULLETIN

BULLETIN OF THE NATIONAL INSTITUTE FOR PERSONNEL RESEARCH
See PSYCHOLOGIA AFRICANA

BULLETIN OF THE NATIONAL SCIENCE MUSEUM. SERIES D. ANTHROPOLOGY
See KOKURITSU KAGAKU HAKUBUTSUKAN

BULLETIN OF THE OXFORD UNIVERSITY INSTITUTE OF ECONOMICS AND STATISTICS
See OXFORD BULLETIN OF ECONOMICS AND STATISTICS

BULLETIN OF THE SOCIAL RESEARCH INSTITUTE
See University of Zambia. Institute for Social Research. BULLETIN

BULLETIN OFFICIEL DE LA LIGUE DES DROITS DE L'HOMME
See LES CAHIERS DES DROITS DE L'HOMME

942
BULLETIN ON ANCIENT INDIAN HISTORY AND ARCHAEOLOGY. no.1– , 1967– . Sangar. Irreg.
Issued by: Department of Ancient Indian History and Archaeology, University.

BULLETIN ON INTERNATIONAL AFFAIRS
See BULLETIN BIBLIOGRAPHIQUE DE DOCUMENTATION INTERNATIONALE CONTEMPORAINE

943
BULLETIN ON ISLAM AND CHRISTIAN–MUSLIM RELATIONS IN AFRICA. v.1– , Jan. 1983– . Birmingham. Quarterly.
Issued by: Centre for the Study of Islam and Christian–Muslim Relations.

944
BULLETIN ON SOVIET AND EAST EUROPEAN AFFAIRS. 3–6, Jan. 1969–Dec. 1970. London. Two no. a year.
Issued by: Institute of Jewish Affairs in association with the World Jewish Congress.
Continues: *Bulletin on Soviet Jewish Affairs.*
Continued by: *Soviet Jewish Affairs* (June 1971–)

945
BULLETIN SIGNALÉTIQUE. 390. PSYCHOLOGIE ET PSYCHOPATHOLOGIE. v.23–31, 1961–1970. Paris. Quarterly.
Issued by: Centre de Documentation Sciences Humaines, Centre National de la Recherche Scientifique. In French.

Continues: *Bulletin Signalétique*. Continued by: *Bulletin Signalétique. 390. Psychologie et Psychopathologie, Psychiatrie.*

946
BULLETIN SIGNALÉTIQUE. 390. PSYCHOLOGIE ET PSYCHOPATHOLOGIE, PSYCHIATRIE. v.32– , 1971– . Paris. Quarterly.
Issued by: Centre de Documentation Sciences Humaines, Centre National de la Recherche Scientifique. In French.
Continues: *Bulletin Signalétique. 390. Psychologie et Psychopathologie.*

947
BULLETIN SIGNALÉTIQUE. 520. PÉDAGOGIE. v.23, 1969. Paris. Quarterly.
Issued by: Centre de Documentation Sciences Humaines, Centre National de la Recherche Scientifique. In French.
Continues, in part: *Bulletin Signalétique. 20. Psychologie, Pédagogie* (1961–68). Continued by: *Bulletin Signálétique. 520. Sciences de l'Éducation* (1970)

948
BULLETIN SIGNALÉTIQUE. 521. SOCIOLOGIE, ETHNOLOGIE, PRÉHISTOIRE ET ARCHÉOLOGIE. v.15–23, 1961–1969. Paris. Quarterly.
Issued by: Centre de Documentation Sciences Humaines, Centre de la Recherche Scientifique. In French.
Continues, in part: *Bulletin Signalétique. 21. Sociologie, Science du Langage*, and, in part: *Bulletin Signalétique C (19–24) Sciences Humaines*. Continued by: *Bulletin Signalétique. 521. Sociologie—Ethnologie, Bulletin Signalétique. 525. Préhistoire*, and: *Bulletin Signalétique. 526. Art et Archéologie; Proche-Orient, Asie, Amérique.*

949
BULLETIN SIGNALÉTIQUE. 521. SOCIOLOGIE—ETHNOLOGIE. v.24– , 1970– . Paris. Quarterly.
Issued by: Centre de Documentation Sciences Humaines, Centre Nationale de la Recherche Scientifique. In French.
Continues: *Bulletin Signalétique. 521. Sociologie, Ethnologie, Préhistoire et Archéologie.*

950
BULLETIN SIGNALÉTIQUE. 525. PRÉHISTOIRE. v.24– , 1970– . Paris. Quarterly.
Issued by: Centre de Documentation Sciences Humaines, Centre National de la Recherche Scientifique. In French.
Continues, in part: *Bulletin Signalétique. 521. Sociologie, Ethnologie, Préhistoire et Archéologie.*

951
BULLETIN SIGNALÉTIQUE. 526. ART ET ARCHÉOLOGIE; PROCHE-ORIENT, ASIE, AMÉRIQUE. v.24– , 1970– . Paris. Quarterly.
Issued by: Centre de Documentation Sciences Humaines, Centre National de la Recherche Scientifique. In French.
Continues, in part: *Bulletin Signalétique. 521. Sociologie, Ethnologie, Préhistoire et Archéologie.*

952
BULLETIN SIGNALÉTIQUE. 528. SCIENCE ADMINISTRATIVE. v.25–31, 1971–1977. Paris. Quarterly.
Issued by: Centre de Documentation Sciences Humaines, Centre National de la Recherche Scientifique. In French.
Continues: *Bulletin Signalétique; Sciences Humaines*. Continued by: *Bulletin Signalétique. 528. Bibliographie Internationale de Science Administrative.*

953
BULLETIN SIGNALÉTIQUE. 528. BIBLIOGRAPHIE INTERNATIONALE DE SCIENCE ADMINISTRATIVE. v.32– , 1978– . Paris. Quarterly.
Issued by: Centre de Documentation Sciences Humaines, Centre National de la Recherche Scientifique. In French.
Continues: *Bulletin Signalétique. 528. Science Administrative.*

954
BULLETIN SIGNALÉTIQUE; SCIENCES HUMAINES. v.1–14, 1947–1960. Paris. Quarterly.
Issued by: Centre de Documentation, Centre Nationale de la Recherche Scientifique. Title varies: 1947–55, *Bulletin Analytique, Troisième Partie. Philosophie.*
Continued by: *Bulletin Signalétique. 390. Psychologie et Psychopathologie, Bulletin Signalétique. 521. Sociologie, Ethnologie, Préhistoire et Archéologie*, and others not pertinent to the scope of this work.

BULLETIN TRIMESTRIEL ÉCONOMIQUE ET STATISTIQUE
See BENELUX; ECONOMISCHE EN STATISTISCH KVARTAALBERICHT

BULLETINS DE LA SOCIÉTÉ D'ANTHROPOLOGIE DE PARIS
See Société d'Anthropologie de Paris. BULLETINS ET MÉMOIRES

BULLETINS ET MÉMOIRES
See Société d'Anthropologie de Paris. BULLETINS ET MÉMOIRES

955
BUNKA. 1– , 1934– . Tokyo, Iwanami Shoten. Monthly, 1934–50; bimonthly, 1951–58; quarterly.
In Japanese; some summaries in English, French, or German. Other title: *Culture*.

956
BUNKA TO SHAKAI. 1957–July 1965. Kyoto. Irreg.
Issued by: Ryukoku Daigaku Shakai Gakkai. In Japanese. Other title: *Culture and Society*.
Continued by: *Shakai to fukushi*.

957
BURAKU MONDAI KENKYŪ. no.1– , 1956– . Kyoto. Semi-annual.
Issued by: Institute of Buraku Problems. In Japanese. Tables of contents also in English.

958
Bureau National d'Ethnologie. BULLETIN. no.1– , 1984– . Port-au-Prince. Two no. a year.
In French; occasionally in English.
Continues: *Bulletin du Bureau d'Ethnologie* (Feb. 1942–198?)

959
Buriatskiĭ Institut Obshchestvennykh Nauk. TRUDY. no.1– , 196?– . Ulan-Ude. Annual.
In Russian.
Indexed: Int. Bibl. Soc. Cul. Anth.

960
BUSINESS ABROAD AND EXPORT TRADE. v.1– , Mar. 29, 1919– . Stroudsburg, Pa., T. Askwell. Frequency varies.
Title varies: 1919–Mar. 20, 1920, *Export Trade*; Mar. 27, 1920–Apr. 29, 1922, *Export Trade and Exporter's Review*; May 6, 1922–Apr. 21, 1923, *Export Trade*; Apr. 28, 1923–Dec. 1932, *Export Trade and Finance*; May 1933–Nov. 4, 1935, *The Export Shipper*; Nov. 11, 1935–Oct. 27, 1951, *Export Trade and Shipper*; Nov. 3, 1952–Apr. 27, 1964, *Export Trade*. Absorbed: *Exporters' Review*, Feb. 28, 1920; *Export Adviser*, June 1932; *Piggott's Bulletin*, Mar. 4, 1933; *Overseas Trader*, Aug. 7, 1939.

BUSINESS AND CONSUMER SURVEY RESULTS *See* EUROPEAN ECONOMY. SUPPLEMENT B. BUSINESS AND CONSUMER SURVEY RESULTS

961
BUSINESS AND ECONOMIC DIMENSIONS. v.1–19, no.4, Apr. 1965–1983. Gainesville, Fla. Quarterly.
Issued by: Bureau of Economic and Business Research, University of Florida.
Indexed: PAIS.

962
BUSINESS & PROFESSIONAL ETHICS JOURNAL. v.1– , fall 1981– . Troy, N.J. Quarterly.
Issued by: Human Dimensions Center, Reusselaer Polytechnic Institute; sponsored by: The University of Delaware and the University of Florida.

963
BUSINESS ECONOMICS. v.1– , summer 1965– . Cleveland, Ohio. Three no. a year.
Issued by: National Association of Business Economists.
Indexed: Bull. Anal. Pol. Ec. Soc.; PAIS; Sage Urb. Stu. Abst.

964
BUSINESS HISTORY REVIEW. v.28– , Mar. 1954– . Boston, Mass. Quarterly.
Issued by: The Harvard Graduate School of Business Administration, Harvard University.
Continues: The Business Historical Society. *Bulletin* (v.1–27, 1926–53)
Indexes: Vols. 36–40, 1962–66, 1v.; v.41–45, 1967–71, 1v.; v.46–50, 1972–76, 1v.
Indexed: Bull. Anal. Pol. Ec. Soc.; Ind. Per. Art. Law 1970; His. Abst.; PAIS; Peace Res. Abst. J.; SSCI.

965
BUSINESS INTERNATIONAL INDEX. Dec. 1982– . New York, Business International Corporation. Quarterly, with annual cumulation.
Continues: *Master Key Index*.

966
BUSINESS PERIODICAL INDEX. v.1– , Jan. 1958– . New York, H.W. Wilson. Monthly, except August, with bimonthly, semi-annual, and cumulative annual index.
Subtitle reads: "A cumulative subject index to English language periodicals in the fields of accounting, advertising and public relations, automation, banking, communications, economics, finance and investments, insurance, labor, management, etc."
Continues, in part: *Industrial Arts Index*.

967
BUSINESS PUBLICATIONS INDEX AND ABSTRACTS. v.1– , 1983– . Detroit, Mich., Gale Research Co. Monthly, with annual cumulation. In two volumes: Abstracts, and Subject/Author Citations.

BUSINESS SURVEY RESULTS *See* EUROPEAN COMMUNITY. SUPPLEMENT B. BUSINESS SURVEY RESULTS

C

CEPAL REVIEW
See United Nations. Economic Commission for Latin America. CEPAL REVIEW

967a
CES REVIEW. 1– , July 1977– . London. Irreg.
Issued by: Centre of Environmental Studies.

CIRES
See CAHIERS IVORIENS DE RECHERCHE ÉCONOMIQUE ET SOCIALE

CJE/RCE
See CANADIAN JOURNAL OF EDUCATION

CPS
See COMPARATIVE POLITICAL STUDIES

CPS RESEARCH PAPERS
See University of London. School of Hygiene and Tropical Medicine. Centre of Population Studies. CPS WORKING PAPERS

CRUG
See Loyola University, Chicago. Center for Research in Urban Government. CRUG

C.S.A.A.R. RESEARCH PAPER
See Griffith University, Brisbane. School of Modern Asian Studies. Centre for the Study of Australian–Asian Relations. RESEARCH PAPER.

CADERNOS
See Centro de Estudos Rurais e Urbanos. CADERNOS

968
CADERNOS DE ESTUDOS BRASILEIROS. 1– , 1972– . Rio de Janeiro.
Issued by: Forum de Ciência e Cultura, Universidade Federal. In Portuguese.

CADERNOS DO TERCEIRO MUNDO
See THIRD WORLD (Mexico City)

969
CADMOS. 1– , spring 1978– . Genève, Centre Européen de la Culture. Quarterly.
Issued by: Institut Universitaire d'Études Européennes de Genève, and Centre Européen de la Culture. In French.
Supersedes: Centre Européen de la Culture. *Bulletin*.
Indexed: Int. Bibl. Pol. Sc.

CAHIERS
See École Pratique des Hautes Études. 6ᵉ Section des Sciences Économiques et Sociales. Laboratoire de Sociologie de la Connaissance. CAHIERS

CAHIERS
See Fondation Nationale de Sciences Politiques. CAHIERS

CAHIERS
See Institut International d'Études Sociales. CAHIERS

CAHIERS
See Université de Bordeaux II. Centre d'Études et de Recherches Ethnologiques. CAHIERS

970
CAHIERS AFRICAINS D'ADMINISTRATION PUBLIQUE. AFRICAN ADMINISTRATIVE STUDIES. no.1– , May 1967– . Tangier.
Issued by: Centre Africain de Formation et de Recherche Administrative pour le Développement. In French, Arabic or English. No.1 preceded by no.0, Nov. 1966.
Indexed: Bull. Anal. Pol. Ec. Soc.; Int. Pol. Sc. Abst.

CAHIERS CANADIENNE DE SOCIOLOGIE
See THE CANADIAN JOURNAL OF SOCIOLOGY

971
CAHIERS CONGOLAIS D'ANTHROPOLOGIE ET D'HISTOIRE. 1– , 1976– . Brazzaville. Annual.
Issued by: Laboratoire d'Anthropologie, Université de Brazzaville. In French; some summaries in English.
Indexed: Bull. Sig. Soc. Eth.

972
CAHIERS CONGOLAIS DE LA RECHERCHE ET DU DÉVELOPPEMENT. 1970–1972. Kinshasa.
Issued by: Centre de Recherche et d'Information Socio-Politiques.
Continues: *Études Congolaises*. Continued by: *Cahiers Zaïrois de la Recherche et du Développement*.

973
LES CAHIERS D'ANALYSE DES DONNÉES. v.1– , 1976– . Paris, Dunod. Quarterly.
Issued by: Le Laboratoire de Statistique de l'Université Pierre-et-Marie-Curie, Centre National de la Recherche Scientifique, and Association pour le Développement et la Diffusion de l'Analyse des Données. In French; summaries in Arabic, English and French.

974
CAHIERS D'ÉTUDE DE SOCIOLOGIE CULTURELLE. no.1– , 1971– . Bruxelles. Irreg.
Issued by: Institut de Sociologie, Université Libre. In French.

975
CAHIERS D'ÉTUDES AFRICAINES. v.1– , Jan. 1960– . Paris, Mouton. Quarterly.
Issued by: 6e Section, Sciences Économiques et Sociales, École Pratique des Hautes Études. In French.
Indexed: Abst. Anth.; Bull. Anal. Pol. Ec. Soc.; Bull. Sig. Soc. Eth.; Int. Bibl. Eco.; Int. Bibl. Pol. Sc.; ABC POL. SCI; Int. Lab. Doc.; LLBA; PAIS; Pop. Ind.; Int. Pol. Sc. Abst.; Soc. Abst.; SSCI.

976
CAHIERS D'ÉTUDES ARABES ET ISLAMIQUES. no.4– , Oct. 1977– . Paris, Sorbonne Nouvelle—Paris III. Three no. a year.
In Arabic or French. Added title: *Majallat al-dirāsāt al-'Arabīyah wa-al-Islāmīyah*. Other title: *Cahiers d'Études Arabes et Islamiques de l'U.E.R. des Langes et Civilisations de l'Indie, de l'Orient et de l'Afrique du Nord*.
Continues: *Cahiers d'Études Arabes et Islamiques de l'U.E.R. des Langes et Civilisations de l'Indie, de l'Orient et de l'Afrique de Nord*.

977
CAHIERS D'ÉTUDES RURALES. no.1– , 1963– . Paris. Irreg.
Issued by: 6e Section, Sciences Économiques et Sociales, École Pratique des Études Sociales. In French.

CAHIERS D'HISTOIRE DE L'INSTITUT DE RECHERCHES MARXISTES
See Institut de Recherches Marxistes. CAHIERS D'HISTOIRE

CAHIERS D'HISTOIRE ET DE POLITIQUE INTERNATIONALE
See CAHIERS D'HISTOIRE ET DE POLITIQUE INTERNATIONALES

978
CAHIERS D'HISTOIRE ET DE POLITIQUE INTERNATIONALES. no.1– , spring 1983– . Genève.
Issued by: Institut Universitaire des Hautes Études Internationales. In French. Other title: *Cahiers d'Histoire et de Politique Internationales*.

979
CAHIERS D'HISTOIRE JURIDIQUE ET POLITIQUE. 1– , 1975– . Tananarive. Irreg.
Issued by: Établissement Supérieur de Droit, d'Économie, de Gestion, et de Sociologie. In French.
Continues: Université de Madagascar. Centre d'Études des Coutumes. *Cahiers*.

CAHIERS D'HISTOIRE MONDIALE
See JOURNAL OF WORLD HISTORY

980
CAHIERS D'OUTRE-MER. v.1– , 1948– . Bordeaux. Quarterly.
Issued by: Institut de Géographie et d'Études Regionales, Université de Bordeaux III, Institut d'Outre-Mer de Bordeaux, and Société de Géographie de Bordeaux. In French; summaries in English and German.
Indexed: Bull. Anal. Pol. Ec. Soc.; Bull. Sig. Soc. Eth.; Int. Bibl. Eco.; Int. Bibl. Soc. Cul. Anth.; Int. Lab. Doc.; PAISFL.

CAHIERS DE DOCUMENTATION EUROPÉENNE
See European Parliament. CAHIERS DE DOCUMENTATION EUROPEENNE

CAHIERS DE L'A.D.E.T.E.M.
See REVUE FRANÇAISE DU MARKETING

CAHIERS DE L'I.S.M.A. SÉRIE AB. ÉCONOMIE DE TRAVAIL
See ÉCONOMIES ET SOCIÉTÉS

CAHIERS DE L'I.S.M.A. SÉRIE AF. HISTOIRE QUANTITATIVE D'ÉCONOMIE FRANÇAIS
See ÉCONOMIES ET SOCIÉTÉS

CAHIERS DE L'I.S.M.A. SÉRIE AG. PROGRÈS ET AGRICULTURE
See ÉCONOMIES ET SOCIÉTÉS

CAHIERS DE L'I.S.M.A. SÉRIE EM. ÉCONOMIE MATHÉMATIQUE ET ÉCONOMETRIE
See ÉCONOMIES ET SOCIÉTÉS

CAHIERS DE L'I.S.M.A. SÉRIE EN. ÉCONOMIE ET L'ÉNERGIE
See ÉCONOMIES ET SOCIÉTÉS

CAHIERS DE L'I.S.M.A. SÉRIE ES. ÉCONOMIE ET SOCIOLOGIE
See ÉCONOMIES ET SOCIÉTÉS

CAHIERS DE L'I.S.M.A. SÉRIE F. DÉVELOPPEMENT, CROISSANCE, PROGRÈS
See ÉCONOMIES ET SOCIÉTÉS

CAHIERS DE L'I.S.M.A. SÉRIE G. ÉCONOMIE PLANIFIÉE
See ÉCONOMIES ET SOCIÉTÉS

CAHIERS DE L'I.S.M.A. SÉRIE HS. HORS SÉRIE
See ÉCONOMIES ET SOCIÉTÉS

CAHIERS DE L'I.S.M.A. SÉRIE K. PRÉVISION ÉCONOMIQUE ET ÉCONOMIE DE L'ENTREPRISE
See ÉCONOMIES ET SOCIÉTÉS

CAHIERS DE L'I.S.M.A. SÉRIE L. ÉCONOMIE RÉGIONALE
See ÉCONOMIES ET SOCIÉTÉS

CAHIERS DE L'I.S.M.A. SÉRIE M. PHILOSOPHIE ET SCIENCES DE L'HOMME
See ÉCONOMIES ET SOCIÉTÉS

CAHIERS DE L'I.S.M.A. SÉRIE MO. POUVOIRS ET RÉGULATIONS MONÉTAIRES
See ÉCONOMIES ET SOCIÉTÉS

CAHIERS DE L'I.S.M.A. SÉRIE P. RELATIONS ÉCONOMIQUES INTERNATIONALES
See ÉCONOMIES ET SOCIÉTÉS

CAHIERS DE L'I.S.M.A. SÉRIE PE. HISTOIRE DE LA PENSÉE ÉCONOMIQUE
See ÉCONOMIES ET SOCIÉTÉS

CAHIERS DE L'I.S.M.A. SÉRIE R. THÉORIES DE LA RÉGULATION
See ÉCONOMIES ET SOCIÉTÉS

CAHIERS DE L'I.S.M.A. SÉRIE S. ÉTUDES DE MARXOLOGIE
See ÉCONOMIES ET SOCIÉTÉS

CAHIERS DE L'I.S.M.A. SÉRIE SG. SÉRIE DE GESTION
See ÉCONOMIES ET SOCIÉTÉS

CAHIERS DE L'I.S.M.A. SÉRIE T. PROBLÈMES ÉCONOMIQUES DE LA RECHERCHE ET DE L'INFORMATION SCIENTIFIQUES ET TECHNIQUES
See ÉCONOMIES ET SOCIÉTÉS

CAHIERS DE L'I.S.M.A. SÉRIE V. HUMANITÉS, ÉCONOMIE, ETHNOLOGIE, SOCIOLOGIE
See ÉCONOMIES ET SOCIÉTÉS

981
CAHIERS DE LA COMMUNICATION. v.1– , Jan./Feb. 1981– . Paris, Bordas-Dunod. Five no. a year.
Issued by: Conseil Français des Études et Recherches sur l'Information et la Communication (C.F.I.R.I.C.) in cooperation with Université Paris I, l'Université Paris II, and Unesco. In French.
Indexed: Int. Bibl. Eco.

CAHIERS DE LA FEMME
See CANADIAN WOMEN'S STUDIES

CAHIERS DE LA FONDATION NATIONALE DE GÉRONTOLOGIE
See GÉRONTOLOGIE ET SOCIÉTÉ

982
CAHIERS DE PHILOSOPHIE POLITIQUE. no.1– , 1983– . Bruxelles, Ousia.
Issued by: Centre de Philosophie Politique, Université de Rheims. In French.

983
CAHIERS DE PSYCHOLOGIE SOCIALE. no.1– , Oct. 1978– . Liège.
Issued by: Service de Psychologie Sociale, Université de Liège. In French.

984
CAHIERS DE SOCIOLOGIE DE L'ART ET DE LITTÉRATURE. no.1– , 1980– . Paris.
Issued by: Département de Sociologie, Université de Paris VIII. In French.

985
CAHIERS DE SOCIOLOGIE ÉCONOMIQUE. no.1–15, June 1959–Nov. 1966; 2. ser. no.1–4, June 1971–1972; n. ser. no.1– , Apr. 1979– . Le Havre. Semi-annual.
Issued by: Institut Havrais de Sociologie Économique et de Psychologie des Peuples, 1959–60; Centre de Recherches et d'Études de Psychologie des Peuples et de Sociologie Économique, Université de Caen, 1961–64; Centre de Recherches et d'Études de Psychologie des Peuples et de Sociologie Économique, Académie de Rouen, 1965; Centre de Recherches et d'Études de Psychologie des Peuples et de Sociologie Économique, Université de Rouen, 1966; Centre Universitaire de Psychologie des Peuples, 1971–72; and Institut Havrais de Sociologie Économique et de Psychologie des Peuples, 1971–. Published as supplement to *Ethnopsychologie*.
Superseded by: *Cahiers de Sociologie Économique et Culturelle. Ethnopsychologie*.

986
CAHIERS DE SOCIOLOGIE ÉCONOMIQUE ET CULTURELLE, ETHNOPSYCHOLOGIE. 1– , June 1984– . Le Havre. Semi-annual.
Issued by: Institut Havrais de Sociologie Économique et de Psychologie des Peuples. In French.
Continues: *Cahiers de Sociologie Économique*.

987
CAHIERS DE SOCIOLOGIE ET DE DÉMOGRAPHIE MÉDICALES. 1– , June 1961– . Paris, Éditions du Centre de Sociologie et de Démographie Médicales.

In French.
Indexed: Bull. Anal. Pol. Ec. Soc.; Bull. Sig. Soc. Eth.; Int. Bibl. Soc.; Soc. Abst.

988
LES CAHIERS DE TUNISIE. v.1– , 1953– . Tunis. Quarterly.
Issued by: Faculté des Lettres et des Sciences Humaines, Université de Tunis. In Arabic, English, French, German, Italian, or Spanish.
Indexed: His. Abst.; Int. Bibl. Soc.; Int. Bibl. Soc. Cul. Anth.

989
CAHIERS DES AMÉRIQUES LATINES. n.ser. 1– , spring 1985– . Paris. Semi-annual.
Issued by: Institut des Hautes Études de l'Amérique Latine, Université de la Sorbonne Nouvelle—Paris III. In French.
Continues: *Cahiers des Amériques Latines. Série Sciences de l'Homme.*

990
CAHIERS DES AMÉRIQUES LATINES. SÉRIE SCIENCES DE L'HOMME. Jan./June 1968–1984?. Paris. Semi-annual.
Issued by: Institut des Hautes Études de l'Amérique Latine. In French; summaries in French, Portuguese and Spanish.
Continued by: *Cahiers des Amériques Latines.*
Indexed: Bull. Anal. Pol. Ec. Soc.; Bull. Sig. Soc. Eth.; Int. Bibl. Eco.; Int. Bibl. Pol. Sc.; Int. Pol. Sc. Abst.

991
LES CAHIERS DES DROITS DE L'HOMME. v.1– , Jan. 1901– . Paris. Semi-annual.
Issued by: Ligue des Droits de l'Homme et du Citoyen. In French. Title varies: 1901–03, *Bulletin Officiel de la Ligue des Droits de l'Homme*; 1914–17, *Bulletin des Droits de l'Homme*. Vols. 30–39, May 1945–Nov. 1949 called new ser. v.11–19. Not published Aug. 1939–May 1945.

992
CAHIERS DES RELIGIONS AFRICAINES. no.1/2– , July 1967– . Kinshasa. Semi-annual.
Issued by: Centre d'Études des Religions Africaines, Université de Kinshasa. In French. Title varies: no.1/2, 1967, *Religions Africaines et Christianisme.*
Indexed: Int. Bibl. Soc. Cul. Anth.

CAHIERS DU BOLSHEVISME
See CAHIERS DU COMMUNISME

CAHIERS DU CENTRE D'ÉTUDES ET DE RECHERCHES DE L'ASSOCIATION DES ANCIENS ÉLÈVES
See HUMANISME ET ENTREPRISE

993
CAHIERS DU COMMUNISME. v.1– , Nov. 21, 1924– . Paris. Monthly.
Issued by: Comité Central du Parti Communiste Français. In French. Title varies: 1924–June 1939, *Cahiers du Bolshevisme*. Supplement called "Bulletin Colonial Français. Dossier de l'Agitateur" accompanies some numbers.
Indexed: Bull. Anal. Pol. Ec. Soc.; Curr. Cont. Soc. Beh. Sc.; His. Abst.; Int. Bibl. Pol. Sc.; Int. Bibl. Soc. Cul. Anth.; Int. Pol. Sc. Abst.; Int. Lab. Doc.; PAIS; Peace Res. Abst. J.

994
CAHIERS DU MONDE HISPANIQUE ET LUSO-BRÉSILIEN. 1– , 1963– . Toulouse-le-Mirail. Two no. a year.
Issued by: Institut d'Études Hispaniques et Luso-Brésiliennes, Université de Toulouse-le-Mirail II. In English or Spanish; occasionally in Portuguese. Some no. are thematic.
Indexed: Bull. Anal. Pol. Ec. Soc.; Bull. Sig. Soc. Eth.; Int. Bibl. Soc. Cul. Anth.

995
CAHIERS DU MONDE RUSSE ET SOVIÉTIQUE. v.1– , May 1959– . Paris, Mouton. Quarterly.
Issued by: Centre d'Études sur l'URSS et l'Europe Orientale et le Domain Turc, École des Hautes Études en Sciences Sociales. In French or English; summaries in English and French. Supplements accompany some numbers (1964–)
Indexes: Vols. 1–20, 1959–79, 1v.
Indexed: Bull. Anal. Pol. Ec. Soc.; Bull. Sig. Soc. Eth.; His. Abst.; Int. Bibl. Soc. Cul. Anth.; Int. Lab. Doc.; Int. Pol. Sc. Abst.; Peace Res. Abst. J.

996
CAHIERS ÉCONOMIQUES DE BRUXELLES. no.1– , Oct. 1958– . Bruxelles. Quarterly (irreg.)
Issued by: Département d'Économie Appliqué, Université Libre de Bruxelles. In English, French, or Dutch.
Indexed: Int. Bibl. Eco.; PAISFL.

997
CAHIERS ÉCONOMIQUES ET MONÉTAIRES. no.1– , Oct. 1976– . Paris. Irreg.
Issued by: La Banque de France. In French.
Indexed: PAISFL.

998
CAHIERS ÉCONOMIQUES ET SOCIAUX. ECONOMIC AND SOCIAL PAPERS. 1– , 1962– . Kinshasa. Four no. a year.
Issued by: Institut des Recherches Économiques et Sociales, Université de Kinshasa.
Indexed: Bull. Anal. Pol. Ec. Soc.; Bull. Sig. Soc. Eth.; Int. Lab. Doc.; Int. Bibl. Soc. Cul. Anth.

CAHIERS INTERNATIONAUX
See RASSEGNA INTERNAZIONALE

999
CAHIERS INTERNATIONAUX D'HISTOIRE ÉCONOMIQUE E SOCIALE. QUADERNI INTERNAZIONALI DI STORIA ECONOMICA E SOCIALE. INTERNATIONAL JOURNAL OF ECONOMIC AND SOCIAL HISTORY. 1– , 1972– . Genève, Librairie Droz. Annual.
Issued by: Istituto Italiano per la Storia dei Movimenti Sociali e delle Strutture Sociali, Naples. In English, French, German, Italian, or Spanish.

1000
CAHIERS INTERNATIONAUX DE SOCIOLOGIE. v.1– , 1946– . Paris, Presses Universitaires de France. Two no. a year (some combined)
Issued by: 6e Section des Sciences Économiques et Sociales, École Pratique des Hautes Études. In French.
Indexed: Bull. Anal. Pol. Ec. Soc.; Bull. Sig. Soc. Eth.; Int. Bibl. Pol. Sc.; Int. Bibl. Soc. Cul. Anth.; Int. Pol. Sc. Abst.; Int. Lab. Doc.; LLBA; Soc. Abst.; SSCI; Urb. Aff. Abst.; Wom. Stu. Abst.

1001
CAHIERS IVORIENS DE RECHERCHE ÉCONOMIQUE ET SOCIALE. no.1– , 1970– . Abidjan. Annual.
Issued by: Université d'Abidjan. In French. Other title: CIRES.

CAHIERS MENSUELLES DE DOCUMENTATION EUROPÉENNE
See European Parliament. CAHIERS DE LA DOCUMENTATION EUROPÉENNE

1002
CAHIERS NORD-AFRICAINS. ÉTUDES SOCIALES NORD-AFRICAINES. no.1– , Jan. 1950– . Paris. Bimonthly.
Indexed: Int. Bibl. Soc. Cul. Anth.

1003
CAHIERS O.R.S.T.O.M. v.3, no.4– , 1966– . Paris. Four no. a year.
Issued by: Office de Recherche Scientifique et Technique d'Outre-Mer. In French.
Continues: *Cahiers O.R.S.T.O.M. Sciences Humaines* (v.1–3, no.3, 1963–66)
Indexed: Bull. Anal. Pol. Ec. Soc.; Bull. Sig. Soc. Eth.

1004
LES CAHIERS RURAUX. 1– , 1953– . Bruxelles. Quarterly.
Issued by: Centre d'Études Rurales. In French.
Indexed: Int. Bibl. Soc. Cul. Anth.

CAHIERS. SÉRIE F. DÉVELOPPEMENT, CROISSANCE, PROGRÈS
See Institut de Science Économique Appliqué. CAHIERS. SÉRIE F. DÉVELOPPEMENT, CROISSANCE, PROGRÈS

1005
CAHIERS VILFREDO PARETO: REVUE EUROPÉENNE D'HISTOIRE DES SCIENCES SOCIALES. 1– , 1963– . Genève, Librairie Droz. Semi-annual.
In English, French, German, Italian, or Spanish.
Indexed: Bull. Anal. Pol. Ec. Soc.; Int. Bibl. Soc.; Int. Pol. Sc. Abst.; Soc. Abst.; SSCI.

1006
CAHIERS ZAÏROIS DE LA RECHERCHE DU DÉVELOPPEMENT. v.17– , 1971– . Lubumbashi, later Kinshasa-Gombe, Presses Universitaires du Zaire. Quarterly.
Issued by: Office National de la Recherche et du Développement, subsequently by: Centre d'Études Socio-Politiques pour l'Afrique Central. In French.
Continues: *Cahiers Congolais de la Recherche et du Développement*. Continued by: *Études Zaïrois*.
Indexed: His. Abst.; Int. Bibl. Soc. Cul. Anth.

1007
CAIRO PAPERS IN SOCIAL SCIENCES. v.1– , Dec. 1977– . Cairo. Frequency varies.
Issued by: Social Research Center, American University in Cairo. Other title: *Buḥūth al-Qāhirah fī al-'Ulum al-Ijtimā'īyah*. Monograph series.

1008
Caisse Centrale de Coopération Économique. RAPPORT D'ACTIVITÉ. 1964– . Paris. Annual.
In French. Published also in English edition: *Annual Report*.

1009
California Institute of International Studies. WORLD AFFAIRS REPORT. v.3– , Mar. 1973– . Stanford, Calif. Quarterly.
Continues: the institute's *Report*.

1010
CALIFORNIA MANAGEMENT REVIEW. v.1– , fall 1958– . Berkeley, Calif. Quarterly.
Issued by: Graduate School of Business Administration, University of California at Berkeley and Los Angeles, and Graduate Graduate School of Administration, Irving.
Indexed: ABC POL SCI; His. Abst.; Int. Bibl. Eco.; PAIS.

1011
CALIFORNIA WESTERN INTERNATIONAL LAW JOURNAL. v.1– , fall 1970– . San Diego, Calif. Annual, 1970–71; semi-annual, 1972–76; three no. a year.
Issued by: California Western School of Law.
Indexes: Vols. 1–10, 1970–80, with v.10.
Indexed: Ind. Leg. Per.

1012
CAMBIO SOCIAL Y MODERNIZACIÓN POLÍTICA. ANUARIO POLÍTICO ESPAÑOL. 1969– . Madrid, Editorial Cuadernos para el Diálogo Edicusa. Annual.
Issued by: Instituto de Técnicas Sociales de la Fundación Fondo Social Universitario. In Spanish.

1013
CAMBRIDGE JOURNAL OF ECONOMICS. 1– , Mar. 1977– . London, Academic Press. Quarterly.
Issued by: Cambridge Political Economy Society.
Indexed: Bull. Anal. Pol. Ec. Soc.; Int. Bibl. Eco.

1014
CAMBRIDGE STUDIES IN CULTURAL SYSTEMS. 1– , 1977– . London, Cambridge University Press. Irreg.
Monograph series.

1015
CAMBRIDGE STUDIES IN SOCIAL ANTHROPOLOGY. 1– , 1967– . London, Cambridge University Press. Irreg.
Monograph series.

1016
CAMPAIGNS AND ELECTIONS. v.1– , spring 1980– . Washington, D.C., F. Reed. Quarterly.
Indexed: Int. Pol. Sc. Abst.; PAIS.

1017
Canada. Department of External Affairs. DOCUMENTS OF CANADIAN EXTERNAL RELATIONS. 1967– . Ottawa, Queen's Printer. Irreg.

1018
Canada. Department of Finance. ECONOMIC REVIEW. 1972– . Ottawa. Annual.
French edition called *Revue Économique* (1975–) is also published.

1019
Canada. Dominion Bureau of Statistics. Government Finance Section. FEDERAL GOVERNMENT FINANCE. FINANCES PUBLIQUES FÉDÉRALES. 1965– . Ottawa. Annual.
In English and French.
Continues: *Financial Statistics of the Government of Canada*, 1953–64.

1020
Canada. Department of Indian Affairs and Northern Development. ANNUAL REPORT. RAPPORT ANNUEL. 1966/67–1969/70. Ottawa. Annual.
In English and French. Formed by the union of: Canada. Department of Indian Affairs and Northern Development. *Annual Report*, and Canada. Ministère des Affaires Indiennes et du Nord Canadien. *Rapport Annuel*.
Supersedes: Canada. Department of Northern Affairs and National Resources. *Annual Report*.
Continued by: Canada. Indian and Northern Affairs Canada. *Annual Report*.

1021
Canada. Statistics Canada. FEDERAL GOVERNMENT ACTIVITIES IN THE HUMAN SCIENCES. ACTIVITÉS DE L'ADMINISTRATION FÉDÉRALE EN SCIENCES HUMAINES. 1972– . Ottawa. Annual.
In English and French.

1022
CANADA IN WORLD AFFAIRS. [1935/39]– . Toronto. One volume every two or three years.
Published under the auspices of the Canadian Institute of International Affairs. Some volumes have also distinctive titles.

1023
CANADIAN AND INTERNATIONAL EDUCATION. ÉDUCATION CANADIENNE ET INTERNATIONALE. v.1– , June 1979– . London, Canada. Semi-annual.
Issued by: Comparative and International Education Society of Canada.
Supersedes: Comparative and International Education Society of Canada. *Papers*.
Indexed: Bull. Sig. Soc. Eth.

1024
CANADIAN ANNUAL REVIEW OF POLITICS AND PUBLIC AFFAIRS. 1971– . Toronto University Press. Annual.
In English or French.
Continues: *Canadian Annual Review* (1960–70)

1025
CANADIAN BUSINESS. v.1– , Feb. 1928– . Montréal. Monthly.
Issued by: Canadian Chamber of Commerce, –1970.
Title varies: 1928–32, *The Commerce of the Nation*.
Indexed: Int. Lab. Doc.; PAIS; Peace Res. Abst. J.

1026
THE CANADIAN BUSINESS REVIEW. v.1– , winter 1974– . Ottawa. Quarterly.
Issued by: Conference Board in Canada.
Indexed: PAIS.

1027
Canadian Centre for Folk Culture Studies. PAPER. 1972– . Ottawa.
Issued by: National Museums of Canada. In English or French; summaries in French. Other title: *Dossier*.

1028
CANADIAN ETHNIC STUDIES. v.1– , 1969– . Calgary. Two no. a year.
Issued by: Research Centre for Canadian Ethnic Studies, University of Calgary. Sponsored by: Canadian Ethnic Studies Association. Other title: *Études Ethniques au Canada*.

1029
CANADIAN GEOGRAPHIC. v.97– . Aug./Sept. 1978– . Ottawa. Bimonthly.
Issued by: Royal Canadian Geographical Society. In English; occasionally in French.
Continues: *Canadian Geographical Journal*.
Indexed: PAIS.

1030
CANADIAN GEOGRAPHICAL JOURNAL. v.1–96, May 1930–1978. Ottawa. Monthly.
Issued by: Royal Canadian Geographical Society. In English; occasionally in French.
Continued by: *Canadian Geographic*.
Indexes: Vols. 1–59, 1930–59, 1v.
Indexed: PAIS; Soc. Sc. Hum. Ind.

1031
CANADIAN HISTORICAL REVIEW. v.1– , Mar. 1920– . Toronto, University of Toronto Press. Quarterly.
Supersedes: *Review of Historical Publications Relating to Canada*.
Indexes: Vols. 1–10, 1920–29, 1v.; v.11–20, 1930–39, 1v.
Indexed: His. Abst.

1032
Canadian Human Rights Commission. ANNUAL REPORT. 1977/78– . Ottawa.
In English and French. French text on the inverted pages.

1033
CANADIAN HUMAN RIGHTS YEARBOOK. ANNUAIRE CANADIEN DES DROITS DE LA PERSONNE. 1983– . Toronto, Carewell Co. Annual.
Issued by: Human Rights and Education Centre, University of Ottawa. In English and French.

CANADIAN INDEX TO PERIODICALS AND DOCUMENTARY FILMS
See CANADIAN PERIODICAL INDEX

1034
Canadian International Development Agency. CANADIANS IN THE THIRD WORLD: CIDA'S YEAR IN REVIEW. STATISTICAL INDEX. 1980/81–1982. Ottawa, later Hull, Quebec. Annual.
Published also in French under the title: *Canadiens dans le Tiers-Monde. Revue Annuel de l'ACDI. Annexe Statistique*. Supplement to: Canadian International Development Agency. *Canadians in the Third World*.
Continues, in part, and continued by: Canadian International Development Agency. *Annual Report*.

1035
CANADIAN JOURNAL OF AFRICAN STUDIES. REVUE CANADIENNE DES ÉTUDES AFRICAINES. v.1– , Mar. 1967– . Montréal. Semi-annual, 1967–69; three no. a year.
Issued by: Committee on African Studies in Canada (Conseil des Études Africaines au Canada), and published by the Loyola College in Montréal. In English or French. Other title: *Journal Canadien des Études Africaines*.
Supersedes: *Bulletin on African Studies in Canada*.
Indexed: Abst. Anth.; Bull. Anal. Pol. Ec. Soc.; Bull. Sig. Soc. Eth.; Int. Bibl. Eco.; Int. Bibl. Pol. Sc.; Int. Bibl. Soc.; Int. Bibl. Soc. Cul. Anth.; Int. Pol. Sc. Abst.; SSCI; Wom. Stu. Abst.

1036
CANADIAN JOURNAL OF AGRICULTURAL ECONOMICS. REVUE CANADIENNE D'ÉCONOMIE RURALE. v.1– , 1952– . Ottawa. Three no. a year, 1952–67; two no. a year.
Issued by: Canadian Agricultural Economics Society. Initially included *Proceedings* of the society published as one of the two issues, later published as an additional issue, supplement.
Indexed: Bull. Anal. Pol. Ec. Soc.; Curr. Cont. Soc. Beh. Sc.; Int. Bibl. Eco.; Int. Bibl. Pol. Sc.; Int. Pol. Sc. Abst.; PAIS; SSCI; Wom. Stu. Abst.

1037
CANADIAN JOURNAL OF BEHAVIOURAL SCIENCE. REVUE CANADIENNE DU COMPORTEMENT. v.1– , Jan. 1969– . Toronto, University of Toronto Press. Quarterly.
Published for: Canadian Psychological Association.
Indexed: Curr. Cont. Soc. Beh. Sc.; Psych. Abst.; SSCI.

1038
CANADIAN JOURNAL OF CRIMINOLOGY. REVUE CANADIENNE DE CRIMINOLOGIE. v.20– , Jan. 1978– . Ottawa.

Issued by: Canadian Association for the Prevention of Crime. In English or French.
Continues: *Canadian Journal of Criminology and Corrections*.
Indexed: Ind. Per. Art. Law.

1039
CANADIAN JOURNAL OF CRIMINOLOGY AND CORRECTIONS. REVUE CANADIENNE DE CRIMINOLOGIE. v.13–19, Jan. 1971–Oct. 1977. Ottawa. Quarterly.
Issued by: Canadian Association for the Prevention of Crime. In English or French.
Continues: *Canadian Journal of Corrections*. v.1–12, 1958–70. Continued by: *Canadian Journal of Criminology*.
Indexed: Ind. Per. Art. Law.

CANADIAN JOURNAL OF DEVELOPMENT STUDIES
See REVUE CANADIENNE D'ÉTUDES DU DÉVELOPPEMENT

1040
CANADIAN JOURNAL OF ECONOMICS. REVUE CANADIENNE D'ÉCONOMIE. v.1– , Feb. 1968– . Toronto, University of Toronto Press. Quarterly.
Issued by: Canadian Economics Association. In English or French; summaries in English and French. Supplements accompany some numbers.
Indexed: Bull. Anal. Pol. Ec. Soc.; Curr. Cont. Soc. Beh. Sc.; Int. Bibl. Eco.; Int. Bibl. Pol. Sc.; Int. Bibl. Soc.; Int. Bibl. Soc. Cul. Anth.; Ind. Per. Art. Law; PAIS; PAISFL; Pop. Ind.; SSCI.

1041
CANADIAN JOURNAL OF ECONOMICS AND POLITICAL SCIENCE. v.1–33, 1935–67. Toronto, University of Toronto Press. Quarterly.
Issued by: Canadian Political Science Association. Other title: *Revue d'Économie et de Science Politique*.
Supersedes: *Contributions to Canadian Economics, Papers and Proceedings* of the Canadian Political Science Association, and *Studies. History and Economics Series* of the University of Toronto. Superseded by: *Canadian Journal of Political Science*.
Indexes: Vols. 1–10, 1935–44, 1v.; v.1–33, 1935–67, 1v.
Indexed: His. Abst.; J. Eco. Lit.; Int. Bibl. Soc. Cul. Anth.; Peace Res. Abst. J.

1042
CANADIAN JOURNAL OF EDUCATION. REVUE CANADIENNE DE L'ÉDUCATION. v.1– , 1976– . Toronto. Quarterly.
Issued by: Canadian Society for the Study of Education. In English or French. Other title: *CJE/RCE*.

1043
CANADIAN JOURNAL OF HISTORY AND SOCIAL SCIENCE. v.5– , Nov. 1969– . Toronto. Quarterly.
Issued by: Ontario History and Social Science Teachers' Association.
Continues: *Canadian Journal of History*, and *History Newsletter*.

1044
CANADIAN JOURNAL OF LATIN AMERICA AND CARIBBEAN STUDIES. REVUE CANADIENNE DES ÉTUDES LATINOAMÉRICAINES ET CARIBES. v.9(no.17)– , 1984– . Ottawa. Semi-annual.
Issued by: Canadian Association for Latin American and Caribbean Studies. In English, French, or Spanish.
Continues: *NS Northsouth. Canadian Journal of Latin American Studies* (1976–83).

1045
CANADIAN JOURNAL OF NATIVE EDUCATION. v.8– , Nov. 1969– . Edmonton. Quarterly.
Issued by: International Education Program, University of Alberta.
Continues: *Indian-ed*.

1046
CANADIAN JOURNAL OF POLITICAL AND SOCIAL THEORY. REVUE CANADIENNE DE THÉORIE POLITIQUE ET SOCIALE. v.1– , winter 1977– . Winnipeg. Three no. a year.
Issued by: Bull. Sig. Soc. Eth.; Int. Bibl. Eco.; Int. Bibl. Pol. Sc.; Int. Pol. Sc. Abst.

1047
CANADIAN JOURNAL OF POLITICAL SCIENCE. REVUE CANADIENNE DE SCIENCE POLITIQUE. v.1– , Mar. 1968– . Toronto, University of Toronto Press. Quarterly.
Issued by: Canadian Political Science Association. Includes lists of theses in political science in Canada.
Supersedes: *Canadian Journal of Economics and Political Science*.
Indexed: ABC POL SCI; Bull. Anal. Pol. Ec. Soc.; Bull. Sig. Soc. Eth.; Int. Bibl. Eco.; Int. Lab. Doc.; Int. Pol. Sc. Abst.; Curr. Cot. Soc. Beh. Sc.; Int. Lab. Doc.; PAIS; Soc. Abst.; SSCI.

1048
CANADIAN JOURNAL OF PSYCHOLOGY. v.1– , Mar. 1947– . Toronto. Quarterly.
Issued by: Canadian Psychological Association.
Supersedes: the association's *Bulletin*.
Indexed: Abst. Soc. Work; LLBA; Peace Res. Abst. J.; Psych. Abst.; SSCI.

1049
CANADIAN JOURNAL OF REGIONAL SCIENCE. LA REVUE CANADIENNE DES SCIENCES RÉGIONALES. v.1– , spring 1978– . Halifax. Semi-annual.
Issued by: Institute of Public Affairs, Dalhousie University.

1050
CANADIAN JOURNAL OF SOCIOLOGY. CAHIERS CANADIENNE DE SOCIOLOGIE. v.1– , spring 1975– . Edmonton. Quarterly.
Issued by: Department of Sociology, University of Alberta.
Indexed: Int. Bibl. Eco.; Soc. Abst.

1051
CANADIAN JOURNAL ON AGING. LA REVUE CANADIENNE DU VIEILLISSEMENT. v.1– , 1982– . Toronto. Quarterly.
Issued by: Canadian Association on Gerontology.

THE CANADIAN MUNICIPAL JOURNAL
See THE MUNICIPAL REVIEW OF CANADA

1052
CANADIAN PARLIAMENTARY REVIEW. v.3, no.4– , winter 1980/81– . Ottawa. Quarterly.
Issued by: Canadian Parliamentary Relations Secretariat in association with the Library of the Parliament. Edition in French called: *Revue Parlementaire Canadienne* is also published.
Continues: *Canadian Regional Review.*

1053
CANADIAN PERIODICAL INDEX. v.1–32, Jan. 1948–1976. Ottawa. Monthly, with annual cumulation.
Issued by: Canadian Library Association, 1948–50, in cooperation with the Canadian Bibliographic Centre, 1952–64; the association with the National Library of Canada. Title varies: *Canadian Index to Periodicals and Documentary Films.*
Supersedes: *Canadian Periodical Index*, 1938–May 1947.

1054
Canadian Political Science Association. Annual Meeting. PAPERS AND PROCEEDINGS OF THE ANNUAL MEETING. v.1–6, 1913–34. Ottawa.
Publication suspended: 1914–29.
Indexes: 1913–35, in: *Canadian Journal of Economics and Political Science*, v.1, pp.131–135.

1055
CANADIAN PSYCHOLOGICAL REVIEW. PSYCHOLOGIE CANADIENNE. v.16– , Jan. 1975– . Montreal, later Calgary. Quarterly.
Issued by: Canadian Psychological Association. In English or French; summaries in English and French.
Continues: *Canadian Psychologist* (v.1–15, 1960–74)
Indexed: LLBA; Psych. Abst.; SSCI.

1056
CANADIAN PUBLIC ADMINISTRATION. ADMINISTRATION PUBLIQUE DU CANADA. v.1– , Mar. 1958– . Toronto. Quarterly.
Issued by: Institute of Public Administration of Canada. In English or French. Title varies: 1958–June 1962, *Journal of the Institute of Public Administration of Canada.*
Indexed: ABC POL SCI; Abst. Anth.; Bull. Anal. Pol. Ec. Soc.; Bull. Sig. Soc. Eth.; Hum. Res. Abst.; Ind. Per. Art. Law; Int. Bibl. Eco.; Int. Bibl. Pol. Sc.; Int. Bibl. Soc.; PAIS; PAISFL; PHRA; Sage Pub. Adm.; SSCI.

1057
CANADIAN PUBLIC POLICY. ANALYSE DE POLITIQUES. v.1– , 1975– . Downsview, University of Toronto Press. Quarterly.
Sponsored by: Canadian Economic Association, the Canadian Political Science Association, the Canadian Association of Law Teachers, the Canadian Sociology and Anthropology Association, the Canadian Association of Geographers, the Canadian Association of Social Work, the Institute of Public Administration of Canada, the Administrative Sciences Association of Canada, and the Canadian Association of Business Economics. In English or French.
Indexed: Int. Bibl. Eco.; Int. Bibl. Pol. Sc.; PAIS; PAISFL; Sage Urb. Stu. Abst.

1058
CANADIAN REVIEW OF SOCIOLOGY AND ANTHROPOLOGY. REVUE CANADIENNE DE SOCIOLOGIE ET D'ANTHROPOLOGIE. v.1– , 1964– . Toronto, University of Toronto Press. Quarterly.
Sponsored by: Canadian Sociology and Anthropology Association. In English or French.
Indexed: Abst. Anth.; Bull. Anal. Pol. Ec. Soc.; Bull. Sig. Soc. Eth.; Curr. Cont. Soc. Beh. Sc.; His. Abst.; Int. Bibl. Eco.; Int. Bibl. Pol. Sc.; Int. Bibl. Soc.; Int. Bibl. Soc. Cul. Anth.; Int. Pol. Sc. Abst.; Psych. Abst.; Soc. Abst.; SSCI; Wom. Stu. Abst.

1059
CANADIAN REVIEW OF STUDIES IN NATIONALISM. REVUE CANADIENNE DES ÉTUDES SUR LE NATIONALISME. 1– , fall 1975– . Charlottetown. Two no. a year.
Issued by: University of Prince Edward Island in cooperation with the Canadian Council. In English, French, German, or Spanish.
Indexed: ABC POL SCI; PAIS.

1060
CANADIAN REVIEW OF STUDIES IN NATIONALISM. BIBLIOGRAPHY. REVUE CANADIENNE DES ÉTUDES SUR LE NATIONALISME. BIBLIOGRAPHIE. 1– , 1974– . Charlottetown. Irreg.
Issued by: University of Prince Edward Island.

1061
CANADIAN SLAVONIC PAPERS. 1– , 1956– . Toronto, University of Toronto Press, subsequently Canadian Association of Slavists. Annual, 1956–68; quarterly.
Issued by: Department of Slavonic Languages and Literatures, University of Toronto, and Canadian Association of Slavists. In English or French. Subtitle reads: "An interdisciplinary quarterly devoted to the Soviet Union and Eastern Europe". Other title: *Revue Canadienne des Slavistes*.
Indexed: Bull. Anal. Pol. Ec. Soc.; His. Abst.; Int. Bibl. Eco.; Int. Bibl. Soc. Cul. Anth.; PAIS.

1062
THE CANADIAN STRATEGIC REVIEW. 1982– . Toronto. Annual.
Issued by: Canadian Institute for Strategic Studies.

1063
CANADIAN WELFARE. 1924– . Ottawa. Bimonthly.
Issued by: Canadian Council on Social Development.

1064
CANADIAN WOMEN'S STUDIES. LES CAHIERS DE LA FEMME. v.1–3, no.2, fall 1978–1981. Scarborough. Quarterly.
Issued by: The Centennial College. In English or French.
Continued by: *Canadian Women Studies*.

1065
CANADIAN YEARBOOK OF INTERNATIONAL LAW. ANNUAIRE CANADIENNE DE DROIT INTERNATIONAL. v.1– , 1963– . Vancouver, University of British Columbia Press. Annual.
Published under the auspices of the Canadian Branch, International Law Association. In English or French.
Indexed: Bull. Anal. Pol. Ec. Soc.; Ind. Leg Per.; Int. Bibl. Pol. Sc.; Int. Pol. Sc. Abst.

CANADIANS IN THE THIRD WORLD; CIDA'S YEAR IN REVIEW. STATISTICAL INDEX
See Canadian International Development Agency. CANADIANS IN THE THIRD WORLD: CIDA'S YEAR IN REVIEW. STATISTICAL INDEX

LES CANADIENS DANS LE TIERS-MONDE
See Canadian International Development Agency. CANADIANS IN THE THIRD WORLD: CIDA'S YEAR IN REVIEW. STATISTICAL INDEX

1066
CANTERBURY MAORI STUDIES. 1– , 1983– . Christchurch. Irreg.
Issued by: Department of Maori, University of Canterbury. In English or Maori.

1067
CAPITAL & CLASS. no.1– , 1977– . Oxford, later London. Three no. a year.
Issued by: Conference of Socialist Economists.
Supersedes: Conference of Socialist Economists. *Bulletin*.

1068
CARAVELLE. 1– , 1963– . Toulouse-le-Mirail. Two no. a year.
Issued by: Institut d'Études Hispaniques, Hispano-Américaines et Luso-Brésiliennes, Université Toulouse-le-Mirail. Chiefly in French or Spanish, occasionally in Portuguese. Some numbers are thematic.

1069
CARIBBEAN BASIC ECONOMIC SURVEY. v.1–7, no.1, Mar./Apr. 1971–Jan./Mar. 1981. Atlanta. Bimonthly (irreg.)
Issued by: Research Department, Federal Reserve Bank of Atlanta. Summaries in Spanish.
Absorbed by: *Economic Review* (Federal Reserve Bank of Atlanta)

1070
CARIBBEAN FINANCE AND MANAGEMENT; CFM. v.1– , summer 1985– . Mona. Semi-annual.
Issued by: Department of Management Studies, University of the West Indies.

1071
CARIBBEAN JOURNAL OF EDUCATION. v.1– , June 1974– . Mona. Semi-annual, 1974–75; three no. a year.
Issued by: School of Education, University of the West Indies.

1072
CARIBBEAN STUDIES. v.1– , Apr. 1961– . Rio Piedras. Quarterly.
Issued by: Instituto de Estudios del Caribes, Universidad de Puerto Rico. In English, French, or Spanish.
Indexed: Abst. Anth.; Bull. Anal. Pol. Ec. Soc.; His. Abst.; Int. Bibl. Eco.; Int. Bibl. Soc. Cul. Anth.; Int. Pol. Sc. Abst.

1073
CARIBBEAN STUDIES. v.1– , 1981– . New York, Gordon and Breach. Irreg.
Indexed: His. Abst.; Int. Bibl. Soc. Cul. Anth.

1074
CARIBBEAN YEARBOOK OF INTERNATIONAL RELATIONS. 1975– . Leiden, A.W. Sijthoff. Annual.
Issued by: Institute of International Relations, University of the West Indies.
Indexed: Int. Bibl. Eco.; Int. Pol. Sc. Abst.

1075
EL CARIBE CONTEMPORÁNEO. no.1– , Mar. 1980– . Mexico, D.F. Three no. a year.
Issued by: Centro de Estudios Latinoamericanos, Faculdad de Ciencias Políticas y Sociales, Universidad Nacional Autónoma de México. In Spanish.
Indexed: PAISFL.

1076
Carnegie Endowment for International Peace. YEARBOOK. 1911–1947. Washington, D.C. Annual.
Vols. for 1917–29 called no.6–18. Supplements accompany some issues.
Continued by: *Annual Report.*

1077
CARPATHICA. 1960– . Bratislava. Irreg.
Issued by: International Commission for the Study of the Popular Culture of the Carpathian Region. Sponsored by: Slovak Academy of Sciences. In English, French, or Russian.

1078
CASE WESTERN RESERVE JOURNAL OF INTERNATIONAL LAW. v.1–10, fall 1968–1978. Cleveland, Ohio. Two no. a year, 1968–77; three no. a year.
Issued by: School of Law, Case Western Reserve University.
Indexed: Bull. Anal. Pol. Ec. Soc.; Ind. Bibl. Eco.; Int. Leg. Per.; SSCI.

1079
CASE STUDIES IN AFRICAN DIPLOMACY. no.1– , 1969– . Dar es Salaam, Oxford University Press.
Issued by: Institute of Public Administration, University College, Dar es Salaam.

CATALOGUE AFRIQUE. ARTICLES CHOISIS SUR LE DÉVELOPPEMENT ÉCONOMIQUE ET SOCIALE
See AFRICA INDEX; SELECTED ARTICLES ON SOCIO-ECONOMIC DEVELOPMENT

1080
CATO JOURNAL. v.1– , spring 1981– . San Francisco, Calif. Three no. a year.
Issued by: Cato Institute.
Indexed: ABC POL SCI; Curr. Cont. Soc. Beh. Sc.; PAIS; SSCI.

1081
CATO POLICY REPORT. v.6, no.5– , June 1984– . Washington, D.C. Bimonthly.
Formed by the union of: *Policy Report* and *Cato's Letter*.

1082
Center for the Study of Presidency. PROCEEDINGS. v.1– , 1971– . New York. Irreg.

CENTER HOUSE BULLETIN
See PRESIDENTIAL STUDIES QUARTERLY

1083
THE CENTER MAGAZINE. 1– , Oct./Nov. 1967– . Santa Barbara, Calif. Bimonthly.
Issued by: The Robert Maynard Hutchins Center for the Study of Democratic Institutions in association with the University of California at Santa Barbara.
Indexed: Curr. Cont. Soc. Beh. Sc.; His. Abst.; Ind. Per. Art. Law; Sage Pub. Adm. Abst.; Wom. Stu. Abst.

1084
Central African States Development Bank. ANNUAL REPORT. 1– , 1976/77– . Brazzaville. Annual.
Some numbers in English and French. Other title: *Rapport Annuel.*

1085
CENTRAL ASIAN SURVEY. v.1– , July 1982– . Oxford, Oxford Microform Publications. Quarterly.

1086
CENTRAL ASIATIC JOURNAL. v.1– , 1955– . The Hague, later Wiesbaden, Harrassowitz. Quarterly.
In English or German. Subtitle reads: "International periodical for the languages, literature, history and archaeology of Central Asia".
Indexed: Abst. Anth.; Bull. Sig. Soc. Eth.; Int. Bibl. Soc. Cul. Anth.

1087
CENTRAL ISSUES IN ANTHROPOLOGY. v.1– , 1979– . Ann Arbor, Mich., later Wichita, Kans. Semi-annual.
Issued by: Central States Anthropological Society.
Indexed: Abst. Anth.; Int. Bibl. Soc. Cul. Anth.; Soc. Abst.

CENTRAL-BLATT
See SOCIAL JUSTICE REVIEW

CENTAL-BLATT AND SOCIAL JUSTICE
See SOCIAL JUSTICE REVIEW

1088
CENTRALLY PLANNED ECONOMIES IN EUROPE. 1985– . Brussels, New York. Irreg.
Issued by: Conference Board.
Continues: *Centrally Planned Economies.*

1089
Centre d'Études Politiques, Économiques et Sociales. DOCUMENTS. 1962–1984. Bruxelles, Tweekerkenstraat. Bimonthly.
In French. No. 1 of each volume has title *Faits et Documents.*
Continued by: *Revue Politique.*

1090
Centre d'Études Sociologiques. TRAVAUX ET DOCUMENTS. 1969– . Paris, Centre National de la Recherche Scientifique. Irreg.
In French.

1091
Centre de Recherches Anthropologiques, Préhistoriques et Ethnographiques. MÉMOIRES. 1– , 1963– . Algiers, Arts et Métiers Graphiques. Irreg.
In French. Monograph series.

1092
Centro Brasileiro de Estudos Demográficos. ESTUDOS E ANÁLISES. v.1–7, 1971–1977. Rio de Janeiro. Annual.
Issued in cooperation with the Instituto Brasileiro de Estatística. In Portuguese.
Continued by: Fundação I.B.G.F. Superintendencia de Estudos Geográficos e Socio-Econômicos. *Boletim Demográfico.*

1093
Centro de Estudios Monetarios Latinoamericanos. BOLETÍN QUINCENAL. v.1–25, 1952?–1979. Mexico, D.F. Semimonthly.
In Spanish. Beginning with Jan. 1958 accompanied by a monthly supplement. Other title: *Aspectos Monetarios Latinoamericanos.*
Continued by: Centro de Estudios Monetarios. *Boletín Mensual.*

1094
Centro de Estudos Rurais e Urbanos. CADERNOS. v.1– , 1968– . São Paulo.
Issued in collaboration with the Fundação de Amapro a Pesquisa do Estado do São Paulo. In Portuguese.
Indexed: Bull. Sig. Soc. Eth.

1095
Centro de Estudios Socio-Económicos. CUADERNO. no.1– , 196?– . Santiago. Irreg.
In Spanish.
Indexed: Int. Lab. Doc.

1096
Centro Latinoamericano de Economía Humana. CUADERNOS. 1– , 1958– . Montevideo. Quarterly.
In Spanish. Other title: *Revista Uruguaya de Ciencias Sociales.* Cover title: *Cuadernos de CLAEH.*
Continues: *Publicación* del Centro Latinoamericano de Economía Humana.

1097
Centro Latinoamericano de Pesquisas em Ciências Sociais. BIBLIOGRAFIA. v.1– , Sept./Oct. 1962– . Rio de Janeiro. Bimonthly.
In Portuguese.

Centro Latinoamericano de Pesquisas em Ciências Sociais. BOLETIM
See AMÉRICA LATINA

1098
Centro Studi Investimenti Sociali. RAPPORTO DELLA SITUAZIONE SOCIALE DEL PAESE. 1– , 1967– . Milano, F. Angeli. Annual.
In Italian. (Collana Censis)

1099
[No entry]

1100
Československa Akademia Věd. Řada Spolecenských Věd. ROZPRAVY. v.1– , 1891– . Praha, Nakladetelstvi Československé Akademie Věd. Irreg.
In Czech; occasionally in English or German. Monograph series.

1101
ČESKOSLOVENSKA ETNOGRAFIE. v.1– , 1953– . Praha. Quarterly.
Issued by: 1956– , Ústav pro Etnografii a Folkloristiku and Kabinet pro Etnografii a Folkloristiku, both of the Československá Akademia Věd. In Czech or Slovak.

1102
ČESKOSLOVENSKA PSYCHOLOGIE. v.1– , 1957– . Praha. Quarterly.
Issued by: Československá Akademia Věd. In Czech or Slovak; summaries in French and Russian. Tables of contents also in French and Russian.
Indexed: LLBA; Psych. Abst.; SSCI.

1103
ČESKÝ LID. 1891–1914; 1924–1935; 1947– . Praha, Nakladetelstvi Československé Akademie Věd. Bimonthly.
Issued by: Etnografický Ústav, Československá Akademia Věd. In Czech; summaries in English, French and German. Vols. 1–32, 1891–1932 issued as *Přiručký Společnosti Československých Narodopiscŭ*; supplement to *Zpravy Společnosti Československých Narodopiscŭ*.
Indexes: Vols. 1–32, 1891–1932.
Indexed: Abst. Anth.; Bull. Sig. Soc. Eth.; His. Abst.; Int. Bibl. Soc. Cul. Anth.

1104
CEYLON JOURNAL OF HISTORICAL AND SOCIAL STUDIES. v.1–10, no.1/2, Jan. 1958–1967. Paradeniya. Two no. a year.
Issued by: Ceylon Historical and Social Studies Publications Board.
Continued by: a publication of the same title.
Indexes: Vols. 1–5, 1958–62, in v.5.
Indexed: Soc. Abst.

1105
CEYLON JOURNAL OF HISTORICAL AND SOCIAL STUDIES. n. ser. v.1– , 1971– . Paradeniya, Ceylon Historical and Social Studies Publications Board. Two no. a year.
Issued by: Department of Sociology, University of Ceylon.
Continues: a publication of the same title.
Indexed: Soc. Abst.

1106
CEYLON JOURNAL OF SCIENCE. SECTION G: ANTHROPOLOGY. v.1– , July 2, 1924– . Colombo.
Title varies: v.1–2, *Ceylon Journal of Science. Section G: Archaeology and Ethnology*.

CEYLON JOURNAL OF SCIENCE. SECTION G: ARCHAEOLOGY AND ETHNOLOGY
See CEYLON JOURNAL OF SCIENCE. SECTION G: ANTHROPOLOGY

CHARACTER AND PERSONALITY
See JOURNAL OF PERSONALITY

CHARITIES
See THE SURVEY (East Stronsburg)

1107
CHATHAM HOUSE ANNUAL REVIEW. v.1– , 1981– . Oxford, Pergamon Press.
Issued by: Royal Institute of International Affairs. Each volume has also a distinctive title.

1108
Chayu Akádemi. CHAYU AK'ADEMI YŎN'GU NONCH'ONG. 1977– . Seoul. Annual.
In Korean. Other title: *The Journal of the Freedom Academy*.

CHAYU AK'ADEMI YŎN'GU NONCH'ONG
See Chayu Akádemi. CHAYU AK'ADEMI YON'GU NONCH'ONG

1109
CHECKLIST OF HUMAN RIGHTS DOCUMENTS. v.1– , Jan./May 1976– . Stanfordville, N.Y., E.M. Coleman Enterprises. Monthly.
Vols. for 1975– are issued by the Torton Law Library in cooperation with the United States Institute of Human Rights.
Supersedes: *Checklist of Human Rights Documents* issued by the Buffalo Law Library, State University of New York.

1110
CHELOVEK I OBSHCHESTVO. no.1– , 1966– . Leningrad. Irreg.
Issued by: Laboratoriia Sotsiologicheskikh Issledovaniĭ Problem Vospitaniia Studenchestva, Nauchno-issledovatel'skiĭ Institut Kompleksnykh Sotsial'nykh Issledovaniĭ. In Russian. (Subseries of the institute's *Uchenye Zapiski*)

1111
CHENG CHIH HSÜEH PAO. 1– , Sept. 1971– . Taipei. Annual.
Issued by: Chung-kuo chen chih hsüeh hui. In Chinese; summaries in English. Vols. for 1970– include *Papers and Proceedings* of the Chinese Association of Political Science. Other title: *The Annals of Political Science*.

1112
CHENG CHIN YÜ FA LÜ. June 1982– . Shanghai, Fu tan hsüeh ch'u pan she.
Issued by: Shang-hai she hui k'o hsüeh yüan fa hsüeh yen chiu so. Other title: *Cheng chih yü fa lü ts'ung k'an*.

CHENG CHIN YÜ FA LÜ TS'UNG K'AN
See CHENG CHIN YÜ FA LÜ

1113
CH'ENG SHIH KUEI HUA. CH'ENG SHIH HUEI HUA PIEN CHI WEI YUAN HUI. 1– , 1982– . Pei-ching, Kai wei yuan hui. Bimonthly.
Sponsored by: Chung-kuo chien chu hsüeh hui, ch'eng shih kuei hua hsüeh shu wei yuan hui. In Chinese. Tables of contents also in English. Other title: *City Planning Review*.

1114
CHI-LIN TA HSÜEH SHE HUI K'O HSÜEH HSÜEH PAO. 1– , Jan. 1980– . Ch'ang-chun, Chi-lin ta hsüeh hsüeh pao pien chi we yüan hui. Bimonthly.
In Chinese. Other title: *Jilindaxue she huikeksue xuebao—Jilin University Journal. Social Science Edition.*
Continues: *Chi Lin ta hsüeh pao; she hui k'o hsüeh pan.*

1115
CHIANG HAI HSÜEH K'AN. 1982– . Nan-ching shih, Chiang hui hsüeh k'an pien chi pu. Bimonthly.
Sponsored by: Chiang-su sheng she hui k'o hsüeh yüan. Chiang-su sheng che hsüeh she hui k'o hsüeh lien ho hui.
Added title-page title: *Jianghai xuekan.*
Continues: *Ch'ün chun lun ts'ung.*

1116
CHILD ABUSE & NEGLECT. v.1– , 1977– . Oxford, Pergamon Press. Quarterly (irreg.)

1117
CHINA ECONOMIC REPORT. v.1– , Oct. 1980– . New York. Quarterly.
Prepared by the Research Unit, International Currency Review.
Indexed: PAIS.

1118
CHINA OFFICIAL ANNUAL REPORT. ENGLISH EDITION. 1981– . Kowloon, Hong Kong, Kingsway International Publications. Annual.
In English; some parts in Chinese. Published also in Chinese.

1119
CHINA OFFICIAL YEARBOOK. 1983–84– . Hong Kong, Dragon Pearl Publications.

1120
THE CHINA QUARTERLY. no.1– , Jan./Mar. 1960– . London.
Issued by: Contemporary China Institute, School of Oriental and African Studies, University of London.
Indexed: ABC POL SCI; Bull. Anal. Pol. Ec. Soc.; His. Abst.; Int. Bibl. Pol. Sc.; Int. Lab. Doc.; Int. Pol. Sc. Abst.; PAIS; Peace Res. Abst. J.; Pop. Ind.; Wom. Stu. Abst.

1121
THE CHINA QUARTERLY. YING WEN CHUNG-KUO CHI K'AN. v.1–6, no.3, 1935–1941. Shanghai.

1122
CHINA REPORT. POLITICAL, SOCIOLOGICAL AND MILITARY AFFAIRS. no.1– , July 18, 1979– . Arlington, Va., Foreign Broadcast Information Service. Irreg.
Continues, in part: *Transactions on People's Republic of China.*

1123
CHINA RESEARCH MONOGRAPH. no.14– , 1979– . Berkeley, Calif. Irreg.
Issued by: Center for Chinese Studies, University of California.
Continues: *China Research Monographs* (1–13, 1967–78)

1124
CHINA URBAN STATISTICS. 1985– . London, Longman Group Ltd; China Statistical Information & Consultancy Service Centre. Annual.

1125
CHINA YEARBOOK. 1957/58–1980. Taipei, China Pub. Co. Annual.
Continues: *China Yearbook (Taipei)* (1937/43–1950). Publication suspended: 1947–49.

1126
CHINESE CULTURE. v.1– , July 1957– . Taipei, United Publishing Center. Irreg.
Issued by: Institute for Advanced Chinese Studies (called 1957–Apr. 1958, Chinese Cultural Research Institute)
Indexed: Bull. Anal. Pol. Ec. Soc.; Int. Bibl. Pol. Sc.; Int. Pol. Sc. Abst.; Int. Bibl. Soc. Cul. Anth.

1127
CHINESE ECONOMIC STUDIES. v.1– , fall 1967– . Armonk, N.Y., M.E. Sharpe. Four no. a year.
Translations of articles from Chinese.
Indexed: Bull. Anal. Pol. Ec. Soc.; Int. Bibl. Eco.; Pop. Ind.

1128
CHINESE EDUCATION. v.1– , spring 1968– . Armonk, N.Y., M.E. Sharpe. Four no. a year.
Translations of articles from Chinese.

CHINESE JOURNAL OF ADMINISTRATION
See CHUNG KUO HSING CHENG

CHINESE JOURNAL OF SOCIOLOGY
See CHUNG-KUO SHE HUI HSÜEH K'AN

1129
CHINESE LAW AND GOVERNMENT. spring 1968– . Armonk, N.Y., M.E. Sharpe. Four no. a year.

Translations of articles from Chinese.
Indexed: Bull. Anal. Pol. Ec. Soc.; PAIS.

1130
THE CHINESE SOCIAL AND POLITICAL SCIENCE REVIEW. v.1–16, no.4, 1916–Jan./Mar. 1941. Peking. Quarterly.
Issued by: Chinese Social and Political Science Association. Contains translations from Chinese. Not published in 1921.
Indexes: Vols. 1–5, in v.5; v.1–20, 1916–37, with v.20.

1131
CHINESE SOCIOLOGY AND ANTHROPOLOGY. v.1– , fall 1968– . Armonk, N.Y., M.E. Sharpe. Four no. a year.
Translations of articles from Chinese.
Indexed: Abst. Anth.; Curr. Cont. Soc. Beh. Sc.; LLBA; Soc. Abst.; SSCI.

1132
CHIRI-KAGAKU. GEOGRAPHICAL SCIENCES. v.1– , 1961– . Hiroshima. Two no. a year.
Issued by: Hiroshima Geographical Association. In Japanese; summaries in English. Tables of contents also in English.

1133
CHIYOK SAHOE KAEBAL NONCH'ONG. 1978– . Changganho-Taegu-si, Han'guk sahoe saop taehak. Chiyok sahoe kaebal yon'guso. Annual.
In Korean; summaries in English. Other title: *Journal of Community Development*. Vol. for 1981 last available for examination.

1134
CHRISTIAN ATTITUDES ON JEWS AND JUDAISM. no.1–69, June 1968–Dec. 1979. London. Quarterly.
Issued by: Institute of Jewish Affairs in association with the World Jewish Congress.
Continued by: *Christian Jewish Relations: A Documentary Survey*.

1135
CHRISTIAN JEWISH RELATIONS: A DOCUMENTARY SURVEY. no.70– , Mar. 1980– . London. Quarterly.
Issued by: Institute of Jewish Affairs in association with the World Jewish Congress.
Continues: *Christian Attitudes on Jews and Judaism*.

1136
CHRISTUS REX: AN IRISH QUARTERLY OF SOCIOLOGY. v.1–25, no.4, Jan. 1947–Oct. 1971. Dublin.
Superseded by: *Social Studies; Irish Journal of Sociology*.
Indexed: Ind. Per. Law 1970; Int. Bibl. Soc. Cul. Anth.; Int. Lab. Doc.

CHRONICLE OF PARLIAMENTARY ELECTIONS
See CHRONICLE OF PARLIAMENTARY ELECTIONS AND DEVELOPMENTS

1137
CHRONICLE OF PARLIAMENTARY ELECTIONS AND DEVELOPMENTS. 1– , July 1966– . Geneva. Annual.
Issued by: Inter-Parliamentary Union, International Center for Parliamentary Documentation (Union Interparlementaire). Published also in French edition. Title varies: v.1–11, 1966–77, *Chronicle of Parliamentary Elections*.

1138
CHRONICLE DE POLITIQUE ÉTRANGÈRE. v.1–27, no.4, Jan. 1948–1974. Bruxelles. Bimonthly.
Issued by: Institut Royal des Relations Internationales. In French.
Continued by: *Studia Diplomatica*.
Indexed: ABC POL SCI; Int. Bibl. Soc. Cul. Anth.; Int. Pol. Sc. Abst.; Int. Lab. Doc.; Peace Res. Abst. J.

CHRONICLE, THE COMMERCIAL & FINANCIAL CHRONICLE, BANKER'S GAZETTE, COMMERCIAL TIMES, RAILWAY MONITOR & INSURANCE JOURNAL
See THE COMMERCIAL AND FINANCIAL CHRONICLE

1139
CHRONIQUES D'OUTRE-MER; ÉTUDES ET INFORMATIONS. Jan. 1951– . Paris, Éditions de la Présidence du Conseil. Monthly.
Issued by: Ministère de la France d'Outre-Mer. In French.
Supersedes: *La France d'Outre-Mer; Études et Informations* (1944–1950)

1140
CHRONOLOGIE ÉCONOMIQUE INTERNATIONALE. 1934–1946; n. ser. 1947– . Paris, Sirey. Annual, 1934–46; monthly.
Issued by: Institut Scientifique de Recherches Économiques et Sociales. In French.

1141
CHRONOLOGY OF ARAB POLITICS. v.1– , Jan./Mar. 1963– . Beirut. Quarterly.

Issued by: Political Studies, Public Administration Department, American University of Beirut.

CHRONOLOGY OF INTERNATIONAL TREATIES AND LEGISLATIVE MEASURES
See League of Nations. CHRONOLOGY OF INTERNATIONAL TREATIES AND LEGISLATIVE MEASURES

1142
CHU HAI SHU YAN HUI HSÜEH CHI SHE HUI KUNG TSO HSÜEH HSI. 1– , June 1971– . Kowloon.
Issued by: Department of Sociology and Social Work, Hsi Institute. In Chinese. Other title: *Sociological Review.*

1143
CH'UAN KUO KAO YUAN HSIAO SHE HUI K'O HSÜEH HSÜEH PAO TSUNG MU LU. 1980– . Ch'ang-choun shih; Chi-lin ta hsüeh she hui k'o hsüeh pao pien chi pu. Annual.
In Chinese.

1144
CHUNG KUNG YEN CHIU. STUDIES ON CHINESE COMMUNISM. 1– , Jan. 1967– . Taipei. Monthly.
Issued by: Fei Ch'ing Yen Chiu. In Chinese.
Title varies: 1–2, 1967–Apr. 1969, *Fei ch'ing yen chiu. Studies on Chinese Communism.*

1145
CHUNG-KUO CHING CHI NIEN CHIEN. ANNUAL ECONOMIC REPORT OF CHINA. 1981– . Hsiang-kan Chung wen hai wai pan. Hsiang-kan hsien tai wen hua sh'i yeh kung ssu. Annual.
Chinese language edition for foreign distribution. Original domestic edition is published by Ching chi kuan litsa chih she. Other title: *Almanac of China's Economy.*

1146
CHUNG-KUO CHING CHI T'E CH'U NIEN CHIEN. YEARBOOK OF CHINA'S SPECIAL ECONOMIC ZONES. 1984– . Hsiang-kang, "Chung-kuo ching chi t'e ch'u nien chien" ch'u pan she. Annual.
In Chinese.

1147
CHUNG-KUO HSING CHENG. THE CHINESE JOURNAL OF ADMINISTRATION. v.1– , 1963– . Taipei. Semi-annual.
Issued by: Cheng-chih ta hsueh kung kung hsing cheng chi ch'i yeh kuan lichung hsin. In Chinese or English.

1148
CHUNG-KUO KUO CHI FA HSÜEH HUI. THE ANNALS OF THE CHINESE SOCIETY OF INTERNATIONAL LAW. Taipei.
Continued by: *Chinese Yearbook of International Law and Affairs.*

1149
CHUNG-KUO SHE HUI HSÜEH K'AN. 1– , 1978– . Taipei, Chung-kuo she hui hsüeh she. Annual.
In Chinese or English. Other title: *Chinese Journal of Sociology.*

1150
CHUNG-KUO SHE HUI K'O HSÜEH YÜAN YEN CHIN SHENG YÜAN HSÜEH PAO. 1985– . Pei-ching, Chung-kuo she hui k'o hsüeh ch'u pan she. Bimonthly.
In Chinese. Other title: *Academic Journal. Graduate School, Chinese Academy of Social Sciences.*
Continues: *Hsüeh hsi yü ssu k'ao.*

1151
CHUNG-KUO SHE K'O HSÜEH—ZHONGGUO SHE HUI KEKSUE. Pei-ching chung-kuo she hui k'o hsüeh ch'u pan she. Bimonthly.
In Chinese. Other title: *Social Sciences in China.*

CHUNG-KUO WAI CHIAP SHIH WU
See FOREIGN AFFAIRS CHINA

CHUNG-KUO YEN CHIU
See ÉTUDES CHINOISES

CHUNG-SHAN TA HSÜEH HSÜEH PAO; SHE HUI K'O HSÜEH
See Guanzhou. Zhongshan Daxue Huebao. CHUNG-SHAN TA HSÜEH HSÜEH PAO; SHE HUI K'O HSÜEH

1152
CHUNG-SO YŎN'GU. SINO-SOVIET AFFAIRS. Mar. 1980– . Seoul, Hanuang Taehakkyo Chung-so Yŏn'guso. Semi-annual, 1980–Dec. 1981; quarterly.
In English or Korean. Formed by the union of: *Soryon Yon'gu* and *Chenguk Munje.*

CHUNG WEN HSÜEH HUI HSÜEH PAO
See University of Singapore Chinese Society JOURNAL

1153
CHUNG YANG MIN TSU HSÜEH YÜAN HSÜEH PAO. ZHONGYANG MINZU XUEYUAN XUEBAO. 1982– . Pei-ching, Kai hsüeh yuan. Quarterly.
In Chinese. Other title: *Journal* of the Central Institute for Nationalities.

1154
CIÊNCIA E SOCIEDADE; TEMAS E DEBATES. 1963–1975. Rio de Janeiro. Irreg.
Issued by: Centro Brasileiro de Pesquisas Físicas. In Portuguese.

1155
CIÊNCIA E TRÓPICO. v.1– , Jan./June 1973– . Recife. Two no. a year.
Issued by: Fundação Joaquim Nabuco de Pesquisas Sociais. In Portuguese; summaries in English.
Indexed: Int. Bibl. Eco.

1156
CIENCIA POLÍTICA. 1– , 4. trimestre 1985– . Bogotá, Tierra Firme. Quarterly.
In Spanish.

1157
CIENCIAS ECONÓMICAS. v.1– , Sept. 1981– . San José, Editorial Universidad de Costa Rica. Semi-annual.
Issued by: Instituto de Investigaciones en Ciencias Económicas, Universidad de Costa Rica and Banco Central de Costa Rica. In Spanish.

1158
CIÊNCIAS ECONÔMICAS SOCIAIS. v.1– , 1965– . São Paulo, Editora Revista dos Tribunais. Semi-annual.
Issued by: Faculdade Municipal de Ciências Econômicas e Administrativas de Osasco. In English or Portuguese.

CIÊNCIAS HUMANAS
See Instituto de Investigaciais Científice de Moçambique. MEMÓRIAS. SERIE C: CIÊNCIAS HUMANAS

CIENCIAS POLÍTICAS Y SOCIALES
See REVISTA MEXICANA DE CIENCIA POLÍTICA

CIÊNCIAS SOCIAIS
See SOCIAL SCIENCES (Moscow)

1159
CIENCIAS SOCIALES. Jan. 1950–1956?. Washington, D.C. Bimonthly.
Issued by: Oficina de Ciencias Sociales y de Asuntos Culturales, Union Panamericana. In Spanish.
Continued by: *Revista Interamericana de Ciencias Sociales*.

1160
CIENCIAS SOCIALES. v.1– , 1958– . Medellin. Irreg.
Issued by: Instituto Colombiano de Investigaciones Sociales. In Spanish.
Indexed: Int. Bibl. Soc. Cul. Anth.

1161
CIENCIAS SOCIALES. v.1–7, no.1, Dec. 1963–Jan./June 1971. Cumana. Two no. a year.
Issued by: Escuela de Ciencias Sociales, Universidad de Oriente. In Spanish.
Indexed: Int. Bibl. Soc. Cul. Abst.; Soc. Abst.

CIENCIAS SOCIALES
See CRÍTICA & [i.e. Y] UTOPIA LATINOAMERICANA. CIENCIAS SOCIALES

CIENCIAS SOCIALES
See SOCIAL SCIENCES (Moscow)

CITAS LATINOAMERICANAS EN SOCIOLOGÍA, ECONOMÍA Y HUMANIDADES
See CLASE; CITAS LATINOAMERICANAS EN SOCIOLOGÍA Y ECONOMÍA

1162
CITTÀ. CRIME E DEVIANZA. 1979– . Milano, Guidicini Paolo Angeli. Semi-annual.
In Italian.

1163
CITY. v.1–6, 1961–1972. Washington, D.C. Bimonthly.
Issued by: National Urban Council.
Indexed: Abst. Soc. Work.; PHRA.

CITY PLANNING REVIEW
See CH'ENG SHIH KUEI HUA

CIUDAD
See ACTA SOCIOLOGICA. SERIE B. CIUDAD

1164
CIUDAD Y TERRITORIO. v.1– , 1970– . Madrid. Quarterly.
Issued by: Instituto Colombiano de Estudios Urbanos, Instituto de Administración Local. In Spanish.

1165
CIVIL LIBERTIES REVIEW. v.1– , fall 1973– . New York, Wiley. Quarterly, 1973–75; bimonthly.
Issued by: American Civil Liberties Union.

1166
CIVIL RIGHTS DIGEST. v.1–11, no.3, spring 1968–spring 1969. Washington, D.C. Quarterly.
Issued by: U.S. Commission on Civil Rights. V.1 preceded by two issues: August 1964 and Sept. 1967.

Continued by: *Perspectives*. (Sup. Docs. no.CR 1.12)

1167
CIVILISATIONS. v.1– , Jan. 1951– . Bruxelles. Quarterly.
Issued by: International Institute of Differing Civilisations (called until 1952 International Institute of Political and Social Sciences). In English or French.
Indexed: ABC POL SCI; Bull. Anal. Pol. Ec. Soc.; Bull. Sig. Soc. Eth.; His. Abst.; Int. Bibl. Eco.; Int. Bibl. Pol. Sc.; Int. Bibl. Soc. Cul. Anth.; Int. Lab. Doc.; Pop. Ind.; Peace Res. Abst. J.

1168
CIVILIZATION OF THE AMERICAN INDIAN. no.1– , 1932– . Norman, Okla., University of Oklahoma Press. Irreg.

1169
LA CIVILTÀ CATTOLICA. Monthly. v.1– , Apr. 1850– . Napoli, later Firenze, Roma. Monthly.
In Italian. Title varies: 1850–52, *La Civiltà Cattolica; Pubblicazione Periodica per Tutta Italia.*
Indexes: Vols. 1–10, 1850–Dec. 1903.
Indexed: Bull. Anal. Pol. Ec. Soc.; Int. Bibl. Pol. Sc.

1170
CIVITAS. v.1–3, 1947–1949; n. ser. v.1– , 1950– . Roma. Monthly, 1947–81; bimonthly.
In Italian. Each no. has a section "Rassegna di politica internazionale". Subtitle reads: "Rivista mensile di studi politici".
Indexed: Bull. Anal. Pol. Ec. Soc.; His. Abst.; Int. Bibl. Soc. Cul. Anth.

1171
CIVITAS. 1– , 1962– . Mannheim, later Mainz, Matthias Grünewald Verlag. Annual.
In German.
Indexed: Bull. Anal. Pol. Ec. Soc.; Int. Bibl. Eco.

1172
CLASE. CITAS LATINOAMERICANAS EN SOCIOLOGÍA Y ECONOMÍA. 1/2– , Jan./June 1976– . Mexico, D.F.
In Spanish. Other title: *Citas Latinoamericanas en Sociología, Economía y Humanidades.*

1173
CLASSE E STATO. 1– , 1965– . Bologna, Stame F. Semi-annual.
In Italian.

1174
CLINICAL SOCIOLOGY REVIEW. 1982– . Providence, R.I. Annual.
Issued by: Clinical Sociology Association.
Indexed: Psych. Abst.

1175
CLIO. v.1– , Jan./Feb. 1933– . Santo Domingo. Bimonthly.
Issued by: Academia Dominicana de la Historia. In Spanish. Publication suspended July 1937–Feb. 1938.
Indexes: Vols. 1–15, 1933–47.

1176
CO-EXISTENCE. v.1– , May 1964– . Glasgow, later Oxford, Pergamon Press, The Hague, M. Nijhoff Publishers. Semi-annual, 1964–82; three no. a year.
Subtitle reads: "An international journal for the comparative study of economics, sociology and politics in a changing world".
Indexed: ABC POL SCI; Bull. Sig. Soc. Eth.; Ind. Per. Art. Law 1970; Int. Bibl. Eco.; Int. Bibl. Pol. Sc.; Int. Bibl. Soc.; Int. Bibl. Soc. Cul. Anth.; Peace Res. Abst. J.; Soc. Abst.; SSCI.

1177
COLLANA DI SCIENZE SOCIALI. 1– , 1975– . Napoli. Irreg.
Issued by: Università di Napoli. In Italian. Monograph series.

COLLECTION OF DECISIONS
See European Commission of Human Rights. COLLECTION OF DECISIONS

1178
COLLECTION SCIENCES SOCIALES. SOCIAL SCIENCE SERIES. no.1– , 1971– . Ottawa, Éditions de l'Université d'Ottawa. Irreg.
In English or French. Monograph series.

1179
COLLECTIVE BEHAVIOR IN SPORT SITUATIONS. 1975– . Waterloo. Three no. a year.
Issued by: SIRLS, Faculty of Kinetics and Leisure Studies, University of Waterloo.

1180
COLLEGIUM ANTHROPOLOGICUM. v.1– , 1977– . Zagreb, School of Biological Anthropology. Semi-annual.
Issued by: Croatian Anthropological Society. In English, French, German, or Spanish; summaries in English.

1181
COLLOQIUM INTERNATIONALE. July 1976– . St. Saphrin, Georgi Pub. Co. Bimonthly.
Issued by: Society of Human Ecology. In English, French, or German; summaries in two of these languages.

1182
THE COLONIAL JOURNAL. v.1–13, June 1907–1920. London. Quarterly.
Title varies: 1907–Apr. 1913, *The Colonial Office Journal*.

THE COLONIAL OFFICE JOURNAL
See THE COLONIAL JOURNAL

1183
THE COLONIAL REVIEW. v.1–10, no.4, Feb. 1939–Dec. 1957. St. Albans. Irreg.
Issued by: Department of Education in Tropical Areas, Institute of Education (called Colonial Department from June 1945 to June 1952), University of London.
Superseded by: *Overseas Quarterly*.

1184
COLORADO COLLEGE PUBLICATION. SOCIAL SCIENCE SERIES. v.1–3, no.2, 1905–1927. Colorado Springs, Colo. Irreg.
Title varies: v.1–2, no.1, *Colorado College Studies*.

COLORADO COLLEGE STUDIES
See COLORADO COLLEGE PUBLICATION. SOCIAL SCIENCE SERIES

1185
COLUMBIA ESSAYS IN INTERNATIONAL AFFAIRS. 1965– . New York, Columbia University Press. Annual.
Issued by: School of International Studies, Columbia University.

1186
COLUMBIA HUMAN RIGHTS LAW REVIEW. v.4– , winter 1972– . New York.
Issued by: School of Law, Columbia University.
Continues: *Columbia Survey of Human Rights Law* (v.1–3, 1967/68–1970/71)
Indexed: Ind. Leg. Per.; PAIS.

COLUMBIA JOURNAL OF INTERNATIONAL AFFAIRS
See JOURNAL OF INTERNATIONAL AFFAIRS

1187
COLUMBIA JOURNAL OF LAW AND SOCIAL PROBLEMS. v.3– , fall 1965– . New York. Annual, 1965–67; semi-annual, 1968–69; three no. a year, 1970–71; quarterly.
Continues: *International Law Bulletin*.
Indexes: Vols. 1–4, 1961–66, in v.4 (it includes also index to *International Law Bulletin*)
Indexed: ABC POL SCI; Ind. Per. Art. Law; Int. Lab. Doc.; PAIS.

1188
THE COLUMBIA JOURNAL OF TRANSNATIONAL LAW. 1– , 1961– . New York. Three no. a year.
Issued by: Columbia Society of International Law.
Indexed: ABC POL SCI; Bull. Anal. Pol. Ec. Soc.; His. Abst.; Ind. Leg. Per.; Int. Bibl. Pol. Sc.; Int. Bibl. Soc.; Int. Lab. Doc.; Int. Pol. Sc. Abst.; SSCI.

1189
THE COLUMBIA JOURNAL OF WORLD BUSINESS. 1– , 1965– . New York, Pergamon Press. Quarterly.
Edited by: Graduate School of Business, Columbia University.
Indexed: Bull. Anal. Pol. Ec. Soc.; Int. Bibl. Eco.; Int. Bibl. Soc. Cul. Anth.; PAIS; SSCI.

COLUMBIA STUDIES IN HISTORY, ECONOMICS AND PUBLIC LAW
See COLUMBIA STUDIES IN THE SOCIAL SCIENCES

1190
COLUMBIA STUDIES IN THE SOCIAL SCIENCES. no.1– , 1891– . New York. Irreg.
Issued by: Columbia University. Title varies: no.1–578, 1891–1955, *Columbia Studies in History, Economics and Public Law*. Monograph series.

1191
COMBATE. v.1–4, no.25, July/Aug. 1958–Nov./Dec. 1962. San José.
Issued by: Instituto Internacional de Estudios Político-Sociales. Includes supplements. In Spanish.

1192
Comité Économique et Social des Communautés Européennes. Service Presse et Information. EXPOSÉ SUR ÉVOLUTION SOCIALE DANS LA COMMUNAUTÉ. 1968– . Luxembourg. Annual.
Published with its *Rapport Générale sur l'Activité des Communautés*. In French. Editions in Dutch, German and Italian are also published.

1193
COMMENTARY. v.1– , Nov. 1945– . New York. Monthly.
Issued by: American Jewish Committee.
Supersedes: *Contemporary Jewish Record*.
Indexed: Bull. Anal. Pol. Ec. Soc.; Int. Bibl. Pol. Sc.

1194
COMMENTARY. v.1– , Aug. 1975– . Singapore. Quarterly.
Issued by: University of Singapore Society.

Supersedes: *Commentary*.
Indexed: ABC POL SCI; His. Abst.; Ind. Per. Art. Law; Int. Bibl. Pol. Sc.; Int. Pol. Sc. Abst.; Peace Res. Abst. J.; Wom. Stu. Abst.; SSCI.

1195
COMMERCE AFRICAIN. AFRICAN TRADE. no.2– , May 1976– . Addis Ababa. Quarterly.
Issued by: Economic Commission for Africa, United Nations. In English and French.
Continues: *Commerçant Africain*.

COMMERCE EXTÉRIEUR. PAYS TIERS
See YEARBOOK OF FOREIGN TRADE STATISTICS. THIRD COUNTRIES

COMMERCE EXTÉRIEUR. SÉRIE B. RESUMÉS ANALYTIQUES
See Organisation for Economic Co-operation and Development. FOREIGN TRADE. SERIES B. ANALYTICAL ABSTRACTS

THE COMMERCE OF THE NATION
See CANADIAN BUSINESS

1196
COMMERCE TODAY. v.1– , Oct. 19, 1970– . Washington, D.C. Biweekly.
Issued by: U.S. Department of Commerce.
Supersedes: *International Commerce*.

THE COMMERCIAL & FINANCIAL CHRONICLE AND HUNT'S MAGAZINE
See THE COMMERCIAL AND FINANCIAL CHRONICLE

COMMERCIAL BANKS
See League of Nations. COMMERCIAL BANKS

1197
THE COMMERCIAL AND FINANCIAL CHRONICLE. v.1– , July 1, 1865– . New York. Weekly, 1965–Aug. 1941; three no. a week, Sept. 1941–Feb. 1942; two no. a week, Feb. 17, 1942–Mar. 1944.
Title varies: 1865–70, *Chronicle, The Commercial & Financial Chronicle, Banker's Gazette, Commercial Times, Railway Monitor and Insurance Journal*; 1871–June 1896, *The Commercial & Financial Chronicle and Hunt's Merchant's Magazine*. Absorbed: *Merchant's Magazine and Commercial Review* on Jan. 7, 1871, *Financial Reporter* on Sept. 4, 1941.

1198
Commission of the European Communities. COMPARATIVE TABLES OF SOCIAL SECURITY SYSTEMS IN THE MEMBER STATES. 1970?– . Luxembourg. Irreg.

1199
Commission of the European Communities. ÉTUDES. SÉRIE AIDE AU DÉVELOPPEMENT. no.1– , 1967– . Luxembourg, Office for Official Publications of the European Communities. Irreg.
In French. Published also in Dutch, German and Italian editions.

1200
Commission of the European Communities. ÉTUDES. SÉRIE POLITIQUE SOCIALE. 1963– . Luxembourg, Office of the Official Publications of the European Communities. Irreg.
In Dutch, French, German, or Italian.

1201
Commission of the European Communities. EURO-BAROMÈTRE. EURO-BAROMETER. no.1– , June 1974– . Brussels.
In English and French.

1202
Commission of the European Communities. EXPOSÉ ANNUEL SUR LES ACTIVITÉS D'ORIENTATION PROFESSIONELLE DANS LA COMMUNAUTÉ. 1968– . Luxembourg, Office for Official Publications of the European Communities. Annual.
In French. Published also in Dutch, German and Italian editions.

1203
Commission of the European Communities. EXPOSÉ SUR L'ÉVOLUTION SOCIALE DANS LA COMMUNAUTÉ. 1968– . Luxembourg. Irreg.
Published with its *Rapport Général sur l'Activité des Communautés*. In French.

1204
Commission of the European Communities. GENERAL REPORT ON THE ACTIVITIES OF THE COMMUNITIES. 1st– , 1967– . Brussels. Annual.
Issued also in French: *Rapport Général sur l'Activité des Communautés*, and in German: *Gesamtbericht über die Tätigkeit der Gemeinschaften*.

1205
Commission of the European Communities. RECHERCHE ET DÉVELOPPEMENT. 1– , 1970– . Luxembourg. Irreg.
In French.

1206
Commission of the European Communities. REPORT ON SOCIAL DEVELOPMENTS. 1979– . Brussels. Annual.
Continues: Commission's *Report on the Development of the Social Situation in the Communities*.

1207
Commission of the European Communities. Directorate for National Economies and Economic Trends. THE ECONOMIC SITUATION IN THE COMMUNITY. Sept. 1961–1977. Brussels, Publishing Services of the European Communities. Quarterly.
Published also in French: *Situation Économique de la Communauté et les Perspectives.*
Superseded by: *European Economy.*

COMMODITY SURVEY
See United Nations. Commission on International Commodity Trade. COMMODITY SURVEY

1208
COMMODITY TRADE AND PRICE TRENDS. TENDANCES DU COMMERCE ET DE PRIX DES PRODUITS DE BASE. TENDENCIAS DEL COMERCIO Y DES LOS PRECIOS DE LOS PRODUCTOS BÁSICOS. 1972– . Washington, D.C. Annual.
Issued by: Development Policy Staff, Commodities and Export Protection Division, World Bank.
Continues: International Bank for Reconstruction and Development. *Commodity Price Trends* (1966–71)

COMMODITY TRADE STATISTICS
See United Nations. Statistical Office. COMMODITY TRADE STATISTICS

COMMODITY TRADE STATISTICS, BY GROUPS OF STANDARD INTERNATIONAL TRADE CLASSIFICATION
See United Nations. Statistical Office. COMMODITY TRADE STATISTICS BY GROUPS OF STANDARD INTERNATIONAL TRADE CLASSIFICATION

1209
COMMON MARKET. v.1– , Nov. 1960– . The Hague. Monthly.
Subtitle reads: "A monthly review of European integration and economic development".
Indexed: Peace Res. Abst. J.

1210
COMMON MARKET LAW REVIEW. v.1– , June 1963– . London, Hackensack, N.J. Quarterly.
Issued by: Europa Institute, University of Leiden.
Indexed: Ind. For. Leg. Per.; Int. Lab. Doc.; Int. Bibl. Pol. Sc.; Int. Pol. Sc. Abst.

1211
THE COMMONWEAL. v.1– , Nov. 12, 1924– . New York. Biweekly.
Indexed: His. Abst.; Peace Res. Abst. J.; Wom. Stu. Abst.

1212
COMMONWEALTH. v.1–9, Jan. 14, 1883–Nov. 1902. New York. Weekly, 1883–1899; monthly.
Subtitle reads: "A monthly magazine and library of sociology". Publication suspended: May 1893–Apr. 1894.

1213
THE COMMONWEALTH & EMPIRE REVIEW. v.1– , Feb. 1901– . London. Monthly, 1901–Oct. 1914– quarterly.
Title varies: 1901–Oct. 1914, *The Empire Review*; 1914–22, *The Empire Review and Journal of British Trade*; 1923–Aug. 1944, *The Empire Review.*

1214
COMMONWEALTH INSTITUTE JOURNAL. v.1– , Feb. 1963– . Oxford, Pergamon Press. Annual.
Issues for 1966–69 called also *Annual Review.* Volume numbering discontinued with v.3, no.2.

1215
COMMONWEALTH JOURNAL. v.1– , May/June 1958– . London. Bimonthly.
Issued by: Royal Commonwealth Society. Title varies: 1958–62, *Journal.*
Supersedes: *United Empire.*

COMMONWEALTH PAPERS
See University of London. Institute of Commonwealth Studies. COMMONWEALTH PAPERS

1216
COMMONWEALTH REVIEW OF THE UNIVERSITY OF OREGON. v.1–23, no.2, Jan. 1919–May 1941. Eugene, Oreg. Bimonthly, 1919–June 1940. Quarterly.
Issued by: College of Social Science and other divisions of the University of Oregon.
Indexes: Vols. 1–3, 1916–July 1918; n. ser. v.1–17, Apr. 1919–Jan. 1936.

COMMUNICATION
See University of Zambia. Institute for Social Research. COMMUNICATION

1217
COMMUNICATION ABSTRACTS. v.1– , Mar. 1978– . Beverly Hills, Calif., Sage Publications. Quarterly.
Published with the cooperation of the School of Communication and Theater, Temple University, Philadelphia.

1218
COMMUNICATION AND SOCIETY. 1– , 1979– . Paris, Unesco. Irreg.
Other title: *Documents on Communication and Society.* Each issue has also a distinctive title.

1219
COMMUNICATION RESEARCH. v.1– , Jan. 1974– . Beverly Hills, Calif., Sage Publications. Quarterly.
Indexed: Hum. Res. Abst.; Psych. Abst.; Sage Pub. Adm. Abst.

1220
COMMUNICATION RESEARCH TRENDS. v.1– , spring 1980– . London. Quarterly.
Issued by: Centre for the Study of Communication and Culture.
Continues: *CSCC News Letter*.

1221
COMMUNICATION, THE MEDIA, SPORT AND LEISURE. 1975– . Waterloo. Three no. a year.
Issued by: SIRLS, Faculty of Human Kinetics and Leisure, University of Waterloo.

1222
COMMUNICATION YEARBOOK. no.1– , 1977– . New Brunswick, N.J., Transaction Books.
Issued by: International Communication Association.

1223
COMMUNICATIONS. v.1– , 1961– . Paris, Éditions du Seuil. Semi-annual.
Issued by: 6e Section Sciences Économiques et Sociales, École Pratique des Hautes Études. In French. Issues are thematic.
Indexed: Bull. Anal. Pol. Ec. Soc.; Bull. Sig. Soc. Eth.; Int. Bibl. Soc. Cul. Anth.; Int. Pol. Sc. Abst.; Soc. Abst.

1224
COMMUNICATIONS. 1– , 1974– . St. Augustin, Verlag Franz Richarz. Three no. a year.
In English, French, or German; summaries in the three languages. Title varies: 1974, *Internationale Zeitschrift für Kommunikationsforschung*.

COMMUNICATIONS
See Académie des Sciences d'Outre-Mer. COMPTES RENDUS TRIMESTRIELLES DES SÉANCES

COMMUNICATIONS
See University of Cape Town. Centre for African Studies. COMMUNICATIONS

1225
COMMUNICATIONS AND DEVELOPMENT. 1– , 1977– . Tehran. Quarterly.
Issued by: Iran Communications and Development Institute.

1226
COMMUNICAZIONI SOCIALI. Jan./Mar. 1979– . Milano, Vita e Pensiero.
Issued by: Scuola Superiore delle Communicazioni Sociali, Università Cattolica del Sacro Cuore. In Italian.
Continues: *Annali della Scuola Superiore delle Communicazioni Sociali*.

1227
COMMUNIST. v.6–23, Mar. 1927–Dec. 1944. New York. Monthly.
Continues: *Workers Monthly*. Continued by: *Political Affairs*.

1228
COMMUNIST AFFAIRS: DOCUMENTS AND ANALYSIS. v.1– , 1982– . Guildford, Butterworth Scientific. Quarterly.
Supersedes: *Documents in Communist Affairs*.

THE COMMUNIST BLOC AND THE WESTERN ALLIANCES: THE MILITARY BALANCE
See International Institute for Strategic Studies. MILITARY BALANCE

1229
THE COMMUNIST INTERNATIONAL. no.1–30, May 1919–1924; n. ser. v.1–17, 1924–1940. Petrograd. Monthly.
Issued by: Executive Committee of the Communist International. Published also in French, German and Russian editions.

1230
COMMUNIST VIEWPOINT. v.1– , Mar./Apr. 1969– . Toronto, Progress Books. Bimonthly.
Issued by: Communist Party of Canada.
Indexed: His. Abst.

1231
COMMUNITIES. 1972– . Louisa, Va. Bimonthly.
Issued by: Community Publications Cooperative. Subtitle reads: "A journal of cooperative living".
Supersedes: *Modern Utopian & Alternatives Newsmagazine*, *Communitarian* and *Communitas*.
Indexed: Sage Urb. Stu. Abst.

COMMUNITIES
See Commission of the European Communities. GENERAL REPORT ON THE ACTIVITIES OF THE COMMUNITIES

1232
COMMUNITY. v.1– , Apr. 1954– . Colombo. Semi-annual.
Suspended: Dec. 1955–Mar. 1958.

1233
COMMUNITY DEVELOPMENT. no.1– , 1958– . Rome. Semi-annual.

Issued by: Federation of Settlements and Neighborhood Centers. In English, French, or Italian. Running title: *International Review of Community Development.*
Indexed: Int. Bibl. Soc. Cul. Anth.

1234
COMMUNITY DEVELOPMENT JOURNAL. v.1– , Jan. 1966– . London, Oxford University Press. Quarterly.
Issued by: Community Development Clearinghouse, University of London. Subtitle reads: "An international forum".
Supersedes: *Community Development Bulletin* (1949–Dec. 1964)
Indexed: Int. Bibl. Eco.; Int. Bibl. Soc. Cul. Anth.

1235
Community Development Society. JOURNAL. v.1– , spring 1970– . Stillwater, Okla., later Urbana, Ill., University of Illinois. Two no. a year.

1236
COMMUNITY PLANNING REVIEW. REVUE CANADIENNE D'URBANISME. v.1–27, no.9, Feb. 1951–Sept. 1977. Ottawa. Quarterly.
Issued by: Community Planning Association of Canada. In English or French.
Supersedes: *Layout for Living and Urbanisme.*

1237
THE COMPANION TO THE NEWSPAPER: AND JOURNAL OF FACTS IN POLITICS, STATISTICS AND PUBLIC ECONOMY. no.1–49, Mar. 1, 1833–Jan. 1, 1837. London, C. Knight. Monthly.

1238
THE COMPARATIVE AND INTERNATIONAL LAW OF SOUTHERN AFRICA. v.1– , Mar. 1968– . Pretoria. Three no. a year.
Issued by: Institute of Foreign and Comparative Law, University of Pretoria.
Indexed: Ind. For. Leg. Per.

1239
COMPARATIVE ECONOMIC STUDIES. v.27– , spring 1985– . Notre Dame, Ind. Quarterly.
Issued by: Association for Comparative Economic Studies.
Continues: the association's (U.S.) *ACES Bulletin.*

1240
COMPARATIVE EDUCATION. 1– , 1964– . Oxford, later Dorchester-on-Thames, Carfax Pub. Co. Three no. a year.
Issued by: Institute of Education, Oxford University.

COMPARATIVE EDUCATION
See VERGLEICHENDE PEDAGOGIK

1241
COMPARATIVE EDUCATION REVIEW. v.1– , June 1957– . Chicago, Ill., The University of Chicago Press. Three no. a year.
Organ of: Comparative and International Education Society.
Indexed: Bull. Anal. Pol. Ec. Soc.; Int. Bibl. Soc.; Int. Lab. Doc.; PAIS; SSCI.

1242
COMPARATIVE GROUP STUDIES. v.1–3, 1970–1972. Beverly Hills, Calif., Sage Publications. Quarterly.
Continued by: *Small Group Behavior.*

1243
COMPARATIVE JUDICIAL REVIEW. v.1– , 1964– . Coral Gables, Fla., Rainforth Foundation. Annual.
Issued by: Pan American Institute of Comparative Law. In English or Spanish.
Indexes: Vols. 1–10, 1964–73, in v.11.

COMPARATIVE LAW REVIEW
See HIKAKU HO ZASSHI

1244
COMPARATIVE LAW YEARBOOK. v.1– , 1977– . Alphen aan den Rijn, Sijthoff & Noordhoff. Annual.
Issued by: Center for International Legal Studies.
Indexed: Ind. For. Leg. Per.

1245
COMPARATIVE POLITICAL ECONOMY AND PUBLIC POLICY SERIES. v.1– , 1975– . Beverly Hills, Calif., Sage Publications. Irreg.
Monograph series.

1246
COMPARATIVE POLITICAL STUDIES. v.1– , Apr. 1968– . Beverly Hills, Calif., Sage Publications. Quarterly.
Other title: CPS.
Indexed: ABC POL SCI; Bull. Anal. Pol. Ec. Soc.; Bull. Sig. Soc. Eth.; Curr. Cont. Soc. Beh. Sc.; His. Abst.; Int. Bibl. Eco.; Int. Bibl. Pol. Sc.; Int. Bibl. Soc.; Int. Pol. Sc. Abst.; PAIS; Sage Pub. Adm. Abst.; Sage Urb. Stu. Abst.; Urb. Stu. Abst.; SSCI.

1247
COMPARATIVE POLITICS. v.1– , Oct. 1968– . Chicago, Ill., The University of Chicago Press. Quarterly.

Sponsored and edited by: Political Science Program of the City University of New York.
Indexed: ABC POL SCI; Bull. Sig. Soc. Eth.; His. Abst.; Ind. Per. Art. Law; Int. Bibl. Eco.; Int. Pol. Sc. Abst.; Int. Bibl. Soc.; Int. Bibl. Soc. Cul. Anth.; Int. Pol. Sc. Abst.; PAIS; PHRA; SSCI; Sage Pub. Adm. Abst.; Urb. Stu. Abst.

1248
COMPARATIVE SOCIAL RESEARCH. v.2– , 1979– . Greenwich, Conn., JAI Press. Annual.
Continues: *Comparative Studies in Sociology* (v.1, 1978).
Indexed: Int. Bibl. Eco.

1249
COMPARATIVE STRATEGY. v.1– , 1978– . New York, Crane Russak, publisher for the Strategic Studies Center. Quarterly.
Issued by: Strategic Studies Center, SRI International.
Indexed: Int. Bibl. Pol. Sc.; Int. Bibl. Soc. Cul. Anth.; Int. Pol. Sc. Abst.; PAIS; SSCI.

1250
COMPARATIVE STUDIES; CROSS-NATIONAL SUMMARIES. no.1– , Mar. 1980– . The Hague. Irreg.
Issued by: International Statistical Institute, Vooburg, and World Fertility Survey, London. Each no. has a distinctive title.

1251
COMPARATIVE STUDIES DOCUMENTS. 1– , 1975– . Pittsburgh, Pa.
Issued by: Comparative Interdisciplinary Studies Section, International Studies Association. Subseries of: its *Occasional Papers*.

1252
COMPARATIVE STUDIES IN OVERSEAS HISTORY. 1– , 1978– . The Hague, Leiden University Press. Irreg.
Issued by: Centre for the History of European Expansion, Leiden.

1253
COMPARATIVE STUDIES IN SOCIETY AND HISTORY. v.1– , Oct. 1958– . Cambridge, New York, Cambridge University Press. Quarterly.
Organ of: Society for the Comparative Study of Society and History. Includes supplements, 1–3, 1961–68.
Indexed: ABC POL SCI; Abst. Anth.; Bull. Anal. Pol. Ec. Soc.; Bull. Sig. Soc. Eth.; His. Abst.; Hum. Res. Abst.; Int. Bibl. Eco.; Int. Bibl. Pol. Sc.; Int. Bibl. Soc.; Int. Bibl. Soc. Cul. Anth.; Int. Pol. Sc. Abst.; Ind. Per. Art. Law; Soc. Sc. Hum. Ind.; Soc. Abst.; SSCI.

COMPARATIVE STUDY OF MIGRATION, URBANIZATION IN RELATION TO THE DEVELOPMENT IN THE ESCAP REGION; COUNTRY REPORTS
See United Nations. Economic and Social Commission for Asia and the Pacific. COMPARATIVE STUDY OF MIGRATION, URBANIZATION IN RELATION TO DEVELOPMENT IN THE ESCAP REGION; COUNTRY REPORTS

COMPARATIVE TABLES OF SOCIAL SECURITY SYSTEMS IN THE MEMBER STATES IN THE EUROPEAN COMMUNITIES
See Commission of the European Communities. COMPARATIVE TABLES OF SOCIAL SECURITY SYSTEMS IN THE MEMBER STATES IN THE EUROPEAN COMMUNITIES

1254
COMPARATIVE URBAN RESEARCH. v.1– , spring 1972– . New Brunswick, N.J., Transaction Periodicals Consortium. Three no. a year.
Official publication of: Committee for Community Research, International Sociological Association.
Indexed: ABC POL SCI; Bull. Anal. Pol. Ec. Soc.; Int. Bibl. Pol. Sc.; Int. Pol. Sc. Abst.; Sage Pub. Adm. Abst.; Sage Urb. Stu. Abst.; Urb. Aff. Abst.

1255
COMPENDIO ESTADÍSTICO CENTROAMERICANO. 1– , 1957– . Guatemala City.
Issued by: Committee on Economic Cooperation in Central America, United Nations, 1–2; Secretaría Permanente del Tratado General de Integración Económica Centroamericana (SIECA), 3– .

COMPILATION OF RECOMMENDATIONS AND RESOLUTIONS ADOPTED
See Council of Europe. Consultative Assembly. TEXTS ADOPTED

COMPTE RENDU
See International Congress of Americanists. PROCEEDINGS

COMPTE-RENDU
See International Institute of Differing Civilizations. COMPTE-RENDU. REPORT

COMPTES NATIONAUX. PRINCIPAUX AGRÉGATES
See Organisation for Economic Co-operation and Development. NATIONAL ACCOUNTS

COMPTES NATIONAUX, SEC AGRÉGATES
See Statistical Office of the European Communities. NATIONAL ACCOUNTS. ESA AGGREGATES

COMPTES NATIONAUX. SEC. TABLEAUX DÉTAILLÉS PAR BRANCHE
See Statistical Office of the European Communities. NATIONAL ACCOUNTS. ESA. DETAILED TABLES BY BRANCH

COMPTES NATIONAUX. TABLEAUX DÉTAILLÉS
See Organisation for Economic Co-operation and Development. NATIONAL ACCOUNTS

COMPTES-RENDUS
See Congrès International d'Anthropologie Criminelle. BERICHT

COMPTES-RENDUS DES SÉANCES
See Académie des Sciences d'Outre-Mer. COMPTES-RENDUS TRIMESTRIELLES

COMPTES-RENDUS MENSUELS DES SÉANCES
See Académie des Sciences d'Outre-Mer. COMPTES-RENDUS TRIMESTRIELLES.

COMPTES-RENDUS TRIMESTRIELLES DES SÉANCES
See Académie des Sciences d'Outre-Mer. COMPTES-RENDUS TRIMESTRIELLES DES SÉANCES

1256
COMPUTER APPLICATIONS. v.5– , 1978– . Nottingham. Quarterly.
Issued by: Department of Geography, University of Nottingham.
Continues: *Computer Applications in the Natural and Social Sciences* (v.1–4, 1969–76)

1257
COMPUTERS AND THE SOCIAL SCIENCES. v.1– , Jan./Mar. 1985– . Osprey, Fla., Paradigm Press. Quarterly.

1258
COMPUTERS, ENVIRONMENT AND URBAN SYSTEMS. v.5, no.1/2– , 1980– . New York, Pergamon Press. Quarterly.
Published in cooperation with the Urban and Regional Information Systems Association. Some issues are thematic.
Continues: *Urban Systems.*

1259
COMUNICAÇÃO & POLÍTICA. v.1– , Mar./May 1983– . São Paulo, Paz e Terra. Quarterly.
In Portuguese or Spanish; summaries in English; some articles in English or French with summaries in Portuguese or Spanish.

1260
COMUNIDAD. 1– , 1966– . Mexico, D.F. Bimonthly.
Issued by: Universidad Iberoamericana. In Spanish.
Indexed: Bull. Anal. Pol. Ec. Soc.; His. Abst.

1261
COMUNIDADES. v.1– , Jan./Feb. 1966– . Madrid. Three no. a year.
Issued by: Instituto de Estudios Sindicales, Sociales y Cooperativos. In Spanish.
Indexed: Bull. Sig. Soc. Eth.; Int. Bibl. Soc.; Int. Bibl. Soc. Cul. Anth.; Int. Lab. Doc.

1262
COMUNITÀ. no.1– , Jan. 1946– . Milano. Three no. a year.
In Italian.
Indexed: Bull. Anal. Pol. Ec. Soc.; Int. Bibl. Soc. Cul. Anth.; Int. Pol. Sc. Abst.; Soc. Abst.

1263
LA COMUNITÀ INTERNAZIONALE. v.1– , Jan. 1946– . Roma. Quarterly.
Issued by: Società Italiana per l'Organizzazione Internazionale. In Italian, occasionally in English or French.
Indexes: Vols. 1–10, 1946–55, 1v.
Indexed: Bull. Anal. Pol. Ec. Soc.; ABC POL SCI; His. Abst.; Int. Pol. Sc. Abst.

CONDITIONS ÉCONOMIQUES EN AFRIQUE
See United Nations. Bureau of Economic Affairs. ECONOMIC DEVELOPMENTS IN AFRICA

1264
CONFLICT. v.1, no.1/2– , 1978/79– . New York, Crane Russak. Quarterly.
Published in cooperation with the Institute for Conflict and Policy Studies.
Indexed: ABC POL SCI; Int. Bibl. Pol. Sc.; Int. Pol. Sc. Abst.; SSCI.

1265
CONFLICT MANAGEMENT AND PEACE SCIENCE. v.5– , fall 1980– . Ithaca, N.Y., World University Division, World Research Center. Semi-annual.
Issued in cooperation with: World University of the World Academy of Science, the Field of Peace Studies and Peace Science, Cornell University, and Peace Science Society (International).
Continues: *Journal of Peace Science.*

Indexed: ABC POL SCI; PAIS; SSCI.

CONFLICT RESOLUTION
See THE JOURNAL OF CONFLICT RESOLUTION

1266
CONFLICT STUDIES. no.1– , Dec. 1969– . London, Current Affairs Research Service Centre. Ten no. a year, 1969– ; bimonthly, –1975; monthly.
Issued by: Institute for the Study of Conflict, London. Published also in French edition under the title: *Monde des Conflits*.
Indexed: Bull. Anal. Pol. Ec. Soc.; Int. Bibl. Pol. Sc.; Int. Pol. Sc. Abst.

CONFLUENCE
See KANO STUDIES; DIRĀSĀT

CONGO AFRIQUE
See ZAÏRE–AFRIQUE

1267
Congrès International d'Anthropologie Criminelle. BERICHT. 1–7, 1885–1911. [Place of publication varies]
Issued by: the congress, also under a variant name: Internationaler Kongress für Kriminal Anthropologie (1911). Title varies: 1st–3rd, 1885–92, *Actes*; 4th–6th, 1896–1906, *Comptes-Rendus*.

1268
CONGRESS & THE PRESIDENCY. v.9– , winter 1981/82– . Washington, D.C., American University. Semi-annual.
Published jointly by: Center for Congressional and Presidential Studies, American University, and U.S. Capitol Historical Society.
Continues: *Congressional Studies*.

1269
CONGRESSIONAL STUDIES. v.7–9, spring 1979–1980. Washington, D.C. Semi-annual.
Issued by: U.S. Capitol Historical Society.
Continues: *Capitol Studies*. Continued by: *Congress & the Presidency*.

CONJONCTURE
See KONJUNKTUR

LA CONJONCTURE; ÉCONOMIE MONDIALE
See ÉTUDES ET CONJONCTURES; ÉCONOMIE MONDIALE

1270
CONJUNCTURA. v.34–40, no, 1, Jan. 1980–Jan. 1986. Rio de Janeiro. Monthly.
Issued by: Instituto Brasileiro de Economia, Fundação Getulio Vargas. In Portuguese. Supplements accompany some numbers.
Continues: *Conjunctura Econômica*.

1271
CONJUNCTURA ECONÔMICA. v.1–33, 1947–1979. Rio de Janeiro. Monthly.
Issued by: Centro de Analise da Conjunctura Econômica do Núcleo da Fundação Getulio Vargas. In Portuguese. Published also as *Economics & Business in Brazil. Conjunctura Econômica* (1–, Apr. 1954–)
Indexed: Int. Lab. Doc.; Peace Res. Abst. J.

CONNECT
See CONNEXION

1272
CONNEXION. v.1– , Jan. 1976– . Paris, Unesco. Quarterly.
Subtitle reads: "Bulletin de l'éducation relative à l'environnement". In French. Published also in English under the title: *Connect*, and in Spanish: *Contacto*.

Conseil de l'Europe
See Council of Europe

1273
Consejo de Arqueología. BOLETÍN. 1– , 1984– . Mexico, D.F. Annual.
Issued by: Instituto Nacional de Antropología e Historia. In Spanish.

1274
THE CONSENSUS. v.1–24, no.2, May 1915–July 1939. Boston, Mass. Four no. a year (irreg.)
Title varies: 1915–May 1919, *The National Economic League Quarterly*.

1275
CONSOMMATION. v.1– , 1954– . Montrouge, Dunod. Quarterly.
Issued by: Centre de Recherche et de Documentation sur la Consommation. In French. Title varies: v.1–4, 1954–57, *Annales de Recherches et de Documentation sur la Consommation*.
Indexed: Int. Bibl. Eco.; PAISFL.

CONSTITUTIONAL AND PARLIAMENTARY INFORMATION
See Inter-Parliamentary Union. CONSTITUTIONAL AND PARLIAMENTARY INFORMATION

1276
THE CONSTITUTIONAL REVIEW. v.1–13, Apr. 1917–1929. Washington, D.C. Quarterly.

Issued by: The National Association for Constitutional Government.

1277
CONSTITUTIONAL YEAR BOOK. v.1–53, 1885–1939. London. Annual.
Issued by: National Union of Conservative and Constitutional Association.

1278
CONSUMER POLICY IN OECD COUNTRIES. 1983– . Paris, 1985– .
Issued by: Organisation for Economic Co-operation and Development. Published also in French as: *Politique à l'Égard des Consommateurs dans les Pays de l'OCDE*.
Continues: the organization's *Annual Report on Consumer Policy in OECD Member Countries* (in 1972 *Consumer Policy in Member Countries*)

CONSUMER SURVEY RESULTS
See EUROPEAN ECONOMY. SUPPLEMENT C. CONSUMER SURVEY RESULTS

1279
CONSUMPTION OF LEISURE AND SPORT. 1975– . Waterloo. Three no. a year.
Issued by: SIRLS, Faculty of Human Kinetics and Leisure Studies, University of Waterloo.

CONTACTO
See CONNEXION

1280
CONTEMPORARY CHINA. TANG-TAI CHUNG-KUO. 1955/56– . Hong Kong, Hong Kong University Press. Annual.
Issued by: Department of Economics and Political Science, University of Hong Kong. Tables of contents also in Chinese.

1281
CONTEMPORARY CRISIS. v.1– , Jan. 1977– . Amsterdam, Elsevier Pub. Co. Quarterly.
Indexed: ABC POL SCI; Bull. Anal. Pol. Ec. Soc.; Int. Bibl. Eco.; Int. Bibl. Pol. Sc.; Int. Pol. Sc. Abst.; Soc. Abst.; SSCI.

1282
CONTEMPORARY EDUCATION. v.39, no.4– , Jan. 1968– . Terre Haute, Ind. Quarterly.
Issued by: School of Education, Indiana State University.
Continues: *Teachers College Journal*.

1283
CONTEMPORARY EDUCATIONAL PSYCHOLOGY. 1– , Jan. 1976– . New York, Academic Press. Quarterly.

1284
CONTEMPORARY FRENCH CIVILIZATION. 1– , Jan. 1976– . Bozeman, Mont. Three no. a year, 1976–84; two no. a year.
Issued by: Montana State University. In English or French.
Indexed: Int. Bibl. Pol. Sc.; Int. Bibl. Soc. Cul. Anth.

CONTEMPORARY INTERNATIONAL RELATIONS
See HSIEN TAI KUO CHI KUAN HSI

1285
CONTEMPORARY JAPAN: A REVIEW OF FAR EASTERN AFFAIRS. v.1– , June 1932– . Tokyo. Quarterly, 1932–38; monthly, Mar. 1939– .
Issued by: Foreign Affairs Association of Japan.
Indexes: Vols. 1–10, 1932–41, 1v.
Indexed: His. Abst.; Int. Bibl. Soc. Cul. Anth.; Int. Pol. Sc. Abst.; Peace Res. Abst. J.

1286
CONTEMPORARY POLICY ISSUES. no.1– , Oct. 1982– . Long Beach, Calif. Irreg.
Issued by: California State University, Long Beach, and Western Economic Association (International)

1287
CONTEMPORARY POLITICAL SOCIOLOGY. v.1– , 1979– . Beverly Hills, Calif., Sage Publications. Irreg.
Each no. has also a distinctive title.

CONTEMPORARY PRACTICE OF THE UNITED KINGDOM IN THE FIELD OF INTERNATIONAL LAW
See BRITISH PRACTICE IN INTERNATIONAL LAW

1288
CONTEMPORARY PSYCHOANALYSIS. v.1– , fall 1964– . New York. Semi-annual.
Issued by: William Alanson White Psychoanalytic Society and William Alanson White Institute of Psychiatry, New York.
Indexed: Abst. Soc. Work.; Psych. Abst.; SSCI.

1289
CONTEMPORARY PSYCHOLOGY. 1– , Jan. 1956– . Washington, D.C. Monthly.
Issued by: American Psychological Association.
Indexed: LLBA; SSCI; Wom. Stu. Abst.

1290
THE CONTEMPORARY REVIEW. v.1– , Jan. 1866– . London. Monthly. Two volumes to a year.
Indexed: His. Abst.; Ind. Per. Art. Law; Int. Bibl. Eco.; Int. Bibl. Pol. Sc.; Int. Bibl. Soc.; Int. Bibl. Soc. Cul. Anth.; Peace Res. Abst. J.; Soc. Abst.; Soc. Sc. Hum. Ind.; Wom. Stu. Abst.

1291
CONTEMPORARY SOCIAL RESEARCH. 1– , 1981– . London, Allen & Unwin. Irreg.
Monograph series.

1292
CONTEMPORARY SOCIAL SCIENCES. v.1– , Jan./Mar. 1972– . New Delhi. Quarterly.
Issued by: Research Foundation.

1293
CONTEMPORARY SOCIOLOGY. 1– , Jan. 1972– . Washington, D.C. Bimonthly.
Issued by: American Sociological Association.
Continues: "Book Review Section" of the *American Sociological Review*.
Indexed: His. Abst.; PAIS; Soc. Abst.; SSCI; Wom. Stu. Abst.

1294
CONTEMPORARY STUDIES IN APPLIED BEHAVIORAL SCIENCES. v.1– , 1983– . Greenwich, Conn., JAI Press. Annual.

1295
CONTINUITY AND CHANGE. v.1– , Mar. 1986– . Cambridge, Cambridge University Press. Three no. a year.
Issued by: Tulane University Law School, and Cambridge Group for the History of Population and Social Structure.

1296
CONTREPOINT. no.1– , May 1970– . Paris. Quarterly, 1972; three no. a year.
In French. Some no. are thematic.
Indexed: Bull. Anal. Pol. Ec. Soc.; Int. Bibl. Pol. Sc.

1297
CONTRIBUCIONES. no.1– , Jan./Mar. 1984– . Buenos Aires. Quarterly.
Issued by: Centro Interdisciplinario de Estudios sobre el Desarrollo Latinoamericano. In Spanish.

1298
CONTRIBUTII LA SOCIOLOGIA CULTURII DE MASA. 1– , 1970– . Bucureşti, Editura Academiei Republicii Socialiste România. Annual.
In Romanian.

CONTRIBUTION À L'HISTOIRE DU SOCIALISME
See PRILOZI ZA ISTORIJU SOCIALIZMA

CONTRIBUTIONS
See University of California, Berkeley, Archaeological Research Facility. CONTRIBUTIONS

1299
CONTRIBUTIONS IN INTERCULTURAL AND COMPARATIVE STUDIES. 1976– . Westport, Conn., Greenwood Press. Irreg.
Monograph series.

CONTRIBUTIONS. SOCIAL SCIENCES
See University of Florida, Gainesville. State Museum. CONTRIBUTIONS. SOCIAL SCIENCES

CONTRIBUTIONS TO A HISTORY OF SOCIALISM
See PRILOZI ZA ISTORIJU SOCIJALIZMA

1300
CONTRIBUTIONS TO AMERICAN ANTHROPOLOGY AND HISTORY. v.1–12(no.1–60), 1931–1960. Washington, D.C. Irreg.
Issued by: Carnegie Institution of Washington. Title varies: v.1–4, *Contributions to American Archaeology*.

CONTRIBUTIONS TO AMERICAN ARCHAEOLOGY
See CONTRIBUTIONS TO AMERICAN ANTHROPOLOGY AND HISTORY

1301
CONTRIBUTIONS TO ASIAN STUDIES. v.1– , Jan. 1971– . Leiden, E.J. Brill. Semi-annual.
Official publication of: Canadian Association for South Asian Studies. Some nos. are monographs.

CONTRIBUTIONS TO ETHNOLOGY AND LINGUISTICS, ARCHAEOLOGY AND PHYSICAL ANTHROPOLOGY OF INDIAN AMERICA
See INDIANA

1302
CONTRIBUTIONS TO INDIAN SOCIOLOGY. no.1–4, Apr. 1957–Apr. 1960; n. ser. no.1– , Dec. 1967– . Paris, Mouton. Annual.
Issued by: 6e Section des Sciences Économiques et Sociales, École Pratique des Hautes Études, and the Institute of Social Anthropology, Oxford. Sponsored by: Research Centre on Social and Economic Development in Asia, Delhi (1967–).

Indexed: Bull. Sig. Soc. Eth.; Int. Bibl. Eco.; Int. Bibl. Soc. Cul. Anth.; Soc. Abst.

1303
CONTRIBUTIONS TO POLITICAL ECONOMY. v.1– , Mar. 1982– . London, New York, Academic Press. Annual.
Published for the Cambridge Political Economy Society.

CONTRIBUTIONS TO THE SOCIOLOGY OF KNOWLEDGE
See BEITRÄGE ZUR WISSENSSOZIOLOGIE

1304
CONTRIBUTIONS TO THE SOCIOLOGY OF LANGUAGE. no.1– , 1971– . The Hague, Mouton. Irreg.
Monograph series. Other title: *Advances in the Sociology of Language.*

CONTRIBUTIONS TO THE SOCIOLOGY OF RELIGION
See BEITRÄGE ZUR WISSENSSOZIOLOGIE. BEITRÄGE ZUR RELIGIONSSOZIOLOGIE

1305
CONTROCORRENTE. v.1– , 1969?– , Milano.
In Italian. Subtitle reads: "Quaderni trimestrali di studi e ricerche su temi e problemi delle scienze umane".
Indexed: Bull. Anal. Pol. Ec. Soc.

1306
CONVERGENCE. CONVERGENCIA. SKHOZHDENIE. v.1– , Mar. 1968– . Toronto. Quarterly.
Subtitle reads: "An international journal of adult education". In English, French, Russian, or Spanish.
Indexes: Vols. 1–10, 1968–71, 1v.
Indexed: Int. Bibl. Soc. Cul. Anth.; SSCI.

CONVERGENCIA
See CONVERGENCE

1307
COOPÉRATION. v.1–42, Jan. 1938–Dec. 1972. Paris. Monthly.
Issued by: Fédération Nationale des Coopératives de Consommation. In French.
Continued by: *Coopération, Distribution, Consommation.*

1308
COOPERATION AND CONFLICT. 1– , 1966– . Stockholm. Four no. a year.
Issued by: Nordic Committee for the Study of International Politics.
Indexed: ABC POL SCI; Bull. Anal. Pol. Ec. Soc.; His. Abst.; Int. Bibl. Eco.; Int. Bibl. Pol. Sc.; Int. Bibl. Soc.; Int. Bibl. Soc. Cul. Anth.; Ind. Per. Art. Law; Int. Pol. Sc. Abst.; PAIS; Soc. Abst.

1309
COOPÉRATION, DISTRIBUTION, CONSOMMATION. v.43– , Jan. 1973– . Paris, S.C.E.L. Monthly (some combined numbers)
In French.
Continues: *Coopération.*

COOPÉRATION ÉCONOMIQUE ET INTÉGRATION ENTRE LES PAYS EN DÉVELOPPEMENT
See ECONOMIC COOPERATION AND INTEGRATION AMONG DEVELOPING COUNTRIES

1310
COOPÉRATION ET DÉVELOPPEMENT. 1– , 1964– . Paris. Bimonthly.
Issued by: Bureau de Liaison de Agents de Coopération Technique. In French.
Indexed: Bull. Sig. Soc. Eth.; Int. Bibl. Soc. Cul. Anth.; Int. Lab. Doc.

1311
COOPERATION IN EDUCATION. 1– , 1972– . Rome. Quarterly.
Issued by: Istituto per la Cooperazione Universitaria. In Italian.
Indexed: Bull. Anal. Pol. Ec. Soc.

1312
CORNELL INTERNATIONAL LAW JOURNAL. v.1– , spring 1968– . Ithaca, N.Y. Annual.
Issued by: Cornell Society of International Law.
Indexed: Ind. Leg. Per.; Ind. Per. Art. Law; PAIS; SSCI.

1313
THE CORNELL JOURNAL OF SOCIAL RELATIONS. 1– , spring 1966– . Ithaca, N.Y. Semi-annual.
Issued by: Department of Sociology, Cornell University.
Indexed: Bull. Anal. Pol. Ec. Soc.; Int. Bibl. Pol. Sc.; Int. Pol. Sc. Abst.; Psych. Abst.; Soc. Abst.; SSCI.

1314
CORRESPONDANCE D'ORIENT. ÉTUDES. 1/2– , 1962– . Bruxelles. Semi-annual (irreg.)
Issued by: Centre pour l'Étude des Problèmes du Monde Musulman Contemporain. In French.
Indexed: Int. Bibl. Soc. Cul. Anth.; Int. Pol. Sc. Abst.

CORRESPONDENZ-BLATT
See Deutsche Gesellschaft für Anthropologie, Ethnologie und Urgeschichte. CORRESPONDENZ-BLATT

1315
COST AND MANAGEMENT. 1926– . Hamilton. Bimonthly.
Issued by: Canadian Society of Cost Accountants and Industrial Engineers. Summaries in English and French.
Indexed: Eco. Abst.

1316
[No entry]

1317
Council of Europe. EUROPEAN TREATY SERIES. no.1– , 1949– . Strasbourg, Publications Section. Irreg.
In English and French. (Série de Traités et Conventions Européennes).

1318
Council of Europe. Consultative Assembly. TEXTS ADOPTED. TEXTES ADOPTÉS. 1st sess.– , Aug. 10–Sept. 8, 1949– . Strasbourg. Irreg.
In English and French. Title varies: 1950, *Compilation of Recommendations and Resolutions Adopted*; 1951, *Recommendations and Resolutions. Recommendations et Resolutions.*
Continued by: Council of Europe. Parliamentary Assembly. *Texts Adopted by the Assembly. Textes Adoptés par l'Assemblée.*

1319
Council of Europe. Parliamentary Assembly. DOCUMENTS. WORKING PAPERS. 1– , Aug. 10–Sept. 8, 1949– . Strasbourg. Irreg.
In English and French. Title varies: 1st–25th sess., 1949–74, Council of Europe. Consultative Assembly. *Documents. Working Papers.*

1320
Council of State Governments. INDEX TO RECENT POLICY POSITIONS OF THE GOVERNING BOARD OF THE COUNCIL OF STATE GOVERNMENTS, GENERAL ASSEMBLY OF THE STATES AND ORGANIZATIONS AFFILIATED WITH THE COUNCIL OF STATE GOVERNMENTS. Nov. 1962– . Chicago, Ill.
Continued by: *Annual Supplement.*

1321
Council on Foreign Relations. STUDIES IN AMERICAN FOREIGN RELATIONS. no.1– , 1941– . New York. Annual.

COUNTRY DEMOGRAPHIC PROFILES. ISP-DP
See United States. Bureau of the Census. COUNTY DEMOGRAPHIC PROFILES. ISP-DP

Cour Européenne des Droits de l'Homme
See European Court of Human Rights

THE COURSE AND PHASES OF THE WORLD ECONOMIC DEPRESSION
See WORLD ECONOMIC SURVEY

1322
Court of Justice of European Communities. RECUEIL DE LA JURISPRUDENCE DE LA COUR. 1954/56– . Luxembourg, Office of the Official Publications of the European Communities. Annual.
Vols. for 1954/55–June/July 1958 issued by the Court of Justice of the European Coal and Steel Community. In Dutch, French, German and Italian.

1323
CRIME & DELINQUENCY. v.6, no.3– , July 1960– . New York. Quarterly.
Issued by: National Council on Crime and Delinquency. Title varies: v.6, no.3–v.21, no.3, July 1960–July 1975, *Crime and Delinquency.*
Continues: *NPPA Journal* (1955–Apr. 1960)
Indexed: Ind. Leg. Per.; Ind. Leg. Per. Law; PAIS; Psych. Abst.; Soc. Work Res. Abst.; Sage Urb. Stu. Abst.; SSCI.

CRIME AND DELINQUENCY
See CRIME & DELINQUENCY

1324
CRIME AND DELINQUENCY ABSTRACTS. v.1–8, no.6, Jan. 1963–1972. Bethesda, Md., National Clearinghouse for Mental Health Information. Irreg.
Issued by: National Institutes for Health, Department of Health, Education and Welfare. Title varies: 1963–June 1966, *International Bibliography on Crime and Delinquency.* Absorbed: *Current Projects in the Prevention, Control and Treatment of Crime and Delinquency.*

1325
CRIME AND JUSTICE BEHAVIOR. v.1– , Mar. 1974– . Beverly Hills, Calif., Sage Publications. Quarterly.
Official publication of the American Association of Correctional Psychologists.
Supersedes: *Correctional Psychologist.*

1326
CRIME AND SOCIAL JUSTICE. 1– , spring/summer 1974– . San Francisco, Calif. Two no. a year.
Issued by: Institute for the Study of Labor and Economic Crisis. Subtitle reads: "A journal of radical criminology". Absorbed: *Issues in Criminology* (1976)

1327
CRIMINAL JUSTICE AND BEHAVIOR. v.1– , Mar. 1974– . Beverly Hills, Calif., Sage Publications. Quarterly.
Official publication of: American Association of Correctional Psychologists. Subtitle reads: "An international journal of correctional psychology".
Supersedes: *Correctional Psychologist.*
Indexed: Curr. Cont. Soc. Beh. Sc.; Hum. Res. Abst.; PAIS; Psych. Abst.; Sage Urb. Stu. Abst.; Soc. Abst.

CRIMINOLOGICA
See CRIMINOLOGY

1328
CRIMINOLOGIE. v.8– , Jan. 1973– . Montréal, Les Presses de l'Université de Montréal. Semi-annual.
In English or French; summaries in the other language, or in German, Russian, Spanish.
Continues: *Acta Criminologica* (1968–74)
Indexed: PAISFL.

1329
CRIMINOLOGY. v.2– , 1970– . Beverly Hills, Calif., Sage Publications. Quarterly.
Continues: *Criminologica* (v.1, 1969)
Indexed: PAIS; Sage Urb. Stu. Abst.

1330
THE CRISIS; A RECORD OF THE DARK AGES. v.1– , 1910– . New York. Ten no. a year.
Organ of: National Association for the Advancement of Colored People.
Indexed: Bull. Anal. Pol. Ec. Soc.; His. Abst.

1331
CRISIS AND CHANGE. 1– , spring 1971– . Boston, Mass. Quarterly.
Issued by: Community Crisis Intervention Project, Laboratory of Community Psychiatry, Department of Psychiatry, Harvard Medical School.

1332
CRITERIO. 1– , 1928– . Buenos Aires. Biweekly.
In Spanish.
Indexed: Bull. Anal. Pol. Ec. Soc.

1333
CRITICA MARXISTA. v.1– , Jan./Feb. 1963–1973. Roma, Editori Riuniti. Bimonthly.
In Italian.
Indexed: Bull. Sig. Soc. Eth.; Int. Bibl. Pol. Sc.; Int. Bibl. Soc.; Int. Bibl. Soc. Cul. Anth.; Soc. Abst.

1334
LA CRITICA SOCIOLOGICA. 1– , spring 1967– . Roma. Quarterly.
Issued by: Istituto de Sociologia. In Italian; summaries in English.
Indexed: Bull. Sig. Soc. Eth.; Int. Bibl. Soc.; Int. Pol. Sc. Abst.; Soc. Abst.

1335
CRÍTICA & [i.e. Y] UTOPIA LATINOAMERICANA DE CIENCIAS SOCIALES. 1– , 1979– . Buenos Aires, El Cid Editor. Irreg.
In Spanish.
Indexed: PAISFL.

1336
CRITICAL INQUIRY. v.1– , Sept. 1974– . Chicago, Ill., The University of Chicago Press. Quarterly.
Indexed: Bull. Sig. Soc. Eth.; Soc. Abst.

1337
CRITICAL PERSPECTIVES ON CONTEMPORARY PSYCHOLOGY. v.1– , spring 1980– . New York. Semi-annual.
Issued by: Graduate Faculty, New School for Social Research.

1338
CRITIQUE OF ANTHROPOLOGY. v.[1]– , spring 1974– . London. Four no. a year, 1974–77; three no. a year.

1339
CRITIQUES DE L'ÉCONOMIE POLITIQUE. no.1– , Apr./June 1971– . Paris, F. Maspero. Quarterly.
In French.

CRITIQUES OF RESEARCH IN THE SOCIAL SCIENCES
See Social Science Research Council. BULLETIN

1340
CRITIQUES RÉGIONALES; CAHIERS DE SOCIOLOGIE ET D'ÉCONOMIE RÉGIONALES. 1– , 1979– . Bruxelles. Four no. a year.
Issued by: Institut de Sociologie, Université Libre de Bruxelles, in cooperation with the Comité pour l'Étude des Problèmes de l'Emploi et du Chômage. In French.

1341
CROISSANCE DES JEUNES NATIONS. no.1– , May 1961– . Paris. Monthly.
In French.
Indexed: Int. Bibl. Pol. Sc.; Int. Bibl. Soc. Cul. Anth.

1342
CROSSROADS; TRENDS AND ISSUES OF CONTEMPORARY SOCIETY. [no.1]– , autumn 1978– . Jerusalem. Quarterly.
Issued by: Israel Research Institute of Contemporary Society. First no. is not numbered.

THE CROWN COLONIST
See NEW COMMONWEALTH

CUADERNO
See Centro de Estudios Socio-económicos. CUADERNO

CUADERNOS
See Instituto Nacional de Antropología. CUADERNOS

CUADERNOS
See Universidad Nacional Autónoma de México. Centro de Estudios Mayas. CUADERNOS

CUADERNOS
See Universidad Nacional de Cuyo. Instituto de Estudios Políticos y Sociales. CUADERNOS

1343
CUADERNOS AMERICANOS. v.1– , Jan./Feb. 1942– . Mexico, D.F. Bimonthly.
In Spanish.
Indexed: ABC POL SCI; Bull. Anal. Pol. Ec. Soc.; Bull. Sig. Soc. Eth.; His. Abst.; Int. Bibl. Eco.; Int. Bibl. Pol. Sc.; Int. Bibl. Soc.; Int. Bibl. Soc. Cul. Anth.; Int. Pol. Sc. Abst.; Peace Res. Abst. J.; Soc. Abst.

1344
CUADERNOS DE ANTROPOLOGÍA SOCIAL Y ETNOLOGÍA. v.1– , Oct. 1970– . Madrid.
In Spanish.

1345
CUADERNOS DE CIENCIA POLÍTICA. no.1– , Aug. 1983– . Santiago, Chile.
Issued by: Instituto de Ciencia Política, Universidad de Chile. In Spanish.

CUADERNOS DE CIENCIA POLÍTICA
See POLÍTICA (Santiago, Chile)

1346
CUADERNOS DE CIENCIAS SOCIALES. no.1– , Jan. 1973– . Tegucigulpa.
Issued by: Departamento de Ciencias Sociales, Universidad Nacional Autónoma. In Spanish.

CUADERNOS DE CLAEH
See Centro Latinoamericano de Economía Humana. CUADERNOS DE CLAEH.

1347
CUADERNOS DE ECONOMÍA. 1– , Sept./Dec. 1963– . Santiago, Chile, Oficina de Publicaciones. Three no. a year.
Issued by: Instituto de Economía, Facultad de Ciencias Económicos y Sociales, Universidad de Chile. In Spanish.

1348
[No entry]

1349
CUADERNOS DE ECONOMÍA. v.1– , 1973– . Barcelona. Three no. a year.
Issued by: Centro de Estudios Económicos y Sociales of C.S.I.C. Some volumes issued with the cooperation of the Departamento di Teoría Económica, Universidad de Barcelona. In Spanish.
Continues: *Cuadernos de Información Económica*, 1966–69, which in turn continues: *Cuadernos de Información Económica y Sociológica*, 1955–64.
Indexed: Bull. Anal. Pol. Sc. Soc.; Int. Bibl. Eco.

1350
CUADERNOS DE ESTUDIOS COOPERATIVOS. 1– , 1958– . Madrid. Four no. a year.
Issued by: Instituto Sindical de Formación Cooperativa. In Spanish.

1351
CUADERNOS DE HISTORIA. v.1– , Sept. 1982– . Caracas, Ediciones de la Faculdad de Humanidades y Educación. Three no. a year.
Issued by: Escuela de Historia y Instituto de Estudios Latinoamericanos, Universidad Católica de Chile. In Spanish.

CUADERNOS DE HISTORIA MUNDIAL
See JOURNAL OF WORLD HISTORY

CUADERNOS DE INFORMACIÓN ECONÓMICA
See CUADERNOS DE ECONOMÍA (Barcelona)

CUADERNOS DE INFORMACIÓN ECONÓMICA Y SOCIOLÓGICA
See CUADERNOS DE ECONOMÍA (Barcelona)

CUADERNOS DE LOS INSTITUTOS
See Universidad Nacional de Córdoba. Faculdad de Derecho y Ciencias Sociales. CUADERNOS DE LOS INSTITUTOS

1352
CUADERNOS DE POLÍTICA EXTERIOR MEXICANA. CIDE. v.1– , 1984– . Mexico, D.F. Annual.
Issued by: Programa de Estudios de la Relaciones Exteriores de Mexico. In Spanish.

CUADERNOS DE POLÍTICA INTERNACIONAL
See REVISTA DE POLÍTICA INTERNACIONAL

CUADERNOS DE POLÍTICA SOCIAL
See REVISTA DE POLÍTICA SOCIAL

1353
CUADERNOS DE RUEDO IBÉRICO. no.1– , 19??– . Paris, Éditions Ruedo Ibérico. Bimonthly.

In Spanish; occasionally articles in French; summaries in English. Issues are thematic.
Indexed: Bull. Anal. Pol. Ec. Soc.; Int. Pol. Sc. Abst.

1354
CUADERNOS DE SOCIOGRAFÍA Y PLANEACIÓN. 1– , 1951– . Tucuman. Irreg.
Issued by: Instituto de Sociografía y Planeación, Universidad. In Spanish; summaries in English. Subseries of the Instituto's *Publicaciones*.

CUADERNOS DEL CELADE
See United Nations. Centro Latinoamericano de Demografía. CUADERNOS DEL CELADE/ CELADE MEMORANDA

CUADERNOS DEL CENtRO LATINOAMERICANO DE ECONOMÍA HUMANA
See Centro Latinoamericano de Economía Humana. CUADERNOS DEL CENTRO LATINOAMERICANO DE ECONOMÍA HUMANA

CUADERNOS DEL INSTITUTO ESPAÑOL DE ESTUDIOS MEDITERRÁNEOS
See Instituto Español de Estudios Mediterráneos. CUADERNOS

CUADERNOS DEL TERCER MUNDO
See THIRD WORLD (Mexico City)

CUADERNOS. SERIE DOCUMENTAL
See Universidad Nacional Autónoma de México. Instituto de Investigaciones Históricas. CUADERNOS. SERIE DOCUMENTAL

1355
CUBA SOCIALISTA. 1– , Sept. 1961– . La Habana. Monthly.
Issued by: Partido Unido de la Revolución Socialista Cubana. In Spanish.
Indexed: Peace Res. Abst. J.

CUBAN STUDIES
See ESTUDIOS CUBANOS

1356
CULTURAL ANTHROPOLOGY. v.1– , Feb. 1986– . Washington, D.C., American Anthropological Association. Quarterly.
Issued by: Society for Cultural Anthropology.

1357
CULTURAL HERMENEUTICS. 1–4, Apr. 1973–Dec. 1977. Dordrecht, D. Reidel Pub. Co. Quarterly.
Continued by: *Philosophy & Social Criticism*.
Indexed: Abst. Anth.

CULTURAS
See CULTURES [English Edition]

1358
CULTURE. v.1– , 1981– . Quebec, Autrement.
Issued by: Canadian Ethnology Society. In English or French. Papers in other languages are also accepted.
Indexed: Abst. Anth.; Bull. Sig. Soc. Eth.; Int. Bibl. Soc. Cul. Anth.

CULTURE
See BUNKA

CULTURE AND LANGUAGE
See KULTURI JA KIELI

1359
CULTURE AND LIFE. 1957– . Moscow. Monthly.
Issued by: Soi͡uz Sovetskikh Obshchestv Druzhby i Kul'turnoĭ Svi͡azi z Zarubezhnymi Stranami. English language version of: *Kul'tura i Zhizn'*. Published also in French. German and Spanish editions.

CULTURE AND SOCIETY
See BUNKA TO SHAKAI

1360
CULTURE AU ZAÏRE ET EN AFRIQUE. REVUE ZAÏROIS DES SCIENCES DE L'HOMME. no.1– , 1973– . Kinshasa. Four no. a year.
Issued by: Office National de la Recherche et du Développement. In French.

1361
CULTURE, MEDICINE AND PSYCHIATRY. v.1– , Apr. 1977– . Dordrecht, Boston, Mass., D. Reidel. Quarterly.
Indexed: Abst. Anth.; Bull. Sig. Soc. Eth.; Int. Bibl. Soc. Cul. Anth.; LLBA; Soc. Abst.; SSCI.

1362
CULTURES [English edition]. v.1–8, no.1, 1975–1982. Neuchâtel, Paris, The Unesco Press and La Baconiere. Quarterly.
Issued by: United Nations Educational, Scientific and Cultural Organization. Issues are thematic. Published also in French; *Cultures*, and in Spanish: *Culturas*, and special versions in Arabic and Russian.
Continued by: *Cultures: Dialogue between the Peoples of the World*.

Indexed: Bull. Sig. Soc. Eth.

1363
CULTURES: DIALOGUE BETWEEN THE PEOPLES OF THE WORLD. v.8, no.3/4– , 1982– . Neuchâtel, The Unesco Press. Quarterly.
Continues: *Cultures.*

1364
CULTURES ET DÉVELOPPEMENT. 1– , 1968– . Louvain. Quarterly.
Issued by: Institut d'Études des Pays en Développement, Université Catholique de Louvain. In French or English.
Supersedes: *Zaïre; Revue Congolaise.*
Indexed: ABC POL SCI; Bull. Anal. Pol. Ec. Soc.; Int. Bibl. Eco.; Int. Bibl. Pol. Sc.; Int. Bibl. Soc.; Int. Pol. Sc. Abst.

CUMULATIVE DIGESTS OF INTERNATIONAL LAW AND RELATIONS
See INTERNATIONAL LAW AND RELATIONS

1365
CURRENT. no.1– , May 1960– . New York. Monthly.
Indexed: ABC POL SCI; Bull. Anal. Pol. Ec. Soc.; Ind. Per. Art. Law; Peace Res. Abst. J.

1366
CURRENT ANTHROPOLOGY. v.1– , Jan. 1960– . Chicago, Ill. Five no a year.
Sponsored by: Wenner–Gren Foundation for Anthropological Research. Includes periodically revised editions of: "International Directory of Anthropological Institutions" and "International Directory of Anthropologists".
Indexed: Abst. Soc. Work; APAIS; Bull. Anal. Pol. Ec. Soc.; Bull. Sig. Soc. Eth.; Int. Bibl. Pol. Sc.; Int. Pol. Sc. Abst.; Peace Res. Abst. J.; Psych. Abst.; Soc. Sc. Hum. Ind.; SSCI; Wom. Stu. Abst.

1367
CURRENT ARCHAEOLOGY. v.1– , Mar. 1967– . London, A. & W. Silkirk. Bimonthly.

1368
A CURRENT BIBLIOGRAPHY OF AFRICAN AFFAIRS. v.1–6, Apr. 1962–1967; n. ser. v.1– , 1968– . Washington, D.C., later Westport, Conn., Greenwood Periodicals, Inc., and Farmingdale, N.Y., Baywood Pub. Co. Monthly.
Issued by: African Bibliographic Center.

1369
CURRENT CONTENTS OF ACADEMIC JOURNALS IN JAPAN. THE HUMANITIES AND SOCIAL SCIENCES. 1974/75– . Tokyo. Annual.
Issued by: Kokusai Bunka Shinkokai.
Continues: *Current Content of Academic Journals in Japan* (1970–76)

1370
CURRENT CONTENTS; SOCIAL AND BEHAVIORAL SCIENCES. v.6, no.2– , Jan. 2, 1974– . Philadelphia, Pa. Weekly.
Issued by: Institute for Scientific Information.
Continues: *Current Contents: Behavioral, Social and Educational Sciences* (v.1–6, no.1, 1962–73)

1371
CURRENT DEVELOPMENTS IN ANTHROPOLOGICAL GENETICS. v.1– , 1980– . New York, Plenum Press.
Each no. has also a distinctive title.

1372
CURRENT ECONOMIC AND INDUSTRIAL RELATIONS INDICATORS. Mar. 1977– . Kingston. Semi-annual.
Issued by: Industrial Relations Centre, Queen's University.

1373
CURRENT HISTORY. v.1– , 1914– . Philadelphia, Pa. Monthly (combined issued May–June)
Absorbed: *Forum*, in 1950.
Indexed: ABC POL SCI; APAIS; Curr. Cont. Soc. Beh. Sc.; His. Abst.; Ind. Per. Art. Law; Int. Bibl. Eco.; Int. Bibl. Pol. Sc.; Int. Bibl. Soc.; Int. Bibl. Soc. Cul. Anth.; Peace Res. Abst. J.; Soc. Abst.; SSCI.

1374
CURRENT ISSUES IN CURRENT EDUCATION. 1– , 1979– . Washington, D.C. Bimonthly (irreg.)
Issued by: American Association for Higher Education.
Supersedes: *Current Issues in Higher Education.*

1375
CURRENT MUNICIPAL PROBLEMS. v.1– , Aug. 1959– . Wilmette, Ill., Callaghan. Quarterly.
Indexed: SSCI.

1376
CURRENT OPINION. v.1–6, no.1, 1973–1978. Williamstown, Mass.
Issued by: Roper Public Opinion Research, Williams College.
Superseded by: *Public Opinion.*

CURRENT POPULATION REPORTS. SERIES P–20. POPULATION CHARACTERISTICS
See United States. Bureau of the Census. Population Division. CURRENT POPULATION REPORTS. P–20. POPULATION CHARACTERISTICS

CURRENT POPULATION REPORTS. SERIES P–26. FEDERAL STATE COOPERATIVE PROGRAM FOR POPULATION ESTIMATES
See United States. Bureau of the Census. Population Division. CURRENT POPULATION REPORTS. SERIES P–26. FEDERAL STATE COOPERATIVE PROGRAM FOR POPULATION ESTIMATES

1377
CURRENT PSYCHOLOGICAL RESEARCH & REVIEWS. v.3– , spring 1984– . New Brunswick, N.J., Transaction Periodicals Consortium. Quarterly.
Formed by the union of: *Current Psychological Research* (v.1–2, 1981–82) and *Current Psychological Reviews* (v.1–2, 1981–82).
Indexed: Curr. Cont. Soc. Beh. Sc.; Psych. Abst.; Soc. Sc. Ind.; SSCI.

1378
CURRENT RESEARCH IN BEHAVIORAL SCIENCES IN ISRAEL. 1977– . Jerusalem. Quarterly.
Issued by: Henrietta Szold Institute. In Hebrew. Tables of contents and index in English.

1379
CURRENT RESEARCH IN BRITAIN. SOCIAL SCIENCES. 1st ed.– , 1985– . Boston Spa. Annual.
Issued by: Lending Division, British Library.

CURRENT RESEARCH IN SOCIAL SCIENCES IN UNIVERSITIES AND COLLEGES
See Indian Council of Social Science Research. CURRENT RESEARCH IN SOCIAL SCIENCES IN UNIVERSITIES AND COLLEGES

1380
CURRENT RESEARCH ON PEACE AND VIOLENCE. v.1– , 1978– . Tampere. Quarterly.
Issued by: Tampere Peace Research Institute.
Supersedes: *Instant Research on Peace and Violence.*
Indexed: Bull. Anal. Pol. Ec. Soc.; Int. Bibl. Pol. Sc.; Int. Pol. Sc. Abst.

CURRENT SCHOOL ENROLLMENT STATISTICS
See United Nations Educational, Scientific and Cultural Organization. CURRENT SCHOOL ENROLLMENT STATISTICS

A CURRENT SELECTED BIBLIOGRAPHY
See SOCIAL SCIENCES IN FORESTRY: A CURRENT SELECTED BIBLIOGRAPHY

1381
CURRENT SOCIOLOGY. LA SOCIOLOGIE CONTEMPORAINE. v.1– , 1952– . Beverly Hills, Calif., Sage Publications. Four no. a year.
Issued by: International Sociological Association. Included as supplement first four volumes of the *International Bibliography of Sociology*. Supplements accompany some numbers (1974–)
Indexed: Bull. Anal. Pol. Ec. Soc.; Int. Bibl. Soc.; Int. Pol. Sc. Abst.; PAIS; Psych. Abst.; Pop. Ind.; Soc. Abst.; SSCI; Urb. Aff. Abst.

CURRENT TRENDS AND POLICIES IN THE WORLD ECONOMY
See WORLD ECONOMIC SURVEY

CYLCHGRAWN HANES CYMRU
See WELSH HISTORY REVIEW

1382
CZECHOSLOVAK ECONOMIC PAPERS. no.1– , 1959– . Prague. Irreg. 1959–62; semi-annual.
Issued by: Ekonomický Ústav, Československa Akademia Věd. In Czech.

D–C DESARROLLO Y COOPERACIÓN
See ENTWICKLUNG UND ZUSAMMENARBEIT

D–C DÉVELOPPEMENT ET COOPÉRATION
See ENTWICKLUNG UND ZUSAMMENARBEIT

DWI–FORSCHUNGSHEFTE
See Institut für Internationale Politik und Wirtschaft. IPW–FORSCHUNGSHEFTE

1383
DADOS. no.1– , 1966– . Rio de Janeiro, Editora Campus. Semi-annual.
Issued by: Instituto Universitario de Pesquisas do Rio de Janeiro. In Portuguese; summaries in English and French.
Indexes: 1966–72, 1v.
Indexed: Bull. Anal. Pol. Ec. Soc.; Int. Bibl. Pol. Sc.; Int. Bibl. Soc. Cul. Anth.; Int. Lab. Doc.; Int. Pol. Sc. Abst.

1384
DAEDALUS. v.1– , May 1846– . Brookline, Mass. Quarterly.
Issued by: Academy of Arts and Sciences. Vols. 9–31 numbered also as n. ser. v.1–23. Title varies: v.1–85, 1846–1958, *Proceedings of the Academy of Arts and Sciences*.
Indexed: ABC POL SCI; Abst. Anth.; Abst. Soc. Work; Bull. Anal. Pol. Ec. Soc.; Bull. Sig. Soc. Eth.; His. Abst.; Hum. Res. Abst.; Int. Bibl. Eco.; Int. Bibl. Soc.; Int. Bibl. Soc. Cul. Anth.; Int. Pol. Sc. Abst.; LLBA; PAIS; PHRA; Peace Res. Abst. J.; Soc. Sc. Hum. Ind.; Soc. Work Res. Abst.; Wom. Stu. Abst.

Dag Hammarskjöld Library
See United Nations. Dag Hammarskjöld Library

A DANISH SOCIOLOGICAL JOURNAL
See SOCIOLOGISKE MEDDELELSER

DARBAI. SERIJA A
See Lietuvos TSR Mokslu Akademija. DARBAI. TRUDY. SERIJA A. VISUOMENĖS MOKSLAI. SOCIAL SCIENCES

1385
DARSTELLUNGEN ZUR INTERNATIONALEN POLITIK UND ENTWICKLUNGSPOLITIK. v.1– , 1980– . Frankfurt am Main, Metzner.
Issued by: Institut für Internationale Gelegenheiten, Universität Hamburg. In German.

1386
DATA RESOURCES REVIEW. v.1–6, 1972–1977. Lexington, Mas s., Data Resources. Quarterly.
Continued by: *Data Resources Review of the U.S. Economy*.

1387
DATA RESOURCES REVIEW OF THE U.S. ECONOMY. v.7– , 1978– . Lexington, Mass., Data Resources. Monthly.
Supplement called "Notes and Technical Appendix" accompany each number.
Continues: *Data Resources Review*.

1388
DE ECONOMÍA. v.1– , Oct./Nov. 1948– . Madrid. Frequency varied; quarterly.
Issued by: Vicesecretaría de Ordenación Económica of the Falange Española Traditionalista y de las Justas Ofensivas Nacional Sindicales. Delegación Nacional Sindicales. In Spanish. Includes supplements.
Indexes: Vols. 1–6(no.1–25/26), 1948–53.

1389
LE DÉBAT. no.1– , May 1980– . Paris, Gallimard. Eleven no. a year.
In French.
Indexed: Int. Bibl. Pol. Sc.; PAIS; PAISFL.

1390
DEBATES. v.1– , Feb. 1977– . Lima.
Issued by: Departamento de Ciencias Sociales, Pontificia Universidad Católica del Perú. In Spanish.

DEBATES OF THE EUROPEAN PARLIAMENT
See OFFICIAL JOURNAL OF THE EUROPEAN COMMUNITIES; DEBATES OF THE EUROPEAN PARLIAMENT

1391
DEBATES SOCIAIS. v.1– , 1965– . Rio de Janeiro. Two no. a year.
Organ of: Comitê Brasileiro del Conferência Internacional do Serviço Social; later, Centro Brasileiro do Cooperação e Intercambio de Serviços Sociais, Comitê Nacional no Brasil Representativo do International Council of Social Welfare. In Portuguese.

DÉBATS; COMPTE-RENDU IN EXTENSO DES SÉANCES
See European Parliament. DÉBATS; COMPTE-RENDU IN EXTENSO DES SÉANCES

DECISIONS TAKEN AT THE MEETINGS
See Organization of American States. Council. DECISIONS TAKEN AT THE MEETINGS

DECOLONIZATIONS
See United Nations. Department of Political Affairs, Trusteeship and Decolonization. DECOLONIZATION

1392
DÉFENSE DE L'OCCIDENT. n. ser. 1– , Dec. 1962– . Paris. Monthly.
In French. Each number has a distinctive title.
Indexed: Bull. Anal. Pol. Ec. Soc.; Int. Bibl. Soc. Cul. Anth.; Peace Res. Abst. J.

DELINQUENCY AND SOCIETY
See 'AVARYYANUTH VE-ḤEVRAH

1393
DEMOCRAZIA E DIRITTO. v.1– , Jan./Mar. 1960– . Roma. Quarterly.
In Italian.
Indexed: Ind. For. Leg. Per.; Int. Pol. Sc. Abst.; PAISFL.

1394
DEMOCRAZIA NAZIONALE. v.1– , Apr. 17, 1977– . Roma, Cosliniente di Destra. Weekly.
In Italian.
Indexed: PAISFL.

1395
DEMOGRAFIA. v.1– , 1958– . Budapest. Quarterly.
Issued by: Központi Sztatistikai Hivatal, 1958–60; Geografiai Elnöksegi Bizottság, Magyar Tudományos Akadémia, and Központi Sztatistikai Hivatal. In Hungarian; summaries in English and Russian. Tables of contents in English and Russian.
Indexed: Bull. Sig. Soc. Eth.; His. Abst.; Int. Bibl. Soc. Cul. Anth.; LLBA; Pop. Ind.; SSCI.

1396
DEMOGRAFÍA Y ECONOMÍA. 1– , 1967– . Mexico, D.F. Three no. a year, 1967–78; quarterly.
Issued by: Colegio del México. In Spanish.
Indexed: Bull. Anal. Pol. Ec. Soc.; Int. Lab. Doc.; Pop. Ind.

1397
LE DÉMOGRAPHE. no.1– , Apr. 1955– . Grivegné, Belgium. Semi-annual, 1955–57; annual.
Issued by: International Union for the Scientific Study of Population. Chiefly in English or French; some articles in Spanish.

1398
DEMOGRAPHIC INDICATORS OF COUNTRIES, ESTIMATES AND PROJECTIONS AS ASSESSED IN 1980– . New York, United Nations [publ. 1982]. Annual.
Issued by: Department of International Economics and Social Affairs, United Nations. (ST/ESA/Ser.A)

1398a
DEMOGRAPHIC YEARBOOK. ANNUAIRE DÉMOGRAPHIQUE. [1]– , 1948– . New York.
Issued by: Statistical Office, United Nations. Accompanied by the supplement called "Special Issue—Historical Supplement". (ST/ESA/STAT/SER R)

DEMOGRAPHIE
See ZEITSCHRIFT FÜR BEVÖLKERUNGSWISSENSCHAFT. DEMOGRAPHIE

1399
DÉMOGRAPHIE AFRICAINE. no.1–28, 1971–Sept./Dec. 1978. Yaoundé. Three no. a year.
Issued by: Institut de Formation et de Recherche Démographiques. Some nos. by: Groupe de Démographie Africaine IDP–INED–INSEE–MICOOP–ORSTOM. In English or French.
Title varies: *La Démographie en Afrique d'Expression Française.*
Continued by: *Bulletin de Liaison de Démographie Africaine* (no.29– , March/Apr. 1979–). Photoduplicated.

DÉMOGRAPHIE ET EMPLOI
See France. Institut National de la Statistique et des Études Économiques. DÉMOGRAPHIE ET EMPLOI

1400
DÉMOGRAPHIE ET SOCIÉTÉS. 1–16, 1960–1972. Paris. Irreg.
Issued by: Centre de Recherches Historiques, École Pratique des Hautes Études. In French.

DÉMOGRAPHIE HISTORIQUE
See HISTORICKÁ DEMOGRAFIE

1401
DEMOGRAPHISCHES JAHRBUCH ÖSTERREICHS. 1975– . Wien. Annual.
Issued by: Österreichisches Statistisches Zentralamt. In German.
Continues: *Natürliche Bevölkerungsbewegung* (1956–74)

1402
DEMOGRAPHY. v.1– , 1964– . Chicago, Ill., later Washington, D.C. Annual.
Issued by: Population Association of America. Summaries in Spanish.
Indexes: Vols. 1–10, 1964–73.
Indexed: Int. Bibl. Soc.; PAIS; Pop. Ind.; SSCI; Wom. Stu. Abst.

1403
DEMOGRAPHY INDIA. v.1– , 1972– . Delhi. Quarterly.
Issued by: Indian Association for the Study of Population.

1404
DEN'GI I KREDIT. 1– , 1942– . Moskva, Izd-vo Finansy. Monthly.
Issued by: Gosudarstvennyĭ Bank S.S.S.R. In Russian.
Indexed: Bull. Anal. Pol. Ec. Soc.

1405
DENVER JOURNAL OF INTERNATIONAL LAW AND POLICY. 1– , fall 1971– . Denver, Colo. Semi-annual.
Issued by: College of Law, University of Denver.
Indexed: Ind. Leg. Per.; Int. Pol. Sc. Abst.; PAIS.

1406
DESARROLLO. 1– , 1965– . Mexico, D.F. Bimonthly.
Issued by: Instituto Mexicano de Estudios Sociales. In Spanish.

DESARROLLO
See DEVELOPMENT (Washington, D.C.)

DESARROLLO
See INTERNATIONAL DEVELOPMENT REVIEW

1407
DESARROLLO ECONÓMICO. 1– , 1958– . Buenos Aires. Quarterly (some combined numbers)—two volumes a year.
Issued by: Instituto de Desarrollo Económico e Social. In Spanish.
Title varies: 1958–60, *Revista de Desarrollo Económico.*
Indexed: Int. Bibl. Eco.; Int. Lab. Doc.; PAISFL.

1408
DESARROLLO INDOAMERICANO. 1– , 1966– . Barranquilla. Six no. a year, 1966–81; four no. a year.
In Spanish.
Indexed: Bull. Anal. Pol. Ec. Soc.; Int. Bibl. Eco.; PAISFL.

1409
DESARROLLO RURAL EN LAS AMÉRICAS. v.1– , 1969– . Bogotá. Three no. a year.
Issued by: Instituto Interamericano de Ciencias Agrícolas, Centro Interamericano de Desarrollo Rural y Reforma Agraria. In Spanish; summaries in English, Portuguese, or Spanish.
Indexed: Int. Bibl. Eco.; Soc. Abst.

1410
DESARROLLO Y SOCIEDAD. no.1– , Jan. 1979– . Bogotá. Three no. a year.
Issued by: Centro de Estudios sobre Desarrollo Económico, Facuidad de Economía, Universidad de los Andes. In Spanish.
Indexed: PAISFL.

Deutsche Akademie der Wissenschaften
See Akademie der Wissenschaften der DDR

1411
DEUTSCHE AUSSENPOLITIK. 1– , 1966– . Berlin, Deutsche Verlag der Wissenschaften. Monthly.
Issued by: Institut für Internationale Beziehungen. In German.
Indexed: Bull. Anal. Pol. Ec. Soc.; His. Abst.; Int. Pol. Sc. Abst.; Peace Res. Abst. J.

1412
DEUTSCHE FINANZWIRTSCHAFT. v.1– , Apr. 1947– . Berlin, Deutsche Zentralverlag. Monthly.
In German. Includes: Apr. 1947–Mar. 1948, Publikationstell der Deutschen Zentralfinanzverwaltung in der Sowjetischen Besatzungszone.

1413
Deutsche Gesellschaft für Anthropologie, Ethnologie und Urgeschichte. CORRESPONDENZ-BLATT. v.1–51, 1870–1920. Braunschweig. Monthly.
In German.

1414
DER DEUTSCHE ÖKONOMIST. v.1–35, no.39(no.1–2587), 1883–Sept. 27, 1935. Berlin, Heymans Verlag. Monthly, Oct. 1922–25; semimonthly, 1926; weekly, 1883–Sept. 1922, 1927–35.
Issued by: Reichsverbad des Deutschen Ein- und Ausfuhrhandels, June 1922–Jan. 1929. In German. Supplements accompany some numbers, 1927–30. Merged into: *Deutsche Volkswirt.*

1415
DEUTSCHE STUDIEN. 1– , 1965– . Bremen, Karl Schumann. Quarterly.
Supersedes: *Ostbriefs.*
Indexed: Bull. Anal. Pol. Ec. Soc.; Peace Res. Abst. J.

1416
DEUTSCHE VERWALTUNG. v.1–22, no.2, 1924–Feb. 15, 1945. Berlin.
Issued by: Nationalsozialistischer Rechtswahrerbund. In German. Absorbed: *Deutsche Verwaltungsblätter.*

1417
DEUTSCHE VERWALTUNGSBLÄTTER: BLÄTTER FÜR ADMINISTRATIVE PRAXIS. 1851–1938. München, C.H. Beck. Frequency varies.
In German. Title varies: 1851–1922, *Blätter für Administrative Praxis*; 1923–33, *Bayerische Verwaltungsblätter: Blätter für Administrative Praxis*. Absorbed by: *Deutsche Verwaltung*.
Indexes: Vols. 1–10, 1851–60, 1v.; v.11–20, 1861–70; v.21–30, 1871–80; v.1–40, 1851–90.

1418
DEUTSCHES ARCHIV FÜR ERFORSCHUNG DES MITTELALTERS. v.1– , 1937– . Cologne, Böhlau Verlag. Two no. a year.
In German.

1419
DEUTSCHES JAHRBUCH FÜR VOLKSKUNDE UND KULTURGESCHICHTE. v.1–12, 1955–1966; n. ser. v.1– , 1967– . Berlin, Akademie Verlag. Two no. a year, 1967–78; annual.
Issued by: Institut für Deutsche Volkskunde, Akademie der Wissenschaften der DDR. In German. Some numbers are combined. Title varies: 1955–69, *Deutsches Jahrbuch für Volkskunde*. Not published, 1970–72. V.16, 1973, called also n.s. v.1.
Indexed: His. Abst.; Int. Bibl. Soc. Cul. Anth.

DEVELOPING COUNTRIES, ECONOMICS AND POLITICS
See RAZVIVAI͡USHCHIESI͡A STRANY; EKONOMIA I POLITIKA

1420
THE DEVELOPING ECONOMIES. 1– , Jan. 1963– . Tokyo. Semi-annual, 1963–66; quarterly.
Issued by: Ajia Keizai Kenkyū-sho. V.1, no.1 preceded by Preliminary issue.
Indexes: Vols. 1–10, 1963–72, 1v.
Indexed: Bull. Anal. Pol. Ec. Soc.

1421
DEVELOPMENT. DÉVELOPPEMENT. DESARROLLO. v.20–22, 1978–1980/84. Washington, D.C. Four no. a year.
Issued by: Society for International Development. In English, French, or Spanish. Other titles: *International Development Review*; *Revue du Développement*; *Revista del Desarrollo Internacional*. Absorbed: *Focus*, *Technical Cooperation*.
Continues: *Revista del Desarrollo Internacional*. Continued by: *Development; Seeds of Change. Village through Global Order*.
Indexed: ABC POL SCI; Int. Pol. Sc. Abst.

1422
DEVELOPMENT AND CHANGE. v.1– , 1969– . The Hague, Mouton, later Beverly Hills, Calif., Sage Publications. Quarterly, 1969–74; three no. a year.
Issued by: Institute of Social Studies, The Hague.
Indexed: ABC POL SCI; Bull. Anal. Pol. Ec. Soc.; His. Abst.; Int. Bibl. Eco.; Int. Bibl. Pol. Sc.; Int. Bibl. Soc.; Int. Lab. Doc.; Int. Pol. Sc. Abst.; SSCI.

1423
DEVELOPMENT AND PEACE. v.1– , spring 1980– . Budapest. Semi-annual.
Issued by: Hungarian Peace Council and World Peace Council.
Indexed: Int. Bibl. Eco.; Int. Pol. Sc.; Int. Bibl. Soc.; Int. Bibl. Soc. Cul. Anth.

1424
DEVELOPMENT DIALOG. no.1– , Nov. 1972– . New York. Semi-annual.
Issued by: Dag Hammarskjöld Foundation with the support of the Swedish International Development Authority.
Indexed: Bull. Anal. Pol. Ec. Soc.

1425
DEVELOPMENT DIGEST. v.1– , July 1962– . Washington, D.C. Quarterly.
Published by: Agency for International Development, U.S. Department of State; prepared by: National Planning Association. Publication suspended: Oct. 1964–Apr. 1965. Title varies: July 1962, *Development Research Review*; Oct. 1962–July 1964, *Development Research Digest*.

DEVELOPMENT FINANCING
See Organization of American States. Public Sector Program. DEVELOPMENT FINANCING

1426
DEVELOPMENT INFORMATION ABSTRACTS. no.1– , Jan. 1981– . New York. Five no. a year, 1981; bimonthly.
Issued by: Information Systems Unit, Department of International Economic and Social Affairs, United Nations. In English, French, or Spanish. Issues for Jan. 1981–Dec. 1982, called nos. 1–11, constitute v.1–2. Other titles: *Bulletin Analytique sur le Développement*; *Resumenes de Información sobre el Desarrollo*.

1427
DEVELOPMENT ISSUE PAPER FOR THE 1980s. no.1– , 1980– . New York. Irreg.
Issued by: United Nations Development Program. Each no. has also a distinctive title.

1428
DEVELOPMENT PAPERS. no.1– , 1981– . Bangkok. Irreg.
Issued by: Economic and Social Commission for Asia and the Pacific, United Nations.

1429
DEVELOPMENT POLICY AND ADMINISTRATION REVIEW. v.1– , Jan./June 1975– . Jaipur. Semi-annual.
Issued by: State Institute of Public Administration.
Indexed: Bull. Anal. Pol. Ec. Soc.; Int. Pol. Sc. Abst.; Sage Pub. Adm. Abst.

DEVELOPMENT RESEARCH DIGEST
See DEVELOPMENT DIGEST

DEVELOPMENT RESEARCH REVIEW
See DEVELOPMENT DIGEST

DEVELOPMENT STUDIES. OCCASIONAL PAPER
See OCCASIONAL PAPER. DEVELOPMENT STUDIES

DEVELOPMENT STUDIES. REGISTER OF RESEARCH IN THE UNITED KINGDOM
See Institute of Development Studies. REGISTER OF RESEARCH IN THE UNITED KINGDOM

1430
DEVELOPMENT STUDIES SERIES. v.1– , 1982– . Dublin, Tycooly International for UN CHS. Irreg.
Issued by: United Nations Centre for Human Settlements. Each no. has also a distinctive title.

DÉVELOPPEMENT
See DEVELOPMENT

DÉVELOPPEMENT
See INTERNATIONAL DEVELOPMENT REVIEW

1431
DÉVELOPPEMENT ET CIVILISATIONS. no.1– , Mar. 1960– . Paris. Quarterly.
Issued by: Institut International de Formation et de Recherche en vue du Développement Harmonisé (called in 1960 Centre International de Formation et de Recherche en vue du Développement Harmonisé). Mainly in French; occasionally in English or Spanish. Supplements accompany some issues.
Indexed: Bull. Sig. Soc. Eth.; Int. Bibl. Soc.; Int. Bibl. Soc. Cul. Anth.; Int. Lab. Doc.

DÉVELOPPEMENT SOCIAL
See SOCIAL DEVELOPMENT. English Edition.

1432
DÉVIANCE ET SOCIÉTÉ. 1977– . Genève, Éditions Médecine et Hygiène. Quarterly.
Issued by: Faculté de Droit, Université de Genève. In French.
Indexed: Bull. Anal. Pol. Ec. Soc.

1433
DEVIANT BEHAVIOR. v.1– , Oct./Dec. 1979– . Washington, D.C., Hemisphere Pub. Co. Quarterly.
Title on cover: An Interdisciplinary Journal on Human Behavior.
Indexed: Psych. Abst.; Soc. Abst.; SSCI.

1434
DIALECTICAL ANTHROPOLOGY. v.1– , 1975– . Amsterdam, Elsevier. Quarterly.
Issued by: New School for Social Research. Includes some special issues.
Indexed: Abst. Anth.; Bull. Sig. Soc. Eth.; Int. Bibl. Soc. Cul. Anth.; Soc. Abst.; SSCI.

1435
DIALEKTICHESKIĬ MATERIALISM. no.1– , 1976– . Moskva. Annual.
Issued by: Institut Nauchnoĭ Informat͡sii po Obshchestvennym Naukam, Akademii͡a Nauk S.S.S.R. In Russian. No.1 covers 1917–25, no.10 –1980. Processed.

1436
DIDAKOMETRY AND SOCIOMETRY. 1– , 1969– . Malmö.
Issued by: Department of Education and Sociological Research, School of Education.

1437
DIFESA SOCIALE. v.1– , 1922– . Roma. Quarterly.
Issued by: Istituto Italiano di Medicina Sociale. In Italian; summaries in English, French, German, Italian, or Spanish.
Indexed: Int. Bibl. Soc. Cul. Anth.; Psych. Abst.

DIFFUSION OF INNOVATIONS IN RURAL SOCIETIES. REPORT
See DIFFUSION OF INNOVATIONS: RESEARCH REPORTS

1438
DIFFUSION OF INNOVATIONS: RESEARCH REPORT. no.1– , 1964– . East Lansing, Mich.
Issued by: College of Communication Arts, Michigan State University. Includes: *Diffusion of Innovations in Rural Societies*.

1439
DINÁMICA ECONÓMICA. v.1– , Oct./Dec. 1958– . La Paz. Bimonthly.
Issued by: Faculdad de Ciencias Económicas, Universidad Mayor de San Andres. In Spanish.

1440
DIOGENES. no.1– , winter 1953– . London. Quarterly.

Issued by: International Council of Philosophy and Humanistic Studies. Issued also in Arabic, French and Spanish editions. Under the auspices of the International Council of Philosophical and Humanities Studies.
Indexed: Abst. Anth.; Bull. Sig. Soc. Eth.; Bull. Anal. Pol. Ec. Soc.; Int. Pol. Sc. Abst.; PAIS; Peace Res. Abst. J.

1441
DIPLOMATIC HISTORY. v.1– , winter 1977– . Wilmington, Del., Scholarly Resources. Quarterly.
Issued by: Society for Historians of American Foreign Relations.

1442
DIRĀSĀT ĀRABĪYAH. ARAB STUDIES. 1– , Nov. 1964– . Beirut, Dar al-Tali'ot. Monthly.
In Arabic. Issued by: Miṣr al-Mus'āṣirah.

DIRĀSĀT KANU
See KANO STUDIES

DIRECTION OF INTERNATIONAL TRADE
See United Nations. Statistical Office. DIRECTION OF INTERNATIONAL TRADE

1443
DIRECTION OF TRADE STATISTICS. YEARBOOK. 1981– . Washington, D.C. Annual.
Issued by: International Monetary Fund. Supplement to: *Direction of Trade Statistics*.
Continues: *Direction of Trade Yearbook*.

1444
DIRECTION OF TRADE YEARBOOK. 1972/73–1973/79. Washington, D.C. Irreg.
Issued by: Statistics Bureau, International Monetary Fund, and International Bank for Reconstruction and Development (–1970/74)
Continues: International Monetary Fund. Statistics Bureau. *Direction of Trade*. Continued by: *Direction of Trade Statistics. Yearbook*.

1445
DIRECTORY OF PAKISTAN'S PERIODICALS IN SOCIAL SCIENCES. 1964– . Karachi. Irreg.
Issued by: Documentation and Information Bureau.

1446
DIRECTORY OF PUBLISHED PROCEEDINGS. SERIES SSH: SOCIAL SCIENCES/HUMANITIES. 1/4– , 1968/71– . Harrison, N.Y., Inter-Dok Corporation. Quarterly.
Supersedes, in part: *Directory of Published Proceedings*.

1447
DIRECTORY OF SOCIAL SCIENCE RESEARCH INSTITUTIONS IN INDIA. 1971– . New Delhi. Irreg.
Issued by: Indian Council of Social Science Research. (Subseries of the Council's *Research Information Series*)

1448
DIRECTORY OF THE THIRD WORLD STUDIES. 1981– . Waltham, Mass., Crossroads Press.
Issued by: African Studies Association.
Continues: *Directory of African & Afro-American Studies in the United States*.

1449
DIRITTO INTERNAZIONALE. 1– , 1937– . Milano. Quarterly.
Issued by: Istituto per gli Studi di Diritto Internazionale. In Italian. Title varies: 1937–41, 1948–59, *Annali di Diritto Internazionale*.
Indexed: Int. Bibl. Pol. Sc.

1450
DIS POLITIKA. FOREIGN POLICY. no.1– , Mar. 1971– . Ankara. Quarterly.
In English or Turkish.

1451
DISARMAMENT. v.1– , May 1978– . New York. Three no. a year.
Issued by: Centre for Disarmament, United Nations. Published also in French and Spanish.
Indexed: PAIS.

DISCUSSION PAPERS
See Policy Studies Institute, London. DISCUSSION PAPER

1452
DISCUSSION PAPERS IN INTERNATIONAL ECONOMICS AND FINANCE. 1– , Jan. 1982– . Rome. Irreg.
Issued by: Research Department, Banca d'Italia.

DISCUSSION PAPERS IN SOCIAL RESEARCH
See University of Glasgow. DISCUSSION PAPERS IN SOCIAL RESEARCH

DISPOSITION OF AGENDA ITEMS
See United Nations. Dag Hammarskjöld Library. INDEX TO PROCEEDINGS OF GENERAL ASSEMBLY

1453
DISSENT. 1– , winter 1954– . New York, Dissent Pub. Co. Quarterly.
Subtitle reads: "A quarterly of Socialist opinion".
Indexed: ABC POL SCI; Abst. Soc. Work; APAIS; His. Abst.; Hum. Res. Abst.; Ind. Per. Art. Law; Int. Bibl. Eco.; Int. Bibl. Pol. Sc.; Bull. Anal. Pol. Ec. Soc.; Bull. Sig. Soc. Eth.; Int. Bibl. Soc.; Int. Bibl. Soc. Cul. Anth.; Int. Pol. Sc. Abst.; PAIS; Peace Res. Abst. J.; PHRA; Soc. Sc. Ind.; Wom. Stu. Abst.

1454
DISSERTATION ABSTRACTS. A, THE HUMANITIES AND SOCIAL SCIENCES. v.27–29, July 1966–June 1969. Ann Arbor, Mich., University Microfilms. Monthly.
Continues, in part: *Dissertation Abstracts* (v.12–26, 1952–66). Continued by: *Dissertation Abstracts International. A. The Humanities and Social Sciences* (v.30–, July 1969–)

1455
THE DITCHLEY JOURNAL. v.1– , autumn 1974– . Enstone. Semi-annual.
Issued by: Ditchley Foundation.
Indexes: Vols. 1–18, in v.8, no.1.
Indexed: Bull. Anal. Pol. Ec. Soc.; Int. Bibl. Eco.; Int. Bibl. Pol. Sc.; Int. Pol. Sc. Abst.; PAIS.

1456
DOCPAL LATIN AMERICAN POPULATION ABSTRACTS. v.1– , June 1977– . Santiago, Chile.
Other title: *Docpal Resumenes sobre Población en América Latina*. (United Nations/Document/E/CEPAL/CELADE)

DOCPAL RESUMENES SOBRE POBLACIÓN EN AMÉRICA LATINA
See RESUMENES SOBRE POBLACIÓN EN AMÉRICA LATINA

DOCPAL RESUMENES SOBRE POBLACIÓN EN AMÉRICA LATINA
See DOCPAL LATIN AMERICAN POPULATION ABSTRACTS

DOCUMENTACIÓN LATINOAMERICANA
See DOKUMENTATIONSDIENST LATEINAMERICA

1457
DOCUMENTATION ÉCONOMIQUE; BIBLIOGRAPHIE TRIMESTRIELLE. [v.1]–5, (no.1–191), May 1934–Nov. 1938; v.6– , 1947– . Paris, Librairie Économique et Technique. Bimonthly, 1934–38, 1947–50; quarterly.
Issued by: Institut de la Statistique et des Études Économiques, and Association de Documentation Économique et Sociale. In French.

DOCUMENTATION ÉCONOMIQUE ET SOCIALE; RÉSUMÉS ANALYTIQUES
See ECONOMISCHE EN SOCIAL DOKUMENTATIE. REFERATEN

DOCUMENTATION INTERNATIONALE DU TRAVAIL
See INTERNATIONAL LABOUR DOCUMENTATION

DOCUMENTATION POLITIQUE INTERNATIONALE
See INTERNATIONAL POLITICAL SCIENCE ABSTRACTS

1458
DOCUMENTATION SUR EUROPE CENTRALE. 1– , 1963– . Louvain. Quarterly.
Issued by: Institut de Recherches de l'Europe Centrale. In French.
Indexed: Int. Bibl. Pol. Sc.

DOCUMENTATION SUR LA RECHERCHE FÉMINISTES DRF
See RESOURCES FOR FEMINIST RESEARCH

1459
DOCUMENTI; LA FAMIGLIA IN UN MONDO CHE CAMBIA. 1– , 1977– . Milano. Five no. a year.
Issued by: Centro Internazionale Studi Famiglia. In Italian.

DOCUMENTOS OFICIALES
See United Nations. General Assembly. OFFICIAL RECORDS

DOCUMENTOS OFICIALES
See United Nations. Trusteeship Council. OFFICIAL RECORDS

DOCUMENTOS OFICIALES DE LA ORGANIZACIÓN DE LOS ESTADOS AMERICANOS; INDICE Y LISTA
See Organization of American States. DOCUMENTOS OFICIALES. INDICE Y LISTA GENERAL

DOCUMENTOS OFICIALES. SUPLEMENTO
See United Nations. Trusteeship Council. OFFICIAL RECORDS. SUPPLEMENT

DOCUMENTS
See Centre d'Études Politiques, Économiques et Sociales. DOCUMENTS

DOCUMENTS AND DECISIONS
See YEARBOOK OF THE EUROPEAN CONVENTION ON HUMAN RIGHTS

DOCUMENTS [AND] DECISIONS [OF THE] EUROPEAN COMMISSION ON HUMAN RIGHTS
See YEARBOOK OF EUROPEAN CONVENTION ON HUMAN RIGHTS

DOCUMENTS INDEX (UNDEX)
See United Nations. Dag Hammarskjöld Library. UNDEX. UNITED NATIONS DOCUMENTS INDEX: SERIES A, SERIES B, AND SERIES C.

DOCUMENTS OF CANADIAN EXTERNAL RELATIONS
See Canada. Department of External Affairs. DOCUMENTS OF CANADIAN EXTERNAL RELATIONS

DOCUMENTS OFFICIELS
See United Nations. Economic and Social Council. OFFICIAL RECORDS

DOCUMENTS OFFICIELS
See United Nations. General Assembly. OFFICIAL RECORDS

DOCUMENTS OFFICIELS
See United Nations. Security Council. OFFICIAL RECORDS

DOCUMENTS OFFICIELS
See United Nations. Trusteeship Council. OFFICIAL RECORDS

DOCUMENTS ON CANADIAN EXTERNAL RELATIONS
See Canada. Department of External Affairs. DOCUMENTS ON CANADIAN EXTERNAL RELATIONS

DOCUMENTS ON COMMUNICATION AND SOCIETY
See COMMUNICATION AND SOCIETY

DOCUMENTS. WORKING PAPERS
See Council of Europe. Parliamentary Assembly. DOCUMENTS. WORKING PAPERS

1460
DOKUMENTATIONSDIENST LATEINAMERICA. v.1– , 1971– . Hamburg. Four no. a year.
Issued by: Dokumentationsleitstelle am Institut für Iberoamerika-Kunde. In German or Spanish. Other title: *Documentación Latinoamericana*.

1461
DOKUMENTE ZUR AUSSENPOLITIK DER REGIERUNG DER DEUTSCHEN DEMOKRATISCHEN REPUBLIK. v.1– , 1954– . Berlin, Rutten & Loening. Annual; later two no. a year.
In German.

1462
LE DOMAIN HUMAIN. THE HUMAN CONTEXT. DER MENSCH UND SEINE WELT. HOMBRE Y SOCIEDAD. IL MONDO VISSUTO DELL'UOMO. v.1– , Aug. 1968–. The Hague, M. Nijhoff. Three no. a year.
In English, French, German, or Spanish.
Indexed: Abst. Anth.; Bull. Sig. Soc. Eth.; Int. Pol. Sc. Abst.; Soc. Abst.

1463
DER DONAURAUM. 1– , 1956– . Wien. Quarterly.
Issued by: Forschungsinstitut für Fragen des Donauraumes, 1956–59; Forschungsinstitut für den Donauraum. In German; some summaries in English. Includes supplements called "Sonderhefte".
Indexed: His. Abst.; Int. Bibl. Eco.; Int. Bibl. Pol. Sc.; Int. Bibl. Soc.; Int Pol. Sc. Abst.; PAISFL.

DONGGUK JOURNAL OF PUBLIC ADMINISTRATION
See HAENGJONG NONJIP. CH'ANGGNHO

1464
DONGYAND MUNHWHA. ORIENTAL CULTURE. 1– , 1960– . Taegu. Annual.
Issued by: Dongang-Muwha-Yongusa, Taegu Daihak. In Korean.

DOSSIER
See Archaeological Survey of Canada. PAPER

DOSSIER
See Canadian Centre for Folk Culture Studies. PAPER

DOSSIERS DE L'ACTION CATHOLIQUE
See Action Populaire. DOSSIERS DE L'ACTION POPULAIRE

1465
DIE DRITTE WELT. 1– , 1973– . Meisenheim am Glen, Arca-Verlagsgesellschaft.
In English, French, or German.
Indexed: Bull. Anal. Pol. Ec. Soc.; Int. Bibl. Eco.

DROIT INTERNATIONAL ET DIPLOMATIE
See INTERNATIONALES RECHT UND DIPLOMATIE

1466
DUQUESNE REVIEW. v.1–18, no.2, spring 1956–1973. Pittsburgh, Pa. Two no. a year.
Issued by: Departments of Economics, Political Science, and Sociology, Duquesne University.
Indexed: Soc. Abst.

1467
DZIEJE NAJNOWSZE. v.1– , 1969– . Warszawa, Państwowe Wydawnictwo Naukowe. Quarterly.
Issued by: Instytut Historii, Polska Akademia Nauk. In Polish; summaries in French and Russian. Tables of contents also in French and Russian.
Supersedes: *Najnowsze Dzieje Polski; Materiały i Studia z Okresu*, 1914–39; *Najnowsze Dzieje Polski. Materiały i Studia z Okresu Drugiej Wojny Światowej* (v.1–12, 1957–68), and *Polska Ludowa: Materiały i Studia* (v.1–7, 1962–68).

E

EAZ ETHNOGRAPHISCH-ARCHÄOLOGISCHE ZEITSCHRIFT
See ETHNOGRAPHISCH-ARCHÄOLOGISCHE ZEITSCHRIFT

1468
E.E.C. AND THE THIRD WORLD; A SURVEY. 1– , 1981– . New York, Holmes & Meier. Annual.
Issued in cooperation with the Overseas Development Institute and the Institute of Development Studies.

1468a
EIA [ENVIRONMENTAL IMPACT ASSESSMENT] REVIEW. v.1– , Mar. 1980– . New York, Plenum Press. Quarterly.

1469
EISS YEARBOOK. ANNUAIRE EISS. 1974/77– . Deventer, Boston, Kluwer, [1979–]. Irreg., 1974/77–79; annual.
Issued by: European Institute for Social Security.

ER ENVIRONMENTAL REVIEW
See ENVIRONMENTAL REVIEW

ERQ
See EDUCATIONAL RESEARCH QUARTERLY

ERS
See EUROPEAN SOCIOLOGICAL REVIEW

ERS. ETHNIC AND RACIAL STUDIES
See ETHNIC AND RACIAL STUDIES

1470
ESCAP/ESPC COUNTRY MONOGRAPH SERIES. no.7– , 1979– . Bangkok. Irreg.
Issued by: Economic and Social Commission for Asia and the Pacific, United Nations.
Continues: *Escap Country Monograph Series* (no.1–6)

E—Z ENTWICKLUNG UND ZUSAMMENARBEIT
See ENTWICKLUNG UND ZUSAMMENARBEIT

EAST AFRICA ECONOMIC REVIEW
See EASTERN AFRICA ECONOMIC REVIEW

1471
EAST AFRICA JOURNAL. v.1–9, no.11, 1964–Nov. 1972. Nairobi. Monthly.
Issued by: East African Institute of Social and Cultural Affairs.
Indexed: Int. Bibl. Soc.; Int. Bibl. Soc. Cul. Anth.; Int. Lab. Doc.

1472
EAST AFRICA JOURNAL OF RURAL DEVELOPMENT. v.1–5, Jan. 1968–1972?. Kampala. Semi-annual.
Continued by: *Eastern Africa Journal of Rural Development.*
Indexed: Int. Bibl. Eco.; Int. Bibl. Soc.; Int. Lab. Doc.; PAIS.

1473
EAST ASIAN CULTURAL STUDIES. v.1– , Mar. 1962– . Tokyo. Quarterly.
Issued by: Centre for East Asian Studies. Occasionally all four nos. are combined in one volume.

EAST ASIAN OCCASIONAL PAPERS
See ASIAN STUDIES AT HAWAII

1474
EAST CENTRAL EUROPE. L'EUROPE DU CENTRE-EST. 1974– . Tempe, Ariz., Russian and East European Publications, later Schlacks, Jr. Two pts. a year, combined into one.
In English, French, German, or Russian. Some issues are thematic.
Indexed: His. Abst.

1475
EAST EUROPEAN QUARTERLY. v.1– , Mar. 1967– . Boulder, Colo. Quarterly.
Issued by: University of Colorado. Some numbers are thematic.
Indexes: Vols. 1–12, 1967–79.
Indexed: Bull. Anal. Pol. Ec. Soc.; Curr. Cont. Soc. Beh. Sc.; His. Abst.; Int. Bibl. Pol. Sc.; PAIS; SSCI.

1476
EASTERN AFRICA ECONOMIC REVIEW. 1969– . Nairobi, East African Literature Bureau. Semi-annual.
Supersedes: *The East African Economics Review* (1954–68)
Indexed: Bull. Anal. Pol. Ec. Soc.; Curr. Cont. Soc. Beh. Sc.; Int. Bibl. Eco.; Ind. Eco.; Int. Bibl. Pol. Sc.; PAIS; Pop. Ind.; SSCI.

1477
EASTERN AFRICA JOURNAL OF RURAL DEVELOPMENT. v.6– , 1973– . Kampala. Semi-annual.

Issued by: Department of Rural Economy and Rural Extension, Makerere University, and the Eastern Africa Agricultural Economics Society.
Continues: *East Africa Journal of Rural Development.*
Indexed: Int. Bibl. Soc. Cul. Anth.

1478
EASTERN ANTHROPOLOGIST. v.1– , Sept. 1947– . Lucknow. Quarterly.
Issued by: Ethnographic and Folk Culture Society.
Indexed: Abst. Anth.; Bull. Anal. Pol. Ec. Soc.; Bull. Sig. Soc. Eth.; Int. Bibl. Soc. Cul. Anth.; Int. Pol. Sc. Abst.; Soc. Abst.; SSCI.

1479
EASTERN ECONOMIST. v.1–79, no.8, May 21, 1943–July 31, 1982. New Delhi, A.P. Agarwala. Biweekly.
Continued by: *The Eastern Economist.*
Indexed: Bull. Anal. Pol. Ec. Soc.

1480
EASTERN EUROPEAN ECONOMICS. v.1– , fall 1962– . Armonk, N.Y., M.E. Sharpe. Quarterly.
Translations of articles from German, Hungarian, Romanian and Slavic languages.
Indexed: Eco. Abst.; Curr. Cont. Soc. Beh. Sc.; Bull. Anal. Pol. Ec. Soc.; Int. Bibl. Eco.; Int. Bibl. Pol. Sc.; Int. Bibl. Soc.; Int. Lab. Doc.; PAIS; Pop. Ind.; SSCI.

1481
THE EASTERN JOURNAL OF INTERNATIONAL LAW. v.1–10, Apr. 1969–Jan. 1979. Madras. Quarterly.
Issued by: Eastern Centre of International Studies.

1482
EASTERN MARKET. v.1– , May 1947– . London. Monthly (some nos. are combined)
Indexed: His. Abst.; Int. Bibl. Eco.; Int. Bibl. Soc. Cul. Anth.; PAIS; Peace Res. Abst. J.

1483
ÉCHANGES INTERNATIONAUX ET DÉVELOPPEMENT. no.1– , Dec. 1971– . Toulouse. Ten no. a year.
Issued by: Institut d'Études Internationales et des Pays en Voie de Développement, Université de Toulouse, and the Association Échanges Internationaux et Développement. In French.

1484
École Française de l'Extrême-Orient. BULLETIN. v.1– , Jan. 1901– . Paris, Imprimerie Nationale. Frequency varies.
In French.
Indexes: Vols. 1–15, 1901–15, 1v.; v.1–20, 1901–20, in v.21; v.21–30, 1921–30, in v.32.

1485
École Pratique des Hautes Études. 6e Section des Sciences Économiques et Sociales. Laboratoire de Sociologie de la Connaissance. CAHIERS. 1– , 1967– . Paris. Irreg.
In French.

1486
THE ECOLOGIST. v.9, no.3– , May/June 1979– . Wadebridge, Ecosystems Ltd. Quarterly.
Subtitle reads: "Journal of the post-industrial age".
Continues: *New Ecologist.*
Indexed: PAIS.

1487
ECOLOGY ABSTRACTS. v.6– , 1980– . London. Monthly.
Issued by: Information Retrieval Ltd. in cooperation with the Unesco Program of Man and the Biosphere.
Continues: *Applied Ecology Abstracts* (v.1–5, 1975–79)

1488
ECONOMETRIC THEORY. v.1– , Apr. 1985– . New York, Cambridge University Press. Three no. a year.

1489
ECONOMETRICA. v.1– , Jan. 1933– . Chicago, Ill., The University of Chicago Press (1981–). Quarterly, 1933–69; bimonthly.
Indexes: Vols. 1–20, 1933–52, 1v.
Indexed: Bull. Anal. Pol. Ec. Soc.; Bull. Sig. Soc. Eth.; Eco. Abst.; Int. Bibl. Eco.; Int. Bibl. Pol. Sc.; Int. Bibl. Soc.; Int. Lab. Doc.; Int. Pol. Sc. Abst.; SSCI.

ECONOMETRICS AND OPERATIONS *See* ÖKONOMIE UND UNTERNEHMUNGSFORSCHUNG

1490
ECONOMÍA. 3. ser. no.50– , Dec. 1965– . Quito. Irreg.
Issued by: Instituto de Investigaciones Económicas, Faculdad de Ciencias Económicas y Administrativas, Universidad Central del Ecuador. In Spanish.
Indexed: Bull. Anal. Pol. Ec. Soc.

1491
ECONOMIA. v.1– , 1977– . Lisboa. Three no. a year.

Issued by: Faculdade de Ciências Humanas, Universidade Católica Portuguesa. In English, French, Portuguese, or Spanish.
Indexed: PAISFL.

1492
ECONOMÍA. v.1– , Dec. 1977– . Lima. Semi-annual.
Issued by: Departamento de Economía, Universidad Católica del Perú. In Spanish.
Indexed: PAISFL.

1493
ECONOMÍA COLOMBIANA. 4. ser. v.1–5, May 1954–Oct. 1958. Bogotá. Monthly.
Issued by: Controloria General de la República. In Spanish.
Superseded by: *Economica Grandcolombiana.*

1494
ECONOMÍA DE AMÉRICA LATINA. no.1– , Sept. 1978– . Mexico, D.F. Semi-annual.
Issued by: Centro de Documentación y Docencia Económicas jointly with the Instituto Económico de América Latina. In Spanish.
Indexed: PAISFL.

1495
ECONOMIA E DESENVOLVIMENTO. v.1– , Mar. 1981– . São Paulo, Cortez Editora. Three no. a year.
In Portuguese.

1496
ECONOMIA E FINANZAS. 1– , 1933– . Lisboa, Librario Portugal. Annual.
Issued by: Instituto Superior de Ciências Econômicas e Finanzieros, Universidade Técnico de Lisboa. In Portuguese.
Indexed: Int. Bibl. Eco.

1497
ECONOMIA E GESTÃO. v.3, no.17– , Aug. 1979– . Lisboa, A. da Cruz Rodrigues. Bimonthly (irreg.)
In Portuguese.
Continues: *Resistência. Serie de Economia* (Lisboa)

1498
ECONOMIA E SOCIALISMO. v.1–5, Apr. 1976–1981; n. ser. v.6(no.55)– . fall 1981– . Lisboa, Libreria Retrand. Quarterly.
In Portuguese.
Indexed: PAISFL.

1499
ECONOMIA E SOCIOLOGIA. 1– , 1966– . [Place of publication varies]. Semi-annual.
Issued by: Instituto Superior Ecônomico e Social. In Portuguese.
Indexed: PAISFL.

1500
ECONOMIA E STORIA. v.1–24, June/Sept. 1954–1979; 2d. ser. v.1– , Jan./Mar. 1980– . Roma, Fratelli Bocca; Milano, A. Giuffrè. Quarterly.
In Italian.

1501
LA ECONOMÍA ESPAÑOLA. 1968– . Madrid, Editorial para il Diálogo. Annual.
Issued by: Dirección General de Política Económica y Previsión, Ministerio de Economía e Comercio (Spain). In Spanish.

1502
ECONOMIA FASCISTA. v.1–3, Feb. 1940–1942. Roma. Monthly.
In Italian.

1503
ECONOMÍA GRANDCOLOMBIANA. v.1–7(no.1–21), Aug. 1959–1963. Bogotá.
Issued by: Controloría General de la República. In Spanish.
Supersedes: *Economía Colombiana.* Superseded by: *Economía Colombiana.*

1504
ECONOMIA INTERNAZIONALE. v.1– , Jan. 1948– . Genova. Quarterly.
Issued by: Istituto di Economia Internazionale, Camera di Comercio, Industria e Agricultura di Genova. In English, French, Italian, or Spanish; summaries in English and Italian.
Indexed: Bull. Anal. Pol. Ec. Soc.; Curr. Cont. Soc. Beh. Sc.; Eco. Abst.; Int. Bibl. Eco.; Int. Bibl. Pol. Sc.; Int. Bibl. Soc.; Int. Lab. Doc.; PAIS; Pop. Ind.

1505
ECONOMIA PUBBLICA. 1– , May 1971– . Milano, F. Angeli. Monthly.
Issued by: Centro Italiani di Ricerche e d'Informazione sull'Economia delle Imprese Pubbliche e di Pubblico Interesse (CIRIEC). In Italian.
Supersedes: *Bolletino dell'Economia Pubblica* (with no.22, Mar./Apr. 1971)
Indexed: PAISFL.

1506
ECONOMÍA SALVADORENA. 1– , 1952– . El Salvador. Two no. a year.

Issued by: Instituto de Estudios Económicos, Faculdad de Economía, Universidad de El Salvador. In Spanish. Other title: *Revista de la Facultad de Economía*.

1507
ECONOMÍA Y ADMINISTRACIÓN. 1–49, 1950–1965. Quito. Irreg.
Issued by: Instituto de Investigaciones Económicas, Universidad Central del Ecuador. In Spanish. Publication suspended in 1961. Title varies: Jan./Mar. 1951, *Boletín Información Económica*; Sept./Nov. 1951–Apr./Dec. 1960, *Boletín Trimestral de Información Económica*.

1508
ECONOMÍA Y ADMINISTRACIÓN. 1– , 1964– . Concepción. Five no. a year.
Issued by: Faculdad de Ciencias Económicas y de Administración, Universidad de Concepción. In Spanish.
Indexed: Bull. Anal. Pol. Ec. Soc.

1509
ECONOMÍA Y CIENCIAS SOCIALES. Sept. 1958–Oct. 1969. Caracas. Four no. a year.
Issued by: Instituto de Investigaciones Sociales, Faculdad de Ciencias Económicas y Sociales, Universidad Central de Venezuela. In Spanish.
Indexed: Bull. Sig. Soc. Eth.; Int. Bibl. Soc.; Int. Pol. Sc. Abst.; Soc. Abst.

1510
ECONOMÍA Y DESARROLLO. no.1– , Jan./Mar. 1970– . La Habana. Bimonthly.
Issued by: Faculdad de Economía, Universidad de La Habana. In Spanish.
Indexed: Int. Lab. Doc.; PAISFL.

1511
ECONOMIC ABSTRACTS. v.1–22, June 1, 1953–1975. The Hague, Nijhoff. Semimonthly.
Issued by: Economic Information Service, Ministry of Economic Affairs (The Netherlands)
Continued by: *Key to Economic Science*.

1512
ECONOMIC ACTIVITY IN CARIBBEAN COUNTRIES. 1976– . Port of Spain.
Issued by: Office for the Caribbean, Economic Commission for Latin America, United Nations.

1513
ECONOMIC AFFAIRS. v.4– , Oct. 1983– . London, Longman in association with the Institute of Economic Affairs. Quarterly.
Continues: *Journal of Economic Affairs*.

ECONOMIC ANALYSIS
See EKONOMSKA ANALIZA

1514
ECONOMIC ANALYSIS AND POLICY. v.1– , Mar. 1970– . St. Lucia. Semi-annual.
Issued by: Queensland Branch, Economic Society of Australia and New Zealand.
Indexed: APAIS; Curr. Cont. Soc. Beh. Sc.; Int. Bibl. Eco.; Int. Bibl. Pol. Sc.; Int. Bibl. Soc.

1515
ECONOMIC ANALYSIS AND WORKERS' MANAGEMENT. v.8, no.3/4– , 1978– . Beograd, Ekonomski Biro. Quarterly.
Issued jointly by: Yugoslav Association of Econometrics and Management with other similar bodies. In English, Macedonian, Russian, Serbo-Croatian, or Slovenian. Tables of contents also in English.
Indexed: PAIS.; SSCI.

1516
ECONOMIC AND FINANCIAL REVIEW. 1– , 1963– . Lagos. Monthly.
Issued by: Central Bank of Nigeria.

1517
ECONOMIC AND FINANCIAL REVIEW. Sept. 1968– . Blantyre. Quarterly.
Issued by: Reserve Bank of Malawi.

1518
ECONOMIC AND INDUSTRIAL DEMOCRACY. v.1– , Feb. 1980– . Beverly Hills, Calif., London, Sage Publications. Quarterly.
Indexed: Int. Bibl. Eco.

1519
ECONOMIC AND POLITICAL WEEKLY. v.1– , 1965– . Bombay, Sameeksha Trust Publications.
Indexed: Bull. Anal. Pol. Ec. Soc.; Int. Bibl. Pol. Sc.; Int. Pol. Sc. Abst.; Soc. Abst.

1520
ECONOMIC AND SOCIAL BULLETIN. v.1– , May 1953– . Brussels. Bimonthly.
Issued by: International Confederation of Free Trade Unions.

1521
Economic and Social Committee of the European Communities. ANNUAIRE. 1960– . Brussels, Service Press et Information. Irreg.
In French.

1522
Economic and Social Committee of the European Communities. BULLETIN. no.1/2/3– , Jan./Feb./Mar. 1974– . Brussels. Monthly.

ECONOMIC AND SOCIAL PAPERS
See CAHIERS ÉCONOMIQUES ET SOCIAUX

ECONOMIC AND SOCIAL PROGRESS IN LATIN AMERICA
See Inter-American Development Bank. ECONOMIC AND SOCIAL PROGRESS IN LATIN AMERICA

1523
Economic and Social Research Council (Gr. Britain). RESEARCH SUPPORTED BY THE ECONOMIC AND SOCIAL RESEARCH COUNCIL. 1984– . London. Annual.
Continues: Social Science Research Council (Gr. Britain). *Research Supported by the Social Science Council.*

1524
The Economic and Social Research Institute, Dublin. REGISTER OF CURRENT SOCIAL SCIENCE RESEARCH IN IRELAND. 1976– . Dublin.

1525
ECONOMIC AND SOCIAL REVIEW. v.1– , Oct. 1969– . Dublin. Quarterly.
Issued by: Economic and Social Research Institute.
Indexed: Bull. Anal. Pol. Ec. Soc.; Int. Bibl. Eco.; Int. Bibl. Pol. Sc.; Int. Bibl. Soc.; Int. Pol. Sc. Abst.; Int. Lab. Doc.; PAIS; SSCI.

ECONOMIC AND SOCIAL STUDIES
See National Institute of Economic and Social Research, London. ECONOMIC AND SOCIAL RESEARCH

ECONOMIC AND SOCIAL SURVEY OF ASIA AND THE PACIFIC
See United Nations. Economic and Social Commission for Asia and the Pacific. ECONOMIC AND SOCIAL SURVEY OF ASIA AND THE PACIFIC

1526
ECONOMIC AND SOCIAL SURVEY OF LATIN AMERICA. 1– , 1961– . Washington, D.C.
Prepared jointly by: the Secretariats of the Organization of American States and the Economic Commission for Latin America.
Continued by: *Social Survey of Latin America.*

ECONOMIC BULLETIN FOR AFRICA
See United Nations. Economic Commission for Africa. ECONOMIC BULLETIN FOR AFRICA

ECONOMIC BULLETIN FOR ASIA AND THE FAR EAST
See United Nations. Economic and Social Commission for Asia and the Pacific. ECONOMIC BULLETIN FOR ASIA AND THE PACIFIC

ECONOMIC BULLETIN FOR ASIA AND THE PACIFIC
See United Nations. Economic and Social Commission for Asia and the Pacific. ECONOMIC BULLETIN FOR ASIA AND THE PACIFIC

ECONOMIC BULLETIN FOR EUROPE
See United Nations. Economic Commission for Europe. ECONOMIC BULLETIN FOR EUROPE

ECONOMIC CONDITIONS IN FRANCE
See Organisation for Economic Co-operation and Development. OECD ECONOMIC SURVEYS: FRANCE

ECONOMIC CONDITIONS IN ITALY
See Organisation for Economic Co-operation and Development. OECD ECONOMIC SURVEYS: ITALY

ECONOMIC CONDITIONS IN MEMBER AND ASSOCIATED COUNTRIES OF THE OECD
See under: Organisation for Economic Co-operation and Development. OECD ECONOMIC SURVEYS; separate entries for the following countries: Austria, Denmark, France, Iceland, Ireland, Italy, Netherlands, Norway, Portugal, Spain, Sweden, Switzerland, United Kingdom, United States

ECONOMIC CONDITIONS IN SWEDEN
See Organisation for Economic Co-operation and Development. OECD ECONOMIC SURVEYS: SWEDEN

ECONOMIC CONDITIONS IN THE UNITED KINGDOM
See Organisation for Economic Co-operation and Development. OECD ECONOMIC SURVEYS: UNITED KINGDOM

1527
ECONOMIC COOPERATION AND INTEGRATION AMONG DEVELOPING COUNTRIES. COOPÉRATION ÉCONOMIQUE ET INTÉGRATION ENTRE LES PAYS EN DÉVELOPPEMENT. 1970–1978– . Ljubljana. Irreg.
Issued by: Research Centre for Cooperation with Developing Countries. In Serbo-Croatian, English, French, or Spanish.

1528
ECONOMIC DEVELOPMENT AND CULTURAL CHANGE. v.1– , Mar. 1952– . Chicago, Ill., The University of Chicago Press. Quarterly.
Issued by: Research Center in Economic Development and Cultural Change, University of Chicago.

Indexes: Vols. 1–15, 1952–67, in v.16, no.2, pt.2.
Indexed: Abst. Anth.; Bull. Anal. Pol. Ec. Soc.; Bull. Sig. Soc. Eth.; ABC POL SCI; Eco. Abst.; Curr. Cont. Soc. Beh. Sc.; His. Abst.; Ind. Per. Art. Law; Int. Bibl. Eco.; Int. Bibl. Pol. Sc.; Int. Bibl. Soc.; Int. Pol. Sc. Abst.; Int. Bibl. Soc. Cul. Anth.; PAIS; Peace Res. Abst. J.; Pop. Ind.; Sage Urb. Stu. Abst.; SSCI.

ECONOMIC DEVELOPMENT IN AFRICA
See United Nations. Economic Commission for Africa. ECONOMIC DEVELOPMENTS IN AFRICA

ECONOMIC DEVELOPMENTS IN THE MIDDLE EAST
See United Nations. Economic Commission for Western Asia. STUDIES ON DEVELOPMENT PROBLEMS IN COUNTRIES OF WESTERN ASIA

ECONOMIC DIGEST
See BANGLADESH DEVELOPMENT STUDIES

1529
ECONOMIC GEOGRAPHY. v.1– , Mar. 1925– . Worcester, Mass. Quarterly.
Issued by: Clark University.
Indexes: Vols. 1–25, 1952–49, 1v.
Indexed: ABC POL SCI; Bull. Anal. Pol. Ec. Soc.; Eco. Abst.; His. Abst.; Int. Bibl. Eco.; Int. Bibl. Pol. Sc.; Int. Pol. Sc. Abst.; PAIS; Peace Res. Abst. J.; Pop. Ind.; Soc. Sc. Hum. Ind.; Soc. Abst.; SSCI; Urb. Aff. Abst.

ECONOMIC GEOGRAPHY
See GEO ABSTRACTS. C: ECONOMIC GEOGRAPHY

1530
ECONOMIC HANDBOOK OF THE WORLD. 1981– . New York, McGraw-Hill for the Center for Social Analysis, State University of New York, Binghampton. The issue for 1982 last examined.

ECONOMIC HISTORY
See ECONOMIC JOURNAL

ECONOMIC HISTORY
See HOSPODRSKE DEJINY

1531
THE ECONOMIC HISTORY REVIEW. v.1–18, Jan. 1927–1948; ser. 2, v.1– , 1948– . Welwyn Garden City, Popper and Co. Three no. a year, 1941–1970; quarterly.
Issued by: Economic History Society. Supplements accompany some numbers.
Indexes: Vols. 1–18, 1927–48; ser.2: v.1–23, 1948–70.
Indexed: Curr. Cont. Soc. Beh. Abst.; His. Abst.; Int. Bibl. Eco.; Int. Bibl. Pol. Sc.; Int. Bibl. Soc.; PAIS; Peace Res. Abst. J.; Pop. Ind.; Soc. Sc. Hum. Ind.

1532
ECONOMIC INQUIRY. v.12– , Mar. 1974– . Los Angeles, Calif., Western Economic Association. Quarterly.
Continues: *Western Economic Journal*.
Indexed: Bull. Anal. Pol. Ec. Soc.; Curr. Cont. Soc. Beh. Sc.; PAIS; PHRA; Pop. Ind.; Sage Urb. Stu. Abst.

1533
THE ECONOMIC JOURNAL. v.1– , Mar. 1891– . London, Macmillan; New York, St. Martin's Press. Quarterly.
Organ of: The Royal Economic Society (1891–1902, called British Economic Association). Includes supplement: Economic History (1–4, 1926–40), and list of doctoral dissertation once a year.
Indexes: Vols. 1–10, 1891–1900, 1v.; v.11–20, 1901–10, 1v.; v.21–30, 1v.; v.1–40, 1891–1930, 1v.
Indexed: Bull. Anal. Pol. Sc.; His. Abst.; J. Eco. Lit.; Int. Bibl. Eco.; Int. Bibl. Pol. Sc.; Int. Bibl. Soc.; Ind. Per. Art. Law; Int. Lab. Doc.; PAIS; Peace Res. Abst. J.; Soc. Sc. Hum. Ind.

1534
ECONOMIC MODELLING. v.1– , Jan. 1984– . Haywards Heath, Butterworth. Quarterly.

1535
ECONOMIC OUTLOOK USA. v.1– , winter 1974– . Ann Arbor, Mich. Quarterly.
Issued by: Survey Research Center, University of Michigan.
Indexed: PAIS; Sage Urb. Stu. Abst.

1536
ECONOMIC PAPERS. v.1– , Apr. 1982– . Sydney. Four no. a year.
Issued by: Economic Society of Australia and New Zealand, New South Wales Branch. Continues a publication of the same title.

1537
ECONOMIC PERSPECTIVES. v.1– , winter 1979– . Chur, New York, Harwood Academic Publishers. Irreg.

1538
ECONOMIC POLICY. 1– , Nov. 1985– . Cambridge, New York, Press Syndicate of the University of Cambridge. Two no. a year.

1539
ECONOMIC RECORD. 1– , 1925– . Melbourne, Melbourne University Press. Quarterly.
Issued by: Economic Society of Australia and New Zealand.
Indexed: Bull. Anal. Pol. Ec. Soc.; Curr. Cont. Soc. Beh. Sc.; Eco. Abst.; Ind. Per. Art. Law; Int. Bibl. Eco.; Int. Bibl. Pol. Sc.; Int. Bibl. Soc.; J. Eco. Lit.; Int. Lab. Doc.; PAIS; Pop. Ind.

ECONOMIC REPORT
See United Nations. Department of Economic and Social Affairs. WORLD ECONOMIC REPORT

ECONOMIC REPORT; SALIENT FEATURES OF THE WORLD ECONOMIC SITUATION
See United Nations. Department of Economic and Social Affairs. WORLD ECONOMIC REPORT

ECONOMIC REPORT; SALIENT FEATURES OF THE WORLD ECONOMICS
See United Nations. Department of Economic and Social Affairs. WORLD ECONOMIC REPORT

1540
ECONOMIC RESEARCH JOURNAL. 1– , 1953– . Manila. Quarterly.
Issued by: Faculty of the Graduate School, University of the East.
Indexed: Int. Lab. Doc.; PAIS.

ECONOMIC RESEARCH SERIES
See Hitotsubashi Daigaku. Keizai Kenkyu. ECONOMIC RESEARCH SERIES

1541
ECONOMIC REVIEW. 1– , 1955– . Jerusalem. Quarterly.
Issued by: Research Department, Bank of Israel.
Indexed: APAIS; Int. Bibl. Eco.; Peace. Res. Abst. J.

1542
ECONOMIC REVIEW. no.1– , July/Aug. 1966– . Djakarta.
Issued by: Indonesia Unit III, Bank Negara.

1543
ECONOMIC REVIEW. v.1– , Apr. 1975– . Colombo. Monthly.
Issued by: Research Department, People's Bank.

ECONOMIC REVIEW
See Canada. Department of Finance. ECONOMIC REVIEW

ECONOMIC REVIEW
See KEIZAI KENKYŪ

ECONOMIC REVIEW
See POLITICAL AND ECONOMIC REVIEW

ECONOMIC REVIEW
See University of Sydney Economics Society. ECONOMIC REVIEW

ECONOMIC REVIEW OF LATIN AMERICA
See United Nations. Economic Commission for Latin America. ECONOMIC REVIEW OF LATIN AMERICA AND THE CARIBBEAN

THE ECONOMIC SCIENCE
See KEIZAI KAGAKU

THE ECONOMIC SITUATION IN THE COMMUNITY
See Commission of the European Communities. Directorate for National Economies and Economic Trends. THE ECONOMIC SITUATION IN THE COMMUNITY

1544
ECONOMIC STUDIES. 1– , 1965– . Aberdeen. Semi-annual.
Issued by: Department of Economics, University of Aberdeen. Title varies: 1965–Oct. 1969, *Journal of Economic Studies*.

ECONOMIC SURVEY: B.L.E.U.
See Organisation for Economic Co-operation and Development. OECD ECONOMIC SURVEYS: BELGIUM–LUXEMBOURG

ECONOMIC STUDIES
See KEIZAIGAKU KENKYŪ

ECONOMIC STUDIES
See STUDIA EKONOMICZNE

THE ECONOMIC STUDIES QUARTERLY
See KIKAN RIRON-KEIZAIGAKU

1545
ECONOMIC STUDIES. no.1– , Dec. 1983– . Paris. Semi-annual.
Issued by: Economics and Statistics Department, Organisation for Economic Co-operation and Development.

ECONOMIC SURVEY OF AFRICA
See United Nations. Economic Commission for Africa. SURVEY OF ECONOMIC AND SOCIAL CONDITIONS IN AFRICA

ECONOMIC SURVEY OF ASIA AND THE FAR EAST
See United Nations. Economic and Social Commission for Asia and the Pacific. ECONOMIC SURVEY OF ASIA AND THE PACIFIC

ECONOMIC SURVEY OF EUROPE
See United Nations. Economic Commission for Europe. ECONOMIC SURVEY OF EUROPE

ECONOMIC SURVEY OF EUROPE SINCE THE WAR
See United Nations. Economic Commission for Europe. ECONOMIC SURVEY OF EUROPE

1546
ECONOMIC SURVEY OF JAPAN. 1949/50– . Tokyo. Frequency varies.
Issued by: 1950/51–1951/52, Economic Stabilization Board; 1952/53–1953/54, Economic Counsel Board; 1954/55–, Economic Planning Agency.
Continues: *Report on Current Economy. Nenji Keizai Hokōku.*

ECONOMIC SURVEY OF LATIN AMERICA
See United Nations. Economic Commission for Latin America. ECONOMIC SURVEY OF LATIN AMERICA AND THE CARIBBEAN

ECONOMIC SURVEY OF LATIN AMERICA AND THE CARIBBEAN
See United Nations. Economic Commission for Latin America and the Caribbean. ECONOMIC SURVEY OF LATIN AMERICA AND THE CARIBBEAN

ECONOMIC SURVEY OF NEW ZEALAND
See NEW ZEALAND ECONOMIC SURVEY

1547
ECONOMIC SURVEY OF THE KOREAN ECONOMY. 1958– . Seoul. Annual.
Issued by: 1958–59, Ministry of Reconstruction; 1962–, Economic Planning Board. Vols. for 1960–61 not published.

ECONOMIC SURVEYS BY THE OECD
See under: Organisation for Economic Co-operation and Development. OECD ECONOMIC SURVEYS separate entries for the following countries: Austria, Canada, Denmark, Finland, France, Germany, Greece, Turkey, Yugoslavia

1548
ECONOMIC THEORY. v.1– , Apr. 1985– . New York, Cambridge University Press. Three no. a year.

1549
ECONOMIC TRENDS. no.1– , Nov. 1953– . London, H.M.S.O. Monthly.
Prepared by: Central Statistical Office in collaboration with the statistics divisions of government departments and the Bank of England.
Indexed: PAIS.

ECONOMIC YEARBOOK
See STATE OF THE WORLD ECONOMY

ECONOMIC YEARBOOK OF TUNISIA
See ANNUAIRE ÉCONOMIQUE DE LA TUNISIE

1550
ECONOMICA. v.1–13(no.1–42), Jan. 1921–Nov. 1933; n. ser. v.1– , Feb. 1934– . London. Three no. a year, 1913–30; quarterly.
Issued by: London School of Economics and Political Science.
Indexes: Vols. 1–7, 1921–27, with v.7; v.1–10, 1934–43, in v.10.
Indexed: Curr. Cont. Soc. Beh. Sc.; Eco. Abst.; Int. Bibl. Eco.; Int. Bibl. Pol. Sc.; Int. Bibl. Soc.; His. Abst.; Int. Lab. Doc.; PAIS; Peace Res. Abst. J.; Pop. Ind.; Soc. Sc. Hum. Ind.; SSCI.

1551
ECONOMICA. v.1– , July/Sept. 1954– . Buenos Aires. Three no. a year.
Issued by: Faculdad de Ciencias Económicas, Universidad Nacional de la Plata. In Spanish. Other title: *Revista de la Faculdad de Ciencias Económicas*, Universidad Nacional de la Plata.
Indexed: Bull. Anal. Pol. Ec. Soc.; Int. Bibl. Eco.

ECONOMICS & BUSINESS IN BRAZIL. CONJUNTURA ECONÔMICA
See CONJUNCTURA ECONÔMICA

1552
ECONOMICS AND FINANCE INDEX TO PERIODICAL ARTICLES, 1947–1971. Boston, Mass., G.K. Hall, 1972.
First Supplement, 1972–1973–1974, Boston, Mass., G.K. Hall, 1976.
Prepared by: Joint Library of the International Monetary Fund and the International Bank for Reconstruction and Development.

1553
ECONOMICS AND PHILOSOPHY. v.1– , Apr. 1985– . London, Cambridge University Press. Semi-annual.

1554
ECONOMICS OF PLANNING. v.3– , Apr. 1963– . Oslo, 1963–77; Birmingham. Three no. a year.

Issued by: Norwegian Institute of International Affairs, 1973–77, Centre for Russian and East European Studies, University of Birmingham, 1978, with financial support of the Swedish Royal Academy of Sciences, State Council for Social Research in Stockholm, Norwegian Research Council for Sciences and the Humanities, and Bank of England, Helsinki. Subtitle reads: "Theory and practice of centrally planned economies and their relations with market economies". Other title: *Ekonomika Planirovaniia.*

Continues: *Øst-Økonomi* (v.1–2, 1961–62)

Indexed: Bull. Anal. Pol. Ec. Soc.

1555

ÉCONOMIE APPLIQUÉE. v.[1]– , Jan./Mar. 1948– . Paris, Presses Universitaires de France. Quarterly.

Issued by: Institut des Sciences Mathématiques et Économiques Appliquées (called until 1975 Institut de Science Économique Appliquée). In English or French. Tables of contents also in English, German, Italian, or Spanish.

Indexed: Bull. Anal. Pol. Ec. Soc.; Bull. Sig. Soc. Eth.; Eco. Abst.; Int. Bibl. Eco.; Int. Lab. Doc.

1556

ÉCONOMIE ET HUMANISME. 1– , 1942– . Lyon, CEDEX. Bimonthly.

Issued by: Centre d'Études des Complexes Sociaux, Association Économie et Humanisme. In French.

Indexed: Bull. Sig. Soc. Eth.; Int. Bibl. Eco.; Int. Bibl. Pol. Sc.; Int. Bibl. Soc. Cul. Anth.; Int. Pol. Sc. Abst.; Peace Res. Abst. J.

1557

ÉCONOMIE ET POLITIQUE. 1– , Apr. 1954– . Paris, Guin. Eleven no. a year.

In French. Subtitle reads: "Revue marxiste d'économie".

Indexed: Bull. Sig. Soc. Eth.; Geo. Abst.; Int. Bibl. Eco.; Int. Bibl. Pol. Sc.; Int. Bibl. Soc.; Int. Lab. Doc.; PAISFL; Peace Res. Abst. J.

ÉCONOMIE ET SOCIOLOGIE RURALES *See* AGRARWIRTSCHAFT UND AGRARSOZIOLOGIE

1558

ÉCONOMIE MÉRIDIONALE. 1– , 1953– . Montpellier. Quarterly.

Issued by: Centre Régional de la Productivité et des Études Économiques, Faculté de Droit et des Sciences Économiques, Université de Montpellier. In French.

Indexed: PAISFL.

1559

ÉCONOMIES ET SOCIÉTÉS. v.1– , Jan. 1967– . Paris, Droz. Monthly.

Issued by: Institut de Sciences Mathématiques et Économiques Appliquées (called until 1975 Institut de Science Économique Appliquée). Includes subseries: *Cahiers de l'I.S.M.A. Série AB. Économie du Travail*; *Cahiers de l'I.S.M.A. Série AF. Histoire Quantitative d'Économie Français*; *Cahiers de l'I.S.M.A. Série AG, Progrès et Agriculture*; *Cahiers de l'I.S.M.A. Série EM. Économie, Mathématique et Économetrie*; *Cahiers de l'I.S.M.A. Série EN. Économie de l'Énergie*; *Cahiers de l'I.S.M.A. Série ES. Économie et Sociologie*; *Cahiers de l'I.S.M.A. Série F. Développement, Croissance, Progrès*; *Cahiers de l'I.S.M.A. Série G. Économie Planifiée*; *Cahiers de l'I.S.M.A. Série HS. Hors Série*; *Cahiers de l'I.S.M.A. Série K. Prévision Économique et Économie de l'Entreprise*; *Cahiers de l'I.S.M.A. Série L. Économie Régionale*; *Cahiers de l'I.S.M.A. Série M. Philosophie et Sciences de l'Homme*; *Cahiers de l'I.S.M.A. Série MO. Pouvoirs et Régulations Monétaires*; *Cahiers de l'I.S.M.A. Série P. Relations Économiques Internationales*; *Cahiers de l'I.S.M.A. Série PE. Histoire de la Pensée Économique*; *Cahiers de l'I.S.M.A. Série R. Théories de la Régulation*; *Cahiers de l'I.S.M.A. Série S. Études de Marxologie*; *Cahiers de l'I.S.M.A. Série SG. Série de Gestion*; *Cahiers de l'I.S.M.A. Série T. Problèmes Économiques de la Recherche et de l'Information Scientifiques et Techniques*; *Cahiers de l'I.S.M.A. Série V. Humanities, Économie, Ethnologie, Sociologie*. In French.

Indexed: Bull. Anal. Pol. Ec. Soc.; Bull. Sig. Soc. Eth.; Int. Bibl. Eco.; Int. Bibl. Soc.; Int. Lab. Doc.; Peace Res. Abst. J.

1560

ÉCONOMIQUE PROSPECTIVE INTERNATIONALE. no.1– , 1980– . Paris, La Documentation Française. Quarterly.

Issued by: Centre d'Études Prospectives et d'Informations Internationales (CEPII). In French.

1561

ECONOMISCH- EN SOCIAAL-HISTORISCH JAARBOEK. v.33– , 1971– . 's-Gravenhage, M. Nijhoff. Irreg. 1971–78; annual.

Issued by: Vereeniging het Nederlandsch Economisch-Historisch Archief. In Dutch.

Continues: *Economisch-Historisch Jaarboek.*

1562

ECONOMISCH EN SOCIAAL TIJDSCHRIFT. VIE ÉCONOMIQUE ET SOCIALE. v.1– , Feb. 1947– . Antwerpen. Five no. a year.

Issued by: Instituut voor Postuniversitai Onderwijs, Universitaire Faculteiten Sint-Ignatius te Antwerpen. In Dutch, English, French, or German. Absorbed: *Vie Économique et Sociale*, in 1962.

Indexed: Bull. Anal. Pol. Ec. Soc.; Int. Bibl. Eco.; J. Eco. Lit.; PAIS.

1563
ECONOMISCH-HISTORISCH JAARBOEK. v.1–32, 1916–1969. 's-Gravenhage, M. Nijhoff. Annual.
Issued by: Vereeniging het Nederlandsch Economisch-Historisch Archief. In Dutch. Title varies: v.1–2, 1916–17, *Economisch-Historisch Jaarboek van Nederland.*
Continued by: *Economisch- en Sociaal-Historisch Jaarboek.*
Indexes: Vols. 1–22, 1916–43, in v.22; v.1–30, 1916–64, in v.30.

ECONOMISCH-HISTORISCH JAARBOEK VAN NEDERLAND
See ECONOMISCH-HISTORISCH JAARBOEK

1564
ECONOMISCHE- EN SOCIALE DOKUMENTATIE. REFERATEN. DOCUMENTATION ÉCONOMIQUE ET SOCIALE. RÉSUMÉS ANALYTIQUES. v.1– , 1966– . Bruxelles. Quarterly.
Organ of: Bibliothek Quetelefons en Centrum voor Informatie en Dokumentatie in Economische en Sociale Wetenschappen (C.I.D.E.S.), Ministerie van Economische Zakenen Energie. Algemeine Directie voor Studien en Dokumentatie. In Dutch, English, French, or German.

1565
THE ECONOMIST. v.1– , Sept. 2, 1843– . London. Weekly (except for combined issued of the last week in Dec. and first week in Jan.)
Includes: Monthly Trade Supplement; Reports of the Joint Stock of Banks of the United Kingdom; and Commercial History and Review.
Indexed: APAIS; Bull. Anal. Pol. Ec. Soc.; Eco. Abst.; Int. Lab. Doc.; PAIS; Pop. Ind.; Peace Res. Abst. J.; Soc. Sc. Hum. Ind.; Wom. Stu. Abst.

1566
DE ECONOMIST. v.1– , Jan. 1852– . Haarlem, Leiden. Bimonthly, 1852–74; quarterly.
Issued by: Nederlandsch Economisch Instituut. In Dutch or English.
Indexes: 1852–62, 1v.; 1877–86, 1852–1902, 1v.
Indexed: PAIS; SSCI.

1567
ECONOMY AND HISTORY. 1– , spring 1959– . Lund. Annual.
Issued jointly by: Institute of Economic History and the Economic History Association, University of Lund.
Indexes: v.1–5, in v.5.
Indexed: His. Abst.; PAIS.

1568
ECONOMY AND SOCIETY. v.1– , 1972– . London, Routledge & Kegan Paul. Quarterly.
Indexed: Bull. Anal. Pol. Ec. Soc.; Int. Bibl. Eco.; Int. Bibl. Pol. Sc.; Int. Bibl. Soc.; Int. Pol. Sc. Abst.; Soc. Abst.; SSCI; Urb. Aff. Abst.

1569
EDUCAÇÃO & SOCIEDADE. v.1– , Sept. 1978– . São Paulo, Cortez & Morae. Three no. a year.
In Portuguese.

1570
LA EDUCACIÓN. v.1– , 1956– . Washington, D.C., Departamento de Asuntos Educativos, Secretaría General de la O.E.A. Four no. a year (some combined), 1955–68; three no. a year.
Issued by: Jan. 1956, Union Panamericana; Apr./June 1956–63, Union's Division de Educación; 1964–, Departamento de Asuntos Educativos. In Spanish.
Indexes: Vols. 1–5(no.1–20), 1956–60, in v.6; v.1–16(no.1–58), 1956–70, issued as no.59.

1571
EDUCATION. v.1– , Sept. 1880– . Boston, Mass. Quarterly.
Indexes: Vols. 1–25, 1v.
Indexed: Psych. Abst.

1572
EDUCATION. v.1– , 1903– . London, Councils and Education Press. Weekly.
Issued by: Association of Education Committees.

1573
L'ÉDUCATION. no.1/2– , Sept. 26, 1968– . Paris. Weekly.
Issued by: Association de l'Éducation. In French.
Supersedes: *Éducation Nationale.*

1574
EDUCATION ABSTRACTS. Mar. 1949–1963?. Paris, Education Clearinghouse, Unesco. Monthly, except July-Aug.
Title varies: Mar.–Aug. 1949, *Fundamental Education; Abstracts and Bibliography*; Sept. 1949–Dec. 1951, *Fundamental Education Abstracts.*

1575
L'ÉDUCATION AFRICAINE. 1– , 1913– . Dakar. Quarterly (irreg.)
Organ of: Afrique Occidentale Française. Issued by: Inspection de l'Enseignement de l'Afrique Occidentale Française, Direction Générale de l'Enseignement. In French. Other title: *Bulletin de l'Enseignement de l'Afrique Occidentale Française.*

EDUCATION & CULTURE
See OPVOEDING EN KULTUUR

1576
EDUCATION AND SOCIETY. v.1– , 1983– . Melbourne, James Nicholas Publishers. Semi-annual.

1577
EDUCATION AND URBAN SOCIETY. v.1– , Nov. 1968– . Beverly Hills, Calif., Sage Publications. Quarterly.
Indexed: ABC POL SCI; Curr. Cont. Soc. Beh. Sc.; Hum. Res. Abst.; Ind. Per. Ar. Law; LLBA; PAIS; PHRA; Soc. Abst.; Soc. Sc. Ind.; SSCI; Urb. Stu. Abst.

ÉDUCATION CANADIENNE ET INTERNATIONALE
See CANADIAN AND INTERNATIONAL EDUCATION

L'ÉDUCATION EN ASIE
See ASIAN EDUCATION

ÉDUCATION ET DÉVELOPPEMENT LOCAL
See ÉDUCATION ET SOCIÉTÉ

1578
ÉDUCATION ET GESTION. no.1– , 1965– . Paris. Two or three no. a year.
Issued by: Institut National d'Administration Scolaire et Universitaire. Includes supplements which are thematic.

1579
ÉDUCATION ET SOCIÉTÉ. ÉDUCATION ET DÉVELOPPEMENT LOCAL. no.1– , May/June 1982– . Paris. Quarterly.
Issued by: Institut National de Formation et de Recherche sur l'Éducation Permanente INFRED. In French.

1580
EDUCATION IN ASIA AND OCEANIA. no.13/14–17, Sept. 1978–Sept. 1980. Bangkok. Annual.
Issued by: Office for Education in Asia and Oceania, United Nations Educational, Scientific and Cultural Organization.
Continues: *Education in Asia; Reviews, Reports and Notes*. Continued by: *Education in Asia and the Pacific*.

1581
EDUCATION IN ASIA AND THE PACIFIC. no.18– , Sept. 1981– . Bangkok.
Issued by: Office for Education in Asia and the Pacific, United Nations Educational, Scientific and Cultural Organization.
Continues: *Education in Asia and Oceania*.

1582
EDUCATION IN ASIA; REVIEWS, REPORTS AND NOTES. no.1–12, Mar. 1972–Sept. 1977. Bangkok. Semi-annual.
Issued by: Regional Office for Education in Asia, United Nations Educational, Scientific and Cultural Organization.
Continued by: *Education in Asia and Oceania*.

1583
EDUCATION INDEX. Jan. 1929– . New York, N.W. Wilson. 1932– , monthly, cumulated annually and triennially.

EDUCATION. SECTION IB. SOCIAL SCIENCE
See Hokkaido Kyoiku Daigaku. HOKKAIDO KYOIKU KIYŌ

1584
EDUCATIONAL DOCUMENTATION AND INFORMATION. v.45(no.178)– , 1971– . Paris, Unesco. Quarterly.
Issued by: Unesco for the International Bureau of Education. Each number is thematic.
Continues: *Bulletin* of the International Bureau of Education.

1585
EDUCATIONAL RECORD. v.1– , 1920– . Washington, D.C. Quarterly.
Issued by: American Council on Education. Supplements accompany some numbers.
Indexed: Int. Bibl. Soc. Cul. Anth.; Psych. Abst.; SSCI.

1586
EDUCATIONAL RESEARCH QUARTERLY. v.1– , spring 1976– . Los Angeles, Calif.
Issued by: School of Education, University of Southern California. Other title: *ERQ*.
Supersedes: *California Journal of Educational Research*.

1587
EDUCATIONAL REVIEW. v.1–76, Jan. 1891–Oct.1928. Garden City, N.Y., Educational Pub. Co. Monthly, except July–Aug.
Merged into: *School and Society*.
Indexes: Vols. 1–25, 1891–May 1903, 1v.; v.26–50, June 1903–Oct. 1915, 1v.

1588
EDUCATIONAL STATISTICS YEARBOOK. v.1– , 1974– . Paris. Annual.
Issued by: Organisation for Economic Co-operation and Development.

1589
EDUCATIONAL STUDIES. v.1– , Mar. 1975– . Dorchester-on-Thames. Three no. a year.

1590
THE EDUCATIONAL TRENDS. v.1– , 1966/67– . Ajmer. Two no. a year, 1966–79; quarterly.
Issued by: Alumni Association of the Regional College of Education. Title varies: v.1–2, 1966/67–1967/68, *Alumnus*.

1591
EESTI NSV AJOLOO KUSIMUSI. VOPROSY ISTORII ESTONSKOĬ SSR. 1– , 1960– . Tartu. Irreg.
Issued by: Tartuskiĭ Universitet. In Estonian or Russian; summaries in Estonian, German, or Russian.

1592
Eesti NSV. Teaduste Akademia. Ajaloo Institut. ARHEOLOGILINE KOGUMIK. 1– , 1955– . Tallin.
In Estonian or Russian, occasionally in German; summaries in the other language; v.2 has also summaries in German.

1593
ÉGYPTE CONTEMPORAINE. v.1– , 1910– . Le Caire, Imprimerie Nationale. Four no. a year, 1910–16; seven no. a year, 1917; six no. a year.
Issued by: Société d'Économie Politique, de Statistique et de Législation. Other title: *Miṣr al-Mus'āsirah*. Initially in French; now in Arabic or English.
Indexes: Vols. 1–50, 1910–59, 1v.
Indexed: Int. Lab. Doc.; PAIS; PAISFL.

EGYPTIAN REVIEW OF INTERNATIONAL LAW
See REVUE ÉGYPTIENNE DE DROIT INTERNATIONAL

1594
[No entry]

1595
EINHEIT. v.1– , June 1946– . Berlin. Monthly.
Issued by: Zentralkommittee der Sozialistischen Einheitspartei Deutschlands. In German. Subtitle reads: "Zeitschrift für Theorie und Praxis des wissenschaftlichen Sozialismus". Supplements accompany some numbers.
Indexed: Bull. Anal. Pol. Ec. Soc.; PAISFL.

1596
DIE EINHEIT DER GESELLWISSENSCHAFTEN. v.1– , 1964– . Tübingen, J.C.B. Moher. Irreg.
In German. Some works are translations into German. Includes subseries: *Studien in den Grenzbereichen der Wirtschafts- und Sozialwissenschaften*. Monograph series.

1597
EKISTICS. v.1– , Oct. 1955– . Athens, Doxiadis Associates. Monthly.
Title varies: no.1, *Tropical Housing and Planning Monthly*.
Indexes: Vols. 1–10(no.1–62), 1955–63, in no.63.
Indexed: Abst. Anth.; Bull. Anal. Pol. Ec. Soc.; Bull. Sig. Soc. Eth.; Int. Bibl. Soc.; PHRA; Sage Urb. Stu. Abst.

1598
EKONOMICHESKAI͡A GEOGRAFII͡A; RESPUBLIKANSKIĬ MEZHVIDOMSTVENNYĬ SBIRNIK. no.22– , 1977– . Kiev, Vidavnit͡svo Kiovskogo Universiteta. Irreg.
Issued by: Kiovskiĭ Gosudarstvennyĭ Universitet. In Russian or Ukrainian.
Continues: *Ekonomicheskai͡a Heohrafii͡a* (no.1–21, 1966–76).

EKONOMICHESKIE ISSLEDOVANII͡A
See STUDIA EKONOMICZNE

EKONOMICHESKIE POLOZHENIE KAPITALISTICHESKIKH STRAN
See MIROVAI͡A EKONOMIKA I MEZHDUNARODNYE OTNOSHENII͡A

EKONOMICHESKIĬ ANALIZ
See EKONOMSKA ANALIZA

1599
EKONOMICHESKOE POLOZHENIE KAPITALISTICHESKIKH I RAZVIVAI͡USHCHIKHSI͡A STRAN. 1962/63– . Moskva.
Issued by: Institut Mirovoĭ Ekonomiki Mezhdunarodnikh Otnosheniĭ, Akademii͡a Nauk SSSR. In Russian.
Continues: *Ekonomicheskoe Polozhenie Kapitalisticheskikh Stran*; *Kon'i͡unkturnyĭ Obzor*.

1600
EKONOMICKÝ CASOPIS. 1– , 1949– . Bratislava, Vieda, Izdavatelstvo Slovenskej Akademii Vied. Four no. a year, 1949–58; six no. a year, 1959–66; ten no. a year, 1967–80; monthly.
In Slovak; summaries in Russian. Tables of contents in English and Russian. Title varies: *Ekonomický Sbornik*.
Indexed: Int. Bibl. Eco.; Int. Lab. Doc.

EKONOMICKÝ SBORNIK
See EKONOMICKÝ CASOPIS

1601
EKONOMIKA I MATEMATICHESKIE METODY. v.1– , Jan./Feb. 1965– . Moskva, Nauka. Bimonthly.

Issued by: T͡Sentral'nyĭ Ekonomichesko-Matematicheskiĭ Institut, Akademii͡a Nauk SSSR. In Russian.
Indexed: Bull. Anal. Pol. Ec. Soc.; Int. Bibl. Eco.

1602
EKONOMIKA I ORGANIZACJA PRACY. v.1– , Jan. 1950– . Warszawa, Państwowe Wydawnictwo Ekonomiczne. Monthly.
Issued by: Instytut Ekonomiki i Organizacji Przemysłu. In Polish. Includes supplement: "Biuletyn Instytutu Ekonomiki i Organizacji Przemysłu".

1603
EKONOMIKA I ORGANIZATSII͡A PROMYSHLENNOGO PROIZVODSTVA. v.1– , 1970– . Novosibirsk, Nauka. Bimonthly, 1970–78; monthly.
Issued by: Sibirskoe Otdelenie, Akademii͡a Nauk SSSR. In Russian.
Indexed: Int. Bibl. Eco.

1604
EKONOMIKA I ZHIZN'. 1959– . Tashkent. Monthly.
Issued by: Gosudarstvennyĭ Planovoĭ Komitet Uzbekhskoĭ SSR. In Russian. Title varies: 1959–63, *Narodnoe Khozi͡aĭstvo Uzbekistana*; 1964–Jan. 1965, *Narodnoe Khozi͡aĭstvo Sredneĭ Azii.*

EKONOMIKA PLANIROVANII͡A
See ECONOMICS OF PLANNING

1605
EKONOMIKA PREDUZECA. v.1–21, 1953–1975. Beograd. Monthly.
Issued by: Savez Ekonomista SR Srbije za Izuchivanje Problematike Prevrednih Preduzeca, Drustvo Ekonomista Srbije. In Serbo-Croatian; summaries in English.
Continued by: *Ekonomika Udruchnog Rada.*

EKONOMIKA PROMYSHLENNOSTI
See REFERATIVNYI SBORNIK. EKONOMIKA PROMYSHLENNOSTI

1606
EKONOMIKA SEL'SKOGO KHOZI͡AĬSTVA. 1– , 1925– . Moskva, "Kolos". Monthly.
Issued by: Ministerstvo Sel'skogo Khozi͡aĭstva S.S.S.R. In Russian. Tables of contents also in Chinese, English, French and German. Title varies: 1925–29, *Puti Sel'skogo Khozi͡aĭstva*; 1930–38, *Sot͡sialisticheskai͡a Rekonstrukt͡sii͡a Sel'skogo Khozi͡aĭstva*; 1939–56, *Sot͡sialisticheskoe Sel'skoe Khozi͡aĭstvo.*
Indexed: Bull. Anal. Pol. Ec. Soc.; Int. Bibl. Eco.

1607
EKONOMIKA UDRUCHNOG RADA. v.22– , Jan. 1974– . Beograd. Monthly.
Issued by: Savez Ekonomista Srbije. In Serbo-Croatian.
Continues: *Ekonomika Preduzeca.*

1608
EKONOMIST. 1858–1861. St. Petersburg.
In Russian. Issued as a supplement to: *Ukazatel'; Ekonomicheskiĭ, Politicheskiĭ i Promyshlennyĭ.*

1609
EKONOMIST. 1– , 1948– . Beograd. Quarterly.
Issued by: Savez Ekonomistov Jugoslavije. In Serbo-Croatian.
Indexed: His. Abst.; Int. Lab. Doc.

1610
EKONOMISTA. v.1– , 1900– . Warszawa, Państwowe Wydawnictwo Naukowe. Bimonthly.
Issued by: Komitet Nauk Ekonomicznych, Polska Akademia Nauk and Polskie Towarzystwo Ekonomiczne. In Polish; summaries in English and Russian. Not published 1939–46. Volume numbering discontinued.

1611
EKONOMSKA ANALIZA. ECONOMIC ANALYSIS. EKONOMICHESKIĬ ANALIZ. v.1–11, 1967–1977. Beograd, Ekonomski Biro. Four no. a year.
Issued by: Jugoslovensko Udruzenje za Ekonometriju i Organizacione Nauke, Institut Ekonomskih Nauk, Beograd, Jugoslovenski Institut za Ekonomska Raziskovanja, Ljubljana, and Ekonomski Institut, Zagreb. In Serbo-Croatian; summaries in English and Russian. Published also in English and Russian editions.
Continued by: *Economic Analysis and Workers Management* (v.12–, 1980–)

1612
EKONOMSKA MISAO. v.1– , Apr. 1968– . Beograd, Privrecni Pregled. Quarterly.
Issued by: Savez Ekonomista Srbije za Pitanja Ekonomske Teorije i Prakse. In Serbo-Croatian; summaries in English and Russian, occasionally in French and Russian.

1613
EKONOMSKA REVIJA. 1– , summer 1950– . Ljubljana. Quarterly.
Issued by: Savez Ekonomistov Slovenije. In Slovenian; summaries in English and French.
Indexes: Vols. 1–10, 1950–59, with v.11.

Indexed: Bull. Anal. Pol. Ec. Soc.; Int. Bibl. Eco.; Int. Lab. Doc.

1614
EKONOMSKI PREGLED. v.1– , 1950– . Zagreb, Izdavacko Preduzece Kultura. Bimonthly, 1950–52; monthly.
Issued by: Drustvo Ekonomista Hrvatske (earlier by Savez Ekonomska Hrvatske). In Serbo-Croatian; summaries in English and Russian.
Indexes: Vols. 1–20, 1950–69, 1v.

1615
ELECTORAL STUDIES. v.1– , Apr. 1982– . Guildford, Butterworth. Three no. a year.
Indexed: His. Abst.; PAIS; SSCI.

1616
EMIGRAZIONE; INFORMAZIONI SOCIALI. 1967– . Roma.
In Italian.
Continues: *Informazioni Sociali per l'Emigrazione.*
Indexed: Bull. Anal. Pol. Ec. Soc.

THE EMPIRE REVIEW
See THE COMMONWEALTH & THE EMPIRE REVIEW

THE EMPIRE VIEW AND JOURNAL OF BRITISH TRADE
See THE COMMONWEALTH & EMPIRE REVIEW

1617
EMPIRICAL ECONOMICS. v.1– , 1976– . Wien, Physica-Verlag. Quarterly.
Issued by: Institut für Höhere Studien und Wissenschaftliche Forschung, Wien.
Indexed: PAIS.

EMPIRICAL SOCIAL RESEARCH
See EMPIRISCHE SOZIALFORSCHUNG

1618
EMPIRISCHE SOZIALFORSCHUNG. 1968– . München, Pullah Verlag Dokumentation. Irreg.
Issued by: Zentralarchiv für Empirische Sozialforschung, Universität zu Köln. In German. Other title: *Empirical Social Research* (A directory of research institutes)

1619
ENCOUNTER. Oct. 1953– . London, Secker & Warburg. Monthly.
Published for the Congress for Cultural Freedom.
Indexed: APAIS; Bull. Anal. Pol. Ec. Soc.; His. Abst.; Int. Bibl. Pol. Sc.; Int. Pol. Sc. Abst.; Ind. Per. Art. Law; Peace Res. Abst. J.; Soc. Sc. Hum. Ind.; Wom. Stu. Abst.

1620
ENERGY POLICY. v.1– , June 1973– . Guildford, IPC Science and Technology Press. Quarterly.
Indexed: Bull. Anal. Pol. Ec. Soc.; Int. Bibl. Eco.; Int. Pol. Sc. Abst.

1621
ENERGY SYSTEMS AND POLICY. v.1– , fall 1974– . New York, Crane Russak. Quarterly.
Indexed: Bull. Anal. Pol. Ec. Soc.; Int. Bibl. Eco.; Int. Bibl. Pol. Sc.; Int. Pol. Sc. Abst.

1622
THE ENGINEERING ECONOMIST. v.1– , June 1955– . Hoboken, N.J. Quarterly.
Issued by: Engineering Economy Committee (called Engineering Economy Committee, June 1953–spring 1956), American Society for Engineering Education, and the Institute of Industrial Engineers.
Indexes: Vols. 1–8, 1955–summer 1963, 1v.

1623
THE ENGLISH HISTORICAL REVIEW. v.1– , Jan. 1886– . London, Longman Group Journal. Quarterly.
Indexes: Vols. 1–20, 1886–1905, 1v.; v.21–30, 1906–15, 1v.; v.31–40, 1916–25, 1v.
Indexed: Soc. Sc. Hum. Ind.

ENGLISH SUPPLEMENT
See LA SPETTATORE INTERNAZIONALE

1624
THE ENGLISHWOMAN'S REVIEW OF SOCIAL AND INDUSTRIAL QUESTIONS. v.[1]–41, no.3, Oct. 1866–July 1910. London. Monthly.
Not published July 1869–Jan. 1873.

1625
ENSAYOS SOBRE POLÍTICA ECONÓMICA. v.1– , Mar. 1982– . Bogotá. Two no. a year.
Issued by: Departamento de Investigaciones Económicas, Banco de la Republica. In Spanish.
Indexed: PAISFL.

1626
ENTWICKLUNG UND ZUSAMMENARBEIT. 1– , 1960– . Bonn. Bimonthly.
Issued by: Deutsche Stiftung für Internationale Entwicklung. In German. Some numbers are combined. Subtitle reads: "Beiträge zur Entwicklungspolitik". Published also in English: *D–C Development and Cooperation*, French: *D–C Développement et Coopération*, and Spanish: *D–C Desarrollo y Cooperación* editions. Other title: *E–Z Entwicklung und Zusammenarbeit.*
Indexed: PAISFL.

1627
ENVIRONMENT. v.11– , Jan./Feb. 1969– . St. Louis, Mo., Committee for Environmental Information. Ten no. a year.
"An official publication of Scientists' Institute for Public Information".
Continues: *Scientist and Citizen.*
Indexed: Curr. Cont. Soc. Beh. Sc.; Eco. Abst.; Ind. Per. Art. Law; Hum. Res. Abst.; SSCI; Urb. Aff. Abst.

1628
ENVIRONMENT AND BEHAVIOR. v.1– , June 1969– . Beverly Hills, Calif., Sage Publications. Quarterly.
Issued by: Environmental Psychology Program, City University of New York.
Indexed: Curr. Cont. Soc. Beh. Sc.; Ind. Per. Art. Law; PAIS; PHRA; Psych. Abst.; Sage Urb. Stu. Abst.; Soc. Abst.; SSCI; Urb. Aff. Abst.

1629
ENVIRONMENT & PLANNING. v.1–5, 1969–1973. London, Pion.
Continued by: *Environment and Planning. A*; *Environment and Planning. B*; *Environment and Planning. C. Government and Policy*; *Environment and Planning. D. Society and Space.*

1630
ENVIRONMENT AND PLANNING. A. v.6– , Jan./Feb. 1974– . London, Pion.
Continues, in part: *Environment & Planning.*
Indexed: Pop. Ind.; Sage Urb. Stu. Abst.

1631
ENVIRONMENT AND PLANNING. B. v.1– , June 1974– . London, Pion. Semi-annual.
Supersedes, in part: *Environment & Planning.*

1632
ENVIRONMENT AND PLANNING. C. GOVERNMENT AND POLICY. v.1– , Jan. 1983– . London, Pion. Quarterly.
Supersedes, in part: *Environment & Planning.*

1633
ENVIRONMENT AND PLANNING. D. SOCIETY AND SPACE. v.1– , Mar. 1983– . London, Pion. Quarterly.
Supersedes, in part: *Environment & Planning.*

1634
ENVIRONMENT AND SOCIAL SCIENCES. ENVIRONNEMENT ET SCIENCES SOCIALES. 1–5, 1972–1973. The Hague, Mouton.
Published with the support of the Maison des Sciences de l'Homme. In English or French.

1635
ENVIRONMENTAL AFFAIRS. v.1– , Apr. 1971– . Brighton, Mass. Four no. a year.
Issued by: Environmental Law Center, Boston College Law School.
Indexes: Vols. 1–10, 1978/79–1982/83, in v.10.
Indexed: Ind. Per. Art. Law; Urb. Aff. Abst.

1636
ENVIRONMENTAL PERIODICALS BIBLIOGRAPHY; INDEXED ARTICLE TITLES. v.2– , Feb. 1973– . Santa Barbara, Calif. Bimonthly, with cumulative annual index.
Issued by: Environment Studies Institute, International Academy at Santa Barbara.
Continues: *Environmental Periodicals; Indexed Article Titles* (v.1, 1972).

1637
ENVIRONMENTAL POLICY AND LAW. v.1– , June 1975– . Lausanne, Elsevier Sequoia. Four no. a year.
Indexed: Bull. Anal. Pol. Ec. Soc.; Int. Bibl. Pol. Sc.; Int. Pol. Sc. Abst.

1638
ENVIRONMENTAL REVIEW. no.1–6, 1976–1978; v.3– , fall 1978– . Pittsburgh, Pa. Three no. a year.
Issued by: American Society for Environmental History. Includes: "Bibliographic Supplement" (fall 1976–). Other title: *ER Environmental Review.*

1639
ENVIRONNEMENT AFRICAIN. v.1– , Dec. 1974– . Dakar. Four no. a year. Some combined nos.
Issued by: IDEP, Environment Training Program (ENDA) in association with the African Institute. Issued also in English: *African Environment.*
Indexed: Bull. Anal. Pol. Ec. Soc.

ENVIRONNEMENT ET SCIENCES SOCIALES
See ENVIRONMENT AND SOCIAL SCIENCES

EPHEMERIS ARCHAIOLOGIKE
See Archaiologike Hetaireia em Athenais. ARCHAIOLOGIKE EPHEMERIS

1640
EPIGRAPHIA INDICA. v.1– , Oct. 1888– . Delhi, Manager of Publications. Quarterly (irreg.); eight no. per volume.
Issued by: 1888–1939, Archaeological Survey of India; 1942–61, Department of Archaeology; Oct. 1962–Jan. 1966, Archaeological Survey of the Republic of India. Vols. for 1894–1920 published as supplement to *Indian Antiquary.* Title varies: 1888–July 1939, *Epigraphia Indica and Record of Archaeological Survey of India.*

EPIGRAPHIA INDICA AND RECORD OF ARCHAEOLOGICAL SURVEY OF INDIA
See EPIGRAPHIA INDICA

1641
EPITHEŌRĒSIS KOINŌNIKON EREUNŌN. 1– , July/Sept. 1969– . Athenai. Quarterly.
Issued by: Ethnikon Kentron Koinōnikōn Ereunōn. In Greek, English, or French; occasionally in German or Italian. Other title: *Greek Review of Social Research.*
Supersedes: *Koinōlogike Skepse.*
Indexed: Soc. Abst.

1642
EPITHEŌRĒSIS OIKONOMIKON KAI POLITIKŌN EPISTĒMON. 1– , 1946– . Athenai, Arguris Papazisi. Four no. a year.
In Greek. Tables of contents also in English. Other title: *Review of Economic and Political Sciences.*

1643
EQUITY. v.1–21, no.2, 1898–Apr. 1919. Philadelphia, Pa. Quarterly.
Issued by: American Proportional Representation League. Title varies: 1898–1913, *Equity Series.*

EQUITY SERIES
See EQUITY

ERGÄNZUNGSHEFTE. BEITRÄGE ZUR BEZIEHUNGSLEHRE
See KÖLNER VIERTELJAHRESHEFTE FÜR SOZIOLOGIE

1644
ERGONOMICS. v.1– , Nov. 1957– . London, Taylor & Francis. Quarterly, 1957; monthly.
Official publication of: Ergonomics Society (called Ergonomics Research Society, 1957–Mar. 1976), the Nederlands Vereiniging voor Ergonomie, and the International Ergonomics Association.
Indexed: PAIS.

ERZIEHUNGSWISSENSCHAFTLICHE VERÖFFENTLICHUNGEN
See Freie Universität, Berlin. Osteuropa Institut. ERZIEHUNGSWISSENSCHAFTLICHE VERÖFFENTLICHUNGEN

1645
ESPACE, POPULATION, SOCIÉTÉS. 1982– . Lille. Semi-annual.
Issued by: Université des Sciences et Techniques de Lille in cooperation with various French and Belgian universities. In French; summaries in English and French.
Indexed: Pop. Ind.

1646
ESPAÑA ECONÓMICA. v.1– , 1893– . Madrid. Weekly.
In Spanish. Suspended with no. 2263–2395, Feb. 4, 1939–Jan. 3, 1942. (Publisher ignored the existence of the mentioned numbers published during the Spanish Civil war). Title varies: 1893–1903, *Estafeta*; 1904–49, *España Económica y Finanziera.* Supplements accompany some numbers.

ESPAÑA ECONÓMICA Y FINANZIERA
See ESPAÑA ECONÓMICA

1647
ÉSPRIT. v.1– , Oct. 1932– . Lyon, Édition Française. Frequency varies, –1983; monthly.
In French. Continuing numbering of issues discontinued in 1976. Initially issues of one year were grouped in two volumes. Suspended Sept. 1941–Nov. 1944.
Indexed: Bull. Sig. Soc. Eth.; His. Abst.; Int. Lab. Doc.; Int. Pol. Sc. Abst.; Peace Res. Abst. J.

1648
ESSAYS IN CONTEMPORARY ECONOMIC PROBLEMS. 1981/1982– . Washington, D.C. Quarterly.
Issued by: American Enterprise Institute for Public Policy Research. Each volume has also a distinctive title.
Continues: *Contemporary Economic Problems.*

1649
EST-OVEST. v.1– , 1970– . Trieste. Quarterly.
Issued by: Istituto di Studi e Documentazione sull'Est Europeo. In Italian.
Indexed: PAISFL.

ESTAFETA
See ESPAÑA ECONÓMICA

1650
ESTRATEGIA. v.1– , Jan. 1969– . Buenos Aires. Bimonthly.
Issued by: Instituto Argentino de Estudios Estratégicos y de las Relaciones Internacionales. In Spanish.
Indexed: Bull. Anal. Pol. Ec. Soc.

ESTUDIO DE LOS MERCADOS PRIMARIOS
See United Nations. Commission on International Commodity Trade. COMMODITY SURVEY

ESTUDIO ECONÓMICO DE AMÉRICA LATINA
See United Nations. Economic Commission for Latin America. ECONOMIC SURVEY OF LATIN AMERICA AND THE CARIBBEAN

ESTUDIO ECONÓMICO DE AMÉRICA LATINA Y DEL CARIBE
See United Nations. Economic Commission for Latin America and the Caribbean. ECONOMIC SURVEY OF LATIN AMERICA AND THE CARIBBEAN

1651
ESTUDIOS ANDINOS. v.1– , 1970– . La Paz. Three no. a year.
Issued by: Instituto Boliviano de Estudios y Acción Social (IBEAS), and the University of Pittsburgh. In Spanish. Includes some translations from English.
Indexed: Int. Bibl. Soc. Cul. Anth.; Int. Lab. Doc.; Int. Pol. Sc. Abst.

1652
ESTUDIOS CENTROAMERICANOS. no.1– , 1965– . Guatemala City.
Issued by: Seminario de Integración Social Guatemalteca, and the Institute of Latin American Studies, University of Texas. In Spanish.

1653
ESTUDIOS COOPERATIVOS. 1– , 1963– . Madrid. Three no. a year.
Issued by: Asociación de Estudios Cooperativos. Co-sponsor: Catedra Libre de Cooperación, Universidad de Madrid. In Spanish.

1654
ESTUDIOS CUBANOS. CUBAN STUDIES. v.5– , Jan. 1975– . Pittsburgh, Pa. Semi-annual.
Issued by: Center for Latin American Studies, University of Pittsburgh.
Continues: *Cuban Studies Newsletter. Boletin de Estudios sobre Cuba.*

1655
ESTUDIOS DE CULTURA MAYA. 1– , 1961– . Mexico, D.F., Libreria Universitaria. Annual.
Issued by: Seminario de Cultura Maya, Universidad Nacional Autónoma de México. In Spanish.

1656
ESTUDIOS DE ECONOMÍA. no.1– , first quarter 1973– . Santiago, Chile. Semi-annual.
Issued by: Departamento de Economía, Faculdad de Ciencias Económicas y Administrativos, Universidad de Chile. In Spanish.
Indexed: Bull. Anal. Pol. Ec. Soc.

1657
ESTUDIOS DE HISTORIA DE LAS INSTITUCIONES POLÍTICAS Y SOCIALES. no.1– , 1966– . Santiago, Chile, Editorial Jurídica de Chile.
Issued by: Faculdad de Ciencias Jurídicas y Sociales, Universidad de Chile. In Spanish. Vol. 2, 1967 last available for examination.
Indexed: His. Abst.

1658
ESTUDIOS DE HISTORIA SOCIAL. no.1– , Apr./June 1977– . Madrid. Quarterly.
Issued by: Instituto de Estudios Laborales y de Securidad; subsequently by Instituto de Estudios de Sociedad y Securidad Social. In Spanish.

1659
ESTUDIOS DE HISTORIA SOCIAL DE ESPAÑA. 1– , 1949– . Madrid.
Issued by: Instituto Balmes de Sociología, Consejo Superior de Investigaciones Científicas. In Spanish.

1660
ESTUDIOS DE HISTORIA SOCIAL, ECONÓMICA Y DEMOGRÁFICA DE ESPAÑA. 1– , 1967– . Madrid. Irreg.
Issued by: Seminario Social y Económica, Faculdad de Filosofía y Letras, Universidad de Madrid. In Spanish.

1661
ESTUDIOS DE HISTORIA SOCIAL Y ECONÓMICA DE AMÉRICA. no.1– , June 1985– . Madrid.
Issued by: Departamento de Historia de América, Faculdad de Filsofía y Letras, Universidad de Alcala de Henares. In Spanish.

1662
ESTUDIOS DEL TERCER MUNDO. v.1– , Dec. 1978– . Mexico, D.F. Four no. a year.
Issued by: El Centro de Estudios Económicos y Sociales del Tercer Mundo (CEESTM). In Spanish.

1663
ESTUDIOS GEOPOLÍTICOS Y ESTRATÉGICOS. no.1– , Jan./Mar. 1979– . Lima. Quarterly.
Issued by: Instituto Peruano de Estudios Geopolíticos y Estrategías. In Spanish.

1664
ESTUDIOS INTERNACIONALES. v.1– , Apr. 1967– . Santiago, Chile. Quarterly.
Issued by: Instituto de Estudios Internacionales, Universidad de Chile. In Spanish.
Indexed: ABC POL SCI; Bull. Anal. Pol. Ec. Soc.; Int. Bibl. Pol. Sc.; Int. Pol. Sc. Abst.; Int. Lab. Doc.; PAISFL.

ESTUDIOS INTERNACIONALES
See REVISTA DE ESTUDIOS INTERNACIONALES

1665
ESTUDIOS LATINOAMERICANOS. 1– , 1972– . Wrocław, Zakład Narodowy im. Ossolińskich. Irreg.
Issued by: Instytut Historii, Polska Akademia Nauk. In English, Portuguese, or Spanish.

1666
ESTUDIOS MIGRATORIOS LATINOAMERICANOS. 1– , Dec. 1985– . Buenos Aires. Three no. a year.
Issued by: Centro de Estudios Migratorios Latinoamericanos. In Spanish.

1667
ESTUDIOS POLÍTICOS. v.1– , Apr./June 1975– . Mexico, D.F. Four no. a year.
Issued by: Centro de Estudios Políticos, Faculdad de Ciencias Políticas y Sociales, Universidad Nacional Autónoma de México. In Spanish.
Indexed: Bull. Anal. Pol. Ec. Soc.; Int. Pol. Sc. Abst.

1668
ESTUDIOS SINDICALES Y COOPERATIVOS. v.1–6, Jan./Mar. 1967–1972. Madrid. Quarterly.
Issued by: Instituto de Estudios Sindicales, Sociales y Cooperativos. In Spanish.
Continued by: *Estudios Sindicales* (v.7–8 (no.25/26–32), Jan./Mar. 1973–Oct./Dec. 1974)
Indexes: no.1–27/28, 1967–73, in no.27/28.
Indexed: Bull. Anal. Pol. Ec. Soc.; Int. Bibl. Eco.; Int. Bibl. Soc.; Int. Lab. Doc.

1669
ESTUDIOS SOBRE LA ECONÓMIA ARGENTINA. 1– , 1969– . Buenos Aires. Four no. a year.
Issued by: Instituto de Investigaciones Económicas y Financieras de la Confederación General Económica. In Spanish.

1670
ESTUDIOS SOCIALES. no.1– , June 1970– . Ciudad de Guatemala.
Issued by: Instituto de Ciencias Políticas y Sociales, Universidad Rafael Landivar. In Spanish.
Indexed: Int. Bibl. Soc. Cul. Anth.

1671
ESTUDIOS SOCIALES. v.1– , Sept. 1982– . Lima.
Issued by: Unidad de Documentación y Publicación Estudios, Universidad Nacional Mayor de San Marcos. In Spanish.

1672
ESTUDIOS SOCIALES CENTROAMERICANOS. v.1– , Jan./Apr. 1972– . San Jose. Three no. a year.
Issued by: Programa Centroamericana de Ciencias Sociales (called earlier Programa Centroamericana de Desarrollo de las Ciencias Sociales). In Spanish.
Indexed: Bull. Anal. Pol. Ec. Soc.; Hist. Abst.; Int. Bibl. Eco.; Int. Bibl. Soc. Cul. Anth.; PAISFL; SSCI.

1673
ESTUDIOS SOCIOLÓGICOS. v.1– , Jan./Apr. 1983– . Mexico, D.F. Three no. a year.
Issued by: Centro de Estudios Sociológicos, Colegio de México. In Spanish.

1674
ESTUDIOS SOCIOLÓGICOS LATINOAMERICANOS. v.1– , 1961– . Madrid. Irreg.
Issued by: Oficina Internacional de Investigaciones Sociales de Feres. In Spanish. Cover title: *América Latina.*

ESTUDOS COLONAIS
See ESTUDOS ULTRAMARINOS

1675
ESTUDOS DE CIÊNCIAS POLÍTICAS E SOCIAIS. 1–89, 1956–1972. Lisboa. Irreg.
Issued by: Centro de Estudos Políticos e Sociais, Junta do Investigaçãos do Ultramar, Ministerio do Ultramar. In Portuguese. Each volume has also a distinctive title.

1676
ESTUDOS DE ECONOMIA. v.1– , Sept./Dec. 1980– . Lisboa. Quarterly.
Issued by: Instituto Superior de Economia, Universidade Técnica de Lisboa. In Portuguese.
Indexed: PAISFL.

ESTUDOS DE ECONOMIA E FINANÇAS
See Instituto Gulbenkian de Ciências. Centro de Economia e Finanças. ARQUIVO B. ESTUDOS DE ECONOMIA E FINANÇAS

1677
ESTUDOS DEMOGRÁFICOS. 1951– . Rio de Janeiro. Irreg.
Issued by: Instituto Brasileiro de Geografia e Estatística, Conselho Nacional de Estatística. In Portuguese.

ESTUDOS E ANÁLISES
See Centro Brasileiro de Estudos Demográficos. ESTUDOS E ANÁLISES

1678
ESTUDOS ECONÔMICOS. v.1– , 1971– . São Paulo. Bimonthly, 1972–73; three no. a year.
Issued by: Instituto de Pesquisas Econômicos (IPE), Faculdade de Economia e Administração, Universidade de São Paulo. In Portuguese.

1679
ESTUDOS POLÍTICOS E SOCIAIS. v.1–7, 1963–1969. Recife. Semi-annual.
Issued by: Instituto de Ciências Políticas e Sociais, Universidade Federal de Pernambuco. In Portuguese.
Indexed: Int. Bibl. Eco.; Int. Bibl. Pol. Sc.; Int. Bibl. Soc.; Int. Lab. Doc.; Int. Pol. Sc. Abst.

1680
ESTUDOS POLÍTICOS E SOCIAIS. no.1– , 1963– . Lisboa. Quarterly.
Issued by: Instituto Superior de Ciências Sociais e Política Ultramarina. In Portuguese, English, or French.
Indexed: Int. Bibl. Eco.; Int. Bibl. Pol. Sc.; Int. Bibl. Soc.; Int. Bibl. Soc. Cul. Anth.; Int. Lab. Doc.; Int. Pol. Sc. Abst.; LLBA.

1681
ESTUDOS SOCIAIS E COOPERATIVOS. v.1–3, 1962–1969. Lisboa.
Issued by: Centro de Estudos Sociais e Cooperativos. In Portuguese; summaries in English, French and German.
Indexed: Int. Bibl. Pol. Sc.; Int. Bibl. Soc.; Int. Lab. Doc.; Int. Pol. Sc. Abst.

1682
ESTUDOS ULTRAMARINOS. v.1– , 1948/49–1962. Lisboa.
Issued by: Instituto Superior de Estudos Ultramarinos (called 1948–54 Escola Superior Colonial), later by: Universidade Técnica de Lisboa. In Portuguese. Title varies: v.1–4, 1948–54, *Estudos Coloniais*.

1683
ETC: A REVIEW OF GENERAL SEMANTICS. v.1– , Aug. 1943– . Bloomington, Ind. Quarterly.
Issued by: International Society for General Semantics.
Indexed: Ind. Per. Art. Law; Int. Bibl. Pol. Sc.; LLBA; Peace Res. Abst. J.; Psych. Abst.; Wom. Stu. Abst.

1684
ETHICS. v.1– , Oct. 1890– . Chicago, Ill., University of Chicago Press. Quarterly.
Title varies: 1890–Jan. 1938, *International Journal of Ethics, devoted to the Advancement of Ethical Knowledge and Practice*.
Indexed: ABC POL SCI; Bull. Anal. Pol. Ec. Soc.; Bull. Sig. Soc. Eth.; Eco. Abst.; Ind. Per. Art. Law; Int. Bibl. Eco.; Int. Bibl. Pol. Sc.; Int. Bibl. Soc.; Soc. Abst.; Soc. Sc. Hum. Ind.; SSCI.

1685
ETHICS IN SCIENCE AND MEDICINE. v.2–7, May 1975–1980. Oxford, Elmsford, N.Y., Pergamon Press. Quarterly.
Continues: *Science, Medicine and Man* (v.1, 1974). Continued by: *Social Science and Medicine. Part F. Medical and Social Ethics*.

1686
ETHNIC AND RACIAL STUDIES. 1– , Jan. 1978– . London, Routledge & Kegan Paul. Quarterly.
Other title: *ERS. Ethnic and Racial Studies*.
Indexed: ABC POL SCI; Bull. Anal. Pol. Ec. Soc.; Int. Bibl. Pol. Sc.; Int. Bibl. Soc. Cul. Anth.; Int. Pol. Sc. Abst.

1687
ETHNICA. no.1– , Jan./June 1971– . Barcelona. Semi-annual.
Issued by: Centro de Etnología Peninsular. In Spanish.
Indexed: Abst. Anth.; Int. Bibl. Soc. Cul. Anth.

1688
ETHNICITY. 1– , Apr. 1974– . New York, Academic Press. Quarterly.
Subtitle reads: "An interdisciplinary journal of the study of ethnic relations".
Indexed: Bull. Anal. Pol. Ec. Soc.; Int. Bibl. Soc. Cul. Anth.; Soc. Abst.

ETHNO-MUSICOLOGY
See ETHNOMUSICOLOGY

ETHNOGRAFIKA
See ETHNOGRAPHIKA

1689
ETHNOGRAPHIA. v.1– , 1890– . Budapest. Bimonthly, 1890–1922; monthly, 1923–30; quarterly.
Issued by: A. Magyar Nemzeti Múzeum. In Hungarian; summaries in English. Tables of contents also in English. Title varies: 1–33, 1890–1922, *Ethnografia*; 34–37, 1923–26, *Népélet*. Vol. 34/35 also as ser.3, v.1.
Indexes: v.1–50, 1890–1939.
Indexed: Int. Bibl. Soc. Cul. Anth.

1690
L'ETHNOGRAPHIE. 1860–1912; n. ser., Oct. 15, 1913– . Paris, P. Geuthner, later Gabalda. Frequency varied; two no. a year.
Issued by: Société d'Ethnographie de Paris. In French; summaries in English and French. Occasionally third no. is published and called "special".
Indexed: Int. Bibl. Soc. Cul. Anth.

ETHNOGRAPHIE SOVIÉTIQUE
See SOVETSKAI͡A ETNOGRAFII͡A

1691
ETHNOGRAPHIKA. v.1– , 1978– . Nauplio, Peloponesiakon Laographikon Hidryma. In English or Greek. Other title: *Ethnografica*.

1692
ETHNOGRAPHISCH-ARCHÄOLOGISCHE ZEITSCHRIFT. 1– , 1960– . Berlin, Deutscher Verlag der Wissenschaften. Two no. a year.

In German. Other title: *EAZ Ethnographisch-Archäologische Zeitschrift.*
Supersedes: *Ethnographisch-Archäologische Forschungen* (v.1–6, 1953·59)
Indexed: Abst. Anth.

1693
ETHNOHISTORY. v.1– , 1954– . Tucson, Ariz. Quarterly.
Issued by: American Society for Ethnohistory.
Indexed: Abst. Anth.; Bull. Sig. Soc. Eth.; Int. Bibl. Soc. Cul. Anth.; Soc. Sc. Ind.

ETHNOHISTORY STUDIES
See AUSTRALIAN ABORIGINAL STUDIES

1694
ETHNOLOGIA AMERICANA. 1– , 1964– . Graz. One or two no. a year.
Issued by: Düsseldorfer Institut für Amerikanische Volkskunde. In German.
Indexed: Int. Bibl. Soc. Cul. Anth.

1695
ETHNOLOGIA EUROPEA. v.1– , 1967– . Göttingen, Verlag Otto Schwartz. Irreg.
In English, French, or German.
Indexed: Abst. Anth.

1696
ETHNOLOGIA FENNICA. FINNISH STUDIES IN ETHNOLOGY. v.1– , 1971– . Helsinki. Annual.
In English, Finnish, or German.

1697
ETHNOLOGIA POLONA. v.1– , 1975– . Wrocław, Zakład Narodowy im. Ossolińskich. Annual.
Issued by: Instytut Historii Kultury Materialnej, Polska Akademia Nauk.

1698
ETHNOLOGIA SCANDINAVICA. 1971– . Lund. Annual.
Issued by: Royal Gustav Adolph Academy. In English or German.
Supersedes: *Folk-Liv.*
Indexed: Int. Bibl. Soc. Cul. Anth.; Bull. Sig. Soc. Eth.

1699
ETHNOLOGIA SLAVICA. 1– , 1969– . Bratislava, Slovenské Pedagogické Nakladatelštvo. Annual; some nos. combined.
Issued by: Filozofická Fakulta, Univerzita Komenského. In English, French, or German; summaries in Bulgarian, Czech, French, Russian, Serbo-Croatian, Slovak, or Wendic. Subseries of: *Zbornik Filozofickéj Fakulty Univerzity Komenského.*

1700
Ethnological Society of London. JOURNAL. v.1–4, 1848–1856; n. ser. v.1, no.2–v.2, no.1, 2, 4, 1868–1869/1870. Edinburgh.
During the interval of 1861–69, *Transactions* of the society took the place of the *Journal.*

1701
Ethnological Society of London. TRANSACTIONS. 1861–1869. London.
The *Transactions* replaced the *Journal* of the society during the interval between the first and second series.

1702
ETHNOLOGIE FRANÇAISE. n. ser. no.1– , 1971– . Paris, G.P. Maisonneuve et Larose. Quarterly.
Issued by: Société d'Ethnographie Française. In French; summaries in English and French.
Supersedes: *Arts et Traditions Populaires*, *Folklore Paysan*, *Le Folklore Vivant*, and the *Annales* of the Société Française d'Ethnologie.
Indexed: Bull. Sig. Soc. Eth.; Int. Bibl. Soc. Cul. Anth.

1703
ETHNOLOGISCHE ZEITSCHRIFT ZÜRICH. 1– , 1970– . Bern, Verlag H. Lang. Two no. a year.
Issued by: 1970–71, Völkerliche Museum der Universität Zürich; Sammlung für Völkerkunde der Universität Zürich. In English, French, or German.
Indexed: Abst. Anth.; Int. Bibl. Soc. Cul. Anth.

1704
ETHNOLOGY. v.1– , 1962– . Pittsburgh, Pa. Quarterly.
Issued by: Department of Anthropology, University of Pittsburgh.
Indexed: Abst. Anth.; Abst. Soc. Work; Bull. Sig. Soc. Eth.; Int. Bibl. Pol. Sc.; Int. Bibl. Soc. Cul. Anth.; Int. Pol. Sc. Abst.; LLBA; Peace Res. Abst. J.; Soc. Sc. Hum. Ind.; SSCI; Wom. Stu. Abst.

ETHNOMEDICINE
See ETHNOMEDIZIN

1705
ETHNOMEDIZIN. ETHNOMEDICINE. v.1– , 1971– . Hamburg, In Kommission Edmund Buske Verlag. Irreg. (two to four no. a year)
In English or German. Subtitle reads: "Zeitschrift für interdisziplinare Forschung".
Indexed: Abst. Anth.; Bull. Sig. Soc. Eth.

1706
ETHNOMUSICOLOGY. v.1– , Dec. 1953– . Middletown, Conn., Wesleyan University Press. Irreg., 1953–55; three no. a year.

Issued by: Society of Ethnomusicology. Title varies: *Ethno-musicology*.
Indexed: Abst. Anth.

1707
ETHNOPSYCHIATRICA. 1– , 1978– . Claix, La Pensée Savage Édition. Semi-annual.
In English or French; summaries in the other language.

1708
ETHNOPSYCHOLOGIE. v.1– , Mar. 1946– . Le Havre. Quarterly.
Issued by: Centre de Recherche et Études de l'Institut Havrais de Psychologie des Peuples et Sociologie Économique and some other research institutions in France. In French. Includes supplement: Cahiers de Sociologie Économique. Other title: *Revue de Psychologie des Peuples*.
Indexed: Bull. Anal. Pol. Ec. Soc.; Bull. Sig. Soc. Eth.; LLBA; Int. Bibl. Soc. Cul. Anth.

1709
ETHNOS. v.1, no.1–12, Apr. 1921–Mar. 1922; ser. 2, v.1, no.1–2, 1922–1923; ser. 3, v.1, no.1–5, 1925. Mexico, D.F. Irreg.
In Spanish. Subtitle reads: "Revista dedicada al studio y mayoramento de la población indígena de México".

1710
ETHNOS. v.1– , 1935– . Lisboa. Irreg.
Issued by: Instituto Português de Arqueologia, Historia e Etnografia. In Portuguese.

1711
ETHNOS. v.1– , Jan. 1936– . Stockholm, Bokforlags Aktiebolaget Thule. Bimonthly, v.1–3; quarterly.
Issued by: Ethnographical Museum of Sweden, and the Swedish Oriental Society.
Indexed: Abst. Anth.; Bull. Sig. Soc. Eth.; His. Abst.; Int. Bibl. Soc. Cul. Anth.; LLBA.

1712
ETHOLOGY AND SOCIOBIOLOGY. v.1– , Oct. 1979– . New York, Elsevier North-Holland. Quarterly.
Indexed: Curr. Cont. Soc. Beh. Sc.; LLBA; Psych. Abst.; Soc. Abst.

1713
ETNOGRAFIA POLSKA. v.1– , 1958– . Wrocław, Zakład Norodowy im. Ossolińskich. Annual.
Issued by: Dział Etnografii, Instytut Historii Kultury Materialnej, Polska Akademia Nauk. In Polish; summaries in English, French, and Russian.
Indexed: Bull. Sig. Soc. Eth.; Int. Bibl. Soc. Cul. Anth.

1714
ETNOGRAFIA SHQIPTARE. no.1– , 1962– . Tirane. Annual.
Issued by: Sektori i Etnografise Instituti i Historise dhe Gjuhesise, Universiteti Shteteror i Tiranes. In Albanian.
Indexed: Bull. Sig. Soc. Eth.

1715
ETNOGRAFICHESKIĬ SBORNIK. 1–6, 1853–1864. St. Petersburg.
Issued by: Russkoe Geograficheskoe Obshchestvo. In Russian.

1716
ETNOIATRIA. 1– , 1967– . Verse. Semi-annual.
Issued by: Istituto Italiano di Etnoiatria. In English, French, German, Portuguese, or Spanish; summaries and reports in English and Italian. Subtitle reads: "Rivista di etnomedicina".

1717
ETNOLOŠKI PREGLED. REVUE D'ETHNOLOGIE. v.1– , 1959– . Beograd.
Issued by: Savez Etnoloških Društva SFR Jugoslavije. In Serbo-Croatian; summaries in English, French, or German. Some texts in the Cyrillic alphabet.

1718
ETNOLOŠKA TRIBINA. 1– , 1978– . Zagreb. Annual (irreg.)
Issued by: Hrvatsko Etnološko Društvo. In Serbo-Croatian; summaries in English.
Supersedes: *Izvjesca*.

ÉTUDE DES MARCHÉS DES PRODUITS DE BASE
See United Nations. Commission on International Commodity Trade. COMMODITY SURVEY

ÉTUDE ÉCONOMIQUE SUR L'ASIE ET L'EXTRÊME-ORIENT
See United Nations. Economic Commission for Asia and the Pacific. ECONOMIC AND SOCIAL SURVEY OF ASIA AND THE PACIFIC

1719
ÉTUDE MENSUELLE SUR L'ÉCONOMIE ET LES FINANCES DE LA SYRIE ET DES PAYS ARABES. 1– , 1958– . Damascus. Monthly.
Issued by: Centre d'Étude et de Documentation Économiques, Financières et Sociales. In French.
Indexed: Int. Bibl. Eco.

ÉTUDE SUR L'ÉCONOMIE MONDIALE
See United Nations. Department of Economic and Social Affairs. WORLD ECONOMIC REPORT

ÉTUDE SUR LA POPULATION ET LA TECHNOLOGIE
See Science Council of Canada. STUDY OF POPULATION AND TECHNOLOGY. PERCEPTIONS

1720
ÉTUDES. 1–3, 1856–1858; n.ser. v.1–3, 1859–1861; ser.3, v.1–13, 1862–1867; ser.4, v.1–6, 1868–1870; ser. 5, v.1–12, 1872–1877; ser. 6, v.1–5, 1878–1880; v.43– , 1888– . Paris. Monthly, 1856–96; semimonthly, 1897–1940; monthly.
Issued by: Pères de la Compagnie Jesus. In French. Publication suspended June 1940–Dec. 1945. Title varies: 1856–96, *Études Religieuses, Philosophiques, Historiques et Littéraires.*
Indexed: Bull. Sig. Soc. Eth.; His. Abst.; Int. Bibl. Eco.; Int. Pol. Sc. Abst.; Wom. Stu. Abst.

ÉTUDES ASIATIQUES
See ASIATISCHE STUDIEN

1721
ÉTUDES BALKANIQUES. v.1– , 1964– . Sofia. Quarterly.
Issued by: Institut za Balkanistika, Bulgarskata Akademiia na Naukite. In English, French, German, or Russian.
Indexed: Bull. Anal. Pol. Ec. Soc.; Bull. Sig. Soc. Eth.; His. Abst.; Peace Res. Abst. J.

1722
ÉTUDES CHINOISES. no.1–3, v.4– , spring 1985– . Paris. Two no. a year.
Issued by: L'Association Française d'Études Chinoises. In French. Other title: *Chung-kuo yen chiu.*

1723
ÉTUDES D'HISTOIRE AFRICAINE. STUDIES IN AFRICAN HISTORY. 1970– . Lubumbashi, Zaire. Annual.
Issued by: Département d'Histoire, Université Nationale du Zaire (called earlier Université Lovanium de Kinshasa) in cooperation with the Musée Royal d'Afrique Centrale. In French.

1724
ÉTUDES DE SOCIOLOGIE ET ETHNOLOGIE JURIDIQUES. v.1–34, 1930–1942. Paris, Éditions Domat-Montchrétien.
In French.

1725
ÉTUDES DE SOCIOLOGIE TUNISIENNE. v.1– , 1968– . Tunis. Annual.
Issued by: Bureau de Recherches Sociologiques. In French.
Indexed: Soc. Abst.

ÉTUDES ÉCONOMIQUES SUR LA SYRIE ET LES PAYS ARABES
See SYRIE ET LE MONDE ARABE

ÉTUDES ET CHRONIQUES DE DÉMOGRAPHIE HISTORIQUE
See ANNALES DE DÉMOGRAPHIE HISTORIQUE

1726
ÉTUDES ET CONJONCTURE; ÉCONOMIE MONDIALE. v.1–8, June 15, 1946–May/June 1953. Paris, Presses Universitaires de France. Monthly, 1946–48; bimonthly.
In French. Title varies: June–Sept. 1946, *La Conjoncture; Économie Mondiale.*
Supersedes, in part: *Point Économique*, and *Revue des Économies Étrangères.* Merged with: *Études et Conjoncture; Économie Française* to form: *Études et Conjoncture.*

1727
ÉTUDES & EXPANSION. no.1– , 1957– . Liège. Frequency varies.
Issued by: Société d'Études et d'Expansion (called 1911–Apr. 1913, Association des Licenciés sortis de l'Université de Liège; Oct. 1913–Mar./July 1961, Société Belge d'Études et d'Expansion). In French. Issue for Oct. 1914 without volume number has title *Le Katanga, Province Belge.* Title varies: 1911–Nov./Dec. 1957, *Bulletin*; 1958–Apr./June 1976, Société d'Études et d'Expansion. *Revue.*

ÉTUDES EN STATISTIQUES
See Banque des États de l'Afrique Centrale. ÉTUDES ET STATISTIQUES

ÉTUDES ETHNIQUES AU CANADA
See CANADIAN ETHNIC STUDIES

ÉTUDES HONGROISES
See REVUE D'HISTOIRE COMPARÉE

ÉTUDES ET DOCUMENTS
See RECHERCHE SOCIALE

1728
ÉTUDES INTERNATIONALES. v.1– , Feb. 1970– . Québec. Presses de l'Université Laval. Quarterly.
Issued by: Institut Canadien des Affaires Internationales, and subsequently by: Centre Québecois des Relations Internationales, Faculté des Sciences Sociales, Université Laval. In French.
Indexed: ABC POL SCI; Bull. Anal. Pol. Ec. Soc.; His. Abst.; Int. Bibl. Pol. Sc.; Int. Lab. Doc.; Int. Pol. Sc. Abst.; PAISFL.

ÉTUDES INTERNATIONALES
See NEDERLANDS GENOOTSCHAP VAN INTERNATIONALEN ZAKEN

1729
ÉTUDES INTERNATIONALES DE PSYCHO-SOCIOLOGIE CRIMINELLE. 1– , July/Sept. 1956– . Paris. Irreg.
Issued by: Société Internationale de la Prophylaxe Criminelle. In French.

1730
ÉTUDES MONGOLES. 1– , 1970– . Nanterre. Annual.
Issued by: 1970, Groupe de Documentation et d'Études Mongoles; 1971–, Centre de Documentation et d'Études Mongoles. In French. Title varies: no.7, 8 and 9, *Études Mongoles et Sibériennes*.
Indexed: Int. Bibl. Soc. Cul. Anth.

ÉTUDES MONGOLES ET SIBÉRIENNES
See ÉTUDES MONGOLES

1731
ÉTUDES POLÉMOLOGIQUES. no.1– , July 1971– . Paris. Quarterly.
Issued by: Institut Français de Polémologie. In French.
Indexed: Bull. Anal. Pol. Ec. Soc.; Bull. Sig. Soc. Eth.; Int. Pol. Sc. Abst.

ÉTUDES RELIGIEUSES, PHILOSOPHIQUES, HISTORIQUES ET LITTÉRAIRES
See ÉTUDES

1732
ÉTUDES RURALES. no.1– , Apr./June 1961– . Paris, The Hague, Mouton. Quarterly.
In French.
Indexed: Bull. Anal. Pol. Ec. Soc.; Bull. Sig. Soc. Eth.; His. Abst.; Int. Bibl. Soc. Cul. Anth.; Int. Lab. Doc.; Soc. Abst.

ÉTUDES. SÉRIE AIDE AU DÉVELOPPEMENT
See Commission of the European Communities. ÉTUDES. SÉRIE AIDE AU DÉVELOPPEMENT

ÉTUDES. SÉRIE POLITIQUE SOCIALE
See European Economic Community. ÉTUDES. SÉRIE POLITIQUE SOCIALE

1733
ÉTUDES SLAVES ET EST-EUROPÉENNES. SLAVIC AND EAST EUROPEAN STUDIES. v.1– , spring 1956– . Montréal, Les Presses de l'Université Laval. Two no. a year (some numbers combined).
Issued by: Centre d'Études Slaves, Université de Montréal, later Centre des Slavists et de Spécialistes Est-Européennes du Canada de l'Est. In English or French.
Indexed: His. Abst.; Int. Bibl. Soc. Cul. Anth.; Wom. Stu. Abst.

1734
LES ÉTUDES SOCIALES. v.1–53, Jan. 15, 1881–June 1933. Paris. Irreg.
Issued by: Union de la Paix Sociale, Société Internationale de Science Sociale. In French. Title varies: v.1–90, no.12, 1881–1930, *Reforme Social*; v.91–95, no.3, 1931–Mar. 1935, *Revue d'Économie Sociale; Suivant la Méthode d'Observation*.

1735
ÉTUDES SOCIALES. 1–8, 1904–1913; n. ser. v.1–5, 1932–34. Bruxelles. Irreg.
Issued by: Institut de Sociologie, Université Libre de Bruxelles. In French. Monograph series.
Supersedes: *Bibliothèque Sociologique* (1903). Superseded by: *Travaux* (1–2, 1921) of the Institut de Sociologie.

ÉTUDES SOCIALES NORD-AFRICAINES
See CAHIERS NORD-AFRICAINS

ÉTUDES SUR LA CONDUITE ANTISOCIALE
See ACTA CRIMINOLOGICA

1736
ÉTUDES TSIGANES. 1– , Apr. 15, 1955– . n. ser. v.1– , 1971– . Paris. Four no. a year.
Issued by: Association des Études Tsiganes. In French.
Indexed: Bull. Sig. Soc. Eth.; Int. Bibl. Soc. Cul. Anth.

1737
ÉTUDES UNIVERSITAIRES SUR L'INTEGRATION EUROPÉENNE. UNIVERSITY STUDIES ON EUROPEAN INTEGRATION. 1967– . Luxembourg, Office des Publications Officielles.
Issued by: European Community Institute for University Studies. Prepared by the Centre d'Études Européennes, Université Catholique de Louvain. In English or French.
Continues: *Recherches et Études Universitaires sur l'Integration Européenne* (no.1–3, 1963–66)

1738
ÉTUDES ZAÏROISES. 1961– . Kinshasa. Semi-annual.
Issued by: Centre Interdisciplinaire pour le Développement et l'Éducation Permanente, Université Nationale du Zaïre. In French.

Continues: *Études Congolaises* (no.1–12, 1961–69, Bruxelles)

1739
EUGENICS: A JOURNAL OF RACE BETTERMENT. v.1–4, no.2, 1928–Feb. 1931. New Haven, Conn.
Issued by: American Eugenics Society.
Superseded by: *People*.

1740
EUGENICS QUARTERLY. v.1–15, Mar. 1959–Dec. 1968. Chicago, Ill.
Issued by: American Eugenics Society.
Supersedes: *Eugenical News*. Continued by: *Social Biology*.
Indexes: Vols. 1–15, 1959–68, in *Social Biology*, v.29 (1982)
Indexed: Int. Bibl. Soc. Cul. Anth.

1741
THE EUGENICS REVIEW. v.1–60, Apr. 1909–1968. London. Quarterly.
Issued by: Eugenics Education Society.
Superseded, in part, by: *Bulletin*, and *Journal of Biosocial Sciences*.
Indexes: Vols. 1–60, in v.60, no.4.
Indexed: Int. Bibl. Soc. Cul. Anth.

1742
EUHEMER. v.1– , Nov./Dec. 1957– . Warszawa, Państwowe Wydawnictwo Naukowe. Six no. a year.
Issued by: Polskie Towarzystwo Religioznawcze. In Polish; summaries in English. Tables of contents also in English and French.
Indexed: Bull. Sig. Soc. Eth.

EURAFRICA
See EURAFRICA ET TRIBUNE DU TIERS-MONDE

1743
EURAFRICA ET TRIBUNE DU TIERS-MONDE. 1– , 1957– . Bruxelles. Frequency varies.
Issued by: Fédération Congolaise des Classes Moyennes, 1958–; Organ of: Chambre de Commerce et d'Industrie Eurafricaine, 1964–66. Title varies: 1957–61, *Eurafrica; Revue de la Fedacol*; May 1961–Feb./Mar. 1963, *Eurafrica; Revue de Chambre et d'Industrie pour le Marché Commun Eurafricain*; Apr./Sept. 1963–Dec. 1963, *Eurafrica*. In French.

1744
EURE; REVISTA LATINOAMERICANA DE ESTUDIOS URBANO REGIONALES. v.1– , Oct. 1970– . Santiago, Chile.
Issued by: Centro de Desarrollo Urbano y Regional, Universidad Católica de Chile. In Spanish.
Supersedes: *Cuadernos de Desarrollo Urbano Regional*.
Indexed: Bull. Anal. Pol. Ec. Soc.

1745
EURO COOPERATION; ECONOMIC STUDIES ON EUROPE. no.1– , June 1972– . Paris. Two or three no. a year.
Issued by: Banco di Roma, Commerz Bank, and Crédit Lyonnais.

EURO-BAROMETER
See Commission of European Communities. EURO-BAROMÈTRE

EURO-BAROMÈTRE
See Commission of European Communities. EURO-BAROMÈTRE

1746
EUROPA. v.1– , Nov. 1977– . Montréal. Semi-annual.
Issued by: Centre Interuniversitaire d'Études Européennes. In English or French.
Indexed: Int. Bibl. Pol. Sc.; Int. Pol. Sc. Abst.

1747
EUROPA-ARCHIV. 1– , 1946/47– . Bonn, Verlag für Internationale Politik. Monthly, 1946–48; semimonthly.
Issued by: Deutsche Gesellschaft für Auswärtige Politik (1953–June 1956, called Institut für Europäisch Politik und Wirtschaft). Issues for 1959– in separately paged sections: "Beiträge und Berichte" and "Dokumente". Subtitle reads: "Zeitschrift für international Politik".
Indexed: ABC POL SCI; Bull. Anal. Pol. Ec. Soc.; His. Abst.; Int. Bibl. Eco.; Int. Bibl. Pol. Sc.; Int. Bibl. Soc.; Int. Pol. Sc. Abst.; PAIS; Peace Res. Abst. J.; Soc. Abst.; SSCI.

1748
EUROPA-ETHNICA. v.1– , 1927/28– . Wien, Wilhelm Braumuller. Quarterly.
Issued by: Föderalistische Union Europäischer Volksgruppen. In English, French, or German. Title varies: 1927/28–1943/44, *Nation und Staat*.

1749
EUROPÄISCHE RUNDSCHAU. 1– , July 1973– . Wien, Europa Verlag. Quarterly.
Issued by: Verein "Europäische Rundschau". In German.
Indexed: PAISFL.

EUROPÄISCHES ARCHIV FÜR SOZIOLOGIE
See ARCHIVES EUROPÉENNES DE SOCIOLOGIE

1750
EUROPE D'OUTRE-MER. no.517– , Feb. 1973– . Paris, Société Nouvelles Éditions France d'Outre-Mer. Eleven no. a year.
In French.
Continues: *Europe, France d'Outre-Mer.*
Indexed: Bull. Anal. Pol. Ec. Soc.; PAISFL.

L'EUROPE DU CENTRE-EST
See EAST CENTRAL EUROPE

1751
EUROPE, FRANCE D'OUTRE-MER. no.1–516, 1923–1972. Paris, Société des Éditions France Outre-Mer. Monthly.
In French. Title varies: no.1–344, 1923–58, *France d'Outre-Mer.*
Continued by: *Europe d'Outre-Mer.*
Indexed: Int. Bibl. Soc. Cul. Anth.; Int. Lab. Doc.; Peace Res. Abst. J.

1752
EUROPEAN BIBLIOGRAPHY OF SOVIET, EAST EUROPEAN AND SLAVONIC STUDIES. 1– , 1975– . Birmingham. Annual.
Issued by: Centre for Russian and East European Studies, University of Birmingham. In English, French, or German.
Supersedes: *Soviet, East European and Slavonic Studies in England.*

1753
European Commission on Human Rights. COLLECTION OF DECISIONS. RECUEIL DE DECISIONS. no.1–46, Jan. 1960–Dec. 1974. Strasbourg.
Issued by: Council of Europe. In English and French.
Continued by: European Commission on Human Rights. *Decisions and Reports* (1975–)

1754
EUROPEAN COMMUNITY [American Edition]. no.1– , Oct. 1954– . Washington, D.C. Frequency varies.
Issued by: Washington Office of the Information Service of the European Communities. Includes supplement: *Business Survey Results.* Title varies: 1954–Mar./Apr. 1958, *Bulletin from the Community for Coal and Steel*; May/June 1958–Mar. 1963, *Bulletin from the European Community* [American Edition].
Indexes: no.1–17, Oct. 1954–Aug. 1956, supplement, no.78 with no.17; no.18–29, Sept. 1956–Apr. 1958, with no.29; no.30–38, May 1958–Nov. 1959, with no. 57.
Indexed: Bull. Anal. Pol. Ec. Soc.; Curr. Cont. Soc. Beh. Sc.; PAIS; Peace Res. Abst. J.

1755
European Conference on Local Authorities. TEXTS ADOPTED. TEXTES ADOPTÉS. 3rd–10th sessions, 1960–1974. Strasbourg.
In English and French. With: European Conference of Local Authorities. *Documents, Working Papers* continues: European Conference of Local Authorities. *Documents and Texts Adopted.*

1756
European Economic Community. ÉTUDES. SÉRIE POLITIQUE SOCIALE. no.1– , 1963– . Bruxelles, Service des Publications des Communautés Européennes. Irreg.
In French. Each no. has also a distinctive title.

1757
EUROPEAN ECONOMIC REVIEW. v.1– , fall 1969– . White Plains, N.Y., M.E. Sharpe. Quarterly, 1969–70; nine no. a year.
Sponsored by: Association Scientifique Européenne d'Économie Appliqué.
Supersedes: *Western European Economics.*
Indexed: Bull. Anal. Pol. Ec. Soc.; Eco. Abst.; Int. Bibl. Eco.; Int. Bibl. Pol. Sc.; Ind. Per. Art. Law; Int. Lab. Doc.; PAIS.

1758
EUROPEAN ECONOMY. no.1– , Nov. 1978– . Luxembourg. Three no. a year.
Issued by: Directorate-General for Economic and Financial Affairs, Commission of the European Communities. In English; published also in French and German editions.
Continues: Commission of the European Communities. Directorate for National Economies and Economic Trends. *The Economic Situation in the Community.*
Includes supplements: (a) *European Economy. Supplement A. Recent Economic Trends* (Jan. 1979–). Monthly (except August). This supplement continues, in part: *Graphs and Notes on the Economic Situation in the Community*, issued by the Commission of the European Communities. (b) *European Economy. Supplement B. Business and Consumer Survey Results* (Jan. 1979–). Monthly (except August). This supplement continues, in part: *Graphs and Notes on the Economic Situation in the Community*; it absorbed *European Economy. Supplement C*, and *European Economy. Supplement C. Economic Prospects—Consumer Survey Results* (Jan. 1979–198?). Continues in part: *Graphs and Notes on the Economic Situation in the Community.* It merged with *European Economy. Supplement B.* Three no. a year. The titles of the three supplements vary slightly.

1759
EUROPEAN JOURNAL OF BEHAVIORAL ANALYSIS AND MODIFICATION. 1– , Apr. 1975– . Wiesbaden, Otto Harrassowitz.

1760
EUROPEAN JOURNAL OF EDUCATION. v.14– , Mar. 1979– . Dorchester-on-Thames, Carfax Pub. Co. Quarterly.
Official journal of: European Cultural Foundation's Institute of Education.
Continues: *Paedagogica Europea.*

1761
EUROPEAN JOURNAL OF POLITICAL RESEARCH. v.1– , Apr. 1973– . Amsterdam, Elsevier. Quarterly.
Official organ of: European Consortium for Political Research.
Indexed: ABC POL SCI; Bull. Anal. Pol. Ec. Soc.; Int. Bibl. Pol. Sc.; Int. Pol. Sc. Abst.

1762
EUROPEAN JOURNAL OF POPULATION. REVUE EUROPÉENNE DE DÉMOGRAPHIE. v.1– , Jan. 1985– . Amsterdam, North-Holland. Quarterly.
Published under the auspices of the European Association for Population Studies. In English or French.
Supersedes: *European Demographic Population Bulletin.*

1763
EUROPEAN JOURNAL OF SOCIAL PSYCHOLOGY. 1– , 1971– . The Hague, Mouton, 1971–77; New York, Wiley. Quarterly.
Indexed: Bull. Anal. Pol. Ec. Soc.; LLBA; Psych. Abst.

EUROPEAN JOURNAL OF SOCIOLOGY
See ARCHIVES EUROPÉENNES DE SOCIOLOGIE

1764
EUROPEAN JUDAISM. v.1– , summer 1966– . Amsterdam, Polak & Van Gennep. Two no. a year.
Indexes: v.1–8, no.1, 1966–73.

1765
EUROPEAN MARXIST REVIEW. no.1– , May 1968– . London, Fourth International Publications.
English-language edition of: *Revista Marxista Europea.*

1766
European Parliament. CAHIERS DE DOCUMENTATION EUROPÉENNE. v.1– , Oct. 1959– . Luxembourg. Irreg, 1959–67; quarterly.
In French. Title varies: *Cahiers Mensuelles de Documentation Européenne.*
Supersedes: the Parliament's *Informations Mensuelles.*
Indexes: v.1–2, 1959–60, with v.1–2.

1767
European Parliament. DÉBATS; COMPTE RENDU IN EXTENSO DES SÉANCES. no.1– , Mar. 19–21, 1958– . Luxembourg.
In French. Issued under French name: Parlement Européen (called no.1–55, Assemblée Parlementaire Européenne)

1768
EUROPEAN RESEARCH. v.1– , 1973– . Deventer, Kluwer. Bimonthly.
Issued by: European Society for Opinion and Marketing Research.
Indexed: PAIS.

1769
EUROPEAN SOCIOLOGICAL REVIEW. v.1– , May 1985– . Oxford, Oxford University Press. Three no. a year.
Other title: *ESR.*

1770
EUROPEAN STUDIES REVIEW. v.1– , Jan. 1971– . London, Macmillan, 1971–73; Beverly Hills, Calif., Sage Publications. Quarterly.
Indexed: Bull. Anal. Pol. Ec. Soc.; Curr. Cont. Soc. Beh. Sc.; His. Abst.; Int. Bibl. Pol. Sc. Abst.; SSCI.

EUROPEAN TREATY SERIES
See Council of Europe. EUROPEAN TREATY SERIES

EUROPEAN YEARBOOK
See ANNUAIRE EUROPÉEN

1771
EUROPEAN YEARBOOK IN LAW AND SOCIOLOGY. 1977– . The Hague, Nijhoff.
In English or French.

1772
EUROSTAT REVIEW. REVUE EUROSTAT. 1970/79– . Luxembourg. Annual.
Issued by: Statistical Office of the European Communities. In English, French, or Dutch.

EUROSTATISTICHE: DATI PER L'ANALISE DELLA CONGIUNTURA
See Statistical Office of the European Communities. EUROSTATISTIK

EUROSTATISTICS DATA FOR SHORT-TERM ECONOMIC ANALYSIS
See Statistical Office of the European Communities. EUROSTATISTIK

EUROSTATISTIQUES; DONNÉES POUR L'ANALYSE DE LA CONJONCTURE
See Statistical Office of the European Communities. EUROSTATISTIK

1773
EVALUATION AND PROGRAM PLANNING. v.1– , Jan. 1978– . Oxford, New York, Pergamon Press. Quarterly.

Other title: *Journal of Evaluation and Program Planning*.
Indexed: Curr. Cont. Soc. Beh. Sc.; Psych. Abst.; SSCI; Soc. Abst.

1774
EVALUATION REVIEW. v.4– , Feb. 1980– . Beverly Hills, Calif., Sage Publications. Bimonthly.
Continues: *Evaluation Quarterly* (v.1–3, 1977–79)
Indexed: PAIS; Sage Urb. Stu. Abst.; Soc. Abst.

1775
EVALUATION STUDIES REVIEW ANNUAL. v.1– , 1976– . Beverly Hills, Calif., Sage Publications.
Indexed: Int. Bibl. Soc. Cul. Anth.

1776
THE EVOLUTION. v.1–3, Jan. 6, 1877–1880? New York. Irreg.
Subtitle reads: "Review of politics, science, literature and art".

1777
ÉVOLUTION. v.1–8(no.1–92), Jan. 15, 1926–Nov./Dec. 1933. Paris. Monthly.
In French. Subtitle reads: "Revue mensuelle des questions intéressant l'apaisement international des peuples".

ÉVOLUTION ÉCONOMIQUE AU MOYEN-ORIENT
See United Nations. Economic and Social Commission for Western Asia. STUDIES ON DEVELOPMENT IN COUNTRIES OF WESTERN ASIA

ÉVOLUTION ÉCONOMIQUE EN AFRIQUE
See United Nations. Economic Commission for Africa. ECONOMIC DEVELOPMENTS IN AFRICA

1778
EXAMINER, AND JOURNAL OF POLITICAL ECONOMY: DEVOTED TO THE ADVANCEMENT OF THE CAUSE OF STATE RIGHTS AND FREE TRADE. v.1–2, Aug. 7, 1833–July 22, 1835. Philadelphia, Pa. Biweekly.
Supersedes: *Country Courier*.

EXCERPTA CRIMINOLOGICA
See ABSTRACTS ON CRIMINOLOGY AND PENOLOGY

1779
EXCERPTA MEDICA. SECTION 22. HUMAN GENETICS. v.1– , Sept. 1962– . Amsterdam. Monthly.

1780
THE EXCHANGE; A HOME AND COLONIAL REVIEW OF COMMERCE, MANUFACTURES AND GENERAL POLITICS. v.1–2, Apr. 1862–Feb. 1863. London. Monthly.

1781
EXPLORATIONS IN ECONOMIC HISTORY. v.7– , fall 1969– . Kent, Ohio, The Kent University Press. Quarterly.
Supplements accompany some numbers.
Continues: *Explorations in Entrepreneurial History*.
Indexed: Curr. Cont. Soc. Beh. Sc.; His. Abst.; Int. Bibl. Eco.; Int. Bibl. Pol. Sc.; Int. Bibl. Soc.; PAIS; Pop. Ind.

1782
EXPLORATIONS IN ETHNIC STUDIES. 1– , Jan. 1978– . Pomona, Calif., NAIES Publications. Semi-annual.
Issued by: National Association of Interdisciplinary Ethnic Studies, and Ethnic Studies Department, California State Polytechnic University.
Indexes: Vols. 1–5, 1978–82, in v.6, no.2 (Author and title index)
Indexed: His. Abst.

THE EXPORT SHIPPER
See BUSINESS ABROAD AND EXPORT TRADE

EXPORT TRADE
See BUSINESS ABROAD AND EXPORT TRADE

EXPORT TRADE AND EXPORTER'S REVIEW
See BUSINESS ABROAD AND EXPORT TRADE

EXPORT TRADE AND FINANCE
See BUSINESS ABROAD AND EXPORT TRADE

EXPORT TRADE AND SHIPPER
See BUSINESS ABROAD

EXPOSÉ ANNUEL SUR LES ACTIVITÉS D'ORIENTATION PROFESSIONELLE DANS LA COMMUNAUTÉ
See Commission of the European Communities. EXPOSÉ ANNUEL SUR LES ACTIVITÉS D'ORIENTATION PROFESSIONELLE DANS LA COMMUNAUTÉ

EXPOSÉ SUR L'ÉVOLUTION SOCIALE DANS LA COMMUNAUTÉ
See Commission of the European Communities. EXPOSÉ SUR L'ÉVOLUTION SOCIALE DANS LA COMMUNAUTÉ

EXTERNAL AFFAIRS
See INTERNATIONAL PERSPECTIVES

F.F. COMMUNICATIONS
See Folklore Fellows. F.F. COMMUNICATIONS

F.S. FEMINIST STUDIES
See FEMINIST STUDIES

1783
FABIAN QUARTERLY. no.1–58, Mar. 1934–summer 1948. London.
Issued by: Fabian Society.

FAITS ET DOCUMENTS
See Centre d'Études Politiques, Économiques et Sociales. DOCUMENTS

1784
FAMILLES DANS LE MONDE. 1– , Apr./May 1948– . Paris. Quarterly.
Issued by: Union Internationale des Organismes Familiaux. Title varies: 1948, the union's *Liaison et Information Bulletin*.

1785
FAMILY PLANNING AND POPULATION. PLANIFICATION FAMILIALE ET POPULATION. spring 1973– . Toronto. Quarterly.
In English or French.

1786
FAMILY PLANNING PERSPECTIVES. v.1– , spring 1969– . New York, New Guttmaker Institute. Bimonthly.
Issued by: Center for Family Planning Program Development, and Technical Assistance Division of Planned Parenthood–World Population.
Indexed: Abst. Anth.; Abst. Soc. Work.; PAIS; Pop. Ind.; PHRA.

1787
FAMILY PRACTICE RESEARCH JOURNAL. v.1– , fall 1981– . New York, Human Sciences Press. Quarterly.
Co-sponsored by: Michigan Academy of Family Physicians, and the Family Health Research, Education and Service Institute.

1788
FAMILY PROCESS. v.1– , Mar. 1962– . New York. Semi-annual, 1962–69; quarterly.
Issued by: 1962–77, The Family Process Nathan W. Ackerman Institute. Subtitle reads: "A multidisciplinary journal of research and treatment".
Indexed: Abst. Soc. Work; Psych. Abst.; Soc. Abst.

1789
FAMILY STUDIES REVIEW YEARBOOK. v.1– , 1983– . Beverly Hills, Calif., Sage Publications.

1790
THE FAR EAST AND AUSTRALIA. 1969– . London, Europa Publications. Annual.

1791
FAR EASTERN AFFAIRS. no.1– , 1974– . Moscow. Quarterly.
Issued by: Akademii͡a Nauk SSSR. Translation of *Problemy Dal'nogo Vostoka*.

THE FAR EASTERN QUARTERLY
See JOURNAL OF ASIAN STUDIES

1792
Federación Latinoamericana de Bancos. REVISTA. no.1– , Oct. 1968– . Bogotá. Four no. a year.
In Spanish.
Indexes: Ind. Gen., no.1–20, 1968–75; Separatos, 1–12, 1970–75. 1v.

FEDERAL GOVERNMENT ACTIVITIES IN THE HUMAN SCIENCES
See Canada. Statistics Canada. FEDERAL GOVERNMENT ACTIVITIES IN THE HUMAN SCIENCES

1793
FEDERAL GOVERNMENT ENTERPRISE FINANCE. 1962– . Ottawa. Annual.
Issued by: Government Finance Section, Public Finance and Transportation Division.
Continues: *Financial Statistics of Federal Government Enterprises. Les Finances Publiques Fédérales.*

FEDERAL GOVERNMENT FINANCE
See Canada. Dominion Bureau of Statistics. Government Finance Section. FEDERAL GOVERNMENT FINANCE

1794
FEDERAL GOVERNMENT FINANCE; REVENUE AND EXPENDITURE; ASSETS AND LIABILITIES. 1965– . Ottawa. Annual.
Issued by: Government Finance Section, Transportation Division. In English and French. Other title: *Les Finances Publiques Fédérales.*
Continues: *Finance Statistics of the Government of Canada.*

1795
Federal Reserve Bank of New York. QUARTERLY REVIEW. v.1– , winter 1976– . New York.
Supersedes: the bank's *Monthly Review.*

1796
FEDERAL RESERVE BULLETIN. 1– , 1915– . Washington, D.C. Monthly.
Issued by: Board of Governors of the Federal Reserve System.
Indexed: Bull. Anal. Pol. Ec. Soc.; Curr. Cont. Soc. Beh. Sc.; Eco. Abst.; Int. Bibl. Eco.; Int. Bibl. Soc.; PAIS.

1797
IL FEDERALISTA. v.17– , 1975– . Pavia, Editrice Libera Federalista. Four no. a year.
Issued by: Movimento Federalista. In Italian. Subtitle reads: "Rivista di politica".
Continues: *Le Fédéraliste* (v.1–16, 1959–74)
Indexed: PAISFL.

FEI CH'ING YEN CHIU
See CHUNG KUNG YEN CHIU

1798
FEMINIST FORUM. 5th issue– , 1982– . Oxford, New York, Pergamon Press.
Issued with: *Women's Studies International Forum.*

1799
FEMINIST ISSUES. v.1– , summer 1980– . Berkeley, Calif., later New Brunswick, N.J., Transaction Periodicals Consortium. Three no. a year.
An English language edition of: *Questions Féministes.*

1800
FEMINIST STUDIES. v.1– , summer 1972– . College Park, Md. Quarterly, 1972–73; three no. a year.
Other title: *FS Feminist Studies.*

1801
FENNOSCANDIA ARCHAEOLOGICA. 1– , 1984– . Helsinki. Annual.
Issued by: Suomen Arkeologinen Seura. In English, Finnish, or Swedish.
Continues: *Fennoscandia Antiqua.*

1802
FIELDIANA; ANTHROPOLOGY. v.1– , Dec. 1895– . Chicago, Ill.
Issued by: Field Museum of Natural History (called Field Columbian Museum of Natural History, 1895–1905). Title varies: v.1–35, 1895–1943, *Anthropological Series.*

1803
FILOSOFII͡A I NAUCHNYĬ KOMMUNIZM. 1974– . Minsk, Izd-vo BGU. Annual.
In Russian.

1804
FILOSOFII͡A I SOT͡SIOLOGII͡A NAUKI I TEKHNIKI. 1983– . Moskva. Annual.
Issued by: Nauchnyĭ Sovet po Filosofskim i Sot͡sial'nym Problemam Nauki i Tekhniki. In Russian. Other title: *Philosophy and Sociology of Science and Technology.*

1805
FINANCE AND DEVELOPMENT. v.5– , Mar. 1968– . Washington, D.C. Quarterly.
Issued by: International Monetary Fund, and the World Bank. Published also in French edition: *Finances & Développement.*
Continues: *Fund and Bank Review; Finance and Development.*
Indexed: His. Abst.; Int. Bibl. Soc. Cul. Anth.; PAIS.

FINANCES & DÉVELOPPEMENT
See FINANCE AND DEVELOPMENT

FINANCES LOCALES
See LOCAL FINANCE

FINANCES PUBLIQUES
See PUBLIC FINANCE

FINANCES PUBLIQUES FÉDÉRALES
See Canada. Dominion Bureau of Statistics. Government Finances Section. FEDERAL GOVERNMENT FINANCE

FINANCIAL AND ECONOMIC JOURNAL
See TS'AI CHING SHIH SHIH

1806
FINANCIAL MANAGEMENT. 1– , 1972– . Albany, N.Y. Quarterly.
Issued by: School of Business, State University of New York at Albany, and Financial Management Association.
Indexed: Bull. Anal. Pol. Ec. Soc.; Int. Bibl. Eco.

1807
FINANCIAL MARKET TRENDS. no.1– , Oct. 1977– . Paris. Five no. a year, 1977–80; three no. a year.
Issued by: Capital Markets Division, Directorate for Financial and Fiscal Affairs, Organisation for Economic Co-operation and Development. Supplements accompany some issues. Some issues are thematic. Issue no.1 preceded by a no. dated June 1977 designated 0. Some volumes are photoduplicated.

FINANCIAL STATISTICS MONTHLY. INTERNATIONAL MARKETS
See Organisation for Economic Co-operation and Development. FINANCIAL STATISTICS MONTHLY. INTERNATIONAL MARKETS

1808
FINANCIAL WORLD. v.1– , Oct. 1902– . New York. Monthly, 1902–Sept. 1905; semimonthly, Oct. 1905–Aug. 1906; weekly.
Subtitle reads: "America's investment business weekly".

1809
FINANSE I KREDIT. v.1– , 1950– . Warszawa, Państwowe Wydawnictwo Naukowe. Monthly.
In Polish.
Indexed: Int. Bibl. Eco.

1810
FINANSI I KREDIT. 1950–1984. Sofiia. Ten no. a year.
Issued by: Ministerstvo na Finansite, Bulgarska Narodna Banka, Derzhavnata Spesovna Kas, and Durzhavna Zastrakhvatele Institut. In Bulgarian.
Continues: *Finansova Misul*, and *Pari i Kredit*. Continued by: *Ikonomika*.

FINANSI I KREDIT SSSR
See FINANSY SSSR

1811
FINANSIJE. v.1– , 1946– . Beograd. Monthly.
Issued by: Savezni Derzavni Sekretariat za Poslove Finansija, and Ministerstvo Finansija FNRJ (1949–). In Serbo-Croatian.

1812
FINANSY SSSR. v.15, no.7– , July 1954– . Moskva, Gosfinizdat. Monthly.
Issued by: Ministerstvo Finansov SSSR. In Russian.
Continues, in part: *Finansi i Kredit SSSR*.
Indexed: Bull. Anal. Pol. Ec. Soc.; Curr. Cont. Soc. Beh. Sc.; His. Abst.; Int. Bibl. Eco.

1813
FINANȚE ŞI CREDIT. v.1– , 1955– . Bucureşti, Editura di Stat pentru Imprimate şi Publicatii. Monthly.
In Romanian.
Indexed: Int. Bibl. Eco.

1814
FINANZARCHIV. 1884– . Tübingen, J.C.B. Mohr. Three no. a year.
In German.
Indexed: Bull. Anal. Pol. Ec. Soc.; Eco. Abst.; Ind. Per. Art. Law; Int. Bibl. Eco.; Int. Bibl. Pol. Sc.; Int. Bibl. Soc.; PAIS; PAISFL; Peace Res. Abst. J.

1815
FINISTERRA. v.1– , 1966– . Lisboa. Two no. a year.
Issued by: Centro de Estudos Geográficos, Faculdade de Letras, Universidade. In Portuguese; some articles in French; summaries in English and French.

FINNISH ECONOMIC JOURNAL
See KANSANTALOUDELLINEN AIKAKAUSKIRJA

FINNISH STUDIES IN ETHNOLOGY
See ETHNOLOGIA FENNICA

1816
FLINDERS JOURNAL OF HISTORY AND POLITICS. 1– , July 1969– . Bedford Park. Annual.
Issued by: Flinders University of South Australia, History and Politics Society, and School of Social Sciences.

1817
THE FLORIDA ANTHROPOLOGIST. v.1– , May 1948– . Gainesville, Fla. Four no. a year (some combined numbers)
Issued by: Florida Anthropological Society.
Indexed: Abst. Anth.; Int. Bibl. Soc. Cul. Anth.

1818
FLORIDA INTERNATIONAL LAW JOURNAL. v.1– , 1984– . Gainesville, Fla. Semi-annual.

THE FLOW OF FINANCIAL RESOURCES TO COUNTRIES IN COURSE OF ECONOMIC DEVELOPMENT
See Organisation for Economic Co-operation and Development. THE FLOW OF FINANCIAL RESOURCES TO LESS-DEVELOPED COUNTRIES

THE FLOW OF FINANCIAL RESOURCES TO DEVELOPING COUNTRIES
See Organisation for Economic Co-operation and Development. THE FLOW OF FINANCIAL RESOURCES TO LESS-DEVELOPED COUNTRIES

1819
FOLIA ARCHAEOLOGICA. 1/2– , 1939– . Budapést, Népmüvelési Propaganda Iroda. Annual.
Issued by: A Magyar Nemzeti Múzeum Évkönyve. In English, German, or Hungarian; summaries in English or German. Title varies: 1939–53, *Archaeologica Hungarica*; 1954, *Magyar Nemzeti*. Other title: *Annales Musei Nationalis Hungarici*.
Indexed: Int. Bibl. Soc. Cul. Anth.

1820
FOLIA GEOGRAPHICA. SERIES GEOGRAPHICA-OECONOMICA. v.1– , 1968– . Wrocław, Zakład Narodowy im Ossolińskich. Annual (irreg.)

Issued by: Komisja Nauk Geograficznych. Oddział w Krakowie, Polska Akademia Nauk. In Polish; summaries in English. Tables of contents also in English.

1821
FOLIA OECONOMICA CRACOVIENSIA. v.1– , 1960– . Kraków, Państwowe Wydawnictwo Naukowe. Four no. a year.
Issued by: Komisja Nauk Ekonomicznych, Oddział w Krakowie, Polska Akademia Nauk. In Polish; summaries in English and Russian. Tables of contents also in English and Russian.

1822
FOLK: DANSK ETNOGRAFISK TIDSKRIFT. v.1– , 1959– . København. Annual.
Issued by: Dansk Etnografisk Forening. In Danish, English, or German.
Indexed: Int. Bibl. Soc. Cul. Anth.

1823
FOLK-LIV. ACTA ETHNOLOGICA ET FOLKLORISTICA EUROPEA. v.1–33/34, 1937–1969/70. Stockholm, Generalstabens Litografiska Anstalts Forlag. Annual, 1937–39; four no. a year.
Issued by: Académie Royale Gustave Adolphe pour Recherches Ethnologiques. In English, a Scandinavian language, or German; summaries in English.
Superseded by: *Ethnologica Scandinavica.*

1824
FOLK-LORE. v.1– , 1890– . London. Quarterly.
Issued by: Folk-Lore Society. Title varies: v.1–68, 1890–1957, *Folk Lore; A Quarterly Review of Myth, Tradition, Institution & Custom, being the Transactions of the Folk-Lore Society and Incorporating The Archaeological Review and the Folk-Lore Journal.*
Indexed: Bull. Sig. Soc. Eth.; Int. Bibl. Soc. Cul. Anth.

1825
FOLKLORE. v.1– , Jan./Feb. 1960– . Calcutta. Bimonthly.
Supersedes: *Indian Folk-Lore.*
Indexed: Abst. Anth.; Int. Bibl. Soc. Cul. Anth.

1826
FOLKLORE AMERICANO. v.1– , Nov. 1953– . Mexico, D.F. Annual.
Issued by: Comite Interamericano de Folklore, Pan American Institute of Geography and History. In Spanish.
Indexed: Int. Bibl. Soc. Cul. Anth.

1827
Folklore Fellows. F.F. COMMUNICATIONS. no.1– , 1911– . Helsingsfors. Annual.
In Finnish.
Indexes: 1–47, 1911–36.

1828
FOLKLORE SUISSE. FOLKLORE SVIZZERO. v.33– , 1943– . Basel. Five or six no. a year.
Issued by: Société Suisse des Traditions Populaires. In French or Italian.
Supersedes, in part: *Schweizer Volkskunde* and continues its volume numbering.
Indexes: Vols. 33–38 included in the index, v.1–45 of *Schweizerisches Archiv für Volkskunde.*
Indexed: Bull. Sig. Soc. Eth.

FOLKLORE SVIZZERO
See FOLKLORE SUISSE

1829
FOMENTO SOCIAL. v.1– , Apr. 1945– . Madrid. Quarterly.
Title varies: v.1–18, 1945–63, *Revista de Fomento Social.*
Indexed: Bull. Sig. Soc. Eth.; Int. Bibl. Eco.; Int. Bibl. Soc.; Int. Bibl. Soc. Cul. Anth.

1830
Fondation Nationale des Sciences Politiques. CAHIERS. no.1– , 1947– . Paris. Irreg.
In French. Monograph series; some of them are doctoral dissertations.

1831
Fondazione Giangiacomo Feltrinelli. ANNALI. v.16– , 1974/75– . Milano, A. Giuffrè. Irreg.
In Italian; summaries in English and French.
Continues: Istituto Giangiacomo Feltrinelli. *Annali.*

1832
Fondazione Italiana per la Storia Administrativa. ANNALI. 1– , 1964– . Milano, A. Giuffrè. Irreg.
In Italian.

1833
Fondazione Italiana per la Storia Administrativa. ARCHIVIO. v.1– , 1963– . Milano, A. Giuffrè. Annual.
In Italian. Consists of: Prima Collana; Monografie, Ricerche Ausiliare, Opere Strumentali, and Seconda Collana; Storici dell'Amministrazione e delle Constituzione.

1834
FONTES ARCHAEOLOGICI POSNANIENSES. ANNALES MUSEI ARCHAEOLOGICI POSNANIENSIS. v.1– , 1950– . Poznán. Annual.
Issued by: Muzeum Archeologiczne in Poznań. In Polish; summaries in French. Title varies: v.1–3, 1950–52, *Fontes Praehistorici. Annales Musei Posnaniensis.*
Indexed: Int. Bibl. Soc. Cul. Anth.

Indexed: Int. Bibl. Soc. Cul. Anth.

1835
FONTES ARCHAEOLOGICI PRAGUENSES. v.1– , 1958– . Pragae.
Issued by: Prehistorické Oddeleni, Narodni Museum in Prague. In Czech, English, or occasionally in another language. Monograph series.

FONTES PRAEHISTORICI POSNANIENSES
See FONTES ARCHAEOLOGICI POSNANIENSES

1836
FORDHAM INTERNATIONAL LAW JOURNAL. v.4– , 1980– . New York. Semi-annual.
Issued by: Fordham University School of Law.
Continues: *Fordham International Law Forum* (v.1–3, 1977–1979/80)
Indexed: Ind. Leg. Per.

1837
FOREIGN AFFAIRS. v.1– , Sept. 15, 1922– . New York. Quarterly; five no. a year.
Issued by: Council on Foreign Relations. Separately paged supplements accompany some numbers.
Supersedes: *Journal of International Relations*.
Indexes: Vols. 1–5, 1922–July 1927, 1v.; v.1–10, 1922–July 1932, 1v.; v.1–25, 1922–July 1947, 1v.; v.1–50, 1922–1972, 1v.
Indexed: ABC POL SCI; Bull. Anal. Pol. Ec. Soc.; Curr. Cont. Soc. Beh. Sc.; His. Abst.; Ind. Per. Art. Law; Int. Bibl. Eco.; Int. Bibl. Pol. Sc.; Int. Lab. Doc.; Int. Pol. Sc. Abst.; PAIS; Peace Res. Abst. J.; Pop. Ind.; SSCI.

1838
FOREIGN AFFAIRS BULLETIN. Aug./Sept. 1961– . Bangkok. Bimonthly.
Issued by: Department of Information, Ministry of Foreign Affairs (Thailand)

1839
FOREIGN AFFAIRS CHINA. CHUNG-KUO WAI CHIAP SHIH WU. v.1– , 1981– . Peking.
Issued by: Information Department, Ministry of Foreign Affairs, The People's Republic of China. Texts of statements and addresses. In Chinese and English.

1840
FOREIGN AFFAIRS REPORTS. v.1– , July/Aug. 1952– . New Delhi. Monthly.
Issued by: Indian Council of Foreign Affairs, and the Asian Relations Organization.
Indexed: Bull. Anal. Pol. Ec. Soc.; Int. Bibl. Pol. Sc.; Int. Pol. Sc. Abst.; Peace Res. Abst. J.

1841
FOREIGN AND COMPARATIVE STUDIES; EASTERN AFRICA. 16– , 1975–197? Syracuse, N.Y. Irreg.
Issued by: Maxwell School of Citizenship and Public Affairs, Syracuse University.
Continues: *Foreign and Comparative Studies*.
Continued by: *Foreign and Comparative Studies. Africa Series*.

FOREIGN AND DOMESTIC COMMERCE
See INTERNATIONAL COMMERCE

FOREIGN LANGUAGE INDEX
See Public Affairs Information Service. FOREIGN LANGUAGE INDEX

1842
FOREIGN POLICY. no.1– , winter 1970/71– . Washington, D.C., National Affairs, Inc. Quarterly.
Issued by: Carnegie Endowment for International Peace.
Indexed: ABC POL SCI; His. Abst.; Ind. Per. Art. Law; Int. Bibl. Eco.; Int. Bibl. Pol. Sc.; Int. Pol. Sc. Abst.; Soc. Abst.; SSCI.

FOREIGN POLICY
See DIS POLITICA

1843
FOREIGN SERVICE JOURNAL. v.1– , Oct. 1924– . Washington, D.C. Monthly.
Issued by: American Foreign Service Association. Title varies: 1924–July 1925, *The American Foreign Service Journal*.
Supersedes: *American Consular Bulletin*.
Indexes: Vols. 1–3, 1924–26, in v.3; v.1–5, 1924–28, in v.5.

FOREIGN TRADE; ANALYTICAL TABLES
See Statistical Office of the European Communities. AUSSENHANDEL; ANALYTISCHE ÜBERSICHTEN

1844
FOREIGN TRADE AND ECONOMIC DEVELOPMENT. 1974– . New York, Distributed by the Columbia University Press. Two or three no. a year.
Issued by: National Bureau of Economic Research.

FOREIGN TRADE. SERIES B. ANALYTICAL ABSTRACTS
See Organisation for Economic Co-operation and Development. FOREIGN TRADE. SERIES B. ANALYTICAL ABSTRACTS

FOREIGN TRADE STATISTICS; ANALYTICAL TABLES
See Statistical Office of the European Communities. STATISTIKEN UBER DEN AUSSENHANDEL: ANALYTISCHE ÜBERSICHTEN

FOREIGN TRADE STATISTICS FOR AFRICA. SERIES A. DIRECTION OF TRADE
See United Nations. Economic Commission for Africa. FOREIGN TRADE STATISTICS. SERIES A: DIRECTION OF TRADE

FOREIGN TRADE STATISTICS FOR AFRICA. SERIES B. TRADE BY COMMODITIES
See United Nations. Economic Commission for Africa. FOREIGN TRADE STATISTICS. SERIES B: TRADE BY COMMODITIES

FOREIGN TRADE STATISTICS FOR AFRICA. SERIES C. SUMMARY TABLES
See United Nations. Economic Commission for Africa. FOREIGN TRADE STATISTICS. SERIES C. SUMMARY TABLES

FOREIGN TRADE STATISTICS OF ASIA AND THE FAR EAST. SERIES A.
See United Nations. Economic and Social Commission for Asia and the Pacific. FOREIGN TRADE STATISTICS OF ASIA AND THE PACIFIC. SERIES A

FOREIGN TRADE STATISTICS OF ASIA AND THE FAR EAST. SERIES B
See United Nations. Economic and Social Commission for Asia and the Pacific. FOREIGN TRADE STATISTICS OF ASIA AND THE PACIFIC. SERIES B.

FOREIGN TRADE STATISTICS OF ASIA AND THE PACIFIC. SERIES A
See United Nations. Economic and Social Commission for Asia and the Pacific. FOREIGN TRADE STATISTICS OF ASIA AND THE PACIFIC.

FOREIGN TRADE STATISTICS OF ASIA AND THE PACIFIC. SERIES B
See United Nations. Economic and Social Commission for Asia and the Pacific. FOREIGN TRADE STATISTICS OF ASIA AND THE PACIFIC

FORESTRY ECONOMICS
See SOCIAL SCIENCES IN FORESTRY

Formosa
See Taiwan

1845
FORO INTERNACIONAL. v.1– , July/Sept. 1960– . Mexico, D.F. Quarterly.
Issued by: Colegio del México. In Spanish.
Indexed: ABC POL SCI; Bull. Anal. Pol. Ec. Soc.; His. Abst.; Int. Bibl. Eco.; Int. Bibl. Pol. Sc.; Int. Pol. Sc. Abst.; PAISFL.

1846
FORSCHUNGEN ZUR ANTHROPOLOGIE UND RELIGIONSGESCHICHTE. 1– , 1978– . Saarbrücken. Quarterly.
Issued by: Universität des Saarlandes. In German. Monograph series.

FORTNIGHTLY ECONOMIC REVIEW
See POLITICAL AND ECONOMIC REVIEW

1847
FORTUNE. v.1– , Feb. 1930– . Jersey City, N.J., now Chicago, Ill. Monthly, 1930–77; biweekly.
Indexes: (general) vols. 1–10, 1930–34, 1v.; v.1–16, 1930–37, 1v.; (vocational): v.1–22, 1930–40; (classified): v.1–34, no.2, 1930–Aug. 1946, 1v.; v.34, no.3–36, Sept. 4, 1946–Oct. 1947.
Indexed: Int. Bibl. Eco.; Int. Lab. Doc.; Int. Pol. Sc. Abst.; PAIS; Peace Res. Abst. J.

1848
THE FORUM. [1]– , 1965– . Washington, D.C. Annual, 1965–66; two no. a year, 1967–69; three no. a year.
Issued by: National War College. Issues for 1965–fall 1967 have no numbering but constitute 1st–4th issues. Cover title: *The National War College Forum*.
Indexed: APAIS; Ind. Leg. Per.; Peace Res. Abst. J.

FOURTH INTERNATIONAL
See INTERNATIONAL SOCIALIST REVIEW

1849
France. Agence Général des Colonies. BULLETIN. v.1–27 (no.1–307), Jan. 1908–Oct./Dec. 1934. Paris. Monthly.
Issued by: Office Colonial, 1908–Aug./Sept. 1919; Agence Économique des Colonies Autonomes et des Territoires Africains sous Mandat, May–Oct./Dec. 1934. Supplements accompany some numbers.
Supersedes: *Feuillé de Renseignements* (1899–1906).

France. Centre National de Recherche Scientifique. Centre de Documentation. BULLETIN SIGNALÉTIQUE
See BULLETIN SIGNALÉTIQUE

1850
France. Institut National de la Statistique et des Études Économiques. DÉMOGRAPHIE ET EMPLOI. no.1– , 1969– . Paris.
In French; summaries in English and Spanish. (its Collection. Serie/D)

1851
France. Ministère de l'Intérieur. REVUE GÉNÉRALE D'ADMINISTRATION. 1878–1928. Paris, Berger-Levrault. Monthly, forming three volumes per year.
In French.

France. Office de la Recherche Scientifique et Technique d'Outre-Mer. CAHIERS O.R.S.T.O.M. *See* CAHIERS O.R.S.T.O.M.

FRANCE/ASIE
See FRANCE—ASIE/ASIA

1852
FRANCE—ASIE/ASIA. v.1– , Apr. 1947– . Tokyo. Monthly (irreg.), 1947–Nov. 1960; bimonthly.
In English or French. Title varies: 1947–Mar./Apr. 1962, *France—Asie*. Subtitle reads: "Bilingual review of Asian cultures and problems". Absorbed: *Asia* (Saigon), Apr./May 1962.
Indexed: His. Abst.; Int. Bibl. Soc. Cul. Anth.; Peace Res. Abst. J.

LA FRANCE D'OUTRE-MER
See EUROPE, FRANCE D'OUTRE-MER

1853
FRANKFURTER HEFTE. 1945– . Remagen-Rolandseck, Verlag Rommerskirchen and Co. Monthly.
In German. Subtitle reads: "Zeitschrift für Kultur und Politik".
Indexed: Bull. Anal. Pol. Ec. Soc.; His. Abst.; Int. Bibl. Pol. Sc.; Int. Pol. Sc. Abst.; PAISFL.

1854
Franklin Foundation. THE INDIVIDUAL AND THE FUTURE OF ORGANIZATIONS. v.7– , 1976/77– . Atlanta, Ga., Publishing Service Division. Irreg.
Issued by: College of Business Administration, Georgia State University.
Continues: *Man and the Future of Organizations* (v.1–6, 1970/71–1976)

1855
Freie Universität Berlin. Osteuropa Institut. BIBLIOGRAPHISCHE MITTEILUNGEN. v.1– , 1954– . Wiesbaden, Harrassowitz (in Kommission). Irreg.
In German.

1856
Freie Universität Berlin. Osteuropa Institut. ERZIEHUNGSWISSENSCHAFTLICHE VERÖFFENTLICHUNGEN. v.1– , 1964– . Berlin, Harrassowitz. Irreg.
In German.

1857
Freie Universität Berlin. Osteuropa Institut. HISTORISCHE VERÖFFENTLICHUNGEN. v.1– , 1954– . Wiesbaden, Verlag Otto Harrassowitz (in Kommission). Irreg.
In German. Includes subseries: *Forschungen zur Europäischen Geschichte.*

1858
FRONTIERS IN SYSTEMS RESEARCH. v.1– , 1979– . Boston, Mass., The Hague, Nijhoff Pub. Irreg.
Subtitle reads: "Implications for the social sciences". Monograph series.

1859
Fundação Instituto Brasileiro de Geografia e Estatística. Departamento de Estudos e Indicadores Sociais. INDICADORES SOCIAIS. RELATORIO. 1979– . Rio de Janeiro, Superintendencia de Estudos Geográficos e Socio-económicos. Departamento de Estudos e Indicadores Sociais.
In Portuguese.

FUNDAMENTAL EDUCATION ABSTRACTS
See EDUCATION ABSTRACTS

FUNDAMENTAL EDUCATION; ABSTRACTS AND BIBLIOGRAPHY
See EDUCATION ABSTRACTS

1860
FUENTES INDÍGENAS DE LA CULTURA NÁHUATL. no.1– , 1958– . Mexico, D.F. Irreg.
Issued by: Instituto de Investigaciones Históricas, Universidad Nacional Autónoma de México. Title varies: v.1–3, 1958–61, *Textos de los Informantes de Sahagun*. In Spanish. Translations from the classic Nahuatl language.

1861
FUNDAMENTALS OF EDUCATIONAL PLANNING. no.1– , 1967– . Paris. Irreg.
Issued by: International Institute for Educational Planning. Published also in French edition.

FURTHER PAPERS ON THE SOCIAL SCIENCES
See Institute of Sociology, London. REPORTS OF THE ANNUAL CONFERENCES

1862
FUTURES. v.1– , Sept. 1968– . Guildford, Iliffe Science and Technology Publications. Quarterly.
Indexed: ABC POL SCI; Bull. Anal. Pol. Ec. Soc.; Curr. Cont. Soc. Beh. Sc.; Int. Bibl. Eco.; Int. Bibl. Pol. Sc.; Int. Bib. Soc.; Int. Pol. Sc. Abst.; Int. Lab. Doc.

1863
FUTURIBLES 2000; ANALYSE ET PRÉVISION. no.1/2–18, winter/spring 1975–Nov./Dec. 1978. Paris. Quarterly, 1975–77; bimonthly.
Issued by: Association Internationale Futuribles. In French; summaries in English and French. Subtitle reads: "Analyse, prévision, prospective". Formed by the merger of: *Analyse et Prévision*, and *Prospectives*.

Indexed: Bull. Anal. Pol. Ec. Soc.; Int. Pol. Sc. Abst.

1864
FUTURIBLES; ANALYSE, PRÉVISION, PROSPECTIVE. no.40– , Jan. 1981– . Paris. Monthly.
Issued by: Association Internationale Futuribles. In French; summaries in English and French. Formed by merger of: *Futuribles 2000*, and *Futuribles*.
Indexed: ABC POL SCI; Curr. Cont. Soc. Beh. Sc.; Int. Bibl. Pol. Sc.; Soc. Abst.

1865
FUTURICS. v.1– , 1977?– . New York, Pergamon Press. Quarterly.
Organ of: Minnesota Futurists, a chapter of World Future Society.
Indexed: Sage Urb. Stu. Abst.

1866
THE FUTURISTS. v.1– , Feb. 1967– . Washington, D.C. Bimonthly.
Issued by: World Future Society. V.1, no.1, preceded by an unnumbered issue dated July 1, 1966.
Indexed: Curr. Cont. Soc. Beh. Sc.; Wom. Stu. Abst.

1867
FUZZY SETS AND SYSTEMS. 1– , 1978– . Amsterdam, North-Holland Pub. Co. Bimonthly.

1868
GPSA JOURNAL. v.1– , 1973– . Atlanta, Ga., Department of Political Science, Emory University. Semi-annual.
Issued by: Georgia Political Science Association and Georgia State University, Atlanta.
Indexed: Bull. Anal. Pol. Ec. Soc.; Int. Bibl. Pol. Sc.

1869
GALLUP OPINION INDEX. no.1–184, June 1965–Jan. 1981. Princeton, N.J., Gallup International. Monthly.
Title varies: no.1–18, 1965–66, *Gallup Political Index*.
Continued by: *Gallup Report*.
Indexed: Bull. Anal. Pol. Ec. Soc.; Ind. Per. Art. Law; Int. Bibl. Pol. Sc.; PAIS.

GALLUP POLITICAL INDEX
See GALLUP OPINION INDEX

1870
GALLUP REPORT. no.185– , Feb. 1981– . Princeton, N.J., The Gallup Poll. Monthly.
Continues: *Public Opinion Index*.
Indexed: PAIS.

1871
GEGENWARTSKUNDE. 1– , 1952– . Opladen, Leske Verlag. Quarterly.
Issued by: Universität Hamburg. In German. Subtitle reads: "Gesellschaft, Staat, Erziehung". Absorbed: *Gesellschaft, Staat, Erziehung*.
Indexed: ABC POL SCI; Bull. Anal. Pol. Ec. Soc.; Int. Bibl. Pol. Sc.; Int. Pol. Sc. Abst.

1872
GENAVA. 1– , 1923– . Genève. Annual.
Issued by: Musée d'Art et d'Histoire. In French. Subtitle reads: "Revue d'archéologie et d'histoire d'art".
Supersedes: the museum's *Compte Rendu*, and *Genève; Cité des Nations*.
Indexed: Int. Bibl. Soc. Cul. Anth.

GENDAI NIHON SHAKAI KAGAKU
See SCIENCES SOCIALES DU JAPON CONTEMPORAIN

1873
GENERAL AGREEMENT ON TARIFFS. GATT ACTIVITIES IN [YEAR]. 1953– . Geneva. Annual.
Editions in English, French and Spanish are published.

GENERAL REPORT ON THE ACTIVITIES OF THE COMMUNITIES
See Commission of the European Communities. GENERAL REPORT ON THE ACTIVITIES OF THE COMMUNITIES

1874
GENERAL SYSTEMS. v.1– , 1956– . Ann Arbor, Mich. Annual.
Issued by: General Systems Research (called in 1956 Society for the Advancement of the General Systems Theory)

1875
GENETIC, SOCIAL AND GENERAL PSYCHOLOGY MONOGRAPHS. v.111, no.1– , Feb. 1985– . Washington, D.C., Heldref Publications. Quarterly.
Continues: *Genetic Psychology Monographs*.

GENEVA-AFRICA
See GENÈVE-AFRIQUE

1876
GENÈVE–AFRIQUE. GENEVA–AFRICA. ACTA AFRICANA. v.1– , 1962– . Genève. Semi-annual.
Issued by: Institut Africain de Genève. In French, occasionally in English.
Indexed: ABC POL SCI; Bull. Anal. Pol. Ec. Soc.; Bull. Sig. Soc. Eth.; His. Abst.; Int. Bibl. Eco.; Int. Bibl. Pol. Sc.; Int. Bibl. Soc.; Int. Bibl. Soc. Cul. Anth.; Int Pol. Sc. Abst.

1877
GENUS. v.1– , June 1934– . Roma. Semi-annual (some combined numbers)
Issued by: Comitato Italiano per lo Studio dei Problemi della Popolazione. In English, French, or Italian.
Indexed: Bull. Sig. Soc. Eth.; Int. Bibl. Soc. Cul. Anth.; Pop. Ind.

1878
GEO ABSTRACTS. ANNUAL INDEX. v.2– , 1977– . Norwich.
Issued by: University of East Anglia. This index is to all sections: A, B, C, D and F of *Geo Abstracts*.
Continues: *Geographical Abstracts. Annual Index* (v.1, 1976)

1879
GEO ABSTRACTS. C: ECONOMIC GEOGRAPHY. 1960–1985. Norwich. Twenty-four no. a year.

Issued by: University of East Anglia. Title varies: 1960–65, *Geomorphological Abstracts*.
Continued by: *Geographical Abstracts. C: Economic Geography*.

1880
GEO ABSTRACTS. D: SOCIAL AND HISTORICAL GEOGRAPHY. 1974–1985. Norwich. Six no. a year.
Issued by: University of East Anglia.
Continues: *Geo Abstracts. D: Social Geography and Cartography*. Continued by: *Geographical Abstracts. D: Social and Historical Geography*.

1881
GEO ABSTRACTS. D: SOCIAL GEOGRAPHY. 1966–1967. Norwich. Annual.
Issued by: University of East Anglia.
Continued by: *Geo Abstracts. D: Social Geography and Cartography*.

1882
GEO ABSTRACTS. D: SOCIAL GEOGRAPHY AND CARTOGRAPHY. 1972–1973. Norwich. Annual.
Issued by: University of East Anglia.
Continues: *Geo Abstracts. D: Social Geography*. Continued by: *Geo Abstracts. D: Social and Historical Geography*.

1883
GEO ABSTRACTS. F: REGIONAL AND COMMUNITY PLANNING. 1972–1985. Norwich. Six no. a year.
Issued by: University of East Anglia.
Continued by: *Geographical Abstracts. F: Regional and Community Planning*.

1884
GEOFORUM. 1– , 1970– . Braunschweig, Pergamon Press. Quarterly.
Subtitle reads: "The international multidisciplinary journal for the rapid publication of research results and critical review articles in the physical, human, and regional geosciences".
Indexed: Pop. Ind.

1885
GEOGRAFIA SPOŁECZNA I EKONOMICZNA. no.1– , 1975– . Wrocław. Irreg.
Issued by: Instytut Ekonomiczny, Uniwersytet Wrocławski. In Polish.
(Subseries of: *Acta Universitatis Wratislaviensis*)

1886
GEOGRAFISKA ANNALER. SERIES B: HUMAN GEOGRAPHY. v.47– , 1965– . Stockholm, The Almquist & Wiksell Periodical Co. Semi-annual.
Issued by: Svenska Sallskapet for Antropologi och Geografi. In English, French, or German; summaries in these three languages.
Continues, in part: *Geografiska Annaler*.

1887
GEOGRAPHIA HELVETICA. SCHWEIZERISCHE ZEITSCHRIFT FÜR LÄNDER UND VOLKSKUNDE. 1– , Jan. 1946– . Zürich. Quarterly.
Issued by: Geographisch Ethnographische Gesellschaft. In French, German, or Italian.
Indexed: Abst. Anth.; Bull. Sig. Soc. Eth.; Int. Bibl. Soc. Cul. Anth.

1888
GEOGRAPHICAL ABSTRACTS. C: ECONOMIC GEOGRAPHY. 1986– . Norwich, Geo Abstracts. Six no. a year.
Issued by: University of East Anglia.
Continues: *Geo Abstracts. C: Economic Geography*.

1889
GEOGRAPHICAL ABSTRACTS. D: SOCIAL AND HISTORICAL GEOGRAPHY. 1986– . Norwich. Six no. a year.
Issued by: University of East Anglia.
Continues: *Geo Abstracts. D: Social and Historical Geography*.

1890
GEOGRAPHICAL ABSTRACTS. F: REGIONAL AND COMMUNITY PLANNING. 1986– . Norwich. Six no. a year.
Issued by: University of East Anglia.
Continues: *Geo Abstracts. F: Regional and Community Planning*.

GEOGRAPHICAL DISTRIBUTION OF FINANCIAL FLOWS TO LESS DEVELOPED COUNTRIES (DISBURSEMENT)
See Organisation for Economic Co-operation and Development. GEOGRAPHICAL DISTRIBUTION OF FINANCIAL FLOWS TO LESS DEVELOPED COUNTRIES (DISBURSEMENT)

1891
THE GEOGRAPHICAL JOURNAL. v.1– , Jan. 1893– . London. Monthly, 1893–1938; bimonthly, 1939–50; quarterly, 1951–72; three no. a year.
Issued by: Royal Geographical Society. Includes supplements: Recent Geographical Literature, Maps and Photographs (no.1– , June 1918–) with its own index: v.1–4. Absorbed: *Proceedings* of the Royal Geographical Society.
Indexes: Vols. 1–20, 1893–1902, 1v.; v.21–40, 1903–?2, 1v.
Indexed: Abst. Anth.; His. Abst.; Int. Bibl. Eco.; Int. Bibl. Soc. Cul. Anth.; Int. Pol. Sc. Abst.; Soc. Sc. Hum. Ind.

1892
THE GEOGRAPHICAL REVIEW. v.1– , jan. 1916– . New York. Monthly.
Issued by: National Geographical Society.
Supersedes: the society's *Bulletin.*
Indexed: His. Abst.; Int. Bibl. Eco.; PAIS; Peace Res. Abst. J.; Soc. Sc. Hum. Ind.

GEOGRAPHICAL SCIENCES
See CHIRI KAGAKU

GEOMORPHOLOGICAL ABSTRACTS
See GEO ABSTRACTS. C: ECONOMIC GEOGRAPHY

1893
THE GEORGE WASHINGTON JOURNAL OF INTERNATIONAL LAW AND ECONOMICS. v.16– , 1981– . Washington, D.C. Three no. a year.
Issued by: George Washington University.
Continues: *Journal of International Law and Economics.*
Indexed: Ind. Leg. Per.; Ind. For. Leg. Per.

1894
THE GEORGIA JOURNAL OF INTERNATIONAL AND COMPARATIVE LAW. v.1– , fall 1970– . Athens, Ga. Annual, 1970; two no. a year, 1972–76; three no. a year.
Supplements accompany some issues.
Indexed: Ind. Leg. Per.; Ind. For. Leg. Per.

1895
GERMAN ECONOMIC REVIEW. v.1–15, 1963–1977. Stuttgart, Wissenschaftliche Verlagsgesellschaft. Quarterly.
Indexed: Bull. Anal. Pol. Ec. Soc.; Curr. Cont. Soc. Beh. Sc.; Eco. Abst.; Pop. Ind.

1896
GERMAN POLITICAL STUDIES. v.1– , 1974– . Beverly Hills, Calif., Sage Publications. Annual.
Sponsored by: German Political Science Association.
Indexed: Int. Pol. Sc. Abst.; PAIS.

1897
GERMAN YEARBOOK OF INTERNATIONAL LAW. JAHRBUCH FÜR INTERNATIONALES RECHT. v.19– , 1976– . Berlin, Duncker & Humblot. Annual.
Issued by: Institut für Internationales Recht, Universität Kiel. In English, French, or German.
Continues: *Jahrbuch für Internationales Recht* (v.3–18, 1950–75)
Indexed: Bull. Anal. Pol. Ec. Soc.; Ind. For. Leg. Per.; Int. Pol. Sc. Abst.

1898
GÉRONTOLOGIE ET SOCIÉTÉ. v.1– , 1972– . Paris. Quarterly.
Issued by: Fondation Nationale de Gérontologie. In French. Issues are thematic. Title varies: 1972–76, *Cahiers de la Fondation de Gérontologie.*

1899
GERONTOLOGIST. v.1– , Mar. 1961– . Washington, D.C. Quarterly, 1961–62; bimonthly.
Issued by: Gerontological Society.
Indexed: Psych. Abst.; Soc. Abst.; Soc. Work Res. Abst.; Wom. Stu. Abst.

GESAMTBERICHT ÜBER DIE TÄTIGKEIT DER GEMEINSCHAFTEN
See Commission of the European Communities. GENERAL REPORT ON THE ACTIVITIES OF THE COMMUNITIES

1900–1999: not used

2000
GESCHICHTE UND GESELLSCHAFT. v.1– , 1975– . Göttingen, Vandenhoek & Ruprecht. Four no. a year.
In German. Issues are thematic.

GESCHIEDENIS EN AARDRIJKSKUNDE. TIJDSCHRIFT VOOR LAGER EN MIDDELBAAR ONDERWIJS
See TIJDSCHRIFT VOOR GESCHIEDENIS

2001
GESELLSCHAFT. Apr. 1924–Mar. 1933. Berlin, J.H.W. Dietz. Monthly.
In German. Subtitle reads: "Internationale Revue für Sozialismus".

2002
GESELLSCHAFT UND POLITIK. 1965– . Wien. Quarterly.
Issued by: Institut für Sozialpolitik und Sozialreform (Wien). Each no. has also a distinctive title.
Continues: *Schriftenreihe des Instituts für Sozialpolitik und Sozialreform.*

GESELLWISSENSCHAFTEN
See Akademie der Wissenschaften der DDR. ABHANDLUNGEN. GESELLWISSENSCHAFTEN

GESELLWISSENSCHAFTEN
See SCIENCES SOCIALES (Moscow)

2003
GESTALT THEORY. v.1– , Oct. 1979– . Darmstadt, Steinkopf. Two double no. a year.

Issued by: Society for Gestalt Theory and Its Applications. In English or German.

2004
GESTION & SOCIÉTÉ. v.2– , 1978– . Casablanca, I.S.C.A.E. Quarterly.
In English or French; summaries in Arabic. Other title: *Tasyir wa al-majtama*.

2005
GHANA SOCIAL SCIENCE JOURNAL. 1– , May 1971– . Legon. Semi-annual.

GIORNALE DEGLI ECONOMISTO
See GIORNALE DEGLI ECONOMISTI E ANNALI DI ECONOMIA

2006
GIORNALE DEGLI ECONOMISTI E ANNALI DI ECONOMIA. v.1–78, Jan. 1886–Nov./Dec. 1938; n. ser. 1– , Jan./Feb. 1939– . Roma, Istituto Editoriale Cisalpino-La Gohardica. Bimonthly, 1886–1938; monthly, 1939–42; bimonthly, 1946– . Not published 1943–45.
In Italian. Title varies: 1886–1909, *Giornale degli Economisti*; 1910–38, *Giornale degli Economisti e Rivista Statistica*. Absorbed: *Annali di Economia*, 1939.
Indexes: (author) v.1–77, 1886–1973, 1v.; (general) v.1–78, 1886–1938.
Indexed: Bull. Anal. Pol. Ec. Soc.; Int. Bibl. Eco.; PAIS; PAISFL.

GIORNALE DEGLI ECONOMISTI E RIVISTA STATISTICA
See GIORNALE DEGLI ECONOMISTI E ANNALI DI ECONOMIA

GLAS
See Srpska Akademija Nauka i Umetnosti. Odeljenie Drustvenih Nauka. GLAS

GLASNIK ETNOGRAFSKOG INSTITUTA SAN
See Srpska Akademija Nauka i Umetnosti. Etnografski Institut. GLASNIK

GLAUBE UND ARBEIT
See SOZIALE REVUE

2007
GLEDISTA. v.1– , 1960– . Beograd. Bimonthly, 1960–61; monthly (except July-Aug.)
Issued by: University of Belgrade, and other institutions. In Serbo-Croatian.
Indexed: Bull. Anal. Pol. Ec. Soc.; Int. Bibl. Eco.

2008
GLOBAL POLITICAL ASSESSMENT. 1– , Oct. 1975/Mar. 1976– . New York, Columbia University Press. Semi-annual.
Issued by: Research Institute on International Change, Columbia University.

GODISNJAK
See Akademija Nauka i Umetnosti Bosne i Hercegovine. Centar za Balkanoloska Ispitivanja. GODISNJAK

2009
GÖTEBORG STUDIES IN POLITICS. no.4– , 1974– . Lund, C.W.K. Gleerup. Irreg.
In English or Swedish. Includes some doctoral dissertations.
Continues: *Studier i Politik. Studies in Politics.*

2010
GOSPODARKA I ADMINISTRACJA TERENOWA. v.1– , Oct. 1960– . Warszawa, Wydawnictwo RSW "Prasa Krajowa". Monthly.
In Polish. Includes supplements.
Indexed: Int. Bibl. Pol. Sc.; Int. Lab. Doc.

2011–2110: not used

2111
GOSPODARKA PLANOWA. v.1– , Nov. 1946– . Warszawa, Państwowe Wydawnictwo Naukowe. Monthly.
Indexed: Bull. Anal. Pol. Ec. Soc.; Int. Bibl. Eco.; Int. Lab. Doc.

2112
GOVERNMENT AND OPPOSITION. v.1– , Oct. 1965– . London, Weidenfeld & Nicolson. Quarterly.
Issued by: Government Department, London School of Economics and Political Science.
Indexed: ABC POL SCI; APAIS; Bull. Anal. Pol. Ec. Soc.; Curr. Cont. Soc. Beh. Sc.; Int. Bibl. Eco.; Int. Bibl. Pol. Sc.; Int. Bibl. Soc.; Int. Pol. Sc. Abst.; PAIS; Sage Pub. Adm. Abst.; Sage Urb. Stu. Abst.; Soc. Abst.; Soc. Sc. Hum. Ind.

GOVERNMENT AND POLICY
See ENVIRONMENT AND PLANNING. C: GOVERNMENT AND POLICY

2113
GOVERNMENT FINANCE REVIEW. v.1– , Apr. 1985– . Chicago, Ill. Bimonthly.
Issued by: Government Finance Officers Association.
Formed by the merger of: *Governmental Finance*, and *Government Financial Resources in Review*.

2114
GOVERNMENT FINANCE STATISTICS YEARBOOK. v.1– , 1977– . Washington, D.C. Annual.
Issued by: Government Finance Statistics Division, Bureau of Statistics, International Monetary Fund.

GOVERNMENT STATISTICS YEARBOOK
See International Monetary Fund. GOVERNMENT STATISTICS YEARBOOK

2115
GOVERNMENTAL FINANCE, v,1–13, Feb. 1972–Dec. 1984. Chicago, Ill. Quarterly.
Issued by: Municipal Finance Officers Association of the United States and Canada.
Supersedes: *Municipal Finance*. Merged with: *Government Financial Resources in Review* to form: *Government Finance Review*.

2116
GREAT IDEAS TODAY. 1961– . Chicago, Ill., Encyclopaedia Britannica. Annual.

2117
GREAT PLAINS JOURNAL. v.1– , fall 1961– . Lawton, Okla. Semi-annual, 1961–77; annual.
Issued by: 1961–69, Great Plains Historical Association; Institute of Great Plains.
Indexed: Abst. Anth.; His. Abst.

2118
GREATER LONDON INTELLIGENCE QUARTERLY. no.26– , Mar. 1974– . London.
Issued by: Greater London Council.
Continues: Greater London Council. Intelligence Unit. *Quarterly Bulletin* (no.1–25, 1968–73)

2119
GREEK OPINION. v.1– , Jan./Feb. 1981– . Athens, Eurodim. Bimonthly.
Includes monographic supplements called: *Greek Opinion. Special Reports on Greek Politics* (no.1, Aug. 1981)

GREEK REVIEW OF SOCIAL RESEARCH
See EPITHĒORESIS KOINŌNIKŌN EREUNŌN

2120
Griffith University, Brisbane. School of Modern Asian Studies. Centre for the Study of Australian–Asian Relations. RESEARCH PAPER. no.1– , Feb. 1980– . Brisbane. Irreg.
Cover title: *C.S.A.A.R. Research Paper*.

2121
GROTIANA. 1980– . Assen, Van Gorcum. Annual.

2122
GROTIUS ANNUAIRE INTERNATIONAL. 1913–1940/41. La Haye, M. Nijhoff.
In Dutch, English, or French.

2123
Grotius Society. TRANSACTIONS. v.4–29, 1918–1943. London, Sweet and Maxwell. Annual.
Includes reports of the 3rd–28th annual general meeting.
Continues: *Problems of the War* (v.1–3, 1915–17). Continued by: Grotius Society. *Transactions for the year . . .*
Indexes: Vols. 1–44, 1915–59 (includes index to: *Problems of the War*, *Transactions*, and *Transactions for the year . . .*)

2124
Grotius Society. TRANSACTIONS FOR THE YEAR . . . v.30–44, 1944–1958/1959. London, Longmans, Green. Annual.
Vol. 1958/59 published under the auspices of the British Institute of International and Comparative Law (incorporating the Grotius Society and the Society of Comparative Legislation & International Law). Vols. for 1944–59 include the *Proceedings* of the International Law Conference.
Continues: Grotius Society. *Transactions*. Absorbed, in part, by: *International and Comparative Law Quarterly*.
Indexes: Vols. 1–44, 1915–59; includes index to *Transactions* under its earlier title.

2125
GROUP AND ORGANIZATION STUDIES. v.1– , 1976– . San Diego, Calif., 1976–83; Beverly Hills, Calif., Sage Publications. Quarterly.
Indexed: Abst. Anth.

2126
GROWTH AND CHANGE. v.1– , Jan. 1970– . Lexington, Ky. Quarterly.
Issued by: Office for Research, College of Business and Economics, University of Kentucky. Subtitle reads: "A journal of regional development".
Indexed: ABC POL SCI; Abst. Anth.; Bull. Anal. Pol. Ec. Soc.; Eco. Abst.; Ind. Per. Art. Law; Int. Bibl. Eco.; Int. Bibl. Soc.; Sage Pub. Adm. Abst.; Sage Urb. Stu. Abst.

THE GROWTH OF WORLD INDUSTRY
See United Nations. Statistical Office. YEARBOOK OF INDUSTRIAL STATISTICS

2127
Guanzhou. Zhongshan Daxue Huebao. CHUNG-SHAN TA HSÜEH HSÜEH PAO; SHE HUI K'O HSÜEH. JOURNAL OF SUN-YAT-SEN UNIVERSITY; SOCIAL SCIENCES. v.1– , Mar. 1955– . Canton. Quarterly.
In Chinese. Tables of contents in English and Russian. The numbering of this series is combined in one sequence with that of the *Natural Science Edition*.

2128
GUATEMALA INDÍGENA. v.1– , Jan./Mar. 1961– . Guatemala City. Quarterly.
Issued by: Instituto Indigenista Nacional. In Spanish. Some combined numbers.

Indexed: Int. Bibl. Soc. Cul. Anth.

2129
GUNTON'S MAGAZINE. v.1–27, 1885–Dec. 1904. New York. Monthly.
Issued by: Institute of Social Economics. Title varies: v.1–12, no.2, 1885–Feb. 1897, *Gunton's Magazine of American Economics and Political Science*; v.12, no.3–v.13, no.3, Mar. 1897–Sept. 1897, *Gunton's Magazine of Practical Economics and Political Science*; v.13, no.4–v.14, no.3, Oct. 1897–Mar. 1898, *Gunton's Magazine of Social Economics and Political Science*.

GUNTON'S MAGAZINE OF AMERICAN ECONOMICS AND POLITICAL SCIENCE
See GUNTON'S MAGAZINE

GUNTON'S MAGAZINE OF PRACTICAL ECONOMICS AND POLITICAL SCIENCE
See GUNTON'S MAGAZINE

GUNTON'S MAGAZINE OF SOCIAL ECONOMICS AND POLITICAL SCIENCE
See GUNTON'S MAGAZINE

2130
GURU NANAK JOURNAL OF SOCIOLOGY. v.1– , Apr./Oct. 1980– . Amritsar.
Issued by: Sociology Department, Guru Nanak Dev University.

Gylyn Akademiiasymyn Habarlary
See Akademii͡a Nauk Kazakhskoĭ SSR

H

2131
HAHR. v.62– , 1982– . Durham, N.C., Duke University Press. Quarterly.
Published in cooperation with the Conference on Latin American History of the American Historical Association.
Continues: *The Hispanic American Historical Review.*
Indexed: Bull. Sig. Soc. Eth.; His. Abst.; Peace Res. Abst. J.

2132
HRAF NEWS. v.1–5, 1961–1965. New Haven, Conn. Quarterly.
Issued by: Human Relations Area Files.
Superseded by: *Behavior Science Notes.*

HABITAT
See HABITAT INTERNATIONAL

2133
HABITAT INTERNATIONAL. v.2, no.5/6– , 1977– . New York, Pergamon Press. Bimonthly.
Published in cooperation with the World Environment and Resources Council (WERC). Subtitle reads: "Journal for the study of human settlements".
Continues: *Habitat* (v.1, 1976)
Indexed: Sage Urb. Stu. Abst.

HACETTEPE BULLETIN OF SOCIAL SCIENCES AND HUMANITIES
See HACETTEPE SOSYAL VE BESERI BILIMLER DERGISI

2134
HACETTEPE SOSYAL VE BESERI BILIMLER DERGISI. 1– , 1969– . Ankara, Hacettepe University Press. Two no. a year.
Issued by: Hacettepe Univeritesi. In Turkish. Also English edition is published under the title: *Hacettepe Bulletin of Social Sciences and Humanities.*
Indexed: Abst. Soc. Work; His. Abst.

2135
HAENGJONG NONJIP. CH'ANGGANHO. 1969– . Seoul, Tongguk Taehakkyo Hengjong Taeghag-won.
In English or Korean. Other title: *Dongguk Journal of Public Administration.*

2136
HAMBURGER JAHRBUCH FÜR WIRTSCHAFTS- UND GESELLSCHAFTSPOLITIK. 1– , 1956– . Tübingen, J.C.B. Mohr (Paul Siebeck)
In German; summaries in English. (Veröffentlichungen der Akademie für Gemeinwirtschaft, Hamburg)
Indexed: Bull. Anal. Pol. Ec. Soc.; Peace Res. Abst. J.

2137
HAMIZRAḤ HE-ḤADASH. NEW EAST. 1– , 1945– . Jerusalem. Four no. a year (some combined numbers)
Issued by: Israel Oriental Society, and Hebrew University. In Hebrew; some articles with summaries in English.
Indexed: ABC POL SCI; His. Abst.; Int. Pol. Sc. Abst.

2138
HANDBOOK OF INTERNATIONAL SOCIOMETRY. v.1–7, summer 1956–1973. Beacon, N.Y., Beacon Press. Irreg.
Title varies: v.1, no.1, *International Journal of Sociometry*; v.1, no.2–v.2, no.2, *International Journal of Sociometry and Sociatry.*
Merged with: *Group Psychotherapy and Psychodrama* to form: *Group Psychotherapy, Psychodrama and Sociometry.*
Indexed: Bull. Sig. Soc. Eth.; Psych. Abst.

2139
HANDBOOK OF LATIN AMERICAN STUDIES. 1– , 1935– . Gainesville, Fla., University of Florida Press. Annual.
Prepared by: Hispanic Division, Library of Congress. Since 1964 divided into two sections: Social Sciences, and Humanities, appearing in alternative years.
Indexes: 1–28, 1936–1966, 1v.

2140
HANDBOOK OF POLITICAL BEHAVIOR. v.1– , 1981– . New York, London, Plenum Press. Irreg.

HANDBUCH FÜR INTERNATIONALES RECHT
See GERMAN YEARBOOK OF INTERNATIONAL LAW

2141
HANDEL ZAGRANICZNY. v.1– , 1955– . Warszawa. Monthly.
Issued by: Polska Izba Handlu Zagranicznego. In Polish; summaries in various languages.
Indexed: Bull. Anal. Pol. Ec. Soc.; Int. Bibl. Eco.

HANDELINGEN
See Akademie van Wetenschappen, Amsterdam. Sociaal Wetenschappelijke Rad. HANDELINGEN

2142
HANG-CHOU TA HSÜEH HSÜEH PAO. CHE HSÜEH SHE HUI K'O HSÜEH PAN. May 1979– . Hang-chou, Kai ta hsüeh. Quarterly.
In Chinese. Other titles: *Journal of Hangzhou Daxue xuebao. Journal of Hangz hou University. Philosophy & Social Science Edition.*

2143
HAN'GUK CHONGCH'I HAKKOE. 1– , 1975– . Seoul, Tong Hakkoe. Irreg.
Issued by: Chae Pungmi Han'gugin Chononch'i, and Hakkoe haptong haksul nonmunjip. In Korean; some articles in English. Other title: *Joint Conference of the Korean Political Scientists in North America.*

2144
HANKUK SAHYOKUAHA—LONTJIB. KOREAN SOCIAL SCIENCE REVIEW. 1– , 1965– . Seoul. Irreg.
Issued by: Hannkuk-Sakhyokuahak—Yeunnku-Oweunn. In Korean. Tables of contents also in English.

2145
HANSISCHE GESCHICHTSBLÄTTER. v.1– , 1871– . Leipzig, later München, Köln, Bohlau Verlag. Annual.
Issued by: Verein für Hansische Geschichte, 1871–1927; Hansischer Geschichtsverein. In German. Issues for 1871–1902 numbered in tables of contents; the 15 numbers, 1903–1918, not numbered; numbers for 1919 numbered v.45.
Indexes: 1871–96, in v.1896; 1871–1925, in v.1925, pp. 349–469; 1926–35, in v.1935, pp. 387–435.

2146
HANZAI GAKU NENPŌ. v.1– , 1960– . Tokyo. Annual.
In Japanese. Other title: *Annales Criminologiae Japonicae.*

2147
HARVARD BUSINESS REVIEW. v.1– , Oct. 1922– . Boston, Mass. Bimonthly.
Issued by: Graduate School of Business Administration, Harvard University. Supplements accompany some issues.
Indexes: Vols. 1–15, 1922–37, with v.16; v.16–25, 1937–47, in v.25; v.26–35, 1946–57, 1v.
Indexed: Bull. Anal. Pol. Ec. Soc.; Bull. Sig. Soc. Eth.; Eco. Abst.; Int. Bibl. Eco.; Int. Lab. Doc.; LLBA; PAIS; PHRA; Psych. Abst.

2148
HARVARD CIVIL LIBERTIES—CIVIL LIBERTIES LAW REVIEW. v.1– , spring 1966– . Cambridge, Mass. Three no. a year, 1966–81; two no. a year.
Issued by: Civil Rights–Civil Liberties Committee, Harvard Law School, Harvard University.
Indexed: Ind. Leg. Per.; PAIS; Sage Urb. Stu. Abst.

2149
HARVARD CONTEMPORARY CHINA SERIES. 1– , 1985– . Cambridge, Mass. Irreg.
Issued by: Council on East Asian Studies, Harvard University. Monograph series.

2150
HARVARD EAST ASIAN MONOGRAPHS. 1– , 1973– . Cambridge, Mass., Harvard University Press. Irreg.
Issued by: East Asian Research Center, Harvard University. Monograph series.

2151
HARVARD EDUCATIONAL REVIEW. v.1– , Feb. 1931– . Cambridge, Mass. Three no. a year, 1931–Oct. 1936; two no. a year.
Issued by: Graduate School of Education, Harvard University. Title varies: 1931–Oct. 1936, *The Harvard Teachers Record.*
Indexed: Abst. Soc. Work.; Bull. Anal. Pol. Ec. Soc.; Bull. Sig. Soc. Eth.; Int. Bibl. Pol. Sc.; Int. Lab. Doc.; Int. Pol. Sc. Abst.; LLBA; PAIS; Psych. Abst.; Wom. Stu. Abst.

2152
HARVARD INTERNATIONAL LAW JOURNAL. v.8– , winter 1967– . Cambridge, Mass. Two no. a year, 1967–70; three no. a year, 1971–81; annual.
Continues: *Harvard International Law Club Journal.*
Indexes: Vols. 1–5, 1959–66, in v.6; v.1–10, 1959–70, in v.10.
Indexed: Ind. Leg. Per.; Ind. For. Leg. Per.; PAIS.

2153
HARVARD JOURNAL OF ASIATIC STUDIES. v.1– , Apr. 1936– . Cambridge, Mass. Irreg.
Issued by: Yenching Institute, Harvard University.
Indexes: Vols. 1–20, 1936–57 (published in 1962)
Indexed: Ind. Per. Art. Law; Int. Bibl. Sc. Cul. Anth.; Soc. Sc. Hum. Ind.

2154
HARVARD JOURNAL OF LAW AND PUBLIC POLICY. v.1– , 1978– . Cambridge, Mass. Annual.
Issued by: Harvard Society for Law and Social Policy.

THE HARVARD TEACHERS RECORD
See THE HARVARD EDUCATION REVIEW

2155
Harvard University. Peabody Museum of Archaeology and Ethnology. MEMOIRS. v.1–12, 1876–1957. Cambridge, Mass. Irreg.

Monograph series.

2156
Harvard University. Peabody Museum of Archaeology and Ethnology. PAPERS. 1– , 1888– . Cambridge, Mass. Irreg.

2157
Harvard University. Russian Research Center. STUDIES. no.1– , 1950– . Cambridge, Mass., Harvard University Press. Irreg.

2158
Harvard–Yenching Institute. STUDIES. v.1– , 1950– . Cambridge, Mass., Harvard University Press. Irreg.

2159
HASTINGS INTERNATIONAL AND COMPARATIVE LAW REVIEW. spring 1977– . San Francisco, Calif. Semi-annual.
Issued by: Hastings College of the Law, University of California.
Indexed: Ind. Leg. Per.; PAIS; Peace Res. Abst. J.

2160
HAUTES ÉTUDES ISLAMIQUES ET ORIENTALES D'HISTOIRE COMPARÉE. 1– , 1971– . Genève, Librairie Droz. Irreg.
Issued by: Centre de Recherches d'Histoire et de Philologie, École Pratique des Hautes Études. In French.

2161
HAUTES ÉTUDES MEDIÉVALES ET MODERNES. 1– , 1964– . Genève, Librairie Droz. Irreg.
Issued by: Centre de Recherches d'Histoire, École Pratique des Hautes Études. In French.

2162
HAWAIIAN ARCHAEOLOGY. v.1– , 1984– . Honolulu. Annual.
Issued by: Society for Hawaiian Archaeology.

2163
THE HAWAIIAN JOURNAL OF HISTORY. v.1– , 1967– . Honolulu. Annual.
Issued by: Hawaiian Historical Society. Subtitle reads: "Devoted to the history of Hawaii, Polynesia and the Pacific area".

Haykalan SSR Gitut'yunneri Akademiia
See Akademiia Nauk Armianskoĭ SSR

2164
ḤAWLĪYĀT, SIYĀSĪYA-AL-SAMAH. 1– , 1982– . Paris, Mu'ssasat Hasad lil-Nashr wa al-Surah. Five no. a year.
In Arabic or English. Other titles: *Annales Politiques*, and *Political Quarterly*.
Indexed: Sage Urb. Stu. Abst.

2165
HEALTH AND POPULATION; PERSPECTIVES AND ISSUES. v.1– , Jan./Mar. 1978– . New Delhi. Quarterly.
Issued by: National Institute of Health and Family Welfare. Absorbed: *NIHAE Bulletin* (1968–), and *Population Research* (1974–).
Indexed: Pop. Ind.

2166
HECATE. v.1– , 1975– . St. Lucia. Semi-annual.
Issued by: English Department, University of Queensland. Subtitle reads: "A women's interdisciplinary journal".

2167
HELINIUM. 1– , 1961– . Wetteren, Éditions Universa. Three no. a year.
In French. Subtitle reads: "Revue consacrée a l'archéologie des Pays-Bas, de la Belgique et du Grand-Duché Luxembourg".
Indexed: Int. Bibl. Soc. Cul. Anth.

2168
HELVETIA ARCHAEOLOGICA. 1– , 1970– . Basel. Quarterly.
Issued by: Schweizerische Gesellschaft für Ur- und Frühgeschichte. In French, German, or Italian.
Supersedes: *Ur-Schweitz*.

2169
HEMISPHERES. no.1– , 1984– . Wrocław, Ossolineun. Annual.
Issued by: Zakład Badania Krajów Pozaeuropejskich, Instytut Historii, Polska Akademia Nauk. In English or French.

2170
Henrietta Szold Institute—National Institute for Research in the Behavioral Sciences. PUBLICATIONS. no.437 [first numbered]– , 1965– . Jerusalem. Irreg.
In Hebrew or occasionally in English. Titles of articles also in English. Includes subseries: *Research Report* (96 [first numbered], 1965).

2171
Henrietta Szold Institute—National Institute for Research in the Behavioral Sciences. Information Retrieval Centre for Research in the Behavioral Sciences. SURVEY ON CURRENT RESEARCH IN BEHAVIORAL SCIENCES. SEKER 'AI MEKHAR SHOTEF BEMADA'E HA-HITNAHAGUT BE-YISRA'EL. 1977– . Jerusalem [Jan. 1979–]. Four no. a year.

In Hebrew; occasionally in English. Titles of articles also in English. Vol. 6 (1983/84) last examined.

2172
HERODOTE. 1– , 1976– . Paris, Éditions François Maspero. Quarterly.
Issued by: Institut des Hautes Études Marocaines. In French. Subtitle reads: "Archives Berbères et Bulletin de l'Institut des Hautes Études Marocaines".
Supersedes: Institut des Hautes Études Marocaines. *Bulletin*. Continued by: *Hesperis Tamuda*.

2173
HESPERIS TAMUDA. v.1– , 1961– . Rabat. Imprimerie de l'Agdal. Three no. a year.
Issued by: Faculté des Lettres et des Sciences Humaines, Université de Rabat. In French. Formed by the merger of: *Hesperis*, and *Tamuda*.
Indexed: Int. Bib. Soc. Cul. Anth.

2174
HIKAKU HŌ ZASSHI. COMPARATIVE LAW REVIEW. REVUE DE DROIT COMPARÉE. 1951–1960; 1968– . Tokyo. Irreg.
Issued by: Nihon Hikaku ho Kenkūjo. In English, German, or Japanese. Some articles originally in foreign languages are translated into Japanese.

HIROSHIMA ECONOMIC STUDIES
See NENPŌ KEIZAGAKU

2175
THE HISPANIC AMERICAN HISTORICAL REVIEW. v.1–61, Feb. 1918–1981. Durham, N.C., Duke University Press. Quarterly.
Published with the cooperation of the Conference on Latin American Historical Association. Publication suspended, 1923–25.
Continued by: *HAHR*.
Indexed: Bull. Sig. Soc. Eth.; His. Abst.; Peace Res. Abst. J.; Soc. Sc. Hum. Ind.

2176
HISPANIC AMERICAN REPORT. v.1–17, no.9, Nov. 1948–Nov. 1964. Stanford, Calif. Monthly, 1948–51; bimonthly.
Issued by: Institute of Hispanic American & Luso-Brazilian Studies, Stanford University, and Hispanic American Society. Title varies: 1–2, Oct. 1948–Dec. 1949, *Hispanic World Report*.

2177
HISPANIC JOURNAL OF BEHAVIORAL SCIENCES. v.1– , Mar. 1979– . Los Angeles, Calif. Quarterly.
Issued by: Spanish Speaking Mental Health Center, University of California at Los Angeles. In English or Spanish.
Indexed: Curr. Cont. Soc. Beh. Sc.; SSCI.

HISPANIC WORLD REPORT
See HISPANIC AMERICAN REPORT

2178
HISTOIRE, ÉCONOMIE ET SOCIÉTÉ. v.1– , 1981– . Paris, Éditions C.D.U. and S.E.D.E.S. Quarterly.
In French.

2179
HISTOIRE ET SOCIÉTÉ CONTEMPORAINES. v.1– , 1983– . Lausanne.
Issued by: Section d'Histoire, Université de Lausanne. In French.

2180
HISTOIRE SOCIALE. SOCIAL HISTORY. 1– , 1968– . Ottawa, Les Éditions de l'Université d'Ottawa and Carleton University. Semi-annual.
Issued by: University of Ottawa. In English or French.
Indexed: Urb. Aff. Abst.

2181
HISTORIA. 1961– . Santiago, Chile. Annual.
Issued by: Instituto de Historia, Universidad Católica de Chile. In Spanish.

2182
HISTORIA NAUK SPOŁECZNYCH. v.1– , 1957– . Warszawa, Państwowe Wydawnictwo Naukowe. Irreg.
Issued by: Komitet Historii Nauki, Polska Akademia Nauk. In Polish; summaries in English, German and Russian. No.1 and 2 called also v.6 in continuing the volume numbering of the superseded publication.
Supersedes, in part: *Studia i Materiały do Dziejów Nauki Polskiej*.

2183
HISTORIA PARAGUAYA. v.7– , 1962– . Asunción. Annual (some annuals are combined).
Issued by: 1962, Instituto Paraguayo de Investigaciones Históricas; 1963–, Academia Paraguaya de Historia. In Spanish.
Continues: *Anuario del Instituto Paraguayo de Investigaciones Históricas* (v.1–6, 1956–62)

2184
HISTORIA Y CULTURA. 1– , 1962– . Montevideo, Departamento de Publicación. Irreg.
Issued by: Universidad de Montevideo. In Spanish.

2185
HISTORIA Y CULTURA. 1– , 1973– . La Paz, Academia Nacional de Ciencias de Bolivia. Irreg.

Issued by: Sección Cultura, Instituto de Estudios Bolivianos, Universidad Mayor de San Andrés, and Sociedad Boliviana de Historia. In Spanish.

HISTORIADORES DE AMÉRICA
See Pan American Institute of Geography and History. Commission on History. HISTORIADORES DE AMÉRICA

2186
HISTORIALLINEN AIKAKAUSKIRJA. 1903– . Helsinki. Quarterly (irreg.)
Issued by: Historian Ystäväin Liitto, 1903–48; Suomen Historiallinen Seura. In Finnish.
Indexes: 1903–52, as no.1a, 1953; 1903–64, 1v.

2187
HISTORIALLINEN ARKISTO. no.1– , 1866– . Helsinki. Irreg.
Issued by: Suomen Historiallinen Seura. In Finnish or Swedish; summaries in English or German.

2188
HISTORICAL ABSTRACTS. 1775–1945; v.1– , Mar. 1955– . New York. Quarterly.

2189
HISTORICAL AND POLITICAL STUDIES. no.1– , Oct. 1969– . Dunedin. Annual.
Issued by: Political Science Society of the University of Otago.

2190
Historical Association of Tanzania. PAPER. no.1– , 1966– . Nairobi, East African Publishing House. Irreg.

HISTORICAL JOURNAL
See SAHAKCHI

2191
HISTORICAL METHODS. v.11– , winter 1978– . Washington, D.C. Quarterly.
Continues: *Historical Methods Newsletter* (v.1–10, 1967–78, Pittsburgh).

2192
HISTORICAL RESEARCH FOR HIGHER DEGREES IN THE UNITED KINGDOM. no.47– , 1985– . London.
Issued by: Institute of Historical Research, University of London. Consists of two parts: Pt. 1, Theses Completed; Pt. 2, Theses in Progress (no.47, 1986).
Continues: *Historical Research for University Degrees*, Pt. 1 and Pt. 2.

2193
HISTORICAL SOCIAL RESEARCH. no.12– , Oct. 1979– . Köln, Quantum. Quarterly.
Published jointly by: Quantum (= Arbeitsgemeinschaft für Quantizierung und Methoden in der Historisch Sozialwissenschaftlichen Forschung e.V.), and Zentrum für Historische Sozialforschung. In English or German. Other title: *Historische Sozialforschung*. Continues, in part: *Historisch-Sozialwissenschaftliche Forschungen*.
Indexed: Hist. Abst.; Int. Pol. Sc. Abst.; Soc. Abst.

HISTORICAL STATISTICS
See Organisation for Economic Co-operation and Development. HISTORICAL STATISTICS

2194
HISTORICAL STUDIES; AUSTRALIA AND NEW ZEALAND. v.1–12 (no.1–48), Apr. 1940–Apr. 1967. Melbourne. Two no. a year.
Issued by: University of Melbourne.
Indexes: Vols. 1–12, 1947–67, in v.12, Apr. 1967.

HISTORICAL STUDIES OF IRAN
See BAR RASIHÂYE TÂRIKHI

2195
HISTORICKÁ DEMOGRAFIE. DÉMOGRAPHIE HISTORIQUE. no.1– , 1967– . Prague. Annual.
Issued by: Komise pro Historickou Demografii pri Historickom Ústavu, Československa Akademia Věd. In Czech; summaries in French. Includes subseries: *Z Historicko-demografickych Studii*, published annually.

2196
HISTORICKÉ STUDIE. v.1– , 1955– . Bratislava, Vydavatelstvo Slovenskej Akademie Vied.
Issued by: Historický Ústav, Slovenska Akademie Vied. In Slovak; summaries in German and Russian. V.1–2 published as supplement to *Historický Casopis*.

2197
HISTORICKÝ SBORNIK. 1, 1953. Praha. Nakl. Československe Akademie Věd. Annual.
Issued by: Historický Ústav, Československá Akadémia Věd. In Czech; summaries in German and Russian. Tables of contents also in German and Russian.
Continued by: *Sbornik Historický*.

2198
HISTORIOGRAFÍA I BIBLIOGRAFÍA AMERICANISTAS. 1954– . Sevilla. Annual.
Issued by: Escuela de Estudios Hispanoamericanos, Consejo Superior de Investigaciones Científicas. In Spanish. Vols. for 1954–68 published as a section of the *Anuario de Estudios Americanos* (Publicaciones de la Escuela de Estudios Latino-Americanos).

HISTORIOGRAFIAS AMERICANAS
See Pan American Institute of Geography and History. Commission on History. GEOGRAFIAS AMERICANAS

HISTORISCHE SOZIALFORSCHUNG
See HISTORICAL SOCIAL RESEARCH

HISTORISCHE VERÖFFENTLICHUNGEN
See Freie Universität Berlin. Osteuropa-Institut. HISTORISCHE VERÖFFENTLICHUNGEN

2199
HISTORISCHE ZEITSCHRIFT. v.1– , 1859– . München, Verlag R. Olden Oldenbour. Frequency varies.
In German. Vols. 37–96 called also neue Folge, v.1–60; v.97–130 called also 3. Folge, v.1–34. Supplements accompany some numbers. Publication suspended: 1944–Mar. 1949.

2200
HISTORISCHES JAHRBUCH. v.1– , 1880– . München, Verlag Karl Alber. Four no. a year, 1880–1963; two no. a year.
In German.
Cumulative table of contents: v.1–34, 1v.

2201
HISTORISK TIDSKRIFT. v.1–18, 1881–1898; 1– , 1899– . Stockholm. Quarterly.
Issued by: Svenska Historiska Föreningen. In Swedish or English; summaries in English. Volume numbering discontinued in 1971.
Cumulative table of contents: 1881–1900, 1v.

2202
HISTORY. v.1–4, Jan. 1912–Dec. 1915; n. ser. v.1– , Apr. 1916– . London. Three no. a year.
Issued by: Historical Association.
Indexed: Soc. Sc. Hum. Ind.

2203
HISTORY AND ANTHROPOLOGY. v.1– , Nov. 1984– . Chur, New York, Harwood Academic. Irreg.

2204
HISTORY AND ARCHAEOLOGY. v.1, no.1/2– , 1980– . Allahabad. Semi-annual.
Issued by: Department of Ancient History, Culture and Archaeology, University of Allahabad.

2205
HISTORY AND POLITICS REVIEW, WESTERN AUSTRALIA. v.1– , 1967– . Nedlands.
Issued by: History and Politics Society, University of Western Australia. The issue for 1967 last examined.
Indexed: Int. Bibl. Pol. Sc.

2206
HISTORY AND THEORY. 1– , 1960– . 's-Gravenhage, Mouton. Quarterly.
Includes supplements called "Beihefte"; a "Beiheft" is either a bibliography on one topic covering a few years or a thematic issue.
Indexed: Curr. Cont. Soc. Beh. Sc.; His. Abst.; Ind. Per. Art. Law; Int. Pol. Sc. Abst.; SSCI.

2207
HISTORY IN AFRICA. 1– , 1974– . Waltham, Mass. Annual.
Issued by: African Studies Association. Subtitle reads: "A journal of method".
Indexed: Curr. Cont. Soc. Beh. Sc.; His. Abst.

2208
HISTORY OF ANTHROPOLOGY. v.1– , 1983– . Madison, Wis., University of Wisconsin Press. Annual.

2209
HISTORY OF EDUCATION. v.1– , Jan. 1972– . London, Taylor & Francis. Two no. a year, v.1–4; three no. a year, v.5–6; quarterly.
Indexed: His. Abst.

2210
HISTORY OF EDUCATION REVIEW, WESTERN AUSTRALIA. v.12– , 1983– . Nedlands. Semi-annual.
Issued by: Australian and New Zealand History of Education Society.
Continues: *ANZHES Jornal.*

2211
HISTORY OF EUROPEAN IDEAS. v.1– , 1980– . Oxford, Toronto, New York, Pergamon Press. Quarterly.
Issues are thematic.

2212
HISTORY OF POLITICAL ECONOMY. v.1– , spring 1969– . Durham, N.C., Duke University Press. Semi-annual.
Indexed: Bull. Anal. Pol. Ec. Soc.; His. Abst.; Eco. Abst.; Int. Bibl. Eco.; SSCI.

2213
HISTORY OF POLITICAL THOUGHT. v.1– , spring 1980– . Exeter, Imprint Academic. Three no. a year.
Occasionally in German.
Indexed: His. Abst.; Int. Bibl. Pol. Sc.; Int. Pol. Sc. Abst.

2214
HISTORY OF RELIGIONS. v.1– , summer 1961– . Chicago, Ill., University of Chicago Press. Semi-annual.

Indexed: Bull. Sig. Soc. Eth.; Int. Bibl. Soc. Cul. Anth.

2215
THE HISTORY OF SOCIOLOGY; HS. v.5, no.2– , spring 1985– . Lawrence, Kans. Two no. a year.
Other title: *HoS*.
Continues: *Journal of the History of Sociology*.
Indexed: Soc. Abst.

2216
HISTORY TODAY. [v.1]– , Jan. 1951– . London. Monthly.
Indexes: 1951–55, 1v.; 1956–60, 1v.; 1961–65, 1v.; 1965–70, 1v.
Indexed: His. Abst.; Peace Res. Abst. J.; Soc. Sc. Hum. Ind.; Wom. Stu. Abst.

2217
Hitotsubashi Daigaku. HITOTSUBASHI DAIGAKU KENKYŪ NENPŌ. SHAKAIGAKU KENKYŪ. no.1– , Oct. 1955– . Tokyo. Annual.
In Japanese.

2218
Hitotsubashi Daigaku. Hitotsubashi Gakkai. ANNALS. v.1–10, Oct. 1950–Dec. 1959. Tokyo. Two no. a year.
Includes supplements (no.1, 1951)
Continued by: *Hitotsubashi Journal of Commerce and Management*; *Hitotsubashi Journal of Arts and Sciences*; *Hitotsubashi Journal of Economics*; *Hitotsubashi Journal of Law & Politics*; *Hitotsubashi Journal of Social Studies*.

2219
Hitotsubashi Daigaku. Keizai Kenkyū. ECONOMIC RESEARCH SERIES. no.1– , 1957?– . Tokyo. Irreg.
Monograph series.

2220
Hitotsubashi Daigaku. Keizai Kenkyū. NIHON KEIZAI TOKEI BUNKEN SENTA. 1– , 1977– . Tokyo. Annual.
In Japanese.

HITOTSUBASHI DAIGAKU KENKYŪ NENPŌ. SHAKAI SHAKAIGAKU KENKYŪ
See Hitotsubashi Daigaku. HITOTSUBASHI DAIGAKU KENKYŪ NENPŌ. SHAKAIGAKU KENKYŪ

2221
HITOTSUBASHI JOURNAL OF COMMERCE AND MANAGEMENT. v.1– , Mar. 1961– . Tokyo. Annual.
Issued by: Hitotsubashi Daigaku. In English; occasionally in German.
Supersedes, in part: Hitotsubashi Daigaku. *Annals*.
Indexed: Bull. Anal. Pol. Ec. Soc.

2222
HITOTSUBASHI JOURNAL OF ECONOMICS. v.1– , Oct. 1960– . Tokyo. Annual.
Issued by: Hitotsubashi Daigaku.
Supersedes, in part: Hitotsubashi Daigaku. *Annals*.
Indexed: Bull. Anal. Pol. Ec. Soc.; Int. Bibl. Eco.; PAIS; SSCI.

2223
HITOTSUBASHI JOURNAL OF LAW & POLITICS. v.1– , Apr. 1960– . Tokyo. Irreg.
Issued by: Hitotsubashi Daigaku. In English; occasionally in German.
Supersedes, in part: Hitotsubashi Daigaku. *Annals*.
Indexed: Int. Bibl. Eco.; Int. Bibl. Pol. Sc.; Int. Pol. Sc. Abst.

2224
HITOTSUBASHI JOURNAL OF SOCIAL STUDIES. v.1– , Aug. 1960– . Tokyo. Irreg.
Issued by: Hitotsubashi Daigaku. In English, Japanese, or occasionally in German.
Supersedes, in part: Hitotsubashi Daigaku. *Annals*.
Indexed: Bull. Anal. Pol. Ec. Soc.; Int. Bibl. Eco.; Int. Bibl. Pol. Sc.

HITOTSUBASHI JOURNAL OF SOCIAL SCIENCES
See HITOTSUBASHI KENKYŪ

2225
HITOTSUBASHI KENKYŪ. no.1– , Aug. 1960– . Tokyo.
Issued by: Hitotsubashi Daigaku Daigakunsei Jichikai. In Japanese. Other title: *Hitotsubashi Journal of Social Sciences*.
Indexed: His. Abst.

2226
HŌ-SHAKAIGAKU. no.1–18, Mar. 1951–Apr. 1966; no.19– , Mar. 1967– . Tokyo, Yukohub. Irreg.
Issued by: Nihon Hō Shakai Gakkai. In Japanese. Other title: *Sociology of Law*.

2227
Hochschule für Ökonomie. WISSENSCHAFTLICHE ZEITSCHRIFT. no.1– , 1960– . Berlin.
In German.

2228
DAS HOCHSCHULWESEN. v.1– , Aug. 1953– . Berlin, Deutscher Verlag der Wissenschaften. Monthly.

Issued by: Staatssekretariat für das Hochschulwesen (Aug. 1953–Feb. 1958, called Staatssekretariat für das Hochschulwesen of the German Democratic Republic). In German.

2229
HŌGAKU KENKYŪ. 1– , 1922– . Tokyo. Monthly.
Issued by: Keiō Gijuku Hagaku Kenkyūkai. In Japanese. Other title: *Journal of Law, Politics and Sociology*.

2230
HOKEI RONSŌ. Dec. 1980– . Morioka-shi, Iwate Kenritsu Morioka Tanki Daigaku.
In Japanese. Added title on title page: *Journal of Law and Economics*.

2231
Hokkaidō Kyoiku Daigaku. HOKKAIDŌ KYOIKU KIYŌ. 1– , 1979– . Sapporo.
In Japanese; with some summaries in English. Other title: *Journal of Hokkaidō University of Education. Section IB; Social Science*.

HOKKAIDŌ KYOIKU KIYŌ
See Hokkaidō Kyoiku Daigaku. HOKKAIDŌ KYOIKU KIYŌ

HOKUTŌ AIJA KENKYŪ
See JOURNAL OF NORTHEAST ASIAN STUDIES

HOMBRE Y SOCIEDAD
See LE DOMAIN HUMAIN

2232
L'HOMME. 1884–1887. Paris. Two no. a month.
In French. Subtitle reads: "Journal illustré des sciences anthropologiques".

2233
HOMME. v.1– , Jan./Apr. 1961– . Paris, Mouton. Three no. a year, 1961–79; quarterly.
Issued by: Laboratoire d'Anthropologie Sociale, Section des Sciences Économiques et Sociales, École Pratique des Hautes Études en Sciences Sociales with the support of the Centre Nationale de la Recherche Scientifique. In French.
Indexes: v.1–23, 1961–83, 1v.
Indexed: Abst. Anth.; Bull. Sig. Soc. Eth.; Int. Bibl. Soc. Cul. Anth.; LLBA; Soc. Abst.; SSCI; Wom. Stu. Abst.

2234
L'HOMME ET HUMANITÉ. 1951– . Paris. Bimonthly.
Issued by: Fédération pour le Respect de l'Homme et de l'Humanité. In French. Continues: *Bulletin* of the Centre de Réflexion sur le Monde non-Occidentale.
Indexed: Bull. Anal. Pol. Ec. Soc.

2235
L'HOMME ET LA SOCIÉTÉ. no.1– , July/Sept. 1966– . Paris, Éditions Anthropos. Three no. a year.
In French. Subtitle reads: "Revue internationale de recherches et de synthèses sociologiques".
Indexed: Bull. Anal. Pol. Ec. Soc.; Bull. Sig. Soc. Eth.; Int. Bibl. Soc.; Int. Lab. Doc.; Int. Pol. Sc. Abst.; Soc. Abst.; Urb. Aff. Abst.

2236
HOMMES ET MIGRATIONS. DOCUMENTS SUR LES TRAVAILLEURS ÉTRANGERS. 1964– . Paris, Études Sociales Nord-Africaines. Irreg.
In French.
Continues, in part: *Études et Migrations* (1950–64)
Indexed: Bull. Anal. Pol. Ec. Soc.; Bull. Sig. Soc. Eth.; Int. Bibl. Soc.; Int. Lab. Doc.

2237
HOMMES ET MIGRATIONS. ÉTUDES. 1964– . Paris, Études Sociales Nord-Africaines. Irreg.
In French.
Continues, in part: *Hommes et Migrations* (1950–64). Processed.

2238
HOMO. 1– , 1949– . Göttingen, Mutterschmidt. Semi-annual, 1949–51; quarterly.
Organ of: Deutsche Gesellschaft für Anthropologie. Vols. 1–6 have subtitle: "Internationale Zeitschrift für die vergleichende Anthropologie"; later vols. "Zeitschrift für die vergleichende Forschung der Menschen". In German.
Indexed: Bull. Sig. Soc. Eth.; Int. Bibl. Soc. Cul. Anth.

2239
HOMO. 1– , 1953– . Toulouse. Annual.
Issued by: Faculté des Lettres et Sciences Humaines, Université de Toulouse-le-Mirail (1971–84). In French. Suspended 1957–64. Subseries of: Université de Toulouse. Faculté des Lettres et Sciences Humaines. *Annales* (until 1984); later of: Université de Toulouse-le-Mirail. Faculté des Lettres et Sciences Humaines. *Annales*.

2240
HONG KONG ECONOMIC PAPERS. 1– , 1960– . Hong Kong, Business Press. Annual.
Issued by: Hong Kong Economic Association.

2241
HONG KONG JOURNAL OF PUBLIC ADMINISTRATION. 1– , June 1979– . Hong Kong. Semi-annual.

Issued by: Department of Political Science, University of Hong Kong. Other title: *Kung Kung Hain Chen Hsüeh* (Dec. 1981–)
Continued by: *Asian Journal of Public Administration.*
Indexed: Int. Bibl. Eco.; Int. Bibl. Pol. Sc.; Int. Pol. Sc. Abst.; Sage Urb. Stu. Abst.

2242
ḤOQUQ-E BASHAR. 1– , 1970– . Tehran. Quarterly.
Issued by: Iranian Committee of Human Rights. In Persian.

HOS
See THE HISTORY OF SOCIOLOGY: HoS

2243
HOSPODARSKE DEJINY. ECONOMIC HISTORY. 1– , 1978– . Praha. Semi-annual.
Issued by: Ústav Československýh Svetovyh Dejin, Československá Akademia Věd. In Czech, English, or Slovak; summaries in English and Russian. Tables of contents also in English and Russian.

2244
HOUSTON JOURNAL OF INTERNATIONAL LAW. v.1– , spring 1978– . Houston, Tex. Semi-annual.
Issued by: University of Houston College of Law.
Indexes: v.1–3, 1978–81, in v.3, no.2.
Indexed: Ind. Leg. Per.

2245
THE HOWARD UNIVERSITY STUDIES IN THE SOCIAL SCIENCES. v.1–5, 1938–1946. Washington, D.C. Irreg.
Monograph series.

2246
HSIA-MEN TA HSÜEH HSÜEH PAO. CHE HSÜEH SHE HUI K'O HSÜEH PAN. v.1– , Sept. 1952– . Hsia-men (Amoy). Two no. a year.
Issued by: Hsia-men ta Hsüeh Yen Chiu Pu. In Chinese; summaries in English. Other title: *Universitatis Amoensis Acta Scientiarum Socialium.*

2247
HSIEN TAI KUO CHI KUAM HSI. CONTEMPORARY INTERNATIONAL RELATIONS. 1– , Oct. 1981– . Pei-ching, Shih ch'in pan she.
In Chinese.

2248
HSING CHIEN-SHE. 1– , 1949– . Pei-ching, Kuand-Ming Jih Pao. Monthly.
Issued by: Chian-Kuo Men Nei Ta-Chieh. In Chinese.

2249
HUA KANG FA K'O HSÜEH PAO. 1– , Apr. 1978– . Taipei, Chung-kuo Wen Hua Hsüeh Yuan.
In Chinese. Other title: *Hwa Kang Journal of Law and Social Science.*

2250
HUMAN AFFAIRS. v.1– , fall 1981– . Kingston, I.B. Tan. Semi-annual.
Subtitle reads: "International journal of social studies".

2251
HUMAN BEHAVIOR AND ENVIRONMENT. ADVANCES IN THEORY AND RESEARCH. v.1– , 1976– . New York, Plenum Press. Annual (irreg.).

2252
HUMAN BIOLOGY. 1929– . Detroit, Mich., Wayne State University Press. Quarterly.
Indexed: Abst. Anth.; Psych. Abst.; Int. Bibl. Soc. Cul. Anth.

HUMAN BIOLOGY SERIES
See AUSTRALIAN ABORIGINAL STUDIES

THE HUMAN CONTEXT
See LE DOMAIN HUMAIN

2253
HUMAN DEVELOPMENT. VITA HUMANA. v.1– , 1958– . Basel, Karger Medical and Scientific Publishers. Bimonthly.
Indexed: Abst. Anth.; Bull. Sig. Soc. Eth.; LLBA; Psych. Abst.; Wom. Stu. Abst.

2254
HUMAN ECOLOGY. v.1– , Mar. 1972– . New York, Plenum Pub. Co. Quarterly, 1972–82; three no. a year.
Indexed: Int. Bibl. Soc. Cul. Anth.

HUMAN GENETICS
See EXCERPTA MEDICA. SECTION 22. HUMAN GENETICS

HUMAN GEOGRAPHY
See GEOGRAFISKA ANNALER. SERIES B: HUMAN GEOGRAPHY

THE HUMAN GEOGRAPHY
See JIMBUN CHIRI

HUMAN GEOGRAPHY
See LUND STUDIES IN GEOGRAPHY. SERIES B: HUMAN GEOGRAPHY

2255
HUMAN HEREDITY. v.1– , 1950– . Basel, New York, Karger. Bimonthly.
Supersedes: *Acta Genetica et Statistica Medica*.
Indexed: Abst. Anth.; Int. Bibl. Soc. Cul. Anth.

2256
HUMAN ORGANIZATION. v.1– , Oct./Dec. 1941– . New York, Lexington, Ky. Quarterly.
Issued by: Institute of Behavioral Science, University of Colorado. Title varies: 1941–fall 1948, *Applied Anthropology*.
Indexed: Abst. Anth.; Bull. Anal. Pol. Ec. Soc.; Bull. Sig. Soc. Eth.; Curr. Cont. Soc. Beh. Sc.; Int. Bibl. Eco.; Int. Bibl. Pol. Sc.; Int. Bibl. Soc.; Int. Pol. Sc. Abst.; Ind. Per. Art. Law; Peace Res. Abst. J.; Psych. Abst.; Sage Pub. Adm. Abst.; Abst. Soc. Work; SSCI; Sage Urb. Stu. Abst.; Wom. Stu. Abst.

2257
HUMAN RELATIONS. v.1– , June 1947– . New York, Plenum Press. Quarterly, 1947–67; bimonthly, 1968–73; quarterly, 1974–75; monthly.
Issued by: Tavistock Institute of Human Relations and the Research Center for Group Dynamics.
Indexed: Abst. Anth.; Abst. Soc. Work; Bull. Sig. Soc. Eth.; Ind. Per. Art. Law; Int. Bibl. Soc.; Int. Bibl. Soc. Cul. Anth.; Int. Pol. Sc. Abst.; Bull. Anal. Pol. Ec. Soc.; PAIS; Psych. Abst.; Sage Pub. Adm. Abst.; Peace Res. Abst. J.; SSCI; Urb. Aff. Abst.; Wom. Stu. Abst.

2258
HUMAN RESOURCES ABSTRACTS. v.1– , Jan./ Feb. 1966– . Ann Arbor, Mich., 1966–74; Beverly Hills, Calif., Sage Publications. Bimonthly, 1966–74; quarterly.
Issued by: Institute of Labor and Industrial Relations, University of Michigan, 1966–74; the Institute and Wayne State University. Cover title: *Poverty and Human Resources Abstracts*. Title varies: v.1–9, 1966–74, *Poverty and Human Resources Abstracts*.

2259
HUMAN RIGHTS. v.1– , Aug. 1970– . Chicago, Ill.
Issued by: Section of Individual Rights and Responsibilities, American Bar Association.
Indexed: Ind. Leg. Per.; Ind. Per. Art. Law; PAIS.

2260
HUMAN RIGHTS. issue 1– , 1983– . Moscow, General Editorial Board for Foreign Publications, Nauka. Annual.
Issued by: Institute of State and Law, USSR Academy of Sciences.
Indexed: Ind. Leg. Per.

2261
HUMAN RIGHTS BULLETIN. no.1–18, July 1969–June/Dec. 1977. Geneva. Bimonthly.
Issued by: Division of Human Rights, United Nations.
Superseded by: *Bulletin of Human Rights*.

2262
HUMAN RIGHTS IN LATIN AMERICA. [8]– , 1983– . Washington, D.C. Annual.
Issued by: Council on Hemispheric Affairs. Reports 1–7 were untitled and unnumbered.

HUMAN RIGHTS JOURNAL
See REVUE DE DROIT DE L'HOMME

2263
HUMAN RIGHTS QUARTERLY. v.3– , Feb. 1981– . Baltimore, Md., Johns Hopkins University Press. Quarterly.
Sponsored by: Division of Behavioral and Social Sciences, University of Maryland. Subtitle reads: "A comparative and international journal of the social sciences, philosophy and law".
Continues: *Universal Human Rights*.
Indexed: ABC POL SCI; Soc. Abst.; SSCI.

2264
THE HUMAN RIGHTS REVIEW. v.1–6, no.3, spring 1976–1981. Three no. a year. London, Oxford University Press. Semi-annual.
Vols. 2–6 issued in association with the British Institute of Human Rights. Absorbed by: *Human Rights Law Journal*.
Indexed: Bull. Anal. Pol. Ec. Soc.; Ind. Leg. Per.; Int. Bibl. Pol. Sc.; Int. Pol. Sc. Abst.; Soc. Abst.; SSCI.

2265
Human Sciences Research Council, Pretoria. Raad vir Geestes-Wetenskaplike Novorsing. RESEARCH FINDINGS. 1975– . Pretoria. Irreg.
In Afrikaans; some volumes in English; summaries in English when text in Afrikaans.

2266
HUMAN SYSTEMS MANAGEMENT. v.1– , Feb. 1980– . Amsterdam, North-Holland Pub. Co. Quarterly.
Indexed: Int. Bibl. Eco.; Int. Pol. Sc. Abst.

2267
HUMANISME ET ENTREPRISE. 1963– . Paris. Bimonthly.
Issued by: Centre d'Études et de Recherches. In French. Title varies: *Cahiers du Centre d'Études et de Recherches de l'Association des Anciens Élèves*.
Indexed: Bull. Anal. Pol. Ec. Soc.; Int. Bibl. Eco.; Peace Res. Abst. J.

2268
THE HUMANIST; A RATIONAL APPROACH TO THE MODERN WORLD. 1885– . London. Frequency varies.
Title varies: 1885–Sept. 1956, *The Literary Guide and Rationalist Review*.
Indexed: Curr. Cont. Soc. Beh. Sc.; Ind. Per. Art. Law; SSCI; Wom. Stu. Abst.

2269
HUMANITAS. v.1–9, no.4, 1971–Dec. 1983. Pretoria. Quarterly.
Issued by: South African Human Science Research Council. In Afrikaans or English.
Supersedes: *Journal for Social Research*.
Indexed: Bull. Sig. Soc. Eth.; Int. Bibl. Soc. Cul. Anth.; Peace Res. Abst. J.; Psych. Abst.; Wom. Stu. Abst.

HUMANITIES
See Asiatic Society of Bangladesh. JOURNAL. HUMANITIES.

THE HUMANITIES AND SOCIAL SCIENCES
See CURRENT CONTENTS OF ACADEMIC JOURNALS IN JAPAN

THE HUMANITIES AND SOCIAL SCIENCES
See DISSERTATION ABSTRACTS. A: THE HUMANITIES AND THE SOCIAL SCIENCES

2270
HUMANITIES INDEX. 1974– . New York, H.W. Wilson. Quarterly with annual cumulation.
Continues, in part: *Social Sciences and Humanities Index*.

2271
HUMANITY AND SOCIETY. v.1– , summer 1977– . Hartford, Conn. Two no. a year, 1977; four no. a year.
Issued by: Association for Humanist Sociology.
Indexed: Soc. Abst.

2272
HUMBOLDT JOURNAL OF SOCIAL RELATIONS. v.1– , fall 1973– . Acta, Calif. Semi-annual.
Issued by: Department of Sociology, Anthropology and Social Welfare, California State University at Humboldt.
Indexed: Abst. Anth.

2273
HUNG-CH'I. 1– , Jan. 1958– . Peking. Biweekly.
Issued by: Chung-kuo-ch'an tang chung yuan wei-yuan-hui. In Chinese.

HWA KANG JOURNAL OF LAW AND SOCIAL SCIENCE
See HUA KANG FA K'O HSÜEH PAO

I

ICSSR JOURNAL OF ABSTRACTS AND REVIEWS
See Indian Council of Social Science Research. ICSSR JOURNAL OF ABSTRACTS AND REVIEWS

ICSSR JOURNAL OF ABSTRACTS AND REVIEWS. ECONOMICS
See Indian Council of Social Science Research. ICSSR JOURNAL OF ABSTRACTS AND REVIEWS. ECONOMICS

ICSSR JOURNAL OF ABSTRACTS AND REVIEWS. GEOGRAPHY
See Indian Council of Social Science Research. ICSSR JOURNAL OF ABSTRACTS AND REVIEWS. GEOGRAPHY

ICSSR JOURNAL OF ABSTRACTS AND REVIEWS. POLITICAL SCIENCE
See Indian Council of Social Science Research. ICSSR JOURNAL OF ABSTRACTS AND REVIEWS. POLITICAL SCIENCE

ICSSR JOURNAL OF ABSTRACTS AND REVIEWS. SOCIOLOGY, SOCIAL ANTHROPOLOGY, CRIMINOLOGY AND SOCIAL WORK
See Indian Council of Social Science Research. ICSSR JOURNAL OF ABSTRACTS AND REVIEWS. SOCIOLOGY, SOCIAL ANTHROPOLOGY, CRIMINOLOGY AND SOCIAL WORK

ICSSR OCCASIONAL MONOGRAPHS IN RESEARCH AND METHODOLOGY
See Indian Council of Social Science Research. ICSSR MONOGRAPHS IN RESEARCH AND METHODOLOGY

IECS
See INDICE ESPAÑOL DE CIENCIAS SOCIALES

2274
IEEE TRANSACTIONS ON SYSTEMS, MEN AND CYBERNETICS. 1972– . New York. Bimonthly.
Issued by: IEEE Systems, Man and Cybernetics Society.
Continues: *IEEE Systems, Man and Cybernetics.*

2275
IFO-STUDIEN; ZEITSCHRIFT FÜR EMPIRISCHE WIRTSCHAFTSFORSCHUNG. 1– , 1955– . Berlin. Quarterly.
Issued by: IFO Institut für Wirtschaftsforschung, München. In German.
Indexed: PAISFL.

IJSGR
See INTERNATIONAL JOURNAL OF SMALL GROUP RESEARCH

I.M.F. SURVEY
See International Monetary Fund. I.M.F. SURVEY

I.M.R. INTERNATIONAL MIGRATION REVIEW
See INTERNATIONAL MIGRATION REVIEW

I.P.A. REVIEW
See Institute of Public Affairs. I.P.A. REVIEW

IPSA MONOGRAFIE REEKS
See IPSO MONOGRAPH SERIES

2276
IPSO MONOGRAPH SERIES. no.1–6, 1976–1981. Pretoria. Irreg.
Issued by: Institute for the Study of Plural Societies, University of Pretoria. Some monographs published as *IPSA Monografie Reeks.*

IPSR INTERNATIONAL POLITICAL SCIENCE REVIEW
See RISP. REVUE INTERNATIONAL DE SCIENCE POLITIQUE

IPW BERICHTE
See Institut für Internationale Politik und Wirtschaft der Deutschen Demokratischen Republik. IPW BERICHTE

IPW FORSCHUNGSHEFTE
See Institut für Internationale Politik und Wirtschaft der Deutschen Demokratischen Republik. IPW FORSCHUNGSHEFTE

I.U.L.A. BULLETIN
See International Union of Local Authorities. I.U.L.A. BULETIN

2277
IBADAN. v.1– , 1957– . Ibadan, University College Press. Three no. a year.
Issued by: University of Ibadan.
Indexed: Int. Bibl. Eco.; Int. Bibl. Soc. Cul. Anth.

2278
IDEAS EN CIENCIAS SOCIALES. v.1– , Jan./Mar. 1984– . Buenos Aires. Quarterly.
Issued by: Universidad de Belgrano. In Spanish.

IKLANTARA
See INDONESIAN PERSPECTIVES

IKLANTARA INDONESIA; ECONOMY & TOURISM
See INDONESIAN PERSPECTIVES

2279
IKONOMIKA. [v.1]– , 1985– . Sofiia, Izd. na Durzhavniia Komiteta za Planirane, Ministrstvo na Finansite, Bulgarskata Narodna Banka, Komiteta za Sotsialna Informatsiia. Monthly.
In Bulgarian. Formed by the union of: *Planovo Stopanstvo* (1968–84) and *Finansi i Kredit* (1950–84)

AL-'ILM WA-AL MUJTAMA
See IMPACT OF SCIENCE ON SOCIETY

2280
IMMIGRANT COMMUNITIES & ETHNIC MINORITIES IN THE UNITED STATES & CANADA. 1– , 1984– . New York, AMS Press. Irreg.

2281
IMMIGRANTS AND MINORITIES. v.1– , Mar. 1982– . London, Frank Cass. Three no. a year.

2282
IMPACT OF SCIENCE ON SOCIETY. v.1– , Apr./June 1950– . Paris, Unesco. Quarterly.
Issued by: United Nations Educational, Scientific and Cultural Organization. Published also in French edition: *Impact; Science et Société*; Spanish: *Impacto*; Arabic: *al-Ilm wa-al mujtama. al-Qahirah Majallat Risālat al Unisku; Markaz Matbu'at al-Unisku* of selected articles (irreg.); and Korean: *Kwahak Kwa Sahoe.*
Indexed: Curr. Cont. Soc. Beh. Sc.; Ind. Per. Art. Law; Int. Bibl. Eco.; Int. Bibl. Pol. Sc.; Int. Bibl. Soc.; Eco. Abst.; Int. Bibl. Soc. Cul. Anth.; Int. Lab. Doc.; Int. Pol. Sc. Abst.; PAIS; Peace Res. Abst. J.; SSCI; Wom. Stu. Abst.

IMPACT. SCIENCE ET SOCIÉTÉ
See IMPACT OF SCIENCE ON SOCIETY

IMPACTO
See IMPACT OF SCIENCE ON SOCIETY

THE IMPERIAL AND ASIATIC QUARTERLY REVIEW AND ORIENTAL AND COLONIAL RECORD
See ASIAN REVIEW

2283
INDEX ISLAMICUS. 1976–1980– . London, Mansell Pub. Ltd. Quinquennial.
Cumulation of: *Quarterly Index Islamicus.*
Continues: *Index Islamicus. Supplement.*

INDEX OF ECONOMIC ARTICLES IN COLLECTIVE VOLUMES
See INDEX TO ECONOMIC ARTICLES IN JOURNALS AND COLLECTIVE VOLUMES

2284
INDEX OF ECONOMIC JOURNALS. v.1–6, 1886–1964/65. Nashville, Tenn., later Homewood, Ill., R.D. Irwin.
Superseded by: *Index to Economic Articles in Journals and Collective Volumes.*

INDEX TO CONFERENCE PROCEEDINGS RECEIVED
See British Library. Lending Division. INDEX TO CONFERENCE PROCEEDINGS RECEIVED

2285
INDEX TO ECONOMIC ARTICLES IN JOURNALS AND COLLECTIVE VOLUMES. v.1– , 1960– . Homewood, Ill., R.D. Irwin. Annual.
Prepared under the auspices of: American Economic Association. Title varies: v.1–7, 1960–65, *Index to Economic Articles in Collective Volumes.*
Supersedes: *Index of Economic Journals* (1886–1960)

2286
INDEX TO FOREIGN LEGAL PERIODICALS. 1960– . Chicago, Ill. Quarterly, with annual and triennial cumulation.
Issued by: American Association of Law Libraries and the Institute of Advanced Legal Studies, London. Subject headings in English with translation into French, German and Spanish.

2287
INDEX TO INDIAN ECONOMIC JOURNALS. 1966– . Calcutta. Monthly.
Issued by: Information Research Academy.

2288
INDEX TO INTERNATIONAL PUBLIC OPINION. 1978/79– . Westport, Conn., Greenwood Press. Annual.

2289
INDEX TO INTERNATIONAL STATISTICS: IIS. v.1– , Jan. 1983– . Washington, D.C. Congressional Information Service. Monthly, with quarterly and annual cumulations.

INDEX TO LATIN AMERICAN PERIODICALS. HUMANITIES AND SOCIAL SCIENCES
See INDICE GENERALE DE PUBLICACIONES PERIÓDICAS LATINOAMERICANAS. HUMANIDADES Y CIENCIAS SOCIALES

2290
INDEX TO LEGAL PERIODICALS. Jan. 1908– . Chicago, Ill. Quarterly, 1908–36; bimonthly, 1937–July 1940; monthly (except Aug. 1940–), with annual and triennial cumulations. Each issue cumulates previous ones in the same volume.
Title varies: v.1–28, 1908–35, *Index to Legal Periodicals and Law Library Journal.*

INDEX TO LEGAL PERIODICALS AND LAW LIBRARY JOURNAL
See INDEX TO LEGAL PERIODICALS

2291
INDEX TO PERIODICAL ARTICLES BY AND ABOUT BLACKS. 1973– . Boston, Mass., G.K. Hall. Annual.
Issued by: Hallie Q. Brown Memorial Library, Central State University, Wilberforce, in cooperation with the Schomburg Collection of the Negro Literature and History. Continues: *Index to Periodicals by and about Negroes* (1966–73)

INDEX TO PROCEEDINGS OF THE ECONOMIC AND SOCIAL COUNCIL
See United Nations. Dag Hammarskjöld Library. INDEX TO PROCEEDINGS OF THE ECONOMIC AND SOCIAL COUNCIL

INDEX TO PROCEEDINGS OF THE GENERAL ASSEMBLY
See United Nations. General Assembly. INDEX TO PROCEEDINGS

INDEX TO PROCEEDINGS OF THE SECURITY COUNCIL
See United Nations. Dag Hammarskjöld Library. INDEX TO PROCEEDINGS

INDEX TO PROCEEDINGS OF THE TRUSTEESHIP COUNCIL
See United Nations. Dag Hammarskjöld Library. INDEX TO PROCEEDINGS OF THE TRUSTEESHIP COUNCIL

INDEX TO RECENT POLICY POSITIONS OF THE GOVERNING BOARD OF THE COUNCIL OF STATE GOVERNMENTS, GENERAL ASSEMBLY OF STATE GOVERNMENTS AND ORGANIZATIONS AFFILIATED WITH THE COUNCIL OF STATE GOVERNMENTS
See Council of State Governments. INDEX TO RECENT POLICY POSITIONS OF THE GOVERNING BOARD OF THE COUNCIL OF STATE GOVERNMENTS AND ORGANIZATIONS AFFILIATED WITH THE COUNCIL OF STATE GOVERNMENTS

2292
INDEX TO SOCIAL SCIENCES & HUMANITIES PROCEEDINGS. Jan./Mar. 1979– . Philadelphia, Pa. Quarterly, with annual cumulation.

2293
INDEX TO THE OFFICIAL JOURNAL OF THE EUROPEAN COMMUNITIES. ALPHABETICAL INDEX. English Edition. Jan. 1980– . Luxembourg, Office for Official Publications of the European Communities. Monthly, with annual cumulation.
Continues, in part: *Index to the Official Journal of the European Communities. Alphabetical Index and Methodology Table.*

2294
INDEX TO THE OFFICIAL JOURNAL OF THE EUROPEAN COMMUNITIES. METHODOLOGICAL TABLE. English Edition. Jan. 1980– . Luxembourg, Office for Official Publications of the European Communities. Monthly, with annual cumulation. Issues for May–Dec. 1980 never published. Each volume called v.2. Published also in other languages of the European Communities.
Continues, in part: *Index to the Official Journal of the European Communities; Alphabetical Index and Methodological Table.*

INDEX TO VIETNAMESE SOCIAL SCIENCE PERIODICALS
See MUC LUC PHAN TIN TAP KHOA HOC XA HOI VIETNAM

2295
INDIA CULTURES QUARTERLY. v.15, no.2–v.35, no.3/4, 1957–1980. Jabalpur. Two, three, or four no. a year.
Issued by: School of Research, Leonard Theological College. V.15, no.2 called also v.1, no.1.
Continues: *Pilgrim.* Continued by: *India Cultures.*
Indexes: vols. 15–24, no.1, 1957–first quarter 1957, 1v.

2296
INDIA QUARTERLY. v.1– , Jan. 1945– . New Delhi, A. Affadorai.
Issued by: Indian Council of World Affairs.
Indexed: ABC POL SCI; Bull. Anal. Pol. Ec. Soc.; His. Abst.; Ind. Bibl. Eco.; Int. Bibl. Pol. Sc.; Int. Bibl. Soc.; Pop. Ind.

2297
Indian Anthropological Society. JOURNAL. v.1– , Mar. 1966– . Calcutta. Semi-annual, 1966–75; three no. a year.
Indexed: Abst. Anth.; Soc. Abst.

2298
INDIAN ANTHROPOLOGIST. 1– , 1971– . New Delhi. Semi-annual.
Issued by: Indian Anthropological Association.
Indexed: Int. Bibl. Soc. Cul. Anth.

2299
INDIAN ARCHAEOLOGY; A REVIEW. 1960– . New Delhi. Annual.
Issued by: Archaeological Survey.
Continues: publication of the same title issued by the Department of Archaeology (1953/54–1959)

2300
INDIAN BEHAVIOURAL SCIENCES ABSTRACTS. 1– , Jan. 1970– . Delhi. Quarterly.
Issued by: Behavioural Sciences Centre. Volumes from 1975 on were not available for examination.

2301
INDIAN COMMUNIST. v.1– , Mar. 1968– . New Delhi. Quarterly.
Issued by: Society for the Study of Communist Affairs in India.

2302
Indian Council of Social Science Research. CURRENT RESEARCH IN SOCIAL SCIENCES IN UNIVERSITIES AND COLLEGES. v.4– , Jan./June 1974– . New Delhi. Two no. a year.
Subseries of the council's *Research Information Series*.

2303
Indian Council of Social Science Research. ICSSR JOURNAL OF ABSTRACTS AND REVIEWS. v.1–3, Jan./Dec. 1972–1974. New Delhi, National Publishing House. Semi-annual.
Continued by: *ICSSR Journal of Abstracts and Reviews. Economics*; *ICSSR Journal of Abstracts and Reviews. Geography*; *ICSSR Journal of Abstracts and Reviews. Political Science*; *ICSSR Journal of Abstracts and Reviews. Sociology, Social Anthropology, Criminology and Social Work*.

2304
Indian Council of Social Science Research. ICSSR JOURNAL OF ABSTRACTS AND REVIEWS. ECONOMICS. v.1– , 1971– . New Delhi. Quarterly.
Continues, in part: Indian Council for Social Science Research. *ICSSR Journal of Abstracts and Reviews*.

2305
Indian Council of Social Science Research. ICSSR JOURNAL OF ABSTRACTS AND REVIEWS. GEOGRAPHY. v.1– , Jan./Dec. 1975– . New Delhi. Semi-annual.
Continues, in part: Indian Council of Social Science Research. *ICSSR Journal of Abstracts and Reviews*.

2306
Indian Council of Social Science Research. JOURNAL OF ABSTRACTS AND REVIEWS. POLITICAL SCIENCE. v.4– , Jan./Dec. 1975– . New Delhi. Semi-annual.
Continues, in part: *Journal of Abstracts and Reviews*.

2307
Indian Council of Social Science Research. JOURNAL OF ABSTRACTS AND REVIEWS. SOCIOLOGY, SOCIAL ANTHROPOLOGY, CRIMINOLOGY AND SOCIAL WORK. v.4– , Jan./June 1975– . New Delhi. Semi-annual.
Continues, in part: *Journal of Abstracts and Reviews*.

2308
Indian Council of Social Science Research. OCCASIONAL MONOGRAPHS. 1– , 1974– . New Delhi. Irreg.
Monograph series. Title varies: *ICSSR Occasional Monographs in Research Methodology*.

2309
INDIAN CULTURE. v.1–13, no.2, July 1934–Oct./Dec. 1946. Calcutta.
Issued by: Indian Research Institute. In English or Hindi.

2310
INDIAN ECONOMIC AND SOCIAL HISTORY REVIEW. v.1– , July/Sept. 1963– . New Delhi, Vikas Publishing House. Quarterly.
Indexed: His. Abst.

2311
THE INDIAN ECONOMIC JOURNAL. v.1– , July 1953– . Bombay, Geetanjali Press. Quarterly.
Issued by: Indian Economic Association, and Department of Economics, University of Bombay.
Indexed: Curr. Cont. Soc. Beh. Sc.; Eco. Abst.; Ind. Per. Art. Law; Int. Lab. Doc.; Pop. Ind.; PAIS; Soc. Abst.; SSCI.

2312
INDIAN ECONOMIC REVIEW. v.1–6, Feb. 1952–Aug. 1963; n. ser. v.1– , Apr. 1966– . Delhi. Semi-annual, 1952; quarterly.
Issued by: Delhi School of Economics, University of Delhi.
Indexed: Bull. Anal. Pol. Ec. Soc.; Int. Bibl. Eco.

2313
INDIAN EDUCATIONAL REVIEW. v.1– , July 1966– . New Delhi. Semi-annual.
Issued by: Indian Council of Educational Research and Training.
Indexed: Psych. Abst.

2314
INDIAN FOREIGN AFFAIRS. v.1– , 1958– . New Delhi. Monthly.
Issued by: Indian Foreign Affairs Association.

THE INDIAN HISTORIAN
See WASSAJA

2315
INDIAN HORIZONS. v.21– , 1972– . New Delhi. Four no. a year.
Issued by: Indian Council for Cultural Relations.
Continues: *Indo-Asian Culture.*
Indexed: Bull. Sig. Soc. Eth.; His. Abst.

2316
INDIAN JOURNAL OF AGRICULTURAL ECONOMICS. v.1– , July 1946– . Bombay. Semi-annual; quarterly.
Issued by: Indian Society of Agricultural Economics.
Indexed: Bull. Anal. Pol. Ec. Soc.; Int. Bibl. Soc. Cul. Anth.; Int. Lab. Doc.; PAIS.

2317
INDIAN JOURNAL OF BEHAVIOUR. v.1– , Oct. 1976– . Mysore, Academy Press. Quarterly.
Subtitle reads: "Interdisciplinary approach".

2318
INDIAN JOURNAL OF COMPARATIVE LAW. v.1– , 1977– . Trivandrum. Semi-annual, 1977–1980; three no. a year.

2319
INDIAN JOURNAL OF COMPARATIVE SOCIOLOGY. 1– , Aug. 1974– . Dharwar. Semi-annual.
Issued by: Forum for Sociologists.

2320
INDIAN JOURNAL OF CRIMINOLOGY. v.1– , 1972?– . Madras. Semi-annual.
Issued by: The Indian Society of Criminology, and Department of Psychology, University of Madras.

2321
INDIAN JOURNAL OF ECONOMICS. v.1– , Jan. 1916– . Allahabad, D.K. Ghose for the Department of Economics and Commerce, University of Allahabad. Four no. a year.
Issued by: Department of Economics and Commerce, University of Allahabad.
Indexed: Bull. Anal. Pol. Ec. Soc.; Int. Bibl. Eco.; Pop. Ind.; SSCI.

2322
INDIAN JOURNAL OF INDUSTRIAL RELATIONS. v.1– , July 1965– . New Delhi. Quarterly.
Issued by: Shri Ram Centre for Industrial Relations and Human Resources.
Indexed: Int. Bibl. Soc.; Int. Lab. Doc.; PAIS.

2323
INDIAN JOURNAL OF INTERNATIONAL LAW. v.1– , July 1960– . New Delhi, M.K. Nawaz. annual, v.1; quarterly.
Official organ of: Indian Society of International Law. Includes a section of official documents.
Indexed: Ind. For. Leg. Per.

2324
INDIAN JOURNAL OF LABOUR ECONOMICS. v.1– , 1958– . Lucknow. Quarterly.
Issued by: Labour Society of Labour Economics.
Indexed: Int. Bibl. Eco.; Int. Bibl. Soc.

2325
THE INDIAN JOURNAL OF MARKETING GEOGRAPHY. v.1– , 1983– . Gorakhpur.
Issued by: The Association of Marketing Geographers of India.

2326
INDIAN JOURNAL OF PHYSICAL ANTHROPOLOGY AND HUMAN GENETICS. v.1– , June 1975– . Lucknow. Semi-annual.
Issued by: Ethnographic and Folk Culture Society.

2327
INDIAN JOURNAL OF POLITICAL SCIENCE. v.1– , July/Sept. 1939– . Calcutta. Quarterly.
Issued by: Indian Political Science Association. Includes the association's "Annual Report".
Indexed: ABC POL SCI; Int. Bibl. Pol. Sc.; Int. Bibl. Soc.; Int. Pol. Sc. Abst.; Soc. Abst.; Wom. Stu. Abst.

2328
THE INDIAN JOURNAL OF POLITICAL SCIENCE. v.1– , Jan. 1977– . Jodhpur. Semi-annual.
Issued by: Department of Political Science, University of Jodhpur.
Indexed: Bull. Anal. Pol. Ec. Soc.; int. Bibl. Pol. Sc.; Int. Pol. Sc. Abst.

2329
INDIAN JOURNAL OF POLITICS. v.1– , Jan./June 1967– . Aligarh. Three no. a year.
Issued by: Department of Political Science, Aligarh Muslim University.
Indexed: ABC POL SCI; Bull. Anal. Pol. Ec. Soc.; Int. Bibl. Pol. Sci.; Int. Pol. Sc. Abst.

2330
INDIAN JOURNAL OF PSYCHOLOGY. v.1– , 1926– . Calcutta. Quarterly (some combined numbers)
Official organ of: Indian Psychological Association.
Indexed: LLBA; Psych. Abst.; Wom. Stu. Abst.

2331
INDIAN JOURNAL OF PUBLIC ADMINISTRATION. v.1– , Jan./Mar. 1955– . New Delhi. Quarterly.
Issued by: Indian Institute of Public Administration.
Indexed: ABC POL SCI; Int. Bibl. Eco.; Int. Bibl. Pol. Sc.; Int. Bibl. Soc.; Int. Pol. Sc. Abst.; Int. Lab. Doc.; PAIS.

2332
INDIAN JOURNAL OF REGIONAL SCIENCE. 1– , 1968– . Kharagpur. Semi-annual.
Issued by: Regional Science Association, and Indian Institute of Technology.

2333
INDIAN JOURNAL OF SOCIAL RESEARCH. v.1– , 1959– . Meerut. Three no. a year, 1959–83; semi-annual.
Issued by: Department of Sociology, J.V. College.
Indexed: Bull. Sig. Soc. Eth.; His. Abst.; Int. Bibl. Eco.; Soc. Abst.; SSCI.

2334
INDIAN JOURNAL OF SOCIAL SCIENCES. 1– , Sept. 1971– . Hyderabad. Three no. a year.
Organ of: Society for the Study of Social Sciences.

2335
INDIAN JOURNAL OF SOCIOLOGY: IJS. 1– , Mar. 1970– . New Delhi, Academic Journals of India. Semi-annual.
Issued by: Indian Academy of Social Sciences.
Indexed: LLBA; Soc. Abst.

2336
INDIAN JOURNAL OF YOUTH AFFAIRS. v.1– , Mar. 1979– . New Delhi, Vishva Yuwak Kendra. Quarterly, 1979; semi-annual.

INDIAN LABOUR GAZETTE
See INDIAN LABOUR JOURNAL

2337
INDIAN LABOUR JOURNAL. v.1– , 1944– . Delhi. Monthly.
Issued by: Labour Bureau of India, Ministry of Labour and Employment. Title varies: 1944–60, *Indian Labour Gazette*.
Indexed: Bull. Anal. Pol. Ec. Soc.; Int. Bibl. Eco.; Int. Bibl. Soc. Cul. Anth.; Int. Lab. Doc.

2338
THE INDIAN MARXIST. v.1– , Feb. 1965– . Varanasa. Semi-annual, 1964–76; three no. a year, 1977; quarterly.
Issued by: National Marxist Association, and the India First Forum.

2339
INDIAN POLITICAL SCIENCE REVIEW. v.1–19, no.1/2, Oct. 1966–Jan./Dec. 1966–1985. Delhi. Quarterly, 1966–81; semi-annual.
Issued by: Department of Political Science, University of Delhi.
Indexed: ABC POL SCI; Curr. Cont. Soc. Beh. Sc.; Int. Bibl. Eco.; Int. Bibl. Pol. Sc.; Int. Bibl. Soc.; Int. Bibl. Soc. Cul. Anth.; Int. Pol. Sc. Abst.; SSCI.

2340
INDIAN PSYCHOLOGICAL ABSTRACTS. v.1– , 1972– . Bombay, New Delhi, Soniaiya Publications. Bimonthly.
Issued under the auspices of: Behavioural Science Centre, Indian Council of Social Science Research, and Indian Psychological Association.

2341
INDIAN PSYCHOLOGICAL REVIEW. v.1– , July 1964– . Agra. Frequency varied, –1986; monthly.
Issued by: Agra Psychological Research Cell.
Indexed: Psych. Abst.; SSCI (1979–).

INDIAN SOCIOLOGICAL BULLETIN
See INTERNATIONAL JOURNAL OF CONTEMPORARY SOCIOLOGY

2342
THE INDIAN YEARBOOK OF INTERNATIONAL AFFAIRS. v.1– , 1952– . Madras. Annual.
Issued by: Indian Study Group of International Affairs, University of Madras.

2343
INDIANA. 1– , 1973– . Berlin, Mann Verlag. Irreg.
Issued by: Ibero-Amerikanische Institut Preussischer Kulturbesitz. In English, German, or Spanish. Supplements called "Beihefte" accompany some issues. Other titles: *Beiträge zur Völker- und Sprachenkunde des Indianischen Amerika*; *Aportes a la Etnología y Lingüística, Arqueología y Antropología Física de la América Indígena*; *Contributions to Ethnology and Linguistics, Archaeology and Physical Anthropology of Indian America*.
Indexed: Int. Bibl. Soc. Cul. Anth.

2344
Indiana Academy of the Social Sciences. PROCEEDINGS OF THE ANNUAL MEETING. 1946– . Indianapolis. Annual.
None published in 1949–55. Vols. 1947/48–1948/49 issued as the academy's *Annals*.

2345
Indiana University. INDIANA UNIVERSITY PUBLICATIONS. SOCIAL SCIENCE SERIES. no.1– , 1939– . Bloomington, Ind., Indiana University Press. Irreg.

Title varies: *Indiana University Social Science Series.* Monograph series.

2346
Indiana University. Folklore Institute. JOURNAL. v.1–19, 1964–Dec. 1982. The Hague, Mouton. Three no. a year.
Continued by: *Journal of Folklore Research.*
Indexed: Abst. Anth.; Bull. Sig. Soc. Eth.; His. Abst.; Int. Bibl. Soc. Cul. Anth.; Soc. Sc. Hum. Ind.

INDIANA UNIVERSITY PUBLICATIONS. SOCIAL SCIENCES SERIES
See Indiana University. INDIANA UNIVERSITY PUBLICATIONS. SOCIAL SCIENCE SERIES

INDIANA UNIVERSITY SOCIAL SCIENCES SERIES
See INDIANA UNIVERSITY PUBLICATIONS. SOCIAL SCIENCES SERIES

INDIANIST YEARBOOK
See ANUARIO INDIGENISTA

INDICADORES ECONÔMICO-SOCIAIS
See Portugal. Instituto Nacional de Estatística. INDICADORES ECONÔMICO-SOCIAIS

INDICADORES ECONÓMICOS Y SOCIALES
See El Salvador. Consejo Nacional de Planificación y Coordinación Económica. Sección de Estudios Económicos. INDICADORES ECONÓMICOS Y SOCIALES

INDICADORES SOCIAIS
See Fundação Instituto Brasileiro de Geografia e Estatística. Departamento de Estudos e Indicadores Sociais. INDICADORES SOCIAIS

INDICATEURS DES ACTIVITÉS INDUSTRIELLES
See Organisation for Economic Co-operation and Development. INDICATORS OF INDUSTRIAL ACTIVITY

INDICATEURS ÉCONOMIQUE AFRICAINS
See United Nations. Economic Commission for Africa. AFRICAN SOCIO-ECONOMIC INDICATORS

INDICATEURS SOCIAUX POUR LA COMMUNAUTÉ EUROPÉENNE
See SOCIAL INDICATORS FOR THE EUROPEAN COMMUNITIES

INDICATORS TO INDUSTRIAL ACTIVITY
See Organisation for Economic Co-operation and Development. INDICATORS OF INDUSTRIAL ACTIVITY

2347
INDICE DE CIÊNCIAS SOCIAIS. v.1– , July 1979– . Rio de Janeiro. Semi-annual, 1979–80; three no. a year.
Issued by: Instituto Universitario de Pesquisas de Rio de Janeiro, IUPERJ, in cooperation with the Instituto de Planejamento Econômico e Social, IPEA. In Portuguese. Processed.

2348
INDICE ECONÓMICO COLOMBIANO. 1951– . Medellín. Annual.
Issued by: Biblioteca, Faculdad de Ciencias Económicas, Universidad de Antioquia. In Spanish.

2349
INDICE ESPAÑOL DE CIENCIAS SOCIALES. SERIE A. PSICOLOGÍA Y CIENCIAS DE L'EDUCACIÓN. v.5– , Jan./Dec. 1981– . Madrid.
Issued by: Centro de Información y Documentación (C.S.I.C.), Instituto de Información y Documentación en Ciencias Sociales y Humanidades (ISOC). In Spanish.
Continues, in part: *Indice Español de Ciencias Sociales* (v.1–4, 1977–80)

2350
INDICE GENERALE DE PUBLICACIONES PERIÓDICAS LATINOAMERICANAS; HUMANIDADES Y CIENCIAS SOCIALES. INDEX TO LATIN AMERICAN PERIODICALS; HUMANITIES AND SOCIAL SCIENCES. v.1–10, no.2, 1961–Apr./June 1970. Metuchen, N.J., Scarecrow Press. Annual.
In Spanish, partly in English. Author, title and subject indexes.

2351
INDICE HISPANOAMERICANO DE CIENCIAS SOCIALES. v.1– , Jan./Feb. 1985– . Bogotá, Indizar Ltola. Bimonthly.
In Spanish.

2352
INDIKATOREN ZUR GESELLWISSENSCHAFTLICHEN ENTWICKLUNG. 1976– . Wien.
Issued by: Österreichische Statistische Zentralamt. In German.

INDIVIDUAL AND THE FUTURE OF ORGANIZATIONS
See Franklin Foundation. INDIVIDUAL AND THE FUTURE OF ORGANIZATIONS

2353
THE INDO-ASIAN CULTURE. v.1–20, July 1952–1971. New Delhi. Four no. a year.

Issued by: Indian Council for Cultural Relations.
Continued by: *Indian Horizons*.
Indexed: Bull. Sig. Soc. Eth.; His. Abst.

2354
Indonesia. Biro Pusat Statistik. INDIKATOR EKONOMI. 1970– . Jakarta. Monthly.
In English and Indonesian.

2355
INDONESIA. 1– , Apr. 1966– . Ithaca, N.Y. Two no. a year.
Issued by: Modern Indonesia Project, Cornell University.
Indexes: no.1–6, 1966–Oct. 1968, in no.6.
Indexed: Int. Bibl. Soc. Cul. Anth.

THE INDONESIAN JOURNAL OF CULTURAL STUDIES
See MADJALAH ILMU-ILMU SASTRA INDONESIA

2356
THE INDONESIAN JOURNAL OF GEOGRAPHY. v.6(no.10)– , June 1976– . Yogyakarta. Semi-annual.
Issued by: Faculty of Geography, Gadjah Mada University.
Continues: *Madjalah Geografi Indonesia*.

THE INDONESIAN JOURNAL OF PUBLIC ADMINISTRATION
See ADMINISTRASI NEGARA

2357
INDONESIAN PERSPECTIVES. no.1– , Aug. 1968– . Djakarta. Monthly.
Title varies: no.1–5, Aug. 1968–Dec. 1968, *Iklantara*; no.6–12, Jan. 1969–July 1969, *Iklantara Indonesia*; *Economy & Tourism*. Suspended with no.13, 1969 through Sept. 1969. In English or Indonesian.

2358
INDONESIAN QUARTERLY. v.1– , Oct. 1972– . Jakarta, Yayasan Proklamasi. Quarterly.
Issued by: Centre for Strategic and International Studies.
Indexed: Bull. Anal. Pol. Ec. Soc.

2359
INDONESIAN REVIEW OF INTERNATIONAL AFFAIRS. v.1– , July 1970– . Djakarta. Annual.
Issued by: Indonesian Institute of International Affairs.

2360
INDUSTRIAL AND LABOR RELATIONS REVIEW. v.1– , 1947– . Ithaca, N.Y. Quarterly.
Issued by: New York School of Labor and Industrial Relations, Cornell University. Special issues appeared in v.1–20, 1947–67.
Indexed: ABC POL SCI; Bull. Anal. Pol. Ec. Soc.; His. Abst.; Int. Bibl. Eco.; Int. Bibl. Pol. Sc.; Int. Lab. Doc.; Int. Pol. Sc. Abst.; PAIS; PHRA; Soc. Abst.

2361
INDUSTRIAL ARCHAEOLOGY. v.1– , May 1964– . Glasgow. Quarterly.
Vols. for 1964–65 published in association with the Newcomen Society. Title varies: 1964–65, *The Journal of Industrial Archaeology*.

INDUSTRIAL MANAGEMENT
See KEY TO TURKISH SCIENCE; APPLIED ECONOMICS

2362
INDUSTRIAL RELATIONS JOURNAL. 1970– . London, Industrial Relations Journal. Two no. a year, 1971; quarterly.
Indexes: Vols. 1–2, 1970–71, in v.2.
Indexed: APAIS; Int. Bibl. Soc. Cul. Anth.; Int. Lab. Doc.

2363
INDUSTRIAL REVIEW OF JAPAN. 1956–1984. Tokyo. Annual.
Supplement to: *Japan Economic Journal*. Other title: *Nihon Jimbun*.
Continued by: *Japan Economic Almanac*.

2364
INDUSTRIAL STATISTICS YEARBOOK. 1982– . New York. Annual.
Issued by: Department of International Economic and Social Affairs, Statistical Office, United Nations.
Continues: *Yearbook of Industrial Statistics*. (ST/ESA/STAT/ser. F)

2365
INDUSTRIALIZATION AND PRODUCTIVITY. 1– , 1970– . New York. Quarterly.
Issued by: United Nations Industrial Development Organization. The issues for 1975 were the last available for examination.

INDUSTRIE ET SOCIÉTÉ
See INDUSTRY AND SOCIETY

2366
INDUSTRIES ET TRAVAUX D'OUTRE-MER. 1– , 1953– . Paris, René Moreau. Monthly.
In French.
Indexed: Bull. Anal. Pol. Ec. Soc.; PAISFL.

INDUSTRIESTATISTIK
See Statistical Office of the European Communities. INDUSTRIESTATISTIK

2367
INDUSTRY AND DEVELOPMENT. GLOBAL REPORT. no.1– , 1978– . New York. Two no. a year.
Issued by: United Nations. Published also in French and Spanish editions.
Indexed: PAIS.

2368
INDUSTRY AND SOCIETY. no.1– , Jan. 8, 1974– . Brussels. Weekly.
Issued by: Directorate of General Information, Commission of the European Communities. Published also in French edition titled: *Industrie et Société*.

2369
INFORMAÇÃO SOCIAL. v.1– , Jan./Mar. 1966– . Lisboa. Quarterly.
Issued by: Direcção Geral de Assistência, Ministerio de Saúde e Assistência. In Portuguese; summaries in English, French and German.
Indexed: Int. Bibl. Soc. Cul. Anth.; Int. Lab. Doc.; Psych. Abst.

2370
INFORMACIONES SOCIALES. v.1– , 1937– . Lima. Quarterly.
Issued by: Departamento de Estudios Sociales y Económicos, Caja Nacional de Seguro Social Obrero. In Spanish.

INFORMATION
See SOCIAL SCIENCE INFORMATION

2371
INFORMATION AND BEHAVIOR. v.1– , 1985– . New Brunswick, N.J., Transaction Books. Annual.

INFORMATION SUR LES SCIENCES SOCIALES
See SOCIAL SCIENCE INFORMATION

INFORMATIONS CONSTITUTIONELLES ET PARLEMENTAIRES
See Inter-Parliamentary Union. INFORMATIONS CONSTITUTIONELLES ET PARLEMENTAIRES

2372
INFORMATIONS SOCIALES. 1– , 1947– . Paris. Biweekly, 1947–53; monthly.
Issued by: Union Nationale des Caisses d'Allocations Familiales. In French. Issue no.9 of 1974 was the latest examined.
Indexed: Bull. Anal. Pol. Ec. Soc.; Bull. Sig. Soc. Eth.; Int. Bibl. Soc. Cul. Anth.; Int. Lab. Doc.

INFORMATIONS STATISTIQUES
See Statistical Office of the European Communities. SOZIALSTATISTIK. STATISTIQUES SOCIALES

2373
INFORMATIQUE EN SCIENCES HUMAINES. v.1– , 1969– . Paris. Bimonthly.
Issued by: Institut des Sciences Humaines Appliqués de Paris. In French.

INFORME
See United Nations. Commission on the Racial Situation in the Union of South Africa. REPORT

INFORME
See United Nations. Commission on the Status of Women. REPORT

INFORME
See United Nations. Economic and Social Council. REPORT OF THE ECONOMIC AND SOCIAL COUNCIL

INFORME
See United Nations. Economic and Social Council. Commission on Human Rights. REPORT

INFORME
See United Nations. Economic Commission for Europe. REPORT

INFORME
See United Nations. Trusteeship Council. OFFICIAL RECORDS (its subseries)

INFORME ANNUAL
See United Nations. Economic Commission for Asia and the Far East. INFORME ANNUAL

INFORME ECONÓMICO MUNDIAL
See United Nations. Department of Economic and Social Affairs. WORLD ECONOMIC REPORT

2374
THE INNER CITY IN CONTEXT. 1– , 1980– . London.
Issued by: Bartlett School of Architecture and Planning, London University College.

INQUIRIES ON MODERN ECONOMIC AND SOCIAL HISTORY
See RECHERCHES D'HISTOIRE ÉCONOMIQUE ET SOCIALE

2375
INQUIRY. 1– , spring 1958– . Oslo, Oslo University Press. Quarterly.
Subtitle reads: "An interdisciplinary journal of philosophy and the social sciences".
Indexed: ABC POL SCI; Curr. Cont. Soc. Beh. Sc.; Int. Bibl. Pol. Sc.; Int. Pol. Sc. Abst.; PAIS; Soc. Abst.; SSCI.

2376
INSTANT RESEARCH ON PEACE AND VIOLENCE. 1971–1977. Tampere. Quarterly.
Issued by: Tampere Peace Research Institute (TAPRI).
Superseded by: *Current Research on Peace and Violence*.
Indexed: Soc. Abst.

Institut Colonial International
See International Institute of Differing Civilizations

2377
Institut de Recherches Marxistes. CAHIERS D'HISTOIRE. n. ser. no.1(35)– , 3e trimestre 1980– . Paris.
In French.
Continues: Institut Maurice Thorez. *Cahiers d'Histoire* (no.1–34, 1934–79)

2378
Institut de Science Économique Appliqué. CAHIERS. SÉRIE F. DÉVELOPPEMENT, CROISSANCE, PROGRÈS. 1– , 1955– . Paris.
In French. Published as the institute's *Publication Mensuelle* or *Publication Trimestrielle*.

2379
Institut Fondamental d'Afrique Noire. BULLETIN. 1–15, Jan. 1939–Oct. 1953. Paris. Quarterly.
The institute's earlier name was: Institut Français d'Afrique Noire.
Supersedes: Comité d'Études Historiques et Scientifiques de l'Afrique Occidentale Française. *Bulletin*. Superseded by two series: *Bulletin. Série A: Sciences Naturales*, and *Série B: Sciences Humaines*.
Indexed: Abst. Anth.; His. Abst.; Int. Bibl. Soc. Cul. Anth.; Int. Lab. Doc.

2380
Institut Fondamental d'Afrique Noire. BULLETIN. SÉRIE B: SCIENCES HUMAINES. Jan./Apr. 1954– . Dakar. Semi-annual (some combined numbers)
In French.
Continues, in part: the institute's *Bulletin*.
Indexed: Bull. Sig. Soc. Eth.

2381
Institut für Gesellschaftspolitik. MITTEILUNGEN. 1970– . Wien, Verlag Ernst Schwartz. Semi-annual.
In German.

2382
Institut für Internationale Politik und Wirtschaft, Berlin. IPW—BERICHTE. v.1– , 1972– . Berlin, Staatsverlag der Deutschen Demokratischen Republik. Quarterly.
In German.

2383
Institut für Internationale Politik und Wirtschaft, Berlin. IPW FORSCHUNGSHEFTE. v.1– , 1966– . Berlin, Staatsverlag der Deutschen Demokratischen Republik. Four no. a year.
In German. Tables of contents also in English and Russian. Each number has also a distinctive title. Title varies: v.1–6, 1966–71, *DWI—Forschungshefte*.

2384
Institut International d'Administration Publique. BULLETIN. v.1– , Jan./Mar. 1967– . Genève. Quarterly.
In French.
Indexed: Int. Lab. Doc.; Int. Pol. Sc. Abst.

2385
Institut International d'Études Sociales. BULLETIN. v.1– , 1966– . Genève. Quarterly.
In French.
Indexed: Bull. Sig. Soc. Eth.; Int. Lab. Doc.

2386
Institut International d'Études Sociales. CAHIERS. 1966–1974. Genève, Librairie Sociale et Économiques. Quarterly (irreg.)
Published in English, French and Spanish editions.
Indexed: Int. Bibl. Pol. Sc.; Int. Lab. Doc.

2387
Institute for Comparative Studies of Culture. PUBLICATIONS. 1955– . Tokyo. Semi-annual.
In English.

2388
Institute for Defense Studies & Analyses. NEWS REVIEW ON CHINA, MONGOLIA AND THE KOREAS. v.1– , Jan. 1971– . New Delhi.
Title varies: v.1, 1971, *News Review on China*.

2389
Institute of British Geographers. TRANSACTIONS AND PAPERS. 1933/34– . London, G. Philip. Semi-annual.
Summaries in English and German. Some numbers have distinctive titles. Publication suspended 1939–45. Issues for 1933/34–38 published in combined numbers with the monographs of the *Publication* series. Title varies: 1933/34–1938, *Transactions*.
Indexes: for 1946–56 in the index to the institute's *Publication*, no.2–22.

2390
Institute of Development Studies. DEVELOPMENT STUDIES REGISTER OF RESEARCH IN THE UNITED KINGDOM. 1971– . Brighton. Biennial.

Continues: *Development Studies Register of UK based Ongoing Research.*

2391
Institute of Family Studies, Melbourne. WORKING PAPER. 1– , 1981– . Melbourne. Irreg.
Each number has also a distinctive title.

INSTITUTE OF HUMAN SCIENCES REVIEW *See* THE URBAN AND SOCIAL CHANGE REVIEW

2392
Institute of International Law. ANNUAIRE DE L'INSTITUT DE DROIT INTERNATIONAL. 1–32, 1874–1925; 1927– . Ghent, later Paris, A. Pedone. Annual.
In French. Suspended, 1914–18, 1926.

2393
Institute of Public Administration. JOURNAL. v.1– , 1980– . Lucknow. Quarterly.
Issued by: Regional Centre for Urban and Environmental Studies, Lucknow University.

2394
Institute of Public Affairs. I.P.A. REVIEW. v.1– , 1947– . Melbourne, Ramsay Ware Pub. Pty. Quarterly.

2395
Institute of Social Studies, The Hague. PUBLICATIONS. SERIES MAJOR. v.1– , 1961– . The Hague. Irreg.
Monograph series.

2396
Institute of Sociology, London. REPORTS OF THE ANNUAL CONFERENCES. 1– , 1935– . London.
The institute was called the Sociological Society through 1929. Title varies: 1935, *Social Sciences*; 1936, *Further Papers on the Social Sciences*; 1937, *Papers on the Social Sciences.*

2397
Instituto de Ciencias Sociales. REVISTA. no.1– , 1961– . Barcelona, Sección de la Prensa, Información y Ediciones. Semi-annual.
In Spanish. The institute is an institution of the Diputación Provincial de Barcelona. Issues are thematic or devoted to certain geographical regions.
Indexed: Bull. Sig. Soc. Eth.; His. Abst.; Int. Bibl. Soc. Cul. Anth.; Int. Pol. Sc. Abst.; Soc. Abst.

2398
Instituto de Investigaciais Científice de Moçambique. MEMÓRIAS. SERIE C: CIÊNCIAS HUMANAS. v.7– , 1965– . Lourenço Marques. Irreg.
In Portuguese.
Continues, in part: Instituto de Investigação Científica de Moçambique. *Memórias.*

2399
Instituto Espanõl de Estudios Mediterráneos. CUADERNOS. no.1– , 1963– . Barcelona. Quarterly.
In Spanish. Vol. for 1971 last available for examination.

2400
Instituto Gulbenkian de Ciência. Centro de Economia e Finanças. ARQUIVO B. ESTUDOS DE ECONOMIA E FINANÇAS. 1– , 1966– . Lisboa. Two no. a year.
In English or French. Monograph series.

2401
Instituto Joaquim Nabuco de Pesquisas Sociais. BOLETIM DO INSTITUTO JOAQUIM NABUCO DE PESQUISAS SOCIAIS. 1–18, 1952–1971. Recife. Annual.
In Portuguese. Vol. 1 issued under a variant name: Instituto Joaquim Nabuco.
Superseded by: *Ciência e Tropico.*

2402
Instituto Nacional de Antropología. CUADERNOS. 1– , 1960– . Buenos Aires. Irreg.
In Spanish.
Indexed: His. Abst.

2403
Instituto Nacional de Antropología e Historia. ANALES. v.1– , 1939/40– . Mexico, D.F., Tall. Graf. de la Editorial Stylo.
In Spanish. Vol. 1 called also v.29 "de la colección" continuing numbering of *Anales* issued 1877–1909 by Museo Nacional, and 1909–38 by Museo Nacional de Arqueología, Historia, Etnología.

Instituto Panamericano de Geografía e Historia *See* Pan American Institute of Geography and History

2404
Institutul de Studii Sud-Est Europene. BULLETIN DE L'INSTITUT POUR L'ÉTUDE DE L'EUROPE SUD-ORIENTALE. v.1–10, 1914–1923. Bucureşti. Quarterly.
In French.
Superseded by: *Revue Historique du Sud-Est Européen.*

2405
THE INSURGENT SOCIOLOGIST. v.1– , 1971– . Four no. a year.

Issued by: Department of Sociology, University of Oregon.
Indexed: Soc. Abst.

2406
LA INTEGRACIÓN LATINOAMERICANA. 1– , Apr. 1976– . Buenos Aires. Monthly.
Issued by: Instituto para Integración de América Latina. In Spanish.
Supersedes: *Boletín de Integración*, and *Revista de la Integración*.
Indexed: Bull. Anal. Pol. Ec. Soc.; Int. Bibl. Eco.

2407
INTÉGRATION AFRICAINE. no.1– , 1977– . Ouagadougou. Quarterly.
Issued by: Communauté Économique de l'Afrique de l'Ouest. In French.

2408
Inter-American Development Bank. ECONOMIC AND SOCIAL PROGRESS IN LATIN AMERICA; ANNUAL REPORT. 1972– . Washington, D.C. Annual.
Continues: the bank's *Socio-Economic Progress in Latin America*.

2409
Inter-American Development Bank. Board of Governors. PROCEEDINGS [OF THE] MEETING. 1960– . Washington, D.C. Annual.
Issued also in Portuguese and Spanish editions: *Anales [de la] Reunión*.

2410
INTER-AMERICAN ECONOMIC AFFAIRS. v.1– , June 1947–39, no.1/2, winter 1985. Washington, D.C., Inter-American Affairs Press. Quarterly.
Issued by: Institute of Inter-American Studies.
Indexes: v.1–3, 1947–50, in v.3.
Indexed: ABC POL SCI; Bull. Anal. Pol. Ec. Soc.; His. Abst.; Int. Bibl. Eco.; Int. Lab. Doc.; PAIS; Soc. Sc. Hum. Ind.

2411
INTER-AMERICAN FOREIGN TRADE. no.1– , 1953– . New York.
Issued by: Chamber of Commerce for Latin America.

INTER-AMERICAN JOURNAL OF PSYCHOLOGY
See REVISTA INTERAMERICANA DE PSICOLOGÍA

2412
INTER-AMERICAN LABOR BULLETIN. v.1– , Feb. 1951– . Washington, D.C.
Issued by: Inter-American Regional of the International Cooperation of Free Trade Unions. Published also in Spanish.

INTER-AMERICAN YEARBOOK OF HUMAN RIGHTS
See ANUARIO INTERAMERICANO DE DERECHOS HUMANOS

2413
INTER-NORD. v.1– , 1960– . Paris. Annual.
Issued by: Centre d'Études Arctiques et Finno-Scandinaves. In English or French.
Indexed: Bull. Anal. Pol. Ec. Soc.

INTER-PARLIAMENTARY BULLETIN
See Inter-Parliamentary Union. BULLETIN INTERPARLEMENTAIRE

2414
Inter-Parliamentary Union. BULLETIN INTERPARLEMENTAIRE. v.1– , Jan./Feb. 1921– . Genève. Bimonthly.
In French. Beginning with issues for 1926 published also in English: *Inter-Parliamentary Bulletin* (v.6–, 1926–), and German: *Interparlamentarische Bulletin*, beginning also with v.6, Jan./Feb. 1926. The German edition ceased with v.20, no.3/4, Dec. 1940.
Indexed: Int. Bibl. Pol. Sc.

2415
Inter-Parliamentary Union. CONSTITUTIONAL AND PARLIAMENTARY INFORMATION. n. ser. 1st–2nd year, 1948–49; 3rd ser. no.1– , Jan. 15, 1950– . Geneva, Association of Secretaries General of Parliaments (1948–July 1957, called Autonomous Section of Secretaries General of Parliaments). Volumes for 1948–49 called n. ser. Include coverage of the period Oct. 1939–1947. French edition began in 1936.

2416
Inter-Parliamentary Union. INFORMATIONS CONSTITUTIONELLES ET PARLEMENTAIRES. no.1–24, Feb. 15, 1936–Dec. 31, 1938; 2nd ser. no. 1–5/6, Feb. 15–Sept. 30, 1939; n. ser. v.1–2, 1948–1949; 3rd ser., no.1– , Jan. 15, 1950– . Genève, Association of Secretaries General of Parliaments. Eight no. a year, 1936–38; annual, 1948–49; quarterly 1950–64.
Issued under French name: Union Interparlementaire. Publication suspended Oct. 1939–47. Published also in English.

2417
Inter-Parliamentary Union. Conference. COMPTE RENDU DE LA CONFÉRENCE. 8th conference– , 1897– . Genève. Annual.

Chiefly in English or French. Title varies: 1906, *Official Report*; 1907, *Bericht*.

2418
INTERAMERICAN JOURNAL OF PSYCHOLOGY. v.14– , 1980– . Austin, Tex. Quarterly.
Published under the auspices of the Interamerican Society of Psychology.
Continues: *Revista Interamericana de Psicología*.

2419
Interamerican Planning Society. REVISTA. v.1–5, Mar. 1967–1971. Oali. Quarterly.
In Spanish; summaries in English. Supplements accompany some numbers. Other titles: *Revista Interamericana de Planificación*; *Journal of the Interamerican Planning Society*.
Continued by: *Revista Interamericana de Planificación*.
Indexed: Int. Bibl. Eco.; Int. Lab. Doc.

2420
INTERCHANGE ON EDUCATION. v.14, no.2– , 1983– . Toronto. Quarterly.
Issued by: Toronto Institute for Studies in Education.
Continues: *Interchange on Educational Policy*.
Indexed: Bull. Anal. Pol. Ec. Soc.; Psych. Abst.

2421
INTERCHANGE ON EDUCATIONAL POLICY. v.9, no.3–v.14, no.1, 1978/79–1983. Toronto. Quarterly.
Issued by: Ontario Institute for Studies in Education.
Continues: *Interchange* (v.1–9, no.2, 1970–1978/79). Continued by: *Interchange on Education*.
Indexed: Bull. Anal. Pol. Ec. Soc.

THE INTERCOLLEGIATE SOCIALIST
See LABOR AGE

2422
INTERCULTURAL STUDIES. INTERKULTURELLE STUDIEN. 1– , 1983– . Brockney. Annual.
Issued by: International Association of Intercultural Studies. In Arabic, English, French, German, or Spanish.

2423
INTERDISCIPLINARIA. v.5– , 1984– . Buenos Aires.
Issued by: Centro Interamericano de Investigaciones Psicológicas y Ciencias Afines. In Spanish; summaries in English.

AN INTERDISCIPLINARY JOURNAL OF HUMAN BEHAVIOR
See DEVIANT BEHAVIOR

2424
INTERDISCIPLINE. v.1– , 1964– . Varanasi. Quarterly.
Issued by: Gandhian Institute of Studies. Title varies: 1964–Dec. 1965, *Social Science Abstracts*.

2425
INTERECONOMICS. v.1– , Jan. 1966– . Hamburg, Welt-Wirtschafts-Archiv. Bimonthly, 1966–69; monthly.
Issued by: 1970–, Institut für Wirtschaftsforschung. In German. Subtitle reads: "Monthly review of international trade and development". English edition.
Supersedes: *Monthly Review of Economic Policy*.
Indexed: Int. Bibl. Eco.; PAIS; Peace Res. Abst. J.

2426
Intergovernmental Committee for Migration. REVIEW OF ACHIEVEMENTS. ICM. 1980– . Geneva, 1981– .
Continues: Intergovernmental Committee for European Migration. *Review of Achievements*.
There are also editions in French and Spanish.

INTERKULTURELLE STUDIEN
See INTERCULTURAL STUDIES

2427
INTERNASJONAL POLITIK. 1947– . Bergen, J.W. Eides. Six no. a year, 1950–60; quarterly, 1961–82; three no. a year.
Issued by: Chr. Michelsen's Instituut for Videnskap og Endsfrihet, later by Uterinskpolitisk Instituut. In Norwegian.
Supersedes a publication of the same title (1937–40).
Indexed: ABC POL SCI; Bull. Anal. Pol. Ec. Soc.; Int. Bibl. Eco.; Int. Bibl. Pol. Sc.; Int. Bibl. Soc. Cul. Anth.; Int. Pol. Sc. Abst.

2428
INTERNATIONAL ABSTRACTS IN OPERATIONS RESEARCH. v.1– , Nov. 1961– . Baltimore, Md. Five no. a year.
Issued by: International Federation of Operational Research Society of America.
Indexes: Vols. 5–8, in v.8.

2429
International Academy of Comparative Law. ACTA ACADEMIAE UNIVERSALIS JURISPRUDENTIARUM COMPARATIVAE. MÉMOIRES DE L'ACADÉMIE INTERNATIONALE DE DROIT COMPARÉ. v.1–2, 1928–1935. Berolini, Paris.

In English, French, German, or Latin.

2430
INTERNATIONAL AFFAIRS. v.1– , Jan. 1922– . London, Dawson. Bimonthly, 1922–39; quarterly (irreg.)
Issued by: Royal Institute of International Affairs (called 1922–Mar. 1926, British Institute of International Affairs). Title varies: v.1–9, 1922–30, *Journal*.
Indexes: *International Affairs Cumulative Index*, 1922–1976, by Lalit Adolphus (Oxford, Learned Information Europe, 1978).
Indexed: ABC POL SCI; Bull. Anal. Pol. Ec. Soc.; Eco. Abst.; Geo. Abst.; His. Abst.; Ind. Per. Art. Law; Int. Bibl. Eco.; Int. Bibl. Pol. Sc.; Int. Bibl. Soc.; Int. Lab. Doc.; Int. Pol. Sc. Abst.; PAIS; Peace Res. Abst. J.; Soc. Sc. Hum. Ind.; SSCI.

2431
INTERNATIONAL AFFAIRS. no.1– , Jan. 1955– . Moscow, Znanye Pub. House. Monthly.
Published also in Russian beginning 1954.
Indexed: ABC POL SCI; Bull. Anal. Pol. Ec. Soc.; Int. Pol. Sc. Abst.; PAIS; Peace Res. Abst. J.

2432
INTERNATIONAL AFFAIRS BULLETIN. v.1– , 1977– . Pretoria. Quarterly.
Issued by: Die Suid-Afrikaanse Institut van Internasjonale Aangeleenthede.

2433
INTERNATIONAL AFRICAN BIBLIOGRAPHY. BIBLIOGRAPHIE INTERNATIONALE AFRICAINE. 1971– . London, Mansell Pub. Ltd. Quarterly.
Issued by: International African Institute. In English or French.

2434
THE INTERNATIONAL AND COMPARATIVE LAW QUARTERLY. v.1– , Jan. 1952– . London. Quarterly.
Issued by: The Society of Comparative Legislation (vols. 1952–58), The British Institute of International and Comparative Law, 1959– , Vol. 1 called 4th series to continue the numbering of the *Journal of Comparative Legislation and International Law*. Formed by the union of: *International Law Quarterly*, and *Journal of Comparative and International Law*. Absorbed: Grotius Society. *Transactions*.
Indexed: ABC POL SCI; Bull. Anal. Pol. Ec. Soc.; Ind. Leg. Per.; Ind. For. Leg. Per.; Int. Bibl. Eco.; Int. Bibl. Pol. Sc.; Int. Bibl. Soc.; Int. Bibl. Soc. Cul. Anth.; Int. Lab. Doc.; Int. Pol. Sc. Abst.; PAIS; Peace Res. Abst. J.; SSCI; Wom. Stu. Abst.

2435
INTERNATIONAL AND COMPARATIVE PUBLIC POLICY. v.1–3/4, winter/spring 1976–1979/80. New York. Irreg.
Issued by: International Public Policy Institute.

INTERNATIONAL ANNALS OF CRIMINOLOGY
See ANNALES INTERNATIONALES DE CRIMINOLOGIE

2436
INTERNATIONAL ANTHROPOLOGICAL AND LINGUISTIC REVIEW. v.1– , 1953– . Miami, Fla. Irreg.
Organ of: International Anthropological and Linguistic Circle.

INTERNATIONAL ARCHIVES OF COOPERATION
See ARCHIVES INTERNATIONALES DE SOCIOLOGIE DE LA COOPÉRATION

2437
INTERNATIONAL ARCHIVES OF ETHNOGRAPHY. INTERNATIONALES ARCHIV FÜR ETHNOGRAPHIE. ARCHIVES INTERNATIONALES D'ETHNOGRAPHIE. v.1– , 1888– . Leiden, E.J. Brill. Irreg.
Organ of: Internationale Gesellschaft für Ethnographie. Supplements accompany some numbers. Title varies: v.1–45, 1888–1947, *Internationales Archiv für Ethnographie*.
Superseded by: *Tropical Man*.

2438
INTERNATIONAL BEHAVIOURAL SCIENTIST. v.1– , Mar. 1969– . Meerut, Sadhna Prakashan. Quarterly.
Official Organ of: Delta Tau Kappa.
Indexed: Bull. Anal. Pol. Ec. Soc.; Int. Pol. Sc. Abst.; Soc. Abst.

2439
INTERNATIONAL BIBLIOGRAPHY OF ECONOMICS. BIBLIOGRAPHIE INTERNATIONALE DES SCIENCES ÉCONOMIQUES. v.1– , 1952– . Paris, Unesco, 1952–59; London, Tavistock Pub., Chicago, Ill., Aldine Pub. Co., 1960–. Annual.
Vol. for 1952 prepared by the Fondation National des Sciences Politiques (Paris) with the assistance of the International Economic Association and the International Committee for Social Science Documentation.

INTERNATIONAL BIBLIOGRAPHY OF HISTORICAL DEMOGRAPHY
See BIBLIOGRAPHIE INTERNATIONALE DE LA DÉMOGRAPHIE HISTORIQUE

2440
INTERNATIONAL BIBLIOGRAPHY OF INCOME AND WEALTH. v.1–10, no.1, Jan./Mar. 1948–Jan./Mar. 1957. New York. Quarterly.
Issued by: International Association for Research in Income and Wealth in cooperation with the Statistical Office of the United Nations.

2441
INTERNATIONAL BIBLIOGRAPHY OF POLITICAL SCIENCE. BIBLIOGRAPHIE INTERNATIONALE DE SCIENCE POLITIQUE. v.1– , 1953– . London, Tavistock Publications, Chicago, Ill., Aldine Pub. Co. Annual.
Prepared by: International Political Science Association in cooperation with the International Council for Social Science Documentation.

INTERNATIONAL BIBLIOGRAPHY OF PSYCHOLOGY
See BIBLIOGRAPHIE INTERNATIONALE DE PSYCHOLOGIE

INTERNATIONAL BIBLIOGRAPHY OF RESEARCH IN THE MARRIAGE AND THE FAMILY
See INVENTORY OF MARRIAGE AND FAMILY LITERATURE

2442
INTERNATIONAL BIBLIOGRAPHY OF SOCIAL AND CULTURAL ANTHROPOLOGY. BIBLIOGRAPHIE INTERNATIONALE D'ANTHROPOLOGIE SOCIALE ET CULTURELLE. v.1– , 1955– . Paris, Unesco, 1955–59; London, Tavistock Publications, Chicago, Ill., Aldine Pub. Co., 1960–. Annual.
Issued by: International Committee for Social Science Documentation in cooperation with the International Congress of Anthropological and Ethnological Sciences.

2443
INTERNATIONAL BIBLIOGRAPHY OF SOCIOLOGY. BIBLIOGRAPHIE INTERNATIONALE DE SOCIOLOGIE. [1]– , 1951– . Paris, Unesco; London, Tavistock Pub. Annual.
Issued by: International Committee for Social Science Documentation. Issues for 1951–54 published as a part of *Current Sociology*.

2444
INTERNATIONAL BIBLIOGRAPHY OF THE HISTORY OF RELIGIONS. 1952– . Leiden, E.J. Brill. Irreg.
Issued by: International Association for the Study of the History of Religions. Other title: *Bibliographie Internationale de l'Histoire des Religions*.

INTERNATIONAL BIBLIOGRAPHY OF THE SOCIAL SCIENCES. BIBLIOGRAPHIE INTERNATIONALE DES SCIENCES SOCIALES
Includes:
INTERNATIONAL BIBLIOGRAPHY OF ECONOMICS. BIBLIOGRAPHIE INTERNATIONALE DES SCIENCES ÉCONOMIQUES;
INTERNATIONAL BIBLIOGRAPHY OF POLITICAL SCIENCE. BIBLIOGRAPHIE INTERNATIONALE DE SCIENCE POLITIQUE;
INTERNATIONAL BIBLIOGRAPHY OF SOCIAL AND CULTURAL ANTHROPOLOGY. BIBLIOGRAPHIE INTERNATIONALE D'ANTHROPOLOGIE SOCIALE ET CULTURELLE;
INTERNATIONAL BIBLIOGRAPHY OF SOCIOLOGY. BIBLIOGRAPHIE INTERNATIONALE DE SOCIOLOGIE

2445
INTERNATIONAL BIBLIOGRAPHY OF THE SOCIOLOGY OF LAW. 1979– . London, New York, Academic Press. Annual.
Continues: *International Journal of Criminology and Penology*.

2446
INTERNATIONAL BIBLIOGRAPHY ON CRIME AND DELINQUENCY. v.1–3, no.8, Jan. 1963–June 1966. Washington, D.C. Three no. a year, 1963–Apr. 1965; eight no. a year.
Issued by: National Research and Information Center on Crime and Delinquency. Prepared by the National Clearinghouse for Mental Health Information, and the U.S. Department of Health, Education and Welfare. Absorbed: *Current Projects in the Prevention, Control of Crime and Delinquency*.
Continued by: *Crime and Delinquency Abstracts*.

2447
International Bureau of Education. BULLETIN. v.1–44 (no.1–177), 1927–1970. Geneva.
Published in English and French editions.
Continued by: *Educational Documentation and Information*.

2448
International Bureau of Education. PUBLICATION. 1– , 1927– . Geneva. Irreg.
In French. Includes: *Annual Education Bibliography*, and *International Yearbook of Education*, issued now by Unesco.

2449
International Bureau of Fiscal Documentation, Amsterdam. BULLETIN FOR INTERNATIONAL FISCAL DOCUMENTATION. BULLETIN DE DOCUMENTATION FISCALE INTERNATIONALE. v.1– , 1946/47– . Amsterdam. Monthly.

In various languages.
Indexed: PAIS.

2450
INTERNATIONAL CANADA. v.1–13, no.2, 1970–Feb. 1982. Toronto. Monthly.
Issued by: Canadian Institute of International Affairs, and Parliamentary Centre for Foreign Affairs and Foreign Trade. Absorbed by: *International Perspectives*.
Supersedes: Canadian Institute of International Affairs (C.I.I.A.), *Monthly Report on Canadian External Relations*.

INTERNATIONAL CENSUS BIBLIOGRAPHY
See University of Texas. Bureau of International Business Research. Population Research Center. INTERNATIONAL CENSUS BIBLIOGRAPHY

2451
INTERNATIONAL CHILD WELFARE REVIEW. v.1– , 1947– . Geneva. Quarterly.
Issued by: International Centre, International Union for the Child Welfare.
Indexed: Abst. Soc. Work.

2452
INTERNATIONAL COMMERCE. v.1– , Oct. 5, 1940– . Washington, D.C., Government Printing Office. Weekly.
Title varies: 1940–June 11, 1962, *Foreign and Domestic Commerce*.
Supersedes: *Commerce Reports* issued by the Bureau of Foreign and Domestic Commerce.

2453
INTERNATIONAL CONCILIATION. no.1– , 1907– . New York. Monthly.
Issued by: American Branch, Association for International Conciliation, 1907–June 1924; Division of Intercourse and Education, Carnegie Endowment for International Peace, July 1922–. No.1 and 2 have no series title.
Indexed: His. Abst.; Int. Bibl. Soc. Cul. Anth.; Int. Pol. Sc. Abst.

2454
International Congress of Americanists. PROCEEDINGS. 1st– , 1875– . [Place of publication varies]
In English, French, German, Portuguese, or Spanish. Title varies: *Actas*, *Akten*, *Anais*, *Compte Rendu*, *Selected Papers*, *Verhandlungen*.

INTERNATIONAL CO-OPERATIVE BULLETIN
See REVIEW OF INTERNATIONAL COOPERATION

2455
International Congress of Local Authorities. PROCEEDINGS. 1–6, 1913–1936. Brussels. Irreg.

2456
INTERNATIONAL CURRENCY REVIEW. v.1– , Feb. 1969– . London. Bimonthly.
Indexed: Bull. Anal. Pol. Ec. Soc.

2457
INTERNATIONAL DEVELOPMENT ABSTRACTS. 1982– . Norwich, Geo Abstracts. Six no. a year.
Issued by: Centre for Development Studies, University of Swansea.

2458
INTERNATIONAL DEVELOPMENT REVIEW. v.1–11, Oct. 1959–1969. Washington, D.C. Two no. a year, 1959–60; quarterly.
Issued by: Society for International Development. Supplements accompany some numbers.
Continued by: *Revista del Desarrollo Internacional*.
Indexes: Vols. 1–3, 1959–61, in v.3.
Indexed: ABC POL SCI; Bull. Anal. Pol. Ec. Soc.; Int. Bibl. Soc. Cul. Anth.; Int. Lab. Doc.; PAIS.

2459
INTERNATIONAL DIRECTORY OF SOCIAL SCIENCE ORGANIZATIONS. 1981/82– . Stockholm, Almquist & Wiksell International.
Compiled and edited by: International Federation of Social Science Organizations (IFSSE). Other title: *Social Science Organizations*.
Continues: *International Directory of Social Science Council*.

INTERNATIONAL ECONOMIC ASSISTANCE TO AFRICA
See United Nations. Economic Commission for Africa. INTERNATIONAL ECONOMIC ASSISTANCE TO AFRICA

2460
INTERNATIONAL ECONOMIC INDICATORS. v.1– , Feb. 1975– . Washington, D.C., Department of Commerce. Quarterly.
Issued by: Bureau of International Economic Policy and Research, U.S. Domestic and International Business Administration. Title varies: v.1–2, 1975–76, *International Economic Indicators and Competitive Trends*.

INTERNATIONAL ECONOMIC INDICATORS AND COMPETITIVE TRENDS
See INTERNATIONAL ECONOMIC INDICATORS

2461
INTERNATIONAL ECONOMIC REVIEW. 1– , 1960– . Osaka, Kansai Keizai Rongo-Kai. Three no. a year.

Issued by: Kansai Economic Federation, and Wharton School of Finance & Commerce, University of Pennsylvania.
Indexed: Bull. Anal. Pol. Ec. Soc.; Eco. Abst.; Int. Bibl. Eco.; PAIS; Peace Res. Abst. J.; Pop. Ind.

INTERNATIONAL ECONOMIC REVIEW
See KUKCHE KYONGJE

INTERNATIONAL ECONOMIC REVIEW
See KUKCHE KYONGJE YŎN'GU

2462
INTERNATIONAL FAMILY PLANNING PERSPECTIVES. 1– , 1979– . New York. Quarterly.
Issued by: Alan Guttmacher Institute for the Planned Parenthood Federation of America Inc., with the assistance of the U.S. Agency for International Development. Chiefly in English; summaries in French. Published also in Spanish: *Perspectivas Internacionales en Planificación Familiar.*
Continues: *International Family Planning; Perspectives and Digest.* V.11, 1985 latest examined.
Indexed: Pop. Ind.

2463
INTERNATIONAL FINANCIAL STATISTICS. v.1– , Jan. 1948– . Washington, D.C. Monthly.
Issued by: International Monetary Fund. Published also in French. *Statistiques Financières Internationales,* and Spanish: *Estadísticas Financieras Internacionales.* Includes supplements called *Supplement Series* (no.1, 1981)
Indexed: PAIS.

2464
THE INTERNATIONAL GALLUP POLLS. PUBLIC OPINION. 1975– . Wilmington, Del., Scholarly Resources. Annual.

INTERNATIONAL INDEX
See SOCIAL SCIENCES AND HUMANITIES INDEX

INTERNATIONAL INDEX TO PERIODICALS
See SOCIAL SCIENCES AND HUMANITIES INDEX

2465
International Institute for Peace and Conflict Research. SIPRI YEARBOOK OF WORLD ARMAMENTS AND DISARMAMENTS. 1968/69–71?. New York, Humanities Press.
Vol. for 1968/69 issued under a variant name of the Institute: Stockholm International Peace Research Institute.
Continued by: *World Armaments and Disarmaments. SIPRI Yearbook.*

2466
International Institute for Population Studies. ANNUAL REPORT. 13– , 1970/71– . Bombay.
Continues: Demographic Training and Research Centre (former name of the International Institute for Population Studies). *Annual Report.*

2467
International Institute for Social History. BULLETIN. 1937–1955. Amsterdam. Three no. a year.
In Dutch, English, French, or German. Other title: *Bulletin of the International Institute of Social History.*
Continued by: *International Review of Social History.*

2468
International Institute for Social History. SOCIAAL HISTORISCHE STUDIEN. PUBLICATIONS ON SOCIAL HISTORY. 1– , 1959– . Assen, Van Gorcum. Irreg.
Monograph series.

2469
International Institute for Strategic Studies. MILITARY BALANCE. 1961/62– . London. Annual.
Earlier name of this institute: Institute for Strategic Studies. Title varies: 1961/62–1962/63, *The Communist Bloc and the Western Alliances; The Military Balance.*

2470
International Institute of Differing Civilizations. ANNUAIRE DE DOCUMENTATION COLONIALE COMPARÉE. YEARBOOK OF COMPARED COLONIAL DOCUMENTATION. 1928– . Bruxelles.

2471
International Institute of Differing Civilizations. COMPTE RENDU. REPORT. 1894– . Bruxelles.
In English or French. Earlier names of the Institute were: 1858–1939, Institut Colonial International; 1949–, International Institute of Political and Social Sciences concerning Countries of Different Civilizations. Vols. for 1894–1928 in French; 1929–58 in English or French. Vols. 1953–59 have also distinctive titles. Vols. 1895–1939 as *Bibliothèque Coloniale Internationale.*

International Institute of Political and Social Sciences concerning Countries of Differing Civilizations
See International Institute of Differing Civilizations

2472
INTERNATIONAL INTERACTIONS. v.1– , 1974– . New York, Gordon and Breach. Quarterly.
Subtitle reads: "A transnational multidisciplinary journal".

2473
INTERNATIONAL JOURNAL. v.1– , Jan. 1946– . Toronto. Quarterly.
Issued by: Canadian Institute of International Relations. Some numbers are thematic.
Indexed: ABC POL SCI; Bull. Anal. Pol. Ec. Soc.; Curr. Cont. Soc. Beh. Sc.; His. Abst.; Int. Bibl. Eco.; Int. Bibl. Pol. Sc.; Int. Bibl. Soc.; PAIS; Peace Res. Abst. J.; Soc. Abst.; SSCI.

2474
THE INTERNATIONAL JOURNAL FOR BIOSOCIAL RESEARCH. v.3, no.2– , 1981– . Tacoma, Wash., Biosocial Publications. Quarterly.
Other title: *International Journal of Biosocial Research.*
Continues: *Journal of Behavioral Ecology. Biosocial.*
Indexed: LLBA; Psych. Abst.; Soc. Abst.

2475
INTERNATIONAL JOURNAL OF AFRICAN HISTORICAL STUDIES. 5– , 1972– . New York, Africana Pub. Co. Quarterly.
Continues: *African Historical Studies.*
Indexed: Bull. Sig. Soc. Eth.

INTERNATIONAL JOURNAL OF AFRICAN STUDIES
See REVISTA INTERNACIONAL DE ESTUDOS AFRICANOS (Lisboa)

2476
INTERNATIONAL JOURNAL OF AGRARIAN AFFAIRS. Oct. 1939–1976. London, Oxford University Press.
Issued by: International Association of Agricultural Economics.

2477
INTERNATIONAL JOURNAL OF AGRICULTURAL ECONOMICS. 1– , 1928– . Aberdeen. Three no. a year.
Issued by: School of Agriculture, Aberdeen, Agricultural Economics Division, Agricultural Economics Society. Summaries in English, French and German. Title varies: 1928–54, *Journal of Proceedings of the Agricultural Society.*

2478
INTERNATIONAL JOURNAL OF ASIAN STUDIES. IJAS. 1– , 1981– . Paris, New Delhi, Concept Pub. House. Annual.
Published under the auspices of Unesco.

2479
INTERNATIONAL JOURNAL OF BEHAVIORAL DEVELOPMENT. IJBD. v.1– , Jan. 1978– . Amsterdam, North-Holland Pub. Co. Quarterly.
Issued by: International Society for the Study of Behavioral Development (ISSBD)
Indexed: Psych. Abst.

2480
INTERNATIONAL JOURNAL OF BEHAVIORAL SOCIAL WORK AND ABSTRACTS. v.1– , 1981– . Oxford, Pergamon Press. Three no. a year.

INTERNATIONAL JOURNAL OF BIOSOCIAL RESEARCH
See THE INTERNATIONAL JOURNAL FOR BIOSOCIAL RESEARCH

2481
INTERNATIONAL JOURNAL OF COMPARATIVE SOCIOLOGY. v.1– , 1960– . Dharwar, later Leiden, E.J. Brill. Quarterly.
Issued by: Department of Social Anthropology, Karnatak University, –v.5, no.2; Department of Sociology, York University (Canada).
Indexed: ABC POL SCI; Bull. Anal. Pol. Ec. Soc.; Bull. Sig. Soc. Eth.; Abst. Anth.; Int. Bibl. Pol. Sc.; Int. Bibl. Soc.; Int. Bibl. Soc. Cul. Anth.; Int. Pol. Sc. Abst.; Soc. Sc. Hum. Ind.; Soc. Abst.; SSCI; Urb. Aff. Abst.

2482
INTERNATIONAL JOURNAL OF CONTEMPORARY SOCIOLOGY. v.1– , Oct. 1963– . Ghaziabad, J.G. Mohan at Intercontinental Press (first seven volumes). Quarterly (in semi-annual combinations).
Edited by: Department of Sociology and Anthropology, Auburn University, Auburn, Ala. Title varies: v.1–7, 1963–70, *Indian Sociological Bulletin.* Issues for 1983 are the last examined.
Indexed: Curr. Cont. Soc. Beh. Sc.; Int. Bibl. Soc.; Int. Pol. Sc. Abst.; Soc. Abst.; SSCI.

2483
INTERNATIONAL JOURNAL OF CRIMINOLOGY AND PENOLOGY. v.1–6, Feb. 1973–Nov. 1978. London, New York, Academic Press. Quarterly.
Continued by: *International Journal of the Sociology of Law.*
Indexed: Psych. Abst.

2484
INTERNATIONAL JOURNAL OF CRITICAL SOCIOLOGY. 1– , Sept. 1974– . New Brunswick, N.J., Transaction Periodicals Consortium. Semi-annual.
Issued by: Jaipur Institute of Sociology.

2485
INTERNATIONAL JOURNAL OF CULTURAL SOCIOLOGY. 1973– . New Brunswick, N.J., Transaction Periodicals Consortium. Semi-annual.

INTERNATIONAL JOURNAL OF ECONOMIC AND SOCIAL HISTORY
See CAHIERS INTERNATIONAUX D'HISTOIRE ÉCONOMIQUE ET SOCIALE

2486
THE INTERNATIONAL JOURNAL OF ENVIRONMENTAL STUDIES. v.1– , Oct. 1970– . London, Gordon and Breach. Quarterly.
Organ of: The College of Technology and Design, Blackburn.
Indexed: Bull. Sig. Soc. Eth.; PAIS; Wom. Stu. Abst.

INTERNATIONAL JOURNAL OF ETHICS; DEVOTED TO THE ADVANCEMENT OF ETHICAL KNOWLEDGE AND PRACTICE
See ETHICS

2487
INTERNATIONAL JOURNAL OF GENERAL SYSTEMS. 1– , 1974– . London, Gordon and Breach. Quarterly.

2488
INTERNATIONAL JOURNAL OF GROUP TENSIONS. v.1– , Jan./Mar. 1971– . Washington, D.C. Quarterly.
Issued by: International Organization for the Study of Group Tensions.
Indexed: Bull. Anal. Pol. Ec. Soc.; Int. Bibl. Soc. Cul. Anth.; Int. Pol. Sc. Abst.; PAIS; Psych. Abst.

2489
INTERNATIONAL JOURNAL OF INTERCULTURAL RELATIONS. v.1– , spring 1977– . New York, Pergamon Press. Quarterly.
Official publication of the Society for Intercultural Education, Training and Research.
Indexed: Psych. Abst.

2490
INTERNATIONAL JOURNAL OF MIDDLE EAST STUDIES. v.1– , Jan. 1970– . London, Cambridge University Press. Quarterly.
Issued by: Near Eastern Center, University of California at Los Angeles.
Indexed: Abst. Anth.; ABC POL SCI; Bull. Anal. Pol. Ec. Soc.; Bull. Anal. Pol. Ec. Soc.; Bull. Sig. Soc. Eth.; His. Abst.; Int. Bibl. Eco.; Int. Bibl. Pol. Sc.; Int. Bibl. Soc.; Int. Bibl. Soc. Cul. Anth.; Int. Lab. Doc.; Int. Pol. Sc. Abst.; PAIS; SSCI.

2491
INTERNATIONAL JOURNAL OF NAUTICAL ARCHAEOLOGY AND UNDERWATER EXPLORATION. v.1– , 1972– . London, Seminar Press. Annual.
Issued by: Institute of Nautical Archaeology, Council for Nautical Archaeology.

2492
INTERNATIONAL JOURNAL OF ORAL HISTORY. v.1– , Feb. 1980– . Westport, Conn., Meckler Pub. Three no. a year.
Indexed: His. Abst.

2493
INTERNATIONAL JOURNAL OF POLICY ANALYSIS AND INFORMATION SYSTEMS. v.4– , Mar. 1980– . New York, Plenum Press. Quarterly.
Continues: *Policy Analysis and Information Systems.*

2494
INTERNATIONAL JOURNAL OF POLITICAL EDUCATION. v.1–6, Sept. 1977–Mar. 1984. Amsterdam, Elsevier Scientific Pub. Co. Quarterly.
Indexed: ABC POL SCI; Int. Bibl. Pol. Sc.; Int. Pol. Sc. Abst.

2495
INTERNATIONAL JOURNAL OF POLITICS. v.1– , spring 1971– . White Plains, later Armonk, N.Y., M.E. Sharpe. Quarterly.
Translations.
Indexed: Bull. Anal. Pol. Ec. Soc.; Int. Bibl. Pol. Sc.; Int. Pol. Sc. Abst.

2496
INTERNATIONAL JOURNAL OF PSYCHOLOGY. JOURNAL INTERNATIONAL DE PSYCHOLOGIE. v.1– , 1966– . Paris, Dunod. Quarterly, 1966–82; bimonthly.
Issued by: International Union of Psychological Science. In English or French.
Indexed: Int. Bibl. Soc. Cul. Anth.; Psych. Abst.

2497
INTERNATIONAL JOURNAL OF PUBLIC ADMINISTRATION. v.1– , 1979– . New York, M. Dekker. Quarterly.
Indexed: Curr. Cont. Soc. Beh. Sc.; Int. Bibl. Eco.; Int. Bibl. Pol. Sc.; Int. Pol. Sc. Abst.; Sage Pub. Adm. Abst.; Sage Urb. Stu. Abst.; Soc. Work. Res. Abst.; SSCI.

2498
INTERNATIONAL JOURNAL OF SMALL GROUP RESEARCH. v.1– , 1985– . Tucson, Ariz. Semi-annual.
Other title: IJSGR.

2499
INTERNATIONAL JOURNAL OF SOCIAL ECONOMICS. v.1– , 1974– . Bradford, M.C.B. Social Economics. Three no. a year.
Issued by: International Institute of Social Economics. Spine title: *Social Economics.*
Indexed: Bull. Anal. Pol. Ec. Soc.; Int. Bibl. Eco.; PAIS.

2500
INTERNATIONAL JOURNAL OF SOCIAL PSYCHIATRY. v.1– , July 1955– . London, The Avenue Pub. Co. Quarterly, 1955–74; three no. a year.
Issued by: Institute of Social Psychiatry.
Indexed: Abst. Soc. Work; Bull. Sig. Soc. Eth.; Int. Bibl. Soc.; Peace Res. Abst. J.; Psych. Abst.; Soc. Abst.; Soc. Work. Res. Abst.; Wom. Stu. Abst.

2501
INTERNATIONAL JOURNAL OF SOCIOLOGY. v.1– , 1971– . White Plains, later Armonk, N.Y., M.E. Sharpe. Quarterly.
Supersedes: *Eastern European Studies in Sociology and Anthropology.*
Indexed: Bull. Sig. Soc. Eth.; Int. Bibl. Soc.; Int. Pol. Sc. Abst.; PAIS; Soc. Abst.

2502
THE INTERNATIONAL JOURNAL OF SOCIOLOGY AND SOCIAL POLICY. v.1– , 1981– . Hull, Barmarick Publications. Three no. a year.
Indexed: Int. Bibl. Soc. Cul. Anth.

2503
INTERNATIONAL JOURNAL OF SOCIOLOGY OF THE FAMILY. v.1– , 1971– . Lucknow, later New Delhi, Vikas Publishing House. Semi-annual.
Edited by: Department of Sociology, Northern Illinois University. Subtitle reads: "Journal of cross-national, cross-cultural and interdisciplinary approach".
Indexed: Curr. Cont. Soc. Beh. Sc.; Pop. Ind.; Soc. Abst.; SSCI.

INTERNATIONAL JOURNAL OF SOCIOMETRY AND SOCIATRY
See HANDBOOK OF INTERNATIONAL SOCIOMETRY

2504
INTERNATIONAL JOURNAL OF SPORT SOCIOLOGY. v.1– , 1970– . Rome. Semi-annual, 1970–75; three no. a year, 1976–; quarterly.
In English, French, or Italian; summaries in English, French, German, Italian, or Spanish.

2505
INTERNATIONAL JOURNAL OF THE SOCIOLOGY OF LANGUAGE. no.1– , 1974– . The Hague, New York, Mouton. Three no. a year, 1974–76; quarterly.
In English or German. Issued also as individual numbers of *Linguistics.*
Indexed: Int. Bibl. Pol. Sc.; Int. Bibl. Soc. Cul. Anth.; Int. Pol. Sc. Abst.; Psych. Abst.

2506
INTERNATIONAL JOURNAL OF TURKISH STUDIES. v.1– , 1979/80– . Madison, Wis. Two no. a year.
Issued by: University of Wisconsin.

2507
INTERNATIONAL JOURNAL OF URBAN AND REGIONAL RESEARCH. v.1– , Mar. 1977– . London, E. Arnold. Three no. a year, 1977–80; quarterly.
Other title: *Revue Internationale de Recherche Urbaine et Regionale.*
Indexed: Int. Bibl. Eco.; PAIS; Urb. Stu. Abst.

2508
INTERNATIONAL JOURNAL OF WOMEN'S STUDIES. v.1– , Jan./Feb. 1978– . Montreal, Eden Press Woman's Publications. Bimonthly; five no. a year.
Indexed: Psych. Abst.

2509
INTERNATIONAL LABOUR DOCUMENTATION. v.1– , 1948?– . Geneva. Irreg., 1948?–Dec. 20, 1956; weekly (irreg.), 1957–70; biweekly, 1971–76; monthly.
Issued by: Library and Documentation Centre, International Labour Office. Includes periodical articles and monographs. Information is arranged in broad subject groups. Indexes in English, French and Spanish. The issues for 1965–76 were reprinted as "cumulative edition" by G.K. Hall, Boston, in 15 volumes. Other title: *Documentation Internationale du Travail.*

2510
International Labour Office. OFFICIAL BULLETIN. v.1–57, Apr. 1919–1974. Geneva.
Includes some supplements.
Continued by: *Official Bulletin. Series* A, B. C. (v.8–, 1975–)

2511
International Labour Office. STUDIES AND REPORTS. 1920–1943; n. ser. 1946– . Geneva.
Consists of the following series: A (Industrial Relations), B (Economic Conditions), C, D, F, G, H, I, K, M, N, O and P, issued by various agencies of ILO.

2512
INTERNATIONAL LABOUR REVIEW. v.1– , Jan. 1921– . Geneva. Monthly.
Organ of: International Labour Office. Includes *Statistical Supplement* (1952–) replaced by *Bulletin of Labour Statistics* in 1961. Published also in French edition: *Revue Internationale du Travail*, and Spanish: *Revista Internacional del Trabajo.*

Indexes: Vols. 1–20, 1921–29, 1v.; v.31–75, 1935–57 (published as International Labour Office. Library. *Bibliographical Contributions*, no.17, 1v.)
Indexed: Eco. Abst.; Bull. Sig. Soc. Eth.; Curr. Cont. Soc. Beh. Sc.; Ind. For. Leg. Per.; Pop. Ind.; Int. Lab. Doc.; Soc. Sc. Hum. Ind.; Wom. Stu. Abst.

INTERNATIONAL LAW AND DIPLOMACY
See INTERNATIONALES RECHT UND DIPLOMATIE

2513
INTERNATIONAL LAW AND RELATIONS. v.1–6, no.13, June 1930–June 1937. Washington, D.C.
Issued by: Graduate School, American University. Title varies: v.1–4, no.16/17, 1930–3?, *Cumulative Digest of International Law and Relations*. Vols. 1–3 consist of 50 nos. each; v.4 of 24 numbers.

2514
INTERNATIONAL LAW QUARTERLY. v.1–4, spring 1947–Oct. 1951. London, Stevens. Quarterly.
Suspended in 1949.
Merged with: *Journal of Comparative Legislation and International Law* to form: *Comparative and International Law Quarterly*.

2515
INTERNATIONAL LAW REPORTS. 1919/22– . London, Butterworth. Irreg.
Issued by: London School of Economics and Political Science, University of London. Vols. 1919/22–1931/32 issued as *Contributions to International Law and Diplomacy*. Title varies: 1919/22–1931/32, *Annual Digest of Public International Law Cases*; 1933/34, 1949, *Annual Digest and Reports of Public International Law Cases*.
Indexes: (tables and index) Vols. 1–35, 1919–67, 1v.

INTERNATIONAL LAW REVIEW
See REVUE DE DROIT INTERNATIONAL DE SCIENCES DIPLOMATIQUES ET POLITIQUES

2516
INTERNATIONAL MARXIST REVIEW. v.1– , June 1971– . London. Quarterly.
Supersedes: *Marxist Review*.

2517
INTERNATIONAL MIGRATION. MIGRATIONS INTERNATIONALES. MIGRACIONES INTERNACIONALES. v.1– , 1963– . The Hague. Quarterly.
Issued by: Intergovernmental Committee for European Migration (ICEM), and the Research Group for European Migration Problems. Summaries in French and Spanish. Title varies: 1963–70, *Migrations Internationales*.
Supersedes: the intergovernmental committee's *Migration*, and the research group's *Bulletin*.
Indexed: Int. Bibl. Soc.; Pop. Ind.

2518
INTERNATIONAL MIGRATION REVIEW. v.1– , fall 1969– . Staten Island, N.Y. Quarterly.
Issued by: Center for Migration Studies in Staten Island, N.Y., in cooperation with the Centro Studi Emigrazione in Rome. Other title: *IMR. International Migration Review*. Called n. ser. in continuation of *International Migration Digest*. Summaries in French, German and Spanish.
Supersedes: *International Migration Digest*.
Indexed: Abst. Anth.; Bull. Anal. Pol. Ec. Soc.; Bull. Sig. Soc. Eth.; His. Abst.; Int. Bibl. Soc.; LLBA; PHRA; Int. Bibl. Soc. Cul. Anth.; PAIS; Pop. Ind.; Sage Urb. Abst.; Soc. Abst.; Urb. Aff. Abst.

2519
International Monetary Fund. ANNUAL REPORT ON EXCHANGE ARRANGEMENTS AND EXCHANGE RESTRICTIONS. 1979– . Washington, D.C. Annual.
Continues: the fund's *Annual Report on Exchange Restrictions*.

2520
International Monetary Fund. BALANCE OF PAYMENTS YEARBOOK. [v.]1– , 1946/47– . Washington, D.C. Annual, 1946/47; monthly with Dec. issue cumulated.

2521
International Monetary Fund. GOVERNMENT STATISTICS YEARBOOK. 1977– . Washington, D.C. Annual.

2522
International Monetary Fund. IMF SURVEY. v.1– , Aug. 14, 1972– . Washington, D.C. Semimonthly (monthly in Dec.)
Published also in French: *Bulletin du FMI*, and Spanish: *Boletín del FMI*.

2523
International Monetary Fund. SELECTED DECISIONS OF THE INTERNATIONAL MONETARY FUND; SELECTED DOCUMENTS. 6th– , 1972– . Washington, D.C. Irreg.
Continues: the fund's *Selective Decisions of the Executive Directors and Selected Documents*.

2524
International Monetary Fund. STAFF PAPERS. 1– , Feb. 1950– . Washington, D.C. Three no. a year, 1950–77; four no. a year.

Summaries in English, French and Spanish.
Indexes: Vols. 1–16, 1950–69, 1v.
Indexed: His. Abst.; Int. Lab. Doc.; J. Eco. Lit.; PAIS.

2525
International Monetary Fund. SUMMARY PROCEEDINGS OF THE ANNUAL MEETING OF THE BOARD OF GOVERNORS. 1st– , 1946– . Washington, D.C.
Title varies: 1946, *Annual Meeting of the Board of Directors. Report of the Executive Directors and Summary Proceedings.*

2526
INTERNATIONAL MONETARY MARKET YEAR BOOK. 1972/73–. Chicago, Ill.
Issued by: Statistical Department, Chicago Mercantile Exchange.

2527
INTERNATIONAL ORGANIZATION. v.1– , Feb. 1947– . Boston, Mass., M.I.T. Press. Quarterly.
Edited at the Stanford University.
Indexed: ABC POL SCI; Bull. Anal. Pol. Ec. Soc.; Curr. Cont. Soc. Beh. Sc.; Eco. Abst.; His. Abst.; Int. Bibl. Pol. Sc.; Int. Bibl. Soc.; Int. Lab. Doc.; Int. Pol. Sc. Abst.; PAIS; Peace Res. Abst. J.; Soc. Abst.; Soc. Sc. Hum. Ind.

2528
INTERNATIONAL PERSPECTIVES. Jan./Feb. 1972– . Ottawa, External Affairs Canada. Bimonthly.
Published also in French: *External Affaires.* Absorbed: *International Canada.*
Indexed: ABC POL SCI; His. Abst.; PAIS; Peace Res. Abst. J.; Soc. Abst.; Soc. Sc. Hum. Ind.

2529
INTERNATIONAL POLITICAL ECONOMY YEARBOOK. v.1– , 1985– . Boulder, Colo., Westview Press. Annual.
Published under the sponsorship of the International Political Economy Section of the International Studies Association at the Brigham Young University.

2530
INTERNATIONAL POLITICAL SCIENCE ABSTRACTS. DOCUMENTATION POLITIQUE INTERNATIONALE. 1951– . Paris. Bimonthly.
Issued by: International Political Science Association. In English and French.

2531
International Political Science Association. WORLD CONGRESS. 1st– , 1951– . [Place of publication varies]. Triennial.
Continues: International Political Science Association. World Conference. *Proceedings.*

2532
INTERNATIONAL POLITICAL SCIENCE REVIEW. 1– , 1980– . Beverly Hills, Calif., Sage Publications. Quarterly.
Issued by: International Political Science Association.
Indexed: Int. Bibl. Eco.; Int. Bibl. Pol. Sc.; Int. Pol. Sc. Abst.

2533
INTERNATIONAL PROBLEMS. v.[1]– , 1960– . Beograd. Annual.
Issued by: International Institute of Politics and Economics. Contents consists of translations from: *Medjunarodni Problemi.*
Indexed: Bull. Anal. Pol. Ec. Soc.; Int. Bibl. Soc. Cul. Anth.; Int. Pol. Sc. Abst.

INTERNATIONAL PROBLEMS
See BE'AYOT BEMLUMIYOT

2534
INTERNATIONAL REGIONAL SCIENCE REVIEW. v.1– , spring 1975– . Philadelphia, Pa. Quarterly.
Issued by: Regional Science Association.
Indexed: Int. Bibl. Soc. Cul. Anth.; Pop. Ind.; Sage. Urb. Stu. Abst.

2535
INTERNATIONAL RELATIONS. v.1– , Apr. 1954– . London. Semi-annual.
Issued by: David Davies Memorial Institute of International Studies.
Indexed: ABC POL SCI; Bull. Anal. Pol. Ec. Soc.; Int. Bibl. Eco.; Int. Bibl. Pol. Sc.; Ind. Per. Art. Law; Int. Bibl. Soc.; Int. Pol. Sc. Abst.; Soc. Abst.

2536
INTERNATIONAL RELATIONS. v.1– , 1967– . Prague. Annual.
Issued by: Institute of International Politics and Economics.
Indexed: Bull. Anal. Pol. Ec. Soc.; Int. Bibl. Pol. Sc.; Int. Bibl. Soc. Cul. Anth.; Int. Pol. Sc. Abst.

2537
INTERNATIONAL RELATIONS. v.1– , Jan. 1974– . London, Gordon and Breach. Quarterly.
Indexed: Int. Bibl. Eco.; Int. Bibl. Pol. Sc.

INTERNATIONAL RELATIONS
See REVUE IRANIENNE DES RELATIONS INTERNATIONALES

2538
INTERNATIONAL REVIEW. v.1–14, no.4/5, 1874–May/June 1883. New York.

2539
INTERNATIONAL REVIEW. v.1–5(no.1–63), Oct. 1913–Dec. 1918; n. ser. v.1–2(no.64–75), 1919. London, War & Peace Ltd. Monthly.
Title varies: 1913–Nov. 1918, *War & Peace*. Merged into: *Contemporary Review*.

2540
INTERNATIONAL REVIEW. 1– , spring 1974– . London, Hulton Publications.
Supersedes: *European Review*.

2541
INTERNATIONAL REVIEW FOR SOCIAL HISTORY. v.1–4, 1936–1939. Leiden, E.J. Brill. Irreg.
Issued by: International Institute for Social History, Amsterdam. In English, French, or German; summaries in two other languages.

2542
INTERNATIONAL REVIEW FOR SOCIAL HISTORY. v.1– , 1956– . Assen, Van Gorcum. Three no. a year.

2543
INTERNATIONAL REVIEW FOR THE SOCIOLOGY OF SPORT. v.19– , 1984– . München, R. Oldenbourg Verlag. Quarterly.
Issued by: International Committee for Sociology of Sport (ICSS). In Chinese, English, French, or German; summaries in two other languages.
Continues: *International Review of Sport Sociology*.

2544
INTERNATIONAL REVIEW OF ADMINISTRATIVE SCIENCES. v.1– , 1928– . Brussels. Quarterly.
Issues for 1947–49 called "nouvelle série" have no volume numbering but constitute v.13–15. Publication suspended, 1940–47. Other title: *Revista Internacional de Ciencias Administrativas*. Published also in French and Spanish editions. Title varies: 1928–56, *Revue Internationale des Sciences Administratives*. Absorbed: *Progress in Public Administration*.
Indexes: 1938–57 (includes index to *Progress in Public Administration*).
Indexed: ABC POL SCI; Eco. Abst.; Ind. Per. Art. Law; Ind. For. Leg. Per.; Int. Bibl. Pol. Sc.; Int. Lab. Doc.; Int. Pol. Sc. Abst.; PAIS; PAISFL.

INTERNATIONAL REVIEW OF COMMUNITY DEVELOPMENT
See COMMUNITY DEVELOPMENT

2545
INTERNATIONAL REVIEW OF CRIMINAL POLICY. REVUE INTERNATIONALE DE POLITIQUE CRIMINELLE. REVISTA INTERNACIONAL DE POLÍTICA CRIMINAL. no.1– , Jan. 1952– . New York, United Nations. Semi-annual.
Issued by: 1952–55, Department of Social Affairs; 1955–, Department of Economic and Social Affairs, and its successor. In English, 1952–July 1953; in English, French and Spanish (ST/SOA/Ser. M.)
Indexed: Ind. For. Leg. Per.; Int. Bibl. Soc.; PAIS.

2546
INTERNATIONAL REVIEW OF EDUCATION. INTERNATIONALE ZEITSCHRIFT FÜR ERZIEHUNGSWISSENSCHAFT. REVUE INTERNATIONALE DE PEDAGOGIE. v.1– , 1955– . The Hague, later 's-Gravenhage, Dordrecht. Quarterly.
Issued by: Unesco Institute for Education, Hamburg. In English, French, or German. Some nos. are thematic.
Indexed: Int. Lab. Doc.; LLBA.

INTERNATIONAL REVIEW OF ETHNOLOGY AND LINGUISTICS
See ATHROPOS (Fribourg)

2547
INTERNATIONAL REVIEW OF HISTORY AND POLITICAL SCIENCE. v.1– , June 1964– . Meerut, Review Publications. Semi-annual, 1964; quarterly.
Indexed: Int. Bibl. Eco.; Int. Bibl. Pol. Sc.; Int. Bibl. Soc.; Int. Pol. Sc. Abst.; Peace Res. Abst. J.; Soc. Abst.; SSCI; Soc. Sc. Hum. Ind.; Wom. Stu. Abst.

2548
INTERNATIONAL REVIEW OF MODERN SOCIOLOGY. 1– , Mar. 1971– . Lucknow, later New Delhi, Vikas Publishing House. Semi-annual.
Subtitle reads: "Journal of cross-national, cross-cultural and interdisciplinary research". Title varies: v.1, 1971–Mar. 1972, *International Review of Sociology*.
Indexed: Curr. Cont. Soc. Beh. Sc.; LLBA; Soc. Abst.; SSCI.

2549
INTERNATIONAL REVIEW OF SOCIAL HISTORY. v.1– , 1956– . Assen, van Gorcum. Three no. a year.
Organ of: International Institute for Social History (Internationaal Instituut voor Sociale Geschiedenis).
Supersedes: International Institute for Social History. *Bulletin*.
Indexed: Bull. Sig. Soc. Eth.; His. Abst.; Int. Bibl. Soc.; Int. Lab. Doc.; Int. Pol. Sc. Abst.; Peace Res. Abst. J.; Soc. Abst.; Soc. Sc. Hum. Ind.; Urb. Aff. Abst.

INTERNATIONAL REVIEW OF SOCIOLOGY
See INTERNATIONAL REVIEW OF MODERN SOCIOLOGY

INTERNATIONAL REVIEW OF SOCIOLOGY
See REVUE INTERNATIONALE DE SOCIOLOGIE

2550
INTERNATIONAL REVIEW OF SPORT SOCIOLOGY. v.1–18, 1966–1983. Warszawa, Państwowe Wydawnictwo Naukowe. Annual, 1966–72; quarterly.
Issued by: Committee for Sociology of Sports, International Council of Sport and Physical Education (Unesco), and International Sociological Education. Summaries in French, German and Russian.
Continued by: *International Review of the Sociology of Sport.*

2551
INTERNATIONAL REVIEW OF THE AESTHETICS AND SOCIOLOGY OF MUSIC. 1970– . Zagreb. Semi-annual.
Issued by: Muzikološki Zavod, Akademija u Zagrebu. In English, French, or German.

INTERNATIONAL REVIEW OF THE HISTORY OF BANKING
See REVUE INTERNATIONALE D'HISTOIRE DE LA BANQUE

2552
INTERNATIONAL SECURITY. v.1– , summer 1976– . Cambridge, Mass., M.I.T. Press. Quarterly.
Vols. for summer 1976–spring 1978 sponsored by the Program for Science and International Affairs, Harvard University; summer 1978–, by the Center for Science and International Affairs, Harvard University.
Indexed: ABC POL SCI; Bull. Anal. Pol. Ec. Soc.; Int. Bibl. Pol. Sc.; Int. Bibl. Soc. Cul. Anth.; Int. Pol. Sc. Abst.; PAIS; SSCI.

2553
INTERNATIONAL SECURITY REVIEW. v.3, no.4– , winter 1983/84– . Boston, Va. Quarterly.
Issued by: Center for International Security Studies, American Security Council Foundation.
Continues: *Journal of International Relations.*
Indexed: PAIS.

2554
INTERNATIONAL SECURITY YEARBOOK. 1983/84– . London, Macmillan, New York, St. Martin's Press. Annual.
Issued by: Center for Strategic and International Studies, Georgetown University.

2555
INTERNATIONAL SMALL BUSINESS JOURNAL. v.2, no.2– , winter 1984– . Wilmslow, Wrodewek Publications. Quarterly.
Summaries in English, French, German and Spanish.
Continues: *European Small Business Journal.*

2556
INTERNATIONAL SOCIAL DEVELOPMENT REVIEW. no.1– , 1968– . New York. Irreg.
Issued by: Social Development Division, Department of Economic and Social Affairs, United Nations. Each no. has also a distinctive title.
Supersedes: the department's *Housing, Building and Planning*, and *Population Bulletin*, and *International Social Service Review.* Subseries of: United Nations. [Document] ST/SOA/ser X).

INTERNATIONAL SOCIAL SCIENCE BULLETIN
See INTERNATIONAL SOCIAL SCIENCE JOURNAL

2557
INTERNATIONAL SOCIAL SCIENCE JOURNAL. v.1– , 1949– . Paris, Unesco. Quarterly.
Issues for 1949 also have title in French. Includes two supplements annually: (1) a list of new periodicals that appeared since the latest edition of the *World List of Social Science Periodicals. List Mondiale des Périodiques dans les Sciences Sociales*, and (2) a list of new institutions established since the latest edition of the *World Index of Social Science Institutions. Répertoire Mondiale des Institutions des Sciences Sociales.* Published also in French: *Revue Internationale des Sciences Sociales*, and Spanish: *Revista Internacional de Ciencias Sociales*, whose no. 1 is a translation of no.3 of 1976. Some articles are translated into Arabic and published under the title: *al-Majallah al-Duwalīyah lil-'ulūm al-ījtimā'īyah.* Title varies: 1949–58, *International Social Science Bulletin.*
Indexed: ABC POL SCI; APAIS; Eco. Abst.; Abst. Anth.; Bull. Sig. Soc. Eth.; Curr. Cont. Soc. Beh. Sc.; Ind. Per. Art. Law; Int. Bibl. Soc. Cul. Anth.; J. Eco. Lit.; Int. Pol. Sc. Abst.; PAIS; Peace Res. Abst. J.; Pop. Ind.; Int. Lab. Doc.; Sage Fam. Stu. Abst.; Sage Urb. Stu. Abst.; Soc. Sc. Hum. Ind.; Soc. Work Res. Abst.; SSCI; Urb. Aff. Abst.

2558
INTERNATIONAL SOCIAL SCIENCE REVIEW. v.57– , winter 1982– . Winfield, Kans. Quarterly.
Organ of: Pi Gamma Mu, International Honor Society.
Continues: *Social Science.*
Indexed: Abst. Soc. Work; Int. Bibl. Soc. Cul. Anth.; Int. Lab. Doc.; Int. Pol. Sc. Abst.; PAIS.

2559
INTERNATIONAL SOCIAL SECURITY REVIEW. v.20– , 1967– . Geneva. Quarterly.
Issued by: General Secretariat of the International Social Security Association.
Continues: International Social Security Association. *Bulletin.*
Indexed: PAIS.

2560
INTERNATIONAL SOCIAL SERVICE REVIEW. no.1–9, Jan. 1956–1963. New York, United Nations. Two no. a year.
Issued by: Department of Economic and Social Affairs, United Nations.
Superseded by: *International Social Development Review* (United Nations. Document. ST/SOA/ser.)

2561
INTERNATIONAL SOCIAL WORK. 1958– . Bombay. Four no. a year.
Issued by: International Conference of Social Work, and International Association of Schools of Social Work.
Indexed: Abst. Soc. Work.; Int. Bibl. Soc.; Int. Lab. Doc.; Wom. Stu. Abst.

INTERNATIONAL SOCIALIST JOURNAL
See REVUE INTERNATIONALE DU SOCIALISME

2562
INTERNATIONAL SOCIALIST REVIEW. v.1–18, no.8, July 1900–Feb. 1918. Chicago, Ill., C.H. Kerr. Monthly.

2563
INTERNATIONAL SOCIALIST REVIEW. v.1– , Mar. 1940– . New York, Fourth International Publishing Association. Frequency varies.
Issued by: National Committee, Socialist Workers Party, May–Nov. 1940. Title varies: May 1940–spring 1956, *Fourth International.*
Supersedes: *The New International.*
Indexed: Int. Bibl. Soc. Cul. Anth.; PAIS; Wom. Stu. Abst.

2564
INTERNATIONAL STATISTICAL REVIEW. REVUE INTERNATIONALE DE STATISTIQUE. v.40– , Apr. 1972– . Edinburgh, Longman. Three no. a year.
Issued by: International Statistical Institute. In English or French; summaries in the same language.
Continues: Institut Internationale de Statistique. *Revue.*
Indexed: Pop. Ind.

INTERNATIONAL STATISTICAL YEAR-BOOK
See League of Nations. STATISTICAL YEAR-BOOK OF THE LEAGUE OF NATIONS

INTERNATIONAL STATISTICS OF LARGE TOWNS
See ANNUAIRE DE STATISTIQUE INTERNATIONALE DES GRANDES VILLES

2565
INTERNATIONAL STUDIES. v.1– , July 1959– . Bombay, later New Delhi, Asia Publishing House. Quarterly.
Issued by: Indian School of International Studies, Jawaharlal Nehru University.
Indexed: ABC POL SCI; Bull. Anal. Pol. Ec. Soc.; His. Abst.; Ind. Per. Art. Law; Int. Bibl. Pol. Sc.; Int. Pol. Sc. Abst.; Peace Res. Abst. J.

2566
INTERNATIONAL STUDIES OF MANAGEMENT AND ORGANIZATION. v.1– , spring 1971– . White Plains, later Armonk, N.Y., M.E. Sharpe. Quarterly.
Translations.
Indexed: PHRA.

2567
INTERNATIONAL STUDIES QUARTERLY. v.1– , Mar. 1967– . Detroit, later Beverly Hills, Calif., Sage Publications, London, Butterworth.
Issued by: Institute for Research on International Behavior, San Francisco State College (1964–66), School of International Relations, University of Southern California (1967–68)
Continues: *Background on Foreign Politics* (1957–winter 1962), *Background* (1962–May 1964)
Indexed: ABC POL SCI; Bull. Anal. Pol. Ec. Soc.; Curr. Cont. Soc. Beh. Sc.; Ind. Per. Art. Law; His. Abst.; Int. Bibl. Eco.; Int. Bibl. Pol. Sc.; Int. Pol. Sc. Abst.; PAIS; Peace Res. Abst. J.; Sage Urb. Abst.

HET INTERNATIONAL TIJDSCHRIFT VOOR DE EUROPAMARKT
See REVUE INTERNATIONALE DU MARCHÉ COMMUN

2568
INTERNATIONAL TRADE FORUM. v.1– , Dec. 1964– . Geneva. Quarterly.
Issued by: International Trade Centre, GATT. Includes supplements. Published in English, French, and Spanish editions. UNCTAD/GATT.

2569
INTERNATIONAL TRADE STATISTICS. 1931/32–1938. Geneva, 1933–1939.
Issued by: League of Nations.

Continued by: *Yearbook of International Trade Statistics.*

2570
INTERNATIONAL TRADE STATISTICS YEARBOOK. ANNUAIRE STATISTIQUE DU COMMERCE INTERNATIONAL. 1983– . New York, United Nations. Annual.
Issued by: Statistical Office, United Nations. In English and French.
Continues: *Yearbook of International Trade Statistics.*

2571
INTERNATIONAL TRADE UNION MOVEMENT. v.1– , Jan. 1921– . Amsterdam. Bimonthly, 1921–23; quarterly, 1924–; monthly.
Issued by: International Federation of Trade Unions. Title varies: *Review of the International Federation of Trade Unions.*

2572
International Union of Local Authorities. I.U.L.A. BULLETIN. v.1–13, July 1949–1961. The Hague. Quarterly.
Supersedes: *L'Administration Locale.* Superseded by: *Local Government throughout the World.*

INTERNATIONAL YEARBOOK FOR THE HISTORY OF RELIGION
See INTERNATIONALES JAHRBUCH FÜR RELIGIONSSOZIOLOGIE

INTERNATIONAL YEARBOOK FOR THE SOCIOLOGY OF KNOWLEDGE AND RELIGION
See INTERNATIONALES JAHRBUCH FÜR WISSENS- UND RELIGIONSSOZIOLOGIE

2573
INTERNATIONAL YEARBOOK OF EDUCATION. 1– , 1933– . Geneva. Annual.
Issued by: Bureau International d'Éducation. Not published 1940–45, 1970–79. Includes section "Annual Bibliography". Other title: *Annuaire International de l'Éducation et de l'Enseignement.* Published also in French edition.

2574
THE INTERNATIONAL YEARBOOK OF FOREIGN POLICY ANALYSIS. v.1– , 1974– . London, Croom Helm; New York, Wiley. Annual.
Indexed: Bull. Anal. Pol. Ec. Soc.

2575
INTERNATIONAL YEARBOOK OF ORGANIZATION STUDIES. 1979– . London, Routledge and Kegan Paul. Annual.
Indexed: Int. Bibl. Eco.

2576
INTERNATIONALES AFRIKA FORUM. v.1– , Jan. 1965– . München, Weltforum Verlag. Ten no. a year.
Issued by: Europäisches Institut für Politische, Wirtschaftliche und Soziale Fragen. In German.
Indexed: Bull. Anal. Pol. Ec. Soc.; Eco. Abst.; Int. Bibl. Eco.; Int. Bibl. Pol. Sc.; Int. Bibl. Soc.; PAISFL; Peace Res. Abst. J.

INTERNATIONALES ARCHIV FÜR ETHNOGRAPHIE
See INTERNATIONAL ARCHIVES OF ETHNOGRAPHY

2577
INTERNATIONALES JAHRBUCH FÜR INTERDISZIPLINARE FORSCHUNG. 1– , 1974– . Berlin, New York, W. de Gruyter.
Issued by: Interdisziplinare Forschungstelle für Anthropologie und Sozialkulturelle Probleme der Wissenschaften, Universität München. In English, French, or German; summaries in these languages.

2578
INTERNATIONALES JAHRBUCH FÜR POLITIK. 1– , Apr. 1954– . München, Isar Verlag. Quarterly.
In English, French, or German.

2579
INTERNATIONALES JAHRBUCH FÜR RELIGIONSSOZIOLOGIE. v.1–8, 1965–1974. Opladen, Westdeutscher Verlag.
In German. Other title: *International Yearbook for the History of Religion.*
Continued by: *Internationales Jahrbuch für Wissen- und Religionssoziologie.*

2580
INTERNATIONALES JAHRBUCH FÜR WISSEN- UND RELIGIONSSOZIOLOGIE. INTERNATIONAL YEARBOOK FOR THE SOCIOLOGY OF KNOWLEDGE AND RELIGION. v.9– , 1975– . Opladen, Westdeutscher Verlag. Annual.
Includes subseries: *Beiträge zur Wissenssoziologie. Beiträge zur Religionssoziologie (Contributions to the Sociology of Knowledge. Contributions to the Sociology of Religion)*
Continues: *Internationales Jahrbuch für Religionssoziologie. International Yearbook for Sociology of Knowledge and Religion.*

2581
INTERNATIONALES RECHT UND DIPLOMATIE. DROIT INTERNATIONAL ET DIPLOMATIE. INTERNATIONAL LAW AND DIPLOMACY. MEZHDUNARODNOE PRAVO I DIPLOMAT͡SIIA. v.1– , 1956– . Cologne, Verlag Wissenschaft und Politik. Irreg.
Mainly in German; occasionally in English, French, or Russian.

Indexed: Abst. Anth.; His. Abst.; Ind. For. Leg. Per.; Int. Pol. Sc. Abst.

DIE INTERNAZIONALES ZEITSCHRIFT DES GEMEINSAMEN MARKETS
See REVUE INTERNATIONALE DU MARCHÉ COMMUN

2582
INTERNATIONALES ZEITSCHRIFT FÜR ERZIEHUNG. v.1–13, no.4/5, Apr. 1931–June/Aug. 1944. Berlin.
In German. Title varies: v.1–3, 1931/32–1933/34, *Internationales Zeitschrift für Erziehungswissenschaft.*

INTERNATIONALES ZEITSCHRIFT FÜR ERZIEHUNGSWISSENSCHAFT
See INTERNATIONAL REVIEW OF EDUCATION (The Hague)

INTERNATIONALES ZEITSCHRIFT FÜR KOMMUNIKATIONSFORSCHUNG
See COMMUNICATIONS

INTERNATIONALES ZEITSCHRIFT FÜR SOZIOLOGIE UND SOZIALPSYCHOLOGIE
See SOCIOLOGIA INTERNATIONALIS

2583
International Institute for Peace and Conflict Research. SIPRI YEARBOOK OF WORLD ARMAMENTS AND DISARMAMENTS. 1968/69–1971. New York, Humanities Press.
Vol. for 1968/69 issued under a variant name of the institute: Stockholm International Peace Research Institute.
Continued by: *World Armaments and Disarmaments. SIPRI Yearbook.*

INTERPARLAMENTARISCHE BULLETIN
See Inter-Parliamentary Union. BULLETIN INTERPARLEMENTAIRE

Interparlamentarische Union
See Inter-Parliamentary Union

2584
INTERPRETATION. 1– , summer 1970– . The Hague, M. Nijhoff, later Flushing, N.Y., Queen's College Press. Three no. a year.
Issued by: City University of New York. Subtitle reads: "A journal of political philosophy".
Indexed: Int. Pol. Sc. Abst.

2585
INTISARI. 1962– . Singapore. Quarterly.
Issued by: Malaysian Sociological Research Institute. Publication suspended, 1975–78.

2586
INVENTORY OF MARRIAGE AND FAMILY LITERATURE. v.1– , 1900/64– . St. Paul, Minn. (publ. in 1967), later Beverly Hills, Calif., Sage Publications. Annual beginning with v.6, 1979.
Issued by: Inventory of Marriage and Family Project, University of Minnesota. V.2 covers 1965–72; v.3, 1973/74; v.4, 1975/76; v.5, 1977/78. Title varies: v.1–2, 1900/64–1965/72, *International Bibliography of Research in the Marriage and the Family.*

2587
INVENTORY OF POPULATION PROJECTS IN DEVELOPING COUNTRIES AROUND THE WORLD. 1973/74– . New York, United Nations. Every three years.
Issued by: Fund for Population Activities, United Nations. Published every three years as v.2 of the *Population Programs and Projects.*

2588
INVESTIGACIÓN ECONÓMICA. 1– , 1940– . Mexico, D.F. Quarterly.
Issued by: Escuela Nacional de Economía, Universidad Nacional Autónoma. In Spanish.
Indexes: Vols. 1–18, 1940–58, 1v.
Indexed: Bull. Anal. Pol. Ec. Soc.; His. Abst.; Int. Bibl. Eco.; Int. Lab. Doc.

2589
IRAN. 1– , 1963– . London. Annual.
Issued by: British Institute of Persian Studies. In Arabic, English, French, or Persian.
Indexed: Int. Bibl. Soc. Cul. Anth.

IRANIAN ECONOMIC REVIEW
See MAJALLE-YI OLUM-IIQTISADI-YI IRAN

IRANIAN REVIEW OF INTERNATIONAL RELATIONS
See REVUE IRANIENNE DES RELATIONS INTERNATIONALES

2590
IRANIAN STUDIES. v.1– , winter 1968– . New Haven, later Philadelphia, Pa. Quarterly.
Issued by: Society for Iranian Studies (called –1968, Society for Iranian Cultural and Social Studies)
Indexed: Bull. Anal. Pol. Ec. Soc.; Int. Bibl. Soc. Cul. Anth.

2591
IRAQ. v.1– , Apr./Nov. 1934– . London, Oxford University Press. Semi-annual.
Issued by: British School of Archaeology in Iraq. In English; occasionally in French or German.
Indexed: Abst. Anth.; Int. Bibl. Soc. Cul. Anth.

IRIS EIREANNAH AN OIDEACHAIS
See THE IRISH JOURNAL OF EDUCATION

2592
IRISH ECONOMIC AND SOCIAL HISTORY. 1– , 1974– . Belfast. Annual.
Issued by: Economic and Social History Society of Ireland.

2593
IRISH HISTORICAL STUDIES. v.1– , Mar. 1938– . Dublin, Dublin University Press. Semi-annual.
Issued by: Irish Historical Society, and Ulster Society for Irish Historical Studies.

2594
IRISH JOURNAL OF AGRICULTURAL ECONOMICS AND RURAL SOCIOLOGY. 1– , 1967– . Dublin. Semi-annual.
Issued by: Educational Research Centre, St. Patrick's College.

2595
IRISH JOURNAL OF EDUCATION. IRIS EIREANNAH AN OIDEACHAIS. v.1– , summer 1967– . Dublin. Two no. a year.
Issued by: Educational Research Centre, St. Patrick's College.
Indexed: Psych. Abst.

2596
IRISH STUDIES IN INTERNATIONAL AFFAIRS. v.1– , 1979– . Dublin. Annual.
Issued by: Royal Irish Academy.

ISIS INTERNATIONAL
See ISIS INTERNATIONAL BULLETIN

2597
ISIS INTERNATIONAL BULLETIN. [1]–21, 1976–1981. Rome, ISIS. Quarterly.
No.20 has title: *ISIS International.*
Continued by: *Women's International Bulletin.*

2598
ISIS INTERNATIONAL WOMEN'S JOURNAL. no.1– , 1984– . Rome. Semi-annual.
Continues: *Women's International Bulletin.*

2599
DER ISLAM; ZEITSCHRIFT FÜR GESCHICHTE UND KULTUR DES ISLAMISCHEN ORIENTS. 1– , 1910– . Strasbourg. Annual, 1910–54; three no. a year, 1955–72; two no. a year.
In English, French, or German. None published Mar. 1942–Feb. 1944, Aug. 1944, Sept. 1946, and 1948.
Indexed: Int. Bibl. Soc. Cul. Anth.

2600
ISLAMIC AND COMPARATIVE LAW QUARTERLY. v.1– , 1981– . New Delhi.
Issued by: Department of Islamic and Comparative Law, Indian Institute of Islamic Studies.

2601
ISLAMIC CULTURE. v.1– , 1927– . Hyderabad. Quarterly.
Issued by: Islamic Culture Board.
Indexed: Bull. Sig. Soc. Eth.; Int. Bibl. Soc. Cul. Anth.

2602
Islamic Development Bank. ANNUAL REPORT. 1975/76– . Jeddah. Annual.

2603
ISLAMIC STUDIES. Mar. 1962– . Karachi. Quarterly.
Issued by: Central Institute of Islamic Studies, Islamic University.

2604
THE ISRAEL ANNUAL OF PUBLIC ADMINISTRATION AND PUBLIC POLICY. 15– , 1976– . Jerusalem. Quarterly.
Issued by: Israel Institute of Public Administration.
Continues: *Public Administration in Israel and Abroad.*
Indexed: Bull. Anal. Pol. Ec. Soc.

2605
THE ISRAEL ECONOMIST. 1– , 1945– . Jerusalem, Kollek & Sons. Monthly.
Title varies: 1945–48, *The Palestine Economist.*
Indexed: Int. Bibl. Soc. Cul. Anth.; PAIS.

2606
ISRAEL SOCIAL SCIENCE RESEARCH. v.1– , 1983– . Beer-Sheva. Semi-annual.
Issued by: The Hubert Humphrey Center for Social Ecology, Ben Gurion University of the Negev.

2607
ISRAEL STUDIES IN CRIMINOLOGY. v.1– , 1971– . Tel-Aviv, Gomeh Pub. House. Annual.
Issued by: Institute of Criminology and Criminal Law, Tel-Aviv University.
Indexed: Psych. Abst.

2608
ISRAEL YEARBOOK ON HUMAN RIGHTS. v.1– , 1971– . Tel-Aviv. Annual.
Published under the auspices of: Faculty of Law, Tel-Aviv University.

Indexed: ABC POL SCI; Int. Bibl. Pol. Sc.; Int. Pol. Sc. Abst.

ISSLEDOVANIIA V OBLASTI PROSVESHCHENIIA
See BADANIA OŚWIATOWE

2609
ISSUES & STUDIES. v.1– , Oct. 1964– . Taipei. Monthly.
Issued by: Institute of International Relations.
Supersedes: *Analysis of Current Chinese Problems*.
Indexed: ABC POL SCI; Bull. Anal. Pol. Ec. Soc.

2610
Istanbul Universitesi. Fakultesi Memuasi. REVUE DE LA FACULTÉ DES SCIENCES ÉCONOMIQUES DE L'UNIVERSITÉ D'ISTANBUL. 1– , 1939– . Istanbul. Bimonthly (some combined numbers)
In French.

2611
Istituto per la Scienza dell'Amministrazione Pubblica. ARCHIVIO. 1– , 1962– ; n. ser. v.1– , 1983– . Milano, Giuffre. Two volumes per year.
In Italian. Each volume has a distinctive title.

2612
ISTORICHESKI PREHLED. 1944– . Sofiia. Five no. a year, 1944–52; bimonthly, 1953–84; monthly.
Issued by: Bulgarsko-Istorichesko Druzhestvo (1944) and later by Institut za Istoriia, Bulgarska Akademiia na Naukite. In Bulgarian. Tables of contents in French in early years; later in English and Russian.
Indexes: 1944–51, 1v.

2613
ISTORICHESKII MATERIALISM. 1917–1925– . Moskva. Beginning with no.10, 1980 (publ. 1982). Annual.
Issued by: Institut Nauchnoi Informatsii po Obshchestvennym Naukam, Akademiia Nauk SSSR. In Russian. Processed.

ISTORIE
See Universitatea "Al-I. Cuza" din Isąi. ANALELE ŞTIINTIFICE. SERIE NOUA. SECTIUNEA IIIa: ISTORIE

ISTORIE—ARHEOLOGIE
See Academia de Ştiinţe Sociale şi Politice. Centrul de Informare şi Documentaire in Ştiinţele Sociale şi Politice. ISTORIE-ARHEOLOGIE

2614
ISTORIIA AFRIKI. 2– , 1979– . Moskva, Nauka. Annual.
In Russian. Vol. 1 issued without series title. Each volume has also a distinctive title. Other title: *African History. Studies and Publications*.

2615
ISTORIIA SSSR. Mar./Apr. 1957– . Moskva, Nauka. Bimonthly.
Issued by: Institut Istorii, Akademiia Nauk SSSR. In Russian. Tables of contents also in English.
Indexed: Bull. Sig. Soc. Eth.; His. Abst.; Int. Bibl. Soc. Cul. Anth.

2616
L'ITALIA NELLA POLITICA INTERNAZIONALE. v.1– , 1972/73– . Milano, Edizioni di Comunità. Annual.
Issued by: Istituto Affari Internazionali. In Italian.

2617
THE ITALIAN YEARBOOK OF INTERNATIONAL LAW. v.1– , 1975– . Napoli, Editoriale Scientifica. Annual, 1975–77; biennial.
Indexed: Bull. Anal. Pol. Ec. Soc.

ITEMS
See Social Science Research Council (U.S.A.). ITEMS

2618
IZSLEDOVANIIA ZA ISTORIATA NA BULGARSKII NAROD. 1– , 1970– . Sofiia.
Issued by: Institut za Istoriia, and Institut za Balkanistika, Bulgarska Akademiia na Naukite. In Bulgarian.

IZVESTIIA
See Bulgarska Akademiia na Naukite. Geografski Institut. IZVESTIIA

IZVESTIIA
See Bulgarska Akademiia na Naukite. Institut za Istoriia. IZVESTIIA

IZVESTIIA
See Bulgarsko Istorichesko Druzhestvo. IZVESTIIA

IZVESTIIA
See Russia. Arkheologicheskaia Komissiia. IZVESTIIA

IZVESTIIA AKADEMII NAUK ARMIANSKOI SSSR. SERIIA OBSHCHESTVENNYE NAUKI
See Akademiia Nauk Armianskoi SSR. IZVESTIIA. SERIIA OBSHCHESTVENNYE NAUKI

IZVESTIIA AKADEMII NAUK AZERBAIDZHANSKOI SSR. SERIIA EKONOMIKI

See Akademii͡a Nauk Azerbaĭdzhanskoĭ SSR. IZVESTII͡A. SERII͡A EKONOMIKI

IZVESTII͡A AKADEMII NAUK AZERBAĬDZHANSKOĬ SSR. SERII͡A ISTORII, FILOSOFII I PRAVA
See Akademii͡a Nauk Azerbaĭdzhanskoĭ SSR. IZVESTII͡A. SERII͡A ISTORII, FILOSOFII I PRAVA

IZVESTII͡A AKADEMII NAUK KAZAKHSKOĬ SSR. SERII͡A EKONOMIKI, FILOSOFII I PRAVA
See Akademii͡a Nauk Kazakhskoĭ SSR. IZVESTII͡A. SERII͡A EKONOMIKI, FILOSOFII I PRAVA

IZVESTII͡A AKADEMII NAUK KAZAKHSKOĬ SSR. SERII͡A ISTORII, ARKHEOLOGII I ETNOGRAFII
See Akademii͡a Nauk Kazakhskoĭ SSR. IZVESTII͡A. SERII͡A ISTORII, ARKHEOLOGII I ETNOGRAFII

IZVESTII͡A AKADEMII NAUK KAZAKHSKOĬ SSR. SERII͡A ISTORII, EKONOMIKI, FILOSOFII I PRAVA
See Akademii͡a Nauk Kazakhskoĭ SSR. IZVESTII͡A. SERII͡A ISTORII, EKONOMIKI, FILOSOFII I PRAVA

IZVESTII͡A AKADEMII NAUK KAZAKHSKOĬ SSR. SERII͡A OBSHCHESTVENNAI͡A
See Akademii͡a Nauk Kazakhskoĭ SSR. IZVESTII͡A. SERII͡A OBSHCHESTVENNAI͡A

IZVESTII͡A AKADEMII NAUK KAZAKHSKOĬ SSR. SERII͡A OBSHCHESTVENNYKH NAUK
See Akademii͡a Nauk Kazakhskoĭ SSR. IZVESTII͡A. SERII͡A OBSHCHESTVENNYKH NAUK (two entries)

IZVESTII͡A AKADEMII NAUK MOLDAVSKOĬ SSR. SERII͡A OBSHCHESTVENNYKH NAUK
See Akademia de Shtiintse a RSS Moldovenest. IZVESTII͡A. SERII͡A OBSHCHESTVENNYKH NAUK

IZVESTII͡A AKADEMII NAUK SSSR. SERII͡A VII. OTDELENIE HUMANITARNYKH NAUK
See Akademii͡a Nauk SSSR. IZVESTII͡A. SERII͡A OTDELENIE OBSHCHESTVENNYKH NAUK

IZVESTII͡A AKADEMII NAUK SSSR. SERII͡A OTDELENIE OBSHCHESTVENNYKH NAUK
See Akademii͡a Nauk SSSR. IZVESTII͡A. SERII͡A OTDELENIE OBSHCHESTVENNYKH NAUK

IZVESTII͡A AKADEMII NAUK SSSR. SERII͡A EKONOMICHESKAI͡A
See Akademii͡a Nauk SSSR. IZVESTII͡A. SERII͡A EKONOMICHESKAI͡A

IZVESTII͡A AKADEMII NAUK SSSR. SERII͡A EKONOMIKI
See Akademii͡a Nauk SSSR. IZVESTII͡A. SERII͡A EKONOMIKI

IZVESTII͡A AKADEMII NAUK TURKMENSKOĬ SSR. SERII͡A OBSHCHESTVENNYKH NAUK
See Akademii͡a Nauk Turkmenskoĭ SSR.

IZVESTII͡A SIBIRSKOGO OTDELENIA AKADEMII NAUK SSSR. SERII͡A EKONOMIKI I PRIKLADNOĬ SOT͡SIOLOGII
See Akademii͡a Nauk SSSR. Sibirskoe Otdelenie. IZVESTII͡A. SERII͡A EKONOMIKI I PRIKLADNOĬ SOT͡SIOLOGII

IZVESTII͡A SIBIRSKOGO OTDELENIA AKADEMII NAUK SSSR. SERII͡A OBSHCHESTVENNYKH NAUK
See Akademii͡a Nauk SSSR. Sirbirskoe Otdelenie. IZVESTII͡A. SERII͡A OBSHCHESTVENNYKH NAUK

J

2619
J.A. JEUNE AFRIQUE. v.19–20 (no.929–990/991), Oct. 25, 1978–Jan. 1980. Paris. Weekly.
Continues: *Jeune Afrique*. Continued by: *Jeune Afrique*.

2620
JASA. v.1– , 1888– . Washington, D.C. Quarterly.
Issued by: American Statistical Association. Title varies: 1888–1921, *Quarterly Publications of the American Statistical Association*; 1922–70, *Journal of the American Statistical Association*.
Indexed: Pop. Ind.

JASO
See Anthropological Society of Oxford. JOURNAL

JBES
See JOURNAL OF BUSINESS AND ECONOMIC STATISTICS

2621
JBR JOURNAL OF BUSINESS RESEARCH. v.5– , Mar. 1977– . New York, Elsevier North-Holland. Quarterly.
Continues: *Journal of Business Research* (v.1–4, 1973–76, Athens, Ga.)

JCR
See JAPANESE CURRENT RESEARCH

J.E.I.
See JOURNAL OF ECONOMIC ISSUES

JET
See THE JOURNAL OF EDUCATIONAL THOUGHT

JHS
See THE JOURNAL OF THE HISTORY OF SOCIOLOGY

JMR
See JOURNAL OF MARKETING RESEARCH

JMS
See JOURNAL OF MANAGEMENT STUDIES

JPMS
See JOURNAL OF POLITICAL AND MILITARY SOCIOLOGY

JPSS
See JOURNAL OF PERSONALITY AND SOCIAL SYSTEMS

JSS
See JOURNAL OF THE SOCIAL SCIENCES (Kuwait)

JAARBOEK
See Africana Society of Pretoria. YEARBOOK. JAARBOEK

JAARBOK REGIONALE STATISTIEK
See Statistical Office of the European Communities. REGIONAL STATISTISK ÅRBOG

JAHRBUCH
See Museum für Volkerkunde, Leipzig. JAHRBUCH

JAHRBUCH
See Schweizerische Gesellschaft für Urgeschichte. JAHRBUCH

2622
JAHRBUCH ASIEN–AFRIKA–LATEINAMERIKA. 1974– . Berlin, Deutscher Verlag des Wissenschaften. Annual.
Issued by: Zentraler Rat für Asien–Afrika–Lateinamerikawissenschaften in DDR. In German.
Continues: *Asien–Afrika–Lateinamerika*.

JAHRBUCH DER AKADEMIE DER WISSENSCHAFTEN DER DDR
See Akademie der Wissenschaften der DDR. JAHRBUCH

2623
JAHRBUCH DER INTERNATIONALEN POLITIK UND WIRTSCHAFT. 1975– . Berlin, Staatsverlag der Deutschen Demokratischen Republik. Annual.
Issued by: Institut für Weltwirtschaft und Internationale Beziehungen, Akademie der Wissenschaften der UdSSR, and Institut für Internationale Beziehungen, Akademie der Staats- und Rechtswissenschaften der DDR. In German.

JAHRBUCH DER SCHWEIZERISCHEN VEREINIGUNG FÜR POLITISCHE WISSENSCHAFT
See ANNUAIRE SUISSE DE SCIENCE POLITIQUE

2624
JAHRBUCH DER SOZIALRECHTS DER GEGENWART. v.1– , 1979– . Berlin, E. Schmidt. Annual.

In German.
Continues: *Sozialordnung der Gegenwart.*

JAHRBUCH DER SOZIALSTATISTIK
See Statistical Office of the European Communities. SOZIALSTATISTIK

2625
JAHRBUCH DER WIRTSCHAFT OSTEUROPAS. YEARBOOK OF EAST-EUROPEAN ECONOMICS. v.1– , 1970– . München, G. Olzog Verlag. Annual.
Issued by: Ost-Europa Institut. In English or German.

2626
JAHRBUCH DES BALTISCHEN DEUTSCHTUMS. 1955– . Lüneber. Annual.
Issued by: Carl-Shirren-Gesellschaft on behalf of the Deutsch-Baltische Landmanschaft. In German.

JAHRBUCH DES INSTITUTS FÜR CHRISTLICHE SOZIALWISSENSCHAFTEN
See JAHRBUCH FÜR CHRISTLICHE SOZIALWISSENSCHAFTEN

2627
JAHRBUCH FÜR AFRIKANISCHES RECHT. ANNUAIRE DE DROIT AFRICAIN. v.1– , 1980– . Heidelberg, G.F. Müller. Annual.
In English, French, or German.

2628
JAHRBUCH FÜR AMERIKASTUDIEN. v.1–18, 1956–1973. Stuttgart, J.B. Metzlerische Verlagsbuchhandlung. Two no. a year.
Issued by: Deutsches Gesellschaft für Amerikastudien. In German.

2629
JAHRBUCH FÜR AUSWÄRTIGE POLITIK. v.1– , 1929– . Berlin, later Frankfurt am Main, P. Keppler Verlag.
In German. Title varies: 1929–31, *Jahrbuch für Auswärtige Politik, International Wirtschaft und Kultur, Welt-Verkehr und Völkerrecht.*

JAHRBUCH FÜR AUSWÄRTIGE POLITIK, INTERNATIONAL WIRTSCHAFT UND KULTUR, WELT-VERKEHR UND VÖLKERRECHT
See JAHRBUCH FÜR AUSWÄRTIGE POLITIK

2630
JAHRBUCH FÜR CHRISTLICHE SOZIALWISSENSCHAFTEN. 1960– . Münster. Annual.
Organ of: Institut für Christliche Sozialwissenschaften, Universität Münster. In German. Title varies: *Jahrbuch des Instituts für Christliche Sozialwissenschaften.*
Indexed: Bull. Anal. Pol. Ec. Soc.; Int. Bibl. Eco.

2631
JAHRBUCH FÜR GESCHICHTE. 1– , 1967– . Berlin, Akademie-Verlag. Annual.
Issued by: Zentralinstitut für Geschichte, Akademie der Wissenschaften der DDR (called earlier Deutsche Akademie der Wissenschaften). In German.

2632
JAHRBUCH FÜR GESCHICHTE DER UdSSR UND DER VOLKSDEMOKRATISCHE LÄNDERN EUROPAS. v.3–12, 1959–1968. Berlin, Rutter & Leoning. Annual.
In German.
Continues: *Jahrbuch für Geschichte der Deutsch–Slavischen Beziehungen und Geschichte Ost- und Mitteleuropas* (v.1–2, 1956–58). Continued by: *Jahrbuch für Geschichte der Sozialistischen Ländern Europas.*
Indexed: Bull. Anal. Pol. Ec. Soc.

2633
JAHRBUCH FÜR GESCHICHTE VON STAAT, WIRTSCHAFT UND GESELLSCHAFT, LATEINAMERIKAS. v.1– , 1964– . Cologne, Böhlau Verlag. Annual.
In German; some articles in French or Spanish; summaries in German.
Indexed: Int. Bibl. Eco.

2634
JAHRBUCH FÜR INTERNATIONALES RECHT. v.1–18, 1948–1975?. Göttingen, Vendenhoek & Ruprecht.
Issued under the auspices of the Forschungsstelle für Völkerrecht und Ausländisches Öffentliches Recht, Universität Hamburg. Institut für Internationales Recht in der Universität Kiel, 1948–195?, and Hans Bredow Institut für Rundfunk und Fernschen der Universität Hamburg. in German or English.
Continued by: *German Yearbook of International Law* (1976–)
Indexed: His. Abst.; Int. Pol. Sc. Abst.

JAHRBUCH FÜR INTERNATIONALES RECHT
See GERMAN YEARBOOK OF INTERNATIONAL LAW

2635
JAHRBUCH FÜR NEUE POLITISCHE ÖKONOMIE. v.1– , 1982– . Tübingen, J.C.B. Mohr. Annual.
In German.

2636
JAHRBUCH FÜR OSTDEUTSCHE VOLKSKUNDE. 1– , 1955– . Marburg. Annual.
Issued by: Kommission für Ostdeutsche Volkskunde. In German. Title varies: v.1–6, 1955–60, *Jahrbuch für Volkskunde der Heimatvertriebenen.*
Indexed: Int. Bibl. Soc. Cul. Anth.

JAHRBUCH FÜR RECHTSVERGLEICHUNG UND GESETZGEBUNG STUDIES
See ANNUARIO DI DIRITTO COMPARATO E DI STUDI LEGISLATIVI

2637
JAHRBUCH FÜR SOZIALWISSENSCHAFT. v.1– , 1950– . Göttingen, Vandenhoek & Ruprecht. Three no. a year.
Issued by: Institut für Europäische Wirtschaftspolitik, Universität Hamburg. In German. V.1 includes "Bibliographie der Sozialwissenschaften" (v.42(n.F. v.1)), separately paged, continued by: *Bibliographie der Sozialwissenschaften* (1968–)
Indexed: Bull. Anal. Pol. Ec. Soc.; Bull. Sig. Soc. Eth.; Int. Bibl. Eco.; Int. Bibl. Pol. Sc.; Int. Lab. Doc.; PAISFL; SSCI.

JAHRBUCH FÜR VOLKSKUNDE DER VETRIEBENEN
See JAHRBUCH FÜR OSTDEUTSCHE VOLKSKUNDE

2638
JAHRBUCH FÜR WIRTSCHAFTSGESCHICHTE. 1960– . Berlin, Akademie-Verlag. Four no. a year.
Issued by: Abteilung Wirtschaftsgeschichte, Institut für Wirtschaftsgeschichte, Akademie der Wissenschaften der DDR; 1966–, by Arbeitsstelle für Wirtschaftsgeschichte. In German.
Indexed: His. Abst.; Int. Bibl. Soc. Cul. Anth.; PAISFL; Peace Res. Abst. J.

JAHRBUCH REGIONAL STATISTIK
See Statistical Office of the European Communities. REGIONAL STATISTISK ÅRBOG

JAHRBUCH SCHWEITZ DRITTE WELT
See ANNUAIRE SUISSE TIERS-MONDE

2639
JAHRBÜCHER NATIONALÖKONOMIE UND STATISTIK. v.1–34, 1863–1879; n. ser. v.35–55 (v.1–21), 1880–1890; 3rd ser. v.56– , 1891– . Jena, F. Manke. Monthly.
Indexes: Vols. 1–7, 1863–66, in v.7; v.1–19, 1863–1872, in v.19; v.1–29, 1863–87, in v.29; Register zu v.1–34, and n. ser. v.1–16 (Jena, Fischer, 1902); General Register for v.76–95 (3rd ser. v.21–40), 1901–10 (Jena, Fischer, 1912)
Indexed: Bull. Anal. Pol. Ec. Soc.; Int. Bibl. Eco.; Peace Res. Abst. J.; Pop. Ind.

JAHRESBERICHT
See Schweizerische Gesellschaft für Urgeschichte. JAHRBUCH

2640
JAHRESBERICHT ÜBER DIE POLITIK DER EUROPÄISCHEN GEMEINSCHAFT UND IHRER MITGLIEDSTAATEN AUF DEM GEBIET DER ENTWICKLUNGSKOOPERATION. 1977/78– . Brüssel, Die Kommission. Annual.
Issued by: Kommission der Europäischen Gemeinschaften. In German.

2641
JAMAICAN ECONOMIC REVIEW. 1984– . Kingston. Annual.
Issued by: Private Sector Organization of Jamaica.

2642
JAPAN ANNUAL OF LAW AND POLITICS. 1– , 1952– . Tokyo. Annual.
Issued by: Nihon Gakujutsu Kaigi Dai Nibu. In English. None published in 1954.

2643
JAPAN ECONOMIC ALMANAC. 1985– . Tokyo, The Japan Economic Journal.
Continues: *Industrial Review of Japan.*

2644
THE JAPAN ECONOMIC JOURNAL. NIHON KEIZAI SHIMBUN. INTERNATIONAL WEEKLY EDITION. v.9– , June 5, 1971– . Tokyo, Nihon Keizai Shinbunsha. Weekly.
Includes annual supplement: *Industrial Review of Japan* (–1984)
Continues: *Nihon Keizai Shimbun. International Weekly.*

2645
JAPAN INTERPRETER. 1– , 1963– . Tokyo. Semi-annual.
Issued by: Center for Japanese and Political Studies. Title varies: v.1–5, 1963–69, *Journal of Social and Political Ideas in Japan.*
Indexed: ABC POL SCI; Bull. Anal. Pol. Ec. Soc.; His. Abst.; Int. Pol. Sc. Abst.; Peace Res. Abst. J.

2646
JAPAN POLITIK UND WIRTSCHAFT. 1976/77– . Hamburg. Annual.
Issued by: Institut für Asienkunde. In German.

2647
JAPAN QUARTERLY. v.1– , Oct./Dec. 1954– . Tokyo, Asahi Shimbun-sha.
Indexed: Bull. Anal. Pol. Ec. Soc.; Int. Bibl. Eco.; Int. Bibl. Pol. Sc.; Int. Bibl. Soc.; Int. Lab. Doc.; Int. Pol. Sc. Abst.; PAIS; Peace Res. Abst. J.; SSCI.

2648
JAPAN QUARTERLY. v.1– , Oct. 1974– . New Delhi.
Issued by: India Committee on Economic Development in India and Japan.
Indexed: Int. Pol. Sc. Abst.

2649
JAPAN SOCIALIST REVIEW. no.1– , Nov. 1, 1961– . Tokyo. Semimonthly, 1961–74; monthly.
Issued by: Japan Socialist Party.
Indexed: Bull. Anal. Pol. Ec. Soc.

2650
THE JAPANESE ANNUAL OF INTERNATIONAL LAW. 1967– . Tokyo.
Issued by: Kokusai Kyokai Nihon Shobu.
Indexed: Bull. Anal. Pol. Ec. Soc.; Ind. For. Leg. Per.; Int. Bibl. Pol. Sc.; Int. Pol. Sc. Abst.

2651
JAPANESE CURRENT RESEARCH. v.1– , Jan. 1986– . Ann Arbor, Mich., University Microfilms. Monthly.
Published in cooperation with the Japanese Technical Information Service. Other title: *JCR*. A companion to: *Japanese Technical Abstracts*.

2652
JAPANESE ECONOMIC STUDIES. v.1– , 1972– . White Plains, Armonk, N.Y., M.E. Sharpe. Quarterly.
Translations from Japanese.

2653
JAPANESE FINANCE AND INDUSTRY: QUARTERLY SURVEY. no.27– , Jan./Mar. 1975– . Tokyo.
Issued by: Industrial Bank of Japan.
Continues: *Quarterly Journal of Japanese Finance & Industry*.
Indexed: PAIS.

JAPANESE JOURNAL OF ETHNOLOGY
See MINZO KUGAKU-KENKYŪ

2654
JAPANESE JOURNAL OF PSYCHOLOGY. SHINRIGAKU KENKYŪ. v.1–3, 1923–1925; n. ser. v.1– , 1926– . Tokyo. Bimonthly.
Issued by: Nihon Shinri Gakkai. In Japanese; summaries in English.
Indexed: Psych. Abst.; SSCI.

JAPANESE PERIODICAL INDEX. HUMANITIES AND SOCIAL SCIENCES SECTION
See ZASSHI KIJI SAKUIN. JINMUN SHAKAI HEN

2655
JAPANESE PSYCHOLOGICAL RESEARCH. no.1– , Mar. 1954– . Tokyo. Quarterly (irreg.)
Issued by: Japanese Psychological Association. In English, French, or German.
Indexed: LLBA; Psych. Abst.

JAPANESE SOCIOLOGICAL REVIEW
See SHAKAIGAKU HYŌRON

2656
JAPANESE YEARBOOK ON BUSINESS HISTORY. 1– , 1984– . Tokyo. Annual.
Issued by: Japan Business History Institute.

2657
JEN LEI HSÜEH PAO. ANTHROPOLOGICA SINICA. 1982– . Pei ching, K'o hsüeh ch'u pan she. Quarterly.
Issued by: Chung-kuo k'o hsüeh yuan ku chi hui tung wu yu ku jen lei yen chen sopien chi. In Chinese.

2658
JEN YU SHE HUI. 1– , 1971/72– . T'aipei, Shih cien wen wu kung she Tsung ching Hsiao. Bimonthly.
In Chinese. Other title: *Man & Society*.

2659
JERNAL ANTROPOLOJI DAN SOSIOLOJI. 1– , 1971/72– . Kuala Lumpur. Annual.
Issued by: Persutuan Kajimanusia & Kajimasharakat, Universiti Kebangsan Malaysia. In English or Malay. Vol. 4, 1975/76 last available for examination.

2660
JERUSALEM JOURNAL OF INTERNATIONAL RELATIONS. 1– , fall 1975– . Jerusalem, The Magness Press. Quarterly.
Issued by: The Leonard Davis Institute of International Studies, The Hebrew University of Jerusalem.
Indexed: ABC POL SCI; Bull. Anal. Pol. Ec. Soc.; Int. Bibl. Pol. Sc.

2661
THE JEWISH JOURNAL OF SOCIOLOGY. v.1– , Apr. 1959– . London, Heinemann on behalf of the World Jewish Congress. Semi-annual.

Indexed: Bull. Sig. Soc. Eth.; Int. Bibl. Soc. Cul. Anth.; Int. Pol. Sc. Abst.; PAIS.

2662
THE JEWISH QUARTERLY. n. ser. v.1– , July 1910– . Philadelphia, Pa., New York.
Issued by: Dropsie University for Hebrew and Cognate Learning. Continues *The Jewish Quarterly Review*. London.
Indexes: Vols. 1–20, 1909–Apr. 1930, 1v.

2663
THE JEWISH QUARTERLY REVIEW. v.1–20, Oct. 1888–July 1908. London.
Issued by: Dropsie University for Hebrew and Cognate Learning.
Continued by: *The Jewish Quarterly*. Philadelphia, New York.

2664
JEWISH SOCIAL STUDIES. v.1– , 1939– . New York. Quarterly.
Issued by: Conference on Jewish Studies.
Indexes: Vols. 1–25, 1939–64, 1v.
Indexed: Abst. Anth.; His. Abst.; Int. Pol. Sc. Abst.; PAIS; Pop. Ind.; Soc. Sc. Hum. Ind.; SSCI.

2665
JEWISH STUDIES JOURNAL. v.1– , first quarter 1948– . Oxford. Quarterly, 1948–71; semi-annual.
Issued by: Oxford Centre for Postgraduate Hebrew Studies.
Indexed: His. Abst.

JIANGHAI ACADEMIC JOURNAL. EDITION OF ECONOMY AND SOCIETY
See CHING CHI SHE HUI PAN

JILINDAXUE SHE HUI KEKSUE XUEBAO—JILIN UNIVERSITY JOURNAL. SOCIAL SCIENCE EDITION
See CHI-LIN TA HSÜEH SHE HUI K'O HSÜEH HSÜEH PAO

2666
JIMBUN CHIRI. 1– , 1948– . Kyōto. Six no. a year.
Issued by: Jimbun Chiri Gakkai. In Japanese. Other title: *The Human Geography*.

2667
JIMBUN GAKUHŌ. v.1– , 1944– . Tōkyō. Quarterly.
Organ of: Tōkyō Toritsu Daigaku Jimbub Gakkai. In Japanese. Other title: *Social and Human Sciences Journal*.
Indexed: His. Abst.; Int. Bibl. Soc.

2668
JINKO MONDAI KENKYŪ. 1– , 1946– . Tōkyō. Quarterly.
Issued by: Jinko Mondai Kenyū-sho, Ministry of Health and Welfare. Other titles: *Annual Report of the Institute of Population Problems*, and *Journal of Population Problems*.

JINRUIGAKU KENKYŪJO
See Nanzan Daigaku, Nagoya. Jinruigaku Kenkyū-jo. JINRUIGAKU KENKYUJO KIYO—NANZAN DAIGAKU JINRUIGAKU KENKYU

2669
JINRUIGAKU ZASSHI. v.1– , 1886– . Tōkyō. Annual.
Issued by: Nippon Jinruigaku Kai. In Japanese. Other title: *Journal of the Anthropological Society of Nippon*.

JOINT ARAB ECONOMIC REPORT
See AL-TAQRIR AL-IQTISADI AL-ARABI AL-MUWAHHAD

JOINT CONFERENCE OF THE KOREAN POLITICAL SCIENCE ASSOCIATION AND THE ASSOCIATION OF POLITICAL SCIENTISTS IN NORTH AMERICA
See HAN'GUK CHONGCH'I HAKKOE

2670
JOINT STUDIES IN PUBLIC POLICY. 1– , 1980– . London, Heinemann.
Issued jointly by: National Institute of Economic and Social Research, Policy Studies Institute, and Royal Institute of International Affairs.

JORDBRUKSEKONOMISKA MEDDELANDEN
See Sweden. Statens Jordbruksnämd. JORDBRUKSEKONOMISKA MEDDELANDEN

2671
JORNAL BRASILEIRO DE SOCIOLOGIA. 1– , 1958– . Recife.
Issued by: Sociedade Brasileira de Sociologia, Faculdade de Filosofia, Universidade Federal de Pernambuco. In Portuguese.
Supersedes: *Revista Pernambucana de Sociologia*.

2672
JORNAL PORTUGUÊS DE ECONOMIA & FINANÇAS. v.1– , 1952?– . Lisboa, Publicações "Economia & Finanças". Monthly.
Issued by: Sociedade de la Economia de la Empresa. In Portuguese.

2673
JOURNAL ASIATIQUE. v.1– , July 1822– . Paris. Quarterly.
Issued by: Société Asiatique. In French. Includes some supplements. Title varies: 1828–35, *Nouveau Journal Asiatique*.
Indexes: ser. 2–3, 1828–42; ser.4–5, 1843–62; ser.6, 1863–72; ser. 7, 1873–82; ser.8, 1883–1892; ser. 9, 1893–1902; ser. 10, 1903–12; ser. 11, 1913–22, 1v.; ser. 12, 1923–32, 1v.; v. 234–40, 1943/45–52, 1v.
Indexed: Bull. Sig. Soc. Eth.; Int. Bibl. Soc. Cul. Anth.

JOURNAL CANADIEN DES ÉTUDES AFRICAINES
See CANADIAN JOURNAL OF AFRICAN STUDIES

2674
JOURNAL DE GÉNÉTIQUE HUMAINE. v.1– , June 1952– . Genève, Éditions Médecine et Hygiène. Quarterly.
Issued by: Fédération Générale de Neurologie. In English, French, or German; summaries in English, French and German.

JOURNAL DE L'HISTOIRE ÉCONOMIQUE ET SOCIALE DE L'ORIENT
See JOURNAL OF THE ECONOMIC AND SOCIAL HISTORY OF THE ORIENT

JOURNAL DE LA SOCIÉTÉ INTERNATIONALE D'ÉTUDES ORIENTALES
See ORIENS

JOURNAL DE PLANIFICATION DU DÉVELOPPEMENT
See JOURNAL OF DEVELOPMENT PLANNING

JOURNAL DE STATISTIQUE ET REVUE ÉCONOMIQUE SUISSE
See SCHWEIZERISCHE ZEITSCHRIFT FÜR VOLKSWIRTSCHAFT UND STATISTIK

2675
JOURNAL DES AFRICANISTES. v.46– , 1976– . Paris. Two no. a year.
Issued by: Société des Africanistes. In French; summaries in English.
Continues: Société des Africanistes. *Journal*, v.1–45, 1931–75.
Indexed: Int. Bibl. Soc. Cul. Anth.

2676
JOURNAL DES ÉCONOMISTES. v.1–37, Dec. 1841–Dec. 1853; 2. ser., v.1–48, Jan. 1854–Dec. 1865; 3. ser., v.1–48, Jan. 1866–Dec. 1877; 4. ser., v.1–48, Jan. 1878–Dec. 1889; 5. ser., v.1–56, Jan. 1890–Dec. 1903; 6. ser., v.1–56, Jan. 1904–Dec. 1917. Paris. Monthly (semimonthly Apr.–Nov. 1848); bimonthly.
Issued by: Société de Statistique de Paris. Includes: "Comptes Rendus" of the society.
Cumulative table of contents, 1841–65 (published in 1883), 1841–91, and 1886–98.

JOURNAL DES MARXISTES AFRICAINS
See JOURNAL OF AFRICAN MARXISTS

JOURNAL FOR SOCIAL RESEARCH
See TYDSKRIF VIR MAATSKAPLIKE NAVORSING

JOURNAL FOR STUDIES IN ECONOMICS AND ECONOMETRICS
See TYDSKRIF VIR STUDIES IN EKONOMIE EN EKONOMETRIE

JOURNAL FOR THE POLITICAL SCIENCES
See POLITEIA

2677
JOURNAL FOR THE STUDY OF JUDAISM IN THE PERSIAN, HELLENISTIC AND ROMAN PERIOD. 1– , Mar. 1970– . Leiden, E.J. Brill. Two no. a year.
In English, French, or German.

2678
JOURNAL FOR THE THEORY OF SOCIAL BEHAVIOUR. v.1– , Apr. 1971– . Oxford, B. Blackwell. Semi-annual, v.1–7; three no. a year.
Indexed: Int. Pol. Sc. Abst.; Soc. Abst.; Urb. Stu. Abst.

2679
JOURNAL FÜR ANGEWANDTE SOZIALFORSCHUNG. v.1–20, July 1961–1980. Wien. Quarterly.
Issued by: Sozialgeschichtliche Studien-Gesellschaft. In German. Title varies: v.1–8, 1961–68, *Meinung*.
Continued by: *Journal für Sozialforschung*.

JOURNAL. HUMANITIES
See Asiatic Society of Bangladesh. JOURNAL. HUMANITIES

JOURNAL INTERNATIONAL DE PSYCHOLOGIE
See INTERNATIONAL JOURNAL OF PSYCHOLOGY

2680
JOURNAL OF ABNORMAL AND SOCIAL PSYCHOLOGY. v.20–69, Apr. 1925–Dec. 1964. Washington, D.C. Quarterly, 1925–54; bimonthly.
Issued by: American Psychological Association.
Continues: *Journal of Abnormal Psychology and Social Psychology*. Continued by: *Journal of Abnormal Psychology*, and *Journal of Personality and Social Psychology*.

JOURNAL OF ABSTRACTS AND REVIEWS
See Indian Council of Social Science Research. ICSSR JOURNAL OF ABSTRACTS AND REVIEWS

2681
JOURNAL OF ABSTRACTS IN INTERNATIONAL EDUCATION. v.1– , 1970– . Toledo, Ohio. Semi-annual.
Issued by: College of Education, University of Toledo. In English or French.

2682
JOURNAL OF ADMINISTRATION OVERSEAS. v.5, no.2–v.19, no.4, Apr. 1966–Oct. 1980. London, HMSO. Quarterly.
Issued by: Administrative Services Branch, Ministry of Overseas Development.
Continues: *Journal of Local Administration Overseas* (1964–Jan. 1966). Continued by: *Public Administration and Development.*
Indexed: ABC POL SCI; Bull. Anal. Pol. Ec. Soc.; Hum. Res. Abst.; Int. Bibl. Eco.; Int. Bibl. Pol. Sc.; Int. Bibl. Soc.; Int. Bibl. Soc. Cul. Anth.; Int. Pol. Sc. Abst.; PAIS; Pop. Ind.; Sage Pub. Adm. Abst.; Sage Urb. Stu. Abst.

2683
JOURNAL OF AFRICAN ADMINISTRATION. v.1–13, Jan. 1949–Oct. 1961. London. Quarterly.
Issued by: African Studies Branch, Colonial Office.
Supersedes: *Digest of African Local Administration.* Superseded by: *Journal of Local Administration Overseas.*

2684
JOURNAL OF AFRICAN AND ASIAN STUDIES. v.1–4, no.1, autumn 1967–Mar./Apr. 1973. Delhi, Prakash Goel et Kay-Kay Printers. Semi-annual.
Issued by: Association for the Study of African and Asian Affairs, and Department of African Studies, University of Delhi. Suspended autumn 1970–72.
Indexed: Int. Bibl. Soc. Cul. Anth.; Int. Pol. Sc. Abst.

2685
JOURNAL OF AFRICAN CIVILIZATIONS. v.1– , Apr. 1979– . New Brunswick, N.J., Transaction Periodicals Consortium. Two no. a year.
Issued by: Douglas College, Rutgers University. Issues are thematic.

2686
JOURNAL OF AFRICAN HISTORY. v.1– , 1960– . London, Cambridge University Press. Quarterly, 1960–84; three no. a year.
In English or French.
Indexed: Abst. Anth.; Bull. Anal. Pol. Ec. Soc.; Bull. Sig. Soc. Eth.; Int. Bibl. Soc. Cul. Anth.; SSCI.

2687
JOURNAL OF AFRICAN MARXISTS. JOURNAL DES MARXISTES AFRICAINS. no.1– , Nov. 1981– . London.
In English or French; summaries in French and Portuguese.

2688
JOURNAL OF AFRICAN STUDIES. 1– , spring 1974– . Los Angeles, Calif., Washington, D.C. Heldref Publications. Quarterly.
Issued by: African Studies Center, University of California at Los Angeles.
Indexed: Bull. Anal. Pol. Ec. Soc.; PAIS.

JOURNAL OF AFRICAN STUDIES
See AFURIKA KENKYŪ

2689
JOURNAL OF AGRICULTURAL ECONOMICS. v.1– , 1928– . Aberdeen, later Ashford. Three no. a year.
Issued by: Agricultural Economics Society, and Agricultural Economics Division School of Rural Economics and Related Studies. Summaries in English, French and German. Title varies: 1928–54, *Journal of Proceedings of the Agricultural Economics Society.*
Indexed: Bull. Anal. Pol. Ec. Soc.; Int. Bibl. Eco.; Int. Bibl. Soc. Cul. Anth.; Int. Lab. Doc.; PAIS; SSCI.

2690
JOURNAL OF AMERICAN ETHNIC HISTORY. v.1– , fall 1981– . New Brunswick, N.J., Transaction Periodicals Consortium. Semi-annual.
Issued by: Immigration History Society.
Indexed: Curr. Cont. Soc. Beh. Sc.; His. Abst.; SSCI.

2691
JOURNAL OF AMERICAN FOLKLORE. v.1– , Apr./June 1888– . Boston, Mass., Washington, D.C. Quarterly.
Official organ of the American Folk-lore Society.
Indexed: Abst. Anth.; Bull. Sig. Soc. Eth.; His. Abst.; Int. Bibl. Soc. Cul. Anth.; Soc. Sc. Hum. Ind.

2692
THE JOURNAL OF AMERICAN HISTORY. v.1–29, 1907–1935. New York.
Issued by: National Historical Society.
Indexes: Vols. 1–7, 1907–1913.

2693
THE JOURNAL OF AMERICAN HISTORY. v.1– , June 1914– . Abilene, Kans., Lincoln, Nebr., Bloomington, Ind. Quarterly.

Issued by: Mississippi Valley Historical Association, Organization of American Historians. Title varies: 1914–Mar. 1964, *The Mississippi Valley Historical Review*.
Indexes: Vols. 1–15, 1914–Mar. 1929, 1v.; v.16–25, June 1929–Mar. 1939, 1v.
Indexed: His. Abst.; Soc. Sc. Hum. Ind.; Wom. Stu. Abst.

2694
JOURNAL OF AMERICAN STUDIES. v.1– , Apr. 1967– . London, Cambridge University Press. Semi-annual, 1967–1970; three no. a year.
Issued by: British Association of American Studies.
Supersedes: British Association of American Studies. *Bulletin*.
Indexed: Bull. Anal. Pol. Ec. Soc.; Curr. Cont. Soc. Beh. Sc.; His. Abst.; Int. Bibl. Eco.; Int. Bibl. Pol. Sc.; Int. Bibl. Soc.; Int. Bibl. Soc. Cul. Anth.; SSCI; Ind. Per. Art. Law.

JOURNAL OF ANCIENT HISTORY
See VESTNIK DREVNEĬ ISTORII

2695
JOURNAL OF ANCIENT INDIAN HISTORY. 1– , 1967/68– . Calcutta. Annual, issued in two parts.
Issued by: Department of Ancient History, University of Calcutta.

2696
JOURNAL OF ANTHROPOLOGICAL ARCHAEOLOGY. v.1– , Mar. 1982– . New York, Academic Press. Quarterly.
Indexed: Abst. Anth.; SSCI.

2697
JOURNAL OF ANTHROPOLOGICAL RESEARCH. v.29– , spring 1973– . Albuquerque, N.Mex. Quarterly.
Issued by: New Mexico University.
Continues: *Southwestern Journal of Anthropology* (v.1–28, 1945–72)
Indexed: Bull. Sig. Soc. Eth.; Int. Bibl. Soc. Cul. Anth.

2698
JOURNAL OF ANTHROPOLOGY. v.1, no.1–3, July 1870–Jan. 1871. London.

2699
THE JOURNAL OF APPLIED BEHAVIORAL SCIENCE. v.1– , Jan./Mar. 1965– . Washington, D.C. Quarterly.
Issued by: National Training Laboratories, National Education Association.
Indexed: ABC POL SCI; Abst. Soc. Work; Bull. Anal. Pol. Ec. Soc.; Bull. Sig. Soc. Eth.; Int. Bibl. Eco.; Int. Bibl. Pol. Sc.; Int. Bibl. Soc.; Int. Pol. Sc. Abst.; Peace Res. Abst. J.; Psych. Abst.; Sage Pub. Adm. Abst.; Soc. Abst.

2700
JOURNAL OF APPLIED ECONOMETRICS. v.1– , Jan. 1986– . Chichester, New York, Wiley. Quarterly.

2701
JOURNAL OF APPLIED SOCIAL PSYCHOLOGY. v.1– , Jan./Mar. 1971– . Washington, D.C., Scripta Pub. Corp. Quarterly.
Organ of: Department of Psychology, Purdue University.
Indexed: Bull. Anal. Pol. Ec. Soc.; Bull. Sig. Soc. Eth.; Ind. Per. Art. Law; LLBA; PHRA; Psych. Abst.; SSCI; Wom. Stu. Abst.

2702
JOURNAL OF ARCHAEOLOGICAL SCIENCE. v.1– , Mar. 1974– . London, Academic Press. Quarterly, 1974–82; bimonthly.
Indexed: Abst. Anth.; Int. Bibl. Soc. Cul. Anth.

2703
JOURNAL OF ASIAN AND AFRICAN STUDIES. v.1– , Jan. 1966– . Leiden, E.J. Brill. Quarterly (some nos combined)
Issued by: Department of Sociology, York University (Canada)
Indexed: ABC POL SCI; Abst. Anth.; Bull. Sig. Soc. Eth.; His. Abst.; Int. Bibl. Pol. Sc.; Int. Bibl. Soc.; Int. Bibl. Soc. Cult. Anth.; Int. Lab. Doc.; Soc. Abst.; SSCI.

JOURNAL OF ASIAN AND AFRICAN STUDIES
See AJIA AFURIKA GENGO BUNKA KENKYŪ

2704
JOURNAL OF ASIAN HISTORY. v.1– , 1967– . Wiesbaden, Harrassowitz. Semi-annual.
In English, French, German, or Russian; summaries in these languages.

2705
JOURNAL OF ASIAN INTEGRATION STUDIES. no.1– , 1973– . London.
Issued by: Asian Club, London School of Economics and Political Science.
Indexed: Bull. Anal. Pol. Ec. Soc.

2706
THE JOURNAL OF ASIAN STUDIES. v.1– , Nov. 1941– . Ann Arbor, Mich. Quarterly, 1941–54; five no. a year, 1955–69; quarterly.
Issued by: Association for Asian Studies (Far Eastern Association, 1941–Feb. 1957). Includes "Bibliography of Asian Studies" (formerly "Far Eastern Bibliography", 1941–Feb. 1957). Title varies: v.1–15, 1941–Sept. 1956, *Far Eastern Quarterly*.
Indexed: ABC POL SCI; Bull. Anal. Pol. Ec. Soc.; Bull. Sig. Soc. Eth.; His. Abst.; Ind. Per. Art. Law; Int. Bibl. Eco.; Int. Bibl. Pol. Sc.; Int. Bibl. Soc. Cul. Anth.; Int. Pol. Sc. Abst.; Int. Lab. Doc.; PAIS; Peace Res. Abst. J.; Pop. Ind.; Soc. Sc. Hum. Ind.; Wom. Stu. Abst.

JOURNAL OF ASIATIC STUDIES
See ASEIA YEUNKU

THE JOURNAL OF ASSOCIATION OF POLITICAL AND SOCIAL STUDIES
See KOKKA-GAKKAI ZASSHI

2707
JOURNAL OF BANKING AND FINANCE. v.1– , June 1977– . Amsterdam, North-Holland Pub. Co. Quarterly.
Published under the sponsorship of the Università di Bergamo.
Indexed: Int. Bibl. Eco.; PAIS.

2708
JOURNAL OF BEHAVIORAL ECONOMICS. v.1– , 1972– . Macomb, Ill. Semi-annual.
Issued by: Center for Business and Economic Research, Western Illinois University.

2709
JOURNAL OF BEHAVIORAL MEDICINE. v.1– , Mar. 1973– . New York, Plenum Press. Quarterly.
Indexed: Psych. Abst.; Soc. Abst.; Soc. Work. Res. Abst.

2710
JOURNAL OF BEHAVIOURAL SCIENCE. v.1– , 1969– . Durban. Quarterly.
Issued by: University of Natal, and Psychology Society.

2711
JOURNAL OF BIOSOCIAL SCIENCE. v.1– , Jan. 1969– . Oxford, Blackwell for the Galton Foundation. Four no. a year.
Issued by: Galton Foundation. Includes "Supplement" (no.1, 1969)
Supersedes: *The Eugenics Review.*
Indexed: Abst. Anth.; APAIS; Int. Bibl. Soc. Cul. Anth.; Pop. Ind.

2712
THE JOURNAL OF BLACK PSYCHOLOGY. v.1– , Aug. 1974– . Cincinnati, Ohio. Semi-annual.
Indexed: Psych. Abst.; Soc. Abst.

2713
JOURNAL OF BLACK STUDIES. v.1– , Sept. 1970– . Beverly Hills, Calif., Sage Publications. Quarterly.
Issued by: Afro-American Center, University of California at Los Angeles.
Indexed: Abst. Soc. Work; Bull. Anal. Pol. Ec. Soc.; Int. Bibl. Eco.; Int. Bibl. Soc.; Int. Pol. Sc. Abst.; Curr. Cont. Soc. Beh. Sc.; PAIS; PHRA; Sage Fam. Stu. Abst.; Sage Urb. Stu. Abst.; Soc. Abst.; SSCI; Soc. Work Res. Abst.; Urb. Aff. Abst.

2714
JOURNAL OF BUSINESS AND ECONOMIC PERSPECTIVES. v.8, no.2– , fall 1982– . Mortin, Tenn.
Issued by: School of Business Administration, University of Tennessee at Mortin.
Continues: *Business and Economic Perspectives.*

2715
JOURNAL OF BUSINESS & ECONOMIC STATISTICS. v.1– , Jan. 1983– . Washington, D.C. Quarterly.
Issued by: American Statistical Association. Other title: *JBES*.

JOURNAL OF BUSINESS ECONOMICS
See LIIKETALOUDELLINEN AIKAKAUSKIRJA

2716
JOURNAL OF BUSINESS ETHICS. JBE. v.1– , Feb. 1982– . Dordrecht, D. Reidel Pub. Co. Quarterly.

2717
THE JOURNAL OF BUSINESS STRATEGY. v.1– , summer 1980– . Boston, Mass., Warren, Gorkham & Lamont. Quarterly.
Indexed: PAIS.

2718
JOURNAL OF CANADIAN STUDIES. REVUE D'ÉTUDES CANADIENNES. v.1– , May 1966– . Peterborough. Quarterly.
In English or French.
Indexed: Abst. Anth.; ABC POL SCI; His. Abst.; Ind. Per. Art. Law; Curr. Cont. Soc. Beh. Sc.; SSCI.

2719
JOURNAL OF CARIBBEAN STUDIES. 1– , winter 1980– . Coral Gables, Fla. Three no. a year.
Issued by: Association of Caribbean Studies. In English, French, or Spanish.

2720
JOURNAL OF CHILDREN IN CONTEMPORARY SOCIETY. v.14– , fall 1981– . New York, Haworth Press. Quarterly.
Partially sponsored by: Carnegie-Mellon University Child Care Center.
Continues: *Children in Contemporary Society.*

2721
JOURNAL OF CHURCH AND STATE. v.1– , Nov. 1959– . Waco, Tex. Three no. a year.
Issued by: J.M. Dawson Studies in Church and State, Baylor University.
Indexes: Vols. 1–25, 1959–83.
Indexed: His. Abst.; PAIS.

2722
JOURNAL OF COLLECTIVE NEGOTIATIONS IN THE PUBLIC SECTOR. Feb. 1972– . Farmingdale, N.Y., Baywood Pub. Co. Quarterly.
Indexed: PAIS.

2723
JOURNAL OF COMMON MARKET STUDIES. v.1– , 1962– . Oxford, Blackwell. Three no. a year.
Indexed: ABC POL SCI; Bull. Anal. Pol. Ec. Soc.; Curr. Cont. Soc. Beh. Sc.; Eco. Abst.; Ind. Per. Art. Law; Int. Bibl. Eco.; Int. Bibl. Pol. Sc.; Int. Bibl. Soc.; Int. Lab. Doc.; Int. Pol. Sc. Abst.; J. Eco. Lit.; PAIS; Soc. Sc. Hum. Ind.; SSCI.

2724
THE JOURNAL OF COMMONWEALTH & COMPARATIVE POLITICS. v.21– , 1974– . London, Frank Cass. Three no. a year.
Continues: *Journal of Commonwealth Political Studies*.
Indexed: ABC POL SCI; Bull. Anal. Pol. Ec. Soc.; His. Abst.; Int. Bibl. Pol. Sc.; Int. Bibl. Soc. Cul. Anth.; Int. Pol. Sc. Abst.; PAIS.

2725
JOURNAL OF COMMONWEALTH POLITICAL STUDIES. v.1– , Nov. 1961– . Leicester, Leicester University Press. Semi-annual.
Continued by: *The Journal of Commonwealth & Comparative Politics*.
Indexed: ABC POL SCI; APAIS; His. Abst.; Int. Bibl. Soc. Cul. Anth.; PAIS; Peace Res. Abst. J.

2726
THE JOURNAL OF COMMUNICATION. v.1– , May 1951– . [Place of publication varied], Philadelphia, Pa., Annenberg School Press. Annual, 1951–53; quarterly.
Issued by: National Society for the Study of Communication, 1951–53; Annenberg School of Communications, University of Pennsylvania.
Indexed: Bull. Sig. Soc. Eth.; His. Abst.; Int. Bibl. Pol. Sc.; Int. Bibl. Soc.; Int. Pol. Sc. Abst.; Psych. Abst.; Sage Fam. Stu. Abst.; Sage Urb. Stu. Abst.; Soc. Abst.

2727
THE JOURNAL OF COMMUNIST STUDIES. v.1– , Mar. 1985– . London, Frank Cass. Quarterly.
Supersedes: *Communist Affairs*.

JOURNAL OF COMMUNITY DEVELOPMENT
See CHIYOK SAHOE KAEBAL NONCH'ONG

JOURNAL OF THE COMMUNTY DEVELOPMENT SOCIETY
See Community Development Society. JOURNAL

2728
JOURNAL OF COMMUNITY PSYCHOLOGY. v.1– , Jan. 1973– . Rutland, Vt., Clinical Psychology Pub. Co. Quarterly.
Supersedes, in part: *Journal of Clinical Psychology*.
Indexed: Psych. Abst.

2729
JOURNAL OF COMPARATIVE ADMINISTRATION. v.1–5, May 1969–Feb. 1974. Beverly Hills, Calif., Sage Publications. Quarterly.
Published in cooperation with Comparative Administrative Group, American Society of Public Administration.
Continued by: *Administration & Society*.
Indexed: ABC POL SCI; Curr. Cont. Soc. Beh. Sc.; Ind. Per. Art. Law; Int. Bibl. Eco.; Int. Bibl. Pol. Sc.; Int. Bibl. Soc.; Int. Bibl. Soc. Cul. Anth.; Hum. Res. Abst.; PAIS; PHRA; Sage Pub. Adm. Abst.; Sage Urb. Stu. Abst.; SSCI; Urb. Aff. Abst.

2730
JOURNAL OF COMPARATIVE ECONOMICS. v.1– , Mar. 1977– . New York, Academic Press. Quarterly.
Issued by: Association for Comparative Economic Studies.
Indexed: Int. Bibl. Eco.; PAIS; Soc. Sc. Ind.; SSCI.

2731
JOURNAL OF COMPARATIVE FAMILY STUDIES. v.1– , autumn 1970– . Calgary. Three no. a year.
Issued by: Department of Sociology and Anthropology, The University of Calgary.
Indexed: Abst. Anth.; Int. Bibl. Soc.; Int. Bibl. Soc. Cul. Anth.; Pop. Ind.; Psych. Abst.; Sage Fam. Stu. Abst.; Soc. Abst.; SSCI.

2732
JOURNAL OF COMPARATIVE LEGISLATION AND INTERNATIONAL LAW. v.1–2, Aug. 1896–Dec. 1897; n. ser. v.1–18 (no.1–41), Mar. 1899–Dec. 1918; ser.3, v.1–35, Apr. 1919–Nov. 1951. London. Two or three no. a year, 1896–1920; quarterly (irreg.)
Issued by: Society of Comparative Legislation. Title varies: 1896–1919, *Journal of the Society of Legislation*.

2733
JOURNAL OF COMPARATIVE PSYCHOLOGY. v.1–39, Feb. 1921–Dec. 1946. Baltimore, Md., Williams & Wilkins. Bimonthly.
Formed by the union of: *Psychobiology* and *Journal of Animal Behavior*.
Continued by: *Journal of Comparative and Physiological Psychology*.

2734
JOURNAL OF COMPARATIVE PSYCHOLOGY. v.40– , 1947. Washington, D.C. Quarterly.

Issued by: American Psychological Association.
Continues: *Journal of Comparative Psychology*.

2735
JOURNAL OF COMPARATIVE SOCIOLOGY AND RELIGION. BULLETIN DE SOCIOLOGIE ET DE RELIGION COMPARÉS. v.6, no.7– , 1979– . Ottawa. Annual.
Issued by: Sociological Research Centre. Each issue has also a distinctive title. In English or occasionally in French.
Continues: *Journal of Comparative Sociology*.

2736
THE JOURNAL OF CONFLICT RESOLUTION. v.1– , Mar. 1957– . Ann Arbor, Mich. Quarterly.
Issued by: Department of Journalism, University of Michigan. Title varies: Mar.–June 1957, *Conflict Resolution*.
Indexes: Vols. 1–12, 1957–68, in v.12.
Indexed: ABC POL SCI; HIS. ABST.; Bull. Anal. Pol. Ec. Soc.; Bull. Sig. Soc. Eth.; Int. Bibl. Pol. Sc.; Int. Bibl. Soc.; Int. Bibl. Soc. Cul. Anth.; Int. Pol. Sc. Abst.; PAIS; Peace Res. Abst. J.; Sage Pub. Adm. Abst.; Hum. Res. Abst.; Soc. Abst.; SSCI; Wom. Stu. Abst.

2737
JOURNAL OF CONSTITUTIONAL AND PARLIAMENTARY STUDIES. v.1– , Jan./Mar. 1968– . New Delhi. Quarterly.
Issued by: Institute of Constitutional and Parliamentary Studies.
Indexed: ABC POL SCI; Bull. Anal. Pol. Ec. Soc.; Int. Bibl. Pol. Sc.; Int. Pol. Sc. Abst.

JOURNAL OF CONSUMER POLICY
See ZEITSCHRIFT FÜR VERBRAUCHERPOLITIK

2738
THE JOURNAL OF CONSUMER RESEARCH. v.1– , June 1974– . Chicago, later Worcester. Quarterly.
Co-sponsored by: American Association of Public Opinion.

2739
JOURNAL OF CONTEMPORARY ASIA. v.1– , autumn 1970– . London. Quarterly.
Indexed: Bull. Anal. Pol. Ec. Soc.; Int. Bibl. Eco.; Int. Bibl. Pol. Sc.; Int. Pol. Sc. Abst.; SSCI.

2740
JOURNAL OF CONTEMPORARY BUSINESS. v.1–11, no.2, winter 1972–second quarter 1982. Seattle, Wash. Quarterly.
Issued by: Graduate School of Business Administration, University of Washington. Each issue has also a distinctive title.
Supersedes: *The University of Washington Business Review*.
Indexed: Bull. Anal. Pol. Ec. Soc.; Int. Bibl. Eco.; PAIS; Sage Pub. Adm. Abst.

2741
JOURNAL OF CONTEMPORARY HISTORY. v.1– , 1966– . London, Weidenfeld and Nicolson. Four no. a year.
Issued by: Institute for Advanced Studies in Contemporary History.
Indexed: ABC POL SCI; Bull. Anal. Pol. Ec. Soc.; Curr. Cont. Soc. Beh. Sc.; His. Abst.; Int. Bibl. Eco.; Int. Bibl. Pol. Sc.; Int. Bibl. Soc.; Int. Bibl. Soc. Cul. Anth.; Peace Res. Abst. J.; SSCI.

2742
JOURNAL OF CROSS-CULTURAL PSYCHOLOGY. v.1– , 1970– . Bellingham, Wash. Quarterly.
Issued by: Center for Cross-Cultural Research, Department of Psychology, Western Washington State University. Summaries in English, French and German.
Indexed: Abst. Anth.; Int. Bibl. Soc.; Int. Bibl. Soc. Cul. Anth.; Psych. Abst.; Sage Urb. Stu. Abst.; Soc. Abst.; Urb. Aff. Abst.

2743
JOURNAL OF CULTURAL AND SOCIAL SCIENCE. 1– , 1966– . Tokushima.
Issued by: College of General Education, University of Tokushima. In English or Japanese. Tables of contents also in English.

2744
JOURNAL OF CULTURAL GEOGRAPHY. v.1– , fall/winter 1980– . Bowling Green, Colo. Semi-annual.
Issued by: Bowling Green State University in cooperation with the Popular Culture Association and the American Culture Association.

2745
THE JOURNAL OF DEVELOPING AREAS. v.1– , Oct. 1966– . Macomb, Ill., Western Illinois University Press. Quarterly.
Issued by: Western Illinois University. In English or French. Includes "Bibliography of Periodicals and Monographs".
Indexed: ABC POL SCI; Bull. Sig. Soc. Eth.; Eco. Abst.; His. Abst.; Ind. Per. Art. Law; Int. Bibl. Eco.; Int. Bibl. Pol. Sc.; Int. Bibl. Soc.; Int. Bibl. Soc. Cul. Anth.; Int. Pol. Sc. Abst.; Hum. Res. Abst.; PAIS; Peace Res. Abst. J.; Sage Pub. Adm. Abst.; Soc. Abst.; SSCI.

2746
JOURNAL OF DEVELOPING SOCIETIES. v.1– , June 1985– . Leiden, E.J. Brill. Semi-annual.
Each issue also has a distinctive title.
Supersedes: *Contributions to Asian Studies.*

2747
JOURNAL OF DEVELOPMENT ECONOMICS. 1– , June 1974– . Amsterdam, North-Holland Pub. Co. Six no. a year forming two volumes.
Indexed: Bull. Anal. Pol. Ec. Soc.; Int. Bibl. Eco.

2748
JOURNAL OF DEVELOPMENT PLANNING. JOURNAL DE LA PLANIFICATION DE DÉVELOPPEMENT. REVISTA DE LA PLANIFICACIÓN DEL DESARROLLO. no.1– , 1969– . New York, United Nations. Annual, 1969–73, 1975–76; two no. a year, 1975–76, 1977–.
Issued by: Department of Economic and Social Affairs, United Nations. Published also in French and Spanish editions (ST/ECA) and (ST/ESA)

2749
JOURNAL OF DEVELOPMENT STUDIES. v.1– , Oct. 1964– . London, Frank Cass. Quarterly.
Issued by: School of Oriental and African Studies, University of London.
Indexed: ABC POL SCI; Curr. Cont. Soc. Beh. Sc.; His. Abst.; Int. Bibl. Eco.; Int. Bibl. Pol. Sc.; Int. Pol. Sc. Abst.; PHRA; Pop Ind.; PAIS; Sage Pub. Adm. Abst.; Sage Urb. Stu. Abst.; Soc. Abst.; SSCI.

2750
JOURNAL OF EASTERN AFRICAN RESEARCH AND DEVELOPMENT. 1– , 1971– . Nairobi, Kenya Literature Bureau, 1979–. Semi-annual; occasionally combined numbers.
In English or Swahili. Not published 1976–78.
Indexed: Soc. Abst.

2751
JOURNAL OF ECONOMETRICS. v.1– , Mar. 1973– . Lausanne, North-Holland Pub. Co. Bimonthly.

2752
JOURNAL OF ECONOMIC ABSTRACTS. v.1–6, Jan. 1963–Dec. 1968. Cambridge, Mass. Quarterly.
Published under the auspices of the American Economic Association.
Continued by: *Journal of Economic Literature.*

2753
THE JOURNAL OF ECONOMIC AFFAIRS. v.1–3, no.4, Oct. 1980–July 1983. London, B. Blackwell in association with the Institute of Economic Affairs.
Continued by: *Economic Affairs* (London)

JOURNAL OF ECONOMIC AND SOCIAL GEOGRAPHY
See TIJDSCHRIFT VOOR ECONOMISCHE EN SOCIALE GEOGRAFIE

JOURNAL OF ECONOMIC AND SOCIAL HISTORY OF THE ORIENT
See JOURNAL OF THE ECONOMIC AND SOCIAL HISTORY OF THE ORIENT

2754
JOURNAL OF ECONOMIC BEHAVIOR & ORGANIZATION. v.1– , Mar. 1980– . Amsterdam, North-Holland Pub. Co. Quarterly.

2755
JOURNAL OF ECONOMIC DYNAMICS AND CONTROL. 1– , 1979– . Amsterdam, North-Holland Pub. Co. Quarterly.
Indexed: SSCI.

2756
JOURNAL OF ECONOMIC HISTORY. v.1– , May 1941– . New York. Semi-annual, 1941–50; quarterly.
Issued by: Economic History Association. Includes dissertation abstracts.
Indexes: Vols. 1–10, 1941–50; v.11–15, 1951–55.
Indexed: Bull. Anal. Pol. Ec. Soc.; Curr. Cont. Soc. Beh. Sc.; His. Abst.; Int. Bibl. Eco.; Int. Bibl. Pol. Sc.; Ind. Per. Art. Law; Int. Bibl. Soc.; Int. Lab. Doc.; PAIS; Pop. Ind.; Soc. Sc. Hum. Ind.; J. Eco. Lit.; SSCI; Wom. Stu. Abst.

2757
JOURNAL OF ECONOMIC ISSUES. v.1, no.1/2– , June 1967– . Austin, Tex. Quarterly.
Sponsored by: Association for Evolutionary Economics, and the University of Texas.
Indexed: Bull. Anal. Pol. Ec. Soc.; Int. Bibl. Eco.; J. Eco. Lit.; PAIS.

2758
JOURNAL OF ECONOMIC LITERATURE. v.7– , Mar. 1969– . Nashville, Tenn. Quarterly.
Issued by: American Economic Association.
Continues: *Journal of Economic Abstracts.*
Indexed: Bull. Anal. Pol. Ec. Soc.; Bull. Sig. Soc. Eth.; His. Abst.; Ind. Per. Art. Law; Int. Bibl. Eco.; PAIS.

2759
JOURNAL OF ECONOMIC PSYCHOLOGY. v.1– , Mar. 1981– . Amsterdam, North-Holland Pub. Co. Quarterly.
Published under the auspices of: Society of European Research in Economic Psychology. In English or French.

Indexed: Psych. Abst.

JOURNAL OF ECONOMIC STUDIES
See ECONOMIC STUDIES

2760
JOURNAL OF ECONOMIC THEORY. 1– , June 1969– . London, New York, Academic Press. Bimonthly, forming two volumes per year.
Indexes: Vols. 1–9, 1969–74, 1v.; v.20–29, in v.29.
Indexed: Int. Bibl. Eco.; J. Eco. Lit.

JOURNAL OF ECONOMICS
See ZEITSCHRIFT FÜR NATIONALÖKONOMIE

2761
JOURNAL OF ECONOMICS AND BUSINESS. v.25– , fall 1972– . New York, North-Holland Pub. Co. Three no. a year, 1972–81; quarterly.
Issued by: School of Business Administration, Temple University, 1972–81; in cooperation with the Graduate Faculty of the School of Business Administration, Temple University.
Continues: *Economic and Business Bulletin.*
Indexed: PAIS.

2762
JOURNAL OF EDUCATION. v.1– , Jan. 2, 1875– . Boston, Mass. Frequency varies.
Formed by the union of: *Maine Journal of Education*, *Massachusetts Teacher*, *R.I. Schoolmaster*, *Connecticut School Journal*, and *College Courant*. Title varies: 1875–78, *The New England Journal of Education*. Absorbed: *Educational Weekly of Indianapolis*, Nov. 1885.

2763
JOURNAL OF EDUCATION POLICY. v.1– , Jan./Mar. 1986– . London, Philadelphia, Pa., Taylor & Francis. Quarterly.

2764
JOURNAL OF EDUCATIONAL RESEARCH. v.1–53, no.1, Jan. 1920–Sept. 1959. Bloomington, Ind., 1920–41; Madison, Wis. Monthly (except. July–Aug.), 1920–32; monthly (except July, Aug., Sept.).
Issued by: American Education Association (called 1920–22, National Association of Directors of Educational Research; Apr. 1922–Feb. 1928, Educational Research Association)
Indexed: Psych. Abst.

2765
JOURNAL OF EDUCATIONAL RESEARCH. v.1– , Nov. 1978– . Karachi. Semi-annual.
Issued by: Organization of Workers in Educational Research.

JOURNAL OF EDUCATIONAL RESEARCH
See JURNAL PENDIDEKAN

JOURNAL OF EDUCATIONAL RESEARCH
See ZEITSCHRIFT FÜR ERZIEHUNGSWISSENSCHAFTLICHE FORSCHUNG

JOURNAL OF EDUCATIONAL SOCIOLOGY
See SOCIOLOGY OF EDUCATION

2766
JOURNAL OF EDUCATIONAL THOUGHT. v.1– , Apr. 1967– . Calgary. Three no. a year.
Issued by: Faculty of Education, University of Calgary. Other title: *JET*.

2767
THE JOURNAL OF EGYPTIAN ARCHAEOLOGY. v.1– , Jan. 1914– . London. Two no. a year, 1914–18; annual.
Issued by: Egyptian Exploration Fund, 1914–18, and the Egypt Exploration Society.
Supersedes: *Archaeological Report.*
Indexes: Vols. 1–20, 1914–34; v.21–40, 1935–54.
Indexed: Brit. Hum. Ind.; Int. Bibl. Soc. Cul. Anth.

2768
JOURNAL OF ENVIRONMENTAL ECONOMICS AND MANAGEMENT. v.1– , May 1974– . New York, Academic Press. Quarterly.
Indexed: PAIS.

JOURNAL OF ENVIRONMENTAL POLICY
See ZEITSCHRIFT FÜR UMWELTPOLITIK

2769
JOURNAL OF ENVIRONMENTAL PSYCHOLOGY. v.1– , Mar. 1981– . London, New York, Academic Press. Quarterly.
Indexed: Psych. Abst.

2770
JOURNAL OF ENVIRONMENTAL SYSTEMS. v.1– , Mar. 1981– . Farmingdale, N.Y., Baywood Pub. Co. Quarterly.
Indexed: Urb. Aff. Abst.

2771
JOURNAL OF ETHIOPIAN STUDIES. v.1– , Jan. 1963– . Addis Ababa. Semi-annual, 1963–80; irreg.
Issued by: Institute of Ethiopian Studies, Haile Selassie University. In Amharic, English, French, or Italian. Title in Amharic precedes English title, 1963–July 1964.
Supersedes: *University College Review.*
Indexes: Vols. 1–14, 1963–80, 1v.
Indexed: Abst. Anth.; Bull. Sig. Soc. Eth.; Int. Bibl. Soc. Cul. Anth.

2772
JOURNAL OF ETHNIC STUDIES. 1– , 1973– . Bellingham, Wash. Quarterly.
Issued by: College of Ethnic Studies, Western Washington University (called earlier Western Washington State College)
Indexed: Curr. Cont. Soc. Beh. Sc.; Int. Bibl. Soc. Cul. Anth.

2773
JOURNAL OF ETHNOBIOLOGY. v.1– , May 1981– . Flagstaff, Ariz. Semi-annual.
Issued by: Center for Western Studies, Society of Ethnobiology.
Indexed: Abst. Anth.

JOURNAL OF ETHNOLOGICAL SOCIETY OF LONDON
See Ethnological Society of London. JOURNAL

2774
JOURNAL OF ETHNOPHARMACOLOGY. v.1– , 1979– . Lausanne, Elsevier Sequoia. Six no. a year, forming two volumes.
Indexed: Bull. Sig. Soc. Eth.; SSCI.

2775
JOURNAL OF EUROPEAN ECONOMIC HISTORY. v.1– , spring 1972– . Rome. Three no. a year.
Issued by: Ufficio Stampa e Relazioni Pubbliche, Banco di Roma.
Indexed: Int. Bibl. Eco.; Pop. Ind.

JOURNAL OF EVALUATION AND PROGRAM PLANNING
See EVALUATION AND PROGRAM PLANNING

JOURNAL OF EXPERIMENTAL RESEARCH IN PERSONALITY
See JOURNAL OF RESEARCH IN PERSONALITY

2776
JOURNAL OF EXPERIMENTAL SOCIAL PSYCHOLOGY. v.1– , Jan. 1965– . New York, Academic Press. Quarterly.
Issued by: Department of Psychology, University of North Carolina. Includes “Supplement” (no.1, 1966–)
Indexed: Int. Bibl. Soc.; Int. Pol. Sc. Abst.; LLBA; Psych. Abst.; Soc. Abst.; Wom. Stu. Abst.

2777
JOURNAL OF FAMILY HISTORY. 1– , autumn 1976– . Minneapolis, Minn. Quarterly.
Issued by: National Council on Family Relations.
Indexed: Pop. Ind.; Sage Urb. Stu. Abst.

2778
THE JOURNAL OF FAMILY WELFARE. v.1– , 1954– . Bombay. Quarterly.
Issued by: Family Planning Association of India.
Indexed: Pop. Ind.

2779
JOURNAL OF FAR EASTERN STUDIES. v.1– , Jan. 1942– . Chicago, Ill., The University of Chicago Press. Quarterly.
Issued by: Department of Oriental Languages and Literature, University of Chicago.
Supersedes: *The American Journal of Semitic Languages and Literatures* (1884–1941)
Indexed: Abst. Anth.; Int. Bibl. Soc. Cul. Anth.; LLBA; Soc. Sc. Hum. Ind.

2780
JOURNAL OF FINANCE. v.1– , Aug. 1946– . New York, Graduate School of Business Administration, New York University. Five no. a year.
Issued by: American Finance Association. Includes dissertation abstracts.
Indexes: Vols. 1–38, 1946–83, 1v.
Indexed: Bull. Anal. Pol. Ec. Soc.; Curr. Cont. Soc. Beh. Sc.; Eco. Abst.; Ind. Per. Art. Law; Int. Bibl. Eco.; Int. Bibl. Pol. Sc.; Int. Bibl. Soc.; J. Eco. Lit.; PAIS; SSCI.

2781
JOURNAL OF FINANCIAL ECONOMICS. v.1– , May 1974– . Amsterdam, North-Holland Pub. Co. Bimonthly.
Published in collaboration with the Graduate School of Management, University of Rochester.
Indexed: Ind. Bibl. Eco.

THE JOURNAL OF FREEDOM ACADEMY
See Chayu A'kademi. YŎN'GU NON'CHONG

2782
THE JOURNAL OF FUTURES MARKETS. v.1– , spring 1981– . New York, Wiley Interscience Journals. Quarterly.
Published in collaboration with the Center for the Study of Futures Markets, Columbia University.
Indexed: PAIS.

JOURNAL OF GAKUKEI COLLEGE. TOKUSHIMA UNIVERSITY. SOCIAL SCIENCE
See Tokushima Daigaku. Gakukei Gakubu. TOKUSHIMA DAIGAKU GAKUKEI KIYŌ SHAKAI KAGAKU

2783
JOURNAL OF GOVERNMENT AND POLITICAL STUDIES. v.1– , Sept. 1976– . Patiala. Semi-annual.
Issued by: Department of Political Science, Punjabi University.
Indexed: Bull. Anal. Pol. Ec. Soc.; Int. Bibl. Pol. Sc.; Int. Pol. Sc. Abst.

JOURNAL OF HANGZHOU DAXUE XUEBAO
See HANG-CHOU TA HSÜEH HSÜEH PAO. CHE HSÜEH SHE HUI K'O HSÜEH PAN

JOURNAL OF HANGZHOU UNIVERSITY. PHILOSOPHY AND SOCIAL SCIENCES EDITION
See HANG-CHOU TA HSÜEH HSÜEH PAO. CHE HSÜEH SHE HUI K'O HSÜEH PAN

2784
JOURNAL OF HEALTH AND SOCIAL BEHAVIOR. v.8– , Mar. 1967– . Washington, D.C. Quarterly.
Issued by: American Sociological Association.
Continues: *Journal of Health and Human Behavior* (v.1–7, 1960–66)
Indexed: Abst. Anth.; Bull. Sig. Soc. Eth.; Int. Bibl. Soc.; Pop. Ind.; Psych. Abst.; Sage Fam. Stu. Abst.; Sage Pub. Adm. Abst.; Sage Urb. Stu. Abst.; Soc. Abst.; Soc. Work Res. Abst.; SSCI; Wom. Stu. Abst.

2785
JOURNAL OF HEALTH ECONOMICS. v.1– , May 1982– . Amsterdam, North-Holland Pub. Co. Three no. a year.

2786
JOURNAL OF HEALTH POLITICS, POLICY AND LAW. v.1– , spring 1976– . Durham, N.C., Duke University Press. Quarterly.
Issued by: University Grants Commission.

2787
THE JOURNAL OF HIGHER EDUCATION. v.1– , Jan. 1930– . Columbus, Ohio. Monthly (except July–Sept.)
Issued by: Ohio State University.

2788
JOURNAL OF HISTORICAL GEOGRAPHY. v.1– , Jan. 1975– . London, New York, Academic Press. Quarterly.

2789
JOURNAL OF HISTORY AND POLITICAL SCIENCE. 1–2, 1971/72–1974/75. Lahore.
Issued by: Departments of History and Political Science, Government College.
Superseded by: *Journal of Political Science*.

2790
JOURNAL OF HISTORY AND THE SOCIAL SCIENCES. v.1–3, 1967–1970. Portland, Oreg. Irreg.
Issued by: Division of History and Social Sciences, Reed College.
Indexed: Soc. Abst.

JOURNAL OF HOKKAIDO UNIVERSITY OF EDUCATION. SECTION IB. SOCIAL SCIENCE
See Hokkaidō Kyoiku Daigaku. HOKKAIDŌ KYOIKU KIYŌ

2791
JOURNAL OF HUMAN ERGOLOGY. v.1– , Sept. 1972– . Tokyo, Center for Academic Publications for the Human Ergology Research Association. Two no. a year.
Indexed: Abst. Anth.

2792
JOURNAL OF HUMAN EVOLUTION. v.1– , Jan. 1972– . London, New York, Academic Press. Bimonthly.
Indexed: Abst. Anth.

2793
JOURNAL OF HUMAN RELATIONS. v.1–21, spring 1952–1973. Wilberforce, Ohio. Quarterly.
Issued by: Central State College.
Indexed: Abst. Soc. Work.; Curr. Cont. Soc. Beh. Sc.; Peace Res. Abst. J.; Psych. Abst.; Soc. Abst.; SSCI.

2794
THE JOURNAL OF HUMAN RESOURCES. v.1– , summer 1966– . Madison, Wis., University of Wisconsin Press. Quarterly.
Issued by: Industrial Relations Research Institute and the Institute for Research on Poverty, University of Wisconsin, and Center for Studies in Vocational and Technical Education. Issues are thematic.
Indexed: Abst. Soc. Work.; Bull. Anal. Pol. Ec. Sc.; Bull. Sig. Soc. Eth.; Ind. Per. Art. Law; Int. Lab. Doc.; J. Eco. Lit.; PAIS; Pop. Ind.

2795
JOURNAL OF HUMANITIES AND SOCIAL SCIENCES. v.1– , June 1978– . Pokhara, Dean's Office. Quarterly.
Issued by: Institute of Humanities and Social Sciences, Tribhuban University. In English or Nepalese.

JOURNAL OF HUMANITIES AND SOCIAL SCIENCES
See AKADEMIKA

JOURNAL OF HUMANITIES AND SOCIAL SCIENCES
See NONMUNJIP; INMUN SAHOE KWAHAK P'YON

2796
JOURNAL OF INDIAN HISTORY. v.1– , Nov. 1921– . London, 1921–Sept. 1924, for the Department of Modern Indian History, University of Allahabad; Trivandrum. Three no. a year.

Issued by: Department of Indian History, University of Allahabad, 1921–46; Department of Modern History, University of Kerala (called 1947–57, University of Travancore). Includes supplements.

2797
JOURNAL OF INDIAN PSYCHOLOGY. v.1– , Jan. 1978– . Waltais, Undhra University Press. Semi-annual.
Indexed: Psych. Abst.

THE JOURNAL OF INDUSTRIAL ARCHAEOLOGY
See INDUSTRIAL ARCHAEOLOGY

2798
THE JOURNAL OF INDUSTRIAL ECONOMICS. v.1– , Nov. 1952– . Oxford, Blackwell. Three no. a year, 1952–78; quarterly.
Indexed: Bull. Anal. Pol. Ec. Soc.; Eco. Abst.; Int. Bibl. Eco.; Int. Lab. Doc.; PAIS; SSCI.

2799
THE JOURNAL OF INDUSTRIAL RELATIONS. v.1– , Apr. 1959– . Sydney. Semi-annual, 1959–63; quarterly.
Issued by: Industrial Relations Society of Australia (1959–July 1964 called Industrial Relations Society).
Indexed: Int. Bibl. Soc.; Soc. Abst.

2800
JOURNAL OF INTER-AMERICAN STUDIES AND WORLD AFFAIRS. v.12– , 1970– . Miami, Fla. Quarterly.
Issued by: Center for Advanced International Studies, University of Miami.
Continues: *Journal of Inter-American Studies.*
Indexed: ABC POL SCI; Bull. Anal. Pol. Ec. Soc.; His. Abst.; Ind. Per. Art. Law; Int. Bibl. Eco.; Int. Bibl. Pol. Sc.; Int. Bibl. Soc.; Int. Lab. Doc.; Int. Pol. Sc. Abst.; Peace Res. Abst. J.; Pop. Ind.; Sage Urb. Stu. Abst.; SSCI.

2801
JOURNAL OF INTERAMERICAN STUDIES. v.1–11, Jan. 1959–1968. Gainesville, Fla., University of Miami Press. Quarterly.
Issued by: Inter-American Academy; sponsored by the Pan American Foundation and the University of Miami; subsequently by: Center for Advanced International Studies, University of Florida at Gainesville. In English, French, Portuguese, or Spanish.
Continued by: *Journal of Inter-American Studies and World Affairs.*

2802
JOURNAL OF INTERCULTURAL STUDIES. v.1– , 1980– . Melbourne, River Seine Publications. Three no. a year.

2803
JOURNAL OF INTERDISCIPLINARY HISTORY. v.1– , autumn 1970– . Cambridge, Mass., M.I.T. Press. Quarterly.
Organ of: School of Humanities and Social Sciences, Massachusetts Institute of Technology.
Indexed: ABC POL SCI; Bull. Sig. Soc. Eth.; Curr. Cont. Soc. Beh. Sc.; His. Abst.; Int. Bibl. Soc. Cul. Anth.; Pop. Ind.; Soc. Abst.; SSCI.

2804
JOURNAL OF INTERDISCIPLINARY MODELLING AND SIMULATION. v.1– , 1978– . New York, Marcel Dekker. Quarterly (irreg.)
Indexed: Curr. Cont. Soc. Beh. Sc.; SSCI.

2805
JOURNAL OF INTERNATIONAL AFFAIRS. v.1– , spring 1947– . New York. Semi-annual.
Issued by: School of International Affairs, Columbia University. Title varies: 1947–51, *Columbia Journal of International Affairs.*
Indexed: ABC POL SCI; Bull. Anal. Pol. Ec. Soc.; Bull. Sig. Soc. Eth.; Curr. Cont. Soc. Beh. Sc.; His. Abst.; Ind. Per. Art. Law; Int. Bibl. Eco.; Int. Bibl. Pol. Sc.; Int. Bibl. Soc.; Int. Bibl. Soc. Cul. Anth.; Int. Pol. Sc. Abst.; PAIS; Peace Res. Abst. J.; Int. Lab. Doc.; SSCI.

2806
JOURNAL OF INTERNATIONAL AND COMPARATIVE SOCIAL WELFARE. v.1– , fall 1984– . Baton Rouge, La., Brij Mohan. Semi-annual.
Issued by: School of Social Work, Louisiana State University (LSU). Co-sponsored by: International Fellowship for Social and Economic Development.

2807
JOURNAL OF INTERNATIONAL ARBITRATION. v.1– , Apr. 1984– . Geneva, D. Thompson and J. Werner. Quarterly.

2808
JOURNAL OF INTERNATIONAL BUSINESS STUDIES. J.I.B.S. v.1– , 1970– . Waco, Tex. Semi-annual, 1970–77; three no. a year.
Issued by: Academy of International Business, and Graduate School of Management, Rutgers University.
Indexed: PAIS.

2809
JOURNAL OF INTERNATIONAL ECONOMICS. v.1– , Feb. 1971– . Amsterdam, North-Holland Pub. Co. Quarterly.
Indexed: Bull. Anal. Pol. Ec. Soc.; Eco. Abst.; Int. Bibl. Eco.

THE JOURNAL OF INTERNATIONAL LAW AND ECONOMIC DEVELOPMENT
See THE JOURNAL OF INTERNATIONAL LAW AND ECONOMICS

2810
THE JOURNAL OF INTERNATIONAL LAW AND ECONOMICS. v.5, no.2–v.15, no.3, 1971–1981. Washington, D.C. Two no. a year, 1971–73; three no. a year.
Issued by: National Law Center, George Washington University.
Continues: *Journal of International Law and Economic Development* (v.2–v.5, no.1, May 1967–spring 1970). Continued by: *George Washington Journal of International Law and Economics.*
Indexes: Vols. 1–5, 1966–Jan. 1971, in v.6, no.1.
Indexed: Ind. Per. Leg.; Ind. For. Leg. Per.; Int. Bibl. Eco.; Int. Bibl. Pol. Sc.; Int. Bibl. Soc.; Int. Lab. Doc.; PAIS; SSCI.

2811
JOURNAL OF INTERNATIONAL MONEY AND FINANCE. v.1– , 1982– . Guildford, Butterworth. Three no. a year.

2812
THE JOURNAL OF INTERNATIONAL RELATIONS. v.1–12, July 1910–Apr. 1922. Worcester, Mass., later Baltimore, Md. Quarterly.
Issued by: Clark University. Title varies: v.1–9, 1910–19, *Journal of Race Development.* Merged into *Foreign Affairs.*

JOURNAL OF INTERNATIONAL STUDIES
See KUKCHE MUNHWA

THE JOURNAL OF JAPANESE ASSOCIATION OF THEORETICAL ECONOMICS
See KIKAN RIRON-KEIZAIGAKU

2813
THE JOURNAL OF JEWISH STUDIES. v.1– , 1st quarter 1948– . Cambridge. Quarterly, 1948–71; semi-annual.
Issued by: Oxford Centre for Postgraduate Hebrew Studies.
Indexed: His. Abst.

2814
JOURNAL OF LABOR ECONOMICS. v.1– , Jan. 1983– . Chicago, Ill., University of Chicago Press. Quarterly.

2815
JOURNAL OF LABOR RESEARCH. v.1– , Jan. 1980– . Fairfax, Va. Semi-annual.
Issued by: Department of Economics, George Mason University.
Indexed: Int. Bibl. Eco.; PAIS.

JOURNAL OF LAND AND PUBLIC UTILITY ECONOMICS
See LAND ECONOMICS

JOURNAL OF LATIN AMERICAN AND CARIBBEAN STUDIES
See BOLETÍN DE ESTUDIOS LATINOAMERICANOS Y DEL CARIBE

2816
JOURNAL OF LATIN AMERICAN STUDIES. v.1– , May 1969– . London, Cambridge University Press. Semi-annual.
Sponsored by: Centres of Institutes of Latin American Studies at the Universities of Cambridge, Essex, Glasgow, Liverpool, London and Oxford.
Indexed: ABC POL SCI; Abst. Anth.; Bull. Anal. Pol. Ec. Soc.; Int. Bibl. Pol. Sc.; Int. Lab. Doc.; Int. Pol. Sc. Abst.; Pop. Ind.

2817
JOURNAL OF LAW AND ECONOMICS. 1– , Oct. 1958– . Chicago, Ill. Annual, 1958–67; semi-annual.
Issued by: Law School, University of Chicago.
Indexes: Vols. 1–10, 1958–67, 1v.; v.11–15, 1968–72, 1v.
Indexed: ABC POL SCI; Bull. Anal. Pol. Ec. Soc.; His. Abst.; Ind. Leg. Per.; Int. Bibl. Eco.; Int. Pol. Sc. Abst.; PAIS; PHRA.

JOURNAL OF LAW & ECONOMICS
See HOKEI RONSŌ

JOURNAL OF LAW AND PUBLIC ADMINISTRATION
See NONMUNJIP

2818
JOURNAL OF LAW AND SOCIETY. v.9– , summer 1982– . Oxford, Martin Robertson. Semi-annual.
Continues: *British Journal of Law and Society.*
Indexed: His. Abst.; Int. Pol. Sc. Abst.; Soc. Abst.; Soc. Work Res. Abst.

2819
JOURNAL OF LAW, ECONOMICS & ORGANIZATION. v.1– , spring 1985– . New Haven, Conn., Yale University Press. Semi-annual.
Other title: *LEO.*

JOURNAL OF LAW, POLITICS AND SOCIOLOGY
See HOGAKU KENKYŪ

2820
JOURNAL OF LEGAL AND POLITICAL SOCIOLOGY. v.1–4, no.3/4, Oct. 1942–summer/winter 1947. New York, Philosophical Library, and International University Press. Semi-annual.

2821
JOURNAL OF LINGUISTICS. v.1– , Apr. 1965– . London, Cambridge University Press. Semi-annual.

Issued by: Linguistic Association of Great Britain.
Indexed: Abst. Anth.; Int. Bibl. Soc. Cul. Anth.; LLBA.

2822
JOURNAL OF LOCAL ADMINISTRATION OVERSEAS. v.1–5, no.1, Jan. 1962–Jan. 1966. London.
Continued by: *Journal of Administration Overseas.*

2823
JOURNAL OF MACROECONOMICS. v.1– , winter 1979– . Detroit, Mich., Wayne State University Press. Quarterly.

2824
JOURNAL OF MAN–ENVIRONMENT RELATIONS. v.1– , summer 1980– . University Park, Pa., Graduate Students in the Program of Man–Environment Relations. Three no. a year.
Issued by: Program of Man–Environment Relations, College of Human Development, Pennsylvania State University.

2825
THE JOURNAL OF MANAGEMENT STUDIES. v.1– , Mar. 1964– . Oxford, B. Blackwell. Three no. a year.
Other title: *JMS Journal of Management Studies.*
Indexed: Curr. Cont. Soc. Beh. Sc.; Bull. Anal. Pol. Ec. Soc.; Eco. Abst.; Int. Bibl. Eco.; Int. Bibl. Soc.; Psych. Abst.

2826
JOURNAL OF MARKETING. v.1– , July 1936– . New York, Brattleboro, Vt., Vermont Printing Co. Quarterly.
Issued by: American Marketing Association. Formed by the union of *American Marketing Journal*, and *National Marketing Review*. Some issues are thematic; some papers of symposia.
Indexed: Bull. Anal. Pol. Ec. Soc.; Bull. Sig. Soc. Eth.; Int. Lab. Doc.; J. Eco. Lit.; PAIS; Psych. Abst.

2827
JOURNAL OF MARKETING RESEARCH. JMR. v.1– , Feb. 1964– . Ann Arbor, Mich., Edwards Brothers. Quarterly.
Issued by: American Marketing Association. Other title: *JMR.*
Indexed: Bull. Anal. Pol. Ec. Soc.; Bull. Sig. Soc. Eth.; Int. Bibl. Eco.; Psych. Abst.

2828
JOURNAL OF MARRIAGE AND THE FAMILY. v.1– , 1939– . Menasha, Wis. Quarterly.
Issued by: National Council on Family Relations. Title varies: 1939–Nov. 1941, *Living*; Feb. 1942–Nov. 1963, *Marriage and Family Living.*
Indexed: APAIS; Bull. Anal. Pol. Ec. Soc.; Bull. Sig. Soc. Eth.; Int. Bibl. Soc.; Int. Bibl. Soc. Cul. Anth.; LLBA; Pop. Ind.; Psych. Abst.; Sage Fam. Stu. Abst.; Soc. Sc. Hum. Ind.; Soc. Abst.; Soc. Work Res. Abst.; SSCI; Wom. Stu. Abst.

2829
JOURNAL OF MATHEMATICAL ECONOMICS. v.1– , 1974– . Lausanne, Elsevier Sequoia. Three no. a year.
Indexed: SSCI.

2830
JOURNAL OF MATHEMATICAL PSYCHOLOGY. v.1– , Feb. 1964– . New York, Academic Press. Semi-annual.

2831
JOURNAL OF MATHEMATICAL SOCIOLOGY. v.1– , 1971– . New York, Gordon and Breach. Semi-annual.
Issued by: Department of Sociology, University of Pittsburgh.
Indexed: Bull. Sig. Soc. Eth.; Int. Bibl. Soc.; Int. Bibl. Pol. Sc.; Soc. Abst.; SSCI.

JOURNAL OF MENTAL HEALTH
See BRITISH JOURNAL OF PSYCHIATRY

2832
JOURNAL OF MEXICAN AMERICAN HISTORY. v.1– , fall 1970– . Santa Barbara, Calif., Joseph Peter Navarro. Two no. a year.

2833
JOURNAL OF MEXICAN AMERICAN STUDIES. v.1– , fall 1970– . Anaheim, Calif. Quarterly.
Issued by: Mexican American Documentation and Educational Research Institute.

2834
JOURNAL OF MIND AND BEHAVIOR. v.1– , spring 1980– . New York. Quarterly.
Issues for summer and winter 1980 were not published.
Indexed: LLBA; Psych. Abst.; SSCI.

2835
THE JOURNAL OF MODERN AFRICAN STUDIES. v.1– , Mar. 1963– . London, Cambridge University Press. Quarterly.
Subtitle reads: "A quarterly survey of politics, economics and related topics in contemporary Africa".
Indexed: ABC POL SCI; Abst. Anth.; Bull. Anal. Pol. Ec. Soc.; His. Abst.; Int. Bibl. Eco.; Int. Bibl. Pol. Sc.; Int. Bibl. Soc.; Int. Bibl. Soc. Cul. Anth.; Int. Lab. Doc.; Int. Pol. Sc. Abst.; LLBA; PAIS; Peace Res. Abst. J.; Pop. Ind.; Sage Urb. Stu. Abst.; Soc. Sc. Hum. Ind.; SSCI; Wom. Stu. Abst.

JOURNAL OF MODERN EDUCATION
See MAJALLAT AL-TARBĪYAH AL-ḤADĪTHAH

2836
JOURNAL OF MODERN HISTORY. v.1– , Mar. 1929– . Chicago, Ill., University of Chicago Press. Quarterly.
Issued by: The University of Chicago in cooperation with the Modern European History Section, American Historical Association.
Indexed: His. Abst.; Int. Bibl. Pol. Sc.; Int. Pol. Sc. Abst.; Peace Res. Abst. J.; Wom. Stu. Abst.

2837
JOURNAL OF MONETARY ECONOMICS. v.1– , Jan. 1975– . Amsterdam, North-Holland Pub. Co. Six no. a year in two volumes.
Published with the cooperation of: Department of Economics and Center for Research in Government Policy Policy and Business, Graduate School, University of Rochester, and Center for Research in Government and Business.
Indexed: Bull. Anal. Pol. Ec. Soc.; PAIS.

2838
JOURNAL OF MONEY, CREDIT AND BANKING. v.1– , Feb. 1969– . Columbus, Ohio, Ohio State University Press. Quarterly.
Includes: "Special issues", symposia and proceedings.
Indexed: Bull. Anal. Pol. Ec. Soc.; Int. Bibl. Eco.; Int. Bibl. Pol. Sc.; J. Eco. Lit.; PAIS.

2839
JOURNAL OF MULTIVARIATE ANALYSIS. v.1– , Apr. 1971– . Bruges, New York, Academic Press. Four no. a year.

2840
JOURNAL OF NEAR EASTERN STUDIES. v.1– , Jan. 1942– . Chicago, Ill., University of Chicago Press. Quarterly.
Issued by: Department of Oriental Languages and Literature, University of Chicago.
Supersedes: *The American Journal of Semitic Languages and Literatures.*
Indexed: Abst. Anth.; Int. Bibl. Soc. Cul. Anth.; LLBA; Soc. Sc. Hum. Ind.

2841
JOURNAL OF NEGRO EDUCATION. v.1– , Apr. 1, 1932– . Lancaster, Pa., later Washington, D.C. Quarterly.
Issued by: Bureau of Educational Research, Howard University.
Indexed: Bull. Sig. Soc. Eth.; His. Abst.; LLBA; PAIS; PHRA; Psych. Abst.; Soc. Abst.; Wom. Stu. Abst.

2842
JOURNAL OF NEGRO HISTORY. v.1– , 1916– . Washington, D.C. Quarterly.
Issued by: The Association for the Study of Negro Life and History.
Indexed: ABC POL SCI; His. Abst.; Int. Bibl. Soc.; Soc. Sc. Hum. Ind.; Wom. Stu. Abst.

2843
JOURNAL OF NONVERBAL BEHAVIOR. v.4– , fall 1979– . New York, Human Sciences Press. Quarterly.
Continues: *Environmental Psychology and Nonverbal Behavior.*

2844
JOURNAL OF NORTHEAST ASIAN STUDIES. TUNG PEI YACHOU YEN CHIU. HOKUTŌ AIJA KENKYŪ. TONGBUK ASEIA YŎN'GU. v.1– , Mar. 1982– . Washington, D.C. Quarterly.
Issued by: Institute for Sino-Soviet Studies, George Washington University.
Indexed: His. Abst.; Int. Bibl. Eco.; Int. Bibl. Pol. Sc.; Int. Bibl. Soc.; Int. Bibl. Soc. Cul. Anth.; Int. Pol. Sc. Abst.; PAIS.

2845
JOURNAL OF ORGANIZATIONAL BEHAVIOR MANAGEMENT. v.1– , summer 1977– . New York, Haworth Press. Quarterly.
Each issue has also a distinctive title.

2846
JOURNAL OF ORIENTAL STUDIES. v.1– , Jan. 1954– . Hong Kong, Hong Kong University Press. Semi-annual.
Issued by: Centre for Asian Studies, University of Hong Kong. In Chinese or English.
Indexes: Vols. 1–5, 1954–60, with v.5–6.

2847
JOURNAL OF PACIFIC HISTORY. v.1– , 1966– . Canberra, Oxford University Press. Annual, 1966–67; quarterly (two double nos.)
Issued by: Australian National University. Occasionally in French.
Indexes: Vols. 1–16, 1966–81.
Indexed: Abst. Anth.; APAIS; His. Abst.; Int. Bibl. Soc. Cul. Anth.; SSCI.

2848
JOURNAL OF PALESTINE STUDIES. v.1– , autumn 1971– . Beirut. Quarterly.
Issued by: Institute of Palestine Studies, and Kuwait University. In English or French.
Indexed: ABC POL SCI; Bull. Anal. Pol. Ec. Soc.; Int. Bibl. Soc. Cul. Anth.; PAIS.

2849
JOURNAL OF PEACE RESEARCH. v.1– , 1964– . Oslo, Universitetsforlaget. Quarterly.
Edited by: International Peace Research Institute, Oslo. Published under the auspices of the International Peace Research Association, Groningen.
Indexed: ABC POL SCI; Curr. Cont. Soc. Beh. Sc.; His. Abst.; Ind. Per. Art. Law; Int. Bibl. Eco.; Int. Bibl. Soc.; Int. Pol. Sc. Abst.; PAIS; Peace Res. Abst. J.; Psych. Abst.; Soc. Abst.; SSCI; Wom. Stu. Abst.

2850
JOURNAL OF PEACE SCIENCE. v.1–4, autumn 1973–spring 1980. Philadelphia, Pa. Semi-annual.
Issued by: Peace Science Division, World Friends Research Center.
Continued by: *Conflict Management and Peace Science*.

2851
JOURNAL OF PEASANT STUDIES. v.1– , Oct. 1973– . London, Frank Cass. Quarterly.
Indexed: His. Abst.; Int. Bibl. Eco.; Int. Bibl. Pol. Sc.; Int. Bibl. Soc. Cul. Anth.; Int. Pol. Sc. Abst.; PAIS.

2852
JOURNAL OF PERSONALITY. v.1– , Sept. 1932– . Durham, N.C., Duke University Press. Quarterly.
Title varies: 1932–Mar./June 1945, *Character and Personality*.
Indexed: Bull. Sig. Soc. Eth.; Psych. Abst.; Soc. Abst.; Soc. Work. Res. Abst.; Wom. Stu. Abst.

2853
JOURNAL OF PERSONALITY. v.1– , Sept./Oct. 1973– . London, F. Cass. Quarterly.
Issued by: Centre of International Area Studies, University of London.
Indexed: Abst. Soc. Work.; Bull. Sig. Soc. Eth.; Int. Bibl. Soc.; Int. Bibl. Soc. Cul. Anth.; Int. Pol. Sc. Abst.; LLBA; Psych. Abst.; Wom. Stu. Abst.

2854
JOURNAL OF PERSONALITY AND SOCIAL PSYCHOLOGY. v.1– , Jan. 1965– . Washington, D.C. Monthly forming two volumes a year.
Issued by: American Psychological Association. Includes "Monograph Supplement".
Supersedes: *Journal of Abnormal and Social Psychology*.
Indexed: Abst. Soc. Work.; Bull. Anal. Pol. Ec. Soc.; Bull. Sig. Soc. Eth.; Ind. Per. Art. Law; Curr. Cont. Soc. Beh. Sc.; Int. Bibl. Eco.; Int. Bibl. Pol. Sc.; LLBA; PAIS; Psych. Abst.; Soc. Abst.; Soc. Work Res. Abst.; Sage Fam. Stu. Abst.; Soc. Abst.; Soc. Sc. Ind.; SSCI; Wom. Stu. Abst.

2855
JOURNAL OF PERSONALITY AND SOCIAL SYSTEMS. v.1–2, no.2/3, Apr. 1977–Sept. 1980. Washington, D.C. Irreg.
Issued by: A.K. Rice Institute. Other title: *JPSS Journal of Personality and Social Systems*.

JOURNAL OF PERSONNEL RESEARCH
See PERSONNEL JOURNAL

2856
JOURNAL OF POLICE SCIENCE AND ADMINISTRATION. v.1– , Jan. 1973– . Gaitherburg, Md. Quarterly.
Issued jointly by: International Association of Chiefs of Police, and Northwestern University School of Law. With: *Journal of Criminal Law & Criminology* supersedes: *Journal of Criminal Law, Criminology and Police Science*.
Indexed: Curr. Cont. Soc. Beh. Sc.; Ind. Per. Art. Law; PAIS; Psych. Abst.; Sage Urb. Stu. Abst.; Urb. Aff. Abst.

2857
JOURNAL OF POLICY ANALYSIS AND MANAGEMENT. v.1– , 1982– . New York, Wiley. Four no. a year.
Issued by: Association of Public Policy Analysis and Management. Formed by the merger of: *Policy Analysis*, and *Public Policy*.
Indexed: ABC POL SCI; Int. Pol. Sc. Abst.; PAIS; Sage Pub. Adm. Abst.; Sage Urb. Stu. Abst.; Soc. Work. Res. Abst.

2858
JOURNAL OF POLICY MODELLING. v.1– , Jan. 1979– . New York, North-Holland Pub. Co. Three no. a year.
Organ of: Society of Policy Modelling.
Indexed: Int. Bibl. Eco.; Int. Pol. Sc. Abst.

2859
JOURNAL OF POLITICAL AND MILITARY SOCIOLOGY. v.1– , spring 1973– . Dekalb, Ill., later New Brunswick, N.J., Transaction Periodicals Consortium. Two no. a year.
Issued by: Department of Sociology, Northern Illinois University. Other title: *JPMS. Journal of Political and Military Sociology*.
Indexed: ABC POL SCI; Bull. Anal. Pol. Ec. Soc.; His. Abst.; Int. Bibl. Pol. Sc.; Int. Pol. Sc. Abst.; PAIS; Sage Pub. Adm. Abst.; Soc. Abst.; Soc. Sc. Ind.; SSCI.

2860
THE JOURNAL OF POLITICAL ECONOMY. v.1– , Dec. 1892– . Chicago, Ill., University of Chicago Press. Quarterly, 1892–1905; monthly (except Aug. and Sept.), 1906–23; bimonthly.

Issued by: Department of Political Economy, University of Chicago, 1892–June 1911; University of Chicago in cooperation with the Western Economic Society, July 1911–July 1970. Issues are thematic.
Indexed: ABC POL SCI; Curr. Cont. Soc. Beh. Sc.; Bull. Anal. Pol. Ec. Soc.; His. Abst.; Ind. Per. Art. Law; Int. Bibl. Eco.; Int. Bibl. Pol. Sc.; Ind. Bibl. Soc.; Int. Lab. Doc.; J. Eco. Lit.; PAIS; Peace Res Abst. J.; Soc. Sc. Hum. Ind.; SSCI; Wom. Stu. Abst.

JOURNAL OF POLITICAL ECONOMY AND COMMERCIAL SCIENCE
See KOKUMIN KEIZAI ZASSHI

2861
JOURNAL OF POLITICAL SCIENCE. v.1– , winter 1978– . Lahore. Semi-annual.
Issued by: Department of Political Sciences, Government College.
Supersedes: *Journal of History and Political Science.*

JOURNAL OF POLITICAL SCIENCE
See CHONGCH'IHAK NONCH'ONG. CH'AGGANHO

JOURNAL OF POLITICAL SCIENCE
See POLITICAL SCIENCE (Wellington)

2862
THE JOURNAL OF POLITICS. v.1– , Feb. 1939– . Gainesville, Fla. Quarterly.
Issued by: Southern Political Science Association in cooperation with the University of Florida.
Supersedes: Southern Political Science Association. *Proceedings.*
Indexed: Curr. Cont. Soc. Beh. Sc.; ABC POL SCI; Bull. Anal. Pol. Ec. Soc.; Ind. Per. Art. Law; Int. Pol. Sc. Abst.; LLBA; PAIS; Soc. Sc. Hum. Ind.

2863
JOURNAL OF POPULATION. v.1–2, spring 1978–winter 1979. New York, Human Sciences Press. Quarterly.
Sponsored by: Division of Population and Environmental Pathology, American Psychological Association.
Continued by: *Population and Environment.*
Indexed: Curr. Cont. Soc. Beh. Sc.; Pop. Ind.; Soc. Abst.; Soc. Work. Abst.; SSCI.

JOURNAL OF POPULATION PROBLEMS
See JINKO MONDAI KENKYŪ

2864
JOURNAL OF POPULATION RESEARCH. v.1– , July/Dec. 1974– . New Delhi. Semi-annual.
Issued by: National Institute of Family Planning.

2865
JOURNAL OF POST KEYNESIAN ECONOMICS. v.1– , fall 1978– . Armonk, N.Y., M.E. Sharpe. Quarterly.
Indexed: Int. Bibl. Eco.

JOURNAL OF PROCEEDINGS OF THE AGRICULTURAL ECONOMICS SOCIETY
See JOURNAL OF AGRICULTURAL ECONOMICS

2866
THE JOURNAL OF PSYCHOANALYTIC ANTHROPOLOGY. v.3, no.3– , summer 1980– . New York. Quarterly.
Issued by: Association for Psychohistory.
Continues: *Journal of Psychological Anthropology* (v.1–3, no.2, winter 1978–spring 1980)
Indexed: Abst. Anth.; LLBA; Psych. Abst.; Soc. Abst.

2867
JOURNAL OF PSYCHOLOGICAL RESEARCH. v.1– , Jan. 1957– . Madras. Three no. a year.
Issued by: Madras Psychology Society, and the Department of Psychology, University of Madras.
Indexed: Psych. Abst.

2868
THE JOURNAL OF PSYCHOLOGY. v.1– , 1935/36– . Worcester, Mass. Quarterly.
Indexed: Psych. Abst.

2869
THE JOURNAL OF PUBLIC ADMINISTRATION. v.1–11, 1938–1949. Wellington. Two no. a year.
Issued by: The New Zealand Institute of Public Administration.
Continued by: *The New Zealand Journal of Public Administration.*

JOURNAL OF PUBLIC ADMINISTRATION
See MADJALAH ADMINISTRASI NEGARA

JOURNAL OF PUBLIC ADMINISTRATION
See THE NEW ZEALAND JOURNAL OF PUBLIC ADMINISTRATION

THE JOURNAL OF PUBLIC ADMINISTRATION
See PUBLIC ADMINISTRATION (London)

2870
JOURNAL OF PUBLIC AND INTERNATIONAL AFFAIRS. v.1– , spring 1979– . Pittsburgh, Pa. Semi-annual.
Issued by: Graduate School of Public and International Affairs, University of Pittsburgh. Issues are thematic.

2871
JOURNAL OF PUBLIC ECONOMICS. v.1– , Apr. 1972– . Amsterdam, North-Holland Pub. Co. Frequency varies, 1972–81; three no. a year.
Indexed: Bull. Anal. Pol. Ec. Soc.; Eco. Abst.; Int. Bibl. Eco.; J. Eco. Lit.; PAIS; Sage Urb. Stu. Abst.

2872
JOURNAL OF PUBLIC POLICY & MARKETING. JPP&M. v.2– , 1983– . Ann Arbor, Mich. Annual.
Issued by: Division of Research, Graduate School of Business Administration, University of Michigan.
Continues: *Journal of Marketing and Public Policy*.

JOURNAL OF PUBLIC UTILITY ECONOMICS
See KŌEKI JIGYŌ KENKYŪ

2873
JOURNAL OF QUANTITATIVE CRIMINOLOGY. v.1– , Mar. 1985– . New York, Plenum. Quarterly.

2874
JOURNAL OF QUANTITATIVE ECONOMICS. v.1– , Jan. 1985– . Delhi. Semi-annual.
Issued by: Indian Econometric Society.

JOURNAL OF RACE DEVELOPMENT
See THE JOURNAL OF INTERNATIONAL AFFAIRS

JOURNAL OF RACIAL AFFAIRS
See TYDSKRIF VIR RASSE-AANGELEENTHEDE

2875
JOURNAL OF REGIONAL POLICY. 1985– . Naples, Isveimer. Quarterly.
Issues for 1985 called also v.5. English edition of *Mezzogiorno d'Europa*.

2876
JOURNAL OF REGIONAL SCIENCE. v.1– , 1958– . Philadelphia, Pa. Quarterly.
Issued by: Regional Science Research Institute in cooperation with the Department of Regional Science, Wharton School, University of Pennsylvania.
Indexes: Vols. 1–8, 1958–68.
Indexed: Bull. Anal. Pol. Ec. Soc.; Curr. Cont. Soc. Beh. Sc.; Int. Per. Art. Law; Int. Bibl. Eco.; Int. Pol. Sc. Abst.; J. Eco. Lit.; PHRA; Sage Urb. Stu. Abst.; Soc. Abst.; SSCI; Urb. Aff. Abst.

2877
JOURNAL OF RELIGIOUS PSYCHOLOGY, INCLUDING ITS ANTHROPOLOGICAL AND SOCIOLOGICAL ASPECTS. v.1–7, May 1904–Dec. 1915. Worcester, Mass., Wilson. Three no. a year, 1904–11; quarterly.
Title varies: 1904–July 1911, *The American Journal of Religious Psychology and Education*.

2878
JOURNAL OF RESEARCH IN CRIME AND DELINQUENCY. v.1– , Jan. 1964– . New York, later Hackensack, N.J. Semi-annual.
Issued by: National Council on Crime and Delinquency, and the Center for Youth and Community Studies, Harvard University.
Indexed: Ind. Per. Art. Law; Soc. Abst.; Soc. Work Res. Abst.; Urb. Aff. Abst.

2879
JOURNAL OF RESEARCH IN PERSONALITY. v.7– , June 1973– . New York, Academic Press. Bimonthly.
Continues: *Journal of Experimental Research in Personality*.
Indexed: Int. Bibl. Soc.; LLBA; Peace Res. Abst. J.; Psych. Abst.

2880
JOURNAL OF RURAL COMMUNITY PSYCHOLOGY. v.1– , spring 1980– . Fresno, Calif.
Issued by: California School of Professional Psychology.
Indexed: Psych. Abst.

2881
JOURNAL OF RURAL DEVELOPMENT. 1– , Nov. 1978– . Seoul. Semi-annual.
Issued by: Korea Rural Economics Institute. In Korean. Tables of contents also in English.

2882
JOURNAL OF RURAL ECONOMICS AND DEVELOPMENT. v.9– , Mar. 1974– . Ibadan. Semi-annual.
Issued by: Department of Agricultural Economics, University of Ibadan.
Continues: *Bulletin of Rural Economics and Sociology*.

2883
JOURNAL OF SOCIAL AND BIOLOGICAL STRUCTURES. v.1– , Jan. 1978– . London, Academic Press. Quarterly.
Subtitle reads: "Studies in human social biology".
Indexed: Int. Bibl. Soc. Cul. Anth.; Psych. Abst.; SSCI.

JOURNAL OF SOCIAL AND POLITICAL IDEAS IN JAPAN
See JAPAN INTERPRETER

2884
JOURNAL OF SOCIAL AND POLITICAL STUDIES. v.2–5, spring 1977–winter 1980. Washington, D.C. Quarterly.

Issued by: Council on American Affairs.
With: *Journal of International Relations* (Boston) continues: *Journal of Social and Political Affairs* (v.1, 1976). Continued by: *The Journal of Social and Economic Studies.*
Indexed: Bull. Anal. Pol. Ec. Soc.; Int. Bibl. Eco.; Int. Bibl. Pol. Sc.; PAIS.

2885
JOURNAL OF SOCIAL DEVELOPMENT IN AFRICA. v.1– , 1986– . Harare. Semi-annual.
Issued by: Department of Sociology, University of Zimbabwe. Two no. a year.

JOURNAL OF SOCIAL FORCES
See SOCIAL FORCES

2886
JOURNAL OF SOCIAL HISTORY. v.1– , fall 1967– . Berkeley, Calif., later Pittsburgh, Pa., Carnegie-Mellon University Press. Quarterly.
Indexed: APAIS; Curr. Cont. Soc. Beh. Sc.; His. Abst.; Ind. Per. Art. Law; Soc. Abst.; Soc. Sc. Ind.; SSCI; Wom. Stu. Abst.

2887
JOURNAL OF SOCIAL HYGIENE. 1–10, Dec. 1914–Dec. 1954; n. ser. 1955– . New York. Quarterly, 1914–Oct. 1922; monthly (except July–Sept.), 1923–54; annual.
Issued by: American Social Hygiene Association. Supplements accompany some issues. Title varies: 1914–Oct. 1921, *Social Hygiene.*

2888
THE JOURNAL OF SOCIAL ISSUES. v.1– , Feb. 1945– . New York, Plenum. Quarterly.
Issued by: Society for the Psychological Study of Social Issues.
Indexed: ABC POL SCI; Abst. Anth.; Abst. Soc. Work; Bull. Anal. Pol. Ec. Soc.; Bull. Sig. Soc. Eth.; Curr. Cont. Soc. Beh. Sc.; His. Abst.; Int. Bibl. Pol. Sc.; Int. Bibl. Soc.; Int. Bibl. Eco.; Int. Lab. Doc.; Int. Pol. Sc. Abst.; Hum. Res. Abst.; LLBA; PAIS; Peace Res. Abst. J.; PHRA; Psych. Abst.; Sage Urb. Stu. Abst.; Soc. Abst.; SSCI; Urb. Aff. Abst.; Wom. Stu. Abst.

2889
JOURNAL OF SOCIAL PHILOSOPHY. v.1–7, Oct. 1935–July 1942. New York. Quarterly.
Subtitle reads: "A quarterly devoted to a philosophic synthesis of the social sciences".

2890
JOURNAL OF SOCIAL POLICY. v.1– , 1972– . Cambridge, Cambridge University Press. Quarterly.
Issued by: Social Administration Association.
Indexed: ABC POL SCI; Bull. Anal. Pol. Ec. Soc.; Int. Bibl. Eco.; Int. Bibl. Pol. Sc.; Int. Bibl. Soc.; Hum. Res. Abst.; PAIS; Sage Pub. Adm. Abst.; SSCI; Urb. Aff. Abst.

2891
JOURNAL OF SOCIAL, POLITICAL AND ECONOMIC STUDIES. v.6– , spring 1981– . Washington, D.C. Quarterly.
Issued by: Council for Social and Economic Studies in cooperation with the Contemporary Economics and Business Association at the George Mason University.
Continues: *Journal of Social and Political Studies.*
Indexed: ABC POL SCI; Int. Bibl. Eco.; Int. Pol. Sc. Abst.; LLBA; PAIS; SSCI.

THE JOURNAL OF SOCIAL PROBLEMS
See SHAKAI MONDAI KENKYŪ

2892
THE JOURNAL OF SOCIAL PSYCHOLOGY. v.1– , Feb. 1930– . Provincetown, Mass., Journal Press. Bimonthly, forming three volumes per year.
Summaries in French and German.
Indexed: Bull. Anal. Pol. Ec. Soc.; Bull. Sig. Soc. Eth.; Curr. Cont. Soc. Beh. Sc.; Soc. Sc. Ind.; Ind. Per. Art. Law; Int. Bibl. Pol. Sc.; Int. Bibl. Soc.; Psych. Abst.; Soc. Work Res. Abst.; SSCI; Wom. Stu. Abst.

2893
JOURNAL OF SOCIAL RESEARCH. v.1– , Sept. 1958– . Ranchi. Semi-annual.
Organ of: Council for Social and Cultural Research, Bihar, and Department of Anthropology, Ranchi University.
Indexed: Bull. Sig. Soc. Eth.

2894
JOURNAL OF SOCIAL SCIENCE. v.1–46, June 1869–Dec. 1909. New York.
Not published in 1908. Other titles: *Journal of Social Science containing Proceedings of the American Association*, and *Journal of Social Science containing the Transactions of the American Association.*
Superseded by: National Institute of Social Sciences. *Journal.*

2895
JOURNAL OF SOCIAL SCIENCE. v.1– , 1972– . Limbe. Annual.
Issued by: Social Science Group Board, Chancellor College, University of Malawi.

2896
JOURNAL OF SOCIAL SCIENCE. 1973– . Kuwait. Quarterly.
Issued by: Kuwait University College of Commerce and Economics.

JOURNAL OF SOCIAL SCIENCE
See SAHOE KWAHAK NONJIP (Seoul)

JOURNAL OF SOCIAL SCIENCE
See SAHOE KWAHAK YON'GU

JOURNAL OF SOCIAL SCIENCE
See SAHOE KWAHAK YŎN'GU (Ch'unch'on-si)

JOURNAL OF SOCIAL SCIENCE
See SHAKAI KAGAKU JANARU

THE JOURNAL OF SOCIAL SCIENCE
See SHAKAI KAGAKU RONSHU

JOURNAL OF SOCIAL SCIENCE
See SHE HUI K'O HSÜEH LUN TS'UNG

JOURNAL OF SOCIAL SCIENCE
See WARASAN SANGKHOSAT

JOURNAL OF SOCIAL SCIENCE CONTAINING PROCEEDINGS OF THE AMERICAN ASSOCIATION
See JOURNAL OF SOCIAL SCIENCE (New York)

JOURNAL OF SOCIAL SCIENCE CONTAINING THE TRANSACTIONS OF THE AMERICAN ASSOCIATION
See JOURNAL OF SOCIAL SCIENCE (New York)

2897
JOURNAL OF SOCIAL SCIENCES. v.1– , 1978– . Peshavar. Biennial.
Issued by: University of Peshavar.

JOURNAL OF SOCIAL SCIENCES
See MAJALLAT AL-'ULUM AL-IJTIMĀ'ĪYAH

2898
THE JOURNAL OF SOCIAL SCIENCES AND HUMANITIES. v.1– , 1977– . Shiraz. Semi-annual.
Issued by: College of Arts and Sciences, Pahlavi University. In English or Persian. Other title: *Majallah-'ulum't va insani.*

2899
THE JOURNAL OF SOCIAL STUDIES. v.1– , Jan. 1978– . Dacca. Quarterly.
Issued by: Centre for Social Studies, University of Dacca.

JOURNAL OF SOCIAL WORK
See SOCIAL CASEWORK

2900
JOURNAL OF SOCIETAL ISSUES. v.1– , 1965– . Melbourne. Semi-annual.
Issued by: Cairmillar Institute.
Indexed: APAIS; Soc. Abst.

2901
JOURNAL OF SOCIOLOGIC MEDICINE. v.1–20, no.3, Feb. 1891–June 1919. Easton, Pa.
Issued by: American Academy of Medicine. Title varies: v.1–5, *Bulletin of the Academy of Medicine.*

2902
JOURNAL OF SOCIOLOGICAL STUDIES. v.1– , Jan. 1982– . Jodhpur. Annual.
Issued by: Department of Sociology, University of Jodhpur.

JOURNAL OF SOCIOLOGY AND ANTHROPOLOGY
See WARSAWSANGHKHOMWITTHAYA-MANUTWITTHAYA

2903
JOURNAL OF SOCIOLOGY AND PSYCHOLOGY. v.1– , 1978– . Singapore.
Issued by: University of Singapore Sociology Society, and Nanyang University Sociology & Psychology Society. V.2, 1979, last examined.

2904
JOURNAL OF SOCIOLOGY AND SOCIAL WELFARE. v.1– , 1973– . West Hartford, Conn. Quarterly.
Issued by: Division of Sociology and Social Welfare, Society for the Study of Social Problems.
Indexed: Psych. Abst.; Soc. Abst.; Soc. Work. Res. Abst.

JOURNAL OF SOUTHEAST ASIA
See REVUE DU SUD-EST ASIATIQUE ET DE L'EXTRÊME-ORIENT

JOURNAL OF SOUTHEAST ASIA AND THE FAR EAST
See REVUE DU SUD-EST ASIATIQUE ET DE L'EXTRÊME-ORIENT

2905
JOURNAL [OF] SOUTHEAST ASIAN HISTORY. v.1–10, no.2, Mar. 1960–Sept. 1969. Singapore. Semi-annual.
Issued by: Department of History, University of Malaya in Singapore. Other title: *Journal, Southeast Asian History.*
Superseded by: *Journal of Southeast Asian Studies.*

2906
JOURNAL OF SOUTHEAST ASIAN STUDIES. v.1– , Mar. 1970– . Singapore, National University of Singapore Press. Semi-annual.
Issued by: Department of History, National University of Singapore.

Supersedes: *Journal [of] Southeast Asian History.*
Indexed: ABC POL SCI; Abst. Anth.; Bull. Anal. Pol. Ec. Soc.; Bull. Sig. Soc. Eth.; His. Abst.; Int. Bibl. Eco.; Int. Bibl. Pol. Sc.; Int. Bibl. Soc. Cul. Anth.; Int. Pol. Sc. Abst.; Soc. Sc. Hum. Ind.; Soc. Abst.

2907
JOURNAL OF SOUTHERN AFRICAN AFFAIRS. 1– , Oct. 1976– . Brunswick, Ohio, Kings Court Communications. Quarterly.
Issued by: Southern African Research Association, and Afro-American Studies, University of Maryland.
Indexed: Abst. Anth.; ABC POL SCI; Bull. Anal. Pol. Ec. Soc.; Int. Bibl. Eco.; Int. Bibl. Pol. Sc.; Int. Bibl. Soc. Cul. Anth.; Int. Pol. Sc. Abst.

2908
JOURNAL OF SOUTHERN AFRICAN STUDIES. v.1– , Oct. 1974– . Oxford, Oxford University Press. Semi-annual.
Indexed: ABC POL SCI; Bull. Anal. Pol. Ec. Soc.; Int. Bibl. Soc. Cul. Anth.; Int. Pol. Sc. Abst.; Soc. Abst.

2909
JOURNAL OF SPECIAL EDUCATION. v.1– , fall 1966– . Philadelphia, Pa. Quarterly.
Indexed: Psych. Abst.

2910
JOURNAL OF SPORT AND SOCIAL ISSUES. v.1– , 1976– . Las Vegas, ARENA. Semi-annual.
Issued by: ARENA, Institute for Sport Sociology and Sport Analysis.

2911
JOURNAL OF SPORT BEHAVIOR. 1978– . Mobile, Ala. Quarterly.
Sponsored by: United States Sports Academy, and later by the University of South Alabama. Summaries in English and French.
Indexed: Psych. Abst.

2912
THE JOURNAL OF STRATEGIC STUDIES. v.1– , May 1979– . London, F. Cass. Three no. a year.
Indexed: Bull. Anal. Pol. Ec. Soc.; Int. Pol. Sc. Abst.

JOURNAL OF STUDIES IN ECONOMICS AND ECONOMETRICS
See TYDSKRIF VIR STUDIES IN EKONOMIE ET EKONOMETRIE

JOURNAL OF THE ACADEMY OF MARKETING SCIENCE
See Academy of Marketing Science. JOURNAL

JOURNAL OF THE AMERICAN ASIATIC ASSOCIATION
See ASIA AND THE AMERICAS

JOURNAL OF THE AMERICAN INSTITUTE OF PLANNERS
See American Institute of Planners. JOURNAL

JOURNAL OF THE AMERICAN PLANNING ASSOCIATION
See American Planning Association. JOURNAL

JOURNAL OF THE AMERICAN STATISTICAL ASSOCIATION
See JASA

JOURNAL OF THE ANTHROPOLOGICAL SOCIETY OF NIPPON
See JINRUIGAKU ZASSHI

JOURNAL OF THE ASIATIC SOCIETY OF BANGLADESH
See Asiatic Society of Bangladesh. JOURNAL

JOURNAL OF THE BEIJING NORMAL UNIVERSITY. SOCIAL SCIENCE EDITION
See PEI-CHING SHIH FAN TA HSÜEH PAO; SHE HUI K'O HSÜEH PAN

JOURNAL OF THE CENTRAL ASIAN SOCIETY
See Royal Society for Asian Affairs. JOURNAL

JOURNAL OF THE CENTRAL INSTITUTE FOR NATIONALITIES
See CHUNG YANG MIN TSU HSÜEH YUAN HSÜEH PAO

JOURNAL OF THE CEYLON BRANCH OF THE ROYAL ASIATIC SOCIETY
See Royal Asiatic Society. Ceylon Branch. JOURNAL

2913
JOURNAL OF THE ECONOMIC AND SOCIAL HISTORY OF THE ORIENT. JOURNAL DE L'HISTOIRE ÉCONOMIQUE ET SOCIALE DE L'ORIENT. v.1– , Aug. 1957– . Leiden, E.J. Brill. Three no. a year.
In English, French, or German. Title varies: Aug. 1957, *Journal of Economic and Social History of the Orient.*
Indexed: His. Abst.; Int. Bibl. Soc. Cul. Anth.

JOURNAL OF THE FOLKLORE INSTITUTE
See Indiana University. Folklore Institute. JOURNAL

2914
JOURNAL OF THE HISTORY OF IDEAS. v.1– , Jan. 1940– . New York, later Philadelphia, Pa. Quarterly.

Issued by: Finely Center, City University, New York, later Temple University, Philadelphia.
Indexed: Curr. Cont. Soc. Beh. Sc.; His. Abst.; Int. Bibl. Pol. Sc.; Int. Pol. Sc. Abst.; LLBA; Peace Res. Abst. J.; Soc. Sc. Hum. Ind.; SSCI.

2915
JOURNAL OF THE HISTORY OF SOCIOLOGY. v.1–5, no.1, fall 1978–1984. Brookline, Mass., J.N. Potter. Semi-annual.
Issued by: Department of Sociology, University of Massachusetts, Campus at Boston. Other title: *JHS*.
Indexed: Soc. Abst.

2916
JOURNAL OF THE HISTORY OF THE BEHAVIORAL SCIENCES. v.1– , Jan. 1965– . Brandon, Vt., Clinical Psychology Pub. Co. Quarterly.
Organ of: Department of Psychology, University of New Hampshire.
Indexed: Abst. Anth.; Bull. Sig. Soc. Eth.; His. Abst.; Ind. Per. Art. Law; Int. Bibl. Soc. Cul. Anth.; Psych. Abst.

JOURNAL OF THE HONG KONG BRANCH OF THE ROYAL ASIATIC SOCIETY
See Royal Asiatic Society. Hong Kong Branch. JOURNAL

JOURNAL OF THE INSTITUTE FOR CROSS-CULTURAL STUDIES
See TONSO MUNKHWA

JOURNAL OF THE INSTITUTE OF PUBLIC ADMINISTRATION OF CANADA
See CANADIAN PUBLIC ADMINISTRATION

JOURNAL OF THE INTERAMERICAN PLANNING SOCIETY
See Interamerican Planning Society. REVISTA

JOURNAL OF THE MALAYAN BRANCH OF THE ROYAL ASIATIC SOCIETY OF GREAT BRITAIN AND IRELAND
See Royal Asiatic Society of Great Britain and Ireland. Malayan Branch. JOURNAL

JOURNAL OF THE MALAYSIAN BRANCH OF THE ROYAL ASIATIC SOCIETY OF GREAT BRITAIN AND IRELAND
See Royal Asiatic Society of Great Britain and Ireland. Malayan Branch. JOURNAL

JOURNAL OF THE NATIONAL INSTITUTE FOR PERSONNEL RESEARCH
See PSYCHOLOGIA AFRICANA

2917: not used

Indexes: Vols. 1–16, 1966–81.
Indexed: Abst. Anth.; APAIS; His. Abst.; Int. Bibl. Soc. Cul. Anth.

2918
JOURNAL OF THE PARLIAMENTS OF THE COMMONWEALTH. v.1–46, Jan. 1920–July 1965. London.
Issued by: United Kingdom Branch, Commonwealth Parliamentary Association (called 1920–48, Empire Parliamentary Association). Title varies: 1920–48, *Journal of the Parliaments of the Empire*.
Continued by: *The Parliamentarian*.

JOURNAL OF THE PARLIAMENTS OF THE EMPIRE
See JOURNAL OF THE PARLIAMENTS OF THE COMMONWEALTH

JOURNAL OF THE POLYNESIAN SOCIETY CONTAINING THE TRANSACTIONS AND PROCEEDINGS OF THE SOCIETY
See Polynesian Society. JOURNAL

THE JOURNAL OF THE POPULATION ASSOCIATION OF KOREA
See HAN'GUK IN'GU HAKKOE CHI

THE JOURNAL OF THE RESEARCH CENTRE
See MAJALLAT MARKAZ AL-BUḤŪTH

JOURNAL OF THE ROYAL AFRICAN SOCIETY
See AFRICAN AFFAIRS

JOURNAL OF THE ROYAL INSTITUTE OF INTERNATIONAL AFFAIRS
See Royal Institute of International Affairs. JOURNAL

JOURNAL OF THE ROYAL SOCIETY FOR ASIAN AFFAIRS
See Royal Society for Asian Affairs. JOURNAL

JOURNAL OF THE ROYAL TOWN PLANNING INSTITUTE
See Royal Town Planning Institute. JOURNAL

JOURNAL OF THE SOCIAL SCIENCE
See SAHOE KWAHAK NONCH'ONG

JOURNAL OF THE SOCIAL SCIENCES
See MAJALLAT AL-'ULUM AL-IJTIMĀ'IYAH

JOURNAL OF THE SOCIAL SCIENCES
See SĀMĀJAKA WIGIĀNA PATTARA

JOURNAL OF THE SOCIETY OF LEGISLATION
See JOURNAL OF COMPARATIVE LEGISLATION AND INTERNATIONAL LAW

JOURNAL OF THE SOCIETY OF STATE GOVERNMENTS
See Society for the Study of State Governments. JOURNAL

JOURNAL OF SOUTHEAST ASIA AND THE FAR EAST
See REVUE DU SUD-EST ASIATIQUE ET DE L'EXTRÊME-ORIENT

2919
JOURNAL OF THE STATISTICAL AND SOCIAL INQUIRY OF IRELAND. 1– , 1861– . Dublin. Irreg.
Issued by: Central Statistical Office, and Statistical and Social Inquiry of Ireland.

JOURNAL OF THE STRAITS BRANCH OF THE ROYAL ASIATIC SOCIETY OF GREAT BRITAIN AND IRELAND
See Royal Asiatic Society of Great Britain and Ireland. Straits Branch. JOURNAL

2920
JOURNAL OF THE THEORY OF SOCIAL BEHAVIOR. v.1– , Apr. 1971– . Oxford, B. Blackwell. Semi-annual, 1971–77; three no. a year.
Indexed: LLBA.

JOURNAL OF THE TIBET SOCIETY
See Tibet Society. JOURNAL

JOURNAL OF THE UNIVERSITY OF TEXAS LAW SOCIETY
See THE TEXAS INTERNATIONAL LAW FORUM

2921
THE JOURNAL OF TRANSPERSONAL PSYCHOLOGY. spring 1969– . Palo Alto, Calif. Semi-annual.
Indexed: Psych. Abst.

2922
THE JOURNAL OF URBAN ANALYSIS. v.1–7, no.1, Oct. 1972–Feb. 1983. London, New York, Gordon and Breach. Semi-annual.
Continued by: *Journal of Urban Analysis and Public Management.*
Indexed: Soc. Abst.

2923
THE JOURNAL OF URBAN ANALYSIS AND PUBLIC MANAGEMENT. v.8– , June 1984– . New York, published for Gordon and Breach by OPA Ltd. Two no. a year.
Continues: *Journal of Urban Analysis.*

A JOURNAL OF URBAN AND RURAL PLANNING THOUGHT
See URBAN AND RURAL PLANNING THOUGHT

2924
JOURNAL OF URBAN ECONOMICS. v.1– , Jan. 1974– . New York, Academic Press. Quarterly, 1974–79; bimonthly.
Indexed: PAIS; SSCI; Urb. Aff. Abst.

2925
JOURNAL OF URBAN HISTORY. v.1– , Nov. 1974– . Beverly Hills, Calif., Sage Publications. Quarterly.
Indexed: ABC POL SCI; Sage Urb. Stu. Abst.

2926
JOURNAL OF WORLD HISTORY. v.1– , July 1953– . Neuchâtel, Éditions de la Baconnière. Semi-annual.
Issued by: Commission Internationale pour une Histoire du Développement Scientifique et Culturel de l'Humanité. In English or French. Other titles: *Cahiers d'Histoire Mondiale*, *Cuadernos de Historia Mundial.*
Indexed: Soc. Sc. Hum. Ind.

2927
JOURNAL OF YOUTH AND ADOLESCENCE. v.1– , June 1972– . New York, Plenum. Quarterly.
Indexed: Psych. Abst.; Soc. Abst.; SSCI.

2928
JOURNAL OFFICIEL DES COMMUNAUTÉS EUROPÉENNES. v.1–10 (no.1–321), Apr. 1958–Dec. 1967. Luxembourg. Semiweekly.
Issued by: Office Central de Vente des Publications des Communautés Européennes. In Dutch, French, German and Italian. Official organ of: European Atomic Energy Committee, European Coal and Steel Community, European Parliament, and the Courts of Justice of the European Communities.
Continues: *Journal Officiel de la Communauté du Charbon et de l'Acier*. Continued by: *Journal Officiel des Communautés Européennes*; *Communications et Informations*, and *Journal Officiel des Communautés Européennes. Législation.*

2929
JOURNAL OFFICIEL DES COMMUNAUTÉS EUROPÉENNES. COMMUNICATIONS ET INFORMATIONS. v.11, no.10, Jan. 11, 1968– . Luxembourg, Office des Publications, Office Central de Vente.
In French. Published also in other official languages of the European Communities. Includes supplements.
Continues, in part: *Journal Officiel des Communautés Européennes.*

2930
JOURNAL OFFICIEL DES COMMUNAUTÉS EUROPÉENNES. LÉGISLATION. v.11, no.51– , Jan. 3, 1968– . Luxembourg, Office des Publications, Office Central de Vente.
In French. Published also in other languages of the European Communities. Includes supplements.
Continues, in part: *Journal Officiel des Communautés Européennes.*

JOURNAL RUSSE D'ANTHROPOLOGIE
See RUSSKIĬ ANTROPOLOGICHESKIĬ ZHURNAL

JOURNAL. SOCIAL SCIENCES
See Karnatak University. JOURNAL. SOCIAL SCIENCES

JOURNAL, SOUTHEAST ASIAN HISTORY
See JOURNAL [OF] SOUTHEAST ASIAN HISTORY

THE JOURNALISM BULLETIN
See JOURNALISM QUARTERLY

2931
JOURNALISM QUARTERLY. v.1– , Mar. 1924– . Iowa City, Iowa.
Issued by: American Association of Teachers of Journalism, American Association of Schools and Departments of Journalism (called earlier Association of American Schools and Departments of Journalism), in cooperation with the American Society of Journalism School Administrators, and Association for Education in Journalism and Mass Communication. Subtitle reads: "Devoted to journalism and mass communication". Title varies: v.1–4, no.3, 1924–Nov. 1927, *The Journalism Bulletin.*
Supersedes: American Association of Teachers of Journalism. *The Monthly News Letter.*
Indexes: Vols. 1–40, 1924–63 (includes index to supplements), 1v.
Indexed: Bull. Sig. Soc. Eth.; His. Abst.; Int. Bibl. Soc. Cul. Anth.; Int. Pol. Sc. Abst.; PAIS; Peace Res. Abst. J.; Wom. Stu. Abst.

JOURNÉES
See Société de Législation Comparée. JOURNÉES

JUGOSLOVENSKI PREGLED
See YUGOSLAV SURVEY

2932
Jugoslavenska Akademija Znanosti i Umjetnosti. Historijski Institut, Dubrovnik. ANALI. v.1–12, 1952–1975. Dubrovnik. Annual.
In Serbo-Croatian; summaries in English and French.
Continued by: Jugoslavenska Akademija Znanosti i Umjetnosti. Historijski Otdel. *Anali.*

2933
Jugoslavenska Akademija Znanosti i Umjetnosti. Centar za Znanstvěni Rad u Dubrovniku. Historijski Otdel. ANALI. no.13/14–15/16, 1976–1978. Dubrovnik. Annual.
In Serbo-Croatian; summaries in English, French or Italian.
Continues: Jugoslavenska Akademija Znanosti i Umjetnosti. Historijski Institut. *Anali.*

2934
Jugoslavenska Banka za Medunarodnu Ekonomensku Saradnju. ANNUAL REPORT. Beograd. Annual.
In English.

2935
JUGOSLAVENSKA REVIJA ZA MEDUNARODNO PRAVO. 1– , 1954– . Beograd. Quarterly.
Organ of: Jugoslovensko Udruzenje za Medunarodno Pravo. In English, French, or Serbo-Croatian. Papers in Serbo-Croatian have summaries in English or French. Each volume includes section "Jugoslavenska Bibliografija iz Medunarodnog Prava".
Indexed: Ind. For. Leg. Per.; Int. Bibl. Soc. Cul. Anth.

2936
JUGOSLAVIJA SSSR. 1– , Nov. 1945– . Beograd. Monthly.
Issued by: Drustvo za Kulturnu Saradnju Jugoslavije sa SSSR. In Serbo-Croatian.

2937
JURNAL ANTROPOLOGI DAN SOSIOLOGI. 1– , 197?– . Selongar. Irreg.
Issued by: Universite Kebangsaan. In Malay.

JURNAL EKONOMI PERTANIAN MALAYSIA
See THE MALAYSIAN JOURNAL OF AGRICULTURAL ECONOMICS

2938
JURNAL PENDIDEKAN. JOURNAL OF EDUCATIONAL RESEARCH. v.1– , Aug. 1970– . Kuala Lumpur. Annual.
Issued by: Fakulti Pendidekan Universiti Malaya. Chiefly in English.

2939
JURNAL PSIKOLOGI INDONESIA. 1– , Mar. 1980– . Jakarta Timur, Penerbit Journal. Three no. a year.
Issued by: Fakultas Psikologi, Universitas Indonesia. In Indonesian.

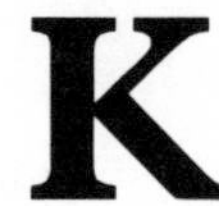

2940
Kagoshima Daigaku. Kyōyōbu. KAGOSHIMA DAIGAKU SHAKAI KAHAKU ZASSHI. 1– , 1978– . Kagoshima. Nine no. a year.
In Japanese. Other title: *Social Science Review of Kagoshima University*.

KAGOSHIMA DAIGAKU SHAKAI KAGAKU ZASSHI
See Kagoshima Daigaku. Kyōyōbu. KAGOSHIMA DAIGAKU SHAKAI KAGAKU ZASSHI

2941
KAJIAN EKONOMI MALAYSIA. MALAYSIAN ECONOMIC STUDIES. v.1– , June 1964– . Kuala Lumpur. Semi-annual.
Issued by: Economic Association of Malaysia in cooperation with the Department of Economics, University of Malaysia. In English.

2942
KALYANI. v.1, no.1/2– , Oct. 1982– . Kalyani. Semi-annual.
Issued by: University of Kelaniya. Subtitle reads: "Journal of humanities and social sciences".

2943
DER KAMPF. v.1–27, no.2, Oct. 1907–Feb. 1934; n. ser. v.1–5, no.9, May 1934–Sept. 1938. Wien, Volksbuchhandlung.
In German. Subtitle reads: "Sozialistische Kampf".
Superseded by: *Sozialistische Kampf*.

2944
KANO STUDIES. DIRĂSĀT KĀNŪ. v.1, no.1–4, 1965–1968; n. ser. v.1– , 1973– . Kano, Oxford University Press. Annual.
Organ of: Faculty of Arts and Islamic Studies, Abdulani Bayero College. In Arabic or English. Subtitle reads: "A journal of Saharan and Sudanic Research". Title varies: 1965, *Confluence*.

2945
KANSAI UNIVERSITY REVIEW OF LAW AND POLITICS. no.1– , Mar. 1980– . Osaka. Annual.
Issued by: Faculty of Law, Kansai University. In English, German, or Italian.
Indexed: Int. Bibl. Pol. Sc.

2946
KANSANTALOUDELLINEN AIKAKAUSKIRJA. FINNISH ECONOMIC JOURNAL. 1905– . Helsinki. Four no. a year.
Issued by: Finnish Economic Association. In Finnish; summaries in English or German. Vols. 29–39 numbered also v.1–15.

2947
Karnatak University. JOURNAL. SOCIAL SCIENCES. 1– , 1965– . Dhrwar. Annual.

2948
THE KASETSART JOURNAL. SOCIAL SCIENCES. WITTHAYSAN KASSETSART. v.1, no.1/2– , 1980– . Bangkok.
Issued by: Kasetsart University. In English or Thai; summaries in English.

2949
KATUNOB. v.1– , 1960– . Magnolia, Ark. Quarterly (irreg.)
Subtitle reads: "A newsletter–bulletin on Mesoamerican anthropology".
Indexed: Int. Bibl. Soc. Cul. Anth.

KAVKASIIS ET'NOGRAP'ULI KREBULI
See Akademii͡a Nauk SSSR. Institut Etnografii. TRUDY. KAVKAZSKIĬ ETNOGRAFICHESKIĬ SBORNIK

KAVKAZSKIĬ ETNOGRAFICHESKIĬ SBORNIK
See Akademii͡a Nauk SSSR. Institut Etnografii. TRUDY. KAVKAZSKIĬ ETNOGRAFICHESKIĬ SBORNIK

KEIŌ ECONOMIC STUDIES
See Keiō Gijuku Daigaku, Tokyo. Keiō Economic Society. KEIŌ ECONOMIC STUDIES

2950: not used

2951
Keiō Gijuku Daigaku, Tokyo. Keio Economic Society. KEIŌ ECONOMIC STUDIES. v.1– , 1963– . Tokyo. Annual, 1963–71; semi-annual.
In English.
Indexed: SSCI.

2952
KEIZAI BUNSEKI FUROKU. 1– , June 1968– . Tokyo, Keizai Kokakucho Kensai Kenkyūjo. Quarterly.
In Japanese. Other title: *Quarterly Supplement to Economic Analysis*.

2953
KEIZAI HYŌRON. 1– , 1946–1951; 1– , 1952– . Tokyo, Nihon Hyoron-sho. Monthly.
In Japanese. Publication suspended from July 1951 and resumed with Jan. 1952. New volume numbering began in 1952.

2954
KEIZAI KAGAKU. 1– , Feb. 1951– . Nagoya. Quarterly.
Issued by: Nagoya Daigaku. Keizaigakubu. In Japanese. Other title: *The Economic Science.*

KEIZAI KEIEI GAKKAI
See Kyoto Sangyo Daigaku. KEIZAI KEIEI GAKKAI

2955
KEIZAI KENKYŪ. v.1– , Jan. 1951– . Tokyo. Quarterly.
Issued by: Hitotsubashi Daigaku. In Japanese; summaries in English. Tables of contents also in English. Other title: *Economic Review.*
Indexed: His. Abst.

2956
KEIZAI RIRON. 1– , 1926– . Wakayama.
Issued by: Wakayama Daigaku Keizai Gakkai. In Japanese; summaries in English. Other title: *The Wakayama Economic Review.*

2957
KEIZAIGAKU KENKYŪ. 1983– . Hiroshima. Annual.
Issued by: Hiroshima Daigaku Daigakuin Keizaigaku Kenkyūka. In Japanese. Other title: *Economic Studies.*

KENKYŪ HOKŌKU SHAKAIGAKU
See Aichi Kyoiku Daigaku. KENKYŪ HOKŌKU SHAKAIGAKU

2958
KEY CONCEPTS IN INTERNATIONAL RELATIONS. 1– , 1983– . London, Boston, Mass., Allen & Unwin. Irreg.
Monograph series.

2959
KEY TO ECONOMIC SCIENCE. v.23–24, Jan. 1, 1976–Dec. 15, 1977. The Hague, M. Nijhoff. Semimonthly.
Issued by: Economische Voorlichtingdienst, Ministerie van Economische Zaken. In Dutch, English, French, or German.
Continues: *Economic Abstracts.* Continued by: *Key to Economic Science and Managerial Sciences.*

2960
KEY TO ECONOMIC SCIENCE AND MANAGERIAL SCIENCES. v.29, no.22– , Nov. 15, 1982– . The Hague, M. Nijhoff. Semimonthly.
Compiled by: Economische Voorlichtingdienst, Ministerie van Economische Zaken.
Continues: *Key to Economic Science.*

2961
KEY TO TURKISH SCIENCE: APPLIED ECONOMICS. v.1–2, Apr. 1969–1970. Ankara, Yenisehir, Turdok. Two no. a year.
Issued by: TBTAK Scientific and Technical Research Council of Turkey. Continued by: *Key to the Turkish Science: Industrial Management* (formerly *Applied Economics*)

2962
THE KIBBUTZ. 1– , 1973– . Tel-Aviv. Annual.
Issued by: Federation of Kibbutz Movements. In English or Hebrew.
Indexed: Soc. Abst.

2963
KIKAN RIRON-KEIZAIGAKU. 1– , 1950– . Tōkyō, Tōkyō Keizai Shimpō-sha. Three no. a year.
Issued by: Riron Keiryo Keizaigakkai Shikanshi. In English or Japanese. Other titles: *The Economic Studies Quarterly; The Journal of Japanese Association of Theoretical Economics.*

2964
KLEIO, v.1– , 1969– . Pretoria. Two or three no. a year.
Issued by: Departement Geschiedenis, Universiteit van Suid-Afrika. In Afrikaans or English.

2965
KNOWLEDGE AND SOCIETY. v.3– , 1981– . Greenwich, Conn., JAI Press. Annual.
Subtitle reads: "Studies in the sociology of culture past and present".
Continues: *Research in Sociology of Knowledge, Sciences and Art* (v.1–2, 1978–79)

2966
KNOWLEDGE, CREATION, DIFFUSION, UTILIZATION. 1– , Sept. 1979– . Beverly Hills, Calif., Sage Publications. Quarterly.

2967
KOBE UNIVERSITY ECONOMIC REVIEW. v.1– , 1955– . Kobe. Annual.
Issued by: Faculty of Economics, Kobe University. In English.
Indexed: Bull. Anal. Pol. Ec. Soc.; Int. Bibl. Eco.; Int. Bibl. Soc. Cul. Abst.

2968
KŌEKI JIGYŌ KENKYŪ. 1– , 1949– . Tōkyō. Quarterly.
Issued by: Kōeki Jigyō Kenkyū. In Japanese. Other title: *Journal of Public Utility Economics.*

KÖLNER VIERTELJAHRESHEFTE FÜR SOZIALWISSENSCHAFTEN
See KÖLNER VIERTELJAHRESHEFTE FÜR SOZIOLOGIE

2969
KÖLNER VIERTELJAHRESHEFTE FÜR SOZIOLOGIE. v.1–12, 1921–1934. München. Quarterly.
Issued by: Forschungsinstitut für Sozialwissenschaften in Köln. In German. Includes supplement, "Ergänzungshefte. Beiträge zur Beziehungslehre". Title varies: v.1–2, 1921–22, *Kölner Zeitschrift für Soziologie und Sozialpsychologie*. Vol.3–12 called also "Neue Folge" of *Kölner Vierteljahreshefte für Sozialwissenschaften*.

2970
KÖLNER VORTRÄGE UND ABHANDLUNGEN ZUR SOZIAL- UND WIRTSCHAFTSGESCHICHTE. no.27– , 1977– . Köln. Irreg.
Issued by: Forschungsinstitut für Sozial- und Wirtschaftsgeschichte, Universität zu Köln. In German.
Continues: *Kölner Vorträge zur Sozial- und Wirtschaftsgeschichte* (no.1–26, 1969–76). Each number has also a distinctive title.

KÖLNER ZEITSCHRIFT FÜR SOZIOLOGIE UND SOZIALPSYCHOLOGIE
See KÖLNER VIERTELJAHRESHEFTE FÜR SOZIOLOGIE

KÖLNER ZEITSCHRIFT FÜR SOZIOLOGIE
See KÖLNER ZEITSCHRIFT FÜR SOZIOLOGIE UND SOZIALPSYCHOLOGIE

2971
KÖLNER ZEITSCHRIFT FÜR SOZIOLOGIE UND SOZIALPSYCHOLOGIE. 1– , 1948/49– . Köln, Westdeutscher Verlag. Quarterly.
Issued by: Forschungsinstitut für Sozial- und Verwaltungswissenschaften in Köln. In German. Vol. 1 also numbered 13 in continuation of *Kölner Viertelsjahreshefte für Soziologie*. Title varies: 1948/49–1953/54, *Kölner Zeitschrift für Soziologie*.
Indexed: Bull. Anal. Pol. Ec. Soc.; Bull. Sig. Soc. Eth.; Int. Bibl. Soc. Cul. Anth.; Int. Pol. Sc. Abst.; LLBA; PAISFL; Peace Res. Abst. J.; Psych. Abst.; Soc. Abst.; SSCI.

2972
KOKKA-GAKKAI ZASSHI. v.1– , 1887– . Tōkyō, Bunkyoku. Nine no. a year.
Issued by: Kokka Gakkai. In Japanese. Other title: *The Journal of the Association of Political and Social Sciences*. Not published Sept. 1944–Dec. 1945.
Indexed: Int. Bibl. Soc. Cul. Anth.

2973
KOKUMIN KEIZAI ZASSHI. v.1– , 1896– . Tōkyō. Monthly.
Issued by: Kōbe Daigaku Keizai Gakkai. In Japanese. Other title: *Journal of Political Economy and Commercial Science*.

2974
KOKURITSU KAGAKU HABUKUTSUKAN. BULLETIN OF THE NATIONAL SCIENCE MUSEUM. SERIES D. ANTHROPOLOGY. v.1– , 1975– . Tōkyō. Annual.
In Japanese or English. Other title: *Kokuritsu Kagaku Habutsukan Kenkyū Hokōku. D-rui: Jinruigaku*.

KOKURITSU KAGAKU HABUTSUKAN KENKYU HOKOKU. D-RUI: JINRUIGAKU
See KOKURITSU KAGAKU HABUTSUKAN

KOLONIAL DEUTSCHE. WISSENSCHAFTLICHE BEIHEFTE
See KOLONIALE RUNDSCHAU

2975
KOLONIALE MONATSBLÄTTER. v.1–16, July 1899–Aug. 1914. Berlin. Twenty no. a year, 1899–1903; monthly.
Issued by: Deutsche Kolonialgesellschaft. In German. Supplements accompany some issues. Title varies: 1899–Dec. 1903, *Beiträge zur Kolonialpolitik und Kolonialwirtschaft*; 1904–Dec. 1912, *Zeitschrift für Kolonialpolitik, Kolonialrecht und Kolonialwirtschaft*.

2976
KOLONIALE RUNDSCHAU. v.1–34, no.2, 1909–Mar. 1943. Berlin.
In German. Numbering begins with v.25, 1933. Title varies: 1923–25, *Kolonial Deutsche. Wissenschaftliche Beihefte*.

2977
KOLONIALE STUDIEN. v.1– , Oct. 1916– . Batavia, 's-Gravenhage, M. Nijhoff. Bimonthly.
Issued by: Vereeniging voor Studie van Koloniaalmaatschappelijke Vraagstuken, Afdeling Sociale Economie van het Koninklijk Bataviaasch Genootschap van Kunsten en Wetenschappen. In Dutch. Supplements accompany some issues, 1936–.
Indexes: Vols. 1–20, 1916–36, with v.20.

2978
KOLONIALES JAHRBUCH. 1–11, 1888–1898. Berlin.
In German.
Superseded by: *Beiträge zur Kolonialpolitik und Kolonialwirtschaft*.

KOMMUNAL FINANZEN
See LOCAL FINANCE

KOMMUNALE RUNDSCHAU
See DER REICHSSTADTBUND

2979
KOMMUNALES JAHRBUCH. 1–7, 1908–1919; n. ser. v.1–3, 1927–1932. Jena.

Issued by: Forschungsinstitut für Sozialwissenschaften, Cologne Universität. In German. Publication suspended, 1915–18.

2980
KOMMUNISMUS UND KLASSENKAMPF. v.1– , 1973– . Frankfurt. Irreg.
Issued by: Zentrales Komitee, Kommunistischer Bund Westdeutschland. In German.
Indexed: Bull. Anal. Pol. Ec. Soc.

2981
KOMMUNIST. 1918– . Vil'nius. Monthly.
Issued by: (post-1944 period) TSentral'nyĭ Komitet Kommunisticheskoĭ Partii, Litovska SSR. In Lithuanian or Russian.
Indexed: Int. Bibl. Ec.

2982
KOMMUNIST. 1924– . Moskva, Izd-vo Pravda. Monthly.
Issued by: TSentral'nyĭ Komitet Kommunisticheskoĭ Partii SSSR. In Russian. Title varies: 1924–52, *Bol'shevik*. In Russian.
Indexed: His. Abst.; Int. Bibl. Pol. Sc.; Int. Bibl. Soc.; Int. Bibl. Soc. Cul. Anth.; Int. Bibl. Eco.; LLBA; Peace Res. Abst. J.

2983
KOMMUNIST. 1926– . Frunze, Izd-vo "Sovetnik Kyrgystan". Monthly.
Issued by: TSentral'nyĭ Komitet Kommunisticheskoĭ Partii Kirgizskoĭ SSR. In Russian.

KOMMUNIST
See LENINJAN UGLOV

KOMMUNIST
See NAŠA STVARDNOST

KOMMUNIST AZERBAĬDZHANA
See AZERBACHAN KOMMUNISTI

KOMMUNIST BELARUSSII
See KOMMUNIST BELORUSSII

2984
KOMMUNIST BELORUSSII. KOMMUNIST BELARUSSII. 1927– . Minsk, Izd-vo "Zvezda". Bimonthly.
Issued by: TSentral'nyĭ Komitet Kommunisticheskoĭ Partii Belorusskoĭ SSR. In White Russian or Russian. Title varies: 1927–52, *Bol'shevik Belarussii*.
Indexed: Int. Bibl. Soc. Cul. Anth.

2985
KOMMUNIST ESTONII. 1945– . Tallin. Monthly.
Issued by: TSentral'nyĭ Komitet Kommunisticheskoĭ Partii Estonii. In Estonian or Russian. Title varies: 1945–52, *Bol'shevik Estonii*.
Indexed: Int. Bibl. Soc. Cul. Anth.

KOMMUNIST GRUZII.
See SAKARTVELOS KOMMUNISTI

2986
KOMMUNIST MOLDAVII. 1956– . Kisenev. Monthly.
Issued by: TSentral'nyĭ Komitet Kommunisticheskoĭ Partii Moldavii. In Moldavian or Russian.
Indexed: Int. Bibl. Soc. Cul. Anth.

2987
KOMMUNIST SOVETSKOĬ LATVII. 1945– . Riga, Latviĭskoe Gazetno-Zhurnal'noe Izdatel'stvo. Monthly.
Issued by: Centrala Komiteja, Latvijas Komunistiska Partija (TSentral'nyĭ Komitet Kommunisticheskoĭ Partii Latviĭskoĭ SSR). In Latvian or Russian. Title varies: 1945–52, *Bol'shevik Sovetskoĭ Latvii*.
Indexed: Int. Bibl. Eco.; Int. Bibl. Soc. Cul. Anth.

2988
KOMMUNIST TADZHIKISTANA. KOMMUNISTE TOCHIKISTON. 1935– . Dushanbe. Monthly.
Issued by: TSentral'nyĭ Komitet Kommunisticheskoĭ Partii Tadzhikskoĭ SSR. In Tadzhik. Title varies: 1945–52, *Bol'shevik Tadzhikistana*.

KOMMUNIST TURKMENISTANA
See TURKMENISTAN KOMMUNISTI

2989
KOMMUNIST UKRAINY. 1925– . Kiev, Izd-vo "Sovetskaia Ukraina". Monthly.
Issued by: TSentral'nyĭ Komitet Kommunisticheskoĭ Partii Ukrainy. In Russian or Ukrainian. Edition in Ukrainian is also published. Title varies: 1925–52, *Bol'shevik Ukrainy*.

KOMMUNISTE TOCHIKISTON
See KOMMUNIST TADZHIKISTANA

2990
KOMMUNISTICHESKIĬ INTERNATSIONAL. v.1–24 [i.e. 25], no.5/6, May 1919–May/June 1943. Moskva. Frequency varies.
Organ of the Executive Committee of the Communist International. In Russian.

2991
KOMUNIST. 1946–1952. Beograd, Borba. Irreg., 1946–47; bimonthly.

Organ of: Centralni Komitet, Savez Komunista Jugoslavije. Title varies: 1946–51, *Partiska Izgradiia.*
Continued by: *Naša Stvarnost.*

Koninklijk Museum voor Miden-Afrika
See Musée Royal de l'Afrique Centrale

Koniklijke Akademie voor Overzeese Wetenschappen
See Académie Royale des Sciences d'Outre-Mer

Koninklije Nederlands Akademie van Wetenschappen
See Akademie van Wetenschappen, Amsterdam

2992
KONJONKTUR. CONJONCTURE. 35– , 1975– . Ankara, Ticaret Bakanligi Konjunktur ve Yayn Müdürülügü. Annual.
In French or Turkish.
Continues: *Turkey. Konjunktur ve Yayn Müdürülügü.*

2993
KONJUNKTUR UND KRISE. 1– , 1957– . Berlin, Akademie Verlag. Quarterly.
Issued by: Institut für Wirtschaftswissenschaften, Deutsche Akademie der Wissenschaften zu Berlin. In German.
Indexed: Int. Bibl. Eco.

KONJUNKTURLÄGET
See THE SWEDISH ECONOMY

2994
KONJUNKTURPOLITIK. 1– , Oct. 1954– . Berlin, Duncker & Humblot. Bimonthly.
In English or German; summaries in English. Subtitle reads: "Zeitschrift für angewandte Wirtschaftsforschung". Includes irregular supplement "Beihefte der Konjunkturpolitik" (1956–)
Indexed: Bull. Anal. Pol. Ec. Soc.; Int. Bibl. Eco.; PAIS; PAISFL.

2995
KOREA & WORLD AFFAIRS. v.1– , spring 1977– . Seoul. Quarterly.
Issued by: Research Center for Research and Unification.
Indexed: Bull. Anal. Pol. Ec. Soc.; Int. Bibl. Eco.; Int. Bibl. Pol. Sc.; Int. Pol. Sc. Abst.

2996
KOREA JOURNAL. v.1– , Sept. 1961– . Seoul. Quarterly.
Organ of: Korean National Commission for Unesco. French edition called *Revue de Corée* is also published.
Indexed: Bull. Anal. Pol. Ec. Soc.; Int. Bibl. Pol. Sc.; Int. Bibl. Soc. Cul. Anth.

KOREA UNIVERSITY JOURNAL. HUMANITIES AND SOCIAL SCIENCES
See KORYO TAEHAKKYO NONMUNJIP SAHOE KWAHAP'YON

2997
KOREAN AFFAIRS. v.1– , Feb./Mar. 1962– . Seoul. Bimonthly.
Issued by: Council on Korean Affairs.

THE KOREAN ECONOMIC JOURNAL
See KYONGJE NONJIP

2998
KOREAN JOURNAL OF COMPARATIVE LAW. v.1– , 1973– . Seoul. Annual.
Issued by: Korean Research Institute of Comparative Law.

2999
KOREAN JOURNAL OF INTERNATIONAL AFFAIRS. v.1– , 1963– . Seoul. Irreg.
Issued by: Korean Association of International Relations.

THE KOREAN JOURNAL OF INTERNATIONAL LAW
See Taehan Kukchepop Hakhoe Nonchong. TAEHAN KUKCHEPOP HAKKOE

3000
KOREAN JOURNAL OF INTERNATIONAL STUDIES. 1– , summer 1970– . Seoul. Quarterly (irreg.)
Issued by: Korean Association of International Studies.
Indexed: Bull. Anal. Pol. Ec. Soc.; Int. Bibl. Pol. Sc.; Int. Pol. Sc. Abst.

KOREAN PERIODICAL INDEX ON SOCIAL SCIENCE
See SAHOE KWAHAK NON MUN KISA SEGIN

3001
KOREAN SOCIAL SCIENCE JOURNAL. v.10– , 1983– . Seoul. Annual.
Issued by: Korean Social Science Council, and the Korean National Commission for Unesco.
Continues: *Social Science Journal.*

KOREAN SOCIAL SCIENCE REVIEW
See HANKUK SAHYOKUAHA-LONTJIB

3002
KOREANA QUARTERLY. v.1– , summer 1959– . Seoul. Four no. a year.
Issued by: Kukche Haksulwon.
Indexed: Int. Bibl. Soc. Cul. Anth.; Int. Pol. Sc. Abst.; Peace Res. Abst. J.

KORRESPONDENZBLATT
See Deutsche Gesellschaft für Anthropologie, Ethnologie und Urgeschichte. KORRESPONDENZBLATT

3003
KORYO TAEHAKKYO NONMUNJIP, INMUN SAHOE KWAHAKP'YON. Seoul, Tong Taehakkyo.
In English or Korean. Other title: *Korea University Journal. Humanities and Social Sciences.*

3004
KÖZGAZDASÁGI SZEMLE. v.1– , 1874– . Budapest.
In Hungarian.
Indexes: Vols. 1–25, 1874–1901.
Indexed: Bull. Anal. Pol. Ec. Soc.; Int. Bibl. Eco.

3005
KREDIT UND KAPITAL. v.1– , 1968– . Berlin, Duncker & Humblot. Quarterly.
In German, occasionally in French; summaries in English and French. Supplements, "Beihefte", accompany some numbers.
Indexed: Int. Bibl. Eco.; PAIS; PAISFL.

3006
KRITIKA SOVREMENNOĬ BURZHUAZNOĬ IDEOLOGII REFORMIZMA I REVIZIONISMA. 1977– . Moskva, 1979– . Annual.
Issued by: Mezhdunarodnai͡a Informat͡sionnai͡a Sistema po Obshchestvennym Naukam. In Russian.
Continues: *Kritika Sovremennykh Burzhuaznykh i Revizionistitskikh Teoriĭ* (1976, publ. 1978)

3007
KRITIKA SOVREMENNOĬ BURZHUAZNOĬ SOT͡SIOLOGII. no.1– , 1976– . Moskva.
Issued by: Institut Sot͡siologicheskikh Isslevodaniĭ, Akademii͡a Nauk SSSR, and Sovetskai͡a Assot͡siatsii͡a. In Russian. Processed.

3008
Kroeber Anthropological Society. PAPERS. no.1– , 1950– . Berkeley, Calif. Irreg.
Indexed: Abst. Anth.; His. Abst.; Int. Bibl. Soc. Cul. Anth.

KSU ECONOMIC AND BUSINESS ADMINISTRATION
See Kyoto Sangyo Daigaku. KEIZAI KEIEI GAKKAI

KSU ECONOMIC AND BUSINESS REVIEW
See Kyoto Sangyo Daigaku. KEIZAI KEIEI GAKKAI

3009
KUKCHE KYONGJE. 1– , 1965– . Seoul, Oemubu. Monthly.
In English or Korean. Other title: *International Economic Review.*
Continues: Korea (South). Oemubu. *Kukche Kyŏngje Wŏlbo.* (Issues for 1972 last available for examination)

3010
KUKCHE KYONGJE YŎN'GU. INTERNATIONAL ECONOMIC REVIEW. 1– , 1984– . Seoul. Sejong Taehak Kukche Kyongje Yon'guso.
In English or Korean.

3011
KUKCHE MUNHWA. 1– , 1964– . Seoul, Songgun'gwan Taehakkyo Pusol Kukche Munhwa Yŏn'guwon. Semi-annual; quarterly.
In English, French, German, or Korean. Other title: *Journal of International Studies.* (Issues for 1966 last available for examination)

AL-KULLĪYAH
See MIDDLE EAST FORUM

3012
KULTURA. 1– , 1968– . Beograd. Quarterly.
Issued by: Zavod za Proucivanje Kulturnog Razvitka. In Serbo-Croatian; summaries in English. Subtitle reads: "Casopis za teoriju i sociologiju kulture i kulturnu politiku".

3013
KULTÚRA ÉS KÖZÖSSÉG. 1– , 1980– . Budapést, Népmüvelési Intézet. Bimonthly.
In Hungarian. Tables of contents also in English and Russian.

3014
KULTURA I SPOŁECZEŃSTWO. v.1– , 1957– . Warszawa, Państwowe Wydawnictwo Naukowe. Quarterly.
Issued by: Wydział Nauk Społecznych, later by Komitet Nauk Społecznych, Polska Akademia Nauk. In Polish.
Indexed: Bull. Anal. Pol. Ec. Soc.; His. Abst.; Int. Bibl. Soc.; Int. Bibl. Soc. Cul. Anth.; Int. Lab. Soc. Soc. Abst.

KUL'TURA I ZHIZN'
See CULTURE AND LIFE

3015
KULTURGEOGRAFI. v.1–28, Feb. 1949–1981. København, I Kommission hos Gyldendalske Boghandel, later Århus, Munksgaard Forlag. Bimonthly.

Issued by: Kulturgeografisk Institut. In Danish; summaries in English.
Continued by: *Geografisk Magasin.*

3016
KULTURI JA KIELI. CULTURE AND LANGUAGE. 1– , 1982– . Tampere. Irreg.
Issued by: Tampereen Yliopiston Kansanperinteen. In English or Finnish.

3017
KULTUURPATRONEN. PATTERNS OF CULTURE. 1959–1981. Delft. Annual.
Issued by: Ethnografisch Museum. In Dutch; some summaries in English. Tables of contents also in English.

KUNG KUNG HSIN CHEN HSÜEH
See HONG KONG JOURNAL OF PUBLIC ADMINISTRATION

3018
THE KUWAIT ECONOMY. 1980–1984– . Kuwait. Annual.
Issued by: Central Bank of Kuwait.

3019
KWAHAK KWA SAHOE. IMPACT OF SCIENCE ON SOCIETY. 7– , 1984– . Seoul, T'ukpyolsi Yunesuk'o Han'guk Wiwenhoe. Quarterly.
Translation of: *Impact of Science on Society.*

3020
KWARTALNIK HISTORII KULTURY MATERIALNEJ. v.1– , July 1953– . Warszawa, Państwowe Wydawnictwo Naukowe. Quarterly.
Issued by: Instytut Historii Kultury Materialnej, Polska Akademia Nauk. In Polish; summaries in English, French and Russian. Includes supplement, "Ergon".
Indexed: Bull. Sig. Soc. Eth.; His. Abst.

3021
KWARTALNIK HISTORII RUCHU ZAWODOWEGO. 1– , Jan. 1962– . Warszawa, Wydawnictwo Związkowe CRZZ. Quarterly.
Issued by: Biuro Historyczne, Centralna Rada Związków Zawodowych. In Polish. Tables of contents in French, German, Polish and Russian. Title varies: 1962–66, *Biuletyn Biura Historycznego CRZZ.*

3022
KWARTALNIK HISTORYCZNY. v.1– , 1887– . Warszawa, Państwowe Wydawnictwo Naukowe. Bimonthly.
Issued by: Instytut Historii, Polska Akademia Nauk. In Polish; summaries in French and Russian. Publication suspended 1940–46.
Indexed: His. Abst.

3023
KWARTALNIK PEDAGOGICZNY. v.1– , 1956– . Warszawa, Państwowe Wydawnictwo Naukowe. Quarterly.
In Polish; summaries in English and Russian.

3024
KYBERNETES. v.1– , 1972– . London, New York, Gordon and Breach. Quarterly.

3025
KYKLOS. v.1– , 1947– . Berlin, Kyklos Verlag. Quarterly.
In English, French, or German.
Indexed: Bull. Anal. Pol. Ec. Soc.; Eco. Abst.; Int. Bibl. Eco.; Int. Bibl. Pol. Sc.; Int. Bibl. Soc.; J. Eco. Lit.; PAIS; Pop. Ind.; SSCI.

3026
KYOIKU SHAKAIGAKU KENKYŪ. Ser. 1–20, May 1951–Oct. 1965; ser. 22– , Oct. 1967– . Tōkyō. Annual.
Issued by: Nippon Kyoiku Shakai Gaku Kai. In Japanese. Other title: *(Japan) Journal of Educational Sociology.*

3027
KYONGJE NONJIP. THE KOREAN ECONOMIC JOURNAL. v.1– , 1962– . Seoul. Quarterly.
Issued by: Soul Taehakkyo Kyongje Yŏn'guso. In English or Korean.

3028
Kyotō Sangyo Daigaku. KEIZAI KEIEI GAKKAI. no.1– , 1974– . Kyoto. Annual.
Other titles: *Ksu Economic and Business Administration*; *Ksu Economic and Business Review.*

3029
KYOTO UNIVERSITY ECONOMIC REVIEW. v.1– , July 1926– . Kyoto. Semi-annual, 1926–July 1933; quarterly, 1934–46; six no. a year.
In English. Subtitle reads: "Memoirs of the Department of Economics in the Imperial University of Kyoto".
Indexes: Vols. 1–10, 1926–July 1933, with v.10.
Indexed: Bull. Anal. Pol. Ec. Soc.; Int. Bibl. Eco.; Int. Lab. Doc.; PAIS.

L

LGA LOCAL GOVERNMENT ADMINISTRATION
See LOCAL GOVERNMENT ADMINISTRATION

LLBA
See LANGUAGE AND LANGUAGE BEHAVIOR ABSTRACTS

3030
LABOR AGE. v.1–22, no.1, Feb. 1913–Feb./Mar. 1933. New York, Labor Publications Society. Four no. a year, 1913–May 1919; monthly (irreg.)
Title varies: 1913–May 1919, *The Intercollegiate Socialist*; Dec. 1919–May 1927, *The Socialist Review*.

LABOR HERALD
See POLITICAL AFFAIRS

3031
LABOR HISTORY. v.1– , 1960– . New York. Quarterly.
Issued by: Tamiment Institute.
Indexed: His. Abst.; Int. Bibl. Soc.; Int. Lab. Doc.; Soc. Sc. Hum. Ind.; Wom. Stu. Abst.

3032
LABOR RELATIONS YEARBOOK. 1965– . Washington, D.C. Annual.
Issued by: Bureau of National Affairs.

3033
Laboratoire d'Anthropologie Sociale. MÉMOIRES. 1– , 1970– . Paris, La Haye, Mouton.
In French. Subseries of: *Cahiers de l'Homme; Ethnologie, Géographie, Linguistique*. n. ser.

3034
LABORATORIO DI SOCIOLOGIA. 1– , 1979– . Roma, La Goliardica. Irreg.
In Italian.

3035
LABOUR AND SOCIETY. v.1– , July 1976– . Geneva. Quarterly.
Issued by: International Institute for Labour Studies. Published also in French: *Travail et Société*.
Supersedes: International Institute for Labour Studies. *Bulletin*.
Indexed: Hum. Res. Abst.; Int. Lab. Doc.; Sage Urb. Stu. Abst.; Soc. Abst.

3036
LABOUR, CAPITAL AND SOCIETY. TRAVAIL, CAPITAL ET SOCIÉTÉ. v.12– , Apr. 1979– . Montreal. Semi-annual.
Issued by: Centre for Developing Area Studies, McGill University. In English or French.
Continues: *Manpower and Unemployment Research*.
Indexed: Sage Urb. Stu. Abst.

LABOUR FORCE STATISTICS (YEARBOOK)
See Organisation for Economic Co-operation and Development. LABOUR FORCE STATISTICS (YEARBOOK)

3037
LABOUR HISTORY. v.1– , 1961– . Canberra. Semi-annual.
Issued by: Australian Society for the Study of Labour History. Title varies: 1961–62, *Bulletin of the Australian Society for the Study of Labour History*.
Indexed: APAIS; His. Abst.; Ind. Per. Art. Law; Int. Lab. Doc.; J. Eco. Lit.; Wom. Stu. Abst.

3038
Lan-chou ta hsüeh pao. She hui ta hsüeh pan. LANDZHOUDAXUE XUEBAO. 1– , 1972– . Lan-chou, Kai ta hsüeh. Quarterly.
In Chinese. Other title: *Lanzhou University. Social Sciences*.

3039
LAND ECONOMICS. v.1– , Jan. 1925– . Chicago, Evanston, Ill.; Madison, Wis., University of Wisconsin Press. Quarterly.
Issued by: Institute for Economic Research (1925–30, called Institute for Research for Land Economics and Public Utilities), 1925–34; Northwestern University, 1935–41. Title varies: 1925–47, *The Journal of Land & Public Utility Economics*.
Indexed: Bull. Anal. Pol. Ec. Soc.; Eco. Abst.; Ind. Per. Art. Law; Curr. Cont. Soc. Beh. Sc.; His. Abst.; Int. Bibl. Eco.; Int. Bibl. Soc.; J. Eco. Lit.; Pop. Ind.; Int. Bibl. Soc. Cul. Anth.; PAIS; Sage Urb. Stu. Abst.; SSCI; Urb. Aff. Abst.

3040
LAND REFORM, LAND SETTLEMENT AND COOPERATIVES. 1972– . Rome. Semi-annual.
Issued by: Food and Agriculture Organization of the United Nations.
Supersedes: *Informations on Land Reform, Land Settlement and Cooperatives* issued by the Rural Institutions and Services Division of FAO.

LANDZHOUDAXUE XUEBAO
See Lan-chou ta hsüeh pao. She hui ta hsüeh pan. LANDZHOUDAXUE XUEBAO

3041
LANGUAGE. v.1– , Mar. 1925– . Baltimore, Md. Quarterly.
Issued by: Linguistic Society of America.
Indexes: Vols. 1–5, 1925–29, with v.4–6; v.6–10, 1930–34, with v.10–11; v.11–15, 1935–39, with v.14–15; v.16–20, 1940–44, with v.20–21; and subsequently every five years.
Indexed: Abst. Anth.; Bull. Sig. Soc. Eth.; Int. Bibl. Soc. Cul. Anth.; Psych. Abst.

3042
LANGUAGE & COMMUNICATION. v.1– , 1981– . Oxford, Pergamon Press. Three no. a year.

LANGUAGE AND EDUCATION
See PRIMARY SOCIALIZATION

3043
LANGUAGE AND LANGUAGE BEHAVIOUR ABSTRACTS. v.1– , Jan. 1967– . New York, Appleton-Century-Crofts. Quarterly.
Issued by: Center for Research on Language and Language Behavior, University of Michigan. Other title: *LLBA Language and Language Behavior Abstracts*.

3044
LANGUAGE IN SOCIETY. v.1– , Apr. 1972– . Cambridge, New York, Cambridge University Press. Semi-annual, 1972–74; three no. a year.
Supplements accompany some numbers.
Indexes: Vols. 1–10, 1972–81.

3045
LANGUAGE IN SOCIETY. 1– , 1979– . Baltimore, Md., University Park Press; Oxford, B. Blackwell. Irreg.
Monograph series.
Indexed: Int. Bibl. Soc. Cul. Anth.

3046
LANGUAGE RESEARCH IN PROGRESS. v.1– , 1965– . Washington, D.C. Semi-annual.
Issued by: Center for Applied Linguistics.

3047
LANGUE. 1– , 1973– . Anvers-sur-Oise. Irreg.
Issued by: Centre d'Analyse et de Sociologie des Langages. In French.

LANZHOU UNIVERSITY. SOCIAL SCIENCES
See Lan-chou ta hsüeh pao. She hui ta hsüeh pan. LANDZHOU DAXUE XUEBAO

3048
LAPORAN. no.1– , 1962/63– . Djakarta. Irreg.
Issued by: Bito Penjlidicon Ekonomi dan Sosial, Universitas Sjah Kuala. In Indonesian; summaries in English.

3049
LATEINAMERIKA. v.1– , 1965– . Rostock, Verlag der Universität Rostock. Semi-annual.
Issued by: Lateinamerika Institut, Universität Rostock. In German or Spanish.

3050
LATIN AMERICA & CARIBBEAN REVIEW. 1985– . Saffron Walden, World of Information. Annual.
Continues: *Latin America & Caribbean.*

3051
LATIN AMERICA; STUDIES BY SOVIET SCHOLARS. 1981– . Moscow, "Social Science Today".
Issued by: Akademii͡a Nauk SSSR. In English.

3051a
THE LATIN-AMERICAN INTEGRATION PROCESS IN . . . 1977– . Buenos Aires. Annual.
Issued by: Inter-American Development Bank and Institute for Latin American Integration. English version of: *Proceso de Integración en América Latina*. Some vols. are for combined years.

3052
LATIN AMERICAN PERSPECTIVES. v.1– , spring 1974– . Riverside, Calif., later Beverly Hills, Calif., Sage Publications. Three no. a year, 1974; quarterly.
Indexed: Abst. Anth.; His. Abst.; Ind. Per. Art. Law; Int. Bibl. Eco.; Int. Bibl. Pol. Sc.; Int. Bibl. Soc.; Int. Bibl. Soc. Cul. Anth.; Int. Lab. Doc.; PAIS; Peace Res. Abst. J.; SSCI; Wom. Stu. Abst.

LATIN AMERICAN POPULATION ABSTRACTS
See RESUMENES SOBRE POBLACIÓN EN AMÉRICA LATINA

3053
LATIN AMERICAN STUDIES SERIES. v.1– , 1965– . Los Angeles, Calif. Irreg.
Issued by: Latin American Center, Institute of Archaeology, University of California at Los Angeles. Monograph series.

3054
LATIN AMERICAN STUDIES WORKING PAPERS. [1]– , 1972– . Bloomington, Ind. Irreg.
Issued by: Latin American Studies Program, Indiana University. In English or Spanish. Some issues are unnumbered.

3055
LATIN AMERICAN URBAN RESEARCH. v.1– , 1970– . Beverly Hills, Calif., Sage Publications. Annual.
Indexed: Bull. Anal. Pol. Ec. Soc.

3056
LATINOAMÉRICA: ANUARIO ESTUDIOS LATINO-AMERICANOS. v.1– , 1968– . Mexico, D.F., Dirección General de Publicaciones. Annual.
Issued by: Faculdad de Filosofía y Letras, Universidad Nacional de Mexico. In Spanish.

3057
LATINSKAI͡A AMERIKA. 1969– . Moskva, Nauka. Monthly.
Organ of: Institut Latinskoĭ Ameriki, Akademii͡a Nauk SSSR. In Russian. Published also in English edition: *Amerika Latina*.
Indexed: Bull. Anal. Pol. Ec. Soc.; Bull. Sig. Soc. Eth.; Int. Bibl. Soc. Cul. Anth.

3058
LATINSKAI͡A AMERIKA V SOVETSKIKH ISSLEDOVANII͡AKH. 1970/71– . Moskva. Irreg.
Issued by: Institut Latinskoĭ Ameriki, Akademii͡a Nauk SSSR. In Russian. (Vol. for 1976 last available for examination)

3059
Latvijas Padomju Socialistikas Republikas Zinatnu Akademija. Vestures Instituts. VESTURES PROBLEMAS. 1– , 1958– . Riga.
In Latvian; summaries in Russian.

LAUFENDE SOZIOLOGISCHE FORSCHUNGEN
See RECHERCHES SOCIOLOGIQUES EN COURS

3060
LAW AND CONTEMPORARY PROBLEMS. v.1– , Dec. 1933– . Durham, N.C., Duke University Press. Quarterly.
Issued by: School of Law, Duke University. Each issue has also a distinctive title.
Indexed: ABC POL SCI; Bull. Anal. Pol. Ec. Soc.; Ind. Leg. Per.; Int. Bibl. Eco.; Int. Bibl. Pol. Sc.; Int. Bibl. Soc.; Int. Lab. Doc.; Int. Pol. Sc. Abst.; J. Eco. Lit.; PAIS; Soc. Abst.; Soc. Sc. Hum. Ind.; SSCI.

3061
LAW AND HISTORY REVIEW. v.1– , spring 1983– . Ithaca, N.Y. Semi-annual.
Issued by: Cornell Law School in cooperation with the American Society for Legal History.

3062
LAW AND HUMAN BEHAVIOR. v.1– , 1977– . New York, Plenum Pub. Corp. Quarterly, 1977–89; bimonthly.
Published in cooperation with the American Psychology—Law Society.
Indexed: Psych. Abst.; Soc. Abst.

3063
LAW AND INTERNATIONAL AFFAIRS. 1– , Jan. 1975– . Dacca. Semi-annual.
Issued by: Bangladesh Institute of Law and International Affairs.

3064
LAW & POLICY. v.6– , Jan. 1984– . Oxford, B. Blackwell for the Baldy Center for Law and Social Policy, State University of New York at Buffalo. Quarterly.
Continues: *Law & Policy Quarterly* (v.1–5, 1979–83)
Indexed: Int. Bibl. Pol. Sc.; Int. Pol. Sc. Abst.

LAW AND POLICY
See POPULATION REPORTS. SERIES E. LAW AND POLICY

LAW AND POLITICAL REVIEW
See BEBJONG-HAKBO

3065
LAW AND PSYCHOLOGY REVIEW. [v.1]– , 1975– . Alabama. Annual.
Issued by: Department of Psychology, School of Law, University of Alabama.
Indexed: Psych. Abst.

3066
LAW & SOCIAL PROBLEMS. v.1– , 1980– . Nashville, Tenn. Annual.
Issued by: Vanderbilt University School of Law.

3067
LAW AND SOCIETY IN THE CARIBBEAN. 1– , 1972– . St. Augustine.
Issued by: Institute of Social and Economic Research, University of the West Indies.

LAW AND SOCIETY NEWSLETTER
See LAW AND SOCIETY QUARTERLY

3068
LAW AND SOCIETY QUARTERLY. v.1– , 1971– . New Delhi. All four nos. are combined in one in some years.
Issued by: Institute of Constitutional and Parliamentary Studies, and Centre for the Study of Law and Society. Title varies: v.1, 1971, *Law and Society Newsletter*.

3069
LAW & SOCIETY REVIEW. v.1– , Nov. 1966– . Denver, Colo., later Beverly Hills, Calif., Sage Publications. Three no. a year, 1966–67; quarterly.
Issued by: Law and Society Association, College of Law, University of Denver.
Indexed: ABC POL SCI; Bull. Anal. Pol. Ec. Soc.; Bull. Sig. Soc. Eth.; His. Abst.; Ind. Leg. Per.; Int. Bibl. Eco.; Int. Bibl. Pol. Sc.; Int. Pol. Sc. Abst.; PAIS; Soc. Abst.; Urb. Aff. Abst.

3070
LAW IN SOCIETY. v.1– , 1964/65– . Zaria. Two no. a year.
Issued by: Law Society, and Faculty of Law, Ahmadu Bello University.

3071
League of Nations. BALANCES OF PAYMENTS. 1931/32–1938 (published 1933–39). Geneva.

3072
League of Nations. CHRONOLOGY OF INTERNATIONAL TREATIES AND LEGISLATIVE MEASURES. v.1–11, 1930–1939/40. Geneva.

3073
League of Nations. COMMERCIAL BANKS. 1913/21–1929/34. Geneva.
Continued by: the league's *Money and Banking*.

3074
League of Nations. MONEY AND BANKING. 1935/36–1942/44. Geneva.
Continues: the league's *Commercial Banks*.

3075
League of Nations. MONTHLY BULLETIN OF STATISTICS. July 1919–1946. Geneva.
Continued by: United Nations. Statistical Office. *Monthly Bulletin of Statistics*.

3076
League of Nations. OFFICIAL JOURNAL. 1920–1940. Geneva.
Vols. for 1920–21 are bilingual: English and French. Beginning with 1922 two editions: English and French were published.

3077
League of Nations. REVIEW OF WORLD TRADE. 1932–1938 (published 1933–39). Geneva.

3078
League of Nations. STATISTICAL YEAR-BOOK OF THE LEAGUE OF NATIONS. 1927–1942/44. Geneva.
Title varies: 1927–29, *International Statistical Year-Book*.

3079
League of Nations. TREATY SERIES. v.1–205, 1920–1946. Geneva.
Continued by: United Nations. Legal Department. *Statement of Treaties and International Agreements Registered or Filed with the Secretariat*.

3080
THE LEAST DEVELOPED COUNTRIES. 1984– . New York, United Nations. Annual.
Prepared by: UNCTAD (United Nations Conference on Trade and Development). Supplements are called "Annex, Basic Data".

3081
THE LEFT INDEX. no.1– , spring 1982– . Santa Cruz, Calif. Quarterly.

THE LEGISLATOR
See STATE GOVERNMENT

3082
LEIPZIGER VIERTELJAHRESSCHRIFT FÜR SÜDOSTEUROPA. v.1–7, no.2/4, Apr. 1937–1943. Leipzig. Quarterly.
In German.

3083
LEISURE, RECREATION AND TOURISM ABSTRACTS. v.6– , Mar. 1981– . Farnham Royal. Quarterly.
Issued by: Commonwealth Agricultural Bureaux, and World Leisure Association.
Continues: *Rural Recreation and Tourism Abstracts*.

3084
LEISURE SCIENCES. 1– , 1977– . London, New York, Taylor & Francis. Quarterly.
Issued by: Institute of Environmental Studies, University of Illinois. Subtitle reads: "An interdisciplinary journal". Some issues are thematic.
Indexed: Hum. Res. Abst.; PAIS; Sage Urb. Stu. Abst.

3085
LENINIAN UGLOV. PO LENINSKOMU PUTI. 1925– . Ereven. Quarterly.
Issued by: T͡Sentral'nyĭ Komitet Kommunisticheskoĭ Partii Armi͡anskoĭ SSR. In Russian. Title varies: 1925–28, 1935–36, *Kommunist* (Erevan); 1932–33, *Partiĭnoe Stroitel'stvo*; 1936–41, *Partrobotnik*; 1945–56, *Partiĭnai͡a Zhizn'*.

LEO
See JOURNAL OF LAW, ECONOMICS & ORGANIZATION

LETTERS AND PROCEEDINGS
See Asiatic Society. JOURNAL

LETTERS AND SCIENCE
See Asiatic Society. JOURNAL

3086
LEVIATHAN. 1973– . Berlin, Westdeutscher Verlag. Quarterly.
In German; summaries in English. Includes supplements called "Sonderhefte". Subtitle reads: "Zeitschrift für Sozialwissenschaft".

Indexed: Int. Bibl. Eco.; Int. Bibl. Pol. Sc.; Int. Pol. Sc. Abst.; PAIS; PAISFL.

3087
LI SHIH YEN-CHIU. 1– , Feb. 1954– . Peking. Six no. a year.
Issued by: Li-Shi Yen-Chiu Wei-Yuan-Hui. Chung-Kuo Ko-Hsueh Yuan. In Chinese.

LIAISON ET INFORMATION BULLETIN
See FAMILLES DANS LE MONDE

3088
LIAUDIES UKIS. NARODNOE KHOZI͡AĬSTVO. 1958– . Vilnius, Zhurnalnoe Gazetnoe Izd-vo pri CK LKP. Monthly.
Issued by: Lietuvos TSR Mokslu Akademija, Sovet Narodnogo Khozi͡aĭstva and Institut Ekonomiki. In Lithuanian.

3089
LIBERATION. v.1– , Mar. 1956– . New York. Monthly.
Indexed: Ind. Per. Art. Law; PAIS; Peace Res. Abst. J.; Wom. Stu. Abst.

LIBYCA: ANTHROPOLOGIE, ARCHÉOLOGIE, PRÉHISTORIQUE
See LIBYCA: ANTHROPOLOGIE, PRÉHISTOIRE, ETHNOGRAPHIE

3090
LIBYCA: ANTHROPOLOGIE, PRÉHISTOIRE, ETHNOGRAPHIE. v.1– , 1953– . Alger. Semi-annual, 1956–57; annual.
Issued by: Centre de Recherches Anthropologiques, Préhistoriques et Ethnographiques. In French. Title varies: v.1–3, 1953–55, *Libyca: Anthropologie, Archéologie, Préhistorique*.

3091
Lietuvos TSR Mokslų Akademija, Vilna. DARBAI. TRUDY. SERIJA A. VISUOMENĖS MOKSLAI. OBSHCHESTVENNYE NAUKI. SOCIAL SCIENCES. 1– , 1955– . Vilnius, VPMLL, Mokslas. Irreg., 1955–71; quarterly.
In Lithuanian or Russian, with summaries in the other language, occasionally in English or German.
Supersedes, in part: the academy's *Žinynas* (1947–52).

3092
LIFESTYLES. v.7– , fall 1984– . New York, Human Sciences Press. Four no. a year.
Some issues have distinctive titles. Subtitle reads: "Changing patterns in marriage, family and intimacy".
Continues: *Alternative Life Styles* (v.1–6, Feb. 1978–summer 1984)

3093
LIIKETALOUDELLINEN AIKAKAUSKIRJA. JOURNAL OF BUSINESS ECONOMICS. 1– , 1952– . Helsinki. Quarterly.
In Finnish; summaries in English or German.

LINGUISTIC SERIES
See AUSTRALIAN ABORIGINAL STUDIES

3094
LINGUISTICS AND LANGUAGE BEHAVIOR ABSTRACTS. LLBA. v.19– , Apr. 1985– . La Jolla, Calif., Sociological Abstracts. Quarterly, cumulated annually.
Continues: *LLBA Language and Language Behavior Abstracts*.

THE LITERARY GUIDE AND RATIONALIST REVIEW
See THE HUMANIST; A RATIONAL APPROACH TO THE MODERN WORLD

3095
LITERATURE OF LIBERTY. v.1– , Jan./Mar. 1978– . San Francisco, Calif. Quarterly.
Issued by: Cato Institute.
Indexed: Int. Bibl. Pol. Sc.

3096
LITUANISTIKA V SSSR. EKONOMIKA. 1– , 1978– . Vil'nius. Annual.
Issued by: Lietuvos TSR Mokslu Akademija. Institut Filosofii, Sot͡siologii i Prava. T͡Sentr Nauchnoĭ Informat͡sii po Obshchestvennym Naukam. In Russian.

3097
LITUANISTIKA V SSSR. ISTORII͡A. 1– , 1977– . Vil'nius. Annual.
Issued by: Lietuvos TSR Mokslu Akademija. Institut Filosofii, Sot͡siologii i Prava. T͡Sentr Nauchnoĭ Informat͡sii po Obshchestvennym Naukam. In Russian.

3098
LIVERPOOL PAPERS IN HUMAN GEOGRAPHY. 1– , 1981– . Liverpool. Irreg.
Issued by: Department of Geography, University of Liverpool. Each number has also a distinctive title. Other title: *Working Paper*.

LIVING
See JOURNAL OF MARRIAGE AND THE FAMILY

3099
LOCAL FINANCE. FINANCES LOCALES. KOMMUNAL FINANZEN. v.1– , Mar. 1972– . The Hague. Bimonthly.

Issued by: International Centre for Local Credit. In English, French, or German; summaries in other two languages.

Supersedes: International Centre for Local Credit. *Bulletin.*

3100
LOCAL GOVERNMENT ADMINISTRATION. v.1– , June 1935– . London. Three no. a year, 1935, 1938; quarterly.

Issued by: British and American Committees, International Union of Local Authorities. Includes also translations of some articles in *L'Administration Locale.*

3101
LOCAL GOVERNMENT ADMINISTRATION. 1– , 1957– . Edgecliffs, Strand Publications.

Issued by: Institute of Public Administration. Other title: *LGA Local Government Administration.*

3102
LOCAL GOVERNMENT POLICY MAKING. INLOGOV. v.9– , summer 1981– . Birmingham. Irreg.

Issued by: Local Government Studies, University of Birmingham.

Continues: *The Corporate Planning Journal.*

3103
LOCAL GOVERNMENT QUARTERLY. v.1– , Mar. 1972– . Dacca. Four no. a year.

Some numbers are combined.

3104
LOCAL GOVERNMENT REVIEW. v.136, no.20– , 1971– . London. Weekly.

Continues, in part: *Justice of the Peace and Local Government Review.*

3105
LOCAL GOVERNMENT REVIEW IN JAPAN. no.7– , 1979– . Tokyo. Annual.

Issued by: Local Government Research and Data Center Jichi Kenshu Kyokail.

Continues: *Local Government Review.*

3106
LOCAL GOVERNMENT STUDIES. 1– , 1971– , n. ser. 1– , Jan. 1975– . London, Charles Knight. Semi-annual.

Issued by: Institute of Local Government Studies, University of Birmingham.

3107
LOCAL GOVERNMENT THROUGHOUT THE WORLD. v.1–5, Feb. 1962–Dec. 1966. The Hague.

Issued by: International Union of Local Authorities.

Supersedes: International Union of Local Authorities. *I.U.L.A. Bulletin.* Continued by: *IULA News Letter.*

3108
LOISIR ET SOCIÉTÉ. SOCIETY AND LEISURE. v.1– , Apr. 1978– . Montréal. Presses Universitaires de l'Université de Québec. Semi-annual.

Issued by: Research Group on Leisure, International Sociological Association. In English and French.

Supersedes: *Society and Leisure.*

3109
A LONDON BIBLIOGRAPHY OF THE SOCIAL SCIENCES. v.1–4, 1931–32; Supplements, v.5– , 1934– . London.

Issued by: London School of Economics and Political Science.

3110
THE LONDON JOURNAL. 1– , May 1975– . London, Longman Group. Semi-annual.

Subtitle reads: "A review of metropolitan society, past and present".

LONDON QUARTERLY AND WORLD AFFAIRS *See* WORLD AFFAIRS (London)

3111
LONG RANGE PLANNING. Sept. 1968– . Oxford, Pergamon Press. Quarterly, 1968–72; bimonthly.

Issued by: Society for Long Range Planning.

Indexes: Vols. 1–2, 1968–June 1970, 1v.

Indexed: Bull. Anal. Pol. Ec. Soc.; Curr. Cont. Soc. Beh. Sc.; Eco. Abst.; Int. Bibl. Eco.; PAIS; SSCI.

3112
LOUGHBOROUGH JOURNAL OF SOCIAL STUDIES. no.1– , 1966– . Loughborough. Semi-annual.

Issued by: Loughborough University of Technology.

Indexed: Int. Bibl. Soc. Cul. Anth.

3113
LOUISIANA STATE UNIVERSITY STUDIES. SOCIAL SCIENCE SERIES. no.1– , 1951– . Baton Rouge, La., Louisiana University Press. Irreg.

Monograph series.

3114
LOYOLA OF LOS ANGELES INTERNATIONAL AND COMPARATIVE LAW JOURNAL. v.4– , 1981– . Los Angeles, Calif. Annual, 1981; three no. a year.

Issued by: Los Angeles Loyola Law School.

Continues: *Loyola of Los Angeles International and Comparative Annual* (v.1–3, 1978–80)

Indexed: Ind. Leg. Per.

3115
Loyola University, Chicago. Center for Research in Urban Government. CRUG. no.1– , July 1965– . Chicago, Ill. Six no. a year.
Title varies: July 1965, *The Machinery and Growth of American Cities*. Each no. has a distinctive title.

3116
LUD. v.1– , 1895– . Wrocław, Zakład Narodowy im. Ossolińskich. Annual.
Issued by: Polskie Towarzystwo Ludoznawcze. In Polish; summaries in English, Polish and Russian. Published: v.1–35, 1895–1937; v.36–, 1939/45.
Indexes: Vols. 1–39, 1895–1950, in v.40.
Indexed: Abst. Anth.; Bull. Sig. Soc. Eth.; Int. Bibl. Soc. Cul. Anth.

3117
LUND STUDIES IN GEOGRAPHY. SER. B. HUMAN GEOGRAPHY. no.1– , 1949– . Lund. Irreg.
Issued by: Department of Geography, University of Lund. In English, French, or German.

3118
LUND STUDIES IN INTERNATIONAL HISTORY. 1– , 1970– . Lund, Laromedesforlagen. Irreg.
Issued by: Department of History, University of Lund. In English or German. Monograph series.

3119
LUSO-BRASILIAN REVIEW. v.1– , 1963– . Madison, Wis. Semi-annual.
Issued by: Department of Spanish and Portuguese, University of Wisconsin.
Indexed: His. Abst.; Int. Bibl. Soc. Cul. Anth.

3120
LA LUTTE DE CLASSES. no.1–51/52, Feb./Mar. 1928–Apr./June 1935. Paris.
In French.
Superseded by: *Quatrième*.

MTG
See ZEITSCHRIFT FÜR SOZIALÖKONOMIE; MENSCH, TECHNIK, GESELLSCHAFT

MAATSKAPLIKE WERK
See SOCIAL WORK

THE MACHINERY AND GROWTH OF AMERICAN CITIES
See Loyola University, Chicago. Center for Urban Government. CRUG

3121
MADJALAH ADMINISTRASI NEGARA. JOURNAL OF PUBLIC ADMINISTRATION. 1– , 1959– . Djakarta. Irreg.
Issued by: Lembaga Administrasi Negara. In English or Indonesian.

3122
MADJALAH GEOGRAFI INDONESIA. v.1–5 (no.1–9), Sept. 1960–1975. Jogkarta.
Issued by: Department of Geography, Gadjah Mada University. In English or Indonesian.
Continued by: *Indonesian Journal of Geography*.

MADJALAH HUKUM ADAT
See SOSIOGRAFI INDONESIA DAN HUKUM ADAT

3123
MADJALAH ILMU-ILMU SASTRA INDONESIA. INDONESIAN JOURNAL OF CULTURAL STUDIES. 1– , Apr. 1963– . Djakarta. Irreg.
Issued by: Jajasan Penerbitan Karya Sastra, Ikatan Sardjana Indonesia, and Departement Urusan Reseach Nasional. In Indonesian.

3124
MAGHREB DÉVELOPPEMENT. no.1–31, Jan. 1977–Apr. 1980. Paris. Ten no. a year, 1977–Apr. 1980. Monthly.
Issued by: Afrique Développement. In French. Photoduplicated.
Indexed: Bull. Anal. Pol. Ec. Soc.

MAGHREB DOCUMENTS
See MAGHREB MACHREK

3125
MAGHREB MACHREK. MONDE ARABE. 1– , 1964– . Paris, La Documentation Française. Bimonthly, 1973–74; quarterly, 1964–72, 1975– .
Issued by: Section Monde Arabe, Centre d'Études et Recherches Internationales, Fondation National des Sciences Politiques. In Arabic or French. Title varies: 1964–72, *Maghreb. Documents*. Other title: *al-Alam al-'Arabī; al Maghrib wa-al-Mashriq*.
Indexed: Bull. Anal. Pol. Ec. Soc.; Int. Bibl. Eco.; Int. Bibl. Pol. Sc.; Int. Pol. Sc. Abst.

MAGYAR NEMZETI HUNGARICA
See FOLIA ARCHAEOLOGICA

3126
MAGYAR PSZICHOLÓGIAI SZEMLE. v.1– , 1926– . Budapest, Akademiai Kiádo. Quarterly.
Organ of: Pszichológiai Bozottságanak, Magyar Tudományos Akadémia. In Hungarian; summaries in English and Russian. Suspended 1942–47.
Indexed: LLBA; Psych. Abst.

3127
THE MAHARASHTRA CO-OPERATIVE QUARTERLY. June 1917– . Bombay, later Maharashtra. Four no. a year.
Issued by: Maharashtra State Cooperative Union (called June 1938–Mar. 1946, Provincial Co-Operative Institute; July 1957–Oct. 1960, Bombay State Cooperative Union). Title varies: 1917–Oct. 1961, *The Bombay Cooperative Quarterly*.
Indexed: Int. Bibl. Soc. Cul. Anth.

3128
MAIN CURRENTS IN INDIAN SOCIOLOGY. 1– , 1976– . Delhi, Vikas Pub. Co. Irreg.

3129
MAIN CURRENTS IN MODERN THOUGHT. Nov. 1940– . New York, Gordon and Breach. Monthly (irreg.), 1940–43; quarterly, 1944–53; five no. a year.
Issued by: Center for Integrative Education. Publication suspended Apr.–Dec. 1943, Apr. 1944–Jan. 1946.

MAIN ECONOMIC INDICATORS
See Organisation for Economic Co-operation and Development. MAIN ECONOMIC INDICATORS

MAIN REGIONAL INDICATORS
See Statistical Office of the European Communities. REGIONAL STATISTICS. MAIN REGIONAL INDICATORS

3130
MAJALLA-YI MARDUMSHINASI. REVUE IRANIENNE D'ANTHROPOLOGIE. 1– , 1336 [i.e. 1958]– . Tehran, Administration Générale des Beaux Arts. Quarterly.

Issued by: Institut d'Anthropologie. In French or Persian.

3131
AL-MAJALLAH AL-'ARABĪYAH LIL-DIFĀ-'AL-IJTIMĀ'Ī. 1969– . Cairo. Two no. a year.
In Arabic. Other title: *Arab Journal for Sociological Defence*.

3132
AL-MAJALLAH AL-DUWALĪYAH LIL-'ULŪM AL-IJTIMĀ-'ĪYAH. 1971– . al-Qāhirah. Quarterly.
Issued by: Majallat Risālat al-Yūnisku. Translations into Arabic of some articles published in the *International Social Science Journal*.

AL-MAJALLAH AL-IJTIMĀ'ĪYAH AL-QAWMĪYAH
See Al-Markaz al-qawmī lil-Buḥūth al-ijtimā'īyah wa-al-qawmīyah. AL-MAJALLAH AL-IJTIMĀ'ĪYAH AL-QAWMĪYAH

AL-MAJALLAH AL-MISRĪYAH LIL-QĀNŪM AL-DUWALĪ
See REVUE EGYPTIENNE DE DROIT INTERNATIONAL

MAJALLAH AL-TŪNĪSĪYAH LIL-'ULŪM AL-IJTIMĀ'ĪYAH
See REVUE TUNISIENNE DES SCIENCES SOCIALES

MAJALLAH PELARAJAN MALAYSIA
See MALAYSIAN JOURNAL OF EDUCATION

MAJALLAH-'ULUM'T VA INSANI
See THE JOURNAL OF SOCIAL SCIENCES AND HUMANITIES (Shiraz)

MAJALLAT AL-DIRĀSĀT AL-'ARABĪYAH WA-AL-ISLĀMĪYAH
See CAHIERS D'ÉTUDES ARABES ET ISLAMIQUES

3133
MAJALLAT AL-DIRĀSĀT AL-SŪDĀNĪYAH. BULLETIN OF SUDANESE STUDIES. v.1– , 1968– . Khartoum. Monthly.
Issued by: Institute of African and Asiatic Studies (called earlier Sudan Research Unit), University of Khartoum. In Arabic or English.

3134
MAJALLAT AL-MAL WA-AL-SHU'UN AL-IJTIMĀ'ĪYAH. 1– , 1950– . Damascus. Bimonthly.

3135
MAJALLAT AL-MU' ARRIKH AL-'ARABĪ. THE ARAB HISTORIAN. 1– , 1975– . Baghdad, al-Amānah al-Āmmah li-Ittiḥad al-Mu'arrikhīn al-Arab.
In Arabic or English.

3136
MAJALLAT AL-TARBĪYAH AL-ḤADĪTHAH. 1– , 1928– . Cairo. Four no. a year.
Issued by: American University of Cairo. In Arabic, English, or French. Other title: *Journal of Modern Education*. Volume for 1971 last available for examination.

3137
MAJALLAT AL-'ULŪM AL-IJTIMĀ'ĪYAH. v.1– , 1974– . al-Kuwayt, al-Kullīyah. Quarterly.
Issued by: Kuwait University. In Arabic or English; summaries in English. Other title: *Journal of the Social Sciences*.
Supersedes: Jāmi'at al-Kuwayt. *Kullīyat* al-Tijārah wa-al-Iqtisād wa-al-'Ulūm al-Siyāsīyah. Majallat Kullīyat al-Tijārah wa-al-Iqtisād wa-al-'Ulūm al-Siyāsīyah.
Indexed: Bull. Anal. Pol. Ec.; Int. Bibl. Eco.; Int. Pol. Sc. Abst.

3138
MAJALLAT MARKAZ AL-BUḤŪTH. 1– , 1982– . al-Riyād, al-Mamlakah al-'Arabīyah al-Sa'udīyah, Wizārat al-Ta'līm al-Ālī, Jāmi'at al-Imām Muḥammad ibn Sa'ūd al-Islāmīyah. Annual.
In Arabic or English. Other title: *The Journal of the Research Centre*.

3139
MAJALLE-YIOLUM IIQTISADI-YI IRAN. 1– , 1976– . Tehran, Quarterly.
Issued by: Institute for Development and Economic Research, Tehran University. In English or French. Other title: *Iranian Economic Review*.

3140
THE MALAYAN ECONOMIC REVIEW. v.1–27, June 1956–Oct. 1982. Singapore. Semi-annual.
Issued by: University of Malaya Economic Society, June 1956; Malayan Economic Society, Apr. 1957–Apr. 1962; and various departments of the University of Singapore. Vol.1, no.2 not published. In English.
Continued by: *Singapore Economic Review*.
Indexed: Bull. Anal. Pol. Ec. Soc.; Int. Bibl. Eco.; Int. Bibl. Soc.; J. Eco. Lit.; Int. Lab. Doc.; PAIS; SSCI.

MALAYSIAN ECONOMIC STUDIES
See KAJIAN EKONOMI MALAYSIA

3141
THE MALAYSIAN JOURNAL OF AGRICULTURAL ECONOMICS. JURNAL EKONOMI PERTANIAN MALAYSIA. v.1– , 1984– . Serdang Selangor. Semi-annual.

Issued by: Malaysian Agricultural Economics Association.

3142
MALAYSIAN JOURNAL OF EDUCATION. MAJALLAH PELAJARAN MALAYSIA. v.1– , June 1964– . Kuala Lumpur, Educational Journal Press. Semi-annual.
In English or Malay.
Indexed: Curr. Cont. Soc. Beh. Sc.

3143
MAN. v.1–54, 1901–1964. London. Monthly (occasionally two nos. combined into one)
Issued by: Royal Anthropological Institute of Great Britain and Ireland.
Continued by a publication of the same title.
Indexed: Int. Bibl. Soc. Cul. Anth.

3144
MAN. n. ser. v.1– , Mar. 1966– . London. Quarterly.
Issued by: Royal Anthropological Institute.
Continues: the institute's: *Journal*, and *Man*.
Indexed: Abst. Anth.; APAIS; Bull. Sig. Soc. Eth.; LLBA; Int. Bibl. Soc. Cul. Anth.; Soc. Abst.; Soc. Sc. Ind.; SSCI; Wom. Stu. Abst.

3145
MAN AND MEDICINE. v.1– , autumn 1975– . New York. Quarterly.
Subtitle reads: "The journal of values and ethics in health care".

MAN & SOCIETY
See JEN YU SHE HUI

MAN AND SOCIETY
See MANUSIA DAN MASYARAKAT

3146
MAN IN NEW GUINEA. v.1–6, Oct. 1968–Dec. 1974. Boroko.
Issued by: Department of Anthropology and Sociology, University of Papua & New Guinea. Processed.
Superseded by: *Research in Melanesia*.
Indexed: Abst. Anth.

3147
MAN IN SOUTHEAST ASIA. no.1– , Feb. 1968– . Brisbane. Three no. a year.
Issued by: Department of Anthropology and Sociology, and the Department of Geography, University of Brisbane. A brief list of research projects. Photoduplicated. No.22/23 last available for examination.

3148
MAN IN THE PACIFIC. 1–9, 1963–1970. Honolulu. Irreg.
Supplement to: *Pacific Anthropologist*.

3149
MANAGEMENT AND LABOR STUDIES. v.1– , June 1975– . Jamshedpur. Semi-annual.
Issued by: Xavier Institute. Subtitle reads: "Prediction, marketing, management, industrial relations, business policy".
Indexed: Psych. Abst.; Sage Pub. Adm. Abst.; Sage Urb. Stu. Abst.

3150
MANAGEMENT IN GOVERNMENT. v.37– . Feb. 1982– . London, HMSO. Quarterly.
Issued by: Managerial Services, Civil Service Department, in collaboration with the Departmental Management Services Officers.
Continues: *Management Services in Government*.

3151
MANAGEMENT INTERNATIONAL REVIEW. [v.]6– , 1966– . Wiesbaden, Betriebswirtschaftlicher Verlag T. Gabler. Bimonthly.
Published under the auspices of the European Foundation for Management Development. In English, French, or German. Issues are thematic.
Continues: *Management International* (v.1–5, 1961–65)
Indexed: Bull. Anal. Pol. Eco. Soc.; Curr. Cont. Soc. Beh. Sc.; Eco. Abst.; Int. Bibl. Eco.; Int. Bibl. Soc.; Int. Bibl. Soc. Cul. Anth.; Int. Lab. Doc.; J. Eco. Lit.; PAIS; SSCI.

3152
MANAGEMENT SCIENCE. v.1– , Oct. 1954– . Baltimore, Md., Waverley Press, later Providence, R.I. Monthly.
Official organ of: Institute of Management Science.
Indexes: Vols. 1–10, 1954–64.
Indexed: Eco. Abst.; Int. Bibl. Eco.; Int. Bibl. Pol. Sc.; Int. Bibl. Soc.; Peace Res. Abst. J.; Sage Urb. Stu. Abst.

3153
MANCHESTER SCHOOL OF ECONOMIC AND SOCIAL STUDIES. v.1– , 1930– . Manchester. Three no. a year.
Issued by: Department of Economics, University of Manchester. Title varies: 1930–31, *The Manchester School of Economics, Commerce and Administration*; 1932–38, *The Manchester School of Economics and Social Studies*.

Indexed: Bull. Anal. Pol. Ec. Soc.; Eco. Abst.; Int. Bibl. Eco.; Int. Bibl. Pol. Sc.; Int. Bibl. Soc.; Int. Lab. Doc.; Int. Pol. Sc. Abst.; J. Eco. Lit.; PAIS; Pop. Ind.; SSCI.

THE MANCHESTER SCHOOL OF ECONOMICS AND SOCIAL STUDIES
See MANCHESTER SCHOOL OF ECONOMIC AND SOCIAL STUDIES

THE MANCHESTER SCHOOL OF ECONOMICS, COMMERCE AND ADMINISTRATION
See MANCHESTER SCHOOL OF ECONOMIC AND SOCIAL STUDIES

3154
MANAGING INTERNATIONAL DEVELOPMENT. MID. [v.]1– , Jan./Feb. 1984– . Armonk, N.Y., M.E. Sharpe. Bimonthly.

3155
MANKIND. v.1– , Mar. 1931– . Sydney. Three no. a year. Volume consists of six numbers.
Issued by: Anthropological Society of New South Wales, and Department of Anthropology, University of Sydney.
Indexed: Abst. Anth.; APAIS; Bull. Sig. Soc. Eth.; Curr. Cont. Soc. Beh. Sc.; His. Abst.; Int. Bibl. Soc. Cul. Anth.; Peace Res. Abst. J.; Soc. Abst.; Soc. Sc. Ind.; SSCI.

3156
THE MANKIND QUARTERLY. v.1– , June 1960– . Edinburgh, later Washington, D.C., The Clivedon Press. Three no. a year.
Issued by: The Council for Social and Economic Studies.
Indexed: Abst. Anth.; Bull. Sig. Soc. Eth.; Int. Bibl. Soc. Cul. Anth.; Pop. Ind.; Soc. Abst.

3157
MANPOWER AND UNEMPLOYMENT RESEARCH. v.9–11, no.2, Apr. 1976–Nov. 1978. Montreal. Semi-annual.
Issued by: Centre for Developing Area Studies, McGill University. In English; occasionally in French.
Continues: *Manpower and Unemployment Research in Africa* (v.1–8, 1968–75). Continued by: *Labour, Capital and Society*.

3158
MANPOWER JOURNAL. 1– , 1965– . New Delhi. Quarterly.
Issued by: Institute for Applied Manpower Research.
Indexed: Abst. Soc. Work.; Bull. Anal. Pol. Ec. Soc.; Int. Bibl. Soc. Cul. Anth.; Int. Lab. Doc.; Peace Res. Abst. J.

3159
MANUSIA DAN MASHARAKAT. no.1– , 1972– . Kuala Lumpur. Annual.
Issued by: Persutuan Antropologi & Sosiologi, Universiti Malaya. In English or Malay. Other title: *Man & Society*.

MARCHÉS COLONIAUX
See MARCHÉS TROPICAUX & MEDITERRANÉENS

MARCHÉS COLONIAUX DU MONDE
See MARCHÉS TROPICAUX & MEDITERRANÉENS

MARCHÉS TROPICAUX DU MONDE
See MARCHÉS TROPICAUX & MEDITERRANÉENS

3160
MARCHÉS TROPICAUX & MEDITERRANÉENS. 1– , Nov. 17, 1945– . Paris. Weekly.
In French. Title varies: v.1–3 (no.1–72), 1945–Mar. 29, 1947, *Marchés Coloniaux*; v.5–12 (no.164–567), Jan. 1949–Sept. 22, 1956, *Marchés Coloniaux du Monde*; v.13–14 (no.582–673), Jan. 5, 1957–Oct. 8, 1958, *Marchés Tropicaux du Monde*.
Indexed: Int. Lab. Doc.; PAISFL; Peace Res. Abst. J.

3161
Al-Markaz al-qawmī lil-Buḥūth al-ijtimā'īyah wa-al-qawmīyah. AL-MAJALLAH AL-IJTIMĀ'ĪYAH AL-QAWMĪYAH. v.1– , Jan. 1964– . Cairo. Three no. a year.
Issued by: National Centre for Sociological and Criminological Research. Other title: *The National Review of Social Sciences*.

3162
MARKSISTSKO-LENINSKAI͡A ETIKA. 1972/73– . Moskva. Annual.
Issued by: Institut Nauchnoĭ Informat͡sii po Obshchestvennym Naukam, Akademii͡a Nauk SSSR. In Russian.

3163
MARKSISTICKA MISAO. 1– , 1975– . Beograd. Bimonthly.
Issued by: Marksisticki Centar Centralnog Komiteta Saveza Komunista Srbije. In Serbo-Croatian.

MARRIAGE AND FAMILY LIVING
See JOURNAL OF MARRIAGE AND FAMILY

3164
MARRIAGE AND FAMILY REVIEW. 1– , Jan./Feb. 1978– . New York, Haworth Press. Quarterly.

Indexed: Psych. Abst.; Sage Fam. Stu. Abst.; Soc. Abst.

MASCA JOURNAL
See University of Pennsylvania. Museum. Applied Science Center for Archaeology. MASCA JOURNAL

3165
AL-MASHRIQ. 1898– . Beirut. Bimonthly.
Issued by: Université-St. Joseph. In Arabic; occasionally articles in European languages. Summaries and index in French.

MAṢRIF AL-'ARABĪ LIL-TAUMĪYAH AL-IQTIṢĀDĪYAH FI AFRIQ'UJĀ
See ARAB COOPERATION WITH AFRICA; A SURVEY

3166
MATECON. v.6– , 1969/70– . Armonk, M.E. Sharpe. Quarterly.
Translations.
Continues: *Mathematical Studies in Economics and Statistics in the USSR and Eastern Europe* (v.1–5, fall 1964–winter/spring/summer 1968/69).
Indexed: Int. Bibl. Eco.; Int. Bibl. Pol. Sc.; Int. Bibl. Soc.; J. Eco. Lit.

MATERIALE ŞI CERCETĂRI ARHEOLOGICE
See Academia de Ştiinţe Sociale şi Politice a Republici Socialiste România. Institutul de Arheologie. MATERIALE ŞI CERCETĂRI ARHEOLOGICE

MATERIALSAMMLUNG
See Agrarsoziale Gesellschaft. MATERIALSAMMLUNG

MATERIAŁY ANTROPOLOGICZNO-ARCHEOLOGICZNE I ETNOGRAFICZNE
See Polska Akademia Umiejetności. Komisja Antropologiczna. MATERIAŁY ANTROPOLOGICZNO-ARCHEOLOGICZNE I ETNOGRAFICZNE

3167
MATERIALY DO UKRAINSKOI ETHNOLOGII. BEITRÄGE ZUR UKRAINISCHEN ETHNOLOGIE. v.11–20, 1909–1919. U L'vovi, Nakl. Naukovoho Tovaristva im. Shevchenka. Irreg.
In Ukrainian.
Continues: *Materialy do Ukrainskoi Ethnologii. Matériaux pour l'Ethnologie Ukraino-Ruthène* (v.1–10, 1899–1908)

3168
MATERIALY I ISSLEDOVANIIA PO ARKHEOLOGII SSSR. 1940– . Moskva, Mezhdunarodnaia Kniga. Irreg.
Issued by: Akademiia Nauk SSSR. In Russian.

3169
MATERIAŁY I PRACE ANTROPOLOGICZNE. v.1– , 1953– . Wrocław, Państwowe Wydawnictwo Naukowe. Irreg.
Issued by: Zakład Antropologii, Polska Akademia Nauk, and Polskie Towarzystwo Antropologiczne. In Czech, English, German, Polish, or Russian.
Supersedes: *Materiały Antropologiczno-Archeologiczne i Etnograficzne* (v.1–14, 1896–1919)
Indexed: Abst. Anth.; Bull. Sig. Soc. Eth.

MATERIALY PO ANTROPOLOGII KAVKAZA
See Akademiia Nauk Gruzinskoĭ SSR, Tiflis. Institut Istorii, Arkheologii i Etnografii. MATERIALY PO ANTROPOLOGII GRUZII I KAVKAZA

MATERIALY PO ARKHEOLOGII GRUZII I KAVKAZA
See Akademiia Nauk Gruzinskoĭ SSR, Tiflis. Institut Istorii, Arkheologii i Etnografii. MATERIALY PO ARKHEOLOGII GRUZII I KAVKAZA

3170
MATERIALY PO ARKHEOLOGII ROSSII. no.1–37, 1866–1918. Petrograd.
In Russian; summaries in French. Nos. 3–37 have also distinctive titles.

3171
MATERIALY PO ETNOGRAFII. v.3– , 1926– . Leningrad. Irreg.
Issued by: Etnograficheskiĭ Otdel Gosudarstvennogo Muzeia. In Russian.
Continues: *Materialy po Etnografii Rossii* (v.1–2, 1910–14)

3172
MATERIAŁY STAROŻYTNE I WCZESNOŚREDNIOWIECZNE. v.1– , 1971– . Wrocław, Zakład Narodowy im. Ossolińskich. Irreg.
Issued by: Państwowe Muzeum Archeologiczne in Warszawa. In Polish; summaries in English and Russian. Tables of contents in English and Russian.
Supersedes: *Materiały Starożytne* (1956–68) and *Materiały Wczesnośredniowieczne* (1949–69)
Indexed: Abst. Anth.; Bull. Sig. Soc. Eth.

3173
MATERIALY Z ANTROPOLOGII UKRAINY. v.1– , 1960– . Kiev, Vid-vo Akademii Nauk Ukrainskoi RSR.

Issued by: Institut Mystoznavstva Fol'kloru, Akademiia Nauk URSR. In Ukrainian.

MATÉRIAUX POUR L'HISTOIRE POSITIVE ET PHILOSOPHIQUE DE L'HOMME
See MATÉRIAUX POUR L'HISTOIRE PRIMITIVE DE L'HOMME

3174
MATÉRIAUX POUR L'HISTOIRE PRIMITIVE DE L'HOMME. v.1–4, Sept. 1864–1868; v.5–6, 8–13 (2. ser. v.1–13), 1869–1882/83; v.18–22 (3. ser. v.1–5), 1884–1888. Paris, Toulouse, Au Musée Histoire Naturelle.
In French. Title varies: 1864–68, *Matériaux pour l'Histoire Positive et Philosophique* (later "*Primitive et Philosophique*") *de l'Homme. Bulletin Mensuelle des Travaux et Découvertes concernant Anthropologie, les Temps Préhistoriques, l'Époque Quaternaire, les Questions de l'Espace et de la Génération spontanée*; 1869–72, *Matériaux pour l'Histoire Primitive et l'Étude du Sol, de la Fauna et de Flora qui Rattachent.*

MATÉRIAUX POUR L'HISTOIRE PRIMITIVE ET L'ÉTUDE DU SOL, DE LA FAUNA ET DE FLORA QUI RATTACHENT
See MATÉRIAUX POUR L'HISTOIRE PRIMITIVE DE L'HOMME

3175
MATHEMATICAL SOCIAL SCIENCES. v.1– , Sept. 1980– . Amsterdam, North-Holland Pub. Co. Quarterly.

3176
MATHEMATICAL STUDIES IN ECONOMICS AND STATISTICS IN THE USSR AND EASTERN EUROPE. v.1–5, fall 1964–winter/spring/summer 1968/69. White Plains, N.Y., International Arts and Sciences Press. Quarterly.
Continued by: *Matecon.*

3177
MATHÉMATIQUES ET SCIENCES HUMAINES. no.1– , 1965– . Paris. Some nos. published by: Gauthier-Villars. Quarterly (irreg.)
Issued by: Centre de Analyse et Mathématique Sociales, Section 6e. Sciences Économiques et Sociales, École des Hautes Études des Sciences Sociales, in cooperation with the Centre National de la Recherche Scientifique. In French. Some nos. have also distinctive titles. Processed.
Indexed: Int. Bibl. Pol. Sc.; Int. Pol. Sc. Abst.; Psych. Abst.

MATSUE
See Akademiia Nauk Gruzinskoĭ SSR. Otdelenie Obshchestvennykh Nauk. MATSUE

3178
MAYOR AND MANAGER. v.1– , Jan. 1958– . Morton Grove, Ill. Quarterly, Sept. 1958–59; monthly, Jan.–June 1958, 1960–.

3179
MAZINGIRA. no.1– , 1977– . Oxford, Pergamon Press. Quarterly.
Issued by: Le Forum Mondial sur l'Environnement et de Développement under the auspices of the United Nations. In French. There are also: English Edition, and Edición en Español.

MEDDELANDEN
See SOCIALA MEDDELANDEN

MEDEDELINGEN DER ZITTINGEN
See Académie Royale des Sciences d'Outre-Mer. Classe des Sciences Morales et Politiques. BULLETIN DES SÉANCES

3180
MEDIA, CULTURE & SOCIETY. v.1– , Jan. 1979– . London, New York, Academic Press. Quarterly.
Indexed: Int. Bibl. Eco.

MEDIA IKATAN KEKERABATAN ANTROPOLOGI
See Universitas Indonesia. Iketan Kekerabatan Antropologi. MEDIA IKATAN KEKERABATAN ANTROPOLOGI

3181
MEDIAEVAL STUDIES. v.1– , 1939– . London, Sheed & Ward. Annual.
Issued by: Pontifical Institute of Medieval Studies. In English; occasionally in French, German, or Latin.
Indexes: Vols. 1–25; v.26–30.

MEDICA ANTHROPOLOGICA
See Soumalainen Tiedeakademia, Helsingfors. TOIMITUKSIA. ANNALES. SERIES A. SECTION 5. MEDICA ANTHROPOLOGICA

3182
MEDICAL ANTHROPOLOGY. v.1– , winter 1977– . Pleasantville, N.Y., Redgrave Pub. Co., later Washington, D.C. Quarterly.
Issued by: Society for Medical Anthropology.
Indexed: Abst. Anth.; Bull. Sig. Soc. Eth.; Int. Bibl. Soc. Cul. Anth.

MEDICAL ANTHROPOLOGY
See SOCIAL SCIENCE & MEDICINE. MEDICAL ANTHROPOLOGY and: SOCIAL SCIENCE & MEDICINE. PART B. MEDICAL ANTHROPOLOGY

3183
MEDICAL ANTHROPOLOGY QUARTERLY. v.14, no.2– , Feb. 1983– . Washington, D.C. Quarterly.
Issued by: Society for Medical Anthropology.
Continues: *Medical Anthropology Newsletter* (v.1–14, no.1, Oct. 1968–Nov. 1982)

3184
MEDICAL BEHAVIORAL SCIENCE. no.1– , 1972– . Winston-Salem, N.C.
Issued by: Wake Forest University. Subtitle reads: "A journal of cross-cultural research".

MEDICAL ECONOMICS
See SOCIAL SCIENCE & MEDICINE. MEDICAL ECONOMICS and: SOCIAL SCIENCE & MEDICINE. PART C. MEDICAL ECONOMICS

MEDICAL GEOGRAPHY
See SOCIAL SCIENCE & MEDICINE. MEDICAL GEOGRAPHY and: SOCIAL SCIENCE & MEDICINE. PART D. MEDICAL GEOGRAPHY

MEDICAL PSYCHOLOGY
See SOCIAL SCIENCE & MEDICINE. MEDICAL PSYCHOLOGY & MEDICAL SOCIOLOGY and: SOCIAL SCIENCE & MEDICINE. PART E. SOCIAL PSYCHOLOGY

MEDICAL SOCIOLOGY
See SOCIAL SCIENCE & MEDICINE. MEDICAL PSYCHOLOGY & MEDICAL SOCIOLOGY and: SOCIAL SCIENCE & MEDICINE. PART A. MEDICAL ANTHROPOLOGY

MEDITERRANEAN COUNTRIES
See YEARBOOK OF FOREIGN TRADE STATISTICS. THIRD COUNTRIES (volume B)

MEDITERRANEAN PEOPLES
See PEUPLES MEDITERRANÉENS

3185
MEDIZIN UND SOZIALWISSENSCHAFTEN. v.1– , 1974– . München, Wien, Baltimore, Md., Urban & Schwarzenberg. Irreg.
In German. Some works are translations from English. Monograph series.

3186
MEDIZINISCHE SOZIOLOGIE. 1– , 1981– . Frankfurt, New York, Campus Verlag. Annual.
In German.

3187
MEDUNARODNI PROBLEMI. 1– , 1949– . Beograd, "Jugoslavija". Quarterly.
Issued by: Institut za Medunarodnu Politiku i Privredu. In Serbo-Croatian. Published also in English edition, 1960–, containing translations of selected articles.
Indexed: Bull. Anal. Pol. Ec. Soc.

MEIJI DAIGAKU SHAKAI KAGAKU KENKYŪJO KIYŌ
See Meiji Daigaku, Tōkyō. Shakai Kagaku Kenkyū. MEIJI DAIGAKU SHAKAI KAGAKU KENKYUJŌ KIYŌ

3188
Meiji Daigaku, Tōkyō. Shakai Kagaku Kenkyū. MEIJI DAIGAKU SHAKAI KAGAKU KENKYŪJO KIYŌ. MEMOIRS OF THE INSTITUTE OF SOCIAL SCIENCES. 1– , 1963– . Tōkyō. Annual.
In Japanese; summaries in English. Vols. 8–9 issued in a combined form, 1971.

MEINUNG
See JOURNAL FÜR ANGEWANDTE SOZIALFORSCHUNG

3189
MELIORA. v.1–12, 1858–1869. London.
Subtitle reads: "A quarterly review of social science in its ethical, economical, political and ameliorative aspects".

MÉMOIRES
See Académie Royale des Sciences d'Outre-Mer. Classe des Sciences Morales et Politiques. MÉMOIRES. VERHANDELINGEN. IN 4°.

MÉMOIRES
See Académie Royale des Sciences d'Outre-Mer. Classe des Sciences Morales et Politiques. MÉMOIRES. VERHANDELINGEN. IN 8°.

MÉMOIRES
See Centre de Recherches Anthropologiques, Préhistoriques et Ethnographiques, Algiers. MÉMOIRES

MÉMOIRES
See Laboratoire d'Anthropologie Sociale. MÉMOIRES

MÉMOIRES
See Société d'Ethnographie. MÉMOIRES

MÉMOIRES DE L'ACADÉMIE INTERNATIONALE DE DROIT COMPARÉE
See International Academy of Comparative Law. ACTA ACADEMIAE UNIVERSITATIS JURISPRUDENTIARUM COMPARATIVAE

MÉMOIRES DE LA SECTION DE GÉOGRAPHIE
See Comité des Travaux Historiques et Scientifiques. Section Geógraphie. MÉMOIRES

MEMOIRS
See Anthropological Society of London. MEMOIRS

MEMOIRS
See American Anthropological Association. MEMOIRS

MEMOIRS
See Harvard University. Peabody Museum of Archaeology and Ethnology. MEMOIRS

MEMOIRS
See University of London. University College. Francis Galton Laboratory of Eugenics. MEMOIRS

MEMOIRS OF THE INSTITUTE OF SOCIAL SCIENCES, MEIJI UNIVERSITY
See Meiji Daigaku, Tōkyō. Shakai Kagaku Kenkyū. MEIJI DAIGAKU SHAKAI KAGAKU KENKYŪJO KIYŌ

MEMORIAS
See Academia Mexicana de la Historia. MEMORIAS

MEMÓRIAS DO INSTITUTO DE INVESTIGACIAIS CIENTÍFICE DE MOÇAMBIQUE. SERIE C. CIÊNCIAS HUMANAS
See Instituto de Investigaciais Científice de Moçambique. MEMÓRIAS. SERIE C. CIÊNCIAS HUMANAS

MEMORIE DI GEOGRAFIA ANTROPICA
See MEMORIE DI GEOGRAFIA ECONOMICA ET ANTROPICA

3190
MEMORIE DI GEOGRAFIA ECONOMICA ET ANTROPICA. v.1–15, 1946–1959; n. ser. 1– , 1963– . Napoli. Annual.
Organ of: Istituto di Geografia, Università di Napoli. In Italian; summaries in English, French, or German. Title varies: v.1–15, 1946–59, *Memorie di Geografia Antropica.*

3191
MENS EN MAATSCHAPPIJ. v.1– , 1925– . Rotterdam, Rotterdam University Press, later Deventer, Van Logus Slaterus. Bimonthly, 1925–70; quarterly.
Issued by: Rotterdam University, and Nederlandse Sociologisch Vereninging. In Dutch; some articles in English. Title varies: v.1–22, *Mensch en Maatschappij.*
Indexes: Vols. 1–25, 1925–50.
Indexed: Bull. Sig. Soc. Eth.; Int. Bibl. Soc. Cul. Anth.; Soc. Abst.; Urb. Aff. Abst.

MENSCH EN MAATSCHAPPIJ
See MENS EN MAATSCHAPPIJ

DER MENSCH UND SEINE WELT
See LE DOMAIN HUMAIN

METHODOLOGICAL AND HISTORIOGRAPHIC PROBLEMS OF HISTORICAL SCIENCE
See METODOLOGICHESKI I ISTORIOGRAFSKI PROBLEMI NA ISTORICHESKATA NAUKA

3192
METODOLOGICHESKI I ISTORIOGRAFSKI PROBLEMI NA ISTORICHESKATA NAUKA. 1– , 1973– . Sofii͡a, Publishing House of the Bulgarian Academy of Sciences. Biennial.
Issued by: Institut za Istorii͡a, Bulgarska Akademii͡a na Naukite. In Bulgarian; summaries in English, French, German and Russian. Other title: *Methodological and Historiographic Problems of Historical Science.*

3193
METODOLOGICHESKIE PROBLEMY OBSHCHESTVENNYKH NAUK. no.1– , 1968– . Leningrad, Izd-vo Leningradskogo Universiteta. Irreg.
In Russian. Title varies: no.1–4, 1968–75, *Metodologicheskie Voprosy Obshchestvennykh Nauk.*

METODOLOGICHESKIE VOPROSY OBSHCHESTVENNYKH NAUK
See METODOLOGICHESKIE PROBLEMY OBSHCHESTVENNYKH NAUK

3194
METRA. v.1– , Mar. 1962– . Paris, Grouppe Metra. Quarterly.
In English, French, German, or Italian.
Indexed: Bull. Sig. Soc. Eth.; Int. Bibl. Soc.; Int. Pol. Soc. Abst.; PAIS; Soc. Abst.

3195
METROECONOMICA. 1– , July 1949– . Trieste, later Bologna, Casa Editrice Licinio Capelli. Three no. a year.
Issued by: Istituto di Economia. In English; book reviews in English or Italian.
Indexed: Eco. Abst.; Geo. Abst.; Int. Bibl. Eco.; Int. Bibl. Pol. Sc.; Int. Bibl. Soc.; Int. Bibl. Soc. Cul. Anth.

3196
MEZHDUNARODNAI͡A ZHIZN'. Apr. 1954– . Moskva. Quarterly, 1954; monthly.
In Russian. Tables of contents also in Chinese, English, French and German.
Indexed: His. Abst.; Int. Bibl. Eco.; Int. Bibl. Pol. Sc.

MEZHDUNARODNOE PRAVO I DIPLOMAT͡SII͡A
See INTERNATIONALES RECHT UND DIPLOMATIE

3197
MEZINARODNI VZTAHY. 1– , 1966– . Praha, Orbis. Quarterly.
Issued by: Mezinarodni Ústav pro Mezinarodnu Politiku a Ekonomii. In Czech; summaries in English, French, German and Russian. Tables of contents also in these languages.
Indexed: Bull. Anal. Pol. Ec. Soc.; Int. Bibl. Eco.; Peace Res. Abst. J.

MEZZOGIORNO D'EUROPA
See JOURNAL OF REGIONAL POLICY

3198
MICHIGAN DISCUSSIONS IN ANTHROPOLOGY. v.1– , fall 1975– . Ann Arbor, Mich. Semi-annual.
Issued by: Department of Anthropology, University of Michigan.
Indexed: Int. Bibl. Soc. Cul. Anth.

3199
MICHIGAN INDEX TO LABOR UNION PERIODICALS. Jan./June 1960–1967. Ann Arbor, Mich. Monthly, with semi-annual cumulation in 1960; with annual cumulation.
Issued by: Bureau of Industrial Relations, University of Michigan. Title varies: 1960–66, *The University of Michigan Index to Labor Union Periodicals.*

3200
MICHIGAN MONOGRAPHS IN CHINESE STUDIES. no.45– , 1982– . Ann Arbor, Mich. Irreg.
Issued by: Center for Chinese Studies, University of Michigan.
Continues: *Michigan Papers in Chinese Studies* (no.1–44, 1968–80)

3201
MICRONESIA. 1– , June 1964– . Agana.
Issued by: Territorial College. In various languages.
Indexed: Abst. Anth.; Int. Bibl. Soc. Cul. Anth.

3202
MICROPOLITICS. v.1– , 1981– . New York, Crane Russak. Quarterly.
Published in cooperation with the Center for the Study of Business and Government, Baruch College—CUNY.
Indexed: ABC POL SCI; Int. Bibl. Soc. Cul. Anth.; Int. Pol. Sc. Abst.

3203
MIDCONTINENTAL JOURNAL OF ARCHAEOLOGY. MCJA. v.1– , Feb. 1976– . Kent, Ohio, Kent State University Press. Semi-annual.
Indexed: Int. Bibl. Soc. Cul. Anth.

3204
MIDDLE EAST ANNUAL REVIEW. 1–6, 1974–1980. Saffron Walden. Annual.
Based on material provided by: The Economist Intelligence Unit.
Continued by: *Middle East Review.*
Indexed: Bull. Anal. Pol. Ec. Soc.

3205
MIDDLE EAST CONTEMPORARY SURVEY. v.1– , 1976/77– . London, New York, Holmes & Meier Pub. Annual.
Issued by: Shiloah Center for Middle Eastern and African Studies, Tel-Aviv University.

3206
MIDDLE EAST FORUM. AL-KULLĪYAH. v.1– , 1925– . Beirut. Quarterly.
Organ of: Alumni Association, American University, Beirut. V.48 of 1972 last available for examination.
Indexed: Int. Bibl. Pol. Sc.; Peace Res. Abst. J.

3207
THE MIDDLE EAST JOURNAL. 1– , 1947– . Washington, D.C. Quarterly (some combined numbers)
Issued by: The Middle East Institute.
Indexed: ABC POL SCI; Abst. Anth.; Bull. Anal. Pol. Ec. Soc.; Bull. Sic. Soc. Eth.; Eco. Abst.; His. Abst.; Ind. Per. Art. Law; Int. Bibl. Eco.; Int. Bibl. Pol. Sc.; Int. Bibl. Soc.; Int. Bibl. Soc. Cul. Auth.; Int. Lab. Doc.; J. Eco. Lit.; PAIS; Peace Res. Abst. J.; Pop. Ind.; Soc. Sc. Hum. Ind.; SSCI.

3208
MIDDLE EAST REVIEW. v.7– , fall 1974– . New Brunswick, N.J., Transaction Periodicals Consortium. Quarterly (some combined numbers)
Issued by: American Academic Association for Peace in Middle East.
Continues: *Middle East Information Series.*
Indexed: Bull. Anal. Pol. Ec. Soc.; Int. Bibl. Pol. Sc.; Int. Pol. Sc. Abst.; LLBA; PAIS; Soc. Abst.

3209
MIDDLE EAST REVIEW. [7]– , 1981– . Saffron Walden, World of Information [publ. 1980]. Annual.
Based on material provided by: The Economist Intelligence Unit. Published also in Arabic, American and German editions.

Continues: *Middle East Annual Review.*

3210
MIDDLE EASTERN STUDIES. v.1– , Oct. 1964– . London, F. Cass. Quarterly.
Indexed: ABC POL SCI; Abst. Anth.; Bull. Anal. Pol. Ec. Soc.; Bull. Sig. Soc. Eth.; Curr. Cont. Soc. Beh. Sc.; Eco. Abst.; His. Abst.; Ind. Per. Art. Law; Int. Bibl. Eco.; Int. Bibl. Pol. Sc.; Int. Bibl. Soc.; Int. Bibl. Soc. Cul. Anth.; PAIS; Peace Res. Abst. J.; Pop. Ind.; Soc. Abst.; Soc. Sc. Ind.; SSCI.

3211
MIDWEST JOURNAL OF POLITICAL SCIENCE. v.1–16, May 1957–1972. Detroit, Mich., Wayne State University Press. Quarterly.
Sponsored by: Midwest Conference of Political Scientists.
Continued by: American Journal of Political Science.
Indexes: v.1–10, 1957–66, in v.11, no.2.
Indexed: His. Abst.; Ind. Per. Art. Law; Int. Pol. Sc. Abst.; Peace Res. Abst. J.

3212
THE MIDWEST QUARTERLY. v.1– , autumn 1959– . Pittsburg, Kans. Quarterly.
Issued by: Pittsburg State University (called earlier Kansas State College). Subtitle reads: "A journal of contemporary thought".
Indexed: His. Abst.; Ind. Per. Art. Law; PAIS; PHRA; Soc. Sc. Hum. Ind.

3213
MIDWEST REVIEW OF PUBLIC ADMINISTRATION. v.1– , 1967– . Parkville, Mo. Semi-annual.
Indexed: ABC POL SCI; Bull. Anal. Pol. Ec. Soc.; Int. Bibl. Pol. Sc.; Sage Urb. Stu. Abst.

MIGRACIONES INTERNACIONALES
See INTERNATIONAL MIGRATION

3214
MIGRACIONES INTERNACIONALES EN LAS AMÉRICAS. v.1– , 1980– . Caracas. Annual.
Issued by: Centro de Estudios de Pastoral y Assistencia Migratoria. In Spanish.

MIGRATIONS INTERNATIONALES
See INTERNATIONAL MIGRATION

3215
MILBANK MEMORIAL FUND QUARTERLY. 1– , 1923– . New York. Quarterly.
Indexed: Bull. Anal. Pol. Ec. Soc.; Bull. Sig. Soc. Eth.; Ind. Per. Art. Law; Int. Bibl. Soc.; Int. Lab. Doc.; PAIS; PHRA; Soc. Sc. Hum. Ind.; Soc. Abst.

MILITARY BALANCE
See International Institute for Strategic Studies. MILITARY BALANCE

3216
MILLENNIUM. [v.1]– , autumn 1961– . London, Millennium Pub. Group. Three no. a year.
Issued by: London School of Economics and Political Science.
Indexed: ABC POL SCI; Brit. Hum. Ind.; Bull. Anal. Pol. Ec. Soc.; His. Abst.; Int. Bibl. Eco.; Int. Bibl. Pol. Sc.; Int. Pol. Sc. Abst.; PAIS.

3217
MILLETLERARASI MUNASEBETLER TÜRK YILLIGI. THE TURKISH YEARBOOK OF INTERNATIONAL RELATIONS. 1– , 1960– . Ankara. Annual.
Issued by: Munasebetler Eustitusu Siyasel Bilgiler Fakultesi, Universitesi. In Turkish.

MILLETLERARASI SARK TETKIKLERI MECMUASI
See ORIENS

3218
MIN TSU HSÜEH PAO. 1– , 1981– . K'un-ming, Yun-nan min tsu ch'n pan she. Annual.
Issued by: Yun-nan sheng min tsu yen chiu so pien. In Chinese.

3219
MINERVA. v.1– , autumn 1962– . London, Macmillan Journals. Quarterly.
Issued by: International Council on the Future of the University.
Indexed: Bull. Anal. Pol. Ec. Soc.; Int. Bibl. Pol. Sc.; Int. Bibl. Soc. Cul. Anth.; Int. Lab. Doc.; Int. Pol. Sc. Abst.; PAIS; Soc. Abst.; Urb. Aff. Abst.

3220
MINORITIES IN AMERICA. 1976– . University Park, Pa., Pennsylvania State University Press. Annual.

3221
MINZOKU-GAKU KENKYŪ. v.1– , 1935– . Tokyo. Four no. a year.
Issued by: Nippon Minzokugaku Tai. In Japanese. Other title: *Japanese Journal of Ethnology.*
Indexed: Abst. Anth.; His. Abst.; Int. Bibl. Soc. Cul. Anth.

MINZOKUGAKUSHI
See ASIAN FOLKLORE STUDIES

3222
MIROVAI͡A EKONOMIKA I MEZHDUNARODNYE OTNOSHENII͡A. 1– , July 1957– . Moskva, Izd-vo "Pravda". Monthly.

Issued by: Institut Mirovoĭ Ekonomiki i Mezhdunarodnikh Otnosheniĭ, Akademiia Nauk SSSR. In Russian. Tables of contents in Chinese, English, French, and German. Includes supplement "Ekonomicheskie polozhenie kapitalisticheskikh stran; kon'iunkturnyĭ obzor".

Indexed: Bull. Anal. Pol. Ec. Soc.; Int. Bibl. Eco.; Int. Pol. Sc. Abst.

3223
MIROVOE KHOZIAĬSTVO. 1928– . Moskva. Annual.

Issued by: Institut Mirovogo Khoziaistva i Mirovoĭ Politiki, Kommunisticheskaia Akademiia, 1928–35; Akademiia Nauk SSSR. In Russian.

3224
MIROVOE KHOZIAĬSTVO I MIROVAIA POLITIKA. v.1–22, 1926–1947. Moskva, "Pravda". Monthly.

Organ of: Institut Mirovogo Khoziaistva i Mirovoĭ Politiki Kommunisticheskoĭ Akademii, 1926–36; Institut Akademii Nauk SSSR, 1936–47. In Russian. Issues for Oct. 1939–Dec. 1942 have also title in English: *World Economics and Politics*. Includes: "Statisticheskoe Prilozhenie", "Mezhdunarodnye Dokumenty", "Diplomaticheskaia Khronika Vtoroĭ Mirovoĭ Voiny", and "Prilozhenie". Absorbed: *Kon'iunktura Mirovogo Khoziaistva* in Oct. 1935, and *Tikhyĭ Okean* in July 1938.

Superseded by: *Voprosy Ekonomiki*.

MIṢR AL-MUS'ĀSIRAH
See EGYPTE CONTEMPORAINE

3225
MISSIOLOGY. v.1– , Jan. 1973– . South Pasadena, Calif. Quarterly.

Issued by: American Society for Missiology.

Supersedes: *Practical Anthropology*.

Indexed: Bull. Anal. Pol. Ec. Soc.; Int. Bibl. Soc. Cul. Anth.

THE MISSISSIPPI VALLEY HISTORICAL REVIEW
See JOURNAL OF AMERICAN HISTORY

3226
DIE MITARBEIT. v.1– , 1952– . Heidelberg, later Göttingen, Verlag Otto Schwartz. Bimonthly, 1952–66; quarterly.

In German.

Indexed: Int. Bibl. Eco.; PAISFL; Peace Res. Abst. J.

MITTEILUNGEN
See Akademie der Wissenschaft, Wien. Prähistorische Kommission. MITTEILUNGEN

MITTEILUNGEN
See Anthropologische Gesellschaft in Wien. MITTEILUNGEN

MITTEILUNGEN
See Berliner Gesellschaft für Anthropologie, Ethnologie und Urgeschichte. MITTEILUNGEN

MITTEILUNGEN
See Institut für Gesellschaftspolitik. MITTEILUNGEN

MITTEILUNGEN
See ZEITSCHRIFT FÜR KULTURAUSTAUSCH

MITTEILUNGEN DER GESELLSCHAFT FÜR VERGLEICHENDE RECHTS- UND STAATSWISSENSCHAFT ZU BERLIN
See ZEITSCHRIFT FÜR VERGLEICHENDE RECHTS- UND STAATSWISSENSCHAFT MIT BESONDERER RÜCKSICHTIGUNG DER RECHTE DER NATUR- UND KULTURVÖLKER

3227
MITTEILUNGEN ZUR ALTEN GESCHICHTE UND ARCHÄOLOGIE IN DER DEUTSCHEN DEMOKRATISCHEN REPUBLIK. v.1– , 1973– . Berlin. Annual.

Issued by: Zentralinstitut für Alte Geschichte und Archäologie, Akademie der Wissenschaft der DDR. In German. Processed.

3228
MITTEILUNGEN ZUR KULTURKUNDE. v.1, 1966. Wiesbaden, F. Steiner. Annual.

Issued by: Frobenius-Institut. In German.

Supersedes: *Paideuma*. Superseded by: *Paideuma*.

3229
MODERN AGE. v.1– , summer 1957– . Chicago, Ill. Quarterly.

Issued by: Foundation for Foreign Affairs.

Indexed: Bull. Anal. Pol. Ec. Soc.; His. Abst.; Int. Bibl. Soc. Cul. Anth.; PAIS; Peace Res. Abst. J.

3230
MODERN ASIAN STUDIES. v.1– , Jan. 1967– . London, Cambridge University Press. Quarterly.

Indexed: ABC POL SCI; Abst. Anth.; Bull. Anal. Pol. Ec. Soc.; Curr. Cont. Soc. Beh. Sc.; His. Abst.; Int. Bibl. Eco.; Int. Bibl. Pol. Sc.; Int. Bibl. Soc.; Int. Bibl. Soc. Cul. Anth.; Int. Lab. Doc.; Int. Pol. Sc. Abst.; SSCI; Wom. Stu. Abst.

3231
MODERN CEYLON STUDIES. v.1– , Jan. 1970– . Paradeniya. Semi-annual.

Issued by: University of Ceylon. Subtitle reads: "A journal of the social sciences".

3232
MODERN CHINA. v.1– , Jan. 1975– . Beverly Hills, Calif., Sage Publications. Quarterly.
Indexed: ABC POL SCI; PAIS.

3233
MODERN LAW AND SOCIETY. v.1– , 1968– . Tübingen. Semi-annual.
Issued by: Institute for Scientific Cooperation. Subtitle reads: "A review of German language and research contributions on law, political science and sociology".

3234
MODERNE WELT. June 1959–1970. Kon-Marienburg, Kiepenheur & Witsch. Quarterly.
Issued by: Arbeitskreis für Ost–West Forschungen. In German.
Indexed: Int. Bibl. Pol. Sc.; Peace Res. Abst. J.

LE MOIS EN AFRIQUE. REVUE FRANÇAISE D'ÉTUDES POLITIQUES AFRICAINES
See REVUE FRANÇAISE D'ÉTUDES POLITIQUES AFRICAINES

MONATSHEFTE FÜR AUSWÄRTIGE POLITIK
See AUSWÄRTIGE POLITIK

3235
LE MONDE D'OUTRE-MER; PASSÉ ET PRÉSENT. SÉRIE D'ÉTUDES. 1– , 1957– . Paris. Irreg.
Issued by: Centre des Recherches Historiques, École Pratique des Hautes Études. In French.
Indexed: Bull. Anal. Pol. Ec. Soc.; Peace Res. Abst. J.

LE MONDE DE ISLAM
See DIE WELT DES ISLAMS

MONDE DES CONFLICTS
See CONFLICT STUDIES

3236
LE MONDE DIPLOMATIQUE. 1– , 1954– . Paris, Le Monde. Monthly.
Subtitle reads: "Le journal de la coopération et des grandes organisations internationales".
Indexed: Bull. Anal. Pol. Ec. Soc.

3237
LE MONDE JUIF. [1]–18, Aug. 1946–1963 (no.1–34/35); n. ser. v.19 (no.36)– , Jan./Mar. 1964– . Paris. Quarterly (irreg.)
Issued by: Centre de Documentation Juive Contemporaine. In French.
Supersedes: Bulletin du Centre de Documentation Juive Contemporaine.
Indexed: Bull. Anal. Pol. Ec. Soc.

3238
MONDES ET CULTURES. v.38– , 1978– . Paris. Quarterly.
Issued by: Académie des Sciences d'Outre-Mer. In French.
Continues: Académie des Sciences d'Outre-Mer. *Comptes Rendus des Séances. Communications.*
Indexed: Int. Bibl. Soc. Cul. Anth.

3239
MONDO APERTO. 1– , 1947– . Roma. Bimonthly.
Issued by: Centro Italiano per le Studi delle Relazioni Economiche Estere e dei Mercati. In Italian.
Indexed: J. Eco. Lit.

MONDO OPERAIO
See MONDOOPERARIO

IL MONDO VISSUTO DELL'UOMO
See LE DOMAIN HUMAIN

3240
MONDOOPERARIO. v.27– , 1974– . Roma, Mondooperario Edizione. Monthly.
In Italian.
Continues: *Mondo Operaio.*
Indexed: Bull. Anal. Pol. Ec. Soc.

3241
MONEDA Y CRÉDITO. 1– , June 1942– . Madrid. Quarterly.
In Spanish.
Indexes: No.1–10, June 1942–Sept. 1944.
Indexed: Bull. Anal. Pol. Ec. Soc.; His. Abst.; Int. Bibl. Eco.

3242
MONETA E CREDITO. [1]– , 1st quarter 1948– . Roma. Quarterly.
Issued by: Banca Nazionale del Lavoro. In Italian.
Indexed: Int. Bibl. Eco.; PAISFL.

MONETARY AND ECONOMIC STUDIES
See Bank of Japan. MONETARY AND ECONOMIC STUDIES

MONEY AND BANKING
See League of Nations. MONEY AND BANKING

3243
MONGOLIAN STUDIES. v.1– , 1974– . Bloomington, Ind., Research Center for Language and Semiotic Studies, Indiana University. Annual.

Issued by: The Mongolia Society. In English, French, or German.
Supersedes: Mongolia Society. *Bulletin*.

MONOGRAPH
See American Academy of Political and Social Science. MONOGRAPH

3244
MONOGRAPH SERIES IN ETHNOMUSICOLOGY. no.1– , 1980– . Los Angeles, Calif. Irreg.
Issued by: Program in Ethnomusicology, Department of Music, University of California at Los Angeles. Other title: *UCLA Monograph Series in Ethnomusicology*.

3245
MONOGRAPH SERIES IN WORLD AFFAIRS. v.1– , 1963– . Denver, Colo. Four no. a year.
Issued originally by: Graduate School of International Studies, University of Denver; later by: Social Science Foundation.
Indexed: SSCI.

MONOGRAPH SUPPLEMENT
See JOURNAL OF PERSONALITY AND SOCIAL PSYCHOLOGY

MONOGRAPHS
See American Ethnological Society. MONOGRAPHS

3246
MONOGRAPHS IN ECONOMIC ANTHROPOLOGY. no.1– , 1983– . Lanham, Md., University Press of America. Irreg.
Issued by: Society for Economic Anthropology.

3247
MONOGRAPHS IN INTERNATIONAL STUDIES. SOUTHEAST ASIA SERIES. no.64– , 1984– . Athens, Ohio. Irreg.
Issued by: Center for International Studies.
Continues: *Papers in International Studies. Southeast Asia Series* (no.1–63, 1968–83)

MONOGRAPHS IN SOCIAL RESEARCH
See National Opinion Research Center. MONOGRAPHS IN SOCIAL RESEARCH

MONTHLY BULLETIN OF STATISTICS
See League of Nations. MONTHLY BULLETIN OF STATISTICS

MONTHLY BULLETIN OF STATISTICS
See United Nations. Statistical Office. MONTHLY BULLETIN OF STATISTICS

MONTHLY JOURNAL OF INSTITUTE OF DEVELOPING ECONOMIES
See AJIA KEIZAI

MONTHLY MARKETING REVIEW
See REVIEW OF MARKETING AND AGRICULTURAL ECONOMIES

3248
MONTHLY PUBLIC OPINION SURVEYS. 1– , 1955– . New Delhi. Monthly.
Issued by: Indian Institute of Public Opinion.
Indexed: Bull. Anal. Pol. Ec. Soc.; Int. Pol. Sc. Abst.

3249
MONTHLY REVIEW; AN INDEPENDENT SOCIALIST MAGAZINE. v.1–12, May 1949–Dec. 1961. New York, Monthly Review Foundation.
Indexed: Bull. Anal. Pol. Ec. Soc.; Bull. Sig. Soc. Eth.; PAIS.

MONTHLY STATISTICS OF FOREIGN TRADE
See Organisation for Economic Co-operation and Development. MONTHLY STATISTICS OF FOREIGN TRADE

MONUMENTOS HISTÓRICOS Y ARQUELÓGICOS
See Pan American Institute of Geography and History. Commission on History. MONUMENTOS HISTÓRICOS Y ARQUEOLÓGICOS

MOROCCAN ANNALS OF SOCIOLOGY
See ANNALES MAROCAINES DE SOCIOLOGIE

3250
Moskovskiĭ Universitet. VESTNIK. SERIIA XII. TEORIIA NAUCHNOGO KOMMUNIZMA. Jan./Feb. 1977– . Moskva, Izd-vo Moskovskogo Gosudarstvennogo Universiteta. Bimonthly.
In Russian.
Continues: Moskovskiĭ Universitet. *Vestnik. Seriia XIII. Teoriia Nauchnogo Kommunizma.*

3251
Moskovskiĭ Universitet. VESTNIK. SERIIA ISTORIIA. 1978– . Moskva. Bimonthly.
In Russian. Tables of contents also in English.
Continues: *Vestnik. Seriia IX. Istoricheskie Nauki* (1960–76)

THE MOSLEM WORLD
See MUSLIM WORLD

MOUVEMENT JURIDIQUE, ÉCONOMIQUE ET SOCIOLOGIQUE
See RUCH PRAWNICZY, EKONOMICZNY I SOCJOLOGICZNY

3252
MOUVEMENT SOCIAL. v.1–78?, 1876–July 1914. Paris.
In French. Title varies: v.1–66, *Association Catholique*.
Indexes: Vols. 1–26, 27–32.

3253
LE MOUVEMENT SOCIAL. no.1– , 1951– . Paris, Les Éditions Ouvrières. Quarterly.
Organ of: Institut Français d'Histoire Française; 1968– with the Centre d'Histoire du Syndicalisme de l'Université de Paris. In French. Title varies: 1951–52, *Bulletin de l'Institut Français d'Histoire Social*; 1953–July/Sept. 1960, *L'Actualité d'Histoire*.
Indexed: Bull. Anal. Pol. Ec. Soc.; Bull. Sig. Soc. Eth.; His. Abst.; Int. Bibl. Soc. Cul. Anth.; Int. Pol. Sc. Abst.

LE MOUVEMENT SOCIOLOGIQUE
See LE MOUVEMENT SOCIOLOGIQUE INTERNATIONAL

3254
LE MOUVEMENT SOCIOLOGIQUE INTERNATIONAL. v.1–11, 1900–1911. Bruxelles.
In French. Title varies: v.1–7, no.1, 1900–06, *Mouvement Sociologique*, a supplement to *Revue Néoscolastique de Philosophie*. Merged with: *Annales de Sociologie*.

3255
LE MOUVEMENT SYNDICAL MONDIAL. May 1951– . Paris, Société Français d'Éditions et de Publications Syndicales Internationales. Semimonthly, 1951–Apr. 1954; monthly.
In French. Includes some supplements.
Supersedes: a publication of the same title issued by: Fédération Syndicale Mondiale.
Indexed: Bull. Anal. Pol. Ec. Soc.

3256
AL-MU'ASHOHIRĀT AL-IḤṢĀ'ĪYAH LIL-'ĀLAM AL-'ARABĪ LIL-FATRAH. STATISTICAL INDICATORS OF THE ARAB WORLD FOR THE PERIOD; 1970–1978– . Beirut [published in 1980 by the Economic Commission for Western Asia, United Nations].
Issued by: Jāmi'at al-Duwal al-'Arabīyah, al-Lajnah al-Iqtiṣādīyah li-Gharbī Āsiyā. In Arabic and English.

3257
MUC LUC PHAN TIN TAP KHOA HOC XA HOI VIETNAM. INDEX TO VIETNAMESE SOCIAL SCIENCE PERIODICALS. Saigon, Hoc Vien Quoc gia Hanh chanh tu vien.
In Vietnamese.

3258
MÜNCHNER STUDIEN ZUR SOZIAL- UND WIRTSCHAFTSGEOGRAPHIE. v.1– , 1966– . München, Verlag Michael Lassleben. Irreg.
Issued by: Wirtschaftsgeographische Institut, Universität München. In German; summaries in English, French and Russian.

3259
MUJER Y SOCIEDAD. v.1– , July 1980– . Lima, Editora Ital Perú.
In Spanish.

3260
IL MULINO. v.1– , Nov. 1951– . Bologna, Società Editrice il Mulino. Monthly, 1951–58; bimonthly.
In Italian.
Indexes: no.1–272, 1951–80, 1v.
Indexed: Bull. Sig. Soc. Eth.; Int. Bibl. Pol. Sc.

3261
MULTICULTURAL EDUCATION ABSTRACTS. v.1– , 1982– . Abingdon, Carfax. Quarterly.

3262
MULTILATERAL TREATIES DEPOSITED WITH THE SECRETARY GENERAL [OF THE UNITED NATIONS]. 1981– . New York, United Nations. Annual.
Continues: *Multilateral Treaties in Respect of which the Secretary General Performs Depository Function* (United Nations. ST/LEG/SER.E/1)

3263
MULTIVARIATE BEHAVIORAL RESEARCH. v.1– , Jan. 1966– . Fort Worth, Tex., Texas Christian University. Quarterly.
Organ of: Society for Multivariate Experimental Psychology, University of Colorado, Boulder.
Indexed: Curr. Cont. Soc. Beh. Sc.; LLBA; Psych. Abst.; SSCI.

3264
MUNDO NUEVO. v.1– , July 1966– . Buenos Aires. Monthly (some combined numbers)
In Spanish.
Indexed: Int. Bibl. Soc. Cul. Anth.; Int. Lab. Doc.

3265
MUNICIPAL MANAGEMENT. v.1– , summer 1978– . Brandon, Vt., Municipal Management Pub. Co. Quarterly.
Indexed: Sage Pub. Adm. Abst.

3266
THE MUNICIPAL REVIEW. 1– , 1930– . London. Monthly.
Issued by: Association of Municipal Authorities.

Supersedes: the association's *Monthly Circular.*

3267
MUNICIPAL REVIEW OF CANADA. v.1– , 1905– . Montreal. Monthly.
Official organ of: Union of Canadian Municipalities. Title varies: v.1–18, no.7, *The Canadian Municipal Journal.*

3268
Musée Social, Paris. ANNALES. Jan. 1902–July 1914. Paris, Librairie A. Rousseau. Monthly.
In French. Vols. for 1902–08 called v.7–13 continuing the numbering of the museum's monthly bulletin published 1899–1909.

3269
Museum für Völkerkunde, Leipzig. JAHRBUCH. v.1– , 1906– . Leipzig, later Berlin, Akademie Verlag.
In German; occasionally in English.
Supersedes: the museum's *Bericht.*

3270
THE MUSLIM WORLD. v.1– , Jan. 1911– . Hartford, London, later New York, Missionary Review Pub. Co. Quarterly.
Issued by: Hartford Seminary Foundation. Subtitle reads: "A quarterly review of history, culture, religions and Christian mission in Islamdom". Title varies: 1911–Oct. 1947, *The Moslem World.*
Indexed: Bull. Anal. Pol. Ec. Soc.; Bull. Sig. Soc. Eth.; Int. Bibl. Soc. Cul. Anth.; Int. Pol. Sc. Abst.

3271
MYŚL MARKSISTOWSKA. v.1– , Jan./Feb. 1985– . Warszawa, RSW "Prasa-Książka-Ruch" Wydawnictwo Współczesne. Bimonthly.
Issued by: Akademia Nauk Społecznych Polskiej Zjednoczonej Partii Robotniczej. In Polish.

N

NILR
See NETHERLANDS INTERNATIONAL LAW JOURNAL

NP
See NUEVA POLITICA

NSP
See NEW POLITICAL SCIENCE

3272
NADA. v.1– , 1964– . Harare. Annual.
Issued by: Ministry of Internal Affairs.
Indexed: His. Abst.

3273
NAGOYA GAKUIN DAIGAKU RONSHU. SHAKAI KAGAKU HEN. 1– , 1964– . Set, Aichi-ken.
Issued by: Sangyo Kagaku Kenkyūjo, Nagoya Gakuin Daigaku. In Japanese. Other title: *Nagoya Gakuin University Review. Social Sciences.*
Continues, in part: *Nagoya Gakuin Daigaku Ronshu.*

NAGOYA GAKUIN UNIVERSITY REVIEW. SOCIAL SCIENCES
See NAGOYA GAKUIN DAIGAKU RONSHU. SHAKAI KAGAKU HEN

3274
NANYANG QUARTERLY. v.1–3, Mar. 1971–1973. Singapore. Ten no. a year.
Issued by: South Seas Society. Summaries in Chinese. Spine title: *Review of Southeast Asian Studies.*
Continued by: *Review of Southeast Asian Studies.*

3275
Nanzan Daigaku, Nagoya. Jinruigaku Kenkyūjo. JINRUIGAKU KENKYŪJO KIYŌ—NANZAN DAIGAKU JINRUIGAKU KENKYŪ. 1– , 1972– Nagoya. Annual.
In English, German, or Japanese. Other title: *Bulletin of the Anthropological Institute.*

3276
Narodna Banka FNRJ. Odeljenie za Analize i Ekonomska Izucivanja. BILTEN ODELJENJA ZA ANALIZE I EKONOMSKA IZUČIVANJA NARODNE BANKE FNRJ. 1946–1959. Beograd. Monthly.
In Serbo-Croatian.
Superseded by: *Statisticki Bilten* (issued by the bank's Sluzba Drustvenog Knjigovodstva)

NARODNA DRZAVA
See NOVA ADMINISTRACJA

3277
NARODNA TVORCHIST TA ETNOGRAFIIA. 1957– . Kiev, Vid-vo Akademiia Nauk SSSR. Quarterly.
Issued by: Institut Mystestvoznavstva, Fol'kloru ta Etnografii, Akademiia Nauk Ukrainskoï SSR, and Ministerstvo Kultury Ukrainskoï SSR. In Ukrainian. Tables of contents also in English. Subtitle reads: "Naukovo-popularnyi zhurnal".
Indexed: Bull. Sig. Soc. Eth.; Int. Bibl. Soc. Cul. Anth.

NARODNI ODBOR
See OPSTINA

NARODNOE KHOZIAĬSTVO
See LIAUDIES UKIS

3278
NARODNOE KHOZIAĬSTVO KAZAKHSTANA. v.1–21, 1926–1963. Alma Ata. Monthly.
Issued by: Gosudarstvennaia Planovaia Komissiia KSSR. In Russian.

3279
NARODNOE KHOZIAĬSTVO SOTSIALISTICHESKIKH STRAN V . . . GODU . . .: SOOBSHCHENIIA TSENTRAL'NYKH STATISTICHESKIKH UPRAVLENIĬ. 1961– . Moskva, Izd-vo Ekonomicheskoï Literatury. Annual.
Issued by: Sektor Statistiki, Institut Ekonomiki Mirovoï Sotsialisticheskoï Sistemy, Akademiia Nauk SSSR. In Russian.

NARODNOE KHOZIAĬSTVO SREDNEĬ AZII
See EKONOMIKA I ZHIZN'

NARODNOE KHOZIAĬSTVO UZBEKISTANA
See EKONOMIKA I ZHIZN'

3280
NARODOPISNY SBORNIK ČESKOSLOVENSKÝ. 1– , 1906– . Praha.
Issued by: Narodopisne Muzeum Československé, and Narodopisna Společnost Československá. In Czech. Other title: *Revue Ethnographique Tchécoslave.*
Supersedes: *Narodopisny Sbornik Československý* (v.1–11, 1897–1905)

Indexes: Vols. 1–20, in v.20.
Indexed: Int. Bibl. Soc. Cul. Anth.

3281
NARODY AZII I AFRIKI. 1– , 1959– . Moskva, Nauka. Bimonthly.
Issued by: Institut Narodov Azii i Afriki, Akademiia Nauk SSSR. In Russian; some summaries in English. Tables of contents also in Chinese, English and French. Title also in Chinese, Hindi and Urdu. Title varies: 1959–61, *Problemy Vostokovedeniia.*
Supersedes: *Sovetskoe Vostokovedenie* (1955–58), and *Sovetskoe Kitaevedenie* (1958)
Indexed: Bull. Anal. Pol. Ec. Soc.; His. Abst.; Int. Bibl. Eco.; Int. Bibl. Pol. Sc.; Int. Bibl. Soc.; Int. Bibl. Soc. Cul. Anth.; Int. Lab. Doc.; Int. Pol. Sc. Abst.

3282
NAŠA STVARNOST; CASOPIS ZA DRUSTVENA PITANJA. v.1–17, Oct. 1946–Nov./Dec. 1963. Beograd. Frequency varies.
Organ of: Centralni Komitet, Savez Komunista (called in 1946–52 Komunisticka Partija Jugoslavije). Title varies: 1946–52, *Komunist.*
Absorbed by: *Socijalizam.*
Indexes: (author) vols. 7–17, 1953–63, with v.17.

3283
AL-NASHRAH AL-SANAWĪYAH LIL-IḤṢĀ'AT AL-TĪJĀRAH AL-KHĀRĪ LIL-BĪLA AL-ARABĪ-YAH 'ALA MUSTWĀ FUṢŪL AL-TAṢNIF AL-DUWALĪ AL-MI'ADDAL. ANNUAL BULLETIN FOR ARAB COUNTRIES FOREIGN TRADE STATISTICS, ACCORDING TO SITC, R DIVISIONS. 1970/73– . al-Quhirah, Majlis al-Ammah, al-Maktab, al-Markazī al Rābi' lil-Iḥṣā'. Annual.
In Arabic and English.

3284
NASIONALE REGISTER VAN NAVORSINGSPROJEKTE. REGISTER OF RESEARCH IN SOUTH AFRICA. 1967– . Pretoria. Annual.
In Afrikaans and English. Issued by: Kantoor van die Wetenskaplike Raadgewewer van die Eerste Minister. Beginning with 1974/75 includes also natural sciences. Processed.

NATION UND STAAT
See EUROPA-ETHNICA

NATIONAL ACCOUNTS, ESA AGGREGATES
See Statistical Office of the European Communities. NATIONAL ACCOUNTS, ESA AGGREGATES

NATIONAL ACCOUNTS. ESA. DETAILED TABLES BY BRANCH
See Statistical Office of the European Communities. NATIONAL ACCOUNTS. ESA. DETAILED. TABLES BY BRANCH

NATIONAL ACCOUNTS STATISTICS. GOVERNMENT ACCOUNTS AND TABLES
See United Nations. Statistical Office. NATIONAL ACCOUNTS STATISTICS. GOVERNMENT ACCOUNTS AND TABLES

NATIONAL ACCOUNTS STATISTICS. MAIN AGGREGATES AND DETAILED TABLES
See United Nations. Statistical Office. NATIONAL ACCOUNTS STATISTICS. MAIN AGGREGATES AND DETAILED TABLES

3285
NATIONAL CIVIC REVIEW. v.48– , 1959– . Worcester, Mass. Monthly (except Aug.)
Issued by: National Municipal League.
Continues: *National Municipal Review.*
Indexed: ABC POL SCI; Bull. Anal. Pol. Ec. Soc.; His. Abst.; Int. Bibl. Pol. Sc.; Int. Pol. Sc. Abst.; PAIS; Sage Urb. Stu. Abst.

3286
National Council on Crime and Delinquency. YEARBOOK. 1915–1953. New York.
Vols. for 1915–46 issued by the council under its earlier name: National Probation Association. Some nos. have also distinctive titles. Title varies: 1915–21, *Annual Report and Proceedings*; 1922–23, *Proceedings of the Annual Conference*; 1924–28, *Proceedings.*

NATIONAL ECONOMIC LEAGUE QUARTERLY
See THE CONSENSUS

3287
NATIONAL EDUCATION. Feb. 1919– . Wellington, later Armi. Monthly (except. Jan.)
Issued by: New Zealand Educational Institute, later the Department of Education, University of New England.
Supersedes: *New Zealand Journal of Education.*

3288
NATIONAL INSTITUTE ECONOMIC REVIEW. no.1– , Jan. 1959– . London. Bimonthly, 1959–61; quarterly.
Issued by: National Institute of Economic and Social Research.
Indexed: Bull. Anal. Pol. Ec. Soc.; Int. Bibl. Eco.; Int. Lab. Doc.; J. Eco. Lit.; PAIS.

3289
National Institute of Economic and Social Research. ECONOMIC AND SOCIAL STUDIES. no.1– , 1946– . London, Cambridge University Press. Irreg.

Monograph series.

3290
National Institute of Social Sciences. JOURNAL. v.1–19, 1915–Dec. 1934. New York.
V.1, no.1 also represents no.47 of the *Journal of the American Social Science Association.*

3291
NATIONAL MUNICIPAL REVIEW. v.1–47, Jan. 1912–1958. Worcester, Mass. Monthly (except July-Aug.)
Issued by: National Municipal League. Vols. 1–6 include Proceedings of the 17th–22nd annual meetings of the National Municipal League, previously included in the *Proceedings of the Conference for Good City Government.* Absorbed: *Equity* in Aug. 1919, *Short Ballot Bulletins* in 1920, *Proportional Representation Review* in May 1932.
Continued by: *National Civic Review.*

3292
National Opinion Research Center. MONOGRAPHS IN SOCIAL RESEARCH. no.1– , 1964– . Chicago, Ill. Irreg.
Monograph series.

NATIONAL REVIEW OF SOCIAL SCIENCES
See al-Markaz al-qawmī lil-Buḥūth al-ijtimā'īyah wa-al-qawmīyah. AL-MAJLLAH AL-IJTIMĀ'ĪYAH AL-QAWMĪYAH

3293
NATIONAL TAX JOURNAL. v.1– , Mar. 1948– . Chicago, Ill., later Sacramento, Calif.
Issued by: National Tax Association.
Supersedes: the association's *Bulletin.*
Indexed: Bull. Anal. Pol. Ec. Soc.; Curr. Cont. Soc. Beh. Sc.; Eco. Abst.; Ind. Leg. Per.; Ind. Per. Art. Law; Int. Bibl. Eco.; Int. Bibl. Pol. Sc.; Int. Bibl. Soc.; Int. Pol. Sc. Abst.; J. Eco. Lit.; PAIS; Urb. Aff. Abst.

THE NATIONAL WAR COLLEGE FORUM
See THE FORUM

NATIONALE REKENINGEN ESER. GEDETAILLEERDE TABELLEN PER BRANCHES
See Statistical Office of the European Communities. NATIONAL ACCOUNTS, ESA DETAILED TABLES BY BRANCH

NATIONALE REKENINGEN. ESER TOTALEN
See Statistical Office of the European Communities. NATIONAL ACCOUNTS, ESA AGGREGATES

3294
NATIONALITIES PAPERS. v.1– , fall 1972– . Charleston, Ill. Semi-annual.
Issued by: Association for the Study of Nationalities (USSR and East Europe) in collaboration with the Shevchenko Scientific Society in America.
Indexed: His. Abst.; Int. Bibl. Soc. Cul. Anth.; Int. Pol. Sc. Abst.

3295
NATIONALØKONOMISK TIDSSKRIFT FOR SAMFUNDSSPØRGSMAAL, ØKONOMI OG HANDEL. v.1– , 1873– . København. Semi-annual, 1873–77; four no. a year, 1878–1951; six no. a year, 1952–72 (issues combine 1/2, 3/4); three no. a year.
Issued by: Nationaløkonomisk Forening. In Danish; summaries in English. Some nos. are combined.
Indexes: Vols. 51–75, 1913–37, with v.75.
Indexed: J. Eco. Lit.; SSCI.

3296
NATO ADVANCED STUDY INSTITUTES SERIES. SERIES B. BEHAVIORAL AND SOCIAL SCIENCES. no.1– , 1974– . Alphen aan den Rijn, Sijthoff & Noordhoff. Irreg.
Published in cooperation with the Nato Scientific Affairs Division. Monograph series.

3297
NATO CHALLENGES OF MODERN SOCIETY. v.1– , 1981– . New York, Plenum Press.
Published in cooperation with the Nato Committee on the Challenge of Modern Society.

3298
NATO REVIEW. v.19, no.5/6– . Brussels. Bimonthly.
Issued by: Information Service, North Atlantic Treaty Organization.
Continues: *Nato Letter.*

3299
NATURE. v.1– , Nov. 4, 1869– . London, New York, Macmillan.
Supplements accompany some numbers.
Indexed: Abst. Anth.; Int. Bibl. Soc. Cul. Anth.; Peace Res. Abst. J.; Psych. Abst.; Wom. Stu. Abst.

NAUCHNI TRUDOVE
See Akademija za Obshchestveni Nauki i Sot͡sialno Upravlenie. NAUCHNI TRUDOVE

NAUCHNYE TRUDY. SERII͡A OBSHCHESTVENNYKH NAUK
See Armi͡anskiĭ Gosudarstvennyĭ Pedagogicheskiĭ Institut. NAUCHNYE TRUDY. SERIIA OBSHCHESTVENNYKH NAUK

3300
NAUCHNYĬ KOMMUNIZM. 1973– . Moskva, Izd-vo Vysshaia͡ Shkola. Bimonthly.
Issued by: Ministerstvo Vysshego i Srednego Spet͡sial'nogo Obrazovanii͡a. In Russian. Subseries of: Nauchnye Trudy Vyssheĭ Shkoly.

3301
NAUKA I SUSPILSTVO. 1– , 1951– . Kiev, Vyd-vo Radianskai͡a Ukraina. Monthly.
In Ukrainian.

3302
NAUKI HUMANISTYCZNO-SPOŁECZNE. no.1–72, 1955–1980. Łódź, Państwowe Wydawnictwo Naukowe. Irreg.
Issued by: Universytet Łódzki. In Polish; summaries in English, French, German and Russian. Subseries of: *Zeszyty Naukowe Uniwersytetu Łódzkiego*, called later *Acta Universitatis Lodziensis*.
Superseded by: *Folia Archaeologica*, *Folia Ethnologica*, *Folia Geographica*, *Folia Historica*, *Folia Iuridica*, *Folia Linguistica*, *Folia Litteraria*, *Folia Oeconomica*, *Folia Paedagogica et Psychologica*, *Folia Philosophica*, *Folia Scientiarum Artium et Librarum*, *Folia Politologica*, *Folia Sociologica*.

3303
NAUKI SPOŁECZNE. 1– , 1964– . Gliwice. Irreg.
Issued by: Politechnika Śląska. In Polish; summaries in English and Russian. Subseries of: Politechnika's *Zeszyty Naukowe*.

3304
NAUKI SPOŁECZNE. no.1– , 1971– . Białystok, Wydawnictwo Wyższej Szkoły Inżynierskiej. Irreg.
Issued by: Wyższa Szkoła Inżynierska. In Polish; summaries in English and Russian. Subseries of: Szkoła's *Zeszyty Naukowe*.

3305
NAUKI SPOŁECZNO-EKONOMICZNE. 1– , 1974– . Łódź. Irreg.
Issued by: Politechnika Łódzka. In Polish; summaries in English, German and Russian. Subseries of: Politechnika's *Zeszyty Naukowe*.

3306
NEDERLANDS GENOOTSCHAP VAN INTERNATIONALEN ZAKEN. ÉTUDES INTERNATIONALES. v.1– , Jan. 1948– . Haarlem, H.D. Tjeenk Willing. Quarterly.
In Dutch, English, or French.

3307
NEDERLANDSCH INDIË OUD & NIEUW. v.1–19, 1916–Mar. 1934. Amsterdam. Monthly.
In Dutch. Other title: *Old and New Netherlands India*.

3308
NEDERLANDS TIJDSCHRIFT VOOR INTERNATIONAAL RECHT
See NETHERLANDS INTERNATIONAL LAW REVIEW.

3309
LA NEF. v.1– , July 1944– . Paris, Librairie Jule Tallandier (Algiers, July-Sept. 1944). Irreg.
Publication suspended: Oct. 1944–Feb. 1945, Aug. 1951–Nov. 1952; Nov. 1956.
Issued for July 1944–June 1956 called no.1–77/78; Dec. 1952–Nov. 1956 called no.1–13; Dec. 1956–Oct. 1959 called no.1–31; Jan./Mar. 1960–Apr./June 1961 called "nouvelle série". In French.
Indexed: Bull. Sig. Soc. Eth.; Int. Bibl. Pol. Sc.; Peace Res. Abst. J.; Wom. Stu. Abst.

3310
NEGRO HISTORY BULLETIN. v.1– , Oct. 1937– . Washington, D.C. Bimonthly.
Issued by: The Association for the Study of Negro Life and History.
Indexed: Bull. Sig. Soc. Eth.; His. Abst.

3311
NEMPŌ GYOSEI KENKYŪ. 1– , 1962– . Tokyo, Keizai Shabo, Kanda Surugadai. Annual.
Issued by: Nippon Gyoseigaku Kai. In Japanese. Other title: *Annals of the Japanese Society of Public Administration*.

3312
NEMPŌ KEIZAGAKU. 1– , 1980– . Hiroshima, Daigaku Keizagakubu.
In Japanese. Other title: *Hiroshima Economic Review*.

3313
NEPALESE ECONOMIC JOURNAL. v.1– , Dec. 1979– . Kathmandu. Three no. a year.
Issued by: Pastar Bank, Bakers Club.

3314
NEPALESE JOURNAL OF POLITICAL SCIENCE. v.1– , May 1979– . Kathmandu, Kirtipur Multiple Campus, Political Science Instruction Committee, Tribhuvan University. Semi-annual.

NÉPÉLET
See ETHNOGRAPHIA

3315
Nepessegtudományi Kutato Intézet. ANNALS OF THE DEMOGRAPHIC RESEARCH INSTITUTE OF THE STATISTICAL OFFICE. 1963–1968. Budapést.

3316
NETHERLANDS INTERNATIONAL LAW

REVIEW. v.1– , 1953/54– . The Hague, M. Nijhoff. Quarterly, 1953–68; annual, 1969; three no. a year.
Published under the auspices of the University Institute for International Law. T.M.C. Asser Instituut. Other title: *NILR*.
Title varies: *Nederlands Tijdschrift voor Internationaal Recht.*
Indexed: Ind. For. Leg. Per.

NETHERLANDS JOURNAL OF ECONOMIC AND SOCIAL GEOGRAPHY
See TIJDSCHRIFT VOOR ECONOMISCHE EN SOCIALE GEOGRAFIE

3317
THE NETHERLANDS JOURNAL OF SOCIOLOGY. v.12– , July 1976– . Amsterdam, Elsevier Scientific Pub. Co. Semi-annual.
Issued by: Netherlands Sociological and Anthropological Society.
Continues: *Sociologia Neerlandica.*
Indexed: Bull. Anal. Pol. Pol. Ec. Soc.; Int. Bibl. Pol. Sc.; Int. Pol. Sc. Abst.; Soc. Abst.; SSCI.

3318
NETHERLANDS YEARBOOK OF INTERNATIONAL LAW. v.1– , 1970– . Leiden, A.W. Sijthoff.
Published jointly with the *Netherlands Law Review* and under the auspices of the Interuniversity Institute for International Law, T.M.C. Asser Institute, The Hague.
Indexes: v.1–10, 1970–79, 1v.
Indexed: Ind. For. Leg. Per.

3319
NEUE GESELLSCHAFT. v.1– , July/Aug. 1954– . Bonn, Verlag Neue Gesellschaft. Bimonthly, 1954–70; monthly.
In German.
Indexed: Bull. Anal. Pol. Ec. Soc.; Int. Bibl. Pol. Sc.; Int. Pol. Sc. Abst.; Peace Res. Abst. J.

3320
NEUE ORDNUNG. v.37– , 1983– . Walberberg, Gesellschaftswissenschaften. Bimonthly.
Issued by: Institut für Gesellschaftswissenschaften. In German.
Continues: *Die Neue Ordnung in Kirche, Staat, Gesellschaft, Kultur* (v.1–36, 1946–82)
Indexed: PAISFL.

3321
NEUE ORDNUNG; MONATSSCHRIFT FÜR GESELLSCHAFTSFRAGEN. v.1–16, no.8/10, 1925–1974. Wien, Amanaus Edition. Monthly.
Issued by: Institut für Gesellschaftswissenschaften. In German; summaries in English. Vol. 16, no.5/7–8/10 lack date. Suspended between Mar. 1938 and Mar. 1946.

3322
NEW AFRICA. v.1– , July 1959– . London. Monthly.
Subtitle reads: "Africa trade & development".
Indexed: Peace Res. Abst. J.

3323
NEW AFRICAN YEARBOOK. WEST & CENTRAL AFRICA. 1983/84– . London, I.C. Magazines. Annual.
"Africa's politics, economics, history, statistics, organization, population, essential dates and figures".
Continues: *New African Yearbook* (1978–82)

3324
NEW APPROACHES TO SOCIAL SCIENCE HISTORY. v.1– , 1981– . Beverly Hills, Calif., Sage Publications. Irreg.
Published in cooperation with the Social History Association. Monograph series.

3325
THE NEW ATLANTIS. v.1– , summer 1969– . Padova, Marsilio Editore. Semi-annual.
In Italian. Subtitle reads: "International journal of urban and regional studies".
Indexed: ABC POL SCI; PHRA.

NEW BABYLON
See STUDIES IN THE BEHAVIORAL SCIENCES

3326
NEW COMMONWEALTH. v.1–49, no.1, Dec. 1931–Oct. 1966. London, Tothill Press. Monthly.
Title varies: 1931–Sept. 1950, *The Crown Colonist.*
Superseded by: *World Development.*

NEW COMMONWEALTH QUARTERLY
See WORLD AFFAIRS (London)

3327
NEW COMMUNITY. v.1– , Oct. 1971– . London. Three no. a year.
Issued by: Community Relations Commission.

3328
NEW DIRECTIONS FOR METHODOLOGY OF SOCIAL AND BEHAVIORAL SCIENCE. no.3– , 1980– . San Francisco, Calif., Jossey-Bass. Irreg.
Continues: *New Directions for Methodology of Behavioral Sciences* (v.1–2, 1979).

3329
THE NEW ECOLOGIST. v.1–9, no.2, 1970–Mar./Apr. 1979. Wadebridge, Ecosystems Ltd.
Continued by: *The Ecologist.*
Indexed: Bull. Anal. Pol. Ec. Soc.

THE NEW ENGLAND JOURNAL OF EDUCATION
See JOURNAL OF EDUCATION

3330
NEW GUINEA RESEARCH BULLETIN. no.1–63, Apr. 1963–1975. Canberra. Irreg.
Issued by: New Guinea Research Unit, Research School of Pacific Studies, Australian National University. Title varies: 1963–66, *New Guinea Research Unit Bulletin.*
Indexed: Abst. Anth.; Int. Bibl. Soc.; Int. Lab. Doc.; Soc. Abst.

NEW GUINEA RESEARCH UNIT BULLETIN
See NEW GUINEA RESEARCH BULLETIN

3331
NEW HUNGARIAN QUARTERLY. v.1– , 1960– . Budapest, Publishing House Lapkiado.
Beginning with v.22, 1981, the title was changed to: *N.H.Q.*
Indexed: Bull. Anal. Pol. Ec. Soc.; Bull. Sig. Soc. Eth.; Int. Bibl. Eco.; Int. Bibl. Pol. Sc.

3332
NEW IDEAS IN PSYCHOLOGY. v.1– , 1983– . Oxford, Pergamon Press. Three no. a year.

NEW KOREA
See SAI CHOSEN

3333
THE NEW LEADER. v.1– , Dec. 3, 1927– . New York, American Labor Conference on International Affairs. Weekly, 1927–61; biweekly.
Official organ of: Social Democratic Federation, Jan. 1944–June 29, 1949. Title varies: 1927–Oct. 6, 1928, *New Leader and American Appeal*; Oct. 13, 1928– Mar. 16, 1935, *New Leader Which is Combined with the American Appeal*. Absorbed: *Russian Affairs*, 1945.
Indexed: Bull. Anal. Pol. Ec. Soc.; His. Abst.; PAIS; Peace Res. Abst. J.; Wom. Stu. Abst.

NEW LEADER WHICH IS COMBINED WITH THE AMERICAN APPEAL
See THE NEW LEADER

NEW LEADERS AND AMERICAN APPEAL
See THE NEW LEADER

3334
NEW LEFT REVIEW. no.1– , Jan./Feb. 1960– . London, New Left Ltd. Bimonthly.
Formed by the merger of: *Universities and Left Review*, and *Reasoner*.
Indexed: Bull. Anal. Pol. Ec. Soc.; Bull. Sig. Soc. Eth.; Int. Bibl. Eco.; Int. Bibl. Pol. Sc.; Int. Bibl. Soc.; Int. Pol. Sc. Abst.; PAIS.

3335
NEW OUTLOOK. v.1– , July 1957– . Tel-Aviv, Tazpiot. Monthly (irreg.)
Issued by: Givat Haviva. Issues for 1957–Feb. 1962 have added title pages in Arabic and Hebrew.
Indexed: Bull. Anal. Pol. Ec. Soc.; Int. Pol. Sc. Abst.; PAIS; Peace Res. Abst. J.

3336
NEW POLITICAL SCIENCE. [no.1]– , spring 1979– . Indianapolis, Ind., later New York. Quarterly.
Issued by: Caucus for a New Political Science, later by: Department of Political Science, Columbia University. Other title: *NPS*.
Indexed: Int. Pol. Sc. Abst.

3337
THE NEW REPUBLIC. v.1– , Nov. 7, 1914– . New York, The Republic Pub. Co. Weekly, except July, Aug., Sept. and Dec. when three no. a month.
Subtitle reads: "A journal of opinion".
Indexed: Bull. Anal. Pol. Ec. Soc.; His. Abst.; Peace Res. Abst. J.; Urb. Aff. Abst.; Wom. Stu. Abst.

3338
NEW SCHOLAR. 1969– . La Jolla, Calif. Semi-annual.
Issued by: University of California at San Diego.
Indexed: ABC POL SCI; His. Abst.; Psych. Abst.; Soc. Abst.

3339
THE NEW SOCIAL SCIENCE REVIEW. v.1–2, Jan. 1865–Oct. 1866. New York.
Title varies: v.1, 1865, *The New York Social Science Review Devoted to Political Economy and Statistics.*

THE NEW YORK SOCIAL SCIANCE REVIEW DEVOTED TO POLITICAL ECONOMY AND STATISTICS
See THE NEW SOCIAL SCIENCE REVIEW

3340
NEW SOCIETY. no.1– , Oct. 1962– . London, New Science Publications. Weekly.
Indexed: Bull. Anal. Pol. Ec. Soc.; Bull. Sig. Soc. Eth.; Int. Lab. Doc.; Peace Res. Abst. J.; Sage Fam. Stu. Abst.; Sage Urb. Stu. Abst.; Soc. Abst.; SSCI; Wom. Stu. Abst.

3341
NEW STATESMAN. v.1–36 (no.1–930), 12 Apr. 1913–21 Feb. 1931; n. ser. no.1–2291, 28 Feb. 1931–June 1988. London. Weekly.

Title varies: 1931–29 June 1957, *The New Statesman and Nation*. Absorbed: *The Nation and Athenaeum*. Supplements accompany some numbers.
Superseded by *New Statesman Society* (1988).
Indexed: APAIS; Bull. Anal. Pol. Ec. Soc.; Peace Res. Abst. J.; Soc. Sc. Hum. Ind.; Wom. Stu. Abst.

THE NEW STATESMAN AND NATION
See NEW STATESMAN

3342
NEW ZEALAND ECONOMIC SURVEY. 1952– . Wellington. Annual.
Issued by: Office of the Minister of Finance. Other title: *Economic Survey of New Zealand*.
Continues: *New Zealand Economy*. The combined issued for 1962/63 last available for examination.

3343
NEW ZEALAND FOREIGN AFFAIRS REVIEW. v.20– , 1970– . Wellington. Monthly, 1970–Jan./Mar. 1976; quarterly.
Issued by: Ministry of Foreign Affairs.
Continues: New Zealand. Department of External Affairs. *External Affairs Review* (v.1–19, Apr. 1951–1969)
Indexed: PAIS.

3344
NEW ZEALAND JOURNAL OF ANTHROPOLOGY. v.1– , 1979– . Dunedin. Annual.
Issued by: New Zealand Archaeological Association in cooperation with the University of Otago.

3345
NEW ZEALAND JOURNAL OF EDUCATIONAL STUDIES. v.1– , May 1966– . Wellington. Quarterly.
Issued by: New Zealand Council for Educational Research.

3346
NEW ZEALAND JOURNAL OF HISTORY. v.1– , Apr. 1967– . Auckland. Semi-annual.
Issued by: Department of History, University of Auckland.
Indexed: APAIS; His. Abst.

3347
THE NEW ZEALAND JOURNAL OF PUBLIC ADMINISTRATION. v.1–39, no.2, May 1938–Sept. 1977. Wellington. Semi-annual.
Organ of: The New Zealand Institute of Public Administration. Title varies: v.1–19, 1938–Mar. 1957, *Journal of Public Administration*.
Continued by: *Public Administration*.
Indexes: Vols. 1–17, 1938–Mar. 1956, 1v.; v.19–29, 1956–67, 1v.
Indexed: ABC POL SCI; Bull. Anal. Pol. Ec. Soc.; Ind. Per. Art. Law; Int. Bibl. Eco.; Int. Bibl. Pol. Sc.; PAIS.

NEWS BULLETIN
See PACIFIC AFFAIRS

NEWS REVIEW ON CHINA, MONGOLIA AND THE KOREAS
See Institute for Defense Studies and Analyses. NEWS REVIEW ON CHINA, MONGOLIA AND THE KOREAS

NEWSLETTER
See Australian Institute of Aboriginal Studies. NEWSLETTER

3348
NIGERIAN ANNUAL OF INTERNATIONAL LAW. 1– , 1976– . Lagos, Oxford University Press. Annual.
Published in cooperation with the Nigerian Society of International Law and Nigerian Institute of International Affairs.

3349
THE NIGERIAN JOURNAL OF DEVELOPMENT STUDIES. v.1– , Apr. 1981– . Enugu. Semi-annual.
Issued by: Economic Development Institute, University of Nigeria, Enugu Campus. Other title: *NJDS*.

3350
NIGERIAN JOURNAL OF ECONOMIC AND SOCIAL STUDIES. v.1– , May 1959– . London, later Ibadan. Three no. a year.
Issued by: Nigerian Economic Society.
Indexed: Int. Bibl. Soc. Cul. Anth.; PAIS; Pop. Ind.; Soc. Abst.

3351
NIGERIAN JOURNAL OF INTERNATIONAL AFFAIRS. v.1– , 1975– . Lagos. Annual.
Issued by: Nigerian Institute of International Affairs.
Indexed: Int. Pol. Sc. Abst.; PAIS.

3352
NIGERIAN JOURNAL OF INTERNATIONAL LAW. v.1– , 1976– . Lagos, Oxford University Press. Two no. a year.
Published in cooperation with the Nigerian Society of International Law and Nigerian Institute of International Affairs.

3353
NIGERIAN JOURNAL OF POLITICAL SCIENCE. NJPS. v.1– , June 1979– . Zaria. Semi-annual.

Issued by: Department of Political Science, Ahmadu Bello University. Publication suspended, 1981–83.

3354
NIGERIAN JOURNAL OF PUBLIC ADMINISTRATION AND LOCAL GOVERNMENT. NJPALG. v.1– , June 1983– . Nsukka. Semi-annual.
Issued by: Sub-Department of Public Administration and Local Government, University of Nigeria, Nsukka.

3355
NIHON BUNKA KENKYŪSHO KENKYŪ HŌKOKU. 1965– . Sendai, Tōhoku Daigaku Bungakubu Nihon Bunka Kenkyūsho. Annual (irreg.)
In Japanese. Other title: *Reports of the Research Institute for Japanese Culture.*
Supersedes: Tōhōku Daigaku, Sendai. Tōhōku Bunka Kenkyūshitsu. *Tōhoku Bunka Kenkyūshitsu Kiyō.*

NIHON JIMBUN
See INDUSTRIAL REVIEW OF JAPAN

NIHON KEIZAI TOKEI BUNKEN SENTA
See Hitotsubashi Daigaku. NIHON KEIZAI TOKEI BUNKEN SENTA

3356
Nihon Kōkogaku Kyōkai. NIHON KŌKOGAKU NEMPŌ. 1– , 1948– . Tokyo, Seibundo Shinko Sha.
In Japanese. Other title: *Archaeologia Japonica.*

NIHON KOKO-GAKU NEMPŌ
See Nihon Koko-gaku Kyokai. NIHON KOKO-GAKU NEMPŌ

3357
Nihon Kokusai Mondai Kenkyujo. ANNUAL REVIEW. v.1– , 1964– . Tokyo. Annual.
Issued by: The Japan Institute of International Affairs.
Continues: *The Japan Annual of International Affairs* (1961–63)

3358
NOMOS. 1– , 1958– . Cambridge, Mass., Harvard University Press, later New York, New York University Press. Irreg.
Organ of: American Society for Political and Legal Philosophy.
Indexed: Bull. Anal. Pol. Ec. Soc.; Int. Pol. Sc. Abst.

3359
NONMUNJIP. 1– , 1973?– . Daejeon, Ch'ungnom Taehakkyo. Pomnyul Haengjong Yŏn'guso. Annual.
In English or Korean. Other title: *Journal of Law and Public Administration.*

3360
NONMUNJIP; INMUN SAHOE KWAHAK P'YON. 1– , 1969– . Seoul, Soul Taehakkyo. Kyoyang Kwajongbu.
In English or Korean. Other title: *Journal of Humanities and Social Sciences.*

3361
NORC. REPORT. no.118– , Oct. 1966– . Chicago, Ill. Irregular biennial.
Issued by: National Opinion Research Center, University of Chicago. Each number has also a distinctive title.
Continues: National Opinion Research Center. *Report* (no.1–117, Dec. 1941–Sept. 1966)

3362
NORD E SUD. v.1– , Dec. 1954– . Napoli, Edizioni Scientifiche Italiane. Monthly (every two numbers combined into one)
Indexed: Bull. Anal. Pol. Ec. Soc.; Bull. Sig. Soc. Eth.; Int. Bibl. Pol. Sc.; Int. Pol. Sc. Abst.

3363
NORDIC JOURNAL OF SOVIET AND EAST EUROPEAN STUDIES. v.1– , 1984– . Uppsala. Quarterly.
Issued by: Nordic Committee for Soviet and East European Studies. In Danish, English, or Swedish.
Continues: *Bidrag till Ostatsforskningen.*

3364
NORDISK ADMINISTRATIVE TIDSSKRIFT. 1– , 1920– . København. Quarterly.
Issued by: Nordisk Administrative Forbund. In Danish; summaries in English.
Indexed: Bull. Anal. Pol. Ec. Soc.; Int. Bibl. Eco.; Int. Bibl. Soc. Cul. Anth.; Int. Pol. Sc. Abst.

3365
NORDISK PSYKOLOGI. v.1– , 1949– . København, E. Munksgaard. Six no. a year, 1949–70; four no. a year.
Organ of: Norsk Psykologforening, and Svenska Psykologsamfundet. In Scandinavian languages. Includes quarterly supplement "Tidskrift—Information".
Indexes: Vols. 1–12, 1949–60, 1v.
Indexed: Psych. Abst.; SSCI.

NORDISK TISKRIFT FOR INTERNATIONAL RET
See NORDISK TIDSKRIFT FOR INTERNATIONAL RET OG JUS GENTIUM

3366
NORDISK TIDSKRIFT FOR INTERNATIONAL RET OG JUS GENTIUM. ACTA SCANDINAVICA JURIS GENTIUM. v.1– , 1930– . København, Ostonyt Nordisk Forlag. Quarterly.
Issued by: Nordisk Samarbeidsnemnd Samfundsforskning. In Scandinavian languages. Title varies: 1–21, 1930–51, *Nordisk Tidskrift for International Ret*. Absorbed: *Jus Gentium* in 1952.
Indexed: Ind. For. Leg. Per.

3367
NOROIS. 1– , 1954– . Paris. Quarterly.
Issued by: a few French universities having interest in the Celtic countries. Some nos. are thematic. In French; summaries in English and French.
Indexed: Bull. Anal. Pol. Ec. Soc.; Int. Bibl. Soc. Cul. Anth.

3368
NORTH AMERICAN ARCHAEOLOGIST. 1981– . Farmingdale, N.Y., Baywood Pub. Co. Four no. a year.
Indexed: Abst. Anth.

NORTHERN RHODESIA JOURNAL
See ZAMBIA JOURNAL

3369
NORVEG. 1– , 1951– . Oslo, H. Aschenkong. Annual.
In English, German, or a Scandinavian language; summaries in English. Subtitle reads: "Journal of Norwegian ethnology".
Indexed: Abst. Anth.; Int. Bibl. Soc. Cul. Anth.

NORWEGIAN JOURNAL OF SOCIAL RESEARCH
See TIDSSKRIFT FOR SAMFUNSFORSKNING

3370
NOTE DI SOCIOLOGIA. v.1– , Jan./June 1979– . Roma, Editrice Beniamino Carucci. Quarterly.
In Italian; summaries in English.

3371
NOTES AFRICAINES. no.1– , 1939– . Dakar. Quarterly.
Issued by: Institut Fondamental d'Afrique Noire, Université de Dakar. In French.
Indexes: no.1–40, 1939–48, supplement to no.40; no.41–49, 1949–63, with no.100.
Indexed: His. Abst.; Int. Bibl. Soc. Cul. Anth.

NOTES ET DOCUMENTS
See United Nations. Centre against Apartheid. NOTES ET DOCUMENTS

NOTICIAS MUNICIPAIS
See REVISTA DE ADMINISTRAÇÃO MUNICIPAL

NOTIZIARIO DELLA ASSOCIAZIONE FRALE; IMPRESSE ITALIANE IN AFRICA
See AFRICA (Rome)

NOVEAU JOURNAL ASIATIQUE
See JOURNAL ASIATIQUE

3372
LA NOUVELLE CRITIQUE. no.1–181, Dec. 1948–Jan. 1967; n. ser. no.1–130 (182–311), Feb. 1967–Jan./Feb. 1980. Paris. Ten no. a year.
In French. Subtitle reads: "Politique, marxisme, culture". Supplements accompany some issues.
Superseded by: *Révolution*.
Indexed: Bull. Sig. Soc. Eth.; Int. Bibl. Soc. Cul. Anth.; LLBA; Peace Res. Abst. J.

3373
LA NOUVELLE REVUE ANTHROPOLOGIQUE. June 1974– . Paris. Four no. a year.
Organ of: Institut International d'Anthropologie. In French.
Continues: *Revue Anthropologique*.

NOUVELLES ARCHÉOLOGIQUES
See ARCHEOLOGICKÉ ROZGLEDY

3374
NOUVELLES D'ARCHÉOLOGIE. 1– , Dec. 1979– . Paris. Quarterly.
Issued by: Maison des Sciences de l'Homme. In French. Preceded by no.0 in July 1979. Accompanied by "Numéros spécials" and supplements.

3375
NOVA ADMINISTRACIJA. 1– , 1948– . Beograd. Monthly.
Issued by: Zavod za Javene-Upravu Montazni. In Serbo-Croatian. Title varies: 1948–52, *Narodna Drzava*.

NOVA ADMINISTRACIJA
See RADNA I DRUSTVENA ZAJEDNICA

3376
NOVAIA I NOVEĬSHAIA ISTORIIA.
1957– . Moskva, Izd-vo Akademii Nauk SSSR. Bimonthly.
Issued by: Institut Istorii, Akademiia Nauk SSSR. In Russian. Tables of contents in English.
Indexed: His. Abst.; Int. Bibl. Pol. Sc.; Int. Bibl. Soc. Cul. Anth.

NOVAIA KOREA
See SAI CHOSEN

3377
NOVYE ISSLEDOVANIIA V PSIKOLOGII. 1973– . Moskva, Pedagogika. Semi-annual.

Issued by: Akademiia Pedagogicheskikh Nauk SSSR. In Russian.
Continues: *Novye Issledovaniia v Psikologii i Rozrastnoĭ Fiziologii* (1970–72)

3378
NOWE DROGI. v.1– , Jan. 1947– . Warszawa, "Ruch". Monthly.
Organ of: Komitet Centralny, Polska Zjednoczona Partia Robotnicza. In Polish. Includes supplements: "Zeszyty Ekonomiczne. Przekłady"; "Zeszyty Filozoficzne "Nowych Dróg" i "Myśli Filozoficznej" " (no.1–2, 1949–52; "Zeszyty Filozoficzne. Przekłady" (one issue, 1954); "Zeszyty Historyczne. Przekłady".
Indexed: Bull. Anal. Pol. Ec. Soc.; His. Abst.; Int. Bibl. Eco.; Int. Lab. Doc.; Peace Res. Abst. J.

3379
NUESTRA AMÉRICA. no.1– , June 1982– . Tunja, Editorial Bolivariana Internacional. Quarterly.
Issued by: Instituto de Estudios para el Desarrollo y la Integración de América Latina. In Spanish.
Indexed: His. Abst.

3380
NUEVA ANTROPOLOGÍA. v.1– , July 1975– . Mexico, D.F. Quarterly.
In Spanish. Volumes for July 1975–July 1976 were issued by the Escuela Nacional de Antropología e Historia.
Indexed: Int. Bibl. Soc. Cul. Anth.

3381
NUEVA POLÍTICA. [v.1]– , Jan./Mar. 1976– . Mexico, D.F. Quarterly.
Issued by: Centro Latinoamericano de Estudios Políticos. In Spanish. Other title: *NP. Nueva Política.*

THE NYASALAND JOURNAL
See Society of Malawi. JOURNAL

OBJETS AFRICAINS
See AFRICAN TARGETS

3382
OBJETS ET MONDES. 1– , spring 1961– . Paris. Quarterly.
Issued by: Musée de l'Homme. In French; summaries in English and French.
Indexed: Abst. Anth.; Bull. Sig. Soc. Eth.; Int. Bibl. Soc. Cul. Anth.

3383
OBSHCHESTVENNYE NAUKI. no.1– , 1974– . Alma-Ata. Annual.
Issued by: Ministerstvo Proshveshcheniia Kazakhskoĭ SSR, and Kazakhskiĭ Pedagogicheskiĭ Institut im. Abaya. In Russian.

3384
OBSHCHESTVENNYE NAUKI. 1976– . Moskva, Nauka. Bimonthly.
Issued by: Sektsiia Obshchestvennykh Nauk, Akademiia Nauk SSSR. In Russian. Includes subsection "Seriia 1. Nauchnogo Kommunizma" (1–, 1979–)
Indexed: Int. Bibl. Eco.; Int. Bibl. Pol. Sc.; Int. Bibl. Soc. Cul. Anth.

OBSHCHESTVENNYE NAUKI
See Akademiia Nauk Armianskoĭ SSR. IZVESTIIA. OBSHCHESTVENNYE NAUKI

OBSHCHESTVENNYE NAUKI
See Akademiia Nauk SSSR. Irkutskiĭ Filial. TRUDY. OBSHCHESTVENNYE NAUKI

OBSHCHESTVENNYE NAUKI
See Lietuvos TSR Mokslų Akademija, Vilnius. DARBAI. TRUDY. SERIJA A. VISUOMENES MOKSLAI

3385
OBSHESTVENNYE NAUKI V MNR. 1– , 1980– . Ulan Bator, Izd-vo Akademii Nauk Mongol'skoĭ Narodnoĭ Respubliki. Annual.
Issued by: Otdelenie Obshchestvennykh Nauk, Akademiia Nauk Mongol'skoĭ Respubliki. In Russian.

3386
OBSHCHESTVENNYE NAUKI V UZBEKISTANE. 1956– . Tashkent. Monthly.
Issued by: Akademiia Nauk Uzbekskoĭ SSR. In Russian or Uzbek.
Indexed: Int. Bibl. Soc. Cul. Anth.

OBZOR EKONOMICHESKOGO POLOZHENIIA EVROPY
See United Nations. Economic Commission for Europe. ECONOMIC SURVEY OF EUROPE

OBZOR EKONOMICHESKOGO POLOZHENIIA EVROPY ZA POSLEVOENNYĬ PERIOD
See United Nations. Economic Commission for Europea. ECONOMIC SURVEY OF EUROPE

OBZOR EKONOMICHESKOGO POLOZHENIIA EVROPY I EKONOMICHESKIKH PERSPECTIV EVROPY
See United Nations. Economic Commission for Europe. ECONOMIC SURVEY OF EUROPE

OCCASIONAL PAPER
See Australian National University. Development Studies Centre. OCCASIONAL PAPER

3387
OCCASIONAL PAPER. DEVELOPMENT STUDIES. no.1– , Jan. 1979– . Norwich. Irreg.
Issued by: School of Development Studies, University of East Anglia. Other title: *Development Studies. Occasional Paper.*

3388
OCCASIONAL PAPER IN INTERNATIONAL BUSINESS. no.1– , 1965– . East Lansing, Mich. Irreg.
Issued by: Institute for International Business Studies, Michigan State University.

OCCASIONAL PAPERS
See American Institute for Marxist Studies. OCCASIONAL PAPERS

OCCASIONAL PAPERS
See Australian National University. Faculty of Asian Studies. OCCASIONAL PAPERS

OCCASIONAL PAPERS
See Royal Anthropological Institute of Great Britain and Ireland. OCCASIONAL PAPERS

OCCASIONAL PAPERS IN ABORIGINAL STUDIES
See AUSTRALIAN ABORIGINAL STUDIES

3389
OCCASIONAL PAPERS IN ARCHAEOLOGY AND HISTORY. 1– , 1970– . Ottawa. Irreg.

Issued by: Department of Indian Affairs and Northern Development (Federal Government)

3390
OCCASIONAL PAPERS IN ETHNIC STUDIES. 1–8, 1977–1979. Detroit, Mich. Irreg.
Issued by: Ethnic Studies Division, Wayne State University.

3391
OCCASIONAL PAPERS IN IMMIGRATION STUDIES. 3– , 1978– . Toronto. Irreg.
Issued by: Multicultural History Society of Ontario.
Continues: *Occasional Papers on Ethnic and Immigration Studies*.

3392
OCCASIONAL PAPERS IN SURVEY RESEARCH. 1– , 1976– . London. Irreg.
Issued by: Survey Unit, Social Science Research Council.

3393
OCCASIONAL PAPERS ON KOREA. no.1– , Apr. 1974– . Seattle, Wash. Irreg.
Issued by: Joint Committee on Korean Studies, American Council of Learned Societies and Social Science Research Council.

3394
OCCASIONAL PAPERS ON MALAYSIAN SOCIOECONOMIC AFFAIRS. 1– , 1974– . Kuala Lumpur. Irreg.
Issued by: University of Malaysia.

3395
OCCASIONAL PUBLICATIONS IN ANTHROPOLOGY. ARCHAEOLOGY SERIES. [no.1]– , 1967– . Greeley, Colo. Irreg.
Issued by: Museum of Anthropology, University of Northern Colorado (1967–70, called Colorado State College)

3396
OCCUPATIONAL INDEX. v.1– , Jan. 1936– . New York. Monthly.

3397
OCEAN DEVELOPMENT AND INTERNATIONAL LAW. v.1, no.3– , fall 1973– . New York, Crane Russak. Quarterly.
Continues: *Ocean Development and International Law Journal* (v.1, no.1–2, 1973). Continued by: *Ocean Development International Law*.
Indexed: Bull. Anal. Pol. Ec. Soc.; Ind. Leg. Per.; Int. Bibl. Pol. Sc.; Int. Pol. Sc. Abst.

3398
OCEANIA. v.1– , Apr. 1930– . Melbourne, later Sydney, Macmillan. Quarterly (irreg.)
Issued by: Australian National Research Council. Subtitle reads: "A journal devoted to the study of the native people of Australia, New Guinea and islands of the Pacific Ocean".
Indexed: Abst. Anth.; APAIS; Bull. Sig. Soc. Eth.; Int. Bibl. Soc. Cul. Anth.; Int. Lab. Doc.; Soc. Sc. Hum. Ind.; Soc. Sc. Ind.; SSCI.

OCHERKI ISTORII RUSKOĬ ETNOGRAFII
See Akademiia Nauk SSSR. Institut Etnografii. TRUDY. n. ser.

OCHERKI ISTORII SOCIJALIZMA
See PRILOZI ZA ISTORIJU SOCIALIZMA

3399
ODENSE UNIVERSITY STUDIES IN HISTORY AND SOCIAL SCIENCES. v.1– , 1970– . Odense, Odense University Press. Irreg.
In Danish; summaries in English or German. Monograph series.

3400
ODI REVIEW. 1–6, 1966–1982. London. Irreg., 1966–73; semi-annual.
Issued by: Overseas Development Institute. Each number has also a distinctive title.
Continued by: *Development Policy Review* (May 1983–)
Indexed: Bull. Anal. Pol. Ec. Soc.; Int. Bibl. Eco.; Int. Pol. Sc. Abst.

3401
OECD ECONOMIC OUTLOOK. 1– , July 1967– . Paris. Semi-annual.
Issued by: Department of Economics and Statistics, Organisation for Economic Co-operation and Development.

OECD ECONOMIC SURVEYS: AUSTRALIA
See Organisation for Economic Co-operation and Development. OECD ECONOMIC SURVEYS: AUSTRALIA

OECD ECONOMIC SURVEYS: AUSTRIA
See Organisation for Economic Co-operation and Development. OECD ECONOMIC SURVEYS: AUSTRIA

OECD ECONOMIC SURVEYS: BELGIUM–LUXEMBOURG
See Organisation for Economic Co-operation and Development. OECD ECONOMIC SURVEYS: BELGIUM–LUXEMBOURG

OECD ECONOMIC SURVEYS: CANADA
See Organisation for Economic Co-operation and Development. OECD ECONOMIC SURVEYS: CANADA

OECD ECONOMIC SURVEYS: DENMARK
See Organisation for Economic Co-operation and Development. OECD ECONOMIC SURVEYS: DENMARK

OECD ECONOMIC SURVEYS: FINLAND
See Organisation for Economic Co-operation and Development. OECD ECONOMIC SURVEYS: FINLAND

OECD ECONOMIC SURVEYS: FRANCE
See Organisation for Economic Co-operation and Development. OECD ECONOMIC SURVEYS: FRANCE

OECD ECONOMIC SURVEYS: GERMANY
See Organisation for Economic Co-operation and Development. OECD ECONOMIC SURVEYS: GERMANY

OECD ECONOMIC SURVEYS: GREECE
See Organisation for Economic Co-operation and Development. OECD ECONOMIC SURVEYS: GREECE

OECD ECONOMIC SURVEYS: ICELAND
See Organisation for Economic Co-operation and Development. OECD ECONOMIC SURVEYS: ICELAND

OECD ECONOMIC SURVEYS: IRELAND
See Organisation for Economic Co-operation and Development. OECD ECONOMIC SURVEYS: IRELAND

OECD ECONOMIC SURVEYS: ITALY
See Organisation for Economic Co-operation and Development. OECD ECONOMIC SURVEYS: ITALY

OECD ECONOMIC SURVEYS: JAPAN
See Organisation for Economic Co-operation and Development. OECD ECONOMIC SUrVEYS: JAPAN

OECD ECONOMIC SURVEYS: NETHERLANDS
See Organisation for Economic Co-operation and Development. OECD ECONOMIC SURVEYS: NETHERLANDS

OECD ECONOMIC SURVEYS: NEW ZEALAND
See Organisation for Economic Co-operation and Development. OECD ECONOMIC SURVEYS: NEW ZEALAND

OECD ECONOMIC SURVEYS: NORWAY
See Organisation for Economic Co-operation and Development. OECD ECONOMIC SURVEYS: NORWAY

OECD ECONOMIC SURVEYS: PORTUGAL
See Organisation for Economic Co-operation and Development. OECD ECONOMIC SURVEYS: PORTUGAL

OECD ECONOMIC SURVEYS: SPAIN
See Organisation for Economic Co-operation and Development. OECD ECONOMIC SURVEYS: SPAIN

OECD ECONOMIC SURVEYS: SWEDEN
See Organisation for Economic Co-operation and Development. OECD ECONOMIC SURVEYS: SWEDEN

OECD ECONOMIC SURVEYS: SWITZERLAND
See Organisation for Economic Co-operation and Development. OECD ECONOMIC SURVEYS: SWITZERLAND

OECD ECONOMIC SURVEYS: TURKEY
See Organisation for Economic Co-operation and Development. OECD ECONOMIC SURVEYS: TURKEY

OECD ECONOMIC SURVEYS: UNITED KINGDOM
See Organisation for Economic Co-operation and Development. OECD ECONOMIC SURVEYS: UNITED KINGDOM

OECD ECONOMIC SURVEYS: UNITED STATES
See Organisation for Economic Co-operation and Development. OECD ECONOMIC SURVEYS: UNITED STATES

OECD ECONOMIC SURVEYS: YUGOSLAVIA
See Organisation for Economic Co-operation and Development. OECD ECONOMIC SURVEYS: YUGOSLAVIA

3402
OECONOMICA POLONA. v.1– , 1974– . Warszawa, Państwowe Wydawnictwo Naukowe. Four no. a year.

Issued by: Komitet Nauk Ekonomicznych, Polska Academia Nauk, and Polskie Towarzystwo Ekonomiczne. In English.

Indexed: Int. Bibl. Eco.; PAIS.

3403
ÖFFENTLICHE VERWALTUNG. 1– , Oct. 1948– . Stuttgart, W. Kohlhammer. Biweekly.
In German.
Indexed: Bull. Anal. Pol. Ec. Soc.; Int. Bibl. Pol. Sc.; Int. Pol. Sc. Abst.; Peace Res. Abst. J.

3404
ÖKONOMETRIE UND UNTERNEHMUNGSFORSCHUNG. ECONOMETRICS AND OPERATIONS RESEARCH. no.1– , 1962– . New York, Springer Verlag. Irreg.
In German; occasionally in English. Monograph series.

3405
ØKONOMI OG POLITIK. 1– , Jan./Mar. 1927– . København, Munksgaards Forlag. Quarterly.
Issued by: Selskabet for Historie of Samfundsøkonomi; later by Institutet for Historie og Samfundsøkonomi. In Danish.
Indexed: Bull. Anal. Pol. Ec. Soc.; His. Abst.; Int. Pol. Sc. Abst.; Peace Res. Abst. J.

Österreichische Akademie der Wissenschaften
See Akademie der Wissenschaften, Wien

3406
Österreichische Gesellschaft für Raumforschung und Landesplanung. BERICHTE. v.1– , 1957– . Wien, Springer Verlag. Quarterly.
In German; summaries in English. Title varies: v.1–8, 1957–64, *Berichte zur Landesforschung* (issued by this society under its earlier name: Österreichische Gesellschaft für Förderung von Landesforschung und Landesplanung)
Indexed: PAISFL.

3407
ÖSTERREICHISCHE HISTORISCHE BIBLIOGRAPHIE. AUSTRIAN HISTORICAL BIBLIOGRAPHY. 1965– . Santa Barbara, Calif., Clio Press. Annual.
Issued by: American Bibliographic Center.

3408
ÖSTERREICHISCHE ZEITSCHRIFT FÜR AUSSENPOLITIK. v.1–22, Oct. 1960–Dec. 1983. Wien, Verlag für Geschichte und Politik. Four no. a year.
Issued by: Österreichische Gesellschaft für Aussenpolitik und Internationale Beziehungen, and Österreichisches Institut für Internationale Politik. In German.
Continued by: Österreichisches Jahrbuch für Internationale Politik.
Indexed: Bull. Anal. Pol. Ec. Soc.; ABC POL SCI; Int. Pol. Sc. Abst.; PAISFL; Peace Res. Abst. J.

3409
ÖSTERREICHISCHE ZEITSCHRIFT FÜR POLITIKWISSENSCHAFT. no.1– , 1972– . Wien, Verlag für Gesellschaftskritik. Quarterly.
Published under the auspices of the Österreichische Gesellschaft für Politikwissenschaft. In German. Tables of contents also in English.
Indexed: Bull. Anal. Pol. Ec. Soc.; Int. Bibl. Pol. Sc.; Int. Pol. Sc. Abst.; PAISFL.

ÖSTERREICHISCHE ZEITSCHRIFT FÜR VERWALTUNG
See ZEITSCHRIFT FÜR VERWALTUNG

3410
ÖSTERREICHISCHE ZEITSCHRIFT FÜR VOLKSKUNDE. v.1–48, 1895–1943; n. ser. v.1– , 1947– . Wien. Six no. a year, 1899–1935; four no. a year.
Issued by: Verein für Volkskunde in Wien. In German. Title varies: 1895–1900, *Zeitschrift für Österreichische Volkskunde*; 1931–35, *Wiener Zeitschrift für Volkskunde*.
Indexed: Bull. Sig. Soc. Eth.

3411
ÖSTERREICHISCHES BANK-ARCHIV. 1– , Jan. 1953– . Wien. Monthly.
Issued by: Österreichische Bankwissenschaftliche Gesellschaft. In German.
Indexed: PAISFL.

3412
Österreichisches Forschungsinstitut für Wirtschaft und Politik. BERICHTE UND INFORMATIONEN. 1946– . Wien. Weekly.
In German. V.26 (1971) last examined.

3413
ÖSTERREICHISCHES JAHRBUCH FÜR INTERNATIONALE POLITIK. v.1– , 1984– . Wien, Böhlau. Annual.
Issued jointly by: Österreichische Gesellschaft für Aussenpolitik und Internationale Beziehungen, and Österreichisches Institut für Internationale Politik. In German.
Supersedes: *Österreichische Zeitschrift für Aussenpolitik.*

3414
ÖSTERREICHISCHES JAHRBUCH FÜR POLITIK. 1977– . München, Verlag für Geschichte und Politik. Annual.

In German.

3415
Österreichisches Kulturinstitut, Rome. Abteilung für Historische Studien. PUBLIKATIONEN. I. ABTEILUNG: ABHANDLUNGEN. v.1– , 1954– . Wien, Verlag der Österreichischen Akademie der Wissenschaften. Irreg.
In English, French, or German.

Office de Recherche Scientifique et Technique d'Outre-Mer. CAHIERS
See CAHIERS O.R.S.T.O.M.

OFFICIAL BULLETIN
See International Labour Office. OFFICIAL BULLETIN

OFFICIAL JOURNAL
See League of Nations. OFFICIAL JOURNAL

3416
OFFICIAL JOURNAL OF THE EUROPEAN COMMUNITIES. INFORMATION AND NOTICES. v.16– , Jan. 15, 1973– . Luxembourg, Office for Official Publications of the European Communities. Irreg.
Danish and English editions began with 1973– and assumed volume numbering of Dutch, French, German and Italian editions.

3417
OFFICIAL JOURNAL OF THE EUROPEAN COMMUNITIES. LEGISLATION. v.16– , Jan. 1, 1973– . Luxembourg, Office for Official Publications of the European Communities. Irreg.
Danish and English editions began publication in 1973– and assumed volume numbering of Dutch, French, German and Italian editions.

OFFICIAL RECORDS
See League of Nations. OFFICIAL JOURNAL

OFFICIAL RECORDS
See United Nations. General Assembly. OFFICIAL RECORDS

OFFICIAL RECORDS
See United Nations. Security Council. OFFICIAL RECORDS

OFFICIAL RECORDS
See United Nations. Trusteeship Council. OFFICIAL RECORDS

OFFICIAL REPORT
See Inter-Parliamentary Union. Conference. COMPTE RENDU DE LA CONFÉRENCE

3418
Oklahoma State University of Agriculture and Applied Science, Stillwater. ARTS AND SCIENCES STUDIES. SOCIAL STUDIES SERIES. no.1– , 1951– . Stillwater, Okla. Irreg.
No.1 issued by the university under its earlier name: Agricultural and Mechanical College. Title varies: no.1, *Arts and Sciences Studies. Social Science Series*.

OLD AND NEW NETHERLANDS INDIA
See NEDERLANDSCH INDIË OUD & NIEUW

3419
DE ONTWIKKELING VAN DE SOCIALE WETENSCHAPPEN IN NEDERLAND. 1– , 1981– . Utrecht, Stichting Grafiet.
In Dutch.

OPENBAR FINANCIEN
See PUBLIC FINANCE

OPERATIONS AND POLICY RESEARCH. ELECTION ANALYSIS SERIES
See Operations and Policy Research, Inc. Institute for the Comparative Study of Political Systems. ELECTION ANALYSIS SERIES

3420
Operations and Policy Research, Inc. Institute for the Comparative Study of Political Systems. OPERATIONS AND POLICY RESEARCH. ELECTION ANALYSIS SERIES. no.1– , 1963– . Washington, D.C. Irreg.

3421
Operations and Policy Research, Inc. Institute for the Comparative Study of Political Systems. OPERATIONS AND POLICY RESEARCH. POLITICAL STUDY SERIES. no.1– , 1964– . Washington, D.C. Irreg.
Title varies: no.1, called *Special Article Series*.

OPERATIONS AND POLICY RESEARCH. POLITICAL STUDY SERIES
See Operations and Policy Research, Inc. Institute for the Comparative Study of Political Systems. POLITICAL STUDY SERIES

3422
OPERATIONS RESEARCH. v.4– , Feb. 1956– . Baltimore, Md. Bimonthly.
Issued by: Operations Research Society of America. Individual numbers are thematic. Supplements accompany some numbers.
Continues: *Journal of the Operations Research Society of America*.

Indexes: Vols. 1–15, 1952–57, 1v.
Indexed: Int. Lab. Doc.; Peace Res. Abst. J.; PHRA; Psych. Abst.

OPERATIONS RESEARCH
See UNTERNEHMUNGSFORSCHUNG

3423
OPŠTINA. no.1– , 1948– . Beograd. Monthly.
Issued by: Zavod za Javnu Upravu. In Serbo-Croatian. Title varies: 1948–63, *Narodni Odbor.* Subtitle reads: "Casopis za pitania drustvenohot samoupravleniia".
Indexed: Bull. Anal. Pol. Ec. Soc.; Int. Bibl. Eco.; Int. Lab. Doc.

3424
OPÚSCULOS SOBRE DESARROLLO ECONÓMICO-SOCIAL. no.1– , 1963– . Madrid. Irreg.
Issued by: Instituto Balmes de Sociología. In Spanish. Monograph series.

3425
OPVOEDING & KULTUUR. EDUCATION & CULTURE. v.1– , Jan. 1976– . Pretoria. Irreg.
Issued by: Department of National Education (Government). In Afrikaans or English.

3426
ORBIS. v.1– , Apr. 1957– . Philadelphia, Pa., University of Pennsylvania Press. Quarterly.
Issued by: Foreign Policy Research Institute in association with the International Relations Graduate Group, University of Pennsylvania.
Indexed: ABC POL SCI; Abst. Anth.; His. Abst.; Ind. Per. Art. Law; Bull. Anal. Pol. Ec. Soc.; Curr. Cont. Soc. Beh. Sc.; Int. Bibl. Eco.; Int. Bibl. Pol. Sc.; Int. Bibl. Soc. Cul. Anth.; LLBA; PAIS; Peace Res. Abst. J.; Sage Pub. Adm. Abst.; Soc. Sc. Hum. Ind.; SSCI.

3427
Organisation for Economic Co-operation and Development. FINANCIAL STATISTICS MONTHLY. INTERNATIONAL MARKETS. STATISTIQUES FINANCIÈRES MENSUELLES. MARCHÉS INTERNATIONAUX. July 1983– . Paris.
In English and French.
Continues: *OECD Financial Statistics. Part 1. Financial Statistics Monthly. International Markets.*

3428
Organisation for Economic Co-operation and Development. THE FLOW OF FINANCIAL RESOURCES TO LESS-DEVELOPED COUNTRIES. 1956/1959– . Paris. Irreg.
Title varies: 1956/59–1960, *The Flow of Financial Resources to Countries in Course of Economic Development*; 1961, *The Flow of Financial Resources to Developing Countries.*

3429
Organisation for Economic Co-operation and Development. FOREIGN TRADE. SERIES B. ANALYTICAL ABSTRACTS. COMMERCE EXTÉRIEUR. SÉRIE B. RÉSUMÉS ANALYTIQUES. Jan./Mar. 1959–1975. Paris. Quarterly.
In English and French. Other title: *OECD Statistical Bulletins.*
Supersedes: *Bulletins Statistiques de l'OEEC. Commerce Extérieur. Serie 4. OEEC Statistical Bulletin. Foreign Trade. Series 4*, 1959–60, issued under the organization's earlier name: Organisation for European Economic Co-operation.
Continued by: *Statistics of Foreign Trade. Series B. Trade by Commodities. Analytical Abstracts. Statistiques du Commerce Extérieur. Série B. Échanges par Produits. Tableaux Analytiques.*

3430
Organisation for Economic Co-operation and Development. GEOGRAPHICAL DISTRIBUTION OF FINANCIAL FLOWS TO LESS DEVELOPED COUNTRIES (DISBURSEMENT). RÉPARTITION GÉOGRAPHIQUE DES RESOURCES FINANCIÈRES MISES À LA DISPOSITION DES PAYS MOINS DÉVELOPPÉS (VERSEMENTS). 1960/1964– . Paris. Irreg.

3431
Organisation for Economic Co-operation and Development. INDICATORS OF INDUSTRIAL ACTIVITY. INDICATEURS DES ACTIVITÉS INDUSTRIELLES. Aug. 1979– . Paris. Quarterly.
Issued by the organization's: Industry Division, Economics Statistics Division, and National Accounts Division. Formed by the merger of: *Short Term Economic Indicators for Manufacturing Industry*, and *Industrial Production* (1965–78). In English and French. This publication was preceded by a sample issue denoted "0".

3432
Organisation for Economic Co-operation and Development. LABOUR FORCE STATISTICS. STATISTIQUES DE LA POPULATION ACTIVE. 1950/1960– . Paris. Annual.
In English and French.
Supersedes: *Manpower Statistics.*

3433
Organisation for Economic Co-operation and Development. MAIN ECONOMIC INDICATORS. PRINCIPAUX INDICATEURS ÉCONOMIQUES. Jan. 1960– . Paris. Monthly.

Jan. 1960–Feb. 1962 issued as Part 1 of its *General Statistics*. Mar. 1962 issued as supplement to its *General Statistics*. Mar. 1965 absorbed its *General Statistics* and the recapitulative tables published in the series A: *Bulletin of Foreign Trade Statistics* (Overall Trade by Countries)

3434
Organisation for Economic Co-operation and Development. MONTHLY STATISTICS OF FOREIGN TRADE. STATISTIQUES MENSUELLES DU COMMERCE EXTÉRIEUR. Jan. 1983– . Paris.
Prepared by the organization's Department of Economics and Statistics. In English and French. On cover: "Series A".
Continues: Organisation for Economic Co-operation and Development. *Statistics of Foreign Trade. Monthly Bulletin. Series A* (1974–82)

3435
Organisation for Economic Co-operation and Development. OECD ECONOMIC SURVEYS: AUSTRALIA. 1972– . Paris. Annual.

3436
Organisation for Economic Co-operation and Development. OECD ECONOMIC SURVEYS: AUSTRIA. 1959– . Paris. Annual.
Title varies: 1961, *Economic Conditions in Member and Associated Countries of the OECD: Austria*; 1962–63, *Economic Surveys by the OECD: Austria*.

3437
Organisation for Economic Co-operation and Development. OECD ECONOMIC SURVEYS: BELGIUM–LUXEMBOURG. 1960– . Paris. Annual.
Title varies: 1963–196?, *Economic Survey: B.L.E.U.*; 1970, 1972–74, *OECD Economic Survey: Belgium-Luxembourg Economic Union*.

3438
Organisation for Economic Co-operation and Development. OECD ECONOMIC SURVEYS: CANADA. 1959– . Paris. Annual.
Title varies: 1963–65, *Economic Surveys by the OECD: Canada*.
Continues, in part: *Economic Conditions in Canada and United States*.

3439
Organisation for Economic Co-operation and Development. OECD ECONOMIC SURVEYS: DENMARK. 1960– . Paris. Annual.
Title varies: 1960–66, *Economic Surveys by the OECD: Denmark*.
Continues, in part: the organization's: *Economic Conditions in Denmark, Iceland, Norway and Sweden*.

3440
Organisation for Economic Co-operation and Development. OECD ECONOMIC SURVEYS: FINLAND. 1969– . Paris. Annual.
Title varies: 1969–70, *Economic Surveys by the OECD: Finland*.

3441
Organisation for Economic Co-operation and Development. OECD ECONOMIC SURVEYS: FRANCE. 1953– . Paris. Annual.
Title varies: 1953–57, *Economic Conditions in France*; 1958–61, *Economic Conditions in Member and Associated Countries*; 1962–65, *Economic Surveys by the OECD: France*.

3442
Organisation for Economic Co-operation and Development. OECD ECONOMIC SURVEYS: GERMANY. 1953– . Paris. Annual.
Title varies: 1953–63, *Economic Surveys by the OECD: Germany*.

3443
Organisation for Economic Co-operation and Development. OECD ECONOMIC SURVEYS: GREECE. 1954?– . Paris. Annual.
Title varies: 1954–62, *Economic Surveys by the OECD: Greece*.

3444
Organisation for Economic Co-operation and Development. OECD ECONOMIC SURVEYS: ICELAND. 1960– . Paris. Annual.
Continues, in part: the organization's: *Economic Conditions in Denmark, Iceland, Norway and Sweden*.

3445
Organisation for Economic Co-operation and Development. OECD ECONOMIC SURVEYS: IRELAND. 1960– . Paris. Annual.
Title varies: 1960–61, *Economic Conditions in Member Countries of the OEEC: Ireland*.
Continues, in part: *Economic Conditions in Ireland and Portugal*.

3446
Organisation for Economic Co-operation and Development. OECD ECONOMIC SURVEYS: ITALY. 1953– . Paris. Annual.
Title varies: 1953–58, *Economic Conditions in Italy*; 1959–62?, *Economic Conditions in Member and Associated Countries of the OEEC: Italy*.

3447
Organisation for Economic Co-operation and Development. OECD ECONOMIC SURVEYS: JAPAN. 1964– . Paris. Annual.

3448
Organisation for Economic Co-operation and Development. OECD ECONOMIC SURVEYS: NETHERLANDS. 1954?– . Paris. Annual.
Title varies: 195?–1961, *Economic Conditions in Member and Associated Countries: Netherlands.*
Continues, in part: *Economic Conditions in Member and Associated Countries of the OEEC: Benelux.*

3449
Organisation for Economic Co-operation and Development. OECD ECONOMIC SURVEYS: NEW ZEALAND. 1975– . Paris. Annual.

3450
Organisation for Economic Co-operation and Development. OECD ECONOMIC SURVEYS: NORWAY. 1960– . Paris. Annual.
Title varies: 1960–61, *Economic Conditions in Member and Associated Countries of OEEC: Norway.*
Continues, in part: the organization's *Economic Conditions in Denmark, Iceland, Norway and Sweden.*

3451
Organisation for Economic Co-operation and Development. OECD ECONOMIC SURVEYS: PORTUGAL. 1960– . Paris. Annual.
Title varies: 1960–61, *Economic Conditions in Member and Associated Countries of the OEEC.*
Continues, in part: the organization's *Economic Conditions in Ireland and Portugal.*

3452
Organisation for Economic Co-operation and Development. OECD ECONOMIC SURVEYS: SPAIN. 1958– . Paris. Annual.
Title varies: 1958, *Economic Conditions in Member and Associated Countries of the OEEC: Spain.*

3453
Organisation for Economic Co-operation and Development. OECD ECONOMIC SURVEYS: SWEDEN. 1954– . Paris. Annual.
Title varies: 1954, *Economic Conditions in Sweden*; 1959–61, *Economic Conditions in Member and Associated Countries of the OEEC: Sweden.*
Continues, in part: the organization's *Economic Conditions in Member and Associated Countries of the OEEC: Denmark, Iceland, Norway, Sweden.*

3454
Organisation for Economic Co-operation and Development. OECD ECONOMIC SURVEYS: SWITZERLAND. 1959– . Paris. Annual.
Title varies: 1959–60, *Economic Conditions in Member and Associated Countries of the OECD: Switzerland.*

3455
Organisation for Economic Co-operation and Development. OECD ECONOMIC SURVEYS: TURKEY. 1954– . Paris. Annual.
Title varies: *Economic Surveys by the OECD: Turkey.*

3456
Organisation for Economic Co-operation and Development. OECD ECONOMIC SURVEYS: UNITED KINGDOM. 1953– . Paris. Annual.
Title varies: 1953–57, *Economic Conditions in the United Kingdom*; 1958–60, *Economic Conditions in Member and Associated Countries of the OECD: United Kingdom.*

3457
Organisation for Economic Co-operation and Development. OECD ECONOMIC SURVEYS: UNITED STATES. 1958– . Paris. Annual.
Title varies: 1958, *Economic Conditions in Member and Associated Countries of the OECD: United States.*
Continues, in part: *Economic Conditions in Canada and United States.*

3458
Organisation for Economic Co-operation and Development. OECD ECONOMIC SURVEYS: YUGOSLAVIA. 1962– . Paris. Annual.
Title varies: *Economic Surveys by the OEEC: Socialist Federal Republic of Yugoslavia.*

3459
Organisation for Economic Co-operation and Development. QUARTERLY LABOUR FORCE STATISTICS. 1983– . Paris.
Issued by: the organization's Department of Economics and Statistics. In English and French.
Continues: *Labour Force Statistics. Quarterly Supplement to the Yearbook.*

3460
Organisation for Economic Co-operation and Development. STATISTICS OF FOREIGN TRADE. SERIES A. OVERALL TRADE BY COUNTRIES. STATISTIQUES DU COMMERCE EXTÉRIEUR. SÉRIE A. COMMERCE TOTAL PAR PAYS. 1960–June 1974. Bimonthly, 1960–64; quarterly.
Title varies: 1960–July 1966, *Statistics of Foreign Trade. Series A. Overall Trade by Origin and Destination. Statistiques du Commerce Extérieur. Série A. Commerce Total par Origine et Destination.*
Continued by: the organization's *Statistics of Foreign Trade. Monthly Bulletin. Series A. Statistiques du Commerce Extérieur. Série A. Statistiques Mensuelles* (July 1974–1982)

3461
Organisation for Economic Co-operation and Development. STATISTICS OF FOREIGN TRADE. SERIES B. ANNUAL TABLES BY REPORTING COUNTRIES. STATISTIQUES DU COMMERCE EXTÉRIEUR. SÉRIE B. ANNUAIRE. TABLEAUX PAR PAYS DÉCLARANTS. 1978– . Paris. Annual.
In English and French.
Continues: the organization's *Foreign Trade Statistics. Series B. Trade by Commodities. Country Summaries*, *Statistiques du Commerce Extérieur. Série B. Résumé par Pays* (1971–77)

3462
Organisation for Economic Co-operation and Development. STATISTICS OF FOREIGN TRADE. SERIES C. TRADE BY COMMODITIES; MARKET SUMMARIES. STATISTIQUES DU COMMERCE EXTÉRIEUR. SÉRIE C. ÉCHANGES PAR PRODUITS: RÉSUMÉ PAR MARCHÉS. 1968– . Paris. Semi-annual with annual cumulation, 1968–69; annual.
In English and French. Sections: *Exports* and *Imports* published in separate volumes.
Continues: Organisation for Economic Co-operation and Development. *Foreign Trade. Series C. Commodity Trade; Detailed Analysis by Products.*
Continued by: Organisation for Economic Co-operation and Development. *Statistics of Foreign Trade. Series C. Trade by Commodities. Market Summaries. Exports and Imports* (1980–)

3463
Organisation for Economic Co-operation and Development. STATISTIQUES DE RESETLÉS PUBLIQUES DES PAYS MEMBRES DE L'OCED. REVENUE STATISTICS OF OECD MEMBER COUNTRIES. 1965/1971– . Paris. Annual.
In English and French. Volume for 1968–70 published under the title: *Revenue Statistics of OECD Member Countries.*

3464
Organisation for Economic Co-operation and Development. Department of Economics and Statistics. NATIONAL ACCOUNTS. COMPTES NATIONAUX. 1980/1981– . Paris. Annual.
Published in two volumes: v.1, *Main Aggregates. Principaux Agrégates*; v.2, *Detailed Tables. Tableaux Détailles*. In English and French.
Continues: *National Accounts Statistics* (1963–80)

3465
Organization of American States. ANNALS. v.1–10, no.2, 1949–July/Sept. 1958. Washington, D.C. Quarterly.
Issued by: Department of International Law and Organization, Pan American Union.
Supersedes, in part: Pan American Union. *Bulletin.*

3466
Organization of American States. BOLETÍN ESTADÍSTICO DE AMÉRICA LATINA. v.1– , Jan./Mar. 1979– . Washington, D.C. Quarterly.
Issued by: General Secretariat. Published also in English: *Statistical Bulletin of the OAS.*

3467
Organization of American States. DOCUMENTOS OFICIALES DE LA ORGANIZACIÓN DE LOS ESTADOS AMERICANOS. LISTA GENERAL. INDICE ANALÍTICO. v.1– , 1960– . Washington, D.C., Department of Publication.
In Spanish. Published also in French and Portuguese.

3468
Organization of American States. SYNTHESIS OF ECONOMIC PERFORMANCE IN LATIN AMERICA. 1978– . Washington, D.C. Annual.
Prepared by: Program of Development Programming of the OAS General Secretariat.

3469
[No entry]

3470
Organization of American States. TREATY SERIES. 1948– . Washington, D.C. Irreg.

3471
Organization of American States. Council. DECISIONS TAKEN AT THE MEETINGS. v.1– , 1948– . Washington, D.C. General Secretariat, Pan American Union. Annual.
Issue for 1948 covers the period May–Dec. 1948. (OEA/SER/G/III/C–sa. Cumulated edition, 1–, 1951–)

3472
Organization of American States. General Assembly. JOURNAL. Washington, D.C. Irreg.
In English and Spanish. (OEA/SER.P.AC/Diario)

3473
Organization of American States. Permanent Council. ACTA DE LA SESIÓN. 1– , Dec. 1948– . Washington, D.C.
Issued by: Consejo de Organización de los Estados Americanos, 1948–Feb. 1949; Consejo, 1949–Feb. 26, 1970; Consejo Permanente, Mar. 9, 1970–. Includes *Protocol* of the Consejo de Organización, *Acta* de la Sesión Ordinaria, and *Acta* de la Sesión Extraordinaria. In Spanish. (OEA/Doc/Ser. G)

3474
Organization of American States. Planning Statistics Program. BOLETÍN ESTADÍSTICO DE LA OEA. v.1, no.4– , Oct./Dec. 1979– . Washington, D.C. Quarterly.
Continues: Organization of American States. Program Development Programming. *Boletín Estadístico de la OEA* (v.1, no.1–3, Jan./Mar.–Mar./Sept. 1979)

3475
Organization of American States. Public Sector Program. DEVELOPMENT FINANCING. v.2–3, June 1978–June./Dec. 1979. Washington, D.C. Semi-annual.
Continues: *Development Financing*, issued by: Development Financing Program.

3476
ORGANIZATION STUDIES. 1– , 1980– . Berlin, New York, W. de Gruyter. Quarterly.
Published in cooperation with the European Group for Organizational Studies (EGOS) and the Maison des Sciences de l'Homme.
Indexed: Int. Bibl. Eco.; Int. Pol. Sc. Abst.; SSCI.

3477
ORGANIZAT͡SII͡A I PLANIROVANIE OTRASLEĬ NARODNOGO KHOZI͡AĬSTVA. no.1– , 1956– . Kiev. Irreg.
Issued by: Nauchno-issledovatel'skiĭ Ekonomicheskiĭ Institut of Gosplan. In Russian.

3478
ORIENS. v.1– , 1948– . Leiden, E.J. Brill. Irreg.
Issued by: International Society for Oriental Research. In English, French, German, or Turkish. Other titles: *Milletlerarasi Tetkikleri Cimeyeti Mecmuasi*; *Journal de la Société Internationale d'Études Orientales*; *Zeitschrift der Internationalen Gesellschaft für Orientforschung*.

3479
ORIENT. v.1– , 1960– . Opladen, Leske Verlag und Budrich. Quarterly.
Issued by: Nah- und Mittelost-Verein Deutsches Orient-Institut; later by: Stiftung Deutsches Übersee-Institut. In English or German; summaries in English. Tables of contents also in Arabic, English and French.
Indexed: Bull. Anal. Pol. Ec. Soc.; Int. Bibl. Eco.; Int. Bibl. Pol. Sc.; Int. Bibl. Soc. Cul. Anth.; Int. Lab. Doc.; PAISFL; Peace Res. Abst. J.

ORIENTAL CULTURE
See DONYANG MUNKWA

3480
THE ORIENTAL ECONOMIST. v.1–53, no.901/902, May 1934–1985. Tokyo, Toyo Keizai Shimpo Shu. Monthly.
English edition of: *Toyo Keizai shimpo*, founded in 1895. Title changed to: *Shukan Toyo Keizai*.
Indexed: Bull. Anal. Pol. Soc.; PAIS; Peace Res. Abst. J.

3481
ORIENTAMENTI SOCIALI. v.1–36, no.3, 1971–Sept./Dec. 1981. Roma. Bimonthly, 1971–78; monthly.
In Italian.
Indexed: Bull. Anal. Pol. Ec. Soc.; Int. Bibl. Soc. Cul. Anth.

3482
ORIENTE MODERNO. 1– , 1921– . Roma. Monthly.
Issued by: Istituto per l'Oriente. In English, French, or Italian. Subtitle reads: "Rivista mensile d'informazione e di studi per la diffusione della conoscenza dell'oriente supra tutto musulmano".
Indexed: Bull. Anal. Pol. Ec. Soc.; His. Abst.; Int. Bibl. Soc. Cul. Anth.; Int. Pol. Sc. Abst.; Peace Res. Abst. J.

ORIGINAL SERIES
See STUDIES IN COMPARATIVE INTERNATIONAL DEVELOPMENT

3483
OSLO STUDIES IN SOCIAL ANTHROPOLOGY. no.1– , 1981– . Oslo, Universitetforlaget; New York, Columbia University Press. Irreg.

3484
OSMANIA JOURNAL OF SOCIAL SCIENCES. v.1– , June 1981– . Hyderabad. Semi-annual.
Issued by: Faculty of Social Sciences, Osmania University.

3485
OST-EUROPA. v.1– , 1951– . Stuttgart, Deutsche Verlags-Anstalt. Monthly.
Issued by: Deutsche Gesellschaft für Ost-Europakunde. In German. Subtitle reads: "Zeitschrift für Gegenwartsfragen des Ostens".
Indexed: ABC POL SCI; Bull. Anal. Pol. Ec. Soc.; Int. Bibl. Eco.; Int. Bibl. Pol. Sc.; Int. Lab. Doc.; Int. Pol. Sc. Abst.; PAISFL; Peace Res. Abst. J.

3486
OSTEUROPA WIRTSCHAFT. v.1– , Aug. 1956– . Stuttgart, Deutsche Verlags-Anstalt. Two no. a year, 1956–61; quarterly.
Issued by: Deutsche Gesellschaft für Osteuropakunde. In English or German; summaries in English and German. Tables of contents in English and German.

Indexes: v.1–6, 1956–61, 1v.
Indexed: Int. Bibl. Soc. Cul. Anth.; Int. Lab. Doc.; PAIS; PAISFL.

3487
OXFORD BULLETIN OF ECONOMICS AND STATISTICS. 1– , 1939– . Oxford, B. Blackwell. Quarterly.
Issued by: Institute of Economics and Statistics, Oxford University. Title varies: 1939–62, *Bulletin of the Oxford University Institute of Statistics*; 1963–72, *Bulletin of the Oxford University of Economics and Statistics*.
Indexed: Bull. Anal. Pol. Ec. Soc.; Curr. Cont. Soc. Beh. Sc.; Eco. Abst.; Int. Bibl. Eco.; Int. Bibl. Pol. Sc.; Int. Bibl. Soc.; J. Eco. Lit.; PAIS; Pop. Ind.; Soc. Abst.; SSCI.

3488
OXFORD ECONOMIC PAPERS. no.1–8, Oct. 1938–Nov. 1947; v.1– , Jan. 1949– . Oxford, Clarendon Press. Irreg., 1938–47; two no. a year, 1949; three no. a year.
Issued by: Department of Economics, University of Oxford. Not published in 1948.
Indexed: Bull. Anal. Pol. Ec. Soc.; Eco. Abst.; His. Abst.; Int. Bibl. Eco.; Ind. Per. Art. Law; Int. Bibl. Pol. Sc.; Int. Lab. Doc.; J. Eco. Lit.; PAIS; Pop. Ind.; SSCI.

3489
OXFORD JOURNAL OF ARCHAEOLOGY. v.1– , Mar. 1982– . Oxford, B. Blackwell. Three no. a year.

3490
OXFORD REVIEW OF ECONOMIC POLICY. v.1– , spring 1985– . Oxford, Oxford University Press. Quarterly.

3491
OXFORD REVIEW OF EDUCATION. v.1– , 1975– . Oxford, Carfax Pub. Co. Three no. a year.

3492
OXFORD STUDIES IN SOCIAL AND LEGAL HISTORY. v.1–9, 1909–1927. Oxford, The Clarendon Press. Irreg.

P & M POLITICS AND MONEY
See POLITICS AND MONEY

PDP WORKING PAPER SERIES
See Battelle Population and Development Program. PDP WORKING PAPER SERIES

PPSJ
See PHILIPPINE POLITICAL SCIENCE JOURNAL

3493
PS. v.1– , winter 1968– . Washington, D.C. Quarterly.
Issued by: American Political Science Association. Other title: *Political Science*.
Indexed: ABC POL SCI; Ind. Per. Art. Law; Int. Bibl. Eco.; Int. Bibl. Pol. Sc.; Int. Bibl. Soc.; SSCI; Wom. Stu. Abst.

PS POLITICAL SCIENCE
See POLITICAL SCIENCE

PSR
See POLICY STUDIES REVIEW

3494
PACIFIC AFFAIRS. 1– , Jan. 1928–1977; [n. ser.] 1– , 1978– . Honolulu. Monthly, 1928–Jan. 1933; bimonthly, 1933; quarterly.
Issued by: Institute of Public Relations. Title varies: Jan.–Apr. 1928, *News Bulletin*. (Earlier called Hawaii Institute of Pacific Relations)
Indexed: Abst. Anth.; ABC POL SCI; His. Abst.; Ind. Per. Art. Law; Int. Bibl. Eco.; Int. Bibl. Pol. Sc.; Int. Bibl. Soc.; Int. Bibl. Soc. Cul. Anth.; PAIS; Peace Res. Abst. J.; Soc. Sc. Hum. Ind.; Wom. Stu. Abst.

3495
PACIFIC ECONOMIC AND SOCIAL REVIEW. v.9– , 1971– . Lahore. Quarterly.
Issued by: Department of Economics, University of Punjab.
Continues: *Punjab University Economist*.

3496
PACIFIC HISTORICAL REVIEW. v.1– , Mar. 1932– . Los Angeles. Quarterly.
Issued by: Pacific Coast Branch, American Historical Association. V.1–2 include *Proceedings* of the 27th–28th annual meetings of the Pacific Coast Branch.
Indexes: Vols. 1–43, 1932–74, 1v.

3497
PACIFIC PERSPECTIVE. 1– , 1972– . Suva. Semi-annual.
Issued by: Institute of Polynesian Studies, and South Pacific Social Science Association, and sponsored by: Polynesian Cultural Center and the Brigham Young University.
Indexed: Int. Bibl. Soc. Cul. Anth.

3498
PACIFIC REVIEW OF ETHNOMUSICOLOGY. v.1– , 1984– . Los Angeles, Calif. Annual.
Issued by: UCLA [i.e. University of California at Los Angeles] Ethnomusicology Students Association.

3499
THE PACIFIC SOCIOLOGICAL REVIEW. v.1–25, spring 1958–Oct. 1982. Beverly Hills, Calif., Sage Publications. Semi-annual; quarterly.
Official publication of: Pacific Sociological Society.
Continued by: *Sociological Perspectives*.
Indexes: Vols. 1–5, 1958–62, with v.5; v.1–10, 1958–67, with v.10.
Indexed: Abst. Soc. Work.; ABC POL SCI; Bull. Anal. Pol. Ec. Soc.; Bull. Sig. Soc. Eth.; Curr. Cont. Soc. Beh. Sc.; Int. Bibl. Pol. Sc.; Int. Bibl. Soc.; Int. Bibl. Soc. Cul. Anth.; Int. Pol. Sc. Abst.; PHRA; SSCI; Soc. Work. Res. Abst.; Soc. Abst.; Sage Urb. Stu. Abst.; Wom. Stu. Abst.

3500
PACIFIC STUDIES. v.1– , Sept. 1977– . Laie. Semi-annual.
Issued by: Institute for Polynesian Studies, Brigham Young University.
Indexed: Int. Bibl. Soc. Cul. Anth.

3501
PACIFIC VIEWPOINT. v.1– , Mar. 1960– . Wellington. Semi-annual.
Issued by: Department of Geography, Victoria University of Wellington. Subtitle reads: "Change, conflict, continuity".
Indexed: Bull. Anal. Pol. Ec. Soc.; Curr. Cont. Soc. Beh. Sc.; Int. Bibl. Soc.; Int. Bibl. Soc. Cul. Anth.; Int. Pol. Sc. Abst.; Soc. Abst.; SSCI.

3502
PAEDAGOGICA EUROPEA. v.1–13, 1965–1978. 's-Hertogenbosch, L.C.G. Malmberg. Annual.
In English, French, or German. Each number has also a distinctive title.
Continued by: *European Journal of Education*.

3503
PAEDAGOGICA HISTORICA: INTERNATIONAL JOURNAL OF THE HISTORY OF EDUCATION. 1– , 1961– . Gent. Two no. a year.

In English, French, German, Italian, or Spanish.
Indexed: Curr. Cont. Soc. Beh. Sc.; His. Abst.

3504
PAEDAGOGICA, PSYCHOLOGICA, SOCIOLOGICA. v.12– , 1971– . Praha, Statni Pedagogické Nakladetelstvi.
Issued by: Filosofická Fakulta, Univerzita Palackého v Olomouci. In Czech or Slovak; summaries in English, German and Russian. Each volume has also a distinctive title.
Continues: *Paedagogica, Psychologica* (v.1–11, 1969–70)

3505
PAIDEIA. v.1– , 1972– . Wrocław, Zakład Narodowy im. Ossolińskich. Annual.
Issued by: Komitet Nauk Pedagogicznych, Polska Akademia Nauk. In English, French, German, or Russian. Subtitle reads: "Międzynarodowy rocznik pedagogiczny".

3506
PAIDEUMA; MITTEILUNGEN ZUR KULTURKUNDE. v.1–11, June 1938–1965; v.13– , 1967– . Wiesbaden, F. Steiner. Annual.
Issued by: Deutsche Kulturforschende Gesellschaft. In German. Publication suspended May 1944–Sept. 1948. Vol. 12 issued as: *Mitteilungen zur Kulturkunde.*
Indexed: Abst. Anth.; Bull. Sig. Soc. Eth.; Int. Bibl. Soc. Cul. Anth.

PAIX ET COEXISTENCE
See COEXISTENCE

3507
PAKISTAN ADMINISTRATION. v.15, no.2– , July 1978– . Lahore. Semi-annual.
Issued by: Administrative Staff College.
Continues: *Pakistan Administrative Staff College Journal* (v.7, no.3–v.15, no.1, Dec. 1969–Jan./June 1978)

PAKISTAN DEVELOPMENT REVIEW
See BANGLADESH DEVELOPMENT STUDIES

3508
PAKISTAN ECONOMIC AND SOCIAL REVIEW. v.9– , 1971– . Lahore. Quarterly.
Issued by: Department of Economic, University of Punjab.
Continues: *Punjab University Review.*

3509
PAKISTAN ECONOMIC JOURNAL. v.1–22, 1949–1973; n. ser. v.1, no. 1&2– , 1972/74– . Dacca. Two no. a year.
Issued by: Pakistan Economic Association, and Department of Economics, Dacca University.

3510
Pakistan Historical Society. JOURNAL. v.1– , Jan. 1953– . Karachi. Quarterly.

3511
PAKISTAN HORIZON. v.1– , Mar. 1948– . Karachi. Quarterly.
Issued by: Pakistan Institute of International Affairs.
Indexed: ABC POL SCI; His. Abst.; Ind. Per. Art. Law; Int. Bibl. Eco.; Int. Bibl. Pol. Sc.; Int. Bibl. Soc.; Int. Lab. Doc.; Int. Pol. Sc. Abst.; Peace Res. Abst. J.

3512
PAKISTAN JOURNAL OF HISTORY AND CULTURE. v.1– , Jan./June 1980– . Islamabad. Semi-annual.
Issued by: National Institute of Historical and Cultural Research.

3513
PAKISTAN JOURNAL OF SOCIAL SCIENCES. v.6, no.2– , July/Dec. 1982– . Islamabad. Semi-annual.
Issued by: Faculty of Social Sciences, Ouaid-i-Azam University.
Continues: *Scrutiny.*

3514
PALAEOHISTORIA. ACTA ET COMMUNICATIONES. v.1– , 1951– . Groningen, J.B. Wolters.
Issued by: Biologisch-Archaeologisch Instituut, Rijksuniversiteit de Groningen. In English, French, or German. Vols. 11–13 are monographs.

PALESTINE ECONOMIST
See THE ISRAEL ECONOMIST

3515
PALESTINE EXPLORATION QUARTERLY. Jan./Mar. 1869– . London. Quarterly, 1869–1940; two no. a year (some combined numbers)
Issued by: Palestine Exploration Fund. Includes: "Quarterly Statement of the Palestine Exploration Fund". Title varies: 1869–1936, Palestine Exploration Fund. *Quarterly Statement.* Absorbed: *Bulletin of the British School of Archaeology*, in 1928.
Indexes: 1869–92; 1893–1910.
Indexed: Abst. Anth.

3516
PAN-AFRICAN JOURNAL. v.1– , winter 1968– . Nairobi, The East African Literature Bureau. Quarterly.
Issued by: Pan-African Institute.
Indexed: His. Abst.

3517
Pan American Institute of Geography and History. BOLETÍN BIBLIOGRÁFICO DE ANTROPOLOGÍA AMERICANA. v.1– , Jan./June 1937– . Mexico, D.F. Frequency varies.
In English or Spanish.

3518
Pan American Institute of Geography and History. PUBLICATION. no.1– , 1949– . Mexico, D.F.
In Spanish or English. Includes the following subseries, each with its own volume numbering: *American Journal of Physical Anthropology*; *Estudios de Historia*; *Monumentos Históricos y Arqueológicos de América*; *Misiones Americanas en los Archivos Europeos*; *Programa de Historia de América*; *Informe del Secretaría General*; *Historiografías*; *Memorias sobre la Ensenanza de la Historia*.

3519
Pan American Institute of Geography and History. Commission on History. BIBLIOGRAFÍAS. v.1– , 1953– . Mexico, D.F. Irreg.
In English, French, Portuguese, or Spanish.

3520
Pan American Institute of Geography and History. Commission on History. HISTORIADORES DE AMÉRICA. v.1– , 1949– . Mexico, D.F. Irreg.
In English, French, Portuguese, or Spanish.

3521
Pan American Institute of Geography and History. Commission on History. HISTORIOGRAFÍAS AMERICANAS. v.1– , 1953– . Mexico, D.F. Irreg.
In Spanish.

3522
Pan American Institute of Geography and History. Commission on History. MONUMENTOS HISTÓRICOS Y ARQUEOLÓGICOS. v.1– , 1950– . Mexico, D.F. Irreg.
In Portuguese or Spanish.

3523
PANORAMA DE LA ECONOMÍA. v.6– , 4. trim. 1969– . Buenos Aires. Quarterly.
In Spanish.
Continues: *Panorama de la Economía Argentina* (v.1–6 (no.1–40), May 1957–1968)
Indexed: Int. Lab. Doc.

3524
PANORAMA DES SCIENCES SOCIALES. 1– , 1979– . El-Karrah. Quarterly.
Issued by: Centre de Recherches en Architecture et Urbanisme, Ministère de l'Enseignement Supérieur et de la Recherche Scientifique. In French; comments in Arabic.

3525
PANORAMA DU MARCHÉ COMMUN. PANORAMA OF THE COMMON MARKET. 1– , Sept. 1959– . Paris, Presseclichés Français. Monthly (irreg.), 1959–60; quarterly.
In English or French; summaries in English and French.

3526
PANORAMA LATINOAMERICANA. no.1– , Nov. 1979– . Moscow, Agencia de Prensa Novosti.
In Spanish.

PANORAMA OF THE COMMON MARKET
See PANORAMA DU MARCHÉ COMMUN

3527
PAŃSTWO I PRAWO. v.1– , 1946– . Warszawa, RSW "Prasa". Monthly.
Issued by: Instytut Nauk Prawnych, Polska Akademia Nauk. In Polish; summaries in English, French and Russian.
Indexed: ABC POL SCI; Bull. Anal. Pol. Ec. Soc.; His. Abst.; Int. Bibl. Eco.; Int. Bibl. Pol. Sc.; Int. Lab. Doc.; Int. Pol. Sc. Abst.

PAPER
See Archaeological Survey of Canada. PAPER

PAPER
See Canadian Centre for Folk Culture Studies. PAPER

PAPER
See Historical Association of Tanzania. PAPER

PAPERS
See Harvard University. Peabody Museum of American Archaeology and Ethnology. PAPERS

PAPERS
See Kroeber Anthropological Society. PAPERS

PAPERS
See Peace Science Society (International). PAPERS

PAPERS AND PROCEEDINGS
See Canadian Political Science Association. Annual Meeting. PAPERS AND PROCEEDINGS

PAPERS AND PROCEEDINGS OF MEETINGS OF THE CHINESE ASSOCIATION OF POLITICAL SCIENCE
See CHENG CHIH HSÜEH PAO

3528
PAPERS IN COMPARATIVE PUBLIC ADMINISTRATION. SPECIAL SERIES. no.1– , 1963– . Washington, D.C. Irreg.

Issued by: Comparative Administration Group, American Society for Public Administration. Some works are in reprint edition.

3529
PAPERS ON ISLAMIC HISTORY. no.1– , 1970– . Philadelphia, Pa., later Carbondale, Ill., Southern Illinois University Press. Irreg.
Issued by: Near East Center, University of Pennsylvania. Co-sponsor: Near Eastern History Group, Oxford. In English or French.

3530
PAPERS ON SOCIAL SCIENCE UTILIZATION. 1– , Oct. 1972– . Loughborough. Irreg.
Issued by: Centre for Utilisation of Social Science Research, Loughborough University of Technology. Each number has also a distinctive title.

PAPERS ON THE SOCIAL SCIENCES
See Institute of Sociology, London. REPORTS OF THE ANNUAL CONFERENCES

3531
PAPERS: REVISTA DE SOCIOLOGÍA. no.1– , 1973– . Barcelona. Irreg.
Issued by: Universidad Autónoma de Barcelona. In Catalan or Spanish. No.1 titled: *Papers; Trabajos de Sociología. Ediciones Peninsola.*

3532
THE PARLIAMENTARIAN. v.47– , Jan. 1966– . London. Quarterly.
Issued by: General Council of the Parliaments of the Commonwealth.
Continues: *Journal of the Parliaments of the Commonwealth.*
Indexed: ABC POL SCI; Bull. Anal. Pol. Ec. Soc.; Int. Bibl. Pol. Sc.; Int. Bibl. Soc. Cul. Anth.; Int. Pol. Sc. Abst.

3533
PARLIAMENTARY AFFAIRS. v.1– , winter 1947– . London, Oxford University Press. Quarterly.
Published in association with the Hansard Society for Parliamentary Government.
Indexed: ABC POL SCI; Brit. Hum. Ind.; Bull. Sig. Soc. Eth.; His. Abst.; Ind. Per. Art. Law; Int. Bibl. Eco.; Int. Bibl. Pol. Sc.; Int. Bibl. Soc.; Int. Pol. Sc. Abst.; PAIS; Peace Res. Abst. J.; Soc. Abst.; SSCI.

3534
PARLIAMENTARY GOVERNMENT. v.1– , Oct. 1979– . Ottawa. Quarterly.
Issued by: Institute for Research on Public Policy. Prepared by: Parliamentary Centre for Foreign Affairs and Foreign Trade. In English and French; French text on inverted pages.

3535
PARLIAMENTARY HISTORY; A YEARBOOK. v.1– , 1982– . Gloucester, Martin's Press.

3536
PARLIAMENTARY STUDIES. 1– , Feb. 1957– . New Delhi. Monthly.
Issued by: Indian Bureau of Parliamentary Studies. Some numbers published in combined form.

PARTIĬNAI͡A ZHIZN′
See LENINIAN UGLOV

PARTIĬNOE STROITEL′STVO
See LENINIAN UGLOV

PARTISKA IZGRADIIA
See KOMUNIST (Beograd)

PARTROBOTNIK
See LENINIAN UGLOV

3537
PAST AND PRESENT. v.1– , 1952– . Oxford. Quarterly.
Issued by: Past and Present Society, Corpus Christi College, Oxford University.
Indexed: Bull. Sig. Soc. Eth.; His. Abst.; Peace Res. Abst. J.; Soc. Abst.; Wom. Stu. Abst.

PATH
See PUBLICATIONS FOR THE ADVANCEMENT OF THEORY AND HISTORY IN PSYCHOLOGY

PATTERNS OF CULTURE
See KULTUURPATRONEN

3538
PATTERNS OF PREJUDICE. v.1– , Jan./Feb. 1967– . London. Bimonthly.
Issued by: Institute of Jewish Affairs. Early issues subtitled: "A bimonthly on international antisemitism, radical right movements and counter activities".
Indexed: Bull. Anal. Pol. Ec. Soc.; His. Abst.; Ind. Per. Art. Law; Int. Bibl. Soc. Cul. Anth.

PAYS COMMUNISTES
See REVUE DES PAYS DE L'EST

PEACE
See PEACE YEAR-BOOK

3539
PEACE AND CHANGE. 1– , fall 1972– . Kent, Ohio. Quarterly.
Sponsored by: Conference on Peace Research in History, and the Consortium on Peace Research, Education and Development.

Indexed: Int. Pol. Sc. Abst.; PAIS; Peace Res. Abst. J.; Sage Pub. Adm. Abst.; Sage Urb. Stu. Abst.

3540
PEACE AND THE SCIENCES. July/Sept. 1964– . Wien. Quarterly.
Issued by: International Institute for Peace, Vienna. Supersedes the institute's: *Nuclear Energy*.
Indexed: Int. Bibl. Pol. Sc.

3541
THE PEACE MOVEMENT. v.1–3, no.1, 1912–July 1914. Berne.
Organ of: The International Peace Bureau in Berne.

3542
PEACE RESEARCH ABSTRACTS JOURNAL. v.1– , June 1964– . Clarkson, later Oakville. Monthly, with annual cumulation.
Issued by: Peace Research Institute. Official publication of the International Peace Research Association. Published with assistance from Unesco.

3543
Peace Science Society (International). PAPERS. v.2–29, 1973–1979/80. Philadelphia, Pa. Annual.
Continues: *Papers* issued by this society under its earlier name: Peace Research Society (International) (v.1–19, 1964–72).

THE PEACE YEAR BOOK
See PEACE YEAR-BOOK

3544
PEACE YEAR-BOOK. 1910– . London.
Title varies: 1910–14, *The Peace Year Book*; 1915–21, *Peace Year Book*; 1927, *Peace*.

3545
PEASANT STUDIES. v.1–10, Jan. 1972–winter 1983. Pittsburgh, Pa., later Salt Lake City, Utah. Quarterly.
Issued by: Department of History, University of Pittsburgh, and the Departments of Anthropology, Economics, and Political Science, the Middle East Center, Center for Historical Population Studies, College of Humanities and Social and Behavioral Sciences of the University of Utah. Title varies: v.1–4, 1972–76, *Peasant Studies Newsletter*.

PEASANT STUDIES NEWSLETTER
See PEASANT STUDIES

3546
PEDAGOGISK FORSKNING. SCANDINAVIAN JOURNAL OF EDUCATIONAL RESEARCH. 1– , 1969– . Oslo, Universitetsforlaget. Quarterly.
In English.

3547
PEDAGOSKI RAD. v.1– , 1946– . Zagreb. Six no. a year, 1946–56; ten no. a year.
Issued by: Pedagosko Drustvo SR Hrvatske, and Pedagosko Knizevni Zbor. In Serbo-Croatian. Tables of contents also in French. Some numbers are combined.

3548
PEI-CHING SHIH FAN TA HSÜEH PAO. SHE HUI K'O HSÜEH PAN. Jul./Sept. 1956– . Pei-ching shih fan ta hsüeh. Bimonthly.
Issued by: Beinjg shi-fan daxue xuebao. In Chinese. Other title: *Journal of Beijing Normal University*.
Continues: *Pei-ching shih ta hsüeh pao; she hui k'o hsüeh pan*.

3549
PENSAMIENTO IBEROAMERICANO. no.1– , Jan./June 1982– . Madrid. Semi-annual.
Issued by: Instituto de Cooperación Iberoamericana de España ICI, y la Comisión Económica de las Naciones Unidas. In Spanish.

3550
PENSAMIENTO POLÍTICO. v.1– , May 1969– . Mexico, D.F. Monthly.
Issued by: Cultura y Ciencia Política. In Spanish. Some numbers are accompanied by supplements.
Indexed: Int. Bibl. Soc. Cul. Anth.

3551
PENSÉE. Feb. 1971– . Portland, Oreg. Ten no. a year.
Issued by: Student Academic Freedom Forum.
Indexed: Bull. Anal. Pol. Ec. Soc.; His. Abst.; Int. Pol. Sc. Abst.; LLBA; Peace Res. Abst. J.; Wom. Stu. Abst.

3552
IL PENSIERO POLITICO. v.1– , 1968– . Firenze, L.S. Olschi. Three no. a year.
Issued by: Istituto di Studi Historico-Politici. In English, French, or Italian.
Indexed: Int. Bibl. Soc. Cul. Anth.; Int. Pol. Sc. Abst.

PERCEPTIONS
See Science Council of Canada. STUDY OF POPULATION AND TECHNOLOGY. PERCEPTIONS

PERIFEREIAKEE STATISTIKES
See Statistical Office of the European Communities. REGIONAL STATISTICS: COMMUNITY'S FINANCIAL PARTICIPATION IN INVESTMENTS

3553
PERSONALITY AND SOCIAL PSYCHOLOGY BULLETIN. v.1, no.2– , Feb. 1975– . Beverly Hills, Calif., Sage Publications. Quarterly.

Issued by: Society for Personality and Social Psychology. V.1, no.1 issued as American Psychological Association. Division of Personality and Social Psychology. *Proceedings*.
Indexed: Psych. Abst.; Soc. Sc. Ind.; Sage Fam. Stu. Abst.

3554
PERSONALITY STUDY AND GROUP BEHAVIOUR. v.1– , Jan. 1981– . Amritsar. Semi-annual.
Issued by: Department of Psychology, Guru Nanak Dev University.

3555
PERSONNEL JOURNAL. v.1– , May 1922– . Baltimore, Md., New York. Eleven no. a year.
Title varies: 1922–Apr. 1927, *Journal of Personnel Research*.
Indexed: Bull. Anal. Pol. Ec. Soc.; Bull. Sig. Soc. Eth.; PHRA; Psych. Abst.; Int. Bibl. Soc. Cul. Anth.; Wom. Stu. Abst.

3556
PERSONNEL PSYCHOLOGY. v.1– , spring 1948– . Durham, N.C. Quarterly.
Indexes: Vols. 1–5, 1948–52, 1v.
Indexed: Bull. Anal. Pol. Ec. Soc.; Bull. Sig. Soc. Eth.; Int. Bibl. Eco.; Int. Lab. Doc.; Psych. Abst.; Wom. Stu. Abst.

PERSPECTIVAS INTERNACIONALES EN PLANIFICACIÓN FAMILIAR
See INTERNATIONAL FAMILY PLANNING PERSPECTIVES

3557
PERSPECTIVES CANADA. English Edition. 5– , 1980– . Ottawa.
Issued by: Office of the Senior Adviser on Integration, Statistics Canada. A French edition with the same title is also published.

3558
PERSPECTIVES IN ORGANIZATIONAL SOCIOLOGY; THEORY AND RESEARCH. 1– , 1982– . Greenwich, Conn., JAI Press. Annual.

3559
PERSPECTIVES IN PERSONALITY. v.1– , 1985– . Greenwich, Conn., JAI Press. Annual.

3560
PERSPECTIVES IN SOCIAL SCIENCES. 1– , 1977– . Calcutta, Oxford University Press. Annual.

3561
PERSPECTIVES ON LOCAL PUBLIC FINANCE AND PUBLIC POLICY. v.1– , 1983– . Greenwich, Conn., JAI Press. Annual.

3562
PERSPECTIVES ON THE AMERICAN SOUTH. v.1– , 1981– . New York, Gordon and Breach. Annual.
"An annual review of society, politics and culture".

PERSPECTIVES POLONAISES
See POLISH PERSPECTIVES

PERSPEKTYWY POLSKIE
See POLISH PERSPECTIVES

3563
PESQUISA E PLANEJAMENTO ECONÔMICO. June 1971– . Rio de Janeiro. Three no. a year.
Issued by: Instituto de Planejamento Econômico e Social (IPEA). In Portuguese.
Indexed: PAISFL.

PEUPLES AFRICAINS
See PEUPLES NOIRS

3564
PEUPLES MEDITERRANÉENS. MEDITERRANEAN PEOPLES. 1– , 1977– . Paris, Éditions Anthropos. Quarterly.
In English or French; summaries in French or English.
Indexed: Bull. Anal. Pol. Ec. Soc.; Bull. Sig. Soc. Eth.; Int. Bibl. Eco.; Int. Bibl. Pol. Sc.; Int. Pol. Sc. Abst.; Soc. Abst.

3565
PEUPLES NOIRS. PEUPLES AFRICAINS. 1978– . Paris, Éditions des Peuples Noirs. Six no. a year.
In French.
Indexed: Bull. Anal. Pol. Ec. Soc.; Int. Bibl. Soc. Cul. Anth.

3566
Philippine Chinese Historical Association. THE ANNALS. 1970– . Manila.
Some articles in Chinese.

3567
PHILIPPINE ECONOMIC JOURNAL. 1– , Jan. 1962– . Manila. Semi-annual.
Issued by: Philippine Economic Society.
Indexed: Bull. Anal. Pol. Ec. Soc.; Geo. Abst.; Int. Bibl. Soc. Cul. Anth.; Pop. Ind.; Soc. Abst.

3568
PHILIPPINE ECONOMY AND INDUSTRIAL JOURNAL. 1– , Aug. 1954– . Manila. Bimonthly.
Title varies: v.1–10, 1954–63, *Philippine Economy Review*.
Indexed: PAIS.

PHILIPPINE ECONOMY REVIEW
See PHILIPPINE ECONOMY AND INDUSTRIAL JOURNAL

3569
PHILIPPINE JOURNAL OF PUBLIC ADMINISTRATION. v.1– , Jan. 1957– . Manila. Quarterly.
Issued by: Institute of Public Administration, University of the Philippines.
Indexed: ABC POL SCI; His. Abst.; Int. Bibl. Pol. Sc.; Int. Bibl. Soc. Cul. Anth.; Int. Bibl. Soc.; Int. Lab. Doc.; Int. Pol. Sc. Abst.; PAIS.

3570
PHILIPPINE POLITICAL SCIENCE JOURNAL. no.1– , June 1974– . Quezon City. Semi-annual (irreg.)
Issued by: Philippine Political Science Association. Running title: *PPSJ*.

3571
PHILIPPINE QUARTERLY OF CULTURE AND SOCIETY. v.1– , Mar. 1973– . Cebu City. Four no. a year.
Issued by: University of San Carlos.
Supersedes: *San Carlos Publications. Series E. Miscellaneous Contributions in the Humanities.*

3572
THE PHILIPPINE REVIEW OF BUSINESS AND ECONOMICS. v.1–16, no.1, June 1964–Mar. 1979. Quezon City. Semi-annual; quarterly (some nos. combined)
Issued by: School of Economics and College of Business Administration, University of the Philippines.
Continued by: *The Philippine Review of Economics and Business* (v.16, no.2–, June 1979–)

THE PHILIPPINE SOCIAL SCIENCE REVIEW
See THE PHILIPPINE SOCIAL SCIENCES AND HUMANITIES REVIEW

3573
THE PHILIPPINE SOCIAL SCIENCES AND HUMANITIES REVIEW. v.1–47, Sept. 1929–1983. Quezon City. Monthly, 1929–Feb./Apr. 1930; quarterly.
Issued by: 1929–35, Philippine Academy of Social Sciences; 1936–50, College of Liberal Arts, University of the Philippines. Publication suspended, 1942–48. Supplements accompany some numbers. Absorbed: *Studies in Social Sciences*, issued by the University of the Philippines, in Aug. 1930. Some numbers are combined.
Indexed: His. Abst.; Int. Bibl. Eco.; Int. Bibl. Soc. Cul. Anth.; Int. Pol. Sc. Abst.

3574
PHILIPPINE SOCIOLOGICAL REVIEW. v.1– , Aug. 1953– . Manila. Quarterly.
Issued by: Philippine Sociological Society.
Indexes: (author/title) 1953–64, in v.12, no.3/4; (subject) quinquenially.
Indexed: Abst. Anth. (through 1972); Soc. Abst.; SSCI.

3575
PHILIPPINE STUDIES. v.1– , June 1953– . Manila, Ateneo de Manila University Press. Quarterly.
Issued by: Society of Jesus in the Philippine Islands.
Indexed: Bull. Anal. Pol. Ec. Soc.; His. Abst.; Int. Pol. Sc. Abst.

3576
THE PHILIPPINE YEARBOOK OF INTERNATIONAL LAW. v.1– , 1966/68– . Manila. Irreg.
Issued by: The Philippine Society of International Law and the College of Law, University of the Philippines.
Supersedes: *The Philippine International Law Journal* (v.1–4, 1962–65)

3577
PHILOSOPHY AND PUBLIC AFFAIRS. v.1– , fall 1971– . Princeton, N.J., Princeton University Press. Quarterly.
Indexed: ABC POL SCI; Bull. Anal. Pol. Ec. Soc.; Int. Bibl. Pol. Sc.; Int. Pol. Sc. Abst.; Soc. Abst.; SSCI; Wom. Stu. Abst.

3578
PHILOSOPHY & SOCIAL CRITICISM. v.5– , Jan. 1978– . Chestnut Hill, Mass. Quarterly (occasionally combined numbers)
Issued by: Department of Philosophy, Boston College. Subtitle reads: "An international, inter-disciplinary quarterly journal".
Continues: *Cultural Hermeneutics*.
Indexed: Soc. Abst.

PHILOSOPHY AND SOCIOLOGY OF SCIENCE AND TECHNOLOGY
See FILOSOFII͡A I SOT͡SIOLOGII͡A NAUKI I TEKHNIKI

3579
PHILOSOPHY OF THE SOCIAL SCIENCES. v.1– , Jan. 1971– . Aberdeen, Wilfrid Laurier University Press. Quarterly.
Issued by: Department of Philosophy, York University (Canada)
Indexed: Bull. Anal. Pol. Ec. Soc.; Bull. Sig. Soc. Eth.; Int. Bibl. Pol. Sc.; Int. Bibl. Soc.; SSCI.

3580
THE PHYLON. v.1– , first quarter 1940– . Atlanta, Ga. Quarterly.
Issued by: Atlanta University. Subtitle reads: "The Atlanta University review of race and culture". Other title: *Phylon Quarterly*.
Indexes: Vols. 1–5, 1940–44, in v.5.

Indexed: Abst. Anth.; Bull. Sig. Soc. Eth.; Bull. Anal. Pol. Ec. Soc.; Int. Bibl. Pol. Sc.; His. Abst.; Int. Bibl. Soc.; Int. Bibl. Soc. Cul. Anth.; Int. Lab. Doc.; Int. Pol. Sc. Abst.; PAIS; PHRA; Psych. Abst.; Sage Urb. Stu. Abst.; Soc. Abst.; Soc. Sc. Hum. Ind.; SSCI; Wom. Stu. Abst.

PHYLON QUARTERLY
See THE PHYLON

PLANIFICATION FAMILIALE ET POPULATION
See FAMILY PLANNING AND POPULATION

THE PLANNER'S JOURNAL
See American Institute of Planners. JOURNAL

3581
PLANNING. 1– , 1909– . Chicago, Ill. Annual.
Issued by: American Society of Planning Officials. Title varies: 1909–42, *Proceedings* of the National Planning Conference.
Indexed: Int. Bibl. Eco.; PHRA; Sage Urb. Stu. Abst.

3582
PLANNING AND ADMINISTRATION. v.1– , winter 1974– . The Hague, International Federation for Housing and Planning. Semi-annual.
Indexed: ABC POL SCI; Bull. Anal. Pol. Ec. Soc.; Sage Urb. Stu. Abst.

3583
PLANNING OUTLOOK. v.1– , 1948– . Newcastle upon Tyne. Three no. a year.
Organ of: School of Town and Country Planning, University of Newcastle upon Tyne.
Indexed: Bull. Anal. Pol. Ec. Soc.; Int. Bibl. Eco.; Int. Bibl. Pol. Sc.; Int. Bibl. Soc.

3584
PLANOVANE HOSPODARSTVI. v.1– , 1948– . Praha, Orbis. Ten no. a year.
Issued by: Statni Urad Planovaci v Praze. In Czech.
Indexed: Bull. Anal. Pol. Ec. Soc.; Int. Bibl. Eco.; Int. Lab. Doc.

3585
PLANOVOE KHOZI͡AĬSTVO. v.1– , 1983– . Moskva, Izd-vo Ekonomika. Monthly.
Issued by: Gosplan SSSR. Gosudarstvennai͡a Planovai͡a Komissii͡a SSSR. In Russian. Title varies: no.1–7, 1923, *Bi͡ulleten' Gosplana*; no.10, *Planovoe Khozi͡aĭstvo. Bi͡ulleten' Gosplana*.
Indexed: Bull. Anal. Pol. Ec. Soc.; Int. Bibl. Eco.; Int. Lab. Doc.

PLANOVOE KHOZI͡AĬSTVO; BIULLETEN' GOSPLANA
See PLANOVOE KHOZI͡AĬSTVO

3586
PLURAL SOCIETIES. 1– , 1970– . The Hague. Quarterly.
Issued by: Stichting Plurale Samenlevingen.
Indexed: ABC POL SCI; Bull. Anal. Pol. Ec. Soc.; Bull. Sig. Soc. Eth.; Int. Bibl. Pol. Sc.; Int. Pol. Sc. Abst.

PO LENINSKOMU PUTI
See LENINJAN UGLOV

POL-DOK
See POLITISCHE DOKUMENTATION

3587
POLICY ANALYSIS. v.1–7, no.2, winter 1975–spring 1981. Berkeley, Calif., University of California Press. Quarterly.
Issued by: Graduate School of Public Policy, University of California, Berkeley. Merged with *Public Policy* to form: *Journal of Policy Analysis and Management*.
Indexed: Bull. Anal. Pol. Ec. Soc.; Int. Bibl. Eco.

3588
POLICY ANALYSIS AND INTERNATIONAL ECONOMICS. 1– , 1982– . Washington, D.C. Irreg.
Issued by: Institute for International Economics. Each number has also a distinctive title.

3589
POLICY AND POLITICS. v.1– , Sept. 1972– . London, later Beverly Hills, Calif., Sage Publications. Quarterly.
Indexed: ABC POL SCI; Bull. Anal. Pol. Ec. Soc.; Int. Bibl. Pol.

POLICY AND RESEARCH REPORT
See The Urban Institute. POLICY AND RESEARCH REPORT

POLICY DEVELOPMENT STUDIES
See United Nations Fund for Population Activities. POLICY DEVELOPMENT STUDIES

3590
POLICY OPTIONS. OPTIONS POLITIQUES. v.1– , Mar. 1980– . Montreal. Quarterly.
Issued by: Institute for Research on Public Policy. In English or French.

3591
POLICY REVIEW. v.1– , spring 1970– . Amsterdam, Elsevier Pub. Co. Quarterly.
Indexed: ABC POL SCI; Bull. Anal. Pol. Ec. Soc.; Int. Bibl. Eco.; Int. Bibl. Pol. Sc.; PAIS; Sage Urb. Stu. Abst.

3592
POLICY SCIENCES. v.1– , spring 1970– . Amsterdam, New York, Elsevier Scientific Pub. Co. Quarterly.
Indexed: ABC POL SCI; Bull. Anal. Pol. Ec. Soc.; Curr. Cont. Soc. Beh. Sc.; Ind. Per. Art. Law; Int. Bibl. Eco.; Int. Bibl. Pol. Sc.; Int. Pol. Sc. Abst.; PHRA; Sage Pub. Adm. Abst.; Soc. Abst.; SSCI; Urb. Stu. Abst.

POLICY SCIENCES RESEARCH JOURNAL *See* CHONCH'AEK KWAHAK YŎN'GU NONCH'ONG

3593
POLICY STUDIES. v.1– , July 1980– . London. Quarterly.
Issued by: Policy Studies Institute.
Indexed: Int. Bibl. Pol. Sc.; PAIS.

3594
POLICY STUDIES ANNUAL REVIEW. v.1– , 1977– . Beverly Hills, Calif., Sage Publications. Annual.

3595
Policy Studies Institute, London. DISCUSSION PAPER. no.1– , 1980– . London. Irreg.
Sponsored by: Anglo-American Foundation for the Study of Industrial Society. Each number has also a distinctive title.

3596
POLICY STUDIES JOURNAL. v.1– , autumn 1972– . Urbana, Ill., University of Illinois. Quarterly, 1972–July 1979; eight no. a year, Sept. 1979–Aug. 1981; quarterly.
Issued by: Policy Studies Organization.
Indexed: ABC POL SCI; Bull. Anal. Pol. Ec. Soc.; Curr. Cont. Soc. Beh. Sc.; Int. Bibl. Eco.; Int. Bibl. Pol. Sc.; Int. Pol. Sc. Abst.; PAIS; Sage Fam. Stu. Abst.; Sage Urb. Stu. Abst.; Soc. Sc. Hum. Ind.

3597
POLICY STUDIES REVIEW. v.1– , Aug. 1981– . Urbana, Ill., Policy Studies Organization. Quarterly.
Edited by: Center for Public Affairs, The University of Kansas. Includes papers of *Symposia*, numbered separately. Other title: *PRS*.
Indexed: ABC POL SCI; Int. Bibl. Soc. Cul. Anth.; Int. Pol. Sc. Abst.; Sage Urb. Stu. Abst.

3598
POLISH PERSPECTIVES. v.1– , May 1958– . Warsaw. Monthly.
In English. Other title: *Perspektywy Polskie*. Published also in French: *Perspectives Polonaises*.
Indexed: Wom. Stu. Abst.

3599
POLISH POLITICAL SCIENCE. 1– , 1981– . Wrocław, Zakład Narodowy im. Ossolińskich. Annual.
Issued by: Polish Association of Political Science. In English.
Supersedes: *Polish Round Table. Yearbook* (v.1–10, 1967–76)

3600
THE POLISH SOCIOLOGICAL BULLETIN. no.1– , June/Dec. 1961– . Warsaw, Zakład Narodowy im. Ossolińskich. Semi-annual.
Issued by: Polskie Towarzystwo Socjologiczne.
Indexed: Bull. Anal. Pol. Ec. Soc.; Bull. Sig. Soc. Eth.; Int. Bibl. Pol. Sc.; Int. Bibl. Soc.; Int. Pol. Sc. Abst.; LLBA; Soc. Abst.; SSCI.

3601
THE POLISH YEARBOOK OF INTERNATIONAL LAW. ANNUAIRE POLONAIS DE DROIT INTERNATIONAL. 1– , 1966/67– . Wrocław, Zakład Narodowy im. Ossolińskich. Annual.
Issued by: Polish Institute of International Affairs, Institute of Legal Affairs of the Polish Academy of Sciences, and the Polish Branch of the International Law Association. In English or French.
Indexed: Ind. For. Leg. Per.

3602
POLITEIA. 1– , 1972– . Caracas. Annual.
Issued by: Instituto de Estudios Políticos, Faculdad de Ciencias Jurídicas y Políticas, Universidad Central de Venezuela. In Spanish.
Indexed: Bull. Anal. Pol. Ec. Soc.; Int. Pol. Sc. Abst.

3603
POLITEIA. TYDSKRIF VIR POLITIEKE WETENSKAPPE. JOURNAL FOR THE POLITICAL SCIENCES. v.1– , 1982– . Pretoria.
In Afrikaans or English.

3604
POLITICA. v.1– , 1968– . Aarhus. Four no. a year.
Issued by: Institut for Statskundskab, Aarhus Universitet. In Danish or English.

3605
POLÍTICA. no.1– , Sept. 1982– . Santiago, Chile. Three no. a year.
Issued by: Instituto de Ciencia Política, Universidad de Chile. In Spanish. Includes: *Cuadernos de Ciencia Política*.
Indexed: PAISFL.

3606
POLÍTICA, ECONOMÍA Y SOCIEDAD. 1– , May/June 1982– . Buenos Aires, Editorial Fepa. Bimonthly.

Issued by: Fundación para el Estudio de los Problemos Argentinos. In Spanish.

3607
POLITICA ED ECONOMIA. v.1–6, no.3/4, July 1957–Mar. 1962; n. ser. v.1– , July/Aug. 1970– . Roma, Riuniti (1970–). Monthly.
In Italian. Formed by the union of: *Rivista Bimestral del CESPE* of *Critica Economica*, *Notizie Economiche* and *Riforma Agraria*.
Indexed: Bull. Anal. Pol. Ec. Soc.; Soc. Abst.

POLÍTICA INTERNACIONAL
See REVISTA DE POLÍTICA INTERNACIONAL

3608
POLITICA INTERNAZIONALE. no.1– , Jan. 1973– . Milano, La Nuova Editrice. Bimonthly.
Issued by: Istituto per le Relazioni tra Italia e Paesi del'Africa, America Latina e Medio Oriente, IPALMO. In Italian.
Indexed: Bull. Anal. Pol. Ec. Soc.; Int. Bibl. Pol. Sc.; Int. Pol. Sc. Abst.

3609
POLITICAL AFFAIRS. [v.1]– , Mar. 1922– . New York, Century Publishers. Monthly.
Organ of: Trade Union Educational League, 1922–24; Workers (Communist) Party of the United States of America, Nov. 1924–Feb. 1927. Issues for 1922–Oct. 1927 were published in Chicago. Subtitle reads: "A magazine devoted to the theory and practice of Marxism-Leninism" (later "Journal of Marxist thought"). Not published Oct. 1948–May 1950. Title varies: 1922–Oct. 1924, *The Labor Herald*; Mar. 1927–Dec. 1944, *The Communist*. Absorbed: *Liberator* and *Soviet Russian Pictorial*.
Indexed: Bull. Anal. Pol. Ec. Soc.; Int. Bibl. Soc. Cul. Anth.; Peace Res. Abst. J.

3610
POLITICAL AND ECONOMIC REVIEW. v.1– , May 1970– . New Delhi. Weekly.
Issued by: Indian National Congress. Title varies: *AICC Economic Review*; *Economic Review*; *Fortnightly Economic Review*.
Indexed: PAIS.

3611
POLITICAL ANTHROPOLOGY. 1– , Mar. 1975– . Assen, Van Gorcum. Quarterly.
Issued by: Bowling Green State University.

3612
POLITICAL ANTHROPOLOGY. v.2– , 1983– . New Brunswick, N.J., Transaction Books. Annual.
Continues: *Political Anthropology Yearbook* (v.1, 1980)

3613
POLITICAL BEHAVIOR. 1– , spring 1979– . New York, Agathon Press. Quarterly.
Indexed: Int. Bibl. Pol. Sc.; Int. Pol. Sc. Abst.

3614
POLITICAL BEHAVIOR ANNUAL. v.1– , 1986– . Boulder, Colo., Westview Press. Annual.

3615
POLITICAL COMMUNICATION AND PERSUASION. v.1– , 1980– . New York, Crane Russak. Quarterly.
Indexed: ABC POL SCI; Int. Pol. Sc. Abst.; PAIS; Soc. Abst.

3616
POLITICAL COMMUNICATION YEARBOOK. 1984– . Carbondale, Ill., Southern Illinois University Press. Annual.

3617
THE POLITICAL ECONOMIST AND JOURNAL OF SOCIAL SCIENCE. no.1–15, Jan. 1856–Apr. 1857. London. Monthly (irreg.)

3618
POLITICAL ECONOMY AND PUBLIC POLICY. v.1– , 1984– . Greenwich, Conn., JAI Press. Annual.

3619
POLITICAL ECONOMY AND THE WORLD-SYSTEM ANNUAL. v.1– , 1978– . Beverly Hills, Calif., Sage Publications. Irreg.
Published in cooperation with the Section of the Political Economy of the World Systems of the American Sociological Association.

3620
THE POLITICAL ECONOMY OF INCOME DISTRIBUTION IN DEVELOPING COUNTRIES. v.1– , 1980– . New York, Holmes & Meier Publishers.
Issued under the auspices of the Research Program in Development Studies, Woodrow Wilson School of Public and International Affairs, Princeton University.

3621
POLITICAL GEOGRAPHY QUARTERLY. v.1– , Jan. 1982– . Guildford, Butterworth Scientific Ltd.

3622
POLITICAL METHODOLOGY. v.1– , winter 1974– . Los Angeles, Calif., Geron—X. Quarterly.

3623
POLITICAL POWER AND SOCIAL THEORY. v.1– , 1980– . Greenwich, Conn., JAI Press. Annual.
Indexed: Int. Bibl. Pol. Sc.; Int. Pol. Sc. Abst.; LLBA.

3624
POLITICAL PSYCHOLOGY. 1– , spring 1979– . New Brunswick, N.J., Transaction Periodicals Consortium. Quarterly.
Issued by: International Society of Political Psychology.
Indexed: Psych. Abst.

3625
THE POLITICAL QUARTERLY. v.1– , Jan. 1930– . London, later Oxford, B. Blackwell. Quarterly.
Indexed: ABC POL SCI; Bull. Anal. Pol. Ec. Soc.; His. Abst.; Int. Bibl. Pol. Sc.; Int. Bibl. Soc.; Int. Bibl. Soc. Cul. Anth.; Int. Lab. Doc.; Int. Pol. Sc. Abst.; PAIS; Peace Res. Abst. J.; Sage Urb. Stu. Abst.; Soc. Sc. Hum. Ind.; SSCI.

POLITICAL QUARTERLY
See ḤAWLĪYĀT, SIYĀSĪYA-AL-SAMAH

3626
POLITICAL SCIENCE. v.1– , Sept. 1948– . Wellington. Semi-annual.
Issued by: Political Science Society, Victoria University College, later School of Political Science and Public Administration (with the Political Science Society, –Sept. 1953). Publication suspended between June 1949 and Mar. 1951 (v.1, no.3–v.3, no.1). Title varies: v.1–3, no.3, Sept. 1948–June 1949, *Journal of Political Science*.
Indexed: ABC POL SCI; Bull. Anal. Pol. Ec. Soc.; Int. Pol. Sc. Abst.; SSCI.

3627
POLITICAL SCIENCE. v.5– , 1978– . New York. Irreg. M. Dekker.
Other title: *PS Political Science*.
Continues: *Political Science and Public Administration* (v.1–4, 1977–78)
Indexed: Int. Pol. Sc. Abst.

POLITICAL SCIENCE
See PS

3628
POLITICAL SCIENCE ABSTRACTS. ANNUAL SUPPLEMENT. 1980– . New York, Plenum. Annual.
Continues: *Political Science, Government & Public Policy Series*. (1973–79, annual usually in 3 vols.)

POLITICAL SCIENCE AND JURISPRUDENCE
See ÁLLAM-ÉS JOGTUDOMÁNYI

POLITICAL SCIENCE, GOVERNMENT & PUBLIC POLICY
See Universal Reference System. POLITICAL SCIENCE, GOVERNMENT & PUBLIC POLICY

3629
POLITICAL SCIENCE QUARTERLY. v.1– , Mar. 1886– . New York. Quarterly.
Issued by: Academy of Political Science. Vols. 4–38, 40–41 include "Record of Political Events, Oct. 1, 1888–Dec. 31, 1925". Subtitle reads: "A review devoted to historical, statistical and comparative study of politics, economics and public law".
Indexes: Vols. 1–15, 1886–1900, 1v.; v.1–30, 1886–1915, 1v.; v.1–45, 1886–1930, 1v.; v.46–65, 1931–50, 1v.
Indexed: ABC POL SCI; Bull. Anal. Pol. Ec. Soc.; His. Abst.; Int. Bibl. Pol. Sc.; Int. Bibl. Eco.; Int. Bibl. Soc.; Int. Pol. Sc. Abst.; J. Eco. Lit.; Int. Bibl. Soc. Cul. Anth.; Hum. Res. Abst.; PAIS; Peace Res. Abst. J.; Sage Urb. Stu. Abst.; Soc. Sc. Hum. Ind.; SSCI.

3630
THE POLITICAL SCIENCE REVIEW. v.1– , Feb. 1962– . Jaipur. Two no. a year.
Issued by: Department of Political Science, University of Rajasthan.
Indexed: ABC POL SCI; Bull. Anal. Pol. Ec. Soc.; Bull. Sig. Soc. Eth.; Int. Bibl. Eco.; Int. Bibl. Pol. Sc.; Int. Bibl. Soc.; Int. Bibl. Soc. Cul. Anth.; Int. Pol. Sc. Abst.

THE POLITICAL SCIENCE REVIEW OF THE KOMAZAWA UNIVERSITY
See SEIJIGAKU RONSHŪ

3631
POLITICAL SCIENTIST. v.1– , July/Dec. 1964– . Ranchi. Semi-annual.
Issued by: Department of Political Science, Ranchi University.
Indexed: Ind. Per. Art. Law; Int. Bibl. Pol. Sc.; Int. Pol. Sc. Abst.; Peace Res. Abst. J.

3632
POLITICAL STUDIES. v.1– , Feb. 1953– . Oxford, Oxford University Press. Three no. a year.
Issued by: Political Studies Association of the United Kingdom, and Leicester Polytechnic School of Social and Community Studies.
Indexed: ABC POL SCI; Bull. Anal. Pol. Ec. Soc.; Curr. Cont. Soc. Beh. Sc.; Bull. Sig. Soc. Eth.; His. Abst.; Ind. Per. Art. Law; Int. Bibl. Eco.; Int. Bibl. Pol. Sc.; Int. Bibl. Soc.; Int. Bibl. Soc. Cul. Anth.; PAIS; Peace Res. Abst. J.; Sage Pub. Adm. Abst.; Sage Urb. Stu. Abst.; Soc. Abst.; Soc. Sc. Hum. Ind.; SSCI.

3633
POLITICAL THEORY. v.1– , Feb. 1973– . Beverly Hills, Calif., Sage Publications. Quarterly.

Indexed: ABC POL SCI; Bull. Anal. Pol. Ec. Soc.; Curr. Cont. Soc. Beh. Sc.; Int. Pol. Sc. Abst.; PAIS; Sage Urb. Stu. Abst.; Soc. Abst.; SSCI.

3634
POLITICHESKOE SAMOOBRAZOVANIE. [v.1]– , 1957– . Moskva, Pravda. Monthly.
Issued by: T͡Sentral'nyĭ Komitet, Kommunisticheskaia͡ Partii͡a Sovetskogo Soi͡uza. In Russian. Title varies: *V Pomoshchi Politicheskomu Samoobrazovaniu͡.*

3635
POLITICKA MISAO. 1– , 1964– . Zagreb. Quarterly.
Issued by: Fakultet Politickih Nauk Sveucilists u Zagrebu. In Serbo-Croatian; summaries in English or French.
Indexed: ABC POL SCI; Bull. Anal. Pol. Ec. Soc.; Int. Bibl. Eco.; Int. Bibl. Pol. Sc.; Int. Bibl. Soc.; Int. Pol. Sc. Abst.

3636
IL POLITICO. v.1– , Apr. 1928– . Pavia. Irreg., 1928–57; quarterly.
Issued by: Istituto di Scienze Politiche, Università de Pavia. In English or Italian. Includes "Notiziario dell'Associazione Italiana". Not published 1942–49. Title varies: 1928–41, *Annali di Scienze Politiche.*
Indexed: ABC POL SCI; Bull. Anal. Pol. Ec. Soc.; His. Abst.; Hum. Res. Abst.; Int. Bibl. Pol. Sc.; Int. Bibl. Soc. Cul. Abst.; Int. Pol. Sc. Abst.; LLBA; PAISFL; Peace Res. Abst. J.

3637
POLITICS. v.1– , May 1966– . Sydney. Two no. a year.
Issued by: Australasian Political Studies Association.
Supersedes: *A.P.S.A. News.*
Indexed: ABC POL SCI; APAIS; Bull. Anal. Pol. Ec. Soc.; Int. Bibl. Soc. Cul. Anth.; Int. Pol. Sc. Abst.; SSCI.

3638
POLITICS. v.1– , Apr. 1981– . Manchester. Semi-annual.
Issued by: Political Studies Association of the United Kingdom.

3639
POLITICS, ADMINISTRATION AND CHANGE. v.5– , 1980– . Dacca. Semi-annual.
Issued by: Centre for Administrative Studies, University of Dacca.
Continues: *Public Administration.*

3640
POLITICS AND MONEY. v.1– , Jan. 1970– . London, Politics and Money Pub. Co. Monthly.
Other title: *P & M. Politics and Money.*

3641
POLITICS & POWER. 1– , 1980– . London, Boston, Mass., Routledge & Kegan Paul. Biennial.

3642
POLITICS & SOCIETY. v.1– , Nov. 1970– . Los Angeles, Calif., Geron—X. Quarterly.
Issued by: Department of Political Science, Columbia University.
Indexed: ABC POL SCI; Bull. Anal. Pol. Ec. Soc.; Ind. Per. Art. Law; Int. Bibl. Eco.; Int. Bibl. Pol. Sc.; Soc. Abst.; SSCI; Urb. Aff. Abst.

POLITIEK JAARBOEK
See L'ANNÉE POLITIQUE

3643
POLITIIKKA. 1– , 1959– . Turku, Valtotieteellisen Yhdistysen Julkaisu. Quarterly.
In English, French, or Swedish; summaries in English.
Indexed: His. Abst.; Int. Bibl. Pol. Sc.; Int. Bibl. Soc. Cul. Anth.; Int. Pol. Sc. Abst.; Peace Res. Abst. J.; Soc. Abst.

3644
POLITIKKON. June 1974– . Pretoria. Two no. a year.
Official organ of: South African Political Science Associatrion. In Afrikaans or English.
Indexed: ABC POL SCI; Bull. Anal. Pol. Ec. Soc.; Int. Bibl. Pol. Sc.; Int. Bibl. Soc. Cul. Anth.; Int. Pol. Sc. Abst.

3645
POLITIQUE. v.1–3, Jan./Mar. 1937–Oct./Dec. 1939; n. ser. no.1/2–27/28, Jan./June 1951–July/Dec. 1957; n. ser. [i.e. 3rd ser] no.1– , Jan./Mar. 1958– . Paris, Compagnie des Éditions Libres Sociales et Économiques. Quarterly.
Published under the auspices of the Académie Internationale de Science Politique et d'Histoire Constitutionelle (1937–39, called Institut International d'Histoire Politique et Constitutionelle). In French. Title varies: 1937–39, *Revue d'Histoire Politique et Constitutionelle*; 1951–57, *Revue Internationale d'Histoire Politique et Constitutionelle.*

POLITIQUE À L'ÉGARD DES CONSUMMATEURS DANS LES PAYS DE L'OECD
See CONSUMER POLICY IN OECD COUNTRIES

3646
POLITIQUE AFRICAINE. 1– , Jan. 1981– . Paris, Korthala. Four no. a year.

Issued by: Association des Chercheurs de Politique Africaine.
In French.
Indexed: Int. Bibl. Soc. Cul. Anth.; Int. Pol. Sc. Abst.

3647
POLITIQUE ÉTRANGÈRE. no.1– , Feb. 1936– . Paris, Éditions Economica. Bimonthly.
Issued by: Institut Français des Relations Internationales. In French. Not published: 1941–45.
Indexed: ABC POL SCI; Eco. Abst.; His. Abst.; Int. Bibl. Eco.; Int. Bibl. Pol. Sc.; Int. Bibl. Soc.; Int. Pol. Sc. Abst.; PAISFL.

3648
POLITIQUE INTERNATIONALE. no.1– , autumn 1978– . Paris. Three no. a year.
In French; summaries in English or Spanish.
Indexed: Bull. Anal. Pol. Ec. Soc.; Int. Bibl. Eco.; Int. Bibl. Pol. Sc.; Int. Bibl. Soc. Cul. Anth.; Int. Pol. Sc. Abst.

POLITISCHE BILDUNG
See POLITISCHE STUDIEN

3649
POLITISCHE DOKUMENTATION. v.1– , 1965– . Berlin. Nine no. a year, 1965–79; monthly, 1980; three no. a year.
Issued by: Leitstelle Politische Dokumentation in association with the Otto-Suhr-Institut of the Freie Universität zu Berlin. Other title: *POL-DOK*. In German. Subtitle reads: "Referatedienst—Deutschsprachige Zeitschriften".
Indexed: PAISFL.

3650
DIE POLITISCHE MEINUNG. June 1956– . Bonn, Osnabrück, Verlag A. Fromm. Bimonthly.
In German.
Indexed: Bull. Anal. Pol. Ec. Soc.; Int. Bibl. Eco.; Int. Bibl. Pol. Sc.; Int. Bibl. Soc.; Int. Pol. Sc. Abst.; PAISFL.

3651
POLITISCHE STUDIEN. no.1– , 1950– . München, G. Olzog Verlag. Bimonthly.
Issued by: Hanns-Seidel-Stiftung. In German. Includes supplement called Beiheft (no.1–, 1964–). Title varies: no.1–16, *Schriftenreihe der Hochschule für Politische Wissenschaften*; no.17–47, *Politische Bildung*.
Indexed: ABC POL SCI; His. Abst.; Int. Bibl. Eco.; Int. Bibl. Pol. Sc.; Int. Bibl. Soc.; Int. Pol. Sc. Abst.; Peace Res. Abst. J.; Soc. Abst.

3652
POLITISCHE VIERTELJAHRESSCHRIFT PVS-LITERATUR. v.20– , Oct. 1979– . Opladen, Westdeutscher Verlag. Monthly.
Issued by: Deutsche Vereinigung für Politische Wissenschaft. In German. It was published as a section of *Politische Vierteljahresschrift* (v.1–19, Oct. 1960–1978)
Indexed: Bull. Anal. Pol. Ec. Soc.; His. Abst.; Int. Bibl. Eco.; Int. Bibl. Pol. Sc.; Int. Pol. Sc. Abst.; Soc. Abst.

3653
POLITY. v.1– , fall 1968– . Amherst, Mass., The University of Massachusetts Press. Quarterly.
Issued by: Northwestern Political Science Association.
Indexes: Vols. 1–3, 1968–71, with v.3; v.4–6, 1971–74, with v.6.
Indexed: ABC POL SCI; Bull. Anal. Pol. Ec. Soc.; His. Abst.; Int. Per. Art. Law; Curr. Cont. Soc. Beh. Sc.; Int. Bibl. Pol. Sc.; Int. Pol. Sc. Abst.; Sage Pub. Adm. Abst.; Sage Urb. Stu. Abst.; Soc. Abst.; SSCI.

3654
POLLS. v.1– , spring 1965– . Amsterdam, Systemen Keesing.
Indexed: Int. Bibl. Soc. Cul. Anth.; Int. Pol. Sc. Abst.; Soc. Abst.

3655
Polska Akademia Nauk. Wydział I: Nauk Społecznych. SPRAWOZDANIA Z PRAC NAUKOWYCH. v.1– , 1958– . Warszawa. Bimonthly.
In Polish.

3656
Polska Akademia Umiejętności. Komisja Antropologiczna. MATERIAŁY ANTROPOLOGICZNO-ARCHEOLOGICZNE I ETNOGRAFICZNE. v.1–14, 1896–1919. Kraków. Irreg.
Supersedes the academy's *Zbiór Wiadomości do Antropologii Krajowej*. Superseded by: *Prace i Materiały Antropologiczne i Etnograficzne*.

3657
Polynesian Society. JOURNAL. v.1– , 1892– . Auckland. Quarterly.
Vols. 1–50 called also no.1–200. Issues for June 1907 to Dec. 1941 published in New Plymouth. Title varies: 1892–1941, *The Journal of the Polynesian Society containing the Transactions and Proceedings of the Society*.
Indexes: Vols. 1–50, 1892–1911, 1v.
Indexed: Bull. Sig. Soc. Eth.; His. Abst.; LLBA.; SSCI.

3658
Pontificia Universidad Católica, Rosario. Facultad de Derecho y Ciencias Sociales. ANUARIO. 1– , 1979– . Rosario. Annual.
In Spanish.

3659
POPULAR GOVERNMENT. v.1– , Jan. 1931– . Chapel Hill, N.C. Irreg.
Issued by: Institute of Government.
Indexes: Vols. 18–22, 1951–56, with v.22.
Indexed: Ind. Per. Art. Law; PAIS; Urb. Aff. Abst.

POPULAR MAGAZINE OF ANTHROPOLOGY
See ANTHROPOLOGICAL REVIEW

3660
POPULATION. v.1– , Jan./Mar. 1946– . Paris, Presses Universitaires de France. Bimonthly.
Issued by: Institut National d'Études Démographiques. In French.
Indexed: Bull. Anal. Pol. Ec. Soc.; Bull. Sig. Soc. Eth.; Int. Bibl. Soc.; Int. Bibl. Soc. Cul. Anth.; Int. Lab. Doc.; PAISFL; Peace Res. Abst. J.; Pop. Ind.; Soc. Abst.; Urb. Aff. Abst.; Wom. Stu. Abst.

3661
POPULATION AND DEVELOPMENT REVIEW. v.1– , Sept. 1975– . New York. Quarterly.
Issued by: Center for Policy Studies, Population Council. Summaries in English, French and Spanish. Monographic supplements accompany some numbers.
Indexed: ABC POL SCI; Bull. Anal. Pol. Ec. Soc.; Geo. Abst.; Int. Bibl. Eco.; Int. Bibl. Soc. Cul. Anth.; PAIS; Pop. Ind.; Sage Urb. Stu. Abst.; Soc. Abst.

3662
POPULATION AND ENVIRONMENT. v.3– , spring 1980– . New York, Human Sciences Press. Quarterly.
Sponsored by: Division of Population and Environmental Psychology (Division 34), American Psychological Association.
Continues: *Journal of Population* (v.1–2, spring 1978–1979).
Indexed: Curr. Cont. Soc. Beh. Sc.; PAIS; Pop. Ind.; Psych. Abst.; Soc. Abst.; SSCI.

POPULATION AND VITAL STATISTICS REPORTS
See United Nations. Statistical Office. POPULATION AND VITAL STATISTICS REPORT

3663
POPULATION BULLETIN. v.1– , Sept. 1945– . Washington, D.C. Frequency varies.
Issued by: Population Reference Bureau. Issues are thematic.
Indexed: Int. Bibl. Soc.; Int. Bibl. Soc. Cul. Anth.; Int. Lab. Doc.; PAIS.

POPULATION BULLETIN
See POPULATION BULLETIN OF THE UNITED NATIONS

POPULATION BULLETIN OF ECWA
See United Nations. Economic Commission for Western Asia. POPULATION BULLETIN OF ECWA

3664
POPULATION BULLETIN OF THE UNITED NATIONS. no.1– , Dec. 1951– . New York.
Issued by: 1951–54, Department of Social Affairs; 1955–80, Department of Economic and Social Affairs; no.13–, 1981–, Department of International Economic and Social Affairs. United Nations. Some combined numbers. Title varies: no.1–2, *Population Bulletin*. (ST/ESA/Ser. N.)

POPULATION BULLETIN OF THe UNITED NATIONS ECONOMIC COMMISSION FOR WESTERN ASIA
See United Nations. Economic Commission for Western Asia. POPULATION BULLETIN OF ECWA

3665
POPULATION EDUCATION IN ASIA NEWSLETTER. no.1– , May 1974– . Bangkok. Two no. a year.
Issued by: United Nations Educational, Scientific and Cultural Organization. Regional Office of Education in Asia and Oceania. Population Education Program Service.
Supersedes: United Nations Educational, Scientific and Cultural Organization. Office for Education in Asia. *Conference Reports*.

3666
POPULATION ET FAMILLE. no.26/27– , Dec. 1972– . Bruxelles. Three no. a year.
Issued by: Centre d'Études de la Population et de Famille with the Department of Demography, University of Montreal, and the Department of Demography, University of Louvain. In French; summaries in English and French. Includes bibliographies of Belgian writings on population.
Continues: *Population et Famille. Bevolking en Gezin* (v.1–8, 1963–71)
Indexed: Bull. Anal. Pol. Ec. Soc.; Bull. Sig. Soc. Eth.; Int. Bibl. Eco.; Pop. Ind.; Soc. Abst.

POPULATION ET FAMILLE
See BEVOLKING EN GEZIN

3667
POPULATION ET SOCIÉTÉS. no.1– , 1968– . Paris, CEDEX. Monthly.
Issued by: Institut National d'Études Démographiques. In French. Subtitle reads: "Bulletin mensuel d'informations démographiques, économiques et sociales".

3668
POPULATION GEOGRAPHY. v.1, no.1/2– , June/Dec. 1979– . Chandigarh. Semi-annual.

Some numbers are issued in combined form.

3669
POPULATION INDEX. v.3– , Jan. 1937– . Princeton, N.J. Quarterly.
Vols. for 1937–48 issued by: School of Public Affairs, Princeton University; later Office of Population Research, Princeton University.
Continues: *Population Literature* (v.1, no.2–v.2, no.4, Mar. 20, 1935–Oct. 20, 1936)
Indexed: PAIS.

3670
POPULATION NEWSLETTER. no.1– , Apr. 1968– . New York, United Nations. Semi-annual.
Issued by: Population Division, Department of International Economic and Social Affairs, United Nations.

POPULATION PERSPECTIVES
See American Universities Field Staff. POPULATION PERSPECTIVES

3671
POPULATION REPORTS. SERIES E: LAW AND POLICY. no.1– , July 1974– . Washington, D.C. Department of Medical and Public Affairs, George Washington University.

3672
POPULATION RESEARCH AND POLICY REVIEW. v.1– , Jan. 1982– . Amsterdam, Elsevier Pub. Co. Three no. a year.
Indexed: Pop. Ind.

POPULATION RESEARCH AND STUDIES
See AL-SUKKAN: BUḤŪT WA-DIRĀSĀT

3673
POPULATION REVIEW. v.1– , Jan. 1957– . Madras. Semi-annual.
Issued by: Indian Institute for Population Studies, later Centre for Population Studies. Some numbers are combined.
Indexed: Int. Lab. Doc.; PAIS.

3674
POPULATION SCIENCES. no.1– , 1979– . Cairo. Annual.
Issued by: International Islamic Center for Population Studies and Research, Al-Azhar University.

3675
POPULATION STUDIES. v.1– , June 1947– . London, London University Press. Quarterly, 1947–Mar. 1951; three no. a year.
Issued by: Population Investigation Committee.
Indexed: Abst. Anth.; Bull. Anal. Pol. Ec. Soc.; His. Abst.; Int. Bibl. Eco.; Int. Bibl. Soc. Cul. Anth.; Int. Lab. Doc.; PAIS; Peace Res. Abst. J.; Pop. Ind.

POPULATION STUDIES
See United Nations. Department of International Economics and Social Affairs. Population Division. POPULATION STUDIES

3676
POPULATION TRENDS. 1– , autumn 1975– . London, HMSO. Quarterly.
Issued by: Office for Population Censuses and Surveys.
Indexed: PAIS; Pop. Ind.; SSCI.

3677
POPULI. v.– , 1974– . New York. Quarterly.
Issued by: United Nations Fund for Population Activities.
Indexed: PAIS; Pop. Ind.; Sage Urb. St. Abst.

3678
Portugal. Instituto Nacional de Estatística. INDICADORES ECONOMICO-SOCIAIS. SOCIAL ECONOMIC INDICATORS. 1973– . Lisboa.
In English and Portuguese. Supplements accompany some numbers.
Continues: *Indicadores Estatísticos a Curto Prozo* (1969–72)

POSEBNA IZDANJA
See Srpska Akademija Nauka i Umetnosti. Odeljenie Drustvenih Nauka. POSEBNA IZDANJA

3679
POUVOIRS. 1– , 1977– . Paris, Presses Universitaires de France. Quarterly.
In French; summaries in English and French.
Indexed: Bull. Anal. Pol. Ec. Soc.; Int. Bibl. Pol. Sc.; Int. Pol. Sc. Abst.

POVERTY AND HUMAN RESOURCES ABSTRACTS
See HUMAN RESOURCES ABSTRACTS

3680
PRACA I ZABEZPIECZENIE SPOŁECZNE. v.1– , Jan. 1959– . Warszawa, Państwowe Wydawnictwo Ekonomiczne. Monthly.
Title varies: v.1, no.1–6, Jan.–June 1959, *Przegląd Ubezpieczeń Społecznych i Zagadnień Socjalnych.*
Supersedes: *Przegląd Zagadnień Socjalnych*, and *Przegląd Ubezpieczeń Społecznych.*
Indexed: Bull. Anal. Pol. Ec. Soc.; Int. Bibl. Eco.

3681
PRACE Z NAUK SPOŁECZNYCH. no.1– , 1975– . Katowice. Irreg.

Issued by: Uniwersytet Śląski w Katowicach. In Polish.
Subseries of: Uniwersytet Śląski w Katowicach. *Zeszyty Naukowe*.

3682
PRACTICAL ANTHROPOLOGY. v.1– , 1953– . New Canaan, Conn., Tarrytown, New York. Bimonthly.
Indexed: Abst. Anth.; Int. Bibl. Soc. Cul. Anth.

PRATSY. SERYIA ETNOGRAFII I FOL'KLORU
See Akademiia Navuk BSSR, Minsk. Institut Mastatvaznavstva, Fol'kloru i Etnografii. PRATSY. SERYIA ETNOGRAFII I FOL'KLORU

3683
PRAXIS CENTROAMERICANA. no.1– , July/Dec. 1982– . Panama City.
Issued by: Centro de Estudio y Acción Social (CEASPA). In Spanish.

3684
PRAXIS INTERNATIONAL. v.1– , Apr. 1981– . Oxford, Blackwell. Quarterly.
In English, French, or German; summaries in the other languages.
Supersedes: *Praxis* (Edition Internationale) (v.1–10, 1965–74, Zagreb, Hrvatsko Filosofska Drustvo)

PREHISTORY AND CULTURE SERIES
See AUSTRALIAN ABORIGINAL STUDIES

3685
PRÉSENCE AFRICAINE. v.1–16, Nov./Dec. 1947–1954; n. ser. no.1– , Apr./May 1955– . Paris, Éditions du Seuil. Bimonthly, no.1–60, 1955–66; quarterly.
Issued by: Société Africaine de Culture. In English or French. Published also in English edition, no.1–60, 1955–66.
Indexed: Bull. Anal. Pol. Ec. Soc.; Bull. Sig. Soc. Eth.; Int. Bibl. Eco.; Int. Bibl. Pol. Sc.; Int. Bibl. Soc.; Int. Bibl. Soc. Cul. Anth.; Int. Lab. Doc.; Int. Pol. Sc. Abst.; PAIS; Peace Res. Abst. J.; Wom. Stu. Abst.

3686
PRESIDENTIAL STUDIES QUARTERLY. v.4, no.2– , spring 1974– . New York. Quarterly.
Issued by: Center for the Study of Presidency.
Continues: *Center House Bulletin*.
Indexed: ABC POL SCI; Int. Bibl. Pol. Sc.; Int. Pol. Sc. Abst.; PAIS; Sage Urb. Stu. Abst.

3687
PREVIDENZA SOCIALE E LAVORO IN ITALIA. 1957– . Roma. Bimonthly.
Issued by: Istituto Nazionale della Previdenza Sociale. In Italian.
Indexed: PAISFL.

3688
PRILOZI ZA ISTORIJU SOCIJALIZMA. 1964–1983. Beograd. Annual (irreg.)
Issued by: Institut za Izucivanje Radnickog Pokreta i Razvoja Socijalisticke Misli, 1964–68; Institut za Sovremennu Istoriju. In Serbo-Croatian. Other titles: *Ocherki Istorii Socijalizma*; *Contributions to a History of Socialism*; *Contributions à l'Histoire du Socialisme*; *Beiträge zur Geschichte des Sozialismus*.

3689
PRIMARY SOCIALIZATION. LANGUAGE AND EDUCATION. 1–6, 1971–1973. London, Routledge & Kegan Paul; Beverly Hills, Calif., Sage Publications. Irreg.
Indexed: Soc. Abst.

PRIMITIVE MAN
See ANTHROPOLOGICAL QUARTERLY

PRINCIPAUX INDICATEURS ÉCONOMIQUES
See Organisation for Economic Co-operation and Development. MAIN ECONOMIC INDICATORS

3690
PROBLEMAS DEL DESARROLLO. 1– , 1969– . Mexico, D.F. Quarterly.
Issued by: Instituto de Investigaciones Económicas. In Spanish.
Indexed: Bull. Anal. Pol. Ec. Soc.; Int. Bibl. Eco.

3691
PROBLEME DE ANTROPOLOGIE. v.1–7, 1954–1963. Bucureşti. Annual.
Issued by: Academia Republicii Populare Romine. In Romanian.
Continued by: *Studii şi Cercetări de Antropologie*.

3692
PROBLEME ECONOMICE. v.1– , Jan./Mar. 1949– . Bucureşti. Frequency varied; quarterly.
Issued by: Institutul de Cercetări Economice, Academia Republicii Populare Romine. In Romanian; summaries in English, French and Russian. Tables of contents also in French.
Indexed: Int. Bibl. Eco.; Pop. Ind.

3693
PROBLEME EKONOMIKE. 20– , Jan./Feb. 1973– . Tirane. Bimonthly.
Issued by: Instituti i Studimeve Ekonomike, Akademia e Shkonkave e RPSL. In Albanian.
Continues: *Ekonomia Popullore* (v.1–19).

3694
PROBLÈMES DE PLANIFICATION. 1– , 1952– . Paris. Irreg.
Issued by: Centre d'Études de Planification Socialiste, École Pratique des Hautes Études des Sciences Sociales. In French. Contains occasionally translations of articles published in socialist countries. Not published 1955–60.

3695
PROBLÈMES SOCIAUX ZAÏROIS. no.96/97– , May/June 1972– . Bruxelles. Bimonthly.
Issued by: Centre d'Exécution des Problèmes Sociaux et Économiques (C.E.P.S.E.). In French. Other title: *Bulletin du Centre des Problèmes Sociaux Congolais*.
Continues: *Problèmes Sociaux Congolais* (no.40–94/95, 1958–72)
Indexed: Bull. Anal. Pol. Ec. Soc.; Int. Bibl. Eco.

3696
PROBLEMI DEL SOCIALISMO. v.1– , Jan. 1958– . Milano, FAE Riviste. Monthly.
Issued by: Fondazione Basso. In Italian. Publication suspended: 1964–Feb. 1965.
Indexes: Vols. 1–6, 1958–63, 1v.; v.7–12, 1965–70, 1v.
Indexed: Bull. Anal. Pol. Ec. Soc.; Int. Bibl. Pol. Sc.; Int. Pol. Sc. Abst.

3697
PROBLEMI NA GEOGRAFII͡ATA. 1– , 1979– . Sofii͡a, Izd-vo na Bulgarskata Akademii͡a na Naukite. Four no. a year.
In Bulgarian; summaries in English. Tables of contents also in English. Other title: *Problems of Geography*.

3698
PROBLEMS OF COMMUNISM. no.1– , 1952– . Washington, D.C. Documentary Studies Section, International Information Administration, 1952; International Information Administration, 1953–78; International Communication Agency, July/August 1982– . Bimonthly, 1958–.
V.1, no.1, preceded by an experimental issue, called no.1, 1952.
Indexed: ABC POL SCI; Bull. Anal. Pol. Ec. Soc.; Eco. Abst.; His. Abst.; Ind. Per. Art. Law; Int. Bibl. Pol. Sc.; Int. Pol. Sc. Abst.; PAIS; Peace Res. Abst. J.; Soc. Abst.; SSCI.

3699
PROBLEMS OF ECONOMICS. v.1– , May 1958– . Armonk, N.Y., M.E. Sharpe. Monthly.
In 1958–59 translations of *Voprosy Ekonomiki*; Nov. 1959–, translations of texts from various sources.
Indexed: Bull. Anal. Pol. Ec. Soc.; Eco. Abst.; Int. Lab. Doc.; PAIS; Peace Res. Abst. J.; SSCI.

PROBLEMS OF GEOGRAPHY
See PROBLEMI NA GEOGRAFII͡ATA

3700
PROBLEMS OF THE SCIENCE OF SCIENCE. v.1–6, 1970–1977/79. Wrocław, Zakład Narodowy im. Ossolińskich. Irreg.
Issued by: Committee of Science of Science, Polish Academy of Sciences. Initially published as special issues of the quarterly: *Zagadnienia Naukoznawstwa*.
Superseded by: *Science of Science*.
Indexed: Bull. Anal. Pol. Ec. Soc.; Soc. Abst.

3701
PROBLEMY ARKHEOLOGII. no.1– , 1968– . Leningrad, Izd-vo Leningradskogo Universiteta. Irreg.
Issued by: Leningradskiĭ Gosudarstvennyĭ Universitet. In Russian.

PROBLEMY DAL'NOGO VOSTOKA
See FAR EASTERN AFFAIRS

3702
PROBLEMY FILOSOFII I SOT͡SIOLOGII. 1– , 1969– . Moskva. Irreg.
Issued by: Filosofski Fakultet, Moskovskiĭ Gosudarstvennyĭ Institut im. M.V. Lomonosova. In Russian.

3703
PROBLEMY MIROVOGO REVOLUT͡SIONNOGO PROT͡SESA. May 1981– . Moskva, Mysl. Annual.
Issued by: Akademii͡a Obshchestvennykh Nauk pri T͡Sentral'nom Komitete, Kommunisticheskai͡a Partii͡a Sovetskogo Soi͡uza. In Russian.

3704
PROBLEMY ORGANIZACJI. 1– , 1963– . Warszawa, Państwowe Wydawnictwo Ekonomiczne. Irreg.
Issued by: Towarzystwo Naukowe Organizacji i Kierownictwa. In Polish.
Indexed: Int. Bibl. Eco.

3705
PROBLEMY RAD NARODOWYCH; STUDIA I MATERIAŁY. 1– , 1964– . Warszawa, Wydawnictwo Prawnicze. Irreg.
Issued by: Instytut Nauk Prawnych, Polska Akademia Nauk. In Polish; summaries in English, French and Russian.

3706
PROBLEMY SPOŁECZNO-GOSPODARCZE I KULTUROWE KRAJÓW POZAEUROPEJSKICH. 1– , 1980– . Warszawa, Państwowe Wydawnictwo Naukowe. Annual.
In Polish. Other title: *Social, Economic and Cultural Problems of Non-European Countries.*

PROBLEMY VOSTOKOVEDENIIA
See NARODY AZII I AFRIKI

PROCEEDINGS
See Academy of Political Science. PROCEEDINGS

PROCEEDINGS
See American Political Science Association. PROCEEDINGS

PROCEEDINGS
See American Society of International Law. PROCEEDINGS OF THE ANNUAL MEETING

PROCEEDINGS
See Asiatic Society. JOURNAL

PROCEEDINGS
See Center for the Study of Presidency. PROCEEDINGS

PROCEEDINGS
See International Congress of Americanists. PROCEEDINGS

PROCEEDINGS
See International Congress of Local Authorities. PROCEEDINGS

PROCEEDINGS
See International Congress of Sociology. PROCEEDINGS

PROCEEDINGS
See National Council on Crime and Delinquency. PROCEEDINGS

PROCEEDINGS
See Royal Anthropological Institute of Great Britain and Ireland. PROCEEDINGS

PROCEEDINGS AND TRANSACTIONS
See Royal Society of Canada. PROCEEDINGS AND TRANSACTIONS

PROCEEDINGS OF STANFORD UNIVERSITY SCHOOL OF LAW
See STANFORD JOURNAL OF INTERNATIONAL STUDIES

PROCEEDINGS OF THE AMERICAN ACADEMY OF ARTS AND SCIENCES
See DAEDALUS

PROCEEDINGS OF THE AMERICAN ORIENTAL SOCIETY
See American Oriental Society. JOURNAL

PROCEEDINGS OF THE AMERICAN POLITICAL SCIENCE ASSOCIATION
See American Political Science Association. PROCEEDINGS

PROCEEDINGS OF THE AMERICAN SOCIETY OF INTERNATIONAL LAW AT ITS. . .ANNUAL MEETING
See American Society of International Law. Annual Meeting. PROCEEDINGS OF THE ANNUAL MEETING

PROCEEDINGS OF THE ANNUAL CONFERENCE
See National Council on Crime and Delinquency. YEARBOOK

PROCEEDINGS OF THE ANNUAL MEETING
See American Society of International Law. PROCEEDINGS OF THE ANNUAL MEETING

PROCEEDINGS OF THE ANNUAL MEETING
See Indiana Academy of the Social Sciences. PROCEEDINGS OF THE ANNUAL MEETING

PROCEEDINGS [OF THE CANADIAN AGRICULTURAL SOCIETY]
See CANADIAN JOURNAL OF AGRICULTURAL ECONOMICS

PROCEEDINGS OF THE MEETING
See Inter-American Development Bank. Board of Governors. PROCEEDINGS OF THE MEETING

PROCEEDINGS OF THE NATIONAL PLANNING CONFERENCE
See PLANNING

PROCÈS-VERBAUX OFFICIELS
See United Nations. Economic and Social Council. OFFICIAL RECORDS

PROCÈS-VERBAUX OFFICIELS
See United Nations. Economic Commission for Europe. REPORT

PROCÈS-VERBAUX OFFICIELS
See United Nations. Trusteeship Council. OFFICIAL RECORDS

PROCESO DE INTEGRACIÓN EN AMÉRICA LATINA
See THE LATIN-AMERICAN INTEGRATION PROCESS IN . . .

PROD TRANSLATIONS
See THE AMERICAN BEHAVIORAL SCIENTIST

PRODUCTION INDUSTRIELLE
See Organisation for Economic Co-operation and Development. INDUSTRIAL PRODUCTION

PROFESSIONAL'NYE SOI͡UZY
See SOVETSKIE PROFSOI͡UZY

3707
PROGRÈS SOCIAL. v.1– , 1926– . Liège. Bimonthly.
Issued by: Association Belge pour le Progrès Social. In English, French, German, or Spanish.
Supersedes: *Lutte contre le Chômage* (1912–26)
Indexed: Int. Bibl. Eco.; Int. Bibl. Soc.; Int. Lab. Doc.

3708
PROGRESS IN COMMUNICATION SCIENCES. v.1– , 1979– . Norwood, N.J., Ablex Pub. Co. Irreg.

3709
PROGRESS IN HUMAN GEOGRAPHY. v.1– , Mar. 1977– . London, Edward Arnold. Quarterly.
Supersedes, in part: *Progress in Geography*.
Indexed: Abst. Anth.; Sage Urb. Stu. Abst.

3710
PROGRESS IN MATHEMATICAL SOCIAL SCIENCES. v.1– , 1975– . Amsterdam, Elsevier Pub. Co. Irreg.
Indexed: Sage. Urb. Stu. Abst.

3711
PROGRESS OF EDUCATION IN ASIAN REGION. 1– , 1972– . Bangkok. Irreg.
Issued by: Unesco Regional Office for Education in the Asian Region. Accompanied by: *Statistical Supplement*.

3712
PROGRESS OF EDUCATION OF SCHEDULE CASTES & SCHEDULED TRIBES. New Delhi. Annual.
Issued by: Ministry of Education and Social Welfare.

3713
PROGRESS REPORTS IN ETHNOMUSICOLOGY. v.1– , 1983/84– . Baltimore, Md.
Issued by: SEMPOD Laboratory, Department of Music, University of Maryland Baltimore County.

3714
THE PROGRESSIVE. v.1– , Dec. 7, 1929– . Madison, Wis., Progressive Pub. Co. Weekly.
Indexed: Int. Bibl. Soc. Cul. Anth.; PAIS; PHRA; Peace Res. Abst. J.; Sage Pub. Adm. Abst.; Sage Urb. Stu. Abst.; Wom. Stu. Abst.

PROPAGANDIST
See AZERBACHAN KOOMUNISTI

3715
PRZEGLĄD HISTORYCZNY. v.1– , 1905– . Warszawa, Państwowe Wydawnictwo Naukowe. Quarterly.
Issued by: Towarzystwo Miłośników Historii. V.1–35, 1905–39; v.36–, Nov. 1946–. In Polish; summaries in French and Russian.

3716
PRZEGLĄD ORIENTALISTYCZNY. no.1– , Jan. 1952– . Warszawa, Państwowe Wydawnictwo Naukowe. Quarterly.
Issued by: Polskie Towarzystwo Orientalistyczne. In Polish. Tables of contents also in French and Russian.
Supersedes: *Myśl Karaimska*.
Indexed: Bull. Sig. Soc. Eth.; His. Abst.; Int. Bibl. Soc. Cul. Anth.

3717
PRZEGLĄD SOCJOLOGICZNY. SOCIOLOGICAL REVIEW. v.1– , 1930– . Wrocław, Zakład Narodowy im. Ossolińskich. Semi-annual.
Issued by: Polski Instytut Socjologiczny, 1930–48; Socjologiczny Ośrodek Łódzki, 1958–. Publication suspended, 1940–45 and 1949–56. During this second suspension *Przegląd Nauk Historycznych i Społecznych* (v.1–7, 1950–56) was published.
Indexed: Bull. Sig. Soc. Eth.; Int. Bibl. Soc.; LLBA; Soc. Abst.

PRZEGLĄD UBEZPIECZEŃ SPOŁECZNYCH I ZAGADNIEŃ SOCJALNYCH
See PRACA I ZABEZPIECZENIA SPOŁECZNE

PSICOLOGÍA Y CIENCIA DE L'EDUCACIÓN
See INDICE ESPAÑOL DE CIENCIAS SOCIALES. SERIE A. PSICOLOGÍA Y CIENCIA DE L'EDUCACIÓN

PSYCHIATRIE SOCIALE
See SOCIAL PSYCHIATRY

3718
PSYCHOANALYSIS AND THE SOCIAL SCIENCES. v.1–5, 1947–1958. New York, International Universities Press.

Superseded by: *Psychoanalytic Study of Society.*

3719
THE PSYCHOANALYTIC STUDY OF SOCIETY. v.1– , 1960– . New York, International University Press; later New Haven, Conn., Yale University Press. Annual.
Supersedes: *Psychoanalysis and the Social Sciences.*

3720
THE PSYCHOHISTORY REVIEW. v.5– , June 1976– . Springfield, Ill. Quarterly.
Issued by: Group for Use of Psychology in History.

3721
PSYCHOLOGIA AFRICANA. v.1– , 1948– . Johannesburg. One or two no. a year.
Issued by: Nasionale Institut vir Personeelnavorsing (National Institute for Personnel Research). In Afrikaans or English. Title varies: 1948–53, *Bulletin of the National Institute for Personnel Research*; 1954–61, *Journal of the National Institute for Personnel Research.*
Indexed: Psych. Abst.

3722
PSYCHOLOGICAL BULLETIN. v.1– , Jan. 1904– . Washington, D.C. Six no. a year, 1904–05; monthly (except Aug. and Sept.), 1906–45; bimonthly.
Issued by: American Psychological Association.
Indexed: Abst. Soc. Work; Bull. Sig. Soc. Eth.; LLBA; Psych. Abst.; Wom. Stu. Abst.

3723
THE PSYCHOLOGICAL INDEX. no.1–42, 1894–1935. New York.

3724
PSYCHOLOGICAL MONOGRAPHS; GENERAL AND APPLIED. v.1–80, no.25 (whole no.1–6333), 1895–19??. Washington, D.C.
Issued by: American Psychological Association. Title varies: v.1–7, 1895–Aug. 1906, *Psychological Review. Monograph Supplements*; v.8–61, Jan. 1907–1947, *Psychological Monographs.*

3725
PSYCHOLOGICAL RESEARCH. v.37– , 1974– . Berlin, New York, Springer. Four no. a year.
Continues: *Psychologische Forschung* (v.1–36, 1921–73).
Indexed: Psych. Abst.

3726
PSYCHOLOGICAL REVIEW. v.1– , Jan. 1894– . Washington, D.C. Bimonthly.
Issued by: American Psychological Association.
Indexed: Psych. Abst.

PSYCHOLOGICAL REVIEW. MONOGRAPH SUPPLEMENTS
See PSYCHOLOGICAL MONOGRAPHS. GENERAL AND APPLIED

3727
PSYCHOLOGICAL STUDIES. 1– , 1956– . Mysore. Semi-annual.
Issued by: Post-Graduate Department of Psychology, University of Mysore.
Indexed: Psych. Abst.; SSCI.

PSYCHOLOGIE CANADIENNE
See CANADIAN PSYCHOLOGICAL REVIEW

PSYCHOLOGIE ET PSYCHOPATHOLOGIE, PSYCHIATRY
See BULLETIN SIGNALÉTIQUE. 390. PSYCHOLOGIE ET PSYCHOPATHOLOGIE, PSYCHIATRIE

3728
PSYCHOLOGIE FRANÇAISE. v.1– , Oct. 1956– . Paris. Quarterly.
Issued by: Société Française de Psychologie. In French.
Indexed: Bull. Anal. Pol. Ec. Soc.; Bull. Sig. Soc. Eth.; Int. Pol. Sc. Abst.; LLBA; Psych. Abst.

3729
PSYCHOLOGIE UND PRAXIS. v.1– , 1956– . Stuttgart, Verlag für Angewandte Psychologie. Quarterly.
Issued by: Psychologische Institut, Universität Würzburg. Subtitle reads: "Wirtschaft, Industrie, Verwaltung". Monographic supplements accompany some numbers.
Indexed: Psych. Abst.

3730
PSYCHOLOGY & SOCIAL THEORY. no.1– , spring/summer 1981– . Ithaca, N.Y., Psychology & Social Theory. Semi-annual.

3731
PSYCHOLOGY OF SOCIAL ISSUES. no.1– , 1982– . Cambridge, Cambridge University Press.

3732
PSYCHOLOGY OF WOMEN QUARTERLY. v.1– , fall 1979– . New York, Human Sciences Press. Quarterly.
Official publication of: Division 35, American Psychological Association.
Indexed: Abst. Anth.; Curr. Cont. Soc. Beh. Sc.; Hum. Res. Abst.; Psych. Abst.; Sage Pub. Adm. Abst.; Sage Urb. Stu. Abst.; Soc.Sc. Ind.; Wom. Stu. Abst.

3733
PSYCHOPATHOLOGIE AFRICAINE. 1– , 1965– . Dakar. Three no. a year.
In French or English; summaries in the other language. Issued by: Société de Psychopathologie et d'Hygiène Mentale de Dakar.
Indexed: Bull. Anal. Pol. Ec. Soc.; Bull. Sig. Soc. Eth.; Int. Bibl. Soc. Cul. Anth.

3734
THE PUBLIC. v.1–24, Jan. 6, 1872–Dec. 1883. New York, The Financial Association. Weekly.
Subtitle reads: "A journal of finance, commercial interest and political science".

3735
PUBLIC ADMINISTRATION. v.1– , Jan. 1923– . London, later Oxford, B. Blackwell. Quarterly, 1923–41; three no. a year, 1942–4?; quarterly.
Issued by: Royal Institute of Public Administration. Issues are thematic. Title varies: 1923–25, *The Journal of Public Administration.*
Indexes: Vols. 1–10, with v.10; v.1–20, 1923–42, 1v.
Indexed: ABC POL SCI; Bull. Anal. Pol. Ec. Soc.; Ind. Per. Art. Law; Int. Bibl. Eco.; Int. Bibl. Pol. Sc.; Int. Bibl. Soc.; Int. Pol. Sc. Abst.; PAIS; Sage Pub. Adm. Abst.; SSCI; Urb. Stu. Abst.

3736
PUBLIC ADMINISTRATION. v.1–2, 1937–Mar. 1939; n. ser. v.1–34, June 1939–1975. Sydney. Quarterly.
Issued by: Australian regional groups of the Australian Institute of Public Administration; v.39–, 1975–, Australian Institute of Public Administration.
Continued by: *Australian Journal of Public Administration.*
Indexes: Vols. n. ser. 1–15, 1937–56, 1v.
Indexed: APAIS; Int. Bibl. Pol. Sc.; Int. Bibl. Soc. Cul. Anth.

3737
PUBLIC ADMINISTRATION. v.40– , Mar./Sept. 1978– . Wellington. Two no. a year.
Issued by: New Zealand Institute of Public Administration.
Continues: *The New Zealand Journal of Public Administration* (v.12–39, no.2, Sept. 1949–Sept. 1977). Superseded by: *Public Sector.*
Indexes: v.1–40, no.2, May 1938–Sept. 1977.
Indexed: Bull. Anal. Pol. Ec. Soc.

3738
PUBLIC ADMINISTRATION ABSTRACTS AND INDEX OF ARTICLES. v.1– , Apr. 1957– . New Delhi. Monthly.
Issued by: Indian Institute of Public Administration. Vol. 16 for 1972 last available for examination.

3739
PUBLIC ADMINISTRATION AND DEVELOPMENT. v.1– , Jan./Feb. 1981– . Chichester, New York, Wiley. Quarterly.
Issued by: Royal Institute of Administration.
Supersedes: *Journal of Public Administration Overseas* (v.1–, Jan. 1962–.)
Indexed: ABC POL SCI; Int. Pol. Sc. Abst.; Int. Bibl. Eco.; PAIS; Sage Urb. Stu. Abst.

3740
PUBLIC ADMINISTRATION IN ISRAEL AND ABROAD. v.1– , 1960– . Jerusalem. Annual.
Issued by: Israel Institute of Public Administration. "An annual collection of translations from Hebrew articles that have appeared in Israel during the year together with other materials".
Indexes: Vols. 1–5, 1960–64, in v.5.

3741
PUBLIC ADMINISTRATION REVIEW. v.1– , autumn 1940– . Chicago, Ill., later Washington, D.C. Quarterly, 1940–66; five no. a year, 1967; bimonthly.
Issued by: American Society for Public Administration for Public Administration.
Indexes: Vols. 1–12, 1940–52, 1v.
Indexed: ABC POL SCI; Abst. Soc. Work.; Bull. Sig. Soc. Eth.; Curr. Cont. Soc. Beh. Sc.; Bull. Anal. Pol. Ec. Pol.; Bull. Sig. Soc. Eth.; His. Abst.; Ind. Per. Art. Law; Int. Bibl. Pol. Sc.; Int. Bibl. Eco.; Int. Bibl. Soc.; Hum. Res. Abst.; Int. Lab. Doc.; Int. Pol. Sc. Abst.; PAIS; PHRA; Pop. Ind.; Sage Pub. Adm. Abst.; SSCI; Soc. Sc. Hum. Ind.; Urb. Aff. Abst.

3742
Public Affairs Information Service. BULLETIN. 1915– . New York, H.W. Wilson. Forty-eight no. a year; quarterly and annual cumulations.
Cumulative indexes: 1–53, 1915–74.

3743
Public Affairs Information Service. FOREIGN LANGUAGE INDEX. v.1– , 1968/71– . New York, H.W. Wilson. Quarterly; beginning with v.2, annual cumulations.
In English, French, German, Italian and Spanish.

3744
PUBLIC BUDGETING & FINANCE. v.1– , spring 1981– . New Brunswick, N.J., Transaction Periodicals Consortium. Quarterly.
Issued by: American Association for Budget and Program Analysis.
Other title: *Budgeting.*
Indexed: PAIS; Sage Pub. Adm. Abst.

3745
PUBLIC CHOICE. v.1– , 1966– . Blacksburg, Va., later Dordrecht, Kluwer, M. Nijhoff. Two no. a year, 1966–68; three no. a year, 1969–73; frequency varies, 1974–84; when six no. a year, they formed two volumes a year; five no. a year, 1985–.

Issued by: Thomas Jefferson Center for Political Economy, University of Virginia, v.1–4; Center for the Study of Public Choice, The Polytechnic Institute, 1970–82; Center for the Study of Public Choice, George Mason University, Fairfax, Va.; at present Department of Economics, University of Arizona, Tucson.
Indexed: ABC POL SCI; Bull. Anal. Pol. Ec. Soc.; Int. Bibl. Eco.; Hum. Res. Abst.; Int. Bibl. Pol. Sc.; Int. Pol. Sc. Abst.; J. Eco. Lit.; LLBA; PAIS; Sage Urb. Stu. Abst.; Soc. Abst.; SSCI.

3746
PUBLIC FINANCE. FINANCES PUBLIQUES. v.1– , 1946– . Amsterdam. Quarterly.
In English; summaries in French and German. Title varies: v.1–4, *Openbar Financien*. Subtitle reads: "International quarterly journal devoted to the study of fiscal policy and related problems".
Indexed: Bull. Anal. Pol. Ec. Soc.; Eco. Abst.; Int. Bibl. Eco.; PAIS.

3747
PUBLIC FINANCE QUARTERLY. v.1– , Jan. 1973– . Beverly Hills, Calif., Sage Publications.
Indexed: Bull. Anal. Pol. Ec. Soc.; Curr. Cont. Soc. Beh. Sc.; Hum. Res. Abst.; Int. Bibl. Eco.; Int. Bibl. Soc.; J. Eco. Lit.; PAIS; Sage Pub. Adm. Abst.; Soc. Sc. Hum. Ind.; Soc. Abst.; SSCI.

3748
PUBLIC INNOVATION ABROAD. v.10, no.2– , Feb. 1986– . Washington, D.C. Quarterly.
Issued by: International Center, Academy for State and Local Government.
Continues: *Urban Innovation Abroad*.

3749
THE PUBLIC INTEREST. no.1– , fall 1965– . New York. Quarterly.
Indexed: ABC POL SCI; Abst. Soc. Work; Bull. Anal. Pol. Ec. Soc.; Curr. Cont. Soc. Beh. Sc.; His. Abst.; Int. Bibl. Pol. Sc.; Int. Bibl. Eco.; Int. Bibl. Soc.; Int. Lab. Doc.; Int. Pol. Sc. Abst.; PAIS; Sage Pub. Adm. Abst.; Soc. Abst.; SSCI; Urb. Aff. Abst.

3750
PUBLIC INTERNATIONAL LAW. v.1– , 1975– . Berlin, New York, Springer Verlag. Semi-annual.
Issued by: Max-Planck Institut für Ausländisches Öffentliches Recht und Völkerrecht.

3751
PUBLIC MANAGEMENT. 1– , 1919– . Chicago, Ill., later Washington, D.C. Monthly.
Issued by: International City Management Association.
Indexed: ABC POL SCI; Bull. Anal. Pol. Ec. Soc.; Bull. Sig. Soc. Eth.; Int. Bibl. Eco.; Int. Bibl. Pol. Sc.; Int. Bibl. Soc.; Hum. Res. Abst.; PAIS; Sage Pub. Adm. Abst.; Wom. Stu. Abst.

3752
PUBLIC OPINION. v.1– , Mar./Apr. 1978– . Washington, D.C. Bimonthly.
Issued by: American Enterprise Institute for Public Policy Research.
Indexed: Bull. Anal. Pol. Ec. Soc.; Int. Bibl. Pol. Sc.; Int. Pol. Sc. Abst.; PAIS.

PUBLIC OPINION
See THE INTERNATIONAL GALLUP POLLS. PUBLIC OPINION

3753
THE PUBLIC OPINION QUARTERLY. v.1– , Jan. 1937– . Princeton, N.J., Princeton University Press. Quarterly.
Issued by: American Association for Public Opinion Research, and School of Public Affairs, Princeton University.
Indexed: ABC POL SCI; Bull. Anal. Pol. Ec. Soc.; Bull. Sig. Soc. Eth.; Curr. Cont. Soc. Beh. Sc.; His. Abst.; Ind. Per. Art. Law; Int. Bibl. Eco.; Int. Bibl. Pol. Sc.; Int. Bibl. Soc.; Int. Lab. Doc.; Int. Pol. Sc. Abst.; LLBA; PAIS; Pop. Ind.; Psych. Abst.; Soc. Abst.; SSCI; Urb. Aff. Abst.; Wom. Stu. Abst.

3754
PUBLIC PERSONNEL MANAGEMENT. 1– , 1940– . Chicago, Ill. Bimonthly.
Issued by: International Personnel Administration Association. Title varies: 1940–71, *Public Personnel Review*.
Indexed: ABC POL SCI; Bull. Anal. Pol. Ec. Soc.; Curr. Cont. Soc. Beh. Sc.; Hum. Res. Abst.; Int. Lab. Doc.; PHRA; Sage Pub. Adm. Abst.; Sage Urb. Stu. Abst.; Sage Urb. Abst.; Urb. Aff. Abst.

PUBLIC PERSONEL REVIEW
See PUBLIC PERSONNEL MANAGEMENT

3755
PUBLIC POLICY. [1]–29, 1940–1981. Cambridge, Mass., Harvard University Press. Quarterly, 1940–68; annual.
Issued by: The John Fitzgerald Kennedy School of Government, Harvard University. Not published 1943–52. Merged with: *Policy Analysis* to form: *Journal of Policy Analysis and Management*.
Indexed: ABC POL SCI; Bull. Anal. Pol. Ec. Soc.; Curr. Cont. Soc. Beh. Sc.; Ind. Per. Art. Law; Int. Bibl. Eco.; Int. Bibl. Pol. Sc.; Int. Bibl. Soc.; J. Eco. Lit.; Sage Urb. Stu. Abst.; Soc. Abst.; SSCI.

3756
PUBLIC POLICY STUDIES. v.1– , 1984– . Greenwich, Conn., JAI Press. Annual.

3757
PUBLIC PRODUCTIVITY REVIEW. 1– , Sept. 1975– . New York. Quarterly.
Issued by: National Center for Productive Public Productivity, John Jay College of Criminal Justice. Co-sponsored by: Section on Management Science, American Society of Public Administration.

3758
PUBLIC WELFARE. v.1– , Jan. 1943– . Chicago, Ill. Quarterly.
Issued by: American Public Welfare Association.
Supersedes: *Public Welfare News* (Mar. 1933–Dec. 1941).
Indexed: Abst. Soc. Work; Bull. Anal. Pol. Ec. Soc.; His. Abst.; Int. Bibl. Soc. Cul. Anth.; PAIS; PHRA; Wom. Stu. Abst.

PUBLICACIÓN
See Pan American Institute on Geography and History. PUBLICACIÓN

PUBLICACIONES
See Academie Dominicana de Historia. PUBLICACIONES

PUBLICATION
See AMERICAN JEWISH HISTORICAL QUARTERLY

PUBLICATION
See International Bureau of Education. PUBLICATION

PUBLICATION HG
See Australian National University. Research School of Pacific Studies. Department of Geography. PUBLICATION HG

PUBLICATIONS
See American Ethnological Society. PUBLICATIONS

PUBLICATIONS
See AMERICAN JEWISH HISTORICAL QUARTERLY

PUBLICATIONS
See Henrietta Szold Institute—National Institute for Research in the Behavioral Sciences. PUBLICATIONS

PUBLICATIONS
See Institute for Comparative Studies of Culture. PUBLICATIONS

PUBLICATIONS
See JASA

PUBLICATIONS D'ARCHÉOLOGIE
See PUBLICATIONS IN ARCHAEOLOGY

PUBLICATIONS D'ETHNOLOGIE
See PUBLICATIONS IN ETHNOLOGY

PUBLICATIONS DU COMITÉ D'ÉTUDES HISTORIQUES ET SCIENTIFIQUES DE L'AFRIQUE OCCIDENTALE FRANÇAISE.
See Institut Fondamental d'Afrique Noire. MÉMOIRES

PUBLICATIONS DU MUSÉE D'ANTHROPOLOGIE ET D'ETHNOGRAPHIE
See Akademii͡a Nauk SSSR. Museĭ Antropologii i Etnografii. SBORNIK MUSEI͡A

3759
PUBLICATIONS FOR THE ADVANCEMENT OF THEORY AND HISTORY IN PSYCHOLOGY. [1]– , 1980– . Norwood, N.J., Ablex Pub. Co.
V.1 issued without volume numbering. Other title: *Path.*

3760
PUBLICATIONS IN AMERICAN ARCHAEOLOGY AND ETHNOLOGY. v.1–50, 1903–1964. Berkeley and Los Angeles, University of California Press.
Indexes: Vols. 1–26, 1903–29 (supplement to v.26)

3761
PUBLICATIONS IN ANTHROPOLOGY. no.1–12, 1952–1969. Lincoln, Nebr. Irreg.
Issued by: Nebraska State Historical Society. Other title: *Nebraska State Historical Society Publications in Anthropology.*

3762
PUBLICATIONS IN ARCHEOLOGY. PUBLICATIONS D'ARCHÉOLOGIE. no.1– , 1970– . Ottawa. Irreg.
Issued by: Publications Division, National Museums of Canada. In English; summaries in French. Monograph series.

PUBLICATIONS OF THE AMERICAN ETHNOLOGICAL SOCIETY
See American Ethnological Society. PUBLICATIONS

PUBLICATIONS OF THE INSTITUTE FOR COMPARATIVE STUDY OF CULTURE
See Institute for Comparative Study of Culture. PUBLICATIONS

3763
PUBLICATIONS ON ASIA. [no.1]– , 1952– .

Seattle, Wash., University of Washington Press. Irreg.
Issued by: Eastern and Russian Institute, School for International Studies, University of Washington. Title varies: no.1–14, *University of Washington Studies on Asia*.

PUBLICATIONS ON SOCIAL HISTORY
See International Institute for Social History. SOCIAAL HISTORISCHE STUDIEN

PUBLICATIONS. SERIES MAJOR
See Institute of Social Studies, The Hague. PUBLICATIONS. SERIES MAJOR

PUBLIKATIONEN. I. ABTEILUNG. ABHANDLUNGEN
See Österreichisches Kulturinstitut, Rome. Abteilung für Historische Studien. PUBLIKATIONEN. I. ABTEILUNG. ABHANDLUNGEN

3764
PUBLIUS. v.1– , 1971– . Philadelphia, Pa. Quarterly.
Issued by: Center for the Study of Federalism, Temple University.
Indexed: ABC POL SCI; Bull. Anal. Pol. Ec. Soc.; PAIS; PHRA; Sage Pub. Adm. Abst.; Sage Urb. Stu. Abst.

3765
PUBLIZISTIK. v.1– , Jan./Feb. 1956– . Bremen, later München, Konstanz, Universitätsverlag. Bimonthly, 1956–63; quarterly.
Issued by: Deutsche Gesellschaft für Publizistik. In German. Subtitle reads: "Zeitschrift für die Wissenschaft von Presse, Rundfunk, Rhetorik, Werbung und Meinungsbildung".
Indexed: Bull. Sig. Soc. Eth.; Int. Pol. Sc. Abst.; Peace Res. Abst. J.; Soc. Abst.

3766
PUNJAB JOURNAL OF POLITICS. v.1– , 1977– . Amritsar. Annual.
Issued by: Department of Political Science, Guru Nanak Dev University.
Indexed: Int. Bibl. Soc. Cul. Anth.; Int. Pol. Sc. Abst.

PUTI SEL'SKOGO KHOZIAĬSTVA
See EKONOMIKA SEL'SKOGO KHOZIAĬSTVA

QER
See QUARTERLY ECONOMIC REVIEW

3767
QUADERNI DI SCIENZE SOCIALI. Aug. 1962– . Milano, A. Giuffrè. Three no. a year.
Issued by: Istituto di Scienze Sociali di Genova. In Italian.
Indexed: Bull. Sig. Soc. Eth.; Int. Bibl. Soc.; Int. Pol. Sc. Abst.; Soc. Abst.

3768
QUADERNI DI SOCIOLOGIA. v.1– , summer 1951–1961; n. ser., 1962– . Torino, Einaudi. Quarterly.
Issued by: Istituto di Sociologia, Università di Torino. In Italian; summaries in English.
Indexed: ABC POL SCI; Bull. Anal. Pol. Ec. Soc.; Int. Bibl. Pol. Sc.; Int. Bibl. Soc.; Int. Pol. Sc. Abst.; Soc. Abst.

QUADERNI INTERNAZIONALI DI STORIA ECONOMICA E SOCIALE
See CAHIERS INTERNATIONAUX D'HISTOIRE ÉCONOMIQUE ET SOCIALE

3769
QUALITATIVE SOCIOLOGY. v.1– , May 1978– . New York, Human Sciences Press. Three no. a year, 1978; quarterly.
Vol. for 1978 published by the University of Baltimore.

3770
QUALITY AND QUANTITY. 1– , Jan. 1967– . Amsterdam, Elsevier North-Holland. Quarterly.
In English or French.
Indexed: Bull. Anal. Pol. Ec. Soc.; Bull. Sig. Soc. Eth.; Int. Bibl. Pol. Sc.; Int. Pol. Sc. Abst.; SSCI.

3771
QUANTITATIVE ANALYSIS OF BEHAVIOR. v.1– , 1981– . Cambridge, Mass., Ballinger. Irreg.
Each volume has also a distinctive title.

3772
QUANTITATIVE HISTORISCHE FORSCHUNG. QUANTITATIVE HISTORY. 1977– . Stuttgart. Annual.
In English or German.
Continued by: *Quantum Documentation.*

QUANTITATIVE HISTORY
See QUANTITATIVE HISTORISCHE FORSCHUNG

3773
QUANTUM DOCUMENTATION. 1978– . Stuttgart, Klett-Cotta. Annual.
Issued by: Informationszentrum Sozialwissenschaften. In German.
Continues: *Quantitative Historische Forschung* (1977). Continued by: *Historische Sozialforschung.*

QUARTERLY BULLETIN OF STATISTICS FOR ASIA AND THE FAR EAST
See United Nations. Economic Commission for Asia and the Pacific. QUARTERLY BULLETIN OF STATISTICS FOR ASIA AND THE PACIFIC

QUARTERLY BULLETIN OF STATISTICS FOR ASIA AND THE PACIFIC
See United Nations. Economic and Social Commission for Asia and the Pacific. QUARTERLY BULLETIN OF STATISTICS FOR ASIA AND THE PACIFIC

3774
QUARTERLY ECONOMIC REVIEW. 1956– . London.
Issued by: Economist Intelligence Unit. This title was followed by names of the main parts of the world in 1956. Later this publication was split into publications covering smaller geographical areas or individual countries. In 1971–76 the titles were changed to *QER* followed by names of countries. In 1977 the title was changed to *Quarterly Economic Review* followed by names of individual countries.

3775
THE QUARTERLY INDEX ISLAMICUS. v.1– , Jan. 1977– . London, Mansell Pub. Ltd.
Issued by: School of Oriental and African Studies, University of London. Subtitle reads: "Current books, articles and papers on Islamic Studies".
Supersedes: *Index Islamicus.*

3776
THE QUARTERLY JOURNAL OF ADMINISTRATION. v.4– , Oct. 1969– . Ibadan, later Ife. Quarterly.
Issued by: Institute of Administration, University of Ife.
Continues: *Administration* (v.1–3, 1966–68)
Indexed: Bull. Anal. Pol. Ec. Soc.; Int. Bibl. Pol. Sc.; Int. Bibl. Soc.; Int. Lab. Doc.; Int. Pol. Sc. Abst.; Sage Pub. Adm. Abst.; Sage Urb. Stu. Abst.

3777
QUARTERLY JOURNAL OF ECONOMICS. v.1– , Oct. 1886– . Cambridge, Mass., Harvard University Press, later New York, Wiley for Harvard University. Quarterly.
Issues are thematic. Monographic supplements accompany some numbers.
Indexes: Vols. 1–10, 1886–July 1896, with v.10; v.1–25, 1886–1911, with v.25; v.1–50, 1886–Aug. 1936, with v.50.
Indexed: Abst. Soc. Work; Bull. Anal. Pol. Ec. Soc.; Curr. Cont. Soc. Beh. Sc.; Eco. Abst.; His. Abst.; Ind. Per. Art. Law; Int. Bibl. Eco.; Int. Bibl. Pol. Sc.; Int. Bibl. Soc.; Int. Lab. Doc.; J. Eco. Lit.; PAIS; Pop. Ind.; Sage Urb. Stu. Abst.; SSCI.

QUARTERLY JOURNAL OF SCIENCE, RELIGION, PHILOSOPHY
See WORLD AFFAIRS QUARTERLY

3778
THE QUARTERLY JOURNAL OF SOCIAL AFFAIRS. v.1– , 1985– . London, Lawrence Erlbaum Associates.
Published for the Social Affairs Committee, Economic and Social Research Council.

3779
QUARTERLY JOURNAL OF STUDIES ON ALCOHOL. 1– , 1940– . New Brunswick, N.J.
Indexes: annual, quinquennial and decennial.
Indexed: Abst. Soc. Work.; Bull. Sig. Soc. Eth.; His. Abst.; Psych. Abst.; Soc. Abst.

QUARTERLY LABOUR FORCE STATISTICS
See Organisation for Economic Co-operation and Development. QUARTERLY LABOUR FORCE STATISTICS

QUARTERLY PUBLICATIONS OF THE AMERICAN STATISTICAL ASSOCIATION
See JASA

QUARTERLY REVIEW
See Banca Nazionale del Lavoro. QUARTERLY REVIEW

QUARTERLY REVIEW
See Federal Reserve Bank of New York. QUARTERLY REVIEW

3780
QUARTERLY REVIEW OF AGRICULTURAL ECONOMICS. v.1–31, no.2/3, Jan. 1948–Apr./July 1978. Canberra. Quarterly.
Issued by: Bureau of Agricultural Economics of Australia.
Superseded by: *Quarterly Review of Rural Economy.*
Indexes: Vols. 4–6, 1951–53, 1v.; v.7–9, 1954–56, 1v.
Indexed: APAIS; Bull. Anal. Pol. Ec. Soc.; Int. Bibl. Soc. Cul. Anth.; J. Eco. Lit.; PAIS.

3781
QUARTERLY REVIEW OF AUSTRALIAN EDUCATION. v.1– , Sept. 1967– . Hawthorn.
Issued by: Australian Council for Educational Research. Some numbers have also distinctive titles.

3782
QUARTERLY REVIEW OF ECONOMICS AND BUSINESS. v.1– , Feb. 1961– . Champaign, Ill., Bureau of Economics and Business Research, University of Illinois. Quarterly.
Journal of the Midwest Economics Association.
Supersedes: *Current Economic Comment.*
Indexed: Bull. Anal. Pol. Ec. Soc.; Curr. Cont. Soc. Beh. Sc.; His. Abst.; Ind. Per. Art. Law; Int. Bibl. Eco.; Int. Bibl. Pol. Sc.; Int. Bibl. Soc.; J. Eco. Lit.; PAIS; Pop. Ind.; Soc. Sc. Ind.; SSCI.

3783
QUARTERLY REVIEW OF RURAL ECONOMY. v.1– , Feb. 1979– . Canberra, Australian Government Publishing Service.
Issued by: Board of Agricultural Economic. V.1 was preceded by the "Introductory issue", 1978.
Supersedes: *Quarterly Review of Agricultural Economics.*

QUARTERLY STATEMENT
See PALESTINE EXPLORATION QUARTERLY

QUARTERLY SUPPLEMENT TO THE ECONOMIC ANALYSIS
See KEIZAI BUNSEKI FUROKU

3784
QUARTERLY SURVEY OF JAPANESE FINANCE & INDUSTRY. v.18– , Jan./Mar. 1966– . Tokyo.
Issued by: Reference and Statistics Centre, Industrial Bank of Japan.
Continues: *Survey of Japanese Finance and Industry.*

QUAZAQ SSR GHYLUM AKADEMIIASYNYNG KHARBOLARY
See Akademii͡a Nauk Kazakhskoĭ SSR. IZVESTII͡A

3785
QUEEN'S QUARTERLY. v.1– , July 1893– . Kingston, The News Publishing House. Quarterly.

Indexed: Bull. Anal. Pol. Ec. Soc.; His. Abst.; Int. Bibl. Soc. Cul. Anth.; Int. Pol. Sc. Abst.; PAIS; Peace Res. Abst. J.; Wom. Stu. Abst.

3786
QUEST. v.1– , 1970– . Three no. a year.
Issued by: City University, London.
Indexed: APAIS; Peace Res. Abst. J.

QUESTIONES ACTUALES DEL SOCIALISMO
See QUESTIONS ACTUELLES DU SOCIALISME

3787
QUESTIONS ACTUELLES DU SOCIALISME. 1– , 1946– . Beograd. Monthly.
In French. Published also in English: *Socialist Thought and Practice*; German: *Sozialistische Theorie und Praxis*; Russian: *So͡tsialisticheskai͡a Mysl' i Praktika*; and Spanish: *Questiones Actuales del Socialismo*.

Indexed: Bull. Anal. Pol. Ec. Soc.; Bull. Sig. Soc. Eth.; Int. Bibl. Pol. Sc.; Int. Bibl. Soc. Cul. Anth.; Int. Lab. Doc.; Int. Pol. Sc. Abst.

3788
QUESTIONS DIPLOMATIQUES ET COLONIALES. v.1–38, Mar. 1897–Aug. 1914. Paris, Éditions Tierce. Semimonthly.
In French.

3789
QUESTIONS FÉMINISTES. 1– , Nov. 1977– . Paris, Éditions Tierce. Quarterly.
In French. Published also in English: *Feminist Issues*.
Continued by: *Nouvelles Questions Féministes*.
Indexed: Bull. Anal. Pol. Ec. Soc.

QUINZAINE URBAINE
See VIE URBAINE

R

REIS
See REVISTA ESPAÑOLA DE INVESTIGACIONES SOCIOLÓGICAS

RHDES
See REVUE D'HISTOIRE ÉCONOMIQUE ET SOCIALE

RIIES BIBLIOGRAPHIC STUDIES
See Smithsonian Institution, Washington, D.C. Institute on Immigration and Ethnic Studies. RIIES BIBLIOGRAPHIC STUDIES

3790
RISP. REVUE INTERNATIONALE DE SCIENCE POLITIQUE. IPRS. INTERNATIONAL POLITICAL SCIENCE REVIEW. v.1– , Jan. 1980– . Beverly Hills, Calif., Sage Publications. Quarterly.
Issued by: International Political Science Association. In English or French. Issues are thematic.

3791
R.S. CUADERNOS DE REALIDADES SOCIALES. 1– , 1973– . Madrid. Three no. a year.
Issued by: Instituto de Sociología Aplicada de Madrid. In Spanish.

RSRI ABSTRACTS
See Regional Science Research Institute. RSRI ABSTRACTS

RUP
See RESEARCH IN URBAN POLICY

3792
RABOCHIĬ KLAS I SOVREMENNYĬ MIR. 1– , 1971– . Moskva, Izd-vo Progres. Bimonthly.
Issued by: Institut Mezhdunarodnogo Rabochego Dvizheniia͡, Akademiia͡ Nauk SSSR. In Russian.
Indexed: Bull. Anal. Pol. Ec. Soc.; Int. Bibl. Eco.

3793
RACE. v.1–16, no.1, 1959–July/Sept. 1974. London, Oxford University Press. Quarterly.
Continued by: *Race and Class.*
Indexes: Vols. 1–5, 1959–Apr. 1965, with v.6.
Indexed: Abst. Anth.; APAIS; Abst. Soc. Work; Bull. Sig. Soc. Eth.; Curr. Cont. Soc. Beh. Sc.; Int. Bibl. Eco.; Int. Bibl. Pol. Sc.; Int. Bibl. Soc.; Ind. Per. Art. Law; Int. Lab. Doc.; PAIS; Psych Abst.; Soc. Abst.; SSCI.

3794
RACE AND CLASS. v.16, no.2– , Oct./Dec. 1974– . London, Oxford University Press. Quarterly.
Issued by: Institute of Race Relations, and the Transnational Institute.
Continues: *Race.*
Indexed: Abst. Anth.; Brit. Hum. Ind.; Bull. Anal. Pol. Ec. Soc.; Curr. Cont. Soc. Beh. Sc.; Ind. Per. Art. Law; Int. Bibl. Eco.; Int. Bibl. Soc.; Int. Bibl. Soc. Cul. Anth.; PAIS; Psych. Abst.; Soc. Abst.; SSCI.

RACE RELATIONS
See RACE RELATIONS JOURNAL

3795
RACE RELATIONS JOURNAL. v.1– , Nov. 1953– . Johannesburg, later Amsterdam, Swets & Zeitlinger. Quarterly (irreg.)
Issued by: Institute of Race Relations. Some numbers have also the title in Afrikaans: *Rasseverhoudings*. Title varies: v.1–17, no.1/2, 1953–70, *Race Relations.*

3796
RACE RELATIONS SURVEY. v.38– , 1984– . Johannesburg. Annual.
Issued by: South African Institute of Race Relations.
Continues: *Survey of Race Relations in South Africa* (v.1–37, 1951/52–1983)

3797
RACE TODAY. v.1– , May 1969– . London. Quarterly, 1969–81; bimonthly.
Issued by: Institute of Race Relations; later by: Race Collective Today.
Supersedes: International Institute of Race Relations. *News Letter.*
Indexed: Bull. Anal. Pol. Ec. Soc.

3798
RADICAL HUMANIST. 1937– . New Delhi. Weekly, 1937–27 March 1949; monthly.
Subtitle reads: "English monthly devoted to dispassionate and scientific study of sociological, philosophical and cultural problems of our time in the spirit of humanism".
Indexed: Bull. Anal. Pol. Ec. Soc.

3799
RADNA I DRUSTVENA ZAJEDNICA. v.1– , Jan./Feb. 1953– . Beograd. Bimonthly, 1953–59; monthly.
Issued by: Biro za Organizaciju Uprave i Privrede, 1953–Jan./Feb. 1959; Savezni Zavod za Javnu Upravu (called 1959–Jan. 1965 Zavod za Javnu Upravu), Mar./Apr. 1959–. Published also in English edition. Other title: *Nova Administracija.*

Indexed: Int. Bibl. Soc. Cul. Anth.

RADOVI
See Akademija Nauka i Umjetnosti Bosne i Hercegovine. Odeljenie Drustvenih Nauka. RADOVI

3800
RAMSES. 1981– . Paris, Éditions Économiques. Annual.
Issued by: Institut Français des Relations Internationales. In French. Published also in English edition called: *Ramses. English.*

RAPPORT
See United Nations. Commission on the Racial Situation in South Africa. REPORT

RAPPORT
See United Nations. Economic and Social Council. REPORT OF THE ECONOMIC AND SOCIAL COUNCIL

RAPPORT
See United Nations. Economic and Social Council. Commission on Human Rights. Sub-Commission on the Prevention of Discrimination and the Protection of Minorities. RAPPORT

RAPPORT
See United Nations. Economic Commission for Central America. Committee on Economic Cooperation in Central America. REPORT

RAPPORT
See United Nations. Economic Commission for Europe. REPORT

RAPPORT
See United Nations. Trusteeship Council. OFFICIAL RECORDS

RAPPORT ANNUEL
See Canada. Indian and Northern Affairs. ANNUAL REPORT

RAPPORT ANNUEL
See Central African States Development Bank. ANNUAL REPORT

RAPPORT ANNUEL
See Social Science Federation of Canada. ANNUAL REPORT

RAPPORT D'ACTIVITÉ
See Caisse Centrale de Coopération Économique. RAPPORT D'ACTIVITÉ

RAPPORT ÉCONOMIQUE; ASPECTS CARACTÉRISTIQUES DE LA SITUATION ÉCONOMIQUE MONDIALE
See United Nations. Department of Economic and Social Affairs. WORLD ECONOMIC REPORT

RAPPORT GÉNÉRAL SUR L'ACTIVITÉ DES COMMUNAUTÉS EUROPÉENNES EN . . .
See Commission of the European Communities. GENERAL REPORT ON THE ACTIVITIES OF THE EUROPEAN COMMUNITIES

RAPPORT SUR L'ÉCONOMIE MONDIAL
See United Nations. Department of Economic and Social Affairs. WORLD ECONOMIC REPORT

RAPPORTO DELLA SITUAZIONE SOCIALE DEL PAESE
See Centro Studi Investimenti Sociali. RAPPORT DELLA SITUAZIONE SOCIALE DEL PAESE

3801
RASSE. v.1–11, no.8, Apr. 1934–1944. Leipzig, B.G. Teubner. Annual, 1934–37; monthly.
In German. Subtitle reads: "Monatschrift der Nordischen Gedanken".

3802
RASSEGNA DELLE RICERCHE SULLA FAMIGLIA ITALIANA. no.1– , 1983– . Milano, Vita e Pensiero. Irreg.
Issued by: Centro Studi e Ricerche sulla Famiglia, Università Cattolica del Sacro Cuore. In Italian. Subtitle reads: "Bolletino di informazione e documentazione".
Indexed: PAISFL.

3803
RASSEGNA DI STUDI ETIOPICI. 1– , Jan./Apr. 1941– . Roma. Annual.
Issued by: Ministerio dell'Africa Italiana in collaboration with Reale Academia d'Italia, 1941–43; Centro di Studi Ethiopici e Cristiano-Orientali, Università di Roma, and Istituto per l'Oriente. In English, French, German, or Italian; summaries in English, French and Italian. Vol. for 1966 last available for examination.

3804
RASSEGNA ECONOMICA. v.1– , 1931– . Napoli. Monthly, 1931–41; quarterly, 1942–59; three no. a year, 1960–66; bimonthly.
Issued by: Banca di Roma. In Italian. Title varies: 1949–54, *Rassegna Economico-Finanziera.*
Indexed: Bull. Anal. Pol. Ec. Soc.; Int. Bibl. Eco.; J. Eco. Lit.; PAISFL.

RASSEGNA ECONOMICO-FINANZIERA
See RASSEGNA ECONOMICA

3805
RASSEGNA INTERNAZIONALE. v.1–7, Apr. 1919–Sept./Oct. 1925. Roma. Monthly.

In Italian. Title varies: 1919–20, *Rassegna Internazionale*; *Supplemento Mensile della Rassegna Nazionale*; 1920–May 1921, *Rassegna Internazionale; Aggregata alla "Union Democratica Central" di Londra*; June 1921–Mar. 1924, *Rassegna Internazionale; Cahiers Internationaux*. In English, French, or Italian. Absorbed: *Rivista delle Colonie*, 1919.

RASSEGNA INTERNAZIONALE; AGGREGATA ALLA "UNION DEMOCRATICA CENTRAL" DI LONDRA
See RASSEGNA INTERNAZIONALE

3806
RASSEGNA INTERNAZIONALE DELL'ARTIGIANATO. 1– , 1951– . Roma. Annual (irreg.)
Issued by: Centro Studi del Problemi dell'Artigianato. In English, French, or Italian. Introductions are in English and French.

RASSEGNA INTERNAZIONALE; SUPPLEMENTO MENSILE DELLA RASSEGNA NAZIONALE
See RASSEGNA INTERNAZIONALE

3807
RASSEGNA ITALIANA DI POLITICA E DI CULTURA. v.1–58, May 15, 1918–1960. Roma. Monthly.
In Italian. Title varies: 1918–31, *Rassegna Italiana Politica e Letteraria*; 1932–49, *Rassegna Italiana Politica, Letteraria e Artistica*. Issues for volumes 1.26 (no.1–301) also numbered: Ser. 1–3, v.1–58. Publication suspended: July 1943–Dec. 1949.

3808
RASSEGNA ITALIANA DI SOCIOLOGIA. 1– , Jan./Mar. 1960– . Roma, Il Mulino. Quarterly, 1960–85; three no. a year.
In Italian; summaries in English. Vol. 6 called also 3rd ser.
Indexed: Bull. Anal. Pol. Ec. Soc.; Bull. Sig. Soc. Eth.; Int. Bibl. Pol. Sc.; Int. Bibl. Soc.; Int. Bibl. Soc. Cul. Anth.; Int. Lab. Doc.; Int. Pol. Sc. Abst.; LLBA; PAIS; Psych. Abst.; Soc. Abst.

RASSEGNA ITALIANA POLITICA E LETTERARIA
See RASSEGNA ITALIANIA DI POLITICA E DI CULTURA

RASSEGNA ITALIANA POLITICA, LETTERARIA E ARTISTICA
See RASSEGNA ITALIANA DI POLITICA E DI CULTURA

3809
RASSEGNA SINDICALE. v.1– , 1963– . Roma. Bimonthly.
Issued by: Confederazione Generale Italiana del Lavoro (CGIL). In Italian. Annual index for the previous half year in Jan. no.1 or 2 of the following year.
Indexed: Bull. Anal. Pol. Ec. Soc.; Int. Bibl. Eco.

RASSENVERHOUDINGS
See RACE RELATIONS JOURNAL

3810
RASY I NARODY. 1– . Moskva. Annual.
Issued by: Institut Etnografii, Akademii͡a Nauk SSSR. In Russian; summaries in English. Subtitle reads: "Sovremennye etnicheskie i rassivye problemy".
Indexed: Int. Bibl. Soc. Cul. Anth.

3811
RAUMFORSCHUNG UND RAUMORDNUNG. v.1– , Oct. 1936– . Heidelberg, later München, Carl Heymanns Verlag. Bimonthly.
Issued by: Bundesforschungsanstalt für Landeskunde und Raumforschung, Bonn, Bad-Godesberg, 1936–44, and Akademie für Raumforschung und Landesplanung, Hanover, 1948–. In German. Publication suspended: 1945–47, 1949, 1951–52.
Indexed: Bull. Anal. Pol. Ec. Soc.; Int. Bibl. Eco.; Int. Bibl. Soc. Cul. Anth.; Int. Lab. Doc.; PAIS; Pop. Ind.

3812
RAZVIVAI͡USHCHIESI͡A STRANY; EKONOMIKA I POLITIKA. 1– , 1976– . Moskva, Institut Nauchnoĭ Informat͡sii po Obshchestvennym Naukam, Akademii͡a Nauk SSSR, i Institut Mirovoĭ Ekonomiki i Mezhdunarodnykh Otnosheniĭ, Akademii͡a Nauk SSSR. Annual.
Issued by: Problemnai͡a Komissii͡a Mnogostoronnogo Sotrudnichestva Akademii Nauk Sot͡sialisticheskikh Stran "Ekonomika i Politika Razvivai͡ushchikhsi͡a Stran". In Russian. Published also in English under the title: *Developing Countries, Economics and Politics*.

3813
RAZZA E CIVILTÀ. v.1– , Mar. 1940– . Roma. Ministerio del Interno. Monthly.
Issued by: Consiglio Superiore e la Direzione per la Demografia e Razza. In Italian.

READERS' GUIDE TO PERIODICAL LITERATURE. SUPPLEMENT
See SOCIAL SCIENCES & HUMANITIES INDEX

3814
REALTÀ ECONOMICA. v.1– , 1969– . Milano. Quarterly.

Issued by: Camera di Comercio, Industria, Artigianato e Agricultura di Milano. In Italian.
Indexed: Bull. Anal. Pol. Ec. Soc.; Int. Bibl. Eco.

RECENT ECONOMIC TRENDS
See EUROPEAN ECONOMY. SUPPLEMENT A

RECHERCHE ET DÉVELOPPEMENT
See Commission of the European Communities. RECHERCHE ET DÉVELOPPEMENT

RECHERCHE OPERATIONELLE
See UNTERNEHMUNGSFORSCHUNG

3815
RECHERCHE SOCIALE. v.1– , 1952– . Paris. Bimonthly.
Organ of: Fondation pour la Recherche Sociale. In French. Issues are thematic. Title varies: 1952–Apr./June 1965, *Études et Documents* (Centre de Recherches Économiques et Sociales).
Indexed: ABC POL SCI; Bull. Anal. Pol. Ec. Soc.; Bull. Sig. Soc. Eth.; Int. Bibl. Eco.; Int. Bibl. Pol. Sc.; Int. Bibl. Soc.; Int. Lab. Doc.; PAISFL.

RECHERCHES D'HISTOIRE ÉCONOMIQUE ET SOCIALE MODERNE
See INQUIRIES ON MODERN ECONOMIC AND SOCIAL HISTORY

3816
RECHERCHES DE PSYCHOLOGIE SOCIALE. v.1– , July 1979– . Paris. Annual.
Issued by: Laboratoire de Psychologie Sociale, Université de Paris 7. In French.

RECHERCHES DÉMOGRAPHIQUES
See Université Catholique de Louvain. RECHERCHES DÉMOGRAPHIQUES

3817
RECHERCHES ÉCONOMIQUES DE LOUVAIN. v.1– , Dec. 1929– . Louvain. Quarterly, 1929–Feb. 1940; eight no. a year, Jan. 1946–1966; five no. a year, 1967–72; quarterly.
Issued by: Institut de Recherches Économiques et Sociales, Université Catholique de Louvain. In French. Title varies: 1929–37, *Bulletin de l'Institut des Sciences Économiques*; 1946–60, *Bulletin de l'Institut de Recherches Économiques et Sociales*. Not published: Feb. 1940–Jan. 1946. Includes supplements.
Indexed: Bull. Anal. Pol. Ec. Soc.; His. Abst.; Int. Bibl. Eco.; PAIS; PAISFL; Pop. Ind.

3818
RECHERCHES ÉCONOMIQUES ET SOCIALES. no.1– , Jan. 1976– . n. ser. no.1– , 1er trimestre 1982– . Paris, Documentation Française. Quarterly.
Issued by: Comité d'Organisation des Recherches Appliquées sur le Développement Économique et Sociale (C.O.R.—D.E.S.). In French.
Indexed: Bull. Anal. Pol. Ec. Soc.

3819
RECHERCHES INTERNATIONALES À LA LUMIÈRE DU MARXISME. Mar./Apr. 1967–1980. Paris, Éditions de la Nouvelle Critique. Bimonthly.
In French. Some numbers have also distinctive titles.
Continues: *Recherches Soviétiques*. Continued by: *Recherches Internationales*.
Indexed: Bull. Anal. Pol. Ec. Soc.; Bull. Sig. Soc. Eth.

3820
RECHERCHES SOCIOGRAPHIQUES. v.1– , Jan./Mar. 1960– . Québec, Presses Universitaires Laval. Quarterly.
Issued by: Département de Sociologie et Anthropologie (called 1960 Département de Sociologie), Université Laval, in cooperation with the Centre de Recherches Sociales, in 1960. in French.
Indexed: Bull. Anal. Pol. Ec. Soc.; Bull. Sig. Soc. Eth.; His. Abst.; Int. Bibl. Soc.; Int. Bibl. Soc. Cul. Anth.; Int. Lab. Doc.; Int. Pol. Sc. Abst.; Soc. Abst.

3821
RECHERCHES SOCIOLOGIQUES. v.1– , June 1970– . Louvain-la-Nueve. Three no. a year.
Issued by: Centre de Recherches Sociologiques, Université Catholique de Louvain. In French.
Indexed: Bull. Anal. Pol. Ec. Soc.; Bull. Sig. Soc. Eth.; Int. Bibl. Soc. Cul. Anth.; Int. Bibl. Soc.; LLBA; Soc. Abst.

3822
RECHERCHES SOCIOLOGIQUES EN COURSE. LAUFENDE SOZIOLOGISCHE FORSCHUNGEN. 1973– . Lausanne. Annual.
Issued by: Société Suisse de Sociologie (Schweizerische Gesellschaft für Soziologie). In French or German.

RECHERCHES SUR L'ÉDUCATION
See BADANIA OŚWIATOWE

3823
RECHERCHES UNIVERSITAIRES SUR L'INTÉGRATION EUROPÉENNE. UNIVERSITY RESEARCH ON EUROPEAN INTEGRATION. no.12– , 1982– . Bruxelles.
Issued by: Commission des Communautés Européennes. In English or French.
Continues: *Études Universitaires sur l'Intégration Européenne*.

3824
RECHT IN OST UND WEST. 1– , Mar. 1957– . Berlin, Verlag Verenigte Druckereien Chmielarz & A.W. Hayn's Erben. Bimonthly.

Issued by: Vereinigung Freitlicher Juristen. In German.
Indexed: Bull. Anal. Pol. Ec. Soc.; Ind. For. Leg. Per.; Int. Bibl. Soc. Cul. Anth.

RECOMMENDATIONS AND RESOLUTIONS
See Council of Europe. Consultative Assembly. TEXTS ADOPTED

RECUEIL DE DÉCISIONS
See European Commission of Human Rights. COLLECTION OF DECISIONS

RECUEIL DE LA JURISPRUDENCE
See Court of Justice of European Communities. RECUEIL DE LA JURISPRUDENCE

RECUEIL DES COURS
See Académie de Droit International, The Hague. RECUEIL DES COURS

REFERATIVNYĬ BIULLETEN' BOLGARSKOĬ NAUCHNOĬ LITERATURY. EKONOMIKA I PRAVO
See ABSTRACTS OF BULGARIAN SCIENTIFIC LITERATURE. ECONOMICS AND LAW

3825
REFERATIVNYĬ SBORNIK. EKONOMIKA PROMYSHLENNOSTI. 1– , 1960– . Moskva, Mezhdunarodnaia Kniga. Monthly.
Issued by: Vsesoiuznyĭ Institut Nauchnoĭ i Tekhnicheskoĭ Informatsii (VINITI), Akademiia Nauk SSSR. In Russian.

3826
REFERENCE SOURCES OF THE SOCIAL SCIENCES AND HUMANITIES. no.1– , 1982– . Westport, Conn., Greenwood Press. Irreg.
Monograph series of bibliographies.

3827
REFLETS ET PERSPECTIVES DE LA VIE ÉCONOMIQUE. 1– , Oct. 1961– . Bruxelles, Recherche et Diffusion Économiques. Semi-annual, 1961–62; six no. a year. Issues of 1974 were the latest examined.
In French.
Indexed: Bull. Anal. Pol. Ec. Soc.; PAISFL.

3828
LA RÉFORME SOCIALE. v.1–53, 1881–June 1933. Paris, Bureaux de la Réforme Sociale.
Issued by: Groupe des Économistes avec la Concourse de la Société d'Économie Sociale, de la Société Bibliographique des Unions de la Paix Sociale, later by: Société d'Économie Sociale et des Unions de Paix Sociale. In French.

LA RÉFORME SOCIALE
See LES ÉTUDES SOCIALES

3829
REFUGEES. no.3– , May/June 1981– . Geneva. Monthly.
Issued by: United Nations High Commissioner for Refugees (UNHCR). Accompanied by supplement: *Refugees Magazine*.

REFUGEES MAGAZINE
See REFUGEES

REGIONAL AND COMMUNITY PLANNING
See GEO ABSTRACTS. F. REGIONAL AND COMMUNITY PLANNING

3830
REGIONAL AND URBAN ECONOMICS. 1–4, May 1971–Oct. 1974. Amsterdam, North-Holland Pub. Co. Quarterly.
Issued by: Netherlands Economic Institute.
Continued by: *Regional Science and Urban Economics*.
Indexed: PAIS.

3831
REGIONAL DEVELOPMENT DIALOGUE. v.1– , spring 1980– . Nagoya. Semi-annual.
Issued by: Centre for Regional Development, Third World Development Problems, United Nations.
Supersedes: *Asian Development Dialogue*.
Indexed: PAIS; Sage Pub. Adm. Abst.

3832
REGIONAL SCIENCE AND URBAN ECONOMICS. v.5– , Feb. 1975– . Amsterdam, North-Holland Pub. Co. Quarterly.
Issued by: Regional Science Department, University of Pennsylvania.
Continues: *Regional and Urban Economics*.
Indexed: Bull. Anal. Pol. Ec. Soc.; Curr. Cont. Soc. Beh. Sc.; Int. Bibl. Eco.; Int. Bibl. Pol. Sc.; Int. Bibl. Soc.; J. Eco. Lit.; PAIS.

3833
Regional Science Research Institute. RSRI ABSTRACTS. 1– , June 1976– . Philadelphia, Pa. Three no. a year.

REGIONAL STATISTICS: COMMUNITY'S FINANCIAL PARTICIPATION IN INVESTMENTS
See Statistical Office of the European Communities. REGIONAL STATISTICS; COMMUNITY'S FINANCIAL PARTICIPATION IN INVESTMENTS

3834
REGIONAL STUDIES. v.1– , May 1967– . New York, Pergamon Press, later Cambridge University Press. Three no. a year.
Issued by: Regional Studies Association.
Indexed: Curr. Cont. Soc. Beh. Sc.; Int. Bibl. Eco.; Int. Bibl. Soc. Cul. Anth.; Int. Lab. Doc.; PAIS; PHRA; Pop. Ind.; Sage Pub. Adm. Abst.; Sage Urb. Stu. Abst.; SSCI.

REGIONALE STATISTIEK
See Statistical Office of the European Communities. REGIONAL STATISTICS: COMMUNITY'S FINANCIAL PARTICIPATION IN INVESTMENTS

REGIONALSTATISTIK (German edition)
See Statistical Office of the European Communities. REGIONAL STATISTICS: COMMUNITY'S FINANCIAL PARTICIPATION IN INVESTMENTS

REGIONALSTATISTIK (Greek edition)
See Statistical Office of the European Communities. REGIONAL STATISTICS: COMMUNITY'S FINANCIAL PARTICIPATION IN INVESTMENTS

REGIONALSTATISTISK
See Statistical Office of the European Communities. REGIONAL STATISTICS: COMMUNITY'S FINANCIAL PARTICIPATION IN INVESTMENTS

3835: not used

3836
REGIONI E COMUNITÀ LOCALI. no.1/2– , Jan./Apr. 1982– . Roma, Stampa Periodica Italiana. Four no. a year.
In Italian. Subtitle reads: "Dottrina, legislazione, giurisprudenza, amministrazione, finanza e credito".

REGISTER OF CURRENT RESEARCH IN SOUTH AFRICA
See NASIONALE REGISTER VAN NAVORSINGSPROJEKTE

REGISTER OF CURRENT SOCIAL SCIENCE RESEARCH IN IRELAND
See The Economic and Social Research Institute. REGISTER OF CURRENT SOCIAL SCIENCE RESEARCH IN IRELAND

REGISTER OF RESEARCH IN THE UNITED KINGDOM
See University of Sussex. Institute of Development Studies. REGISTER OF RESEARCH IN THE UNITED KINGDOM

REGISTER OF SOCIAL SCIENCE RESEARCH IN THE NETHERLANDS
See Akademie van Wetenschappen. Sociaal Wetenschappelijke Informatie- en Dokumentatiecentrum. REGISTER VAN SOCIAAL WETENSCHAPPELIJKE ONDERZOEK

3837
REICH UND LÄNDER. v.1–11, 1927–1937. Karlsruhe, Verlag J. Brown. Monthly.
In German. Eleven supplements titled "Sonderheft" were published.

3838
DER REICHS STÄDTEBUND. v.1–26, no.13, 1907–July 1, 1933. Berlin. Monthly.
In German. Title varies: 1907–27, *Kommunale Rundschau*. Subtitle reads: "Zeitschrift für alle Gebiete der Selbsverwaltung".
Merged into: *Gemeinde*.

REIHE SOZIOLOGIE IN DER SCHWEITZ
See SOZIOLOGIE IN DER SCHWEIZ

3839
REIHE STRUKTUR- UND ENTWICKLUNGSPOLITIK. v.1– , 1979– . Bonn, Verlag Neue Gesellschaft. Irreg.
Issued by: Forschungsinstitut der Friedrich-Ebert-Stiftung. In German. Monograph series.

3840
RELACIONES INTERNACIONALES. n. epoca, v.1– , Apr./June 1973– . Mexico, D.F. Quarterly, 1973–85; three no. a year.
Issued by: Centro de Relaciones Internacionales, Faculdad de Ciencias Políticas y Sociales, Universidad Nacional Autónoma de México. In Spanish. Other title: *Revista del Centro de Relaciones Internacionales*.
Indexed: Bull. Anal. Pol. Ec. Soc.; Int. Bibl. Eco.

3841
RELACIONES INTERNACIONALES. v.1– , Mar. 1980– . Heredia. Semi-annual.
Issued by: Escuela de Relaciones Internacionales, Universidad Nacional. In Spanish.

3842
RELACIONES MÉXICO–ESTADOS UNIDOS; BIBLIOGRAFÍA ANUAL. v.1– , July 1980/June 1981– . Mexico, D.F. Annual.
Issued by: El Colegio del México. In Spanish. Processed.

RELATIONS INTERNATIONALES
See REVUE IRANIENNE DES RELATIONS INTERNATIONALES

3843
RELAZIONI INTERNAZIONALI. v.1– , Jan. 1935– . Milano. Quarterly.
Issued by: Istituto per gli Studi di Politica Internazionale. In Italian.

RELEVÉ DES TRAITÉS ET ACCORDS INTERNATIONAUX ENREGISTRÉS OU CLASSÉS ET INSÉRÉS AU RÉPERTOIRE AU SECRÉTARIAT
See United Nations. Legal Department. STATEMENTS OF TREATIES AND INTERNATIONAL AGREEMENTS REGISTERED OR FILED WITH THE SECRETARIAT

3844
RELIGION AND SOCIETY. v.1– , 1954– . Bangalore. Quarterly.
Issued by: The Christian Institute for the Study of Religion and Society (CISRS). Title varies: v.1–4, 1954–57, Christian Institute for the Study of Society. *Bulletin*.
Indexed: Wom. Stu. Abst.

RELIGIONS AFRICAINES ET CHRISTIANISME
See CAHIERS DES RELIGIONS AFRICAINES

RÉPERTOIRE DES DONNÉS EN SCIENCES SOCIALES
See SOCIAL SCIENCE DATA INVENTORY

3845
RÉPERTOIRE MONDIALE DES INSTITUTIONS DE SCIENCES SOCIALES. WORLD DIRECTORY OF SOCIAL SCIENCE INSTITUTIONS. 1970– . Paris, Unesco. Biennial.
Issued by: Centre de Documentation en Sciences Sociales de Unesco. In English and French. Other title: *Repertorio Mundial de Instituciones de Ciencias Sociales*. In the fourth edition the title is reversed: English, French.

REPERTORIO MUNDIAL DE INSTITUCIONES DE CIENCIAS SOCIALES
See RÉPERTOIRE MONDIAL DES INSTITUTIONS DES SCIENCES SOCIALES

3846
REPLICATIONS IN SOCIAL PSYCHOLOGY. 1– , fall 1979– . Hays, Kans. Quarterly.
Issued by: Fort Hays State University. Subtitle reads: "Journal for the development of empirical foundation".

REPORT
See International Institute of Differing Civilizations. COMPTE-RENDU. REPORT

REPORT
See United Nations. Commission on Human Rights. REPORT

REPORT
See United Nations. Commission on the Racial Situation in the Union of South Africa. REPORT

REPORT
See United Nations. Commission on the Status of Women. REPORT

REPORT
See United Nations. Economic and Social Council. REPORT

REPORT
See United Nations. Economic Commission for Central America. REPORT

REPORT
See United Nations. Economic Commission for Europe. REPORT

REPORT
See United Nations. Section on the Status of Women. REPORT

REPORT
See United Nations. Trusteeship Council. OFFICIAL RECORDS (includes "Report")

REPORT OF THE ECONOMIC AND SOCIAL COUNCIL
See United Nations. Economic and Social Council. REPORT

REPORT ON SOCIAL DEVELOPMENTS
See Commission of the European Communities. REPORT ON SOCIAL DEVELOPMENTS

REPORT ON THE WORLD SOCIAL SITUATION
See United Nations. Department of International Economic and Social Affairs. REPORT ON THE WORLD SOCIAL SITUATION

REPORT ON THE WORLD SOCIAL SITUATION INCLUDING STUDIES OF URBANIZATION IN UNDERDEVELOPED AREAS
See United Nations. Department of International Economic and Social Affairs. REPORT ON THE WORLD SOCIAL SITUATION

REPORT ON THE WORLD SOCIAL SITUATION WITH SPECIAL REFERENCE TO THE PROBLEM OF BALANCED SOCIAL AND ECONOMIC DEVELOPMENT

See United Nations. Department of International Economic and Social Affairs. REPORT ON THE WORLD SOCIAL SITUATION

REPORTS AND PAPERS IN THE SOCIAL SCIENCES
See United Nations Educational, Scientific and Cultural Organization. REPORTS AND PAPERS IN THE SOCIAL SCIENCES

REPORTS OF THE ANNUAL CONFERENCES
See Institute of Sociology, London. REPORTS OF THE ANNUAL CONFERENCES

REPORTS OF THE RESEARCH INSTITUTE FOR JAPANESE CULTURE
See NIHON BUNKAKENKYUSHO. NIHON BUNKAKENKYUSHO KENKYU HOKOKU

3847
REPORTS OF THE WORLD FERTILITY SURVEY. 1– , 1980– . New York. Irreg.
Issued by: Population References Bureau. Each volume has also a distinctive title.

3848
REPORTS ON POPULATION/FAMILY PLANNING. [1]– , Dec. 1969– . New York. Irreg.
Issued by: The International Institute for the Study of Human Reproduction, Columbia University, and the Population Council.

REPORTS ON THE POPULATION OF TERRITORIES
See United Nations. Department of International Economic and Social Affairs. POPULATION STUDIES

REPORTS SERVICE
See American Universities Field Staff. REPORTS SERVICE [and its subseries]

3849
RES PUBLICA. v.1– , 1959– . Bruxelles. Two or three no. a year, 1959–60; four no. a year.
Issued by: Institut Belge de Science Politique. In Dutch, English, or French. Supplements accompany some numbers.
Indexes: Vols. 1–5, 1959–63, with v.6.
Indexed: ABC POL SCI; Bull. Anal. Pol. Ec. Soc.; Bull. Sig. Soc. Eth.; Hum. Res. Abst.; Int. Bibl. Eco.; Int. Bibl. Pol. Sc.; Int. Bibl. Soc. Cul. Anth.; Int. Pol. Sc. Abst.; Soc. Abst.; SSCI.

3850
RESEARCH DIGEST; SUMMARIES OF CURRENT BRITISH RESEARCH ON DEVELOPMENT. no.1– , spring 1978– . Brighton.
Issued by: University of Sussex.

RESEARCH FINDINGS
See Human Sciences Research Council (Raad vir Geestes-Wetenskaplike Novorsing). RESEARCH FINDINGS

3851
RESEARCH IN BRITISH UNIVERSITIES, POLYTECHNICS AND COLLEGES. 1979– . Boston Spa. Annual, in three volumes.
Issued by: Lending Division, British Library.
Continues: *Scientific Research in British Universities and Colleges* (1948–78)

3852
RESEARCH IN CONTEMPORARY AND APPLIED GEOGRAPHY. 1– , 1977– . Binghamton, N.Y. Irreg.
Issued by: State University of New York at Binghamton, N.Y.

3853
RESEARCH IN CORPORATE SOCIAL PERFORMANCE AND POLICY. v.1– , 1978– . Greenwich, Conn., JAI Press. Annual.
Indexed: Int. Bibl. Eco.

3854
RESEARCH IN ECONOMIC ANTHROPOLOGY. v.1– , 1978– . Greenwich, Conn., JAI Press. Irreg.
Includes: *Supplement* (v.1–, 1980–)

3855
RESEARCH IN ECONOMIC HISTORY. v.1– , 1976– . Greenwich, Conn., JAI Press. Annual.

3856
RESEARCH IN EDUCATION. v.1–9, Nov. 1966–Dec. 1974. Washington, D.C., Government Printing Office. Monthly.
Issued by: Educational Resources Information Center (ERIC), Office of Education, Department of Health, Education and Welfare.

3857
RESEARCH IN EDUCATION. no.1– , May 1969– . Manchester, Manchester University Press. Semi-annual.

3858
RESEARCH IN EXPERIMENTAL ECONOMICS. v.1– , 1979– . Greenwich, Conn., JAI Press. Annual.

3859
RESEARCH IN FINANCE. v.1– , 1979– . Greenwich, Conn., JAI Press.

3860
RESEARCH IN HUMAN CAPITAL AND HUMAN DEVELOPMENT. 1– , 1979– . Greenwich, Conn., JAI Press. Annual.
Some numbers are accompanied by: *Supplement* (1–, 1981–), monographs.

3861
RESEARCH IN INTERNATIONAL BUSINESS AND INTERNATIONAL RELATIONS. v.1– , 1986– . Greenwich, Conn., JAI Press. Annual.

3862
RESEARCH IN LABOR ECONOMICS. v.1– , 1977– . Greenwich, Conn., JAI Press. Annual.

3863
RESEARCH IN LAW AND ECONOMICS. v.1– , 1979– . Greenwich, Conn., JAI Press. Annual.

3864
RESEARCH IN LAW AND SOCIOLOGY. v.1–3, 1978–1980. Greenwich, Conn., JAI Press. Annual.
Continued by: *Research in Law, Deviance and Social Control.*

3865
RESEARCH IN LAW, DEVIANCE AND SOCIAL CONTROL. v.4– , 1982– . Greenwich, Conn., JAI Press. Annual.
Continues: *Research in Law and Sociology.*

3866
RESEARCH IN MARKETING. v.1– , 1978– . Greenwich, Conn., JAI Press. Annual.
Indexed: Psych. Abst.

3867
RESEARCH IN MICROPOLITICS. v.1– , 1986– . Greenwich, Conn., JAI Press. Annual.

3868
RESEARCH IN ORGANIZATIONAL BEHAVIOR. v.1– , 1979– . Greenwich, Conn., JAI Press. Annual.
Indexed: Int. Bibl. Eco.; Int. Pol. Sc. Abst.

3869
RESEARCH IN POLITICAL ECONOMY. v.1– , 1977– . Greenwich, Conn., JAI Press. Annual.
Indexed: Int. Bibl. Eco.

3870
RESEARCH IN POLITICAL SOCIOLOGY. v.1– , 1985– . Greenwich, Conn., JAI Press. Annual.
Published in cooperation with the Section on Political Sociology, American Sociological Association.

3871
RESEARCH IN POLITICS AND SOCIETY. v.1– , 1985– . Greenwich, Conn., JAI Press. Annual.
Each volume has also a distinctive title.

3872
RESEARCH IN POPULATION ECONOMICS. v.1– , 1978– . Greenwich, Conn., JAI Press. Annual.
Indexed: Pop. Ind.

3873
RESEARCH IN PUBLIC POLICY ANALYSIS AND MANAGEMENT. v.1– , 1981– . Greenwich, Conn., JAI Press. Annual.
Official organ of: Association for Public Policy Analysis and Management (APPAM).

3874
RESEARCH IN RACE AND ETHNIC RELATIONS. 1– , 1979– . Greenwich, Conn., JAI Press. Annual.
Indexed: Int. Bibl. Soc. Cul. Anth.; Psych. Abst.

3875
RESEARCH IN SOCIAL MOVEMENTS; CONFLICTS AND CHANGE. v.1– , 1978– . Greenwich, Conn., JAI Press. Annual.

3876
RESEARCH IN SOCIAL PROBLEMS AND PUBLIC POLICY. v.1– , 1979– . Greenwich, Conn., JAI Press. Annual.
Indexed: Psych. Abst.

3877
RESEARCH IN SOCIAL STRATIFICATION AND MOBILITY. v.1– , 1981– . Greenwich, Conn., JAI Press. Annual.

3878
RESEARCH IN SOCIOLOGY OF EDUCATION AND SOCIALIZATION. v.1– , 1980– . Greenwich, Conn., JAI Press. Annual.

3879
RESEARCH IN THE HISTORY OF ECONOMIC THOUGHT AND METHODOLOGY. v.1– , 1983– . Greenwich, Conn., JAI Press. Annual.

3880
RESEARCH IN THE SOCIOLOGY OF HEALTH CARE. v.1– , 1980– . Greenwich, Conn., JAI Press. Annual.
Some volumes are accompanied by: *Supplement* (1–, 1981–), monographs.

3881
RESEARCH IN THE SOCIOLOGY OF ORGANIZATIONS. v.1– , 1982– . Greenwich, Conn., JAI Press. Annual.

3882
RESEARCH IN THE SOCIOLOGY OF WORK. v.1– , 1981– . Greenwich, Conn., JAI Press. Annual.

3883
RESEARCH IN URBAN ECONOMICS. v.1– , 1981– . Greenwich, Conn., JAI Press. Annual.

3884
RESEARCH IN URBAN POLICY. v.1– , 1985– . Greenwich, Conn., JAI Press. Annual.
Each volume has also a distinctive title. Other title: *RUP*.

3885
RESEARCH JOURNAL OF PHILOSOPHY & SOCIAL SCIENCES. v.1– , Apr. 1976– . Bombay, Anu Prakashan.

3886
RESEARCH MONOGRAPH SERIES IN THE SOCIAL SCIENCES. no.1– , 1974– . Ottawa, Éditions de l'Université d'Ottawa. Irreg.
Issued by: University of Ottawa. Other title: *Travaux de Recherches en Sciences Sociales*. Monograph series. Includes some Ph.D. theses.

3887
RESEARCH ON AGING. v.1– , Mar. 1979– . Beverly Hills, Calif., Sage Publications. Quarterly.
Subtitle reads: "A quarterly of social gerontology".
Indexed: Sage Urb. Stu. Abst.

3888
RESEARCH ON POPULATION ECOLOGY. 1– , 1952– . Kyoto. Semi-annual.
Issued by: Society of Population Ecology. Supplements accompany some numbers (no.1– , 1981–). Title in Japanese: *Kotaigun Seitaigaku no Kenkyū*.

3889
RESEARCH ON TECHNOLOGICAL INNOVATION, MANAGEMENT AND POLICY. v.1– , 1981– . Greenwich, Conn., JAI Press. Annual.

RESEARCH PAPER
See Griffith University, Brisbane. School of Modern Asian Studies. Centre for the Study of Australasian–Asian Relations. RESEARCH PAPER

3890
RESEARCH PAPER IN ECONOMIC HISTORY. no.1– , 1981– . Canberra. Irreg.

RESEARCH PAPERS
See University of Chicago. Department of Geography. RESEARCH PAPERS

3891
RESEARCH POLICY. v.1– , Nov. 1971– . Amsterdam, North-Holland Pub. Co. Quarterly.
Summaries in French and German. Subtitle reads: "A journal devoted to research policy, research management and planning".
Indexed: Bull. Anal. Pol. Ec. Soc.; Eco. Abst.; Int. Bibl. Eco.; Int. Bibl. Pol. Sc.; Int. Pol. Sc. Abst.

RESEARCH REPORT
See Henrietta Szold Institute—National Institute for Research in the Behavioral Sciences. RESEARCH REPORT

3892
RESEARCH REPORTS IN PUBLIC POLICY. no.1– , Oct. 1975– . Santa Barbara, Calif. Irreg.
Issued by: Urban Economic Program, Community and Organization Institute, University of California, Santa Barbara.

3893
RESEARCH REPORTS IN SOCIAL SCIENCE. 1– , 1959– . Tallahassee, Fla. Semi-annual.
Issued by: Institute for Social Research, The Florida State University.

3894
RESEARCH REPORTS IN THE SOCIAL SCIENCES. 1– , spring 1967– . Notre Dame, Ind. Semi-annual.
Issued by: University of Notre Dame.

RESEARCH SERIES
See University of Chicago. Center for Health Administration Studies. RESEARCH SERIES

RESEARCH SUPPORTED BY THE ECONOMIC AND SOCIAL RESEARCH COUNCIL
See Social Science Research Council (U.K.). RESEARCH SUPPORTED BY THE SOCIAL SCIENCE RESEARCH COUNCIL

RESOLUCIONES APROBADAS
See United Nations. Economic and Social Council. RESOLUTIONS ADOPTED BY THE ECONOMIC AND SOCIAL COUNCIL

RESOLUTIONS ADOPTED BY THE ECONOMIC AND SOCIAL COUNCIL
See United Nations. Economic and Social Council. RESOLUTIONS ADOPTED BY THE ECONOMIC AND SOCIAL COUNCIL

RESOLUTIONS ADOPTED BY THE GENERAL ASSEMBLY
See United Nations. General Assembly. RESOLUTIONS ADOPTED BY THE GENERAL ASSEMBLY

RÉSOLUTIONS ADOPTÉE PAR LE CONSEIL ÉCONOMIQUE ET SOCIAL
See United Nations. Economic and Social Council. RESOLUTIONS ADOPTED BY THE ECONOMIC AND SOCIAL COUNCIL

RESOLUTIONS AND DECISIONS OF THE SECURITY COUNCIL
See United Nations. Security Council. OFFICIAL RECORDS (includes "Resolutions and Decisions")

RÉSOLUTIONS ET DÉCISIONS DU CONSEIL DU SÉCURITÉ
See United Nations. Security Council. OFFICIAL RECORDS (includes "Resolutions and Decisions")

3895
RESOURCE MANAGEMENT AND OPTIMIZATION. 1– , Feb. 1980– . Chur, New York, Harwood Academic Publishers. Quarterly.
Issues are thematic.

3896
RESOURCES FOR FEMINIST RESEARCH. R.F.R. DOCUMENTATION SUR LA RECHERCHE FÉMINISTE. DRF. v.8– , Mar. 1978– . Toronto. Quarterly.
Issued by: Department of Sociology, Ontario Institute for Studies in Education. In English or French. Continues: *Canadian Newsletter of Research on Women.*
Indexed: His. Abst.; Soc. Abst.; Wom. Stu. Abst.

RESUMEN DE LA EVOLUCIÓN ECONÓMICA EN ÁFRICA
See United Nations. Economic Commission for Africa. ECONOMIC DEVELOPMENT IN AFRICA

RESUMEN DE LA EVOLUCIÓN ECONÓMICA EN EL CERCANO ORIENTE
See United Nations. Economic Commission for Western Asia. STUDIES ON DEVELOPMENT IN COUNTRIES IN WESTERN ASIA

RESUMENES ANALÍTICOS Y BIBLIOGRÁFICOS
See REVISTA ANALÍTICA DE EDUCACIÓN

RESUMENES DE INFORMACIÓN SOBRE EL DESARROLLO
See DEVELOPMENT INFORMATION ABSTRACTS

3897
RESUMENES SOBRE POBLACIÓN EN AMÉRICA LATINA. LATIN AMERICAN POPULATION ABSTRACTS. v.1– , June 1977– . Santiago, Chile. Two no. a year.
Issued by: Centro Latinoamericano de Demografía. In Spanish. Other title: *DOCPAL Resumenes sobre Población en América Latina.*

RÉSUMÉS ET ANALYSES DES RENSEIGNEMENTS TRANSMIS AU SECRÉTAIRE GÉNÉRAL
See United Nations. Secretary General. TERRITORIES NON-AUTONOMES; RÉSUMÉS ET ANALYSES DES RENSEIGNEMENTS TRANSMIS AU SECRÉTAIRE GÉNÉRAL

REVENUE STATISTICS OF OECD MEMBER COUNTRIES
See Organisation for Economic Co-operation and Development. STATISTIQUES DE RESETLES PUBLIQUES DES PAYS MEMBERS DE L'OCDE

REVIEW INTERAMERICANA
See REVISTA/REVIEW INTERAMERICANA

3898
REVIEW JOURNAL OF PHILOSOPHY & SOCIAL SCIENCE. v.1– , 1977– . Meerut, Anu Prakashan. Semi-annual.

REVIEW OF ACHIEVEMENTS. ICM
See Intergovernmental Committee for Migration. REVIEW OF ACHIEVEMENTS. ICM

3899
REVIEW OF AFRICAN POLITICAL ECONOMY. 1– , Aug./Nov. 1979– . London, Merlin Press. Three no. a year.
Issued by: Economics Department, University of Keele.
Indexed: Bull. Anal. Pol. Ec. Soc.; PAIS.

3900
REVIEW OF AFRO-AMERICAN ISSUES AND CULTURES. v.1–9, fall 1978–1981. Syracuse, N.Y. Quarterly.
Issued by: Afro-American Studies, Syracuse University.

3901
REVIEW OF AUSTRALIA'S DEMOGRAPHIC TRENDS. 1981–1983. Canberra, Australian Government Publishing Service. Annual.
Issued by: Department of Immigration and Ethnic Affairs. Merged with: *Population Trends* to form: *Australia's Population Trends and Prospects* (1984–)

3902
REVIEW OF BLACK POLITICAL ECONOMY. v.1– , spring/summer 1970– . Atlanta, Ga. (distributed by the Transaction Periodicals Consortium, New Brunswick, N.J.). Three no. a year.
Issued by: National Economic Association, and jointly with the Southern Center for Studies in Public Policy at Clark College.
Indexes: Vols. 1–4, 1970/71–1973/74.

Indexed: Hum. Res. Abst.; PAIS; Sage Urb. Stu. Abst.; SSCI.

REVIEW OF ECONOMIC CONDITIONS IN THE MIDDLE EAST
See United Nations. Economic Commission for Western Asia. STUDIES ON DEVELOPMENT IN COUNTRIES OF WESTERN ASIA

REVIEW OF ECONOMIC ACTIVITY IN AFRICA
See United Nations. Department of Economic and Social Affairs. ECONOMIC DEVELOPMENTS IN AFRICA

REVIEW OF ECONOMIC AND POLITICAL SCIENCES
See EPITHEŌRĒSIS OIKONOMIKON KAI POLITIKŌN EPISTĒMON

3903
REVIEW OF ECONOMIC CONDITIONS. 1954– . Ankara. Bimonthly.
Issued by: Turkiye is Bankasi. In English and Turkish.

REVIEW OF ECONOMIC CONDITIONS IN AFRICA
See United Nations. Economic Commission for Africa. ECONOMIC DEVELOPMENT IN AFRICA

3904
REVIEW OF ECONOMIC CONDITIONS IN ITALY. no.1– , 1979– . Roma. Three no. a year.
Issued by: Banca di Roma.
Continues: *Review of the Economic Conditions in Italy.*
Indexed: Bull. Anal. Pol. Ec. Soc.; PAIS.

REVIEW OF ECONOMIC CONDITIONS IN THE MIDDLE EAST
See United Nations. Economic Commission for Western Asia. STUDIES ON DEVELOPMENT IN COUNTRIES OF WESTERN ASIA

THE REVIEW OF ECONOMIC STATISTICS
See THE REVIEW OF ECONOMICS AND STATISTICS

3905
REVIEW OF ECONOMIC STUDIES. 1– , Oct. 1933– . Edinburgh, Longman. Three or four no. a year (with occasional special issue).
Issued by: London School of Economics and Political Science; 1958–, Society for Economic Analysis. Some numbers contain papers of symposia.
Indexes: Vols. 1–25, 1933–58, 1v.
Indexed: Bull. Anal. Pol. Ec. Soc.; Eco. Abst.; Ind. Per. Art. Law; Int. Bibl. Eco.; Int. Bibl. Pol. Sc.; Int. Bibl. Soc.; J. Eco. Lit.; SSCI.

3906
THE REVIEW OF ECONOMICS AND STATISTICS. v.1– , Jan. 1919– . Cambridge, Mass., Harvard University Press. Monthly, 1919–38; quarterly.
Issued by: Department of Statistics, Harvard University. Title varies: 1919–47, *The Review of Economic Statistics.*
Indexed: Bull. Anal. Pol. Ec. Soc.; Curr. Cont. Soc. Beh. Sc.; Eco. Abst.; His. Abst.; Ind. Per. Art. Law; Int. Bibl. Eco.; Int. Bibl. Soc.; J. Eco. Lit.; PAIS; Peace Res. Abst. J.; Pop. Ind.; Soc. Abst.; SSCI; Wom. Stu. Abst.

3907
REVIEW OF EDUCATION IN INDIA. 1950– . New Delhi. Annual.
Issued by: Department of Education, Ministry of Education and Social Welfare, India. Subseries of its *Publication.*

3908
REVIEW OF EDUCATIONAL RESEARCH. 1– , 1931– . Washington, D.C. Five no. a year.
Issued by: American Educational Research Association.
Indexes: Vols. 1–12, 1931–42, 1v.
Indexed: Int. Bibl. Soc. Cul. Anth.; LLBA; Psych. Abst.

3909
A REVIEW OF ELECTIONS OF THE WORLD. 1963/64– . London.
Issued by: Institute of Electoral Research.
Continues: *A Review of Elections* (1954/58–1961/62)

REVIEW OF FINNISH LINGUISTICS AND ETHNOLOGY
See STUDIA FENNICA

3910
THE REVIEW OF INCOME AND WEALTH. ser. 12– , Mar. 1966– . New Haven, Conn. Quarterly.
Issued by: International Association for Research in Income and Wealth.
Continues the association's *Income and Wealth* and continues its volume numbering.
Indexed: Bull. Anal. Pol. Ec. Soc.; Eco. Abst.; Int. Bibl. Eco.; Int. Lab. Doc.; PAIS.

3911
REVIEW OF INDONESIAN AND MALAYSIAN AFFAIRS. v.17– , winter/summer 1983– . Sydney. Semi-annual.
Issued by: Department of Indonesian and Malaysian Studies, University of Sydney.
Continues: *Review of Indonesian and Malayan Affairs* (v.1–16, Mar. 1967–1983).

Indexed: Bull. Anal. Pol. Ec. Soc.; Int. Bibl. Eco.; Int. Bibl. Pol. Sc.; Int. Pol. Sc. Abst.

3912
REVIEW OF INTERNATIONAL AFFAIRS. v.1– , June 7, 1950– . Beograd, Medunarodna Politika. Semimonthly.
Issued by: Federation of Yugoslav Journalists.
Indexed: Curr. Cont. Soc. Beh. Sc.; PAIS; Peace Res. Abst. J.

3913
REVIEW OF INTERNATIONAL COOPERATION. 2nd–32nd ed., Jan. 1909–Dec. 1939. London. Monthly.
Includes section "Bibliography". Title varies: 1909–Mar. 1928, *International Co-operative Bulletin*.

3914
REVIEW OF INTERNATIONAL STUDIES. no.1– , Jan. 1981– . London, Butterworth. Quarterly.
Issued by: British International Studies Association.
Continues: *British Journal of International Studies*.
Indexed: ABC POL SCI; Int. Bibl. Eco.

3915
REVIEW OF MARKETING AND AGRICULTURAL ECONOMICS. v.1– , Apr. 1937– . Sydney. Monthly, 1937–48; quarterly.
Issued by: Division of Marketing and Agricultural Economics, New South Wales Department of Agriculture. Title varies: 1937–43, *Monthly Marketing Review*.
Indexed: APAIS; Bull. Anal. Pol. Ec. Soc.; Int. Bibl. Eco.; PAIS.

3916
REVIEW OF PERSONALITY AND SOCIAL PSYCHOLOGY. 1– , 1980– . Beverly Hills, Calif., Sage Publications. Annual.
Published in cooperation with the Society for Personality and Social Psychology (Division 8, American Psychological Association)

3917
THE REVIEW OF POLITICS. v.1– , Jan. 1939– . Notre Dame, Ind. Quarterly.
Issued by: University of Notre Dame.
Indexed: Bull. Anal. Pol. Ec. Soc.; Curr. Cont. Soc. Beh. Sc.; ABC POL SCI; His. Abst.; Ind. Per. Art. Law; Int. Bibl. Eco.; Int. Bibl. Pol. Sc.; Int. Bibl. Soc.; Int. Pol. Sc. Abst.; PAIS; Peace Res. Abst. J.; Sage Pub. Adm. Abst.; Soc. Sc. Hum. Ind.; SSCI.

3918
REVIEW OF POPULATION REVIEWS. English Edition. no.7– , Jan./Mar. 1978– . Paris. Quarterly.
Issued by: Committee for International Cooperation in National Research in cooperation with the United Nations Fund for Population Activities. Published also in French edition.

3919
REVIEW OF PUBLIC DATA USE. Dec. 1972– . Arlington, Va. Quarterly.
Issued by: Clearinghouse and Laboratory for Census Data.
Indexed: PAIS; Pop. Ind.; SSCI; Urb. Aff. Abst.

3920
THE REVIEW OF RADICAL POLITICAL ECONOMICS. 1– , May 1969– . Ann Arbor, Mich. Quarterly.
Issued by: Union for Radical Political Economics.
Indexed: Bull. Anal. Pol. Ec. Soc.; Ind. Per. Art. Law; Int. Bibl. Eco.; Int. Bibl. Pol. Sc.; Int. Bibl. Soc.; J. Eco. Lit.; PAIS; SSCI.

3921
THE REVIEW OF REGIONAL STUDIES. 1– , fall 1970– . [Place of publication varies]; at present time Cambridge University Press. Three no. a year.
Issued by: Southwestern Regional Science Association, and the School of Business, University of Alabama at Birmingham.
Indexed: Pop. Ind.

3922
THE REVIEW OF RESEARCH IN BANKING AND FINANCE. v.1– , fall 1985– . Miami, Fla. Semi-annual.
Issued by: International Banking Center, Florida International University.

3923
REVIEW OF RESEARCH IN FUTURE MARKETS. v.1– , 1982– . Chicago, Ill. Three no. a year.
Issued by: Chicago Board of Trade in cooperation with the Chicago Board of Trade Foundation. Title varies: 1982–86, *Review of Future Markets*.

3924
REVIEW OF SOCIAL ECONOMY. v.1– , Dec. 1942– . Milwaukee, Wis., Chicago, Ill. Annual, 1942; semi-annual.
Issued by: Catholic Economic Association, later Association for Social Economics.
Indexed: His. Abst.; Int. Lab. Doc.; J. Eco. Lit.; PAIS; SSCI.

3925
REVIEW OF SOCIAL THEORY. 1– , Sept. 1972– . Columbia, Mo. Semi-annual.
Issued by: Department of Sociology, University of Missouri.
Indexed: Soc. Abst.

3926
REVIEW OF SOUTHEAST ASIAN STUDIES. v.4– , 1974– . Singapore. Quarterly.
Issued by: South Seas Society.

Continues: *Nanyang Quarterly* (v.1–3, 1971–73).

REVIEW OF THE INTERNATIONAL FEDERATION OF TRADE UNIONS
See INTERNATIONAL TRADE UNION MOVEMENT

REVIEW OF WORLD ECONOMICS
See WELTWIRTSCHAFTLICHES ARCHIV

REVIEW OF WORLD TRADE
See League of Nations. REVIEW OF WORLD TRADE

3927
REVIEWS IN ANTHROPOLOGY. v.1– , Feb. 1974– . South Salem, N.Y., Redgrave Pub. Co. Quarterly.
Indexed: Int. Bibl. Soc. Cul. Anth.

3928
REVIEWS IN EUROPEAN HISTORY. v.1– , June 1974– . Westport, Conn., Redgrave Information Resources Corporation. Annual.

REVIEWS OF CURRENT RESEARCH
See Social Science Research Council (Gt. Brit.). REVIEWS OF CURRENT RESEARCH

3929
REVIJA ZA SOCIOLOGIJU. SOCIOLOGICAL REVIEW. v.1– , 1971– . Zagreb. Quarterly.
Issued by: Sociolosko Drustvo Hrvatske. In Serbo-Croatian; summaries in English.
Indexed: Bull. Anal. Pol. Ec. Soc.; Int. Bibl. Pol. Sc.; Int. Pol. Sc. Abst.; Soc. Abst.

REVISTA
See Federación Latinoamericana de Bancos. REVISTA

REVISTA
See Instituto de Ciencias Sociales. REVISTA

REVISTA
See Sociedad Interamericana de Planificación. REVISTA

3930
REVISTA AMERICANA DE DERECHO INTERNACIONAL. v.6–15, Jan. 1912–Oct. 1921. Washington, D.C. Quarterly.
Issued by: Sociedad Americana de Derecho Internacional. Spanish edition of the *American Journal of International Law*. V.1–5 were not published in the Spanish edition. Supplements under the title "Documentos Officiales" accompany v.6–15.
Superseded by: *Revista de Derecho Internacional*.

3931
REVISTA ANALÍTICA DE EDUCACIÓN. v.1– , Mar. 1949– . Paris. Monthly.
Issued by: Centro de Intercambios de Educación, Organización de las Naciones Unidas para la Educación, la Ciencia y la Culture. In Spanish. Title varies: Mar.–Aug. 1949, *Resumenes Analíticos y Bibliográficos*; Sept. 1949–Dec. 1951, *Revista Analítica de Educación Fundamental*. (Unesco/ED, Abstracts)

REVISTA ANALÍTICA DE EDUCACIÓN FUNDAMENTAL
See REVISTA ANALÍTICA DE EDUCACIÓN

REVISTA ANTHROPOLÓGICA
See ANTHROPOLÓGICA

3932
REVISTA ANTROPOLÓGICA. v.1– , Apr. 1983– . Montevideo, Imprenta CBA, Juan Carlos Gomez. Quarterly.
In Spanish.
Indexed: Abst. Anth.

3933
REVISTA ARGENTINA DE ADMINISTRACIÓN PÚBLICA. v.1– , Oct./Dec. 1979– . Buenos Aires.
Issued by: Instituto Nacional de la Administración Pública. In Spanish.

3934
REVISTA ARGENTINA DE CIENCIA POLÍTICA. v.1– , Jan./June 1960– . Buenos Aires, Ediciones de Palma. Semi-annual.
Issued by: Asociación Argentina de Ciencia Política. In Spanish.

3935
REVISTA ARGENTINA DE ESTUDIOS POLÍTICOS. v.1– , July 1945– . Buenos Aires. Three no. a year.
Issued by: Instituto Argentino de Estudios Políticos. In Spanish.

3936
REVISTA ARGENTINA DE POLÍTICA ECONÓMICA Y SOCIAL. 1– , Jan./Mar. 1984– . Buenos Aires. Three no. a year.
Issued by: Instituto de Política Económica y Social (IPES). In Spanish.

3937
REVISTA ARGENTINA DE RELACIONES INTERNACIONALES. v.1– , Jan./Apr. 1975– . Buenos Aires. Three no. a year.
Indexes: Vols. 1–4, 1975–78, in v.5 (no.13)
Indexed: Bull. Anal. Pol. Ec. Soc.

3938
REVISTA BRASILEIRA DE CIÊNCIAS SOCIAIS. v.1–19, no.1, Nov. 1961–spring 1980. Belo Horizonte. Three no. a year.
Issued by: Faculdade de Ciências Econômicas, Universidade de Minas Gerais. In Portuguese.

3939
REVISTA BRASILEIRA DE ECONOMIA. 1– , Sept. 1947– . Rio de Janeiro. Four no. a year (some double issues).
Issued by: Instituto Brasileiro de Economia, Fundação Getulio Vargas. in Portuguese; summaries in English.
Indexed: Bull. Anal. Pol. Ec. Soc.; Int. Bibl. Eco.; Int. Lab. Doc.; PAIS; PAISFL; Soc. Abst.; SSCI.

3940
REVISTA BRASILEIRA DE ESTATÍSTICA. v.1– , Jan./Mar. 1940– . Rio de Janeiro. Quarterly.
Issued by: Conselho Nacional de Estatística, and Sociedade Brasileira de Estatística.
Indexed: Bull. Anal. Pol. Ec. Soc.; Int. Bibl. Eco.; Pop. Ind.

3941
REVISTA BRASILEIRA DE ESTUDOS PEDAGÓGICOS. v.1– , July 1944– . Rio de Janeiro. Quarterly.
Issued by: Centro Brasileiro de Pesquisas do Instituto Nacional de Estudos Pedagógicos. In Portuguese.
Indexes: Vols. 1–16, 1944–51, 1v.

3942
REVISTA BRASILEIRA DE ESTUDOS POLÍTICOS. v.1– , Dec. 1956– . Rio de Janeiro, Livraias Editoras Reunidas. Semi-annual.
Issued by: Faculdade de Direito, Universidade Federal de Minas Gerais. In Portuguese.
Indexes: Vols. 1–21, 1956–66, 1v.
Indexed: ABC POL SCI; His. Abst.; Int. Bibl. Eco.; Int. Bibl. Pol. Sc.; Int. Lab. Doc.; PAISFL.

3943
REVISTA BRASILEIRA DE GEOGRAFIA. v.1– , Jan. 1939– . Rio de Janeiro. Four no. a year.
Issued by: Instituto Brasileiro de Geografia e Estatística. In Portuguese; summaries in English and French.
Indexes: Vols. 1–10, 1939–48, 1v.

3944
REVISTA BRASILEIRA DE HISTORIA. no.1– , Mar. 1981– . Rio de Janeiro. Semi-annual.
Issued by: Associação Nacional dos Profesores Universitarios de Historia (ANPUH). In Portuguese.

3945
REVISTA BRASILEIRA DE POLÍTICA INTERNACIONAL. v.1– , Mar. 1958– . Rio de Janeiro. Quarterly.
Issued by: Instituto Brasileiro de Relações Internacionais. In Portuguese.
Indexed: ABC POL SCI; Bull. Anal. Pol. Ec. Soc.; His. Abst.; Int. Bibl. Eco.; Int. Bibl. Pol. Sc.; Int. Bibl. Soc.; Int. Pol. Sc. Abst.

3946
REVISTA CENTROAMERICANA DE ADMINISTRACIÓN PÚBLICA. no.1– , July/Dec. 1981– . San José. Semi-annual.
Issued by: Instituto Centroamericano de Administración Pública. In Spanish.

3947
REVISTA CENTROAMERICANA DE ECONOMÍA. v.1– , Sept. 1979– . Tegucigalpa. Three no. a year.
Issued by: Universidad Nacional de Honduras. In Spanish.
Indexed: PAISFL.

3948
REVISTA CHILENA DE ANTROPOLOGÍA. no.4– , 1984– . Santiago, Chile.
Issued by: Departamento de Antropología, Faculdad de Filosofía, Humanidades y Educación, Universidad de Chile. In Spanish.
Continues: *Revista Chilena de Sociología y Antropología* ([no.1–3], 1978–80, unnumbered)

3949
REVISTA COLOMBIANA DE ANTROPOLOGÍA. v.1– , June 1953– . Bogotá. Annual.
Organ of: Instituto Colombiano de Antropología. In Spanish. Some numbers accompanied by *Suplemento* (no.1–, 1964–)
Supersedes: *Revista del Instituto Etnológico Nacional*, and *Boletín de Arqueología*.
Indexed: His. Abst.; Int. Bibl. Soc. Cul. Anth.

3950
REVISTA COLOMBIANA DE SOCIOLOGÍA. v.1– , Dec. 1979– . Bogotá.
Issued by: Departamento de Sociologia, Universidad Nacional. In Spanish.

3951
REVISTA CRÍTICA DE CIÊNCIAS SOCIAIS. no.1– , 1983– . Coimbra. Two no. a year.
Issued by: Centro de Estudos Sociais, Faculdade de Economia. In Portuguese.

3952
REVISTA CUBANA DE CIENCIAS SOCIALES. 1– , 1983– . La Habana. Three no. a year.

Issued by: Centro de Estudios Filosóficos, Academia de Ciencias de Cuba. In Spanish; summaries in English.

3953
REVISTA DE ADMINISTRAÇÃO. v.1– , Mar. 1947– . São Paulo. From two to four no. a year.
Issued by: Instituto de Administração, Faculdade de Ciências Econômicas de São Paulo, Universidade de São Paulo. In Portuguese.

3954
REVISTA DE ADMINISTRAÇÃO MUNICIPAL. v.8 (no.44)– , Jan./Feb. 1961– . Rio de Janeiro. Bimonthly.
Issued by: Instituto Brasileiro de Administração Municipal. In Portuguese.
Continues: *Noticias Municipias* (1954–60)
Indexed: Bull. Anal. Pol. Ec. Soc.; Int. Bibl. Eco.

3955
REVISTA DE ADMINISTRAÇÃO PARA O DESENVOLVIMENTO. v.1– , July/Sept. 1977– . Recife. Two no. a year.
Issued by: Instituto Nacional de Administração para o Desenvolvimento (INAD), Universidade Federal de Pernambuco. In Portuguese.

3956
REVISTA DE ADMINISTRAÇÃO PÚBLICA. v.1– , 1961– . Rio de Janeiro. Quarterly.
Issued by: Fundação Getulio Vargas, and Centro de Pesquisas Administrativas, Escola Brasileira de Administração Pública. In Portuguese.
Indexed: ABC POL SCI; Bull. Anal. Pol. Ec. Soc.; Bull. Sig. Soc. Eth.

3957
REVISTA DE ADMINISTRACIÓN PÚBLICA. v.1– , Jan./Apr. 1950– . Madrid. Three no. a year.
Issued by: Instituto de Estudios Políticos. In Spanish.
Indexed: ABC POL SCI; Bull. Anal. Pol. Ec. Soc.; Int. Bibl. Eco.; Int. Bibl. Pol. Sc.; Int. Bibl. Soc.; Int. Pol. Sc. Abst.

3958
REVISTA DE ADMINISTRACIÓN PÚBLICA. 1– , 1956– . Mexico, D.F. Four no. a year (some double numbers)
Issued by: Instituto de Administración Publica, Sección Mexicana del Instituto Nacional de Ciencias Administrativas. In Spanish.
Indexed: Bull. Anal. Pol. Ec. Soc.

3959
REVISTA DE ADMINISTRACIÓN Y DESARROLLO. v.17–18, 1977–1979. Bogotá.
Issued by: Escuela Superior de Administración Pública de Colombia. In Spanish.
Continues: *Administración y Desarrollo*. Continued by: *Administración y Desarrollo*.
Indexes: Vols. 17–18, 1977–79, in *Administración y Desarrollo* (v.30, Dec. 1982)

3960
REVISTA DE ANTROPOLOGIA. June 1953– . São Paulo. Two no. a year.
Issued by: Associação Brasileira de Antropologia (1953–58) and with Sociedade Brasileira de Sociologia (1959–68); Sociedade Brasileira de Antropologia (1969–72) and with Faculdade de Filosofia, Letras Sociais, Universidade de São Paulo (1978–). In Portuguese.
Indexed: Bull. Sig. Soc. Eth.; His. Abst.; Int. Bibl. Soc. Cul. Anth.

3961
REVISTA DE ARQUEOLOGIA. v.1– , July/Dec. 1983– . Rio de Janeiro, Ed. Achiame. Semi-annual.
In English, French, or Portuguese.

3962
REVISTA DE CIÊNCIA POLÍTICA. v.1– , Mar. 1967– . Rio de Janeiro. Quarterly.
Issued by: Instituto de Direito e Ciência Política, Fundação Getulio Vargas. In Portuguese. Title varies: 1958–66, *Revista de Direito Público e Ciência Política*.
Indexed: ABC POL SCI; Bull. Anal. Pol. Ec. Soc.; Int. Bibl. Eco.; Int. Bibl. Pol. Sc.; Int. Bibl. Soc.; Int. Pol. Sc. Abst.; Soc. Abst.

3963
REVISTA DE CIENCIA POLÍTICA. 1979– . Santiago, Chile. Semi-annual.
Issued by: Instituto de Ciencia Política, Pontificia Universidad Católica de Chile. In Spanish.
Indexed: ABC POL SCI; Soc. Abst.

3964
REVISTA DE CIÊNCIA POLÍTICA. no.1– , 1. sem. de 1985– . Lisboa. Two no. a year.
Issued by: Instituto de Estudos Políticos. In Portuguese; occasionally in English or French.

3965
REVISTA DE CIÊNCIAS JURÍDICAS, ECONÔMICAS E SOCIAIS. v.1– , Apr. 1963– . Belem. Semi-annual.
Issued by: Departamento de Educação e Ensino, Universidade Federal do Para. In Portuguese; summaries in English and French, and occasionally in German. Absorbed: *Revista* issued by the university's Faculdade de Ciências Econômicas, Contabeis e Atuariais.

REVISTA DE CIENCIAS JURÍDICAS, POLÍTICAS Y SOCIALES
See REVISTA DE DERECHO Y CIENCIAS POLÍTICAS Y SOCIALES

3966
REVISTA DE CIENCIAS JURÍDICAS Y SOCIALES. no.1–77, 1922–1953. Santa Fé. Four no. a year (some double numbers)
Issued by: Facultad de Ciencias Jurídicas y Sociales, Universidad Nacional del Litoral. In Spanish.
Indexes: no.1–77, 1922–53, 1v.

3967
REVISTA DE CIÊNCIAS SOCIAIS. v.1– , 2. semestro 1970– . Fortaleza-Ceara. Semi-annual. Issues are combined frequently.
Issued by: Departamento de Ciências Sociais e Filosofia, Universidad Federal do Ceara. In Portuguese; summaries in English and French.
Indexed: Bull. Anal. Pol. Ec. Soc.

3968
REVISTA DE CIENCIAS SOCIALES. v.1– , Mar. 1957– . Rio Piedras. Four no. a year.
Issued by: Colegio de Ciencias Sociales, Universidad de Puerto Rico. In Spanish; summaries in English.
Indexed: Bull. Anal. Pol. Ec. Soc.; Int. Bibl. Soc.; Int. Pol. Sc. Abst.; Soc. Abst.

3969
REVISTA DE CIENCIAS SOCIALES. 1–16, 1962–primer semestro 1980. Valparaíso, Chile. Semi-annual.
Issued by: Facultad de Ciencias Jurídicas, Económicas y Sociales, Universidad de Chile, Sede Valparaíso. In Spanish.
Continues: *Revista de Ciencias Sociales*. Continued by: *Revista de Ciencias Sociales* (Universidad de Valparaíso. Facultad de Ciencias Jurídicas y Sociales, no.17–, Seg. semester 1980–)

3970
REVISTA DE DERECHO, CIENCIAS POLÍTICAS Y SOCIALES. Oct. 1957– . Oruro.
Issued by: Facultad de Ciencias Jurídicas, Políticas y Sociales, Universidad Técnica. In Spanish. Title varies: v.1–3, no.1, Oct. 1957–Jan. 1960. *Revista de Ciencias Jurídicas, Políticas y Sociales*. Vol. for 1960 last available for examination.

3971
REVISTA DE DERECHO INTERNACIONAL. v.1–60 (no.1–122), Mar. 1922–June 1952. La Habana. Quarterly.
Issued by: Instituto Americano de Derecho Internacional. In Spanish. Vols. 1–60 called also no.1–31.
Supersedes: *Revista Americana de Derecho Internacional*.

3972
REVISTA DE DERECHO INTERNACIONAL Y CIENCIAS DIPLOMÁTICAS. v.1– , Apr./Dec. 1949– . Rosario. Annual.
Issued by: Departamento de Relaciones Internacionales "Dr. Mario Antelo", Faculdad de Ciencias Económicas, Comerciales y Políticas (later called Facultad de Ciencia Política y Relaciones Internacionales), Universidad Internacional de Rosario. In Spanish. Volume numbering irregular; v.8–10 omitted. Publication suspended 1955–56.
Indexed: Bull. Anal. Pol. Ec. Soc.; Int. Bibl. Pol. Sc.; Int. Pol. Sc. Abst.

REVISTA DE DERECHO INTERNACIONAL Y COMPARADO DE ARIZONA
See ARIZONA JOURNAL OF INTERNATIONAL AND COMPARATIVE LAW

3973
REVISTA DE DERECHO Y CIENCIAS POLÍTICAS. v.1– , 1936– . Lima. Quarterly.
Issued by: Departamentos Académicos y Ciencias Políticas, Universidad Mayo de San Marcos. In Spanish.
Indexed: Bull. Anal. Pol. Ec. Soc.; Int. Pol. Sc. Abst.

3974
REVISTA DE DERECHO Y CIENCIAS POLÍTICAS Y SOCIALES. 1– , 1965– . Trujillo.
Issued by: Faculdad de Derecho, Universidad Nacional de Trujillo. In Spanish.
Indexed: His. Abst.; Int. Bibl. Soc. Cul. Anth.; Int. Pol. Sc. Abst.

REVISTA DE DESARROLLO ECONÓMICO
See DESARROLLO ECONÓMICO

3975
REVISTA DE DESARROLLO URBANO E REGIONAL. v.1– , Aug./Nov. 1982– . Recife.
Issued by: Centro de Estudos do Desenvolvimento Urbano e Regional. In Portuguese.

3976
REVISTA DE DIREITO CONSTITUCIONAL E CIÊNCIA POLÍTICA. v.1– , July 1983– . Rio de Janeiro, Comanhia Editora Forense. Semi-annual.
Issued by: Instituto de Direito Constitucional. In Portuguese.

REVISTA DE DIREITO PUBLICO E CIÊNCIA POLÍTICA
See REVISTA DE CIÊNCIA POLÍTICA

3977
REVISTA DE ECONOMÍA. 1– , 1945– . Córdoba. Annual.
In Spanish. Issued by: Banco de la Provincia de Córdoba.
Indexed: Bull. Anal. Pol. Ec. Soc.

3978
REVISTA DE ECONOMIA. 1– , 1948– . Lisboa. Quarterly.
In Portuguese; occasionally summaries in English.

3979
REVISTA DE ECONOMÍA. v.1– , 1st quarter 1970– . Buenos Aires. Quarterly.
Issued by: Asociación de Economistas Argentinos. In Spanish.

3980
REVISTA DE ECONOMÍA LATINOAMERICANA. 1– , June 1961– . Caracas. Quarterly.
Issued by: Banco Central de Venezuela. In Spanish.
Indexed: Bull. Anal. Pol. Ec. Soc.

3981
REVISTA DE ECONOMIA POLÍTICA. 1– , Jan./Mar. 1981– . São Paulo, Editora Brasiliense. Quarterly.
Issued by: Centro de Economia Política. In Portuguese.
Indexed: PAISFL.

3982
REVISTA DE ECONOMÍA Y ESTADÍSTICA. 1– , 1939– ; n. ser. v.1– , 1957– . Córdoba. Quarterly (irreg.)
Issued by: Facultad de Ciencias Económicas, Universidad Nacional de Córdoba. In Spanish. Title varies: 1948–56, *Revista de la Facultad de Ciencias Económicas*. Publication suspended in 1947.
Indexed: Bull. Anal. Pol. Ec. Soc.

3983
REVISTA DE EDUCACIÓN. n. ser. v.1– , Jan. 1956– . La Plata. Quarterly.
Issued by: Dirección General de Escuelas, Province de Buenos Aires, 1956–Oct. 1958; Ministerio de Educación de Argentina. Some issues are accompanied by supplements called "Edición Especial" or "Edición Complimentaria". In Spanish.

3984
REVISTA DE ESTUDIOS AGRO-SOCIALES. v.1– , Oct./Dec. 1952– . Madrid. Quarterly.
Issued by: Instituto de Relaciones Agrarias. In Spanish.
Indexed: Int. Bibl. Eco.; Int. Lab. Doc.

3985
REVISTA DE ESTUDIOS DE LA ADMINISTRACIÓN LOCAL Y AUTONÓMICA. v.44 (no.225)– , Jan./Mar. 1985– . Madrid. Quarterly.
Issued by: Instituto de Estudios de Administración Local. In Spanish.
Continues: *Revista de Estudios de la Vida Local* (v.1–44, Jan./Feb. 1942–1984)

3986
REVISTA DE ESTUDIOS INTERNACIONALES. Jan./Mar. 1980– . Madrid. Quarterly.
Issued by: Centro de Estudios Internacionales. In Spanish.
Continues: *Revista de Política Internacional*.
Indexed: ABC POL SCI; Int. Bibl. Pol. Sc.; Int. Pol. Sc. Abst.

3987
REVISTA DE ESTUDIOS INTERNACIONALES. no.1– , Mar./June 1985– . La Paz. Three no. a year.
Issued by: Academia Boliviana de Estudios Internacionales. In Spanish. Other title: *Estudios Internacionales*.

3988
REVISTA DE ESTUDIOS POLÍTICOS. v.1– , Jan. 1941– . Madrid. Quarterly, 1941–42; bimonthly (some double numbers)
Issued by: Instituto de Estudios Políticos, later by Centro de Estudios Constitucionales. In Spanish.
Superseded by: *Revista de Economía Política*.
Indexed: ABC POL SCI; Bull. Anal. Pol. Ec. Soc.; Bull. Sig. Soc. Eth.; His. Abst.; Int. Bibl. Eco.; Int. Bibl. Pol. Sc.; Int. Bibl. Soc. Cul. Anth.; Int. Pol. Sc. Abst.; Peace Res. Abst. J.

3989
REVISTA DE ESTUDIOS POLÍTICOS Y SOCIALES. no.1– , Jan./Mar. 1949–1956. Oruro.
Issued by: Faculdad de Ciencias Jurídicas, Políticas y Sociales, Universidad Técnica. In Spanish.
Superseded by: *Revista de Derecho, Ciencias Políticas y Sociales*.

3990
REVISTA DE ESTUDIOS SOCIALES. no.1– , Jan./Feb. 1971– . Madrid. Three no. a year.
Issued by: Centro de Estudios Sociales del Valle de los Caidos. In Spanish.
Supersedes: Fundación de la Santa Cruz del Valle de los Caidos. Centro de Estudios Sociales. *Boletin*.
Indexed: Bull. Anal. Pol. Ec. Soc.

3991
REVISTA DE ETNOGRAFIE ŞI FOLCLOR. v.1– , 1956– . Bucureşti, Editura Academie Republicii Populare Romine. Quarterly, 1974; bimonthly, 1964–73, 1975–.

Issued by: Instituto de Etnografie şi Folclor. In Romanian; summaries in English and Russian; later also in French. Title varies: 1956–63, *Revista de Folclor*.
Indexed: Abst. Anth.; Bull. Sig. Soc. Eth.; Int. Bibl. Soc. Cul. Anth.

3992
REVISTA DE FINANZAS PÚBLICAS. v.37 (no.329)– , Jan./Mar. 1977– . Rio de Janeiro. Quarterly.
Issued by: Secretaria de Economia y Finanzas, Secretaria Geral, Ministério da Fazenda. In Portuguese. Supplements accompany some numbers.
Continues: *Finanzas Públicas*.
Indexed: PAISFL.

REVISTA DE FOLCLOR
See REVISTA DE ETNOGRAFIE ŞI FOLCLOR

REVISTA DE FOMENTO SOCIAL
See FOMENTO SOCIAL

3993
REVISTA DE HISTÓRIA. v.1– , Jan./Mar. 1950– . São Paulo. Quarterly.
In Portuguese.

3994
REVISTA DE HISTORIA. v.1– , Apr. 1960– . Caracas. Irreg.
Issued by: Centro de Estudios Históricos. In Spanish.
Cumulative index every five years.

3995
REVISTA DE HISTORIA DE AMÉRICA. v.1– , Mar./Dec. 1938– . Mexico, D.F., Imprento Mundial. Semi-annual.
Issued by: Instituto Panamericano de Geografía e Historia. In English, Portuguese, or Spanish.
Indexed: His. Abst.

3996
REVISTA DE HISTORIA DE LAS IDEAS. no.1– , 1959– . Quito, Casa de la Cultura Ecuatoriana. Irreg.
Issued by: Comité de las Ideas en América, Instituto Panamericano de Geografía e Historia. In Portuguese or Spanish.

3997
REVISTA DE HISTÓRIA ECONÔMICA E SOCIAL. no.1– , Jan./June 1978– . Lisboa, Sa da Costa Editora. Semi-annual.
In English, French, or Portuguese.

3998
REVISTA DE INSTITUCIONES EUROPEAS. 1– , Jan./Apr. 1974– . Madrid. Two no. a year, 1974; three no. a year.
Issued by: Instituto de Estudios Politicos, 1974–75; Centro de Estudios Constitucionales. In Spanish.

REVISTA DE LA CEPAL
See United Nations. Economic Commission for Latin America. REVISTA DE LA CEPAL

REVISTA DE LA FACULDAD DE CIENCIAS ECONÓMICAS
See Universidad de Buenos Aires. Faculdad de Ciencias Económicas. REVISTA

REVISTA DE LA FACULDAD DE CIENCIAS ECONÓMICAS
See Universidad Nacional de Colombia. Faculdad de Ciencias Económicas. REVISTA DE LA FACULDAD DE CIENCIAS ECONÓMICAS

REVISTA DE LA FACULDAD DE CIENCIAS ECONÓMICAS, UNIVERSIDAD NACIONAL DE CÓRDOBA
See REVISTA DE ECONOMÍA Y ESTADÍSTICA

REVISTA DE LA FACULDAD DE CIENCIAS ECONÓMICAS, UNIVERSIDAD NACIONAL DE LA PLATA
See ECONOMICA

REVISTA DE LA FACULDAD DE DERECHO Y CIENCIAS SOCIALES
See Universidad de Buenos Aires. Faculdad de Derecho y Ciencias Sociales. REVISTA

REVISTA DE LA FACULDAD DE DERECHO Y CIENCIAS SOCIALES
See Universidad de Buenos Aires. Faculdad de Derecho y Ciencias Sociales. REVISTA DE LA FACULDAD DE DERECHO Y CIENCIAS SOCIALES

REVISTA DE LA FACULDAD DE ECONOMÍA
See ECONOMÍA SALVADORENA

3999
REVISTA DE LA INTEGRACIÓN. no.1– , 1967– . Buenos Aires. Semi-annual.
Issued by: Instituto para la Integración de América Latina, Banco Interamericano del Desarrollo. In Spanish. Subtitle reads: "Económia, política, sociología".

4000
REVISTA DE LA INTEGRACIÓN Y DEL DESARROLLO DE CENTROAMÉRICA. no.20– , July 1976– . Tegucigalpa. Semi-annual.
Issued by: Banco Centroamericano de Integración Económica. In Spanish.

Continues: *Revista de la Integración Centroamericana* (1–19, 1971–76).

REVISTA DE LA PLANIFICACIÓN DEL DESARROLLO
See JOURNAL OF DEVELOPMENT PLANNING

4001
REVISTA DE PEDAGOGIE. v.1– , 1952– . Bucureşti, Editura de Stat Didactica şi Pedagogica. Monthly, 1956–58; bimonthly.
Issued by: Institutul de Sţiinte Pedagogice. In Romanian.

4002
REVISTA DE PLANEACIÓN Y DESARROLLO. v.1– , Jan. 1969– . Bogotá. Quarterly.
Issued by: Biblioteca, Departamento Nacional de Planeación, Ministerio de Planificación y Coordinación. In English or Spanish.
Indexed: Bull. Anal. Pol. Ec. Soc.; Int. Bibl. Eco.; PAISFL; Pop. Ind.

4003
REVISTA DE POLÍTICA COMPARADA. no.1– , 1980– . Madrid. Quarterly.
Issued by: Universidad Internacional Menendez Pelayo y Departamento de Derecho Constitutional y Ciencia Política, Universidad de Alcala de Henares. In cooperation, in Jan. 1980, with Catedra de Teoria del Estado y Derecho Internacional, Universidad Nacional de Educación a Distanza; 1980–81, with Departamento de Teoria del Estado y Derecho Constitucional, Universidad Nacional de Educación. In Spanish.

4004
REVISTA DE POLÍTICA INTERNACIONAL. 1– , Jan./Mar. 1951– . Madrid. Quarterly.
Issued by: Instituto de Estudios Políticos. In Spanish. Title varies: 1951–56, *Cuadernos de Política Internacional*; 1957–61, *Política Internacional.*
Supersedes: *Política Social.* Superseded by: *Revista de Estudios Internacionales.*
Indexed: ABC POL SCI; Bull. Anal. Pol. Ec. Soc.; His. Abst.; Int. Bibl. Eco.; Int. Bibl. Pol. Sc.; Int. Bibl. Soc.; Int. Pol. Sc. Abst.

4005
REVISTA DE POLÍTICA SOCIAL. 1– , 1947– . Madrid. Quarterly.
Issued by: Instituto de Estudios Políticos; later by El Centro de Estudios Constitucionales. In Spanish. Title varies: 1949–60, *Cuadernos de Política Social.*
Supersedes: *Revista de Estudios Políticos. Suplemento de Política Social.*
Indexed: His. Abst.; Int. Bibl. Eco.; Int. Bibl. Pol. Sc.; Int. Bibl. Soc.

REVISTA DE REFERATI ŞI RECENZII; ŞTIINŢE ECONOMICE
See Academia Republicii Socialiste România. Centrul de Informare Ştiinţifica. BULETIN DE INFORMARE ŞTIINŢIFICA. ŞTIINŢE ECONOMICE

4006
REVISTA DE SOCIOLOGÍA. Jan./June 1968– . Medellín. Two no. a year.
Issued by: Instituto de Sociología, Faculdad de Ciencias Sociales, Universidad Pontificia Bolivariana. In Spanish.

REVISTA DEL CENTRO DE RELACIONES INTERNACIONALES
See RELACIONES INTERNACIONALES

4007
REVISTA DEL DESARROLLO INTERNACIONAL. REVUE DU DÉVELOPPEMENT INTERNATIONAL. INTERNATIONAL DEVELOPMENT REVIEW. v.12–19, 1970–1977. Washington, D.C. Quarterly.
Issued by: Society for International Development (Rome). In English; summaries in English, French and Spanish.
Continues: *International Development Review* (v.1–11, 1959–69). Continued by: *Development.*
Indexed: ABC POL SCI; PAIS.

REVISTA DEL I.T.A.T.
See REVISTA MEXICANA DEL TRABAJO

REVISTA DEL INSTITUTO DE ESTUDIOS COOPERATIVOS
See Universidad Nacional de la Plata. Instituto de Estudios Cooperativos. REVISTA

REVISTA DEL INSTITUTO NACIONAL DE ANTROPOLOGÍA
See ANTROPOLOGÍA

REVISTA DEL TRABAJO
See REVISTA MEXICANA DEL TRABAJO

4008
REVISTA ECONOMICA. no.1– , May 17, 1974– . Bucureşti. Weekly.
Issued by: Institutul Central de Cercetări Economice, Consiliul Supreme al Dezooltari Economice şi Sociale. In Romanian. Tables of contents also in English and Russian. Formed by the union of: *Viata Economica* with *Probleme Economice.*
Indexed: Bull. Anal. Pol. Ec. Soc.

4009
REVISTA ESPAÑOLA DE ANTROPOLOGÍA AMERICANA. v.1– , 1952– . Madrid. Annual (irreg.).

Issued by: Departamento de Antropología y Etnología Americana, Faculdad de Geografía e Historia, Universidad de Madrid. In Spanish. Title varies: v.1, 1952, *Trabajos y Conferencias*, issued by: Seminario de Estudios Americanistas, Faculdad de Filsofía y Letras, Universidad Complutense de Madrid.

4010
REVISTA ESPAÑOLA DE DERECHO INTERNACIONAL. v.1– , 1948– . Madrid. Three no. a year.
Indexed: Bull. Anal. Pol. Ec. Soc.; His. Abst.; Ind. For. Leg. Per.; Int. Bibl. Pol. Sc.; Int. Pol. Sc. Abst.

4011
REVISTA ESPAÑOLA DE INVESTIGACIONES SOCIOLÓGICAS. no.1– , Jan./Mar. 1978– . Madrid, Itaca Distribuciones Editoriales. Quarterly. In Spanish. Other title: *REIS*.
Indexed: Int. Bibl. Pol. Sc.; Int. Pol. Sc. Abst.

4012
REVISTA ESPAÑOLA DE LA OPINIÓN PÚBLICA. no.1– , May/Aug. 1965– . Madrid. Quarterly.
Issued by: Instituto de la Opinión Pública, Presidencia del Gobierno. In Spanish.
Indexed: Bull. Anal. Pol. Ec. Soc.; His. Abst.; Int. Bibl. Pol. Sc.; Int. Bibl. Soc.; Int. Pol. Sc. Abst.; Psych. Abst.; Soc. Abst.

4013
REVISTA ESPAÑOLA DE PEDAGOGÍA. v.1– , Jan./Mar. 1943– . Madrid. Quarterly (irreg.).
Issued by: Instituto San Jose de Casalanz; later by Instituto de Pedagogía, Consejo Superior de Investigaciones Científicas. In Spanish.

REVISTA HOLANDESA DE GEOGRAFÍA ECONÓMICA Y SOCIAL
See TIJDSCHRIFT VOOR ECONOMISCHE EN SOCIALE GEOGRAFIE

4014
REVISTA INTERAMERICANA DE CIENCIAS SOCIALES. no.1– , Dec. 1976– . Buenos Aires, Huemul. Four no. a year.
Issued by: United Nations Educational, Scientific and Cultural Organization. Spanish edition of the *International Social Science Journal*, beginning with the latter's issue no.4 of 1976.

4015
REVISTA INTERAMERICANA DE EDUCACIÓN. no.1– , Aug. 1945– . Bogotá. Quarterly.
Issued by: Confederación Interamericana de Educación Católica. In Spanish.

4016
REVISTA INTERAMERICANA DE PLANIFICACIÓN. v.6 (no.21)– , Mar. 1972– . Bogotá. Four no. a year.
Issued by: Sociedad Interamericana de Planificación. In Spanish.
Continues: Interamerican Planning Society. *Revista* (v.1–5, 1967–71).
Indexed: Bull. Anal. Pol. Ec. Soc.

4017
REVISTA INTERAMERICANA DE PSICOLOGÍA. INTER-AMERICAN JOURNAL OF PSYCHOLOGY. v.1–13, Mar. 1967–1979. Los Angeles, Calif., later Austin, Tex. Quarterly.
Issued by: Sociedad Interamericana de Psicología (Interamerican Society of Psychology). In English or Spanish; summaries in English and Spanish.
Continued by: *Interamerican Journal of Psychology*.
Indexed: Psych. Abst.

4018
REVISTA INTERAMERICANA DE SOCIOLOGÍA. 1– , July/Sept. 1966– . Mexico, D.F. Three no. a year.
Issued by: Sociedad Mexicana de Geografía y Estadística in cooperation with the Asociación Mexicana de Sociología and the Asociación Internacional de Sociología de la Unesco. In Spanish. Publication suspended.

REVISTA INTERNACIONAL DE CIENCIAS ADMINISTRATIVAS
See INTERNATIONAL REVIEW OF ADMINISTRATIVE SCIENCES

REVISTA INTERNACIONAL DE CIENCIAS SOCIALES
See INTERNATIONAL SOCIAL SCIENCE JOURNAL

4019
REVISTA INTERNACIONAL DE ESTUDOS AFRICANOS. no.1– , Jan./June 1984– . Lisboa, R.J. Dias. Semi-annual.
In Portuguese; summaries in English. Other title: *International Journal of African Studies*.

REVISTA INTERNACIONAL DE ETNOLOGÍA E DE LINGÜÍSTICA
See ANTHROPOS

REVISTA INTERNACIONAL DE POLÍTICA CRIMINAL
See INTERNATIONAL REVIEW OF CRIMINAL POLICY

4020
REVISTA INTERNACIONAL DE SOCIOLOGÍA. [1]– , Jan./Mar. 1943– . Madrid. Quarterly.

Issued by: Instituto Sancho de Muocada, 1943–44; Instituto Balmes de Sociología. In Spanish. Early volumes include "Boletín Bibliográfico de Revistas".
Indexed: Bull. Anal. Pol. Ec. Soc.; His. Abst.; Bull. Sig. Soc. Eth.; Int. Bibl. Eco.; Int. Bibl. Soc. Cul. Anth.; Int. Pol. Sc. Abst.; Pop. Ind.; Wom. Stu. Abst.

REVISTA INTERNACIONAL DEL TRABAJO
See INTERNATIONAL LABOUR REVIEW

4021
REVISTA JAVERIANA. v.1– , Feb. 1934– . Bogotá. Monthly.
Issued by: Facultad de Ciencias Económicas y Jurídicas, Universidad Javeriana. In Spanish.
Indexed: Int. Bibl. Eco.; Int. Bibl. Soc. Cul. Anth.

4022
REVISTA LATINOAMERICANA DE ADMINISTRACIÓN PÚBLICA. v.1– , 1972– . Mexico, D.F., Instituto Nacional de Administración Pública.
Organ of: Asociación Latinoamericana de Administración Pública. In Spanish.

4023
REVISTA LATINOAMERICANA DE ADMINISTRACIÓN PÚBLICA. 1– , 1974– . Bogotá. Quarterly.
Issued by: Asociación Latinoamericana de Administración Pública (ALP) and Escuela Superior de Administración Pública (ESAP). In Spanish.

4024
REVISTA LATINOAMERICANA DE CIENCIA POLÍTICA. v.1– , Apr. 1970– . Santiago, Chile. Three no. a year.
Issued by: Escuela Latinoamericana de Ciencia Política y Administración Pública. In Spanish.
Indexed: Bull. Anal. Pol. Ec. Soc.; Int. Bibl. Pol. Sc.; Int. Bibl. Soc. Cul. Anth.; Int. Lab. Doc.; Int. Pol. Sc. Abst.; Soc. Abst.

4025
REVISTA LATINOAMERICANA DE ESTUDIOS EDUCATIVOS. v.9– , 1979– . Mexico, D.F. Quarterly.
Issued by: Centro de Estudios Educativos. In Spanish.
Continues: Centro de Estudios Educativos. *Revista*.

4026
REVISTA LATINOAMERICANA DE PSICOLOGÍA. v.1– , 1969– . Bogotá. Three no. a year.
In Spanish.
Indexed: Psych. Abst.

4027
REVISTA LATINOAMERICANA DE SOCIOLOGÍA. v.1–8, no.2, 1965–1975. Buenos Aires. Three no. a year.
Issued by: Instituto Torcuato di Tella, Centro Investigaciones Sociales. In Spanish.
Indexed: Bull. Sig. Soc. Eth.; Int. Bibl. Soc.; Int. Lab. Doc.; Int. Pol. Sc. Abst.; Soc. Abst.

REVISTA MARXISTA EUROPEA
See EUROPEAN MARXIST REVIEW

4028
REVISTA MEXICANA DE CIENCIA POLÍTICA. v.1–13, July/Sept. 1955–1966; n. epoca, v.14–21 (no.50–80), 1967–1975. Mexico, D.F. Quarterly.
Issued by: Facultad de Ciencias Políticas y Sociales, Universidad Nacional Autónoma de México. In Spanish. Title varies: v.1–13 (no.1–50), 1955–Oct./Dec. 1961, *Ciencias Políticas y Sociales*.
Continued by: *Revista de Ciencias Políticas y Sociales*.
Indexes: No.1–80, 1955–75, 1v.
Indexed: ABC POL SCI; Bull. Sig. Soc. Eth.; Int. Lab. Doc.; Int. Pol. Sc. Abst.

4029
REVISTA MEXICANA DE CIENCIAS POLÍTICAS Y SOCIALES. v.21 (no.81)– , July/Sept. 1975– . Mexico, D.F. Quarterly.
Issued by: Facultad de Ciencias Políticas y Sociales, Universidad Nacional Autónoma de México. In Spanish.
Continues: *Revista Mexicana de Ciencia Política*.
Indexed: ABC POL SCI; Bull. Anal. Pol. Ec. Soc.

4030
REVISTA MEXICANA DE LA ANÁLISIS DE LA CONDUCTA. 1– , 1975– . Mexico, D.F., Editorial Trilica. Semi-annual.
Issued by: Universidad Nacional Autónoma de México. In English or Spanish.

4031
REVISTA MEXICANA DE POLÍTICA EXTERIOR. 1– , Oct./Dec. 1983– . Mexico, D.F., IMRED, 1984– .
Issued by: Instituto Matias Romero de Estudios Diplomáticos. In Spanish.

4032
REVISTA MEXICANA DE SOCIOLOGÍA. v.1– , Mar./Apr. 1939– . Mexico, D.F. Bimonthly, 1939; quarterly.
Issued by: Instituto de Investigaciones Sociales, Universidad Nacional Autónoma de México. In English or Spanish.

Indexed: Bull. Anal. Pol. Ec. Soc.; Bull. Sig. Soc. Eth.; Int. Bibl. Pol. Sc.; Int. Bibl. Soc.; Int. Lab. Doc.; Int. Pol. Sc. Abst.; Psych. Abst.; Soc. Abst.

4033
REVISTA MEXICANA DEL TRABAJO. v.1–33, Aug. 1937–June/July/Aug. 1948; v.1–6, Sept. 1948–May/June 1951; 4. epoca, v.1–May/Nov. 1953; 5. epoca, v.1– , 1954–1964; 6 epoca, v.1– , 1965– . Mexico, D.F. Quarterly.
Issued by: Secretaría del Trabajo y Prevision Social. In Spanish. Title varies: 1937–40, 1947–51, *Revista del Trabajo*. Other title: *Boletín de I.T.A.T.*
Indexed: Int. Bibl. Soc.; Int. Lab. Doc.

4034
REVISTA PARAGUAYA DE SOCIOLOGÍA. v.1– , Sept./Dec. 1964– . Asunción. Three no. a year (some combined numbers)
Issued by: Centro Paraguayo de Estudios Sociológicos. In Spanish.
Indexed: Bull. Sig. Soc. Eth.; Int. Bibl. Soc.; Int. Lab. Doc.; LLBA; Psych. Abst.; Soc. Abst.

4035
REVISTA PERUANA DE DERECHO INTERNACIONAL. 1– , 1941– . Lima. Two no. a year.
Issued by: Sociedad Peruana de Derecho Internacional. In Spanish.
Indexed: Bull. Anal. Pol. Ec. Soc.; Ind. For. Leg. Per.; Int. Bibl. Soc. Cul. Anth.; Int. Pol. Sc. Abst.; PAISFL.

4036
REVISTA/REVIEW INTERAMERICANA. v.6– , spring 1976– . Hato Rey, Interamerican University Press. Quarterly.
In English or Spanish.
Continues: *Revista Interamericana. Interamerican Review.*
Indexed: Int. Bibl. Soc. Cul. Anth.

4037
REVISTA ROMÂNĂ DE STUDII INTERNATIONALE. 1967– . Bucureşti. Quarterly.
Issued by: Asociatia de Drept International şi Relatii Internationăle din Republica Socialista România. In Romanian. Issued also in French edition: *Revue Roumaine d'Études Internationales.*

4038
REVISTA URUGUAYA DE CIENCIAS SOCIALES. v.1–3, Apr./June 1972–1974. Montevideo, Libreria Antiquaria Americana.
Organ of: Centro de Investigaciones Sociales de Montevideo. In Spanish.

REVISTA URUGUAYA DE CIENCIAS SOCIALES
See Centro Latinoamericano de Economía Humana. CUADERNOS

4039
REVISTA URUGUAYA DE DERECHO CONSTITUCIONAL Y POLÍTICA. v.1– , June/July 1984– . Montevideo. Bimonthly.
In Spanish.

4040
REVISTA URUGUAYA DE DERECHO INTERNACIONAL. v.1– , 1972– . Montevideo.
Issued by: Asociación Uruguaya de Derecho Internacional (Filial de la International Law Association). In Spanish.

4041
REVISTA URUGUAYA DE ESTUDIOS INTERNACIONALES. v.1– , July/Aug./Sept. 1982– . Montevideo. Quarterly.
Issued by: Instituto de Estudios Internacionales. In Spanish; summaries in English.

4042
REVISTA VENEZOLANA DE SOCIOLOGÍA Y ANTROPOLOGÍA. 1– , 1960– . Caracas.
In Spanish.
Indexed: Soc. Abst.

4043
REVOLUTIONARY WORLD. v.1– , 1973– . Amsterdam, B.R. Grüner Pub. Co. Five no. a year.
Indexed: Bull. Anal. Pol. Ec. Soc.; Int. Bibl. Soc. Cul. Anth.; Int. Pol. Sc. Abst.

REVOLUT͡SII͡A PRAVA
See SOVETSKOE GOSUDARSTVO

REVUE
See Action Populaire. REVUE

REVUE
See ÉTUDES & EXPANSION

REVUE
See REVUE DE DROIT INTERNATIONAL ET DE DROIT COMPARÉE

REVUE
See Université Libre de Bruxelles. Institut de Sociologie. REVUE

4044
LA REVUE ADMINISTRATIVE. 1– , Jan./Feb. 1948– . Paris. Bimonthly.
In French.

Indexed: ABC POL SCI; Bull. Anal. Pol. Ec. Soc.; Int. Bibl. Eco.; Int. Bibl. Pol. Sc.; Int. Bibl. Soc.; Int. Pol. Sc. Abst.

4045
REVUE AFRICAINE DE DÉVELOPPEMENT. v.1– , 1974– . Kinshasa, Presses Universitaires du Zaïre.
Issued by: Université Nationale du Zaïre. In English or French.

4046
REVUE ALGÉRIENNE DES SCIENCES JURIDIQUES, ÉCONOMIQUES ET POLITIQUES. [v.1]– , Jan. 1974– . Alger. Quarterly.
Issued by: Faculté de Droit et des Sciences Économiques, Université d'Alger; Institut de Droit et des Sciences Administratives. In French.
Indexed: Ind. For. Leg. Per.; Int. Lab. Doc.; Int. Pol. Sc. Abst.

REVUE ANNUELLE DU SOCIALISME INTERNATIONAL
See ALMANACH DE LA QUESTION SOCIALE

4047
REVUE ANTHROPOLOGIQUE. v.1– , 1891–1942; n. ser. 1955– . Paris, F. Alcan. Annual.
Issued by: 1921–40, Institut International d'Anthropologie; École d'Anthropologie de Paris. In French. Title varies: 1891–1910, *Revue d'École d'Anthropologie de Paris.*
Continued by: *La Nouvelle Revue Anthropologique.*
Indexes: Vols. 1–10, 1891–1900, 1v.; v.11–20, 1901–10, 1v.

4048
REVUE ARCHÉOLOGIQUE. v.1–16, Apr. 1844–Sept. 1859; n. ser. v.1–44, Jan. 1860–Dec. 1882; 3. ser. v.1– , Jan. 1883– . Paris. Two no. a year.
In French.
Indexes: Table décennale, 1860–69.
Indexed: SSCI.

4049
REVUE BELGE DE DROIT INTERNATIONAL. BELGIAN REVIEW OF INTERNATIONAL LAW. BELGISCH TIJDSCHRIFT VOOR INTERNATIONALE RECHT. v.1– , 1965– . Bruxelles, Éditions de l'Institut de Sociologie. Semi-annual.
Issued by: Centre de Droit International, Université de Louvain, and Centre de Droit International et de Sociologie Appliquée au Droit International de l'Université Libre de Bruxelles. In English, Flemish, or French.
Supersedes: Revue de Droit International et de Législation Comparée.
Indexed: Bull. Anal. Pol. Ec. Soc.; Ind. For. Leg. Per.; Int. Bibl. Pol. Sc.; Int. Bibl. Soc. Cul. Anth.; Int. Lab. Doc.; Int. Pol. Sc. Abst.; PAISFL.

4050
REVUE BELGE DE LA SÉCURITÉ SOCIALE. v.1– , Jan. 1959– . Bruxelles. Monthly (irreg.)
Issued by: Ministère de Prévoyance Sociale. In French. Includes legislative acts.
Supersedes a publication of the same title and *Revue des Allocations Familiales* issued by the Office National de Coordination des Allocations Familiales.
Indexed: Int. Bibl. Eco.

REVUE BULGARE D'HISTOIRE
See BULGARIAN HISTORICAL REVIEW

REVUE CANADIENNE D'ÉCONOMIE
See THE CANADIAN JOURNAL OF ECONOMICS

REVUE CANADIENNE D'ÉCONOMIE RURALE
See CANADIAN JOURNAL OF AGRICULTURAL ECONOMICS

4051
REVUE CANADIENNE D'ÉTUDES DU DÉVELOPPEMENT. CANADIAN JOURNAL OF DEVELOPMENT STUDIES. v.1– , May 1980– . Ottawa, Éditions de l'Université d'Ottawa. Semi-annual.
In English or French.
Indexed: Int. Bibl. Eco.; Int. Bibl. Soc. Cul. Anth.; Int. Pol. Sc. Abst.

REVUE CANADIENNE D'URBANISME
See COMMUNITY PLANNING REVIEW

REVUE CANADIENNE DE CRIMINOLOGIE
See CANADIAN JOURNAL OF CRIMINOLOGY

REVUE CANADIENNE DE CRIMINOLOGIE
See CANADIAN JOURNAL OF CRIMINOLOGY AND CORRECTIONS

REVUE CANADIENNE DE L'ÉDUCATION
See CANADIAN JOURNAL OF EDUCATION

REVUE CANADIENNE DE SCIENCE POLITIQUE
See CANADIAN JOURNAL OF POLITICAL SCIENCE

REVUE CANADIENNE DE SOCIOLOGIE ET D'ANTHROPOLOGIE
See CANADIAN JOURNAL OF SOCIOLOGY AND ANTHROPOLOGY

REVUE CANADIENNE DE THÉORIE POLITIQUE ET SOCIALE
See CANADIAN JOURNAL OF POLITICAL AND SOCIAL THEORY

REVUE CANADIENNE DES ÉTUDES AFRICAINES
See CANADIAN JOURNAL OF AFRICAN STUDIES

REVUE CANADIENNE DES ÉTUDES LATINOAMERICAINES ET CARIBES
See CANADIAN JOURNAL OF LATIN AMERICAN AND CARIBBEAN STUDIES

REVUE CANADIENNE DES SCIENCES DU COMPORTEMENT
See CANADIAN JOURNAL OF BEHAVIOURAL SCIENCES

REVUE CANADIENNE DES SCIENCES RÉGIONALES
See CANADIAN JOURNAL OF REGIONAL STUDIES

REVUE CANADIENNE DES SLAVISTES
See CANADIAN SLAVONIC PAPERS

REVUE CANADIENNE SUR LE NATIONALISME
See CANADIAN REVIEW OF STUDIES IN NATIONALISM

4052: not used

4053
REVUE COLONIALE INTERNATIONALE. 1–5, July 1885–1887. Amsterdam.
Issued by: Association Coloniale Nederlandaise. In English, French, or German.

REVUE D'ALLEMAGNE
See REVUE ALLEMAGNE ET DES PAYS DE LANGUE ALLEMAGNE

4054
REVUE D'ALLEMAGNE ET DES PAYS DE LANGUE ALLEMAGNE. v.1– , 1969– . Strasbourg, later Paris, A. Colin. Quarterly.
Issued by: Société d'Études Allemandes, and Centre d'Études Germaniques, Université des Sciences Juridiques, Politiques et Sociales de Strasbourg. In French or German. Under the auspices of the Centre National de la Recherche Scientifique. Some numbers have distinctive titles. Other title: *Review d'Allemagne*.
Indexed: Bull. Anal. Pol. Ec. Soc.; Bull. Sig. Soc. Eth.; His. Abst.; Int. Bibl. Pol. Sc.; Int. Pol. Sc. Abst.

4055
REVUE D'ANTHROPOLOGIE. 1–6, 1872–1877; ser. 2, v.1–8, 1878–1885; ser.3, v.1–4, 1886–1888. Paris.
In French. Merged with: *Matériaux pour l'Histoire de l'Homme* and *Revue d'Ethnographie* to form: *L'Anthropologie*.
Indexes: 1872–89, in ser. 3, v.4.

REVUE D'ARCHÉOLOGIE ET D'HISTOIRE SYRIENNES
See ANNALES ARCHÉOLOGIQUES ARABES SYRIENNES

4056
REVUE D'ASSYROLOGIE ET D'ARCHÉOLOGIE ORIENTALE. v.1– , 1884– . Paris, Two no. a year. Presses Universitaires de France.
In French.

REVUE D'ÉCOLE D'ANTHROPOLOGIE DE PARIS
See REVUE ANTHROPOLOGIQUE

REVUE D'ÉCONOMIE ET DE SCIENCE POLITIQUE
See CANADIAN JOURNAL OF ECONOMICS AND POLITICAL SCIENCE

4057
REVUE D'ÉCONOMIE POLITIQUE. 1– , 1887– . Paris, Éditions Sirey. Monthly, 1887–1910; bimonthly.
In French. Suspended in May 1940, v.54, no.3; v.54, no.4/6 covers July 1940–Dec. 1944.
Indexes: Vols. 1–20, 1887–1906, 1v.
Indexed: Bull. Anal. Pol. Ec. Soc.; Bull. Sig. Soc. Eth.; His. Abst.; Int. Bibl. Eco.; Int. Lab. Doc.; PAISFL.

4058
REVUE D'ÉCONOMIE RÉGIONALE ET URBAINE. 1– , 1978– . Paris, Institut d'Économie Régionale. Five no. a year.
Issued by: Associations des Directeurs d'Instituts et de Centres Universitaires d'Études Économiques Régionales (ADICUEER). In French; summaries in English and French.
Indexed: Bull. Anal. Pol. Ec. Soc.; Int. Bibl. Eco.; PAISFL; Pop. Ind.

REVUE D'ÉCONOMIE SOCIALE
See LES ÉTUDES SOCIALES

4059
REVUE D'ETHNOGRAPHIE. v.1–8, 1882–1889. Paris, Ernst Leroux. Annual.

Published under the auspices of the Ministère de l'Instruction Publique et des Beaux-Arts. In French.
In French. Merged with: *Revue d'Anthropologie* to form: *Anthropologie*.

4060
REVUE D'ETHNOGRAPHIE ET DE SOCIOLOGIE. v.1–5, 1910–Mar. 1914. Paris.
Issued by: Institut Ethnographique International de Paris. In French.
Supersedes: *Revue d'Études Ethnographiques et Sociologiques*.

REVUE D'ETHNOLOGIE
See ETNOLOSKI PREGLED

REVUE D'ÉTUDES CANADIENNES
See JOURNAL OF CANADIAN STUDIES

4061
REVUE D'ÉTUDES COMPARATIVES EST-OUEST. v.6– , Mar. 1975– . Paris, Éditions du Centre Nationale de la Recherche Scientifique. In French; summaries in English. Subtitle reads: "Économie, planification, organisation".
Continues: *Revue de l'Est* (1969–74)
Indexed: ABC POL SCI; Bull. Anal. Pol. Ec. Soc.; Int. Bibl. Eco.; Int. Bibl. Pol. Sc.; Int. Pol. Sc. Abst.

4062
REVUE D'ÉTUDES SUD-EST EUROPÉENNES. v.1– , 1963– . Bucharest. Four no. a year.
Issued by: Institutul de Studii Sud-Est Européennes, Academia Republicii Socialiste România. In English, French, German, Italian, or Russian.

REVUE D'HISTOIRE ANCIENNE
See VESTNIK DREVNEĬ ISTORII

4063
REVUE D'HISTOIRE COMPARÉE. v.1–26, 1923–1948. Paris, Les Presses Universitaires de France. Two no. a year.
Published under the auspices of the Institut Hongrois de Paris, Hungarian Academy of Sciences, 1943–45. In French. Title varies: v.1–15, 1923–37, *Revue des Etudes Hongroises*.

4064
REVUE D'HISTOIRE D'AMÉRIQUE FRANÇAISE. 1947– . Montréal. Quarterly.
Issued by: Institut d'Histoire d'Amérique Française. In French.
Indexes: Vols. 1–10, 1947–57, in v.10, no.4; v.21–30, June 1967–Mar. 1977, with no. for Mar. 1977.
Indexed: His. Abst.

4065
REVUE D'HISTOIRE DE LA PHILOSOPHIE ET D'HISTOIRE GÉNÉRALE DE LA CIVILISATION. n. ser. no.1–44, Jan. 15, 1933–Oct./Dec. 1946. Paris. Quarterly (irreg.)
Issued by: Faculté des Lettres, Université de Lille. In French.
Continues: *Revue d'Histoire de Philosophie*. Continued by: *Revue des Sciences Humaines*.

REVUE D'HISTOIRE DES COLONIES
See REVUE FRANÇAISE D'HISTOIRE D'OUTRE-MER

REVUE D'HISTOIRE DES COLONIES FRANÇAISES
See REVUE FRANÇAISE D'HISTOIRE D'OUTRE-MER

REVUE D'HISTOIRE DES DOCTRINES ÉCONOMIQUES ET SOCIALES
See REVUE D'HISTOIRE ÉCONOMIQUE ET SOCIALE

4066
REVUE D'HISTOIRE DIPLOMATIQUE. 1– , 1887– . Paris, Éditions A. Pedone. Quarterly.
Issued by: Société d'Histoire Générale et Histoire Diplomatique (called 1887–1923 Société d'Histoire Diplomatique). In French.
Indexes: Table décennale, Vols. 1–10, 1887–96, in v.10; v.1–77, 1887–1963, 1v.

4067
REVUE D'HISTOIRE ÉCONOMIQUE ET SOCIALE. v.1–6, 1908–1913. Paris, Marcel Rivière. Quarterly.
Issued by: Centre Nationale de la Recherche Scientifique. In French. Each no. includes "Bibliographie". Other title: *RHDES*. Title varies: v.1–5, *Revue d'Histoire des Doctrines Économiques et Sociales*.
Indexed: Bull. Anal. Pol. Ec. Soc.; Bull. Sig. Soc. Eth.; His. Abst.; Int. Bibl. Soc. Cul. Anth.

4068
REVUE D'HISTOIRE ET DU CIVILISATION DU MAGHREB. 1– , 1965– . Algiers. Three or four no. a year.
Issued by: Faculté des Lettres et Sciences Humaines, Université d'Alger. In Arabic or French.
Indexed: Int. Bibl. Soc. Cul. Anth.

4069
REVUE D'HISTOIRE MODERNE ET CONTEMPORAINE. v.1– , 1954– . Paris, Presses Universitaires de France. Quarterly.
Issued by: Société d'Histoire Moderne. In French.

Supersedes: *Revue d'Histoire Moderne* (v.1–15, 1926–40)
Indexed: Bull. Anal. Pol. Ec. Soc.; His. Abst.; Peace Res. Abst. J.

REVUE D'HISTOIRE POLITIQUE ET CONSTITUTIONELLE
See POLITIQUE

REVUE D'HISTOIRE URBAINE
See URBAN HISTORY REVIEW

REVUE DE CORÉE
See KOREA JOURNAL

REVUE DE DROIT COMPARÉ
See HIKAKU HO ZASSHI

4070
REVUE DE DROIT DE L'HOMME. HUMAN RIGHTS JOURNAL. 1968– . Strasbourg, Éditions A. Pedone. Quarterly.
Issued by: Institut International des Droits de l'Homme. In French.
Indexed: Bull. Anal. Pol. Ec. Soc.; Ind. For. Leg. Per.; Int. Pol. Sc. Abst.

4071
REVUE DE DROIT INTERNATIONAL DE SCIENCES DIPLOMATIQUES ET POLITIQUES. 1– , July 1923– . Genève, A. Sotticher. Quarterly.
Issued by: International Law Association. In English or French. Other title: *International Law Review* (v.4, no.2/3–). Includes section "Bulletin Bibliographique". Title varies: v.1–4, no.2/3, 1923–Apr./Sept. 1926, *Revue de Droit International des Sciences Diplomatiques, Politiques et Sociales*.

REVUE DE DROIT INTERNATIONAL DES SCIENCES DIPLOMATIQUES, POLITIQUES ET SOCIALES
See REVUE DE DROIT INTERNATIONAL DE SCIENCES DIPLOMATIQUES ET POLITIQUES

4072
REVUE DE DROIT INTERNATIONAL ET DE DROIT COMPARÉ. v.1– , 1908– . Bruxelles. Quarterly.
Issued by: Institut Belge de Droit Comparé (1908–1914, called Institut de Droit Comparé). In French. Publication suspended: 1915–21 and 1940–48. Title varies: 1908–14, 1925–39, *Revue*.
Indexed: Bull. Anal. Pol. Ec. Soc.; Ind. For. Leg. Per.; Int. Bibl. Pol. Sc.

4073
REVUE DE DROIT INTERNATIONAL ET DE LÉGISLATION COMPARÉE. v.1–30, 1869–1898; 2. ser. v.1–16, 1899–1914; 3. ser. v.1–20, 1920–1939?. Bruxelles. Quarterly, 1869–77; six no. a year (irreg.), 1878–1928; four no. a year.
Issued by: Institute of International Law. In French.
Indexes: Vols. 1–25, 1869–93, 1v.; v.26–ser. 2, v.16, 1894–1914, 1v.

4074
REVUE DE L'EST. v.1–5, July 1970–1974. Paris, Éditions de Centre National de Recherche Scientifique. In English or French. Subtitle reads: "Économie et techniques de planification, droit et sciences sociales".
Continued by: *Revue d'Études Comparatives Est-Ouest*, v.6–, March. 1975–.
Indexed: Bull. Sig. Soc. Eth.; Int. Lab. Doc.; Int. Pol. Sc. Abst.

REVUE DE L'HISTOIRE DES COLONIES FRANÇAISES
See REVUE FRANÇAISE D'HISTOIRE D'OUTRE-MER

4075
LA REVUE DE L'OCCIDENT MUSULMAN ET DE LA MÉDITERRANÉE. v.1– , 1946– . Aix-en-Provence. Semi-annual.
Issued by: Association pour l'Étude des Sciences Humaines en Afrique du Nord, Institut de Recherches Méditerranées. In French. Title varies: 1946–61, *Revue de la Méditerranée*.
Indexed: Bull. Anal. Pol. Ec. Soc.; Bull. Sig. Soc. Eth.; Int. Bibl. Pol. Sc.; Int. Bibl. Soc. Cul. Anth.; Int. Pol. Sc. Abst.

REVUE DE LA FACULTÉ DES SCIENCES ÉCONOMIQUES DE L'UNIVERSITÉ D'ISTANBUL
See Istanbul Universitesi. Iktisad Fakultesi Memuasi. REVUE DE LA FACULTÉ DES SCIENCES ÉCONOMIQUES DE L'UNIVERSITÉ D'ISTANBUL

REVUE DE LA MÉDITERRANÉE
See LA REVUE DE L'OCCIDENT MUSULMAN ET DE LA MÉDITERRANÉE

REVUE DE LA POLITIQUE D'ENVIRONNEMENT
See ZEITSCHRIFT FÜR UMWELTPOLITIK

REVUE DE LINGUISTIQUE ET D'ETHNOLOGIE FINNOIS
See STUDIA FENNICA

REVUE DE PLANIFICATION DE L'ÉDUCATION DANS LES PAYS ARABES
See SAHĪFAT-TAKHITIT ATTARAWI FI EL BILAD EL-ARABIYAT

REVUE DE PSYCHOLOGIE DES PEUPLES
See ETHNOPSYCHOLOGIE

4076
REVUE DE PSYCHOLOGIE ET DES SCIENCES DE L'ÉDUCATION. v.1– , 1965– . Louvain. Quarterly.
Organ of: Groupe de Louvain. In French; summaries in Dutch, English and French.

REVUE DE SOCIOLOGIE
See RIVISTA DI SOCIOLOGIA

REVUE DE SOCIOLOGIE
See SOCIOLOGICKÁ REVUE

REVUE DE SOCIOLOGIE
See SOSYOLOJI DERGISI

4077
REVUE DES ÉTUDES COOPÉRATIVES. v.1–20 (no.1–79), Oct. 1921–July/Sept. 1947; [v.]22 (no.80)– , Apr./June 1950– . Paris. Quarterly.
Issued by: Institut Français de la Coopération. In French. Publication suspended between Jan./Mar. 1940 and July 1946. Merged with: *L'Année Politique, Économique et Coopérative* and *Res Publica* to form: *L'Année Politique, Économique et Coopérative*. The publication was brought to the present title with the number for Apr./June 1950.
Indexed: Bull. Anal. Pol. Ec. Soc.; Bull. Sig. Soc. Eth.; Int. Bibl. Soc. Cul. Anth.; Int. Lab. Doc.

REVUE DES ÉTUDES HONGROISES
See REVUE D'HISTOIRE COMPARÉE

4078
REVUE DES ÉTUDES JUIVES. no.1– , 1880– . Paris. Quarterly.
Issued by: Société des Études Juives. Supported by: Centre National de la Recherche Scientifique and Le Fonds Social Juif Unifié. In French. Some numbers are thematic; some have subtitle: "Historia Judaica".
Indexes: Vols. 1–25, 1880–1892, with v.25.

4079: not used

REVUE DES ÉTUDES SUD-EST EUROPÉENNES
See REVUE D'ÉTUDES SUD-EST EUROPÉENES

4080
REVUE DES PAYS DE L'EST. v.1– , 1960– . Bruxelles, Éditions de l'Université Libre de Bruxelles. Semi-annual.
Issued jointly by: Centre National pour l'Étude des Etats de l'Est, and Centre d'Étude des Pays de l'Est. In French. Title varies: v.1–3, 1960–63, *Pays Communistes*; v.4–8, 1963–67, *Bulletin du Centre d'Étude des Pays de l'Est*; v.9–12, 1968–71, *Revue du Centre d'Étude des Pays de l'Est et du Centre National pour l'Étude des États de l'Est*.
Indexed: Bull. Anal. Pol. Ec. Soc.; Int. Bibl. Eco.; Int. Bibl. Pol. Sc.; Int. Pol. Sc. Abst.; PAISFL; Soc. Abst.

4081
REVUE DES SCIENCES SOCIALES. v.1–7, 1956–1964. Bucharest.
Issued by: Academia de la Republica Popolare Romine. In English, French, German, or Russian.
Supersedes: *Revue des Sciences Sociales*. Continued by: *Revue Roumaine des Sciences Sociales* with the following subseries titles: *Série de Philosphie et Logique*; *Série de Psychologie*; *Série de Sociologie*; *Série des Sciences Économiques*; *Série des Sciences Juridiques*; and the contents on international studies to be continued by: *Revue Roumaine d'Études Internationales*.
Indexed: His. Abst.

REVUE DES TRAVAUX [ET COMPTES-RENDU DE SES SÉANCES] DE L'ACADÉMIE DES SCIENCES MORALES ET POLITIQUES
See Académie des Sciences Morales et Politiques. REVUE DES TRAVAUX ET COMPTES RENDUS DE SES SÉANCES

4082
LA REVUE DIPLOMATIQUE ET COLONIALE; POLITIQUE, LITTÉRATURE, FINANCIÈRE. v.1–62, 1878–June/Aug. 1939. Paris. Weekly (irreg.), 1878–Feb. 1913; two no. a month (irreg.)
In French. Title varies: 1878–1934, *La Revue Diplomatique, Politique, Économique, Littérature, Financière*.

LA REVUE DIPLOMATIQUE, POLITIQUE, ÉCONOMIQUE, LITTÉRATURE, FINANCIÈRE
See LA REVUE DIPLOMATIQUE ET COLONIALE; POLITIQUE, LITTÉRATURE, FINANCIÈRE

REVUE DU CENTRE D'ÉTUDE DES PAYS DE L'EST ET DU CENTRE NATIONAL POUR L'ÉTUDE DES ÉTATS DE L'EST
See REVUE DES PAYS DE L'EST

REVUE DU CHAMBRE ET D'INDUSTRIE POUR LA MARCHÉ COMMUN EURAFRICAIN
See EURAFRICA ET TRIBUNE DU TIERS-MONDE

REVUE DU DÉVELOPPEMENT
See DÉVELOPPEMENT

REVUE DU DÉVELOPPEMENT INTERNATIONAL
See REVISTA DEL DESARROLLO INTERNACIONAL

4083
REVUE DU DROIT PUBLIC ET DE LA SCIENCE POLITIQUE EN FRANCE ET À L'ÉTRANGER. v.1– , 1894– . Paris, Librairie Générale du Droit et de Jurisprudence. Quarterly.
Published in cooperation with the Centre National de la Recherche Scientifique. In French.
Indexes: Vols. 67–74, 1951–58, with v.74.
Indexed: Bull. Anal. Pol. Ec. Soc.; Bull. Sig. Soc. Eth.; Ind For. Leg. Per.; Int. Bibl. Eco.; Int. Bibl. Pol. Sc.; Int. Bibl. Soc.; Int. Lab. Doc.; Int. Pol. Sc. Abst.; PAISFL.

REVUE DU SUD-EST ASIATIQUE
See REVUE DU SUD-EST ASIATIQUE ET DE L'EXTRÊME-ORIENT

4084
REVUE DU SUD-EST ASIATIQUE ET DE L'EXTRÊME-ORIENT. JOURNAL OF SOUTHEAST ASIA AND THE FAR EAST. v.1– , 1961–1970. Bruxelles, Éditions de l'Institut de Sociologie. Four no. a year, 1961–65; two no. a year.
Issued by: Institut de Sociologie, Université Libre de Bruxelles; later Conseil du Sud-Est Asiatique et de l'Extrême-Orient. In French. Title varies: 1961–67, *Revue du Sud-Est Asiatique. Journal of Southeast Asia.*
Superseded by: *Asia Quarterly; A Journal from Europe.*
Indexed: Int. Bibl. Soc.; Soc. Abst.

4085
REVUE DU TRAVAIL. 1– , 1896– . Bruxelles. Monthly.
Issued by: Service d'Études du Ministère de l'Emploi et du Travail. In French. The edition in Flemish is called *Arbeidsblad.*
Indexed: Bull. Anal. Pol. Ec. Soc.; Bull. Sig. Soc. Eth.; Int. Bibl. Eco.; Int. Lab. Doc.; PAISFL.

4086
REVUE ÉCONOMIQUE. v.1– , May 1950– . Paris, Presses de la Fondation Nationale des Sciences Politiques. Five no. a year, 1950–51; bimonthly.
Edited jointly by: Centre National de la Recherche Statistique, École des Hautes Études Sociales, and Fondation National des Sciences Politiques. Some numbers are thematic.
Cumulative index every ten years.
Indexed: Int. Bibl. Eco.; PAIS; PAISFL.

4087
REVUE ÉCONOMIQUE ET SOCIALE. v.1– , 1943– . Lausanne. Quarterly.
Organ of: Bâtiment des Facultés des Sciences Humaines (BFSH), Société des Études Économiques et Sociales. In French.
Indexed: Bull. Anal. Pol. Ec. Soc.; Int. Bibl. Eco.; Int. Bibl. Pol. Sc.; Int. Bibl. Soc.; Int. Lab. Doc.; Int. Pol. Sc. Abst.; PAISFL.

4088
REVUE ÉCONOMIQUE FRANÇAISE. v.1– , Oct. 1878– . Paris. Quarterly.
Issued by: Société de Géographie Commerciale (called earlier Société de Géographie Commerciale et d'Études Coloniales). In French. Publication suspended Jan./Mar. 1940–Oct./Dec. 1948. Vol.63– called also "quatrième série". Title varies: 1878–1920, Société de Géographie Commerciale de Paris. *Bulletin.*
Indexed: Bull. Anal. Pol. Ec. Soc.; PAISFL.

4089
REVUE ÉCONOMIQUE INTERNATIONALE. v.1–32, Mar. 1904–Mar. 1940. Bruxelles. Monthly.
Published by: Institut Économique International, 1935–40. In French. Publication suspended July 1919–Apr. 1920.
Indexes: Vols. 1–10, 1904–13, 1v.; v.12–16, 1920–24, iv.

4090
REVUE ÉGYPTIENNE DE DROIT INTERNATIONAL. v.1– , 1945– . Cairo. Annual.
Issued by: Egyptian Society of International Law. In Arabic, English, or French. There is also an English edition called: *Egyptian Review of International Law.* Other title: *al-Majallah al-Miṣrīyah li i-qānūm al-duwalī.*
Indexes: Vols. 1–15, 1945–60, 1v.
Indexed: Ind. For. Leg. Per.

REVUE ETHNOGRAPHIQUE
See Société d'Ethnographie. MÉMOIRES

REVUE ETHNOGRAPHIQUE TCHÉCOSLAVE
See NARODOPISNY VESTNIK

REVUE EUROPÉENNE DE DÉMOGRAPHIE
See EUROPEAN JOURNAL OF POPULATION

REVUE EUROSTAT
See EUROSTAT REVIEW

4091
REVUE FRANÇAISE D'ADMINISTRATION PUBLIQUE. 1– , 1977– . Paris, Berger Levrault. Quarterly.

Issued by: Institut International Publique. In French; summaries in Arabic, English and Spanish. Title varies: *Bulletin de l'Institut des Hautes Études d'Outre-Mer.*

Indexed: Bull. Anal. Pol. Ec. Soc.; Int. Bibl. Eco.; Int. Bibl. Pol. Sc.

4092
REVUE FRANÇAISE D'ÉTUDES POLITIQUES AFRICAINES. no.13–167/169, Jan. 1967–Nov./Dec. 1979/Jan. 1980. Paris, Société Africaine d'Édition. Monthly.

In French.

Continues: *Le Mois en France*. Continued by: *Mois en France*.

Indexed: Bull. Anal. Pol. Ec. Soc.; Int. Bibl. Soc. Cul. Anth.; Int. Lab. Doc.; Int. Pol. Sc. Abst.

4093
REVUE FRANÇAISE D'HISTOIRE D'OUTRE-MER. v.1– , 1913– . Paris. Frequency varies.

Issued by: Société Française d'Histoire d'Outre-Mer (1913–58, called Société d'Histoire des Colonies Françaises). In French. Title varies: 1913–34, *Revue d'Histoire des Colonies Françaises*; 1934–58, *Revue d'Histoire des Colonies*. Publication suspended 1939, no.4–1945. V.33 dated 1940–46.

Indexes: Vols. 1–25, 1913–32, 1v.

Indexed: Bull. Anal. Pol. Ec. Soc.; Bull. Sig. Soc. Eth.; His. Abst.; Int. Bibl. Pol. Sc.

4094
REVUE FRANÇAISE DE FINANCES PUBLIQUES. 1– , 1983– . Paris, Librairie Générale de Droit et de Jurisprudence. Quarterly.

In French. Each number has also a distinctive title.

4095
REVUE FRANÇAISE DE PÉDAGOGIE. 1– , Oct./Dec. 1967– . Paris. Four no. a year.

Issued by: Institut Pédagogique Nationale. Summaries in French; in English, Russian, or Spanish.

Indexed: Bull. Anal. Pol. Ec. Soc.

4096
REVUE FRANÇAISE DE SCIENCE POLITIQUE. v.1– , Jan./June 1951– . Paris, Presses de la Fondation des Sciences Politiques. Quarterly, 1951–63; bimonthly.

Issued by: Fondation Nationale de Sciences Politiques, and Association Française des Sciences Politiques. In French; summaries in English, French, German, Russian, or Spanish.

Indexed: ABC POL SCI; Bull. Anal. Pol. Ec. Soc.; Bull. Sig. Soc. Eth.; Int. Bibl. Eco.; Int. Bibl. Pol. Sc.; Int. Bibl. Soc.; Int. Lab. Doc.; PAISFL; Peace Res. Abst. J.; Soc. Abst.; SSCI.

4097
REVUE FRANÇAISE DE SOCIOLOGIE. v.1– , Jan./Mar. 1960– . Paris. Quarterly.

Issued by: Centre Nationale de la Recherche Scientifique. In French; summaries in English, German, Russian and Spanish. Supplements accompany some numbers.

Supersedes: *Recherches Sociologiques*.

Indexes: Vols. 1–10, 1960–69, 1v.

Indexed: Bull. Anal. Pol. Ec. Soc.; Bull. Sig. Soc. Eth.; Int. Bibl. Pol. Sc.; Int. Bibl. Soc.; Int. Lab. Doc.; Int. Pol. Sc. Abst.; Peace Res. Abst. J.; Pop. Ind.; Psych. Abst.; SSCI.

4098
REVUE FRANÇAISE DU MARKETING. Cahier no.1– , 1953?– . Paris.

Issued by: Association pour le Développement des Techniques et d'Exploitation des Études des Marchés. In French. Title varies: no.1–9, *Cahiers de l'A.D.E.T.E.M.*

Indexed: Bull. Anal. Pol. Ec. Soc.; Bull. Sig. Soc. Eth.; Psych. Abst.

REVUE GÉNÉRALE D'ADMINISTRATION *See* France. Ministère de l'Intérieur. REVUE GÉNÉRALE D'ADMINISTRATION

4099
REVUE GÉNÉRALE DE DROIT INTERNATIONAL PUBLIC. v.1– , 1894– . Paris, A. Pedone. Bimonthly.

In French. Includes supplements titled "Bibliographie générale de droit international public" in v.26–33, also ser.2, v.1–8, 34–46, and ser.3, v.1–13.

Indexed: Bull. Anal. Pol. Ec. Soc.; Ind. For. Leg. Per.; Int. Bibl. Pol. Sc.; Int. Pol. Sc. Abst.; Peace Res. Abst. J.

4100
REVUE GÉOGRAPHIQUE DES PYRÉNÉES ET DU SUD-OUEST. v.1– , Jan. 1930– . Toulouse. Four no. a year.

Issued by: Instituts de Géographie des Facultés des Lettres de Toulouse et de Bordeaux. Published under the auspices of the Centre National de la Recherche Scientifique. In French.

Indexes: Vols. 1–10, 1930–40.

Indexed: Bull. Sig. Soc. Eth.

4101
REVUE HELLÉNIQUE DE DROIT INTERNATIONAL. v.1– , 1948– . Athens. Quarterly.

Issued by: Institut Hellénique de Droit International et Étranger. In English, French, or German.

Indexed: Int. Bibl. Pol. Sc.; Int. Pol. Sc. Abst.

4102
REVUE HISTORIQUE. v.1– , Jan./June 1876– . Paris, Presses Universitaires de France. Quarterly.
In French.

4103
LA REVUE INDIGÈNE; ORGANE DES INTÉRÊTS DES INDIGÈNES AU COLONIES ET DES PROTECTORATS. v.1–27, Jan. 30, 1906–Jan./Apr. 1932. Paris. Monthly.
In French.
Indexes: Table des matières, vols. 2–3, 1907–08, in v.3; v.9–14, 1914–19, with v.14–15.

4104
REVUE INDO-CHINOISE. Aug. 1893–Dec. 1903; n. ser. v.1–44, Jan. 1904–Dec. 1925. Hanoi. Frequency varies.
In French. Numbers are combined frequently. Merged into *Extrême-Asie* in July 1926.

4105
REVUE INTERNATIONALE D'ACTION COMMUNAUTAIRE. INTERNATIONAL REVIEW OF COMMUNITY DEVELOPMENT. no.1 (41)– , Mar. 1979– . Montréal, Les Éditions Coopératives Albert Saint-Martin. Semi-annual.
Issued by: Forum International d'Action Communautaire. In French; summaries in English, French and Spanish.
Continues: *Community Development*.
Indexed: Int. Pol. Sc. Abst.; Soc. Abst.

REVUE INTERNATIONALE D'ETHNOLOGIE ET DE LINGUISTIQUE
See ANTHROPOS

4106
REVUE INTERNATIONALE D'HISTOIRE DE LA BANQUE. INTERNATIONAL REVIEW OF THE HISTORY OF BANKING. RIVISTA INTERNAZIONALE DI STORIA DELLA BANCA. 1– , 1968– . Genève, Librairie Droz. Quarterly.
Issued by: Institut International d'Histoire de la Banque. In English, French, German, Italian, or Spanish.
Indexed: His. Abst.

REVUE INTERNATIONALE D'HISTOIRE POLITIQUE ET CONSTITUTIONELLE
See POLITIQUE

REVUE INTERNATIONALE DE LA SÛRETÉ ET DE LA SÉCURITÉ
See INTERNATIONAL SECURITY REVIEW

REVUE INTERNATIONALE DE PÉDAGOGIE
See INTERNATIONAL REVIEW OF EDUCATION

REVUE INTERNATIONALE DE POLITIQUE CRIMINELLE
See INTERNATIONAL REVIEW OF CRIMINAL POLICY

REVUE INTERNATIONALE DE SCIENCE POLITIQUE
See RISP. REVUE INTERNATIONALE DE SCIENCE POLITIQUE

4107
REVUE INTERNATIONALE DE SOCIOLOGIE. INTERNATIONAL REVIEW OF SOCIOLOGY. v.1–47, Jan./Feb. 1893–Sept./Dec. 1939; n. ser. 2, v.1–7, 1954/1957–1971. Roma. Three no. a year.
Issued by: École de Perfectionnement en Sociologie et en Sciences Sociales, Università di Roma, International Association for the Advancement of Ethnology and Eugenics, Comité Italien pour l'Étude des Problèmes de la Population, Istituto di Statistica, Facoltà di Scienze Statistiche, Demografia e Affuriali, Università di Roma. In English, French, German, Italian or Spanish.
Indexes: 1893–1902, v.10, pp. 946–960; 1913–22, 1v.
Indexed: Int. Bibl. Soc.; Int. Pol. Sc. Abst.; Soc. Abst.

REVUE INTERNATIONALE DE STATISTIQUE
See INTERNATIONAL STATISTICAL REVIEW

REVUE INTERNATIONALE DES SCIENCES ADMINISTRATIVES
See INTERNATIONAL REVIEW OF ADMINISTRATIVE SCIENCES

4108
REVUE INTERNATIONALE DES SCIENCES SOCIALES. v.1– , 1949– . Paris, Unesco. Quarterly.
In French. Published also in English: *International Social Science Journal*.
Indexed: Bull. Anal. Pol. Ec. Soc.; Int. Pol. Sc. Abst.

4109
REVUE INTERNATIONALE DU MARCHÉ COMMUN. v.1– , Apr. 1958– . Bruxelles. Bimonthly.
In English, Flemish, French, German, or Italian. Other titles: *Die Internationale Zeitschrift des Gemeinsamen Markets*; *Het International Tijdschrift voor de Europamarkt*; *Rivista Internazionale del Mercato Commune*.

REVUE INTERNATIONALE DU RECHERCHE URBAINE ET RÉGIONALE
See INTERNATIONAL JOURNAL OF URBAN AND REGIONAL RESEARCH

4110
REVUE INTERNATIONALE DU SOCIALISME. v.1– , 1964– . Milano. Bimonthly.
In French. Published also in English edition: *International Socialist Journal*.

REVUE IRANIENNE D'ANTHROPOLOGIE
See MAJALLA-YI MARDUMSHINASI

4111
REVUE IRANIENNE DES RELATIONS INTERNATIONALES. IRANIAN REVIEW OF INTERNATIONAL RELATIONS. no.1– , summer 1974– . Téhéran. Irreg.
Issued by: Centre des Hautes Études Internationales, Université de Téhéran. In English or French.
Title varies: 1974, *Relations Internationales. International Relations*.
Indexed: Bull. Anal. Pol. Ec. Soc.; PAIS.

REVUE JURIDIQUE ET POLITIQUE D'OUTRE-MER
See REVUE JURIDIQUE ET POLITIQUE, INDÉPENDANCE ET COOPÉRATION

REVUE JURIDIQUE ET POLITIQUE DE L'UNION FRANÇAISE
See REVUE JURIDIQUE ET POLITIQUE, INDÉPENDANCE ET COOPÉRATION

4112
REVUE JURIDIQUE ET POLITIQUE, INDÉPENDANCE ET COOPÉRATION. v.1– , Jan./Mar. 1947– . Paris. Quarterly.
Issued by: Institut International de Droit d'Expression Française. In French. Title varies: 1947–59, *Revue Juridique et Politique de l'Union Française*; 1959–64, *Revue Juridique et Politique d'Outre-Mer*.
Indexed: ABC POL SCI; Ind. For. Leg. Per.; Int. Bibl. Pol. Sc.; Int. Lab. Doc.; Int. Pol. Sc. Abst.

4113
REVUE LIBANAISE DES SCIENCES POLITIQUES. no.1– , 1970– . Beirut.
Issued by: Association Libanaise des Sciences Politiques. In French.
Indexed: Int. Pol. Sc. Abst.; Soc. Abst.

REVUE NÉERLANDAISE DE GÉOGRAPHIE ÉCONOMIQUE ET SOCIAL
See TIJDSCHRIFT VOOR ECONOMISCHE EN SOCIALE GEOGRAFIE

REVUE ORIENTALE
See Société d'Ethnographie. MEMOIRES

REVUE ORIENTALE ET AMÉRICAINE
See Société d'Ethnographie. MEMOIRES

REVUE OUEST-AFRICAINE D'ARCHÉOLOGIE
See WEST AFRICAN JOURNAL OF ARCHAEOLOGY

REVUE PARLEMENTAIRE CANADIENNE
See CANADIAN PARLIAMENTARY REVIEW

4114
REVUE POLITIQUE DES IDÉES ET DES INSTITUTIONS. v.1–59, Oct. 1912–1970. Paris. Semimonthly.
In French.
Indexed: Int. Bibl. Pol. Sc.; Int. Bibl. Soc. Cul. Anth.; Peace Res. Abst. J.

4115
REVUE POLITIQUE ET PARLEMENTAIRE. v.1– , July 1894– . Paris, A. Colin. Bimonthly.
In French. Each number includes section "Bibliographie". Title varies: 1895–Mar. 1896, *Revue Politique et Parlementaire; Questions Politiques, Sociales et Législatives*.
Indexed: Bull. Anal. Pol. Ec. Soc.; Bull. Sig. Soc. Eth.; Int. Bibl. Eco.; Int. Bibl. Pol. Sc.; Int. Pol. Sc. Abst.; PAISFL; Peace Res. Abst. J.

REVUE POLITIQUE ET PARLEMENTAIRE: QUESTIONS POLITIQUES, SOCIALES ET LÉGISLATIVES
See REVUE POLITIQUE ET PARLEMENTAIRE

4116
REVUE ROUMAINE D'ÉTUDES INTERNATIONALES. 1/2– , 1967– . Bucharest, Editura Academiei Republicii Socialiste România. Semi-annual, 1967–69; quarterly, 1970–80; bimonthly.
Issued by: Association de Droit International et Relations Internationales de la Republique Socialiste de Roumanie. In English, French (mainly), or Russian. Summaries in English and Russian. Published also in Romanian: *Revista Romana de Studii Internationale*.
Indexed: Bull. Anal. Pol. Ec. Soc.; His. Abst.; Int. Bibl. Pol. Sc.

4117
REVUE ROUMAINE D'HISTOIRE. v.1– , 1962– . Bucharest, Éditions de la Académie de la Republique Socialiste de Roumanie.
In French.

Indexed: His. Abst.; Peace Res. Abst. J.

4118
[No entry]

4119
REVUE ROUMAINE DES SCIENCES SOCIALES. SÉRIE DE PSYCHOLOGIE. v.8– , 1964– . Bucharest, Editura Academiei Republicii Socialiste România. Two no. a year, 1964; four no. a year.
Issued by: Académie de la République Socialiste de Roumanie. In English, French, German, Russian, or Spanish.
Continues, in part: *Revue Roumaine des Sciences Sociales.*
Indexed: LLBA; Psych. Abst.

4120
REVUE ROUMAINE DES SCIENCES SOCIALES. SÉRIE DE SOCIOLOGIE. v.10/11– , 1966/67– . Bucharest, Editura Academiei Republicii Socialiste România. Annual.
Issued by: Académie des Sciences Sociales et Politiques de la Republique Socialiste de Roumanie. In English, French, German, or Russian.
Continues, in part: *Revue Roumaine des Sciences Sociales.*
Indexed: Bull. Anal. Pol. Ec. Soc.; Int. Bibl. Eco.; Int. Bibl. Soc.; Int. Pol. Sc. Abst.

4121
REVUE ROUMAINE DES SCIENCES SOCIALES. SÉRIE DES SCIENCES ÉCONOMIQUES. v.13– , 1969– . Bucharest, Editura Academiei Republicii Socialiste România. Two no. a year.
Issued by: Académie des Sciences Sociales et Politiques de la République Socialiste de Roumanie. In English, French, or Russian.
Continues, in part: *Revue Roumaine des Sciences Sociales.*

REVUE SCANDINAVE DE SOCIOLOGIE
See ACTA SOCIOLOGICA

4122
REVUE SOCIALISTE. v.1–59, Jan. 1885–Jan. 1914. Paris. Monthly.
Issued by: Parti Socialiste et Cercle d'Études Socialistes Jean Jaurès. In French. Title varies: 1885–Dec. 1909, *La Revue Socialiste.*
Continued by: *Revue Socialiste* (1946–)

LA REVUE SOCIALISTE
See REVUE SOCIALISTE

LA REVUE SUISSE D'ART ET D'ARCHÉOLOGIE
See ZEITSCHRIFT FÜR SCHWEIZERISCHE ARCHÄOLOGIE UND KUNSTGESCHICHTE

REVUE SUISSE D'ÉCONOMIE POLITIQUE ET DE STATISTIQUE
See SCHWEIZERISCHE ZEITSCHRIFT FÜR VOLKSWIRTSCHAFT UND STATISTIK

REVUE SUISSE D'HISTOIRE
See SCHWEIZERISCHE ZEITSCHRIFT FÜR GESCHICHTE

REVUE SUISSE DE PSYCHOLOGIE ET DE PSYCHOLOGIE APPLIQUÉE
See SCHWEIZERISCHE ZEITSCHRIFT FÜR PSYCHOLOGIE UND IHRE ANWENDUNGEN

REVUE SUISSE DE SOCIOLOGIE
See SCHWEIZERISCHE ZEITSCHRIFT FÜR SOZIOLOGIE

REVUE TIERS-MONDE
See TIERS MONDE

LA REVUE TOCQUEVILLE
See Tocqueville Society. THE TOCQUEVILLE REVIEW

4123
REVUE TUNISIENNE DES SCIENCES SOCIALES. v.1– , Sept. 1964/65– . Tunis. Quarterly, 1964/65–1976; semi-annual, 1977–86; annual.
Issued by: Centre d'Études et de Recherches Économiques et Sociales, Université de Tunis. In French; occasionally in Arabic. Other title: *al-Majallah al-Tūnisīyah alil-'ulūm al-ijtimā'īyah.* Vol. for 1982 last available for examination. Some issues are combined.
Indexed: Bull. Anal. Pol. Ec. Soc.; Bull. Sig. Soc. Eth.; Int. Bibl. Eco.; Int. Bibl. Soc.; Int. Lab. Doc.; LLBA; Pop. Ind.

REVUE TURQUE D'ANTHROPOLOGIE
See TÜRK ANTROPOLOGI MEMUASI

REVUE ZAÏROISE DES SCIENCES DE L'HOMME
See CULTURE AU ZAÏRE ET EN AFRIQUE

RHODES–LIVINGSTONE COMMUNICATIONS
See University of Zambia. Institute for Social Research. COMMUNICATION

4124
RHODES–LIVINGSTONE JOURNAL; HUMAN RELATIONS IN BRITISH CENTRAL AFRICA. no.1–38, June 1944–1965. Cape Town, Oxford University Press.
No.1–4 published by the Rhodes–Livingstone Institute in Livingstone.

Superseded by: *African Social Research.*

4125
RHODESIAN HISTORY. v.1–8, 1970–1978. Salisbury (now Harare). Annual.
Issued by: Central African Historical Association.

4126
RHODESIAN JOURNAL OF ECONOMICS. v.1–10, Aug. 1967–Dec. 1976. Salisbury (now Harare). Quarterly.
Issued by: Rhodesian Economic Society.
Superseded by: *Zimbabwe Journal of Economics.*
Indexed: PAIS.

4127
RICERCHE DI SOCIOLOGIA DELL'EDUCAZIONE E PEDAGOGIA COMPARATA. 1– , 1974– . Messina, Peloritana Editrice. Irreg.
Issued by: Istituto di Pedagogia, Università di Messina. In Italian. Monograph series.

4128
LA RIFORMA SOCIALE. v.1–46, no.2, 1894–Mar./Apr. 1935. Torino, Einaudi. Monthly, 1894–1907, 1911–31; bimonthly, 1908–10, 1932–35.
In Italian. Includes some supplements.
Superseded by: *Rivista di Storia Economica.*

4129
RIVISTA BANCARIA. 1– , 1920– . Milano. Bimonthly.
Issued by: Istituto di Cultura Bancaria. In Italian.
Indexed: PAISFL.

4130
RIVISTA DI ANTROPOLOGIA. v.1– , 1891– . Roma. Two no. a year; frequently one volume.
Issued by: Istituto Italiano di Antropologia, Società Romana di Antropologia, 1893–1937; Istituto Italiano di Antropologia. In Italian. Includes "Supplemento". Title varies: 1–16, 1893–1910, the society's *Atti.*
Indexed: Int. Bibl. Soc. Cul. Anth.

4131
RIVISTA DI DIRITTO INTERNAZIONALE. v.1– , 1906– . Padova, later Milano, A. Giuffrè. Bimonthly, 1906–10; quarterly.
In Italian, English, or French. Issues for 1912– called also ser.2. Publication suspended: Jan.–Dec. 1911 and 1944–52.
Indexes: Vols. 1–17, 1906–25, 1v.
Indexed: Ind. For. Leg. Per.

4132
RIVISTA DI ECONOMIA AGRARIA. v.1– , May 1946– . Roma. Quarterly.
Issued by: Istituto Nazionale di Economia Agraria. In Italian. Subtitle reads: "Studi di economia agraria, politica agraria, sociologia rurale".
Indexes: Vols. 1–8, 1946–63, with v.8; v.9–19, 1954–64, 1v.
Indexed: Bull. Anal. Pol. Ec. Soc.; Bull. Sig. Soc. Eth.; Int. Bibl. Soc.; Soc. Abst.

4133
RIVISTA DI ETNOGRAFIA. v.1–27, Dec. 1946–1973. Napoli, Il Consiglio. Quarterly (irreg.); annual.
In Italian.
Superseded by: *Etnologia, Antropologia Culturale.*

4134
RIVISTA DI MATEMATICA PER LE SCIENZE ECONOMICHE E SOCIALI. v.1– , 1. semestre 1978– . Milano. Semi-annual.
Issued by: Associazione per la Matematica Applicata alle Scienze Economiche e Sociali (A.M.A.S.E.S.). In English, French, or Italian; summaries in English, French and Italian.

4135
RIVISTA DI POLITICA ECONOMICA. 1– , 1911– . Roma, Servizio Italiano Pubblicazioni Internazionali. Monthly (some combined numbers).
In Italian; occasionally articles translated from English.
Indexed: Bull. Anal. Pol. Ec. Soc.; Int. Bibl. Eco.

4136
RIVISTA DI PSICOLOGIA SOCIALE E ARCHIVO ITALIANO DI PSICOLOGIA GENERALE E DEL LAVORO. 1– , 1952– . Cagliari. Quarterly.
Issued by: Istituto di Psicologia e Sociologia, Università di Cagliari. In Italian. Title varies: 1952–53, *Archivo Italiano di Psicologia Generale e del Lavoro.*
Indexed: Int. Bibl. Eco.; Int. Bibl. Soc. Cul. Anth.; Psych. Abst.

4137
RIVISTA DI SCIENZA POLITICA. v.1– , Apr. 1971– . Bologna, Il Mulino. Three no. a year.
In Italian.

4138
RIVISTA DI SCIENZE PREHISTORICHE. v.1– , 1946– . Firenze. Two no. a year.
In English, French, or Italian.
Indexed: Abst. Anth.

4139
RIVISTA DI SOCIOLOGIA. v.1–4, 1894–June 1897. Roma. Three no. a year.
In Italian.

4140
RIVISTA DI SOCIOLOGIA. v.1–10, no.2/3/4, July/Aug. 1927–June/Dec. 1940. Milano. Quarterly (irreg.)

V.1–9, 1927–39, called also ser. 2; v.6–7, no.1, 1932–34, have also secondary title: *Revue de Sociologie*. Ser. 2, no.3–5/6 have cover title: *Rivista di Sociologia et Archives de Sociologie*; v.8, 1938, called also ser. 3. Publication suspended Apr. 1934–Dec. 1937. In English, French, or Italian.

4141
RIVISTA DI SOCIOLOGIA. v.1–16, 1963–1978. Roma. Quarterly.
Issued by: Istituto di Sociologia, Libera Università Internazionale degli Studi Sociali pro Deo. In English, French, or Italian.
Indexes: Vols. 1963–66.
Indexed: Bull. Anal. Pol. Ec. Soc.; Int. Bibl. Soc.; Int. Pol. Sc. Abst.; Soc. Abst.

RIVISTA DI SOCIOLOGIA ET ARCHIVES DE SOCIOLOGIE
See RIVISTA DI SOCIOLOGIA (Milano)

4142
RIVISTA DI STUDI POLItICI INTERNAZIONALI. 1– , 1934– . Firenze, Casa Editrice Sansoni. Quarterly.
In Italian.
Indexes: Vols. 1–10, 1934–43, in v.10.
Indexed: ABC POL SCI; Bull. Anal. Pol. Ec. Soc.; His. Abst.; Int. Bibl. Pol. Sc.; Int. Lab. Doc.; Int. Pol. Sc. Abst.

RIVISTA INTERNAZIONALE DEL MERCATO COMMUNE
See REVUE INTERNATIONALE DU MARCHÉ COMMUN

4143
RIVISTA INTERNAZIONALE DI SCIENZE ECONOMICHE E COMMERCIALI. v.1– , Sept./Oct. 1954– . Padova, CEDAM. Bimonthly, 1954–55; monthly.
Published under the auspices of Università Commerciale "Luigi Bocconi". In English, French, or Italian.
Indexed: Bull. Anal. Pol. Ec. Soc.; Int. Bibl. Eco.; J. Eco. Lit.; PAIS.

4144
RIVISTA INTERNAZIONALE DI SCIENZE SOCIALI. v.1–106, Jan. 1895–Dec. 1926; n. ser. 1927–29; ser. 3, v.1– , 1930– . Roma, later Milano, Vita e Pensiero. Frequency varies; quarterly, 1977–.
Issued by: Società Cattolica Italiana per gli Studi Scientifici. In Italian. Title varies: 1893–1933, *Rivista Internazionale di Scienze Sociali e Discipline Ausiliare*.
Indexed: Bull. Anal. Pol. Ec. Soc.; Bull. Sig. Soc. Eth.; His. Abst.; Int. Bibl. Eco.; Int. Bibl. Soc.; Int. Pol. Sc. Abst.; LLBA; Soc. Abst.

RIVISTA INTERNAZIONALE DI SCIENZE SOCIALI E DISCIPLINE AUSILIARE
See RIVISTA INTERNAZIONALE DI SCIENZE SOCIALI

RIVISTA INTERNAZIONALE DI STORIA DI BANCA
See REVUE INTERNATIONALE D'HISTOIRE DE LA BANQUE

RIVISTA ITALIANA DI DEMOGRAFIA E STATISTICA
See RIVISTA ITALIANA DI ECONOMIA, DEMOGRAFIA E STATISTICA

4145
RIVISTA ITALIANA DI ECONOMIA, DEMOGRAFIA E STATISTICA. v.1– , Jan. 1947– . Roma. Four no. a year (two double numbers)
Issued by: Società Italiana di Economia, Demografia e Statistica. In Italian. Title varies: 1947–Jan./June 1950, *Rivista Italiana di Demografia e Statistica*.

RIVISTA ITALIANA DI POLITICA, LETTERARIA E ARTISTICA
See RASSEGNA ITALIANA DI POLITICA E DI CULTURA

4146
RIVISTA ITALIANA DI SCIENZA POLITICA. v.1– , Apr. 1971– . Bologna, Il Mulino. Three no. a year.
In Italian; summaries in English.
Indexed: ABC POL SCI; Bull. Anal. Pol. Ec. Soc.; His. Abst.; Int. Bibl. Pol. Sc.; Int. Pol. Sc. Abst.; LLBA; Soc. Abst.

4147
RIVISTA ITALIANA DI SOCIOLOGIA. v.1–25, no.2, July 1897–Jan./June 1921. Roma.
In Italian.

LA RIVISTA STORICA SVIZZERA
See SCHWEIZERISCHE ZEITSCHRIFT FÜR GESCHICHTE

RIVISTA SVIZZERA D'ARTE ET D'ARCHEOLOGIA
See ZEITSCHRIFT FÜR SCHWEIZERISCHE ARCHÄOLOGIE UND KUNSTGESCHICHTE

ROCKY MOUNTAINS SOCIAL SCIENCE JOURNAL
See SOCIAL SCIENCE JOURNAL (Fort Collins)

4148
ROCZNIK PRAWA MIĘDZYNARODOWEGO. 1949– . Warszawa. Annual.

Issued by: Polski Instytut Spraw Międzynarodowych. In Polish.

4149
ROCZNIKI DZIEJÓW SPOŁECZNYCH I GOSPODARCZYCH. v.1– , 1931– . Poznań. Annual.
Issued by: Komisja Nauk Społecznych, Poznańskie Towarzystwo Przyjaciół Nauk. In Polish; summaries in French. Other title: *Annales d'Histoire Sociale et Économique*. Published: v.1–7, 1931–39; v.8–, 1939/46–.
Indexed: His. Abst.

4150
ROCZNIKI HISTORYCZNE. v.1– , 1925– . Poznań, Państwowe Wydawnictwo Naukowe. Irreg.
Issued by: Wydział Historii i Nauk Społecznych, Poznańskie Towarzystwo Przyjaciół Nauk. In Polish; summaries in French and Russian. Publication suspended: 1940–45.

4151
ROCZNIKI NAUK SPOŁECZNYCH. v.1– , 1973– . Lublin. Annual.
Issued by: Towarzystwo Naukowe Katolickiego Uniwersytetu Lubelskiego. In Polish; summaries in English. Other titles: *Annales des Sciences Sociales*; *Annals of Social Sciences*.

4152
THE ROMANIAN JOURNAL OF SOCIOLOGY. v.1–6, 1962–1971. Bucharest, Publishing House of the Academy of the Romanian People's Republic.
Issued by: the academy's National Committee of Sociology. In English, French, or Romanian. Title varies: 1964–65, *The Rumanian Journal of Sociology*.
Indexed: Int. Bibl. Soc.

4153
ROMANIAN SCIENTIFIC ABSTRACTS. SOCIAL SCIENCES. v.1–, no.1/2– , Jan./Feb. 1964– . Bucharest. Monthly, 1964–70; bimonthly, 1971–75; semi-annual.
Issued by: Centrul de Informare şi Documentare in Ştiinţele Sociale Republici Socialiste România; subsequently by: Academia de Ştiintç Sociale şi Politice a şi Politice Academia Republicii Socialiste România. In English. Other title: *Rumanian Scientific Abstracts. Social Sciences*. Published also in Russian: *Rumynskiĭ Biulleten' Nauchnoĭ Informatsii. Obshchestvennye Nauki*.

4154
ROUND TABLE. v.1–71 (no.1–284), 1910–Oct. 1981. London, Professional and Scientific Publications. Quarterly.
Indexes: Vols. 1–25 (no.1–100), 1910–35, 1v.
Indexed: ABC POL SCI; Bull. Anal. Pol. Ec. Soc.; Curr. Cont. Soc. Beh. Sc.; His. Abst.; Int. Bibl. Pol. Sc.; Int. Pol. Sc. Abst.; Int. Lab. Doc.; PAIS; Peace Res. Abst. J.

ROUTES DE LA PAIX
See COEXISTENCE (The Hague)

4155
Royal Anthropological Institute of Great Britain and Ireland. JOURNAL. v.1–95, no.2, 1871–1965. London.
Supersedes: *Journal of the Ethnological Society of London*. Merged into *Journal of the Anthropological Society of London* and *Journal of Anthropology*.
Superseded by: *Man*.

4156
Royal Anthropological Institute of Great Britain and Ireland. OCCASIONAL PAPERS. no.1– , 1902– . London. Irreg.
Monograph series.

4157
Royal Anthropological Institute of Great Britain and Ireland. PROCEEDINGS. London. Annual.
Indexed: Int. Bibl. Soc. Cul. Anth.

Royal Anthropological Institute of Great Britain and Ireland. Library. ANTHROPOLOGICAL INDEX TO CURRENT PERIODICALS RECEIVED IN THE LIBRARY OF THE ROYAL ANTHROPOLOGICAL INSTITUTE OF GREAT BRITAIN AND IRELAND
See ANTHROPOLOGICAL INDEX

4158
Royal Asiatic Society of Great Britain and Ireland. JOURNAL. 1–20, 1834–1863; n. ser. 1–21, 1864–1889; [ser.3]– , 1889– . London. Four no. a year; occasionally combined in two double numbers.
Supersedes: the society's *Transactions* (1–3, 1823–33)
Indexes: 1834–1922, in *Centenary*, v.1923; v.1920–29; v.1930–39.
Indexed: His. Abst.

4159
Royal Asiatic Society of Great Britain and Ireland. Ceylon Branch. JOURNAL. v.1–38, 1845–1949; n. ser. v.1–15, 1950–1971. Colombo. Two no. a year.
Continued by: Royal Asiatic Society. Sri Lanka Branch. *Journal*.
Indexes: Vols. 1–11, 1845–90.

4160
Royal Asiatic Society of Great Britain and Ireland. China Branch. TRANSACTIONS. 1–6, 1847–1859. London.

4161
Royal Asiatic Society of Great Britain and Ireland. Hong Kong Branch. JOURNAL. v.1–2, 1960/61–1962. Hong Kong. Annual.

4162
Royal Asiatic Society of Great Britain and Ireland. Korea Branch. TRANSACTIONS. 1– , 1900– . Seoul.
Index to monographs 1–16 in v.17; index to titles and authors of papers, 1–25, in v.25.

4163
Royal Asiatic Society of Great Britain and Ireland. Malayan Branch. JOURNAL. 1– , 1923–1963. Singapore. Two no. a year, 1923–33; three no. a year.
Supersedes: Royal Asiatic Society of Great Britain and Ireland. Straits Branch. *Journal* (v.1–86, 1878–Nov. 1922). Continued by: the society's Malaysian Branch. *Journal.*
Indexes: v.5 contains index to the society's Straits Branch. *Journal*, and *Notes and Queries*.

ROYAL ONTARIO MUSEUM ARCHAEOLOGY MONOGRAPH
See ARCHAEOLOGY MONOGRAPHS

4164
Royal Society for Asian Affairs. JOURNAL. v.1– , 1914– . London. Quarterly, 1914–Oct. 1933; three no. a year.
Former name of the society was Royal Central Asian Society. Title varies: 1914–Apr. 1931 (v.1–18, pt.2) *Journal of the Central Asian Society*.

4165
Royal Society of Canada. PROCEEDINGS AND TRANSACTIONS. series 1, 1–12, 1882/83–1894; series 2, v.1–12, 1895–1906; series 3, v.1–56, 1907–62; series 4, v.1– , 1963– . Ottawa. Irreg.
Separately paged parts 1 and 2 of *Proceedings* contain material on the social sciences.
Indexes: Series, 1882/83–1894, in series 1, v.12; series 1 and 2, 1882/83–1906, 1v.; series 1–3, 1882/83–1942, 1v.
Indexed: His. Abst.

4166
Royal Town Planning Institute. JOURNAL. v.1– , 1914– . London. Ten no. a year.
Indexed: Bull. Sig. Soc. Eth.; PAIS; PHRA.

4167
Royal Western Australian Historical Society. JOURNAL AND PROCEEDINGS. 1927– . Nedlands. Annual.

ROZPRAVY ČESKOSLOVENSKE AKADEMIE VĚD. RADA SPOLEČENSKYCH VĚD
See Československa Akademia Věd. Rada Společenských Věd. ROZPRAVY

4168
RUCH PRAWNICZY, EKONOMICZNY I SOCJOLOGICZNY. v.1– , 1921– . Warszawa, Państwowe Wydawnictwo Naukowe. Quarterly.
Issued by: Uniwersytet im. A. Mickiewicza, Poznań, and Wyższa Szkoła Ekonomiczna, Poznań. V.1–19, 1921–39; v.20–, Jan. 1958–. Some early volumes have also title: *Mouvement Juridique, Économique et Sociologique*. In Polish. Tables of contents also in English and Russian. Title varies: v.20–21, no.2, 1958–59, *Ruch Prawniczy i Ekonomiczny*.
Indexed: Int. Bibl. Eco.

RUCH PRAWNICZY I EKONOMICZNY
See RUCH PRAWNICZY, EKONOMICZNY I SOCJOLOGICZNY

THE RUMANIAN JOURNAL OF SOCIOLOGY
See THE ROMANIAN JOURNAL OF SOCIOLOGY

RUMANIAN SCIENTIFIC ABSTRACTS. SOCIAL SCIENCES
See ROMANIAN SCIENTIFIC ABSTRACTS. SOCIAL SCIENCES

4169
RUMANIAN STUDIES. 1– , 1970– . Leiden, E.J. Brill. Irreg.
Issued by: Department of History, University of Illinois. Subtitle reads: "An international annual of the humanities and social sciences".

RUMYNSKIĬ BIU͡LLETEN' NAUCHNOĬ INFORMAT͡SII. OBSHCHESTVENNYE NAUKI
See ROMANIAN SCIENTIFIC ABSTRACTS. SOCIAL SCIENCES

4170
RURAL AFRICANA. no.1–31, Mar. 1967–1976; n. ser. no.1– , spring 1978– . East Lansing, Mich. Quarterly.
Issued by: African Studies Center, Department of Political Science, Michigan State University.
Indexed: PAIS; Pop. Ind.

4171
RURAL COMMUNITY STUDIES IN EUROPE. v.1– , 1981– . Oxford, Pergamon Press. Annual.
Issued by: European Coordination Centre for Research and Documentation in Social Sciences.

4172
RURAL DEVELOPMENT ABSTRACTS. v.1– , Mar. 1978– . Farnham Royal. Quarterly.

Issued by: Commonwealth Agricultural Bureaux.

4173
RURAL DEVELOPMENT WORKING PAPER. no.86– . Canberra. Irreg.
Issued by: National Centre for Development Studies, The Australian National University.
Continues: Australian National University. National Centre for Development Studies. *Working Paper*.

4173a
RURAL INSTITUTIONS AND PLANNED CHANGE. 1–8, 1969–1975. Geneva. Irreg.
Issued by: Research Institute for Social Development, United Nations. Each no. has also a distinctive title.

4174
RURAL SOCIOLOGY. v.1– , Mar. 1936– . Baton Rouge, La., later Brookings, S.Dak. Quarterly.
Issued by: Section of Rural Sociology, American Sociological Association, later by: Rural Sociological Society, and the Department of Rural Sociology, South Dakota State University; at present time: University, Pa.
Indexes: v.1–20, 21–30, 31–70.
Indexed: Abst. Anth.; Abst. Soc. Work.; His. Abst.; Bull. Anal. Pol. Ec. Soc.; Bull. Sig. Soc. Eth.; His. Abst.; Int. Bibl. Eco.; Int. Bibl. Soc.; Int. Lab. Doc.; Int. Pol. Sc. Abst.; PAIS; PHRA; Pop. Ind.; Psych. Abst.; Sage Fam. Stu. Abst.; Sage Urb. Stu. Abst.; Soc. Abst.; Soc. Sc. Abst.; SSCI; Wom. Stu. Abst.; Soc. Work. Res. Abst.

4175
Russia. Arkheologicheskaia͡ Komissii͡a. IZVESTII͡A. no.1–66, 1901–1918. Petrograd.
In Russian. Includes supplement: "Pribavlenie", 1–12.
Indexes: no.1–20, 1901–06, in no.20.

4176
Russia (1923– , U.S.S.R.). Treaties. SBORNIK DEĬSTVUIU͡SHCHIKH DOGOVOROV, SOGLASHENIĬ I KONVENT͡SIĬ ZAKLIU͡CHENNYKH SSSR C INOSTRANNYMI GOSUDARSTVAMI. no.1–36, 1935–1980. Moskva, Gosudarstvennoe Izd-vo Literatury.
In Russian.

4177
Russia (1923– , U.S.S.R.). Treaties. SBORNIK MEZHDUNARODNIKH DOGOVOROV SSSR. no.36– , 1980– . Moskva.
Issued by: Ministerstvo Inostrannykh Del SSSR. In Russian.
Continues: Russia (1923– , U.S.S.R.). Treaties. *Sbornik Deĭstvuiu͡shchikh Dogovorov, Soglasheniĭ i Konvent͡siĭ Zakliu͡chennykh SSSR c Inostrannymi Gosudarstvami*.

4178
THE RUSSIAN REVIEW. v.1– , Nov. 1941– . Stanford, Calif. Semi-annual, 1941–48; quarterly.
Sponsored by: Hoover Institution on War, Revolution and Peace.
Indexed: Bull. Anal. Pol. Ec. Soc.; His. Abst.; PAIS; Peace Res. Abst. J.; Soc. Sc. Hum. Ind.

4179
RUSSKIĬ ARKHEOLOGICHESKIĬ ZHURNAL. v.1–19, 1900–1930. Moskva. Quarterly.
Issued by: Antropologicheskiĭ Otdel Obshchestva Liu͡biteleĭ Estestvoznanii͡a, Antropologii i Etnografii, 1900–24; Antropologicheskiĭ Institut (later Nauchno-issledovatel'skiĭ Institut Antropologii), Moskovskiĭ Universitet. In Russian. Other title: *Journal Russe d'Anthropologie*.
Continued by: *Antropologicheskiĭ Zhurnal*.

S

SA SOCIOLOGICAL ANALYSIS
See SOCIOLOGICAL ANALYSIS

S.E.E.
See TYDSKRIF VIR STUDIES IN EKONOMIE EN EKONOMETRICS

SIPRI YEARBOOK OF WORLD ARMAMENTS AND DISARMAMENTS
See International Institute for Peace and Conflict Research. SIPRI YEARBOOK OF WORLD ARMAMENTS AND DISARMAMENTS

4180
SRM ABSTRACTS. v.1– , summer 1979– . Rotterdam. Annual.
Issued by: SRM Documentation Centre, Erasmus University. Other title: *Social Research Methodology Abstracts*.
Continues, in part: *SRM Abstracts Bulletin*.

SSIP MITTEILUNGEN
See Society for the Study of International Problems. SSIP MITTEILUNGEN

4181
SAECULUM. v.1– , 1950– . Freiburg, Verlag Karl Alber. Four no. a year.
In German. Subtitle reads: "Jahrbuch für Universalgeschichte".
Indexes: Vols. 1–18, 1950–67, 1v.

4182
SAGE ANNUAL REVIEW OF SOCIAL AND EDUCATIONAL CHANGE. v.1– , 1977– . Beverly Hills, Calif., Sage Publications.

4183
SAGE FAMILY STUDIES ABSTRACTS. v.1– , Feb. 1979– . Beverly Hills, Calif., Sage Publications. Quarterly.

4184
SAGE INTERNATIONAL YEARBOOK OF FOREIGN POLICY STUDIES. v.1– , 1973– . Beverly Hills, Calif., Sage Publications. Annual.
Issues beginning with v.4 (1979) are thematic.
Indexed: Bull. Anal. Pol. Ec. Soc.; Int. Pol. Sc. Abst.

4185
SAGE PROFESSIONAL PAPERS IN CONTEMPORARY POLITICAL SOCIOLOGY. v.1– , 1976– . Beverly Hills, Calif., Sage Publications. Eight no. a year.
Each issue is thematic and has also a distinctive title.

4186
SAGE PUBLIC ADMINISTRATION ABSTRACTS. 1– , Apr. 1974– . Beverly Hills, Calif., Sage Publications. Quarterly.

4187
SAGE RACE RELATIONS ABSTRACTS. v.1– , Nov. 1975– . Beverly Hills, Calif., Sage Publications. Three no. a year.
Published on behalf of the Institute of Race Relations.
Supersedes: *Race Relations Abstracts*.

4188
SAGE SERIES ON AFRICAN MODERNIZATION AND DEVELOPMENT. v.1– , 1976– . Beverly Hills, Calif., Sage Publications. Irreg.
Monograph series.

4189
SAGE SERIES ON ARMED FORCES AND SOCIETY. v.1– , Mar. 1971– . Beverly Hills, Calif., Sage Publications. Irreg.
Sponsored by: Inter-University Seminar on Armed Forces and Society. Monograph series.

4190
SAGE UNIVERSITY PAPERS—QUANTITATIVE APPLICATIONS IN THE SOCIAL SCIENCES. no.1– , 1976– . Beverly Hills, Calif., Sage Publications. Irreg.

4191
SAGE URBAN STUDIES ABSTRACTS. 1– , Feb. 1973– . Beverly Hills, Calif., Sage Publications. Quarterly.

4192
SAGE YEARBOOKS IN POLITICS AND PUBLIC POLICY. 1– , 1975– . Beverly Hills, Calif., Sage Publications.
Sponsored by: Policy Studies Organization.
Indexed: Bull. Anal. Pol. Ec. Soc.; Int. Bibl. Eco.; Int. Pol. Sc. Abst.

4193
SAGE YEARBOOKS IN WOMEN'S POLICY STUDIES. 1– , 1976– . Beverly Hills, Calif., Sage Publications.
Indexed: Bull. Anal. Pol. Ec. Soc.

4194
SAHAK YŎN'GU. v.1– , Aug. 1958– . Seoul, Hah'guk Sa Hakkoe. Two to four no. a year.
In Korean; summaries in English. Added title-page title: *Sahak yuenku*. Other title: *Study of History*.

SAHAK YUENKU
See SAHAK YŎN'GU

4195
SAHAKCHI. 1– , 1967– . Seoul. Annual.
In English or Korean. Other title: *Historical Journal*.

4196
SAHĪFAT-TAKHTIT AL-TARBAWI FI EL BILAD EL-ARABIYAT. REVUE DE PLANIFICATION DE L'ÉDUCATION DANS LES PAYS ARABES. 1– , 1963– . Beirut. Three no. a year.
In Arabic; summaries in English and French. Tables of contents also in French.

4197
SAHOE KWAHAK. 1– , 1964– . Seoul, Pusŏl Sahoe Kwahak Yŏn'guwŏn. Annual (irreg.)
Issued by: 1964–69, Songgyum'gwan Taehakkyo; 1970–, Sanggyum'gwam Taehakkyo Pusŏl Sahoe Kwahak Yŏn'guso. In English or Korean. Other title: *Social Science Review*.

4198
SAHOE KWAHAK. 1977– . P'yongyang. Bimonthly.
Issued by: Sahoe Kwahak Ch'up'ansa. In Korean.

4199
SAHOE KWAHAK. 1979– . Taegu-si, Yongnam Taehakkyo. Sahoe Kwahak Yŏn'guso. Annual.
In English, German, or Korean. Other title: *Social Science*.
Indexed: His. Abst.

4200
SAHOE KWAHAK KWA CHONG'AEK YŎN'GU. 1972– . Seoul.
Issued by: Taehakkyo Kwahak Yŏn'gusŏ. In English or Korean. Other title: *Social Science and Policy Research*.

4201
SAHOE KWAHAK NON MUN KISA SEGIN. 1977–1980– . Seoul, Kikchoe Tosogwan. Irreg.
In Korean. Other title: *Korean Periodical Index on Social Science*.

4202
SAHOE KWAHAK NONCH'ONG. 1– , 1982– . Busan.
Issued by: Kukche Taehak Sahoe Kwahak Yŏn'gusŏ. In Korean. Other title: *Journal of the Social Science*.

4203
SAHOE KWAHAK NONJIP. v.1– , 1965– . Seoul. Annual.
Issued by: *Yonse Taehakkyo Kwahak Yŏn'gusŏ*. In Korean; some summaries in English. Other title: *Yonsei Social Science Review*.

4204
SAHOE KWAHAK NONJIP. 1– , 1972– . Seoul. Annual.
Issued by: Koryo Taehakkyo Ch'onggyong Taehak. In Korean; some summaries in English. Other title: *Journal of Social Science*.

4205
SAHOE KWAHAK NONMUNJIP. 1– , 1976– . Seoul. Annual.
In Korean. Other title: *The Social Science Review*.

4206
SAHOE KWAHAK YŎN'GU. 1– , 1975?– . Ch'unch'on-si. Two no. a year.
Issued by: Ch'unon-si. In Korean. Other title: *Journal of Social Science*.

4207
SAHOE KWAHAK YŎN'GU. 1– , 1981– . Gyonsan. Two no. a year.
Issued by: Yongnam Taehakkyo Pusŏl Sahoe Kwahak Yŏn'gusŏ. In English, German, or Korean. Other title: *Journal of Social Science*.

4208
SAHOE KWAHAK YŎN'GU. 1978– . Kwangjusi. Annual.
Issued by: Choson Taehakkyo Sahoe Kwahak Yŏn'gusŏ. In Korean. Other title: *Social Science Research*.

4209
SAHOE SIMNIHAK YŎN'GU. 1– , 1982– . Seoul.
In Korean; summaries in English. Other title: *Studies on Social Psychology*.

4210
SAHOEHAK YŎN'GU. v.1– , 1962– . Seoul. Annual (irreg., v.10 in 1984).
Issued by: Sahoek-hoe, Mullikwa Taehak, Ihwa Yoja Taehakkyo Sinch'on-dong. In Korean. Tables of contents also in English.

4211
SAI CHOSEN. v.1– , 1951– . Pyongyang, New Korea Press. Monthly.

In Chinese, English, Korean and Russian. Other titles: *New Korea*; *Novaia Korea*; *Hain ch'ao-hsia*.

4212
SAKARTVELOS KOMUNISTI. KOMMUNIST GRUZII. 1– , 1930– . Tbilisi. Monthly.
Issued by: TSentral'nyĭ Komitet Kommunisticheskoĭ Partii Gruzinskoĭ SSR. In Georgian.

4213
El Salvador. Consejo Nacional de Planificación y Coordinación Económica. Sección de Investigaciones Estadísticas. INDICADORES ECONÓMICOS Y SOCIALES. Jan./June 1975– . San Salvador, Departamento de Programación General, 1976– . Semi-annual.
In Spanish.
Continues a publication of the same title issued by: Sección de Estadísticas Económicas.

4214
SĀMĀJAKA WIGIĀNA PATTARA. JOURNAL OF THE SOCIAL SCIENCES. Jan./Feb. 1966– . [Punjab]. Semi-annual.
Issued by: Punjab University. In Punjabi.

4215
SANGKHOMSAT PORITHAT. v.1– , 1953/54– . Bangkok. Quarterly, 1953–60; monthly.
Issued by: Samakhom Sankhomsat haeng Prahet Thai. In Thai. Other title: *The Social Science Review*.

4216
Saudi Arabia. Maslahat al-Iksa'at al-Ammah. THE STATISTICAL INDICATOR. 1st– , 1976– . Riyadh. Annual.
In Arabic and English.

4217
SAUDI ARABIA POLITICAL INSTITUTIONS AND REGIONAL DEVELOPMENT. 1983?– . Beirut, Research & Pub. House. Annual.
Continues, in part: *Saudi Arabia Yearbook*.

4218
SAUDI ARABIA; RECORD OF ECONOMIC DEVELOPMENT. 1983– . Beirut, Research & Pub. House.
Continues, in part: *Saudi Arabia Yearbook*.

4219
SAUDI ARABIA YEARBOOK. 1979/80–1980/81. Beirut, Research & Pub. House.
Continued by: *Saudi Arabia; Political Institutions and Regional Development*, and *Saudi Arabia; Record of Economic Development*.

4220
SAVANNA. 1– , June 1972– . Zaria. Two no. a year.
Issued by: Department of Geography, Ahmadu Belo University. Subtitle reads: "Journal of environmental and social sciences".
Indexed: Geo. Abst.; Int. Bibl. Soc. Cul. Anth.

SBORNIK DISTVUIUSHCHIKH DOGOVOROV, SOGLASHENIĬ I KONVENTSIĬ ZAKLIUCHENNYKH SSSR S INOSTRANNYMI GOSUDARSTVAMI
See Russia (1923– , U.S.S.R.). Treaties. SBORNIK DISTVUIUSHCHIKH DOGOVOROV, SOGLASHENIĬ I KONVENTSIĬ ZAKLIUCHENNYKH SSSR S INOSTRANNYMI GOSUDARSTVAMI

SBORNIK FILOZOFICKÉJ FAKULTY UNIVERZITY KOMENSKÉHO MARXIZMUS-LENINIZMUS
See Univerzita Komenshého. Ústav Marxizmu-Leninizmu. VĚDECKÝ KOMUNIZMUS

4221
SBORNIK HISTORICKÝ. v.2– , 1953– . Praha, Academia, Nakl. Československé Akademie Věd. Annual.
Issued by: Historický Ústav, Československá Akademie Věd. In Czech; summaries in German and Russian. Processed.
Continues: *Historický Sbornik*.

SBORNIK MEZHDUNARODNIKH DOGOVOROV SSSR
See Russia (1923– , U.S.S.R.). Treaties. SBORNIK MEZHDUNARODNIKH DOGOVOROV SSSR

SBORNIK MUZEIA ANTROPOLOGII I ETNOGRAFII
See Akademiia Nauk SSSR. Muzeĭ Antropologii i Etnografii. SBORNIK MUZEIA

SBORNIK MUZEIA ANTROPOLOGII I ETNOGRAFII IMENI PETRA VELIKOGO PRI AKADEMII NAUK SOIUZA SOVETSKIKH SOTSIALISTICHESKIKH RESPUBLIK
See Akademiia Nauk SSSR. Muzeĭ Antropologii i Etnografii. SBORNIK MUZEIA

SBORNIK MUZEIA ANTROPOLOGII I ETNOGRAFII PRI IMPERATORSKOĬ AKADEMII NAUK
See Akademiia Nauk SSSR. Muzeĭ Antropologii i Etnografii. SBORNIK MUZEIA

SBORNIK NAUCHNYKH TRUDOV. SERIIA OBSHCHESTVENNYKH NAUK
See Armianskiĭ Pedagogicheskiĭ Institut. NAUCHNYE TRUDY. SERIIA OBSHCHESTVENNYKH NAUK

4222
SCANDINAVIAN ECONOMIC HISTORY REVIEW. v.1– , 1953– . Copenhagen. Two no. a year.
Issued by: Scandinavian Society for Economic and Social History and Historical Geography.
Indexes: Vols. 1–10, 1953–62, 1v.
Indexed: His. Abst.; Int. Bibl. Eco.; PAIS.

SCANDINAVIAN JOURNAL OF DEVELOPING COUNTRIES
See SCANDINAVIAN JOURNAL OF DEVELOPMENT ALTERNATIVES

4223
SCANDINAVIAN JOURNAL OF DEVELOPMENT ALTERNATIVES. v.2– , Mar. 1983– . Stockholm, Bethany Books. Quarterly.
Issued in cooperation with the Institute of Alternative Development Research in Oslo.
Continues: *Scandinavian Journal of Developing Countries* (v.1, no.3–4, Sept.–Dec. 1982) which in turn continues: *Scandinavian Journal on the Developing Countries* (v.1, no.1–2, 1982)

4224
SCANDINAVIAN JOURNAL OF ECONOMICS. v.78– , 1976– . Stockholm, distributed by: Almqvist and Wiksell. Quarterly.
Issued by: Department of Economics, University of Stockholm.
Continues: *The Swedish Journal of Economics. Ekonomisk Tidskrift* (1965–76).
Indexed: Bull. Anal. Pol. Ec. Soc.; Int. Bibl. Eco.; J. Eco. Lit.; PAIS; SSCI.

SCANDINAVIAN JOURNAL OF EDUCATIONAL RESEARCH
See PEDAGOGISK FORSKNING

4225
SCANDINAVIAN JOURNAL OF HISTORY. 1– , 1976– . Stockholm, Almqvist & Wiksell International. Quarterly.
Issued by: Historical Association of Denmark, Finland, Norway and Sweden.

4226
SCANDINAVIAN JOURNAL OF PSYCHOLOGY. v.1– , 1960– . Stockholm, Almqvist & Wiksell. Quarterly.
Issued by: Psychological associations of Denmark, Finland, Norway and Sweden. Includes monographic supplement called "Supplementum" (no.1, 1982)
Indexed: Psych. Abst.

4227
SCANDINAVIAN JOURNAL OF SPORT SCIENCES. v.1– , Aug. 1979– . Helsinki. Two no. a year.
Issued by: Finnish Society for Research in Sport and Physical Education.

SCANDINAVIAN JOURNAL ON THE DEVELOPING COUNTRIES
See SCANDINAVIAN JOURNAL OF DEVELOPMENT ALTERNATIVES

4228
SCANDINAVIAN PERIODICAL INDEX IN ECONOMICS AND BUSINESS. SCANP. 1978– . Helsinki. Annual, 1978–84; two no. a year.
Issued by: Arhus School of Business Administration Library, Copenhagen School of Economics and Business Administration Library, Norwegian School of Economics and Business Administration Library, and Stockholm School of Economics Library.

4229
SCANDINAVIAN POLITICAL STUDIES. v.1–2, 1966–1977; n. ser. v.1– , 1978– . Helsinki, later Oslo, Beverly Hills, Calif., Sage Publications. Annual, 1966–77; quarterly.
Issued by: Finnish Political Studies Association, Institute of Political Studies of the University of Helsinki, and other Scandinavian associations.
Indexed: ABC POL SCI; Bull. Anal. Pol. Ec. Soc.; Int. Bibl. Eco.; Int. Bibl. Pol. Sc.; Int. Pol. Sc. Abst.; Soc. Abst.; Soc. Sc. Hum. Ind.

4230
SCANDINAVIAN REVIEW. v.1– , 1913– . New York. Bimonthly, v.1–7, monthly, v.8–10; quarterly.
Issued by: American Scandinavian Foundation.
Title varies: v.1–62, 1913–74, *The American Scandinavian Review.*
Indexed: His. Abst.; Ind. Per. Art. Law; Int. Bibl. Soc. Cul. Anth.; PAIS; Peace Res. Abst. J.

SCANDINAVIAN REVIEW OF SOCIOLOGY
See ACTA SOCIOLOGICA. SCANDINAVIAN REVIEW OF SOCIOLOGY

SCANDINAVISCHE ZEITSCHRIFT FÜR SOZIOLOGIE
See ACTA SOCIOLOGICA

SCHMOLLERS JAHRBUCH FÜR GESETZGEBUNG, VERWALTUNG UND VOLKSWIRTSCHAFT
See SCHMOLLERS JAHRBUCH FÜR WIRTSCHAFT UND SOZIALWISSENSCHAFTEN

SCHMOLLERS JAHRBUCH FÜR GESETZGEBUNG, VERWALTUNG UND VOLKSWIRTSCHAFT IM DEUTSCHEN REIHE

See SCHMOLLERS JAHRBUCH FÜR WIRTSCHAFTS- UND SOZIALWISSENSCHAFTEN

4231
SCHMOLLERS JAHRBUCH FÜR WIRTSCHAFTS- UND SOZIALWISSENSCHAFTEN. v.1–91, 1877–1971. Berlin, Duncker & Humblot. Quarterly, 1877–1924; bimonthly.
Title varies: 1877–1912, *Jahrbuch für Gesetzgebung, Verwaltung und Volkswirtschaft im Deutschen Reihe*; 1913–44, *Schmollers Jahrbuch für Gesetzgebung, Verwaltung und Volkswirtschaft im Deutschen Reihe*; 1949–68, *Schmollers Jahrbuch für Gesetzgebung, Verwaltung und Volkswirtschaft*. Not published 1945–48.
Supersedes: *Jahrbuch für Gesetzgebung, Verwaltung und Rechtspflege des Deutschen Reiches*.
Continued by: *Zeitschrift für Wirtschafts- und Sozialwissenschaften*.

4232
THE SCHOMBURG CENTER JOURNAL. v.2– , winter 1983– . New York.
Issued by: Schomburg Center for Research in Black Culture.
Continues: Schomburg Center for Black Culture. *Journal* (v.1, 1982).

4233
SCHOOL AND SOCIETY. v.1–100, Jan. 2, 1915–Oct. 1972. New York. Monthly.
Issued by: Society for the Advancement of Education.
Continued by: *Intellect* (v.101–, 1973–)

4234
SCHOOL REVIEW. v.1– , Jan. 1893– . Ithaca, later Chicago, Ill., University of Chicago Press. Monthly (except July–Aug.); quarterly.
Subtitle reads: "A journal for research, theory and philosophical inquiry in education and related disciplines".
Indexes: Vols. 1–10, 1893–1902, 1v.

SCHRIFTEN
See Akademie der Wissenschaften der DDR. Zentralinstitut für Geschichte. SCHRIFTEN

SCHRIFTEN
See Universitat Münster. Institut für Christliche Sozialwissenschaften. SCHRIFTEN

4235
SCHRIFTEN ZU GESCHICHTE UND KULTUR DES ALTEN ORIENT. v.1– , 1971– . Berlin, Akademie-Verlag. Irreg.
Issued by: Zentralinstitut für Alte Geschichte und Archäologie, Akademie der Wissenschaften der DDR. In German. Monograph series.

4236
SCHRIFTEN ZUR MITTELSTANDFORSCHUNG. v.1– , 1962– ; n. ser., v.1– , 1984– . Wiesbaden, Verlag Otto Schwartz. Irreg.
Issued by: Institut für Mittelstandforschung. In German. Monograph series.

4237
SCHRIFTEN ZUR UR- UND FRÜHGESCHICHTE. v.1– , 1953– . Berlin, Akademie-Verlag. Irreg.
Issued by: Zentralinstitut für Alte Geschichte und Archäologie, Akademie der Wissenschaften der DDR. In German.
Continues: Akademie der Wissenschaften, Berlin. Sektion für Vor- und Frühgeschichte. *Schriften*.

SCHRIFTENREIHE DER HOCHSCHULE FÜR POLITISCHE WISSENSCHAFTEN
See POLITISCHE STUDIEN

4238
SCHWEIZER JAHRBUCH DES ÖFFENTLICHEN LEBENS. ANNUAIRE SUISSE DE LA VIE PUBLIQUE. 1958/59– . Basel, Hans Heinemann. Annual.
In French or German. Includes a section on the Principality of Liechtenstein.

4239
Schweizerische Gesellschaft für Urgeschichte. JAHRBUCH. ANNUAIRE. Frauenfeld. Irreg.
In French, German, or Italian. Title varies: 1908–37, *Jahresbericht*. Earlier name of the issuing body was: Schweizerische Gesellschaft für Ur- und Frühgeschichte.
Indexes: Vols. 1–25, 1908–33, 1v.

4240
Schweizerische Institut für Auslandsforschung. SOZIALWISSENSCHAFTLICHE STUDIEN. v.1– , 1953– ; n. ser. v.5– , 1977– . Zürich.
In German.

SCHWEIZERISCHE POLITIK IN JAHRE . . .
See ANNÉE POLITIQUE SUISSE

4241
SCHWEIZERISCHE ZEITSCHRIFT FÜR GEMEINNUTZIGKEIT. 1–18, 1862–1879. Zürich. Bimonthly.
Issued by: Schweizerische Gemeinnutzige Gesellschaft. In French or German.

4242
SCHWEIZERISCHE ZEITSCHRIFT FÜR GESCHICHTE. REVUE SUISSE D'HISTOIRE. RIVISTA STORICA SVIZZERA. 1– , 1951– . Zürich. Quarterly.
Organ of: Vereinigung Schweitzer Archivar. Issued by: Allgemeine Geschichtsforschende Gesellschaft der Schweitz. In French or German. Includes supplement "Beihefte" (no.1–, 1943–)
Indexed: His. Abst.

SCHWEIZERISCHE ZEITSCHRIFT FÜR INTERNATIONALE WIRTSCHAFTSBEZIEHUNGEN
See AUSSENWIRTSCHAFT

SCHWEIZERISCHE ZEITSCHRIFT FÜR LÄNDER UND VOLKSKUNDE
See GEOGRAPHIA HELVETICA

4243
SCHWEIZERISCHE ZEITSCHRIFT FÜR PSYCHOLOGIE UND IHRE ANWENDUNGEN. REVUE SUISSE DE PSYCHOLOGIE APPLIQUÉE. v.1– , 1942– . Bern, Huber.
In French or German. Supplements called "Beiheft" (no.1–, 1945–) accompany some numbers.

4244
SCHWEIZERISCHE ZEITSCHRIFT FÜR SOZIOLOGIE. REVUE SUISSE DE SOCIOLOGIE. 1– , Nov. 1975– . Genève. Three no. a year.
Issued by: Schweizerische Gesellschaft für Soziologie. In English, French, or German; summaries in these languages.
Indexed: Int. Pol. Sc. Abst.; LLBA; Sage Fam. Stu. Abst.; Soc. Abst.

4245
SCHWEIZERISCHE ZEITSCHRIFT FÜR VOLKSWIRTSCHAFT UND STATISTIK. REVUE SUISSE D'ÉCONOMIE POLITIQUE ET DE STATISTIQUE. 1– , 1865– . Bern. Irreg., 1897–1914; quarterly, 1865–96, 1914–.
Issued by: Schweizerische Gesellschaft für Statistik und Volkswirtschaft. In English, French, or German. Title varies: 1916–44, *Zeitschrift für Schweizerische Volkswirtschaft; Journal de Statistique et Revue Économique Suisse*.
Indexed: Int. Bibl. Eco.; Int. Bibl. Soc. Cul. Anth.; Int. Lab. Doc.; Int. Pol. Sc. Abst.; PAIS; PAISFL; Pop. Ind.

4246
SCHWEIZERISCHES ARCHIV FÜR VOLKSKUNDE. v.1– , 1897– . Basel. Quarterly (irreg.)
Issued by: Schweizerische Gesellschaft für Volkskunde. In German.
Indexes: Vols. 1–45, 1897–1948, 1v. (supplement to v.46); includes index to v.1–38 of *Schweizer Volkskunde* and to v.35–38 of *Folklore Suisse*.
Indexed: Int. Bibl. Soc. Cul. Anth.

4247
SCHWEIZERISCHES JAHRBUCH FÜR INTERNATIONALES RECHT. ANNUAIRE SUISSE DE DROIT INTERNATIONAL. v.1– , 1944– . Zürich, Schalthess Polygraphischer Verlag.
Issued by: Schweizerischer Vereinigung für Internationales Recht. In French or German.
Indexed: Ind. For. Leg. Per.

SCHWEIZERISCHES JAHRBUCH FÜR POLITISCHE WISSENSCHAFT
See ANNUAIRE SUISSE DE SCIENCE POLITIQUE

4248
SCIENCE. v.1– , Nov./Dec. 1979– . Washington, D.C. Bimonthly.
Issued by: American Association for the Advancement of Science.
Indexed: Abst. Anth.; Ind. Per. Art. Law; Int. Lab. Doc.; LLBA; Peace Res. Abst. J.; Psych. Abst.; Soc. Abst.

SCIENCE ADMINISTRATIVE
See BULLETIN SIGNALÉTIQUE. 528. SCIENCE ADMINISTRATIVE

4249
SCIENCE AND CULTURE. v.1– , June 1935– . Calcutta. Monthly.
Issued by: Indian Science News Association. Subtitle reads: "A monthly journal of natural and cultural sciences".
Indexed: Peace Res. Abst. J.; Soc. Abst.

4250
SCIENCE AND PUBLIC AFFAIRS. no.1– , 1986– . London.
Issued by: Royal Society.

4251
SCIENCE AND PUBLIC POLICY. v.1– , 1970– . New York. Irreg.
Subseries of: New York Academy of Sciences. *Annals*.

4252
SCIENCE & PUBLIC POLICY. v.1– , Jan. 1974– . London. Monthly, 1974–75; bimonthly.
Issued by: Science Policy Foundation.
Supersedes: *Science Policy*, and *Science Policy News*.
Indexed: Bull. Anal. Pol. Ec. Soc.; Int. Bibl. Eco.

4253
SCIENCE & SOCIETY. v.1–15, fall 1936–fall 1951. New York. Quarterly.

Issued by: John Jay College, City University of New York. Subtitle reads: "An independent journal of Marxism".
Indexes: Vols. 1–25, 1936–61, 1v.
Indexed: ABC POL SCI; Bull. Anal. Pol. Ec. Soc.; Bull. Sig. Soc. Eth.; His. Abst.; Int. Bibl. Pol. Sc.; Int. Bibl. Soc.; Int. Pol. Sc. Abst.; PAIS; Soc. Sc. Hum. Ind.; Soc. Abst.; Wom. Stu. Abst.

4254
SCIENCE AND SOCIETY. v.1– , 1978– . West Lafayette, Ind. Irreg.
Subtitle reads: "A Purdue University series in science, technology and human values".
Indexed: ABC POL SCI; Curr. Cont. Soc. Beh. Sc.; Bull. Sig. Soc. Eth.; Ind. Per. Art. Law; His. Abst.; Int. Bibl. Eco.; Int. Bibl. Pol. Sc.; Int. Lab. Doc.; Int. Pol. Sc. Abst.; Int. Bibl. Soc.; J. Ec. Lit.; Peace Res. Abst. J.; Soc. Abst.; Soc. Sc. Hum. Ind.; SSCI; Wom. Stu. Abst.

4255
Science Council of Canada. STUDY OF POPULATION AND TECHNOLOGY. PERCEPTIONS. 1– , Nov. 1975– . Ottawa. Irreg.
Published also in French edition: *Étude sur la Population et la Technologie. Perceptions*. Monograph series.

4256
SCIENCE ET PAIX. no.1– , 1973– . Bruxelles. Quarterly.
Issued by: International Peace Research Association. In French.

4257
SCIENCE FOR PEOPLE. v.1– , 1973– . London. Quarterly.
Issued by: British Society for Social Responsibility in Science.

SCIENCE, MEDICINE AND MAN
See ETHICS IN SCIENCE AND MEDICINE

4258
SCIENCE OF SCIENCE. v.1– , 1980– . Wrocław, Zakład Narodowy im. Ossolińskich. Four no. a year.
Issued by: Committee of Science of Science, Polish Academy of Sciences. Summaries in French, German and Russian.
Continues: *Problems of the Science of Science*.

4259
SCIENCE POLICY STUDIES AND DOCUMENTS. no.1– , 1965– . Paris. Irreg.
Issued by: United Nations Educational, Scientific and Cultural Organization. In English or French. Monograph series.

4260
LA SCIENCE SOCIALE, SUIVANT LA MÉTHODE D'OBSERVATION. v.1–18, 1886–1903; v.19–38 (2. période, 1–144 fasc.;, 1904–1924; v.4–42 (3. période, 1–9 fasc.0, 1925–27; v.43 (4. période, 10 fasc.), 1928. Paris. Monthly, 1886–1915; annual, 1916–24; quarterly, 1925–26; annual, 1927–28.
Beginning with 1904 issued in the form of monographs. In French.
Continues with its own title and numbering as individual issues of *Études Sociales*.

4261
SCIENCE, TECHNOLOGY & HUMAN VALUES. no.25– , fall 1978– . Cambridge, Mass., M.I.T. Press, later New York, Wiley. Quarterly.
Issued by: Program on Science, Technology and Public Policy, Harvard University; co-sponsored by the Science, Technology and Society, Massachusetts Institute of Technology and the John F. Kennedy School of Government, Harvard University.
Continues: *Newsletter on Science, Technology and Public Policy*.

SCIENCES ADMINISTRATIVES
See BULLETIN SIGNALÉTIQUE. 528. BIBLIOGRAPHIE INTERNATIONALE DE SCIENCE ADMINISTRATIVE

SCIENCES DE L'HOMME
See ANNUAIRE CNRS. SCIENCES DE L'HOMME

SCIENCES HUMAINES
See Institut Fondamental d'Afrique Noire. BULLETIN. SÉRIE B. SCIENCES HUMAINES

4262
SCIENCES POLITIQUES. v.1–59, 1886–1936; n. ser. no.1–16, Mar. 1937–Feb. 1940. Paris. Quarterly, 1886–1911, 1921–36; bimonthly, 1894–1920, 1938–40. Two volumes per year, 1912–19.
In French. Title varies: v.1–13, 1886–98, École Libre des Sciences Politiques. *Annales*; v.14–25, 1899–1910, *Annales des Sciences Politiques*.
Indexes: Vols. 1–10, 1886–95, in v.10; v.11–20, 1896–1905, in v.20; v.21–48, 1906–25, in v.48; v.49–58, 1926–35, in v.58.

4263
SCIENCES SOCIALES. v.1– , 1970– . Moscow, Mezhdunarodnai͡a Kniga. Quarterly, 1970; bimonthly.
In French. Published also in English: *Social Sciences*; in German: *Gesellschaftswissenschaften*; in Portuguese: *Ciências Sociais*; and in Spanish: *Ciencias Sociales*.
Indexed: Bull. Anal. Pol. Ec. Soc.; Bull. Sig. Soc. Eth.; Int. Bibl. Eco.; Int. Bibl. Pol. Sc.; Int. Pol. Sc. Abst.

SCIENCES SOCIALES AU CANADA
See SOCIAL SCIENCES IN CANADA

4264
SCIENCES SOCIALES DU JAPON CONTEMPORAIN. Nov. 1981– . Paris. Semi-annual.
Issued by: Centre de Recherche sur le Japon Contemporain, École des Hautes Études en Sciences Sociales [et] Centre Nationale de la Recherche Scientifique. Centre de Documentation en Sciences Humaines. In French; summaries in English. Other title: *Gendai Nihon Shakai Kagaku.*
Continues: *Économie et Politique du Japon Contemporain.*

4265
SCIENTIFIC AMERICAN. v.1–14, Aug. 28, 1845–June 25, 1859; n. ser. v.1– , July 2, 1859– . New York. Weekly, 1845–Oct. 15, 1921; monthly.
Absorbed: *People's Journal*, Nov. 1954; and *Scientific American Monthly*, Nov. 1921.
Indexes: v.178, no.5–v.197, May 1948–Dec. 1957.
Indexed: Abst. Anth.; Abst. Soc. Work.; Bull. Anal. Pol. Ec. Soc.; Ind. Per. Art. Law; Int. Bibl. Soc.; Int. Lab. Doc.; LLBA; Int. Pol. Sc. Abst.; Pop. Ind.; Psych. Abst.; Sage Urb. Stu. Abst.; Soc. Abst.; Soc. Work. Res. Abst.

SCIENTIFIC REPORTS
See World Fertility Survey. SCIENTIFIC REPORTS

4266
SCIENTOMETRICS. v.1– , Jan. 1979– . Amsterdam, Elsevier Scientific Pub. Co. Bimonthly.
Subtitle reads: "An international journal for all quantitative aspects of science of science and social policy".
Indexed: Soc. Abst.

4267
SCOTTISH HISTORICAL REVIEW. v.1– , Oct. 1903– . Edinburgh, later Aberdeen, The Aberdeen University Press. Quarterly, 1903–July 1928; semi-annual.
Issued by: Company of Scottish History.
Supersedes: *The Scottish Antiquary.*
Indexes: Vols. 1–12, 1903–16, 1v.; v.13–25, 1916–28, 1v.

4268
SCOTTISH STUDIES. 1– , 1957– . Edinburgh. Semi-annual.
Issued by: School of Scottish Studies, University of Edinburgh.
Indexed: Abst. Anth.; Int. Bibl. Soc. Cul. Anth.

4269
SCRIPTA MERCATURAE. v.1– , 1961– . München, Scripta Mercaturae Verlag. Semi-annual.
In German; summaries in English and French. Subtitle reads: "Zeitschrift für Wirtschafts- und Sozialgeschichte".

SÉANCES ET TRAVAUX
See Académie des Sciences Morales et Politiques. REVUE DES TRAVAUX ET COMPTES RENDUS DE SES SÉANCES

4270
SEGREGATION AND DISCRIMINATION IN SPORT. 1975– . Waterloo. Three no. a year.
Issued by: SIRLS, Faculty of Human Kinetics and Leisure, University of Waterloo.

4271
SEIJIGAKU RONSHŪ. 1974– . Tokyo.
Issued by: Komazawa Daigaku Hogakubu. In Japanese. Other title: *The Political Science Review of Komazawa University.*

SEKER AL MEHKAR SHOTEF BEMADA'E HA-HITNAHAGUT BE-YISRA'EL
See Henrieta Szold Institute—National Institute for Research in the Behavioral Sciences. Information Retrieval Centre for Research in the Behavioral Sciences. SEKER AL MEHKAR SHOTEF BEMADA'E HA-HITNAHAGUT BE-YISRA'EL

SELECTED DECISIONS OF THE INTERNATIONAL MONETARY FUND: SELECTED DOCUMENTS
See International Monetary Fund. SELECTED DECISIONS OF THE INTERNATIONAL MONETARY FUND; SELECTED DOCUMENTS

SELECTED PAPERS
See International Congress of Americanists. PROCEEDINGS

SELECTED SOVIET ANNOTATED BIBLIOGRAPHIES: ASIA, AFRICA AND LATIN AMERICA
See SOVIET PERIODICAL ABSTRACTS: ASIA, AFRICA AND LATIN AMERICA

SELECTED SOVIET ANNOTATED BIBLIOGRAPHIES: SOVIET SOCIETY
See SOVIET PERIODICAL ABSTRACTS: SOVIET SOCIETY

4272
THE SEOUL NATIONAL UNIVERSITY ECONOMIC REVIEW. Dec. 1967– . Seoul. Semi-annual.
Issued by: Institute of Economic Research, Seoul National University. In English or German.

4273
SERIE, ECONOMÍA Y SOCIOLOGÍA AGRARIAS. no.1– , 1971– . Madrid. Irreg.
Issued by: Instituto Nacional de Investigación Agrarias. In Spanish; summaries in English.
Supersedes: Annales del Instituto de Investigaciones Agrarias.

SERIE DE CULTURA NÁHUATL. ESTUDIOS DE CULTURA NÁHUATL
See Universidad Nacional Autónoma de México. Instituto de Investigaciones Históricas. SERIE DE CULTURA NÁHUATL. ESTUDIOS DE CULTURA NÁHUATL

SERIE DE CULTURA NÁHUATL. FUENTES
See Universidad Nacional Autónoma de México. Instituto de Investigaciones Históricas. SERIE DE CULTURA NÁHUATL. FUENTES

SERIE DE CULTURA NÁHUATL. MONOGRAFÍAS
See Universidad Nacional Autónoma de México. Instituto de Investigaciones Históricas. SERIE DE CULTURA NÁHUATL. MONOGRAFÍAS

SERIE DE CULTURAS MESOAMERICANAS
See Universidad Nacional Autónoma de México. Instituto de Investigaciones Históricas. SERIE DE CULTURAS MESOAMERICANAS

SERIE HISTORIADORES Y CRONISTAS DE INDIAS
See Universidad Nacional Autónoma de México. Instituto de Investigaciones Históricas. SERIE DE HISTORIADORES Y CRONISTAS DE INDIAS

4274
SÉRIE SCIENCES DE L'HOMME. no.1–29/30, Jan./June 1968–Jan./Dec. 1984. Paris. Semi-annual.
Issued by: Institut des Hautes Études de l'Amérique Latine, Université de la Sorbonne Nouvelle. In French.
Continued by: *Cahiers des Amériques Latines* (1985–)

SERIES: DOCUMENTS ON AMERICAN FOREIGN RELATIONS
See AMERICAN FOREIGN RELATIONS; A DOCUMENTARY RECORD

SERIES GEOGRAPHICA ET ETHNOGRAPHICA
See ACTA HUMBOLDTIANA

SERIES IN SOCIAL STUDIES. OCCASIONAL PAPER
See University, Harare. Department of Sociology. SERIES IN SOCIAL STUDIES. OCCASIONAL PAPER

SERIES MARXISTICA-LENINISTICA
See ACTA MARXISTICA DEBRECINA

4275
SERIES ON THE DEVELOPMENT OF SOCIETIES. 1– , 1976– . The Hague, M. Nijhoff. Irreg.
Issued by: Institute of Social Studies. Monograph series.

SERIES SSH. SOCIAL SCIENCES/HUMANITIES
See DIRECTORY OF PUBLISHED PROCEEDINGS. SERIES SSH. SOCIAL SCIENCES/HUMANITIES

4276
SERII͡A EKONOMIKA I PRIKLADNAI͡A SOT͡SIOLOGII͡A. no.1– , 1985– . Novosibirsk, Izd-vo Kultura. Three no. a year.
In Russian.
Continues: *Izvestii͡a Sibirskogo Otdelenii͡a Akademii Nauk SSSR. Serii͡a Ekonomiki i Prikladnoĭ Sot͡siologii.*

SERII͡A EKONOMIKI
See Akademii͡a Nauk Azerbaĭdzhanskoĭ SSR. IZVESTII͡A. SERII͡A EKONOMIKI

SERII͡A ISTORII, ARKHEOLOGII, EKONOMIKI, FILOSOFII I PRAVA
See Akademii͡a Nauk Kazakhskoĭ SSR. IZVESTII͡A. SERII͡A ISTORII, ARKHEOLOGII, EKONOMIKI, FILOSOFII I PRAVA

SERII͡A ISTORII, FILOSOFII I PRAVA
See Akademii͡a Nauk Azerbaĭdzhanskoĭ SSR. IZVESTII͡A. SERII͡A ISTORII, FILOSOFII I PRAVA

SERII͡A ISTORII͡A
See Moskovskiĭ Universitet. VESTNIK. SERII͡A ISTORII͡A

SERII͡A OBSHCHESTVENNAI͡A
See Akademii͡a Nauk Kazakhskoĭ SSR. IZVESTII͡A. SERII͡A OBSHCHESTVENNAI͡A

SERII͡A OBSHCHESTVENNYKH NAUK
See Akademia de Shtiint͡se a RSS Moldovenest. BULETINUL. IZVESTII͡A. SERII͡A OBSHCHESTVENNYKH NAUK

SERII͡A OBSHCHESTVENNYKH NAUK
See Akademii͡a Nauk Azerbaĭdzhanskoĭ SSR. SERII͡A OBSHCHESTVENNYKH NAUK

SERIIA OBSHCHESTVENNYKH NAUK
See Akademiia Nauk Kazakhskoĭ SSR. IZVESTIIA. SERIIA OBSHCHESTVENNYKH NAUK

SERIIA OBSHCHESTVENNYKH NAUK
See Akademiia Nauk SSSR. Sibirskoe Otdelenie. IZVESTIIA. SERIIA OBSHCHESTVENNYKH NAUK

SERIIA OBSHCHESTVENNYKH NAUK
See Akademiia Nauk SSSR. Turkmenskiĭ Filial. IZVESTIIA. SERIIA OBSHCHESTVENNYKH NAUK

SERIIA OBSHCHESTVENNYKH NAUK
See Akademiia Nauk Turkmenskoĭ SSR. IZVESTIIA. SERIIA OBSHCHESTVENNYKH NAUK

SERIIA OBSHCHESTVENNYKH NAUK
See Akademiia Navuk Belorusskoĭ SSR. IZVESTIIA. SERIIA OBSHESTVENNYKH NAUK

SERIIA OBSHCHESTVENNYKH NAUK
See Eesti NSV. Teaduste Akademia. IZVESTIIA. SERIIA OBSHCHESTVENNYKH NAUK

4277
SERVICE SOCIAL DANS LE MONDE. 1935– . Bruxelles. Frequency varied; quarterly.
Issued by: Catholic International Union for Social Service. In French. Title varies: *Bulletin d'Information.*
Indexed: Bull. Anal. Pol. Ec. Soc.

4278
SERVICES MONDIAUX D'INFORMATION EN SCIENCES SOCIALES. WORLD SOCIAL SCIENCE INFORMATION SERVICES. 1– , 1976– . Paris, The Unesco Press. Irreg.
Monograph series of reference works.

4279
SHAKAI KAGAKU JANARU. 1960– . Tokyo. Annual.
In Japanese; some articles in English. Other title: *The Journal of Social Science.* (Series: Kokusai Kirisutokyo-Daigaku, Tokyo Kokusai Kirisutokyo-Daigaku, Gakuho)

4280
SHAKAI KAGAKU KENKYŪ. v.1– , 1951– . Tokyo. Bimonthly.
Issued by: Tokyo Daigaku Shakai Kagaku Kenkyū-sho. In Japanese. Other title: *Social Science Journal.*
Indexed: His. Abst.

SHAKAI KAGAKU KENKYŪJO EIBUN HOKOKU
See Tokyo Daigaku. Shakai Kagaku Kenkyūjo. ANNALS

4281
SHAKAI KAGAKU RONSHŪ. no.1– , 1954– . Tokyo. Annual.
Issued by: Tokyo Daigaku. Bungakubu. In Japanese. Some numbers have title: *Shakaikagaku Ronshū.* Other title: *The Journal of Social Science.* (Series: Tokyo Kyoiku Daigaku. Bungakubu. Tokyo Kyoiku Bungakubu Kiyo)
Indexed: His. Abst.; Int. Bibl. Eco.; Int. Bibl. Pol. Sc.; Int. Bibl. Soc.

4282
SHAKAI KAGAKU RONSHŪ. no.1– , 1958– . Saitama. Semi-annual.
Issued by: Saitama Daigaku Keizai Gakkai. In Japanese. Other title: *The Social Science Review.*
Indexed: Int. Bibl. Eco.; Int. Bibl. Pol. Sc.; Int. Bibl. Soc.

4283
SHAKAI MONDAI KENKYŪ. v.1– , July 1951– . Osaka. Quarterly (irreg.).
Issued by: Shakai Mondai Kenkyū Kai. In Japanese. Other title: *The Journal of Social Problems.*

4284
SHAKAI SHISŌ SHI KENKYŪ. 1– , 1977– . Kyoto, Minerubua Shobo.
Issued by: Shakai Shisō Shigakkai Shiso Shigakkai Nempō. In Japanese. Other title: *Annals of the Society for the History of Social Thought.*

4285
SHAKAIGAKU HYŌRON. v.1– , July 1948– . Tokyo. Quarterly.
Issued by: Nihon Shakai Gakkai, and the Department of Sociology, Tokyo University. In Japanese; summaries in English. Other title: *Japanese Sociological Review.*
Indexed: Int. Bibl. Soc.

4286
SHAKAIGAKU KENKYŪ. no.1–27, July 1950–July 1966; no.28– , July 1967– . Tohoku.
Issued by: Tohoku Shakaigaku Kenkyu-kai, and Tohoku Daigaku. In Japanese. Tables of contents also in English. Other title: *The Study of Sociology.*

SHAKAIGAKU KENKYŪ
See Hitotsubashi Daigaku. HITOTSUBASHI

4287
SHAKAIGAKU NENSHI. no.1–8, Apr. 1956–Dec. 1965; no.9– , Dec. 1967– . Tokyo. Three no. a year.

Issued by: Waseda Daigaku Shakai Gakkai. In Japanese. Other title: *Annual Bulletin of Sociology*.

SHAKAIKAGAKU RONSHŪ
See SHAKAI KAGAKU RONSHŪ

4288
SHE HUI HSÜEH-CHIEN. 1927–1938.
In Chinese. Vol. 10 includes abstracts in English and French. Other title: *The Sociological World*.
Superseded by: *Yon-chin she hui k'o hsüeh*.

4289
SHE HUI K'O HSÜEH LUN TS'UNG. v.1– , Apr. 1950– . Taipei.
Issued by: T'aiwan ta hsüeh fa hsüeh yuan. In Chinese or English. Other title: *Journal of Social Science*.

4290
SHIMONOSEKI SHŌKEI RONSHŪ. 1957– . Shimonoseki-shi. Three no. a year.
Issued by: Shimonoseki Gakkai. In Japanese; some articles in English or German.

SHINRIGAKU KENKYŪ
See JAPANESE JOURNAL OF PSYCHOLOGY

4291
SHISŌ. 1921– . Tokyo, Iwanami Shoten Publishers. Monthly.
In Japanese. Other title: *Thought*.
Indexed: His. Abst.; Int. Bibl. Pol. Sc.; Int. Bibl. Soc.; Peace Res. Abst. J.

4292
Siam Society. JOURNAL. v.1– , 1904– . Bangkok. Irreg.
Vols. 32–35, 1940–44 issued by the society under the name: Thailand Research Society. Early volumes in French, German or Siamese; now in English, occasionally in French.
Indexes: Vols. 1–10, 1904–13, in v.10; v.1–25, 1904–32, 1v.
Indexed: Int. Bibl. Soc. Cul. Anth.

SIBIRSKIĬ ETNOGRAFICHESKIĬ SBORNIK
See Akademii͡a Nauk SSSR. Institut Etnografii. TRUDY. n. ser.

4293
SIGNS; JOURNAL OF WOMEN IN CULTURE AND SOCIETY. v.1– , autumn 1975– . Chicago, Ill., University of Chicago Press. Quarterly.
Issued by: Barnard College.
Indexes: Vols. 1–10, 1975–85, 1v. (Supplement to summer issue, 1986)
Indexed: Abst. Anth.; Bull. Anal. Pol. Ec. Soc.; Bull. Sig. Soc. Eth.; Soc. Abst.

4294
SIMULATION AND GAMES. v.1– , Mar. 1970– . Beverly Hills, Calif., Sage Publications. Quarterly.
Subtitle reads: "An international journal of theory design and research".
Indexed: ABC POL SCI; Bull. Anal. Pol. Ec. Soc.; Int. Bibl. Eco.; Int. Bibl. Pol. Sc.; Int. Bibl. Soc.; Int. Pol. Sc. Abst.; PAIS; PHRA; Psych. Abst.; Sage Urb. Stu. Abst.; Soc. Abst.; Soc. Sc. Ind.; SSCI.

4295
SINGAPORE ECONOMIC REVIEW. v.28– , Apr. 1983– . Singapore, Economic Society of Singapore. Semi-annual.
Issued by: Economic Society of Singapore, and Department of Economics and Statistics, University of Singapore.
Continues: *Malayan Economic Review*.

4296
SINGAPORE JOURNAL OF EDUCATION. v.1– , Aug. 1978– . Singapore, Federal Publications Ltd. Irreg.
Issued by: Institute of Education. In English or Malay.

SINO-SOVIET AFFAIRS
See CHUNG-SO YON'GU

4297
SINOPSIS DE LA EVOLUCIÓN ECONÓMICA DE AMÉRICA LATINA. 1979– . Washington, D.C. Annual.
Issued by: Organización de los Estados Americanos. Secretaría General. In Spanish. Other title: *Sinopsis del Desarrollo Económico de América Latina*.

SINOPSIS DEL DESARROLLO ECONÓMICO DE AMÉRICA LATINA
See SINOPSIS DE LA EVOLUCIÓN ECONÓMICA DE AMÉRICA LATINA EN . . .

4298
SINTESE. n. ser. v.1– , Jan./June 1974– . Rio de Janeiro, Edições Loyola.
Issued by: Sociedade Brasileira de Educação, 1974–76; Centro João XXIII (R.J.), Sociedade Brasileira de Educação. In Portuguese.
Continues: *Sintese Política, Econômica e Social* (v.1–9, no.1–33, 1959–67)

4299
SISTEMA. no.1– , Jan. 1973– . Madrid. Three no. a year.

Organ of: Instituto de Técnicas Sociales, Fundación Fondo Social Universitario in cooperation with CEDIS, Centro de Estudios, Documentación y Información Socialista de la Fundación Pablo Iglesias. In Spanish.
Indexed: Int. Bibl. Eco.; Int. Bibl. Pol. Sc.; Int. Pol. Sc. Abst.; PAISFL.

4300
SISYPHUS. v.1– , 1981– . Warszawa, Państwowe Wydawnictwo Naukowe. Irreg.
Issued by: Instytut Filozofii i Socjologii, Polska Akademia Nauk. In English.

4301
AL-SĪYĀSAH AL-DAWLIYAH. 1– , July 1965– . al-Qāhirah, Mu'assasat al-Akram. Quarterly.
In Arabic, English, French, or German.

SIYASAL BILGILER FAKULTESI DERGISI
See Universite, Ankara. SIYASAL BILGILER FAKULTESI DERGISI

SIYASAL BILGILER OKULU
See Universite, Ankara. SIYASAL BILGILER FAKULTESI DERGISI

SKHOZHDENIE
See CONVERGENCE

SKRIFTER
See Svenska Sallskapet for Antropologi och Geografi. SKRIFTER

4302
SLAVERY AND ABOLITION. v.1– , May 1980– . London, Frank Cass. Three no. a year.

4303
SLAVIA ANTIQUA. v.1– , 1948– . Warszawa, Państwowe Wydawnictwo Naukowe. Annual.
Issued by: Katedra Archeologii Polskiej, Uniwersytet im. A. Mickiewicza, and Katedra Archeologii Słowiańskiej, Uniwersytet Warszawski. In Czech, English, French, Italian, Polish, or Russian; summaries in English, French, or Russian.
Indexed: Int. Bibl. Soc. Cul. Anth.

SLAVIC AND EAST EUROPEAN STUDIES
See ÉTUDES SLAVES ET EST-EUROPÉENNES

4304
SLAVIC AND EUROPEAN EDUCATION REVIEW. no.1– , 1977– . Bowling Green, Ohio. Semi-annual.
Issued through the cooperation of the Education Committee of the American Association for the Advancement of Slavic Studies and die Arbeitsstelle für Vergleichende Bildungsforschung, Ruhr-Universität, Bochum.

4305
SLAVIC REVIEW. v.1– , 1945– . Seattle, Wash. Semi-annual, 1945–47; quarterly.
Organ of: American Association for the Advancement of Slavic Studies. Vols. Aug. 1955–Dec. 1957 published for the Committee of American Scholars. Title varies: 1945–Sept. 1961, *The American Slavic and East European Review*.
Indexed: ABC POL SCI; Bull. Anal. Pol. Ec. Soc.; His. Abst.; Ind. Per. Art. Law; Int. Bibl. Eco.; Int. Bibl. Pol. Sc.; Int. Bibl. Soc. Cul. Anth.; Int. Lab. Doc.; Int. Pol. Sc. Abst.; Peace Res. Abst. J.; Soc. Sc. Hum. Ind.; Wom. Stu. Abst.

4306
SLAVONIC AND EAST EUROPEAN REVIEW. v.1– , 1922– . London, Cambridge University Press. Semi-annual.
Issued by: School of Slavonic and East European Studies, University of London.
Indexed: Abst. Anth.; His. Abst.; Soc. Sc. Hum. Ind.; Wom. Stu. Abst.

4307
SLEZSKÝ SBORNÍK. ACTA SILESIACA. 1878– . Praha, Nakladatelstvi C.S.A.V. Quarterly.
Issued by: Slezský Ústav, Československá Akademia Věd. In Czech; summaries in English, French, German and Russian.
Supersedes: Matica Opavska. *Vestnik*.
Indexes: 1878–1952; 1953–62.
Indexed: His. Abst.; Int. Bibl. Soc. Cul. Anth.

4308
SLOAN MANAGEMENT REVIEW. v.12– , fall 1970– . Cambridge, Mass. Three no. a year.
Issued by: Alfred P. Sloan School of Management, Massachusetts Institute of Technology. Some issues are thematic.
Continues: *IMR Industrial Management Review*.
Indexes: Vols. 1–14, 1960–73, in v.15.
Indexed: Bull. Anal. Pol. Ec. Soc.; Eco. Abst.; PAIS; Soc. Abst.

SLOVAK ETHNOGRAPHY
See SLOVENSKY NARODOPIS

4309
SLOVENSKA ARCHEOLOGIA. 1– , 1953– . Bratislava. Annual, 1953–55; two no. a year.
Issued by: Slovenska Akademia Vied. In Slovak; summaries in English, Russian, and occasionally in other languages.
Indexed: Int. Bibl. Soc. Cul. Anth.

4310
SLOVENSKI ETNOGRAF. v.1– , 1948– . Ljubljana. Annual (irreg., 1983–).

Issued by: Etnografski Muzej in Ljubljana. In Serbo-Croatian; summaries in English, French, and occasionally in other languages.
Indexed: Bull. Sig. Soc. Eth.

4311
SLOVENSKÝ NÁRODOPIS. SLOVAK ETHNOGRAPHY. v.1– , 1953– . Bratislva. Quarterly.
Issued by: Slovenska Akademia Vied. In Slovak; summaries in English, French, German and Russian.

4312
SMALL BUSINESS IN JAPAN. 1976– . Tokyo. Annual.
Issued by: Small and Medium Enterprise Agency (MITI).

SMALL INDUSTRY BULLETIN FOR ASIA AND THE FAR EAST
See United Nations. Economic Commission for Asia and the Pacific. SMALL INDUSTRY BULLETIN FOR ASIA AND THE PACIFIC

SMALL INDUSTRY BULLETIN FOR ASIA AND THE PACIFIC
See United Nations. Economic and Social Commission for Asia and the Pacific. SMALL INDUSTRY BULLETIN FOR ASIA AND THE PACIFIC

4313
SMITH COLLEGE STUDIES IN SOCIAL WORK. 1– , Sept. 1930– . Northampton, Mass. Three no. a year.
Organ of: Smith College School for Social Work.
Indexed: Abst. Soc. Work.; Bull. Sig. Soc. Eth.; His. Abst.; Ind. Per. Art. Law; PAIS; Psych. Abst.

4314
SMITHSONIAN CONTRIBUTIONS TO ANTHROPOLOGY. v.1– , 1965– . Washington, D.C. Irreg.
Issued by: Smithsonian Institution. Monograph series.
Indexed: Abst. Anth.; Int. Bibl. Soc. Cul. Anth.

4315
Smithsonian Institution. Institute on Immigration and Ethnic Studies. RIIES BIBLIOGRAPHIC STUDIES. no.1– , 1976– . Washington, D.C. Irreg.

4316
Smithsonian Institution. International Program for Population Analysis. Interdisciplinary Communications Program. ANNOTATED BIBLIOGRAPHY. v.1– , 1973– . Washington, D.C. Semi-annual.

4317
SOCIAAL GEOGRAFISCHE STUDIES. no.1– , 1955– . Assen, van Gorcum. Irreg.
In Dutch. Monograph series.

SOCIAAL-HISTORISCHE STUDIEN
See International Institute for Social History. SOCIAAL-HISTORISCHE STUDIEN

SOCIAAL KOMPAS
See SOCIAL COMPAS

4318
SOCIAAL MAANSBLAD-ARBEID. v.9– , 1954– . Alphen aan den Rijn, Samson Uitgiverij. Monthly.
In Dutch.
Continues: *Sociaal Maansblad* (v.1–8, 1946–53).
Indexed: Bull. Anal. Pol. Ec. Soc.; Int. Bibl. Eco.; Int. Bibl. Soc. Cul. Anth.; Int. Lab. Doc.

4319
SOCIAL ACTION. v.1–39, Mar. 1935–Dec. 1972. Boston, Mass., Chicago, Ill., The Pilgrim Press. Semimonthly.
Subtitle reads: "A quarterly review of social trends".
Indexed: Bull. Sig. Soc. Eth.; Int. Bibl. Soc.; Int. Lab. Doc.; PAIS; Peace Res. Abst. J.

4320
SOCIAL ANALYSIS. no.1– , Feb. 1979– . Adelaide. Three no. a year.
Issued by: Department of Sociology, University of Adelaide. Subtitle reads: "Journal of culture and social practice".
Indexed: Int. Bibl. Soc. Cul. Anth.

4321
SOCIAL AND ECONOMIC STUDIES. v.1– , Feb. 1953– . Mona. Quarterly.
Issued by: Institute of Social and Economic Research, University of the West Indies. Supplements accompany some numbers.
Indexed: Bull. Sig. Soc. Eth.; His. Abst.; Int. Bibl. Soc.; Int. Bibl. Soc. Cul. Anth.; Int. Lab. Doc.; J. Eco. Lit.; PAIS; Peace Res. Abst. J.; Pop. Ind.; Psych. Abst.; SSCI.

SOCIAL AND HISTORICAL GEOGRAPHY
See GEO ABSTRACTS. D. SOCIAL AND HISTORICAL GEOGRAPHY

SOCIAL AND HISTORICAL GEOGRAPHY
See GEOGRAPHICAL ABSTRACTS. D. SOCIAL AND HISTORICAL GEOGRAPHY

SOCIAL AND HUMAN SCIENCES JOURNAL
See JINBUN GAKUHO

SOCIAL ANTHROPOLOGY SERIES
See AUSTRALIAN ABORIGINAL STUDIES

4322
SOCIAL BEHAVIOR AND PERSONALITY. 1– , 1972– . Wellington, Historical Services Ltd. Semi-annual.
Issued by: Society for Personality Research.
Indexed: Psych. Abst.

4323
SOCIAL BIOLOGY. v.16– , 1969– . Chicago, Ill., The University of Chicago Press. Quarterly.
Issued by: Society for the Study of Human Biology.
Continues: *Eugenics Quarterly* (v.1–15, 1954–68)
Indexes: Cumulative table of contents of the *Eugenics Quarterly* (v.1–15) and *Social Biology* (v.16–29) in v.29 (1982), pp.399–436.
Indexed: Abst. Anth.; Bull. Sig. Soc. Eth.; Int. Bibl. Soc.; Psych. Abst.; Pop. Ind.; Soc. Abst.; Urb. Aff. Abst.; Wom. Stu. Abst.

4324
SOCIAL BIOLOGY AND HUMAN AFFAIRS. v.45– , 1980– . London. Two no. a year.
Issued by: British Social Biology Council.
Continues: *Biology and Human Affairs.*

4325
SOCIAL CASEWORK. v.1– , Mar. 1920– . New York. Monthly (except Aug. and Sept.)
Issued by: Family Service Association of America. Title varies: *Journal of Social Work.*
Indexed: Bull. Sig. Soc. Eth.; His. Abst.; Int. Bibl. Soc.; Psych. Abst.; PHRA; SSCI; Soc. Work Res. Abst.

4326
SOCIAL CHANGE. 1– , Apr. 1971– . New Delhi. Three no. a year.
Issued by: Council for Social Development.

4327
SOCIAL CHANGE. v.1– , 1973– . New York, Gordon and Breach. Quarterly.
Issued by: Center for the Study of Social Change.
Supersedes: *Human Relations Training News.*

4328
SOCIAL COGNITION. v.1– , 1982– . New York, Guilford Press. Quarterly.

4329
SOCIAL COMPAS. 1– , May/June 1953– . Louvain. Bimonthly (irreg.), 1966; quarterly.
Issued by: Katholiek Sociaal-Kerkelijk Instituut, The International Catholic Institute for Social Research (Roomsch-Katholieke Centraal Bureau voor Oderwijs en Opvoeding, 1953–59); International Federation of Catholic Institutes for Socio-Religious Research, Centre de Recherches Socio-Religieuses, Université Catholique de Louvain, 1961–65; Katholiek Sociaal-Kerkelijk Instituut and the Centre de Recherches Socio-Religieuses, 1966–. Early issues in Dutch, or German, French, English; recent issues in English or French. Title varies: 1953–55, *Sociaal Kompas.*
Indexes: Vols. 1–10, 1953–63, in v.10.
Indexed: Bull. Sig. Soc. Eth.; Bull. Anal. Pol. Ec. Soc.; Int. Pol. Sc. Abst.; Lang & Lang. Beh. Abst.; SSCI.

4330
SOCIAL CONCEPT. v.1– , May 1982– . Denver, Colo., Social Concepts. Three no. a year.

4331
SOCIAL DEVELOPMENT. English Edition. v.1– , Jan. 1972– . Ottawa. Irreg.
Issued by: Canadian Council on Social Development. Published also in French edition: *Développement Social.* Some no. combine English and French editions, titled *Social Development. Développement Social.* In combined editions text is in English and French.

SOCIAL DEVELOPMENT. DÉVELOPPEMENT SOCIAL
See SOCIAL DEVELOPMENT. English Edition.

4332
SOCIAL DYNAMICS. no.1– , June 1975– . Cape Town. Semi-annual.
Issued by: Faculty of Social Science, University of Cape Town.
Indexed: Int. Bibl. Soc. Cul. Anth.; Soc. Abst.

SOCIAL ECONOMIC INDICATORS
See Portugal. Instituto Nacional de Estatística. INDICADORES ECONÔMICO-SOCIAIS

SOCIAL, ECONOMICAL AND CULTURAL PROBLEMS OF NON-EUROPEAN COUNTRIES
See PROBLEMY SPOŁECZNO-GOSPODARCZE I KULTUROWE KRAJÓW POZAEUROPEJSKICH

SOCIAL ECONOMICS
See INTERNATIONAL JOURNAL OF SOCIAL ECONOMICS

4333
SOCIAL EDUCATION. v.1– , 1937– . Washington, D.C. Seven or eight no. a year.

Issued by: National Council for the Social Studies.
Indexed: His. Abst.; His. Abst.; Ind. Per. Art. Law; SSCI.

4334
SOCIAL EPISTEMOLOGY; JOURNAL OF KNOWLEDGE, CULTURE AND POLICY. v.1– , Jan./Mar. 1987– . London, Taylor & Francis. Quarterly.

4335
SOCIAL FORCES. v.1– , 1922– . Chapel Hill, N.C., University of North Carolina Press. Bimonthly, 1922–Sept. 1924 (actually five no. a year in each volume); quarterly.
Issued by: University of North Carolina; vols. for Sept. 1973–June 1977 issued in association with the Southern Sociological Society. Title varies: v.1–3, 1922–24, *The Journal of Social Forces.*
Indexes: Vols. 1–50, 1922–72, 1v.
Indexed: ABC POL SCI; Abst. Anth.; Abst. Soc. Work; Bull. Anal. Pol. Ec. Soc.; His. Abst.; Ind. Per. Art. Law; Int. Bibl. Pol. Sc.; Int. Bibl. Soc.; Int. Bibl. Soc. Cul. Anth.; Int. Pol. Sc. Abst.; PAIS; Pop. Ind.; Psych. Abst.; Sage Fam. Stu. Abst.; Sage Urb. Stu. Abst.; Soc. Abst.; Soc. Work. Res. Abst.; Wom. Stu. Abst.

SOCIAL GEOGRAPHY
See GEO ABSTRACTS. D: SOCIAL GEOGRAPHY

SOCIAL GEOGRAPHY AND CARTOGRAPHY
See GEO ABSTRACTS. SECTION D. SOCIAL GEOGRAPHY AND CARTOGRAPHY

4336
SOCIAL HISTORY. 1– , Jan. 1976– . London, Methuen and Co. Three no. a year.
Issued by: Department of Economic and Social History, University of Hull.

SOCIAL HISTORY
See HISTOIRE SOCIAL

4337
SOCIAL HISTORY OF CANADA. 1971– . Toronto, University of Toronto Press. Irreg.
Early volumes not numbered. Includes some theses and reprints. Monograph series.

SOCIAL HYGIENE
See JOURNAL OF SOCIAL HYGIENE

4338
SOCIAL INDICATORS. 1973– . Washington, D.C. Triennial.
Issued by: Office of Management and Budget, Statistical Policy Division.

SOCIAL INDICATORS, AUSTRALIA
See Australia. Bureau of Statistics. SOCIAL INDICATORS, AUSTRALIA

4339
SOCIAL INDICATORS FOR THE EUROPEAN COMMUNITIES. INDICATEURS SOCIAUX POUR LA COMMUNAUTÉ EUROPÉENNE. 1960/78– . Luxembourg, 1980– .
Issued by: Statistical Office of the European Communities.
Continues, in part: Statistical Office of the European Communities. *Sociale Indikatoren for de Europeiske Faelles-skaber.* In English and French. Also editions in Danish, Dutch, and German/Italian are published.

4340
SOCIAL INDICATORS NEWSLETTER. no.1–5, Mar. 1973–1984. Washington, D.C. Irreg.
Issued by: Social Science Research Council (U.S.A.). Center for Coordination of Research on Social Indicators.
Continued by: *Social Indicators Network News: SINET* (no.6, fall 1984).

4341
SOCIAL INDICATORS RESEARCH. v.1– , May 1974– . Dordrecht, Boston, Mass., D. Reidel Pub. Co. Eight no. a year, forming two volumes.
Subtitle reads: "Quality of life measurement".
Indexed: Curr. Cont. Soc. Beh. Sc.; Hum. Res. Abst.; Sage Urb. Stu. Abst.; SSCI; Urb. Stu. Abst.

4342
SOCIAL ISSUES IN THE SEVENTIES. 1– , 1973– . London, Tavistock Pub. Irreg.
Monograph series.

4343
SOCIAL JUSTICE REVIEW. v.1– , Apr. 1908– . St. Louis, Mo. Monthly, 1908–June 1938; monthly (except July–Aug. when bimonthly), 1939–57; bimonthly.
Issued by: Catholic Central Union of America. V.1 in German; v.2–38 in English or German. Subtitle reads: "Pioneer journal of Catholic Social Action". Title varies: 1908–Mar. 1909, *Centralblatt*; Apr. 1909–Mar. 1940, *Central-Blatt and Social Justice.*

4344
SOCIAL NETWORKS. 1– , Aug. 1978– . Lausanne, Elsevier Sequoia. Quarterly.
Published in cooperation with the International Network for Social Network Analysis (INSNA). Subtitle reads: "International journal of structural analysis".
Indexed: Int. Bibl. Soc. Cul. Anth.; LLBA; Sage Urb. Stu. Abst.; Soc. Abst.; SSCI.

4345
SOCIAL PHILOSOPHY & POLICY. v.1– , 1983– . Oxford, B. Blackwell. Two no. a year.
Issues are thematic.

4346
SOCIAL PLANNING, POLICY & DEVELOPMENT ABSTRACTS. v.6– , June 1984– . San Diego, Sociological Abstracts. Semi-annual.
Continues: *Social Welfare, Social Planning/Policy & Social Development* (v.1–5, no.2, 1979–Dec. 1983)

4347
SOCIAL POLICY. v.1– , May/June 1970– . White Plains, later Armonk, N.Y., M.E. Sharpe. Bimonthly.
Indexed: ABC POL SCI; Curr. Cont. Soc. Beh. Sc.; Bull. Anal. Pol. Ec. Soc.; Int. Bibl. Pol. Sc.; LLBA; PHRA; Sage Pub. Adm. Abst.; Sage Urb. Stu. Abst.; Soc. Abst.; SSCI; Wom. Stu. Abst.

4348
SOCIAL POLICY & ADMINISTRATION. v.13– , spring 1979– . Oxford, B. Blackwell. Three no. a year.
Continues: *Social and Economic Administration* (v.1–2, 1967–winter 1978).
Indexed: Curr. Cont. Soc. Beh. Sc.; PAIS; SSCI.

4349
SOCIAL PRAXIS. v.1– , 1973– . Amsterdam, Mouton. Quarterly.
Indexed: Curr. Cont. Soc. Beh. Sc.; SSCI.

4350
SOCIAL PROBLEMS. v.1– , June 1953– . Brooklyn. Quarterly, 1953–71/72; five no. a year.
Official organ of: Society for the Study of Social Problems.
Indexed: Abst. Soc. Work; Bull. Anal. Pol. Ec. Soc.; Bull. Sig. Soc. Eth.; Ind. Per. Art. Law; Curr. Cont. Soc. Beh. Sc.; Int. Bibl. Eco.; Int. Bibl. Pol. Sc.; Int. Bibl. Soc.; Int. Lab. Doc.; Int. Pol. Sc. Abst.; Hum. Res. Abst.; Int. Bibl. Soc. Cul. Anth.; PAIS; Peace Res. Abst. J.; PHRA; Psych. Abst.; Sage Pub. Adm. Abst.; SSCI; Urb. Stu. Abst.; Wom. Stu. Abst.

4351
SOCIAL PROCESS IN HAWAII. v.27– , 1979– . Honolulu. Annual.
Issued by: Department of Sociology, University at Hawaii at Manos.
Continues: *Social Process.*

4352
SOCIAL PSYCHIATRY. 1– , 1974– . New York, Grune & Stratton. Annual.
Organ of: American Association for Social Psychiatry.

4353
SOCIAL PSYCHIATRY. SOZIALPSYCHIATRIE. PSYCHIATRIE SOCIALE. v.1– , Aug. 1966– . Berlin, Springer Verlag. Quarterly.
In English, French, or German; summaries in English, French and German.
Indexed: Psych. Abst.

4354
SOCIAL PSYCHOLOGY. v.41, Mar.–Dec. 1978. Washington, D.C. Quarterly.
Issued by: American Sociological Society.
Continues: *Sociometry.* Continued by: *Social Psychology Quarterly.*
Indexed: Bull. Anal. Pol. Ec. Soc.; Psych. Abst.; SSCI; Soc. Work. Res. Abst.

4355
SOCIAL PSYCHOLOGY QUARTERLY. v.42– , Mar. 1979– . Washington, D.C.
Issued by: American Sociological Association.
Continues: *Social Psychology.*
Indexed: Int. Bibl. Pol. Sc.; Int. Pol. Sc. Abst.; Psych. Abst.; Soc. Sc. Ind.; SSCI.

SOCIAL RESEARCH METHODOLOGY ABSTRACTS
See SRM ABSTRACTS

4356
SOCIAL RESPONSIBILITY; BUSINESS, JOURNALISM, LAW, MEDICINE. v.10– , 1984– . Lexington, Va. Annual.
Issued by: Washington and Lee University.
Continues: *Social Responsibility: Journalism, Law, Medicine* ([v.1]–9, 1974–83)

4357
SOCIAL REVIEW. no.1– , Sept. 1978– . Cape Town. Eight no. a year.
Issued by: Social Science Agency.

4358
SOCIAL SCIENCE. v.1–56, Nov. 1925–autumn 1981. Winfield, Kans. Quarterly.
Issued by: National Social Science Honour Society Pi Gamma Mu.
Continued by: *International Social Science Review.*
Indexes: Vols. 21–25, 1946–Oct. 1950, in v.27; v.26–30, 1951–Oct. 1955, 1v.
Indexed: Abst. Soc. Work; Bull. Anal. Pol. Ec. Soc.; Bull. Sig. Soc. Eth.; His. Abst.; Int. Bibl. Eco.; Int. Bibl. Soc.; Int. Pol. Sc. Abst.; PAIS; Peace Res. Abst. J.; Pop. Ind.; Soc. Abst.; SSCI.

4359
SOCIAL SCIENCE. 1– , 1924– . Toledo, Ohio, Social Science Pub. Co. Quarterly.
Issued by: University of Toledo.
Indexed: His. Abst.; Soc. Abst.

SOCIAL SCIENCE
See Hokkaido Kyoiku Daigaku. HOKKAIDO KYOIKU KIYŌ

SOCIAL SCIENCE
See SAHOE KWAHAK

SOCIAL SCIENCE
See SOCIAL SCIENCE REVIEW (New York)

SOCIAL SCIENCE
See Tokushima Daigaku. Gakubei Gakubu. TOKUSHIMA DAIGAKU KIYŌ SHAKAI KAGAKU

4360
SOCIAL SCIENCE ABSTRACTS. v.1–5, no.1, Mar. 1929–Jan. 1933. Menasha, Wis.
Indexes: Vols. 1–4, in v.5, no.1.

SOCIAL SCIENCE ABSTRACTS
See INTERDISCIPLINE

SOCIAL SCIENCE ABSTRACTS
See Tokyo Daigaku. Shakai Kagaku Kenkyōjo. ANNALS

4361
SOCIAL SCIENCE & MEDICINE. v.1–11, Apr. 1967–1977. Oxford, Pergamon Press. Quarterly.
In English, French, German, or Spanish; summaries in one of these languages.
Continued by: *Social Science & Medicine. Medical Anthropology*; *Social Science & Medicine. Medical Economics*; *Social Science & Medicine. Medical Geography*; and *Social Science & Medicine. Medical Psychology and Medical Sociology.*
Indexed: Abst. Anth.; Bull. Sig. Soc. Eth.; Int. Bibl. Soc.; Int. Pol. Sc. Abst.; Psych. Abst.; Soc. Abst.; Urb. Aff. Abst.; Wom. Stu. Abst.

4362
SOCIAL SCIENCE & MEDICINE. v.16– , 1982– . Oxford, Pergamon Press.
Formed by the union of: *Social Science & Medicine. Part A. Medical Sociology*; *Part B. Medical Anthropology*; *Part C. Medical Economics*; *Part D. Medical Geography*; *Part E. Medical Psychology*; and *Part F. Medical & Social Ethics.*

4363
SOCIAL SCIENCE & MEDICINE. MEDICAL ANTHROPOLOGY. v.12–13, no.2, Jan. 1978–July 1979. Oxford, New York, Pergamon Press. Quarterly.
Continues, in part: *Social Science & Medicine.* Continued by: *Social Science & Medicine. Part B. Medical Anthropology.*

4364
SOCIAL SCIENCE & MEDICINE. MEDICAL ECONOMICS. v.12–13, no.3, June 1978–Oct. 1979. Oxford, New York, Pergamon Press. Quarterly.
Continues, in part: *Social Science & Medicine.* Continued by: *Social Science & Medicine. Part C. Medical Economics.*

4365
SOCIAL SCIENCE & MEDICINE. MEDICAL GEOGRAPHY. v.12–13, no.2, Mar. 1978–July 1979. Oxford, New York, Pergamon Press. Twenty-six no. a year.
Continues, in part: *Social Science & Medicine.* Continued by: *Social Science & Medicine. Part D. Medical Geography.*

4366
SOCIAL SCIENCE & MEDICINE. MEDICAL PSYCHOLOGY AND MEDICAL SOCIOLOGY. v.12–14, no.2, Jan. 1978–1980. Oxford, New York, Pergamon Press.
Continues, in part: *Social Science & Medicine.* Continued by: *Social Science & Medicine. Part A. Medical Sociology*, and *Part E. Medical Psychology.*

4367: not used

4368
SOCIAL SCIENCE & MEDICINE. PART A. MEDICAL SOCIOLOGY. v.15, 1981. Oxford, New York, Pergamon Press.
Continues, in part: *Social Science & Medicine. Medical Psychology and Sociology.* Merged with: *Social Science & Medicine. Part B. Medical Anthropology*; *Part C. Medical Economics*; *Part D. Medical Geography*; *Part E. Medical Psychology*; and *Part F. Medical & Social Ethics* to form: *Social Science & Medicine.*

4369
SOCIAL SCIENCE & MEDICINE. PART B. MEDICAL ANTHROPOLOGY. v.13, no.3–v.15, no.4, Sept. 1979–Oct. 1981. Oxford, Pergamon Press. Quarterly.
Continues: *Social Science & Medicine. Medical Anthropology.* Merged with: *Social Science & Medicine. Part A. Medical Sociology*; *Part C. Medical Economics*; *Part D. Medical Geography*; *Part E. Medical Psychology*; and *Part F. Medical & Social Ethics* to form: *Social Science & Medicine.*

4370
SOCIAL SCIENCE & MEDICINE. PART C. MEDICAL ECONOMICS. v.13, no.4–v.15, no.4, Dec. 1979–Dec. 1981. Oxford, New York, Pergamon Press. Quarterly.

Continues: *Social Science & Medicine. Medical Economics*. Merged with: *Social Science & Medicine. Part A. Medical Sociology*; *Part B. Medical Anthropology*; *Part D. Medical Geography*; *Part E. Medical Psychology*; and *Part F. Medical & Social Ethics* to form: *Social Science & Medicine*.

4371
SOCIAL SCIENCE & MEDICINE. PART D. MEDICAL GEOGRAPHY. v.13, no.3–v.15, no.4, Nov. 1979–Nov. 1981. Oxford, New York, Pergamon Press. Twenty-six no. a year.
Continues: *Social Science & Medicine. Medical Geography*. Merged with: *Social Science & Medicine. Part A. Medical Sociology*; *Part B. Medical Anthropology*; *Part C. Medical Economics*; *Part E. Medical Psychology*; and *Part F. Medical & Social Ethics* to form: *Social Science & Medicine*.

4372
SOCIAL SCIENCE & MEDICINE. PART E. MEDICAL PSYCHOLOGY. v.15, 1981. Oxford, New York, Pergamon Press. Quarterly.
Continues, in part: *Social Science & Medicine. Medical Psychology & Medical Sociology*. Merged with: *Social Science & Medicine. Part A. Medical Sociology*; *Part B. Medical Anthropology*; *Part C. Medical Economics*; *Part D. Medical Geography*; and *Part F. Medical & Social Ethics* to form: *Social Science & Medicine*.

4373
SOCIAL SCIENCE & MEDICINE. PART F. MEDICAL & SOCIAL ETHICS. v.15– , Jan. 1981– . Oxford, New York, Pergamon Press. Quarterly.
Continues, in part: *Social Science & Medicine*. Merged with: *Social Science & Medicine. Part A. Medical Sociology*; *Part B. Medical Anthropology*; *Part C. Medical Economics*; *Part D. Medical Geography*; and *Part E. Medical Psychology* to form: *Social Science & Medicine*.

4374
SOCIAL SCIENCE AND THE MODERN HISTORIAN. 1978– . Greenwich, Conn., JAI Press. Irreg.

SOCIAL SCIENCE BIBLIOGRAPHY, INDIA
See ASIAN SOCIAL SCIENCES BIBLIOGRAPHY WITH ANNOTATIONS AND ABSTRACTS

SOCIAL SCIENCE BIBLIOGRAPHY, INDIA, PAKISTAN
See ASIAN SOCIAL SCIENCE BIBLIOGRAPHY WITH ANNOTATIONS AND ABSTRACTS

4375
SOCIAL SCIENCE DATA INVENTORY. RÉPERTOIRE DES DONNÉES EN SCIENCES SOCIALES. 1– , 1977– . Ottawa.
Issued by: Data Clearinghouse for the Social Sciences.

4376
Social Science Federation of Canada. ANNUAL REPORT. 1976/77– . Ottawa.
In English and French. Added title: *Rapport Annuel*.
Continues: Social Science Research Council. *Annual Report*.

4377
SOCIAL SCIENCE HISTORY. v.1– , fall 1976– . Pittsburgh, later Beverly Hills, Calif., Sage Publications. Quarterly.
Organ of: Social Science History Association, subsequently Center for International Studies, University of Pittsburgh.
Indexed: Sage Urb. Stu. Abst.

4378
SOCIAL SCIENCE INFORMATION. no.1–29, May 1954–Dec. 1961; n. ser. v.1– , Apr. 1962– . Paris, Mouton, 1962–73; Beverly Hills, Calif., Sage Publications. Bimonthly.
Issued by: International Social Science Council. In English or French. Other title: *Information sur les Sciences Sociales*. Title varies: 1954–61, *Information*; 1962–66, *Social Sciences Information*.
Indexed: Int. Bibl. Soc.; Soc. Abst.

4379
SOCIAL SCIENCE INFORMATION STUDIES: SSIS. v.1– , Oct. 1980– . Borough Green, Butterworth. Quarterly.
Indexed: Int. Bibl. Eco.

4380
THE SOCIAL SCIENCE JOURNAL. v.1– , Apr. 1963– . Fort Collins, Colo. Three no. a year, 1975–81; quarterly.
Organ of: Western Social Science Association. Title varies: v.1–11, 1963–75, *Rocky Mountains Social Science Journal*.
Indexed: Abst. Soc. Work; Bull. Anal. Pol. Ec. Soc.; Curr. Cont. Soc. Beh. Sc.; Eco. Abst.; His. Abst.; Ind. Per. Art. Law; Int. Bibl. Eco.; Int. Bibl. Soc.; Int. Pol. Sc. Abst.; PAIS; Peace Res. Abst. J.; PHRA; Soc. Abst.; SSCI; Wom. Stu. Abst.

4381
SOCIAL SCIENCE JOURNAL. 1973– . Seoul. Annual.
Issued by: Korean National Commission for Unesco.
Indexed: Bull. Anal. Pol. Ec. Soc.; Int. Bibl. Soc.; Int. Pol. Sc. Abst.

SOCIAL SCIENCE JOURNAL
See SHAKAI KAGAKU KENKYŪ

4382
SOCIAL SCIENCE METHODOLOGY. no.1– , 1966– . Birmingham. Irreg.
Issued by: Faculty of Commerce and Social Science, University of Birmingham. Subseries of *Discussion Papers*.

SOCIAL SCIENCE METHODOLOGY ABSTRACTS
See SRM ABSTRACTS

4383
SOCIAL SCIENCE MICROCOMPUTER REVIEW. v.3– , spring 1985– . Durham, N.C., Duke University Press. Quarterly.
Issued by: The Social Science Research and Instruction Computing Laboratory of North Carolina State University.
Continues: *Social Science Micro Review* (v.2, no.1, 2, 4, 1983–84)

4384
SOCIAL SCIENCE MONOGRAPHS. 1–22, 1953–1963. Canberra. Irreg.
Issued by: National Australian University. Monograph series.

SOCIAL SCIENCE ORGANIZATIONS
See INTERNATIONAL DIRECTORY OF SOCIAL SCIENCE ORGANIZATIONS

4385
SOCIAL SCIENCE PROBINGS. v.1– , Mar. 1984– . New Delhi, People's Pub. House. Quarterly.

4386
SOCIAL SCIENCE QUARTERLY. v.1– , June 1920– . Austin, Tex., University of Texas Press. Quarterly.
Issued by: Southwestern Social Science Association in cooperation with the University of Texas. Title varies: 1920–23, *Southwestern Political Science Quarterly*; 1923–31, *Southwestern Political and Social Science Quarterly*; 1931–68, *Southwestern Social Science Quarterly*.
Indexed: ABC POL SCI; Abst. Anth.; Bull. Anal. Pol. Ec. Soc.; Curr. Cont. Soc. Beh. Sc.; His. Abst.; Int. Bibl. Eco.; Int. Bibl. Pol. Sc.; Int. Bibl. Soc.; Int. Pol. Sc. Abst.; J. Eco. Lit.; PAIS; Peace Res. Abst. J.; Pop. Ind.; Sage Fam. Stu. Abst.; Sage Urb. Stu. Abst.; Sage Pub. Adm. Abst.; Soc. Abst.; SSCI.

4387
SOCIAL SCIENCE RESEARCH. 1971– . Port Moresby. Annual.
Issued by: Department of Social Development and Home Affairs.

4388
SOCIAL SCIENCE RESEARCH. v.1– , Apr. 1972– . New York, Seminar Press. Quarterly.
Subtitle reads: "A quarterly journal of social science methodology and quantitative research".
Indexed: Int. Pol. Sc. Abst.; J. Eco. Lit.; LLBA; Pop. Ind.; Psych. Abst.; Soc. Sc. Ind.

SOCIAL SCIENCE RESEARCH
See SAHOE KWAHAK YŎN'GU (Kwangjusi)

4389
Social Science Research Council (U.K.). RESEARCH SUPPORTED BY THE SOCIAL SCIENCE RESEARCH COUNCIL. 1968– . London. Annual.

4390
Social Science Research Council (U.K.). REVIEW OF CURRENT RESEARCH. 1– , 1968– . London, Heinemann Educational Books. Irreg.

4391
Social Science Research Council (U.S.A.). BULLETIN. no.1– , Dec. 1930– . New York. Irreg.
Issued by: the council's Committee on Appraisal of Research.

4392
Social Science Research Council (U.S.A.). ITEMS. v.1– , Mar. 1947– . New York. Quarterly.
Indexes: Vols. 1–20, 1947–66, with v.22, no.2.
Indexed: Int. Bibl. Soc. Cul. Anth.; Int. Lab. Doc.

4393
SOCIAL SCIENCE REVIEW. v.1–3, no.4, 1887–1901. New York.
Title varies: v.1, 1887, *Social Science*.

4394
THE SOCIAL SCIENCE REVIEW. no.1– , fall 1961– . New York. Two no. a year.
Issued by Social Science Division, Queen's College.
Indexed: Soc. Abst.

4395
SOCIAL SCIENCE REVIEW. v.1– , Mar. 1976– . Bangkok.
Issued by: Social Science Administration of Thailand. Vol. for 1978 last available for examination.
Continues: *Journal of Social Science Association of Thailand*.

4396
SOCIAL SCIENCE REVIEW. no.1– , Sept. 1979– . Colombo. Quarterly.
Issued by: Social Scientists Association of Sri Lanka.

SOCIAL SCIENCE REVIEW
See SAHOE KWAHAK (Seoul)

THE SOCIAL SCIENCE REVIEW
See SAHOE KWAHAK NONMUNJIP (Seoul)

THE SOCIAL SCIENCE REVIEW
See SANGKHOSAT PORITHAT

THE SOCIAL SCIENCE REVIEW
See SHAKAI KAGAKU RONSHŪ (Saitama)

4397
SOCIAL SCIENCE REVIEW AND JOURNAL OF THE SOCIAL SCIENCES. 1–2, 1862–1863; n. ser. v.1–6, no. 32, 1864–1866. London.

SOCIAL SCIENCE REVIEW OF KAGOSHIMA UNIVERSITY
See Kagoshima Daigaku. Kyoyobu. KAGOSHIMA DAIGAKU SHAKAI KAGAKU ZASSHI

SOCIAL SCIENCE SERIES
See LOUISIANA STATE UNIVERSITY STUDIES. SOCIAL SCIENCE SERIES

SOCIAL SCIENCE SERIES
See UNIVERSITY OF MISSOURI STUDIES. SOCIAL SCIENCE SERIES

4398
SOCIAL SCIENCE STUDIES. v.1–40, 1924–1942. Chicago, Ill. Irreg.
Issued by: University of Chicago. V.1–7 lack series numbering; v.2–3 and 5–7 lack series title. Monograph series.

4399
SOCIAL SCIENCE STUDIES. v.1–4, Jan. 1971–1974. London, Macmillan Journals.
Continued by: *Social Sciences of Science*.

SOCIAL SCIENCE YEARBOOK OF POLITICS
See SOZIALWISSENSCHAFTLICHES JAHRBUCH FÜR POLITIK

4400
SOCIAL SCIENCES. 1– , 1970– . Moscow, Mezhdunarodnaia͡ Kniga. Bimonthly, 1970; quarterly.
Issued by: Akademii͡a Nauk SSSR. Published also in French: *Sciences Sociales*; in Portuguese: *Ciências Sociais*; and in Spanish: *Ciencias Sociales*. "Special supplement" published irregularly.

SOCIAL SCIENCES
See CURRENT RESEARCH IN BRITAIN. SOCIAL SCIENCES

SOCIAL SCIENCES
See Institute of Sociology, London. REPORTS OF THE ANNUAL CONFERENCES

SOCIAL SCIENCES
See Karnatak University. JOURNAL. SOCIAL SCIENCES

SOCIAL SCIENCES
See KASETSART JOURNAL

SOCIAL SCIENCES
See Lietuvos TSR Mokslų Akademija, Vilna. DARBAI. TRUDY. SERIJA A. VISUOMENĖS MOKSLAI. SOCIAL SCIENCES

SOCIAL SCIENCES
See ROMANIAN SCIENTIFIC ABSTRACTS. SOCIAL SCIENCES

4401
SOCIAL SCIENCES AND HUMANITIES INDEX. v.1–61, no.4, 1907/15 Mar. 1974. New York, H.W. Wilson. Quarterly.
Title varies: 1907/15–1916/19, *Readers' Guide to Periodical Literature. Supplement*; 1920/23–1952/53, *International Index to Periodicals*; 1956–Mar./Apr. 1965, *International Index*.
Superseded, in part, by: *Social Sciences Index*.

SOCIAL SCIENCES AND POLICY RESEARCH
See SAHOE KWAHAK KWA CHONGCH'AEK YŎN'GU

4402
SOCIAL SCIENCES CITATION INDEX. 1973– . Philadelphia, Pa. Three no. a year and annual cumulation.
Issued by: Institute for Scientific Information. The index consists of three sections: "Citation Index", "Source Index", and "Permuterm Subject Index". Includes "SSCI Citation Report" (first published for 1977 in 1978).

4403
SOCIAL SCIENCES IN CANADA. SCIENCES SOCIALES AU CANADA. v.1– , 1971– . Ottawa, Social Sciences Research Council. Quarterly.
In English and French (the latter on inverted pages)

SOCIAL SCIENCES IN CHINA
See CHUNG-KUO SHE K'O HSÜEH—ZHONGGUO SHE HUI KEKSUE

4404
SOCIAL SCIENCES IN FORESTRY. A CURRENT SELECTED BIBLIOGRAPHY. no.1– , June 1963– . Blacksburg, Va. Irreg.

Issued by: Division of Forestry and Wildlife, Virginia Polytechnic Institute and State University.
Title varies: 1–24, 1963–1971, *Forestry Economics*, issued by the Department of Forestry Economics, Syracuse University.

4405
SOCIAL SCIENCES IN SOCIALIST COUNTRIES. v.1– , 1978/79– . Moscow.
Issued by: Institut Nauchnoĭ Informatsii po Obshchestvennym Naukam, Akademiia Nauk SSSR.

4406
SOCIAL SCIENCES INDEX. June 1974/75– . New York, H.W. Wilson. Quarterly with annual cumulation.
Supersedes, in part: *Social Sciences and Humanities Index*.

SOCIAL SCIENCES INFORMATION
See SOCIAL SCIENCE INFORMATION

4407
SOCIAL SECURITY ABSTRACTS. v.1– , 1965– . Geneva. Irreg.
Issued by: General Secretariat of the International Security Association. The edition of 1974/75 last examined.

SOCIAL SECURITY IN THE NORDIC COUNTRIES
See SOCIAL TRYGGLET I DE NORDISKA LÄNDERNA

4408
SOCIAL SERVICE REVIEW. v.1– , Mar. 1927– . Chicago, Ill., University of Chicago Press. Quarterly.
Issued by: School of Social Service Administration, University of Chicago.
Indexes: Vols. 1–40, 1927–66, 1v.
Indexed: Abst. Soc. Work; His. Abst.; Hum. Res. Abst.; Int. Bibl. Eco.; Int. Bibl. Soc. Cul. Anth.; PAIS; PHRA; Psych. Abst.; Wom. Stu. Abst.

SOCIAL STATISTICS
See Statistical Office of the European Communities. SOZIALSTATISTIK

SOCIAL STUDIES
See AL-ABḤĀTH AL-IJTIMĀ'ĪYAH

4409
SOCIAL STUDIES IN OCEANIA AND SOUTH AND SOUTH EAST ASIA. v.1– , 1977– . Copenhagen.
Issued by: National Museum of Denmark.

4410
SOCIAL STUDIES: IRISH JOURNAL OF SOCIOLOGY. v.1– , Jan. 1972– . Kildare. Bimonthly.
Issued by: Department of Sociology, St. Patrick's College. Jan. 1972 issue preceded by: v.0, no.0, Oct. 1971.
Supersedes: *Christus Rex Journal*.
Indexed: His. Abst.; PAIS; Peace Res. Abst. J.; SSCI.

4411
SOCIAL STUDIES OF SCIENCE. v.5– , 1975– . Beverly Hills, Calif., Sage Publications. Quarterly.
Continues: *Social Studies* (v.1–4, 1971–74)

SOCIAL STUDIES SERIES
See Oklahoma State University of Agriculture and Applied Science, Stillwater. ARTS AND SCIENCES STUDIES. SOCIAL STUDIES SERIES

4412
SOCIAL SURVEY OF LATIN AMERICA. 1962– . Washington, D.C., Pan American Union. General Secretariat of the Organization of American States. Annual.
Prepared by: Department of Social Affairs, Pan American Union.
Continues: *Economic and Social Survey of Latin America* (1961)

4413
SOCIAL THEORY AND PRACTICE. v.1– , spring 1970– . Tallahassee, Fla. Quarterly.
Issued by: Center for Social Philosophy, Department of Philosophy, University of Tallahassee. Subtitle reads: "An international and interdisciplinary journal of social philosophy".
Indexed: ABC POL SCI; Bull. Anal. Pol. Ec. Soc.; Bull. Sig. Soc. Eth.; Ind. Per. Art. Law; Int. Bibl. Eco.; Int. Bibl. Pol. Sc.; Int. Bibl. Soc. Cul. Anth.; LLBA; Soc. Abst.

4414
SOCIAL TRENDS. no.1– , 1970– . London, Government Statistical Service.
Issued by: Central Statistical Office.
Indexed: Bull. Anal. Pol. Ec. Soc.

4415
SOCIAL TRYGGLET I DE NORDISKA LÄNDERNA. 1962– . Stockholm. Biennial.
Issued by: Nordic Statistical Secretariat. In Danish, Norwegian or Swedish. Some issues called in English: *Social Security in the Nordic Countries*. Volumes covering earlier years are translated from: *Social Trygglet i de Nordiska Länderna*, *Social Sikkorhet i de Nordiske Land*, or *Social Trygglet i de Nordiske Lande*. Other title: *Social Security in the Nordic Countries*, or *Statistical Reports of the Nordic Countries* (Nordisk Statistics Skrift Series).

4416
SOCIAL WELFARE. v.1– , 1954– . New Delhi, Publication Division. Monthly.
Organ of: Central Social Welfare Board.
Indexed: Bull. Anal. Pol. Ec. Soc.; Int. Lab. Doc.

4417
SOCIAL WORK. Apr. 1939– . London. Quarterly.
Issued by: The Family Welfare Association (called until Oct. 1945 Charity Organisation Society)
Supersedes: *Charity Organisation Quarterly*.

4418
SOCIAL WORK. v.1– , Jan. 1956– . New York. Quarterly.
Issued by: National Association of Social Workers.
Indexed: Abst. Soc. Work; His. Abst.; Int. Bibl. Soc. Cul. Anth.; Int. Lab. Doc.; PAIS; Psych. Abst.; Sage Urb. Stu. Abst.; Wom. Stu. Abst.

4419
SOCIAL WORK. MAATSKAPLIKE WERK. v.1– , 1965– . Stellenbosch. Quarterly.
In Afrikaans or English.
Indexed: Int. Bibl. Soc. Cul. Anth.

4420
SOCIAL WORK RESEARCH & ABSTRACTS. v.13, no.2– , summer 1977– . New York. Quarterly.
Issued by: National Association of Social Workers.
Continues: *Abstracts for Social Workers*.
Indexed: Psych. Abst.

4421
SOCIAL WORK WITH GROUPS. v.1– , 1977– . New York, Haworth Press. Four no. a year.
Indexed: Psych. Abst.; Soc. Work Res. Abst.; SSCI.

4422
SOCIALA MEDDELANDEN. 1– , 1903– . Lund. Eight no. a year (some combined numbers)
Issued by: Kungl. Sociostyselsen. In Swedish. Title varies: 1903, *Meddelanden*.
Indexed: Int. Bibl. Soc. Cul. Anth.

4423
SOCIALE WETENSCHAPPEN. v.1– , Oct. 1957– . Tilburg. Quarterly.
Issued by: Instituut voor Arbeidsvraagstukken, Hoogleraren Katholieke Economische Hogeschool te Tilburg. In Dutch.

4424
SOCIALISM; THEORY AND PRACTICE. no.1– , 1978– . Moscow, Novosti Press Agency. Quarterly.
Published also in French and Spanish editions. Subtitle reads: "Soviet monthly digest of theoretical and political press".

4425
SOCIALISME. v.1– , May 1945– . Genève. Monthly.
Issued by: Parti Suisse du Travail. In French. Subtitle reads: "La politique, l'économie".

4426
SOCIALISME. [v.1]– , Jan. 1954– . Bruxelles. Bimonthly (irreg.)
In French.
Supersedes: *Les Cahiers Socialistes*.
Indexed: Bull. Anal. Pol. Ec. Soc.; Int. Bibl. Pol. Sc.; Int. Pol. Sc. Abst.

4427
SOCIALIST AFFAIRS. v.2– , 1970– . London, Socialist International Presses. Monthly, 1970–74; bimonthly.
Continues: *Socialist International Information*.
Indexed: Bull. Anal. Pol. Ec. Soc.

4428
SOCIALIST ECONOMIC REVIEW. 1981– . London, Merlin Press. Annual.

4429
SOCIALIST PERSPECTIVE. 1973– . Calcutta. Quarterly.
Issued by: Council for Political Studies. Subtitle reads: "A quarterly journal of social services".

4430
SOCIALIST REVIEW. v.1–17, no.2, Jan. 1932–spring 1940. New York. Quarterly, 1932–35; monthly, Mar.–Aug. 1936; bimonthly.
Title varies: v.1–4, no.3, 1932–Nov. 1935, *American Socialist Quarterly*; v.5–6, no.1, Mar. 1936–May 1937, *American Socialist Monthly*. V.4, no.4, never published.

4431
SOCIALIST REVIEW. v.8 (no.37)– , Jan./Feb. 1978– . Oakland, Calif., Agenda Pub. Co. Bimonthly.
Continues: *Socialist Revolution*.
Indexed: Int. Bibl. Pol. Sc.

THE SOCIALIST REVIEW
See LABOR AGE

4432
SOCIALIST REVOLUTION. v.1–8 (no.1–36), Jan./Feb. 1970–1977. San Francisco, Calif., Agenda Pub. Co. Bimonthly.

Continued by: *Socialist Review.*
Indexed: APAIS; Bull. Anal. Pol. Ec. Soc.; Int. Bibl. Pol. Sc.; Int. Pol. Sc. Abst.; SSCI.

4433
SOCIALIST THOUGHT AND PRACTICE. no.1– , June 1961– . Beograd, Izdavacki Zavod Jugoslavija. Monthly.
Published also in French: *Questions Actuelles du Socialisme* (1946–); German: *Sozialistische Theorie und Praxis*; Russian: *Sotsialisticheskaia Mysl' i Praktika*; and Spanish: *Questiones Actuales del Socialismo.*
Indexed: Bull. Anal. Pol. Ec. Soc.; Bull. Sig. Soc. Eth.; Int. Bibl. Pol. Sc.; Int. Bibl. Soc. Cul. Anth.; Int. Lab. Doc.; Int. Pol. Sc. Abst.

4434
SOCIALISTICKÁ EKONOMICKÁ INTEGRACE. v.1– , 1973– . Praha, Československa Tisková Kancelor. Monthly.
Issued by: Council for Mutual Economic Assistance in cooperation with APN. In Czech.

SOCIALNI VĚDY
See Brnenske Univerzita. Filozofická Fakulta. SBORNI PRACI. RADA G. SOCIALNI VĚDY

4435
SOCIALT TIDSSKRIFT. 1925– . København, I Kommission hos Thaning & Appel. Irreg.
Issued by: Socialministeriet (of Denmark). In Danish.
Indexes: Beretning index, 1917–68, in v.46, no.8–9.
Indexed: Bull. Anal. Pol. Ec. Soc.; Int. Bibl. Soc.

4436
SOCIEDAD E DESARROLLO. Jan./Mar. 1972– . Santiago, Chile, Prensa Latinoamericana. Quarterly.
Issued by: Centro de Estudios Socioeconómicos (CESO), Universidad de Chile. In Spanish; summaries in English.

Sociedad Interamericana de Planificación
See Interamerican Planning Society

4437
SOCIETAS. v.1– , winter 1971– . Oshkosh, Wis. Quarterly.
Issued by: Conference Group for Social and Administrative History. Subtitle reads: "A review of social history".

4438
Societatea de Ştiinţe Istorice din Republica Socialistă România. STUDII ŞI ARTICOLE DE ISTORII. v.2– , 1968– . Bucureşti.
In Romanian.
Continues: Societatea de Ştiinţe Istorice şi Filologie din Republica Socialista România. *Studii şi Articole de Istorie.*

4439
Société Belge d'Études Coloniales. BULLETIN. 1–32, Mar./Apr. 1874–Dec. 1925. Bruxelles.
In French. Vols. 22–25, 1915–18 not published.
Merged with: *Congo; Revue Belge de la Colonie Belge.*
Indexes: 1893–1914.

4440
Société Belge d'Études Géographiques. BULLETIN. v.1– , May 1931– . Louvain. Semi-annual.
Issued by: Belgische Vereniging voor Aardrijkskundige Studies. In Flemish or French; summaries in English and French.
Indexes: Vols. 1931–40, 1941–50.

4441
Société d'Anthropologie de Paris. BULLETINS ET MÉMOIRES. 1859– . Paris, Doin. Four no. a year.
In French. Issued in numbered series; the last series, 13, started in 1974. Title varies: 1859–99, *Bulletins de la Société d'Anthropologie de Paris. Mémoires* were issued as a separate series from 1860 to 1902.
Indexes: 1859–99, 1v.

4442
Société d'Économie et des Sciences Sociales. BULLETIN. 1865–1885. Paris, Bureau de la Réforme Sociale.
Issued by: the society under an earlier name: Société Internationale des Études Pratiques d'Économie Sociale. In French.
Superseded by: *Réforme Sociale.*

4443
Société d'Ethnographie. MÉMOIRES. 1–13, 1895–1975; ser. 2, v.1–7, pt. 3, 1875–1902. Paris.
In French. Added title-page title: *Revue Orientale et Américaine* (v.9 also as *Revue Orientale*; v.11 as *Revue Ethnographique*)

4444
Société de Législation Comparée. JOURNÉES. v.1–71, 1869/72–Oct./Dec. 1948. Paris. Frequency varies.
In French. Publication suspended 1940–44.
Superseded by: *Revue Internationale de Droit Comparé* (1949–)
Indexes: 1869–80, 1v.

4445
Société des Africanistes. JOURNAL. v.1–45, 1931–1975. Paris. Annual, 1931–47; two no. a year.

Published in cooperation with the Centre Nationale de la Recherche Scientifique. In French.
Continued by: *Journal des Africanistes*.
Indexed: Abst. Anth.; Bull. Sig. Soc. Eth.; Int. Bibl. Soc. Cul. Anth.

4446
Société des Américanistes. JOURNAL. v.1–5, 1895–190?; n. ser. 1– , 1903– . Paris, Au Siège de la Société Musée de l'Homme. Annual.
In English, French, German, or Spanish. Includes section "Bibliographie Américaniste", 1914–64.
Indexes: 1895–1946, 1v.
Indexed: His. Abst.; Int. Bibl. Pol. Sc.; Int. Bibl. Soc.

4447
Société des Études Indo-Chinoises. BULLETIN. v.1– , 1925– . Paris, Saigon, Paris. Semi-annual.
Issued with the cooperation of the Musée National de Vietnam. In French, occasionally in Vietnamese.
Supersedes: Comité Agricole et Industrielle de la Cochinchina. *Bulletin*.
Indexes: of the superseded work (1883–1923) and this work, v.1–46, 1925–71, in v.46, no.4, 1971.
Indexed: Abst. Anth.; Bull. Sig. Soc. Eth.; Int. Bibl. Soc. Cul. Anth.

4448
Société des Océanistes. JOURNAL. v.1– , 1945– . Paris. Annual.
Issued in cooperation with the Musée de l'Homme. In English or French.
Indexed: Abst. Anth.; Bull. Sig. Soc. Eth.; His. Abst.; Int. Bibl. Soc. Cul. Anth.

SOCIÉTÉ ET IDÉOLOGIES
See SOCIÉTÉ. MOUVEMENTS SOCIAUX ET IDÉOLOGIES. 1e série. ÉTUDES

4449
SOCIÉTÉ. MOUVEMENTS SOCIAUX ET IDÉOLOGIES. 1e série. ÉTUDES. 1– , 1960– . Paris, Mouton. Irreg.
Issued by: Division des Affaires Culturelles, École Pratique des Hautes Études. In French. Title varies: v.1–6, *Société et Idéologies*.

4450
Société Préhistorique Française. BULLETIN. v.1–60, 1904–1963. Paris. Monthly.
In French.
Continued, in part, by: the society's *Bulletin. Comptes Rendus des Séances Mensuelles*.

4451
SOCIÉTÉS. 1– , 1976– . Toulouse, Université de Toulouse-le-Mirail, Service des Publications. Four no. a year.
In French. Subseries of: Université de Toulouse-le-Mirail. *Annales*.
Indexed: Bull. Anal. Pol. Ec. Soc.

4452
SOCIÉTÉS AFRICAINES, MONDE ARABE & CULTURE ISLAMIQUE; MÉMOIRES DU CERMAA. no.1– , 1981– . Paris. Annual.
Issued by: Institut National des Langues et Civilisations Orientales. In French.

4453
SOCIETY. v.9, no.4– , Feb. 1972– . New Brunswick, N.J., Transaction Periodicals Consortium. Monthly (July/Aug. and Nov./Dec. when bimonthly)
Issued by: Rutgers State University.
Continues: *Transactions, Social Science and Modern Society*.
Indexed: Bull. Anal. Pol. Ec. Soc.; Curr. Cont. Soc. Beh. Sc.; Int. Pol. Sc. Abst.; Peace Res. Abst.; PHRA; Soc. Abst.; SSCI; Soc. Work. Res. Abst.

4454
SOCIETY AND CULTURE. 1– , July 1970– . Calcutta. Semi-annual.
Issued by: Institute of Social Studies. Vol. for 1972 last available for examination.
Indexed: Psych. Abst.

4455
SOCIETY AND LEISURE. v.1–8, no.4, 1969–1976. Prague. Two no. a year, 1969; four no. a year.
Issued by: European Centre for Leisure and Education. Subtitle reads: "Bulletin of sociology of leisure, education and culture".
Superseded by: *Loisir et Société*.
Indexed: Bull. Anal. Pol. Ec. Soc.; Bull. Sig. Soc. Eth.

SOCIETY AND LEISURE
See LOISIR ET SOCIÉTÉ

SOCIETY AND SPACE
See ENVIRONMENT AND PLANNING. D. SOCIETY AND SPACE

4456
Society for Medical Anthropology. SPECIAL PUBLICATION. no.1– , 1979– . Washington, D.C. Irreg.

4457
Society for the Psychological Study of Social Issues. BULLETIN. v.1–3, no.1, Sept. 1936–Aug. 1944. New York.
Some numbers are published as a section of the *Journal of Social Psychology*.

4458
Society for the Study of International Problems. SSIP MITTEILUNGEN. no.1–39, summer 1954–1974. Kiel, Die Studienkreis.
In English, French, or German.
Continued by: the society's *SSIP Bulletin.*

4459
Society for the Study of Labour History. BULLETIN. v.1– , 1960– . Edinburgh. Semi-annual.
Indexed: Bull. Sig. Soc. Eth.; His. Abst.; Peace Res. Abst. J.

4460
Society for the Study of State Governments. JOURNAL. v.1– , Jan./June 1968– . Varanasi. Quarterly.
Indexed: PAIS.

4461
Society of Malawi. JOURNAL. v.1– , 1948– . Blantyre. Three no. a year, 1948; semi-annual.
Title varies: 1948–June 1955, *Nyasaland Journal.*
Indexed: Abst. Anth.; His. Abst.

4462
SOCIJALIZAM. v.1– , 1958– . Beograd, Kultura. Bimonthly.
Issued by: Centralni Komitet, Savez Komunista Jugoslavije. In Serbo-Croatian. Tables of contents also in English and Russian.
Indexed: Int. Bibl. Pol. Sc.; Int. Pol. Sc. Abst.

4463
SOCIJALNA POLITIKA I SOCIJALNI RAD. v.7– , 1971– . Beograd. Annual.
Issued by: Institut za Socijalnu Politiku, and Drustvo Socijalnih Radnika SR Serbije. In Serbo-Croatian; summaries in English.
Continues: *Socijalni Radnik.*

SOCIO-ECONOMIC AND HISTORICAL SCIENCES
See ACTA MANILANA. SERIES B. SOCIO-ECONOMIC AND HISTORICAL SCIENCES

4464
SOCIO-ECONOMIC PLANNING SCIENCES. v.1– , Sept. 1967– . Oxford, New York, Pergamon Press. Bimonthly.
Issued by: Graduate Center, City University of New York.
Indexed: ABC POL SCI; Bull. Anal. Pol. Ec. Soc.; Geo. Abst.; Int. Bibl. Eco.; Int. Bibl. Pol. Sc.; Int. Bibl. Soc.; Int. Lab. Doc.; Int. Pol. Sc. Abst.; PAIS; Pop. Ind.; Soc. Abst.; SSCI.

4465
SOCIOLOGIA. v.1–28, Mar. 1939–1966. São Paulo. Quarterly.
Issued by: Fundação Escola de Sociologia e Politica de São Paulo. Subtitle reads: "Revista dedicada a teoria e pesquisa das ciências sociais". In English, French, Portuguese, or Spanish.
Indexed: Int. Bibl. Soc.; Soc. Abst.

4466
SOCIOLOGIA. v.1– , 1967– . Roma. Three no. a year.
Issued by: Istituto di Luigi Sturzo. In Italian. Subtitle reads: "Rivista di scienze sociali".
Supersedes: *Bolletino di Sociologia dell'Istituto Luigi Sturzo.*
Indexed: Bull. Anal. Pol. Ec. Soc.; Bull. Sig. Soc. Eth.; Int. Bibl. Eco.; Int. Bibl. Pol. Sc.; Soc. Abst.

4467
SOCIOLOGIA. v.1– , 1969– . Bratislava, Vydavatelstve SAV. Four no. a year, 1969–71; bimonthly.
Issued by: Sociologický Ústav, Slovenska Akademia Vied. In Czech; summaries in English and Russian.

4468
SOCIOLOGIA DEL DIRITTO. 1– , 1974– . Milano, A. Giuffrè. Semi-annual.
Issued by: Commissione Permanente di Sociologia del Diritto, Centro Nazionale de Prevenzione e Difesa Sociale. In Italian; summaries in English.

4469
SOCIOLOGIA DEL LAVORO. no.1– , Mar. 1978– . Bologna, Angeli. Three no. a year.
Issued by: Centro Internazionale di Documentazione e Studi Sociologici sui Problemi del Lavoro, Istituto de Sociologia, Università a Bologna. In Italian.

4470
SOCIOLOGIA DELL'ORGANIZAZIONE. 1– , Jan./June 1973– . Padova, F. Angeli. Semi-annual.
In Italian.

4471
SOCIOLOGIA DELLA COMMUNICAZIONE. v.1– , 1982– . Milano, F. Angeli. Semi-annual.
In Italian.

4472
SOCIOLOGIA DELLA LETTERATURA. v.1– , 1975– . Roma, Bulzoni. Semi-annual.
In Italian.

4473
SOCIOLOGIA E RICERCHA SOCIALE. v.1– , June 1980– . Roma, Goliardica. Three no. a year.
In Italian.

4474
SOCIOLOGÍA EN MÉXICO. Apr. 1951–Oct. 1969. Mexico, D.F.
Issued by: Seminario Mexicano de Sociología. In Spanish.

4475
SOCIOLOGIA INDICA. v.1, no.1/2– , May 1977– . Calcutta. Two no. a year; some combined numbers.
Issued by: Indian Institute of Sociology. Vol. for 1979 last available for examination.

4476
SOCIOLOGIA INTERNATIONALIS. INTERNATIONALES ZEITSCHRIFT FÜR SOZIOLOGIE UND SOZIALPSYCHOLOGIE. v.1– , 1963– . Berlin, Duncker & Humblot. Two no. a year.
In various languages; summaries in English, French, German and Spanish.
Indexed: Bull. Sig. Soc. Eth.; Int. Bibl. Soc.; Int. Pol. Sc. Abst.; Soc. Abst.

4477
SOCIOLOGIA NEERLANDICA. v.1–11, winter 1962/63–Jan./July 1976. Assen, Van Gorcum. Semi-annual.
Issued by: Netherlands Sociological Society and (1972–76) Netherlands' Sociological and Anthropological Society. In English; summaries in French, German, and occasionally in Spanish.
Continued by: *Netherlands Journal of Sociology*.
Indexed: Bull. Sig. Soc. Eth.; Int. Bibl. Soc.; Int. Pol. Sc. Abst.; Soc. Abst.; Urb. Aff. Abst.

4478
SOCIOLOGIA RELIGIOSA. no.1– , 1959– . Padova, Milano, Memo Editore. Semi-annual.
In English, French, Italian, or Spanish.
Indexed: Int. Bibl. Soc.; Soc. Abst.

4479
SOCIOLOGIA RURALIS. spring 1960–1969. Assen, Van Gorcum. Semi-annual.
Issued by: European Society for Rural Sociology. In English, French, or German; summaries in English, French and German.
Indexed: Bull. Anal. Pol. Ec. Soc.; Bull. Sig. Soc. Eth.; Int. Bibl. Soc.; Int. Lab. Doc.; Int. Pol. Sc. Abst.; PAIS; PAISFL; Soc. Abst.

4480
SOCIOLOGICAL ABSTRACTS. v.1– , Jan. 1952– . New York, later San Diego, Calif., Sociological Abstracts. Six no. a year; the sixth no. consists of annual indexes (author, subject, and list of publications).
Includes separately numbered supplements (beginning with 1962–): "Abstracts of Papers delivered at the Annual Meetings of . . .": Eastern Sociological Society, Georgia Sociological and Anthropological Association, Illinois Sociological Association, Midwest Sociological Society, North Central Sociological Association, Pennsylvania Sociological Association, Southern Association of Agricultural Scientists. Rural Sociology Section, Southern Sociological Society, Southwestern Sociological Association; and American Society of Criminology, American Sociological Association, Association for the Humanist Sociology, Association for the Sociology of Religion, Canadian Sociology and Anthropology Association, International Society for Research on Aggression, International Symposium on Victimology, World Congress of Sociology; and International Review of Publications in Sociology, Newsletter of International Sociological Association, Newsletter of the International Society for the Sociology of Knowledge.

4481
SOCIOLOGICAL ANALYSIS. v.1– , Mar. 1940– . Worcester, Mass., later River Forest, Ill. Quarterly.
Issued by: American Catholic Sociological Society. Subtitle reads: "A journal of sociology of religion". Title varies: 1940–63, *The American Catholic Sociological Review*. Other title: *SA Sociological Analysis*.
Indexed: Bull. Anal. Pol. Ec. Soc.; Curr. Cont. Soc. Beh. Sc.; His. Abst.; Int. Pol. Sc. Abst.; LLBA; Pop. Ind.; Soc. Abst.; SSCI; Wom. Stu. Abst.

SOCIOLOGICAL ANALYSIS
See SOCIOLOGICAL ANALYSIS & THEORY

4482
SOCIOLOGICAL ANALYSIS & THEORY. v.1– , Oct. 1970– . Beverly Hills, Calif., Sage Publications. Three no. a year.
Issued by: Department of Sociological Studies, University of Sheffield. Title varies: v.1–3, 1970–73, *Sociological Analysis*.
Indexed: Bull. Anal. Pol. Ec. Soc.

4483
SOCIOLOGICAL BULLETIN. v.1– , 1952– . New Delhi. Semi-annual.
Issued by: Indian Sociological Society, and Centre for the Study of Social Systems, Jawaharlal Nehru University.
Indexed: Bull. Sig. Soc. Eth.; His. Abst.; Int. Bibl. Soc.; Int. Lab. Doc.; Soc. Abst.; SSCI.

SOCIOLOGICAL CONTRIBUTIONS
See SOZIOLOGISCHE ARBEITEN

4484
SOCIOLOGICAL INQUIRY. v.1– , 1930– . Urbana, Ill. Semi-annual, 1930–52; quarterly.

Issued by: National Sociology Honor Society, Alpha Kappa Delta. Title varies: *AKD Quarterly*; *Alpha Kappa Delta Quarterly*.
Indexed: Abst. Anth.; Bull. Anal. Pol. Ec. Soc.; Bull. Sig. Soc. Eth.; Abst. Soc. Work; Int. Bibl. Soc.; Soc. Abst.; SSCI.

4485
SOCIOLOGICAL METHODOLOGY. 1969– . San Francisco, Calif., Jossey-Bass. Annual.
Issued by: American Sociological Association.
Indexed: Int. Pol. Sc. Abst.

4486
SOCIOLOGICAL METHODS AND RESEARCH. v.1– , Aug. 1972– . Beverly Hills, Calif., Sage Publications. Quarterly.
Issued by: Department of Sociology, Queen's College, City University of New York.
Indexed: Int. Bibl. Soc.; LLBA; PAIS; Sage Urb. Stu. Abst.; Soc. Abst.; SSCI; Urb. Aff. Abst.

4487
SOCIOLOGICAL MICRO-JOURNAL. 1– , 1967– . Copenhagen. Annual.
Issued by: Sociologisk Institut, Københavns Universitet. In English, French, or German.
Indexed: Soc. Abst.

4488
SOCIOLOGICAL PRACTICE. 1– , spring 1976– . New York, Human Sciences Press. Semi-annual.
Indexed: Soc. Abst.

4489
THE SOCIOLOGICAL QUARTERLY. v.1– , Jan. 1960– . Carbondale, Ill., later Greenwich, Conn., JAI Press. Quarterly.
Issued by: Midwest Sociological Society, subsequently Department of Sociology, University of Missouri, Columbia.
Supersedes: *The Midwest Sociologist* (1938–59).
Indexes: 1974–83.
Indexed: ABC POL SCI; Bull. Anal. Pol. Ec. Soc.; Int. Bibl. Soc.; Int. Bibl. Soc. Cul. Anth.; Int. Pol. Sc. Abst.; PAIS; Pop. Ind.; Psych. Abst.; Soc. Sc. Hum. Ind.; Soc. Sc. Ind.; Soc. Abst.; SSCI; Soc. Work. Res. Abst.; Wom. Stu. Abst.

4490
SOCIOLOGICAL REVIEW. v.1–44, 1908–1952; n. ser. v.1– , July 1953– . Manchester, London, Keele. Quarterly, 1908–40; irreg., 1940–45; three no. a year.
Issued by: Institute of Sociology, 1908–52; University College of North Staffordshire.
Supersedes: *Sociological Papers of the Institute of Sociology*.
Indexes: Vols. 1953–75, 1v.
Indexed: Brit. Hum. Ind.; Bull. Anal. Pol. Ec. Soc.; Bull. Sig. Soc. Eth.; Int. Bibl. Pol. Sc.; Int. Bibl. Soc.; Int. Bibl. Soc. Cul. Anth.; Int. Pol. Sc. Abst.; Pop. Ind.; Psych. Abst.; Sage Fam. Stu. Abst.; Sage Urb. Stu. Abst.; Soc. Abst.; SSCI; Urb. Aff. Abst.

SOCIOLOGICAL REVIEW
See CHU HAI SHU YAN HUI HSÜEH CHI SHE HUI KUNG TSO HSÜEH HSI

SOCIOLOGICAL REVIEW
See PRZEGLĄD SOCJOLOGICZNY

SOCIOLOGICAL REVIEW
See REVIJA ZA SOCIOLOGIJU

SOCIOLOGICAL REVIEW
See SOCIOLOGICKÁ REVUE

SOCIOLOGICAL REVIEW
See SOCIOLOGICKÝ CASOPIS

SOCIOLOGICAL REVIEW
See SOSYLOJII DERGISI

4491
SOCIOLOGICAL SPECTRUM. v.1– , Jan. 1981– . Washington, D.C., Hemisphere Pub. Corp. Quarterly.
Issued by: Mid-South Sociological Association. Formed by the union of: *Sociological Forum* (v.1–3, 1978–80) and *Sociological Symposium* (v.1–8, fall 1968–1975)
Indexed: Soc. Abst.

4492
SOCIOLOGICAL STUDIES IN ROMAN HISTORY. v.1– , 1978– . London, Cambridge University Press. Irreg.
Monograph series.

4493
SOCIOLOGICAL STUDIES OF CHILD DEVELOPMENT. v.1– , 1986– . Greenwich, Conn., JAI Press. Annual.

THE SOCIOLOGICAL WORLD
See SHE HUI HSÜEH-CHIEN

4494
SOCIOLOGICAL YEARBOOK ON RELIGION IN BRITAIN. v.1–8, 1968–1975. London, SCM Press. Annual.
Issued by: London School of Economics and Political Science, University of London. Includes a section "Bibliography of works in the sociology of British religion".

Indexed: Bull. Anal. Pol. Ec. Soc.; Bull. Sig. Soc. Eth.; Int. Bibl. Soc.

4495
SOCIOLOGICKÁ REVUE. REVUE DE SOCIOLOGIE. SOCIOLOGICAL REVIEW. SOZIOLOGISCHE REVUE. 1–15, 1930–1948. Brno.
Issued by: Sociologický Seminar, Masarykova Universita, and Masarykova Sociologická Společnost. In Czech; summaries in English, French, or German.

4496
SOCIOLOGICKÝ ČASOPIS. v.1– , 1965– . Praha. Six no. a year.
Issued by: Vědecke Kolegium Filozofie, subsequently Filozofický Ústav, Československá Akademia Věd. In Czech and Slovak; summaries in English, French, German and Russian. Other title: *Sociological Review.*
Indexed: Bull. Anal. Pol. Ec. Soc.; Bull. Sig. Soc. Eth.; Int. Bibl. Soc.; Int. Lab. Doc.; Int. Pol. Sc. Abst.; LLBA; Psych. Abst.; Soc. Abst.; SSCI.

4497
SOCIOLOGIE A HISTORIE ZEMĚDĚLSTVI. v.1–10, June 1965–1974. Praha. Two no. a year.
Issued by: Ústav Vědecko-Technických Informaci, Ministerstvo Zemědělstvi, Lesniho a Vodniho Hospodarstvi. In Czech; summaries in English, German and Russian. Subseries of: Sbornik UVTI (Ústav Vědecko-Technických Informaci)
Continued by: *Sociologie Zemědělstvi.*
Indexed: Soc. Abst.

LA SOCIOLOGIE CONTEMPORAINE
See CURRENT SOCIOLOGY

4498
SOCIOLOGIE DU DÉVELOPPEMENT. v.1– , 1968– . Paris, Éditions Gauthier-Villars.
In French. Subseries of: *Collection* de l'Institut d'Économie Régionale du Sud-Ouest, and of: *Techniques Économiques Modernes.* V.1 is no.27 of *Techniques Économiques Modernes.*

4499
SOCIOLOGIE DU TRAVAIL. 1– , Oct./Dec. 1959– . Paris, Éditions du Seuil. Quarterly.
Issued by: Association pour le Développement de la Sociologie du Travail. In French.
Indexed: Bull. Anal. Pol. Ec. Soc.; Bull. Sig. Soc. Eth.; Int. Bibl. Eco.; Int. Bibl. Soc.; Int. Lab. Doc.; Int. Pol. Sc. Abst.; PAISFL; Urb. Aff. Abst.

4500
SOCIOLOGIE ET DROIT SLAVES. no.1–9, Dec. 1945–1948. Paris.
Issued under the auspices of the Institut International de Sociologie and Société de Législation Comparée in cooperation with several institutes of the University of Paris. In French.

4501
SOCIOLOGIE ET SOCIÉTÉS. v.1– , May 1969– . Montréal, Les Presses de l'Université de Montréal. Two no. a year.
In French; summaries in English, French and Spanish.
Indexed: Bull. Anal. Pol. Ec. Soc.; Bull. Sig. Soc. Eth.; Int. Bibl. Soc.; Int. Lab. Doc.; Int. Pol. Sc. Abst.; LLBA; Psych. Abst.; PAIS; PAISFL; Soc. Abst.; SSCI.

4502
SOCIOLOGIE; REVISTA DE REFERATI ŞI RECENZII. 1964– . Bucureşti. Bimonthly.
Issued by: Centrul de Informare in Ştiinţe Sociale şi Politice. In Romanian.
Continues, in part: *Revista Referati şi Recenzii; Filosofie, Logica, Sociologie, Psikologie*, and continues its volume numbering. In Romanian.

4503
SOCIOLOGIE ROMÂNIEI. v.1–7, 1940–1946. Bucureşti. Irreg.
Issued by: Institutul Social Roman. In Romanian. Monograph series.

4504
SOCIOLOGIE ZEMĚDĚLSTVI. 1– , 1975– . Praha. Semi-annual.
Issued by: Ústav Vědecko-Technických Informaci, and Československa Akademie Zemědělska. In Czech; summaries in English and Russian.
Supersedes: *Sociologie a Historie Zemědělstvi.*
Subseries of: *Sbornik UVTIZ—Sociologie.*

4505
SOCIOLOGIJA. v.1– , 1959– . Beograd. Quarterly.
Issued by: Jugoslovenske Udrizenje za Sociologiju. In Serbo-Croatian; summaries in English. Tables of contents also in English.
Supersedes, in part: *Jugoslovenski Casopis za Filozofiju i Sociologiju.*
Indexed: Bull. Anal. Pol. Ec. Soc.; Bull. Sig. Soc. Eth.; Int. Bibl. Soc.; Int. Pol. Sc. Abst.; Soc. Abst.

4506
SOCIOLOGIJA SELA. v.1– , July/Sept. 1963– . Zagreb. Quarterly.
Issued by: Ágrarni Institut. In Serbo-Croatian; summaries in English and Russian. Tables of contents also in English and Russian.
Indexed: Bull. Anal. Pol. Ec. Soc.; Bull. Sig. Soc. Eth.; Int. Bibl. Soc.; LLBA; Soc. Abst.

4507
SOCIOLOGISCH JAARBOEK. 1985– . Deventer, Van Logum Slaterns.
Issued by: Stichting Interuniversitair voor Sociaal-Wetenschappelijk Onderzoek te Amsterdam (SISWO). In Dutch.

4508
SOCIOLOGISCHE GIDS; TIJDSCHRIFT VOOR SOCIOLOGIE EN SOCIAAL ONDERZOEK. 1953– . Meppel, J.A. Boom en Zoon. Bimonthly.
In Dutch, English, French, or German; summaries in English.
Indexed: Int. Bibl. Soc.; Soc. Abst.

4509
SOCIOLOGISK FORSKNING. 1– , 1964– . Uppsala. Quarterly.
Issued by: Sveriges Socioloforbund. In Swedish.
Indexed: Int. Bibl. Soc.; Soc. Abst.; SSCI; Urb. Aff. Abst.

4510
SOCIOLOGISKE MEDDELELSER. A DANISH SOCIOLOGICAL JOURNAL. Ser. 1– , 1952– . København. One or two no. a year.
Issued by: Statistisk-Økonomisk Laboratorium, Sociologisk Institut, Københavns Universitet. In English or one of the Scandinavian languages; summaries in one language other than the language of the text.
Indexed: Int. Bibl. Soc.; Soc. Abst.

4511
SOCIOLOGUS; ZEITSCHRIFT FÜR EMPIRISCHE SOZIOLOGIE UND ETHNOLOGISCHE FORSCHUNG; A JOURNAL OF EMPIRICAL SOCIOLOGY, SOCIAL PSYCHOLOGY AND ETHNIC RESEARCH. n. ser. v.1– , 1951– . Berlin, Duncker & Humblot. Two no. a year.
In German.
Continues: *Sociologus*, and *Archiv für Anthropologische Völkerforschung und Kolonialen Kulturwandel*.
Indexed: Bull. Anal. Pol. Ec. Soc.; Bull. Sig. Soc. Eth.; Int. Bibl. Soc.; Int. Bibl. Soc. Cul. Anth.; Int. Pol. Sc. Abst.; PAISFL; Soc. Abst.

4512
SOCIOLOGUS; ZEITSCHRIFT FÜR VÖLKERPSYCHOLOGIE UND SOZIOLOGIE. 1–9, Mar. 1925–Dec. 1933. Leipzig, Hirschfeld. Quarterly.
In German. Title varies: 1925–Dec. 1931, *Zeitschrift für Völkerpsychologie und Soziologie*.
Continued by: *Sociologus; Zeitschrift für Empirische Soziologie und Ethnologische Forschung*.

4513
SOCIOLOGY. v.1– , Jan. 1967– . Oxford, Clarendon Press. Three no. a year, 1967–79; six no. a year.
Issued by: British Sociological Association.
Indexed: Brit. Hum. Ind.; Bull. Anal. Pol. Ec. Soc.; Bull. Sig. Soc. Eth.; Int. Bibl. Soc.; Int. Lab. Doc.; Int. Bibl. Pol. Sc.; Int. Pol. Sc. Abst.; LLBA; Soc. Abst.; SSCI; Urb. Aff. Abst.; Wom. Stu. Abst.

SOCIOLOGY AND SOCIAL ANTHROPOLOGY
See Indian Council of Social Science Research. JOURNAL OF ABSTRACTS AND REVIEWS. SOCIOLOGY AND SOCIAL ANTHROPOLOGY

4514
SOCIOLOGY & SOCIAL RESEARCH. v.1– , 1916– . Los Angeles, Calif. Bimonthly, 1951–59/60; quarterly.
Issued by: University of Southern California, Los Angeles. Title varies: v.1–5 (no.1–19), *Studies in Sociology. Sociological Monographs*; v.6–11, *Journal of Applied Sociology*. Absorbed: *News Notes of Southern California Sociological Society*, in Oct. 1921, and *Bulletin of Social Research* of the Department of Sociology, University of Southern California, in Sept. 1927.
Indexed: Abst. Soc. Work; Bull. Anal. Pol. Ec. Soc.; Bull. Sig. Soc. Eth.; His. Abst.; Int. Bibl. Eco.; Int. Bibl. Soc.; Int. Bibl. Pol. Sc.; Int. Bibl. Soc. Cul. Abst.; Int. Pol. Sc. Abst.; PAIS; Pop. Ind.; Psych. Abst.; Soc. Sc. Hum. Ind.; Soc. Abst.; Soc. Work. Res. Abst.; SSCI.

4515
SOCIOLOGY, LAW AND LEGAL THEORY. 1– , 1974– . Rotterdam, Rotterdam University Press.

4516
SOCIOLOGY OF EDUCATION. v.1– , Sept. 1927– . Washington, D.C. Monthly, 1927–63; quarterly.
Issued by: Department of Sociology, University of California, Berkeley. Title varies: v.1–36, 1927–Mar. 1963, *The Journal of Educational Sociology*.
Indexed: Int. Bibl. Soc.; PAIS; Psych. Abst.; Soc. Abst.; Soc. Sc. Ind.; SSCI.

4517
SOCIOLOGY OF EDUCATION ABSTRACTS. v.1– , 1965– . Liverpool. Quarterly.
Issued by: School of Education, University of Liverpool; and Department of Social Science and Education, and Department of Sociology, Edgehill College of Education.

4518
SOCIOLOGY OF HEALTH & ILLNESS; A JOURNAL OF MEDICAL SOCIOLOGY. v.1– , June 1979– . London, Routledge & Kegan Paul. Quarterly.
Indexed: LLBA; Psych. Abst.; Soc. Abst.; SSCI.

SOCIOLOGY OF LAW
See HO-SHAKAIGAKU

4519
SOCIOLOGY OF PLAY AND GAMES. 1975– . Waterloo. Three no. a year.
Issued by: SIRLS, Faculty of Human Kinetics and Leisure Studies, University of Waterloo.

4520
SOCIOLOGY OF SPORT AND LEISURE ABSTRACTS; A REVIEW OF SOCIAL SCIENCE LITERATURE. 1– , 1980– . Amsterdam, Elsevier Scientific Pub. Co. Three no. a year.

4521
SOCIOLOGY OF SPORT JOURNAL. v.1– , Mar. 1984– . Champaign, Ill. Quarterly.
Issued by: North American Society for the Sociology of Sport (NASS).
Indexed: LLBA.

4522
SOCIOLOGY OF THE SCIENCES. 1– , 1977– . Dordrecht, D. Reidel. Annual.
Monograph series.
Indexed: Soc. Abst.

4523
SOCIOLOGY OF WORK AND OCCUPATIONS. 1– , Feb. 1974– . Beverly Hills, Calif., Sage Publications. Quarterly.
Indexed: Int. Bibl. Soc.; Psych. Abst.; Sage Fam. Stu. Abst.; Soc. Abst.

4524
SOCIOLOGY WORKING PAPERS. 1972– . Singapore. Monthly.
Issued by: Department of Sociology, University of Singapore. Each issue has also a distinctive title.

4525
SOCIOLOŠKI PREGLED. v.1– , 1965– . Beograd. Three no. a year.
Issued by: Srpska Sociološka Drustvo. In Serbo-Croatian; summaries in English and French.
Indexed: Soc. Abst.

4526
SOCIOMETRY. v.1–40, July/Oct. 1937–Dec. 1977. Washington, D.C., American Sociological Association. Quarterly.
Issued by: Department of Sociology, University of California at Los Angeles.
Continued by: *Social Psychology*.
Indexed: Abst. Soc. Work; Bull. Anal. Pol. Ec. Soc.; Bull. Sig. Soc. Eth.; Int. Bibl. Soc.; Int. Pol. Sc. Abst.; Peace Res. Abst. J.; Pop. Ind.; Psych. Abst.; Soc. Abst.; SSCI; Urb. Aff. Abst.; Wom. Stu. Abst.

4527
SOCJOLOGIA MORSKA. v.1– , 1985– . Wrocław, Zakład Narodowy im. Ossolińskich. Irreg.
Issued by: Komisja Socjologii Morskiej, Oddział w Gdańsku, Polska Akademia Nauk. In Polish; summaries in English.

4528
SOCJOLOGIA WYCHOWANIA. 1– , 1976– . Toruń. Irreg.
Issued by: Uniwersytet Mikołaja Kopernika in Toruń. In Polish; summaries in English. Subseries of: *Acta Universitatis Nicolai Copernici. Nauki Humanistyczno-Społeczne*.

4529
SOCJOLOGICZNE PROBLEMY PRZEMYSŁU I KLASY ROBOTNICZEJ. 1– , 1966– . Warszawa, Państwowe Wydawnictwo Naukowe. Irreg.
Issued by: Zakład Badań Społecznych Przemysłu i Klasy Robotniczej, Wyzsza Szkoła Nauk Społecznych przy KC PZPR. In Polish.

4530
SONDAGES. v.1– , June 1939– ; n. ser. Oct. 1944– . Paris, éditions de Chancelier. Quarterly.
Issued by: Institut Français d'Opinion. In French. Title varies: 1939–Aug. 1945, *Bulletin d'Information*. Publication suspended 1941–Aug. 1944. Subtitle reads: "Revue française de l'opinion publique".
Indexed: Bull. Anal. Pol. Ec. Soc.; Bull. Sig. Soc. Eth.; Int. Bibl. Soc.; Soc. Abst.

SONDERBAND
See ZEITSCHRIFT FÜR AGRARGESCHICHTE UND AGRARSOZIOLOGIE

SONDERHEFT
See DER DONAURAUM

SONDERHEFT
See LEVIATHAN

SONDERHEFT
See REICH UND LÄNDER

SONDERREIHE
See Statistical Office of the European Communities. SOZIALSTATISTIK

SONGLIAO JOURNAL. PHILOSOPHY AND SOCIAL SCIENCE
See SUNG LIAO HSÜEH K'AN. SHE HUI K'O HSÜEH PAN. SONG LIAO XUE KAN

SOOCHOW JOURNAL OF SOCIAL AND POLITICAL SCIENCES
See TUNG WU CHIH SHE HUI HSÜEH PAO

4531
SOSHIOROJI. v.1– , Jan. 1952– . Kyoto. Semi-annual.
Issued by: Shakaigaku Kenkyu–kai. In Japanese.

4532
SOSIALØKONOMEN. v.1– , 1947– . Oslo, Sosialøkonomist Samfun. Frequency varies.
Issued by: Norske Socialøkonomers Forening. In Norwegian; occasionally in English.
Supersedes: *Stimulator*.

SOSIOGRAFI INDONESIA
See SOSIOGRAFI INDONESIA DAN HUKUM ADAT

4533
SOSIOGRAFIA INDONESIA DAN HUKUM ADAT. v.1– , 1959– . Jogjakarta, Jajasan Pembina Hukum Adat. Semi-annual.
In Indonesian; some special issues in English. Title varies: v.1, 1959, *Sosiografi Indonesia*; v.2, 1960, *Madjalah Hukum Adat*.

4534
SOSIOLOGIA. v.1– , 1964– . Helsinki. Quarterly.
Issued by: Westermarck-Seuran Julkaisa. Includes some doctoral dissertations in sociology. In Finnish.
Indexed: Int. Bibl. Soc.; Soc. Abst.

4535
SOSYOLOJI DERGISI. SOCIOLOGICAL REVIEW. REVUE DE SOCIOLOGIE. ZEITSCHRIFT FÜR SOZIOLOGIE. 1– , 1942– . Istanbul. Irreg.
Issued by: Edibiyat Fakultesi Yayinlari, Istanbul Universitesi. In English, French, or German.

SOTSIALISTICHESKAIA MYSL' I PRAKTIKA
See QUESTIONS ACTUELLES DU SOCIALISME SOCIALIST THOUGHT AND PRACTICE

SOTSIALISTICHESKAIA REKONSTRUKTSIIA SEL'SKOGO KHOZIAISTVA
See EKONOMIKA SEL'SKOGO KHOZIAISTVA

4536
SOTSIALISTICHESKII TRUD. 1– , 1956– . Moskva. Monthly.
Issued by: Gosudarstvennyi Komitet Soveta Ministrov SSSR po Voprosam Truda i Zarabotnoi Platy. In Russian.

4537
SOTSIALISTICHESKOE KHOZIAISTVO. v.1–8, no.1–3, 1923–1930. Moskva, Gos. Izd-vo.
Vols. 6–8 issued by: Institut Ekonomiki Rossiiskoi Assotsiatsii Nauchno-Issledovatel'skikh Institutov Obshchestvennykh Nauk. In Russian. Formed by the union of: *Narodnoe Khoziaistvo*, and *Finansy i Ekonomika*. Absorbed by: *Problemy Ekonomiki*, in 1930.

SOTSIALISTICHESKOE SEL'SKOE KHOZIAISTVO
See EKONOMIKA SEL'SKOGO KHOZIAISTVA

4538
SOTSIAL'NAIA STRUKTURA SEL'SKOGO NASELENIIA. no.1– , 1976– . Moskva. Irreg.
Issued by: Institut Sotsiologicheskikh Issledovanii, Sovetskaia Sotsiologicheskaia Assotsiatsiia. In Russian.

4539
SOTSIOLOGICHESKI PROBLEMI. 1– , 1969– . Sofiia, Publishing House of the Bulgarian Academy of Sciences. Bimonthly.
Issued by: Institut po Sotsiologiia, Bulgarska Akademiia na Naukite. In Bulgarian; summaries in English and Russian. Tables of contents also in English and Russian. Co-sponsored by: Bulgarska Sotsiologicheskaia Asotsiatsiia.
Supersedes: *Sotsiologicheski Izsledovaniia* (v.1, 1968)

4540
SOTSIOLOGICHESKIE ISSLEDOVANIIA. 1– , 1966– . Sverdlovsk. Irreg.
Issued by: Ural'skii Gosudarstvennyi Universitet. In Russian.

4541
SOTSIOLOGICHESKIE PROBLEMY OBRAZOVANIIA I DUKHOVNOI KULTURY. no.1– , 1975– . Sverdlovsk. Irreg.
Issued by: Sverdlovskii Pedagogicheskii Institut. In Russian.

4542
SOTSIOLOGICHESKIE PROBLEMY UPRAVLENIIA NARODNYM KHOZIAISTVOM. no.1– , 1968– . Sverdlovsk. Irreg.

Issued by: Ukrainskiĭ Nauchnyĭ T͡Sentr, Ukrainskiĭ Filial, Akademii͡a Nauk SSSR. In Russian.

4543
SOT͡SIOLOGICHESKIĬ SBORNIK. 1– , 1970– . Makhal-Kala. Irreg.
Issued by: Institut Istorii, I͡Azyka i Literatury, Dagestanskiĭ Filial, Akademii͡a Nauk SSSR. In Russian.

4544
SOT͡SIOLOGII͡A KUL'TURY. no.1– , 1974– . Moskva, Izd-vo Sovetskai͡a Rossii͡a. Annual.
Issued by: Otdel Sot͡siologicheskikh Issledovaniĭ, Nauchno-Issledovatelskiĭ Institut Kultury. In Russian. (Subseries of: Nauchno-Issledovatelskiĭ Institut Kul'tury. Otdel Sot͡siologicheskikh Issledovaniĭ. *Trudy*)

4545
Soumalainen Tiedeakademia, Helsingfors. TOIMITUKSIA. ANNALES. SERIES A. SECTION 5. MEDICA ANTHROPOLOGICA. no.1– , 1943– . Helsinki.
In English, French, or German. Title varies no.1–68, *Medica Anthropologica*.

4546
SOUNDINGS. v.51– , spring 1968– . Nashville, Tenn. Quarterly.
Issued by: Society for Values in Higher Education, and Vanderbilt University.
Indexed: LLBA; Soc. Abst.

4547
SOUTH AFRICAN INTERNATIONAL. v.1– , July 1970– . Johannesburg. Quarterly.
Issued by: South African Foundation.
Indexed: Bull. Anal. Pol. Ec. Soc.; Int. Bibl. Eco.; Int. Bibl. Pol. Sc.; Int. Pol. Sc. Abst.

4548
THE SOUTH AFRICAN JOURNAL OF AFRICAN AFFAIRS. v.1–9, 1971–1979. Pretoria. Four no. a year; some combined numbers.
Continued by: *Africa Insight*.

4549
THE SOUTH AFRICAN JOURNAL OF ECONOMICS. v.1– , Mar. 1933– . Johannesburg. Quarterly.
Issued by: Economic Society of South Africa. In Afrikaans; summaries in English. Other title: *Suid-Afrikaanse Tydskrif vir Ekonomie*.
Supersedes: *The Journal of the Economic Society of South Africa*.
Indexed: Bull. Anal. Pol. Ec. Soc.; Curr. Cont. Soc. Beh. Sc.; Ind. Per. Art. Law; Eco. Abst.; Int. Bibl. Eco.; Int. Bibl. Pol. Sc.; Int. Bibl. Soc.; J. Eco. Lit.; PAIS; Pop. Ind.; Soc. Abst; SSCI.

4550
SOUTH AFRICAN JOURNAL OF LABOUR RELATIONS. v.1– . Pretoria. Quarterly.
Issued by: Institute of Labour Relations, University of South Africa.

SOUTH AFRICAN JOURNAL OF PEDAGOGY
See SUID-AFRIKAANSE TYDSKRIF VIR PEDAGOGIE

SOUTH AFRICAN JOURNAL OF SOCIOLOGY
See SUID-AFRIKAANSE TYDSKRIF VIR SOCIOLOGIE

4551
SOUTH AFRICAN JOURNAL ON HUMAN RIGHTS. v.1– , May 1985– . Braamfontein, Ravan Press. Three no. a year.

4552
SOUTH AFRICAN YEARBOOK OF INTERNATIONAL LAW. v.1– , 1975– . Pretoria. Annual.
Issued by: VerLoren van Themaat Centre for International Law, University of South Africa. In English. Other title: *Suid-Afrikaanse Jaarboek vir Volkereg*.

4553
SOUTH ASIA RESEARCH. no.1– , May 1981– . London. Semi-annual.
Issued by: South Asia Centre, School of Oriental and African Studies, University of London.

4554
SOUTH ASIA SOCIAL SCIENCE ABSTRACTS. 1952–1958. Calcutta. Seven no. a year.
Issued by: United Nations Educational, Scientific and Cultural Organization. South Asia Science Co-operation Office, 1952–53; Research Centre on Social and Economic Development in Southern Asia, 1954–58.

SOUTH ASIA SOCIAL SCIENCE BIBLIOGRAPHY
See ASIAN SOCIAL SCIENCE BIBLIOGRAPHY WITH ANNOTATIONS AND ABSTRACTS

4555
SOUTH ASIAN ANTHROPOLOGIST. v.1– , Mar. 1980– . Ranchi. Semi-annual.
Organ of: Sarat Chandra Roy Institute of Anthropological Studies.
Indexed: Int. Bibl. Soc. Cul. Anth.

4556
SOUTH ASIAN REVIEW. 1– , Nov. 1967– . London. Quarterly.
Issued by: Royal Society for India, Pakistan and Ceylon. Title varies: v.1–2, 1967–June 1969, *Asian Review.*
Indexed: Int. Lab. Doc.; Int. Pol. Sc. Abst.

4557
SOUTH ASIAN STUDIES. 1– , 1966– . Jaipur. Bimonthly.
Issued by: South Asian Studies Centre, Department of Political Sciences, University of Rajastan.
Indexed: Int. Bibl. Soc. Cul. Anth.

4558
SOUTH-EAST ASIAN JOURNAL OF SOCIAL SCIENCES. 1973– . Singapore, Chopmen Enterprises. Semi-annual.
Issued by: Department of Sociology, National University of Singapore. Formed by the union of: *South-East Asian Journal of Sociology*, and *Southeast Asian Journal of Economic Development and Social Change*. Absorbed: *Southeast Asia Ethnicity and Development Newsletter*.
Indexed: Bull. Anal. Pol. Ec. Soc.

4559
SOUTHEAST ASIA JOURNAL. v.6, no.2– , 1972/73– . Iloilo City. Two no. a year.
Issued by: University Research Center, Central Philippine University.
Continues: *Southeast Asia Quarterly* (v.1–6, no.1, 1966–70)

4560
SOUTHEAST ASIAN AFFAIRS. 1974– . Singapore, Heinemann Educational Books (Asia). Bimonthly.
Issued by: Institute of Southeast Asian Studies.
Indexed: Bull. Anal. Pol. Ec. Soc.; Int. Bibl. Pol. Sc.; Int. Pol. Sc. Abst.

4561
SOUTHEAST ASIAN JOURNAL OF EDUCATION STUDIES. v.14, no.1/2– , Dec. 1977– . Singapore, Pan Pacific Book Distributors. Semi-annual.
Continues: *Malaysian Journal of Education.*

SOUTHEASTERN ASIA SOCIAL SCIENCE BIBLIOGRAPHY
See ASIAN SOCIAL SCIENCE BIBLIOGRAPHY WITH ANNOTATIONS AND ABSTRACTS

4562
SOUTHEASTERN POLITICAL REVIEW. v.9– , spring 1981– . Carrolton, Ga. Semi-annual.
Issued by: Georgia Political Science Association.
Continues: *GPSA Journal.*
Indexed: Int. Pol. Sc. Abst.

4563
SOUTHERN AFRICA TODAY. v.1– , Sept. 1984– . Pretoria. Quarterly, 1984; bimonthly.
Issued by: Department of Foreign Affairs.

SOUTHERN ASIA SOCIAL SCIENCE BIBLIOGRAPHY (WITH ANNOTATIONS AND ABSTRACTS)
See ASIAN SOCIAL SCIENCE BIBLIOGRAPHY WITH ANNOTATIONS AND ABSTRACTS

4564
SOUTHERN ECONOMIC JOURNAL. v.1– , 1933– . Chapel Hill, N.C. Quarterly.
Issued by: Southern Economic Association, and University of North Carolina.
Indexed: Bull. Anal. Pol. Ec. Soc.; Curr. Cont. Soc. Beh. Sc.; Eco. Abst.; His. Abst.; Ind. Per. Art. Law; Int. Bibl. Eco.; Int. Bibl. Pol. Sc.; Int. Bibl. Soc.; J. Eco. Lit.; PAIS; Peace Res. Abst. J.; Pop. Ind.; Sage Urb. Stu. Abst.; SSCI.

4565
THE SOUTHERN JOURNAL OF EDUCATIONAL RESEARCH. v.1– , Jan. 1967– . Hattiesburg, Miss. Quarterly.
Issued by: College of Education and Psychology, University of Southern Mississippi.
Continued by: *Educational and Psychological Research.*

4566
THE SOUTHERN QUARTERLY. v.1– , 1962– . Hattiesburg, Miss. Quarterly.
Issued by: University of Southern Mississippi. Subtitle reads: "A scholarly journal in the humanities and the social sciences".
Indexed: Bull. Anal. Pol. Ec. Soc.; His. Abst.; Ind. Per. Art. Law; Int. Bibl. Eco.; Int. Bibl. Pol. Sc.; Int. Bibl. Soc.; Int. Pol. Sc. Abst.; Soc. Abst.

4567
SOUTHERN RURAL SOCIOLOGY. v.1– , 1984– . Starkville, Miss. Semi-annual.
Issued by: Rural Sociology Section, Southern Association of Agricultural Scientists.
Supersedes: Southern Association of Agricultural Scientists. Rural Sociology Section. *Rural Sociology in the South.*

4568
SOUTHWESTERN JOURNAL OF ANTHROPOLOGY. v.1–28, spring 1945–1972. Albuquerque, N. Mex., University of New Mexico Press. Quarterly.

Issued by: University of New Mexico, and Laboratory of Anthropology, Santa Fe.
Supersedes: *New Mexico Anthropologist*. Continued by: *Journal of Anthropological Research*.
Indexed: Abst. Anth.; Abst. Soc. Work; Bull. Sig. Soc. Eth.; His. Abst.; LLBA.

THE SOUTHWESTERN POLITICAL AND SOCIAL SCIENCE QUARTERLY
See SOCIAL SCIENCE QUARTERLY

THE SOUTHWESTERN POLITICAL SCIENCE QUARTERLY
See SOCIAL SCIENCE QUARTERLY

THE SOUTHWESTERN SOCIAL SCIENCE QUARTERLY
See SOCIAL SCIENCE QUARTERLY

4569
SOVETSKAI͡A ANTROPOLOGII͡A. v.1–3, 1957–1959. Moskva, Izd-vo Moskovskogo Universiteta. Quarterly.
In Russian. Tables of contents also in English.
Superseded by: *Voprosy Antropologii* (1960–)

4570
SOVETSKAI͡A ARKHEOLOGII͡A. 1957– . Moskva, Izd-vo Akademii Nauk SSSR. Quarterly.
Issued by: Institut Arkheologii (earlier Institut Istorii Materialnoĭ Kul'tury), Akademii͡a Nauk SSSR. In Russian.
Indexed: Abst. Anth.; His. Abst.; Int. Bibl. Soc. Cul. Anth.

4571
SOVETSKAI͡A ETNOGRAFII͡A. 1– , 1931– . Moskva, Izd-vo Akademii Nauk SSSR. Quarterly, 1931, 1937, 1946–56; irreg., 1938–45; bimonthly, 1932–36, 1957–.
Issued by: Institut Etnografii im. H. Mikluho-Maklai͡a, Akademii͡a Nauk SSSR. In Russian; summaries in English. Tables of contents also in French. Vols. for 1946–47 have also title: *Ethnographie Soviétique*.
Supersedes: *Etnografii͡a*.
Indexes: Vols. 1946–55, 1v.; 1956–60, with v. 1961; 1961–65, with v. 1965; 1966–70, with v.1971, no.6.
Indexed: Abst. Anth.; Bull. Anal. Pol. Ec. Soc.; Bull. Sig. Soc. Eth.; LLBA.

4572
SOVETSKAI͡A PEDAGOGIKA. July 1937– . Moskva, Izd-vo Pedagogika. Monthly.
Issued by: Akademii͡a Pedagogicheskikh Nauk SSSR. In Russian. Includes section "Bibliografii͡a".
Indexed: Psych. Abst.

SOVETSKAI͡A PEDAGOGIKA [English]
See SOVIET EDUCATION

4573
SOVETSKAI͡A TORGOVLI͡A. 1941– . Moskva, Gostorgizdat. Monthly.
In Russian.
Continues: *Voprosy Sovetskoĭ Torgovlii*.
Indexed: Bull. Anal. Pol. Ec. Soc.; Int. Bibl. Eco.

4574
SOVETSKIE PROFSOI͡UZY. 1947– . Moskva, Profizdat. Biweekly.
"Zhurnal VCSPS". Title varies: 1947–52, *Profesionalnye Soiuzy*.

4575
SOVETSKIĬ EZHEGODNIK MEZHDUNARODNOGO PRAVA. 1958– . Moskva, Izd-vo Akademii Nauk SSSR.
Issued by: Sovetskai͡a Assot͡siat͡sii͡a Mezhdunarodnogo Prava. In Russian; summaries in English. Tables of contents also in Chinese, English, French and German. Vols. for 1958– have added title: *Soviet Yearbook of International Law*.
Indexed: Ind. For. Leg. Per.; Int. Bibl. Pol. Sc.

4576
SOVETSKOE GOSUDARSTVO. 1927–1938. Moskva. Monthly.
In Russian. Title varies: 1927–29, *Revoli͡ut͡sii͡a Prava*; 1930–31, *Sovetskoe Gosudarstvo i Revoli͡ut͡sii͡a Prava*.
Continued by: *Sovetskoe Gosudarstvo i Pravo*.

4577
SOVETSKOE GOSUDARSTVO I PRAVO. 1939– . Moskva, Izd-vo Nauka. Ten no. a year, 1956; eight no. a year, 1953–55; monthly, 1939–52, 1957–.
Issued by: Institut Gosudarstva i Prava, Akademii͡a Nauk SSSR. In Russian. Tables of contents in English and French. Publication suspended, May 1941–Dec. 1945.
Continues: *Sovetskoe Gosudarstvo*.
Indexed: Bull. Anal. Pol. Ec. Soc.; His. Abst.; Ind. For. Leg. Per.; Int. Bibl. Eco.; Int. Bibl. Pol. Sc.; Int. Lab. Doc.; Int. Pol. Sc. Abst.

SOVETSKOE GOSUDARSTVO I REVOLUT͡SII͡A PRAVA
See SOVETSKOE GOSUDARSTVO

SOVETSKOE KITAEVEDENIE
See NARODY AZII I AFRIKI

4578
SOVETSKOE SLAVOVEDENIE. 1– , 1965– . Moskva, Izd-vo Nauka. Bimonthly.

Issued by: Institut Slavi͡anovedenii͡a, called now Institut Slavi͡anovedenii͡a i Balkanistiki, Akademii͡a Nauk SSSR. In Russian.
Indexed: Bull. Sig. Soc. Eth.; His. Abst.; Int. Bibl. Soc. Cul. Anth.

SOVETSKOE VOSTOKOVEDENIE
See NARODY AZII I AFRIKI

4579
SOVIET AND EASTERN EUROPEAN FOREIGN TRADE. v.1– , Jan./Feb. 1965– . Armonk, N.Y., M.E. Sharpe. Bimonthly, 1965; quarterly.
Translations. Title varies: 1965–66, *American Review of Soviet and Eastern European Foreign Trade.*
Indexed: Bull. Anal. Pol. Ec. Soc.; Int. Bibl. Eco.; PAIS.

4580
SOVIET ANTHROPOLOGY AND ARCHAEOLOGY. v.1– , summer 1962– . White Plains, Armonk, N.Y., M.E. Sharpe. Quarterly.
Indexed: Abst. Anth.; Bull. Sig. Soc. Eth.; Int. Bibl. Soc. Cul. Anth.

SOVIET CULTURE
See SURVEY

4581
SOVIET ECONOMY. v.1– , Jan./Mar. 1985– . Silver Spring, Md., V.H. Winston. Quarterly.
Published in association with the Joint Committee on Soviet Studies, American Council of Learned Societies and the Social Science Research Council.

4582
SOVIET EDUCATION. v.1– , Nov. 1958– . White Plains, Armonk, M.E. Sharpe. Monthly.
Translation, selective, of *Sovetskai͡a Pedagogika.*
Indexed: PAIS.

4583
SOVIET ETHNOGRAPHIC STUDIES. SES. 1– , 1982– . Moscow, "Social Sciences Today".
Issued by: Editorial Board, USSR Academy of Sciences. Each number has also a distinctive title.

4584
SOVIET GEOGRAPHY; REVIEW & TRANSLATION. v.1– , Jan./Feb. 1960– . New York. Monthly (except July and Aug.)
Issued by: American Geographical Society.

4585
SOVIET JEWISH AFFAIRS. no.1– , June 1971– . London. Two no. a year.
Issued by: Institute of Jewish Affairs in association with the World Jewish Congress.
Supersedes: *Bulletin on Soviet and East European Affairs.*
Indexed: Bull. Anal. Pol. Ec. Soc.

4586
SOVIET LAW AND GOVERNMENT. v.1– , summer 1962– . White Plains, Armonk, N.Y., M.E. Sharpe.
Translations from Russian.
Indexed: Bull. Anal. Pol. Ec. Soc.; Ind. Per. Art. Law; PAIS.

4587
SOVIET PERIODICAL ABSTRACTS. ASIA, AFRICA AND LATIN AMERICA. v.1–6, no.3/4, May 1961–June 1967. New York, White Plains, N.Y. Quarterly.
Issued by: Soviet and East European Research and Translation Service; May 1962–, Slavic Languages Research Institute. Title varies: 1961–6?, *Selected Soviet Bibliographies. Asia, Africa and Latin America.*

4588
SOVIET PERIODICAL ABSTRACTS. SOVIET SOCIETY. v.1–6, no.3/4, May 1961–June 1967. White Plains, N.Y. Quarterly.
Issued by: Slavic Languages Research Institute. Title varies: v.1, 1961–Mar. 1962, *Selected Soviet Annotated Bibliographies. Soviet Society.*

4589
SOVIET PSYCHOLOGY. v.5– , 1967– . White Plains, Armonk, N.Y., M.E. Sharpe. Quarterly.
Translations.
Supersedes, in part: *Soviet Psychology and Psychiatry* (v.1–4, fall 1962–spring/summer 1966)
Indexed: Psych. Abst.

4590
THE SOVIET REVIEW. v.1– , Aug. 1960– . New York, White Plains, Armonk, N.Y., M.E. Sharpe. Quarterly.
Translations.
Supersedes: *Soviet Highlights.*
Indexed: Pop. Ind.; Soc. Abst.

SOVIET SOCIETY
See SOVIET PERIODICAL ABSTRACTS. SOVIET SOCIETY

4591
SOVIET SOCIOLOGY. v.1– , 1962– . White Plains, Armonk, N.Y., M.E. Sharpe. Quarterly.
Translations.
Indexed: Bull. Sig. Soc. Eth.; Curr. Cont. Soc. Beh. Sc.; Int. Bibl. Soc.; Pop. Ind.; PAIS; Sage Urb. Stu. Abst.; Soc. Abst.; SSCI.

4592
SOVIET STUDIES. v.1– , June 1949– . Oxford, B. Blackwell. Quarterly.
Issued by: Department for Study of Social and Economic Institutions of USSR, later called Institute of Soviet and East European Studies, University of Glasgow. Subtitle reads: "A quarterly journal of the social and economic institutions of the USSR".
Indexed: ABC POL SCI; Bull. Anal. Pol. Ec. Soc.; Bull. Sig. Soc. Eth.; Curr. Cont. Soc. Beh. Sc.; His. Abst.; Ind. Per. Art. Law; Int. Bibl. Eco.; Int. Bibl. Pol. Sc.; Int. Bibl. Soc.; Int. Lab. Doc.; Int. Pol. Sc. Abst.; J. Eco. Lit.; PAIS; Soc. Sc. Hum. Ind.; Soc. Abst.; SSCI.

4593
SOVIET STUDIES IN HISTORY. v.1– , summer 1962– . White Plains, Armonk, N.Y., M.E. Sharpe. Quarterly.
Translations.

SOVIET SURVEY
See SURVEY (London)

Soviet Union
See Russia (1923–, USSR)

4594
SOVIET WOMAN. no.1– , Nov./Dec. 1945– . Moskva. Bimonthly, 1945–53; monthly.
Issued by: Soviet Women's Antifascist Committee, and the Central Council of Trade Unions of USSR.
Indexed: Peace Res. Abst. J.; Wom. Stu. Abst.

SOVIET YEARBOOK OF INTERNATIONAL LAW
See SOVETSKIĬ EZHEGODNIK MEZHDUNARODNOGO PRAVA

SOVIETICA
See STUDIES IN SOVIET THOUGHT

4595
SOVREMENNAI͡A ZARUBEZHNAI͡A FILOSOFII͡A I SOT͡SIOLOGII͡A. no.1– , 1974– . Moskva. Annual.
Issued by: Institut Nauchnoĭ Informat͡sii po Obshchestvennym Naukam, Akademii͡a Nauk SSSR. In Russian.

SOVREMENNYĬ VOSTOK
See AZII͡A I AFRIKA SEGODNI͡A

4596
SOWJETUNION. 1973– . München, Hauser. Annual.
Issued by: Bundesinstitut für Ostwissenschaftliche und Internationale Studien. In German.
Indexed: His. Abst.

4597
SOWJETWISSENSCHAFT. GESELLSCHAFTSWISSENSCHAFTLICHE BEITRÄGE. no.1– , 1954– . Berlin, Verlag Kultur und Fortschritt. Monthly, 1956–80; bimonthly.
Issued by: Gesellschaft für Deutsch–Sowjetische Freundschaft. In German.
Indexed: Bull. Anal. Pol. Ec. Soc.; Bull. Sig. Soc. Eth.; Int. Bibl. Pol. Sc.; PAISFL.

4598
SOZIALE BEWEGUNGEN. GESCHICHTE UND THEORIE. v.1– , 1984– . Frankfurt, New York, Campus. Annual.
In German. Each number has also a distinctive title.
Supersedes: *Jahrbuch Arbeiterbewegung. Geschichte und Theorie.*

4599
SOZIALE PRAXIS. v.1–52, Jan. 1892–1943. Berlin, Leipzig.
Organ of: Verband Deutscher Gewerberichte. In German. Title varies: 1892–Mar. 1895, *Sozialpolitisches Centralblatt*; Apr. 1895–Mar. 1910, *Soziale Praxis*; Aug. 1910–Dec. 1927, *Soziale Praxis und Archiv für Volkswohlfahrt.*

SOZIALE PRAXIS UND ARCHIV FÜR VOLKSWOHLFAHRT
See SOZIALE PRAXIS

4600
SOZIALE REVUE. v.1–33, no.2, 1901–June 1933. München. Bimonthly.
In German. Title varies: 1917–18, *Glaube und Arbeit.*

4601
SOZIALE WELT. v.1– , Oct. 1949– . Göttingen, Otto Schwartz. Quarterly.
Issued by: Arbeitsgemeinschaft Sozialwissenschaftlicher Institut, 1949–60; Sozialforschungstelle an der Universität Münster, Sitz Dormund on behalf of der Arbeitsgemeinschaft Sozialwissenschaftlicher Institut. In German. Includes supplements called "Sonderband" (no.1, 1982–)
Indexes: Vols. 11–30, 1960–79, 1v.
Indexed: LLBA; PAISFL; Soc. Abst.

4602
SOZIALER FORTSCHRITT. 1– , Jan. 1952– . Berlin, Duncker & Humblot. Monthly.
Issued by: Gesellschaft für Sozialen Fortschritt. In German.
Indexed: Int. Bibl. Eco.

4603
SOZIALISTISCHE ARBEITSGEMEINSCHAFT. 1– , 1957– . Berlin, Verlag die Wirtschaft. Eight no. a year.

Issued by: Institut für Arbeitsökonomik und Arbeitsschutzforschung. In German. Subtitle reads: "Theoretische Zeitschrift für Arbeitswissenschaftliche Disziplinen".
Supersedes: *Arbeitsökonomik.*

4604
SOZIALISTISCHE POLITIK. 1969– . Berlin, Verlag Sozialistische Politik. Bimonthly.
In German.
Supersedes: *Berliner Zeitschrift für Politologie.*
Indexed: Int. Pol. Sc. Abst.

SOZIALISTISCHE THEORIE UND PRAXIS
See QUESTIONS ACTUELLES DU SOCIALISME
SOCIALIST THOUGHT AND PRACTICE

SOZIALPOLITISCHES CENTRALBLATT
See SOZIALE PRAXIS

SOZIALPSYCHIATRIE
See SOCIAL PSYCHIATRY

SOZIALSTATISTIK; JAHRBUCH
See Statistical Office of the European Communities. SOZIALSTATISTIK.

4605
SOZIALWISSENSCHAFT UND MEDIZIN. v.1– , 1983– . Erlangen, Permed Fachbuch-Verlagsgesellschaft. Irreg.
In German.

SOZIALWISSENSCHAFTLICHE STUDIEN
See Schweizerische Institut für Auslandforschung. SOZIALWISSENSCHAFTLICHE STUDIEN

SOZIALWISSENSCHAFTLICHE STUDIEN
See Universität Hamburg. Seminar für Sozialwissenschaften. SOZIALWISSENSCHAFTLICHE STUDIEN

4606
SOZIALWISSENSCHAFTLICHES JAHRBUCH FÜR POLITIK. SOCIAL SCIENCES YEARBOOK FOR POLITICS. v.1–6, 1969–1976. München, Wien, Günter Olzog Verlag. Annual (irreg.)
In German.
Indexed: Bull. Anal. Pol. Ec. Soc.; Int. Pol. Sc. Abst.

SOZIALWISSENSCHAFTLICHES LITERATURBLATT
See BIBLIOGRAPHIE DER SOZIALWISSENSCHAFTEN

4607
SOZIOLOGIE IN DER SCHWEITZ. 1– , 1974– . Stuttgart, Hans Huber. Irreg.
Issued by: Schweizerische Gesellschaft für Soziologie. In German. Other title: *Reihe Soziologie in der Schweitz.*

4608
SOZIOLOGISCHE ARBEITEN. TRAVAUX SOCIOLOGIQUES. SOCIOLOGICAL CONTRIBUTIONS. 1– , 1966– . Bern, Stuttgart, Hans Huber. Annual.
Issued by: Schweizerische Gesellschaft für Praktische Sozialforschung. In English, French, or German.

SOZIOLOGISCHE REVUE
See SOCIOLOGICKÁ REVUE

SPECIAL ARTICLE SERIES
See Operations and Policy Research. Institute for Comparative Study of Political Systems. OPERATIONS AND POLICY RESEARCH. POLITICAL STUDY SERIES

SPECIAL PUBLICATION
See Society for Medical Anthropology. SPECIAL PUBLICATION

SPECIAL STUDIES SERIES
See United Nations. Unit on Apartheid. SPECIAL STUDIES SERIES

4609
THE SPECTATOR. v.1– , July 5, 1828– . London. Weekly.
Title varies: 1828–60, *The Spectator; Weekly Review.*
Indexed: Peace Res. Abst. J.; Wom. Stu. Abst.

THE SPECTATOR; WEEKLY REVIEW
See THE SPECTATOR

4610
LO SPETTATORE INTERNAZIONALE. v.1– , Jan./Feb. 1966– . Bologna, Il Mulino. Four no. a year.
Issued by: Istituto Affari Internazionali. In Italian. Published also in English edition called: "English Supplement".
Indexed: Bull. Anal. Pol. Ec. Soc.; Int. Bibl. Eco.; Int. Bibl. Pol. Sc.; Int. Bibl. Soc. Cul. Anth.; Int. Pol. Sc. Abst.

4611
SPÓŁDZIELCZY KWARTALNIK NAUKOWY. v.1– , 1967– . Warszawa, Zakład Wydawniczy Centrali Rolniezej Spółdzielni. Quarterly.
Issued by: Naczelna Rada Spółdzielcza. In Polish; summaries in English and Russian. Includes supplements: "Cooperative Scientific Quarterly" and "Kvartal'nyĭ Nauchno-Kooperativnyĭ Zhurnal".

Indexed: Int. Bibl. Eco.

SPOMENIK
See Srpska Akademija Nauka i Umetnosti. Odeljenie Drustvenih Nauka. SPOMENIK

4612
SPORT AS A MACRO-SOCIAL SYSTEM. 1975– . Waterloo. Three no. a year.
Issued by: SIRLS, Faculty of Human Kinetics and Leisure Studies, University of Waterloo. Processed.

4613
SPORTS OCCUPATIONS AND CARRIER PATTERNS. 1975– . Waterloo. Three no. a year.
Issued by: SIRLS, Faculty of Human Kinetics and Leisure Studies, University of Waterloo. Processed.

SPRAWOZDANIA Z PRAC NAUKOWYCH
See Polska Akademia Nauk. Wydział I: Nauk Społecznych. SPRAWOZDANIA Z PRAC NAUKOWYCH

4614
SPRAWY MIĘDZYNARODOWE. v.1– , Oct. 1948– . Warszawa. Monthly.
Issued by: Polski Instytut Spraw Międzynarodowych. In Polish. Tables of contents also in English and Russian.
Indexed: Bull. Anal. Pol. Ec. Soc.; His. Abst.; Int. Bibl. Eco.; Int. Bibl. Pol. Sc.; Peace Res. Abst. J.

4615
SRI LANKA JOURNAL OF SOCIAL SCIENCES. v.1– , June 1978– . Colombo. Semi-annual.
Issued by: Social Science Research Centre, National Social Science Council of Sri Lanka.

4616
Srpska Akademija Nauka i Umetnosti. Etnografski Institut. GLASNIK. 1– , 1952– . Beograd.
Early volumes issued by the institute under the academy's earlier name: Srpska Akademija Nauka. In Serbo-Croatian; summaries in English, French, or German.
Indexed: Bull. Sig. Soc. Eth.

4617
Srpska Akademija Nauka i Umetnosti. Odeljenie Drustvenih Nauka. GLAS. 1887– ; n. ser. 1951– . Beograd. Irreg.
In Serbo-Croatian, occasionally in French or German; summaries in English, French, German, or Russian. Issued under the earlier name: 1887–1941, Srpska Kraljevska Akademija; 1946–61, Srpska Akademija Nauka. Publication suspended: 1914–20, 1942–45.
Indexed: His. Abst.

4618
Srpska Akademija Nauka i Umetnosti. Odeljenie Drustvenih Nauka. POSEBNA IZDANJA. 1888– . Beograd.
Former names of the academy: 1887–1941, Srpska Kraljevska Akademija; 1946–61, Srpska Akademija Nauka. In Serbo-Croatian; summaries in English, French, German, or Russian. Publication suspended 1915–22, 1944–45.

4619
Srpska Akademija Nauka i Umetnosti. Odeljenie Drustvenih Nauka. SPOMENIK. n. ser. 1950– . Beograd. Irreg.
In Serbo-Croatian; summaries in English, French, German, or Russian.

4620
SSU-CH'UAN TA-HSÜEH-HSÜEH PAO; SHE-HUI K'O-HSÜEH. 1– , 1955– . Ssu-Chu'uan. Four no. a year.
Issued by: Ssu-Ch'uan ta-hsüeh. In Chinese. Tables of contents also in English and Russian. Other title: *Szechuan University Journal; Social Sciences Edition.*

4621
DER STAAT. v.1– , 1962– . Berlin, Duncker & Humblot. Quarterly.
In German. Subtitle reads: "Zeitschrift für Staatslehre, Öffentliches Recht und Verfassungsgeschichte". Supplements, "Beihefte", accompany some numbers.
Indexed: ABC POL SCI; Bull. Anal. Pol. Ec. Soc.; Ind. For. Leg. Per.; Int. Bibl. Eco.; Int. Bibl. Pol. Sc.; Int. Bibl. Soc. Cul. Anth.; Int. Pol. Sc. Abst.; PAISFL; Peace Res. Abst. J.

4622
STAATS- UND SOZIALWISSENSCHAFTLICHE FORSCHUNGEN. v.1–26 (no.1–189), 1879–1916. Leipzig. Irreg.
In German. Monograph series.

STAATSHANDBUCH FÜR GESETZGEBUNG, VERWALTUNG UND STATISTIK DES NORDDEUTSCHEN BUNDES UND DES DEUTSCHEN ZOLLVEREIN
See ANNALEN DES DEUTSCHEN REICHS FÜR GESETZGEBUNG, VERWALTUNG UND VOLKSWIRTSCHAFT

4623
DER STÄDTETAG. n. ser. v.1– , July/Aug. 1948– . Stuttgart, W. Kohlhammer. Monthly.
Organ of: Präsidium des Deutschen Städtetages, Hauptgeschäftsstelle des Deutschen Städtetages, Verbunds Kommunaler Vereinigungsbetriebe. In German.

Continues: *Gemeindestag* (1927–June 1943)
Indexed: Bull. Anal. Pol. Ec. Soc.; Int. Bibl. Soc. Cul. Anth.; PAISFL.

STAFF PAPERS
See International Monetary Fund. STAFF PAPERS

4624
STANFORD JOURNAL OF INTERNATIONAL STUDIES. v.3–15, 1968–1979. Stanford, Calif. Annual.
Issued by: School of Law, Stanford University.
Continues: *Proceedings of the Stanford University School of Law* (v.1–2). Continued by: *Stanford Journal of International Law*.
Indexed: Bull. Anal. Pol. Ec. Soc.; Ind. Per. Art. Law; Int. Bibl. Eco.; Int. Bibl. Soc. Cul. Anth.

4625
STANFORD MATHEMATICAL STUDIES IN THE SOCIAL SCIENCES. v.1–9, 1958–1964. Stanford, Calif., Stanford University Press. Irreg.
Issued by: Stanford University. Includes: *Symposium on Mathematical Methods in the Social Sciences*. Monograph series.

4626
STANOVNISTVO. v.1– , Jan./Mar. 1963– . Beograd. Quarterly (some combined numbers)
Issued by: Institut Drustvenih Nauka, Centra za Demografska Istrazivanja. In Serbo-Croatian; summaries in English. Tables of contents also in English, French, or Russian.

4627
STARINAR. v.1–9, 1884–1892; n. ser. 1–5, 1906–1912; ser. 3, v.1–14, 1923–39; ser. 4, v.1– , 1950– . Beograd.
Issued by: 1884–1939, Srpsko Arkheolosko Drustvo; 1950–, Arheoloski Institut, Srpska Akademija Nauka i Umetnosti. In Serbo-Croatian.
Indexed: Int. Bibl. Soc. Cul. Anth.

4628
STATE & LOCAL GOVERNMENT REVIEW. v.8– , Jan. 1976– . Athens, Ga. Three no. a year.
Issued by: Institute of Government, University of Georgia.
Continues: *Georgia Government Review*.
Indexed: ABC POL SCI; Sage Urb. Stu. Abst.

4629
STATE GOVERNMENT. v.1– , Jan. 1926– . Denver, Chicago, Ill., Lexington, Ky. Monthly, 1926–58; quarterly.
Issued by: American Legislators' Association, 1926–30; Council of State Governments. Title varies: Jan. 1926, *The American Legislator*; Feb. 1926–Nov. 1929, *The Legislator*.
Indexed: ABC POL SCI; PAIS; Sage Pub. Adm. Abst.; Sage Urb. Stu. Abst.; Soc. Sc. Inst.

4630
STATE GOVERNMENT ADMINISTRATION. 1– , 1966– . Des Moines, Iowa. Monthly.
Organ of: National Society of State Legislators.
Indexed: ABC POL SCI.

4631
STATE OF THE WORLD ECONOMY. 1980– . Paris. Annual.
Issued by: International Chamber of Commerce in association with the Trade Policy Research Centre. Other title: *Economic Yearbook*.
Continues, in part: International Chamber of Commerce. *Annual Review*.

STATEMENT OF TREATIES AND INTERNATIONAL AGREEMENTS REGISTERED OR FILED WITH THE SECRETARIAT
See United Nations. Legal Department. STATEMENT OF TREATIES AND INTERNATIONAL AGREEMENTS REGISTERED OR FILED WITH THE SECRETARIAT

STATISTICA REGIONALE
See Statistical Office of the European Communities. REGIONAL STATISTICS: COMMUNITY'S FINANCIAL PARTICIPATION IN INVESTMENTS

4632
STATISTICAL ABSTRACTS OF LATIN AMERICA. [1]– , 1955– . Los Angeles, Calif., UCLA Latin American Center Publications. Annual.
Vols. 1965–66 issued as: University of California at Los Angeles. Center for Latin American Studies. *Reference Series*.

STATISTICAL AND ECONOMIC BULLETIN FOR AFRICA
See United Nations. Economic Commission for Africa. STATISTICAL AND ECONOMIC BULLETIN FOR AFRICA.

STATISTICAL AND ECONOMIC INFORMATION BULLETIN FOR AFRICA
See United Nations. Economic Commission for Africa. STATISTICAL AND ECONOMIC BULLETIN FOR AFRICA

STATISTICAL BULLETIN FOR LATIN AMERICA
See United Nations. Economic Commission for Latin America. BOLETIN ESTADISTICO DE AMERICA LATINA

STATISTICAL BULLETIN OF THE OAS
See Organization of American States. BOLETIN ESTADISTICO DE AMERICA LATINA

THE STATISTICAL INDICATOR
See Saudi Arabia. Maslahat al-Iksa'at al-Ammah. THE STATISTICAL INDICATOR

STATISTICAL INDICATORS FOR ASIA AND THE PACIFIC
See United Nations. Economic and Social Commission for Asia and the Pacific. STATISTICAL INDICATORS FOR ASIA AND THE PACIFIC

4633
STATISTICAL INDICATORS OF SHORT TERM ECONOMIC CHANGES IN EEC COUNTRIES. v.1– , Oct. 1959– . Geneva. Monthly.
Issued by: Economic Commission for Europe, United Nations.

STATISTICAL INDICATORS OF THE ARAB WORLD FOR THE PERIOD: 1970–1978–
See AL-MU'ASHOHIRAT AL-IHSA'IYAH LIL-ALAM AL-ARABI LIL FATRAH

STATISTICAL JOURNAL OF THE UNITED NATIONS ECONOMIC COMMISSION FOR EUROPE
See United Nations. Economic Commission for Europe. STATISTICAL JOURNAL

4634
Statistical Office of the European Communities. ACP YEARBOOK OF FOREIGN TRADE STATISTICS. ACP ANNUAIRE DU COMMERCE EXTÉRIEUR. 1970–1976– . Luxembourg. Annual.
In English and French.
Continues: Statistical Office of the European Communities. *Annuaire des Statistiques du Commerce Extérieur, Synthèse.*

4635
Statistical Office of the European Communities. ASSOCIÉS, STATISTIQUE DU COMMERCE EXTÉRIEUR. ANNUAIRE. 1959–1969. Luxembourg.
In French; summaries in Dutch, English, French, German and Italian. Title in English: *Associates. Foreign Trade Statistics: Yearbook.* Issued in volumes A–L, each on a different subject field.

4636
Statistical Office of the European Communities. BALANCES OF PAYMENTS. GEOGRAPHICAL BREAKDOWN. BALANCES DES PAIEMENTS. VENTILATION GÉOGRAPHIQUE. 1970/74– . Luxembourg.
In English and French. Published also in two other editions: German/Italian and Dutch/Danish.
Continues in part: *Balances of Payments, Yearbook*, volumes of which covered the years 1958–1969.

4637
Statistical Office of the European Communities. BALANCES OF PAYMENTS. GLOBAL DATA. BALANCES DES PAIEMENTS. DONNÉES GLOBALES. 1970/1981– . Luxembourg. Irreg. 1970–84; annual.
In English and French. Published also in German/Italian, and Dutch/Danish editions.
Continues, in part: *Balances of Payments*, which covered the years 1958–74.

4638
Statistical Office of the European Communities. EUROSTATISTIK: DATEN ZUR KONJUNKTURANALYSE. EUROSTATISTICS: DATA FOR SHORT-TERM ECONOMIC ANALYSIS; EUROSTATISTIQUES: DONNÉES POUR L'ANALYSE DE LA CONJONCTURE. EUROSTATISTICHE: DATI PER L'ANALISI DELLA CONGIUNTURA. 1979– . Luxembourg. Monthly.
In English, French and German.

4639
Statistical Office of the European Communities. INDUSTRIESTATISTIK. STATISTIQUES INDUSTRIELLES. STATISTICHE DELL'INDUSTRIA. STATISTIKEN VAN DE INDUSTRIE. 1959– . Brussels. Quarterly, with annual cumulation.
In Dutch, English, French, German and Italian. Title varies: 1959–61, *Zahlen zur Industriewirtschaft*, published as a supplement series to the office's *Statistische Informationen.*

4640
Statistical Office of the European Communities. NATIONAL ACCOUNTS, ESA AGGREGATES. COMPTES NATIONAUX, SEC AGRÉGATES. NATIONALE REKENINGEN, ESER TOTALEN. 1st ed.– , 1960/1974– . Luxembourg, 1979– .
In Dutch, English and French.

4641
Statistical Office of the European Communities. NATIONAL ACCOUNTS. ESA. DETAILED TABLES BY BRANCH. COMPTES NATIONAUX. SEC. TABLEAUX DÉTAILLÉS PAR BRANCHE. NATIONALE REKENINGEN. ESER. GEDETAILLEERDE TABELLEN PER BRANCHE. 1970/1976– . Luxembourg. Irreg. 1970–83; annual.
In English and French. This is one of five related series on the European System of Integrated Economic Accounts issued by the same office. Other series included is: *National Accounts, ESA Aggregates.*

Continues: *National Accounts*, 1959–69.

4642
Statistical Office of the European Communities.
REGIONAL STATISTICS: COMMUNITY'S FINANCIAL PARTICIPATION IN INVESTMENTS. STATISTIQUES RÉGIONALES; CONCOURS FINANCIERS DE LA COMMUNAUTÉ AUX INVESTISSEMENTS. 1972– . Luxembourg, Eurostat. Irreg.
In English and French. Other titles: *Regionalstatistik: Perifereiakes Statistikes; Regionalstatistisk: Faelleskabets Økonomiske Bistand til Investiringer; Regionalstatistik: Finanzbeiträge der Gemeinschaft für Investitionen; Statistica Regionale: Contributi Finanziari della Comunità agli Investimenti Regionale; Statistiek: Financiële Bijdragen van der Gemeenschap aan de Investeringen.*

4643
Statistical Office of the European Communities.
REGIONAL STATISTISK ÅRBOG. JAHRBUCH REGIONAL STATISTIK. YEARBOOK OF REGIONAL STATISTICS. ANNUAIRE DES STATISTIQUES RÉGIONALES. ANNUARIO DE STATISTICHE REGIONALE. JAARBOK REGIONALE STATISTIEK. 1981–1985. Luxembourg. Annual; not published in 1982.
Issued by: Regional and Financial Statistics Division of the Statistical Office of the European Communities.
In Dutch, English, French, German and Italian. Titles in some languages vary slightly.
Supersedes: *Regional Statistics* (1971, 1972), *Regional Statistics—Population, Employment, Living Standards* (1975, 1977, 1979), and *Regional Statistics—Main Regional Indicators* (1978). Continued by: *Regions. Statistical Yearbook* (1986–).

4644
Statistical Office of the European Communities.
SOZIALSTATISTIK. STATISTIQUES SOCIALES. 1960– . Bruxelles.
In English, French and German. Title varies: 1960–61, no.2, *Informations Statistiques. Statistiques Sociales*; 1961, no.3–1962, no.2, *Statistiques Sociales*. In 1970 titles were: *Jahrbuch der Sozialstatistik* and *Annuaire de Statistiques Sociales*. Some numbers are accompanied by supplements called "Sonderreihe. Série Speciale".

4645
Statistical Office of the European Communities.
STATISTIKEN ÜBER DEN AUSSENHANDEL: ANALYTISCHE ÜBERSICHTEN, EINFAHR. STATISTIQUES DU COMMERCE EXTÉRIEUR: TABLEAUX ANALYTIQUES, IMPORTATIONS. FOREIGN TRADE STATISTICS: ANALYTICAL TABLES, IMPORTS. 1958– . Brüssel. Annual, 1958–59; semi-annual, 1960; quarterly; each issue cumulative during the calendar year.
In French and German. The title changed in subsequent years, e.g. 1970, *Commerce Extérieur; Foreign Trade; Aussenhandel; Commercio Estero; Buitenlanelse Handel; Udenrigshandel.*

STATISTICAL PAPERS [Series A–V]
See United Nations. Statistical Office. STATISTICAL PAPERS

4646
STATISTICAL REFERENCE INDEX. 1980– . Washington, D.C., Congressional Information Service. In two volumes: *Abstracts* and *Index*.

STATISTICAL REPORTS OF THE NORDIC COUNTRIES
See SOCIAL TRYGGHET I DE NORDISKA LÄNDERNA

STATISTICAL YEAR-BOOK OF THE LEAGUE OF NATIONS
See League of Nations. STATISTICAL YEAR-BOOK OF THE LEAGUE OF NATIONS.

STATISTICAL YEARBOOK
See United Nations. Economic Commission for Africa. STATISTICAL YEARBOOK

STATISTICAL YEARBOOK
See United Nations. Educational, Scientific and Cultural Organization. STATISTICAL YEARBOOK

STATISTICAL YEARBOOK
See United Nations. Statistical Office. STATISTICAL YEARBOOK

STATISTICAL YEARBOOK OF ASIA AND THE FAR EAST
See STATISTICAL YEARBOOK OF ASIA AND THE PACIFIC

4647
STATISTICAL YEARBOOK OF ASIA AND THE PACIFIC. 1968– . Bangkok. Annual.
Issued by: Economic and Social Commission for Asia and the Pacific (whose earlier name was: Economic Commission for Asia and the Far East). United Nations.
Title varies: 1968–1972, *Statistical Yearbook for Asia and the Far East*. (Subseries of: United Nations/Document/E/CN)

STATISTICAL YEARBOOK OF LATIN AMERICA
See ANUARIO ESTADÍSTICO DE AMÉRICA LATINA Y DEL CARIBE

STATISTICAL YEARBOOK OF LATIN AMERICA AND THE CARIBBEAN
See ANUARIO ESTADÍSTICO DE AMÉRICA LATINA Y DEL CARIBE

STATISTICHE DELL'INDUSTRIA
See Statistical Office of the European Communities. STATISTIQUES INDUSTRIELLES

STATISTICS OF FOREIGN TRADE. SERIES B. ANNUAL TABLES BY REPORTING COUNTRIES
See Organisation for Economic Co-operation and Development. STATISTICS OF FOREIGN TRADE. SERIES B. ANNUAL TABLES BY REPORTING COUNTRIES

STATISTICS OF FOREIGN TRADE. SERIES C. TRADE BY COMMODITIES, MARKET SUMMARIES
See Organisation for Economic Co-operation and Development. STATISTICS OF FOREIGN TRADE. SERIES C. TRADE BY COMMODITIES, MARKET SUMMARIES

STATISTICHESKOE PRILOZHENIE
See MIROVOE KHOZIA͡ISTVO I MIROVAI͡A POLITIKA

STATISTIKEEN VAN DE INDUSTRIE
See Statistical Office of the European Communities. STATISTIQUES INDUSTRIELLES

STATISTIKEN ÜBER DEN AUSSENHANDEL: ANALYTISCHE ÜBERSICHTEN, EINFAHR
See Statistical Office of the European Communities. STATISTIKEN ÜBER DEN AUSSENHANDEL: ANALYTISCHE ÜBERSICHTEN, EINFAHR

STATISTIQUE DU COMMERCE EXTÉRIEUR
See Statistical Office of the European Communities. ASSOCIÉS, STATISTIQUE DU COMMERCE EXTÉRIEUR. ANNUAIRE

4648
STATISTIQUE INTERNATIONALE DES GRANDES VILLES. INTERNATIONAL STATISTICS OF LARGE TOWNS. Series A–B–C–D–E. 1954–1970. La Haye.
Issued by: Institut International de Statistique. In five parts; each with separate title page and separate pagination: A. Population; B. Logement; C. Données Économiques; D. Services Publiques. E. Statistique Culturelle et des Sports. In English and French.

STATISTIQUES AFRICAINES DU COMMERCE EXTÉRIEUR. SÉRIE A. ÉCHANGES PAR PAYS
See United Nations. Economic Commission for Africa. FOREIGN TRADE STATISTICS FOR AFRICA. SERIES A. DIRECTION OF TRADE

STATISTIQUES AFRICAINES DU COMMERCE EXTÉRIEUR. SÉRIE B. ÉCHANGES PAR PRODUITS
See United Nations. Economic Commission for Africa. FOREIGN TRADE STATISTICS FOR AFRICA. SERIES B. TRADE BY COMMODITY

STATISTIQUES AFRICAINES DU COMMERCE EXTÉRIEUR. SÉRIE C. TABLEAUX RÉCAPITULATIFS
See United Nations. Economic Commission for Africa. FOREIGN TRADE STATISTICS. SERIES C. SUMMARY TABLES

STATISTIQUES DE LA POPULATION ACTIVE
See Organisation for Economic Co-operation and Development. LABOUR FORCE STATISTICS

STATISTIQUES DE RESETLÉS PUBLIQUES DES PAYS MEMBRES DE L'OCDE
See Organisation for Economic Co-operation and Development. STATISTIQUES DE RESETLÉS PUBLIQUES DES PAYS MEMBRES DE L'OCDE

STATISTIQUES DES EFFECTIFS SCOLAIRES
See United Nations Educational, Scientific and Cultural Organization. Department of Social Sciences. CURRENT SCHOOL ENROLLMENT STATISTICS

STATISTIQUES DU COMMERCE EXTÉRIEUR. SÉRIE A. COMMERCE TOTAL PAR PAYS
See Organisation for Economic Co-operation and Development. STATISTICS OF FOREIGN TRADE. SERIES A. OVERALL TRADE BY COUNTRIES

STATISTIQUES DU COMMERCE EXTÉRIEUR. SÉRIE B. ANNUAIRE TABLEAUX PAR PAYS DÉCLARANTS
See Organisation for Economic Co-operation and Development. STATISTIQUES FOR FOREIGN TRADE. SERIES B. ANNUAL TABLES BY REPORTING COUNTRIES

STATISTIQUES DU COMMERCE EXTÉRIEUR. SÉRIE C. ÉCHANGES PAR PRODUITS. RESUMÉ PAR MARCHÉ
See Organisation for Economic Co-operation and Development. STATISTICS OF FOREIGN TRADE. SERIES C. TRADE BY COMMODITIES. MARKET SUMMARIES

STATISTIQUES DU COMMERCE EXTÉRIEUR. TABLEAUX: IMPORTATIONS
See Statistical Office of the European Communities. STATISTIKEN ÜBER DEN AUSSENHANDEL. ANALYTISCHE ÜBERSICHTEN

STATISTIQUES FINANCIÈRES DE L'OCDE. 1re PARTIE. STATISTIQUES FINANCIÈRES MENSUELLES. MARCHÉS INERNATIONAUX

See Organisation for Economic Co-operation and Development. OECD FINANCIAL STATISTICS. PART 1. FINANCIAL STATISTICS MONTHLY. INTERNATIONAL MARKETS.

STATISTIQUES FINANCIÈRES INTERNATIONALES
See INTERNATIONAL FINANCIAL STATISTICS

STATISTIQUES INDUSTRIELLES. ANNUAIRE
See Statistical Office of the European Communities. STATISTIQUES INDUSTRIELLES

STATISTIQUES MENSUELLES DU COMMERCE EXTÉRIEUR
See Organisation for Economic Co-operation and Development. MONTHLY STATISTICS OF FOREIGN TRADE

STATISTIQUES RÉGIONALES
See Statistical Office of the European Communities. REGIONAL STATISTICS; COMMUNITY'S FINANCIAL PARTICIPATION IN INVESTMENTS

STATISTIQUES SOCIALES
See Statistical Office of the European Communities. SOZIALSTATISTIK

STATISTISCH JAARBOEK VAN DE SOCIALE ZEKKERHEID
See ANNUAIRE STATISTIQUE DE LA SÉCURITÉ SOCIALE

STATISTISCH KVARTALBERICHT
See BENELUX; BULLETIN TRIMESTRIELLE DE STATISTIQUE

4649
STATISTISCHE ZEITSCHRIFT FÜR VOLKSWIRTSCHAFT UND STATISTIK. REVUE SUISSE D'ÉCONOMIE POLITIQUE ET DE STATISTIQUE. 1– , 1864– . Bern.

4650
STATSØKONOMISK TIDSSKRIFT. 1– , 1877– . Oslo, H. Aschenhong (W. Nygaard). Six no. a year, –1950; quarterly, 1951–73; annual, 1974–76; two no. a year.
Issued by: Styret for Statsøkonomisk Forening. In Norwegian.
Indexed: Int. Bibl. Eco.; J. Eco. Lit.

4651
STATSVETENSKAPLIG TIDSSKRIFT. v.1– , Nov. 1897– . Lund, later Uppsala, Almqvist & Wiksell. Five no. a year (some combined numbers).
Issued by: Fahlbecksa Kollegium. In Swedish. Title varies: 1897–1963, *Statsvetenskaplig Tidsskrift for Politik, Statistik-Ekonomi*.
Indexed: ABC POL SCI; Bull. Anal. Pol. Ec. Soc.; His. Abst.; Int. Bibl. Pol. Sc.; Int. Pol. Sc. Abst.; Peace Res. Abst. J.

STATSVETENSKAPLIG TIDSKRIFT FOR POLITIK, STATISTIK-EKONOMI
See STATSVETENSKAPLIG TIDSSKRIFT

ŞTIINŢE SOCIALE ŞI UMANISTE
See Universitatea din Galati. BULETINUL. ŞTIINŢE SOCIALE ŞI UMANISTE

STOCKHOLM STUDIES IN HUMAN GEOGRAPHY
See ACTA UNIVERSITATIS STOCKHOLMIENSIS

4652
STORIA E POLITICA. v.1– , Jan. 1962– . Milano, A. Giuffrè. Quarterly.
Issued by: Istituto di Studi Storici e Politici, Facoltà di Scienze Politiche, Università di Roma. In Italian.
Indexed: ABC POL SCI; His. Abst.; Int. Bibl. Pol. Sc.; Int. Pol. Sc. Abst.

4653
STRATEGIC REVIEW. v.1– , spring 1973– . Cambridge, Mass. Quarterly.
Issued by: United States Strategic Institute, Washington, D.C.
Indexed: Bull. Anal. Pol. Ec. Soc.; Int. Bibl. Pol. Sc.; Int. Pol. Sc. Abst.; PAIS.

4654
STRATEGIE. no.1– , 1964– . Paris. Quarterly.
Issued by: Centre d'Études de Politique Étrangère. In French.
Indexed: Int. Bibl. Pol. Sc.; Int. Pol. Sc. Abst.; Peace Res. Abst. J.

4655
STRATÉGIQUE. no.1– , 1. trimestre 1979– . Paris. Quarterly.
Issued by: Fondation pour les Études de Défense Nationale. In French.
Indexed: Int. Bibl. Pol. Sc.; Int. Bibl. Soc. Cul. Anth.; Int. Pol. Sc. Abst.

4656
STUDI DI SOCIOLOGIA. v.1– , Jan./Mar. 1963– . Milano, Vita e Pensiero. Quarterly.
Issued by: Università Cattolica del Sacro Cuore. In English, French, or Italian.
Indexes: Vols. 1–5, 1963–67, in v.6.

Indexed: Bull. Sig. Soc. Eth.; Int. Bibl. Soc.; LLBA.

4657
STUDI DI SOCIOLOGIA DELLA RELIGIONE. 1– , 1967– . Roma.
Issued by: Centro Internazionale di Studi Umanisti.

4658
STUDI ECONOMICI. v.1– , Apr. 1941– . Napoli. Quarterly, 1941–48; bimonthly, 1949–; three no. a year.
Issued by: Facoltà di Economia e Comercio, Università di Napoli, in association with the Laboratorio di Statistica, Istituto Universitario Navale. In Italian. Title varies: 1941–49, *Studi Economici, Finanzieri, Corporativi*, and *Studi Economici e Aziendali*.
Indexed: Bull. Anal. Pol. Ec. Soc.; Int. Bibl. Eco.

STUDI ECONOMICI E AZIENDALI
See STUDI ECONOMICI

STUDI ECONOMICI, FINANZIERI, CORPORATIVI
See STUDI ECONOMICI

4659
STUDI EMIGRAZIONE. ÉTUDES MIGRATIONS. v.1– , Oct. 1963– . Roma, Morceliana Editrice. Three no. a year.
Issued by: Centro Studi Emigrazione. In English, French, German, Italian, or Spanish; summaries in English and French.
Indexed: Bull. Anal. Pol. Ec. Soc.; Int. Bibl. Soc.; Int. Bibl. Soc. Cul. Anth.; Int. Lab. Doc.; PAISFL; Pop. Ind.

4660
STUDI INTERNAZIONALI DI ECONOMIA FINANZIERIA. v.1– , Jan./Feb. 1961– . Roma, Edizioni Lessina. Monthly.
Official organ of: Istituto per l'Economia Europea. In Italian.
Supersedes: *Rassegna Internazionale di Economia e Finanza*.

4661
STUDI PARLIAMENTARI E DI POLITICA CONSTITUZIONALE. 1– , 1962– . Roma, Edistudio. Quarterly.
In Italian; summaries in English and French.
Indexed: Int. Bibl. Pol. Sc.; Int. Pol. Sc. Abst.

4662
STUDIA DEMOGRAFICZNE. v.1– , 1963– . Warszawa, Państwowe Wydawnictwo Naukowe. Quarterly.
Issued by: Komitet Nauk Demograficznych, Polska Akademia Nauk. In Polish; summaries in English and Russian.
Indexed: Int. Bibl. Eco.; Int. Lab. Doc.; Pop. Ind.

4663
STUDIA DIPLOMATICA. v.27, no.5/6– , Sept./Nov. 1974– . Bruxelles. Bimonthly.
Issued by: Institut Royale des Relations Internationales, Centre Universitaire de Recherche Indépendant. In French or English.
Continues: *Chronique de Politique Étrangère*.
Indexed: ABC POL SCI; Bull. Anal. Pol. Ec. Soc.; Int. Bibl. Pol. Sc.; Int. Pol. Sc. Abst.; PAISFL.

4664
STUDIA EKONOMICZNE. v.1– , 1959– . Warszawa, Polskie Wydawnictwa Gospodarcze.
Issued by: Zakład Nauk Ekonomicznych, Polska Akademia Nauk. In Polish; summaries in English and Russian. Other titles: *Economic Studies*, *Ekonomicheskie Issledovaniia*, and *Szkice Ekonomiczne*.
Supersedes a publication of the same title (1935–39).
Indexed: Int. Bibl. Eco.

4665
STUDIA FENNICA. REVUE DE LINGUISTIQUE ET D'ETHNOLOGIE FINNOIS. REVIEW OF FINNISH LINGUISTICS AND ETHNOLOGY. 1– , 1935– . Helsinki, Suomalaisen Kirjallisunnden Seura. Annual.
In French. Issues are thematic.
Indexed: Int. Bibl. Eco.; Int. Bibl. Soc. Cul. Anth.

4666
STUDIA HISTORICA UPPSALIENSIA. 1– , 1960– . Stockholm, Almquist & Wiksell. Irreg.
Issued by: Historiska Institutionen, Uppsala Universitet. In English, French, German, Norwegian, or Swedish; summaries in English, French and German.

4667
STUDIA I MATERIAŁY Z DZIEJÓW NAUKI POLSKIEJ. SERIA A. HISTORIA NAUK SPOŁECZNYCH. no.1– , 1957– . Warszawa, Państwowe Wydawnictwo Naukowe.
Issued by: Zakład Historii Nauki i Techniki, Polska Akademia Nauk. In Polish; summaries in English, French, German and Russian.
Supersedes, in part: *Studia i Materiały z Dziejów Nauki Polskiej* (v.1–4, 1953–56)

4668
STUDIA NAUK POLITYCZNYCH. v.1– , 1968– . Warszawa, Państwowe Wydawnictwo Naukowe. Annual, 1968–71; quarterly.

Issued by: Centralny Ośrodek Metodyczny Studiów Nauk Politycznych, Uniwersytet Warszawski. In Polish; summaries in English and Russian. Tables of contents also in English, French and Russian.
Indexed: Bull. Anal. Pol. Ec. Soc.; Int. Pol. Sc. Abst.

4669
STUDIA PSYCHOLOGICA ET PAEDAGOGICA. 1– , 1946– . Lund, C.W.K. Gleerup Verlag. Irreg.
In English or Swedish. Includes subseries: *Studia Psychologica et Paedagogica. Series Altera* (1–, 1947–)

4670
STUDIA SOCIALIA. 1955– . Roma. Irreg.
Issued by: Istituto di Scienze Sociali, Pontificia Università Gregoriana. In various languages.

4671
STUDIA SOCJOLOGICZNE. no.1– , 1961– . Warszawa, Państwowe Wydawnictwo Naukowe. Quarterly.
Issued by: Instytut Filozofii i Socjologii, Polska Akademia Nauk. In Polish; summaries in English and Russian. Tables of contents also in English and Russian.
Indexed: Bull. Sig. Soc. Eth.; Int. Bibl. Soc.; Int. Lab. Doc.; Int. Pol. Sc. Abst.; Int. Bibl. Soc. Cul. Anth.; Psych. Abst.; Soc. Abst.

4672
STUDIA Z SOCJOLOGII MŁODZIEZY I WYCHOWANIA. 1– , 1973– . Kraków, Państwowe Wydawnictwo Naukowe. Irreg.
Issued by: Uniwersytet Jagielloński. In Polish; summaries in English and Russian. Subseries of: the university's *Zeszyty Naukowe. Prace Socjologiczne.*

STUDIEN IN DEN GRENZBERICHTEN DER WIRTSCHAFTS- UND SOZIALWISSENSCHAFTEN
See DIE EINHEIT DER GESELLWISSENSCHAFTEN

4673
STUDIEN ZUM DEUTSCHTUM IN OSTEN. 1962– . Bonn. Irreg.
Issued by: Kommission für das Studium der Deutschen Geschichte und Kultur in Osten, and der Rheinischen-Friedrich-Wilhelms-Universität, Bonn. In German.

4674
STUDIEN ZUM POLITISCHEN SYSTEM DER BUNDESREPUBLIC DEUTSCHLAND. v.1– , 1973– . Königstein, Verlag Anton Hain. Irreg.
In German.

STUDIEN ZUR KULTURKUNDE
See Universität Frankfurt am Main. Frobenius Institut. STUDIEN ZUR KULTURKUNDE

4675
STUDIER I NORSK ARKEOLOGI. 1– , 1953– . Göteborg, Arkeologiska Museet.
Issued by: Arkeologiska Museet, and Göteborgs Universitet. In English or Swedish. 1–2 published as *Skrifter* of the Arkeologiska Museet. Other title: *Studies in North European Archaeology.*

STUDIES
See Harvard University. Russian Research Center. STUDIES

STUDIES
See Harvard–Yenching Institute. STUDIES

STUDIES AND REPORTS. NEW SERIES [Series A and other series]
See International Labour Office. STUDIES AND REPORTS

STUDIES IN AFRICAN HISTORY
See ÉTUDES D'HISTOIRE AFRICAINE

STUDIES IN AMERICAN FOREIGN RELATIONS
See Council on Foreign Relations. STUDIES IN AMERICAN FOREIGN RELATIONS

4676
STUDIES IN BANKING & FINANCE. v.1– , 1985– . Amsterdam. Annual.
Issued by: Office of Official Publications of the European Communities. Supplement to: *Journal of Banking and Finance*. Other title: *Studies in Banking and Finance.*

4677
STUDIES IN COMMUNICATION. v.1– , 1980– . Greenwich, Conn., JAI Press. Annual.

4678
STUDIES IN COMPARATIVE COMMUNISM. v.1– , July/Oct. 1968– . Los Angeles, Calif. Quarterly.
Issued by: School of Politics and International Relations, later by the Klein Smid Institute of International Affairs of the school, University of Southern California.
Supersedes: *Communist Affairs.*
Indexes: Vols. 1–10, 1968–77, in the winter 1977 issue; v.11–15, 1978–82, in the winter 1982 issue.
Indexed: ABC POL SCI; Bull. Anal. Pol. Ec. Soc.; Curr. Cont. Soc. Beh. Sc.; His. Abst.; Ind. Per. Art. Law; Int. Bibl. Pol. Sc.; Int. Bibl. Soc.; Int. Pol. Sc. Abst.; PAIS; SSCI.

4679
STUDIES IN COMPARATIVE INTERNATIONAL DEVELOPMENT. v.1– , 1965– . St. Louis, Mo., later New Brunswick, N.J., distributed by: Transaction Periodicals Consortium. Three no. a year.
Issued by: Social Science Institute, Washington University. Vol.1 called *Original Series.*
Indexed: ABC POL SCI; Bull. Sig. Soc. Eth.; Int. Bibl. Soc.; Int. Lab. Doc.; Int. Pol. Sc. Abst.; PAIS; Sage Urb. Stu. Abst.; Soc. Abst.

4680
STUDIES IN COMPARATIVE LOCAL GOVERNMENT. v.1– , summer 1967– . The Hague, Nijhoff. Two no. a year.
Published under the auspices of the International Union of Local Authorities.
Indexed: Int. Bibl. Pol. Sc.

4681
STUDIES IN DEVELOPMENT AND PLANNING. v.1– , 1973– . Rotterdam, Rotterdam University Press. Irreg.
Monograph series.

4682
STUDIES IN FAMILY PLANNING. no.1– , July 1963– . New York. Monthly (with combined June/July and Aug./Sept. numbers).
Issued by: Population Council. Supplements accompany some numbers.
Indexes: no.1–30, 1v.; no.1–50, 1v.
Indexed: Bull. Anal. Pol. Ec. Soc.; Geo. Abst.; Int. Bibl. Soc. Cul. Anth.; Pop. Ind.

4683
STUDIES IN HIGHER EDUCATION. 1– , 1976– . Dorchester-on-Thames, Carfax. Semi-annual.
Indexed: Psych. Abst.

4684
STUDIES IN HISTORICAL AND POLITICAL SCIENCE. 1– , 1882/1883– . Baltimore, Md., Johns Hopkins University Press. Irreg.
Issued by: Johns Hopkins University. Monograph series. V.5 never published.

STUDIES IN INTERNATIONAL AFFAIRS
See Washington Center of Foreign Policy Research. STUDIES IN INTERNATIONAL AFFAIRS

4685
STUDIES IN INTERNATIONAL ECONOMIC RELATIONS. no.1– , 1963– . Cambridge, Mass. Irreg.
Issued by: National Bureau of Economic Research. Monograph series.

4686
STUDIES IN IRISH ECONOMIC AND SOCIAL HISTORY. [1]– , 1984– . Dublin.
Issued by: Economic and Social History Society of Ireland.

4687
STUDIES IN ISRAELI SOCIETY. v.1– , 1980– . New Brunswick, N.J., Transaction Periodicals Consortium.
Sponsored by: Israeli Sociological Society.

4688
STUDIES IN LATIN AMERICAN POPULAR CULTURE. v.1– , 1982– . Las Cruces, N.Mex. Annual.
Issued by: New Mexico State University.

4689
STUDIES IN LATIN AMERICAN ETHNOHISTORY & ARCHAEOLOGY. v.1– , 1983– . Ann Arbor, Mich.
Issued by: Museum of Anthropology, Regents of the University of Michigan (Memoirs of the Museum of Anthropology, University of Michigan)

4690
STUDIES IN MEDIEVAL AND RENAISSANCE HISTORY. v.1– , 1964– . Vancouver. Annual.
Issued by: Committee for Medieval Studies, University of British Columbia.

STUDIES IN METHODS
See United Nations. Department of International Economic and Social Affairs. STUDIES IN METHODS

4691
STUDIES IN PHILOSOPHY AND SOCIAL SCIENCES. v.1–9, 1932–1941. Frankfurt am Main, later New York. Three no. a year.
In German, 1932–39.
Title varies: v.1–8, no.1/2, 1932–Apr. 1939, *Zeitschrift für Sozialforschung.*
Supersedes: *Archiv für die Geschichte des Sozialismus und der Arbeitsbewegung.*

4692
STUDIES IN POPULATION AND URBAN GEOGRAPHY. no.1– , 1975– . Westport, Conn., Greenwood Press. Irreg.
Issued by: International Population and Urban Research, University of California at Berkeley.

4693
STUDIES IN RACE AND NATIONS. v.1–6, no.3, 1969/70–1975. Denver, Colo. Quarterly.
Issued by: Center on International Race Relations, University of Denver.

4694
STUDIES IN SCIENCE AND CULTURE. v.1– , 1983– . Newark, Del., University of Delaware Press. Annual.
Sponsored by: Center for Science and Culture, University of Delaware.

4695
SOCIAL STUDIES IN SOCIAL HISTORY. 1– , 1976– . The Hague. Irreg.
Issued by: International Institute for Social History. Monograph series.

STUDIES IN SOCIOLOGY. SOCIOLOGICAL MONOGRAPHS
See SOCIOLOGY & SOCIAL RESEARCH

4696
STUDIES IN SOVIET THOUGHT. v.1– , 1961– . Dordrecht, D. Reidel Pub. Co. Annual, 1961; eight no. a year, in two vols.
Issued by: Ost-Europa Institut, University of Fribourg, Center for East Europe, Russia and Asia of Boston College, and Seminar for Political Theory and Philosophy, University of Münich. Title varies: v.1, *Sovietica*. In English, French, or German.
Indexed: ABC POL SCI; Bull. Anal. Pol. Ec. Soc.; His. Abst.; Int. Bibl. Eco.; Curr. Cont. Soc. Beh. Sc.; Int. Pol. Sc. Abst.; SSCI.

4697
STUDIES IN SYMBOLIC INTERACTION. v.1– , 1978– . Greenwich, Conn., JAI Press. Annual.
Supplements accompany some numbers (1, 1985–)

4698
STUDIES IN THE BEHAVIORAL SCIENCES. 1– , 1968– . The Hague, Mouton. Irreg.
Published in cooperation with: 6e Section. Economics and Social Sciences, École Pratique des Hautes Études. Sorbonne. At head of the series title: *New Babylon.*

4699
STUDIES IN THE HISTORY AND ARCHAEOLOGY OF JORDAN. 1– , 1982– . Amman.
Issued by: Department of Antiquities, Kingdom of Jordan. In Arabic, English, or French.

STUDIES IN THE HISTORY OF NETHERLANDS
See ACTA HISTORIAE NEERLANDICAE

4700
STUDIES IN THE STRUCTURE OF POWER; DECISION MAKING IN CANADA. 1– , 1965– . Toronto, University of Toronto Press. Irreg.
Issued by: Social Science Research Council of Canada. Monograph series.

4701
STUDIES IN THE THIRD WORLD SOCIETIES. no.1– , 1976– . Williamsburg, Va., Boswell Print & Pub. Co. Quarterly.
Issued by: Department of Anthropology, College of William and Mary.

4702
STUDIES IN TRANSNATIONAL LEGAL POLICY. no.1– , 1972– . Washington, D.C. Irreg.
Issued by: American Society of International Law. Other title: *Occasional Papers.*

4703
STUDIES IN URBAN GEOGRAPHY. 1– , 1969– . New York. Irreg.
Issued by: American Geographical Society of New York.

STUDIES OF ANTISOCIAL BEHAVIOR
See ACTA CRIMINOLOGICA

4704
STUDIES OF DEVELOPING COUNTRIES. 1– , 1963– . Assen, Van Gorcum. Irreg.
In Dutch or English. Some works are in revised editions. Monograph series.
Supersedes: *Non-European Societies.*

4705
STUDIES OF LAW IN SOCIAL CHANGE AND DEVELOPMENT. 1977– . Uppsala. Irreg.
Issued by: Institutet Nordiska Afrika. Co-sponsored by: International Legal Center in New York.

STUDIES ON CHINESE COMMUNISM
See CHUNG KUNG YEN CHIU

STUDIES ON DEVELOPMENT PROBLEMS IN SELECTED COUNTRIES IN THE MIDDLE EAST
See United Nations. Economic Commission for Western Asia. STUDIES ON DEVELOPMENT IN COUNTRIES OF WESTERN ASIA

STUDIES ON DEVELOPMENT PROBLEMS IN WESTERN ASIA
See United Nations. Economic Commission for Western Asia. STUDIES ON DEVELOPMENT IN COUNTRIES OF WESTERN ASIA

4706
STUDIES ON INTERNATIONAL RELATIONS. no.1–15, 1973–1980. Warsaw. Two no. a year.
Issued by: Polski Instytut Spraw Międzynarodowych.
Indexed: Bull. Anal. Pol. Ec. Soc.; Int. Pol. Sc. Abst.; PAIS.

STUDIES ON SELECTED DEVELOPMENT PROBLEMS IN VARIOUS COUNTRIES OF THE MIDDLE EAST
See United Nations. Economic Commission for Western Asia. STUDIES ON DEVELOPMENT IN COUNTRIES OF WESTERN ASIA

STUDIES ON SOCIAL PSYCHOLOGY
See SAHOE SIMNIHAK YON'GU

4707
STUDIES ON THE LEFT. v.1–7, no.2, fall 1959–Mar./Mar. 1967. Madison, Wis. Three no. a year, 1959–62; quarterly.
Indexed: Soc. Abst.

4708
STUDIES ON THE SOVIET UNION. v.1–5, July 1957–1960; n. ser. v.1– , 1961– . München. Quarterly.
Issued by: Institute for the Study of USSR. Absorbed: *Vestnik*, *Belorussian Review*, *East Turkic Review*, and *Ukrainian Review*.
Indexed: Bull. Sig. Soc. Eth.; His. Abst.; PAIS; Peace Res. Abst. J.

4709
STUDIES ON WOMEN ABSTRACTS. v.1– , 1983– . Abingdon, Carfax Pub. Co. Four no. a year.

STUDII: REVISTA DE ISTORIE
See Academia Republicii Socialiste România. STUDII: REVISTA DE ISTORIE

STUDII ŞI ARTICOLE DE ISTORIE
See Societatea de Ştiinţe Istorice din Republica Socialista România. STUDII ŞI ARTICOLE DE ISTORIE

4710
STUDII ŞI CERCETĂRI DE ANTROPOLOGIE. v.1– , 1964– . Bucureşti, Editura Academiei R.S.R. Semi-annual.
Issued by: Academia Republicii Socialiste România. In French or Romanian; summaries in English and French.
Continues: *Probleme de Antropologie*.

4711
STUDII ŞI CERCETĂRI DE ISTORIE VECHE ŞI ARHEOLOGIE. v.25– , 1974– . Bucureşti, Editura Academiei Socialiste România. Four no. a year.
Issued by: Institutul de Arheologie, Academia de Ştiinţe Sociale şi Politice a Republicii Socialiste România. In Romanian; summaries in French or German.
Continues: *Studii şi Cercetări de Istorie Veche* (v.1–24, 1950–73)
Indexes: Vols. 1–35, 1950–84, in v.36, 1–2 (Jan./June 1985)

4712
STUDII ŞI CERCETĂRI ECONOMICE. 1– , 1964– . Bucureşti. Semi-annual.
Issued by: Institutul de Ştiinţe Economice "Vladimir Ilicin Lenin". In Romanian; summaries in English, French and Russian.
Indexed: Bull. Anal. Pol. Ec. Soc.

4713: not used

STUDII ŞI MATERIALE DE ISTORIE MODERNE
See Academia de Ştiinţe Sociale şi Politice a Republicii Socialiste România. Istitutul de Istorie "N. Iorga". STUDII ŞI MATERIALE DE ISTORIE MODERNE

4714
STUDIUM GENERALE. v.1–24, Oct. 1947–Dec. 1947. Berlin, New York, Springer. Monthly.
In English or German. Subtitle reads: "Zeitschrift für interdisziplinare Studien".
Indexes: v.1–15, 1947–62, 1v. v.1–20, 1947–67, 1v.

STUDY OF HISTORY
See SAHOEK YŎN'GU

STUDY OF POPULATION AND TECHNOLOGY. PERCEPTIONS
See Science Council of Canada. STUDY OF POPULATION AND TECHNOLOGY. PERCEPTIONS

THE STUDY OF SOCIOLOGY
See SHAKAIGAKU KENKYU

4715
STUDYING ORGANIZATIONS. v.2– , 1982– . Beverly Hills, Calif., Sage Publications.

4716
STUTTGARTER GEOGRAPHISCHE STUDIEN. v.1– , 1924– . Stuttgart. Two or three no. a year.
Issued by: Geographisches Institut, Universität Stuttgart. In German.

SUBJECT INDEX TO CURRENT LITERATURE
See Australian Public Affairs Information Service. SUBJECT INDEX TO CURRENT LITERATURE

4717
THE SUBJECT INDEX TO PERIODICALS. 1915/16–1961. London. Annual, 1915/16–1953; quarterly.
Volumes for 1923–25 never published.

Continued by: *British Humanities Index*, and *British Technology Index*.

4718
SUDAN JOURNAL OF DEVELOPMENT RESEARCH. v.1– , Feb. 1977– . Khartoum. Semi-annual.
Issued by: Economic and Social Research Council.

4719
SUDAN JOURNAL OF ECONOMIC AND SOCIAL STUDIES. v.1– , summer 1974– . Khartoum, Khartoum University Press. Semi-annual.
Issued by: Faculty of Economic and Social Sciences, University of Khartoum.
Indexed: PAIS.

4720
SUDAN RESEARCH INFORMATION BULLETIN. v.1–9, 1965–1978. Khartoum. Irreg.
Issued by: Library and Documentation Centre, Institute of African and Asian Studies, University of Khartoum. Processed.
Continued by: *Jami'at al-Khartoum. Ma'had al-Dirāsāt al-Afriquiyah wa-al Asiyawiyah. Research Bulletin of the Institute of African and Asian Studies.*

4721
SUDAN SOCIETY. v.1– , 1962– . Khartoum. Annual.
Issued by: Social Studies Society, and the Faculty of Economic and Social Studies, University of Khartoum. In Arabic or English. Other title: *Al-Mujtama.*
Indexed: Int. Bibl. Soc. Cul. Anth.

4722
SÜDOSTEUROPA-MITTEILUNGEN. 1961– . München. Quarterly.
Issued by: Südosteuropa-Gesellschaft. In German.

SUID-AFRIKAANSE JAARBOEK VIR VOLKEREG
See SOUTH AFRICAN YEARBOOK OF INTERNATIONAL LAW

4723
SUID-AFRIKAANSE TYDSKRIF VIR DIE PEDAGOGIEK. SOUTH AFRICAN JOURNAL OF PEDAGOGY. v.1– , 1967– . Pretoria. Semi-annual.
Issued by: Faculty of Education, University of Pretoria. In Afrikaans, or occasionally in English.

SUID-AFRIKAANSE TYDSKRIF VIR EKONOMIE
See THE SOUTH AFRICAN JOURNAL OF ECONOMICS

4724
DIE SUID-AFRIKAANSE TYDSKRIF VIR SOCIOLOGIE. SOUTH AFRICAN JOURNAL OF SOCIOLOGY. no.1– , Nov. 1970– . Pretoria. Semi-annual.
Issued by: South African Sociological Association, and the Department of Sociology, University of Pretoria. In Afrikaans, Dutch or English.
Indexed: LLBA; Soc. Abst.

4725
AL-SUKKAN; BUḤŪTH WA-DIRĀSĀT. POPULATION RESEARCHES AND STUDIES. 1– , Oct. 1971– . al-Qāhirah, Markaz al-Abbath wa-al-Dirāsāt al-Sukkaniyah, al-Jihaz al-Markazi lil Ta'bi'ah al-'Ammah wa-al-Ihsa. Quarterly, 1971–Oct. 1972; semi-annual.
In Arabic or English. Numbers for 1971–Apr. 1972 have Arabic title only.

SUMMARY OF PROCEEDINGS OF THE ANNUAL MEETING OF THE BOARD OF GOVERNORS
See International Monetary Fund. SUMMARY PROCEEDINGS OF THE ANNUAL MEETING OF THE BOARD OF GOVERNORS

SUMMARY OF RECENT ECONOMIC DEVELOPMENTS IN AFRICA
See United Nations. Economic Commission for Africa. ECONOMIC DEVELOPMENTS IN AFRICA

SUMMARY OF RECENT ECONOMIC DEVELOPMENTS IN THE MIDDLE EAST
See United Nations. Economic Commission for Western Asia. ECONOMIC DEVELOPMENTS IN WESTERN ASIA

SUN YAT-SEN UNIVERSITY. JOURNAL. SOCIAL SCIENCES
See Guangzhou. Zhongshan. Daxue Huebao. CHUNG-SHAN TA HSÜEH HSÜEH PAO: SHE HUI K'O HSÜEH. JOURNAL OF SUN-YAT-SEN UNIVERSITY: SOCIAL SCIENCES

4726
SUNG LIAO HSÜEH K'AN. SHE HUI K'O HSÜEH PAN. SONG LIAO XUE KAN. 1983– . Ssu-p'ing shih fah hsüeh yuan. Quarterly.
In Chinese. Other title: *Songliao Journal. Philosophy & Social Science.*

4727
SUOMEN ANTROPOLOGISEN SEURAN TOIMITUKSIA. 1– , 1977– . Helsinki. Irreg.
Issued by: Suomen Antropologinen Seura. In Finnish.

SUPPLEMENT A, B, C
See EUROPEAN ECONOMY

SUPPLEMENT TO THE STATISTICAL YEARBOOK AND THE MONTHLY BULLETIN OF STATISTICS
See United Nations. Statistical Office. SUPPLEMENT TO THE STATISTICAL YEARBOOK AND MONTHLY BULLETIN OF STATISTICS

SUPPLEMENTO MENSILE DELLA RASSEGNA NAZIONALE
See RASSEGNA INTERNAZIONALE

4728
SUPREME COURT ECONOMIC REVIEW. v.1– , 1980– . New York, Macmillan; London, Collier Macmillan. Annual.
Issued by: The Law and Economics Center, Emory University.

4729
THE SURVEY. v.1–68, Dec. 1897–1939; v.85–88, no.5, May 1949–May 1952. East Stronsburg, Pa., Survey Association. Weekly; in some years, biweekly.
Title varies: v.1–15, no.5, 1897–Oct. 1905, *Charities; a weekly review of local and general philanthropy*; v.15, no.5–v.21, Nov. 1905–Mar. 1909, *Charities and the Commons*. From Oct. 1921 through May 1922, one weekly issue each month is called "Graphic Number"; from June 1922 through 1932, the periodical consists of two numbers each month: "Graphic Number" and "Midmonthly Number". Jan. 1933–Dec. 1948, published as two separate periodicals; *Survey Graphic* and *Survey Midmonthly*. They united in Jan. 1949 to form *Survey*.

4730
SURVEY. no.1– , Jan. 1961– . London, Survey. Quarterly.
Published in cooperation with the Congress for Cultural Freedom, no.1–77, 1956–70, International Association for Cultural Freedom, no.78–, and under the auspices of the London School of Economics and Political Science. Title varies: no.1–8, Jan.–Sept. 1956, *Soviet Culture*; no.9–19, Oct. 1956–Sept. 1957, *Soviet Survey*; no.20–21/23, Oct.–Nov./Dec. 1957, *Survey; An Analysis of Cultural Trends in the Soviet Orbit*. No.78 called also v.16, no.1.
Indexed: ABC POL SCI; Bull. Anal. Pol. Ec. Soc.; Bull. Sig. Soc. Eth.; Int. Bibl. Pol. Sc.; Int. Pol. Sc. Abst.; PAIS.

4731
SURVEY. 1970– . Sarajevo. Quarterly.
Issued by: University of Sarajevo. Contains translations of articles in Serbo-Croatian into English, French, or German.

SURVEY; AN ANALYSIS OF CULTURAL TRENDS IN THE SOVIET ORBIT
See SURVEY

4732
SURVEY OF BRITISH AND COMMONWEALTH AFFAIRS. v.1– , Jan. 6, 1967– . London. Biweekly.
Prepared by: Central Office of Information for British Information Services.
Supersedes: *Commonwealth Survey*.

4733
SURVEY OF CURRENT BUSINESS. /1/– , Aug. 1, 1921– . Washington, Government Printing Office. Monthly.
Issued Aug. 1921–July/Dec. 1925 as monthly supplement to *Commerce Reports* of the Bureau of Foreign and Domestic Commerce. Issues for 1921–May 1931 are numbered 1–117 and constitute v.1–11, no.5. Issued by: 1921–May 1929 by the Bureau of Foreign and Domestic Commerce and Bureau of the Standards; June 1929–June 1930 by the Bureau of Commerce; July 1930–Jan. 1947, Bureau of Foreign and Domestic Commerce; Feb. 1947– by the Office of Business Economics.

SURVEY OF ECONOMIC AND SOCIAL CONDITIONS IN AFRICA
See United Nations. Economic Commission for Africa. SURVEY OF ECONOMIC AND SOCIAL CONDITIONS IN AFRICA

4734
SURVEY OF INTERNATIONAL AFFAIRS. 1920/23–1963. London, Oxford University Press. Irreg.
Issued by: Royal Institute of International Affairs. Some volumes have also distinctive titles.

4735
SURVEY OF JAPANESE FINANCE AND INDUSTRY. v.1–17, June 1949–1965. Tokyo. Monthly, 1949–53; bimonthly.
Issues for Nov.–Dec. 1949 not published.
Continued by: *Quarterly Journal of Japanese Finance & Industry*.

SURVEY OF PRIMARY COMMODITY MARKETS
See United Nations. Commission on International Commodity Trade. COMMODITY SURVEY

4736
A SURVEY OF RACE RELATIONS IN SOUTH AFRICA. v.1–37, 1951/52–1983. Johannesburg. Annual.
Issued by: South African Institute of Race Relations. Information for the period 1946–50 included in the institute's *Annual Report*.
Continued by: *Race Relations Survey*.

A SURVEY OF THE ECONOMIC SITUATION AND PROSPECTS OF EUROPE
See United Nations. Economic Commission for Europe. ECONOMIC SURVEY OF EUROPE

SURVEY ON CURRENT RESEARCH IN THE BEHAVIORAL SCIENCES
See Henrieta Szold Institute—The National Institute for Research in the Behavioral Sciences. Information Retrieval Centre for Research in the Behavioral Sciences. SEKER 'AI MEHKAR SHOTEF BE-MADA'E HA-HITNAHAGUT BE-YISRA'EL. SURVEY ON CURRENT RESEARCH IN THE BEHAVIORAL SCIENCES

4737
SURVIVAL. v.1– , Mar./Apr. 1959– . London. Bimonthly.
Issued by: Institute for Strategic Studies.
Indexes: Vols. 1–8, 1959–65, 1v.
Indexed: Int. Bibl. Pol. Sc.; Int. Pol. Sc. Abst.

4738
Svenska Sallskapet for Antropologi och Geografi. SKRIFTER. 1878–1880. Lund.
In Swedish.
Supersedes: *Tidskrift for Antropologi och Kulturhistorie*. Superseded by: *Ymer*.

4739
Sweden. Statens Jordbruksnämd. JORDBRUCKSEKONOMISKA MEDDELANDEN. v.1– , July 1939– . Stockholm. Monthly.
In Swedish, 1939–50; in English or Sweden, 1951–. Issued by: 1939–June 1950, Kommess Kolegium (with Statens Jordbrucksnamnd, July–Nov. 1939; with Statens Medelskommission, Dec. 1939–June 1950).
Indexed: Int. Bibl. Eco.

4740
THE SWEDISH ECONOMY. Feb. 1961– . Stockholm, Government Publishing House. Irreg., 1962–63; quarterly, 1961, 1965–.
Issued by: Konjunkturinstitutet. This publication is an English edition of *Konjunkturläget*.
Continues, in part: the institute's *Meddelanden*.
Indexed: Bull. Anal. Pol. Ec. Soc.; Int. Bibl. Eco.; PAIS.

4741
THE SWEDISH JOURNAL OF ECONOMICS. v.66–77, Mar. 1965–1975. Stockholm, Almquist & Wiksell. Quarterly.
Some numbers are thematic; some are papers of symposia.
Continues: *Ekonomisk Tidskrift* (v.1–68, 1899–1966). Continued by: *Scandinavian Journal of Economics*.
Indexed: Bull. Anal. Pol. Ec. Soc.; Eco. Abst.; His. Abst.; Curr. Cont. Soc. Beh. Sc.; Int. Bibl. Soc.; Int. Lab. Doc.; J. Eco. Lit.; PAIS; Pop. Ind.; SSCI.

THE SWISS REVIEW OF INTERNATIONAL RELATIONS
See AUSSENWIRTSCHAFT

4742
SWISS REVIEW OF WORLD AFFAIRS. v.1– , Jan. 1951– . Zürich, Neue Zürcher Zeitung. Monthly.
Indexed: APAIS; Bull. Anal. Pol. Ec. Soc.; Peace Res. Abst. J.

4743
SYMBOLIC INTERACTION. 1– , fall 1977– . Minneapolis, Minn., ISSS Press. Quarterly, 1977–80; semi-annual.
Issued by: Society for the Study of Symbolic Interaction (ISSS).
Indexed: Psych. Abst.

4744
SYMBOLON. v.1–6, 1960–1968; n. ser. v.1– , 1972– . Stuttgart, Schwabe. Annual.
In German.

SYMPOSIUM ON MATHEMATICAL METHODS IN THE SOCIAL SCIENCES
See STANFORD MATHEMATICAL STUDIES IN THE SOCIAL SCIENCES

4745
SYNTEZA. June 1968–1981. Bratislava. Bimonthly.
Issued by: Československý Vyskumny Ústav Prace a Socialnych Veci. In Czech or Slovak; summaries in Dutch, English, French and Russian.
Continued by: *Economics of Labor*.
Indexed: Int. Lab. Doc.; Psych. Abst.

4746
SYNTHESE. 1936– . Amsterdam, D. Reidel Pub. Co. Nine no. a year, collected in three volumes.
In Dutch, English, French, or German. Subtitle reads: "An international journal devoted to present day cultural and scientific life".
Indexed: Curr. Cont. Soc. Beh. Sc.; LLBA; SSCI.

SYNTHESIS OF ECONOMIC PERFORMANCE IN LATIN AMERICA
See Organization of American States. SYNTHESIS OF ECONOMIC PERFORMANCE IN LATIN AMERICA

4747
SYRIE ET MONDE ARABE. 1– , 1954– . Damascus. Monthly.

Issued by: Office Arabe de Presse et de Documentation. In French. Title varies: 1954–65, *Études Économiques sur la Syrie et les Pays Arabes*. Processed.
Indexed: Bull. Anal. Pol. Ec. Soc.; PAIS; PAISFL.

4748
SYSTEMATICS. v.1– , June 1963– . Kingston upon Thames, Cheltenham, Coombe Spring Press. Quarterly.
Issued by: Institute for Comparative Study of History, Philosophy and the Sciences.

4749
SYSTEMS ANALYSIS, MODELLING, SIMULATION. v.1– , 1984– . Berlin, Akademie-Verlag.

4750
SYSTEMS RESEARCH. 1– , 1983/84– . Oxford, Pergamon Press. Quarterly.
Issued by: International Federation for Systems Research.

4751
SZCZECIŃSKIE ROCZNIKI NAUKOWE. NAUKI SPOŁECZNE. v.1– , 1986– . Wrocław, Zakład Narodowy im. Ossolińskich. Irreg.
In Polish. Tables of contents also in English and Russian. (Subseries of: Szczecińskie Towarzystwo Naukowe. *Annales*)

SZECHAN UNIVERSITY JOURNAL; SOCIAL SCIENCES EDITION
See SSU-CH'UAN TA-HSÜEH-HSÜEH PAO; SHE-HUI K'O-HSÜEH

SZKICE EKONOMICZNE
See STUDIA EKONOMICZNE

4752
SZOCIOLÓGIA. 1972– . Budapést. Quarterly.
Issued by: Szociológiai Bizottságának Folyóirata Magyar Tudományos Akadémia. In Hungarian; summaries in English and Russian. Tables of contents also in English and Russian.
Indexed: Bull. Anal. Pol. Ec. Soc.; Bull. Sig. Soc. Eth.; Int. Bibl. Soc.; Int. Bibl. Soc. Cul. Anth.; LLBA.

4753
SZOCIOLÓGICA. 1– , 1974– . Szeged, Az MTA Szociológiai Bizottságának Folyóirata. Four no. a year.
Issued by: Central Library, Attila Jozsef University at Szeged. In Hungarian.
Indexed: Soc. Abst.

T

TESG
See TIJDSCHRIFT VOOR ECONOMISCHE EN SOCIALE GEOGRAFIE

TSSS
See TILLAGE SYSTEMS & SOCIAL SCIENCE

TABLEAUX ANALYTIQUES DU COMMERCE EXTÉRIEUR
See ANALYTISKE TABELLER VERDRØRENDE UDENRIGSHANDEL (NIMEXE)

TABLOS ANALÍTICAS DE COMERCIO EXTERIOR
See ANALYTISKE TABELLER VERDRØRENDE UDENRIGSHANDEL (NIMEXE)

4754
Taehan Kukchepop Hakoe Nonchong. TAEHAN KUKCHEPOP HAKKOE. 1– , Feb. 1956– . Seoul. Annual, 1956–57; semi-annual.
In English or Korean. Other title: *The Korean Journal of International Law*.

4755
TAHQIQĀT-I EQTEṢĀDI. 1– , 1961– . Tehrān. Bimonthly.
Issued by: Faculty of Economics, Institute for Economic Development and Research, University of Tehrān. In Persian.

4756
T'AIWAN CHING CHI YEN CHIU YUEH K'AN. TAIWAN ECONOMIC RESEARCH MONTHLY. 1978– . Taipei.
In Chinese.

TAIWAN ECONOMIC RESEARCH MONTHLY
See T'AIWAN CHING CHI YEN CHIU YUEN K'AN

TANG-TAI CHUNG KUO
See CONTEMPORARY CHINA

TANGANYIKA NOTES AND RECORDS
See TANZANIA NOTES AND RECORDS

4757
TANZANIA EDUCATIONAL JOURNAL. no.1– , 1964– . Dar es Salaam. Three no. a year.
Issued by: Ministry of National Education, and National Union of Tanzania Workers (N.U.T.A.). Occasionally in Swahili.

4758
TANZANIA NOTES AND RECORDS. no.1– , Mar. 1936– . Dar es Salaam, Government Printer. Semi-annual.
Issued by: Tanzania Society. Title varies: 1936–Mar. 1966, *Tanganyika Notes and Records*.
Indexed: His. Abst.

4759
AL-TAQRĪR AL-IQTIṢĀDĪ AL-'ARABĪ AL-MUWAḤḤAD. 1980– . Abu Ẓaby, Ṣundūq al-Naqd al-'Arabī lil-Inmā' al-Iqtiṣādī wa-al-Ījtima'ī. Annual.
Issued in cooperation with al-Amānah al-'Āmmah li-Jāmi'at al Duwal al 'Arabīyah. In Arabic. Other title: *Joint Arab Economic Report*.

THE TARIF REVIEW
See AMERICAN ECONOMIST

4760
TÁRSADALMI SZEMLE. 1– , Jan. 1946– . Budapest, Kultura. Monthly.
Issued by: Magyar Szocialista Munkáspárt (MSZMP). In Hungarian; summaries in English, French, German and Russian.
Indexed: His. Abst.; Int. Bibl. Eco.; Int. Bibl. Pol. Sc.; Peace Res. Abst. J.

4761
TÁRSADALOMKUTATAS. 1– , 1983– . Budapést, Akadémiai Kiadó. Quarterly.
"A Magyar Tudományos Akadémia Gazdasag-és Jogtudományok Osztályanok folyoirata". In Hungarian.

4762
TÁRSADALOMTUDOMANYI KÓZLEMENYEK. 1st– , Oct. 1971– . Budapést.
Issued by: Társadalomtudományi Intézet. In Hungarian.
Indexed: Int. Bibl. Pol. Sc.

TASYIR WA-MAJTAMA
See GESTION & SOCIÉTÉ

TAVOLE ANALITICHE DE COMMERCIO ESTERO
See ANALYTISKE TABELLER VERDRØRENDE UDENRIGSHANDEL (NIMEXE)

4763
TAX POLICY. [v.]1– , Nov. 1933– . Princeton, N.J. Monthly.
Issued by: Tax Institute of America (1933–40 called Tax Policy League). Some numbers in v.1–4 have title: *Taxbits*.

Indexed: Ind. Per. Art. Law; PAIS; Urb. Aff. Abst.

TAXBITS
See TAX POLICY

TEACHER EDUCATION
See TEACHER EDUCATION IN NEW COUNTRIES

4764
TEACHER EDUCATION IN NEW COUNTRIES. 1– , May 1960– . London, Oxford University Press. Three no. a year.
Issued by: Institute of Education, University of London. Title varies: v.1–8, 1960–Feb. 1968, *Teacher Education*.

4765
TECHNIQUES NOUVELLES EN SCIENCES DE L'HOMME. GIS TECHNIQUES NOUVELLES EN SCIENCES DE L'HOMME. v.1– , 1984– . Paris, Les Belles Lettres.
Issued in cooperation with the Centre National de la Recherche Scientifique. In French. (Annales Littéraires de l'Université de Besançon)

TECHNOLOGICAL FORECASTING
See TECHNOLOGICAL FORECASTING AND SOCIAL CHANGE

4766
TECHNOLOGICAL FORECASTING AND SOCIAL CHANGE. v.1– , June 1969– . New York, American Elsevier Pub. Co. Frequency varies; eight no. a year.
Title varies: v.1, 1969/70, *Technological Forecasting*.
Indexed: Bull. Anal. Pol. Ec. Soc.; Int. Bibl. Eco.; Int. Bibl. Pol. Sc.; Int. Bibl. Soc.; Int. Pol. Sc. Abst.

4767
TECHNOLOGY AND CULTURE. v.1– , winter 1959– . Chicago, Ill., The University of Chicago Press. Quarterly.
Issued by: Society for the History of Technology, and Case Institute of Technology. Includes "Current Bibliography in the History of Technology", an annual section arranged by historical periods and subject groups.
Indexes: v.1–10, 1959–69.
Indexed: Abst. Anth.; His. Abst.; LLBA; Soc. Abst.; Soc. Sc. Ind.; SSCI; Wom. Stu. Abst.

4768
TECHNOLOGY IN SOCIETY. v.1– , spring 1979– . New York, Oxford, Pergamon Press. Quarterly.
Indexed: Curr. Cont. Soc. Beh. Sc.; Soc. Abst.

4769
TELOS. v.1– , spring 1968– . St. Louis, Mo. Quarterly.
Issued by: Washington University, St. Louis. Subtitle reads: "A quarterly journal of radical thought".
Indexed: Int. Pol. Sc. Abst.; LLBA; Soc. Abst.

4770
TEMAS DE ETNOMUSICOLOGÍA. 1– , 1984– . Buenos Aires.
Issued by: Instituto Nacional de Musicología. In Spanish.

4771
TEMPLE INTERNATIONAL AND COMPARATIVE LAW JOURNAL. v.1– , fall 1985– . Philadelphia, Pa. Semi-annual.
Issued by: Temple University School of Law.

TENDANCES DU COMMERCE ET LES PRIX DES PRODUITS DE BASE
See COMMODITY TRADE AND PRICE TRENDS

4772
TEORÍA Y PRAXIS. v.1– , 1967– . Caracas. Quarterly.
In Spanish. Subtitle reads: "Revista Venezolana de Ciencias Sociales".

4773
TEORIE ŞI PRACTICA ECONOMICA. STUDII ŞI CERCETĂRI DE CALCUL ECONOMIC ŞI CIBERNETICA ECONOMICA. v.1– , 1981– . Bucureşti. Quarterly.
Issued by: Academia de Studii Economice. In Romanian. Tables of contents also in English, French, and Russian.

TEORIIA NAUCHNOGO KOMMUNIZMA
See Moskovskiĭ Universitet. VESTNIK. SERIIA XIII. TEORIIA NAUCHNOGO KOMMUNIZMA

4774
TERRA AMERIGA. 1– , 1964– . Genova. Quarterly.
Issued by: Associazione Italiana di Studi Americanisti. In English, French, Italian, Portuguese, or Spanish.
Indexed: Bull. Sig. Soc. Eth.; Int. Bibl. Soc. Cul. Anth.

TERRITOIRES NON-AUTONOMES; RESUMÉS ET ANALYSES DES RENSEIGNEMENTS TRANSMIS AU SECRÉTAIRE GÉNÉRAL
See United Nations. Secretary General. TERRITOIRES NON-AUTONOMES; RÉSUMÉS ET ANALYSES DES RENSEIGNEMENTS TRANSMIS AU SECRÉTAIRE GÉNÉRAL

TERRITORIOS NO AUTÓNOMOS; RESUMENES Y ANÁLISIS DE LA INFORMACIÓN TRANSMITIDA AL SECRETARIO GENERAL
See United Nations. Secretary General. TERRITOIRES NON-AUTONOMES: RÉSUMÉS ET ANALYSES DES RENSEIGNEMENTS TRANSMIS AU SECRÉTAIRE GÉNÉRAL

4775
TERRORISM. 1– , Sept. 1977– . New York, Crane Russak. Quarterly.
Issued by: State University of New York at Oneonta.
Indexed: Soc. Abst.

4776
TERZO MONDO. THIRD WORLD. v.1– , July/ Sept. 1968– . Milano. Quarterly.
Issued by: Centro Studi Terzo Mondo. In Italian.
Indexed: Bull. Anal. Pol. Ec. Soc.; Bull. Sig. Soc. Eth.; Int. Bibl. Soc. Cul. Anth.; Int. Pol. Sc. Abst.

4777
THE TEXAS INTERNATIONAL LAW JOURNAL. v.7– , summer 1971– . Austin, Tex. Three no. a year.
Other title: *Journal of the University of Texas Law Society*.
Continues: *Texas International Law Forum* (v.1, no.2–v.6, no.2, Jan. 1965–winter 1971)
Indexes: Vols. 1–10, 1965–75, in v.10; v.11–15, 1976–80, in v.15.
Indexed: Ind. For. Leg. Per.

TEXTES ADOPTÉS
See Council of Europe. Consultative Assembly. TEXTS ADOPTED

TEXTES ADOPTÉS
See European Conference of Local Authorities. TEXTS ADOPTED

TEXTES ADOPTÉS PAR L'ASSEMBLÉ
See Council of Europe. Parliamentary Assembly. TEXTS ADOPTED BY THE ASSEMBLY

TEXTOS DE LOS INFORMANTES DE SAHAGUN
See FUENTES INDÍGENAS DE LA CULTUR NÁHUATL

TEXTS ADOPTED
See Council of Europe. Consultative Assembly TEXTS ADOPTED

TEXTS ADOPTED
See European Conference of Local Authorities. TEXTS ADOPTED

4778
THAI JOURNAL OF DEVELOPMENT AND ADMINISTRATION. v.11– , 1970– . Bangkok. Four no. a year.
Issued by: Thammasat University. In English or Thai.
Continues: *The Thai Journal of Public Administration* (v.1–10, 1960–70)

4779
THEORY AND DECISION. v.1– , Oct. 1970– . Dordrecht, D. Reidel Pub. Co. Quarterly.
Subtitle reads: "An international journal for philosophy and methodology of the social sciences".
Indexed: Bull. Sig. Soc. Eth.; Int. Bibl. Pol. Sc.; Int. Pol. Sc. Abst.; Psych. Abst.; Soc. Abst.; SSCI.

4780
THEORY AND RESEARCH IN SOCIAL EDUCATION. v.1– , Oct. 1973– . East Lansing, Mich.; later Graduate School of Education, Rutgers University, New Brunswick, N.J. Two no. a year, 1973–76; quarterly.

4781
THEORY AND RESEARCH IN SOCIAL INDICATORS. v.1– , Oct. 1973– . East Lansing, Mich., Michigan State University Press.
Issued by: National Council for Social Studies.

4782
THEORY AND SOCIETY. v.1– , 1974– . Amsterdam, Elsevier Scientific Pub. Co. Quarterly.
Subtitle reads: "Renewal of critique in social theory".
Indexed: Bull. Anal. Pol. Ec. Soc.; Int. Bibl. Pol. Sc.; Int. Bibl. Soc.; Int. Pol. Sc. Abst.; LLBA; PAIS; Soc. Abst.; SSCI.

THIRD WORLD
See TERZO MONDO

4783
THIRD WORLD AFFAIRS. 1985– . London. Annual.
Issued by: Third World Foundation for Social and Economic Studies.

4784
THIRD WORLD PLANNING REVIEW. v.1– , spring 1979– . Liverpool, Liverpool University Press. Semi-annual, 1979–80; quarterly.
Issued by: Department of Civic Design, The University of Liverpool.
Indexed: Curr. Cont. Soc. Beh. Sc.; Geo. Abst.; Int. Bibl. Eco.; PAIS; Sage Pub. Adm. Abst.; Soc. Abst.; SSCI.

4785
THIRD WORLD QUARTERLY. v.1– , Jan. 1979– . London. Quarterly.

Issued by: Third World Foundation.
Indexed: Int. Bibl. Eco.; Int. Bibl. Pol. Sc.; Int. Bibl. Soc. Cul. Anth.; Int. Pol. Sc. Abst.; PAIS.

THOUGHT
See SHISŌ

4786
Tibet Society. JOURNAL. 1981– . Bloomington, Ind.
In English, French, German, or Tibetan.
Supersedes: Tibet Society. *Bulletin*.

4787
TIDSKRIFT FÖR ANTROPOLOGI OCH KULTURHISTORIA. v.1–3 (no.1–16), 1873–1877. Stockholm.
Issued by: Svenska Sallskapet för Antropologi och Geografi (its earlier name: Antropologiska Sallskapet i Stockholm).
Superseded by: the society's *Skrifter*.

4788
TIDSSKRIFT FOR POLITISK ØKONOMIE. 1– , 1973– . København. Quarterly.
Issued by: Institute of Economics and Planning, Roskilde University Centre. In Danish.

4789
TIDSSKRIFT FOR SAMFUNNSFORSKNING. v.1– , 1960– . Oslo, Universitetsforlaget. Quarterly.
Issued by: Institutt for Samfunnsforskning, University of Oslo. In Danish or Swedish; summaries in English. Other title: *Norwegian Journal for Social Research*.
Indexed: Bull. Sig. Soc. Eth.; His. Abst.; LLBA.

4790
TIERRA NUEVA. 1972– . Bogotá. Quarterly.
Issued by: Centro de Estudios para el Desarrollo e Integración de América Latina. In Spanish.

4791
TIERS MONDE. v.1– , Jan./June 1960– . Paris, Presses Universitaires de France. Quarterly.
Organ of: Institut d'Étude du Développement Économique et Sociale, Université de Paris I. In French. Title on cover: *Revue Tiers-Monde*.
Indexed: Bull. Anal. Pol. Ec. Soc.; Int. Bibl. Eco.; Int. Bibl. Pol. Sc.; Int. Bibl. Soc.; Int. Lab. Doc.; Int. Pol. Sc. Abst.; PAISFL; Pop. Ind.

4792
TIJDSCHRIFT VOOR ECONOMIE EN MANAGEMENT. v.20– , 1975– . Leuven. Quarterly.
Issued by: Fakulteit der Economische en Toegpaste Economische Wetenschappen, Katholieke Universiteit te Leuven. In English or Flemish.
Continues: *Tijdschrift voor Economie* (v.1–19, 1956–74)

4793
TIJDSCHRIFT VOOR ECONOMIE EN SOCIOLOGIE. v.1–5, 1935–1939. Gent. Annual.
Organ of: Vereeniging voor Economische Wetenschappen. In Dutch.

4794
TIJDSCHRIFT VOOR ECONOMISCHE EN SOCIALE GEOGRAFIE. 1– , Jan. 15, 1910– . Rotterdam, Van Vaesberge. Monthly.
Issued by: Nederlandse Vereniging voor Economische en Sociale Geografie (called earlier: Nederlandsch Vereniging voor Economische Geografie). In Dutch or English. Other titles: *TESG*; *Journal of Economic and Social Geography*; *Revue Néerlandaise de Géographie Économique et Social*; *Revista Holandesa de Geografía Económica y Social*. Vols. 8–9 include separately paged supplements called "Economisch Geografische Merelrevue". Vols. 35, no.8–v.36, Aug. 1944–Dec. 1945 not published.
Indexes: Vols. 1–25, 1910–34, in v.35.
Indexed: APAIS; Bull. Sig. Soc. Eth.; Int. Bibl. Eco.; PAIS; Pop. Ind.; SSCI.

TIJDSCHRIFT VOOR ECONOMISCHE GEOGRAFIE
See TIJDSCHRIFT VOOR ECONOMISCHE EN SOCIALE GEOGRAFIE

4795
TIJDSCHRIFT VOOR GESCHIEDENIS. v.1– , 1886– . Groningen. Annual, 1886–1918; bimonthly, 1919–21; quarterly.
In Dutch or English. Title varies: 1886–91, *Tijdschrift voor Geschiedenis*; 1892–93, *Geschiedenis en Aardrijskunde. Tijdschrift voor lager en middelbar onderwijs*; 1894–1919, *Tijdschrift voor Geschiedenis, Land- en Volkenkunde*.
Indexes: Vols. 35–44, 1920–29; v.45–54, 1930–39.

TIJDSCHRIFT VOOR GESCHIEDENIS, LAND- EN VOLKENKUNDE
See TIJDSCHRIFT VOOR GESCHIEDENIS

4796
TIJDSCHRIFT VOOR NEDERLANDSCH INDIË. v.1–24, 1838–1862; n. 2. ser. v.1–4, 1863–66; n. ser. v.1–5, 1867–71. n. [ser.] 4., 1– , 1872– . Batavia. Monthly.
In Dutch. Title varies: 1838–47, *Tijdschrift voor Neerland's Indië*.

TIJDSCHRIFT VOOR NEERLAND'S INDIË
See TIJDSCHRIFT VOOR NEDERLANDSCH INDIË

4797
TIJDSCHRIFT VOOR OPVOEKUNDE. v.1– , 1909– . Nijmegen, Standaart Boekhandel. Bimonthly.
In Dutch. Title varies: 1909–19, *Vlaams Opvoekunding Tijdschrift*; 1919–55, *Tijdschrift voor Zielkunde en Opvoedingsleer*.
Indexed: Soc. Abst.

4798
TIJDSCHRIFT VOOR SOCIALE GESCHIEDENIS. 1– , May 1975– . Ghent. Three no. a year, 1975–79; quarterly.
Issued by: Nederlands Vereiniging to Bevefening van de Sociale Geschiedenis (NVSG). In Dutch.

4799
TIJDSCHRIFT VOOR SOCIALE WETENSCHAPPEN. 1– , 1956– . Ghent. Quarterly.
Issued by: Studieen Onderzoekcentrum voor Sociale Wetenschappen, later by Seminarie voor Sociologie, Rijksuniversiteit, Ghent. In Dutch, English, or French; some summaries in English, French, or German.

4800
TIJDSCHRIFT VOOR STAATHUITSHOUDKUNDE IN STATISTIEK. 1–12, 1841–1855; 13–24 (2. ser. 1–12 deel), 1856–64; 25–28 (3. ser. 1–4 deel), 1865–75. Zwolle.
In Dutch.

4801
TIJDSCHRIFT VOOR ZEEGESCHIEDENIS. v.1– , Apr. 1982– . Den Haag, M. Nijhoff. Semi-annual.
Issued by: Nederlandse Vereniging voor Zeegeschiedenis. In Dutch or English.
Supersedes: *Medelingen van de Nederlandse Vereniging voor Zeegeschiedenis*.

TIJDSCHRIFT VOOR ZIELKUNDE EN OPVOEDINGSLEER
See TIJDSCHRIFT VOOR OPVOEKUNDE

4802
TILLAGE SYSTEMS & SOCIAL SCIENCE. v.1– , Mar. 1981– . Lexington, Ky.
Issued by: Department of Sociology and Office of International Programs for Agriculture, College of Agriculture, University of Kentucky. Other title: *TSSS*.

THE TOCQUEVILLE REVIEW
See Tocqueville Society. THE TOCQUEVILLE REVIEW

4803
Tocqueville Society. THE TOCQUEVILLE REVIEW. LA REVUE TOCQUEVILLE. v.1– , fall 1979– . Charlottesville, Va. Two no. a year.
In English or French.
Indexed: Int. Bibl. Pol. Sc.; Int. Pol. Sc. Abst.

4804
TŌHOKU PSYCHOLOGICA FOLIA. v.1– , 1933– . Sendai. Four no. a year, semi-annual.
Organ of: Faculty of Arts and Letters, Department of Psychology, Tohoku University. In English. Four issues were sometimes published in one cumulative volume.
Indexed: LLBA; Psych. Abst.

TOID SOCIOLOGIA ALALTO
See TRUDY PO SOT͡SIOLOGII

TOIMITUKSIA. ANNALES. SERIES A. SECTION 5. MEDICA ANTHROPOLOGICA
See Soumalainen Tiedeakademia, Helsingfors. TOIMITUKSIA

4805
Tokushima Daigaku. Gakugei Gakubu. TOKUSHIMA DAIGAKU KIYŌ SHAKAI KAGAKU. 1– , 1952– . Tokushima. Annual.
In Japanese; summaries in English. Other title: *Journal of Gakukei College, Tokushima University. Social Science*.
Indexes: Vols. 1–10, 1952–60, with v.10.

TOKUSHIMA DAIGAKU KIYŌ SHAKAI KAGAKU
See Tokushima Daigaku. Gakukei Gakubu. TOKUSHIMA DAIGAKU GAKUKEI KIYŌ SHAKAI KAGAKU

4806
Tōkyō Daigaku. Shakai Kagaku Kenkyūjo. ANNALS. no.1– , 1953– . Tokyo. Annual (irreg.)
Beginning with no.9 the journal includes articles and abstracts. Title varies: no.1–6, 1953–65, *Social Science Abstracts*.
Indexed: PAIS.

4807
TŌKYŌ JOSHI DAIGAKU SHAKAIGAKKAI KIYŌ-KEIZAI TO SHAKAI. no.1– , Oct. 1965– . Tokyo. Annual.
Issued by: Tokyo Women's University Sociological Society. In Japanese.

TONGBUK ASEA YŎN'GU
See JOURNAL OF NORTHEAST ASIAN STUDIES

4808
TONGSO MUNKWA. CHAAGGANHO. 1967– . Taegu-si, Kyemong Taehak Tongso Munkwa Yŏn'guso.

In Korean. Other title: *Journal of the Institute for Cross-Cultural Studies.*

4809
TOOLS AND METHODS OF COMPARATIVE RESEARCH. no.1–3, 1964–1966. New Haven, Conn., Yale University Press.
Issued by: International Social Science Committee, and International Committee for Social Science Documentation. Includes proceedings of conference. Monograph series: Subseries of: *Publications of the International Social Science Council.*

4810
TOOLS & TILLAGE. v.1– , 1968– . Copenhagen. Four no. a year.
Issued by: National Museum of Denmark. In English or German; summaries in the other language.
Indexed: Abst. Anth.

4811
TOR. v.1– , 1948– . Stockholm, Gustavianum. Annual (occasionally biennial)
Issued by: 1948–58, Museum for Nordiske Fornsaker, Uppsala Universiteit; 1959–74, Institutionen for Nordisk Fornkunskap, Uppsala Universiteit. In Swedish; summaries in English, French and German.

4812
TOWN PLANNING REVIEW. v.1– , 1910– . Liverpool, Liverpool University Press. Quarterly.
Issued by: Department of Civil Design, Liverpool School of Architecture, University of Liverpool.
Indexed: Curr. Cont. Soc. Beh. Sc.; Ind. Per. Art. Law; Int. Bibl. Soc.; PAIS; Sage Urb. Stu. Abst.; SSCI.

4813
TŌYŌ KEIZAI SHIMPŌ. 1917–1944. Tokyo.
In Japanese. Published also in English: *The Oriental Economist*. Absorbed: *Sekai Keizai Nenkan*, in 1937.
Continued by: *Shukan Tōyō Keizai.*

TRABAJOS Y CONFERENCIAS
See REVISTA ESPAÑOLA DE ANTROPOLOGÍA AMERICANA

TRANSACTIONS
See American Philosophical Association. TRANSACTIONS

TRANSACTIONS
See Ethnological Society of London. TRANSACTIONS

TRANSACTIONS
See Grotius Society. TRANSACTIONS

TRANSACTIONS
See Institute of British Geographers. TRANSACTIONS AND PAPERS

TRANSACTIONS
See Royal Asiatic Society of Great Britain and Ireland. TRANSACTIONS

TRANSACTIONS
See Royal Asiatic Society of Great Britain and Ireland. China Branch. TRANSACTIONS

TRANSACTIONS
See Royal Asiatic Society of Great Britain and Ireland. Korea Branch. TRANSACTIONS

TRANSACTIONS
See Westermarck Society. TRANSACTIONS

TRANSACTIONS
See World Congress of Sociology. TRANSACTIONS

TRANSACTIONS AND PAPERS
See Institute of British Geographers. TRANSACTIONS AND PAPERS

TRANSACTIONS OF THE ASIATIC SOCIETY OF JAPAN
See Asiatic Society of Japan. TRANSACTIONS

TRANSACTIONS OF THE GROTIUS SOCIETY
See Grotius Society. TRANSACTIONS

4814
TRANSAFRICA FORUM. v.1– , summer 1982– . New Brunswick, N.J., Transaction Periodicals Consortium. Quarterly.
Subtitle reads: "A journal of opinion on Africa and the Caribbean".

4815
TRANSAFRICAN JOURNAL OF HISTORY. v.1– , Jan. 1971– . Nairobi, Kenya Literature Bureau. Two no. a year.
Issued by: Department of History, Makerere University. Processed.

TRAVAIL, CAPITAL ET SOCIÉTÉ
See LABOUR, CAPITAL AND SOCIETY

TRAVAIL ET SOCIÉTÉ
See LABOUR AND SOCIETY

TRAVAUX
See Action Populaire. REVUE

TRAVAUX DE L'INSTITUT D'ETHNOGRAPHIE
See Akademii͡a Nauk SSSR. Institut Etnografii. TRUDY. n. ser.

TRAVAUX DE L'INSTITUT D'ÉTUDES IRANIENNES DE L'UNIVERSITÉ DE LA SORBONNE NOUVELLE

See Université de la Sorbonne Nouvelle. Institut d'Études Iraniennes. TRAVAUX

TRAVAUX DE RECHERCHE EN SCIENCES SOCIALES
See RESEARCH MONOGRAPH SERIES IN THE SOCIAL SCIENCES

TRAVAUX ET COMMUNICATIONS
See Académie des Sciences Morales et Politiques. TRAVAUX ET COMMUNICATIONS

TRAVAUX ET DOCUMENTS
See Centre d'Études Sociologiques. TRAVAUX ET DOCUMENTS

TRAVAUX ET MÉMOIRES
See Académie des Sciences d'Outre-Mer. TRAVAUX ET MÉMOIRES

TRAVAUX SOCIOLOGIQUES
See SOZIOLOGISCHE ARBEITEN

TREATIES AND OTHER INTERNATIONAL ACT SERIES
See United States. Department of State. TREATIES AND OTHER INTERNATIONAL ACT SERIES

TREATY SERIES
See League of Nations. TREATY SERIES

TREATY SERIES
See Organization of American States. TREATY SERIES

4816
TRENDS IN DEVELOPING COUNTRIES, 1969–1973. Washington, D.C. Irreg.
Issued by: International Bank for Reconstruction and Development.

4817
TRENDS IN EDUCATION. no.1– , 1966– . London, HMSO. Quarterly.
Prepared by: Department of Education and Science.

4818
TRENDS IN SOUTHEAST ASIA. no.1– , 1971– . Singapore. Irreg.
Issued by: Institute of Southeast Asian Studies.

4819
EL TRIMESTRE ECONÓMICO. v.1– , Jan. 1934– . Mexico, D.F. Quarterly.
Issued by: Fondo de Cultura Económica, and Instituto de Cooperación Iberoamericana. In Spanish. Publication suspended Jan.–Mar. 1938.
Indexes: Vols. 1–10, 1934–44, with v.10; v.1–18, 1934–51, with v.18; v.1–30, 1934–63, with v.30; v.1–40, 1934–75, with v.40.
Indexed: Bull. Anal. Pol. Ec. Soc.; Int. Bibl. Eco.; Int. Lab. Doc.; J. Eco. Lit.; PAISFL.

TROPICAL HOUSING AND PLANNING MONTHLY BULLETIN
See EKISTICS

4820
TROPICAL MAN. v.1– , 1968– . Leiden, E.J. Brill. Annual.
Organ of: Anthropology Department, Royal Tropical Institute, Amsterdam. In English or French.
Supersedes: *International Affairs of Ethnography.*
Indexed: Bull. Sig. Soc. Eth.

TRUDY
See Akademii͡a Nauk SSSR. Institut Etnografii. TRUDY. n. ser.

TRUDY
See Akademii͡a Nauk Tadzhikskoĭ SSR. Otdel Ekonomiki. TRUDY

TRUDY
See Buri͡atskiĭ Institut Obshchestvennykh Nauk. TRUDY

TRUDY AKADEMII NAUK LITOVSKOĬ SSR. SERII͡A A. OBSHCHESTVENNYE NAUKI
See Lietuvos TSR Mokslų Akademija. DARBAI. SERIJA A. VISUOMENĖS MOKSLAI

TRUDY KAFEDR OBSHCHESTVENNYKH NAUK
See Barnaul'skiĭ Gosudarstvennyĭ Pedagogicheskiĭ Institut. TRUDY KAFEDR OBSHCHESTVENNYKH NAUK

TRUDY. NOVAIA SERII͡A
See Akademii͡a Nauk SSSR. Institut Etnografii. TRUDY. n. ser.

TRUDY. OBSHCHESTVENNYE NAUKI
See Akademii͡a Nauk SSSR. Irkutskiĭ Filial. TRUDY. OBSHCHESTVENNYE NAUKI

4821
TRUDY PO SOT͡SIOLOGII. TOID SOT͡SIOLOGIA ALALTO. 1– , 1968– . Tartu.
Issued by: Sot͡siologia Laboratorium, Ulikool. In Estonian and Russian; summaries in English and Russian.

4822
TS'AI CHING SHIH SHIH. FINANCIAL AND ECONOMIC JOURNAL. 1983– . Ch'usung k'an hao. T'aipei-shih, Ts'ai ching shih shih k'an she. Monthly.
In Chinese. Other title: *Ts'ai ching shih shih tsa chih.*

TS'AI CHING SHIH SHIH TSA CHIH
See TS'AI CHING SHIH SHIH

4823
Tudomány-Egyetem, Budapést. ANNALES. SECTIO PHILOSOPHICA ET SOCIOLOGICA. v.1– , 1966– . Budapést. Annual.
In English, French, German, or Russian.
Continues: *Annales Universitatis Budapestinensis. Sectio Philosophica.*
Indexed: Int. Bibl. Soc.

4824
Tudományos Ismeretterjesztó Társulat. VALÓSÁG. v.1– , 1958– . Budapést, Gondolat Kónyv-Lapkiadó és Terjezstó Vállahat. Monthly.
In Hungarian.
Indexed: LLBA; Soc. Abst.

TUEDDIADAU CYMDEITHASAI
See WELSH SOCIAL TRENDS

TUNG PEI YACHOU YEN CHIU. HOKUTŌ AJIA KENKYŪ
See JOURNAL OF NORTHEAST ASIAN STUDIES

4825
TUNG WU CHIH SHE HUI HSÜEH PAO. no.1– , 1977– . Taipei. Annual.
Issued by: Tung Wu ta Hsüeh. In Chinese or English. Other title: *Soochow Journal of Social and Political Sciences.*

4826
TUNISIE ÉCONOMIQUE. n. ser. no.1– , 1961– . Tunis. Quarterly.
Issued by: Union Tunisienne de l'Industrie, du Commerce. In French.

4827
TÜRK ANTROPOLOGI MEMUASI. REVUE TURQUE D'ANTHROPOLOGIE. Oct. 1925– . Istanbul, Maarif Matbasi. Semi-annual (irreg.)
Issued by: Türk Antropologi Muessesesi, later Enstitusii, Istanbul Universitesi; 1939–, Antropologi ve Etnologi Enstituts of the Tarih Dilve Cografya Fakultesi, in Ankara. In 1925–28 in Ottoman Turkish. In Turkish.

4828
TURKISH ECONOMIC REVIEW FOR FINANCE, INDUSTRY, TRADE. 1– , 1961– . London, Publishing and Distributing Co. Monthly.
Issued by: Union of Chambers of Commerce, Industry and Commodity Exchange of Turkey. In English.
Indexed: Int. Bibl. Soc. Cul. Anth.

4829
TURKISH PUBLIC ADMINISTRATION ANNUAL. v.1– , 1974– . Ankara.
Issued by: Institute of Public Administration for Turkey and the Middle East.
Indexed: Bull. Anal. Pol. Ec. Soc.

4830
TURKISH YEARBOOK OF HUMAN RIGHTS. v.1– , 1979– . Ankara. Annual.
Issued by: Human Rights and Documentation Centre, Institute for Public Administration for Turkey and the Middle East. In English or French. Other title: *Annuaire Türc sur les Droits de l'Homme.*

THE TURKISH YEARBOOK OF INTERNATIONAL RELATIONS
See MILLTLERARASI MUNASEBETLER TURK YILLIGI

Turkmen S.S.R. Ylymar Akademiiasy
See Akademiia Nauk Turkmenskoĭ SSR

4831
TURKMENISTAN KOMMUNISTI. KOMMUNIST TURKMENISTANA. 1925– . Ashkhabad. Monthly.
Issued by: TSentral'nyĭ Komitet Kommunisticheskoĭ Partii Turkmenskoĭ SSR. In Turkmen. Title varies: 1925–32, *Bol'shevik.* In Russian or Turkmen.

4832
TYDSKRIF VIR MAATSKAPLIKE NAVORSING. JOURNAL OF SOCIAL RESEARCH. 1– , July 1950– . Pretoria. Semi-annual.
Issued by: Departement van Oderwys, Kuns en Wetenskop, Nasionale Raad vir Sociale Navorsing. In Afrikaans or English. Title in Afrikaans precedes title in English, v.1–3, no.1.
Continued by: *Humanitas.*

TYDSKRIF VIR POLITIKIE WETENSKAPPE
See POLITEIA

4833
TYDSKRIF VIR RASSE-AANGELEENTHEDE. [1]– , 1949– . Pretoria. Quarterly.
Issued by: Suid-Afrikaanse Buro vir Rasse-aangeleenthede (SABRA). In Afrikaans or English. Other title: *Journal of Racial Affairs.*

4834
TYDSKRIF VIR STUDIES IN EKONOMIE EN EKONOMETRIE. JOURNAL FOR STUDIES IN ECONOMICS AND ECONOMETRICS. no.6– , Dec. 1979– . Stellenbosch. Three no. a year.
Issued by: Buro vir Ekonomiese Onderzoek, Universiteit Stellenbosch. In Afrikaans or English. Other title: *S.E.E.*
Continues: *Tydskrif vir Studies in Ekonomie en Ekonometrie* (no.1–5, 1977–June 1979)

U

UCLA MONOGRAPH SERIES IN ETHNOMUSICOLOGY
See MONOGRAPH SERIES IN ETHNOMUSICOLOGY

UNDEX. UNITED NATIONS DOCUMENTS INDEX. SERIES A, SERIES B, SERIES C
See United Nations. Dag Hammarskjöld Library. UNDEX. UNITED NATIONS DOCUMENTS INDEX

UNDOC: CURRENT INDEX; UNITED NATIONS DOCUMENTS INDEX
See United Nations. Dag Hammarskjöld Library. UNDOC: CURRENT INDEX; UNITED NATIONS DOCUMENTS INDEX

4835
UCHENYE ZAPISKI KAFEDR OBSHCHESTVENNYKH NAUK. 1– , 1967– . Dunshabe.
Issued by: Tadzhikskiĭ Gosudarstvennyĭ Universitet, and Tadzhikskiĭ Politekhnicheskiĭ Institut. In Russian.

4836
THE UGANDA JOURNAL. v.1– , Jan. 1934– . Kampala. Quarterly, 1934–Apr. 1940; semi-annual.
Issued by: Uganda Society (called 1934–35, Uganda Literary and Scientific Society). Publication suspended May 1942–Mar. 1946.
This publication was reprinted for the period 1934–1946 (no.1–2) by the Johnson Reprint Corp. in 1971.
Indexes: Vols. 1–20, 1934–56, supplement to v.22, no.1.

4837
UKRAINIAN QUARTERLY. v.1– , Oct. 1944– . New York.
Issued by: Ukrainian Congress Committee of America. Subtitle reads: "A journal of East European and Asian affairs".
Indexes: Vols. 1–10, 1944–54, 1v.
Indexed: Bull. Sig. Soc. Eth.; His. Abst.; Int. Bibl. Soc. Cul. Anth.; PAIS.

4838
UKRAINSKYI ISTORYCHNYI ZHURNAL. 1– , 1957– . Kiev. Monthly.
Issued by: Instytut Istorii, Akademii͡a Nauk Ukrainskoi RSP, and Komunistychna Partii͡a Ukrainy. In Ukrainian; summaries in English and Russian.

4839
UNESCO YEARBOOK ON PEACE AND CONFLICT STUDIES. 1980– . Westport, Conn., Greenwood Press; Paris, Unesco.

Union Interparlementaire
See Inter-Parliamentary Union

4840
THE UNION OF SOUTH AFRICA FINANCE & TRADE REVIEW. v.1– , Jan. 1951– . Pretoria. Two no. a year.

4841
UNITED ASIA. v.1– , May/June 1948– . Bombay, United Asia Publications. Monthly (irreg.)
Indexed: His. Abst.; Int. Bibl. Pol. Sc.; Int. Pol. Sc. Abst.; PAIS; Peace Res. Abst. J.

4842
United Nations. Centre against Apartheid. NOTES AND DOCUMENTS. no.1– , Jan. 1976– . New York. Two no. a year.
Supersedes: United Nations. Unit on Apartheid. *Notes and Documents*, 1973–75.

4843
United Nations. Centro Latinoamericano de Demografía. CUADERNOS DEL CELADE/ CELADE MEMORANDA. no.1– , Feb. 1979– . Santiago, Chile. Irreg.
In Spanish.

4844
United Nations. Commission on Human Rights. REPORT. 1st sess.– , Jan. 27/Feb. 10, 1947– . New York.
Issued as a supplement to the *Official Records* of the Economic and Social Council. Accompanied by "Addenda" and "Corrigenda". Issued also in French: *Rapport*, and Spanish: *Informe*. (E, E/CN.4)

4845
United Nations. Commission on International Commodity Trade. COMMODITY SURVEY. 1955– . New York. Annual.
Published also in French *Étude des Marchés des Produits de Base*, and Spanish: *Estudio de los Mercados Primarios*. Title varies: 1955–56, *Survey of Primary Commodity Markets*. (E/CN.13.St/ECA)

4846
United Nations. Commission on International Trade Law. YEARBOOK. v.1– , 1968/70– . New York. (A/ CN.9/Ser.A)

Editions in English, French, Russian, and Spanish.

4847
United Nations. Commission on the Racial Situation in the Union of South Africa. REPORT. 1953– . New York. Irreg.
Published also in French: *Rapport*, and Spanish: *Informe*. Issued as supplement to the *Official Records* of the General Assembly.

4848
United Nations. Commission on the Status of Women. REPORT. 1st sess.– , Feb. 10–24, 1947– . New York. Irreg.
Issued also in French: *Rapport*, and Spanish: *Informe*. Includes supplements: "Addenda" and "Corrigenda". Reports for 1950– issued as supplements to the *Official Records* of the Economic and Social Council. (E.E/CN.6)

4849
United Nations. Dag Hammarskjöld Library. INDEX TO PROCEEDINGS OF THE ECONOMIC AND SOCIAL COUNCIL.
Continues in the printed form the mimeographed series called *Agenda Items*. (ST/LIB/Ser.b)

4850
United Nations. Dag Hammarskjöld Library. INDEX TO PROCEEDINGS OF THE GENERAL ASSEMBLY. 5th sess.– , 1950/51– . New York.
Continues the mimeographed series called: *Disposition of Agenda Items*.

4851
United Nations. Dag Hammarskjöld Library. INDEX TO PROCEEDINGS OF THE SECURITY COUNCIL. 19th– , 1964– . New York.

4852
United Nations. Dag Hammarskjöld Library. INDEX TO PROCEEDINGS OF THE TRUSTEESHIP COUNCIL. 11th– , 1952– . New York.
Continues the mimeographed series titled *Disposition of Agenda Items*. (ST/LIB/Ser.B)

4853
United Nations. Dag Hammarskjöld Library. UNITED NATIONS DOCUMENTS INDEX. v.1–13, 1950–1962. New York. Eleven no. and annual cumulation.

4854
United Nations. Dag Hammarskjöld Library. UNITED NATIONS DOCUMENTS INDEX: CUMULATIVE CHECKLIST. v.14– , 1963– . New York.
Supersedes the monthly issues of the *United Nations Documents Index* and continues its volume numbering.

4855
United Nations. Dag Hammarskjöld Library. INDEX; UNITED NATIONS DOCUMENTS INDEX. SERIES A: SUBJECT INDEX; SERIES B: COUNTRY INDEX; SERIES C: LIST OF DOCUMENTS ISSUED. v.1–9, 1970–1978. New York.
The three sections continue: *Documents Index*, and they merged to form: UNDOC. (ST.LIB/ Ser.B)

4856
United Nations. Dag Hammarskjöld Library. UNDOC: CURRENT INDEX; UNITED NATIONS DOCUMENT INDEX. v.1– , Jan./Feb. 1979– . New York. Monthly (except July–Aug.) with annual cumulation. The introductory number called "Sample Issue" was published in 1979.
Formed by the union of: *Undex. United Nations Documents Index. Series A: Subject Index; Series B: Country Index; Series C: List of Documents Issued*. (ST/ LIB/Ser.M)

4857
United Nations. Department of Economic and Social Affairs. WORLD ECONOMIC REPORT. 1945/ 47–1976. New York.
Issued by: Bureau of Economic Affairs, 1954/ 47–1951. Title varies: *Economic Report*. Issued also in French: *Rapport sur l'Économie Mondiale*, and Spanish: *Informe Económico Mundial*.
Continued by: *World Economic Survey*. (ST/ECA)

4858
United Nations. Department of International Economic and Social Affairs. Population Division. POPULATION STUDIES. no.1– , 1948– . New York. Irreg.
No.1–20 issued by: Department of Social Affairs (no.4, 8–9 with the Statistical Office); no.21, by the Bureau of Social Affairs. Population Branch; no.23, by the department's Population Branch. Title varies: no.1–2, *Reports on the Population on Territories*. (ST/ SOA/Ser.A)

4859
United Nations. Department of International Economic and Social Affairs. REPORT ON THE WORLD SOCIAL SITUATION. 1957– . New York. Quadrennial.
Vols. 1957–60 prepared by the United Nations Bureau of Social Affairs in cooperation with the International Labour Office and other organizations; 1960–77, Department of Economic and Social Affairs. Title varies: 1957, *Report on the World Social Situation including Studies of Urbanization in Underdeveloped Areas*; 1958, *Report on the World Social Situation with Special Reference to the Problem of Balanced Social and Economic Development*. (E/CN.5) and (ST/ESA)

4860
United Nations. Department of International Economic and Social Affairs. STUDIES IN METHODS. no.1– , Sept. 1950– . New York. Irreg. (St/ESA/STAT/Ser.P)

4861
United Nations. Department of Political Affairs, Trusteeship and Decolonization. DECOLONIZATION. no.1– , June 1974– . New York.

Issues for 1974–75 called also v.1–2. Other titles: *Décolonisation*, *Decolonización*.

4862
United Nations. Economic and Social Commission for Asia and the Pacific. COMPARATIVE STUDY OF MIGRATION, URBANIZATION IN RELATION TO THE DEVELOPMENT IN THE ESCAP REGION; COUNTRY REPORTS. no.1– , 1980– . New York. Irreg.

4863
United Nations. Economic and Social Commission for Asia and the Pacific. ECONOMIC AND SOCIAL SURVEY OF ASIA AND THE PACIFIC. 1947– . Bangkok. Annual.

Issued by: 1947–74, Economic Commission for Asia and the Far East. Title varies: 1947–73, *Economic Survey of Asia and the Far East*. (E/CN.11) (ST/ESCAP)

4864
United Nations. Economic and Social Commission for Asia and the Pacific. ECONOMIC BULLETIN FOR ASIA AND THE PACIFIC. v.1– , 1949– . Bangkok. Three no. a year, 1949–73; quarterly.

Issued by: 1951, Commission's Secretariat; 1952, Research and Statistics Division. Until 1956 fourth issue was "Survey". Since 1957 "Survey" has been a separate publication. Some nos. in English and French. Each issue has a distinctive title. Issued also in French: *Étude Économique sur l'Asie et l'Extrême-Orient*. Title varies: 1949–73, *Economic Bulletin for Asia and the Far East*. (E/CN.11) (ST/ESCAP)

4865
United Nations. Economic and Social Commission for Asia and the Pacific. FOREIGN TRADE STATISTICS OF ASIA AND THE PACIFIC. SERIES A. v.4– , 1965– . Bangkok, publ. 1968. Annual.

Issued by: 1965–73, Economic Commission for Asia and the Far East.

Continues, in part: *Foreign Trade Statistics of Asia and the Far East*. (E/CN.11) (ST/ESCAP)

4866
United Nations. Economic and Social Commission for Asia and the Pacific. FOREIGN TRADE STATISTICS OF ASIA AND THE PACIFIC. SERIES B. v.4– , 1965– . Bangkok, publ. 1968. Annual.

Issued by: 1964–73, Economic Commission for Asia and the Far East.

Continues, in part: *Foreign Trade Statistics of Asia and the Far East*. (E/CN.11) (ST/ESCAP)

4867
United Nations. Economic and Social Commission for Asia and the Pacific. QUARTERLY BULLETIN OF STATISTICS OF ASIA AND THE PACIFIC. v.1– , 1971– . Bangkok.

Issued by: 1971–73, Economic Commission for Asia and the Far East. In English and French. Title varies: v.1–3, no.2, 1971–Sept. 1973, *Quarterly Bulletin of Statistics of Asia and the Far East*. (E/CN.11); 1974– (ST/ESCAP/STAT)

4868
United Nations. Economic and Social Commission for Asia and the Pacific. SMALL INDUSTRY BULLETIN FOR ASIA AND THE PACIFIC. no.1– , June 1963– . Bangkok. Annual.

Issued by: 1963–73, Economic Commission for Asia and the Far East. In English; often summaries in French. Title varies: no.1–11, 1963–73, *Small Industry Bulletin for Asia and the Far East*.

Supersedes: *Industrial Development Series*. (ST/ESCAP/Ser.M)

4869
United Nations. Economic and Social Commission for Asia and the Pacific. STATISTICAL INDICATORS FOR ASIA AND THE PACIFIC. 1983– . Bangkok. Irreg. (average four no. a year)

United Nations. Economic and Social Commission for Asia and the Pacific
See also: United Nations. Economic Commission for Asia and the Far East

United Nations. Economic and Social Commission for Asia and the Pacific
See STATISTICAL YEARBOOK FOR ASIA AND THE PACIFIC

4870
United Nations. Economic and Social Council. OFFICIAL RECORDS. 1st sess.– , Jan. 23, 1946– . New York.

In English and French; beginning with 10th sess., Feb. 1950 a separate edition in French has been published, in Mar. 1950–Apr. 30, 1954 called *Procès-verbaux*, and subsequently *Documents Officiels*, and Spanish edition called *Documentos Oficiales*. (E/CN.4)

4871
United Nations. Economic and Social Council. REPORT OF THE ECONOMIC AND SOCIAL COUNCIL. Jan. 23/Oct. 3, 1946– . New York.
Issued also in French: *Rapport* and Spanish: *Informe*. (United Nations. General Assembly. *Official Records*. Supplement A)

4872
United Nations. Economic and Social Council. RESOLUTIONS ADOPTED BY THE ECONOMIC AND SOCIAL COUNCIL. 3rd sess.– , Sept. 11, 1946– . New York.
In 1946–53 in English and French. Beginning with the 16th sess., June/Aug. 1953 a separate edition in French was established. Issued also in Spanish: *Resoluciones Aprobadas* (Jan./Feb. 1946–). (A)

United Nations. Economic and Social Office in Beirut *See* United Nations. Economic Commission for Western Asia

4873
United Nations. Economic Commission for Africa. AFRICAN SOCIO-ECONOMIC INDICATORS. INDICATEURS ÉCONOMIQUES AFRICAINS. 1970– . Addis Ababa. Annual.
In English and French. Title varies: 1970–1982, *African Economic Indicators*. (E/CN.14)

4874
United Nations. Economic Commission for Africa. ECONOMIC BULLETIN FOR AFRICA. 1–11, Jan. 1961–1976. Addis Ababa. Annual.
Published also in French: *Bulletin Économique pour l'Afrique*. Each number accompanied by separately paged section of statistical appendix called "African Statistics" which became *Statistical Bulletin for Africa*. (E/CN.14)

4875
United Nations. Economic Commission for Africa. ECONOMIC DEVELOPMENT IN AFRICA. 1949/50– . Addis Ababa. Annual.
Issued by: 1949/50–1950/51, Department of Economic Affairs; 1951/52, Secretary General; 1953/54, Department of Economic and Social Affairs. Published also in French: *Évolution Économique en Afrique*. Issued in 1949/50–1950/51 as supplement to *World Economic Report* (later *World Economic Survey*). Title varies: 1949/50, *Review of Economic Conditions in Africa*; 1950/51, *Summary of Recent Economic Developments in Africa*, 1951/52, *World Economic Situation*.

4876
United Nations. Economic Commission for Africa. FOREIGN TRADE STATISTICS FOR AFRICA. SERIES A. DIRECTION OF TRADE. STATISTIQUES AFRICAINES DU COMMERCE EXTÉRIEUR. SÉRIE A. ÉCHANGES PAR PAYS. no.1– , 1962– . New York. Semi-annual.
In English and French. Title varies: 1960–61, *African Trade Statistics. Statistical Bulletins. Series A. Direction of Trade. Statistiques Africaines du Commerce Extérieur. Bulletins Statistiques. Série A. Commerce par Pays d'Origine et Destination*. (E/CN.14/Stat/Ser.A)

4877
United Nations. Economic Commission for Africa. FOREIGN TRADE STATISTICS FOR AFRICA. SERIES B. TRADE BY COMMODITY. STATISTIQUES AFRICAINES DU COMMERCE EXTÉRIEUR. SÉRIE B. ÉCHANGES PAR PRODUITS. no.1– , 1960– . New York. Semi-annual.
In English and French. The second number of each year is a cumulation for the year. Title varies: 1960–61, *African Trade Statistics. Statistical Bulletins. Series B. Statistiques Africaines du Commerce Extérieur. Bulletins Statistiques. Série B. Échanges par Produits*. (E/CN.14/STAT/Ser.B)

4878
United Nations. Economic Commission for Africa. FOREIGN TRADE STATISTICS FOR AFRICA. SERIES C. SUMMARY TABLES. STATISTIQUES AFRICAINES DU COMMERCE EXTÉRIEUR. SÉRIE C. TABLEAUX DE CAPITULATIFS. no.1– , 1977– . New York.
In English and French. Vol. 1 covers the period 1966/76. (E/CN.14/STAT/Ser.C)

4879
United Nations. Economic Commission for Africa. INTERNATIONAL ECONOMIC ASSISTANCE FOR AFRICA. 1954/58– . New York. Irreg. (E/CN.14)

4880
United Nations. Economic Commission for Africa. STATISTICAL AND ECONOMIC INFORMATION BULLETIN FOR AFRICA. BULLETIN D'INFORMATION STATISTIQUE ET ÉCONOMIQUE POUR L'AFRIQUE. 1–12, 1972–1979. Addis Ababa. Irreg.
In English or French; summaries in the other language.
Supersedes: *Quarterly Statistical Bulletin for Africa. Bulletin Trimestrielle de Statistique pour l'Afrique*. Continued by: *Statistical Information Bulletin for Africa*. (no.13–) (E/CN.14/STAT)

4881
United Nations. Economic Commission for Africa. STATISTICAL YEARBOOK. ANNUAIRE STATISTIQUE. 1970–1973. Addis Ababa. Annual.

Continues: *Statistical Bulletin for Africa*. Continued by: *African Statistical Yearbook*. (E/CN.14/STAT)

4882
United Nations. Economic Commission for Asia and the Far East. FOREIGN TRADE STATISTICS FOR ASIA AND THE FAR EAST. v.1–7, 1961–1968. New York. Annual.
Continued by: *Foreign Trade Statistics of Asia and the Pacific. Series A*, and *Foreign Trade Statistics of Asia and the Pacific. Series B*. (E/CN.11/STAT)

4883
United Nations. Economic Commission for Central America. Committee on Economic Cooperation in Central America. REPORT. 1952/53– . New York. Annual.
Published also in French: *Rapport*. (E/CN.12/A; E/CN.12/CCE)

4884
United Nations. Economic Commission for Europe. ECONOMIC BULLETIN FOR EUROPE. v.1– , first quarter 1949– . Geneva, 1949–82; Oxford, Pergamon Press. Two no. a year.
It supplements: *Economic Survey of Europe*.
Indexed: PAIS; Pop. Ind.

4885
United Nations. Economic Commission for Europe. ECONOMIC SURVEY OF EUROPE. 1947– . Geneva, 1949. Annual (when consisting of two parts, pt.2 has a distinctive title).
Title varies: 1947, *A Survey of the Economic Situation and Prospects of Europe*; 1962, *Economic Survey of Europe since the War*. Published also in Russian: *Obzor Ekonomicheskogo Polozhenii͡a Evropy*. Occasionally accompanied by supplements with distinctive titles. (E/ECE)

4886
United Nations. Economic Commission for Europe. REPORT. 1947/48– . New York. Annual.
Issued also in French: *Rapport* (1949–50, *Procès-verbaux officiels*), and Spanish: *Informe*. (E/ECE)

4887
United Nations. Economic Commission for Europe. STATISTICAL JOURNAL OF THE UNITED NATIONS ECONOMIC COMMISSION FOR EUROPE. v.1– , June 1982– . Amsterdam, North-Holland Pub. Co. Quarterly.
(E/ECE)

4888
United Nations. Economic Commission for Latin America. BOLETÍN ESTADÍSTICO DE AMÉRICA LATINA. v.1–8, Mar. 1964–1972. New York. Semi-annual, 1964–72; three no. a year.
In Spanish. Published also in English: *Statistical Bulletin for Latin America*.
Supersedes: *Boletín Económico de América Latina. Suplemento Estadístico*, and *Supplement* of the *Economic Bulletin for Latin America*. Continued by: *Anuario Estadístico de América Latina*, 1973–85, which has been continued by: *Anuario Estadístico de América Latina y del Caribe*.

4889
United Nations. Economic Commission for Latin America and the Caribbean. CEPAL REVIEW. 1st semester 1976– . Santiago, Chile. Three no. a year.
Published also in Spanish: *Revista de la CEPAL*.
Supersedes: *Economic Bulletin for Latin America* (1956–74). (E/CEPAL/G)
Indexed: PAIS.

4890
United Nations. Economic Commission for Latin America and the Caribbean. ECONOMIC SURVEY OF LATIN AMERICA AND THE CARIBBEAN. 1948– . New York, 1949. Annual.
Published also in Spanish: *Estudio Económico de América Latina y del Caribe*. Title varies: 1949–81, *Economic Survey of Latin America*. (E/CN.12); 1974– (E/CEPAL)

4891
United Nations. Economic Commission for Latin America and the Caribbean. REVISTA DE LA CEPAL. no.1– , 1 semester 1976– . Santiago, Chile. Three no. a year.
In Spanish. Published also in English: *Cepal Review*.
Supersedes: *Boletín Económico de América Latina*. (E/CEPAL)

4892
United Nations. Economic Commission for Western Asia. POPULATION BULLETIN OF ECWA. no.18–26, June 1980–June 1985. Beirut. Semi-annual.
Continues: *Population Bulletin of the United Nations Economic Commission for Western Asia* (no.1–17, June 1971–Dec. 1979). (E/ECWA)

4893
United Nations. Economic Commission for Western Asia. STUDIES ON DEVELOPMENT IN COUNTRIES OF WESTERN ASIA. 1949/50– . Beirut. Annual.
Issued by: 1949/50–1952/53, Department of Economic Affairs; 1953/54–1971/72, Bureau of Economic Affairs. Published also in French: *Évolution Économique du Moyen-Orient*. Title varies: 1949/50, 1951/52, *Review of Economic Conditions in the Middle East*; 1950/51, 1952/53, *Summary of Recent Economic Development in the Middle East*.

4894
United Nations. General Assembly. INDEX TO PROCEEDINGS OF THE GENERAL ASSEMBLY. 5th sess.– , Sept. 19, 1950–Nov. 5, 1951– . New York, [1953].
Prepared by: Dag Hammarskjöld Library of the United Nations. (ST/LIB/Ser.B/A)

4895
United Nations. General Assembly. OFFICIAL RECORDS. 1st sess.– , Jan. 10, 1946– . New York.
Issued also in French: *Documents Officiels*, and Spanish: *Documentos Oficiales* (some numbers have title: *Actas Oficiales*). Documents for some sessions are accompanied by supplements.
(A/31/PV 1–).

4896
United Nations. Section on the Status of Women. REPORT. 1– , 1947– . New York. Annual.
Published also in French and Spanish. Included as *Supplement* to the *Official Records* of the Economic and Social Council.

4897
United Nations. General Assembly. RESOLUTIONS ADOPTED BY THE GENERAL ASSEMBLY. 1st sess.– , Jan. 10–Feb. 14, 1946– . New York.
In English and French first three sessions. Documents for 1st–4th sessions issued as supplements to the *Official Records*. Some numbers accompanied by "Addenda". (A)

4898
United Nations. International Law Commission. YEARBOOK. 1949– . New York, 1956.
Issued also in Spanish: *Anuario*. (A/CN.4/Ser.A)

4899
United Nations. Legal Department. STATEMENTS OF TREATIES AND INTERNATIONAL AGREEMENTS REGISTERED OR FILED WITH THE SECRETARIAT. RELEVÉ DES TRAITÉS ET ACCORDS INTERNATIONAUX ENREGISTRÉS OU CLASSÉS ET INSÉRÉS AU RÉPERTOIRE AU SECRÉTARIAT. Dec. 1946/Mar. 1947– . New York. Monthly.
(ST/LEG/Ser.A)

4900
United Nations. Secretariat. YEARBOOK ON HUMAN RIGHTS. 1946– . New York. Annual.
Continues: League of Nations, *Treaty Series. Publication of Treaties and International Engaments [sic] Registered with the Secretariat of the League of Nations* (1920–46)

4901
United Nations. Secretary General. TERRITOIRES NON-AUTONOMES: RÉSUMÉS ET ANALYSES DES RENSEIGNEMENTS TRANSMIS AU SECRÉTAIRE GÉNÉRAL. 1946– . New York. Annual.
Issues for 1951 accompanied by special volumes. Published also in English: *Territories non-autonomous*, and Spanish: *Territorios no autónomos* (1949–). (ST/TRI/SER.A)

4902
United Nations. Security Council. OFFICIAL RECORDS. DOCUMENTS OFFICIELS. 1st year, Jan. 17, 1946– . New York.
In English and French through 1964; afterward separate editions in English and French. Includes supplements. Includes subseries: *Resolutions and Decisions of the Security Council. Résolutions et Décisions du Conseil de Sécurité*. 1962–64 bilingual in English and French; later two separate editions. (S/INF)

4903
United Nations. Statistical Office. COMMODITY TRADE STATISTICS. no.7– , Sept. 1951– . New York. Irreg. (about 32 issues a year)
Subseries of: U.N. Statistical Office. *Statistical Papers. Ser. D.* In English and French, No.1–6 and until v.11 in English and French; beginning with v.12 in English only.
Continues: *Summary of World Trade Statistics* (no.1–6, 1951). (ST/ESA/STAT/SER.D.)

4904
United Nations. Statistical Office. DIRECTION OF INTERNATIONAL TRADE. Jan./Mar. 1950–Jan. 1963. New York. Monthly, cumulated quarterly, semi-annually and annually.
Issued in cooperation with the: International Monetary Bank and International Bank for Reconstruction and Development. (ST/STAT/SER.T.). Supplements accompany some issues.

4905
United Nations. Statistical Office. MONTHLY BULLETIN OF STATISTICS. BULLETIN MENSUELLE DE STATISTIQUE. v[1]– , Jan. 1947– . New York.
In English and French. Some volumes are accompanied by supplements which are continued by: *Supplement to the Statistical Yearbook and the Monthly Bulletin of Statistics*.

4906
United Nations. Statistical Office. NATIONAL ACCOUNTS STATISTICS. ANALYSIS OF MAIN AGGREGATES. 1982– . New York, 1985–. Annual.
With: *National Accounts Statistics. Government Accounts and Tables* and *National Accounts Statistics. Main Aggregates and Detailed Tables*, continues: United Nations. Statistical Office. *Yearbook of National Accounts Statistics*.

4907
United Nations. Statistical Office. NATIONAL ACCOUNTS STATISTICS. GOVERNMENT ACCOUNTS AND TABLES. 1982– . New York. Annual.
With: *National Accounts Statistics. Analysis of Main Aggregates* and *National Accounts Statistics. Main Aggregates and Detailed Tables*, continues: United Nations. Statistical Office. *Yearbook of National Accounts Statistics*.

4908
United Nations. Statistical Tables. NATIONAL ACCOUNTS STATISTICS. MAIN AGGREGATES AND DETAILED TABLES. 1982– . New York. Annual.
With: *National Accounts Statistics. Analysis of Main Aggregates* and *National Accounts Statistics. Government Accounts and Tables*, continues: *Yearbook of National Accounts Statistics*.

4909
United Nations. Statistical Office. POPULATION AND VITAL STATISTICS REPORTS. v.[1]– , Jan. 1949– . New York. Monthly, 1949; quarterly.
In English only. Supplements *Demographic Yearbook*. Subseries of: U.N. Statistical Office. *Statistical Papers. Ser.A*. (ST/STA/SER.A)

4910
United Nations. Statistical Office. STATISTICAL PAPERS. 1950– . New York. Irreg.
Includes following subseries: *Series A: Population and Vital Statistics Reports*; *Series B: Statistical Notes*; *Series C: Sample Surveys of Current Interest*; *Series D: Commodity Trade Statistics*; *Series E: National Accounts*; *Series F: Studies in Methods*; *Series G: Trade by Country*; *Series J: World Energy Supplies*; *Series K: Compendium of Social Statistics*; *Series M: International Standard Industrial Classification*; *Series N: Compendium of Housing Statistics*; *Series O: Yearbook of Account Statistics*; *Series P: The Growth of World Industry*; *Series R: Demographic Yearbook*; *Series S: Statistical Yearbook*; *Series U: Yearbook of Construction Statistics*; *Series V: United Nations Statistical Pocketbook of World Statistics in Brief*.

4911
United Nations. Statistical Office. STATISTICAL YEARBOOK. ANNUAIRE STATISTIQUE. v.1– , 1949– . New York. Annual.
In English and French. (ST/ESA/STAT/SER.S)

4912
United Nations. Statistical Office. SUPPLEMENT TO THE STATISTICAL YEARBOOK AND THE MONTHLY BULLETIN OF STATISTICS. 1967– . New York.
Supersedes: supplements to the *Monthly Bulletin of Statistics*.
(ST/ESA/STAT/SER.S)

4913
United Nations. Statistical Office. YEARBOOK OF INDUSTRIAL STATISTICS. 1950–1981. New York.
Title varies: 1950–73, *The Growth of World Industry*. Consists of two volumes: (1) General Statistics, (2) Commodity Production Data. (ST/ESA/STAT/SER.P)

4914
United Nations. Statistical Office. YEARBOOK OF INTERNATIONAL TRADE STATISTICS. 1950–1982. New York. Annual (two volumes)
In English and French.
Supersedes: *International Trade Statistics*. Continued by: *International Trade Statistics Yearbook*. (ST/ESA/STAT/SER.G)

4915
United Nations. Statistical Office. YEARBOOK OF NATIONAL ACCOUNTS STATISTICS. ANNUAIRE DE STATISTIQUES DES COMPTABILITÉS NATIONALES. 1957–1981. New York. Annual.
In English and French.
Supersedes: U.N. Statistical Office. *Statistics of National Income and Expenditure*. Continued by: U.N. Statistical Office. *National Accounts Statistics* in three series: (1) *Analysis of Main Aggregates*, (2) *Government Accounts and Tables*, and (3) *Main Aggregates and Detailed Tables*.

4916
United Nations. Trusteeship Council. OFFICIAL RECORDS. 1st sess.– , Mar. 26, 1947– . New York.
Issued also in French: *Documents Officiels* (Jan. 19/Apr. 4, 1950–; in 1950–Mar. 25, 1954, as *Procès-Verbaux Officiels*), and Spanish: *Documentos Oficiales*. Supplements accompany some documents. Includes subseries: *Report*, published also in French: *Rapport*, and Spanish: *Informe*. (A)

4917
United Nations. Unit on Apartheid. SPECIAL STUDIES SERIES. 1– , 1967– . New York. Irreg.
In English, French and Spanish editions; some numbers only in English.
Continued by: Centre against Apartheid. *Special Studies Series*. (ST/PSCA/SER.A)

4918
UNITED NATIONS DISARMAMENT YEARBOOK. v.1– , 1976– . New York.
Issued by: United Nations Centre for Disarmament. (DC/SER.A)

UNITED NATIONS DOCUMENTS INDEX
See United Nations. Dag Hammarskjöld Library. UNITED NATIONS DOCUMENTS INDEX

UNITED NATIONS DOCUMENTS INDEX; CUMULATIVE CHECKLIST
See United Nations. Dag Hammarskjöld Library. UNITED NATIONS DOCUMENTS INDEX; CUMULATIVE CHECKLIST

4919
United Nations Educational, Scientific and Cultural Organization. STATISTICAL YEARBOOK. ANNUAIRE STATISTIQUE. 1963– . Paris.
In English and French. Other title: *Anuario Estadístico*.
Continues: *Basic Facts and Figures*.

4920
United Nations Educational, Scientific and Cultural Organization. Department of Social Sciences. CURRENT SCHOOL ENROLLMENT STATISTICS. STATISTIQUES DES EFFECTIFS SCOLAIRES. no.1– , 1955– . Paris. Annual.
In English and French.

4921
United Nations Educational, Scientific and Cultural Organization. REPORTS AND PAPERS IN THE SOCIAL SCIENCES. no.1– , 1955– . Paris. Irreg.
(Unesco [Document] SS/CH)

4922
United Nations Fund for Population Activities. POLICY DEVELOPMENT STUDIES. no.1– , 1979– . New York. Irreg.

4923
THE UNITED NATIONS YEARBOOK. 1946/47– . New York. Annual.
Issued by: Department of Public Information, United Nations.

4924
United States. Department of Commerce. Bureau of Economic Analysis. SURVEY OF CURRENT BUSINESS. [v.1]– , Aug. 1, 1921– . Washington, D.C., Government Printing Office. Monthly.

4925
United States. Bureau of the Census. COUNTRY DEMOGRAPHIC PROFILES. ISP-DP-1– , Apr. 1973– . Washington, D.C., Government Printing Office. Irreg.

4926
United States. Bureau of the Census. Population Division. CURRENT POPULATION REPORTS. SERIES P–20. POPULATION CHARACTERISTICS. no.1– , 1947– . Washington, D.C. Irreg.

4927
United States. Bureau of the Census. Population Division. CURRENT POPULATION REPORTS. FEDERAL STATE COOPERATIVE PROGRAM FOR POPULATION ESTIMATES. SERIES P–26. no.1– , July 1969– . Washington, D.C., Government Printing Office. Irreg.

4928
United States. Department of State. TREATIES AND OTHER INTERNATIONAL ACT SERIES. 1946– . Washington, D.C., Government Printing Office. Irreg.

4929
United States. Department of State. Historical Division. AMERICAN FOREIGN POLICY CURRENT DOCUMENTS. 1981– . Washington, D.C., Government Printing Office.
Continues: publication of the same title for the years 1956–1980.

4930
United States. Department of State. Historical Office. AMERICAN FOREIGN POLICY CURRENT DOCUMENTS. 1956–1980. Washington, D.C., Government Printing Office.
Continues: its *American Foreign Policy Basic Documents*, 1950–55.
Continued by: publication of the same title, 1981–.

4931
UNITED STATES CONTRIBUTIONS TO INTERNATIONAL ORGANIZATION. 1951/52– . Washington, D.C., Government Printing Office.
Issued by: Bureau of International Organization Affairs.

4932
THE UNITED STATES IN WORLD AFFAIRS. AN ACCOUNT OF AMERICAN FOREIGN RELATIONS. 1931– . New York, Simon and Schuster. Annual.
Issued by: Council for Foreign Relations.

4933
Universal Reference System. POLITICAL SCIENCE, GOVERNMENT & PUBLIC POLICY. v.1–10, 1965–1967. Princeton, N.J., Princeton Research Pub. Co., 1965–69. 10v.
Continued by: *Annual Supplement*, 1967–79, and *Political Science Abstracts*, 1980–. (New York, IFI Plenum)

4934
Universidad Central de Venezuela. Instituto de Antropología e Historia. ANUARIO. v.1– , 1964– . Caracas.
In Spanish.

4935
Universidad Central de Venezuela. Instituto de Estudios Hispanoamericanos. ANUARIO. 1974– . Caracas. Annual.
In Spanish. Monograph series.

4936
Universidad de Buenos Aires. Facultad de Ciencias Económicas. REVISTA DE LA FACULTAD DE CIENCIAS ECONÓMICAS. 1– , Mar. 1948– . Buenos Aires.
In Spanish.
Supersedes: *Revista de Ciencias Económicas*.

4937
Universidad de Buenos Aires. Facultad de Derecho y Ciencias Sociales. REVISTA DE LA FACULTAD DE DERECHO Y CIENCIAS SOCIALES. v.1– , Oct./Dec. 1922– . Buenos Aires. Quarterly.
In Spanish. Publication suspended 1933–45. Absorbed: Universidad de Buenos Aires. Facultad de Derecho y Ciencias Sociales. Seminario de Ciencias Jurídicas y Sociales. *Boletin Mensual*.
Supersedes: Universidad de Buenos Aires. Facultad de Derecho y Ciencias Sociales. *Anales de la Facultad de Derecho y Ciencias Sociales* (1902–19).

4938
Universidad de Chile, Santiago. Facultad de Ciencias Jurídicas y Sociales. ANALES. 1–150, 1843–1922; 2nd ser. v.1–8, 1923–1930; 3rd ser. 1931–1957; 4th ser. v.1, 1958– . Santiago. Annual (occasionally additional issues).
In Spanish.

4939: not used

Universidad de Córdoba
See Universidad Nacional de Córdoba

4940
Universidad Nacional Autónoma de México. Centro de Estudios Mayas. CUADERNOS. no.1– , 1969– . Mexico, D.F. Irreg.
In English or Spanish. Monograph series.

4941
Universidad Nacional Autonoma de Mexico. Instituto de Investigaciones Historicas. CUADERNOS. SERIE DOCUMENTAL. no.1– , 1963– . Mexico, D.F. Irreg.
In Spanish.

4942
Universidad Nacional Autónoma de México. Instituto de Investigaciones Históricas. SERIE DE CULTURA NÁHUATL. ESTUDIOS DE CULTURA NÁHUATL. v.1– , 1958– . Mexico, D.F. Irreg.
In Spanish.

4943
Universidad Nacional Autónoma de México. Instituto de Investigaciones Históricas. SERIE DE CULTURA NÁHUATL FUENTES. 1– , 1958– . Mexico, D.F. Irreg.
In Spanish.

4944
Universidad Nacional Autónoma de México. Instituto de Investigaciones Históricas. SERIE DE CULTURA NÁHUATL. MONOGRAFÍAS. no.1– , 1959– . Mexico, D.F. Irreg.
In Spanish.

4945
Universidad Nacional Autónoma de México. Instituto de Investigaciones Históricas. SERIE DE CULTURAS MESOAMERICANAS. 1– , 1967– , Mexico, D.F. Irreg.
In Spanish.

4946
Universidad Nacional Autónoma de México. Instituto de Investigaciones Históricas. SERIE DE HISTORIADORES Y CRONISTAS DE INDIAS. no.1– , 1967– . Irreg.

4947
Universidad Nacional de Colombia. Facultad de Ciencias Económicas. REVISTA DE LA FACULTAD DE CIENCIAS ECONÓMICAS. v.1– , Jan. 1965– . Bogotá. Two no. a year.
In Spanish.

4948
Universidad Nacional de Córdoba. Facultad de Derecho y Ciencias Sociales. BOLETÍN. no.1– , Sept./Oct. 1937– . Córdoba, Dirección de Publicaciones Universitarias. Five no. a year, 1937–48; four no. a year.
In Spanish.

4949
Universidad Nacional de Córdoba. Facultad de Derecho y Ciencias Sociales. CUADERNOS DE LOS INSTITUTOS. no.1– , 1957– . Córdoba, Dirección de Publicaciones Universitarias. Irreg.
In Spanish.

4950
Universidad Nacional de Cuyo, Mendoza. Instituto de Estudios Políticos y Sociales. CUADERNOS. no.1– , 1957– . Mendoza. Irreg.
In Spanish.

4951
Universidad Nacional de la Plata. Facultad de Ciencias Jurídicas y Sociales. ANALES. v.1– , 1926– . La Plata. Irreg.

In Spanish.

4952
Universidad Nacional de la Plata. Instituto de Estudios Cooperativos. REVISTA DEL INSTITUTO DE ESTUDIOS COOPERATIVOS. 1– , July/Sept. 1958– . La Plata.
In Spanish.

4953
UNIVERSIDAD Y DESARROLLO. v.1–7, Jan./May 1980– . La Paz. Quarterly.
Issued by: Comité Ejecutivo, Universidad Boliviana. In Spanish. Publication suspended: July 1980–Oct. 1982.

4954
UNIVERSIDAD Y SOCIEDAD. no.1– , spring 1981– . Madrid. Three no. a year.
Issued by: Centro Regional de Madrid asociado a Universidad Nacional de Educación a Distancia (UNED). In Spanish.

4955
Universidade de São Paulo. Instituto de Estudos Brasileiros. REVISTA. no.1– , 1966– . São Paulo.
In Portuguese.

4956
Università di Palermo. Facoltà di Economia e Comercio. ANNALI. v.1– , 1947– . Palermo, Editrice Lila, later Abbaco. Two no. a year.
In Italian.
Indexed: Int. Bibl. Eco.; Int. Lab. Doc.

4957
Universität Frankfurt am Main. Frobenius Institut. STUDIEN ZUR KULTURKUNDE. v.1– , 1933– . Stuttgart, A. Schroder. Irreg.
In German. The institute was earlier called: Forschungsanstalt für Kultur & Morphologie; Forschungsinstitut für Kulturmorphologie. Subseries of its *Veröffentlichungen*.

4958
Universität Halle. WISSENSCHAFTLICHE ZEITSCHRIFT; GESELLSCHAFTS- UND SPRACHWISSENSCHAFTLICHE REIHE. v.1– , 1951/52– . Halle. Bimonthly.
In German. Vols. 1–2 numbered also in sequence with *Wissenschaftliche Zeitschrift: Mathematisch-Naturwissenschaftliche Reihe*.
Indexed: His. Abst.; LLBA.

4959
Universität Hamburg. Seminar für Sozialwissenschaften. SOZIALWISSENSCHAFTLICHE STUDIEN. v.1– , 1960– . Stuttgart, Fischer.
In German.

4960
Universität Münster. Institut für Christliche Sozialwissenschaften. SCHRIFTEN. v.1– , 1955– . Münster, Verlag Aschendorf. Irreg.
In German.

4961
UNIVERSITAS. no.1– , 1951– . Bogotá. Annual, 1951–52; semi-annual.
Issued by: Faculdad de Ciencias Jurídicas y Socioeconómicas, Pontificia Universidad Católica in Bogotá. In Spanish.

4962
UNIVERSITAS ECONÓMICA. v.1– , June 1977– . Bogotá. Two no. a year.
Issued by: Faculdad de Ciencias Económicas y Administrativas, Pontificia Universidad Javeriana. In Spanish.

4963
UNIVERSITAS INDONESIA. v.1– , Feb. 1960– . Djakarta. Irreg.
Issued by: Lembaga Penjelidikan Ekonomi dan Masjarakat. Warta Research.
In English or Indonesian.

4964
Universitas Indonesia. Ikatan Kekarabatan Antropologi. MEDIA IKATAN KEKARABATAN ANTROPOLOGI. no.1– , 1973– . Jakarta.
In English or Indonesian.

4965
Universitatea Bucureşti. ANALELE. SOCIOLOGIE. no.1–22, 1951–1973. Bucureşti. Annual.
In various languages; summaries in French and Russian.

4966
Universitatea Bucureşti. BULETIN INFORMARE ŞTIINŢIFICA: FILOZOFIE, LOGICA, SOCIOLOGIE, PSIHOLOGIE. 1964– . Bucureşti. Monthly.
Issued jointly by: Universitatea, and Centrul de Documentare Ştiinţifica, Academia Republicii Socialiste România. In Romanian.

4967
Universitatea din Galati. BULETINUL. ŞTIINŢE SOCIALE ŞI UMANISTE. no.1– , 1978– . Galati. Annual.
In English, French, or Romanian. Some summaries in English or French. Tables of contents in English, French and German.

4968
Universitatea din Iaşi. ANALELE ŞTIINŢIFICE. SECTIUNEA 3.B 1. ŞTIINŢE SOCIALE: FILOZOFICE, ECONOMICE ŞI JURIDICE. n. ser. 1962–1968. Iaşi. Annual.
In Romanian; summaries in French and Russian.
Supersedes, in part: *Analele Ştiinţifice*. Ser. B. Continued by: *Analele Ştiinţifice. Part B: Ştiinţe Filozofice*; *Part C: Ştiinţe Economice*, and *Part D. Ştiinţe Juridice*.

4969
Universitatea din Iaşi. ANALELE ŞTIINŢIFICE. SECTIUNEA III. PART C. ŞTIINŢE ECONOMICE. v.15– , 1969– . Iasi.
In Romanian; summaries in English, French, or Russian.
Continues, in part: *Analele. Sectiunea III. Ştiinţe Sociale*.

4970
Universitatea din Iaşi. ANALELE ŞTIINŢIFICE. SERIE NOUA. SECTIUNEA IIIa: ISTORIE. n. ser. v.15– , 1969– . Iaşi. Annual.
In Romanian.
Continues, in part: Universitatea. *Analele. Ştiinţe. Sectiunea III. Ştiinţe Sociale*.

UNIVERSITATIS AMOENSIS ACTA SCIENTIARUM SOCIALIUM
See HSIA-MEN TA HSÜEH PAO. CHE HSÜEH SHE HUI K'O HSÜEH PAN

4971
Universite, Ankara. SIYASAL BILGILER FAKULTESI DERGISI. 1– , 1943– . Ankara, Ajans Turk Maulbasi. Irreg.
In Turkish. Vol. for 1943 has title: *Siyasal Bilgiler Okulu*.

4972
Université Catholique de Louvain. Département de Démographie. RECHERCHES DÉMOGRAPHIQUES. no.[1]– , Mar. 1980– . Louvain-la-Neueve. Irreg.
In French.

4973
Université d'Abidjan. ANNALES. SÉRIE F: ETHNOSOCIOLOGIE. v.1– , 1965– . Abidjan, Centre d'Édition et de Diffusion Africaines.
In French.
Indexed: Bull. Sig. Soc. Eth.

4974
Université d'Abidjan. ANNALES. SÉRIE K. SCIENCES ÉCONOMIQUES. v.1– , 1978– . Abidjan. Annual.
In French.

4975
Université d'Aix-en-Provence. Faculté de Droit et des Sciences Économiques. ANNALES. nouv. ser. no.52– , 1960/61– . Aix-en-Provence.
In French.

4976
Université d'Aix-Marseille. Faculté de Droit et de Science Politique. ANNALES. [v.]58– , 1972– . Paris, Presses Universitaires de France.
In French.
Continues: Université d'Aix-en-Provence. Faculté de Droit et des Sciences Économiques. *Annales*.

4977
Université de Bordeaux II. Centre d'Études et de Recherches Ethnologiques. CAHIERS. 1972– . Bordeaux. Annual.
In French.

4978
Université de Bordeaux III. Centre de Recherches sur l'Amérique Anglophone. ANNALES. n. ser. 1976– . Bordeaux. Annual.
In French.

4979
Université de la Sorbonne Nouvelle. Institut d'Études Iraniennes. TRAVAUX. 1966– . Paris, C. Klincksieck.
In French.

4980
Université de Liège. Faculté de Droit, d'Économie et des Sciences Sociales. ANNALES. 1– , 1956– . Liège. Four no. a year.
In French.
Indexed: Int. Bibl. Pol. Sc.

4981
Université de Madagascar. Faculté de Droit et des Sciences Économiques. ANNALES. SÉRIE LETTRÉS ET SCIENCES HUMAINES. 1– , 1963– . Tananarive.
In French. Title varies: 1963, *Annales Malgaches*.

4982
Université de Toulouse I. Sciences Sociales. ANNALES. 1– , 1953– . Toulouse. Annual.
In French.

4983
Université Libre de Bruxelles. Institut de Sociologie. REVUE. 1– , July 1920– . Bruxelles, Éditions de l'Université Libre de Bruxelles. Bimonthly, 1920–May 1926; quarterly (forming two volumes annually)
In French. Publication suspended Apr. 1940–1947.
Supersedes: the institute's *Bulletin*.
Indexed: Bull. Sig. Soc. Eth.; Int. Bibl. Soc.; Int. Pol. Sc. Abst.; Soc. Abst.

4984
Universitet i Bergen. Historisk Museum. ARKEOLOGISKE RAPPORTER. no.1– , 1980– . Bergen.
In Norwegian. Other title: *Arkeologiske Rapporter fra Historisk Museum.*

Universitet in Moskva
See Moskovskiĭ Universitet

University College of Nairobi
See University of Nairobi

UNIVERSITY JOURNAL: HUMANITIES AND SOCIAL SCIENCES SERIES
See NONMUNJIP INMUN SAHOE KWAHAK P'YON (Pusan)

4985
University of California, Berkeley. Archaeological Research Facility. CONTRIBUTIONS. no.1– , Sept. 1965– . Berkeley, Calif. Annual.

4986
University of Cape Town. Centre for African Studies. COMMUNICATIONS. no.1– , 1977– . Cape Town. Irreg.
Monograph series.
Supersedes: University of Cape Town. School of African Studies. *Communications* (1936–76)

4987
University of Chicago. Center for Health Administration. RESEARCH SERIES. no.1–33, 1957–1973. New York, later Chicago, Ill. Irreg.
Monograph series.

4988
University of Chicago. Department of Geography. RESEARCH PAPERS. 1– , 1948– . Chicago, Ill. Irreg.
Monograph series. Includes some doctoral dissertations.

4989
University of Florida, Gainesville. State Museum. CONTRIBUTIONS. SOCIAL SCIENCES. no.1–16, 1956–1970. Gainesville, Fla. Irreg.
Continued by: University of Florida, Gainesville. State Museum. *Contributions. Anthropology and History.*

4990
UNIVERSITY OF FLORIDA MONOGRAPHS. SOCIAL SCIENCES. no.1– , winter 1959– . Gainesville, Fla. Irreg.
Issued by: University of Florida.

4991
University of Glasgow. DISCUSSION PAPERS IN SOCIAL RESEARCH. no.1– , 1979– . Glasgow. Irreg.

4992
University of London. Institute of Commonwealth Studies. COMMONWEALTH PAPERS. no.1– , 1954– . London, Athlone Press. Irreg.
Monograph series.

4993
University of London. London School of Hygiene and Tropical Medicine. Centre for Population Studies. CPS RESEARCH PAPERS. no.1– , Apr. 1982– . London. Irreg.
Indexed: Pop. Ind.

4994
University of London. University College. Francis Galton Laboratory of Eugenics. MEMOIRS. 1–42, 1907–1966. London. Irreg.
Monograph series.

4995
THE UNIVERSITY OF MANILA JOURNAL OF EAST ASIATIC STUDIES. v.1– , Oct. 1951– . Manila. Quarterly.

4996
UNIVERSITY OF MIAMI HISPANIC-AMERICAN STUDIES. no.1–21, Nov. 1939–1965. Coral Gables, Fla., University of Miami Press. Irreg.
Continued by: *Hispanic-American Studies.*

THE UNIVERSITY OF MICHIGAN INDEX TO LABOR UNION PERIODICALS
See THE MICHIGAN INDEX TO LABOR UNION PERIODICALS

4997
UNIVERSITY OF MISSOURI STUDIES. SOCIAL SCIENCE SERIES. v.1–3, no.3, 1905–1921. Columbia, Mo. Irreg.
Issued by: University of Missouri.
Continues: *University of Missouri Studies.* Continued by: *University of Missouri Studies.*

4998
University of Pennsylvania. Museum. Applied Science Center for Archaeology. MASCA JOURNAL. v.1– , Dec. 1978– . Philadelphia, Pa. Semi-annual.

4999
University of Singapore Chinese Society. JOURNAL. no.1– , Dec. 1961– . Singapore. Annual.
In Chinese or English. Other title: *Chung wen hsüeh hui hsüeh pao.*

5000
University of Singapore Social Science Society. JOURNAL. v.1– , 1961– . Singapore. Annual.

5001
University of Sussex. Institute of Development Studies. ANNUAl REPORT. HANDBOOK. 1980– . Brighton.
Continues: its *Annual Report . . . Research Review of Quinquennium; Handbook.*

5002
University of Sussex. Institute of Development Studies. REGISTER OF RESEARCH IN THE UNITED KINGDOM. 1975/76– . Brighton. Biennial.
Continues: its *Development Studies. Register of U.K. Based Ongoing Research.*

5003
University of Sydney Economics Society. ECONOMIC REVIEW. July 1955– . Sydney. Three no. a year.

5004
University of Texas. Bureau of International Business Research. Population Research Center. INTERNATIONAL CENSUS BIBLIOGRAPHY. no.1–6, 1965–1967. Austin, Tex.
Continued by: *Supplement* listing censuses currently taken and reporting additions to the first six numbers.

5005
University of the Witwatersrand. African Studies Institute. A.S.I. COMMUNICATIONS. no.1– , 1974– . Johannesburg. Irreg.

5006
University of Toronto. Institute for Quantitative Analysis of Social and Economic Policy. ANNUAL REPORT. 1– , 1976– . Toronto.
Supersedes: its *Newsletter.*

5007
University of Washington, Seattle. PUBLICATIONS IN THE SOCIAL SCIENCES. v.1–13, 1924–1942. Seattle, Wash. Irreg.
Monograph series.

UNIVERSITY OF WASHINGTON STUDIES ON ASIA
See PUBLICATIONS ON ASIA

5008
University of Wisconsin. ECONOMICS AND POLITICAL SERIES. v.1–9, no.3, 1904–1918. Madison, Wis. Irreg.
Monograph series.

5009
University of Yaoundé. Faculté des Lettres et Sciences Humaines. ANNALES. v.2 (no.52)– , 1975– . Yaoundé.
In French.
Continues: Université Fédéral de Cameroun. Faculté des Lettres et Sciences Humaines. *Annales.*

5010
University of Zambia. Institute for Social Research. BULLETIN. 1– , 1966– . Lusaka. Annual.
Supersedes: Rhodes–Livingstone Institute. *Proceedings* (1958–63).

5011
University of Zambia. Institute of African Research. COMMUNICATION. no.7– , 1971– . Lusaka. Irreg.
Continues: University of Zambia. Institute for Social Research. *Communication* (no.1–6, 1966–70).

5012
University of Zimbabwe. Department of Sociology. SERIES IN SOCIAL STUDIES. OCCASIONAL PAPER. no.1– , 1974– . Harare.
Supersedes: its *Occasional Paper.*

UNIVERSITY RESEARCH ON EUROPEAN INTEGRATION. English Edition
See ÉTUDES UNIVERSITAIRES SUR L'INTÉGRATION EUROPÉENNE

5013
Univerzita Komenského. Ustav Marxizmu-Leninizmu. VĚDECKÝ KOMUNIZMUS. 1– , 1978– . Bratislava, Slovenske Pedagogické Nakladatel'stvo. Annual.
In German, Russian, or Slovak; summaries in the other languages. Subseries of: *Zbornik Ústavu Marxizmu-Leninizmu Univerzity Komenského.*

Uniwersytet Łódzki. ZESZYTY NAUKOWE. SERIA 1. NAUKI HUMANISTYCZNO-SPOŁECZNE
See NAUKI HUMANISTYCZNO-SPOŁECZNE

5014
DIE UNTERNEHMUNG. v.1– , Mar. 1947– . Bern, Verlag P. Haupt. Quarterly, 1947–49; bimonthly.
Issued by: Vereinigung Schweizerischer Betriebswirtschafter. In German.
Indexed: PAISFL.

5015
UPPSALA STUDIES IN EDUCATION. 1– , 1976– . Stockholm. Distributed by Almqvist & Wiksell. Irreg.

Issued by: Pedagogiska Institutionen, Uppsala Universitet. In English or Swedish; summaries in English. Subseries of: *Acta Universitatis Uppsaliensis*. Monograph series.
Supersedes: *Studia Scientiae Paedagogicae Uppsaliensia*.

5016
URBAN ABSTRACTS. no.1– , Apr. 1974– . London. Monthly.
Issued by: Greater London Council.
Supersedes: *Planning & Transportation Abstracts*.

5017
URBAN AFFAIRS ABSTRACTS. [1]– , Aug./Dec. 1971– . Washington, D.C. Weekly, with quarterly and annual cumulations.
Issued by: National League of Cities, and the United States Conference of Mayors. Issues for 1971 are not numbered but constitute vol. 1.

5018
URBAN AFFAIRS ANNUAL REVIEW. v.1– , 1967– . Beverly Hills, Calif., Sage Publications. Annual.
Issued by: Department of Urban Affairs, University of Wisconsin at Milwaukee. Each volume has also a distinctive title.
Indexed: Bull. Anal. Pol. Ec. Soc.; Int. Bibl. Eco.

5019
URBAN AFFAIRS PLANNING THOUGHT. v.1– , Apr. 1958– . New Delhi.
Issued by: Institute of Town Planners.

5020
URBAN AFFAIRS QUARTERLY. v.1– , Sept. 1961– . Ann Arbor, Mich., later Beverly Hills, Calif., Sage Publications. Quarterly.
Indexed: ABC POL SCI; Bull. Anal. Pol. Ec. Soc.; Curr. Cont. Soc. Beh. Sc.; Hum. Res. Abst.; Ind. Per. Art. Law; Int. Bibl. Eco.; Int. Bibl. Pol. Sc.; Int. Bibl. Soc.; Int. Pol. Sc. Abst.; PAIS; Sage Pub. Adm. Abst.; Sage Urb. Stu. Abst.; SSCI; Urb. Aff. Abst.

5021
URBAN AND RURAL PLANNING THOUGHT. v.1–21, 1958–1978. Delhi. Quarterly.
Issued by: School of Town and Country Planning. Title varies: *Journal of Urban and Rural Planning Thought*.
Superseded by: *SPA Journal of School of Planning and Architecture* (v.1–, 1979–).

5022
THE URBAN AND SOCIAL CHANGE REVIEW. v.1– , 1967– . Chestnut Hill, Mass. Semi-annual.
Issued by: Institute of Human Sciences, Boston College. Title varies: 1967–68, *Institute of Human Sciences Review*.
Indexed: ABC POL SCI; Abst. Soc. Work.; Bull. Anal. Pol. Eco. Soc.; Eco. Abst.; His. Abst.; Int. Pol. Sc. Abst.; LLBA; Soc. Abst.; SSCI.

5023
URBAN ANTHROPOLOGY. v.1– , spring 1972– . Brockport, N.Y., Plenum Pub. Co. Two no. a year, 1972–74; quarterly.
Issued by: Institute for the Study of Man. Absorbed: *Urban Anthropology Newsletter*.
Indexes: Vols. 1–10, 1971–81, in v.10, no.4. Tables of contents of v.1–10, in v.10, pp. 385–416.
Indexed: Abst. Anth.; Curr. Cont. Soc. Beh. Sc.; Int. Bibl. Soc. Cul. Anth.; PHRA; Soc. Abst.; Sage Urb. Stu. Abst.; SSCI.

5024
URBAN ECOLOGY. v.1– , June 1975– . Amsterdam, Elsevier Scientific Pub. Co. Quarterly.
Sponsored by: International Association for Ecology.

5025
URBAN EDUCATION. v.1– , summer 1964– . Buffalo, N.Y.; beginning with v.4, Beverly Hills, Calif., Sage Publications. Quarterly.
Indexed: Curr. Cont. Soc. Beh. Sc.; PAIS; Sage Pub. Adm. Abst.; Sage Urb. Stu. Abst.; SSCI.

5026
URBAN GEOGRAPHY. v.1– , Jan./Mar. 1980– . Silver Spring, Md., V.H. Vinston. Quarterly.
Indexed: Int. Bibl. Eco.

5027
URBAN HISTORY REVIEW. REVUE D'HISTOIRE URBAINE. no.1– , Feb. 1972– . Ottawa. Three no. a year.
Issued by: History Division, National Museum of Man.
Indexed: Sage Urb. Stu. Abst.

5028
URBAN HISTORY YEARBOOK. 1974– . Leicester, Leicester University Press.

5029
URBAN INDIA. v.1– , Sept. 1981– . New Delhi. Quarterly.
Issued by: National Institute of Urban Affairs.

5030
The Urban Institute. POLICY AND RESEARCH REPORT. v.9– , fall 1979– . Washington, D.C. Quarterly.

Continues: *Search*.
Indexed: Sage Urb. Stu. Abst.

5031
URBAN LIFE. v.1– , Apr. 1972– . Beverly Hills, Calif., Sage Publications. Quarterly.
Title varies: v.1–3, 1972–Jan. 1975, *Urban Life and Culture*. Subtitle reads: "A journal of bibliographic research".
Indexed: Abst. Anth.; Curr. Cont. Soc. Beh. Sc.; Int. Bibl. Soc. Cul. Anth.; PAIS; PHRA; Sage Urb. Stu. Abst.; Soc. Abst.; SSCI; Urb. Aff. Abst.

URBAN LIFE AND CULTURE
See URBAN LIFE

5032
URBAN STUDIES. v.1– , May 1964– . Edinburgh, Longman Group. Journals Department. Semi-annual, 1964–70; three no. a year.
Issued by: Centre for Urban and Regional Research, and Glasgow University.
Indexed: Bull. Anal. Pol. Ec. Soc.; Curr. Cont. Soc. Beh. Sc.; His. Abst.; Ind. Per. Art. Law; Int. Bibl. Eco.; Int. Bibl. Soc.; Int. Pol. Sc. Abst.; J. Eco. Lit.; PAIS; PHRA; Sage Urb. Stu. Abst.; Soc. Abst.; SSCI.

5033
URBAN STUDIES YEARBOOK. 1– , 1983– . Sydney, Allen & Unwin. Annual.

5034
URBANISM PAST & PRESENT. no.1– , winter 1975/76– . Milwaukee, Wis. Semi-annual.
Issued by: College of Letters and Science, University of Wisconsin—Milwaukee.
Supersedes: Urban History Group. *Newsletter*.
Indexed: Sage Urb. Stu. Abst.

5035
URBANISTICA. v.1– , 1932– . Torino, Edizioni Urbanistica. Quarterly.
Official organ of: Istituto Nazionale d'Urbanistica. In Italian.
Indexed: Bull. Anal. Pol. Ec. Soc.

5036
L'U.R.S.S. ET LES PAYS DE L'EST. REVUE DE REVUES. v.[1]–9, no.5, May 1960–1968. Paris, Centre National de la Recherche Scientifique. Quarterly.
Issued by: Centre de Recherches sur L'U.R.S.S. et les Pays de l'Est, Université de Strasbourg. In French.

5037
URUGUAYO ECONÓMICO. v.1– , Oct. 1979– . Montevideo.
Issued by: Asesoria Económico-Finanziera, Ministerio de Economía y Finanzas. In Spanish.

5038
U.S.S.R. AND THIRD WORLD. v.1– , Dec. 7, 1970/Jan. 10, 1971– . London. Eight no. a year.
Issued by: Central Asian Research Centre. Subtitle reads: "A Survey of Soviet and Chinese relations with Africa, Asia and Latin America".

5039
UTAFITI. 1– , 1976– . Nairobi, East African Literature Bureau. Semi-annual.
Issued by: Faculty of Arts and Social Sciences, University of Dar es Salaam.
Indexed: Int. Bibl. Eco.

V POMOSHCHI POLITICHESKOMU OBRAZOVANIIU
See POLITICHESKOE SAMOOBRAZOVANIE

5040
VAESTONTUTKIMUKSEN VUOKSIKIRJA. YEARBOOK OF POPULATION RESEARCH IN FINLAND. 6th ed.– , 1960– . Helsinki. Vaestontutki Muslaitos.
In English. Continues: *Vaestoluton Vuoksirja.*

5041
VANDERBILT JOURNAL OF TRANSNATIONAL LAW. v.5– , winter 1971– . Nashville, Tenn. Semi-annual.
Issued by: School of Law, Vanderbilt University.
Continues: *The Vanderbilt International* (v.1–4, 1967–70).
Indexed: Ind. For. Leg. Per.; Ind. Leg. Per.; PAIS.

VĚDECKÝ KOMUNIZMUS
See Univerzita Komenského. Ústav Marxizmu-Leninizmu. VĚDECKÝ KOMUNIZMUS

5042
VERFASSUNG UND RECHT IN ÜBERSEE. v.1– , 1968– . Hamburg. Quarterly.
Issued by: Forschungsstelle für Völkerrecht der Universität Hamburg, and Hamburger Gesellschaft für Volkerrecht und Auswärtige Politik. Published jointly by: Institut für Internationale Angelegenheiten der Universität Hamburg, and Hamburger Gesellschaft für Völkerrecht und Auswärtige Politik. In German.
Indexed: Bull. Anal. Pol. Ec. Soc.; Int. Bibl. Eco.; Int. Bibl. Pol. Sc.; Ind. For. Leg. Per.; Int. Pol. Sc. Abst.; PAISFL.

5043
VERGLEICHENDE PEDAGOGIK. COMPARATIVE EDUCATION. v.1– , 1965– . Berlin. Quarterly.
Issued by: Deutsches Pedagogisches Zentralinstitut, Akademie der Pedagogischen Wissenschaften der Deutschen Demokratischen Republik. In German; summaries in English, French and Russian.
Supersedes a monograph series with the same title.

VERHANDELINGEN
See Académie Royale des Sciences d'Outre-Mer. Classe des Sciences Morales et Politiques. MEMOIRES

VERHANDELINGEN
See Académie Royale des Sciences d'Outre-mer. Classe des Sciences Morales et Politiques. MÉMOIRES. VERHANDELINGEN. IN 4°

VERHANDELINGEN
See Académie Royale des Sciences d'Outre-mer. Classes des Sciences Morales et Politiques. MÉMOIRES. VERHANDELINGEN. IN 8°

VERHANDLUNGEN
See International Congress of Americanists. PROCEEDINGS

5044
VERITAS. v.1– , Jan. 15, 1931– . Buenos Aires. Monthly.
In Spanish. Title varies: v.1–34, 1931–64, *Veritas Argentina.*
Indexed: Bull. Anal. Pol. Ec. Soc.

VERÖFFENTLICHUNGEN
See Akademie der Wissenschaften, Berlin. Institut für Deutsche Volkskunde. VERÖFFENTLICHUNGEN

VERÖFFENTLICHUNGEN
See Akademie der Wissenschaften, Wien. Ethnologische Kommission. VERÖFFENTLICHUNGEN

VERÖFFENTLICHUNGEN
See Akademie der Wissenschaften, Wien. Kommission für Wirtschafts-, Sozial- und Stadtgeschichte. VERÖFFENTLICHUNGEN

VERÖFFENTLICHUNGEN
See Akademie der Wissenschaften der DDR. Zentralinstitut für Alte Geschichte und Archäologie. VERÖFFENTLICHUNGEN

VERÖFFENTLICHUNGEN DER KOMMISSION FÜR SOZIAL- UND WIRTSCHAFTSWISSENSCHAFTEN
See Akademie der Wissenschaften. Philosophisch-Historische Klasse. Kommission für Sozial- und Wirtschaftswissenschaften. VERÖFFENTLICHUNGEN

VERÖFFENTLICHUNGEN DES INSTITUTS FÜR INTERNATIONALES RECHT, UNIVERSITÄT KIEL
See ABHANDLUNGEN ZUR FORTSCHREITENDEN KODIFIKATION DES INTERNATIONALES RECHT

5045
DIE VERWALTUNG. v.1– , spring 1968– . Berlin, Duncker & Humblot. Quarterly.
In German.

Indexed: ABC POL SCI; Bull. Anal. Pol. Ec. Soc.; Bull. Sig. Soc. Eth.; Int. Bibl. Eco.; Int. Bibl. Pol. Sc.; Int. Bibl. Soc.; Int. Bibl. Soc. Cul. Anth.; Int. Pol. Sc. Abst.; PAISFL.

VERZAMELING
See Académie Royale des Sciences. Classe des Sciences Morales et Politiques. MEMOIRES VERHANDELINGEN. IN 8°

5046
VESTNIK ARKHEOLOGII I ISTORII. 1–23, 1885–1918. Petrograd.
Issued by: Arkheologicheskiĭ Institut. In Russian. Absorbed: *Sbornik Arkheologicheskogo Instituta* in 1885; the latter was revived as a separate publication in 1898.

5047
VESTNIK DREVNEĬ ISTORII. JOURNAL OF ANCIENT HISTORY. 1– , 1937– . Moskva, Izd-vo Nauka. Quarterly.
Issued by: Institut Vseobshcheĭ Istorii, Akademii͡a Nauk S.S.S.R. (no.1–106 by Institut Istorii). In Russian; summaries in English begin with no.99. No.1–20, 83–90 have also title in French: *Revue d'Histoire Ancienne*. No.21–82 lack English title.
Indexes: no.1–34, 1v.; no.35–54, in no.58; no.55–74, in no.75.

VESTNIK MOSKOVSKOGO UNIVERSITETA. SERII͡A XIII. TEORII͡A NAUCHNOGO KOMMUNIZMA
See Moskovskiĭ Universitet. VESTNIK. SERII͡A XII. TEORII͡A NAUCHNOGO KOMMUNIZMA

VESTNIK. SERII͡A XIII. TEORII͡A NAUCHNOGO KOMMUNIZMA
See Moskovskiĭ Universitet. VESTNIK. SERII͡A XII. TEORII͡A NAUCHNOGO KOMMUNIZMA

VESTNIK MOSKOVSKOGO UNIVERSITETA. SERII͡A ISTORII͡A
See Moskovskiĭ Universitet. VESTNIK. SERII͡A ISTORII͡A

VESTNIK OBSHCHESTVENNYKH NAUK
See Akademii͡a Nauk Armi͡anskoĭ S.S.R. VESTNIK OBSHCHESTVENNYKH NAUK

5048
VESTNIK STATISTIKI. 1– , 1949– . Moskva, Izd-vo Statistika. Monthly.
Issued by: T͡Sentralnoe Statisticheskoe Upravlenie Soveta Ministrov S.S.S.R. In Russian.
Indexed: Bull. Anal. Pol. Ec. Soc.; Pop. Ind.

5049
VESTNIK VYSSHEĬ SHKOLY. v.1– , Apr. 1940– . Moskva. Monthly.
Issued by: Vsesoi͡uznyĭ Komitet po Delam Vyssheĭ Shkoly; later by Ministerstvo Vysshego Obrazovanii͡a; in recent years, Ministerstvo Vysshego i Srednego Spet͡sial'nogo Obrazovanii͡a SSSR. In Russian.

VESTSI AKADEMIĬ NAVUK BELARUSKOI SSR
See Akademii͡a Navuk Beloruskoi SSR. VESTSI AKADEMIĬ NAVUK BELARUSKOI SSR

VESTSI AKADEMIĬ NAVUK BSSR. SERYIA HRAMADSKIKH NAVUK
See Akademii͡a Navuk Belaruskoi SSR. VESTSI SERYIA HRAMADSKIKH NAVUK

VESTURES PROBLEMAS
See Latvijas Padomju Socialistickas Republikas Zinatnu Akademija. Vestures Instituts. VESTURES PROBLEMAS

5050
VIE ÉCONOMIQUE ET SOCIALE. 1924–1961. Antwerp. Five no. a year.
Issued by: École Supérieur de Commerce St. Ignace. In French. Title varies: 1–11, 1924–Nov. 1933, École Supérieur de Commerce St. Ignace. *Bulletin d'Études et d'Informations*; v.10, no.12–v.11, no.7/8, Dec. 1933–July/Aug. 1934 as the Institut Supérieur de Commerce St. Ignace's *Bulletin d'Études et d'Informations*.

LA VIE ÉCONOMIQUE ET SOCIALE
See ECONOMISCH- EN SOCIAAL TIJDSCHRIFT

5051
VIE SOCIALE. no.1– , Jan. 1964– . Paris, CEDIAS. Monthly (except Aug./Sept.). Some combined numbers.
Issued by: Centre d'Études des Documentation, d'Information et d'Action Sociales (CEDIAS). Office Central des Oeuvres de Bienfaisance. in French.
Supersedes: *Cahiers du Musée Social*, Paris.
Indexed: Bull. Anal. Pol. Ec. Soc.; Bull. Sig. Soc. Eth.; Int. Bibl. Soc. Cul. Anth.; Int. Lab. Doc.

5052
VIE URBAINE. v.1–16, Mar. 1919–Sept./Dec. 1939; n. ser. no.55– , Jan./Mar. 1950– . Paris. Quarterly.
Issued by: Institut d'Urbanisme, Université de Paris Val-de-Marne. In French; summaries in English and French. Supplement titled *Quinzaine Urbaine* accompanies some numbers beginning with Jan. 1921. Not published 1924–25, 1931, 1940–Dec. 1949. Vol. 1–7, 1919–28 also as no.1–35; v.8–16, Jan. 1930–39 also as no.1–59.

Indexed: Bull. Anal. Pol. Ec. Soc.; Bull. Sig. Soc. Eth.; Int. Bibl. Soc. Cul. Anth.

5053
VIERTELJAHRESHEFTE FÜR ZEITGESCHICHTE. 1– , Jan. 1953– . Stuttgart, Deutsche Verlags-Anstalt. Quarterly.
Issued by: Institut für Zeitgeschichte, München. In German. Includes a section "Bibliographie zur Zeitgeschichte" in each number.
Indexed: PAISFL.

5054
VIERTELJAHRESHEFTE ZUR WIRTSCHAFTSFORSCHUNG. v.1– , 1926– . Berlin, Duncker & Humblot. Quarterly.
Issued by: Institut für Konjunkturforschung, later by Deutsches Institut für Wirtschaftsforschung. In German. Includes supplement "Erganzungsheft".
Indexed: Bull. Anal. Pol. Ec. Soc.; Int. Bibl. Eco.

VIERTELJAHRSCHRIFT FÜR SOCIAL- UND WIRTSCHAFTSGESCHICHTE
See VIERTELJAHRSCHRIFT FÜR SOZIAL- UND WIRTSCHAFTSGESCHICHTE

5055
VIERTELJAHRSCHRIFT FÜR SOZIAL- UND WIRTSCHAFTSGESCHICHTE. v.1– , 1903– . Leipzig, Stuttgart, Wiesbaden, F. Steiner Verlag.
In German. Title varies: v.1–8, no.1/2, 1901–11, *Vierteljahrschrift für Social- und Wirtschaftsgeschichte*. Includes supplement "Bibliographie der Sozial- und Wirtschaftsgeschichte" and "Beihefte" (or "Beiheft"). Not published, 1945–48.
Supersedes: *Zeitschrift für Social- und Wirtschaftsgeschichte*.
Indexes: Vols. 1–20, 1903–28, in v.20.
Indexed: His. Abst.; PAIS; Peace Res. Abst. J.; Pop. Ind.

VIERTELJAHRESSCHRIFT FÜR VERGLEICHENDE RECHTS- UND STAATSWISSENSCHAFT
See ZEITSCHRIFT FÜR VERGLEICHENDE RECHTS- UND STAATSWISSENSCHAFT MIT BESONDERER BERÜCKSICHTIGUNG DER RECHTE DER NATUR- UND KULTURVÖLKER

5056
VIERTELJAHRESSCHRIFT FÜR VOLKSWIRTSCHAFT, POLITIK UND KULTURGESCHICHTE. (Jahr. 1–30), v.1–120, 1863–1893. Berlin.
In German. Title varies: 1863–75, *Vierteljahresschrift für Volkswirtschaft und Kulturgeschichte*.
Superseded by: *Zeitschrift für Literatur und Geschichte der Staats-Wissenschaften*, later called *Vierteljahresschrift für Staats- und Volkswirtschaft für Literatur und Geschichte der aller Länder*.

VIERTELJAHRESSCHRIFT FÜR VOLKSWIRTSCHAFT UND KULTURGESCHICHTE
See VIERTELJAHRESSCHRIFT FÜR VOLKSWIRTSCHAFT, POLITIK UND KULTURGESCHICHTE

5057
VIERTELJAHRESSCHRIFT FÜR WISSENSCHAFTLICHE PHILOSOPHIE UND SOZIOLOGIE. v.26–49, 1902–1916. Leipzig. Quarterly.
In German.
Continues: *Vierteljahresschrift für Wissenschaftliche Philosophie* (1877–1901).
Indexes: v.1–30, 1877–1906, 1v.

5058
VIITORUL SOCIAL; REVISTA DE SOCIOLOGIE ŞI ŞTIINŢE POLITICE. v.1– , 1972– . Bucureşti, Editura Académiei Republicii Socialiste România. Quarterly.
Issued by: Comitetul National de Sociologie, Academia de Ştiinţe Sociale şi Politice and Asociatia Romana de Ştiinţe Politice. In Romanian.
Indexed: Bull. Anal. Pol. Ec. Soc.; Int. Bibl. Soc.; Int. Pol. Sc. Abst.; LLBA; Soc. Abst.

5059
VIRGINIA JOURNAL OF INTERNATIONAL LAW. v.3– , 1963– . Charlottesville, Va. Semi-annual; three no. a year, 1970/71–1971/72; quarterly.
Issued by: John Basset Moore Society of International Law.
Continues: *Journal* issued by the same society.
Indexes: (Author–title) vols. 1–4, 1960–64, in v.4; (subject) v.1–6, 1960–66, in v.6; v.11–13, 1970–73, in v.13.
Indexed: Ind. For. Leg. Per.; Ind. Leg. Per.

VITA HUMANA
See HUMAN DEVELOPMENT

VLAAMS OPVOEKUNDING TIJDSCHRIFT
See TIJDSCHRIFT VOOR OPVOEKUNDE

5060
VOLKSKUNDE; TIJDSCHRIFT VOOR NEDERLANDSCH FOLKLORE. 1– , 1888– . Ghent. Monthly, 1888–1938; quarterly, 1940/41– .
In Dutch. Not published in 1939.
Indexes: 1888–1914, 1v.; 1888–1938; 1936–60.
Indexed: Int. Bibl. Soc. Cul. Anth.

5061
VOPROSY ANTROPOLOGII; NAUCHNYE STATI I MATERIALI. no.1– , 1960– . Moskva, Izd-vo Moskovskogo Universiteta.

Issued by: Moskovskiĭ Gosudarstvennyĭ Universitet. Tables of contents also in English.
Supersedes: *Sovetskaia Antropologiia* (1957–59)
Indexed: Bull. Sig. Soc. Eth.

5062
VOPROSY EKONOMICHESKOĬ I POLITICHESKOĬ GEOGRAFII ZARUBEZHNYKH STRAN. [1]– , 1971– . Moskva. Irreg.
Issued by: Institut Latinskoĭ Ameriki, Akademiia Nauk S.S.S.R., and Geograficheskiĭ Fakul'tet, Moskovskiĭ Universitet. In Russian.

5063
VOPROSY EKONOMIKI. 1– , Mar. 1948– . Moskva, Pravda. Monthly.
Issued by: Akademiia Nauk SSSR. Institut Ekonomiki. In Russian.
Indexed: Bull. Anal. Pol. Ec. Soc.; Int. Bibl. Eco.; Pop. Ind.

5064
VOPROSY FILOSOFII. 1– , 1947– . Moskva, Pravda. Monthly.
Issued by: Institut Filosofii, Akademiia Nauk S.S.S.R. In Russian; summaries in English.
Indexed: Bull. Anal. Pol. Ec. Soc.; His. Abst.; Int. Bibl. Eco.; Int. Bibl. Pol. Sc.; Int. Pol. Sc. Abst.; Psych. Abst.

5065
VOPROSY FILOSOFII I SOTSIOLOGII. no.1– , 1969– . Leningrad, Izd-vo Leningradskogo Universiteta. Annual.
In Russian.

5066
VOPROSY ISTORII. v.1– , July 1945– . Moskva, Pravda. Monthly.
Issued by: Institut Istorii, Akademiia Nauk S.S.S.R. In Russian.
Supersedes: *Istoricheskiĭ Zhurnal.*
Indexed: His. Abst.; Int. Bibl. Eco.; Int. Bibl. Pol. Sc.

VOPROSY ISTORII ESTONSKOĬ SSR
See EESTI NSV AJOLOO KUSIMUSI

5067
VOPROSY ISTORII K.P.S.S. 1– , 1957– . Moskva, Pravda. Monthly.
Issued by: Institut Marksizma-Leninizma pri TSentral'nom Komitete Kommunisticheskoĭ Partii Sovetskogo Soiuza. In Russian. Tables of contents also in Chinese and English.
Indexed: Bull. Anal. Pol. Ec. Soc.

5068
VOPROSY OBSHCHESTVENNYKH NAUK. no.1– , 1970– . Kiev, Izd-vo Kievskogo Universiteta.
In Russian.

5069
VOPROSY PSIKOLOGII. 1– , 1955– . Moskva, Izd-vo Proshveshcheniia. Bimonthly.
Issued by: Akademiia Pedagogicheskikh Nauk RSFSR. In Russian; summaries in English.

5070
VOPROSY SOTSIOLOGII I OBSHCHESTVENNOĬ PSIKHOLOGII. 1– , 1970– . Moskva.
Issued by: Moskovskiĭ Universitet. In Russian.

5071
VOPROSY TEORII GOSUDARSTVA I PRAVA. v.1– , 1968– . Saratov.
Issued by: Saratovskiĭ IUridicheskiĭ Institut. In Russian.

5072
VOPROSY TEORII I METODOV SOTSIOLOGICHESKIKH ISSLEDOVANIĬ. 1– , 1964– . Moskva, Izd-vo Moskovskogo Universiteta. Irreg.
Issued by: Kafedra Metodiki Konkretnykh Sotsialnykh Issledovaniĭ, Moskovskiĭ Gosudarstvennyĭ Universitet.

VUOKSIKIRJA
See Taloustieteellinen Seura. VUOKSIKIRJA

WSI MITTEILUNGEN
See Wirtschafts- und Sozialwissenschaftliches Institut des Deutschen Gewerkschaftsbundes. WSI MITTEILUNGEN

WSR WESTERN SOCIOLOGICAL REVIEW
See WESTERN SOCIOLOGICAL REVIEW

WWI MITTEILUNGEN
See Wirtschaftswissenschaftliches Institut für Gewerkschaften. WWI MITTEILUNGEN

THE WAKAYAMA ECONOMIC REVIEW
See KEIZAI RIRON

WAR AND PEACE
See INTERNATIONAL REVIEW

WITTHAYSAN KASSERTAT
See KASSERTAT JOURNAL

5073
WAR & SOCIETY. v.1– , May 1983– . New York, Holmes & Meier Pub., Duntroon, W. Australia. Annual.
Issued by: Department of History, University of New South Wales.
Indexed: His. Abst.

5074
WARASAN SANGKHOMSAT. 2504[i.e. 1961]– . Bangkok, Khana Ratthasat, Chulalonggkon Mahawitthayalai. Three no. a year.
Text chiefly in Thai. Other title: *Journal of Social Science*.

5075
WARTA DEMOGRAFI. 1– , 1960– . Jakarta, Pusat. Quarterly.
Issued by: Lembaga Demografi, Fakultas Economi, Universitas Indonesia. Chiefly in Indonesian; some articles in English.

5076
WASEDA ECONOMIC PAPERS. 1– , 1955– . Tokyo. Annual (irreg.)
Issued by: Graduate Division of Economics, Waseda University. In Japanese; some articles in English.

5077
WASEDA JOURNAL OF ASIAN STUDIES. v.1– , 1979– . Tokyo. Annual.
Issued by: International Division, Waseda University.

THE WASEDA JOURNAL OF THE SOCIAL SCIENCES
See WASEDA SHAKAI KAGAKU KENKYŪ

5078
WASEDA POLITICAL STUDIES. no.1– , 1957– . Tokyo. Annual (irreg.).
Issued by: Graduate Division of Political Science, Waseda University. In Japanese.
Indexed: Bull. Anal. Pol. Ec. Soc.; Int. Pol. Sc. Abst.

5079
WASEDA SEIJI KEIZAIGAKU ZASSHI. 1– , 1925– . Tokyo. Bimonthly.
Issued by: Seiji Keizai Gakkai, Waseda Daigaku. In Japanese.
Indexed: Int. Bibl. Soc. Cul. Anth.

5080
WASEDA SHAKAI KAGAKU KENKYŪ. 1– , 1967– . Tokyo.
Issued by: Shakai Kagakubu Gakkai, Waseda Daigaku. In Japanese. Other title: *The Waseda Journal of the Social Sciences*.

5081
Washington Center of Foreign Policy Research. STUDIES IN INTERNATIONAL AFFAIRS. no.1– , 1967– . Baltimore, Md., Johns Hopkins University Press. Irreg.
Monograph series.

5082
THE WASHINGTON MONTHLY. Feb. 1969– . Washington, D.C.
Indexed: ABC POL SCI; Bull. Anal. Pol. Ec. Soc.; Hum. Res. Abst.; Ind. Per. Art. Law.; PAIS; PHRA; Int. Pol. Sc. Abst.; Sage Pub. Adm. Abst.; Wom. Stu. Abst.

5083
THE WASHINGTON QUARTERLY. v.1, no.4– , autumn 1978– . Washington, D.C.
Issued by: Center for Strategic and International Studies, Georgetown University.
Continues: *Washington Review of Strategic and International Studies* (v.1, no.1–3, 1978)
Indexed: ABC POL SCI; Int. Bibl. Pol. Sc.; Int. Pol. Sc. Abst.; PAIS; SSCI.

5084
WASSAJA. THE INDIAN HISTORIAN. v.13– , Mar. 1980– . San Francisco, Calif. Semi-annual.

Issued by: American Indian Historical Society.
Continues: *Indian Historian.*
Indexed: SSCI.

5085
WELSH HISTORY REVIEW. CYLCHGRAWN HANES CYMBRU. v.1– , 1960– . Cardiff, University of Wales Press. Annual.
Issued by: 1960–61, on behalf of the History and Law Committee of the Board of Celtic Studies, University of Wales.

5086
WELSH SOCIAL TRENDS. no.1– , 1977– . Cardiff. Annual.
Issued by: Welsh Office. Title in Welsh: *Tuediadau Cymdeithasal.*

5087
DIE WELT DES ISLAMS. THE WORLD OF ISLAM. LE MONDE DE ISLAM. v.1–25, no.1/3, 1913–1943; n. ser., v.1– , 1951– . Leiden, E.J. Brill. Irreg. (up to four no. a year)
In Arabic, English, French, or German. Published in Berlin, 1913–43. Publication suspended: 1920–22, 1944–50.
Indexes: Vols. 1–17, 1913–36, in v.18.

WELTBIBLIOGRAPHIE DER SOZIALEN SICHERKEIT
See BIBLIOGRAPHIE UNIVERSELLE DE SÉCURITÉ SOCIALE

5088
WELTWIRTSCHAFT. no.1– , 1950– . Tübingen, J.C.B. Mohr. Semi-annual.
Issued by: Institut für Weltwirtschaft (called 1921–33, Institut für Weltwirtschaft und Seeverkeher), Universität Kiel. In German or English.
Indexed: Bull. Anal. Pol. Ec. Soc.; PAISFL.

5089
WELTWIRTSCHAFTLICHES ARCHIV. v.1– , Jan. 1913– . Tübingen, J.C.B. Mohr. Quarterly.
Issued by: Institut für Weltwirtschaft, Universität Kiel. In English or German; summaries in English, French, German, Italian, or Spanish. Other title: *Review of World Economics.*
Indexed: Eco. Abst.; J. Eco. Lit.; PAIS; Bull. Anal. Pol. Ec. Soc.; Int. Bibl. Eco.; Pop. Ind.

5090
WEST AFRICAN ECONOMIC JOURNAL. v.1– , Mar. 1980– . Ibadan, Heinemann Educational Books. Biennial.
Issued by: West African Economic Association. In English or French.

5091
WEST AFRICAN JOURNAL OF ARCHAEOLOGY. v.1– , 1971– . Ibadan, Ibadan University Press. Annual.
Issued by: West African Archaeological Association. Sponsored by a few West African universities, the National Museum of Ghana, and some government departments. In English or French. Other title: *Revue Ouest-Africaine d'Archéologie.*
Supersedes: *West African Archaeological Newsletter* (Dec. 1964–1969)

5092
WEST AFRICAN JOURNAL OF EDUCATION. 1– , 1957– . Ibadan. Quarterly.
Issued by: Institute of Economics, University of Ibadan.

5093
WEST AFRICAN JOURNAL OF SOCIOLOGY AND POLITICAL SCIENCE. v.1– , Oct. 1975– . Exeter. Quarterly (irreg.)
Issued by: Department of Politics, University of Exeter.
Indexed: Bull. Anal. Pol. Ec. Soc.

5094
WEST EUROPEAN POLITICS. 1– , Feb. 1978– . London, F. Cass. Three no. a year.
Indexed: ABC POL SCI; Int. Bibl. Eco.; Int. Pol. Sc. Abst.; LLBA; PAIS.

5095
THE WEST INDIES YEARBOOK. 1926/27–1976/77. London. Annual.
Title varies: 1926/27–1935, *Anuario Comercial de las Antillas y Países de Caribe. The Yearbook of the Bermudas, The Bahamas, British Guiana, British Honduras and the British West Indies*; 1936–48, *The West Indies Yearbook*; 1948/49–1952, *The Year Book of the West Indies and the Countries of the Caribbean.* Published in Montreal in 1939–1941/42.
Continued by: *The Caribbean Year Book.*

5096
WEST–OST-JOURNAL. no.1– , Oct. 1968– . Wien, Jupiter Verlagsgesellschaft. Six no. a year.
Issued by: Donaueuropäisches Institut. In German. Subtitle reads: "Unabhängige wirtschaftspolitische Zeitschrift".

5097
Westermarck Society. TRANSACTIONS. v.1– , 1947– . Copenhagen, Munkshaard, subsequently Helsinki.
Indexed: Soc. Abst.

5098
WESTERN CANADIAN JOURNAL OF ANTHROPOLOGY. v.1– , 1969– . Edmonton. Three or four no. a year.
Issued by: Anthropology Club, University of Alberta.
Supersedes: *Alberta Anthropologist.*
Indexed: Abst. Anth.

5099
WESTERN EUROPEAN EDUCATION. v.1– , spring 1969– . Armonk, N.Y., M.E. Sharpe. Quarterly.
Issues are thematic. Translations.

5100
THE WESTERN POLITICAL QUARTERLY. v.1– , 1948– . Salt Lake City, Utah. Quarterly.
Issued by: Institute of Government, University of Utah. Official journal of: Western Political Science Association, The Pacific Northwest Political Science Association, Southern California Political Science Association, and Northern California Political Science Association.
Indexed: ABC POL SCI; Bull. Anal. Pol. Ec. Soc.; Bull. Sig. Soc. Eth.; Curr. Cont. Soc. Beh. Sc.; His. Abst.; Ind. Per. Art. Law; Int. Bibl. Eco.; Int. Bibl. Pol. Sc.; Int. Pol. Sc. Abst.; PAIS; Peace Res. Abst. J.; Sage Pub. Adm. Abst.; Soc. Sc. Ind.; Sage Urb. Stu. Abst.; SSCI; Wom. Stu. Abst.

5101
WESTERN SOCIOLOGICAL REVIEW. v.5– , 1974– . Logan, Utah. Annual.
Issued by: Department of Sociology, Utah State University. Co-sponsored by: Utah Sociological Society. Title on cover: *WSR Western Sociological Review.*
Continues: *Utah State University Journal of Sociology.*

5102
WIADOMOŚCI ARCHEOLOGICZNE. v.1– , 1873– . Warszawa, Państwowe Wydawnictwo Naukowe. Quarterly.
Issued by: Państwowe Muzeum Archeologiczne in Warsaw. In Polish; summaries in English and Russian. Other title: *Bulletin Archéologique Polonais.* Not published: 1883–1919, 1940–47. Vol. 16 repeated numbering.
Indexed: Abst. Anth.

5103
WIENER ETHNOLOGISCHE BLÄTTER. 1– , 1970– . Wien. Irreg.
Issued by: Institut für Völkerkunde, Universität Wien. In German. Each number has also a distinctive title.
Indexed: Int. Bibl. Soc. Cul. Anth.

5104
WIENER VÖLKERKUNDLICHE MITTEILUNGEN. v.1– , 1953– . Wien. Two no. a year.
Issued by: Österreichische Ethnologische Expeditions- und Forschungsgesellschaft, and Völkerkundliche Arbeitsgemeinschaft in Wien. In English or German; summaries in English or German.
Indexed: Int. Bibl. Soc. Cul. Anth.

WIENER ZEITSCHRIFT FÜR VOLKSKUNDE *See* ÖSTERREICHISCHE ZEITSCHRIFT FÜR VOLKSKUNDE

5105
WIRTSCHAFT UND GESELLSCHAFT. v.1– , 1975– . Wien, Wirtschaftsverlag. Quarterly.
Issued by: Kammer für Arbeiter und Ungestellte für Wien. In German.
Indexed: Bull. Anal. Pol. Ec. Soc.; Int. Bibl. Eco.; Int. Pol. Sc. Abst.; PAISFL.

5106
WIRTSCHAFT UND RECHT. v.1– , 1949– . Zürich, Fussili. Quarterly.
In French or German. Subtitle reads: "Zeitschrift für Wirtschaftspolitik und Wirtschaftsrecht mit Einschluss der Sozial- und Arbeitsrechtes".
Indexed: Bull. Anal. Pol. Ec. Soc.; Int. Bibl. Eco.; Int. Bibl. Soc. Cul. Anth.; PAISFL.

5107
Wirtschafts- und Sozialwissenschaftliches Institut des Deutschen Gewerkschaftsbundes. WSI MITTEILUNGEN. v.25– , 1972– . Cologne. Monthly.
In German.
Continues: Wirtschaftswissenschaftliches Institut der Gewerkschaften. *WWI Mitteilungen.*

5108
WIRTSCHAFTSDIENST. 1– , Aug. 9, 1916– . Hamburg, Verlag Weltarchiv. Weekly, 1916–43; monthly.
Issued by: 1916–Aug. 1, 1919, Zentralstelle of the Hamburgisches Kolonialinstitut; Aug. 8, 1919–, the Hamburgisches Weltwirtschaftsarchiv (HWWA), Institut für Wirtschaftsforschung. In German.
Indexes: Vols. 1–35, 1913– Apr. 1932, 1v.; v.30–50, July 1932–Nov. 1939, 1v.
Indexed: Bull. Anal. Pol. Ec. Soc.; Int. Bibl. Eco.; Peace Res. Abst. J.; PAIS; PAISFL; Soc. Abst.

5109
WIRTSCHAFTSGEOGRAPHISCHE STUDIEN. v.1– , 1977– . Wien. Semi-annual.

Issued by: Österreichische Gesellschaftsforschung. In German; summaries in English.

5110
WIRTSCHAFTSKONJUNKTUR. 1– , 1949– . Berlin, Duncker & Humblot. Quarterly, 1949–73; monthly.
Issued by: IFO–Institut für Wirtschaftsforschung, München. In German. Issues for 1949–54 in two parts; pt.1, Text, pt.2, Zahlenübersichten.
Indexed: PAISFL.

5111
WIRTSCHAFTSWISSENSCHAFT. v.1– , July/Aug. 1953– . Berlin, Verlag die Wissenschaft.
In German; summaries in English, German and Russian.
Indexed: Int. Bibl. Soc. Cul. Anth.; PAISFL.

5112
Wirtschaftswissenschaftliches Institut der Gewerkschaften. WWI MITTEILUNGEN. v.1–24, 1948–1971. Cologne. Monthly.
In German.
Continued by: Wirtschafts- und Sozialwissenschaftliche Institut des Deutschen Gewerkschaftsbundes. *WSI Mitteilungen.*

5113
WISCONSIN INTERNATIONAL LAW JOURNAL. v.1– , 1982– . Madison, Wis. Annual.
Issued by: University Law School, University of Wisconsin, in conjunction with the Wisconsin International Law Society's annual symposium at the University of Wisconsin Law School.

5114
WISSENSCHAFT UND WELTBILD. 1– , Jan. 1948– . Wien, Verlag Herold. Quarterly.
In German. Subtitle reads: "Zeitschrift für interdisziplinare Forschung".

WISSENSCHAFTLICHE ZEITSCHRIFT DER HOCHSCHULE FÜR ÖKONOMIE "BRUNO LEUSCHNER"
See Hochschule für Ökonomie, Berlin. WISSENSCHAFTLICHE ZEITSCHRIFT

5115
WISSENSCHAFTLICHE ZEITSCHRIFT DER UNIVERSITÄT ROSTOCK. GESELLSCHAFTS- UND SPRACHWISSENSCHAFTLICHE REIHE. 1– , 1951/52– . Rostock. Ten no. a year.
In German; summaries in English, French, German and Russian. Tables of contents also in English, French, German and Russian.

WISSENSCHAFTLICHE ZEITSCHRIFT; GESELLSCHAFTS- UND SPRACHWISSENSCHAFTLICHE REIHE
See Universität Halle. WISSENSCHAFTLICHE ZEITSCHRIFT; GESELLSCHAFTS- UND SPRACHWISSENSCHAFTLICHE REIHE

5116
WISSENSCHAFTLICHE ZEITSCHRIFT. GESELLSCHAFTS WISSENSCHAFTLICHE REIHE. v.34– , 1985– . Leipzig. Six no. a year.
Issued by: Universität Leipzig. In German. Tables of contents also in English, French and Russian.
Continues: *Wissenschaftliche Zeitschrift. Gesellschafts- und Sprachwissenschaftliche Reihe* (v.18–33, 1969–84)

WITTHAYSAN KASSETART
See KASSETSART JOURNAL

5117
WOMEN & HISTORY. no.1– , spring 1982– . New York, Haworth Press. Quarterly.
Published in cooperation with the Institute for Research on History.
Indexed: Int. Pol. Sc. Abst.

5118
WOMEN & POLITICS. v.1– , spring 1980– . New York, Haworth Press. Quarterly.
Indexed: ABC POL SCI; His. Abst.; Int. Bibl. Pol. Sc.; Int. Pol. Sc. Abst.; LLBA; PAIS; Soc. Abst.; Stu. Wom. Abst.; Urb. Aff. Abst.

5119
WOMEN AND WORK. v.1– , 1985– . Beverly Hills, Calif., Sage Publications. Annual.

5120
WOMEN IN A CHANGING SOCIETY. 1– , 1979– . Bombay, Allied Publ.

5121
WOMEN STUDIES ABSTRACTS. v.1– , winter 1972– . Rush, N.Y., Rush Pub. Co. Quarterly, with annual cumulation.
Indexed: PAIS.

5122
WOMEN, WORK AND DEVELOPMENT. 1– , 1982– . Geneva.
Issued by: International Labour Office.

5123
WOMEN'S INTERNATIONAL BULLETIN. 22– , 1982– . Rome, ISIS. Quarterly.
Continues: *ISIS International Bulletin.*

5124
WOMEN'S STUDIES. v.1– , 1972– . London, Gordon and Breach. Three no. a year (irreg.), 1972–1986; quarterly.

Indexed: Soc. Abst.; Wom. Stu. Abst.

5125
WOMEN'S STUDIES INTERNATIONAL FORUM. v.5– , 1982– . Oxford, Pergamon Press. Bimonthly.
Includes supplement "Feminist Forum".
Continues: *Women's Studies International Quarterly* (v.1–4, 1978–82).
Continued by: *Women's Studies International.*
Indexed: Psych. Abst.

5126
WOMEN'S STUDIES QUARTERLY. v.9– , spring 1981– . Old Westbury, N.Y., Feminist Press.
Published in cooperation with the National Women's Studies Association.
Continues: *Women's Studies Newsletter* (v.1–8, 1972–80)

WOMEN'S WORK AND HOUSEHOLD SYSTEMS
See ANTROPOLOGISKA STUDIER

5127
WORD. v.1– , Apr. 1945– . New York. Three no. a year.
Issued by: International Linguistic Association (called earlier Linguistic Circle of New York). In English, French, or German. Monographic supplements accompany some issues.
Indexes: Vols. 1–12, 1945–56, 1v.
Indexed: Abst. Anth.; Int. Bibl. Soc. Cul. Anth.; LLBA.

5128
WORK AND OCCUPATIONS. v.9– , Feb. 1982– . Beverly Hills, Calif., Sage Publications. Quarterly.
Continues: *Sociology of Work and Occupations* (v.1–8, 1974–81)
Indexed: LLBA; Pop. Ind.; Psych. Abst., Sage Fam. Stu. Abst.; Sage Urb. Stu. Abst.

WORKING PAPER
See Institute of Family Studies, Melbourne. WORKING PAPER

WORKING PAPER
See LIVERPOOL PAPERS IN HUMAN GEOGRAPHY

WORKING PAPERS
See Boston University. African Studies Center. WORKING PAPERS

5129
WORKING PAPERS FOR A NEW SOCIETY. v.1–8, no.3, spring 1973–May/June 1981. Cambridge, Mass., Trusteeship Institute. Bimonthly.
Continued by: *Working Papers Magazine* (July/Aug. 1981–)
Indexed: PAIS.

5130
WORKING PAPERS IN AFRICAN STUDIES. no.1– , 1976– . Brookline, Mass. Irreg.
Issued by: African Studies Center, Boston University. Each number has also a distinctive title.

5131
WORKING PAPERS IN AFRICAN STUDIES. no.1– , 1984– . Uppsala. Irreg.
Issued by: African Studies Programme, Department of Cultural Anthropology, University of Uppsala.

5132
WORKING PAPERS IN COMPARATIVE SOCIOLOGY. no.5– . Auckland. Irreg.
Issued by: Department of Sociology, University of Auckland.
Continues: the university's *Papers in Comparative Sociology* (no.1–4, 1974)

5133
WORKING PAPERS IN CULTURE AND COMMUNICATION. v.1– , 1974– . Philadelphia, Pa. Semi-annual.
Issued by: Department of Anthropology, Temple University.
Continued by: *Temple University Working Papers in Culture and Communications.*

5134
WORKING PAPERS IN U.S. MEXICAN STUDIES. 1– , 1981– . La Jolla, Calif.
Issued by: Program in United States–Mexican Studies, University of California, San Diego. In English or Spanish.

5135
WORKING PAPERS ON CARIBBEAN SOCIETY. SERIES A. NEW PERSPECTIVES IN THEORY AND ANALYSIS. no.1– , 1978– . St. Augustine. Irreg.
Issued by: Department of Sociology, University of the West Indies.

5136
WORKING PAPERS ON CARIBBEAN SOCIETY. SERIES C. RESEARCH FINDINGS. no.1– , 1978– . St. Augustine. Irreg.
Issued by: Department of Sociology, University of the West Indies.

5137
WORLD AFFAIRS. v.1– , June 1837– . Washington, D.C. Monthly (irreg.), June 1838–Apr. 1929; quarterly, 1837–Mar. 1938; Aug. 1929–.

Numbering irregular: v.19–33 also as new series, v.1–15; v.39–46 omitted in numbering. Title varies: v.1–94, no.1, *Advocate of Peace*.
Supersedes: *The American Advocate of Peace*.
Indexed: ABC POL SCI; Bull. Anal. Pol. Ec. Soc.; Int. Bibl. Pol. Sc.; Int. Pol. Sc. Abst.; PAIS; Peace Res. Abst. J.

5138
WORLD AFFAIRS. v.1–12, no.3, Apr./June 1935–Oct. 1946; n. ser. v.1–5, Jan. 1947–Oct. 1951. London, Stevens. Quarterly.
Issued by: London Institute of World Affairs (called earlier, 1935–1940, New Commonwealth Institute; July 1940–Apr. 1943, New Commonwealth Institute of World Affairs). Contains occasionally articles in French or German. Title varies: 1935–Apr. 1943, *New Commonwealth Quarterly*; July 1943–Oct. 1946, *London Quarterly of World Affairs*.

WORLD AFFAIRS INTERPRETER
See WORLD AFFAIRS QUARTERLY

5139
WORLD AFFAIRS QUARTERLY. v.1–30, spring 1930–Jan. 1960. Los Angeles, Calif.
Issued by: 1930, Institute of Religions, Science and School of Philosophy; 1931–Apr. 1932, Science, Religion, Philosophy Pub. Co.; June 1932–Jan. 1950, Los Angeles University of International Relations; Apr. 1950–Jan. 1960, University of Southern California (Oct. 1955–Jan. 1960, under the auspices of the School of International Relations). Title varies: spring 1930–Apr. 1932, *Quarterly Journal of Science, Religion, Philosophy*; July 1932–July 1955, *World Affairs Interpreter*.

WORLD AFFAIRS REPORT
See California Institute of International Studies. WORLD AFFAIRS REPORT

WORLD AGRICULTURAL ECONOMICS ABSTRACTS
See WORLD AGRICULTURAL AND RURAL SOCIOLOGY ABSTRACTS

5140
WORLD AGRICULTURAL ECONOMICS AND RURAL SOCIOLOGY ABSTRACTS. v.1– , Apr. 1959– . Farnham Royal. Quarterly, 1959–72; monthly, with annual cumulation and Geographical Index.
Issued by: Commonwealth Agricultural Bureaux. Title varies: 1959, *World Agricultural Economics Abstracts*.

5141
WORLD ARCHAEOLOGY. v.1– , June 1969– . London, Routledge & Kegan Paul. Three no. to a volume; two volumes a year.
Issues are thematic.
Indexed: Abst. Anth.; APAIS; Bull. Sig. Soc. Eth.; Int. Bibl. Soc. Cul. Anth.; SSCI.

5142
WORLD ARMAMENTS AND DISARMAMENTS; SIPRI YEARBOOK. 1972– . Stockholm, Almqvist & Wiksell.
Continues: *SIPRI Yearbook of World Armaments and Disarmaments*.
Indexes: 1968–79, 1v.

5143
World Bank. World Bank Research Program. ABSTRACTS OF CURRENT STUDIES. Oct. 1981– . Washington, D.C. Annual.

WORLD BIBLIOGRAPHY OF SOCIAL SECURITY
See BIBLIOGRAPHIE UNIVERSELLE DE SÉCURITÉ SOCIALE

5144
WORLD COMMODITY OUTLOOK. 1983– . London. Annual.
Issued by: The Economist Intelligence Unit.

WORLD CONGRESS
See International Politics Association. WORLD CONGRESS

5145
World Congress of Sociology. TRANSACTIONS. 2nd– , 1951– . [Place of publication varies]. Quadrennial.
Issued by: International Sociological Association. Transactions of the first congress were not published.
Indexed: Soc. Abst.

5146
WORLD DEVELOPMENT. v.1– , Feb. 1973– . Oxford, Pergamon Press. Monthly (some combined numbers).
Subtitle reads: "The multidisciplinary interdisciplinary journal devoted to the study and promotion of world development".
Supersedes: *New Commonwealth*.
Indexed: LLBA; PAIS; Soc. Sc. Ind.

5147
WORLD DEVELOPMENT INDICATORS. 1978– . Washington, D.C. Annual.
Issued by: World Bank.

5148
WORLD DEVELOPMENT REPORT. 1978– . Oxford, Oxford University Press. Annual.
Issued by: World Bank.

WORLD DIRECTORY OF SOCIAL SCIENCE INSTITUTIONS
See RÉPERTOIRE MONDIALE DES INSTITUTIONS DES SCIENCES SOCIALES

5149
WORLD ECONOMIC OUTLOOK. May 1980– . Washington, D.C. Annual, 1980–Apr. 1984; semi-annual.
Issued by: International Monetary Fund. Issues from 1980 to 1984 were published as part of *Occasional Papers* (no.9, 27, 32).

WORLD ECONOMIC REPORT
See United Nations. Department of Economic and Social Affairs. WORLD ECONOMIC REPORT

5150
WORLD ECONOMIC REVIEW. v.1– , Jan. 1979– . Philadelphia, Pa. Semi-annual.
Issued by: Wharton Econometric Forecasting Associates.

5151
WORLD ECONOMIC SURVEY. [v.1]–11, 1931/32–1942/44. Geneva.
Issued by: Economic, Financial and Transit Department, League of Nations.

5152
WORLD ECONOMIC SURVEY. 1955– . New York. Annual.
Issued by: Department of International Economic and Social Affairs, United Nations. Some volumes accompanied by monographic supplements and *Current Trends and Policies in the World Economy.*
Continues: *World Economic Report.*

WORLD ECONOMICS AND POLITICS
See MIROVOE KHOZI͡AĬSTVO I MIROVAI͡A POLITIKA

5153
THE WORLD ECONOMY. v.1– , Oct. 1977– . London, Oxford, B. Blackwell for Trade Policy Research Centre. Quarterly.
Issued by: Trade Policy Research Centre.
Includes: "Lectures in Commercial Diplomacy".
Indexed: ABC POL SCI; Bull. Anal. Pol. Ec. Soc.; Int. Bibl. Eco.; PAIS; SSCI.

5154
World Fertility Survey. BASIC DOCUMENTATION. no.1– , Mar. 1975– . Vooburg.
Issued in cooperation with the Information Office, International Statistical Office.
Indexed: Sage Urb. Stu. Abst.

5155
World Fertility Survey. SCIENTIFIC REPORTS. 1977– . The Hague. Irreg.
Issued by: International Union for the Study of Population in cooperation with the International Statistical Office.

WORLD INDEX OF SOCIAL SCIENCE INSTITUTIONS
See RÉPERTOIRE MONDIAL DES INSTITUTIONS DES SCIENCES SOCIALES

5156
WORLD MARXIST REVIEW. v.1– , Sept. 1958– . Toronto, Progress Books. Monthly.
North American edition of: *Problems of Peace and Socialism.* Published also in Prague in Amharic, Arabic, Bengali, Bulgarian, Czech, Danish, Finnish, French, German, Greek, Gujarati, Hebrew, Hindi, Hungarian, Indonesian, Italian, Japanese, Malayan, Mongolian, Norwegian and Oriya editions.
Indexed: Ind. Per. Art. Law; PAIS; Soc. Sc. Ind.; Wom. Stu. Abst.

5157
WORLD MEETINGS. SOCIAL & BEHAVIORAL SCIENCES, HUMAN SERVICES & MANAGEMENT. v.7, no.2– , spring 1971– . Chestnut Hill, Mass., World Meetings Information Center. Quarterly.
Continues: *World Meetings. Social & Behavioral Sciences, Education & Management.*

THE WORLD OF ISLAM
See DIE WELT DES ISLAMS

5158
WORLD OUTLOOK. 1982– . London. Annual.
Issued by: The Economist Intelligence Unit.

5159
WORLD POLICY FORUM. [1]– , spring 1983– . New York. Annual.
Issued by: World Policy Institute.

5160
WORLD POLICY JOURNAL. v.1– , fall 1983– . New York. Quarterly.
Issued by: World Policy Institute.
Indexed: Curr. Cont. Soc. Beh. Sc.; Int. Pol. Sc. Abst.; PAIS; SSCI; Soc. Abst.

5161
WORLD POLITICS. v.1– , Oct. 1948– . Princeton, N.J., Princeton University Press. Quarterly.
Issued by: Yale Institute of International Studies, Yale University (v.1–4, 1948–51); Center for International Studies, Princeton University.

Indexed: ABC POL SCI; Bull. Anal. Pol. Ec. Soc.; Bull. Sig. Soc. Eth.; Curr. Cont. Soc. Beh. Sc.; His. Abst.; Int. Bibl. Eco.; Int. Bibl. Pol. Sc.; Int. Bibl. Soc. Cul. Anth.; Int. Lab. Doc.; Int. Pol. Sc. Abst.; PAIS; Peace Res. Abst. J.; Pop. Ind.; SSCI.

5162
WORLD POPULATION. June 1973– . Washington, D.C. Biennial.
Issued by: Bureau of the Census, Department of Commerce, U.S.A. Vols. 1973–75 issued by the International Statistical Programme Center. (Sup. Doc no.3.205/3:WP)

5163
WORLD REVIEW. v.1– , Mar. 1962– . Brisbane, Jacaranda Press. Three no. a year.
Published under the auspices of the Australian Institute of International Affairs, Queensland Branch.
Indexed: APAIS; Peace Res. Abst. J.

WORLD SOCIAL SCIENCE INFORMATION SERVICES
See SERVICES MONDIAUX D'INFORMATION EN SCIENCES SOCIALES

5164
WORLD SURVEY OF EDUCATION. 1955– . Paris, Unesco. Triennial.
Continues: *World Handbook of Educational Organization and Statistics.*

5165
THE WORLD TODAY. v.1– , July 1945– . London, Oxford University Press. Monthly.
Issued by: Information Department, Royal Institute of International Affairs.
Supersedes: *Bulletin of International News.*
Indexed: ABC POL SCI; Bull. Anal. Pol. Ec. Soc.; Curr. Cont. Soc. Beh. Sc.; His. Abst.; Ind. Per. Art. Law; Int. Bibl. Eco.; Int. Bibl. Pol. Sc.; Int. Lab. Doc.; Int. Pol. Sc. Abst.; PAIS; Peace Res. Abst. J.; Pop. Ind.; Soc. Sc. Ind.; SSCI.

5166
WORLD YEARBOOK OF EDUCATION. 1965– . London, Kogan Page; New York, Nichols Pub. Co. Annual.
Issued in association with the Institute of Education, University of London, and Teachers College, Columbia University, New York.
Continues: *Year Book of Education.*

5167
WRITINGS ON AMERICAN HISTORY. 1906– . New York, New Haven, Washington, 1921–. Annual.

5168
WYCHOWANIE OBYWATELSKIE. 1967– . Warszawa, Wydawnictwa Szkolne i Pedagogiczne. Ten no. a year.
Issued by: Ministerstwo Oświaty i Wychowania. In Polish.

YACHOU KUNG HSING CHENG HSÜEH
See THE ASIAN JOURNAL OF PUBLIC ADMINISTRATION

5169
YAGL-AMBU. 1– , Mar. 1974– . Port Moresby. Two no. a year.
Issued by: Department of Economics, University of Papua New Guinea. Subtitle reads: "Papua and New Guinea journal of the social sciences and the humanities".

5170
YALE ECONOMICS ESSAYS. 1– , spring 1961– . New Haven, Conn. Quarterly.
Issued by: Yale University.

5171
THE YALE JOURNAL OF INTERNATIONAL LAW. v.10– , 1984– . New Haven, Conn. Semi-annual.
Issued by: Yale Law School.
Continues: *Yale Journal of Public Order.*

5172
THE YEAR BOOK FOR SOCIAL POLICY IN BRITAIN. 1971– . London, Routledge & Kegan Paul. Annual.
Indexed: Int. Bibl. Soc.; Int. Pol. Sc. Abst.

5173
YEAR BOOK OF EDUCATION. 1932–1964. London, Evans. Annual.
Published in association with the Institute of Education, University of London. Each volume has also a distinctive title.
Continued by: *World Year Book of Education.*

THE YEAR BOOK OF THE BERMUDAS, THE BAHAMAS, BRITISH GUIANA, BRITISH HONDURAS AND THE BRITISH WEST INDIES
See THE WEST INDIES YEARBOOK

5174
A YEAR BOOK OF THE COMMONWEALTH. 1969–1986. London, H.M. Stationery Office.
Supersedes: *Commonwealth Office Year Book*, and *Commonwealth Relations Office Year Book*. Continued by: *The Commonwealth Yearbook.*

5175
THE YEAR BOOK OF WORLD AFFAIRS. v.1– , 1947– . London, Stevens. Annual.
Published under the auspices of the London Institute of World Affairs. Published also in U.S. edition.
Indexes: Vols. 1–10, 1947–56, in v.10; v.1–25, 1947–71, in v.25.
Indexed: Ind. Per. Art. Law; Int. Bibl. Pol. Sc.; Int. Pol. Sc. Abst.; Soc. Abst.

5176
YEAR BOOK OF WORLD PROBLEMS AND HUMAN POTENTIAL. 1st ed.– , 1976– . Brussels. Irreg.
Issued by: Secretariats of the Union of International Associations.

YEARBOOK
See Africana Society of Pretoria. YEARBOOK

YEARBOOK
See Carnegie Endowment for International Peace. YEARBOOK

YEARBOOK
See National Council on Crime and Delinquency. YEARBOOK

YEARBOOK
See United Nations. Commission on International Trade. YEARBOOK

YEARBOOK
See United Nations. International Law Commission. YEARBOOK

YEARBOOK OF CHINA'S SPECIAL ECONOMIC ZONES
See CHUNG-KUO CHING CHI T'E CH'U NIEN CHIEN

YEARBOOK OF COMPARATIVE COLONIAL DOCUMENTATION
See International Institute of Differing Civilizations. ANNUAIRE DE DOCUMENTATION COLONIALE COMPARÉE

YEARBOOK OF COMPARATIVE LAW AND LEGISLATIVE STUDIES
See ANNUARIO DI DIRITTO COMPARATIVO E DI STUDI LEGISLATIVI

YEARBOOK OF EAST EUROPEAN ECONOMICS
See JAHRBUCH DER WIRTSCHAFT OSTEUROPAS

5177
YEARBOOK OF FINNISH FOREIGN POLICY. 1– , 1973– . Helsinki. Annual.
Issued by: Finnish Institute of International Affairs.
Indexed: Int. Bibl. Pol. Sc.; Int. Pol. Sc. Abst.

5178
YEARBOOK OF FOREIGN TRADE STATISTICS. THIRD COUNTRIES. Luxembourg, Eurostat. Annual.
Issued by: Statistical Office of the European Communities. In English and French. Published in two volumes: *Volume A. Foreign Trade. Third Countries. ACP Countries*, and *Volume B Mediterranean Countries*. [The acronym ACP denotes African countries, Caribbean area, and Pacific area countries.] Cross-references are listed on a separate sheet.

YEARBOOK OF INDUSTRIAL STATISTICS
See United Nations. Statistical Office. YEARBOOK OF INDUSTRIAL STATISTICS

5179
YEARBOOK OF INTERNATIONAL COMMODITY STATISTICS. 1984–1986. New York, United Nations.
Issued by: United Nations Conference on Trade and Development.
Continued by: *UNCTAD Commodity Yearbook*.

5180
YEARBOOK OF INTERNATIONAL COMMUNIST AFFAIRS. 1966– . Stanford, Calif. Annual.
Issued by: Hoover Institution on War, Peace and Revolution.

5181
YEARBOOK OF INTERNATIONAL ORGANIZATIONS. 1st ed.– , 1948– . Bruxelles. Annual.
Issued by: Union of International Organizations. Published also in French: *Annuaire des Organisations Internationales*. Title varies: 1948–50, *Annuaire des Organisations Internationales*. Beginning with 1983 published in three volumes. Text in English, with instructions in English, French and German.

YEARBOOK OF INTERNATIONAL TRADE STATISTICS
See United Nations. Statistical Office. YEARBOOK OF INTERNATIONAL TRADE STATISTICS

YEARBOOK OF NATIONAL ACCOUNTS STATISTICS
See United Nations. Statistical Office. YEARBOOK OF NATIONAL ACCOUNTS STATISTICS

YEARBOOK OF POPULATION RESEARCH IN FINLAND
See VAESTONTUTKIMUKSEN VUOKSIKIRJA

YEARBOOK OF REGIONAL STATISTICS
See Statistical Office of the European Communities. REGIONAL STATISTISK ÅRBOG

YEARBOOK OF THE DEPARTMENT OF FOLKLORE
See ARTES POPULARES

5182
YEARBOOK OF THE EUROPEAN CONVENTION ON HUMAN RIGHTS. 1– , 1955/57– . The Hague, Nijhoff.
Issued by: European Commission on Human Rights, and European Court on Human Rights. Title varies: 1955/57, *Documents and Decisions*, European Commission on Human Rights. Other title: *Annuaire de la Convention Européenne des Droits de l'Homme*.

YEARBOOK OF THE INTERNATIONAL LAW COMMISSION
See United Nations. International Law Commission. YEARBOOK OF THE INTERNATIONAL LAW COMMISSION

YEARBOOK OF THE NATIONAL ACCOUNTS STATISTICS
See United Nations. Statistical Office. YEARBOOK OF NATIONAL ACCOUNTS STATISTICS

5183
YEARBOOK OF THE UNITED NATIONS. 1946/47– . New York. Annual.

YEARBOOK OF THE WEST INDIES & COUNTRIES OF THE CARIBBEAN
See THE WEST INDIES YEARBOOK

5184
YEARBOOK OF WORLD AFFAIRS. 1947– . London, Sweet & Maxwell, Stevens.
Issued by: London Institute of World Affairs.

YEARBOOK ON HUMAN RIGHTS
See United Nations. Secretariat. YEARBOOK ON HUMAN RIGHTS

YING WEN CHUNG-KUO CHI K'AN
See CHINA QUARTERLY

5185
YIVO ANNUAL OF JEWISH SOCIAL SCIENCE. v.1– , 1946– . New York. Two no. a year.
Issued by: Yivo Institute for Jewish Research (called 1946–54, Yiddish Scientific Institute)

Indexed: His. Abst.

5186
YMER. v.1– , 1881–1965. Stockholm, Generalstabens Litografiska Anstaltsforlag. Four no. a year.
Issued by: Svenska Sällskapet för Antropologi och Geografi. In Swedish.
Supersedes: Svenska Sällskapet för Antropologi och Geografi. *Skrifter*. Superseded by: *Ymer [Arsbok]*.
Indexes: Vols. 1–30, 1881–1910; v.31–45, 1911–25, 1v.; v.46–70, 1926–50, 1v.

5187
YMER [ARSBOK] 1966– . Stockholm, Generalstabens Litografiska Anstalts Förlag. Annual.
In Swedish.
Supersedes: *Ymer*.

5188
Yokohama Kokuritsu Daigaku. YOKOHAMA KOKURITSU DAIGAKU JIMBUN KIYŌ. 1– , 1953– . Tetsugaku, Shakai Kagaku. Annual.
Issued by: Department of Sociology, Yokohama University. In Japanese; summaries in English. Other title: *Yokohama National University. Humanities. Section 1. Philosophy and Social Sciences*.

YOKOHAMA KOKURITSU DAIGAKU JIMBUN KIYŌ
See Yokohama Kokuritsu Daigaku. YOKOHAMA KOKURITSU DAIGAKU JIMBUN KIYŌ

YOKOHAMA NATIONAL UNIVERSITY. HUMANITIES. SECTION 1. PHILOSOPHY AND SOCIAL SCIENCES
See Yokohama Kokuritsu Daigaku. YOKOHAMA KOKURITSU DAIGAKU JIMBUN KIYŌ

5189
YONSE HAENGJONG NONCH'ONG. no.1– , 1973– . Seoul, Yonse Taehakkyo Henjong Taehagwon.
In English or Korean. Other title: *Yonsei Journal of Public Administration*.

5190
YONSE NOCH'ONG. 1– , 1962– . Seoul, Yonse Taehakkyo Taehagwon. Annual (in two or more volumes)
In English, French, or Korean. Other title: *Yonsei Nonch'ong*.

YONSEI JOURNAL OF PUBLIC ADMINISTRATION
See YONSE HAENGJONG NONCH'ONG

YONSEI NONCH'ONG
See YONSE NONCH'ONG

YONSEI SOCIAL SCIENCE REVIEW
See SAHOE KWAHAK NONJIP

5191
YOUTH AND POLICY. v.1– , summer 1982– . Newcastle upon Tyne. Quarterly.
Subtitle reads: "The journal of critical analysis".

5192
YOUTH AND SOCIETY. v.1– , Sept. 1969– . Beverly Hills, Calif., Sage Publications. Quarterly.
Indexed: Abst. Soc. Work; Curr. Cont. Soc. Beh. Sc.; Hum. Res. Abst.; PHRA; Sage Fam. Stu. Abst.; Sage Urb. Stu. Abst.; Soc. Abst.; SSCI; Wom. Stu. Abst.

5193
YOUTH IN SOCIETY. no.1– , Sept./Oct. 1973– . Leicester. Bimonthly.
Issued by: National Youth Bureau. Includes "Youth in Society Training Bulletin" previously called "Youth Service Information Centre Training Bulletin". Absorbed: *YSTC Digest*.

5194
YUGOSLAV SURVEY. 1– , Apr. 1960– . Belgrad, Jugoslovenska Stvarnost. Quarterly.
Issued also in Serbo-Croatian edition titled *Jugoslovenski Pregled*.
Indexed: Bull. Sig. Soc. Eth.; Int. Bibl. Eco.; Int. Bibl. Pol. Sc.; Int. Lab. Doc.

Z

ZFG
See ZEITSCHRIFT FÜR GESCHICHTSWISSENSCHAFT

5195
ZA SOCIALISTICESKUJU SELSKOCHOZZIAJNUJU NAUKU. RADA B. EKONOMICKA. 1– , 1952– . Praha. Four no. a year (some combined numbers).
Issued by: Československa Akademia Zemedelskych Věd. In Czech.

5196
ZAHRANIČNI POLITIKA. v.1–17, no.10, Feb. 1922–1939. Praha, Orbis. Two vols. a year.
In Czech.

5197
ZAÏRE–AFRIQUE. 1– , 1961– . Kinshasa. Ten no. a year.
Issued by; Centre d'Études pour l'Action Sociale, and later also by the Institution de Droit Publique. In French. Subtitle reads: "Économie, culture, vie sociale". Title varies: 1961–65, *Documents pour l'Action*; 1966–Oct. 1971, *Congo Afrique*.
Indexed: Bull. Anal. Pol. Ec. Soc.; Int. Bibl. Eco.; Int. Bibl. Soc. Cul. Anth.

5198
ZAMBEZIA. 1– , 1969– . Harare. Annual.
Issued by: University of Zimbabwe. Includes monographic supplements.

5199
THE ZAMBIA JOURNAL. 1– , June 1950– . Livingstone. Two no. a year.
Issued by: Livingstone Museum. Title varies: 1950–64, *Northern Rhodesia Journal*.

5200
ZAMBIAN PAPERS. 1– , 1966– . Manchester, Manchester University Press. Annual.
Issued by: Institute of Social Research, University of Zambia.
Supersedes: *Rhodes–Livingstone Papers*.
Indexed: Bull. Anal. Pol. Ec. Soc.

5201
ZARUBEZHNYĬ MIR; SOT͡SIAL'NO-POLITICHESKIE I EKONOMICHESKIE PROBLEMY. 1981– . Kiev, Nakl. Dumka.
Issued by: Institut Sot͡sial'nykh i Ekonomicheskikh Problem Zarubezhnykh Stran, Akademii͡a Nauk Ukrainskoĭ S.S.R. In Russian or Ukrainian; summaries in English.

5202
ZASSHI KIJI SAKUIN, JINMUN SAKAI HEN. v.1– , 1948– . Tokyo. Monthly, 1948–74; semi-annual, 1975; quarterly.
In Japanese. Other title: *Japanese Periodical Index. Humanities and Social Sciences Section.*

ZBORNIK. SPOLECENSKÉ VEDY. MARKSIZMUS-LENINIZMUS
See Univerzita Komenského. Filozoficka Fakulta. ZBORNIK. SPOLECENSKÉ VEDY. MARKSIZMUS-LENINIZMUS

ZBORNIK USTAVU MARXIZMU-LENINIZMU UNIVERZITY KOMENSKÉHO
See Univerzita Komenského. Ústav Marxizmu-Leninizmu. VĚDECKY KOMUNIZMUS

5203
ZBORNIK ZA DRUSTVENE NAUKE. 11– , 1955– . Novy Sad, Matica Srpska. Three no. a year, 1955–69; annual.
In Serbo-Croatian; summaries in English. Tables of contents in English.
Continues: Zbornik Matice Srpske. Odeljenie, *Serija Drustvenih Nauka*.
Indexes: no.1–20, 1950–58, with no.20; no.21–30, 1958–61, with no.30; no.60–70, 1976–81, with no.70.

ZEITSCHRIFT DER INTERNATIONALEN GESELLSCHAFT FÜR ORIENTFORSCHUNG
See ORIENS

5204
ZEITSCHRIFT DES VEREINS FÜR VOLKSKUNDE. NEUE FOLGE DER ZEITSCHRIFT FÜR VÖLKERPSYCHOLOGIE UND SPRACHWISSENSCHAFT. v.1–37/38, 1891–1927/28. Berlin, later Stuttgart, Verlag Kohlhammer. Quarterly, 1891–1926; irreg., 1928–61; two no. a year.
Issued by: Deutsche Gesellschaft für Volkskunde. In German.
Superseded by: *Zeitschrift für Volkskunde*.
Indexes: Vols. 21–32, 1911–22, in v.30/32.

5205
ZEITSCHRIFT FÜR AGRARGESCHICHTE UND AGRARSOZIOLOGIE. 1– , Apr. 1953– . Frankfurt am Main, DLG Verlag. Semi-annual.

Issued by: Gesellschaft für Agrargeschichte, and Die Deutsche Landwirtschaftsgesellschaft. In German. Includes supplement titled *Sonderband* (1–, 1958–)

Indexed: Int. Bibl. Soc.; PAIS; Soc. Abst.

5206

ZEITSCHRIFT FÜR ARCHÄOLOGIE. v.1– , 1967– . Berlin, VEB Deutscher Verlag der Wissenschaften. Two no. a year.

Organ of: Institut für Ur- und Frühgeschichte, Deutsche Akademie der Wissenschaften zu Berlin. In German. Tables of contents also in English, French, and Russian.

Indexed: Abst. Anth.; Int. Bibl. Soc. Cul. Anth.

5207

ZEITSCHRIFT FÜR AUSLANDISCHES ÖFFENTLICHES RECHT UND VÖLKERRECHT. 1– , 1929– . Berlin, Verlag W. Kohlhammer.

Issued by: Max-Planck Institut für Auslandisches Recht und Völkerrecht. In German, English and French; summaries in English. Publication suspended between Sept. 1944 and Feb. 1950.

5208

ZEITSCHRIFT FÜR BALKANOLOGIE. v.1– , 1962– . Wiesbaden, Harrassowitz. Two no. a year.

Chiefly in German; some articles in English, French, or Italian.

Indexed: Int. Bibl. Soc. Cul. Anth.

5209

ZEITSCHRIFT FÜR BETRIEBSWIRTSCHAFT. 1– , 1924– . Berlin, Betriebswirtschaftlicher Verlag Th. Gabler. Six no. a year, 1924–52; monthly 1953–; four no. a year.

In German. Publication suspended, 1943–49.

5210

ZEITSCHRIFT FÜR DAS GESAMTE GENOSSENSCHAFTSWESEN. 1950– . Göttingen, Vandenhoeck und Ruprecht. Four no. a year.

In German.

Indexed: Int. Bibl. Eco.; PAISFL.

5211

ZEITSCHRIFT FÜR DAS GESAMTE KREDITWESEN. v.1– , May 1950– . Frankfurt am Main, Fritz Knap Verlag. Semi-monthly.

In German. Contains articles translated from *The Journal of Finance and Credit*.

5212

ZEITSCHRIFT FÜR DEMOGRAPHIE UND STATISTIK DER JUDEN. 1–17, 1905–1923; n. ser. v.1–3, 1924–1926. Berlin. Monthly.

In German.

5213

ZEITSCHRIFT FÜR DIE BEVÖLKERUNGSWISSENSCHAFT. DEMOGRAPHIE. [v.1]– , 1976– . Wiesbaden, later Boppard am Rhein, Harald Boldt Verlag. Quarterly.

Issued by: Bundesinstitut für Bevölkerungsforschung. In German. Tables of contents also in English, French and Russian.

Indexed: Int. Bibl. Eco.; PAISFL.

5214

ZEITSCHRIFT FÜR DIE GESAMTE STAATSWISSENSCHAFT. 1– , 1844– . Tübingen, J.C.B. Mohre. Quarterly.

In German. Includes supplements "Ergänzungsheft", 1–53, 1901–20. Not published 1945–47.

Indexes: Vols. 1–20, 1844–94, with v.50; v.1–60, 1844–1904, with v.60; v.1–80, 1844–1926, 1v.

Indexed: Bull. Anal. Pol. Ec. Soc.; Int. Bibl. Eco.; Int. Pol. Sc. Abst.; PAIS; PAISFL; Peace Res. Abst. J.

ZEITSCHRIFT FÜR EINGEBORENEN SPRACHEN
See AFRIKA UND ÜBERSEE; SPRACHE, KULTUREN

ZEITSCHRIFT FÜR EMPIRISCHE SOZIOLOGIE UND ETHNOLOGISCHE FORSCHUNG
See SOCIOLOGUS: ZEITSCHRIFT FÜR VÖLKERPSYCHOLOGIE UND SOZIOLOGIE

5215

ZEITSCHRIFT FÜR ERZIEHUNGSWISSENSCHAFTLICHE FORSCHUNG. JOURNAL OF EDUCATIONAL RESEARCH. 1– , 1967– . München, Manz Verlag. Four no. a year.

In German.

5216

ZEITSCHRIFT FÜR ETHNOLOGIE. v.1– , 1869– . Berlin. Frequency varies.

Issued by: Berliner Gesellschaft für Anthropologie, Ethnologie und Urgeschichte, and Deutsche Gesellschaft für Völkerkunde. In German. Includes the society's *Verhandlungen*. Title varies: v.1, 1869, *Zeitschrift für Ethnologie und ihre Hülfswissenschaften als Lehre von Menschen in seinen Beziehungen zur Natur und zur Geschichte*. Publication suspended: 1945–49.

Indexes: Vols. 1–20, 1869–88; v.21–34, 1889–1902.

Indexed: Abst. Anth.; Bull. Anal. Pol. Ec. Soc.; Bull. Sig. Soc. Eth.

ZEITSCHRIFT FÜR ETHNOLOGIE UND IHRE HÜLFSWISSENSCHAFTEN ALS LEHRE VON MENSCHEN IN SEINEN BEZIEHUNGEN ZUR NATUR UND ZUR GESCHICHTE
See ZEITSCHRIFT FÜR ETHNOLOGIE

5217
ZEITSCHRIFT FÜR GEOPOLITIK. v.1– . Jan. 1924– . Heidelberg, Vowinckel. Monthly.
In German. Includes monthly supplement "Welt-Rundfunk" (v.14–), bimonthly supplement "Staatenwirtschaft; Beiträge zur Staats-handeln in den Aussenwirtschaften". Absorbed: *Weltpolitik und Weltwirtschaft* in Jan. 1927.

5218
ZEITSCHRIFT FÜR GESCHICHTSWISSENSCHAFT. 1– , 1953– . Berlin, VEB Deutscher Verlag der Wissenschaften. Eight no. a year, 1953–68; monthly.
In German; summaries in English, French, Russian and Spanish. Includes supplement titles "Beiheft" published irregularly (1–, 1954–)
Indexes: every ten years.
Indexed: Bull. Anal. Pol. Ec. Soc.

5219
ZEITSCHRIFT FÜR HISTORISCHE FORSCHUNG. v.1– , 1974– . Berlin, Duncker & Humblot. Two no. a year, 1974–76; three no. a year, 1977–78; quarterly.
In German.

ZEITSCHRIFT FÜR KOLONIALPOLITIK, KOLONIALE RECHT UND KOLONIAL WIRTSCHAFT
See KOLONIALE MONATSBLÄTTER

ZEITSCHRIFT FÜR KOLONIALSPRACHEN
See AFRIKA UND ÜBERSEE; SPRACHEN, KULTUREN

5220
ZEITSCHRIFT FÜR KOMMUNALWIRTSCHAFT. v.1–23/24, Nov. 26, 1910–Dec. 25, 1933. Oldenburg.
In German. Title varies: *Zeitschrift für Kommunalwirtschaft und Kommunalpolitik*. Merged with: *Zentralblatt für die Öffentlichen Verwaltungen* to form *Zeitschrift für Öffentliche Wirtschaft*.

ZEITSCHRIFT FÜR KOMMUNALWIRTSCHAFT UND KOMMUNALPOLITIK
See ZEITSCHRIFT FÜR KOMMUNALWIRTSCHAFT

5221
ZEITSCHRIFT FÜR KULTURAUSTAUSCH. v.1– , Nov. 1951– . Stuttgart. Quarterly.
Issued by: Institut für Auslandsbeziehungen. In German. Title varies: v.1–12, no.1, 1951–Jan./Mar. 1962, *Mitteilungen*.
Indexed: PAISFL.

5222
ZEITSCHRIFT FÜR MARKT-, MEINUNGS- UND ZUKUNFTSFORSCHUNG. VIERTELJAHRESBERICHTE ZUR THEORIE UND PRAXIS. v.1– , 1957– . Tübingen, Demokrit Verlag und Wickerinstitut. Quarterly.
Issued by: Wicker Institut für Markt- und Meinungsforschung. In English or German; summaries in English, French, or Spanish. Supplements are titled "Die Ergänzung zur Zeitschrift".
Supersedes: *Zeitschrift für Markt- und Meinungsforschung*.
Indexed: PAISFL.

5223
ZEITSCHRIFT FÜR NATIONALÖKONOMIE. JOURNAL OF ECONOMICS. v.1– , 1929– . Wien, J. Springer. Irreg.
In English, French, German, Italian, or Spanish; summaries in English and French.
Indexed: Int. Bibl. Eco.; PAIS.

ZEITSCHRIFT FÜR ÖSTERREICHISCHE VOLKSKUNDE
See ÖSTERREICHISCHE ZEITSCHRIFT FÜR VOLKSKUNDE

5224
ZEITSCHRIFT FÜR OPERATIONS RESEARCH. Includes Series A. *Theorie*; and Series B. *Praxis*. v.16– , 1972– . Würzburg, Physica Verlag. Each series three no. a year; 1972–82, quarterly.
Organ of: Deutsche Gesellschaft für Operations Research. In German.
Continues, in part: *Unternehmungsforschung*.

5225
ZEITSCHRIFT FÜR OSTFORSCHUNG. v.1– , 1952– . Hamburg, N.G. Elweert. Quarterly.
Issued by: Johann Gottfried Herder-Forschungsrat. In German; summaries in English. Subtitle reads: "Ländern und Völker in ostlichen Europa".
Indexed: His. Abst.; Int. Bibl. Soc. Cul. Anth.; Peace Res. Abst. J.

5226
ZEITSCHRIFT FÜR PARLAMENTSFRAGEN. June 1970– . Opladen, West Deutscher Verlag. Quarterly.
Issued by: Deutsche Vereinigung für Parlamentsfragen. In German.

Indexed: Bull. Anal. Pol. Ec. Soc.; Int. Bibl. Eco.; Int. Bibl. Pol. Sc.; Int. Bibl. Soc.; Int. Pol. Sc. Abst.

5227
ZEITSCHRIFT FÜR POLITIK. v.1–34, Nov. 1907–1944; n. ser. v.1– , 1954– . Berlin, München. Quarterly.
Issued by: Deutsche Auslandswissenschaftliche Institut; n. ser. by: Vereinigung für die Wissenschaft der Politik and Hochschule für Politische Wissenschaft. In German.
Indexed: ABC POL SCI; Bull. Anal. Pol. Ec. Soc.; His. Abst.; Int. Bibl. Eco.; Int. Bibl. Pol. Sc.; Int. Bibl. Soc.; Int. Pol. Sc. Abst.; Int. Lab. Doc.; PAIS; PAISFL; SSCI.

5228
ZEITSCHRIFT FÜR RASSENKUNDE UND DIE GESAMTE FORSCHUNG AM MENSCHEN. v.1–14, no.2, Jan. 18, 1935–July 1944. Stuttgart, F. Enke. Bimonthly.
In English, French, or German. Title varies: 1935–Nov. 1936, *Zeitschrift für Rassenkunde und ihre Nachgebiete*.

ZEITSCHRIFT FÜR RASSENKUNDE UND IHRE NACHGEBIETE
See ZEITSCHRIFT FÜR RASSENKUNDE UND DIE GESAMTE FORSCHUNG AM MENSCHEN

5229
ZEITSCHRIFT FÜR RECHTSSOZIOLOGIE. v.1– , Sept. 1980– . Wiesbaden, Westdeutscher Verlag. Semi-annual.
In German.
Indexed: LLBA.

5230
ZEITSCHRIFT FÜR SCHWEIZERISCHE ARCHÄOLOGIE UND KUNSTGESCHICHTE. 1– , 1959– . Zürich. Three or four no. a year.
Issued by: Schweizerische Landesmuseum. In French, German, or Italian. Other titles: *Revue Suisse d'Art et d'Archéologie*; *Revista Svizzera d'Arte e d'Archeologìa*.
Supersedes: *Anzeiger für Schweizerische Altertumskunde*.
Indexed: Int. Bibl. Soc. Cul. Anth.

ZEITSCHRIFT FÜR SCHWEIZERISCHE VOLKSWIRTSCHAFT
See SCHWEIZERISCHE ZEITSCHRIFT FÜR VOLKSWIRTSCHAFT UND STATISTIK

5231
ZEITSCHRIFT FÜR SOCIAL- UND WIRTSCHAFTSGESCHICHTE. v.1–7, 1893–1900. Weimer, E. Felber.
In German.
Superseded by: *Vierteljahrschrift für Social- und Wirtschaftsgeschichte*.

ZEITSCHRIFT FÜR SOZIALFORSCHUNG
See STUDIES IN PHILOSOPHY AND SOCIAL SCIENCE

5232
ZEITSCHRIFT FÜR SOZIALÖKONOMIE; MENSCH, TECHNIK, GESELLSCHAFT. v.15 (no.43)– , Dec. 1979– . Hamburg. Quarterly.
Issued by: Stiftung für Personliche Freiheit und Soziale Sicherheit and Sozialwissenschaftliche Gesellschaft. In German. Other title: *MTG*.
Continues: *Mensch, Technik, Gesellschaft*.

5233
ZEITSCHRIFT FÜR SOZIALPSYCHOLOGIE. 1– , 1970– . Frankfurt am Main, Akademische Verlagsgesellschaft. Quarterly.
In English or German.
Indexed: Bull. Sig. Soc. Eth.; Psych. Abst.

5234
ZEITSCHRIFT FÜR SOZIALWISSENSCHAFT. v.1–12, 1898–1909; n. ser. v.1–12, 1910–1921. Berlin. Monthly.
In German. Includes supplement: "Statistische Übersichten über die Allgemeine Wirtschaftslage".

5235
ZEITSCHRIFT FÜR SOZIOLOGIE. 1– , Jan. 1972– . Bielefeld, F. Enke Verlag. Quarterly.
Issued by: Fakultat der Soziologie, Universität Bielefeld. In English or German.
Indexed: Bull. Anal. Pol. Ec. Soc.; Bull. Sig. Soc Eth.; Curr. Cont. Soc. Beh. Sc.; Int. Pol. Sc. Abst.; Soc. Abst.; SSCI.

ZEITSCHRIFT FÜR SOZIOLOGIE
See SOSYOLOJI DERGISI

5236
ZEITSCHRIFT FÜR STAATSSOZIOLOGIE; POLITIK, WIRTSCHAFT, KULTUR, ERZIEHUNG. v.1–18, no.4, 1953–1971. Freiburg, Themis Verlag. Quarterly.
In German.

5237
ZEITSCHRIFT FÜR UMWELTPOLITIK. v.1– , May 1978– . Frankfurt am Main, Deutscher Fachverlage. Quarterly.
In English, French, or German. Other titles: *Journal of Environmental Policy*; *Revue de la Politique d'Environnement*.

Indexed: Int. Bibl. Eco.

5238
ZEITSCHRIFT FÜR UNTERNEHMENSGESCHICHTE. v.22– , 1977– . Wiesbaden, F. Steiner Verlag. Three no. a year.
Issued by: Gesellschaft für Unternehmensgeschichte. In German.
Continues: *Tradition.*
Indexed: Int. Bibl. Eco.

5239
ZEITSCHRIFT FÜR VERBRAUCHERPOLITIK. JOURNAL OF CONSUMER POLICY. 1–5, 1st quarter 1977–1982. Neuwied, H. Luchterhand. Quarterly.
In German.
Continued by: *Journal of Consumer Policy.*
Indexed: Int. Bibl. Eco.

5240
ZEITSCHRIFT FÜR VERGLEICHENDE RECHTS- UND STAATSWISSENSCHAFT MIT BESONDERER RÜCKSICHTIGUNG DER RECHT DER NATUR- UND KULTURVÖLKER. v.1–2, no.3/4, 1895–1897. Berlin.
In German. Title varies: 1895–96, *Mitteilungen der Gesellschaft für Vergleichende Rechts- und Staatswissenschaft zu Berlin*; v.2, no.1/2, 1896, *Vierteljahresschrift für Vergleichende Rechts- und Staatswissenschaft.*

5241
ZEITSCHRIFT FÜR VERGLEICHENDE RECHTSWISSENSCHAFT, EINSCHLIESSLICH DER ETHNOLOGISCHEN RECHTSFORSCHUNG. 1– , 1878– . Stuttgart, F. Enke. Quarterly.
In German. Vols. 53–55 issued in cooperation with the Akademie für Deutsches Recht. Publication suspended 1945–52.
Indexes: Vols. 1–20, 1878–1907, in v.20; v.21–50, 1908–36, in v.50.

5242
ZEITSCHRIFT FÜR VERWALTUNG. v.1– , Jan. 1868– . Wien, M. Perles. Weekly, 1868–1918; biweekly, 1919; semi-monthly.
In German. Title varies: 1868–Nov. 21, 1918, *Österreichische Zeitschrift für Verwaltung.*
Indexes: Vols. 1–40, 1868–1907, 1v.

5243
ZEITSCHRIFT FÜR VÖLKERPSYCHOLOGIE UND SPRACHWISSENSCHAFT. v.1–20, 1860–1890. Berlin.
In German.
Continued by: *Zeitschrift des Vereins für Volkskunde.*
Indexes: Vols. 1–20, 1860–89, in v.20.

5244
ZEITSCHRIFT FÜR VÖLKERRECHT. v.1–26, no.3, 1906–1944. Breslau. Bimonthly.
In German. Includes monographic supplements called "Beihefte". Title varies: 1906–13, *Zeitschrift für Völkerrecht und Bundesstaatsrecht.*

ZEITSCHRIFT FÜR VÖLKERPSYCHOLOGIE UND SOZIOLOGIE
See SOCIOLOGUS

ZEITSCHRIFT FÜR VÖLKERRECHT UND BUNDESSTAATSRECHT
See ZEITSCHRIFT FÜR VÖLKERRECHT

5245
ZEITSCHRIFT FÜR WIRTSCHAFTS- UND SOZIALWISSENSCHAFTEN. v.92– , 1972– . Berlin, Duncker & Humblot. Quarterly, 1974–76; bimonthly.
Issued by: Gesellschaft für Wirtschafts- und Sozialwissenschaften. Verein für Socialpolitik. In German.
Continues: *Schmollers Jahrbuch für Wirtschafts- und Sozialwissenschaften.*
Indexed: ABC POL SCI; Bull. Anal. Pol. Ec. Soc.; Bull. Sig. Soc. Eth.; Eco. Abst.; Int. Bibl. Eco.; Int. Bibl. Pol. Sc.; Int. Bibl. Soc.; Int. Pol. Sc. Abst.; PAISFL.

5246
ZEITSCHRIFT FÜR WIRTSCHAFTSGEOGRAPHIE ANGEWANDTE UND SOZIALGEOGRAPHIE. 1– , 1957– . Hagen, later Frankfurt, Buchenverlag. One issue every six weeks.
In German; occasionally articles in English or French. Includes supplements called "Beihefte" (1–, 1974–).
Indexed: PAISFL.

5247
ZEITSCHRIFT FÜR WIRTSCHAFTSPOLITIK; WIRTSCHAFTSPOLITISCHE CHRONIK. v.30– , 1981– . Cologne. Three no. a year.
Issued by: Institut für Wirtschaftspolitik, Universität Köln. In German.
Continues: *Wirtschaftspolitische Chronik; Zeitschrift für fremden Verkehr.*
Indexed: PAISFL.

5248
ZENTRALASIATISCHE STUDIEN. 1– , 1967– . Wiesbaden, Harrassowitz. Annual, 1967–79; two no. a year.

Issued by: Seminar für Sprache und Kulturwissenschaft Zentralasien, Universität Bonn. In German.

5249
ZENTRALBLATT DER BULGARISCHEN LITERATUR. GESCHICHTE ARCHÄOLOGIE UND ETHNOGRAPHIE. v.1– , 1958– . Sofia. Annual, 1958–62; semi-annual.
Issued by: Centre for Scientific Information and Documentation, Bulgarian Academy of Sciences. Volumes for 1958 issued by the academy's Abteilung für Wissenschaftliche Information und Dokumentation; 1959–62, by the Zentralstelle für Wissenschaftliche Information und Dokumentation. Absorbed the section "Ethnographie" of *Bulletin d'Analyses Littéraire, Ethnographie* in 1963. In German or French. Title varies: 1958–62, *Bulletin d'Analyses de la Littérature Scientifique Bulgare. Histoire et Archéologie. Zentralblatt der Bulgarischen Wissenschaftlichen Literatur. Geschichte und Archäologie*. Section "Histoire et Ethnographie" is in French; section "Archäologie" in German.

ZENTRALBLATT DER BULGARISCHEN WISSENSCHAFTLICHEN LITERATUR. GESCHICHTE UND ARCHÄOLOGIE
See ZENTRALBLATT DER BULGARISCHEN LITERATUR. GESCHICHTE, ARCHÄOLOGIE UND ETHNOGRAPHIE

ZENTRALBLATT FÜR ARBEITSWISSENSCHAFT UND SOZIALE BETRIEBSPRAXIS
See ARBEIT UND LEISTUNG

ZESZYTY NAUKOWE POLITECHNIKI ŚLĄSKIEJ
See NAUKI SPOŁECZNE (Gliwice)

ZESZYTY NAUKOWE UNIWERSYTETU ŁÓDZKIEGO. SERIA 1. NAUKI HUMANISTYCZNO-SPOŁECZNE
See NAUKI HUMANISTYCZNO-SPOŁECZNE

ZHOUGYANG MINZU HUEYUAN XUEBAO
See CHUNG YANG MIN TSU HSÜEH YUAN HSÜEH PAO

5250
ZIMBABWE JOURNAL OF ECONOMICS. v.1– , Mar. 1979– . Harare. One no. a year; four nos. forming a volume.
Supersedes: *Rhodesian Journal of Economics*.

5251
ZION. v.1– , Aug. 1935– . Jerusalem. Quarterly.
Issued by: World Zionist Organization, and Historical Society of Israel. In Hebrew; summaries in English. Subtitle reads: "A quarterly for research in Jewish history".
Supersedes: *New Judea*.
Indexed: His. Abst.

5252
ZIVOTNE PROSTREDIE. 1967– . Bratislava, Publishing House of the Slovak Academy of Sciences. Six no. a year.
Issued by: Slovenska Akademie Vied. In Slovak; summaries in English, German and Russian.

5253
DIE ZUKUNFT. Mar. 1946– . Wien, Sozialistischer Verlag. Biweekly, 1946–76; monthly.
Issued by: Sozialistischer Partei Österreichs. The issuing body considers this publication as a revival of *Kampf*, formerly published in Vienna (Oct. 1907–Feb. 1934). In German. Subtitle reads: "Sozialistische Monatsschrift für Politik, Wirtschaft, Kultur".
Indexed: His. Abst.; Bull. Anal. Pol. Ec. Soc.; Peace Res. Abst. J.

5254
ZYCIE SZKOŁY WYŻSZEJ. no.1– , Jan. 1953– . Warszawa, Państwowe Wydawnictwo Naukowe. Monthly.
Issued by: Ministerstwo Szkolnictwa Wyższego. In Polish. Occasionally includes supplement titled: "Zycie Szkoły Wyższej. Zeszyty Specjalne" (translated articles).

APPENDIX 1

Membership of the Social Sciences Group

There is no unanimous agreement concerning the membership of the group of the social sciences. The following listing from some well-known sources—all of them under collective editorship—demonstrates the lack of any agreement.

The *Encyclopaedia of the Social Sciences* (1930–33), edited by E.R.A. Seligman, allocates the members of the social sciences group into two categories: (a) full members: political science, economics, history, jurisprudence, anthropology, penology, sociology and social work (op. cit., v.1, pp.3–5); (b) "semi-social sciences": ethics, education, psychology, and philosophy (op. cit., v.1, pp.5–7); and (c) recognizes a category of sciences "some of the natural, others cultural, which have well defined and increasingly recognized social implications": biology, geography, linguistics, and art (op. cit., v.1, p.7).

In the more recent *International Encyclopedia of the Social Sciences* (New York, Macmillan and Free Press, 1968), the decision concerning the inclusion of individual disciplines was based on the research of human behavior. According to this work there are two groups of the social sciences: (1) anthropology, political science, economics, sociology, psychology, and history; and (2) geography, law, psychiatry, and statistics (op. cit., v.14, p.482).

The New Encyclopaedia Britannica. Macropaedia (15th ed., 1974) includes in the social sciences: cultural anthropology, sociology, economics, political science, and comparative law (op. cit., v.27, p.365).

Some differences are found also when guides to the social sciences are examined. In *A Reader's Guide to the Social Sciences* (2nd ed., 1970), edited by Bert H. Hoselitz, included are: history, geography, political science, economics, sociology, and anthropology. In *Sources of Information in the Social Sciences* (3rd ed., 1980), edited by William B. Webb, included are: history, economics and business, sociology, anthropology, education, and political science.

Two works surveying current research were consulted for this purpose. In the first work, *Main Trends in the Social and Human Sciences. Part 1* (Paris, Unesco, 1970), included are: sociology, political science, psychology, economics, demography, anthropology, and linguistics. Two studies in this work are important in connection with the membership in the social sciences, both by Jean Piaget: "General Problems of Interdisciplinary Research and Common Mechanisms" (op. cit., pp.467–528), and "The Place of Sciences of Man in the System of Sciences" (op. cit., pp.1–57). The second work, *Current Appraisals of Behavioral Sciences* (Revised edition, 1973), edited by Rollo Handy, and E.G. Harwood for the Behavioral Research Council, surveys concepts and progress of the following sciences: psychology, anthropology, sociology, political science, economics, history, jurisprudence, and linguistics.

In addition to the views of social scientists, the findings of the project in the Library of the University at Bath, under the leadership of Dr. Maurice Line, which investigated problems connected with the use of the library resources by social scientists, are recorded here.[1] The following disciplines were included: sociology, political science, economics, anthropology, law, history, education and psychology, and social work. Comments on two of the disciplines are indicative of the close relationships between various disciplines in this group. "Education was included as the relationship between educational research and practice and other disciplines, especially psychology and sociology, appeared to be particularly close and important." Reasons given for the inclusion of social work were the combination of research and application: "all persons concerned with the social sciences as a main area of work, whether the work consisted of research, teaching, administration or practice."

The views that were summarized are presented in Table 1 which demonstrates statistically which social sciences are considered more important.

Reference

1. *Information Requirements of Researchers in the Social Sciences*. Maurice B. Line, Project Head. Bath, 1971. University, Bath. Library. Investigation into Information Requirements of the Social Sciences. *Research Report*, no.1.

Table 1 *Membership in the Social Sciences Group*

Social Science	Enc. Soc. Sc.	Int. Enc. Soc. Sc.	Enc. Brit.	Reader's Guide	Sources Infor.	Main Trends	Beh. Sc.	Lib.	Total	SSB
Political science	X	X	X	X	X	X	X	X	8	X
International relations			X						1	
Economics	X	X	X	X	X	X	X	X	8	X
Anthropology	X	X		X	X	X	X	X	7	
Cultural anthropology			X						1	X
Sociology	X	X	X	X	X	X	X	X	8	X
History	X	X		X	X	X	X	X	7	Y
Law/Jurisprudence	X	Y						X	3	
Comparative law			X						1	X
International law									0	X
Social work	X							x	2	
Ethics	Y							X	2	
Education	Y				X			X	3	Y
Psychology	Y	X			X		X	X	5	Y
Philosophy	Y								1	
Psychiatry		Y							1	
Statistics		Y							1	
Biology	Z								1	
Geography	Z	Y		X					3	Y
Linguistics	Z						X		2	
Art	Z								1	

Enc. Soc. Sc.	*Encyclopaedia of the Social Sciences*
Int. Enc. Soc. Sc.	*International Encyclopedia of the Social Sciences*
Enc. Brit.	*The New Encyclopaedia Britannica. Macropaedia*
Reader's Guide	*A Reader's Guide to the Social Sciences*
Sources Infor.	*Sources of Information in the Social Sciences*
Main Trends	*Main Trends in the Social and Human Sciences. Part 1*
Beh. Sc.	*Current Appraisals of Behavioral Sciences*
Lib.	*Information Requirements of Researchers in the Social Sciences*
SSB	*Social Sciences: An International Bibliography of Serial Literature, 1830–1985*
X	Main social sciences
Y	Semi-social sciences
Z	Containing social science implications

APPENDIX 2

The Development of Social Sciences: A Panoramic View

The scope of this bibliography covers the span of time from deductive social philosophy, called also in the eighteenth century moral philosophy, when the individual social sciences emerged and began to flourish until the present time when owing to the impact of interdisciplinary research a new image of the social sciences has appeared. It was thought that a panoramic view of the development of ideas would be useful for a beginner. This panoramic sketch is limited to listing the names of outstanding contributors, the dates of their lives, the titles of their most important works, followed by their publication dates, and brief statements pointing out the basic ideas. This view includes works published between the sixteenth and nineteenth centuries in Europe or North America in monographic form. This selection is limited to the six disciplines which are the subject of this bibliography. This list is a kind of micro supplement concerning ideas published in works of monographic form to the bibliography, which is limited to serial literature. It will be a time map of concepts which have been replenished and further elaborated in periodical literature.

Economics

Economics was the first discipline which emerged from social philosophy. Its name was originally political economy, coined by Antoine de Montchrestien (1576–1621), known also as Sieur de Watterville, the author of *Traité de l'économie politique* (1615). He did not develop any system of economics.

The reason for this priority in establishing an independent discipline stemmed from the great interest of post-medieval man in the acquisition of wealth. Mercantilists were the first practitioners and conceptualists of the interest in wealth. Thomas Mun (1571–1641), the author of *England's Treausure by Foreign Trade* (1664) and *A Discourse of Trade from England into East Indies* (1621), recommended a favorable balance of trade. William Petty (1623–87), another mercantilist, the author of the *Treatise of Taxes and Contributions* (1662), investigated the concept of interest and the theory of rent. Following the decline of mercantilism physiocrats developed their own theory of wealth based on agriculture. François Quesnay (1694–1774) in his articles in the *Encyclopédie* formulated this system. Another physiocrat, Anne Robert Jacques Turgot (1727–81), a lawyer, theologian, and public servant in the economic sector, the author of *Réflexions sur la formation et la distribution des richesses* (1788), and Étienne Bonnot de Condillac (1714–80), a philosopher, theologian, and physiocrat, the author of *Le Commerce et le Gouvernement considéres relativement l'un à l'autre* (1776), were interested in utility. The honor of establishing the science of political economy is attributed to Adam Smith (1723–90), a Scotsman, professor of moral philosophy at the University of Glasgow, the author of the *Inquiry into the Nature and Causes of the Wealth of Nations* (1776); he dealt in his work with the concept of value, value of labor, market price, real and nominal prices, rent, profit, wages and their effect on the growth of population, and was against regulation of the market by government; he did not formulate a theoretical system. Jean Baptiste Say (1767–1832), a businessman, in his *Lettres à M. Malthus sur différents sujets d'économie politique* (1820) systematized economic ideas developed before him with emphasis on the theory of value, services as immaterial goods, and the concept of equilibrium; he favored the private market. The next significant step in the development of the theory of economics was made by David Ricardo (1772–1823), the author of *Principles of Political Economy and Taxation* (1817); he investigated Smith's concept of capital cumulation, analyzed the theory of value, value of labor, wages, profit, rent; he was for the taxation of proprietors of land. Thomas Albert Malthus (1776–1834), a theologian and mathematician, the author of *Essay on the Principle of Population, as it affects the Future Improvement of Society with Remarks on the Speculation of Mr. Goodwin, Mr. Condorcet and other Writers* (1798), used reasoning similar to Ricardo's. Jeremy Bentham (1748–1832), the author of *An Introduction to the Principles of Morals and Legislation*

(1789), developed the principle of utility expressed in the phrase "the greatest happiness of the greatest number", which can be achieved in the laissez-faire economy. Nassau William Senior (1790–1864), a lawyer who became the first professor of economics at Oxford University in 1925, the author of *An Outline of the Science of Political Economy* (1836), discussed the concept of utility. John Stuart Mill (1806–73), the philosopher, in his *Principles of Political Economy with some of their Applications to Social Philosophy* (1848) organized concepts developed earlier by other thinkers with emphasis on the theory of production and distribution and on international trade. Although he based his system on the laissez-faire principle, he kept his system open to alleviate the situation of the poor. Antoine Augustin Cournot (1801–77), a mathematician and philosopher, was the founder of mathematical economics in his *Recherches sur les principes de la théorie des richesses* (1838) and of the exchange value. William Stanley Jevons (1835–82), a logician and economist, the author of *The Theory of Political Economy* (1871), discussed the marginal utility theory as also did Marie-Esprit Leon Walras (1834–1910), a self-educated economist, and professor of economics at the University of Lausanne, the author of *Éléments d'économie pure, ou Théorie de la richesse sociale* (1874).

A few socialist and utopian philosophers and economists were well known. Among them was Claude Henri Saint-Simon (1760–1825), a prolific writer, who considered ways of changing the structure of society and its government into one that would be controlled and where everybody would work. He publicized his ideas in a kind of journal published at regular intervals; although they carried the same title, they were really a series of his brochures, e.g. *L'Industrie* (1816–18), *L'Organisateur* (1829–30), *Du Système industriel* (1821–22), and others. He conceived a socialist system based mainly on collective agriculture operated by communities and a rigid distribution of earnings. Pierre Joseph Proudhon (1809–65), the author of *Système des contradictions économiques, ou Philosophie de la misère* (1848, 2 vols.), put forward an alternative to the economy of his day based on equality of the distribution of wealth generated by labor. Robert Owen (1771–1858), a factory owner, was the author of *A New View of Society, or Essays on the Principle of the Formation of the Human Character and the Application of the Principle to Practice* (1813).

Karl Marx (1818–83), who did not belong to the utopians, in cooperation with Friedrich Engels (1820–95) spelled out the principles of an economic order—originally envisioned by Proudhon—both in the *Communist Manifesto* (1848) and in a more detailed elaboration in *Das Kapital* (v.1, 1867; v.2–3, edited by Engels, 1885–94) in which he argued for the elimination of private property and as a result the abolition of social classes.

An extensive increase in the number of new concepts is witnessed during the last quarter of the nineteenth century. Among the most important were those developed by: John Bates Clark (1847–1938), who in his *Distribution of Wealth* (1899) used the method of marginal analysis and dealt with the concepts of land, capital goods, social capital and diminishing returns; Alfred Marshall (1842–1924), who discussed the concept of value, demand and market equilibrium, and refined the law of diminishing utility in his *Principles of Economics* (1890); and Vilfredo Pareto (1848–1923), who discussed the general theory of equilibrium in his *Manuale di economia politica* (1906).

Political Science

Following the collapse of the medieval political order many thinkers in France, Italy, Scotland and England searched for a basis for a new type of political organization. Niccolò Machiavelli (1469–1527), the author of *Il Principe* (1513), was interested rather in practical politics in his native Florence. He separated politics from ethics, and advised the ordinary citizen to live according to public spirit and social morale, but the prince (using the term in the contemporary political structure of Florence) has to be expedient. Jean Bodin (1530–96), a Jesuit, philosopher of history, trained in law, the author of *Les Six livres de la république* (1579) and *Methodus ad facilem historiarum cognitionem* (1566), presented in the latter the view that governmental institutions should be studied in order to formulate the system of political theory. He assumed in his *Les Six livres de la république* that the law of nature was the basis of human social relations. The state was created by wars among family groups. The sovereignty of the state is not limited by laws; the hereditary monarchy was the best type of government. He supported the divine right of kings. He pointed out the impact of geographical factors on human affairs. His fragments of a political theory, not a system, are the earliest ones in modern history. Roberto Francisco Romolo Bellarmino (1542–1621), the author of *Tractatus de potestate Sumni Pontificis in rebus temporaralibus* (1610), placed the final authority in the people. Thomas Hobbes (1588–1679), the author of *Elements of Law* (1640), *De cive* (1642), and *Leviathan* (1651), favored the absolute authority of the monarch or one assembly of men to whom all men transfer their wills in order to avoid the state of "bellum omnium contra omnes", that is, for self-interest. The absolute monarchy is responsible to God only both in spiritual and secular affairs. Algernon Sydney (1622–83), the author of the posthumously published *Discourses concerning Government* (1698), argued, in opposition to Hobbes's view, that authority rests on the consent of people. Samuel Pufendorf (1632–94), an international jurist, the author of *De jure naturae et gentium* (1672), started with the assumption of natural law, considered the government's authority as limited by moral restraints, and thought that people might restrict the sovereign's authority concerning certain activities. Giambattista Vico (1668–1744), a jurist and philosopher, the author of *De universi juris uno principio et fino uno* (1720), saw both the government and law as conditioned by the historical development of a given society; he envisaged this development in three stages: theocratic, aristocratic, and democratic. John Locke (1632–1704), a philosopher empirically oriented in his thinking, the author of *Two Treatises of Government* (1690), envisaged the life of early people in natural conditions in freedom and equality having some basic natural rights like that of liberty and property. People may make a social contract to create a body politic but they retain their basic rights, of which the most important is that a majority of people may rebel against sovereignty. He was for the separation of ecclesiastical affairs from civilian government and for the elimination of church authorities' power in secular affairs. He made a distinction between legislative and executive powers. He favored social welfare and religious toleration. Benedict Spinoza (1632–77), the philosopher, author of *Tractatus theologico-politicus* (1670), formulated a theory of social contract different from Hobbes's. If such a contract is not expedient it should cease to exist. Rebellion against the sovereign is justified. He was for an aristocratic republic, and wanted to secure liberty; the power of the state is limited. Charles Louis de Secondat Montesquieu (1689–1755), the author of *De l'esprit des lois, ou du rapport que les lois dérivant avoir avec la constitution de chaque gouvernement, les mœurs, le climat, la religion, le commerce, etc.* (1748), favored an empirical method and a historical approach as methods of research. He saw positive law as a result of historical circumstances in relation to the rational natural law. Institutions should be based on the attitudes of people and historical tradition and not imposed on people. He was for maintaining liberty, and for separating legislative power from the government's executive power. Governments can be grouped in three categories: despotisms (without law), monarchies (society governed by law), and republics (political power belongs to the people). He is considered as a precursor of comparative law studies. Henry Home Kames (1696–1782), a Scottish lawyer and moral philosopher, the author of *Six Sketches of the History of Man* (1776), believed in innate racial characteristics (on the basis of travellers' reports) but that human character is independent of these factors. He considered democracy as contradictory to nature, and a republic or limited monarchy as the best form of government. Jean Jacques Rousseau (1712–1778) was born in Geneva but lived in France. He was not a rationalist although he lived in the age of French rationalism. He was acquainted with the ideas of Pufendorf, Locke, and Montesquieu. In Rousseau's *Discours sur l'origine et les fondemens de l'inégalité parmi les hommes* (1775) and *Du contrat social* (1762) early man is conceived as "a noble savage" living in a state of nature without a state organization and based on emotions of self-interest. But when evils arise man needs to achieve his happiness; therefore both the civil society and state are desirable. Their creation is based on the "general will" of people. David Hume (1711–76), a philosopher, utilitarian, and founder of utilitarian ethics, was the author of *Political Discourses* (1752), *Treatise on Human Nature* (1739–40), and *Of the Original Contract* (1748). He rejected the concept of natural law and of social contract as not supported by evidence, and looked toward history and psychology as ways of constructing a system of political philosophy. According to him states were not originated by contracts but by the use of force and existed because they were necessary and useful. This is consistent with the selfish nature of man. Jeremy Bentham (1748–1832) was a utilitarian who opposed the theory of social contract. His utilitarian ideals can be achieved at best under fully representative government, elected by secret ballot. Colonies should have their own governments. John Stuart Mill (1806–73), a utilitarian, was the author of *On Liberty* (1859), *Consideration on Representative Government* (1861), and *Utilitarianism* (1861). He foresaw dangers even when democratic majority government is in power because such a government may not be impartial in treating minorities; he was for equal rights for women and for trade unions, and conceived the idea of common ownership. He did not follow the laissez-faire principle of other utilitarians, considering the living of man on his own as a condition of personal freedom. He may be considered one of the forerunners of the welfare state.

In addition to monarchists and utilitarians there were two other groups of thinkers who should be mentioned as contributors to the political science theory: idealists and collectivists. Among the idealists were: Immanuel Kant (1724–1804), the author of *Political Rights* (1793); Johann Gottlieb Fichte (1762–1814), the author of *Zur Theoretischen Philosophie* (1845, 2 vols.); Friedrich Schelling (1775–1854); and Georg Wilhelm Hegel (1770–1831), the author of *Vorlesungen über die Philosophie der Geschichte* (1837). Hegel formulated the concept of the three-stage dialectical development of human society, the dominant role being taken by the monarchical state. The form of government is not chosen by the people; this is necessitated by a historical process.

In the group of collectivists, socialists, and utopians the best-known in France were: Claude Henri Saint-Simon (1760–1825); Charles Fourier (1772–1837), the author of *Le nouveau monde industriel et sociétaire de l'invention du procédé de l'industrie attrayante et naturelle distribuée en séries passionnées* (1829); Noel Babeuf (1760–97); François Louis Auguste Blanqui (1805–81), the author of *Critique sociale* (1885); Louis Blanc (1811–82), the author of *Organisation du travail* (1839); and Pierre Joseph Proudhon (1809–47). In Scotland, there was Robert Owen (1771–1858), the author of *A New View of Society* (1813). At the turn of the nineteenth and twentieth centuries a group called the Fabians played an important role in England. They included Beatrice Webb (1859–1942), who jointly with her husband Sidney Webb (1859–1947) wrote a number of works on labor.

Cultural Anthropology

Anthropology embraces two subdisciplines: physical and cultural anthropology; the latter includes ethnology and prehistoric archaeology. Both branches of cultural anthropology had forerunners. Charles Montesquieu (1689–1755) in his *De l'esprit des lois* (1748) was interested in the role of natural and civil law in human society. Henry Home Kames (1696–1782) in his *Six Sketches of the History of Man* (1776) was interested in the development of society. David Hume (1711–76) in his *Treatise about Human Nature* (1739–40) and Adam Smith (1723–90) assumed that societies are natural systems and social activities are natural; both of them were in opposition to the concepts of Rousseau's and Hobbes's formulations of the human societies and states. Some thinkers in the search for sources of information about societies turned their attention to the recorded facts on such matters as subsistence and social classes, among them Adam Ferguson (1723–1816), a Scottish moral philosopher and historian, who in his *Essay on the History of Civil Society* (1767), grouped societies into four categories: hunters, shepherds, agriculturalists accompanied by the development of the alphabetic script, and civilized societies engaged in commerce. These are also stages in development. He was influenced by Montesquieu's and Lord Kames's ideas. Marie Jean Antoine Nicolas Caritat, Marquis de Condorcet (1743–94), the author of *Esquisse d'un tableau historique des progrès de l'esprit humain* (1794), elaborated the idea of progress, which was a uniform historical process similar to processes in nature, "la mathématique sociale". These stages of development of knowledge were: pastoralism, agriculture, and the invention of the alphabetic script. The study of a social system may be accompanied by studying the interdependent parts of that system. These stages resemble the Adam Smith's stages of development. Henry Sumner Maine (1822–88), professor of civil law, the author of *Ancient Law* (1861), considered kinship, not contiguity, as the basis of common political action in early societies. The individual gradually substitutes family. Adolph Bastian (1826–1905), an anthropologist and evolutionist, the author of *Der Mensch in der Geschichte* (1860), presented the idea that the human mind functions according to a constant system. Some of the early contributors to social sciences relied on the Old Testament, Greek and Roman works and on reports and diaries of travellers and missionaries in the newly discovered lands. But in the nineteenth century scholars started to use new methods for studying social institutions and culture. These new methods spread in Europe and North America. Very important and exercising great influence were works published during the 1860s. Among them were: Johann Jacob Bachofen's (1815–87) *Das Mutterrecht* (1861); John F. McLennan's (1822–88) *Primitive Marriage* (1865), in which the concepts of exogamy and endogamy, polyandry and levirate were formulated; Henry Louis Morgan's (1818–81) *Systems of Consanguinity and Affinity of the Human Family* (1871), a study of types of families; and Edward Tylor's (1832–1917) *Researches into the Early History of Mankind* (1865) and *Primitive Culture* (1871), the latter probably the best-known work of that period. The birth of modern ethnology can be placed in that decade and has often been linked to Tylor's work. The works just mentioned were based on the evolutionary theory, but this was rejected when results of research in the field were cumulated and verified. It was succeeded by historical schools, by the diffusionist theory, whose origins lie in Friedrich Ratzel's (1854–1904) *Anthropogeographie* (2nd ed., 1899), Fritz Graebner's (1877–1934) *Die Methode der Ethnologie* (1911), and by works which appeared in the twentieth century. Some influential twentieth-century writers are William Halse Rivers (1864–1922), Emile Durkheim (1858–1917), a sociologist, Lucien Levy-Bruhl (1857–1939), a philosopher, Wilhelm Max Wundt (1832–1920), a social psychologist, Edward Alexander Westermarck (1862–1939), Francis Galton (1822–1911), Wilhelm Schmidt (1868–1954), and Franz Boas (1858–1942).

Sociology

Contributors are listed in chronological order without any attempt to group them by ideology or methodology. Niccolò Machiavelli (1469–1527) was the author of *Il Principe* (1513), in which he indicated the role of the psychological factor in the activities of the prince. Jean Bodin (1530–1596), the author of *Les Six livres de la république* (1579), considered the family to be the foundation of various associations and of the state. Society has its own complex inner structure. John Locke (1632–1704), the author of the *Second Treatise on Government* (1690), perceived human society at its beginning as free and guided by the principle of equality.

Giovanni Battista Vico (1668–1754), a philosopher and jurist, the author of *Scienza nuova* (1725), formulated the concept of the development of man through three stages: gods, heroes, and men. Adam Ferguson (1723–1816), a lawyer, the author of *An Essay on the History of Civil Society* (1767) and *Principles of Moral and Political Science* (1792), advised that man should be studied as he is, and thought that man has gone through three stages: savagery, barbarism, and civilization. David Hume (1711–76), an economist and moral philosopher, the author of *A Treatise of Human Nature* (1739) and *Inquiry concerning Human Understanding* (1748), pointed out the role of emotions and instincts in human activities. Adam Smith (1723–90), an economist and moral philosopher, the author of *The Theory of Moral Sentiments* (1759), formulated his theory of the sympathy of the individual which is modified by the social group in which the individual lives. Sympathy creates mutuality, and that creates a whole and human society. Charles Louis de Secondat, Baron de la Brède et de Montesquieu (1689–1755), a lawyer, in his *De l'esprit des lois, ou du rapport que les lois derivent avoir avec la constitution de chaque gouvernement, les moeurs, le climat, la religion, le commerce, etc.* (1748) thought that each society has its own law of development. Research should uncover that law and uncover the network of social institutions; the knowledge of such laws would help people to perform their duties satisfactorily. Society is formed under the impact of the environment including climate and by the human psychological factor. Marie Jean Antoine Nicolas Caritat, Marquis de Condorcet (1743–94), a mathematician, in his *Esquisse d'un tableau des progrès de l'esprit humain* (1794) visualized social development up to his time in nine stages (based on Fontenelle's (1657–1757) *Politique de tout cabinets de l'Europe*); in the forthcoming tenth state human society will achieve its perfection. He developed the concept of social mathematics to be used in future developments, and hoped that scientific methods would lead to the continuous improvement of society. Claude Henri de

Saint-Simon (1760–1825), the author of *La physiologie sociale* (1813), considered the methods used in the natural sciences as appropriate for the study of human society. Georg Wilhelm Hegel (1770–1830) in his *Vorlesungen über die Philosophie des Geschichte* (1837) contributed indirectly toward understanding the need for sociology.

The title of the founder of sociology is attributed to Auguste Comte (1798–1857), a philosopher of the positivist school, the author of the *Plan des travaux scientifiques nécessaires pour réorganiser la société* (1822) and of the basic work *Cours de philosophie positive* (1830–1842, 6 vols.), which is an outline of the general system of the hierarchy of sciences (mathematics, astronomy, physics, chemistry, biology, and sociology). Sociology occupies the last place because it was developed later than the other sciences, has a lower level of generality, is more complex, and will serve in practical life. Sociology was considered by Comte to be a positivist science because its findings can be verified empirically, and its laws allow for the prediction of processes. Comte named this new discipline sociology although he first used the term social physics. His sociology absorbed many then current concepts. Comte's sociology dealt with mankind, not with nations. He discerned social statics, which deals with teh study of interrelationships among various parts of the system (family, religion, property, language, and state), and social dynamics, which is the formulation of the theory of progress based on regularities in all fields of social life; this law of regular activities, he thought, determines the development of society in three stages: theological, metaphysical, and positive, which are characteristic of mankind, not of individual nations. John Stuart Mill (1806–73), a logician, economist, and politician, the author of *System of Logic Ratiocinative and Inductive* (1843), discussed in "Book 6, On the Moral Sciences" methods that could be used in research on society. The best method selected by him was "the concrete deductive method", which consists of three operations: collection of facts and induction, procedure of inference, and verification. Conclusions reached by the other sciences of society, psychology and ethology should be included in the science of society. Only then is a complete sociological explanation possible. Mill followed Comte's concept of the three stages of historical development. Another contributor at that time was Herbert Spencer (1820–1903), an evolutionist, trained in engineering but self-educated in the social sciences, the author of *The Principles of Sociology* (1876–96, 3 vols.), *Descriptive Sociology* (1893–1910) (in ten parts), and *The Study of Sociology* (1873). Society is a whole composed of institutions which are closely related to each other. In order to understand social institutions one has to know their history. There are similarities and differences between societies and organisms. Society is a collective of individuals, which are subject to evolution which is determined both by physical determinants such as climate, soil, and physical characteristics of the individual, and culture. Lambert Adolphe Jacques Quételet (1796–1874), a mathematician, the author of *Sur l'homme et le développement de ses facultés; physique sociale* (1835), *Physique sociale, ou Essai sur le développement des facultés de l'homme* (1869, 2 vols.) and *Du Système social et des lois qui le régissent* (1848), tried to explain various social systems using statistics of the distribution of properties.

Karl Marx (1818–83) was the author of *The German Ideology* (1846), written jointly with Friedrich Engels (1820–95), which contains basic explanation of the concept of society; *The Holy Family* (1844), which also written with Engels deals with the concept of social bonds; *Communist Manifesto* (1848), which constructs the history of the class struggle generated by the division of labor; and *Das Kapital* (v.1, 1867; v.2–3, edited by Engels, 1885 and 1894 respectively). The most important of Marx's views pertaining to the science of society can be summarized as follows: methods should be empirical, applicable to the whole of nature including human society; they will reveal all laws, and these can be incorporated in dialectical materialism. The same laws will also apply to the study of human society, which is a system of intertwined institutions, beginning with material basis, property relations, division of labor and social classes, the family, religion, military institutions, and the state, together forming a structural-functional whole. Society is not static but a changing process, and its particular stages are the results of conflicts; historical aspects, then, cannot be excluded. Achievements are cumulative in historical process, and this development follows a definite pattern moving toward the elimination of conflict.

In the last quarter of the nineteenth century a number of important works were published. Ludwig Gumplowicz (1838–1909), a sociologist, jurist, and social Darwinist, was the author of *Der Rassenkampf* (1883), *Grundriss der Soziologie* (1885), and *Die Soziologische Staatsidee* (1892). Gumplowicz considered racial conflict as a matter of culture not of biology; wanted to discover universal rules governing societies by studying these societies rather than by adapting concepts from other sciences; and viewed social conflict as a cause of social change. Lester Frank Ward (1841–1913), an evolutionist, was the author of *Dynamic Sociology* (1895), which was a study of social psychology, *Outlines of Sociology* (1898), and *Pure Sociology* (1903). Franklin H. Giddings (1855–1931) was the author of *Principles of Sociology* (3rd ed., 1896) and *The Theory of Socialization* (3rd ed., 1897). William Graham Sumner (1840–1910), an evolutionist, was the author of *Folkways* (1906), while Vilfredo Pareto (1848–1923), an engineer, scientist, and economist, devised some sociological models most of which had an economic background, such as economic equilibrium; his works were published in the twentieth century. Émile Durkheim (1858–1918), a sociologist, was the author of *De la division du travail social* (1893), *Les Règles de la méthode sociologique* (1895), *Le Suicide* (1897), and further works published in the twentieth century. He considered social facts as if they were things; a sociologist should be free from the impact of any ideology when involved in research. Relations among human beings and institutions are durable. As a result of socialization processes the individual accepts the cultural patterns of his group. He formulated the concepts of mechanical and organic solidarity. He excluded biological and psychological explanations. His social morphology is the study of physical conditions of society. Other sociologists such as Georg Simmel, Max Weber, and Charles H. Cooley belong to the twentieth century.

Closely related to sociology has been social psychology, which was of consideration to David Hume in his *Inquiry concerning Human Understanding* (1748) and *A Treatise on Human Nature* (1739–40), and to Adam Smith (1723–90), the author of *The Theory of Moral Sentiments* (1759), in which he formulated his theory that sympathy plays a role in the formations of morals. John Stuart Mill (1806–73) was the author of *System of Logic Ratiocinative and Inductive*. In his view psychology can make use of physiology. Psychology should follow the rules of observation and experimentation. Wilhelm Max Wundt (1832–1920) was the author of *Völkerpsychologie* (1900–20). Gustave le Bon (1841–1931), in *Psychologie des foules* (1895), considered crowds a characteristic of modern societies. Gabriel Tarde (1843–1904), the author of *L'Opinion et la foule* (1901), studied the phenomenon of immitation. William McDougall (1871–1938), John Broadus Watson (1878–1958), and Sigmund Freud (1856–1939) were authors of works published in the twentieth century.

International Public Law

In this work 'international' is limited to adjusting disagreements and conflicts of a political nature. There is no institution that would enact international legal acts. International public law consists of principles of law which are recognized by a large number of civilized nations and is based on treaties, bilateral and multilateral agreements, which may be general or particular, international custom, and judicial decisions and opinions of qualified public lawyers of various nations. On the basis of these decisions and opinions the International Court of Justice makes its decisions. Even the General Assembly of the United Nations is not an authority to formulate new laws because its resolutions are not binding legally beyond the United Nations.

The need for international public law was felt for centuries, and preceded modern times. There were some important contributors to international law. One of them was Francisco de Vitoria (1486?–1546), the author of *Reflectiones theologicae* (1557), in which he called for establishing such a law. Francisco Suarez (1548–1617), a Spanish jesuit, the author of lectures on such a law (1601–02) and later the author of *Tractatus de legibus* (1672), made a distinction between natural law and international law which is based on a custom. Alberico Gentili (1552–1608), an Italian living in England, was the author of *De iure de belli* (1598), a work which influenced Grotius' ideas. Hugo Grotius (1583–1645), a Dutch lawyer whose name appears sometimes as Huigh de Groot, in his work *De jure pacis et belli* (1632) called for international law that would prevent committing cruelties during wars. Richard Zouche (1590–1661), the author of *Iuris et iuridici fecialis, sive iuris inter gentes, et questionum de eodem explication, quod quae ad pacem & bellum inter diversos principes out populos spectant, ex praecipuis historico-iure-peritis, exhibentur* (1650), wanted to base international law on positivism not on the natural law. Samuel Pufendorf (1632–94), a German jurist, the author of *De iure naturae et gentium* (1672) and *De officio hominis et civis* (1728), considered international law to be a part of the natural law. Christian Wolff (1679–1754), a German philosopher, the author of *Institutiones iuris naturae et gentium in quibus hominis natura continuo nexu omnes obligationes et iura deductuntur* (1750), introdued the concept of acquired rights resulting from human laws. Emerich de Vattel (1714–67), a Swiss philosopher, the author of *Les droits des gens, ou Principes de la loi naturelle appliqués a la conduite & aux affaires des nations et de sovereigns* (1758), considered international law as based upon general consent. Jeremy Bentham (1748–1832), a philosopher, jurist, and utilitarian, the author of *Principles of Morals and Legislation* (1789), called for the creation of international law.

Comparative Law

Comparative law presents some difficulties in defining its subject matter. The meaning of comparative law is reflected in the phrase "comparative legal traditions". The meaning of the latter indicates the fact that comparative law is a search for elements of substantive law, or infrastructure of legal systems, e.g. ancient Roman and European law, Anglo-American common law, Muslim law, or socialist law. The studies of comparative law are undertaken in search of relationships among concepts embedded in legal systems of a given family of laws and the values, norms and standards of a given society. Harold C. Gutteridge, the author of *Comparative Law. An Introduction to the Comparative Method of Legal Study and Research* (2nd ed., Cambridge, Cambridge University Press, 1949), defined the nature of comparative law as a study of a given law and the actor, individual and his social group or other social groups in relation to accepted standards. Society defines the accepted understanding of what are certain norms and standards and the individual's actions, status, and role in relationships with social groups. Jerome Hall, in his *Comparative Law and Social Theory* (Louisiana University Press, 1963), defined comparative law as "a composite of social knowledge of positive law, distinguished by the fact that, in its general aspect, it is intermediate between the knowledge of particular laws and legal institutions on one side, and the universal knowledge of them at the other extreme" (p.33).

There were not many forerunners of comparative law, although the interest in comparative law is old. One may cite the Roman "Laws of the Twelve Tables", from the fifth century B.C., to point out the antiquity of comparative law. In modern times Montesquieu is considered as the precursor of comparative law because he emphasized that law should not be viewed as an abstraction but against the social environment in which it acts and its history (Gutteridge, op. cit., p.12). Other contributors to comparative law studies were Henry James Sumner Maine (1822–88), a jurist, the author of *Village Communities in the East and the West* (1871), *The Early History of Institutions* (1875), and *Dissertations on Early Law and Custom* (1874), and Roscoe Pound (1870–1964), the author of *Interpretation of Legal History* (1923). The International Congress of Comparative Law held in Paris in 1900 created an extensive interest in comparative law; the number of new journals published in this field in the twentieth century indicates this interest.

Conclusion

This panoramic view of the development of concepts in the social sciences forms the basic information concerning their development, especially for their beginnings. But their development during later stages was connected with other factors too, such as the setting up of chairs for teaching these sciences in universities, the formation of professional clubs, societies and institutes and their regular meetings, and the part played by professional journals. The pattern of development of these factors has varied from country to country.

The first chair of economics and commerce was established at the University of Halle in 1727, even before Adam Smith's *Inquiry into the Nature and Causes of Wealth of Nations* was published in 1776. The chair of economics in the University of Naples was established in 1754, at Modena in 1772, at Oxford in 1825, and at Edinburgh in 1870; while in the United States the chair of economics (combined with moral philosophy) was established in Columbia College in 1818, and at Harvard an exclusive chair in economics was established in 1850. The lectureship in anthropology was established at the University of Cambridge in 1884. The chair for sociology was established in the University of Indiana in 1885, at Chicago in 1892, and at Harvard in 1938.

The role played by professional clubs, associations, organizations, and institutes has been growing constantly. A few examples of organizations which have survived to the present time are the American Philosophical Society (founded 1743), the American Association for the Advancement of Science (1848), the International Institute of Differing Civilizations (1894), and the National Institute of Social Sciences (1899). Some examples in individual disciplines are the Société d'économie politique (1842), the American Economic Association (1885), the Royal Economic Society in London (1890), the American Academy of Political and Social Science (1880), the Royal Institute of International Affairs (1920), the Académie Internationale de Science Politique et d'Histoire Constitutionelle (1936), the Fondation Nationale des Sciences Politiques (1945), the Anthropology Section of the British Association (1834), the Ethnological Society, England (1844), the Société d'Ethnographie (1859), Die Anthropologische Gesellschaft, Wien (1870), the Royal Anthropological Institute of Great Britain and Ireland (1843), the Anthropological Society of Tokyo (1884), the American Sociological Society (1906), the Deutsche Gesellschaft für Soziologie (1910), the British Sociological Association (1951), and the International Sociological Association (1949).

The growth of serial literature in the social sciences—which is such an important medium of diffusion of scholarly information in our time—was slow. Periodicals except those on economics (in its broad meaning) appeared rarely and their growth in numerical terms was slow until 1890. Their rate of increase was roughly 1 percent per decade until the 1880s; from the 1890s onwards growth was on an increased scale, which increased again during the 1920s. Following World War Two, the 1950s witnessed an extensive increase of growth.

Subject Index